BUSINESS LAW
PRINCIPLES AND CASES

JOHN W. WYATT, S.J.D.

Professor of Business Law
University of Florida
Member of the Florida and Federal Bars

MADIE B. WYATT, A.B., LL.B.

Member of the Florida and Federal Bars

Fifth Edition

McGraw-Hill Book Company

New York   St. Louis   San Francisco   Auckland   Düsseldorf   Johannesburg
Kuala Lumpur   London   Mexico   Montreal   New Delhi   Panama
Paris   São Paulo   Singapore   Sydney   Tokyo   Toronto

This book was set in Times Roman by Black Dot, Inc.
The editors were Thomas H. Kothman and Joseph F. Murphy;
the designer was J. E. O'Connor;
the production supervisor was Thomas J. LoPinto.
Kingsport Press, Inc., was printer and binder.

BUSINESS LAW: PRINCIPLES AND CASES

567890KPKP7987

Library of Congress Cataloging in Publication Data

Wyatt, John Walton, date
    Business Law: principles and cases.

    Includes texts of the 1972 Uniform commercial code
and the Uniform partnership act.
    1. Commercial law—United States. I. Wyatt,
Madie B., joint author. II. American Law Institute.
Uniform commercial code. 1975. III. National
Conference of Commissioners on Uniform State Laws.
Uniform partnership act. 1975. IV. Title.
KF889.W9 1975   346′.73′07   74-13708
ISBN 0-07-072145-9

CONTENTS

TABLE OF CASES

PREFACE

This book originated as an attempt to present the fundamental principles of law which students should understand before they enter their professions. This purpose has continued to dominate the content of the fifth edition. It is not the purpose of this book to prepare the students to be their own attorneys or to be experts in legal procedure or to draft their own legal documents. The purpose is to present legal rules in such a way that the students will acquire a knowledge of law, apply this knowledge to their future profession, and seek the aid of an attorney when it becomes appropriate to do so.

This edition continues the organization of division of chapters into textual material and selected cases. The organization of some of the chapters has been changed, however, and some new chapters have been added. The new chapters are Chapter 48, "Securities Regulation," Chapter 49, "Antitrust: Monopolies, Restraints of Trade, Conspiracies," and Chapter 50, "Labor Relations." These chapters present both the federal and the state law, including fair trade laws, right-to-work laws, workmen's compensation, unemployment compensation, social security, and blue sky laws.

The former chapters, Chapter 42, "Introduction to Corporations," and Chapter 43, "Corporation: Relation to Promoters," have been combined into a new chapter, Chapter 42, "Corporations: Introduction; Promoters." The former Part Three, "Agency," has been changed to Part Seven, "Agency," and immediately precedes Part Eight, "Business Organizations," followed by Part Nine, "Securities Regulation; Antitrust; Labor Relations," so as to achieve an orderly continuity of subjects.

The material on the Uniform Commercial Code has been rewritten to reflect the changes made in the 1972 Official Text. The vast majority of these changes, however, affect Part Six, "Secured Transactions." A sincere effort has been made to simplify and clarify these chapters by introducing this material to the students through specific illustrations, and many new illustrations have been added so as to clarify the principle of law involved. Some of the rules in Article 2, "Sales," have been interspersed with the chapters in Part Two, "Contracts," in order to give the students a realistic and accurate view of the law of contracts.

The majority of the section references to the Code and the Partnership Act have been included in the textual material for ready reference to the Uniform Commercial Code and the Uniform Partnership Act in the Appendixes. Some of the problems at the end of the chapters are new, some have been deleted, and others have been rewritten for faster reading. Some new cases are included in this edition, and others have been deleted.

The material in this edition has been carefully researched by reading the leading professional publications in the field of business law and the decisions which have been reported since the publication of the fourth edition.

As students will note, we have retained the use of generic masculine pronouns in text references to individuals whose gender is not otherwise established. We wish to emphasize that we have done so solely for succinctness of expression and intend such references to apply equally to men and women.

This edition benefits from the constructive suggestions of many teachers in the colleges and universities where the fourth edition has been used. We express our grateful appreciation for these suggestions without in any way attempting to impose any responsibility on these teachers for any possible shortcomings in this book. We owe special thanks to our students at the University of Florida, whose suggestions and comments have been invaluable. We are particularly indebted to Mrs. Betty Taylor, law librarian, and the entire law library staff of the University of Florida for their cooperation in writing this edition.

Acknowledgment is gratefully made to the American Law Institute and the National Conference of Commissioners on Uniform State Laws for permission to reproduce the Uniform Partnership Act and the Official Text of the 1972 Uniform Commercial Code.

John W. Wyatt
Madie B. Wyatt

Part

1

INTRODUCTION

1
NATURE AND SOURCE OF BUSINESS LAW

The task of defining law is not an easy one. Neither is the task of choosing any one definition from among the many which have already been formulated by scholarly authors. A well-recognized definition, however, is the one given by Blackstone in his *Commentaries on the Laws of England.* Law is there defined as "a rule of civil conduct, prescribed by the supreme power of a state, commanding what is right and prohibiting what is wrong." For purposes of business law, it will suffice to say that this book will be devoted to the principles of law which are applied to the more common business transactions. Before turning to a study of these principles, however, it will be useful to review quickly the development of law in earlier centuries and examine briefly the source of law and the present-day American judicial system.

ORIGIN OF LAW

Development of the Common Law The time in which the common law was developed in England is one of the most fascinating periods in legal history. Before the Norman Conquest in 1066, feudal and other local courts administered a diversity of local customs which had been handed down for generations. After the

Conquest—especially during the reign of Henry II (1154–1189)—these courts gave way to the King's Courts. Royal judges went from London to all parts of the realm, seeking to discover and apply the customs having the widest vogue. Uniformity crystallized about the middle of the thirteenth century as a result of the enforcement of the doctrine of stare decisis. This doctrine declares that once a decision is reached by a superior court in a particular case it becomes a precedent, and all other cases of a similar kind are to be decided according to the same rule. The royal judges, therefore, gradually forged a law that was "common" to all England.

A brief review of the early common-law actions, the forms under modern statutes, and the various meanings of the term "common law" may give a clearer understanding of the development of the common law.

(1) *Common-Law Actions* Technical forms of actions were highly important under the strict common-law practice. They were known as actions ex contractu—from a contract—and actions ex delicto—from a tort.

The principal actions ex contractu were known as account, assumpsit, debt, and covenant. Account was used against a person who, by reason of some fiduciary relation, such as a guardian, should render an account to another; assumpsit was used for the recovery of damages for the breach of a simple contract where the sum due was uncertain as well as certain; debt was used to recover a certain specific sum of money, such as an undisputed debt; and covenant was used for the recovery of damages for the breach of a contract under seal.

The principal actions ex delicto were known as case, detinue, replevin, ejectment, and trover. The action of case, which was variously known as "case," "action on the case," and "trespass on the case," was used to recover damages for some indirect injury; detinue was used to recover personal property from one who acquired possession of the property rightfully, but retained the property without right; replevin was used to recover personal property where the taking, as well as the withholding, was wrongful; ejectment was used to recover the possession of real property; trespass de bonis—for goods carried away—was used to recover damages for injury to personal property when the property was carried away; trespass quare clausum—wherefore he broke the close—was used to recover damages for unlawful entry upon the land of the plaintiff; trespass vi et armis—with force and arms—was used to recover damages when the injury was against the plaintiff; and trover was used to recover damages for the conversion of personal property.

(2) *Forms under Statutes* The technical common-law forms of action are of interest historically, but they have been abolished in the states which have adopted the code practice. In other states, they have been abolished or modified. The code procedure had its origin in New York in 1848, and has been followed by many of the states. There are minor differences in steps of practice, but one action, known as the "civil action," has been substituted for the numerous common-law forms of action. This does not mean, however, that the substantive law underlying the common-law actions has been abolished. The fundamental and

substantial distinctions upon which the old common-law actions were based have not been changed.

(3) *Meanings of Common Law*   We should keep in mind that the term common law has various meanings, depending upon the sense in which the term is being used. The term is used to characterize the case law as distinguished from the law enacted by legislative bodies; it is used to denote the common-law system of jurisprudence in contrast to the civil-law system; and another use of the term is to distinguish the common law from equity.

Development of Equity   Adhering to precedent became such a habit in early common-law courts of England that later courts were unequal to the task of providing all the rights and remedies necessary in a later and more complex civilization. It then became a frequent practice for an aggrieved person to petition the King for relief which the common-law courts could not give. The King was supreme and could exercise the prerogative of taking cases out of the regular courts. The petitions brought before the King were entrusted to the chancellor, who, when the burden of compensating for the inadequacies of the common-law courts became too heavy, organized a court of equity. Equity and the common law, therefore, are both case law. But equity was flexible in contrast to the rigidity of common law. Among many other things, the chancellor was often able to take into consideration all the circumstances of a case in reaching a decision; he could exercise preventive measures by issuing injunctions against a threatened wrong; and he could settle the rights of all the parties.

(1) *Maxims of Equity*   It is clear that justice, rather than custom, is the basis of equity. This assertion is obvious by a resort to the following principal maxims of equity: Equity will not suffer a wrong without a remedy; equity regards the substance rather than the form; equity abhors a forfeiture; equity considers that done which ought to be done; where there are equal equities, the first in time will prevail; equity assists ignorance, but not carelessness; he who comes into equity must come with clean hands; he who seeks equity must do equity; equality is equity; equity aids the vigilant, not those who sleep on their rights, upon which maxim the doctrine of laches was founded.

Laches is an equitable doctrine which is intended to discourage stale demands. Each case must be decided on the facts of the particular case, but laches may be defined as such delay in asserting a right, taken in conjunction with other circumstances causing prejudice to the other party, as will operate as a bar for recovery. Laches does not, however, arise from mere delay or lapse of time. The party against whom laches is sought to be invoked must, in addition to the time element, be aware of his rights and fail to assert them. Suppose a debtor made an assignment of all of his property to the payment of a few of his creditors. These creditors obviously received more than they were entitled to receive. A creditor who received nothing but who made no inquiry of the transaction for five or six years would no doubt be guilty of laches and prevented from setting aside the transaction.

(2) *Equitable Remedies*   A court of equity will grant relief only when

there is no remedy at law or where the remedy at law is inadequate. A decree for money damages, therefore, will not be granted by a court of equity. Where a court of equity has taken jurisdiction of the subject matter of litigation, however, the court will do complete justice between the parties. A court of equity, therefore, will permit a recovery of damages if the complainant is entitled to both equitable relief and damages.

The courts of equity have developed a large number of remedies. Those of outstanding importance, which will appear throughout the chapters that follow, will be briefly described at this time.

(a) *Accountings* The jurisdiction of the courts of equity is exercised in a great variety of cases for an accounting, but particularly in those involving a fiduciary and trust relationship and those wherein a charge of fraud is made. Prominent examples are those between the beneficiaries and the trustee in a trust estate, and in the winding up of a partnership.

(b) *Partition* A suit for a partition of property is available when the property is held by two or more persons as co-owners, each owning an undivided interest. The co-owners may make a voluntary partition by mutual consent. If they fail to partition the property by mutual consent, any one may apply for a partition by judicial proceedings.

(c) *Specific Performance* A decree for specific performance is a means of compelling a person to do precisely what he ought to have done under the terms of the contract. Equity will not grant a decree for specific performance, however, if money damages awarded by a court of law would be adequate. Specific performance is ordinarily granted when the subject matter of the contract is of a special nature which cannot be readily replaced.

(d) *Quieting Title or Removal of Cloud from Title* A cloud on a title is an outstanding claim which impairs the title to the property. Suits in equity, therefore, may be maintained against persons, such as one who holds an apparent judgment lien, or one who claims to have a mortgage on the premises.

(e) *Cancellation or Re-formation of Contracts* Courts of equity will grant a decree for the cancellation or rescission of a contract where the injured party entered into the contract because of unreality of consent, such as fraud, misrepresentation, duress, undue influence, and mistake.

(f) *Injunction* Injunction is distincly an equitable remedy, which is used to restrain a person or persons from committing an act which appears to be against equity or conscience. It commonly refers to preventative relief. It has been used in many instances, such as to prevent interference with waters; to prevent the infringement of a copyright or a patent; to prevent unfair use of trade-marks and trade names; to restrain illegal monopolies; and, more recently, in connection with labor disputes.

(3) **Chancery and Common-Law Courts** During the development of equity, the chancery and common-law courts were kept separate and apart. This is also true in a few of the states in this country today. The separation of the two courts, however, has been abolished in most of the states. The prevailing practice today is to have a single court that will act as a court of law and as a court of

equity. This would depend, of course, upon whether or not the relief sought could be granted by a court of law or a court of equity. This does not mean that the substantive distinction between actions at law and suits in equity has been abolished. The legal and equitable remedies available must still be adhered to in applying the relief allowable.

Development of the Law Merchant The common-law courts and, to a lesser extent, the equity courts were not concerned with the practices of the trader. Therefore, in order to obtain quick relief and to protect themselves against the lawlessness and piracy of the times, the traders organized guilds whose membership was made up of all merchants trading in the market town. They established merchants' courts and administered a private law of commerce. The rules pronounced in these merchants' courts became known as the "law merchant." This law was gradually accepted by the common-law courts and is the origin of our insurance law, negotiable-instruments law, partnership law, and the law of sales.

The Civil Law The civil law, as distinguished from the common law, is the system of jurisprudence which was administered in the Roman Empire. The laws which were compiled and promulgated A.D. 529 by order of Emperor Justinian have supplied much of the foundation for the legal system in those countries which adopted the civil-law system. Roman influence is perceptible in the Napoleonic Code, and the French civil law has been used as a pattern for many Continental European and Latin American countries. One should not suppose that the two systems of jurisprudence are entirely different. Many cases today would reach the same result under the common law and the civil law. But the civil law is statutory, and the judges, in theory at least, decide each case on its independent merits by applying the law as it is enacted into the code and not in conformity with precedent. The terms "common law" and "civil law" are used to differentiate the system of jurisprudence developed in England from the system developed in Continental Europe. The characteristic feature of the civil law today, however, is its codified form.

American Law The English colonists brought to this country the common law of England, into which the system of equity that had been developed by the chancellors and the law merchant had become incorporated. The original thirteen states adopted this law, and the other states followed their example as they entered the Union. It should be mentioned, however, that the state of Louisiana was a part of the territory ceded to this country by France, and retained the civil law in effect at the time the grant was made. A few traces of the civil law will also be found in those states founded by people of the civil-law countries. But with these minor exceptions, business law in the United States had its origin in the English common-law system of jurisprudence.

CLASSIFICATIONS OF LAW

The various ways of classifying law depend upon the purpose in view. The classifications that follow are general and relatively simple.

Public and Private Law   Public law is that branch of law which is concerned with the state, including constitutional, administrative, and criminal law. Private law, as used in contradistinction to public law, includes that part of the law which is administered between private individuals. Suppose Brown commits a crime. He has committed a public wrong. He will, therefore, be proceeded against in a criminal action. Suppose Brown breaches his contract with Smith. He has violated a private right. Smith may, therefore, bring a civil action in his own name against Brown for damages for the breach.

Substantive and Adjective Law   Substantive law is that part of the law which the courts are established to administer. Substantive law regulates rights and duties. Adjective, or procedural, law provides a method for enforcing and maintaining rights and duties. Suppose Brown and Smith enter into a contract by the terms of which Brown agrees to render certain services for Smith, for which services Smith agrees to pay Brown $1,000. The substantive law will determine whether or not the contract is enforceable. The substantive law, in other words, determines whether or not Smith can compel Brown to perform the services. If Brown has performed the services, the substantive law will determine whether or not Brown can compel Smith to pay for the services so performed. If the contract is enforceable, the adjective law will determine how the contract may be enforced. Adjective law, in other words, embraces the pleadings and other papers prepared by the lawyer and the final judgment or decision rendered by the court.

Written and Unwritten Law   The important distinction between written and unwritten law is that unwritten law emanates from the judicial branch of the government and written law emanates from the legislative branch of the government. Written law includes constitutions, statutes, municipal ordinances, treaties, and the rules and regulations of the various governmental agencies. The unwritten law, frequently referred to as "common law" or "case law," consists of court decisions. The common law, however, grew up in unwritten form. The term "unwritten law," therefore, is used to characterize the law developed by the courts as unwritten law in contrast to the law enacted by legislative bodies as written law. This characterization of case law as unwritten law is somewhat misleading because the decisions of all courts of major importance are published in official volumes. The case law, therefore, turns out not to be unwritten law except in the sense that, unlike a statute, it has never been textually enacted.

SOURCE OF LAW

The written and the unwritten law described above are the source of our law today. These sources, therefore, will be used as a basis for the material presented in this book.

Constitutions and Statutes   The Constitution of the United States provides that the Constitution, the law of the United States made in pursuance thereof, and all treaties made under the authority of the federal government shall be the supreme law of the land. Each state also has its own constitution, which is the fundamental law of that particular state.

Each state, upon entering the Federal Union, retained all the power and sovereignty except that which was delegated to the federal government. We have, therefore, a dual system consisting of the United States Government and the state governments.

Statutes are enacted by Congress and the state legislatures. All laws, however, are subordinate to the United States Constitution and may be declared unconstitutional and invalid if they are not in accordance with it.

Ordinances   The appropriate officials, ordinarily the city commissioners or councilmen, have the authority to enact ordinances, or laws, for the purpose of regulating the activities in cities, towns, and villages. The ordinances are generally enacted for the preservation of the health, morals, safety, and welfare of dwellers in municipalities. They have been enacted to protect the community from innumerable things, such as nuisances, fire hazards, and storage of inflammable materials. They have also been enacted to regulate things, such as advertising billboards, construction of buildings, and the use of streets and sidewalks, or, more specifically, the vehicles thereon.

Public Administrative Law   At about the turn of the century both the national and state governments undertook in earnest to regulate the field of private business. This obviously enlarged the function of the governments and necessitated the formation of some kind of commission to perform the new duties thus acquired. The result was what is now commonly known as "administrative agencies." The number and scope of these agencies began to grow during the first quarter of the century, increasing rather gradually until about 1933. At that time, and for a decade thereafter, they mushroomed. A few administrative agencies are created by and receive their powers from constitutional provisions. The vast majority of them, however, are created by legislative enactments. The power of an agency, therefore, depends upon the statute which created it. This power may be administrative, legislative, judicial, or investigatory; it may, and probably often does, include all of these. The primary function of an agency is to carry out the purpose of the legislative enactment which created it. To that end it is endowed with power to hear and determine controversies and to issue orders. Its orders have the effect of a judgment or decree rendered by a regularly established court. The aggrieved party may request that the orders be reviewed, or the victorious party may request that they be enforced by a court. The process of adjusting the exercising of the agencies' powers to the traditional system of American law and courts is as yet unfinished. But the orders of the administrative agencies are, nevertheless, a prolific source of present-day law.

Uniform State Laws   The American Law Institute, an organization composed of a number of prominent lawyers, judges, and law teachers, has prepared and published a number of pamphlets and books containing nonstatutory rules of law in an attempt, among other things, to clarify and simplify the law. The publications, which are known as the "Restatement of the Law," are in the nature of a textbook or encyclopedia. They cover topics such as agency, contracts, property, torts, trusts, and many others. It is in no way derogatory of the fine public service rendered by the Institute to say that these Restatements are not the law unless and until they have been adopted by the courts. The courts have, however, frequently resorted to the Restatement in reaching a decision. The National Conference of Commissioners on Uniform State Laws must be given credit for a great portion of the statutory law which affects present-day business transactions. The Conference is composed of commissioners from each of the states, the District of Columbia, and Puerto Rico. Its chief purpose is the promotion of uniformity in state laws and judicial decisions throughout the United States. Some of the important acts which the conference has drafted in the field of commercial law are the Sales Act, the Negotiable Instruments Law, the Bills of Lading Act, the Warehouse Receipts Act, the Stock Transfer Act, the Conditional Sales Act, the Trust Receipts Act, the Partnership Act, and the Limited Partnership Act. However, all of these acts except the Partnership and the Limited Partnership Acts have been superseded by the Uniform Commercial Code.

Uniform Commercial Code   The Uniform Commercial Code is the result of a project of the National Conference of Commissioners on Uniform State Laws and the American Law Institute and is the first effort to promulgate a comprehensive act covering the entire field of commercial transactions. This tremendous undertaking was in reponse to a widespread movement for a substantial revision of the prior uniform acts and integrating them in view of present commercial practices. The Code, therefore, is presented as a unified whole, rather than in a series of separate uniform acts. The history of the law of commercial transactions has never undergone such a sweeping codification and rewriting. It has involved long and tedious hours of study by many experts in various fields of law and business.

The drafts were considered by committees of the Conference and the Institute, and the first edition of the Uniform Commercial Code was published in 1952. Supplement No. 1 was published in January, 1955, which amended various sections of the 1952 edition. During 1956 and 1957, in the light of recommendations of various state agencies and private groups who undertook exhaustive study of the Code, the Code was reconsidered. The result was the publication of the Code under the title 1957 Official Edition, which was revised in 1962. The latest edition of the Uniform Commercial Code is known as the 1972 Official Edition. It is to be realized, however, that the exact interpretations of the Code will not be found in the Code itself, but rather in the court decisions interpreting the Code.

The Code consists of eleven articles. Article 1, "General Provisions," states the purpose of the Code as follows: "To simplify, clarify, and modernize the law governing commercial transactions; to permit the continued expansion of commercial practices through custom, usage and agreement of the parties; and to make uniform the law among the various jurisdictions."

Article 2, "Sales," is a revision of the Uniform Sales Act. Quite a number of rules pertaining to the sale of goods, however, are appropriate to the law of contracts. These rules, therefore, will be interspersed throughout Part 2 of this book, "Contracts."

Article 3, "Commercial Paper," is a revision of the Uniform Negotiable Instruments Law. Article 4, "Bank Deposits and Collections," adopts many of the rules of the American Bankers Association Code. Article 5, "Letters of Credit," is a codification of the rules as developed by the decided cases. Article 6, "Bulk Transfers," is a codification of the bulk sales laws as enacted by the states. Article 7, "Documents of Title," is a consolidation and revision of the Uniform Warehouse Receipts Act, the Uniform Bills of Lading Act, and the provisions of the Uniform Sales Act relating to negotiation of documents of title. Article 8, "Investment Securities," is a negotiable-instruments law dealing with securities, and is a revision of a portion of the Uniform Negotiable Instruments Law and the Uniform Stock Transfer Act. Article 9, "Secured Transactions," supersedes legislation dealing with such security devices as chattel mortgages, conditional sales, trust receipts, factor's liens, and assignments of accounts receivable. Articles 10 and 11 provide for the repeal of prior legislation and the transition to and the effective date of the Code.

The Code has been enacted and is presently effective in the District of Columbia, the Virgin Islands, and all of the states except Louisiana.

PROBLEMS

1   Explain how the royal judges forged a law that was "common" to all England.

2   Explain how the law merchant was developed.

3   What is the distinction between the "written" and the "unwritten" law?

4   What is the distinction between the common-law forms of action of ex contractu and ex delicto?

5   What is the distinction between specific performance and injunction?

6   What is meant by the doctrine of stare decisis?

7   When will a court of equity grant a decree for the cancellation or rescission of a contract?

8   The buyer and the seller entered into a contract for the purchase and sale of a valuable antique clock. The seller breached the contract. What equitable remedy is available to the buyer?

9   What is the purpose of the Uniform Commercial Code?

10   Was the civil law a part of the early common law of England?

THE JUDICIAL SYSTEM

The framers of the Constitution of the United States, who planned our federal form of government, vested the judicial power of the government in one Supreme Court and "in such inferior courts as the Congress shall from time to time ordain and establish." The states were left free to provide any system of courts they might choose. The federal judicial power, therefore, is vested in the United States courts and the judicial power of the states is vested in courts of their own creation. This division of power quite obviously has resulted in different judicial systems—the federal judicial system and the state judicial systems—each with its own separate courts.

The procedure in federal and state courts is quite similar. The power of the federal courts to hear and determine controversies, however, is ordinarily limited to federal questions; the power of the state courts is much broader. The courts, in a few instances, have concurrent jurisdiction. It should be pointed out that the words "court" and "judge" are frequently used synonymously in statutes and in legal writings. A judge, while presiding over a court, is by courtesy called "the court." The word is also used to mean all persons assembled under authority of law for the administration of justice.

THE FEDERAL COURTS

The federal system of courts is traditionally classified as constitutional courts and legislative courts. This classification, however, is subject to some controversy. Article III, section 1, of the United States Constitution provides: "The judicial Power of the United States shall be vested in one supreme Court, and in such inferior Courts as the Congress may from time to time ordain and establish." Article I, section 8, clause 9, gives Congress the power "To constitute Tribunals inferior to the supreme Court." The United States Supreme Court, therefore, is obviously a constitutional court. The traditional theory, however, is that courts created by Congress pursuant to Article III, section 1, are constitutional courts and that courts created by Congress pursuant to Article I, section 8, clause 9, are legislative courts. Irrespective of this classification, the federal judicial system is composed of the United States Supreme Court, the courts of appeals, the district courts, and the various special courts which have been created by Congress from time to time.

The Supreme Court   The United States Supreme Court was organized pursuant to the Judiciary Act of September 24, 1789, and under existing law consists of a Chief Justice of the United States and eight associate justices. It has original jurisdiction of cases affecting ambassadors, public ministers, consuls, and those in which the states may be a party. The greater part of the work of the Supreme Court, however, is done by virtue of its appellate jurisdiction. Decisions made by the courts of appeals, the courts of the District of Columbia, the state courts, and, in a few instances, the federal district court may be reviewed by the Supreme Court. The power of the Supreme Court to review decisions of the state courts, however, is limited to those which involve a federal question. Nevertheless, the Supreme Court has the power to invalidate any federal or state statute by declaring it to be contrary to the United States Constitution.

Courts of Appeals   The United States is divided into eleven judicial circuits, with a court of appeals in every circuit. The *first* circuit includes Maine, Massachusetts, New Hampshire, Puerto Rico, Rhode Island; the *second,* Connecticut, New York, Vermont; the *third,* Delaware, New Jersey, Pennsylvania, Virgin Islands; the *fourth,* Maryland, North Carolina, South Carolina, Virginia, West Virginia; the *fifth,* Alabama, Canal Zone, Florida, Georgia, Louisiana, Mississippi, Texas; the *sixth,* Kentucky, Michigan, Ohio, Tennessee; the *seventh,* Illinois, Indiana, Wisconsin; the *eighth,* Arkansas, Iowa, Minnesota, Missouri, Nebraska, North Dakota, South Dakota; the *ninth,* Alaska, Arizona, California, Idaho, Montana, Nevada, Oregon, Washington, Guam, Hawaii; the *tenth,* Colorado, Kansas, New Mexico, Oklahoma, Utah, Wyoming. The *eleventh* circuit, which is not designated by number, is called and includes the District of Columbia. These courts are not endowed with any original jurisdiction but have appellate jurisdiction to review final decisions of the district courts. The judicial code also empowers these courts to review orders issued by certain federal agencies. These courts, therefore, may enforce, modify, or set aside orders issued by the Federal Trade Commission, the

Interstate Commerce Commission, the Federal Power Commission, the National Labor Relations Board, and other federal agencies. In the federal judicial system, a court of appeals is the court of last resort in the ordinary run of cases.

The District Courts   The United States is divided into judicial districts. The more populous states are divided into two or more districts, but every state constitutes at least one judicial district with one district court. These courts are the trial courts in the federal judicial system and have jurisdiction over all crimes and offenses against the United States. The federal district courts unquestionably have a wider jurisdiction over civil actions than any other court of first instance, which includes all cases arising under the United States Constitution and federal laws. A few of the important subjects covered by these laws are bankruptcy, admiralty, internal revenue, interstate commerce, national banks, patents, copyrights, and trade-marks. An action may also be filed in these courts where the amount in controversy exceeds $10,000, exclusive of interests and costs, and arises under the United States Constitution or other laws or treaties of the United States, or where the parties are citizens of different states.

Special Courts   The special courts which have been created by Congress include the court of claims, court of military appeals, the tax court, the customs court, and the court of customs and patent appeals.

THE STATE COURTS

The state courts vary in accordance with the needs of the particular state. In some states the law courts, the equity courts, the criminal courts, and various other courts are all separate and distinct and have different rules of practice. In other states, two or more of these courts have been merged into one. Special courts are found in all states to meet municipal and other particular problems. The state judicial systems, nevertheless, follow a fairly uniform pattern.

Lower Courts   These are various courts, such as municipal courts, county courts, police courts, traffic courts, courts of small claims, and justices of the peace. These courts have jurisdiction as indicated by their title, and are frequently referred to as "lower courts." The justices of the peace courts, which are presided over by a justice, open the door of justice near the homes of people and afford an inexpensive remedy for minor grievances. The jurisdiction of the courts of small claims is limited to relatively low maximum amounts which vary from one state to another, but the jurisdiction generally extends to tort claims as well as contractual claims.

Circuit Courts   The highest trial court, which is known variously as the circuit court, the superior court, the district court, and the court of common pleas, has general jurisdiction over civil, criminal, and equity matters. These courts may serve as appellate courts for the lower courts. Their jurisdiction frequently extends to two or three counties.

District Courts of Appeals   The function of these courts, which are intermediate courts of appeals, is to review decisions rendered in the lower and circuit courts. Some state systems have intermediate courts with jurisdiction for all classes of cases. Other state systems have intermediate courts with jurisdiction over specified classes of cases, such as a court of criminal appeals. In all states, however, an appeal may be taken to the state court of final resort.

Supreme Court of the State   In every state there is one court of final resort. This court is commonly known as the supreme court and, unless the legislature has provided for an intermediate court of appeals, has appellate jurisdiction over all controversies arising in the state trial courts. This court is always a court of record, and, unless a case can be taken to the Supreme Court of the United States because a federal question is involved, the decision of the state supreme court is final.

JUDICIAL PROCEDURE

The procedure for litigating a judicial controversy is prescribed by statute and varies in details from state to state. A summary of the characteristics common to different states as well as to the federal courts will, however, give a somewhat accurate description of the general method followed throughout the United States.

Instituting the Proceeding   A person who institutes a legal proceeding is, in most states, called the plaintiff or complainant, and the person against whom the proceeding is brought is called the defendant or respondent. The parties in an action at law are sometimes designated as plaintiff and defendant in contradistinction to the parties in a suit in equity, who are designated as complainant and respondent. This distinction has lost its importance in modern practice but is carefully observed in some of the older cases.

Jurisdiction   Jurisdiction, broadly stated, is the power of a court to hear and determine a controversy. The meaning of the word "jurisdiction," however, depends upon the sense in which the word is being used. A probate court would obviously have no jurisdiction over crimes. The jurisdiction of the courts in this respect has been previously mentioned. It now remains to discuss the manner in which the persons and property may be brought within the control of the court.

(1) *Persons*   The plaintiff voluntarily submits to the control of the court by filing his initial pleading, and the defendant is brought within the control of the court by a service of a writ of process, frequently known as a summons. The summons advises the defendant that an action has been started against him and that judgment will be taken by default unless he enters a defense within a specified time. The summons is usually accompanied by a copy of the initiatory pleading, labeled variously the "declaration," "petition," or "complaint," which contains a statement of the alleged claim.

The particular method of serving the summons upon the defendant is regulated by statutory enactments or by rules of the court. The two most widely used methods are actual, or personal, service and substituted, or constructive, service. Personal service means the actual delivery of the summons, or a copy thereof, to the person to whom it is directed or to some person who is authorized to receive it in his behalf. Constructive service means that the defendant is notified of the commencement of the action by some form of notice by mail or by publication. This method is used when the address of the defendant is unknown, when the defendant hides or conceals himself, or when the defendant is a nonresident of the state.

Service of process upon nonresident motorists and foreign corporations, as well as the method of reaching the property of a nonresident defendant, is worthy of mention.

(a) *Nonresident Motorists* The nonresident motorist who is at fault in an automobile accident has presented a particular problem, because he might leave the state before he could be served with process. This meant that the injured plaintiff might be compelled to travel to the place where the defendant could be found and institute his proceeding there in order to serve the defendant with process. Statutes have been enacted, therefore, which provide that service of process may be made upon some state officer, usually the secretary of state. These statutes require the state officer to mail a notice of the action to the defendant at his last known address. In justification of these statutes, it has been said that the operation of an automobile upon the highways by a nonresident amounts to consent by the nonresident to accept process through some designated state official.

(b) *Foreign Corporations* A corporation chartered in one state and doing business in another state is known as a foreign corporation. Such a corporation must comply with certain prerequisites before doing intrastate business in the other state. These prerequisites are discussed in Chapters 42 to 47, on corporations. It should be mentioned at this time, however, that a foreign corporation must appoint some local agent upon whom process may be served so that a personal judgment may be obtained against the foreign corporation.

(2) *Property* A court has jurisdiction over all property, real or personal, within its borders. This is true irrespective of whether the owner is a resident or nonresident.

(a) *Writ of Attachment* The law with respect to imprisonment of debtors which was generally recognized in the colonies at the time of the Revolution underwent a change. Imprisonment for debt was abolished toward the middle of the last century. It then became necessary to formulate some substitute for imprisonment for debt, which resulted in the enactment of attachment statutes.

Suppose plaintiff, an unsecured creditor, learns that defendant, his debtor, is planning to abscond or hide his assets in some manner in order to avoid paying his debt. The plaintiff may, in these circumstances, ask the court to issue a writ of attachment. The plaintiff may do this before he institutes his proceedings, at the time of service of process, during the pretrial proceedings, or at any other time prior to judgment. The early statutes permitted the issuance of a writ of attachment where it was shown that the defendant had concealed himself within the state to avoid service of process, or where the defendant was a nonresident, or had departed from the state. The statutes differ greatly in their details, but it is not uncommon to find a statute which authorizes an attachment when the debtor has assigned, disposed of, or secreted or is about to assign, dispose of, or secrete property with intent to defraud his creditors.

The attachment itself is an order by the court addressed to the sheriff, or other officer, to levy upon and seize property of the debtor. It is a method of seizing the property of a debtor in advance of final judgment and holding it in order to satisfy a judgment if a judgment is finally obtained. The attachment also subjects the property of the debtor in those instances where personal service cannot be obtained upon the debtor to the payment of a claim of a creditor.

(b)   *Attaching Property of Nonresidents*   The court cannot award the plaintiff a personal judgment for money damages if the defendant is a nonresident of the state and has been given notice of the proceedings by publication. The court may, however, attach any property belonging to the defendant which is within the jurisdiction of the court to satisfy the claim of the plaintiff. The claim of the plaintiff, however, must be reduced to a judgment before such property can be sold in satisfaction of the judgment claim. This is a type of judgment which is against the property of the debtor and is known as a judgment "in rem" or "quasi in rem."

Pretrial Proceedings   The defendant may desire not to defend the action against him, in which case a judgment is entered by default in favor of the plaintiff. The defendant, however, may desire to defend the action but finds it advantageous to make certain preliminary objections before answering the complaint. He may claim by way of defense that the facts stated in the complaint do not constitute a cause of action or that the action was brought in the wrong court, or he may assert various other defenses. The merits of these objections will be presented to and argued before the judge, who will dismiss the action, permit the plaintiff to amend the complaint, or overrule the objections. If the objections are overruled, the defendant must file an answer stating the facts supporting his defense. Or the answer may also allege a claim against the plaintiff—a counterclaim—and the plaintiff will then assert objections to the counterclaim, which must be disposed of by legal maneuvers similar to those used to dispose of the objections of the complaint. The disposition of all preliminary objections, however, leaves the issues in dispute for litigation. The attorney for the plaintiff then notifies the clerk of the court to place the case on the court calendar. In many states, the judge and the attorneys have a pretrial conference to determine the exact issues that remain in dispute, thus eliminating unnecessary litigation during the trial of the case.

The Trial   The parties may elect to waive the right to a jury trial; in an equity case, findings of fact may be made by the court without a jury. In criminal cases, however, and certain other cases such as torts and breach of contract, a jury is usually impaneled to find the facts, apply the law as declared by the court, and render a verdict. The first important step in the trial is the impaneling of a jury. The attorneys examine the prospective jurors, and if good cause is shown why a juror cannot give a fair and impartial verdict, he is challenged for cause and excused from the jury. The peremptory challenge, which does not require that any cause be shown, may also be used to excuse a juror, but the number of peremptory challenges that may be used is limited. When the jury box is filled, the jurors are required to take an oath to perform their duties as jurors.

The attorneys make an opening statement of what they expect to prove by the trial. The plaintiff and his witnesses testify upon direct examination, and each is subject to cross-examination by the attorney for the defendant. The defendant and his witnesses then testify upon direct and cross-examination. In each instance, however, there may be redirect examination and re-cross-examination. When the testimony is concluded, the attorney for the plaintiff and the attorney for the defendant each make a final argument to the jury, each summarizing the evidence and urging a verdict in favor of his client. The judge then instructs the jury as to the law in order to help the jurors reach a decision on the facts. The decision they reach is called the "verdict" and is read by the judge in open court.

The plaintiff or the defendant may argue against the verdict. The plaintiff, for example, may argue that the amount of the damages assessed against the defendant is inadequate. But assuming there is no argument, the court will ordinarily enter a judgment in compliance with the verdict.

Enforcement of Judgments   It is quite obvious that some method must be provided for enforcing the judgment if the defendant refuses to pay the amount due the plaintiff. Two common remedies for accomplishing this result are the issuance of a writ of execution for the seizure and sale of property of the judgment debtor and a garnishment proceeding.

(1)   *Writ of Execution*   The principles governing the levy of a writ of execution and a writ of attachment are very similar. The writ of execution in satisfaction of a judgment, however, is not issued until after a money judgment has been rendered. The statutes also commonly give the defendant an opportunity to pay the debt voluntarily. It is generally provided, therefore, that the writ of execution shall not issue against the property of the defendant for a short time after the judgment has been rendered.

(2)   *Garnishment*   The function of garnishment is to make available for the payment of one's debts certain property which is in the possession of some third person. This method of enforcing a judgment is ordinarily used when the defendant has no money or property in his possession, but money or property is due him from some third person. The successful plaintiff, in these circumstances, may institute garnishment proceedings to satisfy his judgment. The third person against whom garnishment proceedings are brought is called the garnishee.

Appellate Procedure   One or both of the parties may appeal to a superior court, which court may review, reverse, correct, or affirm the decision of the lower court. The record of the lower court, or a history of the case, is filed with the superior court. Both parties then submit briefs consisting of decisions reached in similar cases. In an effort to persuade the superior court that his contention is the correct one, each party's attorney points out what he believes constitute errors committed by the lower court. The points are frequently argued orally before the court. The members of the superior court consider the case, and one member renders the decision of the majority, writing a supporting opinion which is published in one of several reports. The decision may take various forms. The appellate court may affirm the decision of the lower court; it may reverse the lower court; it may write an opinion and instruct the lower court to enter a judgment in accordance with the opinion; or it may remand the case for a new trial.

The Reported Decision   The decisions and opinions of the appellate court are found in state reports and also in a series of reporters embracing the whole United States and comprising the National Reporter System. This system divides the states into seven regional reporter groups: North Western, South Western, North Eastern, South Eastern, Atlantic, Pacific, and Southern. The decisions of the United States district courts are reported in the Federal Supplement, and the decisions of the United States courts of appeals are reported in the Federal Reporter. The decisions of the United States Supreme Court are found in several reporters.The one used in this book is the United States Reports.

The cases in this book were taken from these reports and are presented in the following order: (1) the title of the case, (2) the book or volume in which it is reported, (3) a description of the parties to the action, (4) a summary of the facts, (5) excerpts from the opinion of the court, and (6) the decision.

The title of the case consists of the names of the parties to the litigation. At the present time, it is common practice to retain the names of the parties in the order in which they originally appeared in the trial court. In the early reporters and in some jurisdictions today, however, the names of the parties are reversed when the defendant appeals the case. The names of the parties on appeal, therefore, may appear either in the order in which they appeared in the lower court or in reverse order. The citation to the regional reporter in which the case is found follows the title of the case. The parties to the appeal are designated as appellant and appellee. The lower-court description of the parties is indicated in parentheses if the names of the parties were reversed on appeal.

Let us illustrate with the case on page 54. *Simmerman v. Fort Hartford Coal Co.* is the title of the case; 221 S.W.2d 442 indicates that the case is reported in volume 221 of the South Western Reporter, second series, page 442. The case was decided in Kentucky in 1949. Mrs. Jesse R. Simmerman, the defendant in the lower court, appealed the case, and the names of the parties were reversed. The facts of the case have been rewritten, and those facts which are not necessary to explain the principle of law involved have been omitted. References to citations appearing in the opinion of the court have also been omitted.

Full Faith and Credit   The framers of the United States Constitution wanted to help transform the states into a nation, and one of the many ways to accomplish this result was to include a provision in the Constitution which states that "full faith and credit shall be given in each state to the public acts, records, and judicial proceeding of every other state." In pursuance of its powers, therefore, Congress prescribed methods whereby records should be authenticated. Recognition by the other states would therefore be required. For example, a valid personal judgment rendered in New York, when properly authenticated, must be recognized by California or any other sister state. This means that a judgment which has been entered in one state may be carried into another state in which the defendant has property. The property may then be subjected to a forced sale in order to satisfy or pay the judgment. Full faith and credit does not apply to judgments rendered in foreign nations.

Res Judicata   Res judicata is a part of most, if not all, of the legal systems of all the civilized people of the world. Litigation would be endless without it. Public tranquility, justice, and expedience, as well as the best interest of the parties, make this doctrine immanently desirable.

Res judicata may be defined in the following language: A final judgment, rendered by a court of competent jurisdiction, is binding and conclusive on the parties with respect to the rights, questions, and issues. These rights, questions, and issues may not again be litigated by the parties in the same court or any other court of competent jurisdiction. This doctrine obviously protects persons from the harassment and vexation of litigious opponents. Certainty, dignity, and respect for judicial decisions are thereby made possible.

A judgment which is res judicata in the state in which it was rendered is therefore res judicata in a sister state under the full faith and credit clause of the Constitution. A judgment may be attacked, however, if the court which rendered it did not have jurisdiction over the defendant, the subject matter, or the controversy, or if it was rendered because of fraud, perjury, or collusion of the witnesses or the jurors.

PROBLEMS
1   What is meant by the word "jurisdiction"?
2   How may process be served on a nonresident motorist?
3   How may a summons be served upon the defendant?
4   What is meant by full faith and credit?
5   When may the property of a nonresident of a state be sold to satisfy a judgment?
6   Explain how the plaintiff is brought within the control of the court.
7   What is the distinction between personal service and constructive service of a summons?
8   Enumerate two common remedies for the enforcement of judgments.
9   Is it essential that every case be tried by a jury?
10   What is meant by res judicata?

3

THE NATURE OF
TORTS AND CRIMES

It is necessary to insert at this point a chapter on torts and crimes since acts which may constitute a tort or crime are found in the chapters that follow.

TORTS

The law of torts pertains to civil wrongs. Broadly speaking, a tortious act, for which a person may be liable in a civil action, is the commission or omission by one person, without right, of an act which results in injury to the person, property, or reputation of another person. This definition, however, is not exclusive. A tort and a tortious act may be defined variously. A tort defined as a breach of a duty which the law of the state, as distinguished from a contract, has imposed is more appropriate to a study of business law.

A few common specific torts have been selected for the purpose of illustrating more clearly the nature of the law of torts.

Negligence   The word "negligence" has been defined often and variously, but seldom satisfactorily. Inevitably, terms used in the definition themselves require extensive definition. It is quite clear, however, that the word "negligence" signifies a failure to use reasonable care. A failure by one person to use reasonable care will give rise to an action for damages by the injured party; a failure to use reasonable care on the part of the injured party will defeat the action on grounds of contributory negligence. Law books are filled with cases in which compensation is sought for injuries that result from accidents, and the usual argument pertains to the negligence of the respective parties. The cases include automobile accidents, railway accidents, and accidents on sidewalks and in every other conceivable place. An action for negligence, however, is predicated on the breach of some duty on the part of one person to protect another against injury, and the negligence of the respective parties is determinative of the liability for the breach of that duty. Perhaps the duty an owner of premises owes to trespassers, licensees, and invitees provokes a sufficient portion of the litigation to justify particular attention.

The general rule says an owner owes no duty to a trespasser other than that of refraining from willfully injuring him. The rule, however, is not without its many exceptions: Many courts have held an owner is under a duty to notify trespassers of known perils. Many courts have adopted the "attractive nuisance" doctrine. This doctrine provides that an owner who maintains upon his premises a condition which is dangerous to children of tender years and which may reasonably be expected to attract children of tender years is under a duty to exercise reasonable care to protect them.

It is generally said that the owner of premises is under a duty to a licensee—a person who enters upon the property of another for his own convenience, benefit, or pleasure—to refrain from being actively negligent. It is also generally said that an owner in occupation of premises, who directly or impliedly invites others to enter the premises for some purpose of advantage to him, violates his duty to the invitee when he negligently allows conditions to exist which imperil the safety of persons coming upon the premises. The extent of his duty, as a general rule, is to use ordinary care to have his premises in a reasonably safe condition. This rule precludes the possibility of the owner's being an insurer of the safety of the invitee. Recovery is ordinarily denied, however, if it appears that the injured person could have avoided the injury by the exercise of due care.

The law is further extended by the fact that it is often difficult to distinguish between an invitee and a licensee. [*Arthur v. Standard Engineering Co.*, p. 25.]

Conversion A conversion signifies an unlawful act which deprives a person of possession of his personal property. It may consist in an unlawful taking by such means as force, theft, or fraud. A person who comes lawfully into the possession of personal property of another, however, may thereafter commit a tortious act which will constitute conversion. An unqualified refusal by a bailee to surrender the property to the rightful owner upon his demand amounts to conversion. A person in lawful possession may also commit conversion through the misuse or abuse of the property. An improper disposal, delivery, or transfer of possession to one not authorized by the owner to receive the property, therefore, is a conversion of the property. [*Harlan v. Shank Fireproof Warehouse Co.*, p. 26.]

Nuisance The word "nuisance" denotes that class of wrongs arising from an unwarranted use of property lawfully occupied by one person which restricts the ordinary use of property lawfully occupied by another person. It is practically impossible to enumerate the various unwarranted uses of property that may be classified as nuisances. Moreover, what constitutes a nuisance at a particular time and place may not constitute a nuisance at another time and place. Loud and boisterous noises, for example, shouting and singing, especially at nighttime, may be a nuisance. The pollution of air with noxious fumes, gases, vapors, smoke, and soot may be a nuisance. A business enterprise and occupation, although lawful in itself, may be a nuisance. When the question of a nuisance arises, the courts are frequently confronted by the problem of striking a balance between the interests of the private-property owner and those of a growing industry. [*Kentucky & W. Va. Power Co. v. Anderson*, p. 27.]

Assault and Battery Statutory definitions of assault, usually declaratory of the common law, describe the act as an unlawful attempt, coupled with a present ability, to commit a violent injury upon the person of another. A battery is the actual unlawful use of force or violence. Some courts hold that an intent to do harm is the essence of an assault; others hold that actual intent is not an essential element of assault if the conduct is such as to convey to the mind of the victim a well-grounded fear of violence. In a civil action of assault and battery, the element of intent is usually held to be immaterial provided the act causing the injury was wrongful. Ordinarily, the fact that the act itself was wrongful and unlawful will sustain a civil action for assault and battery.

False Imprisonment It is sometimes assumed that false imprisonment is limited to unlawful arrest of a person without a proper warrant. This assumption is erroneous. False imprisonment may easily result from any acts which deprive a person of his personal liberty, provided the detention is unlawful. It is well settled that the essence of an action for false imprisonment is the unlawfulness of the detention. It is likewise well settled that an owner of property has the right to take action by confinement in defense of his property. The problem to be solved, therefore, revolves around the dividing line between those factual situations when a person is or is not justified in detaining a suspect. It is quite clear that actual physical force is not a prerequisite to false imprisonment. [*Parrott v. Bank of America Nat'l Trust & Sav. Ass'n*, p. 28.]

Defamation The word "defamation" is understood to mean the offense of injuring the reputation of a person by libel or slander. Libel is malicious publication tending to injure the reputation of a person and expose him to public hatred, contempt, or ridicule; it may be expressed either in printing or writing, by signs or pictures; it may be against the memory of one who is dead or the reputation of one who is alive. Slander is confined to defamatory words spoken. It is not necessary that the defamatory statement be made known to the general public. The requirement of "publication" is satisfied if it is communicated to only one person other than the person defamed. The statement need not be made in a direct and open manner, but if it conveys a degrading imputation, it is defamatory. To put the words in the form of a question, or to accompany the words with an injunction of secrecy, will in no wise render them any less libelous.

Certain communications, however, are privileged—one which would be defamatory except for the circumstances under which it was made—and for that reason are not within the rules imposing liability for defamation. Privileged communications may be either absolute or conditional. The law, in order to promote the public welfare, recognizes legislative and judicial proceedings as absolutely privileged. Members of the legislature, judges of courts, jurors, lawyers, and witnesses, therefore, may generally speak their minds freely during the course of procedure without incurring the risk of criminal prosecution or an action for the recovery of damages provided their statements are relevant to the case. The communications which the law recognizes as conditionally privileged, however, are broader in scope. Any communication made in good faith on any subject in which the person communicating has an interest, or in reference to which he has a duty, is privileged if made to a person having a corresponding interest or duty. The defense of conditionally privileged communications is not available to a person, however, unless both the person by whom it is made and the person to whom it is made have an interest or duty in respect to the communication, nor is it available if the words were spoken from some motive other than the right and duty which created the privilege. As a general rule, therefore, in order to justify a defamatory statement, not only must the statement be true, but it must have been made without malice from good motives and for justifiable ends.

Deceit The word "deceit" is the name of the action brought to recover damages for fraud. Deceit consists of any false representations by which one person deceives another who has no means of detecting the fraud, and which results in damage to the latter. The false representation may be made by the positive assertion of a falsehood, a concealment of the truth, or the creation of a false impression. It may be written or oral; it may be made by any trick or device. It is quite clear, however, that an intent to deceive is an indispensable element to a tort action of deceit for the recovery of damages. Deceit is an inescapable portion of the law of contracts and sales. Fraud and deceit, therefore, are given more complete treatment in discussing the law of contracts in Chapter 9, "Reality of Consent."

Trespass The more significant forms of trespass are trespass to the person, trespass to chattels, and trespass to realty. Assault, battery, and false imprisonment are forms of trespass to the person. Conversion is a form of trespass to chattels. Nuisance is a form of trespass to land. A person commits trespass if he erects or maintains buildings, fences, or any structure projecting over the land of another. Driving cattle over another person's land or causing dirt to roll on it are acts constituting a trespass. Broadly stated, any unlawful act which interferes with the person, property, or relative rights of another person is a trespass.

Replevin   Replevin is a possessory action. It is a proceeding by statute for the recovery of the possession of a chattel. The action at common law was used to recover personal property where the taking, as well as the withholding, was wrongful. This rule, however, has been changed. The action now lies to recover possession of chattels that are unlawfully detained, and is founded on the claim that the defendant wrongfully withholds the chattels sought to be recovered. The action is not one to determine claims sounding in tort, but it is founded upon a tortious detention. It is a proceeding partly in rem to regain possession of the chattels and partly in personam to recover damages for the detention. It should be pointed out, however, that the primary relief sought in replevin is the return of the property in specie. Damages are ordinarily merely incidental. A number of statutory proceedings exist in some states which partake of the nature of replevin. A quite prominent proceeding is known as "claim and delivery." As a general rule, however, replevin is the proper remedy to recover the possession of every kind of chattel.

CRIMES

The law of crimes pertains to offenses against the state. The offense, however, may be a tort as well as a crime. Assault and battery, for example, may be both a tort and a crime. The common law of England as to crimes was brought to America by the colonists, but it is probably not now in practical operation in any of the states. All crimes against the United States are statutory in character; they are either enumerated and defined by congressional enactment or are found in the Constitution. The statutes of every state, moreover, define the various crimes and prescribe the punishment for each.

Crimes include treason, felonies, and misdemeanors. The Federal Constitution provides that treason against the United States "shall consist only in levying war against them, or in adhering to their enemies, giving them aid and comfort." Apart from treason, all other crimes are either felonies or misdemeanors. State statutes, for the most part, declare whether or not any particular offense shall be considered a felony or a misdemeanor. The distinction most commonly given is that all crimes punishable by death or by imprisonment in the state prison are felonies and all other crimes are misdemeanors. The statutory definitions of crimes are not uniform. A felony, however, implies a crime of a graver or more atrocious nature than crimes designated as misdemeanors. Offenses such as murder, arson, and grand larceny are commonly classified as felonies. Offenses such as drunkenness, disorderly conduct, and assault are commonly classified as misdemeanors.

CASES

Arthur v. Standard Engineering Co.,   193 F.2d 903 (D.C. 1951). Action by John H. Arthur, plaintiff, against Standard Engineering Company, defendant. Plaintiff was an employee of an electrical subcontractor. Defendant was a steamfitting subcontractor, whose employees constructed a rude scaffold for their own use in accomplishing their part of the work. Plaintiff and other electrical workers asked and received the permission of the defendant-company to use the scaffold. Plaintiff was using the scaffold when the long supporting board broke, and he fell about 15 feet and sustained serious injuries. He thereupon brought this action to recover damages from the steamfitting subcontractor whose employees constructed the scaffold.

Wilbur K. Miller, Circuit Judge: It is well settled that an invitor owes his invitee the duty of furnishing him with reasonably safe premises or appliances and will be held liable for injuries caused by a negligent failure to perform the duty. . . . It is equally well established that a licensor is not liable in damages for the injuries of a mere licensee, unless the injuries were the result of the licensor's active negligence. . . .

The case turns, therefore, on the question whether an employee of a subcontractor is in the legal status of a licensee or that of an invitee when he uses, either by permission expressly given or implied from established custom, a scaffold erected by the employees of another subcontractor for their own use.

The Supreme Court said in *Bennet v. Louisville & N. Railroad Co.* . . . "The principle . . . appears to be that invitation is inferred where there is a common interest or mutual advantage, while a license is inferred where the object is the mere pleasure or benefit of the person using it. . . ."

We adopt, therefore, the mutual benefit test for determining whether the plaintiff was a licensee or an invitee. . . .

The true test under the mutual advantage theory is whether the owner of a scaffold or other appliance receives benefit or advantage from the permitted use by another of that particular piece of equipment. If so, the user is an invitee; if not, he is a licensee. . . . We conclude that plaintiff was a licensee. [DECISION FOR DEFENDANT]

Harlan v. Shank Fireproof Warehouse Co., 29 N.E.2d 1003 (Ind. 1951). Action by Gertrude Harlan, plaintiff, against Shank Fireproof Warehouse Company, defendant. Plaintiff delivered to the warehouse and storage building of the defendant in Indianapolis, Indiana, certain household goods and other personal property for storage. About one month thereafter, the defendant shipped by freight all the goods so stored to Los Angeles, California, and notified the plaintiff that the goods were there. The reason for such shipment is not entirely clear, but the evidence disclosed that the shipment was made without authority, knowledge, or consent of the plaintiff. Plaintiff brought an action to recover damages for the unauthorized shipping of the property.

Stevenson, Justice: This court has frequently had occasion to recite the elements which constitute conversion.

Conversion, as a tort, consists either in the appropriation of the personal property of another to the party's own use and benefit, or in its destruction, or in exercising dominion over it, in exclusion and defiance of the rights of the owner or lawful possessor, or in withholding it from his possession, under a claim and title inconsistent with the owner's. . . . The essence of every conversion is the wrongful invasion of the right to, and absolute dominion over, the property of another.

Clearly, the acts involved in taking the plaintiff's household furnishings out of storage in Indianapolis, Indiana, and shipping them to Los Angeles, California, without the order or approval of the plaintiff, were the exercise of an unauthorized dominion and control over such property. This, in our opinion, amounts to a conversion. [DECISION FOR PLAINTIFF]

Kentucky & W. Va. Power Co. v. Anderson, 156 S.W.2d 857 (Ky. 1941). Action by James P. Anderson, plaintiff, against Kentucky & West Virginia Power Co., Inc., defendant. Plaintiff acquired a five-room frame dwelling in 1927. Defendant acquired the adjoining lot in 1936 and erected an electric substation about seven feet from plaintiff's fence and fifteen feet from his house. There are four transformers, but only three are used at a time. Each consists in part of an iron core surrounded by a series of coils. The current is reduced by induction. The core is magnetized and demagnetized 120 times a second, and this causes vibration or pulsation, which produces a constant humming or buzzing. Persons in the house were annoyed and disturbed in their conversations and sleep, and the use of the radio was practically destroyed. Plaintiff thereupon brought an action to recover damages on the ground of nuisance, and the court instructed the jury that the right of recovery of damages depended upon whether or not "the noises constantly and continuously emanating from the transformers" were of "such character and degree as to produce actual physical discomfort and annoyance to a person of ordinary health and of normal or average sensibilities, occupying the home of the plaintiff on his property adjoining the property of the defendant."

Stanley, Commissioner: There can be no doubt but that commercial and industrial activities which are lawful in themselves may become nuisances if they are so offensive to the senses that they render the enjoyment of life and property uncomfortable. It is no defense that skill and care have been exercised and the most improved methods and appliances employed to prevent such result. Of course, the creation of trifling annoyances and inconvenience does not constitute an actionable nuisance, and the locality and surroundings are of importance. The determining factor when noise alone is the cause of complaint is not its intensity or volume. It is that the noise is of such character as to produce actual physical discomfort and annoyance to a person of ordinary sensibilities, rendering adjacent property less comfortable and valuable. If the noise does that, it can well be said to be substantial and unreasonable in degree; and reasonableness is a question of fact dependent upon all the circumstances and conditions. There can be no fixed standard as to what kind of noise constitutes a nuisance. It is true some witnesses in this case say they have not been annoyed by the humming of these trans-formers, but the fact is not conclusive as to the non-existence of the cause of complaint, the test being the effect which is had upon an ordinary person who is neither sensitive nor immune to the annoyance concerning which the complaint is made. In the absence of evidence that the complainant and his family are supersensitive to distracting noises, it is to be assumed that they are persons of ordinary and normal sensibilities. [DECISION FOR PLAINTIFF]

Parrott v. Bank of America Nat'l Trust & Sav. Ass'n, 217 P.2d 89 (Cal. 1950). Action by Zella M. Parrott against Bank of America National Trust & Savings Association and others, defendants. A customer of the Los Angeles Shatto-Wilshire branch of the defendant bank reported to the branch manager that she had made a deposit of $500, consisting of $280.30 in cash and the remainder in the form of five checks; that she did not have her passbook at the time and was not certain whether she had received a duplicate deposit slip, but, in any case, she could not find it; that she returned with her passbook later and requested the same teller with whom she made the deposit to make the entry; and that the teller informed her that she could find no record of the deposit. The branch manager thereupon pointed out the plaintiff, who was employed as a teller, and asked if she was the teller. The customer said "yes."

At about 3 P.M., plaintiff was summoned to the desk of the branch manager and, in the presence of the bank inspector and the branch manager, was told by the inspector that the deposit was missing and that he believed it had been made. Plaintiff denied any knowledge of it. The inspector said he believed she had taken the cash deposit and had destroyed the checks, inasmuch as they had not cleared. He told plaintiff that it would look very bad for her and that the only assumption he could arrive at was that she was guilty and that the best thing for her to do would be to admit it and agree to make restitution. Otherwise the matter would be turned over to the FBI and the bank would prosecute and that it would be in the papers, her folks would find out about it, and it would be very expensive and embarrassing. Plaintiff denied taking the money throughout this interview, and she stated that she did not understand why she should sign a confession and make restitution. The inspector told plaintiff that if she signed a confession and made restitution, the bank would probably drop the matter. By this time, plaintiff was nervous, frightened, and crying and agreed to sign a confession. It was then decided that plaintiff should go to the downtown office to sign the confession. It was then about 4:30 or 5 P.M.

As plaintiff left the bank with the inspector, she felt faint and stumbled. The inspector helped her into his car. They drove to the downtown office, but after a telephone conversation with her fiancé, she refused to sign the confession. The inspector told her it would be far better to sign a confession and make restitution, but plaintiff refused. This interview lasted until 6:30 or 6:45 P.M.

Several days thereafter, the customer reported that she had been mistaken and that she had found the deposit. Plaintiff then brought this action to recover damages for false imprisonment.

White, Justice: The use of actual physical force in detaining a person is not a prerequisite to unlawfully violating the personal liberty of another. All that is necessary to make out a charge of false imprisonment is that the individual be restrained of his liberty without any sufficient complaint or authority therefor, and it may be accomplished by words or acts which such individual fears to disregard. Temporary detention is sufficient, and the use of actual physical force is not necessary. . . . Any unlawful exercise of force, or express or implied threat of force, by which in fact any person is deprived of his liberty and compelled to remain where he does not wish to remain is a false imprisonment. . . . It should be noted that while it is true that where a person has reasonable grounds to believe that another is taking his property *as distinguished from those cases where the offense has been completed,* he is justified in detaining the suspect for a reasonable length of time for the purpose of investigation in a reasonable manner. The evidence in the instant case clearly discloses that plaintiff was not detained for the purpose of investigation, but, on the contrary, was detained for the purpose of securing a confession to the theft of money at a prior time and to obtain restitution of said money from plaintiff. . . . The jury was entitled to reasonably infer from the above evidence that the bank officials had not proceeded carefully and had not acted upon probable cause. [DECISION FOR PLAINTIFF]

PROBLEMS

1 Explain the duty that an invitor owes to his invitee.

2 What is meant by the "attractive nuisance" doctrine?

3 What is the distinction most commonly given between a misdemeanor and a felony?

4 Is trespass limited to the trespass to chattels?

5 What is the distinction between an absolute and a conditionally privileged communication?

6 Allen contended that slander may not be committed unless the defamatory statement is made to the general public. Is this contention correct?

7 Jones built a structure projecting over certain real estate belonging to Smith. Does this unlawful act constitute conversion?

8 What is the distinction between assault and battery?

9 What is the distinction between the law of torts and the law of crimes?

10 Why are judicial proceedings recognized by the law as being privileged?

Part

2

CONTRACTS

4
INTRODUCTION TO CONTRACTS

Simply stated, a contract is a binding agreement to do or to refrain from doing some lawful thing. Before studying the law of contracts, however, it is necessary to be familiar with (1) the kinds of contracts, (2) the distinction between real and personal property, and (3) the essential elements of a contract. The meaning of these words and terms will become more clear as you proceed with the study of the law of contracts.

CLASSIFICATION

Contracts may be classified in various ways depending upon the element in them which is emphasized. They may be grouped (1) as to formality—formal or simple; (2) as to enforceability—valid, void, voidable, or unenforceable; (3) as to compliance—executed or executory; (4) as to reciprocal obligations—unilateral or bilateral; and (5) as to intent—express or implied. One further kind of contract should be mentioned: the quasi contract.

Formal or Simple   Formal contracts include contracts of record, contracts under seal, and negotiable instruments. All others are called simple contracts and, unless they belong to a class of contracts required to be evidenced by a writing, may be oral or written.

racts of record are those entered on the records of courts of competent jurisdiction and include recognizances and judgments. The element of promise, however, is lacking in a judgment, and for this reason judgments are sometimes omitted in the classification of formal contracts.

Under early common law, a contract under seal meant that the obligor had affixed his own private seal to the document by making an imprint on a wafer, soft wax, or some other substance with a signet ring or other device. An agreement was not enforceable unless it was in the form of a sealed instrument. The significance of the seal, however, is historical because the common-law definition of what constitutes a seal has been extended to include the written letter "L.S." (*locus sigilli*), the written word "seal," or even a scroll or scrawl; and in most states the distinction in terms between sealed and unsealed contracts has been abolished. The Code abolishes the law of seals with respect to a contract for sale or an offer to buy or sell goods.

The Code classifies negotiable instruments as checks, promissory notes, drafts, and certificates of deposit. Negotiable instruments are discussed in detail in Part 4, "Commercial Paper."

Valid or Void A valid contract contains all the essential elements of a contract. A void contract lacks one or more of the essential elements of a contract. Such a contract produces no legal obligation and is, therefore, invalid.

Voidable Contracts A voidable contract is one in which one or both parties thereto have the power to avoid the legal relation created by the contract. Infancy, fraud, duress, undue influence, and some kinds of illegality are all sufficient ground for refusing to perform. Unless it is rescinded, however, a voidable contract imposes on the contracting parties the same obligations as a valid contract. A voidable contract should not be confused with a void contract.

Unenforceable Contracts An unenforceable contract may create an obligation but cannot be enforced by legal proceedings. Verbal contracts which are required to be in writing and contracts which have lost their remedy, because the time required by the statute of limitations for bringing an action has expired, are unenforceable. Contracts with the government are likewise unenforceable, if no remedy is provided by law, because of the doctrine of sovereign immunity.

The statutes of limitations are statutory enactments which permit the debtor to say that the obligation cannot be enforced. It is frequently said that the debt continues but the remedy is barred. The effect of the statutes is to furnish the debtor with a defense which prevents the creditor, after the lapse of a specified time, from suing on the debt. The purpose of the statutes is usually said to be the suppression of stale claims which are difficult to prove because proper evidence is lost by the death or removal of witnesses, or because evidence has become obscure in a defective memory through lapse of time. These statutes, nevertheless, have the effect of compelling the exercise of a right to enforce a claim within a reasonable time and of remedying the general inconvenience resulting from delay in asserting a legal right. The statutes differ widely, but a few generalizations are possible.

In a few states, no distinction is made between the different kinds of debts. In the majority of states, however, the time limit varies from two to eight years on an open account and from five to twenty years on bonds, promissory notes, and written contracts. Section 2–725 of the Code fixes the statutory period of time at four years with respect to contracts for the sale of goods. The parties themselves may reduce the period to not less than one year, but they may not extend it. The individual state statute should be examined to determine the exact time limit for bringing an action on any particular type of debt.

Executed or Executory The term "executed contract" denotes a contract that has been fully carried out by the contracting parties and is in contrast to an "executory contract," which is yet to be performed. The term "executed contract," however, is ambiguous if used in this sense because it is not properly a contract at all, except reminiscently. An agreement, however, may be executed on the part of one party and executory on the part of the other. A contract to purchase on credit, followed by delivery, is executed on the part of the seller and executory on the part of the buyer. A contract of this nature, however, is executory because something remains to be done, namely, payment by the buyer of the purchase price.

Unilateral or Bilateral A unilateral contract is one in which, although a legal obligation is created, one party receives as consideration for his promise the performance or forbearance of some act. An offer of a reward by one party may be a unilateral promise or a unilateral offer, but a contractual relationship is not established until the actual performance of the act, at which time a legal obligation is created. A unilateral contract is sometimes referred to as "a promise for an act," or "an act for a promise."

A bilateral contract, on the other hand, is one in which each party receives as consideration for his promise, a promise from the other party. The contract immediately becomes obligatory because of the mutual promises. A bilateral contract is sometimes referred to as "a promise for a promise."

Express or Implied The distinction between these two kinds of contracts is in the way mutual assent is manifested. The terms of an express contract are stated by the parties. The terms of a contract implied in fact are inferred from the acts of the parties. To illustrate, a seller makes an offer to sell goods, which the buyer accepts by taking them, and although no words are uttered by the buyer, a mutual intent to contract is present if both parties know that payment is expected. A contract implied in fact is a true contract and has the same legal effect as an express contract. The term "implied contract," however, has confused judicial thought because it is sometimes used with reference to contracts implied in law, or quasi contracts.

Quasi Contracts It is important to distinguish between contracts implied in fact and contracts implied in law because, as will be seen, the legal relations under a true contract and the legal relations imposed by law are different. The factual situations that give rise to a contract implied in fact and a quasi contract are different. The measure of damages is different. Quasi-contractual obligations do not rest upon the express or implied assent of the parties but are imposed by the law to prevent injustice, irrespective of the intention of the parties, and are not properly contracts at all. The cases that have been classified as quasi contracts are of infinite variety, and when for some reason recovery cannot be had on a true contract, recovery is often allowed on the basis of a quasi contract. [*Old Men's Home, Inc. v. Lee's Estate*, p. 36.]

REAL AND PERSONAL PROPERTY

The dividing line between real and personal property is not always easy to draw. It is frequently said, however, that real property consists of things which are immovable, and that personal property consists of things which are movable. This distinction used in a broad sense is useful, but it will be seen that many kinds of property classed as personal property are not, strictly speaking, movable. It will suffice for the present to define real property as land and those things firmly attached to the land and to define personal property as all other objects and rights capable of being owned.

Article 2 of the Commercial Code provides special rules for a contract to sell goods, and section 2–105 defines goods as "all things which are movable at the time of identification to the contract for sale." Section 2–106 provides that a "contract for sale" includes both a present sale of goods and a contract to sell goods at a future time. This subject is discussed in Part 3, "Sales," but many of the provisions pertain to subjects which are ordinarily included in the law of contracts. These provisions are interspersed throughout Part 2, "Contracts." This means that there will be one set of rules pertaining to the general law of contracts and another set of rules pertaining to the sale of goods. This distinction should be kept in mind.

ESSENTIALS

In order for the contract to be enforceable, there must be an agreement—both offer and acceptance—supported by consideration, entered into by parties having capacity to contract, the objective of which is legal. These four requirements will be discussed, in the order indicated, in the four chapters immediately following.

CASES

Old Men's Home, Inc. v. Lee's Estate, 4 So.2d 235 (Miss. 1941). Action by Old Men's Home, Incorporated, plaintiff, against Lee's Estate, defendant. Lee, the decedent, obtained care and maintenance at the Old Men's Home by false and fraudulent representations that he was a pauper with no one to care for him. While he was at the home, he was so old and infirm that he was unable to perform any kind of work. The home furnished him board, lodging, clothing, laundry, nursing care, and medical attention. At the time he entered the home, however, and continuously thereafter up to the time of his death, he had to his credit in a bank something over $5,000. The home brought this action for reimbursement for room, board, and care furnished him for thirty-eight months at $30 per month.

 Anderson, Justice: It is true . . . that there was no express contract on the part of Lee to pay the Home anything if it turned out he had procured its services through false and fraudulant representations as to his financial condition; nevertheless, we hold that by reason of such representations the law imposed an obligation on him to make the Home whole. The law denominates it as quasi or constructive contract. Such contracts rest upon the equitable principle that a person shall not be allowed to enrich himself unjustly at the expense of another. It is an obligation which the law creates, in the absence of any agreement, when and because the acts of the parties or others have placed in the possession of one person money, or its equivalent, under such circumstances that in equity and good conscience, he ought not to retain it. . . . The foundation of the principle is equity and good conscience. [DECISION FOR PLAINTIFF]

PROBLEMS

1 Plaintiff and defendant entered into an oral contract by the terms of which the plaintiff promised to sell to the defendant and the defendant promised to purchase from the plaintiff ten quarts of milk for $4.50. The plaintiff delivered the milk but defendant refused to pay. Classify the contract as to formality, enforceability, reciprocal obligations, compliance, and intent.

2 Plaintiff sued the defendant for breach of contract but was unable to recover because defendant was entitled, upon the ground of duress, to avoid liability on the contract. Is this contract more accurately classified as voidable or unenforceable?

3 A statute provided that an action upon any instrument of writing can only be commenced within five years. Plaintiff and defendant entered into a written agreement on January 1, 1940, whereby plaintiff sold and delivered merchandise to the defendant for which the defendant agreed to pay one year after date. On January 1, 1950, plaintiff sued the defendant for breach of contract but was unable to recover for the merchandise sold and delivered. Why?

4 Plaintiff, while in the XYZ Store where he had a charge account, saw a shelf containing cigarettes marked $4.80 per carton. He picked up a carton of cigarettes, held it up so that a clerk of the store saw him. The clerk nodded his approval, and plaintiff walked out of the store with the carton of cigarettes. Had a contract been entered into? If so, upon what theory of the law of contracts?

5 Brown built a fireplace in his home from brick. After completion of the fireplace he had several bricks remaining. He stored these remaining bricks in his garage. Classify the brick in the fireplace and the garage as to real and personal property.

AGREEMENT

An agreement, which is the result of an offer and acceptance, is a manifestation of mutual assent by the parties to the agreement. The assent may be clearly expressed in words or writing. In the absence of such an expression, however, it must be gathered from the outward conduct of the parties; the secret intention of the parties is not material in the law of contracts. It is essential to completion of the mutual assent that the offeror make a proposal which is communicated to, and accepted by, the offeree. The ultimate agreement must be sufficiently definite and certain to enable the court to collect from the circumstances the full intention of the parties and to ascertain the damages in case of breach. The rules of law pertaining to the agreement logically divide themselves into (1) formation of offers, (2) termination and duration of offers, and (3) acceptance of offers.

FORMATION OF OFFERS
An offer is a proposal made by one party to another party to enter into a contract. It may be written; it may be oral; it may be implied in fact. It is essential, however, that it be made with the intent to enter into a contract, that it be communicated to the offeree, that it be definite and certain, and that it not be an invitation to negotiate.

Intention   Persons who enter into social engagements are not thinking of legal obligations, although concededly an intent is present, and their true intent will be respected by the law. It is also true that if the parties to a supposed agreement indicate that their words are merely a joke, no legal obligation will be created. Statements or assertions made in jest, or under strain or stress of great excitement, are usually held not to be offers because one is not reasonably justified in relying on them. The courts, when the intent of the parties is litigated, apply the "reasonable man" standard as a means of determining the presence or absence of contractual intent.

Communication   The offer, whether made by words, a writing, or conduct, must be communicated to the offeree. The communication of the offer means more than that the offeree learned of the offer. The offer must be brought home to the offeree by some act of the offeror, which act had for its purpose the communication of the offer to the offeree. An offer is not communicated when a person tells some third person that he intends to make an offer to a proposed offeree, and the third person, without authority, conveys the information to the proposed offeree. [*Jersey City v. Town of Harrison*, p. 49.]

Definiteness   An offer should be literally definite and certain as to such essential terms as the time of performance, the price to be paid, the work to be done, or the identification of the subject matter. This is particularly true when acceptance is to be made merely by an affirmative answer. The absence of literally definite terms, however, does not always render the contract indefinite for, in law, that is certain which will be rendered certain. The measure of the acceptor's undertaking would be a reasonable time where an offer is made to perform definite services without mentioning the time of performance. If the offer fails to mention the period of credit extension in a sale on credit, usage and custom could be resorted to in order to determine what is a reasonable time. The contract must fail for indefiniteness, however, if the parties attempt to state the time of performance or terms of credit extension but do so in such a vague and uncertain manner that their intention cannot be determined. Under the Code, requirement and output agreements do not fail for indefiniteness.

(1) *Requirement and Output Contracts*   Requirement and output contracts are specifically recognized by section 2–306 of the Code. A requirement contract is one whereby the buyer promises to purchase all his requirements from the seller in exchange for the promise of the seller to supply all the needs of the buyer. An output contract is one whereby the seller promises to sell all his production to the buyer in exchange for the promise of the buyer to purchase all the output of the seller.

Pre-Code decisions were not entirely uniform with respect to requirement and output contracts. The decisions which held that offers to furnish such articles as shall be needed, required, or consumed were indefinite apparently did so on the reasoning that the buyer was free to fix the quantity term in the agreement. Under the Code, however, neither the buyer nor the seller is free to fix the quantity term.

The buyer and the seller are limited to the actual good faith requirement or output of the parties. The party who will determine quantity, therefore, is required to operate his plant or conduct his business in good faith and according to commercial standards of fair dealing in the trade.

Suppose a building contractor and a manufacturer entered into a requirements-and-output contract. The requirement of good faith would undoubtedly prevent the building contractor from demanding a greater quantity of materials than is needed and reselling rather than consuming them. The requirement of good faith would also undoubtedly prevent the manufacturer from abnormally expanding his plant and demanding that the contractor accept the increased production.

Suppose one party to the contract sells or abandons his business prior to the time stated in the contract. The pre-Code law indicated that there is an obligation to stay in business unless to do so would be economically unjustified, as where it would result in destruction of the business, in the case of the buyer, or where a confiscatory tariff makes it impossible to continue production, in the case of the seller. A mere desire to be rid of the business or to avoid risk of loss, however, would not justify cessation. The Code seems to be in accord with these rules, namely, that good faith business reasons will excuse cessation.

(2) *Open-Price Agreements* Section 2–305 recognizes two situations where the price is not fixed by the contract. The first is where the parties intend to be bound even though the price is not settled. Suppose a buyer determines that he will need fifty large refrigerators for a chain of restaurants which he intends to begin operating six months from the date of entering into the contract and finds a seller who is willing to sell the refrigerators. Suppose further that both parties agree that $25,000 is a fair price for the refrigerators at the present time. They both know, however, that the price of refrigerators may fluctuate over a six-month period. They thereupon enter into a contract obligating the seller to deliver and the buyer to accept the refrigerators at the end of six months and leave the price term open. In these circumstances, the price will be a reasonable price if the price is to be agreed upon by the parties and they fail to agree, or if the price is to be fixed in terms of some agreed market standard, or if it is to be fixed by some third person or agency that fails to fix the price. The agreement may provide that one of the parties is to fix the price, and a price so fixed in good faith will be honored. If he refuses to fix the price, the other party may fix a reasonable price or treat the contract as canceled.

The second situation is where the parties do not intend to be bound until after the price is fixed. In these circumstances, there is no contract if the price is not fixed. The Code, however, expressly declares that in such case "the buyer must return any goods already received or if unable so to do must pay their reasonable value at the time of delivery and the seller must return any portion of the price paid on account."

Invitations to Negotiate In the transaction of business it is often to the advantage of the contracting parties to negotiate over terms of the agreement. Each party frequently attempts to induce the other party to make the offer. It may be that each party will make several offers before an agreement is reached by an offer and acceptance. An offer, however, must be distinguished from an invitation to negotiate. Acceptance of an offer will give rise to a contract. A reply to an invitation to negotiate, on the other hand, is an offer only and will not create a contract unless, and until, it is accepted by the other party. The particular acts or conduct of the parties and the circumstances attending the transaction will determine whether a definite proposal has been made. General proposals by public notice provoke a substantial portion of the litigation concerning the distinction between invitations to negotiate and offers.

(1) *Public Works* Contracts for the performance of public works are ordinarily awarded to contractors by public bidding. A notice is sometimes mailed to prospective bidders, but it is more commonly published in newspapers or posted in some conspicuous place. The method of bidding and the awarding of the contract are controlled by statute; unless the statute provides otherwise, the authorized board or officer advertising for bids is free to reject any bid, and the contractor responding to the advertisement is free to withdraw his bid at any time prior to acceptance. The statutes in most states provide that the public work must be let to the "lowest bidder" or to the "lowest and best bidder." These statutes are usually interpreted to mean that, although any bid may be rejected, if any contract for public work is consummated it must be awarded to the lowest responsible bidder. The contract, however, is not entered into until the offer of the prospective contractor is accepted by some board or officer authorized to enter into contracts for public works.

(2) *Auctions* Putting up property—other than goods as defined by the Code—for sale by auction is an invitation to the assembled persons to make their offers by bidding. The acceptance of the offer takes place in some customary manner, as by the auctioneer's letting his hammer fall or announcing that the property is "sold." The bidder, prior to that time, may withdraw his offer, and the auctioneer may withdraw the property from sale. If the auctioneer has announced, or if it has been advertised, that the property will be sold "without reserve," however, the announcement binds the auctioneer, and he is obliged to accept the highest bid.

Section 2–328 of the Code follows the pre-Code law in general with respect to goods as defined by the Code. A few provisions have been added. Suppose a bid is made while the hammer is falling in acceptance of a prior bid. The Code provides that the auctioneer in his discretion may either reopen the bidding, in which case the new bid is accepted as a continuation of the bidding, or accept the bid on which the hammer was falling as the closing bid. The Code accepts the view that goods subject to sale may be withdrawn at any time before they are actually "put up" for bidding. This is true irrespective of whether the auction is with or without reserve. If the sale is without reserve, the auctioneer cannot withdraw the goods once bids are called for unless there is no bid within a reasonable time. The Code also provides that a seller, either personally or by his agent, who intends to make bids at an auction must give notice that the liberty to do so has been reserved. In the absence of such notice, the buyer has the option of avoiding the sale or taking the last good faith bid.

(3) *Advertisements* Quotation of a price of goods for sale published in newspapers, periodicals, by circulars sent out by mail, displays in show windows, and other means of advertising are ordinarily general invitations to negotiate. A contract will not result from a statement by an intending purchaser, therefore, that he will take a specified quantity of the goods at that price. The wording of an advertisement may signify clearly an intention to make an offer, but as a general rule, the person who responds to a general advertisement is the offeror. [*Lefkowitz v. Great Minneapolis Surplus Store*, p. 49.]

Irrevocable Offers An offer may be irrevocable either by statute or by contract. A good illustration of an offer made irrevocable by statute is a bid for some public work made to the state. This type of statute usually declares that the bid shall be irrevocable for a stated period of time. An offer made irrevocable by contract is known as an option. An option, however, should not be confused with an offer which limits the time for acceptance—sometimes referred to as a "continuing offer." This type of offer clearly stipulates in its terms that it shall expire within a specified time. The offer, therefore, automatically terminates by the lapse of the time specified. The power of revocation, nevertheless, remains with the offeror. An option is not revocable. The most common form of option is a promise, supported by sufficient consideration, to sell property for a stipulated price within a specified period of time. The option imposes no obligation upon the purchaser. He may use his own discretion as to whether or not he will accept the terms specified. An option, however, is not revocable at the pleasure of the seller. The two important distinguishing characteristics between an option and a continuing offer are, first, the option must be based upon a sufficient consideration, and, second, it is not revocable at the pleasure of the seller. [*Schenley v. Kauth*, p. 51.]

Firm Offer Section 2–205 of the Code pertains to a firm offer made by a merchant. The expression "firm offer" means an irrevocable offer. It should not be presumed, therefore, that the word "firm" refers to a firm, such as a partnership. Section 2–104 defines the word "merchant." The word, broadly speaking, means a person who by his occupation holds himself out as having knowledge or skill peculiar to the practices or goods involved in the transaction.

Section 2–205 makes a rather drastic change with respect to a merchant who makes a written, signed, and current offer to buy or sell goods with the assurances that the offer will be held open for a stated time. The offer is not revocable, for lack of consideration, during the time so stated. If no specific time is stated, the offer is not revocable for a reasonable time. In no event, however, may such period of irrevocability exceed three months. This section also provides that the clause containing the offer must be signed separately by the offeror if the offeree provides the form on which the offer is contained.

TERMINATION AND DURATION OF OFFERS

An offer may be terminated by an acceptance; such a termination carries into effect the object of the offer and changes it into a contract. Prior to acceptance, however, neither the offeror nor the offeree has obligated himself to the other party. The offeree has the power to accept the offer at any time before it is terminated, and, until it is terminated, it is possible for the offer to ripen into a contract through a properly communicated acceptance. This possibility should be remembered. The offeror has the privilege of revoking the offer, and he should withdraw the offer if for any reason he decides not to enter into the contract.

The ways, other than by acceptance, in which an offer may be terminated are revocation, express terms, implied terms, rejection or counteroffer, operation of law, and lapse of time.

Revocation   An offer may be revoked by the offeror, irrespective of stipulations to the contrary, at any time before its acceptance. To be effective, revocation of the offer must be received by the offeree before he has accepted. Communication of the revocation may be through any kind of notice. The sale of the property covered by the offer will constitute notice provided such sale is known by the offeree. Public offers, as a general rule, may be withdrawn by publishing the revocation as fully, and so far as possible, in the same way that the original offer was communicated to the offeree.

Express Terms   An offer which limits the time for acceptance—sometimes referred to as a "continuing offer"—should not be confused with an option. An offer which clearly stipulates in its terms that it shall expire within a specified time automatically terminates by the lapse of the time specified.

Implied Terms   An offer, in the absence of an express limitation, ordinarily expires after a reasonable time has elapsed. The interpretation given the words "reasonable time" depends on the various factual situations, but the method of communication and the nature of the property are important factors. An offer made in conversation, in the absence of words or circumstances indicating a contrary intention, ordinarily would not extend beyond the time of the conversation. An offer communicated by wire would indicate an immediate reply was expected. An offer to sell or buy property with a rapidly fluctuating market price would expire more quickly than an offer to sell or buy property with a more stable price. The same is true of an offer to sell goods of a perishable nature as compared with an offer to sell goods of a more durable nature.

Rejection and Counteroffer   The offeree is under no obligation to reply to the offer. He may, nevertheless, reply to the offer by rejection or counteroffer. He may reject the offer by notifying the offeror that he does not wish to accept; the offer cannot thereafter be revived by any act on his part. The rejection, to be effective, must be received by the offeror. The offeree may, therefore, create a contract by delivering an acceptance to the offeror before the latter receives the rejection. This is commonly accomplished by dispatching the rejection through the regular course of the mails and thereafter transmitting the acceptance by telephone or wire. A counteroffer is made when the offeree replies to the offer by indicating that he desires to enter into a contract on terms different from those made by the offeror. A counteroffer reverses the relationship of the parties. A contract results, however, if, after a counteroffer has been mailed, the offeree can deliver an acceptance to the offeror prior to his receipt of the counteroffer.

The reply of the offeree, however, does not necessarily have to be either a rejection or a counteroffer. The offeree may reply in various ways. He may state that he desires to postpone his decision or that he seeks further information. Such a reply has no effect on the offer, and it remains alive until it is otherwise terminated.

Operation of Law As a gereral rule, termination of an offer by operation of law applies to those situations where the completion of the contract is rendered impossible without fault on the part of the offeror or the offeree. An offer may lapse, therefore, if either of the parties becomes incapacitated prior to acceptance. The death or insanity of the offeror or the offeree will terminate the offer, as will the destruction of the specific subject matter. The termination of an offer by operation of law imposes no obligation on the offeror, or on anyone in his behalf in case of death or insanity, to notify the offeree that the offer is terminated. Notification may be advisable, however, from a practical point of view. [*New Headley Tobacco Warehouse Co. v. Gentry's Ex'r*, p. 52.]

Lapse of Time An offer which does not specify a definite time of duration will lapse after a reasonable time. The courts, in deciding what is a reasonable time, take into consideration such matters as the nature of the contract proposed, the usages of business, and all the other circumstances of the case. A telegram offering to sell stock which fluctuates rapidly on the stock market would obviously lapse at a much earlier time than an offer to sell farmland with a more firmly established price. It is thus clear that the rules for determining the meaning of a reasonable time are very flexible.

ACCEPTANCE OF OFFERS

Acceptance of an offer is the manifested assent of the offeree to comply with the terms of the offer. A contract then arises from which neither party can withdraw at pleasure. The acceptance of the offer can only be made by the offeree, but any conduct on his part which expresses an intent to be bound by the offer is sufficient to constitute an acceptance. The offeror has the right and power to impose any condition he may desire as to the acceptance. He may prescribe the time within which the offer may be accepted, the place and manner of acceptance, or the means of communicating the acceptance. Assuming that the offeror has not prescribed any conditions for acceptance, however, it is appropriate to observe how the acceptance may be expressed by words, how it may be inferred from silence or inaction, and how unilateral offers may be accepted.

Acceptance Expressed by Words   The acceptance of an offer by a reciprocal promise, oral or written, must be communicated to the offeror. The communication, however, is apparent when the contracting parties are in the presence of each other. The formation of an oral agreement is ordinarily completed in the course of a personal interview between the contracting parties, and the formation of a written agreement is completed when the instrument is signed and delivered.

(1)   *Acceptance by Signing*   A complex problem arises when one of the parties contends that an unsigned draft or memorial which contemplated the signature of both parties constituted the contract. The mere failure subsequently to embody the terms of the contract, which have been agreed upon in all respects, into a signed contract does not prevent the formation of a binding contract. If it is clearly understood that the terms of the proposed contract are to be signed before it is binding, no final contract will result until the contract is put in writing and signed. It may be that the draft is viewed as a convenient memorial of the contract. The intention of the parties is controlling. All doubt could be eliminated by incorporating in the agreement a condition to the effect that the agreement would not be binding until it was properly reduced to writing and signed by the contracting parties.

As a general rule, however, the signature to the contract serves as the manifestation of an intent to make a contract. All contracts, therefore, should be carefully read before they are signed; if one is ignorant of the language in which the document is written, he should have the contract read and explained to him. A person who, in the absence of fraud or similar circumstances, signs a document has naturally indicated assent by his action. He is, therefore, bound by its terms. [*Simmerman v. Fort Hartford Coal Co.*, p. 54.]

(2)   *Constructive Communication*   The completion of a contract when the parties are at a distance from one another presents problems of a unique character. The acceptance may be delayed or lost through some mistake or accident on the part of the transmitting agency. The more tiresome problem which confronted the courts for many years, however, was how to determine some exact moment which could be established for the actual formation of the contract. This problem was solved by the adoption of the doctrine of "constructive communication." An acceptance made by correspondence, according to this doctrine, is constructively communicated to the offeror as soon as the offeree places his acceptance with the authorized transmitting agency, properly addressed and stamped, or paid for, as the case may be. In accordance with the general rule that the offeror may impose any desired conditions of acceptance, he may state that the letter of acceptance will be effective only if it is received "in my office by twelve o'clock, June 1," and an attempted acceptance received by the offeror in any other manner will not be effective. The offeror may designate any transmitting agency he desires, therefore, and, if the acceptance by mail is authorized, the contract is completed at the moment the offeree deposits the letter of acceptance in the post office or a United States mailbox. If acceptance by telegraph is authorized, the contract is completed at the moment the offeree delivers the telegram of acceptance to the telegraph company for transmission. If the offeror fails to designate a transmitting agency, it is implied that the offeree is authorized

to use the same medium of transmission as the offeror used for the offer. It should not be presumed, however, that an implied authorization to accept by letter precludes the offeree from accepting by telegraph. The offeree may accept by telegram, but it is effective only if and when it is received by the offeror. The expression "received by the offeror" ordinarily means that the acceptance must be delivered to the residence or place of business of the offeror; if the offeror is absent at the time, the necessary communication is nevertheless completed.

The contract is formed, therefore, as soon as the acceptance is placed in the proper channel of communication by the offeree. After that time, neither an attempted revocation of the offer by the offeror nor an attempted rejection of the offer by the offeree will discharge the parties from their contractual obligations. The fact that a revocation is actually received by the offeree or a rejection is actually received by the offeror will have no effect on the rule. It is within the power of the offeror to state in his offer that the acceptance shall be ineffective unless it is actually received. In the absence of such a statement, however, any possible loss due to the fault of the transmitting agency is placed on the offeror.

(3) *Withdrawal of Letter from Mail* The rule of the postal laws and regulations which permits a depositor—the offeree—to withdraw a letter from the mail presents the question as to the effect of the withdrawal upon the acceptance of offers. The question, however, has not been litigated to any great extent. The majority of the courts hold that an acceptance deposited in the mail is effective even though the offeree intercepts the letter.

Silence or Inaction Manifestation of assent by means other than words or signature may be equally binding upon the parties. The determination to accept, however, must be manifested in some manner; the determination alone will not suffice. The offeree, therefore—in the absence of circumstances that impose a duty to speak, act, or forbear—does not become a party to the contract merely because he refuses or neglects to reply to the offer. The offeror may have stated in his offer that silence on the part of the offeree would constitute an acceptance, but it is beyond the power of the offeror alone to force the offeree into a contractual obligation. Silence or inaction, as a general rule, does not amount to a manifestation of assent to the offer except in a few instances where the law imposes a duty to speak. Silence as a mode of manifesting assent may be inferred when the offeror has changed his position to his injury in reliance on the silence. The offeree, therefore, might avoid legal entanglements by either rejecting or accepting the offer. This is particularly true when the parties have had previous dealings.

(1) *Previous Dealings* The offeree by his conduct on previous occasions may give the offeror reason to understand that his silence is an acceptance. In these circumstances, a duty is imposed on the offeree to communicate a rejection of the offer to the offeror. Previous dealings coupled with an exercise of dominion over the subject matter of the contract, therefore, will ordinarily constitute a manifestation of assent to the offer.

(2) *Retention of Property* Silence as an acceptance is applicable if the offeree takes the benefit of goods or services under circumstances indicating that

they were offered with the expectation of pay. The offeree may not have had previous dealings with the offeror, or ordered the goods for which compensation is sought, yet if he continues to receive and use them in circumstances where he had no right to suppose they were a gratuity, he will have agreed by implication to pay for their value. The offeree may have solicited the offer under circumstances that will justify the offeror in interpreting silence as an acceptance.

Acceptance of Offer for Unilateral Contract It will be remembered that a unilateral contract is defined as a promise for an act. Suppose Brown says to Jones, "I will give you $20 if you will mow my lawn." The early cases held that the promise was not legally binding until the act was fully performed. It will also be remembered that the offeror may revoke his offer at any time prior to acceptance. Under the early cases, therefore, Brown could revoke his offer even though Jones had almost completed mowing the lawn. This creates an obvious hardship on the offeree. The courts today attempt to arrive at justice between the parties, and sometimes allow the offeree to recover on a quasi contract if there has been a benefit to the offeror. The courts also hold that the start of the performance is an accepted bilateral contract where there is doubt as to whether the offer is bilateral or unilateral. There is also an increased willingness on the part of some courts to enforce a promise where (1) the promisee has suffered a substantial change, (2) the promisor actually made the promise which was the cause of the promisee's reliance, and (3) the detrimental reliance by the promisee was foreseen by the promisor. The law, however, is not well settled.

Subsection 2–206(2) of the Code purports to give the offeror protection by providing that the offeror may treat the offer as lapsed unless the offeree notifies the offeror that the offer has been accepted "where the beginning of a requested performance is a reasonable mode of acceptance." The offeree, therefore, should notify the offeror that he has started performance. The offeror, without such notice, may regard the silence of the offeree as a rejection.

Acceptance of Ambiguous Offers It is unquestionably true that the offeror may prescribe any condition to his offer as he desires and the acceptance by the offeree can only be made in accordance with the condition. This rule leaves the offeree in a dilemma where the offer is so ambiguous that he cannot determine what he is required to do to make an effective acceptance. Section 2–206(1) provides that an offer may be accepted in any manner and by any medium reasonable in the circumstances unless a specific mode of acceptance is unambiguously indicated. The problem of ambiguous offers is frequently the result of orders calling for prompt shipment. Suppose the offeror sends the following telegram to the offeree: "Send 200 typewriters Friday." Must the offeree accept by a telegraphic acceptance? Section 2–206 provides a special rule for this problem by providing that the offer may be accepted by either a prompt promise to ship or by a prompt or current shipment.

This section could, however, create a new problem relating to accommodating substitutes. Suppose a seller does not have the precise goods which the buyer has ordered, but has available similar goods and ships them as an accommodation to the buyer. Such accommodation shipments were treated as counteroffers under pre-Code law. Suppose now that the seller in the illustration above elects to accept the offer by shipping similar goods as an accommodation. It is possible to characterize an accommodation shipment as nonconforming goods. Such a characterization would result in both an acceptance and a breach. It may be difficult to determine in any given case whether the nonconforming shipment is an acceptance and a breach or an accommodating substitute. This result can be prevented. This section of the Code makes it mandatory that the seller notify the buyer that the shipment is not an acceptance, but is made only as an accommodation to the buyer. The shipment of goods without such notification to the buyer is an acceptance.

Additional Terms in Acceptance or Confirmation   Under pre-Code law, a counteroffer is made when the offeree proposes additional or different terms in his acknowledgment of the offer made by the offeror. Under the Code, however, additional or different terms do not necessarily prevent a contract from being created. A contract results if the conduct of both parties recognizes the existence of a contract. The problem at hand, however, is to determine the terms of the contract.

Section 2–207 provides that if the seller and the buyer are both merchants, the additional terms become a part of the contract unless (1) the offer expressly limits acceptance to the terms of the offer, (2) they materially alter it, or (3) notification of objection to them has already been given or is given within a reasonable time. Unless both parties are merchants, however, the additional terms do not become a part of the contract unless the express agreement of the offeror is obtained.

The problem of a conflict in the terms of a proposed contract will ordinarily arise where the buyer—the offeror—uses his own form in his order and the seller—the offeree—uses his own form in his acknowledgment of the order. Suppose both the buyer and the seller are merchants—as will ordinarily be the case—and that the buyer-merchant sends a written order to the seller-merchant offering to purchase 100 boxes of Fancy Packed Grade A Oranges at $14 a box to be delivered at the buyer's place of business in lots of twenty boxes on Monday for five weeks. Suppose further that the seller accepted the offer but that his written acceptance contained a clause providing for delivery at the seller's warehouse, a clause fixing the seller's standard credit term, and a clause reserving to the seller the right to cancel upon the failure of the buyer to meet any invoice when due. Is there a contract? If so, what are the terms of the contract?

There is a conflict in the delivery term, but the seller did not expressly condition his acceptance. A contract has resulted, therefore, on the buyer's delivery term. But there are also additional terms. The clause fixing the credit term would not ordinarily materially alter the contract. The seller's credit term, therefore, would become a part of the contract. The clause reserving to the seller the right to cancel upon failure of the buyer to meet any invoice when due would ordinarily materially alter the contract. This clause, therefore, would not become a part of the contract. [*Application of Doughboy Industries, Inc.*, p. 55.]

Neither the seller nor the buyer is compelled to enter into a contract on terms to his disliking. The offeror could include a clause in conspicuous type limiting the acceptance to the exact terms of the offer. The offeree could likewise include a clause in conspicuous type limiting his acceptance to his additional or different terms. This then becomes the Code counteroffer.

CASES

Jersey City v. Town of Harrison,   62 Atl. 765 (N.J. 1905). Action by the Mayor and Aldermen of Jersey City, plaintiffs, against the town of Harrison and others, defendants. On July 7, 1903, the members of the town council of the town of Harrison adopted by unanimous vote a resolution authorizing the president of the council and the town clerk to execute a contract with the municipal authorities of Jersey City for a supply of water. The town council, however, never directed that the resolution be transmitted to Jersey City, or gave anyone authority to present the resolution to Jersey City. The authorities of Jersey City procured in some unexplained way a certified copy of the resolution and prepared and signed a paper purporting to be such a contract as was called for in the resolution. The paper was presented to the town council of Harrison, and a demand was made on behalf of Jersey City that it should be executed by the officials of the town of Harrison who were named in the resolution. This demand was refused. Plaintiffs claim that a contract came into existence when the paper, drawn in accordance with the terms of the resolution and executed so as to bind Jersey City, was tendered to the town of Harrison. This action was brought for breach of contract.

Magie, Chancellor: A proposition for a contract, to be competent to be accepted, must be communicated to the party with whom the contract is proposed. It will not be sufficient that the latter acquire knowledge of it unless the knowledge is acquired with the express or implied intention of the proposing party. An owner of land, contemplating a sale thereof, might direct his stenographer or other agent to draft a contract for sale to a particular person on specified terms. If the owner has not communicated, or intended to communicate, the proposed contract to that person, the latter having acquired knowledge thereof, could not, by acceptance, bring the owner into a contractual relation of sale. The owner might leave his uncommunicated draft in his agent's hands without liability and retract his agency and abandon his plan at any time. Until communicated, there is no efficacious proposal which could be accepted. In like manner the resolution never having been communicated to Jersey City by any act of the town of Harrison did not constitute a proposal and could not be raised to a binding contract by any acceptance. [DECISION FOR DEFENDANTS]

Lefkowitz v. Great Minneapolis Surplus Store, Inc.,   86 N.W.2d 689 (Minn. 1957). Action by Morris Lefkowitz, plaintiff, against Great Minneapolis Surplus Store,

Inc., defendant. Defendant published the following advertisement in a Minneapolis newspaper on April 6, 1956:

SATURDAY 9 A.M. SHARP
3 BRAND NEW
FUR COATS
Worth to $100.00
First Come
First Served
$1
EACH

The defendant again published the following advertisement in the same newspaper on April 13, 1956:

SATURDAY 9 A.M.
2 BRAND NEW PASTEL
MINK 3-SKIN SCARFS
Selling for $89.50
Out they go
Saturday. Each . . . $1.00
1 BLACK LAPIN STOLE
Beautiful,
worth $139.50 . . . $1.00
FIRST COME
FIRST SERVED

Murphy, Justice: The record supports the findings of the court that on each of the Saturdays following the publication of the above-described ads the plaintiff was the first to present himself at the appropriate counter in the defendant's store and on each occasion demanded the coat and the stole so advertised and indicated his readiness to pay the sale price of $1. On both occasions, the defendant refused to sell the merchandise to the plaintiff, stating on the first occasion that by a "house rule" the offer was intended for women only and sales would not be made to men, and on the second visit that plaintiff knew defendant's house rules. . . .

With reference to the offer of the defendant on April 13, 1956, to sell the "1 BLACK LAPIN STOLE . . . worth $139.50. . . . " the trial court held that the value of this article was established and granted judgment in favor of the plaintiff for that amount less the $1 quoted purchase price.

The defendant contends that a newspaper advertisement offering items of merchandise for sale at a named price is a "unilateral offer" which may be withdrawn without notice. He relies upon authorities which hold that, where an advertiser publishes in a newspaper that he has a certain quantity or quality of goods which he wants to dispose of at certain prices and on certain terms, such advertisements are not offers which become contracts as soon as any person to whose notice they may come signifies his acceptance by notifying the other that he will take a certain quantity of them. Such advertisements have been construed as an invitation for an offer of sale on the terms stated, which offer, when received, may be accepted or rejected and which therefore does not become a contract of sale until accepted by the seller; and until a contract has been so made, the seller may modify or revoke such prices or terms. . . .

Where the offer is clear, definite, and explicit, and leaves nothing open for negotiation, it constitutes an offer, acceptance of which will complete the contract. . . .

Whether in any individual instance a newspaper advertisement is an offer rather than an invitation to make an offer depends on the legal intention of the parties and the surrounding circumstances. We are of the view on the facts before us that the offer by the defendant of the sale of the Lapin fur was clear, definite, and explicit, and left nothing open for negotiation. The plaintiff having successfully managed to be the first one to appear at the seller's place of business to be served, as requested by the advertisement, and having offered the stated purchase price of the article, he was entitled to performance on the part of the defendant. We think the trial court was correct in holding that there was in the conduct of the parties a sufficient mutuality of obligation to constitute a contract of sale.

The defendant contends that the offer was modified by a "house rule" to the effect that only women were qualified to receive the bargains advertised. The advertisement contained no such restriction. This objection may be disposed of briefly by stating that, while an advertiser has the right at any time before acceptance to modify his offer, he does not have the right, after acceptance, to impose new or arbitrary conditions not contained in the published offer. [DECISION FOR PLAINTIFF]

Schenley V. Kauth, 122 N.E.2d 189 (Ohio 1953). Action by Mabel St. Clair Schenley, plaintiff, against Florence I. Graber, defendant. Defendant deeded 7½ acres of a 10-acre tract of land to plaintiff at a price of $325 per acre and, as a part of the same transaction, gave plaintiff the following written option:

June 17, 1941

Mabel St. Clair Schenley:

As a consideration of your purchase of 7½-acre tract belonging to me, located in Franklin Township, Summit County, Ohio, I hereby give you the option to purchase the remaining 2½-acres belonging to me, which joins your 7½-acre tract to the north, at the same price per acre as you are paying for the 7½-acre tract; namely $325 per acre.

This option is granted to you only in the event I desire to sell the 2½-acre tract.

Very truly yours,
Florence I. Graber.

Florence I. Kauth was formerly Florence I. Graber.

Several years after these transactions, defendant told plaintiff "that she would decide after she came back from California whether or not she was going to sell that property." When she returned from California, she stated that she did not want to sell. Defendant did, however, thereafter sell the property to a third person, without notice to the plaintiff, for a price substantially greater than $325 per acre. Plaintiff thereupon brought this action for breach of contract.

Doyle, Justice: It is principally claimed by the defendant that the trial court erred in precluding her from offering oral testimony to the effect "that the instrument so signed by her was intended and understood by the parties to remain in force and effect for only a reasonable length of time," and that whether or not a reasonable length of time had elapsed was a question for the jury. To this claim, we now direct our attention.

It is generally held that a written option, signed by an optionor, founded on valid consideration, which gives an optionee the right to purchase real property at a stipulated price in the event the owner of the land desires to sell, constitutes a contract. The law may be succinctly stated as follows:

"A contract is a promise or a set of promises for the breach of which the law gives a remedy, or the performance of which the law in some way recognizes as a duty." I Restatement of the Law of Contracts, Section 1. . . .

It is thus obvious that the written instrument here under consideration has all the essentials of a valid contract. The consideration shown to exist precludes a revocation by the offeror; a definite price is stated for the property; and it is adequately described.

Whether a jury question is ever presented in the determination of what is a reasonable time within which a unilateral contract to sell must be accepted by an optionee in situations where no specific time for acceptance is incorporated, we neither consider nor decide. The contract before us does not require it. Nor do we decide whether oral testimony of the parties would be admissible to determine the question.

Our conclusions in the foregoing paragraph are based upon the fact that the contract before us fixes a definite time when the optionee must exercise the option—to wit, when the optionor desires to sell. It is apparent that the optionor desired and decided to sell, because she did in fact sell to a third person, without notifying the optionee. In so doing, she breached her contract to sell the property for the stipulated price to the optionee, if the optionee agreed to buy, at a time when she desired to sell; and, as a consequence thereof, she must respond in damages. The question of a reasonable length of time is not in the case. [DECISION FOR PLAINTIFF]

New Headley Tobacco Warehouse Co. v. Gentry's Ex'r, 212 S.W.2d 725 (Ky. 1948). Action by New Headley Tobacco Warehouse Company, plaintiff, against the Executor of the Estate of P. T. Gentry, defendant. On September 1, 1932, P. T. Gentry executed a lease to property in Lexington to plaintiff for a term of twenty-one years and six months. The contract contained no provision for extension or renewal. Nearly ten years thereafter, P. T. Gentry addressed the following letter to plaintiff.

"In the event you build within the next five years (from March 1st, 1942) an addition to your warehouse at a cost of not less than $25,000 on the property you have under lease from me, I agree,

"First, to extend your present lease so you will have a total term of twenty-two years (22 years) from March 1st of the year the addition is built."

P. T. Gentry died on September 29, 1945, and the lessee had not made any response or started construction of the building prior to his death. On April 16, 1946, plaintiff mailed a letter addressed to the defendant accepting the offer to extend the lease. The defendant refused to extend the lease, and plaintiff thereupon brought this action seeking a judicial declaration of the plaintiff's right to the extension of the lease.

Stanley, Commissioner: We have, first, a simple offer without consideration to make a bilateral contract. Ordinarily an option for the extension or renewal of a lease given for a good consideration runs with the land and is not terminated by the death of the offeror or optionor but is binding on his successors. . . . The form of the proposal in the instant case did not purport to be a grant upon consideration of an option to extend the lease. It was a mere voluntary offer, submitted without consideration, and under no contractual duty. It imposed no obligation on either party and could, therefore, be withdrawn at any time before acceptance. . . .

The offer having been subject to withdrawal or revocation by the lessor personally any time before he died, the question is as to the effect of his death upon the right of the optionee, the lessee, to accept it thereafter before the end of the five year period, as he undertook to do.

In the making of a contract there must be two minds, at least, concurring at the moment of its completion. But this cannot occur if there be but one of the contracting parties in existence. Hence, the death of a party who had the right of revocation or withdrawal of an offer to contract renders the completion impossible and terminates the negotiations or proceedings at the very point where they were when he died. So, an acceptance by the optionee or the other party subsequent to that event is ineffectual to close the bargain. Therefore, the death of a party while the contract is being made, even though only a single act remains to be done, renders the completion of the contract impossible.

The effect of death upon a revocable offer is thus stated in Restatement of Contracts, sec. 48: "A revocable offer is terminated by the offeror's death or such insanity as deprives him of legal capacity to enter into the proposed contract." This rule has been criticized on the ground that under the modern view of the formation of contracts, it is not the actual meeting of the minds of the contracting parties that is the determining factor, but rather the apparent state of mind of the parties embodied in an expression of mutual consent; so that the acceptance by an offeree of an offer, which is apparently still open, should result in an enforceable contract notwithstanding the prior death of the offeror unknown to the offeree. On the other hand, it has been forcibly suggested that ordinarily the condition is implied in an offer that the offeror will survive to supervise the performance if death is ineffective even though the acceptor be ignorant of the offeror's death. These conflicting views, however, were given consideration in the preparation of the Restatement, and the rule announced was adopted as representing the weight of authority and professional opinion. [DECISION FOR DEFENDANT]

Simmerman v. Fort Hartford Coal Co., 221 S.W.2d 442 (Ky. 1949). Action by Fort Hartford Coal Company (plaintiff below), appellee, against Jesse R. Simmerman (defendant below), appellant. Appellant executed to appellee a lease covering certain coal lands for a period of five years, which lease contained the following clause: "That at any time during the life of this lease, or any extension thereof, the party of the second part has the option to purchase said coal." Appellee, during the term of the lease, notified appellant of its election to exercise its option to purchase the coal, and appellant declined to sign the deed giving appellee the coal and mining rights under the lands. This action was then brought for specific performance.

Knight, Justice: At the time this contract was entered into in 1935, appellant was sixty years of age. Her husband, R. E. L. Simmerman, was a lawyer until his death in 1930. . . . She has one child, a daughter, Winifred Simmerman, who has a college education, is apparently a woman of intelligence, and has always lived with her mother. Appellant, according to her proof, had always lived a sheltered life and during the life of her husband and of her father, she had no financial responsibilities nor any opportunities to acquire any business experience. Her husband became involved in the failure of the Bank of Hartford, which failed in 1926, and her father's estate was also involved in the failure. She contends that the worries she went through in connection with the liquidation of the bank's affairs together with illness, which began in 1924 and has continued up to the present time, rendered her unfit to transact any important business. She says she had to quit school while quite young because of poor health. On the whole she pictures herself as uneducated, inexperienced in business, in poor health and distressed in mind and body, and was therefore not in a position to cope with an experienced business man like Mr. Holt, president of appellee, when the contract was executed in 1935. On the otherwise, it is shown that she is a woman of average, or more than average, intelligence who managed her estate in a capable manner, and it was shown by the records of the county clerk's office that she had bought, sold and mortgaged property in numerous transactions both before and after the time of the execution of the contract here involved. . . .

There is also sharp conflict in the testimony as to whether or not Mrs. Simmerman had an opportunity to read or study the contract after it was drawn up. Miss Simmerman testified that the two copies of the contract came to her mother in a plain envelope postmarked "Owensboro"; that they were received late in the afternoon; that she only glanced through them herself but did not let her mother read them because she had had a nervous attack that evening. . . .

It is the rule in this state that a party who can read and has an opportunity to read the contract which he signs must stand by the words of the contract unless he is misled as to the nature of the writing which he signs or his signature is obtained by fraud. As was said by this court in the case of *J. I. Case Threshing Machine Co. v. Mattingly,* 142 Ky. 581, 134 S.W. 1131, quoting with approval a case from the U.S. Supreme Court (*Upton v. Tribilcock,* 91 U.S. 45):

It will not do for a man to enter into a contract, and, when called upon to respond to its obligations, to say that he did not read it when he signed it, or did not know what it contained. If this were permitted, contracts would not be worth the paper on which they are written. But such is not the law. A contractor must stand by the words of his contract; and, if he will not read what he signs, he alone is responsible for his omission.

Under these authorities and the evidence on this phase of the case, we agreed with the opinion of the chancellor that the defense interposed by Mrs. Simmerman that she did not read the contract, did not know its contents and was overreached in its execution is not sustained. [DECISION FOR APPELLEE]

Application of Doughboy Industries, Inc., 233 N.Y.S.2d 488 (1962). This is a petition by Doughboy Industries, Inc., petitioner, against The Pantasote Company, respondent, to stay an arbitration proceeding.

Doughboy Industries, the buyer, mailed two purchase orders to The Pantasote Company, the seller, for the purchase of 20,000 pounds of film to be delivered in the future on specified dates. In addition, further quantities were ordered on a "hold basis," that is, subject to increase, decrease, or cancellation by the buyer. The seller orally accepted the purchase orders, and suggested immediate shipment of the first part of the order. The buyer agreed, and the seller shipped 10,000 pounds of the film. The seller then mailed written acknowledgments of the orders to the buyer. The buyer later sent change orders with respect to the orders on a "hold basis." A dispute then arose as to whether the buyer was bound to accept all the goods on a "hold basis." The buyer wished to have the dispute determined by court litigation, and the seller wished to have the dispute determined by arbitration.

Breitel, Justice: This case involves a conflict between a buyer's order form and a seller's acknowledgment form, each memorializing a purchase and sale of goods. The issue arises on whether the parties agreed to arbitrate future disputes. The seller's form had a general arbitration provision. The buyer's form did not. The buyer's form contained a provision that only a signed consent would bind the buyer to any terms thereafter transmitted in any commercial form of the seller. The seller's form, however, provided that silence or a failure to object in writing would be an acceptance of the terms and conditions of its acknowledgment form. The buyer never objected to the seller's acknowledgment, orally or in writing. In short, the buyer and seller accomplished a legal equivalent to the irresistible force colliding with the immovable object. . . . Of interest in the case is that both the seller and buyer are substantial businesses—a "strong" buyer and a "strong" seller. This is not a case of one of the parties being at the bargaining mercy of the other. . . .

Although the purchase orders called for written acceptances and return or attached acknowledgments by the seller no one paid any attention to these requirements. Neither party, orally or in writing, objected to the conditions printed on the other's commercial form. . . .

The problem of conflicting commercial forms is one with which there has been much concern before this, and a new effort at rational solution has been made. The Uniform Commercial Code reflects the latest legislative conclusions as to what the law ought to be. It provides:

Section 2–207. Additional Terms in Acceptance or Confirmation

(1) A definite and seasonable expression of acceptance or a written confirmation which is sent within a reasonable time operates as an acceptance even though it states terms additional to or different from those offered or agreed upon, unless acceptance is expressly made conditional on assent to the additional or different terms.

(2) The additional terms are to be construed as proposals for addition to the contract. Between merchants such terms become part of the contract unless:

　(a) the offer expressly limits acceptance to the terms of the offer;

　(b) they materially alter it; or

　(c) notification of objection to them has already been given or is given within a reasonable time after notice of them is received.

(3) Conduct by both parties which recognizes the existence of a contract is sufficient to establish a contract for sale although the writings of the parties do not otherwise establish a contract. In such case the terms of the particular contract consist of those terms on which the writings of the parties agree, together with any supplementary terms incorporated under any other provisions of this Act.

The arbitration clause, whether viewed as a material alteration under subsection (2), or as a term nullified by a conflicting provision in the buyer's form, would fail to survive as a contract term. In the light of the New York cases, at least, there can be little question that an agreement to arbitrate is a material term, one not to be injected by implication, subtlety or inveiglement. And the conclusion is also the same if the limitation contained in the offer (the buyer's purchase order) is given effect, as required by subsection 2(a) of the new section. [DECISION FOR PETITIONER]

PROBLEMS

1　Defendant was the owner of a set of old double harness, worth perhaps $15, which was taken from his premises without his knowledge. He offered a reward for the return of the harness, and a few days afterward a boy named Wilt found part of the harness in a berry patch. Defendant gave the boy a quarter and told him that he would give him a dollar to find the rest. The defendant, on this occasion, was very excited and, using rough language and epithets concerning the thief, said: "I will give $100 to any man who will find out who the thief is, and I will give a lawyer $100 for prosecuting him." He asserted that he would not have a second-class lawyer, either, and that he would not hire a cheap lawyer but a good lawyer. The plaintiff, a few days later, informed the defendant that a man called Red John Smith, who had been adjudged insane, had taken the harness. The remainder of the harness was then found, and this action was brought to recover the $100 claimed as a reward. Is there a valid contract?

2　Plaintiff, knowing that the defendant needed mink pelts over thirty inches in length, delivered to the defendant four or five times during 1963 and 1964 mink pelts of this kind and always received payment therefor. On February 18, 1965, plaintiff delivered 1,000 mink pelts, all over thirty inches in length, to defendant, who did not notify plaintiff that he either rejected or accepted the pelts. The pelts, nevertheless, remained at the defendant's place of business for a few months and were then destroyed. This action was brought to recover the alleged value of the pelts. Is plaintiff entitled to recover?

3　On July 18, a written order was signed by the defendant and delivered to plaintiff directing plaintiff to deliver immediately on board cars, certain farm machinery consigned to defendant at Neola, Iowa. The machinery was shipped on July 20. On July 21, defendant sent a telegram canceling the order, and refused to accept the machinery when it arrived at Neola. Plaintiff brought an action for breach of contract. Defendant contended that the plaintiff failed to communicate an acceptance of the offer prior to revocation. Is defendant's contention correct?

4   Defendants were contemplating the construction of a building, and sought the advice of plaintiffs, who were architects. Although nothing was said about the fee of the architects, the defendants consulted with the plaintiffs for several times. The negotiations continued over a three-month period and finally culminated when the plaintiffs, without being specifically authorized to do so, delivered to the defendants five sets of complete architectural blueprints and an eleven-page pamphlet of specifications for the construction of the building. Defendants accepted the plans and specifications and never offered or attempted to return them. Do you think plaintiffs will be able to recover compensation for the services rendered?

5   On October 5, 1923, defendant purported to execute an oil and gas lease, at which time it was agreed that the president of the plaintiff, an oil company, who was out of town, should have ten days from October 5 within which to execute the lease. The lease was sent to the Conrad Banking Company, the agreed depositary, for execution by the president of the plaintiff. On October 11, the defendant withdrew the papers from the Conrad Banking Company, which company communicated the fact to the office of the plaintiff. The president of the plaintiff, on October 11, offered to execute the contract, but the defendant contended that the offer had been withdrawn. The plaintiff brought suit for specific performance. Had the offer been revoked?

6   Brown, Jr., the executor of the estate of Brown, Sr., wrote a letter to Jones, a broker engaged in the business of buying and selling shares of stock, offering to sell 200 shares of the XYZ Company, which shares were a part of the assets of the estate of Brown, Sr., at $100 per share. Brown, Jr., also gave assurances in the letter that the offer would be held open for thirty days. The next day, Brown, Jr., sold the shares of stock to Smith, also a broker, for $150 per share. Ten days after Jones received the letter, he learned that the shares had been sold by Brown, Jr., to Smith. Jones then contended that the offer made by Brown, Jr., was a firm offer and was not revocable for thirty days. Is this contention of Jones correct?

7   The employer company, in January, 1950, issued and distributed a booklet entitled "Know Your Company" to its employees in which the following appears: "It has been customary since 1937 for the company to make a year-end payment to employees. The amount of such payment, if any, depends upon the earnings available from operations and is entirely at the discretion of the Board of Directors." Certain of the employees did not receive a year-end payment in 1956. These employees contend that the language in the booklet was an offer which was accepted by the employees when they continued in the employment in reliance upon the offer. Do you agree with this contention?

8   Defendant wrote a letter dated January 2 to plaintiff and offered to sell his portable typewriter to plaintiff for $75 provided plaintiff accepted the offer on or before January 7. Plaintiff replied by letter stating: "Your offer to sell your portable typewriter is rejected." Plaintiff then changed his mind and sent defendant a telegram stating: "I hereby accept your offer to purchase your portable typewriter for $75." The telegram was dispatched and received on January 5, and the letter was received on January 6. Defendant refused to sell the typewriter to plaintiff, and plaintiff brought an action for breach of contract. Should he recover?

6
CONSIDERATION
THe AcT

The history of the law of contracts reveals that at a very early date sealed written agreements were enforceable. The prevailing rule today is that a contract, whether oral or written, is not binding in the absence of "consideration." The consideration, moreover, must be *sufficient* in the sense that it has legal value in the eyes of the law. A few exceptions to the rule are discussed throughout the pages of this chapter, but these exceptions have incentives other than the presence or absence of a seal.

Conceding the necessity of consideration, however, does not solve the more difficult problem of defining the word. The generally accepted definition of the word is that the promisee suffers a legal detriment or the promisor receives a legal benefit. This definition, however, is not broad enough to embrace all situations. A few contracts are enforceable even though there is no detriment to the promisee or benefit to the promisor. Consideration is sometimes thought of as the price requested by the promisor and received in exchange for the promise. The theory of consideration is clearly predicated on the idea that the promisor bargains for and receives something in exchange for his promise.

The classical concept of consideration is to the effect that the promise of one person and the consideration of another must be the motive for each other, wholly or in part. The promisor must be induced by the consideration to make the promise and the consideration must have been induced by the express or implied promise of the promisor. This is a two-way proposition, and if one-half is lacking, there is not sufficient consideration to create a contract. Suppose a father merely promises his son a gift of $10,000 on his next birthday. Suppose further, the son, in reliance on this promise, purchases an expensive new convertible the next day. The father is under no duty to make the gift to the son since the fortuitous detriment to the son did not in any way induce the father to make the promise. If the father, however, had bargained for the detriment on the part of the son, the promise would be enforceable.

The mutual promises in a bilateral contract—a promise for a promise—constitute the consideration. Each party, therefore, is both a promisor and a promisee. In a unilateral contract—a promise for an act—one party is a promisor and the other is a promisee. Consideration is obvious in the sale of goods for cash. The contract is made and performed simultaneously, and each party receives something in exchange for something given. Consideration, however, is not always so apparent. But it is quite clear that consideration may be an act, a forbearance, or a return promise. It seems that the best way to approach the problem of explaining consideration, therefore, is (1) to present some specific promises, acts, and forbearances that may or may not constitute consideration, (2) to discuss some miscellaneous kinds of consideration that may or may not support a contract, (3) to explain how some claims are settled with or without considera-tion, and (4) to explain when consideration is or is not necessary in modification, rescission, and waiver.

PROMISES, ACTS, FORBEARANCES

Mutual Promises   The promise of both the promisor and the promisee must be legally binding or the contract is void for lack of consideration. The general rule is that the mutual promises must be stated in such terms that both parties are bound and that an action could be maintained by each against the other for a breach of the contract. This is the doctrine of mutuality of obligation. A party who promises to perform but who reserves to himself the option to perform or not to perform has not made an enforceable promise because there is no promise to enforce. Brown, promising to sell his automobile to Smith "unless I decide not to sell the automobile," has, in fact, promised nothing. With similar reasoning, an agreement which provides that one party reserves the right to cancel the agreement at his pleasure imposes no liability on the party if he takes advantage of the reservation clause and terminates the contract. Suppose a buyer promises to buy from a seller "such goods as I may wish, desire, or order." The promise is too indefinite to determine what has been promised. A promise too indefinite to be sufficient consideration, however, may become definite. A unilateral contract requires no mutuality of obligation. If certain goods are actually sold and delivered, therefore, the contract becomes a valid unilateral contract by performance.

Forbearance of Legal Right Forbearance alone will not constitute consideration. Forbearance, or the promise to forbear, must be given in exchange for the promise of the other person. Forbearance to do a thing which a person is legally entitled to do, or which is not contrary to public policy, is a sufficient consideration. The right may be against a third person as well as against the promisor. A person who refrains to litigate a claim may enforce the promise for which the forbearance was given. The rule, however, cannot be extended to claims made in bad faith, and a person who refrains from bringing suit when he has no intention to sue, or when he knows the claim is unenforceable, cannot enforce the promise of the other person. A promise to forbear suit upon any claim that is clearly illegal, irrespective of the intention, cannot be enforced. The contract itself is void.

   An express or implied promise given in exchange for a forbearance, however, is enforceable. The forbearance on the part of the promisee is sufficient consideration to make the promise given therefor enforceable. [*Zimmerman Ford, Inc. v. Cheney*, p. 67.]

Life Employment Contracts A contract which promises an employee life employment for a consideration in addition to the services to be rendered entitles the employee to an option as to when the term shall end. The employer, however, is not entitled to such an option. The general rule, therefore, that both parties must be bound or neither is bound has led to controversy over the question of whether or not a contract by an employer to give an employee employment for life is enforceable. In contracts for life employment, the employee ordinarily does give consideration in addition to the services incident to the employment. The controversy, however, revolves around the question as to what constitutes consideration in order to prevent termination of the contract without good cause at the will of the employer. The courts are divided as to whether or not such acts as the giving up of a business or profession constitute consideration. They are, nevertheless, fairly uniform in holding that a release by an injured employee of his claim against the employer for personal injuries previously sustained will constitute consideration.

Performance of Pre-existing Duty The performance of, or the promise to perform, that which a person is already under legal obligation to do is not sufficient consideration to support a promise to pay therefor. This is clearly true if the obligation is imposed by statute. The promise to pay a certain sum of money to a police officer to make an arrest is unenforceable. The act requested may be over and beyond the legal duty of the officer, in which case a promise to pay therefor is enforceable. The rule, however, is not limited to statutory obligations.

   With respect to building contracts, it is uniformly held that a person who promises to pay a contractor an additional sum if the contractor will complete the construction work in accordance with the terms of the contract will not be legally bound to pay the promised sum. The contractor is ordinarily required to perform in accordance with the contract even if he encounters unforeseen difficulties which neither party could have foreseen.

In employment contracts, special or extra services not covered by an existing contract of employment will constitute consideration for the promise of the employer to pay higher wages. A promise by an employer, however, to pay an employee additional compensation merely to work for the duration of the contract is unenforceable. [*C. H. Davis & Co. v. Morgan*, p. 68.]

A few courts permit recovery for the performance of a pre-existing contractual obligation. These courts take the view that the original contract has been cancelled, a new agreement has been entered into, and the promise of one party becomes the consideration for the promise of the other. The majority rule, however, is that the performance of a pre-existing contractual obligation is not sufficient consideration.

Estoppel   The doctrine of estoppel, broadly stated, is an impediment raised by the law which prevents a person from alleging or denying certain facts in consequence of his own previous allegations or acts. It should not be presumed, however, that the doctrine is limited to the law of consideration. It is equally applicable to other branches of law, such as agency and corporations. It seems appropriate at this point to mention two kinds of estoppel: (1) equitable estoppel, or estoppel in pais, and (2) promissory estoppel.

(1)   *Equitable Estoppel*   Equitable estoppel arises when a person by his acts or representations, or by his silence when he ought to speak, induces another person to believe certain facts to exist and such other person rightfully relies and acts on such belief to his prejudice. The doctrine also holds that, as between two innocent parties, the one who makes a fraud possible must bear the loss resulting from such fraud. An illustration should be helpful: Suppose Brown purchased certain furniture from The Furniture Company on an installment contract. Suppose further that the contract contained a recital that Brown "acknowledges delivery and acceptance of" the furniture, but that the furniture was not delivered. Suppose further that The Furniture Company assigned the sales contract to The Finance Company, which did not know of the nondelivery of the furniture, and that The Finance Company brought an action against Brown to collect the installments due. If the action had been brought by The Furniture Company, Brown could assert a failure of consideration. In an action by The Finance Company, however, Brown would be estopped from denying the furniture's delivery. To pursue the illustration one step further: Suppose The Finance Company knew, or should have known, that The Furniture Company did not deliver the furniture. The Finance Company would be prevented from invoking estoppel against Brown. In this situation, The Finance Company would not be an innocent party, or, as it is sometimes stated, would not be acting in good faith. The doctrine of estoppel cannot be used to perpetrate a fraud.

(2)   *Promissory Estoppel*   Promissory estoppel is applied to the formation of contracts. It is used when the promisee, relying on a gratuitous promise, suffers a detriment. Legal scholars, however, have debated for decades whether an estoppel may be a substitute for consideration. When the doctrine is applied, however, it is generally essential that the induced action, although not bargained

for, be of a definite and substantial character, and the promisee must suffer irreparable detriment in justifiable reliance on the promise. [*Feinberg v. Pfeiffer Co.*, p. 69.]

MISCELLANEOUS TYPES OF CONSIDERATION

Moral Consideration   It is a well-settled general rule that a mere moral obligation arising from mere ethical motives will not furnish sufficient consideration for an executory promise. A promise by Brown to pay a debt previously contracted by Smith, therefore, would be unenforceable. The general rule, however, is subject to limitations and exceptions. The courts have found little trouble in enforcing a moral obligation arising from, or connected with, what was once a legal liability. Promises made by a person (1) to pay a debt which is barred by the statute of limitations, (2) to pay a debt which is discharged in bankruptcy, and (3) pertaining to charitable subscriptions are prominent illustrations of an enforceable new promise coupled with moral consideration.

    (1)   *Statute of Limitations*   Statutes of limitations have been enacted in all states which provide that actions on contracts must be brought within a stated number of years. The courts have held, however, that a new promise to pay a debt barred by law is enforceable. Such a promise may not only be oral, but implied by an acknowledgment or admission of the debt coupled with an intention to pay. A voluntary part payment of the debt after the statute has run amounts to an acknowledgment of the debt. Mere expressions of good intentions will not be construed as a new promise. The promise, therefore, must be stated in sufficiently clear terms so that the court can determine from the circumstances the presence or absence of an intention to revive the old debt. The courts have generally treated the old debt as the consideration for the new promise of the debtor. Probably of more importance today is the fact that most state legislatures have enacted statutes which provide that a promise to pay a debt barred by the statute of limitations must be in writing. A few courts apply the statute strictly and, in the absence of a writing signed by the person sought to be bound, will not enforce a new oral promise to pay a debt which is barred.

    (2)   *Bankruptcy*   A discharge in bankruptcy excuses the debtor from paying certain debts. A more extensive discussion of this subject will be found in Chapter 62, "Bankruptcy." It is necessary to mention it at this time for the purpose of illustrating a well-recognized legal situation involving consideration: A promise made by a debtor to pay a debt which has been barred by a discharge in bankruptcy is enforceable without any new consideration. The promise may be made orally, but it must be express or directly implied from the terms used; it must be clear and explicit. The promise cannot be implied simply from conduct, such as a voluntary part payment, and some statutes require a written promise.

    (3)   *Subscription Agreements*   It is still recognized that consideration is necessary to make charitable subscriptions binding. A variety of theories, nevertheless, have been advanced to achieve the desired result. Some courts hold

the promise is binding on the doctrine of promissory estoppel. The rule most generally applied is that the consideration is supplied where the promisee, in justifiable reliance on the promise, has altered his position to his injury. If the promisee, therefore, expends money or incurs enforceable liabilities, the subscription is rendered enforceable. The subscription, however, stands as a mere offer which may be revoked at the will of the donor and will be terminated by the death or insanity of the subscriber until such time as the promisee has so acted to his injury on the subscription.

To illustrate: Brown and several other subscribers sign a subscription agreement whereby they promise to give $1,000 each to some charitable organization. The organization commences the erection of the proposed building. Brown then refuses to pay his subscription. Brown will nevertheless be held liable on his promise to pay the $1,000. The line of reasoning generally applied by the courts is that the charitable organization, in reliance on the subscription, suffered a detriment by executing a contract for the erection of the building. The organization did this by becoming liable for the contract price.

Good Consideration   The term "good consideration" is sometimes used synonymously with "sufficient consideration," but in the proper use of the words, a good consideration pertains to a promise founded on a natural duty or love and affection. Such promises are said to be supported by good consideration, which is not sufficient to make a contract binding. An executed gift cannot be set aside because of the absence of consideration. A mere promise to make a gift, however, without anything more, is not enforceable.

Past Consideration   A "past consideration" is not sufficient to make a contract enforceable. The cases which are based on a past consideration, however, should be distinguished from those in which a new promise is made to pay a past debt or obligation, still existing and enforceable. Suppose Brown employs Smith to landscape the yard around his residence and no price is agreed upon. A promise to pay a reasonable compensation therefor will be implied. Suppose further that, after the landscaping is completed, Brown and Smith agree that $500 is the price to be paid and Brown promises to pay this amount. The promise is enforceable. It is thus clear that this line of cases is quite different from the past-consideration cases. The promise of an employer to pay a previously retired employee $200 per month for life or the promise of a son to pay a doctor for services previously rendered his mother are examples of a past consideration. The promise is unenforceable if a person receives a gratuitous benefit and, at a later date, the benefited person, or some person in his behalf, makes a promise to the person who bestowed the benefit to pay therefor. [*Brown v. Addington*, p. 70.]

Adequate Consideration   An "adequate consideration" pertains to the value of the property bargained for but is relatively unimportant in the law of contracts. The courts make no attempt to determine what value the parties may have attached to the thing with which they have parted. The parties may agree to buy and sell property at a price which, in the absence of government control, is above or below the market value. Three exceptions to the rule are well recognized, and the courts frequently inquire into the adequacy of the consideration when (1) there is an exchange of money of the same medium of exchange, that is, 1 cent for $1; or (2) there is an exchange of goods of the same kind and quality at the same time and place; or (3) the contract is sought to be avoided on the ground of fraud.

One other feature requires mention. The common practice of reciting $1 as consideration may or may not be held sufficient to sustain a promise. If the $1 was, in fact, the consideration agreed upon, the courts will not change the contractual terms for the parties. A few courts hold, moreover, that the recital of a consideration estops the contracting parties from later contradicting the recital. But a recital of the receipt of a fictitious consideration—when in fact there was no consideration, promised, or paid, at all—ordinarily will not create a binding contract. [*Allen v. Allen*, p. 71.]

SETTLEMENT OF CLAIMS

The settlement of claims by a substituted agreement constitutes a new contractual relation and is ordinarily based upon a new contract. The elements are essentially the same as in the original contract and include competent parties, legal subject matter, assent, and sufficient consideration. Troublesome questions arose in earlier days with respect to assent and consideration. It is well settled today, however, that assent may be implied from the conduct of the parties. It is also well settled that the "surrender of a right to sue upon a claim" is a sufficient consideration. The courts of today, as will be seen, have little trouble in discovering some circumstance that can be construed as a sufficient consideration to support a promise in a substituted agreement.

Payment of a Lesser Sum   It has been the general rule for a long time that a promise made by a creditor to his debtor to discharge a liquidated, or undisputed, debt by the acceptance of a lesser sum of money is, without anything more, unenforceable. The debtor is obligated to pay the entire debt, and if he promises to pay a lesser sum, he has done nothing more than that which he is already required to do contractually. The hardship of the rule has been lessened by statute in a number of states. These statutes generally declare, in effect, that part payment, when expressly accepted by the creditor in writing in satisfaction of the debt, though without any new consideration, extinguishes the debt. It is also possible that the creditor intended to make a gift of the remainder due on the debt. If the evidence clearly shows that this is the intention of the creditor, the courts generally hold that the debt is extinguished without any new consideration.

The decisions clearly indicate the extremes to which the courts will go in order to hold creditors to their settlements. These decisions have led to the rule that the creditor and the debtor may enter into an agreement for the discharge of the debt whereby the debtor pays or promises to pay, a lesser sum coupled with some new consideration.

The courts are not concerned with the adequacy of the new consideration which may be even of slight value. It has been held sufficient consideration if payment is made before maturity, or at a place other than the one designated for payment. It is also true that a new note secured by a mortgage, or a note which is indorsed by a third person, will suffice. An unsecured note of the debtor for less than is admittedly due, however, is only a new promise to pay less than is due and will not release the debtor of his obligation to pay the entire debt.

Satisfaction Recital   Suppose a debtor sends a check marked "paid in full," or in similar terms, to his creditor in payment of a debt. The acceptance and cashing of such a check may or may not discharge the debt. The answer depends upon whether there was an unliquidated or honestly disputed debt. A debtor who sends a check so marked in the hope that the creditor will accept it as fully satisfying a debt over which there is no honest dispute will not thereby discharge the debt. The creditor may cash the check and sue for the balance. A check so marked, however, will operate as a discharge of the debt (1) if the claim is unliquidated, or is honestly disputed, and (2) if it is cashed by the creditor or the creditor retains it for an unreasonable length of time. In doubtful situations, it probably would be wiser for a creditor who intends to insist upon full payment to return the check. [*Burgamy v. Davis*, p. 71.]

Accord and Satisfaction, Compromise and Settlement   An "accord and satisfaction" and a "compromise and settlement" are broad terms which are generally applied to the settlement of all claims. A compromise and an accord are both agreements for the settlement of a previously existing claim by a substituted performance. The distinction lies in the fact that an accord may be the settlement of a claim that is disputed or undisputed, while a compromise must be the settlement of a claim that is disputed. Stated otherwise, any claim may be discharged by some substituted performance that is agreed upon, but only disputes may be compromised.

An accord and satisfaction is the settlement of a dispute or the satisfaction of a claim by means of a new contract between the contracting parties. When the agreement is executed and satisfaction has been made, it is called an accord and satisfaction. The accord is the agreement for giving and taking a thing in satisfaction of the claim; the satisfaction is the actual giving and taking of the thing. A debtor owes $1,000 to his creditor. The debtor and the creditor enter into an agreement whereby the debtor agrees to deliver, and the creditor agrees to accept, a certain automobile in full satisfaction of the debt. The delivery of the automobile to the creditor is the satisfaction and therefore discharges the debt by an accord and satisfaction.

A compromise and settlement is the settlement of an honestly disputed debt. Such a debt is one in which the amount of the claim cannot be ascertained; it may be one in which the amount is fixed but there is a disagreement as to whether or not it has been paid; or it may be one in which the amount of the original debt was fixed but the balance due cannot be ascertained. Any sum given and accepted will discharge the claim, and the surrender of the right to sue upon the claim constitutes consideration for a promise to settle for less.

Composition with Creditors   An agreement made between a debtor and his creditors whereby the creditors agree with one another and with the debtor to receive a certain proportion of the sum due the creditors is known as a "composition with creditors." The courts have consistently held such agreements to be binding, and have advanced various theories to sustain their holdings. The consideration is generally said to be the promise of each creditor to the other to discharge a portion of his claim. A composition with creditors is a voluntary agreement, and a creditor who does not join in the composition does not lose his right to collect the whole sum due from the debtor. A promise by the debtor to a creditor who was a party to the composition to pay the balance is not enforceable since there is no debt to revive.

MODIFICATION, RESCISSION, WAIVER

Modification   The parties to a contract may modify the contract by entering into an entirely new contract relating to the same subject or by introducing new terms into the old contract. The new contract ordinarily consists of new terms and so much of the old contract as remains unchanged. The sufficiency of the consideration seems to be governed by the rules that govern an original contract. The requirement of consideration for modifying agreements, however, has been dispensed with by statute in some states.

Section 2–209 of the Code provides that an agreement modifying a contract, if made in good faith, needs no consideration to be binding. The requirement of the Statute of Frauds must be satisfied if the contract as modified is for the sale of goods for the price of $500 or more. The original contract may also contain a no-modification-unless-in-writing clause. If such a clause is contained in the original contract, the modification or rescission is required to be in writing. A merchant who supplies a form which contains such a clause must be signed separately by the consumer. With these exceptions, the modification may be made orally. [*Skinner v. Tober Foreign Motors*, p. 72.]

This section also provides that an ineffective attempt at modification or rescission can operate as a waiver. An oral modification which should be in writing, therefore, can operate as a waiver.

Mutual Rescission   A contract which has not been fully performed on either side—a wholly executory contract—may be rescinded by the parties who agreed to enter into the contract provided superior rights of third persons have not intervened. Such an agreement is called "mutual rescission." The agreement to rescind must possess all the elements requisite to the formation of a valid contract; it may be made orally; it may be in writing; or it may be shown by conduct indicating such a purpose. The discharge of one party from an obligation to perform further is a sufficient consideration for the discharge of the other party from his obligation to perform further. For this reason a contract which has been fully performed by one of the parties cannot be rescinded unless the one who has not performed gives some consideration to the party who has performed. Suppose Brown agrees to perform certain services for Jones and that Jones agrees to pay for the services. Brown and Jones may mutually rescind the agreement so long as the services have not been performed and the money has not been paid. If Brown should perform the services, however, a promise by Brown that Jones need not pay for the services would not be binding without consideration.

A claim to the right of restitution is often made in the mutual rescission of a partially performed bilateral contract. The courts attempt to decide the claim in accordance with the intention of the parties. Mutual rescission, as distinguished from the "remedy of rescission," does not require that the parties be restored to their original status. The mutual agreement to rescind, therefore, should eliminate doubt by the inclusion of a clause which provides for restitution if that is the intention of the parties.

Waiver   The word "waiver" is frequently defined as the voluntary relinquishment of a known right. Suppose Brown enters into a contract with a building contractor for the construction of a building to be completed no later than January 31. Suppose further that Brown, prior to completion, promises the contractor that he will accept completion by February 28. This promise of Brown requires consideration or it may be retracted unless the contractor materially changes his position in reliance on the promise. So if Brown fails to make a timely retraction, he will be estopped from alleging a breach of contract. This is a waiver before breach. A waiver after breach ordinarily requires no consideration to be binding. Suppose Brown accepts delivery of certain furniture on the 20th of the month which should have been delivered on the 10th. He is said to have waived his right to delivery on the 10th. In this illustration, however, Brown did not make a promise. He had an election to accept the furniture or refuse acceptance and bring an action to recover damages for the breach.

CASES

Zimmerman Ford, Inc. v. Cheney   271 N.E.2d 682 (Ill. 1971). Action by Zimmerman Ford, Inc. (plaintiff below), appellee, against Franklin Cheney and Winnie Ambrose (defendants below), appellants, under a confession clause of an automobile installment sales contract. The Circuit Court entered judgment against both the buyer and cosigner of the sales contract. Defendant, Winnie Ambrose, appeals from a judgment in the amount of $1,495. She claims there was a lack of consideration for her signature.

Seidenfeld, Justice: The evidence showed that Franklin Cheney, a grandson of Winnie Ambrose, entered into a retail installment sales contract with plaintiff to purchase an automobile. A cosigner was required, and the contract was returned to the plaintiff by Cheney with the purported additional signature of Winnie Ambrose. Later Cheney defaulted in his payments, and the collecting bank notified plaintiff that Winnie Ambrose's signature was a forgery. Thereafter plaintiff obtained Mrs. Ambrose's signature on a "replacement contract," which the trial court found to be identical in its terms with the original contract.

Mrs. Ambrose testified that she was given a blank form and was told only that it was "about the car" and that her grandson could not keep the car if she did not sign. She acknowledged that she knew when she signed the contract that the purported signature on the first contract was not hers. There was testimony that when she signed the contract, Mrs. Ambrose said she would do anything to help keep her grandson out of trouble. At another point in her testimony, Mrs. Ambrose acknowledged that she was asked if she would sign papers so the boy could keep the car and that she signed for that reason.

On these facts, defendant argues that she received no consideration to support her promise to pay the pre-existing debt of Cheney. However, we find sufficient evidence of mutual consideration, consisting of plaintiff's implied promise to forbear from repossessing the car in exchange for defendant's promise to pay if the grandson did not. An agreement to forbear need not be in express terms or for an exact period of time; the terms may be gathered from the surrounding circumstances from which forbearance for a reasonable time may be implied. [DECISION FOR PLAINTIFF]

C. H. Davis & Co. v. Morgan   43 S.E. 732 (Ga. 1903). Action by A. M. Morgan, plaintiff, against C. H. Davis & Company, defendant. Davis & Company employed Morgan for one year at $40 per month. After the contract had been in force for some time, Morgan received an offer of $65 per month from a company in Florida. He mentioned that fact to Davis. At that time, according to Morgan's testimony, Davis stated, "I will add $10 a month from the time you began, and owe you $120 when your time is up." Davis & Company discharged Morgan two or three weeks before the end of the term because the latter had gone to Florida for several days without their consent. Morgan brought this action for the extra compensation promised.

Lamar, Justice: If the promise contemplated that Davis & Co. were to pay Morgan $10 per month for that part of the year which had already passed, and as to which there had been a settlement, it was manifestly nudum pactum; for a past transaction, the obligation of which has been fully satisfied, will not sustain a new promise. . . . The employer, therefore, received no consideration for his promise to give the additional money at the end of the year. Morgan had agreed to work for 12 months at the price promised, and if during the term he had agreed to receive less, the employer would still have been liable to pay him the full $40 per month. On the other hand, the employer would not be forced to pay more than the contract price. He got no more services than he had already contracted to receive, and according to an almost unbroken line of decisions the agreement to give more than was due was a nudum pactum, and void, as having no consideration to support the promise.

. . . Had there been a rescission or formal cancellation of the old contract by mutual consent, and if a new contract with new terms had been made; or if there had been any change in the hours, services, or character of work, or other consideration to support the promise to pay the increased wages it would have been enforceable. But, as it was, Morgan proved that Davis promised to pay more for the performance of the old contract than he had originally agreed. Such a promise is not binding. [DECISION FOR DEFENDANT]

Feinberg v. Pfeiffer Co., 322 S.W.2d 163 (Mo. 1959). Action by Anna Sacks Feinberg, plaintiff, against Pfeiffer Company, defendant. Plaintiff began working for the defendant, a manufacturer of pharmaceuticals, in 1910, when she was seventeen years of age. By 1947 she had attained the position of bookeeper, office manager, and assistant treasurer of the defendant-company. On December 27, 1947, at a meeting of the board of directors, the chairman, among other things, pointed out that Mrs. Feinberg had given the corporation many years of long and faithful service and that she had served the corporation devotedly with exceptional ability and skill. After due discussion and consideration, and upon motion duly made and seconded, it was:

Resolved, that the salary of Anna Sacks Feinberg be increased from $350.00 to $400.00 per month and that she be afforded the privilege of retiring from active duty in the corporation at any time she may elect to see fit so to do upon retirement pay of $200.00 per month for the remainder of her life.

Plaintiff continued to work for the defendant-company through June 30, 1949, on which date she retired. The defendant-company thereafter paid her the sum of $200 each month. These payments continued until April 1, 1956, at which time the defendant-company reduced the retirement pay to $100. Plaintiff declined to accept the reduced amount and brought this action to recover retirement pay in accordance with the resolution quoted above.

Doerner, Commissioner: Plaintiff concedes that a promise based upon past services would be without consideration, but contends that . . . her change of position, i.e., her retirement, and the abandonment by her of her opportunity to continue in gainful employment, made in reliance on defendant's promise to pay her $200 per month for life . . .

Section 90 of the Restatement of the Law of Contracts states that "A promise which the promisor should reasonably expect to induce action or forbearance of a definite and substantial character on the part of the promisee and which does induce such action or forbearance is binding if injustice can be avoided only by the enforcement of the promise." This doctrine has been described as that of "promissory estoppel."

Was there such an act on the part of the plaintiff, in reliance upon the promise contained in the resolution, as will estop the defendant, and therefore create an enforceable contract under the doctrine of promissory estoppel? We think there was. . . .

At the time she retired plaintiff was 57 years of age. At the time the payments were discontinued she was over 63 years of age. It is a matter of common knowledge that it is virtually impossible for a woman of that age to find satisfactory employment, much less a position comparable to that which plaintiff enjoyed at the time of her retirement. [DECISION FOR PLAINTIFF]

Brown v. Addington   52 N.E.2d 640 (Ind. 1944). Action by Francis W. Brown, administrator of the estate of William E. Brown (plaintiff below), appellant, against Claude L. Addington (defendant below), appellee. Claude L. Addington became homeless when he was eight years old, and William E. Brown, his uncle, took him into his home and fed, clothed, and educated him in the public schools. The uncle received no remuneration. When the uncle reached an advanced age he became apprehensive that he might not have the means to provide for his needs during the remainder of his life. He then requested his nephew, in consideration of the board and lodging furnished as mentioned above, to assist him during his old age by payment to him of $100 per year for the remainder of his life. To this the nephew agreed and executed the following writing:

July 20, 1929

I, Claude L. Addington, remembering and appreciating the many favors and acts of kindness, rendered to me, during the years that have passed, by my beloved uncle William E. Brown, and desiring to express my gratitude to him in something more than empty words, hereby promise and pledge that I will pay to my said uncle William E. Brown, the sum of One Hundred Dollars ($100.00) during each year that the said William E. Brown shall live. Payment to be made on or about the first day of January of each said year, beginning with the year 1930.

(Signed) Claude L. Addington.

When the uncle died, the appellant brought this action against the appellee to recover $1,100, the amount alleged to be due under the contract.

Crumpacker, Chief Judge: By the great weight of authority a past consideration, if it imposed no legal obligation at the time it was furnished, will support no promise whatever. A past consideration is insufficient, even though of benefit to the promisor, where the services rendered or things of value furnished were intended and expected to be gratuitous.

Nowhere in the appellant's third paragraph of complaint is it alleged that the board and lodging furnished by said decedent to the appellee were furnished for any expected remuneration or that the appellee accepted them with any agreement or understanding that he was to pay for them. On the contrary, the reasonable construction of the pleading indicates that appellant's decedent had no thought of remuneration until he had reached old age and feared that he had insufficient means to meet his needs during the remainder of his life. Thus it would seem that the consideration, as pleaded, imposed no legal obligation on the appellee at the time it was furnished and was intended by the decedent and expected by the appellee to be gratuitous. [DECISION FOR APPELLEE]

Allen v. Allen   133 A.2d 116 (D.C. 1957). Action by Louis Gregory Allen in his own behalf and as administrator of the Estate of William Kenneth Allen (plaintiff below), appellants, against Jerome Donald Allen and Dorothy M. Allen (defendants below), appellees. In 1898, the appellees, who are brother and sister, became tenants in common of certain improved real estate by deed of conveyance from their aunt. The appellees agreed to provide their father and mother a comfortable home on the premises for as long as they lived. By 1938, the father had died and the family consisted of appellees, their mother, and three brothers who were born after the 1898 conveyance. In that year, appellees, at the request of the mother, entered into a written agreement with her whereby "in consideration of the sum of One ($1.00) Dollar to them paid by Julia A. Allen [the mother], the receipt whereof is hereby acknowledged," they promised and agreed that, in the event of the sale of the property during their lifetime, they would divide the proceeds equally among themselves and their three brothers.

The mother died in 1951, and in 1953 appellees sold the property for $15,000. The suits were then brought by one of the three brothers, one suit being on his own behalf and the other as administrator of a deceased brother's estate, each claiming one-fifth share of the $15,000.

Hood, Associate Judge: The testimony was that the one dollar mentioned in the agreement as consideration was never paid by the mother to appellees and that they received no consideration whatever for signing, that they signed in order to please their mother, and that one of appellees even paid the lawyer's fee of $10 for preparing the agreement. We think it is plain from this testimony, and implicit in the trial court's reference to the "stated payment of One ($1.00) Dollar" as the only consideration, that the one dollar not only was not paid but was never intended to be paid. . . .

Adequacy of consideration is not required and if one dollar is intended as the consideration and paid and accepted as such, it is sufficient consideration. However, a stated consideration which is a mere pretense and not a reality is not sufficient; because if in fact no consideration was intended and none given, recital of a consideration cannot make the promise enforceable. . . .

On the evidence here, the court found no actual but only a stated consideration. We conclude, therefore, that the promise of the appellees was without consideration and unenforceable. [DECISION FOR APPELLEES]

Burgamy v. Davis   313 S.W.2d (Tex. 1958). Action by Emory F. Burgamy (plaintiff below), appellant, against Paul E. Davis (defendant below), appellee. Appellant brought an action against appellee to recover the sum of $328.73, which he claimed was the balance due on a construction contract. The facts are found in the opinion of the court.

Renfro, Justice: Findings of fact and conclusions of law were filed by the trial court.

The court found: Appellant and appellee entered into an oral contract by the terms of which appellant was to furnish material and labor, on a cost plus basis, for plumbing modifications in a house owned by appellee. Prior to completion of the contract, appellant made demand on appellee for the sum of $328.73, which appellee paid on March 19, 1957. About the 22nd of March, appellant completed the job and made demand for an additional $537.45. About the first of April, a dispute in good faith arose between appellant and appellee as to the amount due appellant. Thereafter, while the dispute still existed, appellee delivered a check in the sum of $208.73 to appellant, with the words, "Payment of account in full," written on the check. The check was intended to be in full payment of the disputed claim. Appellant accepted and received the amount of the check. . . .

It is well settled that when an account is made the subject of a bona fide dispute between the parties as to its correctness, and the debtor tenders his check to the creditor upon condition that it be accepted in full payment, the creditor must either refuse to receive the check or accept the same burdened by its attached condition. If he accepts the check and cashes the same, he impliedly agrees to the condition, although he may expressly notify the debtor that he is not accepting the same with the condition, but is only applying the same as a partial payment on account.

When appellant, knowing appellee was disputing in good faith the amount of the claim, received the check marked "Payment of account in full," he was given the option either to accept the check as full payment or to return the check to appellee, unaccepted, and hold appellee for his full claim. He chose to accept and deposit the check to his account. Under the findings of the trial court, there was a valid accord and satisfaction. [DECISION FOR APPELLEE]

Skinner v. Tober Foreign Motors   187 N.E.2d 669 (Mass. 1963). Action by William H. Skinner, et al., plaintiffs, v. Tober Foreign Motors, Inc., defendant.

Plaintiffs purchased an airplane from the defendant. The installment contract provided for payments of $200 per month over a period of twenty-four months with a payment of $353.34 on the twenty-fifth month. The engine developed trouble prior to the due date of the first payment which necessitated either the rebuilding of the engine or the installation of a new one at a cost of $1,400. After discussion between plaintiffs and officers of the defendant, it was agreed that defendant would install a new engine and reduce the monthly payments to $100 for the first year. After approximately five months, the president of the company told plaintiffs that the monthly payments would have to be $200 per month. Plaintiffs did not agree, and defendant's president took possession of the airplane. Plaintiffs thereupon brought an action for damages.

Spalding, Justice: If the oral modification was controlling, the plaintiffs were not in default in their payments. The defendant argues that the oral modification is unenforceable and invalid because of the Statute of Frauds and because it was not supported by consideration. The short answer to the first point is that the defense of the Statute of Frauds is not available to the defendant, for it was not pleaded. As to the oral modification not being supported by consideration, the answer may be found in section 2–209(1) which provides that an "agreement modifying a contract within this Article needs no consideration to be binding." If the oral modification to the written contract was valid and binding—and we hold that it was—the defendant had no right to take possession of the plane. [DECISION FOR PLAINTIFFS]

PROBLEMS

1 Plaintiff, an employee of the Royster Guano Company, defendant, lost his right arm in the service of the defendant in the year 1914. Following the injury, he entered into a settlement with defendant under the terms of which, in consideration of the release of his claim for damages, he was paid $700 and promised a "life time job at top wages for common labor." He was furnished employment pursuant to the terms of the contract until June, 1932, when he was discharged in violation of the terms of the settlement. The plaintiff then brought an action for breach of the contract. Is the alleged contract void for indefiniteness and lack of mutuality?

2 Lorenzo Beach had presented to him a subscription paper in the following words:

"We, the undersigned, agree to pay the sum set opposite our respective names, for the purpose of erecting a new M.E. church in this place, said sums to be paid as follows: One-third to be paid when contract is let, one-third when building is enclosed, one-third when building is completed. Probable cost of said church from ten thousand dollars ($10,000) to twelve thousand dollars ($12,000)."

To which he attached and subscribed the following:

"Dr. Beach gives this subscription on the condition that the remainder of eight thousand dollars is subscribed.

"Lorenzo Beach . . . . $2,000."

About one year thereafter, Lorenzo Beach was adjudged insane. After the adjudication of his insanity, the other subscriptions for the total amount of $8,000 toward the building of the church were obtained. After the building was completed, Lorenzo Beach died. Is the estate of Lorenzo Beach liable on the subscription agreement?

3 Moss was indebted to Gardner in the amount of $500, but Moss was insolvent and unable to pay the debt. Gardner therefore brought an action against Moss and recovered a judgment for $500. Moss and Gardner thereafter entered into an agreement whereby Moss paid Gardner the sum of $150 and gave him a promissory note for the sum of $100 secured by a mortgage on his house and lot, and Gardner delivered to Moss a writing which stated that the $150 and the secured promissory note were accepted by him in full satisfaction of the judgment. In about six months thereafter Moss inherited $10,000 from his grandfather. Moss then paid Gardner the amount of the promissory note, and Gardner brought an action to recover the remaining $250. Should Gardner recover?

4 Brown, a contractor, entered into a contract with Jones, a homeowner, whereby Brown agreed to construct a swimming pool for Jones for a price of $8,000, at which time Jones paid Brown $500 as a part payment. Brown thereafter wrote a letter to Jones stating that he would not be able to construct the pool because of other business commitments. Brown also returned the part payment of $500 to Jones. Jones replied by letter stating that it was agreeable with him to cancel the contract. About two weeks thereafter, Brown contended that the cancellation of the contract was void and that he was prepared to begin construction of the pool. Is the contention of Brown correct?

5 Defendant's brother was shot and killed while returning to his home in Bell County. At the close of the burial services, defendant announced publicly that he would give $200 for the arrest and conviction of the person who killed his brother. Plaintiff, who was a deputy sheriff of Bell County at that time, learned of the offer of reward. Plaintiff then made a personal inquiry of defendant, and received the promise of defendant to pay plaintiff $200 if he would secure the arrest and conviction of the guilty person. Plaintiff thereafter arrested the guilty person, who was convicted. Plaintiff brought an action to recover the $200. Do you think he should recover?

6 Brown, who was in financial difficulty, owed Hunt $10,000, Finley $8,000, and Jones $6,000. The parties, therefore, entered into an agreement whereby Brown agreed to sell all of his assets and distribute the proceeds pro rata among the creditors, and the creditors agreed among themselves and with Brown to accept the proceeds in settlement of the debt. The assets of Brown were thereafter sold and the proceeds distributed according to the agreement. Brown thereafter gave each of the creditors his promissory note for the amount of the unpaid balance. Brown now contends that the notes are unenforceable. Is this contention correct?

7 Plaintiff left a quantity of negotiable bearer bonds for safekeeping in the vault of the defendant-bank. About a year thereafter, plaintiff approached an officer of the bank and stated to him that he felt that his bonds were not safe in the vault and that he desired to remove them to another bank for safekeeping. The officer stated that, in order to assure their safety, the bonds would be placed in the safe where the money of the bank was kept. Plaintiff thereupon left his bonds with the defendant-bank. The bonds, however, were not placed in the safe, and they were thereafter stolen from the vault. Defendant contends that the promise was without consideration and therefore unenforceable. Do you agree with this contention?

8 Defendant, who borrowed $500 from plaintiff, failed to repay the $500 when the loan became due. Plaintiff thereupon promised defendant: "If you will pay $400, I will accept such part payment as a discharge of the total amount due." Defendant relied on the promise and paid the $400 to plaintiff, who thereafter brought an action to recover the remaining $100. Do you think plaintiff will recover the $100?

7
CAPACITY OF PARTIES

A contract entered into between competent persons requires no comment. Such a contract is a binding agreement insofar as capacity of parties is concerned. A contract entered into by an incapacitated person, however, produces legal consequences that require particular attention. This chapter will be devoted to persons with limited contractual capacity, namely, (1) infants and (2) other persons with limited capacity.

INFANTS
The common law defines an infant, or minor, as any person—male or female—who has not attained the age of twenty-one years. There is a definite trend, however, to reduce the legal age to eighteen years. Congress has enacted legislation giving all persons aged eighteen and over the right to vote in national elections. Many of the state legislatures have also recently altered the common-law definition of a minor. In some states, the disability of nonage has been removed for all persons aged eighteen and over. In other states, the disability of nonage has been removed for all persons aged eighteen and over for some particular purpose, such as entering into business contracts, but not for the purpose of holding public office or serving on juries. It should be pointed out,

however, that these state statutes are not uniform. The statutes of the particular state, therefore, should be examined to determine the law of the particular state. This does not mean that contracts of a person under the age of eighteen are void. Infants have full power to enter into binding agreements. The vast majority of their contracts, however, are voidable and are therefore subject to the contingency of being disaffirmed or ratified. But it would be a mistake to assume that an infant can use the privilege of disaffirmance to escape all liability. Infants are liable upon a quasi contract for the reasonable value of the necessaries of life; they are liable for their torts; and a few contracts of an infant are enforceable. The law does not recognize fractions of days, and for this reason a person attains his majority on the first second of the day preceding the day he reaches his age of majority. [*Erwin v. Benton*, p. 80.]

Disaffirmance and Ratification   The disaffirmance of a contract is a manifestation by the infant of an intent not to perform, and the ratification of a contract is a manifestation of an intent to perform. The contract, however, must be disaffirmed or ratified in its entirety or not at all, because an infant cannot disaffirm the detriments and ratify the benefits. The fact that an infant possesses all the appearances of an adult will not deprive him of his right of disaffirmance, but restrictions are sometimes imposed on the privilege of disaffirmance. The power of disaffirmance, nevertheless, is undoubtedly the greatest protection afforded infants.

(1)   *Time of Disaffirmance or Ratification*   The contract may be disaffirmed by the infant at any time during his minority or within a reasonable time after reaching majority. The contract, however, cannot be ratified by the infant until he attains his majority or a reasonable time thereafter because ratification of a contract by a minor would, in effect, give rise to another voidable contract. No definite rules can be stated to draw a dividing line between what is and what is not a reasonable time. It is a question of fact to be determined by the jury considering all the circumstances. "A reasonable time" may be several years if the subject matter was of a diuturnal nature but it would not be if the article was of a perishable nature. [*Merchants' Credit Bureau v. Akiyama*, p. 80.]

An exception to the general rule is made with respect to real estate. As a general rule, an infant cannot disaffirm a sale of real estate until he reaches his majority. In some states the infant may, nevertheless, recover possession of the property prior to disaffirmance, or in other states he may at the time of disaffirmance recover from the adult for use of the property during his infancy.

(2)   *Acts of Disaffirmance and Ratification*   A few states require ratification to be in writing, and a few states hold that unless an infant is aware of his right to disaffirm, ratification will not result from the acts of a minor. As a general rule, however, any words or acts by the infant which clearly indicate an intent to repudiate the contract or to be bound by the contract would operate as a disaffirmance or ratification, as the case may be. An acceptance of the benefits incident to ownership, such as dividends paid on stock, would indicate a ratification, whereas a return of the stock would indicate a disaffirmance. An

expression of a willingness to perform would indicate a ratification, whereas a refusal to perform would indicate a disaffirmance. A distinction is made between the infant as seller and the infant as purchaser. An infant who sold certain land to a purchaser and who, after reaching his majority, resells the land to a third person would indicate a disaffirmance of the sale to the first purchaser. An infant who purchases land from the seller and who, after reaching his majority, resells the land to a third person would indicate a ratification of the purchase from the seller. A distinction must be made, however, between a wholly executory contract and a wholly executed contract. Continued silence would indicate an intent to disaffirm a wholly executory contract, but continued silence would indicate an intent to ratify a wholly executed contract.

(3) *Restrictions on Disaffirmance*   The restrictions imposed on the privilege of disaffirmance are based on justice but compared with the advantages afforded the minor are of little significance. It is clear that the infant may disaffirm a wholly executory contract. It is also clear that if only the infant has performed, he may disaffirm and recover the money or property he has paid or transferred to the adult. Some conflict exists, however, in those situations where the contract is wholly executed or where only the adult has performed and the infant has spent or squandered what he has received and consequently cannot make restitution. A few jurisdictions will not permit a disaffirmance unless the infant can return the consideration or its equivalent. As a general rule, however, the minor must return whatever he has in his possession of the consideration under the contract but, if the consideration has been destroyed, he may nevertheless disaffirm the contract and recover the consideration with which he has parted. An infant may recover whatever property he has parted with even if it is in the hands of an innocent third-party purchaser, but the rule is inapplicable to the sale of goods. Section 2–403 of the Code provides that a person with a voidable title has the power to transfer a good title to a good faith purchaser for value. Suppose Brown, who purchased an automobile from an infant, resold the automobile to Jones. The infant could not recover the automobile from Jones. Recovery of property may also be denied an infant who has entered into a partnership agreement because, although he may withdraw from the partnership, in many states he cannot avoid the payment of the firm's debts to the extent of the capital which he has invested.

Liability for Necessaries   The family relationship of the minor and parent is important in determining the circumstances under which an infant is liable for necessaries because the parent is under a duty to support the minor; the parent is also entitled to any compensation which the infant earns unless the minor is emancipated. Emancipation—whereby the parent surrenders the right to the care, custody, and earnings of the minor and renounces parental duties—may be inferred from the conduct of the parent, for example, where he leaves the minor to support himself, or in some states by the minor's marriage. But emancipation of a minor without anything more does not remove the incapacity of the minor to make enforceable agreements. In some of the states, however, a minor may have his disability of nonage removed by judicial proceedings. The decree of the court will then give the minor full contractual capacity.

In view of the fact, first, that the contract of the infant may be disaffirmed by the infant and, secondly, that the parent is not liable on a contract made by the minor unless the parent joins in the contract or the minor is acting as agent for the parent, it was decided at an early date to hold the infant liable in quasi contract for the reasonable value of necessaries furnished him. This rule is intended to eliminate the possibility that the infant might find himself in the position of needing the necessaries of life with no one willing to sell to him.

Necessaries relate to the subsistence of the infant and consist of such things as food, clothing, lodging, medical attention, and, to a certain extent, education. Ornaments, objects used for pleasure, and ordinarily contracts relating to property or business of the minor are not classed as necessaries. The fact that a particular item is classed as a necessary does not mean that the item will be considered a necessary for which the minor will be held liable. The station in life of the infant is an important factor in determining whether or not the particular item is necessary because things necessary for one person may not be necessary to another. The necessaries must be actually supplied; consequently, an executory contract for necessaries may be disaffirmed. The necessaries must be needed by the infant. If the parent is supplying necessaries or if the quantity furnished the minor is too large, those purchased by the infant are not necessary to him.

As a general rule, however, a minor who has no other means of obtaining the necessaries of life except by pledging his own personal credit is liable in quasi contract, after proper consideration is given to his station in life, for the reasonable value of any necessaries furnished him, and he cannot repudiate this liability placed upon him by law. The minor, however, need not pay the contract price but rather the reasonable value of the necessaries so furnished to him for his use by the adult.

Liability for Torts As a general rule, an infant tort-feasor is liable in a civil action to the injured person to the same extent as an adult for his tortious acts of violence or other pure tort. This general rule, however, does not completely exonerate the parent. The parent is liable, therefore, if the tortious act is committed, expressly or impliedly, at the direction of the parent or if the parent subsequently ratifies the tortious act of the child. It is well settled that the parent is not liable for the tortious acts of his minor child merely because of parental reasons. [*Gissen v. Goodwill*, p. 81.]

False Representations Is the minor liable if he makes a false representation in connection with a contract? The answer to the problem abounds in a conflict of authority. The weight of authority holds that the infant may disaffirm the contract. Many of the courts today, however, will hold the infant liable for any resulting damage, on one theory or another. It is thus clear that a troublesome problem arises when an infant commits a tort in connection with the contract. This is due to the fact that it is difficult to establish the tort liability without giving effect to the contract. It is well settled that a breach of contract cannot be treated as a tort in order to hold the infant liable, but if the tort is a legal wrong independant of the contract, the adult can recover against the infant.

Most of the cases arise when the infant makes a false representation with respect to his age. Suppose an infant, by misrepresenting his age, induces an adult to enter into a contract. The difficulty the courts have had in separating the tort from the contract has resulted in a conflict in the law. A few jurisdictions have held that infants who misrepresent their age are estopped from denying the validity of the contract. On the contrary, a few jurisdictions have gone so far in favor of infants as to absolve them of any and all liability. Some state legislatures have solved the problem by enacting statutes which provide that an infant cannot disaffirm a contract if the infant misrepresented his age and the adult believed him capable of contracting.

As a general rule, however, the infant will be permitted to disaffirm the contract, but the privilege of disaffirmance is so encumbered with restrictions that it loses much of its importance. The infant may be required to make restitution before disaffirming the contract, or the infant may disaffirm the contract and recover the money, less proper offsets for diminution in value of the chattel, paid under it. If a minor brings a suit in equity, the equitable maxim "he who seeks equity must do equity" is generally applied. It is also true that an infant who misrepresents his age and thereby induces an adult to enter into a contract may be held liable in tort of deceit, and liability in deceit is now generally recognized and enforced. [*Byers v. Lemay Bank & Trust Co.*, p. 82.]

OTHER PERSONS OF LIMITED CAPACITY

Insane Persons   Contracts of an insane or mentally incompetent person are generally voidable. A person who is afflicted with temporary insanity may ratify or disaffirm previously made agreements upon becoming sane, as may the personal representatives or heirs of the estate of the incompetent after death. It must be shown, however, that some mental defect rendered the person incapable of understanding the nature and consequences of the act. The prevailing view, moreover, is that when a contract is made in ignorance of the insanity, in perfect good faith, and no advantage has been taken of the incompetent, the contract cannot be disaffirmed by the incompetent unless the parties can be restored to their original position. A person who has been judicially declared insane will have a judicially appointed guardian who is under a duty to transact all business for the estate of the insane person. The guardian may ratify or disaffirm previously made agreements by the incompetent. The finding of insanity and the appointment of the guardian are matters of public record and any attempted contract by the insane person thereafter is void. An incompetent is ordinarily required to pay a reasonable value for necessaries on the theory of a quasi contract.

Intoxicated Persons   A person who is so intoxicated that he does not understand the nature of the transaction is treated much the same as an insane person. He may affirm an executory agreement or disaffirm an executed agreement when he becomes sober but he is bound quasi-contractually for necessaries. Contracts of intoxicated persons differ in at least two respects from those of an infant and an insane person: first, drunkenness is generally held to be no defense against a third person who has subsequently and in good faith purchased the property; secondly, a few jurisdictions hold that since intoxication is a voluntary act the drunkard should suffer the consequences unless someone has knowingly taken advantage of the drunkard's condition. A habitual drunkard who has been declared incapable of transacting his own business and has a judicially appointed guardian is, for all practical purposes, treated the same way as an insane person who has been judicially declared insane.

CASES

Erwin v. Benton　878 S.W. 291 (Ky. 1905). Action by C. P. Erwin, et al., plaintiffs, against J. W. Benton, et al., defendants, to determine the validity of a local option election.

The purpose of the election, which was held on June 8, 1904, was to determine whether spiritous liquors should be sold in the town of Calhoun, Kentucky. A number of votes were contested, and one vote was contested on the ground that the voter had not reached his majority.

O'Rear, Justice:　One voter was born June 9, 1883. The election was held on June 8, 1904. Consequently the day following the election was his "birthday." The question is, when did he become 21 years old?

The question has frequently arisen, though it seems to have been before this court but once, and there it was assumed, without discussion or citation of authority, that one is 21 years old on the day preceding the twenty-first anniversary of his birth. The conventional fixing of 21 years by common law when man's estate of full responsibility is begun has been adopted generally where the common law has gone. It was adopted in deference to considerations of expediency similar to those upon which rest the maxim that the law takes no notice of a fraction of a day. If it were said that 21 years must actually pass before one is of full age, it would follow that he would be more than 21 in fact before he attained to the privileges which the common law gives to one who is just 21 years old. The law notes no fraction of any day. In law a man is 21 years old on the day preceding his twenty-first birthday, and may then do whatever is allowed an adult to do. Hence one born on June 9, 1883, at 11:59 p.m., is deemed in law to have been born on the first moment of that day. By like rule, on the first moment of June 8, 1904, he is encompassed 21 complete years, although as a matter of fact, we see that he lacks 47 hours and 58 minutes of having done so. This illustrates one extreme of the possibilities of the rule. But it is supported by the great majority of the adjudged cases; indeed, the courts seem quite unanimous on the point. [THE COURT HELD THE VOTER WAS ENTITLED TO VOTE]

Merchants' Credit Bureau v. Akiyama　230 Pac. 1017 (Utah 1924). Action by Merchants' Credit Bureau, plaintiff, against Kaoru Akiyama, a minor, and

Gohachi Akiyama, defendants. On January 1, 1921, Gohachi Akiyama, the father, and Kaoru Akiyama, his son and a minor, signed a note in favor of the plaintiff for $2,722.25. In August, 1923, the note was past due, and an action was brought against the defendants. The defendant, Gohachi Akiyama, did not appear, and judgment by default was entered against him. This action, therefore, is prosecuted against Kaoru Akiyama, who pleads his infancy as a defense. The minor became of age on September 20, 1923, and on January 15, 1924, disaffirmed the note. The point in dispute is whether or not the minor had disaffirmed the note within a reasonable time after reaching his majority.

Frick, Justice: It is manifest that in this class of cases no hard and fast rule can be stated regarding the precise time within which a minor may disaffirm his contract. Much depends upon the intelligence of the minor, his means of knowledge, the nature of his relation to the transaction, and the purpose to be attained thereby. In all cases it is, however, always indicated by the courts that, unless it is made to appear that the minor was fully advised of his rights after attaining his majority, the law deals leniently with him with respect to the time within which he may disaffirm. In view of that, there is great diversity among the decisions respecting the time within which disaffirmance is permitted as a matter of law. As before stated, however, no case has been found where the minor was denied the right to disaffirm as a matter of law within a period of time as short as the one in question here. Indeed, in all the cases from four to ten times the time that elapsed in this case was held to be timely.

Kaoru, it seems, was working at times and attending school at times to acquire an education. Nothing is made to appear that he possessed any knowledge whatever respecting his rights until informed of them by his counsel. Moreover, he signed the note with his father, who, it may be assumed, exercised some influence over him. It therefore would be a reproach to the law to deny Kaoru the right to disaffirm the note in question, in view of the facts and circumstances disclosed by this record. [DECISION FOR DEFENDANT]

Gissen v. Goodwill 80 So.2d 701 (Fla. 1955). Action by Julius Gissen (plaintiff below), appellant, against Albert Goodwill and wife (defendants below), appellees. Appellant alleged in his complaint that at the time of his injury, he was employed as a clerk at the Gaylord Hotel in the City of Miami Beach, Florida, and the appellees were residing as business invitees at the same hotel; that the minor child, Geraldine Goodwill, eight years of age, "did willfully, deliberately, intentionally and maliciously" swing a door "with such great force and violence against the plaintiff so that a portion of the middle finger on the left hand was caused to be instantaneously severed and fell to the floor." It is further averred that "owing to a lack of parental discipline and neglect in the exercise of needful parental influence and authority, the appellees carelessly and negligently failed to restrain the child, whom they knew to have dangerous tendencies and propensities of a mischievous and wanton disposition. Said parents, nevertheless, thereby sanctioned, ratified and consented to the wrongful act committed by Geraldine Goodwill against the appellant herein."

Kanner, Associate Justice: It is a basic and established law that a parent is not liable for the tort of his minor child because of the mere fact of his paternity. However, there are certain broadly defined exceptions wherein a parent may incur liability: (1) Where he intrusts his child with an instrumentality which, because of the lack of age, judgment, or experience of the child, may become a source of danger to others. (2) Where a child, in the commission of a tortious act, is occupying the relationship of a servant or agent of its parents. (3) Where the parent knows of his child's wrongdoing and consents to it, directs or sanctions it. (4) Where he fails to exercise parental control over his minor child, although he knows or in the exercise of due care should have known that injury to another is a probable consequence.

Analyzing this problem in the light of the exceptions for parent liability enumerated, one may note that the exceptions relating to instrumentality intrusted to a child, to master and servant or agent relationship, and to parental consent or sanction of a tortious act by the child do not bear upon the circumstances here involved. It is only the fourth category which may be logically analyzed for the purpose of determining whether legal culpability might be attached to the parents of the child here concerned, and it is on this exception to the general rule that the appellant relies.

In the Restatement of the Law, sec. 316, pp. 858, 859, on the subject of Torts, dealing with the duty of the parent to control the conduct of his child, it is said,

A parent is under a duty to exercise reasonable care so to control his minor child as to prevent it from intentionally harming others or from so conducting itself as to create an unreasonable risk of bodily harm to them, if the parent (a) knows or has reason to know that he has the ability to control his child, and (b) knows or should know of the necessity and opportunity for exercising such control. . . .

In the instant case, the cause of action sought to be established fails in that the negligence charged with relation to parental restraint is not claimed to flow from the commission of an act or course of conduct which the child habitually engaged in and which led to the appellant's injury. It is nowhere claimed that the child here involved had a propensity to swing or slam doors at the hazard of persons using such doors. The deed of a child, the enactment of which results in harm to another and which is unrelated to any previous act or acts of the child, cannot be laid at the door of the parents simply because the child happened to be born theirs. However, a wrongful act by an infant which climaxes a course of conduct involving similar acts may lead to the parents' accountability. A deed brought on by a totally unexpected reaction to a situation which is isolated of origin and provocation could not have been foretold or averted and hence could not render the parents responsible. [DECISION FOR APPELLEES]

Byers v. Lemay Bank & Trust Co., 282 S.W.2d 512 (Mo. 1955). Action by Russell Byers (plaintiff below), appellant, against Lemay Bank & Trust Company (defendant below), appellee. Plaintiff, a minor, worked at many places, bought and sold automobiles, and banked with defendant. He applied for his first loan in

November, 1950, and talked with the president of the defendant-company. The president asked him his age, and plaintiff said he was twenty-three years old. A number of loans were made to plaintiff by the defendant-company, each note being secured by a chattel mortgage, and plaintiff paid the notes. On February 19, 1952, plaintiff borrowed $6,500 from defendant-company, signed a note therefor, and secured its payment by a chattel mortgage on five automobiles. The note was not paid on its due date, and the president of the defendant-company called on plaintiff at his car lot. Plaintiff informed the president that the automobiles had been disposed of; that he did not know where they were; that he did not have the money; and that he could not help it that they were subject to defendant's mortgage.

The defendant-company thereafter applied $4,134, which amount was on deposit in plaintiff's checking account, in part payment of the notes. Plaintiff thereupon brought an action for the amount of his bank deposit. Defendant filed a counterclaim, which was based on a tort for deceit. The answer charged "plaintiff fraudulently represented that he was 23 years of age, and that defendant, being deceived and entrapped thereby, loaned to plaintiff $6,500, for which plaintiff executed to defendant his said note of February 19, 1952, and, as security therefor, his chattel mortgage on five automobiles, representing to defendant that he was the sole owner of said automobiles, and that plaintiff disposed of said automobiles without the knowledge or consent of defendant."

Bohling, Commissioner: Protecting those lacking in experience and immature mind from designing adults developed in the common law of feudal England. The purpose is to shield minors against their own folly and inexperience and against unscrupulous persons, but not to give minors a sword with which to wreak injury upon unsuspecting adults. With the advancement of civilization, the spread of education, and modern industrial conditions minors attain a high state of sophistication. Many earn their own livelihood and are more worldly-wise than their parents. Plaintiff's father testified plaintiff never came to him for fatherly advice. The common law is said to be a growing institution, keeping pace with social and economic conditions. The protection of adults against depredations by minors knowingly employing fraudulent methods outweighs the interests of such minors, and adults should have available the remedies not founded on contract for their protection. Every case involving a contract to which a minor is a party should not necessarily be forced into the Procrustean bed of the rule that allows a minor to escape responsibility for his other acts upon exercising the privilege of rescinding his contract at his will. Plaintiff was not a toddler, or a teen-ager, but an "old" infant, cunning enough to conceive and perpetrate a fraud upon experienced adults.

Different results have been reached in different jurisdictions and in some instances within the same jurisdiction on the responsibility of a minor who, as an inducement for an adult to contract with him, misrepresents that he is of age and deceives the adult by his false statement to the adult's resulting injury. Some jurisdictions tend to uncompromisingly permit minors to rescind their contracts. A number of jurisdictions hold that a minor is not estopped by misrepresentations as to his age in actions in law and a lesser number where the suit is in equity; and a greater number apply estoppel where the suit is in equity. An apparently increasing number of jurisdictions hold the infant liable in tort for inducing the contract by misrepresentations that he is of age. Liability ex delicto and liability ex contractu are based on different principles and involve different measures of recovery. If an infant is liable for his torts generally, the better reasoned decisions hold he is liable for his deceit in misrepresenting his age. His deceit induces the contract. It does not involve the subject matter of a contract. The recovery is the damage resulting to the defrauded person and not the contract consideration. He is not held liable on the contract in form or substance.

Plaintiff argues that he was only asked his age, and that since defendant did not ask him to show his service card, or ask him where he was born, or ask him for his birth certificate, defendant did not exercise reasonable diligence and may not successfully assert it was misled by plaintiff's statement. We do not agree. The misrepresentation is the vital part. All the elements of a deceit are present. Plaintiff stated his age was 23. Plaintiff knew this was untrue. Plaintiff made the statement with the intent that defendant act upon it. Defendant acted upon the statement in the manner contemplated by plaintiff. Defendant suffered actual damage by reason of plaintiff's misrepresentation as to his age, and the damage was the natural and probable consequences of plaintiff's fraud. [DECISION FOR DEFENDANT]

PROBLEMS

1 Defendant, a female infant seventeen years of age, purchased from the plaintiff-corporation, a large department store, certain merchandise consisting of dresses, accessories, jewelry, and men's clothing. She was married about two months thereafter, at which time she attained her majority due to the statute of the particular state. Approximately three weeks after her marriage, plaintiff brought an action to recover for the merchandise on the grounds (a) that the merchandise constituted necessaries and (b) that defendant ratified the contract by her failure, subsequent to her marriage, to return the merchandise. Defendant then sought the advice of an attorney and learned for the first time that she had a right to disaffirm a contract. She immediately returned the merchandise to the plaintiff-corporation, which corporation refused to accept the merchandise. Do you think plaintiff is entitled to recover on either of the grounds mentioned above?

2 Brown rented certain premises from Smith, who was insane at the time. The lease creating the rental agreement contained a provision which gave Brown an option to purchase the property at a stated price. After the death of Smith, his son was appointed the administrator of the estate. The son thereafter accepted several installments of rent. Brown attempted to enforce the option to purchase the property, but the son contended that the option was void because of the insanity of his father. Decide.

3 Jones, nineteen years of age, purchased groceries on credit from Davis, a grocer, for an agreed price of $20. Two days later, Jones gave notice to Davis that he disaffirmed the contract since he had just learned that an infant has such a right. Davis nevertheless brought an action against Jones for $18, the reasonable value of the groceries. He alleged and proved that the groceries were necessaries. Is Davis entitled to recover $18 in view of the fact that the infant gave notice of the disaffirmance? Explain.

4 Plaintiff, an adult, purchased a used automobile from defendant, who was seventeen years of age, for $1,200. Plaintiff paid $500 at the time of the purchase, and promised to pay the balance with interest in thirty days. Plaintiff employed a mechanic to repair the automobile and used it for a few days. Plaintiff then notified the defendant that he disaffirmed the contract, tendered the return of the automobile to defendant, and requested the return of the $500. Is plaintiff entitled to disaffirm the contract and the return of the $500?

5 Plaintiff, who was sixteen years of age, entered into a contract with defendant for the purchase of an automobile on a layaway plan. The price of the automobile was $1,200. Plaintiff agreed to make weekly payments of $10 each, and defendant agreed to deliver the automobile when $120 had been paid. Plaintiff paid $90 under this arrangement, but was unable to make any further payments because she had lost her position as a clerk. The automobile was sold to another purchaser by defendant several months thereafter at the then approximate value of $800. Plaintiff then brought an action to recover the $90 which she had paid. What amount, if any, do you think plaintiff should recover?

6 Plaintiff, an infant of the age of sixteen years, entered into a contract with defendant for a course of instruction in voice consisting of thirty-six lessons. At the time of signing the contract, plaintiff paid the defendant the sum of $250. Plaintiff received fourteen of the lessons and then disaffirmed the contract. Plaintiff claims that she is entitled to have the $250 returned to her. Defendant resists the claim on the ground that plaintiff neither returned nor offered to return the benefits received under the contract. Decide.

7 Brown, an insane person who appeared normal and had not been judicially declared insane, borrowed $10,000 from Smith. Brown, to secure the loan, executed a mortgage on his house and lot. He squandered the money, and was then pronounced judicially insane. Will the guardian of Brown succeed in attempting to have the mortgage removed as an encumbrance on the house and lot without paying the debt to Smith? Explain.

8
ILLEGALITY

This concluding chapter on the essential elements of a contract discusses (1) the types of illegality and (2) the remedies for illegality.

TYPES OF ILLEGALITY

It may be well to mention at the outset that the object of an agreement may be the commission of an act which is criminal, tortious, opposed to public policy, adverse to the best interests of society, or forbidden by statute or common law. Irrespective of the source which declares the object to be illegal, the validity of an agreement is destroyed if the purpose of the parties is to accomplish or aid an unlawful object. It should be kept in mind, however, that the statutes and principles of law vary from state to state. This leads to the inevitable result that an agreement may be legal in one state but illegal in another. The following sections embrace those types of illegality which prevail generally throughout the United States.

Crimes and Civil Wrongs It is clear that an agreement which has for its object the commission of a crime is illegal. Obvious examples are agreements to commit murder, robbery, arson, burglary, and assault and battery. It is likewise clear that an agreement which has for its object the commission of a civil wrong against a third person is illegal. Examples are agreements to commit fraud, libel, slander, conversion, trespass, and nuisance. It should not be presumed, however, that the rule is limited to statutory wrongs. Any agreement which provides that one person shall inflict injury to another person or destroy the property of another person is illegal.

Sunday Laws   The common law does not prohibit the making of contracts on Sunday, but most state legislatures have enacted Sunday laws, or blue laws. In some states contracts within the scope of the "ordinary calling" of the parties are illegal, and in other states all contracts made on Sunday are void. It is uniformly provided, however, that acts which must be done on Sunday if done at all to protect health, life, or property do not violate the Sunday statutes. These acts are usually referred to as works of necessity or charity. The terms of the contract may be agreed upon on Sunday but if the contract is not entered into until a weekday the contract is not illegal. Many of the courts have held that although a contract made on Sunday may be illegal, it will be purged of its illegality if it is affirmed on a weekday.

Wagers   A wagering contract, by which the parties promise to pay a certain sum of money or transfer certain property upon the determination of an uncertain event or a fact in dispute, is illegal except when modified by statute. State statutes are variously framed, and a specified type of wagering may be permitted in one state but forbidden in another. Raffles, door prizes, and similar schemes are often approved when used to raise money for a charitable purpose but as a general rule any scheme which invites a number of persons to pay a consideration for an opportunity to win a prize awarded solely by chance is declared to be illegal.

Risk-bearing contracts, such as an insurance contract in which the insured party has an interest to protect, are legal and valid. The risk of loss is merely transferred to one engaged in the business of risk bearing. It is generally agreed, however, that an insurance contract in which the contracting party has no interest in the thing insured at the time the contract is made is a wager upon the life or property of another and is, therefore, a gambling transaction and illegal.

The question frequently arises whether or not a person who lends money which is used for gambling purposes may recover from the borrower. It is clear that a person who advances money and takes an active part in the gambling transaction is a joint wrongdoer and cannot recover the money advanced. It is likewise clear that a person who shares in the proceeds of the gambling transaction cannot recover. But the lender of money which is subsequently used for the purpose of gambling may recover from the borrower if the lender had no knowledge that the money was to be used for an unlawful purpose.

Statutes have been enacted in many states which enable the loser in a gambling transaction to recover from the winner the money or property lost and paid over to the winner. In the absence of such a statute, however, the courts generally will not allow the loser to recover from the winner the money paid over to the winner in a gambling transaction. [*Gilbert v. Berkheiser*, p. 93.]

Usury The taking, or the contracting to take, a greater rate of interest than is allowed by law is known as usury. As a general rule, the essential elements of usury are found in an agreement entered into (1) with the intention to violate the law; (2) for a loan or forbearance of money, express or implied; (3) with the understanding that the principal is to be repaid; and (4) that a greater profit than is authorized by law shall be paid or agreed to be paid for the loan. The first element may be implied if all the others are expressed in the contract.

The statutes of the various states provide for a legal rate of interest which ordinarily ranges from 5 to 8 percent. The legal rate is not necessarily the maximum rate. Small-loan associations are frequently permitted to exact a higher rate of interest than the legal rate. The rule is also well established that a sale of property on credit at a price which exceeds the cash price by more than the legal rate of interest does not constitute usury. [*Morris v. Capitol Furniture & Appliance Co.*, p. 109.]

Corporations are also sometimes given the power to borrow money by the sale of bonds at a rate higher than the legal rate. State statutes, as a general rule, permit the maximum amount of interest to be deducted from principal at the time the loan is made. A note which is antedated or which is made out in excess of the value loaned, however, is ordinarily distinguished from the deduction of interest.

A few of the colorable methods devised for making usurious loans are situations where the lender requires the borrower to purchase property at an excessive price; or where the lender, as seller, turns over to the borrower, as buyer, certain property, and the latter promises to pay in the future a sum greater than the actual value of the property plus an amount in excess of the maximum rate; or where the lender requires the borrower to sell property at a price much less than its true value with an option to repurchase it at a higher price, and the difference between the two prices exceeds the maximum interest rate.

It seems well settled that a lender may require a borrower to pay actual and necessary fees and expenses for preparing, acknowledging, and recording papers connected with the loan, but if such fees or charges are fictitious they will be held to be usurious. An agent employed by the borrower may collect an agent's fee or commission for negotiating the loan, but a lender of money cannot collect such a commission in addition to the maximum rate of interest.

The courts are careful to examine contracts tainted with usury. An agreement for a loan of money may be in outward appearances a legal transaction, but if any collateral agreement or unusual charges reveal the loan was made under such circumstances that the lender will receive more than the maximum rate, it will be held to be usurious. If a contract is found to be usurious, the relief awarded the debtor is not uniform. Depending on the particular state, the results are generally divided into three categories, namely (1) the entire contract is void, (2) all the interest is uncollectible, and (3) only the excess interest is uncollectible.

Federal Consumer Credit Protection Act, 1968 The purpose of this act, more commonly known as the Truth in Lending Act, is to ensure a disclosure of credit terms so that the consumer will be able to compare the various credit terms available. The act is only a disclosure statute. It does not, therefore, set rates or establish ceilings. The act covers intrastate as well as interstate transactions, but it is provided that any state which enacts a statute substantially similar to the Truth in Lending Act and has adequate provision for enforcement is exempt from the provisions of the act. Adoption of the Uniform Consumer Credit Code by any state, therefore, should exempt that state from the coverage of the act. This discussion, however, will be devoted to the Truth in Lending Act.

The Federal Reserve Board is authorized to carry out the purposes of the act, and, pursuant to this authorization, the Board has promulgated regulation Z. The provisions of the act and regulation Z are specific and detailed, and no attempt is made to discuss all the provisions of the act. The following brief discussion, however, should create an awareness of the trend toward consumer credit protection.

The act and regulation Z provide that only *consumer credit* is covered. The consumer is defined to be a natural person, and the subject of the credit transaction covered is defined to be money, property, or services to be used primarily for personal, family, household, or agricultural purposes. All installment creditors are generally covered, including banks, savings and loan associations, department or retail stores, credit card issuers, automobile dealers, credit unions, consumer finance companies, mortgage bankers, and people who perform services, such as doctors or plumbers, if they regularly extend credit. Loans made by one friend to another are exempt by implication. Transactions, other than real estate mortgages, where the amount exceeds $25,000 are also exempt from the act.

Consumer credit is generally divided into three types: (1) the open-end credit, as where the creditor permits a line of credit on a revolving credit card; (2) the closed-end sales, such as installment sales; and (3) the closed-end loan, such as loans by banks and finance companies.

The act and regulation Z require disclosure at various stages of a consumer credit transaction, such as the advertising stage, the confirmation stage, and the monthly or other billing stage. The disclosure must be made clearly and conspicuously. The terms of the finance charge and the annual percentage rate must be more conspicuous than the other disclosures. If the interest rate is $1\frac{1}{2}$ percent per month, it must be shown as 18 percent per year. The seller or lender is also required to disclose in the contract the amount of the loan or debt, all charges and allowances, and the balance which will have to be paid. Included are such items as the cash price, the down payment or amount allowed as a trade in, the balance due, amounts payable, service charges, and interest.

Agreements to Interfere with Justice   An agreement which exposes public officials to corrupt influences is illegal. Any person who agrees to use his influence to interfere with the proper conduct of an executive, legislative, or judicial officer cannot enforce the agreement. Examples of agreements which are illegal because they are opposed to public policy are those between a candidate and another whereby the candidate promises to divide the emoluments of the public office if the other person will aid him in obtaining the office; agreements to influence, through bribery or other corruption, a judge, juror, witness, or members of a board of pardons; an agreement whereby a public official promises to vote for or against a given measure or to award a contract to a named contractor with the understanding that the official is to participate in the proceeds; or an agreement, generally known as the lobbying contract, to use corrupt influence or bribery on members of lawmaking bodies to procure or prevent the enactment of legislation. A contract for strictly professional services, however, whereby a person interested in proposed legislation employs an agent or attorney to collect facts and to fairly and openly explain the proposal to members of the legislature is not illegal.

Restraint of Trade   A contract which has for its purpose the restraint of trade and nothing more is illegal and void. A contract to monopolize trade, to suppress competition, or not to compete in business, therefore, cannot be enforced when the sole purpose of the agreement is to eliminate competition. Let us suppose a contract by the terms of which one person promises to pay a sum of money to another person with the understanding that the latter will not construct and operate a store. Although the first person may have parted with his money and the other person may subsequently have operated the business, the courts will not interfere with the agreement. The person who has parted with his money has no legal remedy.

A contract in partial restraint of trade, however, is enforceable provided the restraint is ancillary to the contract and is reasonable. The courts, when called upon to decide whether or not a particular restraint is reasonable or unreasonable, will consider the nature of the business, the extent of the trade, the relation of the parties to one another, and all other surrounding circumstances. The duration of, and the area covered by, the restraint are always important considerations.

The purchaser of a business may, and often does, bind a seller not to engage in the same business within a designated territory for a specified time. A contract of this nature is for the protection of a purchaser of good will, and the courts will sustain the contract if the restriction is no greater in time and territory than is necessary to protect the purchaser. The courts also sustain similar contracts by professional men who employ and instruct employees. To hold otherwise would permit an employee to set up a rival business in the vicinity and use the confidential knowledge acquired through his employment with the possible result of a loss of business to the employer.

Partial restraints are not only imposed by the purchaser of a business upon the seller but also by an employer upon an employee, such as those imposed by the members of a partnership upon a retiring partner, or by a vendor of real property upon the vendee. In all instances, however, the restrictive negative covenant must be ancillary to a valid affirmative covenant and be reasonably necessary for the protection of the covenantee. [*Mattis v. Lally,* p. 93.]

REMEDIES FOR ILLEGALITY

The courts will not as a general rule come to the assistance of a person who in pari delicto—equally at fault—with another person desires to carry out an illegal object. This rule applies to indirect enforcement as well as direct enforcement. The courts will not, therefore, award damages for the breach of an illegal agreement any more than they will assist the parties in carrying into effect their illegal objects. Three classes of cases, however, wherein assistance is sometimes rendered to a contracting party are worthy of mention. The first class embraces contracts governed by the rule of in pari delicto. The second class rests upon a disaffirmance of the agreement before it is executed and permits a contracting party to repudiate the agreement while it is still executory. A third class embraces contracts in which the legal part of the contract can be separated from the illegal part.

Rule of in Pari Delicto   The courts draw a line of demarcation between illegal agreements in which the parties are in pari delicto—both parties are equally wrong—and those in which the parties are not in pari delicto—the guilt rests chiefly upon one. Generally in those cases where the parties are not in pari delicto the law will render relief to the more innocent party, and in those cases where the parties are in pari delicto the courts will not render relief to either party. [*Miller v. Miller*, p. 94.]

(1)   *Violation of Statute*   Contracting parties who enter into agreements in violation of a statute enacted for the protection of the public, or a specified group of the public, are as a general rule not in pari delicto because ordinarily only one of the parties violates its provisions. The statute may provide, as do the usurious statutes, a remedy for the protected party. The lender is the guilty party and is not allowed to take advantage of the statute; the borrower is the protected party and may do so. The statutes, however, do not always provide the remedy. The courts, therefore, look to the purpose of the statute for the proper remedy. A statute may prohibit an officer or director of a corporation from borrowing money from the corporation in order to protect the stockholders from dishonesty of the officers. A loan made in violation of the statute would be illegal, but the courts, in order to carry out the purpose of the statute, would enforce the contract and require the officer to repay the loan.

The validity of contracts entered into in violation of a statute arises more frequently in that class of cases where the statute prohibits the carrying on of a particular trade, business, or occupation without first procuring the required license or certificate. A few statutes provide that contracts of unlicensed persons are void. The usual type of statute, however, merely provides that the license must be procured and prescribes the steps to be taken in procuring it. The rule which has been adopted for interpreting this type of statute provides that the contract is unaffected if the requirement of the license is merely a revenue measure, but the contract is unenforceable if the requirement of the license is for the protection of the public. The courts, in deciding this class of cases, look to the statute as a whole and give especial attention to the evil, if any, which the statute seeks to prevent and the amount of money exacted from the applicant for the license.

(2)   *Participation in Illegal Agreement*   The rule of in pari delicto operates

so as to permit one party who innocently or through a mistake of fact participates in an illegal contract to recover from the other party. Services which have been performed under an illegal agreement will serve to illustrate this rule. A messenger who, under the impression that he is delivering goods the sale of which is lawful, delivers goods the sale of which is unlawful could ordinarily recover for his services as messenger.

The law is rather divided on the question of whether an agreement is rendered unenforceable by the mere fact that one party knows the intention of the other to further an illegal object by means of the agreement. In general, an agreement which is capable of being performed in a legal manner will not be rendered unenforceable merely because one of the parties intends to perform it in an illegal manner. A person who shares in the benefits of the illegal agreement, however, would be denied a remedy because he is deemed to be a participant in the unlawful intention. A vendor who makes a sale of goods which is lawful would not be prevented from recovering the purchase price by the fact that he knows the vendee is engaged in an unlawful purpose as well as a lawful purpose, provided the vendor did not participate in the unlawful object further than by selling the article. A vendor who sells intoxicating liquor, in a state where the sale is lawful, which is transported and sold by the vendee in a second state where the sale is unlawful could, under ordinary circumstances, recover the purchase price if the vendee were engaged in legally operating a saloon in the first state while illegally transporting the intoxicating liquor into the second state.

It is uniformly held that a contracting party who participates in an illegal agreement because of reasons such as fraud, undue influence, or duress is not in pari delicto and may have a remedy against the other party.

Repentance and Rescission For the purpose of encouraging the abandonment of illegal agreements, the courts permit a contracting party to disavow an executory illegal agreement. Illegal objects may be arrested, therefore, before they are completed. An agreement by the terms of which money has been deposited with a stakeholder as a bet upon the outcome of some event may be repudiated at any time before the happening of the event. The money may be recovered from the stakeholder. The rule is not restricted to wagers. A contracting party usually may repudiate any illegal agreement at any time prior to performance and recover money paid or goods delivered under the contract.

Contracts Partly Illegal An agreement which consists of several promises some of which are illegal and some of which are legal is not enforceable if the promises are indivisible. The contract is enforceable to the extent of the legal promises if the contract is of such a nature that the legal promises can be segregated from the illegal promises. The question frequently arises with respect to recovery for the sale of merchandise. A contract to sell various articles at separate prices would ordinarily be divisible, but if the contract was to sell the articles for a gross price the contract would ordinarily be indivisible. It is immaterial whether the illegality is at common law or by statute. The agreement will, as a general rule, be unenforceable if the unlawful and the lawful parts of the agreement cannot be separated. [*Parker v. Claypool*, p. 95.]

CASES

Gilbert v. Berkheiser   196 N.W. 653 (Minn. 1924). Action by Edward A. Gilbert (plaintiff below), appellant, against F. L. Berkheiser (defendant below), respondent. On the morning of October 5, 1921, appellant entered the M. M. Glasser Company, a grocery jobbing house, and asked the price of cane sugar. Respondent, an officer of that company, informed him that it was worth $6.25 per hundredweight. A debate arose between the parties as to whether or not sugar could be bought for that price on thirty days' time anywhere in town. Appellant argued for the affirmative. Respondent argued for the negative. A bet of $100 was made on the proposition; each party wrote a check on his bank for this amount and placed it on the table. Appellant lost. Respondent thereupon took the checks from the table and went to the bank and drew the cash on the check issued by appellant who in no manner attempted to stop payment on the check. The appellant then brought this action to recover the $100 contending, among other things, that the contract was void and that there was no delivery.

   Quinn, Justice: The transaction was a bet or wager, upon a chance, which amounted to gambling, within the meaning of the law. A bet is the wager of money or property upon an incident by which one or both parties stand to win or lose by chance. In the instant case respondent took a chance and wagered his money upon the proposition that the appellant could not buy cane sugar at $6.25 per cwt., on 30 days' time. He won the bet and took the check in payment therefor upon which he received the money. The parties built their own nest, with which they must be content. The law will leave them where it found them. There was a sufficient delivery of the checks. When two gamblers place the wager on the table at which they are sitting, while determining who the winner is, it is not necessary for the loser to pick up the coin or other article and hand it to the winner, in order to constitute a delivery of the wager. It is sufficient if the winner reaches over and scoops in the pillage. [DECISION FOR RESPONDENT]

Mattis v. Lally   82 A.2d 155 (Conn. 1951). Suit by Edward J. Mattis, plaintiff, against William F. Lally, defendant. Defendant owned and operated in Rockville a business known as Lally's Barber Shop. In September, 1948, he sold the shop "together with all good will" to plaintiff for $1,500. The bill of sale contained the following restrictive clause:

The seller agrees in and for the consideration above named, that he will not engage in the barbering business for a period of five years from this date in the City of Rockville . . . or within a radius of one mile from Market Street in Said City . . . either directly or indirectly on his own account or as partner, stockholder, employee or otherwise.

After the sale, defendant went to work for plaintiff as a barber in his old shop. He worked there for about nine months, after which time he set up a one-chair barbershop in his own home which was not more than 300 yards from the shop he had sold to plaintiff. The business of plaintiff then did not justify hiring another assistant except on Saturdays, and he had to work harder and his net receipts were less. Plaintiff brought this suit for an injunction to restrain defendant from operating his one-chair barbershop in his home.

Baldwin, Judge: This is a contract in restraint of trade. The test of its validity is the reasonableness of the restraint it imposes. To meet this test successfully, the restraint must be limited in its operation with respect to time and place and afford no more than a fair and just protection to the interests of the party in whose favor it is to operate, without unduly interfering with the public interest.

The plaintiff bought all the equipment in the defendant's shop "together with all good will." Good will in the sense here used means an established business at a given place with the patronage that attaches to the name and the location. It is the probability that old customers will resort to the old place. Having paid for "good will," the plaintiff was entitled to have reasonable limitations placed upon the activities of the defendant to protect his purchase. If the plaintiff could hold the patronage of the defendant's old customers and secure that of others who might be looking for the services of a barber at the established location, he would be reasonably assured of carrying on a business profitably. If, however, the defendant should open up another shop in the immediate vicinity, it was to be expected that his old personal customers and others would seek his services.

. . . The defendant may practice his vocation anywhere except in the limited area of one town and part of another. The rest of the state and the world is open to him. To excuse him from the performance of his agreement would amount to returning to him a large part of what he has sold and would work a real hardship on the plaintiff. Nor was there any unwarranted interference with the public interest. The public is not being deprived of the defendant's services as a barber except in the area where the plaintiff is offering the same kind of service. [INJUNCTION GRANTED]

Miller v. Miller   296 S.W.2d 684 (Ky. 1956). Action by Ewell C. Miller, plaintiff, against Alton Miller, defendant, to recover on two promissory notes executed by defendant but which had been marked "Paid" by plaintiff and delivered to defendant.

Defendant testified, in effect, that plaintiff conspired with him in obtaining tires and in recapping tires for him without certificates in violation of the law pertaining to the Office of Price Administration; that he took the responsibility for the action with the result that he was fined $2,080; and that the notes were delivered back to him in settlement for taking the responsibility for the OPA trouble.

Plaintiff explained the delivery of the notes by testifying that he redelivered the notes to defendant because defendant was in the process of refinancing his transportation business and was attempting to borrow $30,000; that defendant could not obtain the loan unless he could remove the notes from his financial statement; and that he delivered the notes to defendant to enable him to obtain the loan.

Moremen, Judge: When we return to the facts of the instant case, we find that one or the other of the brothers had not found truth to be expedient because practically every statement made by one is controverted by the other. In any event, we feel that the action of both parties has been tainted with illegality and we, as certainly did the jury, believe that the courts should not aid them in getting their house in order. The rule deducible from many adjudications of this court is that any conduct or contract of an illegal, vicious or immoral nature cannot be the proper basis for a legal or equitable proceeding. Inevitably the parties are left in a dilemma which they themselves have devised. [DECISION FOR DEFENDANT]

Parker v. Claypool   78 So.2d 124 (Miss. 1955). Action by L. E. Parker, plaintiff, against J. B. Claypool, defendant, to recover on a note dated and payable in Louisiana.

Defendant, who was in Shreveport, Louisiana, one evening desired to play the game of poker with persons other than plaintiff, but he wanted the plaintiff to stand good for any losses to the extent of $3,500. Plaintiff agreed to do this, and at about 1:30 A.M., plaintiff agreed to stand good for an additional $2,500. Defendant lost both the $3,500 and the $2,500 in the game with the other participants, making a total of $6,000. Plaintiff paid this amount to the winners on the next day, and defendant executed and delivered to plaintiff his promissory note for the sum of $10,473.14. The trial judge rendered a judgment for only $4,255.93, which represented principal, interest, and attorney's fee on such amount of the money as had been advanced to the defendant with which to buy oil and gas leases and royalties.

McGhee, Chief Justice: It seems to be well settled by the decisions of the courts of Louisiana, as well as of this Court, and others that one advancing money to another with which to pay gambling losses *already incurred* is entitled to recover of the borrower any sum or sums so advanced, even though the lender knows for what purpose the money is being borrowed from him, provided he did not aid or abet the borrower in engaging in the gambling operation.

In the instant case it was not shown that the plaintiff owned or operated the gambling place, although he did stand good for the money that the defendant might lose in this poker game, and he did so in advance of the sustaining of such losses by the defendant. He enabled the defendant to engage in the game since the record discloses that the other gamblers would not have played with him without their winnings from the defendant being guaranteed in advance by the plaintiff. The plaintiff paid the defendant's losses to those who had won from him, and he did so on the following day. The defendant was under no legal obligation to pay these losses, but the plaintiff felt morally bound to make good his promise to take care of them.

If the illegal portion of a promissory note sued on is separable from the remainder of the consideration of the note, the plaintiff may recover the legal portion of the obligation. [JUDGMENT AFFIRMED]

PROBLEMS

1 Plaintiff made application to the state liquor control board for a license to sell beer. The license was denied. A friend who worked for the state told plaintiff: "I think I can get the license but it will cost you $450, and if I can't get the license I will return the money." The friend was unable to procure the license but refused to return $450. Plaintiff then brought an action to recover $450. Do you think he will succeed?

2 Plaintiff, a certified public accountant residing in Beaumont, Texas, brought an action in Louisiana to recover fees for professional services rendered to defendant in the state of Louisiana. Plaintiff was a registered certified public accountant in the state of Texas, but had not procured a certificate as such in Louisiana. The defendant contends that the plaintiff cannot recover for any services rendered in the state of Louisiana in the practice of his profession because he is not registered as such in Louisiana as required under the statute. Has plaintiff forfeited his right to recover because of having entered into an unlawful contract?

3 The defendant kept a billiard saloon and a bar for the sale of intoxicating liquor. The billiard saloon was licensed but the sale of liquor was illegal. The plaintiff was employed by the defendant at a fixed salary to work generally in and about the saloon but there was no special agreement as to whether he should or should not sell liquor or what his particular duty should be. He worked generally in and about the saloon, taking care of the room and the billiard tables, building the fires, tending bar, and waiting upon customers. Plaintiff brought an action to recover pay for services rendered. Can plaintiff recover for the legal services?

4 Shirley was indicted on the charge of operating a gaming house. The sheriff, at the time he arrested Shirley, seized $260, which Shirley admitted he won in a gaming transaction. The money was turned over to the clerk of the court, and after Shirley was convicted and paid his fine, he petitioned the court for the return of the $260. Will he succeed?

5 A partnership, doing business in only seven northern metropolitan counties in New Jersey, was organized for the purpose of manufacturing and selling burial vaults. The partnership agreement contained the following provision: "In the event the said partnership is terminated by reason of one partner voluntarily retiring, the partner so retiring shall not, at any time carry on the said business of manufacturing and selling burial vaults within the state of New Jersey for a period of five years." Do you think this provision would be enforceable?

6 Defendant and the First Bank entered into an agreement by the terms of which the First Bank loaned defendant the sum of $5,000 for a term of three months with interest at the rate of 6 percent. The agreement also contained a provision which required defendant to leave the sum of $4,000 as a deposit with the First Bank during the period of the loan. Discuss whether or not you think this provision renders the agreement usurious.

7 Linder, who was interested in developing a subdivision, met with Abbot, a contractor. They discussed the probable cost of different kinds of houses, the plans and specifications, and other preliminary subjects. This meeting was held on Sunday, at which time they agreed to have a further meeting on Wednesday. At the meeting on Wednesday, they concluded the discussion and also entered into a contract for the construction of the houses for the subdivision. Abbot thereafter refused to proceed with the construction of the houses, and Linder brought an action for breach of contract. What defense, if any, is available to Abbot?

8 Duke and Dunn were arguing over the outcome of a football game, and each bet $100 that his favorite team would win. They gave Durham the $200 to hold until the game was played. Then Durham was to give the $200 to the man whose team won. Before the game was played, Duke changed his mind. Duke thereupon called off the wager and demanded the return of his $100 from Durham, who refused to return the money. Would Duke prevail in an action to recover the $100 from Durham?

9
REALITY OF CONSENT

The preceding four chapters discussed the essential elements of a contract. It is now appropriate to consider several possibilities: that the validity of a contract might be affected by the fact that the consent of the parties to the contract was not a real expression of their intent; that the parties to the contract may be denied judicial relief because the contract belongs to that class of contracts required to be in writing; that the contract may have created rights which third parties may enforce. These problems will be discussed, in the order indicated, in this and the following two chapters. This chapter will discuss the possible causes for unreality of consent. These are fraud, misrepresentation, duress, undue influence, unconscionable or oppressive contracts, and mistake.

FRAUD AND DECEIT
The word "fraud"embraces all multifarious means resorted to by one individual to get advantage over another. Attention is here directed to "actionable fraud," which entitles a person to bring an action at law for damages based upon fraud and is called an "action for deceit." Fraud is in fact the only one of the possible five causes of unreality of consent which gives a remedy not only of rescission but also of action in tort for damages. The essential elements of actionable fraud may be summarized as (1) the misrepresentation of a material fact, (2) relied upon by

the other party, (3) made with knowledge of its falsity, (4) with the intention to deceive, (5) which results in injury to the other party. For purposes of clarity in explaining fraud, the requirements of the representation are stressed: the representation must be false; it must be of a fact; it must be of a material fact; it must be relied upon; it must be made with knowledge of its falsity; and it must be made with an intent to deceive. [*Meyer v. Brown*, p. 105.]

Representation Must Be False A false representation is a misrepresentation. It may be made by words, writings, or conduct. The controlling factor in determining whether or not any given statement or conduct is a misrepresentation is the impression the statement or conduct created on the mind of a reasonable person and not what the defrauding person meant or claims that he meant. The most obvious form of misrepresentation is an unequivocal falsehood, but any statement made with reckless disregard of its truth or falsity, or any half-truth, trick, or conduct, constitutes a misrepresentation if it creates a false impression on the mind of a reasonable person. Artful concealment and silence amounting to a suppression of the truth are misrepresentations as equally as an unequivocal falsehood.

(1) *Silence* Silence or nondisclosure in and of itself is not a misrepresentation. In the absence of a duty to speak, therefore, a person is not required to disclose his superior information. A duty is not imposed upon a person to disclose information for the mere reason that the person with whom he is dealing would like to have the information. This question has frequently been litigated with respect to the sale of land, and it is uniformly held that a prospective purchaser who knows that there is a mine or other valuable substance on the land of another is not under a duty to disclose his superior knowledge.

The law imposes a duty on a person to speak if one of the parties knows that certain facts are not true and also knows that the other party believes the facts to be true. A person who has innocently misstated a fact is under a duty to inform the other person of the misrepresentation when he learns of the falsity of the statement. Brown, who was unaware that he was insolvent, made an application to purchase goods on credit from Jones. He therefore stated in the application that he was solvent. Brown later made an examination of his finances and learned that his liabilities greatly exceeded his assets and that he would be unable to pay for the goods. After learning this fact, Brown would be under a duty to inform Jones of his insolvency. A person who occupies a fiduciary relationship to another person is required to disclose all information in his possession which is material to the particular transaction. The agent owes such a duty to his principal, the guardian to the ward, the attorney to the client—any person who occupies a fiduciary relationship to someone else. The gist of silence as constituting misrepresentation is the producing of a false impression upon the mind of the other person.

(2) *Concealment* Silence and concealment are similar in that they both imply the nondisclosure of some fact that should be revealed. Any active or artful concealment for the purpose of defrauding another is sufficient ground for an

action for deceit. The owner of property with a known defect which is not apparent upon inspection—a latent defect—is under a duty to speak. [*Weikel v. Sterns*, p. 106.]

Representation Must Be of a Fact   A misrepresentation, in order to constitute fraud, must be a statement of a past or present fact and not a mere expression of opinion. The distinction between a statement of fact and an expression of opinion is lacking in precision. Broadly speaking, however, an opinion includes expressions in the nature of expectations, predictions, beliefs, or promises, whereas a fact includes statements more in the nature of something in actual existence. The following situations will more clearly illustrate the distinction between an opinion and a fact.

(1) *Dealers' Talk*   A good illustration of an expression of opinion is known as "dealers' talk." A seller is allowed considerable latitude in "puffing" his goods; such words of commendation and praise are a form of opinion. If he leaves the realm of generalities and becomes specific, however, his assertion is one of fact. A distinction is made in this connection between a representation as to the value of an article and a representation with respect to an extrinsic fact affecting value. An assertion that an article is worth so much is an expression of opinion, but a statement that the article cost so much is one of fact.

(2) *Opinion of an Expert*   The opinion of an expert is treated as a statement of fact since the expert has superior knowledge in comparison with the other person. An expert, therefore, cannot escape liability on the basis of the distinction between an opinion and a fact. A rule with respect to nonexpert representations as to the law, however, should be mentioned. The law is presumably a matter of common knowledge, and a statement made with respect to a matter of common knowledge is an opinion. The rule makes this distinction: a misrepresentation of local or state law is treated as an opinion, but a misrepresentation of foreign laws or the laws of a sister state is treated as one of fact. This distinction, however, is not applicable to an expert.

(3) *Past or Present Fact*   A representation will not constitute fraud unless it relates to a past or present fact. The underlying reason for the rule is that representations with respect to the future must necessarily be understood by the person to whom they are addressed to be an expression of strong belief only. A prophecy, it is said, is a subject of which knowledge in its strict sense cannot be had. A representation as to what will happen in the future, therefore, is an opinion unless it is coupled with a misstatement as to some past or present fact.

(4) *Statement of Intention*   Closely allied to statements with respect to the future are statements of intention. A statement of intention to do a certain thing in the future will constitute fraud where it is shown that the person making the statement had no such intention. This is a false assertion of a presently existing fact in the mind of the party at the time of making the statement. [*Whitcomb v. Moody*, p. 107.]

Representation Must Be Material   Misrepresentation of a fact is material when it is the substantial inducement for entering into a contract. The test most uniformly applied is that a misrepresentation of a fact is material if it induces a person to enter into a contract that he would not have entered into except for the misrepresentation. This test emphasizes the distinction between an opinion and a fact, and is sometimes stated: an expression of opinion has no moving influence or should have no moving influence on the conduct of the contracting party. The rules which differentiate an opinion from a fact, therefore, permeate all the elements of fraud. More precisely, the distinction between a material and an immaterial representation is not whether the fraud was material to the contract entered into but whether the fraud was material to the inducement which brought about the contract.

Representation Must Be Relied Upon Reliance is inseparable from materiality. The rule that a misrepresentation to be material must be an inducement to enter into the contract implies of necessity that a person must rely on the misrepresentation. It is well settled that fraud will not result unless the misrepresentation is relied on by the injured party. A person who decides as the result of his own investigation will not be heard to say he relied on the misrepresentation. Some courts hold that a person is negligent who does not make his own investigation when the information is available for ascertaining the truth or falsity of the statement, but the rule is limited to those cases which require no expense or undue hardship in making the investigation. Persons who have an equal means of knowledge or who "deal on an equal footing," as is sometimes stated, are generally denied relief for the reason that they are not justified in relying on the misrepresentation.

Representation Must Be Made with Knowledge In an action for deceit the plaintiff must prove scienter, that is, that the defendant made the representation knowing at the time that it was false. Knowledge or absence of knowledge of the falsity of the representation is ordinarily proved from the representation itself and the attendant circumstances. An important problem arises, however, when a person states that he knows a certain fact is true when in reality he does not know whether it is true, and subsequently learns that it is false. In this connection the requirement of scienter is usually satisfied where it is proved that the person has asserted to be true as his own knowledge a material fact which is susceptible of accurate knowledge. When the representation is one upon which accurate knowledge cannot be predicated, however, the assertion is interpreted to be a belief or prophecy. In these circumstances the assertion falls within that class of statements designated as opinions.

Representation Must Be Made with Intent An intent to deceive is an essential element of fraud. A contracting party will be deemed to have intended the natural consequences of his acts. He will be deemed to have intended the fraud, therefore, where his representations operate to defraud another. A representation qualified with such words as "I think" or "I believe" clearly negates an intention to defraud. But the assertion of belief must in truth be the belief of the seller, or he will be deemed to have intended the fraud. [*Thomson v. Pentecost*, p. 107.]

MISREPRESENTATION, DURESS, UNDUE INFLUENCE

Misrepresentation The word "misrepresentation" in its broadest sense is sometimes used to include an intentional false statement. The word is used here, however, to denote a misstatement of a material fact unaccompanied by fraud. The rules which have been formulated for determining the circumstances under which a contract may be rescinded for fraud and deceit are equally applicable to misrepresentation except for the following very important distinctions: First, a false representation, in the case of fraud and deceit, is made with knowledge of its falsity; a misrepresentation lacks this element of knowledge which necessarily precludes an intent to deceive. Secondly, fraud is ground for an action for deceit; the injured party, therefore, may recover damages for fraud. Pecuniary damages are not recoverable for misrepresentation; the remedy for misrepresentation is rescission.

Duress A contract entered into under duress can be avoided on the ground that there was no real consent. The modern test of duress is whether the acts of violence or threats employed for the purpose of overcoming the mind of the contracting person did in fact cause that person to contract contrary to his free will. Acts of violence may be physical injury, such as beating; imprisonment, depriving a person of his liberty; or the unlawful retention of property. Any threat of injury to a person, his property, or his loved ones, which puts a person in such fear that his act is not voluntary, will constitute duress. Most of the adjudicated cases revolve around a threat to prosecute criminally the contracting party or some close relative. A threat to prosecute a criminal action against a relative, whether the relative is guilty or innocent, will constitute duress. A person, however, who is in fact guilty of a crime by which he is indebted to another person and who enters into a contract for the purpose of suppressing a criminal action therefor cannot rescind the contract. The theory of this rule is that a person has a legal right to collect a debt that is due, and a threat to prosecute a civil suit to collect an unpaid debt is not duress. [*Kronmeyer v. Buck*, p. 108.]

Undue Influence The essence of undue influence is the mental coercion of one person over another. It prevents the influenced person from acting intelligently, understandingly, and voluntarily; it constrains him to do what he would not have done if he had been left to his own judgment and volition. An instrument executed under undue influence in fact expresses the will of the dominating person rather than that of the dominated person. A contract entered into under circumstances which show that one person took unfair advantage of another because of superior knowledge derived from a fiduciary relationship or from overmastering influence may be rescinded.

UNCONSCIONABLE OR OPPRESSIVE CONTRACTS

The courts will not relieve a party to a contract merely because he has made a bad bargain, but in many cases have given relief where an unconscionable advantage has been taken of one of the parties. It may be that the person was illiterate, or ignorant, or that there was great inequality in the bargain, thereby rendering the contract oppressive to one of the parties. This principal has been incorporated in the Code by section 2–302. The word "unconscionable" is not defined by the Code, but the purpose is to prevent oppression, unfair surprise, and grossly unfair bargains. [*Morris v. Capitol Furniture & Appliance Co.*, p. 109.]

MISTAKE

A mistake may be defined as an act done under an erroneous conviction which would not have been done without such a conviction. A mistake can only exist when neither party has been influenced by any misconduct on the part of the other party and in this respect is easily distinguishable from other causes of unreality of consent. Numberless mistakes occur which have no bearing upon the consent of the parties. A mistake in the performance of the contract would clearly have no effect on the validity of the contract, but a mistake in the formation of the contract may prevent reality of consent. The mistake, however, must be concerned with a present or past fact, and it must be material. A mistake which affects the validity of the contract may be unilateral. Ordinarily, however, it is mutual.

Unilateral Mistake   A mistake is unilateral if only one of the parties entertains an erroneous belief. As a general rule, a person who makes a mistake to his own injury will be required to show that he was free of negligence before he can assert the invalidity of the contract. A person who is unable to read but signs a document without having it read to him, or a person who can read but did not read the document, cannot avoid the contract simply by showing that he neglected to do so. It should not be presumed that the courts will allow one person knowingly to take advantage of the mistake of another, but generally a party to a contract cannot avoid it on the ground that he made a mistake when the other party has no notice of the mistake and acts in good faith.

   A conflict of authority prevails as to the right of one party to avoid liability on the ground that he made a mistake in computation. The mistake may be so gross that it would be impossible to escape the attention of the other party. In these circumstances the injured party may invoke the rule which permits rescission when the mistake is clearly apparent to the other person prior to acceptance. In the majority of cases, the mistake in computation, like other unilateral mistakes, is not of such magnitude as to direct the attention of the other party to it. The general rule, therefore, which prevents the rescission of a contract on the ground that the mistake could have been avoided with a reasonable degree of care is ordinarily applied to mistakes in computation.

Mutual Mistake   The mistake is mutual when it is entertained by both the contracting parties. A mutual mistake of a material fact is ground for relief in both law and equity. The mistake to be material must be of a fact which was the efficient cause of the agreement, and, as a general rule, one party must be no more at fault than the other. The words "material fact," however, take on a slightly different meaning when used with respect to a mistake than when used with respect to misrepresentation and fraud. In all instances the fact, to be material, must be the substantial inducement for entering into the contract. In the case of mistake, however, the fact itself is the moving influence rather than any representations made by the other party.

The natural outcome of a wholly executory contract entered into under a mutual mistake of fact is the mutual abandonment of the contract. The majority of the cases which come before the courts embrace mistakes which are not discovered prior to performance in whole or in part. These mistakes are here divided for convenience as (1) those which prevent the existence of a valid contract and (2) those which pertain to the re-formation of written agreements.

(1) *Existence of the Contract* A mutual mistake of a material fact which will prevent the existence of the contract may arise in a variety of situations. A few of the more prominent factual circumstances will illustrate the rule. It may be that the parties do not mean the same thing or that the language used is subject to two meanings and each party interprets it differently; for example, an agreement for the sale and purchase of a house on Main Street in a city which has two streets by that name would be invalid if the house the buyer intended to purchase was on one Main Street and the house the seller intended to sell was on the other Main Street. It may be that the parties mean the same thing but form untrue conclusions as to the nature of the subject matter: an agreement entered into for the sale and purchase of a certain identified case of apples which in fact contains potatoes would be invalid. The parties obviously meant the same thing but there was a mutual mistake as to the nature of the subject matter. It may be that the subject matter of the agreement was destroyed prior to entering into the agreement: an agreement for the sale and purchase of a house which, unknown to both parties, was destroyed by fire prior to their entering into the agreement would be invalid. The same rule would be applicable if the subject matter for any other reason was not in existence at the time of entering into the contract.

The rule is otherwise, however, where the parties are merely ignorant as to, or unaware of, the value of the subject matter. This rule may be illustrated by the case where A found a pretty stone and sold it to B for $1.00. Neither A nor B knew the value of the stone. It was then learned that the stone was an uncut diamond having a value of $900. A was not permitted to rescind the contract and recover the stone.

(3) *Re-formation of Written Agreement* A written instrument which does not express the intention of the parties because of a mutual mistake as to the legal effect of the words used may be re-formed to express the true intention of the parties. A person who has entered into an ambiguous contract, however, cannot avoid his obligation by showing that he erred in his understanding of its terms. The mistake of a scrivener in reducing the agreement to writing may be re-formed. The parties may intend to contract for the sale of "Whiteacre," but the written agreement may describe the property as "Blackacre." The instrument could be re-formed so that the written contract in its altered form would express the true

agreement of the parties. An error in the description of the land conveyed by deed presents a rather difficult problem. The intervention of rights of third parties may prevent re-formation, or the parole-evidence rule which forbids the introduction of evidence to vary the terms of the written agreement might be invoked. All written instruments should be carefully verified before they are signed. Neither party to a contract, however, can claim a right or relief superior to the other when both parties to the transaction have acted in ignorance of a material fact. The courts will re-form a written instrument if that method of relief will best serve the justice of the particular case.

CASES

Meyer v. Brown   312 S.W.2d 158 (Mo. 1958). Action by L. H. Meyer, plaintiff, against Ted A. Brown, defendant, for damages arising from alleged fraud and misrepresentations in the sale of a large lot of used storage batteries by defendant to plaintiff. Plaintiff's petition alleged that he purchased a number of storage batteries from defendant for the sum of $5,750; that defendant represented to plaintiff that there were at least 3,000 batteries in the lot; that such representation was false and defendant knew it was false; that plaintiff relied thereon and purchased the batteries upon the assumption that defendant's statements in regard to the number were true; that in truth and fact there were only 1,786 batteries in the lot, and the reasonable value of the shortage (1,214) was $3,000.

Plaintiff testified that he was sixty-one years old; that he visited defendant's place of business for the purpose of trying to buy some batteries; that he saw some in defendant's paint and body shop stacked up in a pile approximately sixty feet long, eight feet high, and six feet wide; that some of the batteries were so heavy one man could not lift or load them; that he then had his son Otto come over; that they measured the pile, and Otto, in defendant's presence, said: "There ain't but about 1,800"; that defendant replied: "There was 2,800 a year ago, and we invoiced them and had 2,800 a year ago, and we have been putting more on the pile ever since; there ought to be 3,000 or 3,500"; that "I just took his word; that was all there was to it"; that on the following day they started loading the batteries; that by count the number totaled only 1,786; that on discovery of this fact he looked for defendant but did not find him; that defendant told him "lots of times" there were at least 3,000 batteries in the pile. . . .

Maughmer, Commissioner: The essential and fundamental elements of an action for fraud have many times been stated by our appellate courts. The rule, as stated in 37 C.J.S. Fraud, Sec. 3, page 215, is as follows: "Comprehensively stated, the elements of actionable fraud consist of: (1) A representation. (2) Its falsity. (3) Its materiality. (4) The speaker's knowledge of its falsity or ignorance of its truth. (5) His intent that it should be acted on by the person and in the manner reasonably contemplated. (6) The hearer's ignorance of its falsity. (7) His reliance on its truth. (8) His right to rely thereon. (9) And his consequent and proximate injury."

There must be substantial evidence as to each of these essential elements, otherwise a plaintiff is not entitled to go to the jury and a recovery would not be permitted to stand.

It is true, of course, that where a party fails to avail himself of means of knowledge readily within his reach equally available to him, he cannot effectively complain if he is defrauded.

For the plaintiff to move and count what he thought were some 3,000 batteries—some heavier than one man could lift—in defendant's occupied business premises, would have required the expenditure of time and money. The actual number of batteries was a latent fact not readily discoverable by plaintiff and he was not possessed of equal knowledge thereof. Moreover, he had a plain, positive and unequivocal statement and representation from the defendant that there were at least 3,000 batteries in the pile. From the record before us we believe and rule that plaintiff had the right to rely upon the alleged misrepresentations and that a submissible case was made for the jury on each of the essential elements of fraud. [DECISION FOR PLAINTIFF]

Weikel v. Sterns   134 S.W. 908 (Ky. 1911). Action by W. A. Sterns and wife, plaintiffs, against Fred Weikel, defendant. Weikel owned a lot on the front of which he built a drugstore, with a residence flat overhead. Sewage from the drugstore and the residence flat ran into a pit which he had dug at the back of the lot under a stable. After some years, he tore the stable down and erected in its place a dwelling house. The pipe from the drugstore building continued to empty into the pit, which he had covered with clay. He sold the dwelling house to plaintiffs to be used for rental purposes, but the tenant which the plaintiffs put in the property vacated it in two weeks because of the odor. Finally, after some months, plaintiffs discovered the existence of the pit, had it cleaned out, the pipe disconnected, and the pit filled with clay. This action was brought for deceit.

Hobson, Chief Justice: It is insisted for Weikel that an action for deceit does not lie, unless the fraud was knowingly practiced, or there was an intentional suppression of facts, where the defendant was in duty bound to disclose them. But a man must be presumed to intend the necessary consequences of his own voluntary act. The voluntary doing of an act which necessarily results in injury to another, where the party knows the facts and had reason to know that the injury will result, will sustain an action for fraud. . . . The house which Weikel had built was built for a residence. He knew, when he sold it to Sterns, that Sterns was buying it to rent to another as a residence. He knew the pit full of sewage was in the cellar, and a reasonable man situated as he was must have known that such a pit, with a pipe running into it carrying in water and more sewage every day in a cellar under a house, would render that house unfit for a residence. To sell such a house without disclosing the situation, when the purchaser would have no means of knowing the facts from the pit being covered up as it was, was to practice fraud upon him.

It is insisted that Weikel acted in good faith and without knowledge of the real condition of things; but the proof shows that he knew enough facts to put a reasonable man on notice, and when he sold an innocent purchaser the house, causing him a loss by reason of the concealment of the facts, the loss should fall on him, and not on the purchaser. [DECISION FOR PLAINTIFFS]

Whitcomb v. Moody   49 S.W.2d 513 (Tex. 1932). Suit by Mrs. Mary E. Whitcomb, plaintiff, against C. H. Moody, defendant. Plaintiff was the owner of a block of land known as "Whitcomb's Place," located in the residential distract of the city of Groesbeck. The land was divided into lots suitable for residential purposes, one of which was sold to the defendant. At the time of the sale defendant represented that he intended to use the lot for residential purposes, but soon after the sale he started the construction of a hamburger stand on the lot. This suit was brought to rescind the deed of sale.

Alexander, Justice: We understand the rule to be that, where a party procures the making of a contract by means of false representations of a material existing fact, and such representation actually induces the other party to enter into the agreement, and injury results thereby, the contract may be canceled or set aside on account of such fraud. It has been said that a man's state of mind is as much a state of facts as the state of his digestion. A misrepresentation as to a party's then intention or as to the present state of his mind is as much a misrepresentation of an existing fact as would be a misrepresentation of any other existing fact, and if by means of such misrepresentation a party is induced to execute a deed to land which he would not have otherwise executed, and is injured thereby, he is entitled to have the deed canceled. . . .

If in this case the defendant fraudulently represented that he then intended to use the property being purchased for the purpose of erecting a home thereon, but in truth and in fact did not then so intend, but then intended to use it for business purposes, his representation was a misstatement of a then existing fact and would form the basis of fraud authorizing a cancellation of the contract. [DECISION FOR PLAINTIFF]

Thomson v. Pentecost   92 N.E. 1021 (Mass. 1910). Action by Thomson and another, plaintiffs, against Pentecost, defendant. The plaintiffs, who were unfamiliar with the dairy business, leased for one year a dairy from the defendant who orally represented that the dairy was making approximately $2,000 a year. The plaintiffs requested a statement from the books of the defendant. The written statement showed a profit of $2,165 and was accompanied by the following letter: "As promised I send you an estimate of the products and expenses of my dairy farm which I think is conservative. I think well managed the farm at present will net $2,000.00 and carefully and systematically handled in 2 years time will add from $500 to $1,000 to the amount." The plaintiffs lost money on the dairy, and after a period of several months learned that the dairy had never made any money while the defendant had it. This action of deceit was brought for damages.

Sheldon, Justice: The fact that in the written paper which he gave to the plaintiffs he called what he said an "estimate" and used the words "I think," could not avail him, if the jury found, as upon the rulings made their verdict shows that they did find, that he intended the plaintiffs to understand and orally represented to them that these statements of actual facts were taken from his books. The attention of the jury was carefully and particularly called to this question, and it now must be regarded as settled by their verdict. [DECISION FOR PLAINTIFFS]

Kronmeyer v. Buck   101 N.E. 935 (Ill. 1913). Suit by Kronmeyer and Staehle, complainants, against Buck, defendant. Defendant was in the business of selling building materials, sewer pipe, and coal, and employed Kronmeyer, who was authorized to and did receive cash for merchandise sold. Kronmeyer, unaware that he did not have the esteem and confidence of his employer, was called by McNaughton, attorney for the defendant, to come to his office. Kronmeyer testified that when he arrived at the office, the attorney spoke in a harsh tone of voice, accusing him of stealing from Buck and, pointing to the county jail which was nearby, said he would send him to jail unless the matter was adjusted. Buck also came to the office and accused Kronmeyer of having stolen $10,000 from him. Kronmeyer was excited and frightened at the charges and threats of his accusers but denied having taken any money from his employer. Kronmeyer then deeded a residence worth $5,000, subject to a $1,500 mortgage, to defendant. He executed a note for $1,500. The attorney asked Kronmeyer if he had any friends who would sign the note with him, and Kronmeyer asked his sister, Mrs. Staehle, to sign the note. He told her Buck accused him of stealing and said if he did not get the note signed he would have to go to jail. Mrs. Staehle signed the note. This suit was brought to rescind the deed and to compel a refund of the proceeds of the note.

 Vickers, Justice: We have no hesitation whatever in holding that the execution of the note by Mrs. Staehle was procured by duress. She was an innocent third party. There can be no pretense that she was indebted to Buck in any amount. The first intimation that she had of any trouble was when her brother approached her in a highly excited manner and told her Buck claimed he had been stealing from him and that unless he got this note executed he would have to go to jail. She signed the note to keep her brother from going to jail and under the belief that if she did sign it he would be saved from imprisonment and prosecution. . . .

 The execution of the note and deed by Kronmeyer stands upon a different footing. Duress is not available as a defense against a note or other instrument executed by one who is, in fact, guilty of misappropriating the money of another, although the execution of the instrument is obtained by threatened prosecution, if the instrument is executed in payment of a debt honestly due. In such case the law regards the existence of a debt, and not the threatened prosecution, as the consideration. The authorities support the proposition that where a deed or mortgage is executed to secure an amount of money actually due as the result of transactions having a criminal aspect, equity will not set aside such conveyance even though their execution was procured by threats of criminal prosecution. . . .

 The case at bar does not fall within the rule of the foregoing authorities, for the reason, as we have already sought to show, the evidence of the existence of the debt is extremely doubtful, and there is no evidence that tends to prove the existence of a debt of more than $17. The evidence in this record shows that McNaughton accused Kronmeyer of embezzlement. . . . If Kronmeyer was, in fact, innocent, and when confronted with a charge of this kind by a lawyer whom he had always regarded as a friend, executed the instruments in question to avoid a prosecution for a crime which he had not committed, then there was both fraud and duress and a total failure of consideration. . . .

Courts of equity, in order to relieve against a great hardship where one has been induced to convey real estate for little or no consideration, will seize upon circumstances of oppression, fraud or duress for the purpose of administering justice in the case in hand. [DECISION FOR COMPLAINANTS]

Morris v. Capitol Furniture & Appliance Co.,   280 A.2d 775 (D.C. 1971). Action by Capitol Furniture & Appliance Co., Inc., appellee (plaintiff below), against Mary C. Morris, appellant (defendant below), to recover the sum of $406, which sum represented the balance due for certain household goods purchased under a conditional sales contract. Appellant contended that the goods were grossly overpriced; that she had already paid their fair market value; that the contract terms were unconscionable; and that the sales price plus the credit charge for the goods constituted a usurious loan. The trial court entered judgment for appellee, concluding as a matter of law that the contract was neither unconscionable nor constituted a usurious loan.

Pair, Associate Judge: The issues raised on this appeal are whether (1) the contract terms are unconscionable and (2) the contract was a time sale transaction or a loan and forbearance at usurious interest.

The cash price of the household goods was $594.85. The sales tax was $17.85. The contract provided that if appellant elected not to pay the cash price she would be required to pay, in addition, a "credit charge" of $219.30. Thus the total price of the goods under the alternative agreement, including the sales tax, was $832.00, payable over a two-year period in weekly installments of $12.00. In answer to interrogatories submitted by appellant, appellee stated that the goods in question were purchased at a cost to it of $234.35.

Relying upon Williams v. Walker-Thomas Furniture Co., 350 F.2d 445 (D.C. 1965), appellant urges that because the sales price ($594.85) represents a markup of more than 100%, the contract was "unconscionable" and under the laws of this jurisdiction unenforceable. This court has held, consistent with Williams v. Walker-Thomas Furniture Co., *supra,* that the absence of a meaningful choice on the part of the parties to a contractual arrangement plus contract terms which are unreasonably favorable to the other party, must be proven in order to sustain the defense of "unconscionability."

The trial court, in its opinion and order dated October 26, 1970, stated specifically that:

Since this contract was a new and independent one, defendant was free to indulge in comparative shopping. Consequently, an essential element of unconscionability, that is, "[t]he absence of meaningful choice" was not present in the instant case. . . .

Although afforded a reasonable opportunity to do so, the defendant has not presented this court with evidence as to the commercial setting, purpose and effect of this contract which would lead the court to a finding of unconscionability.

Appellant contends next, as she did at trial, that the arrangement whereby she obligated herself to pay, over an extended period, a total of $832.00 for merchandise available to her at a cash price of $594.85 constituted a usurious loan. Appellant relies upon so much of the trial court's opinion and order as reads:

Over a two-year period, $219.00 is the credit charge for $612.70 [sic], amounting to 35.7924 or 35⁴/₅% interest. This is 17.9% *interest* for a one-year period and thus within the 18% limit permitted by the law of the jurisdiction. [Emphasis added.]

The transaction in this case falls squarely within the guide lines of the traditional time-price sale. The rule is well established that a bona fide sale of property on credit at a price which exceeds the cash price by more than the legal rate of interest does not constitute usury, since the seller is privileged to fix one price for cash and another for credit. Thus in District of Columbia v. Hamilton Nat. Bank, 76 A.2d 60 (D.C. 1950), we held as we do in this case:

[T]hat "the sale at a *Time Price* to the original purchaser, under a conditional sale agreement providing for monthly installments and including charges for . . . financing and other related services for the privilege of buying on time rather than by cash, is not violative of the usury statute." . . .

Because appellant does not allege that she was induced by fraud, duress or coercion or that she had no meaningful choice when she entered into the contract, we must assume that she elected not to pay the cash price and, preferring additional time to pay for the merchandise, intelligently agreed to pay the $219 credit charge.

Appellant urges vigorously that this court abandon the time-price doctrine and hold, on the authority of *State v. J. C. Penny Co.,* 179 N.W.2d 641 (Wis. 1970), that the credit charge was, in fact, interest. In that case the Supreme Court of Wisconsin held that the 1¹/₂% monthly service charge on a revolving charge account was usurious. However provocative may be that decision and appellant's insistence that we should apply its reasoning to the factual situation in this case, we are not persuaded that the doctrine of District of Columbia v. Hamilton Nat. Bank, *supra,* and the cases which followed it, should be disturbed. [DECISION FOR APPELLEE]

PROBLEMS

1 Stapleton listed certain real estate with a real estate broker for sale at a price of $8,500 in cash. Mendoza and his wife were interested in purchasing the property. The broker told them that it was unnecessary for them to see a lawyer because a contract had been prepared providing for a payment of $500 in cash and the balance in monthly payments of $38. The Mendozas, who were Mexicans by descent and who were not familiar with American business practice, paid the $500 and signed the contract. The contract was neither read by the Mendozas nor read to them. The next day an attorney advised the

Mendozas that they would have to pay an additional $8,000 in cash. They then notified the broker that they had signed the contract under a misunderstanding as to its contents and that it was impossible for them to carry out its terms. Are the Mendozas entitled to rescind the contract?

2 The plaintiff, a student at the Des Moines Commercial College, contended that the defendants represented to her that she could "complete a course in shorthand and typewriting and obtain a position in eight weeks' time under the expert individual instruction of the defendants' school" and that the representations were false. In a letter plaintiff received before entering the school, she was told, "You can take this entire course in from eight to twelve weeks." Is plaintiff entitled to rescind the contract and recover the amount paid as tuition?

3 Lewis, a retail jeweler, applied to Green, a wholesaler, for the purchase of jewelery on credit. Green replied by letter, stating: "It will be necessary to know how you stand." Lewis then furnished Green with a financial statement which showed that he had $50,000 in merchandise and $10,000 on deposit in the First Bank. On the strength of this statement, Green sold jewelry on credit to Lewis. Green then learned that Lewis had $50,000 in merchandise and $10,000 on deposit in the First Bank, but that he also owed $40,000 and was in financial difficulties. What remedy, if any, is available to Green?

4 Plaintiff, a building contractor, made a bid of $50,050 for the construction of a school building. On the day designated for awarding the bid, plaintiff attended the meeting of defendants when his bid and eight others were opened. Plaintiff was awarded the contract and he left the meeting. He then found that in computing the figures on which his bid was made he failed to include an item of $5,000. The following day he notified defendants of his error and said it was due to a defect in, and the manner in which he manipulated, his adding machine. He then requested that he be permitted to withdraw his bid, which was refused. Is plaintiff entitled to rescind the bid?

5 Plaintiff, the owner of certain real estate, executed a coal lease to the defendant whereby he was to receive five cents per ton royalty for coal mined, or $300 per year provided the royalty did not amount to that sum. Both plaintiff and defendant erroneously believed that there was coal underlying the tract of land, which fact turned out to be false. Is plaintiff entitled to recover the stipulated yearly sum?

6 Defendant, who was anxious to purchase plaintiff's 320-acre farm for the oil and gas it contained, told plaintiff that he desired to purchase the farm for agricultural purposes. Plaintiff, who knew nothing about the gas and oil, thereupon signed a deed conveying the farm to defendant. Plaintiff later learned that the farm contained valuable gas and oil, and brought an action to rescind the deed. Defendant contended that a prospective purchaser who knows there is valuable substance on the land of another is not under a duty to disclose his superior knowledge. Decide.

7 Plaintiff, a prospective purchaser, visited a dwelling which had been offered for sale by the defendant, the owner of the dwelling. Plaintiff, while inspecting the basement accompanied by the defendant, inquired about the joists in the basement. The defendant answered that "they are as good as new." A few days thereafter, plaintiff purchased the dwelling for $18,000. When plaintiff moved into the dwelling an inspection of the basement disclosed that the joists had been completely ravaged by termites and provided inadequate support for the floor above; that paint or whitewash had been applied to the joists in a heavy layer; and that strips of wood were used to cover some of the more severe termite damage. What remedy, if any, is available to the plaintiff?

10

CONTRACTS REQUIRED
TO BE IN WRITING

In early English history it was common practice to establish a contract through the testimony of hired witnesses. A wholly fictitious contract could be established in this manner. Perjury was prevalent. The innocent victim was often defrauded through court action. In 1677 in an effort to eliminate this corrupt practice, Parliament passed a statute for the prevention of frauds and perjuries. This statute is known as the "Statute of Frauds." The English Statute of Frauds is usually not considered as extending to this country but similar statutes have been enacted by legislatures of the several states. The distinguishing characteristic of these statutes is the provision that no action can be brought on certain specified classes of contracts unless they are reduced to writing and signed by the party sought to be bound thereby. These statutes are characterized by the expression "contracts required to be in writing." This expression does not mean that a formal written contract is essential but does mean that some note or memorandum is necessary in order to obtain relief in a judicial proceeding under certain specified classes of contracts. These contracts are said to be "within the statute."

Turning now from the historical background of the Statute of Frauds, it is significant to observe (1) the various classes of contracts that are within the statute, (2) the requirements that are necessary to satisfy the statute with respect to the note or memorandum, and (3) those few instances where a person may obtain judicial relief under the doctrine of part performance.

CLASSES OF CONTRACTS

The classes of contracts which are embraced within the English statute and which have been re-enacted by the several state legislatures may be summarized as including (1) an agreement by an executor or administrator to answer for the debt of the decedent out of the estate of the executor, (2) an agreement to answer for the debt or default of another, (3) an agreement made upon consideration of marriage, (4) an agreement not to be performed within the space of one year, (5) an agreement for the sale of land, and (6) an agreement for the sale of goods, wares, and merchandise above a specified amount. This latter class of contracts, namely, sale of personal property, will be discussed in the last pages of this chapter in order to illustrate more clearly the changes made by the Uniform Commercial Code.

The American statutes require many special classes of contracts other than those specified in the celebrated English statute to be in writing. Familiar illustrations are a promise to revive a debt barred by bankruptcy, a promise to extend the statute of limitations, and an agreement for the commission of a real estate broker. The assignment of wages is sometimes embraced within the statute. Although the statutes vary from state to state, the principles of law pertaining to those classes of contracts which are most frequently required to be in writing are fairly uniform. It is also well established by court decisions that an oral agreement to reduce to writing a contract which is within the Statute of Frauds is unenforceable. [*Lee Wilson & Co. v. Springfield,* p. 121.]

Promise by Executor   This section of the statute was designed solely to protect the estate of the executor or administrator who is under no duty to use his personal funds for the benefit of the estate. A special promise by an executor to pay the debts of the decedent out of the estate of the executor is within the statute. A promise of the executor to pay for whatever expenses are necessary to administer the affairs of the estate of the decedent out of the estate of the decedent, however, is without the statute.

Promise to Answer for the Debt of Another   A special promise by one person to answer for the debt or default of another person is within the statute. The promise is in the nature of a guaranty, and there must be a liability of another which is guaranteed. The distinction between those promises which are within the statute and those which are without the statute is said to be the distinction between a collateral promise and an original—or—primary promise. Conceding this distinction, however, does not solve the problem because the dividing line between a collateral promise, which is within the statute, and an original promise, which is without the statute, is difficult to draw. The following tests may be helpful: A promise (1) made to the creditor, (2) which is relied on by the the creditor, (3) to answer for a present or prospective liability of a third person, (4) out of the property of the promisor, (5) the immediate object of which is for the benefit of a third person, but (6) which does not extinguish the liability of the third person, will ordinarily be collateral, within the statute, and required to be in writing. It should be emphasized, however, that a collateral promise is made only in those instances where the promise of the guarantor is collateral to the promise of some other person. It should also be emphasized that the guarantor is liable only if the other person fails to perform.

This distinction between a collateral promise and an original one may be illustrated by a situation where credit is extended. Suppose Brown and Smith enter Jones Grocery Store so that Brown may purchase groceries. Suppose further that Smith says to Jones: "If Brown does not pay you, I will." This is a collateral promise, within the statute, and required to be in writing to be enforceable. Suppose, however, that Smith had said to Jones: "Let Brown have the groceries, and I will pay you." This is an original promise, without the statute, and is not required to be in writing to be enforceable.

The words "payment guaranteed" and "collection guaranteed" are frequently used in promising to answer for the debt of another person. A person guaranteeing payment of a debt undertakes to pay the debt upon default of the principal debtor. A person guaranteeing collection of a debt undertakes to pay the debt on the condition that the creditor first make use of the ordinary legal means to collect it from the debtor. The promise, irrespective of whether payment or collection is guaranteed, is a collateral promise, within the statute, and required to be in writing.

Original promises other than the one in the above illustration which are worthy of mention are promises creating a joint debt, those made for the benefit of the promisor, and those which extinguish the liability.

(1) *Promises Creating Joint Debts* An oral promise, the effect of which is to incur a joint debt with another, is enforceable. The debt, as between the promisor and the third person, may be the debt of the third person only. The promise is nevertheless held to be an original promise. Suppose Brown and Smith enter Jones Department Store, where Brown desires to purchase certain merchandise. Suppose further that Jones will not sell the merchandise to Brown unless Smith consents to an arrangement whereby the merchandise is to be charged to Brown and Smith jointly. Suppose still further that Smith consents to this arrangement. This is an original undertaking on the part of Smith, without the statute, and is not required to be in writing to be enforceable.

(2) *Promises for the Benefit of the Promisor* Promises are sometimes made to pay the debt of another person when in fact the main purpose of the promisor is to subserve his own interest. Suppose Brown is in possession of and is using a delivery truck which belongs to Smith and that the truck is encumbered with a chattel mortgage in favor of Brown. Suppose further that Jones, another creditor of Smith, is threatening to attach the truck to satisfy his claim against Smith. Suppose still further that Brown says to Jones: "I will pay the debt which Smith owes you if you refrain from attaching the truck." The oral promise is not required to be in writing to be enforceable. The theory is that the promisor, under the pretext of a guarantor, is engaging to pay a debt of his own rather than the debt of another person. As a general rule, therefore, the promise is an original one, without the statute, and is not required to be in writing to be enforceable if the

promisor has an immediate business or pecuniary interest in the transaction to the extent that he obtains a substantial benefit to himself.

(3) *Extinguishment of Liability* The courts are not in harmony with respect to a promise to pay a pre-existing debt of another. There are, however, two well-recognized situations which are without the statute. The first situation which is without the statute is a promise made to the debtor which is based upon sufficient consideration. Suppose Brown is the owner of a house and lot which is encumbered by a mortgage to secure a debt of $12,000 in favor of Jones. Suppose further that Brown sells this house and lot to Smith and that Smith assumes the mortgage and promises Brown to pay the debt. The oral promise is enforceable. It should be pointed out, however, that the promise is made to the debtor and that the debtor is not necessarily discharged.

The second situation which is without the statute is where the old debtor is entirely released and discharged. Suppose Brown owes Jones $500. Suppose further that Smith promises Jones that he will pay the $500 provided he will discharge Brown, and that Jones accepts the promise in substitution for and discharge of the debt owed by Brown. The promise of Smith is original and without the statute. The original debtor, Brown, is released, and the promisor, Smith, is the new debtor. Simply stated, this is a novation and is merely a substitution of a new debtor in place of the old debtor. In these circumstances, it is said that a novation creating a new contract has been fashioned and the promise is without the statute. [*La Duke v. Barbee,* p. 122.]

Agreement in Consideration of Marriage This clause of the statute applies to promises in consideration of marriage. Mutual promises to marry, or engagement contracts, are without the statute. This section of the statute also embraces promises by a third person. A promise by a father to his daughter to pay a certain sum of money in consideration of the prospective marriage, therefore, would be within the statute.

The Year Clause Contracts which cannot be performed within a year are within the Statute of Frauds. The typical American statute contains a provision which applies to "agreements not to be performed within the space of one year from the making thereof." The words "from the making" are interpreted to exclude the day on which the contract is made. The year, therefore, begins with the following day and ends at the close of the anniversary of the day on which the contract is made. It should be mentioned that the time begins to run from the day the contract is entered into and not from the time that performance of it is to be entered upon. A contract for a period of longer than one year, therefore, is within the statute even though performance is to begin in the future. These rules seem simple enough, but they are difficult in application when the time of performance is not definitely stated.

(1) *Performance Dependent on a Contingency* The terms of some agreements provide for performance upon the happening of some contingency. An oral agreement to employ a person until he has recovered from some injury would be

enforceable because the injured person may possibly recover within a year. An oral agreement to construct a building would be enforceable because the construction work might possibly be completed within a year. An oral agreement which is contingent upon the duration of human life would likewise be enforceable because the death of a person may possibly occur within a year. This rule has frequently been applied to contracts for personal services, and it is uniformly held that a contract to give one employment for as long as he lives is without the statute. The general rule, broadly stated, is that, although performance may possibly extend longer than one year, the contract is nevertheless without the statute if it is capable of being performed within a year.

(2) *Performance on One Side Only*   Contracts are sometimes performed on one side within a year but are incapable of performance on the other side within a year. Some jurisdictions interpret the statute to mean "full performance on both sides" and will not enforce oral contracts that are performed on one side only. Generally, an oral contract which has been performed on one side will be enforced if the performance has been accepted by the other party. This is particularly true if nothing remains to be done except the payment of money. An oral contract, therefore, whereby money is lent but, by the terms of the agreement, repayment thereof is extended by installments beyond the one-year period would be enforceable.

Contracts for the Sale of Real Estate   This clause of the statute provides that contracts for the sale of land, or for any interest therein, shall be in writing. The words "an interest in land" are interpreted to include, not only the fee-simple title, but an easement, a lease, contracts to mortgage, and contracts to sell real estate. Many state statutes expressly provide that leases for more than one year must be in writing. A license, which is authority to perform some act on the land of another—as where Brown is given permission to cross the land of Smith in order to fish in a stream—is not an interest in land.

The chief controversy concerning the interpretation of "an interest in land" has revolved around the sale of crops and other products of land. A crop which is produced by labor and cultivation has usually been considered a chattel, while growing grass, timber, and minerals have usually been considered an interest in land. It is generally held that all industrial crops and things attached to or forming a part of the land which are agreed to be severed before title is to pass are not an interest in land. The contract may, nevertheless, be within the Statute of Frauds inasmuch as the price may be sufficient to bring the promise within the section of the statute respecting the sale of goods.

Sale of Goods   Section 2–107 of the Code provides that a contract for the sale of minerals or the like or a structure or its materials to be removed from realty is a contract for the sale of goods if they are to be severed by the seller. It is thus clear that if the buyer is to do the severing, the contract is one affecting land. The contract must, therefore, be in writing to be enforceable. The Code also provides that growing crops or other things attached to the realty, other than minerals or the like, which can be severed without material harm is a contract for the sale of goods regardless of who is to effect the severance. With respect to timber to be cut, it is provided that the timber is a sale of goods whether the timber is to be severed by the buyer or the seller. It is conceivable that a rose bush or growing crops could be removed without material harm. It is also conceivable that wall-to-wall carpeting placed over a hardwood floor would fall within the definition of goods. The courts might find, however, that carpeting placed over a concrete floor is within the definition of "an interest in land." It would depend on the facts of the particular case.

Real Estate Brokers   The provisions of the general Statute of Frauds pertaining to real property do not apply to a contract of employment by which one person acts as the broker of another in negotiating a sale or purchase of real property. A broker whose misconduct is so gross as to be fraudulent would undoubtedly be answerable to his employer for damages, and a broker who, in violation of his oral contract, purchases the land in his own name may be compelled to convey the land to his principal. A contract of employment for the sale and purchase of real property should, nevertheless, be reduced to writing. A provision in the terms of employment stating that the broker is to receive land in return for his services would bring the contract within the provisions of the statute. Similarly, a provision in the terms of employment requiring the broker to take title in his own name would likewise bring the contract within the statute. Furthermore, in many states, statutes have been enacted which expressly require contracts for the employment of another as agent in negotiating the purchase or sale of real property to be in writing. These possibilities lead to the conclusion that contracts of employment by which one person is to act as the broker of another in negotiating a sale of real property may justifiably be classified among those contracts that are required to be in writing. Statutes in many states provide that a contract for compensation for procuring a purchaser for real property must be in writing. Under these statutes, the vast majority of the decisions hold that the broker cannot recover on a quasi contract for services rendered if his contract does not satisfy the statute.

FORM OF WRITING

The Statute of Frauds does not require that the contract be reduced to a formal written document, nor is any particular form of language necessary. All that is required is a written note or memorandum thereof signed by the party sought to be bound or his duly authorized agent. It is not necessary that both parties sign the writing. Consequently one party to the agreement may be bound but the other is not. This is a rule of the Statute of Frauds and should not be confused with the rule of mutuality, which is to the effect that in a bilateral contract both parties must be bound or neither is bound.

Memorandum   A formal contract would obviously satisfy the statute. Any writings, however, which accurately state the contract are sufficient. Letters, telegrams, receipts or any kind of note that shows the names or description of the parties and the consideration, are all that is required. The memorandum may consist of several documents, but these must be physically attached to one another or so incorporated by reference that the courts can gather therefrom the intention of the parties and enforce the intended agreement. A few of the early decisions held the parties to a high degree of certainty in the description of land. It is generally held today, however, that no more particular description is necessary in a contract for the sale of real estate than in one relating to personal property. [*Wozniak v. Kuszinski*, p. 122.]

Signature   A few statutes require that the signature be placed at the end of the writing but, as a general rule, the signature need not be at the end of the document. The printed name of the party sought to be charged at the top or in the body of the memorandum is sufficient. The signature may also be stamped; it may be by mark, initials, or by Christian name alone. The person signing the memorandum, however, must intend that the signature authenticate the paper as his own act. [*First Nat'l Bank v. Laperle*, p. 124.]

DOCTRINE OF PART PERFORMANCE

At an early date the courts recognized the possibility of the Statute of Frauds's defeating its very purpose—to prevent fraud—if the statute were applied literally to all situations. The necessity of preventing the statute from becoming an agent of fraud, therefore, gave rise to the doctrine of part performance. The basis of the doctrine is that it would be a fraud to permit a person to escape performance of his part of an oral agreement after he had permitted another person to perform in reliance upon the agreement. The doctrine is based upon equitable principles, and, while it is not confined to any particular class of contracts, it is usually invoked for contracts for the sale of land and for services.

Sale of Land   A diversity of opinion is found in the cases with respect to the sufficiency of acts which will constitute part performance in order to take an oral contract for the sale of land out of the Statute of Frauds so as to permit it to be enforced by specific performance. Some of the courts have said that delivery of possession pursuant to an oral agreement is such part performance as will take the case out of the statute. A reading of the cases, however, reveals that other acts, such as payment of the purchase price or improvements, were involved in the particular cases before the courts. It seems quite clear that the courts will enforce a parol agreement for the sale of land where the purchaser has paid the purchase price, has taken possession of the premises in pursuance of the agreement, with the knowledge and consent of the owner, and has made lasting and valuable improvements. A person, therefore, who, in reliance upon an oral contract for the sale of land, has so far altered his position that he would be defrauded unless the contract were executed may be granted specific performance of the oral contract.

    If the circumstances of the particular case do not warrant specific performance, a vendee who enters the premises under an oral contract for the purchase of land and makes valuable improvements is usually entitled to recover the purchase money paid and the value of the improvements made by him while in possession under the oral contract if the vendor refuses to convey title to the land. The courts allow this recovery on the theory of quasi contract.

Services Rendered It is generally recognized that an employee who has rendered services to an employer in reliance on a contract unenforceable because of the Statute of Frauds may recover on a quasi contract for the rendition of such services when he is discharged without cause. When the employer, therefore, accepts and receives the benefit of such services, the employee may recover the reasonable value of the services rendered under the oral contract. [*Wise v. Midtown Motors, Inc.*, p. 124.]

Extent of the Doctrine It should not be presumed that the doctrine of part performance can be used as an instrument to escape the formalities required by the Statute of Frauds. The courts are uniform in holding that the statute is a perfect defense to an action for breach of the oral contract. A person, therefore, who enters into an oral contract of a class that is required to be in writing cannot sue on the contract successfully. He is left to his remedy on the theory of quasi contract. Specific performance is rarely granted, and damages for breach of the oral contract are never allowed.

Sale of Goods Section 2–201 provides that a contract for the sale of goods for the price of $500 or more is not enforceable unless it is evidenced by some writing. Special provision is made with respect to (1) the form of the contract, (2) specially manufactured goods, (3) part payment and acceptance, (4) admissions in court, (5) contracts between merchants, and (6) modifications of contracts.

(1) *Form of the Contract* Section 2–201 makes it clear that an informal and incomplete writing is sufficient to satisfy the Statute of Frauds. This is true even though some of the important terms, such as the price, the time and place of delivery, and the general quality of the goods, or warranties, are not expressed in the writing. The writing, however, must (a) indicate that a contract for the sale of goods has been entered into between the parties, (b) bear the signature or other reasonable authentication by the party against whom enforcement is sought, and (c) contain a statement of the quantity of the goods. The Code specifically provides that the contract is not enforceable beyond the quantity of goods shown in the memorandum.

(2) *Specially Manufactured Goods* The Code makes provision for the enforceability of oral contracts where the goods are to be made specially for the buyer. The oral contract is enforceable if it is shown that (a) the goods are to be made specially for the buyer, (b) the goods are not suitable for sale in the ordinary course of the business of the seller, and (c) the seller, before receiving notice of any repudiation of the contract, has made a substantial beginning of their manufacture or, if he is not a manufacturer, has made commitments for their procurement.

(3) *Part Payment and Acceptance* An oral contract is enforceable only with respect to goods which have been received and accepted or for which payment has been made and accepted. Receipt and acceptance of a part of the goods by the buyer or receipt and acceptance of a part payment by the seller constitute an admission that a contract exists. In those instances where the court can make an apportionment, therefore, the seller can recover the agreed price of any goods actually delivered and accepted. The buyer may likewise force the seller to deliver the apportionable part of the goods for which payment has been made and accepted. Suppose the buyer ordered fifty typewriters of a specific type of trade name for $200 each. Suppose further that the seller delivered and the buyer accepted ten of the typewriters. The seller could recover the agreed price of the ten typewriters from the buyer. If the buyer paid for and the seller accepted the agreed price for the ten typewriters, the buyer could force the seller to deliver the ten typewriters. Part payment and acceptance, however, will not make the oral contract enforceable for any quantity if the subject matter is not apportionable. If the contract is apportionable, delivery and acceptance of a part of the goods will make the contract enforceable only to the extent of the quantity delivered and accepted. [*Bagby Land & Cattle Co. v. California Livestock Comm'n Co.*, p. 125.]

Section 2–606 provides that acceptance of the goods occurs when the buyer, after a reasonable opportunity to inspect the goods, signifies to the seller that the goods are conforming or that he will accept them in spite of their nonconformity, or if the buyer does any act inconsistent with the seller's ownership. Acceptance will ordinarily be signified by the receipt and retention of, and the payment for, the goods by the buyer.

The "part payment" provision by the buyer requires delivery of something that is accepted by the seller as part performance. Part payment may be made by money or check, or it may consist of goods or services. The part payment, however, must be delivered by the buyer and accepted by the seller irrespective of the method of payment.

(4) *Admissions in Court* Section 2–201 provides that an oral contract is enforceable if the party against whom enforcement is sought makes a statement in court admitting that he has entered into a contract for the sale of goods. This includes admissions made in pleadings, testimony, or otherwise in court, and is evidential only against the party making the admission of the facts so admitted. The contract is not enforceable, therefore, beyond the quantity of the goods admitted.

(5) *Letters of Confirmation* Suppose the seller and the buyer, who are both merchants, enter into an oral contract for the sale of goods. Suppose further that the seller sends a letter of confirmation stating all the terms of the contract. The buyer is required to object in writing within ten days after receiving the confirmation if he wishes to retain the protection of the Statute of Frauds. The rule would also be applicable if the buyer is the sender of the confirmation. The effect of this provision is to take away from the receiver of the confirmation the defense of the Statute of Frauds unless he objects in writing within ten days. This

makes it possible for a merchant to be bound even though he does not sign a memorandum, pays nothing for the goods, and has not accepted any part of the goods.

(6) *Modification, Rescission, Waiver* Section 2–209, which pertains to modification, rescission, and waiver, provides that the requirements of the Statute of Frauds must be satisfied if the contract as modified is within its provisions. For example, a contract for the sale of goods for $200 would not have to meet the requirements of the Statute of Frauds. A new contract modifying the contract so that the price term was increased to $600, however, would have to meet the requirements of the Statute of Frauds. Modification or rescission is intended to include abandonment or other changes by mutual consent.

CASES

Lee Wilson & Co. v. Springfield 321 S.W.2d 775 (Ark. 1959). Action by Lee Wilson & Company (plaintiff below), appellant, against Baker D. Springfield, his wife, Ethel Springfield, and his sister Jane Springfield, and Cecil Earls (defendants below), appellees. The complaint alleges in substance that appellee Baker D. Springfield, hereinafter referred to as Baker, owned a 460-acre farm; that he approached appellant with the idea of selling the land and the farm equipment if he could realize as much as $35,000 after the payment of debts and taxes; that appellee Jane Springfield owns a 490-acre farm adjoining Baker's property, which property appellant would have the right to rent for $25 per acre; and that Baker thereafter entered into a deal to sell the property, both real and personal, to appellee Earls for the sum of $214,000 and to rent him Jane Springfield's land. The complaint then asked that a temporary restraining order be issued enjoining appellees from going through with the deal whereby the sale would be made to Earls.

Robinson, Justice: Appellant insists that it entered into a valid contract concerning the purchase of the land and $30,000 worth of farming equipment and acquired the option of leasing Baker's sister's land and that it has the right to enforce such contract in a court of equity, notwithstanding the Statute of Frauds. . . .

While conceding that oral contracts for the sale of real estate cannot be enforced in some circumstances, appellant says that here there was an oral contract to make an enforceable contract and that such oral contract is not within the purview of the Statute of Frauds. . . .

It is appellant's theory that it has a right to buy the land and equipment for $214,000. It is clear from the complaint that there has been no delivery of any property whatever; that nothing was paid to bind the bargain and no memorandum in writing of any kind was made concerning the transaction. In these circumstances, if the Statute of Frauds is not applicable, then it is completely meaningless. . . . A contract for sale of land or interest therein must be in writing. A quotation from 49 Am. Jur. 368 is peculiarly applicable here:

While there are intimations to the contrary of the rule in a few scattered decisions, the general rule is that an oral agreement to reduce to writing a contract which is within the scope of the operation of the Statute of Frauds, or to sign an agreement which the Statute of Frauds requires to be in writing, is invalid and unenforceable. Neither promise is enforceable unless the Statute is satisfied. In other words, a parol agreement invalid under the Statute is not aided by a further parol agreement to reduce the principal agreement to writing. To allow the enforcement of such an agreement would be tantamount to taking the main contract out of the Statute, and as has been said, it is absurd to say that an oral promise in relation to certain subject matter is invalid, but that a promise that the party will thereafter bind himself with respect to the subject matter is valid. Such a construction would be a palpable evasion of the Statute, and let in all the evils against which it is directed. [DECISION FOR APPELLEES]

La Duke v. John T. Barbee & Co., 73 So. 472 (Ala. 1916). Action by John T. Barbee & Company, plaintiff, against Tom La Duke, defendant. The partnership of Hall & Tarpey bought a shipment of whisky from plaintiff which was placed in the place of business of the partnership. Thereafter, about June 13, 1912, Hall & Tarpey sold their business, including their goods, fixtures, and accounts, to the defendant. At that time there was an unpaid balance of $73.25 on the shipment of whisky. On August 5, 1913, the account was still unpaid, and the plaintiff brought this action to recover this unpaid balance. Jerry Tarpey was the only witness introduced. He testified as to the nature of the transaction.

Mayfield, Justice: This sole witness also testified that:

The original debt between Barbee & Co. and Hall & Tarpey was for $146.50. When we quit business, Hall & Tarpey paid Barbee & Co. one-half of this amount, and the agreement was between all three parties that La Duke would assume the balance of the debt, and Barbee & Co. agreed to this contract and released us. This contract was made when we sold out our business to Tom La Duke, at New Decatur, Ala. Barbee & Co. knew of the contract and agreed to it.

. . . Where the original debtor is entirely released or discharged, and the obligation or promise of another is substituted in place of that of the discharged debtor, a new debt is thereby created, binding on the substituted debtor, which is not affected by the provisions of the Statute of Frauds, declaring "every special promise to answer for the debt, default or miscarriage of another" void unless it is reduced to writing. A promise to pay the pre-existing debt of another, made upon a new and valuable consideration, beneficial to the promisor, is not within the statute. If the original debtor is released on the promise of a third party to pay the debt, the new debt is binding upon the promisor; it is his own debt and is no longer the debt of another. [DECISION FOR PLAINTIFF]

Wozniak v. Kuszinski, 90 N.W.2d 456 (Mich. 1958). Action by Stefan Wozniak and wife (plaintiffs below), appellants, against Josephine Kuzinski (defendant below), appellee. Defendant displayed a "for sale" card in the window of her home, the correct address of which is 1503 Joy Avenue, Jackson, Michigan, and negotiations for the purchase of the house were thereafter opened by plaintiffs with defendant. After discussing price and terms, defendant signed the following writing:

August 15, 1955

Received of Stefan and Karolina Wozniak Three Hundred and no/100 Dollars for deposit on purchase of Prop. known as 1503 Joy.

Previous balance	$6,050.00
Amount paid	300.00
Balance due	5,750.00

Balance on delivery of deed and abstract.

(Signed by defendant Josephine Kuszinski)

Defendant later refused to complete the deal, and plaintiffs sought specific performance for the purchase and sale of the real estate.

Black, Justice: This court has "recently evidenced" a disposition "to liberalize its interpretation of the statute of frauds. . . . "

Professor Grismore, noting this new course of the judiciary in his "Principles of the Law of Contracts," Sec. 261, p. 449, said:

Preliminary to this discussion [of the Statute of Frauds] it is worthy of observation that the tendency, in general, has been to interpret the statute in such a way as to narrow the scope of its operation as much as possible. This result has been accomplished not only by resolving all ambiguities in the phraseology of the statute in such a way as to exclude as many cases as possible from its operation, but also by excluding cases which are within the language, on the ground that they are not within the purpose or spirit of the statute. In fact, in recent years there has been a tendency to doubt the wisdom of the statute as applied to modern conditions and to advocate its outright repeal.

It is not to be gainsaid that our quoted commitment to the rule of evidentiary supplementation, of an otherwise insufficient memorandum relating to sale of real estate, partially eviscerates Sec. 8 of our statute of frauds as once understood and interpreted. Such being the case, it is advisable that the fact and effect be openly heralded, and that we firmly announce that which is to be in this field of law relating to rights in and titles to land. Whether the old interpretation of said Sec. 8, or the new one, is best for society remains and will remain debatable. The change having taken place, we can only say that equity can and will, given appealing equities arrayed against perfidy or fast dealing, prevent most of the frauds that Sec. 8 of this venerable statute was intended to frustrate. . . .

Since the street address of the home is given correctly in the memorandum, and since defendant Josephine Kuszinski owned the property answering such address and the record is clear that the parties were intending to deal with respect to it and no other, we are constrained to hold that the description given in the memorandum was appropriately supplemented. As was said in 49 Am. Jur., Statute of Frauds, Sec. 348, p. 657:

"A description is sufficient if when read in the light of the circumstances of possession, ownership, situation of the parties, and their relation to each other and to the property, as they were when the negotiations took place and the writing was made, it identifies the property." [DECISION FOR PLAINTIFFS]

First Nat'l Bank v. Laperle, 86 A.2d 635 (Vt. 1952). Action by the First National Bank of St. Johnsbury, plaintiff, against Marie J. Laperle, defendant. The plaintiff and the defendant entered into the following agreement:

Received of Mrs. Marie Laperle the sum of Five Hundred Dollars ($500.00), as a down payment on a $25,000 cash offer for the Calvin E. Brown store building located at 99 Eastern Avenue, St. Johnsbury, Vermont, and all stock in trade and fixtures located in said store. . . .

> The First National Bank
> St. Johnsbury, Vt.
> By L. B. Wood, Cashier

Attest,
Mrs. Marie J. Laperle
St. Johnsbury, Vt.
June 2, 1950.

The plaintiff brought this suit for specific performance. The defendant claimed that the contract failed to comply with the Statute of Frauds because she did not sign the paper within the meaning of the statute.

Jeffords, Justice: The signing required by the statute is a signature to the memorandum placed there with the intention of authenticating the writing. If that is the intention it is generally held that it is not essential that the signature be at the end of the memorandum in any particular place thereon.

. . . It is clear from all the circumstances that when she signed she did so not merely as a witness but as a party with the intention of authenticating the writing, or, as the chancellor found, that in affixing her signature under the word "attest" she indicated her agreement and confirmation of the arrangement. This finding amounts to one of intent to authenticate. [DECISION FOR PLAINTIFF]

Wise v. Midtown Motors, Inc., 42 N.W.2d 404 (Minn. 1950). Suit by Frank E. Wise, plaintiff, against Midtown Motors, Inc., defendant. The evidence showed that plaintiff was a highly skilled automobile motor tune-up mechanic and that in October, 1947, Clarence Rexeisen, an official of the defendant, orally offered plaintiff in behalf of defendant three years' employment as a tune-up mechanic and supervisor in St. Paul at an annual salary of $4,500 for the first year, $5,000 for the second year, and $5,500 for the third year; that plaintiff accepted the offer and performed the services agreed upon from November, 1947, until June, 1948, at which latter date he was discharged. Plaintiff concedes that he cannot maintain action against defendant's objection that it is void under the Statute of Frauds, but contends he is entitled to recover the reasonable value of the services rendered.

Peterson, Justice: It is well settled that where the employer-defendant repudiates an oral contract which is within the Statute of Frauds, and therefore unenforceable, plaintiff may recover the reasonable value of the services rendered under the contract. There is a conflict of opinion as to whether the unenforceable contract measures the right of recovery so far as it has been performed or is merely admissible as an admission of the parties relative to that question for whatever evidentiary worth it possesses under the circumstances of the particular case.

. . . According to sound principle and the weight of authority, where an employer-defendant repudiates a contract of employment as unenforceable under the Statute of Frauds, the employee is entitled to recover the reasonable value of the services rendered by him thereunder. [DECISION FOR PLAINTIFF]

Bagby Land & Cattle Co. v. California Livestock Comm'n Co.,   439 F.2d 315 (Tex. 1971). Action by Bagby Land and Cattle Company, appellee (plaintiff below), against California Lifestock Commission Company, appellant (defendant below), to recover the price for cattle sold and delivered.

Bagby Land was engaged in the business of purchasing large quantities of Mexican cattle and bringing them across the Texas border for sale. In November, 1968, California Livestock began purchasing cattle from Bagby Land for resale to third persons. California Livestock made daily oral orders for cattle available at the border at the time of the order, and payment was customarily made immediately by draft. In November and December, California Livestock purchased approximately 1,600 cattle from Bagby Land in this manner. Of the 1,600, however, Bagby Land inadvertently failed to invoice eighty. California Livestock thereafter orally agreed to purchase 2,000 to be delivered in January, 1969. Of this 2,000, Bagby Land delivered 222 cattle to California Livestock, and then failed to deliver any more.

California Livestock demanded delivery of the remaining 1,778 cattle, and refused to pay for the eighty cattle previously delivered until further delivery was made. Bagby Land refused to deliver the cattle, and brought an action to recover the price of the eighty cattle. California Livestock counterclaimed for delivery of the 1,778 cattle. The lower court awarded judgment in favor of Bagby Land for the price of the eighty cattle, and dismissed the counterclaim of California Livestock on the ground that it was barred by the Statute of Frauds. This appeal followed. California Livestock contended that delivery of the 222 cattle was "part performance" of the contract, which performance was sufficient to take the entire contract out of the Statute of Frauds.

Gewin, Circuit Judge: California Livestock seeks to show on several grounds that the admittedly oral contract does not come within the statute of frauds. First, it argues that delivery of 222 of the 2000 head of cattle contracted for was "part performance" of the contract and is sufficient to take the entire contract out of the statute of frauds. We cannot agree. Under Section 2.201(c) (3) of the Texas Business and Commerce Code an otherwise invalid contract "is enforceable . . . (3) with respect to goods . . . which have been received and accepted." Although we have found and are cited to no Texas cases interpreting this recently adopted legislation, we have no hesitancy in holding that the effect of this statute is to validate an oral agreement only as to those goods actually received and accepted by the buyer. While the UCC Comments on this section are not final authority, we treat them as authoritative support for this holding, particularly in the absence of other precedents:

2. "Partial performance" as a substitute for the required memorandum can validate the contract only for the goods which have been accepted or for which payment has been made and accepted.

Receipt and acceptance either of goods or of the price constitutes an unambiguous overt admission by both parties that a contract actually exists. If the court can make a just apportionment, therefore, the agreed price of any goods actually delivered can be recovered without a writing or, if the price has been paid, the seller can be forced to deliver an apportionable part of the goods. The overt actions of the parties make admissible evidence of the other terms of the contract necessary to a just apportionment. This is true even though the actions of the parties are not in themselves inconsistent with a different transaction such as a consignment for resale or a mere loan of money.

California Livestock's acceptance of 222 cattle delivered pursuant to the alleged contract does not, therefore, give rise to the right to have delivery of any other cattle for which it orally contracted. Section 2.201(c) (3) does not sustain the contention made. [DECISION FOR APPELLEE]

PROBLEMS

1 Brown, an orange grower, in a telephone conversation with a processor of frozen orange juice, agreed to sell to the processor 3,000 boxes of oranges at $6.00 per box. Brown delivered 1,000 boxes of oranges to the processor, who accepted the 1,000 boxes. Two weeks later, the price of oranges on the open market had dropped to $5.50 per box. Brown then shipped the remaining 2,000 boxes of oranges to the processor, but he refused to accept the 2,000 boxes. What amount, if any, would Brown be able to recover from the processor?

2 The defendant orally agreed with the plaintiff that, if plaintiff would occupy and improve a certain eighty-acre tract for a period of four years, at the expiration of that time the defendant would deed the land to the plaintiff. The plaintiff accepted the offer and moved upon the land, which was unimproved, and proceeded to improve the same by erecting a dwelling house, barn, fences, etc., and cultivating a portion of the land. About one year later, the plaintiff and the defendant had some words which led to blows, and the defendant ordered the plaintiff to leave the premises, which he did. Is plaintiff entitled to recover from the defendant the value of the improvements which he placed upon the land?

3 The plaintiff and the defendant, a railway company, entered into an oral contract by which it was agreed that if the plaintiff would grade the ground for a switch and put on the ties at a certain point on the defendant's railroad, the defendant would put down the rails and maintain the switch for the plaintiff's benefit for shipping purposes as long as he needed it. In accordance with this agreement, the plaintiff graded the ground for the switch and put down the ties, and the defendant put down the iron rails and established the switch. The plaintiff thereafter sawed and shipped large quantities of lumber until the defendant, about ten years later, tore up the switch and ties and thereby destroyed the transportation facilities. The plaintiff brought an action for breach of contract. The defendant pleaded that the contract was within the Statute of Frauds. Decide.

4 On December 20, 1967, Brown, the landlord, entered into an oral agreement with Smith, the tenant, whereby Brown agreed to lease forty acres of farmland to Smith. The lease agreement provided that Smith might have possession of the farmland as a tenant for a term beginning on December 15, 1968, and ending on January 15, 1969, at a monthly rental of $125. On December 15, 1968, Smith refused to comply with the terms of the lease agreement, and Brown brought an action for breach of contract. Does Brown have a good cause of action?

5 Carroll, the decedent, owed Price $5,000 during his lifetime. James, who was the executor of the estate of Carroll, orally promised Price that he would pay the $5,000, even if he had to pay it personally. James, in accordance with the provisions of a statute, paid the funeral expenses and the expenses of the last illness. There were then no more assets in the estate of Carroll. Price brought an action against James to recover the $5,000 on his promise to pay the $5,000. Will he recover?

6 The Safety Company entered into a contract with Adams to sell and install a fire alarm system for $2,200. The written contract was an order form filled out by the seller. The buyer signed the contract, but the signature of the seller did not appear on the order form. The equipment was installed by the seller. The buyer, however, refused to pay the purchase price. The seller brought an action against the buyer for the purchase price, and the buyer defended the action on the ground that since the contract was not signed by the seller there was not sufficient evidence of a writing to be enforceable. Discuss whether the seller has a good cause of action.

7 Plaintiff and the vice-president of the defendant-corporation entered into an oral contract by the terms of which plaintiff agreed to buy and the corporation agreed to sell certain merchandise for the sum of $15,000. At the same time, the vice-president recorded the order in detail on a printed blank which contained the printed name of the corporation. The corporation thereafter refused to deliver the merchandise, and plaintiff brought an action for breach of contract. The corporation contends the Statute of Frauds is a perfect defense because there was no memorandum in writing signed by the corporation. Decide.

8 Fox, the seller, orally agreed to sell two vats to Moss for the price of $1,600, of which sum Moss paid $100 at the time the contract was entered into. It was also agreed that Moss would pay the balance of $1,500 at the time the vats were delivered. When Fox tendered delivery of the vats, Moss refused to accept the vats and to pay the balance of $1,500. Although Fox admitted that the subject matter of the contract was worth more than $500 and that there was no written evidence that the contract for sale had been entered into, he contended that he was entitled to recover by reason of the part payment by Moss. Discuss whether the part payment makes the total contract enforceable.

11

RIGHTS OF THIRD PARTIES

A person who seeks to maintain an action on a contract will ordinarily be required to have privity of contract; that is, the plaintiff must be a party to the contract. It has been settled law for a long time, however, that a person may sue on a contract under exceptional circumstances although he is neither a promisor nor a promisee. These exceptional circumstances may arise if the makers of the contract provide that performance shall be for the benefit of some third person or if one of the original parties to the contract transfers his interest to some third person in the way of assignment. Third persons, therefore, may acquire rights under a contract either (1) as a beneficiary or (2) as an assignee.

THIRD-PARTY BENEFICIARY

A few states adhere to the rule that a person who is a stranger to the contract and to the consideration has no rights under the contract. These states limit the action on the contract to the original contracting parties. A valid promise for the benefit of a third person may, of course, be enforced by the promisee. The vast majority of the states, moreover, permit beneficiaries to sue.

Third-party beneficiaries are generally classified as creditor beneficiaries, donee beneficiaries, and incidental beneficiaries. Most of the states today allow either the donee beneficiary or the creditor beneficiary to sue on the contract;

some states allow both to sue. The incidental beneficiary is not allowed to sue. Some of the decisions, however, make no reference to either a creditor beneficiary or a donee beneficiary. These decisions hold that a third person for whose *direct* benefit a contract was entered into may enforce the contract. A few statutes provide that a contract made *expressly* for the benefit of a third person may be enforced by the third person. The general rule, however, permits the creditor beneficiary and the donee beneficiary to enforce the contract. It is not a requisite that his name be mentioned in the contract; it is sufficient if the contract was entered into for the direct benefit of the beneficiary. The law is by no means uniform throughout the United States but it may be stated as a general rule that in most states a person for whose direct benefit a contract was entered into may sue on the contract even though he paid nothing for it and was not a party to the contract. [*Johnson v. Holmes Tuttle Lincoln-Mercury, Inc.*, p. 135.]

Creditor Beneficiary   A contract made for the benefit of a third person who is a creditor of the promisee is a "creditor-beneficiary contract." At this point, it seems necessary to distinguish between a novation involving a third party, the assignment of a contractual right, and a creditor-beneficiary contract.

Assume a contract which has created a debtor-creditor relationship, and the debtor delegates his duty of paying to some third person. If the creditor joins in the transaction and releases the debtor from further liability, there is a novation—the substitution of a new debtor in the place of the old debtor. Assume again a contract which has created a creditor-debtor relationship, and the creditor transfers his interest to a purchaser. This gives the purchaser the right to sue the debtor and is called an "assignment." Assume again a contract which has created a creditor-debtor relationship, and the debtor transfers his interest in a retail shop in which the fixtures are encumbered by a mortgage to a purchaser who assumes the debt. The transfer gives the creditor the right to sue the purchaser, and is called a creditor-beneficiary contract.

The following is a good illustration of a creditor-beneficiary contract: Suppose Brown purchases certain household furniture from Smith for $5,000 and that he makes a down payment of $1,000 and agrees to pay the unpaid balance at the rate of $100 a month. Suppose further that Brown then sells the furniture to Jones, who pays Brown $800 for his equity in the furniture and promises him that he will pay the unpaid balance to Smith at the rate of $100 a month until the debt is paid in full. Smith is a creditor beneficiary of the contract entered into between Brown and Jones. Under ordinary circumstances, Smith could recover the debt from Jones although he was not a party to the contract. Smith would not, however, lose his original right to recover the debt from Brown. [*Dick v. Woolson*, p. 137.]

Donee Beneficiary   The characteristic features of a donee-beneficiary contract and a creditor-beneficiary contract are similar except that the purpose of the donee-beneficiary contract is to make a gift to some third person. The donee-beneficiary contract, however, differs from the creditor-beneficiary contract in that the creditor beneficiary may sue either of the parties to the contract, whereas the donee beneficiary can only recover from the person who has promised to perform for the benefit of the donee. A merchant may sell merchandise to a purchaser for $100 on thirty days' credit, and the purchaser promises that at the end of that period he will pay the $100 to some designated person as a gift from the merchant. The donee beneficiary can recover, if at all, only from the purchaser. Another example of a donee beneficiary contract is a life insurance policy. The insurer and the insured are the contracting parties, and the beneficiary named in the policy is the third-party donee. This type of contract ordinarily gives the beneficiary the right to recover from the insurer.

Incidental Beneficiary   A contract which is entered into primarily for the benefit of the contracting parties and which may incidentally benefit some third person is an incidental-beneficiary contract. The contracting parties cannot be sued by such third person. It is a simple matter to visualize many contracts from which may flow an incidental benefit to third persons. An agreement to erect a new building may incidentally benefit the surrounding property owners. The abandonment of the project, however, would not give such property owners the right to sue either of the contracting parties for its breach. [*Isbrandtsen Co. v. Local 1291,* p. 138.]

Rescission   The general rule which permits a third-party beneficiary to sue upon a contract poses the further question: are contracting parties who have entered into a contract for the benefit of a third person permitted thereafter to rescind the agreement? Some courts have pronounced the rule that an agreement cannot be rescinded by the contracting parties without the consent of the beneficiary. The most widely adopted rule, however, is that parties who have entered into a contract for the benefit of a third person may rescind the contract at any time before it is accepted, adopted, or acted upon by the third party.

ASSIGNMENT
A third-party beneficiary and an assignee of a contract are similar in that neither is an original contracting party. These two classes of parties, however, should not be confused with each other because their rights and duties are dissimilar. The rights of a third-party beneficiary are created at the time the contract is entered into; the rights of an assignee can only arise subsequent to the making of the contract when one of the contracting parties transfers his rights arising out of the contract to some third person. The third person is the assignee. An assignment, in the broadest use of the word, may include a transfer of property. The word "assignment," however, is ordinarily limited in its application to rights in property as distinguished from the particular item of property. The problems to be inquired into are (1) the form and notice of the assignment, (2) the contractual rights that may be assigned and the duties that may be delegated, and (3) the effect that such a change in the contractual relation will have on the parties involved.

Form and Notice of the Assignment   An assignment is sometimes required by statute to be in some designated form but, in the absence of statute, no special form is necessary to effect a valid assignment. Any language, oral or written, will be sufficient if it expresses a clear intent of the assignor to effect the transfer. It is frequently stated as a general rule that an assignment need not comply with the fundamental requisites of contracts generally. It is true that neither consideration nor assent is a requisite of a valid assignment, but assignments which are held valid without consideration and assent are ordinarily transfers by gift. An analysis of the contests concerning ordinary business contracts clearly reveals that both consideration and assent are not only desirable but necessary to the enforcement of the assignment in many instances. The absence of consideration may defeat a claim in contests between assignees, and, in accordance with the general rule that an incompleted gift may be revoked, the assignor may rescind the assignment at any time before it is acted upon by the debtor. Aside from legal consequences, an irregular assignment may suggest an attempt to defraud creditors, and the courts are apt to view such an assignment with suspicion if there is the slightest savor of fraud. It is enough to say that ordinary business assignments should comply with the requisites which are applicable to contracts generally—legality of object, capacity of parties, consideration, and assent—in order to avoid possible troublesome litigation.

The notice of the assignment is necessary to establish the claim of the assignee. A few states require that assignments be recorded but, in the absence of statute, the obligor-debtor has no means of learning of the assignment except through notice. Before taking an assignment, the prospective assignee should determine if there are any outstanding claims against the subject matter which is proposed to be assigned. This is particularly true in construction contracts because of the possibility of outstanding claims of laborers and materialmen. A search of the records in those states that require recording may reveal any outstanding claims, but otherwise an inquiry should be made of the obligor-debtor to determine if he has had notice of a prior assignment. If there are no outstanding claims, the assignee should immediately notify the debtor of the assignment. The failure to give notice becomes important in an action between the assignee and other assignees of the same debt or between the assignee and the debtor.

In an action between successive assignees of the same debt wherein no assignee has an intrinsic superior right to that of the other, the order of priority will be determined by the order of the execution of the assignment. A subsequent assignee may, however, defeat a prior assignee by first giving notice to the debtor. A few courts hold that the assignee prior in point of time is superior to a subsequent assignee who first gives notice. The majority of the courts, however, hold that the assignee who first gives notice has a prior right irrespective of whether or not his assignment was first in time.

In an action between the assignee and the debtor, the failure to give notice may defeat the action. The debtor, in the absence of notice, is discharged from his debt if he pays the assignor. A creditor-assignor, however, who makes an assignment of a debt and thereafter accepts performance from the debtor may be compelled to turn the proceeds over to the assignee. A subsequent assignee, however, who was the first to give notice cannot be compelled to turn the proceeds over to an assignee who was first in point of time but who failed to give notice. In these circumstances, the assignee has no recourse against the debtor or the subsequent assignee. He is left to his remedy in an action for damages against the assignor. A debtor, however, who pays the assignor after receiving notice of the assignment is nevertheless liable to the assignee. The notice has the effect of imposing a duty on the debtor to pay the assignee. [*Fidelity Mut. Life Ins. Co. v. City Nat'l Bank,* p. 139.]

Contractual Rights That May Be Assigned   Most of the controversy pertaining to contractual rights that may be assigned has revolved around the following types:

   (1)   *Money Due or to Become Due*   The right to the payment of money is perhaps the most common right that may be assigned. The assignment of a matured claim for money is uniformly recognized. An assignment of money not yet due but which has a potential existence may also be assigned and will operate on the fund as soon as it is acquired. In accordance with this rule, it is uniformly held that future book accounts which are to arise in pursuance of an existing contract, as between a dealer and a customer, have a potential existence and may be assigned.

   The Code continues this law by providing that rights, such as a right to damages for breach or the right to payment of an "account" may be assigned. Section 9–318, however, goes a step further by providing that a clause in a contract which attempts to prohibit or restrict the assignment of the account or the money to be earned under the contract is ineffective. Under the Code, therefore, an assignment would be effective even if it were made to an assignee who had full knowledge that an attempt had been made to prohibit assignment.

   (2)   *Salaries and Wages*   The relationship of an employer and employee insofar as unpaid wages already earned are concerned is that of debtor and creditor, and the right of the employee to those wages may be assigned. Future earnings may also be assigned if a person is under a contract of employment. The assignment is valid even though the contract of hiring is for an indeterminate period. In accordance with the general rule that a mere expectancy is not assignable, however, an assignment of future wages to be earned under a contract to be entered into subsequently is not valid. Compensation already earned by a public officer may validly be assigned, but as a general rule salaries or fees of a public officer cannot be assigned before they are earned. Statutory provisions have been enacted in many jurisdictions which prescribe requisites which must be complied with in order to make an assignment of wages effective. It may be that only a portion of the wages may be assigned, or that the assignment must be in writing, or that it must be recorded or acknowledged before an officer, or that notice must be given the employer. In the absence of a controlling statute, however, an employee may assign his wages. Some courts go a step further and hold that the employee may assign his wages notwithstanding a contract with the employer to the contrary.

(3)   ***Personal Contracts***   Contracts for personal services or those which involve a confidential relation are not assignable. A contract with an artist to paint a picture, a physician to render personal services, or an author to write a book are well-known illustrations of contracts that are nonassignable. As applied, the rule forbids an assignment by either party to the contract. An employer may not assign a contract for the performance of personal duties that gives the assignee the right to services of a person who has never agreed to serve him.

Contracts are frequently entered into on the basis of an honorable reputation of one of the contracting parties. Therefore, the terms of a contract which indicate that reliance was placed on the character and credit of one of the parties cannot be assigned. It is not always easy to segregate those assignments which will fail from those which will not fail because performance is or is not too personal in nature. In borderline cases, resort will be had to the intention of the parties. A provision in the contract that it shall bind and benefit the respective heirs, executors, successors, or "assigns" of the parties to the contract is an indication that the parties intended that it should be assignable. The use of such words, however, is not conclusive upon the question of assignability of personal contracts. An assignment of a contract which involves personal skill or confidence is valid only if the other contracting party assents or ratifies the assignment.

The rule that the right to performance under a personal contract may not be assigned does not operate to prohibit the assignment of the money earned under the contract. A person, therefore, who has performed a contract involving personal skill and confidence may assign his rights to the money earned.

(4)   ***Nonpersonal Contracts***   Up to this point, two types of assignments have been considered, (a) the right to the payment of money and (b) assignments which are prohibited because of the personal nature of the contract. A large number of, if not most, ordinary business contracts may be assigned. The expression "the contract is assignable" is used to mean that the assignor may assign his beneficial rights under the contract and delegate the performance of his duties thereunder to another.

The distinguishing quality of assignable contracts is their nonpersonal feature. A contract which is of such a nature that performance of the duty by another person will be substantially the same as performance by the obligor may be delegated. The terms of building contracts which require performance to meet certain specifications and other construction and engineering work which requires no personal skill may be delegated. A contractor frequently assigns his rights and delegates his duties to a subcontractor; that is, he assigns his right to receive the money and delegates the performance of the work. The subcontractor has the same privilege. Subcontractors ordinarily perform the obligations but frequently assign the right to receive the money. The contractor-assignor nevertheless, remains liable if the subcontractor-assignee fails to perform. [*Edgewood Lumber Co. v. Hull*, p. 140.]

Prohibition against Assignments   The parties may expressly agree that the rights under a contract shall not be assignable, and the courts will generally recognize the prohibition. Prohibition against assignment, however, may be implied with respect to close personal relations. An agreement to serve as a private secretary would not be assignable by the secretary without the consent of the employer, nor by the employer without the consent of the secretary.

Effect of the Assignment   The assignment of a contract transfers the benefits subject to the burdens. The rights and duties of the assignor are fixed by the terms of the contract. It remains, therefore, to determine the extent to which these rights and duties may be transferred to the assignee.

The assignee takes the assignment subject to all the defenses which could have been set up against the assignor. The assignee cannot maintain an action against the obligor if the assignor could not have done so. A contract which is unenforceable in the hands of the assignor because of fraud, duress, or any other cause is likewise unenforceable in the hands of the assignee. The fact that the assignee takes the assignment subject to defenses does not mean, however, that the assignee has no recourse against the assignor if the claim cannot be realized against the obligor. The assignment of a chose in action carries with it certain implied warranties and defenses.

(1)   *Implied Warranties*   The implied warranties which the assignment of a chose in action for a consideration carries with it have not been explicitly defined by the courts. The extent of the warranties that are implied on the part of the assignor must depend upon the facts of the particular case. Certain implied warranties have, however, been developed by the courts over a period of years. The assignment, as a general rule, carries with it an implied warranty that the chose assigned is a valid and genuine claim. The assignor impliedly warrants, therefore, that the parties had capacity to enter into the contract; that it was based on sufficient consideration; and that it is not based upon illegality in its inception. The assignee, therefore, may bring an action against the assignor if the claim proves invalid. The cases also hold that the assignor impliedly warrants that he will do nothing to impede or prevent collection by the assignee. There is, however, no implied warranty that the debtor, or obligor, will pay the debt.

(2)   *Defenses*   It is a well-settled general rule that the assignee takes the debt subject to all the defenses which the debtor may have had against the assignor at the time of the assignment and arising thereafter prior to notice of the assignment. The rule is sometimes stated: The assignee "stands in the shoes" of the assignor. The most common defenses consist of failure of consideration, illegality, payment, fraud, and incompetency. Suppose Brown owes Smith $100. If Smith should bring an action against Brown to collect this debt, it is obvious that Brown could assert the defense of payment, or any of the other defenses in order to defeat the action. Suppose further that Smith should assign the debt to Jones and that Jones brought the action against Brown to collect the debt. It is quite clear that Brown could assert the defense of payment against Jones, the assignee. To pursue the illustration one step further: Suppose that Brown owed Smith $100, that Smith assigned the debt to Jones, and that Brown made a payment of $10 on account of the debt to Smith prior to receiving notice of the assignment. If Jones,

the assignee, should bring an action against Brown to collect the $100, Brown could assert the payment of $10 as a defense.

Sale of Goods   Section 2–210 of the Code pertaining to delegation of performance and assignment of rights does not attempt to lay down rules with respect to such questions as the form of the assignment, the need or effect of the notice of the assignment, nor the rights of successive assignees. The section does, however, recognize that both delegation of performance and assignment of rights are normal incidents of a contract for the sale of goods. It is provided that all the rights of the seller or of the buyer may be assigned unless (1) such assignment would materially change the duty of the other party, materially increase the burden of risk imposed upon him by such contract, or materially impair his chances of obtaining return performance or (2) the parties have included a clause in the contract prohibiting assignment of performance.

The parties to a sales contract frequently do not distinguish between assignment of rights and delegation of performance. This section, therefore, provides guides for interpreting contract provisions with respect to assignability and delegability. An assignment in general terms, such as "the contract" or "all my rights under the contract," is to be construed as an assignment of rights and a delegation of performance. The original promisor, however, does not escape from his obligation to the obligee by delegating performance to a third person. The nonassigning original party, moreover, may demand assurances from the assigning party that the delegated performance will be properly performed. A prohibition of assignment in general terms, such as "the contract," is to be construed as barring only the delegation of performance. The obligor may not, however, perform through a delegate "if the obligee has a substantial interest in having his original promisor perform." This could be the situation with respect to specially manufactured goods when the obligee is relying on the special skill or knowledge of the obligor. This is true even in the absence of an agreement prohibiting performance.

Rights which are no longer executory, such as a right to damages for breach of contract, may be assigned. This is true even though the agreement prohibits assignment.

CASES

Johnson v. Holmes Tuttle Lincoln-Mercury, Inc.,   325 P.2d 193 (Cal. 1958). Action by Willie Mae Johnson and Fletcher Jones, plaintiffs, against Holmes Tuttle Lincoln-Mercury, Inc., defendant. Phillip R. Caldera and his wife purchased a new Mercury automobile from defendant on November 23, 1953. The evidence revealed that one of defendant's salesmen had agreed with Caldera at the time the Mercury was purchased to procure full coverage insurance for Caldera, including public liability and property damage, for the operation of the Mercury; that shortly after the Mercury was purchased, Caldera was involved in an accident; and that plaintiffs were injured. Plaintiffs then brought an action against Caldera to recover damages for the injuries sustained, and judgments were entered in favor of plaintiff Johnson for $4,413.89 and in favor of plaintiff Jones for $2,070. The judgments were unsatisfied, and plaintiffs, on the contention that they were third-party beneficiaries of the agreement to procure the insurance, brought this action against the defendant for breach of contract.

Vallee, Justice: Defendant contends plaintiffs were not third-party beneficiaries. "A contract made expressly for the benefit of a third person, may be enforced by him at any time before the parties thereto rescind it." Civ. Code, Sec. 1559. Where one person for a valuable consideration engages with another to do some act for the benefit of a third person, and the agreement thus made has not been rescinded, the party for whose benefit the contract or promise was made, or who would enjoy the benefit of the act, may maintain an action against the promisor for the breach of his engagement. While the contract remains unrescinded, the relations of the parties are the same as though the promise had been made directly to the third party. Although the party for whose benefit the promise was made was not cognizant of it when made, it is, if adopted by him, deemed to have been made to him. He may sue on the promise. Where a promise is made to benefit a third party on the happening of a certain contingency, the third party may enforce the contract on the occurrence of that contingency. The action by a third party beneficiary for the breach of the promisor's engagement does not rest on the ground of any actual or supposed relationship between the parties but on the broad or more satisfactory basis that the law, operating on the acts of the parties, creates the duty, establishes a privity, and implies the promise and obligation on which the action is founded.

It is not necessary that the beneficiary be named and identified as an individual; a third party may enforce a contract if he can show he is a member of a class for whose benefit it was made. It is no objection to the maintenance of an action by a third person that a suit might be brought also against the one to whom the promise was made.

The test for determining whether a contract was made for the benefit of a third person is whether an intent to benefit a third person appears from the terms of the contract. If the terms of the contract necessarily require the promisor to confer a benefit on a third person, then the contract, and hence the parties thereto, contemplate a benefit to the third person. The parties are presumed to intend the consequences of a performance of the contract. It is held that a person injured may sue on a contract for the benefit of all members of the public who are injured since the happening of the injury sufficiently determines his identity and right of action.

There is no escape from the conclusion that the agreement between defendant and Caldera was not for the sole benefit of the latter but that it was intended to inure to the benefit of third persons who might be protected by a full coverage policy. The intent to confer a benefit on anyone to whom Caldera might become liable as a result of a hazard incident to ownership and operation of the Mercury is obvious. This is precisely what Caldera wanted as a means of obtaining a benefit to himself. . . . The jury finding that there was a third party beneficiary contract breached by defendant to plaintiffs' damage is amply supported by the evidence. [DECISION FOR PLAINTIFFS]

Dick v. Woolson,   235 P.2d 119 (Cal. 1951). Action by John Dick, plaintiff, against Leigh Woolson, Builders Supply Corporation, and Corporation Management, Inc., defendants. Plaintiff entered into a contract to sell a going business to defendant Woolson for a consideration of $25,000. The payment terms were $5,000 on the signing of the agreement, $5,000 in ninety days, and the remainder in equal monthly installments. On May 31, 1947, Woolson assigned the sales contract to defendant Corporation Management, Inc., which assumed all the liabilities and obligations under the contract. On June 4, 1947, Corporation Management assigned the sales contract to defendant Builders Supply Corporation, which company assumed the contractual liabilities and obligations. Plaintiff received the $5,000 payment due in ninety days and the first two monthly installments. On March 18, 1948, plaintiff had received no other payments and brought this action for the remaining payments which were overdue. The defendant Woolson did not appear at the trial, defendant Builders Supply Corporation was shown to be insolvent, and the defendant Corporation Management contended that the second assignment operated as a rescission of the agreement between the defendant Woolson and Corporation Management. Judgment was granted against all three defendants, and defendants Builders Supply Corporation and Corporation Management appeal.

    Shinn, Presiding Justice: Plaintiff was a creditor under the contract with Woolson, was creditor beneficiary under a contract between Woolson and Management, and a creditor beneficiary under the contract between Management and Builders.

    . . . The basis of the action against Management is that it assumed Woolson's obligation and is thus liable to plaintiff, the creditor beneficiary of the assumption contract.

    . . . Where the obligations of a contract are assumed, the creditor under the original contract may sue the assuming party on the theory that he is an express beneficiary of the assumption contract. . . . However, until the creditor beneficiary has accepted the benefit or has detrimentally acted in reliance thereon, the assuming party may rescind. But as long as the assuming promisor continues to retain the consideration from the original promisee, the contract for the benefit of the third party cannot be rescinded or revoked.

    Management concedes that when it assumed the obligations of the sales contract from Woolson on May 31, 1947, plaintiff became a third party beneficiary, but contends that this assumption contract was rescinded by it. If true, this would relieve Management of liability to plaintiff. At the trial, Management advanced the claim that the assignment of June 4, 1947, from Management to Builders, operated as a rescission by Management and a new assignment from Woolson to Builders. This contention was substantially disproved by the terms of the contract of assignment dated June 4, 1947, which was an express assignment by Management to Builders in clear and unambiguous terms. The contract may not be construed as a rescission of the Woolson-Management agreement. It is completely inconsistent with any theory of rescission. There is no basis for the contention that it did not embody the agreement of the parties. There was no other evidence in the record as to recission. Nothing was ever restored to Woolson. [DECISION FOR PLAINTIFF]

Isbrandtsen Co. v. Local 1291, 204 F.2d 495 (Pa. 1953). Action by Isbrandtsen Company, Inc., against Local 1291 of International Longshoremen's Association. The Philadelphia Marine Trade Association, of which Lavino Shipping Company was a member, and Local 1291 of the International Longshoremen's Association entered into an agreement which provided, among other things, that there was to be no work stoppage pending arbitration of disputes which might arise.

Here are the facts briefly stated: Isbrandtsen Company, Inc., was the time charterer of a ship called the *Nyco* and, in turn, chartered the ship to the Scott Paper Company. Under the terms of the charter, Scott Paper Company was to load and unload the vessel, but Scott Paper Company hired Lavino Shipping Company to do the unloading. When the vessel reached its destination, the employees of Lavino started to unload it, and during the unloading stopped work contrary to the provisions of the contract mentioned above.

Isbrandtsen Company claimed that it had suffered loss by the delay in unloading and brought an action against Local 1291 to recover damages.

Goodrich, Judge: Our question then becomes, is Isbrandtsen to be included as one who may sue for damages suffered by breach of this contract?

It may aid in understanding the problem if it is kept in mind just how far away Isbrandtsen stands from the actual parties to the contract. Signatories were, as said above, Philadelphia Marine Trade Association and Local 1291. Lavino Shipping is a member of that Association. Scott made its contract for unloading the vessel with Lavino. Scott in turn chartered this vessel from Isbrandtsen. Isbrandtsen is, then, three steps away from the contracting party. . . .

We can see no possibility that Isbrandtsen can be a creditor beneficiary of this labor union. The labor union was a complete stranger to Isbrandsten so far as this transaction is concerned. Neither owed the other anything. And, therefore, there was no obligation on the part of either to do anything to or for the other. Nor do we see any possibility of making out of this situation a donee beneficiary relationship. . . . The contract recited that the Association was acting on behalf of its members who employ longshoremen. Lavino is one of these members. But it does not appear that either Scott or Isbrandtsen was a member. . . .

We do not think, therefore, that in view of this business setting any statement by the marine association that it intended its agreement with the labor union to benefit all the world who might be helped by the faithful performance of the contract would give these remote parties rights against one who broke it. It may well be that Isbrandtsen suffered a loss of use of its boat because a strike stopped the unloading of the *Nyco*. It also may be that the people who had cargo to ship on the next voyage lost a market by the delay. And it may be that the people who did not get the goods on the next voyage, on time, lost a profitable bargain on that account. But neither in contract nor in tort have duties extended very far beyond the immediate parties to the facts out of which a course of action is said to arise. . . .

The question was thoughtfully considered by the district judge. He concluded that Isbrandtsen was but "an incidental beneficiary" and in this conclusion he was right. [DECISION FOR LOCAL 1291]

Fidelity Mut. Life Ins. Co. v. City Nat'l Bank, 95 F. Supp. 276 (1950). Action by the Fidelity Mutual Life Insurance Company, plaintiff, against City National Bank, Marjorie H. Ave Lallemant and Donald P. Ave Lallemant, defendants. The defendants Donald P. Lallemant and Marjorie H. Lallemant, husband and wife, entered into a separation agreement for a division of their property. At the time of the execution and delivery of the separation agreement, the husband also executed, acknowledged, and delivered a formal assignment of his Fidelity Mutual Life Insurance policy to his wife. The assignment was on a form furnished by the insurance company. The husband agreed to deliver the policy to his wife within the next ten days. On October 27, 1948, William Hughes Lewis, attorney for the wife, notified the insurance company by letter that there had been an assignment of its policy to Marjorie H. Lallemant by Donald P. Lallemant, the insured. On November 9, 1948, the insurance company answered this letter, fixing the number of the policy as 657697, and acknowledged that it had received notice of the assignment by the letter of October 27. The policy was not delivered as promised. On March 4, 1949, Donald P. Lallemant executed a note for $5,000 in favor of the defendant bank and made a formal assignment on the insurance company form, assigning the policy to the bank to secure the loan. The assignment was transmitted to the insurance company where it was filed on March 15, 1949. The plaintiff has filed this action to determine which of the two claimants is entitled to the cash surrender value of the insurance policy. The cash surrender value of the policy has been paid into court and the plaintiff has been dismissed as a party.

Watkins, District Judge: The separation agreement, the collateral assignment, and the two letters exchanged between attorneys (letter from Lewis to the insurance company giving notice of assignment, dated October 27, and letter from Keesey replying thereto, dated November 9) when considered in the light of existing facts and surrounding circumstances, plainly show that it was the intention of Lallemant to make, and his wife to receive, an assignment of all of his interest in this $48,000 insurance policy bearing number 657697. It is also clear that the insurance company believed and intended the notice of assignment to apply to this particular policy. . . . Its identity could not be questioned.

Any language, however informal, if it shows the intention of the owner of the chose in action to at once transfer it, so that it will be the property of the transferee, will be sufficient to vest the title in the assignee. No particular form is necessary. While the chose in action must be identified, no greater particularity is required than is actually necessary to do this, with the aid of the attendant and surrounding circumstances. . . . Here the separation agreement and the formal assignment on the form prescribed by the insurance company, with notice to the debtor created an equitable assignment in Policy No. 657697. . . .

There are two views with reference to the effect of notice to the obligor as affecting priority between two successive assignees of the same chose in action. The majority rule is stated as follows:

The question which of the assignees of a chose in action by express assignments from the same person—the one whose assignment is prior in time, or the one who first gives notice to the debtor—has the prior right, is one in respect to which there is much conflict of authority. In most jurisdictions the assignee first giving notice of his claim to the debtor is preferred, unless he takes a later assignment with notice of a previous one or without a valuable consideration. . . .

Regardless of which rule is applied, the assignee who is not only first in point of time in securing his assignment, but is also first to give notice to the debtor, is of course entitled to priority. . . . Here the wife was the first assignee in point of time and first to give notice to the debtor. . . .

For the reason stated above, the wife, as first assignee, is now best in right, and has an equitable lien on the fund now in the Registry of the Court, and this fund should be decreed to her, less the costs of this proceeding. [DECISION FOR DEFENDANT MARJORIE H. AVE LALLEMANT]

Edgewood Lumber Co. v. Hull, 223 S.W.2d 210 (Tenn. 1949). Action by Edgewood Lumber Company, for its use and benefit and in the name of E. J. Flautt and Rolland R. Markey, plaintiff; against H. M. Hull and Chester Hull, a partnership doing business under the name of H. M. Hull & Son, defendant.

Defendant entered into a written contract with Flautt & Markey, a partnership, by the terms of which the defendant agreed to cut certain timber and manufacture it into lumber. Flautt & Markey agreed to pay a fixed price for the lumber so manufactured. Flautt & Markey also agreed to advance certain sums of money to the defendant for the purchase of machinery and equipment. The contract was afterwards assigned by Flautt & Markey to the plaintiff. The defendants abandoned the contract, at which time there was a balance due and owing the plaintiff in the amount of $3,454.19, over and above all credits for lumber. Plaintiff brought an action to recover the balance due and for damages. Defendants contend, among other things, that the contract between defendants and Flautt & Markey was not assignable.

Howell, Judge: This assignment or transfer by Flautt & Markey to the Edgewood Lumber Company is filed and made an exhibit in the case. It does not contain any provision against its assignability.

The contract contains nothing to indicate that there was any reliance upon any personal skill, trust or confidence in Flautt & Markey. All they were bound to do was to advance money and to pay for the lumber manufactured by the defendants. In addition the defendants knew of the assignment and continued to carry out their contract and to receive payments from the Edgewood Lumber Company. They cannot now be heard to complain. The rule is stated in Vol. 4

American Jurisprudence, page 238, section 11, as follows: "In the absence of an express provision against assignments, a contract which does not involve personal skill, trust, or confidence is assignable without the consent of the other party, whereas contracts which do involve those qualities are not assignable; but if the other party to such a contract assents thereto, a valid assignment may be made. Moreover, the assignment of such a contract may be ratified by the other party." [DECISION FOR PLAINTIFF]

PROBLEMS

1 Defendant insurance company issued a policy of insurance to the insured against loss by theft of an automobile. The policy provided that no assignment of interest under this policy shall be or become binding unless the written consent of the insurer is indorsed thereon. The automobile was stolen and never recovered. The insured assigned the claim under the policy to the plaintiff, who brought an action to recover the proceeds of the policy. Will the plaintiff recover?

2 Faure, a dealer in automobile tires bearing his name, gave to Paige and Linder the exclusive agency in the United States, except the cities of Boston and New York and certain adjacent territories, to sell automobile tires manufactured by and for Faure and bearing his name. The contract was for a period of one year with an option to renew from year to year. About six months thereafter, Linder sold his interest in the contract to Paige who sometime in November requested a renewal of the contract for another year. Did Linder's assignment to Paige of all of his interest in the contract justify Faure in refusing, at the request of Paige, to renew the contract for another year?

3 Plaintiff, the owner and operator of a railroad, entered into a contract with the Lumber Company whereby plaintiff agreed to construct a branch line from his main track to a designated point within the boundary lines of land owned by the Lumber Company. Plaintiff thereafter sold, conveyed, and assigned all of his railway lines, equipment, rights of way, franchises and contracts, including the contract with the Lumber Company, to the defendant. The defendant, however, refused to construct the branch line. The Lumber Company recovered a judgment against the plaintiff in the sum of $18,000 for breach of contract. May the plaintiff recover from the defendant the damages the plaintiff sustained by reason of the failure of the defendant to carry out the assigned contract?

4 The City of Clifton and defendant, an electric company, entered into a contract whereby the defendant agreed to keep the lamps installed along Randolph Avenue, in the City of Clifton, lighted continuously from dusk to dawn. At about 2 A.M., in fog and rain, the plaintiff was riding in an automobile operated by her husband. The automobile was driven onto a safety isle in the center of Randolph Avenue and collided with an unlighted electric pole thereon, causing injuries to plaintiff. The plaintiff brought an action and alleged that the defendant breached the contract and that she sustained the injuries as a result of the breach. Do you think she will recover on a basis of a breach of contract?

5 The Midland Chautauqua System entered into a contract with defendants, certain citizens of Mankato, Kansas, whereby Midland agreed to conduct a five-day chautauqua at Mankato. Midland agreed to furnish the talent, lecturers, musicians, musical organizations, trained junior leader for children, entertainers, a tent, and other necessary equipment. The defendants agreed to furnish the grounds, a piano, and other necessary materials. Midland thereafter assigned the contract to the Standard Chautauqua System, and defendants refused to perform their agreement in any particular. Do you think Standard is entitled to recover damages for breach of contract?

6 Bass owned and operated a very profitable seed and feed store, which Bass had developed into a profitable business over the years including valuable "goodwill." Rogers approached Bass and proposed a sale of the business. The two finally agreed that, as a part of the consideration of the sale, Rogers would pay Bass the sum of $100,000 and would also pay a bill to the X Chemical Company of $10,000 which Bass owed. The promise of Rogers to Bass to pay the $10,000 to the X Chemical Company was oral. Rogers thereafter paid the $100,000 to Bass, and the latter executed a deed to the land on which the business was located and a bill of sale to the inventory and delivered both to Rogers. (a) Explain whether or not the X Chemical Company has a good cause of action against Rogers for the $10,000. (b) Explain whether or not Bass has a good defense if the X Chemical Company brings an action against Bass for the $10,000.

7 Decedent, who several years prior to his death met with his sister and brothers at an attorney's office for the purpose of executing his will, stated that he wanted his property, including his insurance, to be divided equally among his sister and brothers. Decedent further asked his sister, if she were designated as beneficiary of his insurance, if she would accordingly distribute the proceeds. To this she agreed. After the death of decedent, the insurance proceeds were paid to the sister, who refused to make a distribution to her brothers. What are the rights, if any, of the brothers?

8 Defendant bought certain items of furniture from the Furniture Mart for the sum of $250. He made a small payment in cash and signed a conditional sales contract whereby he agreed to pay the balance in thirty days. His home was not ready for immediate occupancy, and the dealer informed him that the articles would be set back, marked sold, and delivered immediately upon his request. The dealer then assigned the sales contract to the plaintiff. A few days thereafter, defendant went to the store for the purpose of directing delivery of the furniture but found that the Furniture Mart had been sold, and the new owner refused to deliver the furniture. Defendant, therefore, refused to pay the balance due on the contract when it became due. Plaintiff thereupon brought this action to recover the balance due. Decide.

PERFORMANCE

The formation of contracts and the requirements for the validity of contracts have been discussed in previous chapters. It now seems appropriate to discuss the rules applicable to the adjustment of the rights and duties of contracting parties when complete performance under the contract has been interrupted. This chapter, therefore, will be devoted to (1) conditions, (2) the doctrine of substantial performance, (3) partial performance, (4) performance of divisible contracts, and (5) excuses for nonperformance.

CONDITIONS

A condition is a clause in a contract which has for its object to suspend, rescind, or modify the principal obligation. It seems best to approach the problem of conditions with respect to their classification. Contracts containing express conditions pertaining to the approval of a third person, personal satisfaction, and time of performance will then be discussed.

Conditions Classified Conditions may be classified variously, but they are classified with regard to their function as conditions subsequent, concurrent, and precedent.

    (1) ***Conditions Subsequent*** A clause in a contract which gives one of the

parties the option of treating the contract as discharged upon the breach of the condition is a condition subsequent. A typical illustration is found in an insurance policy which provides that the insured shall give the insurer notice of a loss by fire within a stated period. The right to recover is lost if the condition is breached. Another type of condition subsequent is found in sales contracts. A seller may sell property with the understanding that it may be returned if it does not comply with certain specifications. The property is vested in the buyer subject to the right of rescission.

(2) *Conditions Concurrent*   A clause in a contract which requires that both parties are to act simultaneously is called a condition concurrent. A typical illustration is found in contracts of sale where payment and delivery are to be contemporaneous. The buyer cannot demand possession until he is ready to perform nor can the seller demand payment until he is ready to deliver the goods. Although actual performance is unnecessary, the party seeking relief must be ready and willing to perform. A tender of performance, however, is all that is necessary as a right to recover.

(3) *Conditions Precedent*   A condition precedent calls for the occurence of some event or the performance of some act before there is a duty of immediate performance of the promise which is so conditioned. Performance is suspended pending the occurrence of the condition, and the failure of the condition to occur will give the party against whom it operates the right to rescind the contract. In some circumstances, the contract is naturally terminated. Neither party, therefore, has a cause of action against the other party for breach of contract. A builder may agree to perform certain construction work for the owner if the city council passes a pending ordinance by a specified date. The builder is under no obligation to perform unless the council passes the ordinance, thereby causing the event to happen. A more common illustration in business would be a merchant who, during early spring, orders ladies' hats and gloves to be delivered by September 1 of the same year. Delivery by September 1 is a condition precedent which must happen before the merchant is under a duty to accept and pay for the merchandise.

PERFORMANCE OF EXPRESS CONDITIONS

Contracting parties have practically unlimited power to make such contracts as they wish to make; they may bind themselves in any manner and to any extent they please; they may make performance of any condition a condition precedent; and they may stipulate with one another that failure to perform the condition shall put an end to the contract. It is sometimes difficult to determine, however, whether or not a term in a contract was intended as a condition which would entitle the party to whom it was made to be discharged from his liabilities under the contract because of its breach. The courts will not make a new contract for the parties but they will attempt to ascertain from the contract the intention of the parties by construing the wording of the contract in the light of the circumstances under which the contract was made.

Approval of Third Person A promise may be expressly conditioned upon the approval of some third person, and the approval of the person so designated therefore becomes a condition precedent to a recovery of the price. A condition of this kind is frequently found in building and construction contracts which provide that the payments are conditioned on the production by the builder of a certificate of a named architect. The courts will deny the contractor the right to recover if he fails to comply with the condition, provided the architect has some reason for withholding the certificate and is acting honestly. In such contracts, therefore, there is an implied condition that the person designated shall act with good faith toward both the contracting parties. The contractor, however, will be excused if the owner induces the architect not to give the certificate. The contractor, as a general rule, will also be excused if the architect fraudulently withholds the certificate or refuses to examine the work. The same is true if the architect specified in the contract dies or otherwise becomes incapable of acting. The contract may be so framed that the owner can protect himself by a promise of the builder to build according to the plans and specifications and in a workmanlike manner. In these circumstances, if the condition precedent requiring the production of an architect's certificate before payment is excused, the builder would nevertheless be required to fulfill his main obligation.

Satisfaction as a Condition A condition in a contract frequently provides that one person must perform some act to the satisfaction of the other person. The performance required may be such performance as would satisfy the personal satisfaction of the other person, or it may be such performance as would satisfy a reasonable man. If the performance is such that it must satisfy the personal satisfaction of the other person, the latter's own determination—if made in good faith—is final and conclusive. This type of satisfaction involves personal taste, such as painting a portrait or writing a novel, and the person to whom the article is to be supplied is the sole judge of the quality of the work done. No one, therefore, has the right to investigate his reasons for accepting or rejecting the work unless he acts in bad faith. The dissatisfaction must be honest dissatisfaction. If he is actually satisfied with the performance but says he is not satisfied solely to escape liability, he is acting in bad faith. His conduct, therefore, is fraudulent.

In contracts to do work to the personal satisfaction of the other party, however, a line is drawn between those contracts where fancy or taste is involved and those contracts where operative fitness or mechanical utility is involved. In this latter class of contracts the satisfaction agreed upon is interpreted to apply to workmanship, salability, and similar considerations rather than personal satisfaction, and the term "reasonably satisfactory" is applicable. The work must be done in a workmanlike manner or, as it is sometimes stated, as well as could be expected, and the right to accept or reject the work on merely personal reasons is denied. [*Haymore v. Levinson*, p. 151.]

Time of Performance A provision in a contract as to the time for performance is effective, and, if time is expressly made a condition precedent, a failure by one party to perform within the time limit will discharge the other party from performance. Any clause which provides in unequivocal terms that the contract shall be void if it is not fulfilled within a specified time will have that effect. The words "time is of the essence" are frequently used to indicate that a condition precedent is intended. The courts, however, look to the intent of the parties, and the use of such words is not strictly applied when they are contrary to the meaning of the contract or the intention of the parties. Conversely if such words are omitted from the terms of the contract, a condition precedent may nevertheless be implied. A condition may be implied when the time for performance is specified in the contract although it is not expressly made the essence of the contract. An option contract and a contract the subject of which is of a perishable nature are illustrations of contracts that may be discharged on the basis of an implied condition if they are not performed within the time specified. In the absence of a stipulation as to time, a reasonable time is implied. The nature of the subject of the contract and all the other attendant factors in the particular circumstances of the case are considered in determining what may be or may not be a reasonable time.

DOCTRINE OF SUBSTANTIAL PERFORMANCE
The doctrine of substantial performance was conceived to dispense with the injustice of the harsh rule which prohibited recovery when there was a trivial and innocent departure from the terms of the contract. This rule established the principal of law that substantial performance accompanied by good faith is all that is required in order to entitle a person to recover on the contract. No precise formula has been found to define substantial performance, but the doctrine is not broad enough to include deviations from the general plan of the contract which would prevent the parties from accomplishing the object of their contract. As applied to building contracts the doctrine does not include deviations so essential in character that they cannot be remedied without partially reconstructing the building. The inadvertent installation of some material, however, which has a different trade name but is equal in quality to that specified in the contract would constitute substantial performance. A person seeking relief under the doctrine must show that he attempted in good faith to perform his full obligation and that the obligation was performed except for some minor details. In these circumstances, he may recover the contract price less the amount of the minor deficiencies.

One of the requisites of the doctrine of substantial performance is good faith. An intentional deviation in bad faith, therefore, is uniformly held to be an exception of the doctrine. A willful variance in bad faith, although it may be slight and relatively unimportant, will defeat recovery on the contract. The doctrine was not fashioned to aid a person who intentionally and deliberately deviates from the terms of the contract. A builder who willfully substitutes material different from that specified in the contract with an intention to reduce costs could not recover on the contract. A person who has unknowingly accepted less than substantial performance may recover the damages which have resulted from the breach. [*Rockland Poultry Co. v. Anderson*, p. 152.]

PARTIAL PERFORMANCE

The doctrine of substantial performance must be clearly distinguished from partial performance. Recovery is not allowed on the contract or on a quasi contract where a person has partially—but not substantially—performed an entire contract unless the failure to perform the remainder of the contract is excused. An owner could not be compelled to accept a partially constructed building from a building contractor. The contractor, however, may recover on a quantum meruit if he has been prevented from performing by the owner. The builder could also recover for the benefit conferred, usually measured by the value of labor and materials furnished, where the owner accepts the partially constructed building. The theory of the cases for permitting recovery for part performance where one party accepts partial performance or prevents complete performance by the other party is that the latter has waived full performance. If the contract is apportionable, recovery is allowed where an apportionable part of the contract is completed.

PERFORMANCE OF DIVISIBLE CONTRACTS

An entire contract is one in which there is only one agreement covering all of the terms. The words "entire contract," however, are used to mean an "indivisible" contract as distinguished from a "divisible" contract. A contract which provides for two or more separate performances and counterperformances each of which can be set off against the other is divisible. A contract which provides that complete performance is to be rendered on one side before or at the time that complete performance is rendered on the other side is entire. If a seller promises to deliver thirty pairs of gloves to the purchaser and the purchaser promises to pay $1.00 upon the delivery of each pair of gloves, the contract is divisible. If the contract calls for thirty pairs of gloves for $30 and payment of the entire price is to be made after the last delivery, the contract is entire.

The intention of the parties is controlling, but contracts are often entered into without any thought as to the entirety or divisibility of the contract. When the question arises, the answer may be found by determining (1) whether the contract embraces one or more subjects, (2) whether the consideration is entire or apportioned, (3) whether the obligation is due to one or more persons, and (4) whether the obligation is due at the same time or at several different times. Contracts for services and those which fix the compensation in installment payments present the most difficulty. The distinction, nevertheless, is significant. Performance of one of the acts in a divisible contract imposes an immediate duty on the other party to perform his part of that particular division. Performance of a part of an entire contract, as a general rule, imposes no immediate duty on the other party to perform.

Contracts for Services An entire contract for services is ordinarily not difficult to classify, but the courts are reluctant to treat performance of the whole labor as a condition precedent to the discharge of the employer's obligation to pay when the benefit of the labor has been accepted. Some courts allow recovery on quantum meruit and hold that the employer is liable to pay the fair value of the benefits resulting from partial performance of the contract. It should not be presumed, however, that the rule which prevents recovery on a contract for the partial performance of an entire contract when the failure to complete the contract is voluntary has been abandoned by the courts. The employer will not be liable for the partial performance if the contract involves performance of services of such a nature that the employer can reject what has been done and refuse to receive any benefit from the part performance. Moreover, many courts take the view that the acceptance of benefits is immaterial and hold that an employee who voluntarily abandons the contract cannot recover for its partial performance on the theory of quantum meruit when the employer is willing to complete its performance. This rule is particularly applicable when compensation is something other than the payment of money. In these circumstances full or substantial performance of the promise is usually held to be a condition precedent to the right to maintain an action for the services rendered.

Installment Contracts   Contracts which fix compensation at a certain amount per unit for work done and those which fix compensation in installment payments cannot be accurately classified as either divisible or entire contracts. Some courts hold such contracts to be divisible; other courts hold such contracts to be entire. [*New Era Homes Corp. v. Forster*, p. 153.]

EXCUSES FOR NONPERFORMANCE
A contract which, at the time it is entered into, is impossible to perform is void; there is no contract to discharge. The majority of such contracts are invalid, however, because of a lack of consideration or a mutual mistake of a material fact. This discussion is limited to impossibility which arises subsequent to the making of the contract. Subsequent impossibility, in and of itself, does not discharge the contract. The contracting parties at the time of entering into the contract, therefore, should protect themselves against any contingency that may arise in the future. This safeguard is important because those instances where the law will operate to discharge the contract are limited to situations where performance is rendered impossible by acts of God or inevitable accident, acts of the other party, or by law.

Impossibility Created by Unavoidable Accident   Impossibility created by an act of God or an unavoidable accident will not, as a general rule, discharge the contract. This rule is subject to some well-established exceptions, but it should not be presumed that the exceptions operate to excuse nonperformance merely because performance has become impossible. It is quite clear that a contracting party may bind himself by an absolute promise to perform things which subsequently become impossible or to pay damages for the nonperformance. Closely related to "impossibility" is "impracticability," which is discussed in Chapter 17, "Sales: Performance."

(1) **Assumption of Risk**   The general theory is that when a party by his own contract creates a duty upon himself, which he might have provided against by his contract, he is bound to make it good. This theory is applied when the promisor has indicated an intent to assume the risk, irrespective of whether the impediment is caused by unavoidable accident or comes from an act of God. [*Berg v. Erickson,* p. 154.]

(2) **Destruction of Specific Thing**   In the absence of a showing that there was an intent to assume the risk, the destruction of the subject matter of the contract by acts of God may discharge the contract. The destruction, however, must be of the specific property or of something to be derived from a particular source. It may be stated, as a general rule, that when the continued existence of a specific thing is essential to the performance of a contract, the destruction of the thing will terminate the contract.

A manufacturer may contract to deliver to a retailer a specified number of manufactured articles. The destruction by fire of the factory in which the manufacturer expects to manufacture the articles will not excuse performance because, although an undue hardship will undoubtedly result, performance is possible from some other source. If the contract had provided that the articles were to be manufactured in a particular factory and that particular factory was destroyed, nonperformance would be excused. A few courts go a step further and hold that the manufacturer will be excused if it can be assumed that the articles were to be manufactured in the particular factory.

The rule is frequently applied to growing crops. A grower may contract to sell and deliver a specified amount of produce to a retailer at a future date. If the production of the subject matter of the contract is prevented because of inevitable accident, such as drought, plant disease, or excessive rains, the grower will nevertheless be obligated to secure the produce from some other source to fulfill the contract or to answer in damages. If the contract had been to grow the produce on a particular tract of land, he would have been excused because the specific thing essential to the performance of the contract would have been destroyed.

(3) **Death or Inability**   The rules respecting the destruction of the subject matter are, for the most part, equally applicable to the death or inability of one of the contracting parties. When the continued existence of a particular person is essential to the performance of the contract the death of the person will terminate the contract.

Nonperformance of a contract is excused by the death or physical incapacity of the promisor when the contract calls for performance of such a personal character that it can be performed only by the promisor. It is also sufficient cause for not fulfilling the contract if the well-founded fear of illness or death is such as to render it unsafe. The parties might expressly provide that incapacity or risk of danger would not excuse nonperformance, and, in some instances, the risk of danger is regarded as assumed from the nature of the contract. It is a general rule, however, that death of the person excuses nonperformance of a contract to render personal services, but that death of the person does not excuse nonperformance when the services are of such a character that they may be performed by a personal representative.

Impossibility Created by Other Party   A contracting party who has prevented the other party from performing the contract will not be permitted to recover from the other party or to plead his own act which has prevented the performance as a defense in order to defeat recovery by the other. This rule is based upon the principal of law that he who prevents a thing may not avail himself of the nonperformance which he has occasioned. Nonperformance of a promise is excused, therefore, if performance is prevented by the conduct of the adverse party. An implied condition arises in every contract that neither party will interfere with the other in the performance of the contract, and, should such interference take place, the party prevented from performing is not only excused from nonperformance but may bring an action to recover damages. [*Overton v. Vita-Food Corp.*, p. 155.]

Impossibility Created by Law   A condition is implied in every contract that the promisor shall not be compelled to perform if performance is rendered impossible by law. The extent to which the general rule is applicable when the subject matter of the contract is put under government control, however, is not clear. The rule with respect to the imposition of governmental restrictions, which is sometimes referred to as the "doctrine of commercial frustration," is impossible to state in general terms which are not too broad. The restrictions imposed during World War II were a fruitful source for application of the doctrine, but the results left no clear-cut dividing line between the meaning of the words "frustration" and "termination." The prevailing view is probably to the effect that the contractual obligation will revive again—provided no greater burdens are imposed upon either of the parties by subsequent performance—when the restrictions are removed, but that the parties are discharged if it appears that the restriction will remain in effect for a substantial part or all of the contract period.

    Statutory enactments of a permanent nature which render performance illegal ordinarily terminate the contract. A contract which is legal in its inception, therefore, but which becomes illegal by subsequent statutory enactment is terminated as soon as the statute becomes effective. In this connection the constitutional prohibition against the impairment of contract obligations by state laws should be kept in mind. A state law which declares usurious and void contracts already existing and bearing interest at a rate which was legal at the time the contracts were made impairs the obligation of contracts and is unconstitutional. The prohibition, however, does not restrict the power of the state to protect public health, public morals, or public safety. Parties who enter into contracts, perfectly lawful at the time, to sell liquor, operate a brewery, or carry on a lottery are subject to impairment by a change of policy on the part of the state.

CASES

Haymore v. Levinson,   328 P.2d 307 (Utah 1958). Action by Arnold Haymore and Blaine H. Haymore, plaintiffs, against Reuben J. Levinson and Yetta Levinson, defendants. Defendants contracted to purchase a house from plaintiff Arnold Haymore, a building contractor, who was in the process of constructing the house. The purchase price was $36,000, and the contract contained a provision that $3,000 of the purchase price was to be placed in escrow to be held until "satisfactory completion of the work." When the construction was finished, Haymore requested the release of the $3,000. Defendants stated that they were not satisfied with certain of the items and refused to release the money. After some discussion and attempts to satisfy defendants, this action was brought to recover the $3,000 held in escrow.

 Crockett, Justice: The defendants' position is in essence that the words "satisfactory completion of the work" are to be given a subjective meaning: i.e., that it is a matter of their choice and unless they are satisfied and so declare, the money is not payable; whereas the plaintiffs assert that it means only that the work must meet a standard reasonable under the circumstances.

 The adjudicated cases recognize that contracts wherein one party agrees to perform to the satisfaction of the other fall into two general classes: the first is where the undertaking is to do something of such a nature that pleasing the personal taste, fancy or sensibility of the other, which cannot be readily determined by objective standards, must reasonably be considered an element of predominant importance in the performance. In such cases the covenant that something will be done to the satisfaction of the favored party ordinarily makes him the sole judge thereof and he may give or withhold his approval as he desires.

 The other class of cases involves satisfaction as to such things as operative fitness, mechanical utility or structural completion in which the personal sensibilities just mentioned would not reasonably be deemed of such predominant importance to the performance. As to such contracts the better considered view, and the one we adhere to, is that an objective standard should be applied: that is, that the party favored by such a provision has no arbitrary privilege of declining to acknowledge satisfaction and that he cannot withhold approval unless there is apparently some reasonable justification for doing so.

 Building contracts such as the one in question generally fall within the second class of contracts above discussed. In regard to them it is plain to be seen that giving the word "satisfactory" an entirely subjective meaning might produce unconscionable results. The favored party could, upon any whim or caprice, and without reason, refuse to acknowledge satisfaction and thereby escape his obligations under the contract. The ends of justice are obviously better served by the application of the objective standard which only requires the work to be completed in a reasonably skillful and workmanlike manner in accordance with the accepted standards, in the locality. If in the light of such standards, it would meet the approval of reasonable and prudent persons, that should be sufficient.

The above view is consonant with our recent holding that a clause in a contract for the furnishing of heat was to be within the lessor's "sole judgment," could not be arbitrarily applied to justify the furnishing of entirely inadequate heat, but was subject to a sensible interpretation in relation to the reasonable needs of the lessees under the circumstances.

The trial court correctly adopted and applied the standard to which we give our approval herein. In doing so it found that the plaintiff had completed the original list of items attached to the contract in a satisfactory manner. [DECISION FOR PLAINTIFF]

Rockland Poultry Co. v. Anderson, 91 A.2d 478 (Me. 1952). Action by Rockland Poultry Company, plaintiff, against Thomas M. Anderson, defendant. The plaintiff and the defendant entered into a contract by the terms of which the defendant agreed to construct for plaintiff a building for the sum of $11,476 "with ample and sufficient foundations, drainage systems for poultry business, gutters on floors and sufficient windows for ample and sufficient light. Said Thomas M. Anderson to furnish all material and labor and to complete and make for said Poultry Company a good, strong substantial building of first class material." The plaintiff paid the defendant the agreed sum of $11,476, but contends that defendant did not build the building as promised "in that said building did not have ample and sufficient foundations, but that said foundations were weak and faulty and have since sagged and settled, whereby the floors are cracked, the walls settled and the roof, by reason thereof, warped and bent so that water does not drain from it in a proper manner and that said building was not the strong substantial building that defendant agreed and contracted to erect." The plaintiff brought this action for breach of the terms of the contract, and the defendant contended, among other things, that the contract had been substantially complied with.

Fellows, Justice: The plaintiff, however, claims that the verdict for the defendant is manifestly wrong because the admitted facts entitled the plaintiff to some damages even if those damages are comparatively small.

A careful examination of the record convinces the Court that this claim of the plaintiff is correct. The jury verdict for the defendant is plainly wrong. The damages may not be large, as the plaintiff states in its brief, but the plaintiff is entitled to something for improper construction of the floor under the terms of the contract, which is proved by the admissions of the defendant, to the effect that the floor is not the good and substantial one he promised. There is no conflicting evidence on that point, for the defendant admits liability in an amount sufficient to make the floor "good, strong and substantial" as the contract required. The contract provided for a good building with "ample and sufficient foundations," and the evidence does not show that to build such a floor was impossible. The defendant's expert witness stated that to build in that building a good floor "you would have to excavate four or five feet." It might be difficult but it was not impossible. It might cost the contractor more than he expected, but he was bound by his contract.

Where a construction contract provides that a certain thing be done in a certain manner, or to obtain a certain result, it must be done by the contracting party if it is not impossible, and if it is not prevented by act of God or of the other party. There must be "substantial performance."

Where a contractor departs from his contract but there is a benefit to the other party and the other accepts, or uses, the subject matter of the contract, the contractor is entitled to receive a fair and reasonable value for services, not exceeding the contract price. The other party may be entitled to damages for failure to perform according to contract. [DECISION FOR PLAINTIFF]

New Era Homes Corp. v. Forster, 86 N.E.2d 757 (N.Y. 1949). Action by New Era Homes Corporation, plaintiff, against Engelbert Forster and another, defendants. Plaintiff entered into a written agreement with defendants to make alterations to defendants' home. The reference to price and payment was as follows:

All above material, and labor to erect and install same to be supplied for $3,075.00 to be paid as follows:
$150.00 on signing of contract.
$1,000.00 upon delivery of materials and starting of work,
$1,500.00 on completion of rough carpentry and rough plumbing,
$425 upon job being completed.

The contract with respect to the first item was completed, but when the rough carpentry and plumbing were finished, the defendants refused to pay the installment of $1,500. The plaintiff stopped work and brought suit for the $1,500 on the theory that since all the necessary rough carpentry and rough plumbing work had been done, the time had arrived for it to collect $1,500. Defendants conceded their default but argue that plaintiff was not entitled to the $1,500 third payment but to such amount as it could establish by way of actual loss sustained from defendants' breach. The jury by its verdict, however, gave plaintiff its $1,500. Defendants appealed.

Desmond, Judge: The whole question is as to the meaning of so much of the agreement as we have quoted above. Did that language make it an entire contract, with one consideration for the doing of the whole work, and payments on account at fixed points in the progress of the job, or was the bargain a severable or divisible one in the sense that, of the total consideration $1,150 was to be the full and fixed payment for "delivery of materials and starting the work," $1,500 the full and fixed payment for work done up to and including "completion of rough carpentry and rough plumbing," and $425 for the rest? We hold that the total price of $3,075 was the single consideration for the whole of the work, and that the separately listed payments were not allocated absolutely to certain parts of the undertaking, but were scheduled part payments, mutually convenient to the builder and the owner. That conclusion, we think, is a necessary one from the very words of the writing, since the arrangement there stated was not that separate items of work be done for separate amounts of money, but that the whole alteration project, including material and labor, was "to be supplied for $3,075.00." There is nothing in the record to suggest that the parties had intended to group, in this contract, several separate engagements, each with its own separate consideration. They did not say, for instance, that the price for all the work up to the completion of rough carpentry and plumbing was to be $1,500. They did agree that at that point $1,500 would be due, but as a part payment on the whole price. . . .

We find no controlling New York case, but the trend of authority in this State, and elsewhere, is that such agreements express an intent that payment be conditioned and dependent upon completion of all the agreed work. We think that is the reasonable rule—after all, a house-holder who remodels his home is, usually, committing himself to one plan and one result, not a series of unrelated projects. The parties to a construction or alteration contract may, of course, make it divisible and stipulate the value of each divisible part. But there is no sign that these people so intended. It follows that plaintiff, on defendant's default, could collect . . . in contract for the value of what plaintiff had lost—that is, the contract price, less payments made and less the cost of completion. [DECISION ON APPEAL FOR DEFENDANTS]

Lewis, Judge (dissenting):   A contract is entire or divisible depending upon the intention of the parties to be gathered from the agreement itself and the circumstances surrounding its execution. . . .

The parties to the written agreement here in suit were careful to provide that the contract price was to be paid in specified installments which, after the initial payment, were in varying amounts payable upon completion of designated stages of the work. The contracting parties thus indicated their intent to be that the part to be performed by the plaintiff was to consist of several distinct and separate items accordingly to fall due when each specified stage of the work should be completed. . . . Concluding, as I do, that such a contract is divisible in character . . . I would affirm the judgment.

Berg v. Erickson,   234 Fed. 817 (Kan. 1916). Action by J. C. Berg, plaintiff, against John Erickson, defendant.

Sanborn, Circuit Judge: John Erickson, a resident of Kansas, made a written contract with J. C. Berg, a resident of St. Francis, Texas, on April 16, 1913, to pasture for him 1,000 steers and to "furnish plenty of good grass, water, and salt during the grazing season of 1913" to them for $7 per head, which Berg agreed to pay. Erickson furnished the grass, water and salt to them during May and June, but the most severe drought which had been known in that part of Kansas subsequently prevailed, and on account of that drought it was impossible for Erickson to furnish, and he failed to furnish, plenty of good grass for the cattle during July, August and September, to the damage of Berg in the sum of about $20,000; and the main question in this case is whether Erickson is liable to pay these damages to Berg on account of his breach of his contract, or is absolved from liability for them by the impossibility of performance which resulted from the drought after the contract was made.

. . . Was the contract of these parties an absolute agreement by Erickson to furnish plenty of good grass to the cattle during the grazing season of 1913, or a contract to furnish good grass unless by an unprecedented drought it should become impossible for him to do so?

. . . Berg was a resident of St. Francis, Tex. He had never had any experience of Kansas grass. He sought pasturing for 1,000 cattle. He went from Texas to Kansas and applied to Erickson for this pasturing. Before the contract was made Erickson showed him the pastures into which he proposed to put the cattle and into which they were subsequently driven. Berg looked at the pastures and made no objection to them. Erickson told him he would guarantee the pastures. After this inspection and conversation Erickson made the contract to furnish plenty of good grass to the cattle during the grazing season of 1913. . . .

In view of these facts, the situation of these parties when this contract was made, the circumstances surrounding them, and the unqualified undertaking of Erickson expressed in the agreement converge with compelling power to force the mind to the conclusion that the minds of these contracting parties met in the intention that Erickson should, and that he did, guarantee plenty of good grass for these cattle in these pastures where he put them during the entire grazing season, without exempting or intending to exempt himself from liability in the case of any impossibility of performance that might result from an unprecedented drought, fire, or other act of God or accident. . . .

The general rule is that one who makes a positive agreement to do a lawful act is not absolved from liability for a failure to fulfill his covenant by a subsequent impossibility caused by an act of God, or an unavoidable accident, because he voluntarily contracts to perform it without any reservations or exceptions, which, if he desired, he could make in his agreement, and thereby induces the other contracting party, in consideration of his positive covenant, to enter into and become bound by the contract. [DECISION FOR PLAINTIFF]

Overton v. Vita-Food Corp.,   210 P.2d 757 (Cal. 1949). Action by Paul Overton (plaintiff below), respondent, against Vita-Food Corporation and M. H. Lewis (defendants below), appellants. On February 5, 1942, appellant and respondents entered into a written contract by which appellants employed respondent to serve as its president from January 1, 1942, to December 31, 1946. The contract provided that respondent should devote as much time as might be necessary in the interest of the corporation and perform all duties as the managing director or the board of directors might direct from time to time and that he should receive as compensation for his services a salary of $250 a month. The contract contained the following contingencies clause:

Said employment shall be totally suspended and no services shall be rendered or required of Overton and the salary of Overton shall not accrue, become owing or due for the period or periods during which any or all of the following occur: The plant or plants of the Corporation are out of production from causes incident to or resulting from the present and prospective emergent conditions, or other causes beyond the reasonable control of the Corporation, such as, but without limitation to, transportation delays or interruptions, strikes, and acts of God.

Respondent brought this action to recover compensation for services rendered in 1945 and 1946. Appellant contended that its plants were out of production within the meaning of the contract in 1945 and 1946 and therefore no salary was due respondent.

Vallee, Justice: The contract says that the employment shall be suspended if the plant or plants are out of production "from causes incident to or resulting from the present and prospective emergent conditions, or other causes beyond the reasonable control of the Corporation, such as, but without limitation to, transportation delays or interruptions, strikes, and acts of God." . . . The court found on substantial evidence that the fact that appellant was out of production in 1945 and 1946 was not due to "emergent conditions" but was due to the fact that appellant by selling a trade-mark for $200,000 "voluntarily placed it out of its power to meet the provisions of the so-called 'production clause.'" Having voluntarily placed itself out of production so as to prevent its performance of the contract, appellant will not be permitted to deny liability thereon. Where a party to a contract prevents the fulfillment of a condition precedent or its performance by the adverse party, he cannot rely on such condition to defeat his liability. . . . Since appellant was not out of production from one of the causes specified in the contract, respondent's employment was not suspended. [DECISION FOR RESPONDENT]

PROBLEMS

1 The plaintiff seeks to recover the sum of $1,000 from defendant, which sum was offered by defendant as first prize in a word-building contest. Plaintiff claims that she is entitled to the first prize because she submitted the largest correct list of words made from the letters in the word "determination." Plaintiff submitted thirty-six more correct words than any other contestant. She intentionally submitted several incorrect words, however, and stated in her letter of transmittal that she did not follow the rule which prohibited obsolete, dialectic, or foreign words. Did the plaintiff substantially perform so that she is entitled to the $1,000?

2 Plaintiff, a private boarding school, entered into a contract with defendant by the terms of which the daughter of defendant was enrolled in the school for a period of nine months for the sum of $1,800 fee for tuition payable half yearly in advance. The daughter was unable to return to the school after the first semester because she developed defective eyesight, rendering her unable to attend school. Plaintiff brought an action to recover $900 as tuition for the second half of the school year. Decide.

3 The plaintiff and the defendant entered into a contract whereby the plaintiff promised to work and manage defendant's hog farm. The plaintiff was to have the use of the farmhouse, a garden, half the chickens and eggs, and pasture for a cow. The contract provided that the plaintiff "is to receive further compensation of $1 per hundred of all pigs raised upon the farm at the time of sale, not less than five months of age." The plaintiff performed properly for about five months, at which time he quit. Plaintiff brought an action for the value of his services. Is he entitled to recover anything except his share of the eggs and poultry and the proceeds from the sale of pigs?

4 Defendant's husband owned and operated a ladies' dress shop. He owed $8,000 to the plaintiff on a note, which was long overdue. Plaintiff and defendant entered into negotiations whereby it was agreed that the plaintiff would finance the defendant to the extent of $15,000, including the $8,000 owed by defendant's husband. This agreement resulted in a written instrument whereby the defendant guaranteed payment of the $8,000 note. The defendant thereafter was unable to operate the shop due to the failure of the plaintiff to extend the necessary credit. Is the defendant liable on the $8,000 note?

5 On or about June 13, 1947, defentant, as seller, and plaintiff, as purchaser, entered into a contract for the sale and purchase of 800 bags of Texas New Crop U.S. No. 1 black-eye peas to be grown and shipped from the locality of Dilley, Texas, on or before June 30, 1947. An unexpected torrential rainfall of five to six inches, however, fell at about the time the crop was to be harvested, and, as a result thereof, U.S. No. 1 black-eye peas were not procurable in the latter part of June, 1947, in the Dilley section of Texas. Does the defense of destruction of the subject matter of the contract by an act of God apply to the situation presented under the facts of this case?

6 Brown, who desired to build a house, employed an architect to draw the plans and specifications. The plans and specifications were complete and detailed. Brown then entered into a contract with a contractor whereby the contractor agreed to build the house according to the plans and specifications for the sum of $45,000. The house was about one-half completed when the contractor died. Brown insists that the executor of the estate of the contractor is obligated to employ the services of another contractor and complete the construction of the house. The executor contends that death of the contractor excused nonperformance. Do you agree with this contention?

7 The buyer and the seller entered into a written contract by the terms of which the seller agreed to install a steam heater in the house of the buyer. The contract contained the following provision: "The seller guarantees this apparatus for heating by steam to be constructed in a good, thorough, and workmanlike manner, to work entirely noiseless, and to give entire satisfaction to the buyer." The buyer contends the heater does not work to his entire satisfaction. He concedes, however, that the heater is reasonably satisfactory. How would you decide the case? Discuss the rules of law ordinarily used in deciding this class of cases.

13
REMEDIES, DAMAGES, INTERPRETATION

This chapter will discuss a summary of (1) the remedies available to an injured party for a breach of contract, (2) the damages that may be awarded to an injured party, (3) the interpretation of contracts, and (4) the joint, several, or joint and several liability.

REMEDIES

A remedy is the means by which a contractual right may be enforced or the violation of a right may be prevented or compensated. Some of the remedies have already been discussed, namely, a remedy on the theory of quasi contract to recover any money or property to which plaintiff is entitled; and a remedy to recover on quantum meruit for what he deserves. The most common remedy for a breach of contract—an action for damages—will be discussed momentarily. It now seems appropriate to discuss briefly the remedies of (1) rescission, (2) specific performance, and (3) injunction.

Rescission   It will be remembered that rescission of the contract is the proper remedy for incapacity of parties and unreality of consent. A breach which is incidental and subordinate to the main purpose of the contract, however, does not warrant a rescission of the contract. The injured party is still bound to perform his part of the agreement, and his only remedy for the breach consists of the damages he has suffered therefrom. A material breach defeats the purpose of the contract and warrants rescission and gives the injured party the right to rescind the contract or to treat it as a breach of the entire contract and maintain an action for the total breach. The effect of a lawful rescission of a contract is to put an end to it for all purposes and put the parties, insofar as possible, into the same position they were in prior to the making of the contract. A person who elects to rescind the contract cannot thereafter maintain an action for damages for the breach. The Code provides, however, that the aggrieved party who rescinds the contract does not thereby lose his right to damages in a contract for the sale of goods. A person who ratifies the contract cannot thereafter rescind the contract. [*Wolin v. Zenith Homes, Inc.,* p. 164.]

Specific Performance A decree for specific performance is a means of compelling a person to do precisely what he ought to have done under the terms of the contract. Contracts which are unfair and inequitable, however, will not be enforced. Contracts for personal services will not be enforced; to enforce such contracts would be unconstitutional. Contracts for the breach of which the injured party can be compensated in money damages likewise will not be enforced. The measure of damages, however, is frequently difficult to determine accurately. Specific performance will be granted, therefore, if more complete justice can be accomplished by requiring performance of the contract than by awarding compensatory damages for the breach. The courts will also grant specific performance for the sale of land and for the sale of antique chattels not obtainable elsewhere, such as heirlooms, famous paintings, and antique coins. Suppose Brown, the owner of an antique clock which Jones wished to purchase, entered into a contract with Jones by the terms of which Brown agreed to sell and Jones agreed to purchase the clock. Suppose further that Brown breached the contract by refusing to sell the clock. Assuming a similar clock could not be purchased elsewhere, Jones could ask the court for a decree of specific performance and compel Brown to sell and deliver the clock to him.

Injunction An injunction is an order of the court requiring a person to do some act or to restrain him from doing some act. Injunctions, with reference to the terms of their command, are classified as affirmative injunctions and negative injunctions. Affirmative injunctions, which are of a mandatory nature, command a person to do some particular act, or restrain a person from permitting his wrongful act to continue and compel him to undo it. Suppose Brown was the owner of a house and lot having a common passageway to the highway and that Jones, who also used the passageway, erected a fence across the passageway, thereby preventing Brown from having ingress or egress to the highway. A mandatory injunction could be used to compel Jones to remove the obstruction.

Negative injunctions are of a preventative nature and prohibit a person, or command him, to refrain from doing some particular act. A negative injunction prevents a course of action which violates the rights of another person, such as building a shopping center in violation of a zoning ordinance. [*Mantell v. International Plastic Harmonica Corp.*, p. 165.]

DAMAGES

The word "damages" is used here to signify the money compensation awarded for a loss which results from a breach of contract. A party to a contract who is injured by its breach is entitled to compensation for the injury sustained. He is entitled, so far as it can be done by the payment of money, to be placed in the same position he would have occupied if the contract had been performed. He is not entitled to be placed in a better position. As a general rule, therefore, he is limited in his recovery to the loss he has actually suffered because of the breach.

Nominal and Actual Damages   A breach of a valid contract entitles the injured party to at least nominal damages. Nominal damages is some trifling sum—frequently $1—in recognition of a technical infraction by the defendant of the plaintiff's right. The recovery for a breach of contract may be limited to nominal damages if there is no proof of actual damages, if the damages are not susceptible of proof or are too speculative to form a basis for legal recovery, or if there is no basis for establishing any measure of damages. Actual or compensatory damages—the terms are synonymous—are such as will compensate the injured party for the injury sustained and is the most frequent award rendered for a breach of contract. The term "actual damages," however, is broad in scope and includes not only general damages but any damages that may arise from the special circumstances of the case.

General and Special Damages   General damages, as distinguished from special damages, are those that are traceable to, and are the probable and necessary result of, the injury. In addition to general damages, the party injured by the breach of the contract is entitled to recover special damages which arise from circumstances peculiar to the case. The special circumstances, however, must be communicated to, or at least known by, the other party at the time the contract is entered into. Notice subsequent to the formation of the contract, although prior to its breach, is not sufficient. This rule is based upon the theory that the damages, in the absence of communication, cannot be fairly considered to have been within the "contemplation of the parties" as part of the consequences which might result from its breach when the contract was made.

Liquidated Damages and Penalties   Liquidated damages and special damages are similar in that they are both made known at the time the contract is entered into, but in the ascertainment of the award the two are quite different. Liquidated damages are the amount of compensation which the contracting parties agree, when the contract is entered into, shall be paid in case of breach. The amount of damages is, therefore, fixed and not subject to change. The chief problem in the ascertainment of damages is not the distinction between special damages and liquidated damages but the distinction between liquidated damages and penalties. A penalty is a sum inserted in a contract, not as a measure of compensation for its breach, but by way of security for actual damages and involves the idea of punishment. No precise rules have been established for determining whether an agreed sum is for liquidated damages or for a penalty. A sum named in the contract which is unconscionable or excessive and out of all proportion to the actual damages will ordinarily be regarded as a penalty. Conceding the difficulty in determining whether a stipulation is for liquidated damages or for a penalty, the distinction is nevertheless important. The contracting parties are bound by an agreement for liquidated damages, but a defaulting party may be relieved of an agreement to pay a stated sum as a penalty. [*King Motors, Inc. v. Delfino,* p. 166.]

Avoidable Damage or Consequences   A person injured by a breach of a contract is required to exercise reasonable care to minimize the resulting damages. He cannot recover for that which he might reasonably have avoided. The repudiation by the buyer of a contract for the sale of perishable fruit or vegetables would impose upon the seller the duty to make reasonable efforts to resell the produce. The repudiation by the landlord of a contract to repair a leaky roof would impose a duty upon the tenant to use reasonable efforts to remove any articles that might be damaged by the water coming through the roof. It is generally held to be the duty of a discharged employee to use reasonable efforts to obtain other employment of a like nature in the same locality, but he is not under a duty to accept employment of a different nature or to seek employment in a different locality. As a general rule, the plaintiff cannot recover from the defendant those damages which plaintiff might have avoided by the exercise of a reasonable effort without undergoing undue risk, humiliation, or expense. [*Barron G. Collier, Inc. v. B. Deutser Furniture Co.,* p. 167.]

Section 2–704 of the Code gives the manufacturer-seller the option to either complete manufacture or to cease manufacture of unfinished goods when the buyer breaches the contract. If he elects to complete manufacture, he may resell the goods. If he elects to cease manufacture, he may resell the partially manufactured goods for scrap or salvage. In either event, he may recover as damages any loss from such resale. If resale is not practicable, he may bring an action for the price. The manufacturer-seller is required, however, to exercise reasonable commercial judgment for the purpose of avoiding a loss.

INTERPRETATION

The interpretation of a contract is the process of ascertaing the intention of the makers of the contract. The interpretation of a poorly drawn written contract or the establishment of a valid oral contract by oral evidence, however, is all too frequently a challenge to the witnesses, the lawyers, the judge, and the jury. The consequences of attempting to interpret or establish such contracts at the trial of the case by offers to introduce and attempts to exclude evidence are so obvious that further comment would be superfluous. The significance of reducing important agreements to well-drawn written contracts cannot be overemphasized. This precaution, however, necessitates a brief examination of the parol-evidence rule and some of the rules pertaining to construction of contracts.

Parol-Evidence Rule   This rule is designed to exclude evidence which would vary or contradict a completely written contract, and might, therefore, prevent the court from discovering the meaning of the written contract. The courts have, over a period of time, developed many rules to guide them in the interpretation of the language used by contracting parties in their written agreements.

The court decisions reveal that evidence is admissible to translate the technical meaning of a word into a popular meaning but not to give a definition different from the technical meaning; to identify the persons or property mentioned in the contract; to show typographical or clerical errors made in reducing the agreement to writing; to explain a business custom which was known or should have been known by both parties. The parties are supposed to have entered into the agreement with reference to such persons, property, or custom. If the contract contains ambiguities, illegible erasures, words that are blurred, or language that is suseptible of more than one interpretation, evidence is not only admissible but is necessary to clarify the uncertainty. A word or phrase which does not have a fixed meaning may be explained by oral testimony, but a word or phrase which has a fixed meaning may not be given a meaning different from its ordinary one. The rule, of course, does not exclude proof that the contract was entered into under a mutual mistake, or that a person was induced by fraud, duress, or undue influence to enter into the contract; nor does it exclude proof of a new oral contract made subsequently to the writing which modifies the written agreement. It merely excludes evidence of prior or contemporaneous oral agreements which would vary the written contract.

The rule rests upon the presumption that the parties have incorporated every material item or term into the written contract and operates to exclude any evidence that might tend to substitute a new and different contract from the one agreed upon by the contracting parties. Ordinarily any evidence may be introduced to show the intention of the parties whenever the object of the contract cannot be ascertained from the language employed. Broadly stated, any evidence is admissible which will not vary, alter, or contradict the terms of the written agreement. [*Grubb v. Rockey,* p. 168.]

Construction of Contracts   The construction of a contract is the process of determining the meaning of the written words contained in the contract. The law has, therefore, devised certain rules of construction. These rules are ordinarily classified as primary and secondary rules.

(1) *Primary Rules*   The primary rules may be briefly summarized as follows: (a) Unless the circumstances show that a special meaning should be attached to the language, the common or normal meaning of the language will be given; (b) unless usage shows a contrary intention, technical terms or words will

be given their technical meaning; and (c) words will be given the meaning which best effectuates the intention of the contracting parties,

(2) *Secondary Rules* An application of the primary rules does not always clearly effectuate the meaning of the language. The courts will then resort to an application of the secondary rules, the most important of which are as follows: (a) The writing will govern if there is a conflict between the printed and written words; (b) obvious mistakes of writing, punctuation, or grammar will be corrected; (c) the words will generally be construed most strongly against the party using them; (d) the meaning which will render the contract valid will be given if the contract is susceptible of two meanings; and (e) in case of doubt, the interpretation given by the parties is the best evidence of their intention.

JOINT AND SEVERAL CONTRACTS

The intention of the contracting parties determines whether a contract with two or more persons on either or both sides is to be construed as several, joint, or joint and several.

Several Liability Two or more persons may contract collectively in such a way that each makes a separate promise to perform some act. If Brown and Jones "promise severally" to perform some act for Smith, their presumed intention is to create several obligations. Smith could recover from either Brown or Jones.

Joint Liability If Brown and Jones "promise jointly" to perform some act for Smith, their presumed intention is to create a joint obligation. A discharge of one joint obligor, as by an accord and satisfaction or by a release, discharges both of them. Statutes in many states, however, have been enacted which provide in effect that a joint debtor may compromise his liability without the others being discharged. Many states have also enacted statutes which provide in effect that contracts which by the common law are joint shall be joint and several.

Section 3–118 of the Code provides that a negotible instrument which is signed by two or more persons as makers, acceptors, drawers, or indorsers who sign in the same capacity and as a part of the same transaction are liable jointly and severally. This is true even though the note reads "I promise to pay." Suppose a promissory note contains the language "I promise to pay" and that Brown and Jones both sign the note as makers. Their liability would be joint and several.

Joint and Several Liability A joint obligation by Brown and Jones is created as well as two several obligations, one by Brown and one by Jones, when they "promise jointly and severally" to perform some act for Smith. Smith may enforce the promise against Brown and Jones jointly, or he may enforce the promise against Brown and Jones separately at different times. Suppose Smith brings an action against Brown on his several liability, receives a judgment, and Brown pays the judgment. The joint obligation of Brown and Jones is discharged as well as the several liability of Brown and Jones.

CASES

Wolin v. Zenith Homes, Inc., 146 A.2d 197 (Md. 1959). Action by Frank Wolin and wife, plaintiffs, against Zenith Homes, Inc., defendant, to rescind a contract. Plaintiffs purchased a newly constructed house from defendant and became dissatisfied with it because of certain structural defects. Plaintiffs thereupon made certain complaints to defendant, and attempts were made to remedy the defects. Plaintiffs then notified defendant by registered mail that another contractor, at their request, had inspected the house and had made certain recommendations. The letter concluded with a warning that "irrespective of what is done, we are not waiving the provisions of our contract of purchase and the supplemental agreement signed at the time we settled for the house." About a week thereafter, plaintiffs demanded a rescission of the contract and cancellation of the deed. No further effort was made to remedy the defects. Plaintiffs thereupon brought this action for rescission of the contract for the purchase of the house.

Horney, Judge: The Wolins contend that they were not so much misled by the general assurances as to the structural stability of the foundation walls and the ultimate dry condition of the basement walls and floor as by the positive statements that the foundation walls were free of substantial defects and that there was a bed of gravel under the concrete floor. Subsequently it was discovered that the foundation walls were only eight inches thick instead of twelve inches as was required by the county building code, and that there was no gravel under the basement floor. The Wolins insist that these specific misrepresentations were ones which they could not have ascertained prior to the execution of the contract of sale and the delivery of the deed. Apparently the unlawful width of the foundation walls had not been discovered by the building inspector who had made ten inspections and finally approved the construction prior to the settlement date. It was also subsequently discovered that the subsurface water level outside the basement was only one foot below the surface and that the house had been built in a swamp. However, even if we assume, without deciding, that such misrepresentations were in fact false, that they were material and that the purchasers relied on them to their detriment, it is clear that the Wolins, by their conduct after the discovery of such false and fraudulent material representations, elected to ratify the transaction rather than rescind it.

In this State, as well as in other jurisdictions, it is settled that when a party to a contract discovers a fraud has been perpetrated upon him, he is put to a prompt election to rescind the contract or to ratify it and claim damages. Acts by a purchaser which constitute acquiescence, ratification or estoppel will preclude him from rescinding the contract. In the Telma case we said, 157 Md. at page 413, 146 Atl. at page 222:

Upon the discovery . . . of the fraudulent misrepresentations, the purchaser had to elect between two rights. He was put to the choice of repudiating or ratifying the conveyance, although the transaction had been fully completed by conveyance and payment. If he adopted the first alternative, he repudiated the conveyance and sought its rescission and a restoration of his situation before the contract; but if he chose the second, he ratified the grant but could obtain damages to redress the injury inflicted by the false and fraudulent representation. These rights were inconsistent and mutually exclusive, and the discovery put the purchaser to a prompt election.

It seems that in some instances even silence may indicate ratification.

In a case such as this where the purchasers, instead of exercising the right to rescind the contract promptly upon the discovery of false and fraudulent misrepresentations, notified the seller they were not waiving the provisions of the contract of purchase and supplemental agreement, demanded that the seller make certain repairs then accepted such repairs as had been made, it is clear the purchasers expressly elected to enforce the contract and supplemental agreement, and could not thereafter repudiate the transaction even though they should afterwards discover other circumstances connected with the same false and fraudulent misrepresentations. [DECISION FOR DEFENDANT]

Mantell v. International Plastic Harmonica Corp.,   55 A.2d 250 (N.J. 1947). Suit by S. Carl Mantell and others, complainants, against International Plastic Harmonica Corporation and Peter Christian Christensen, its president, and Finn H. Magnus, its vice-president, defendants. The complainants and the defendant corporation entered into an agreement on July 3, 1945, for a term of two years whereby the defendant appointed complainants as its "general distributors" of plastic harmonicas. The complainants were allotted an exclusive distributorship in the regional area of the states of New York, Pennsylvania, Delaware, Maryland, Virginia, West Virginia, and the District of Columbia, except for a few minor designated exceptions. The agreement also provided that the corporation "shall deliver to the distributors, and the latter shall take, during every month beginning with July, 1945, all of the harmonicas produced" by it, but not to exceed 30,000 per month. This suit was brought to enjoin the corporation from competing with complainants in the specified area and from selling harmonicas to persons other than complainants until the specified minimum quantities were supplied complainants.

Heher, Justice   This was an appropriate case for negative restraint as an indirect means of enforcement of the contract. The contract granted to complainants an exclusive franchise to vend in the assigned field a new harmonica of radically different design and composition to be manufactured under letters patent controlled by the defendant corporation, and there was an entirely reasonable prospect of a profitable yield if there were deliveries of the product in keeping with the contract, and thus the franchise was a valuable property right entitled to protection by equitable process if the remedy at law was inadequate. It was not, as we have seen, an ordinary contract of sale. Complainants had undertaken performance of the contract; and thereby there came into being the nucleus of a market and good will and the foundation of a lawful business monopoly that would have yielded a substantial return if the promised articles of commerce had been made available. The law does not afford a certain, complete and sufficient remedy in such circumstances. The commodity was not procurable elsewhere; and thus the development of the market and the successful operation of the business depended upon performance by the manufacturer. Nonperformance made for irreparable injury. It would have been well nigh impossible to ascertain the full damages ensuing from the breach of the contract, as an established business of this nature would in all human likelihood have been convertible to other profitable kindred uses even after the particular agreement had been terminated. And the provision of the goods was an indispensable requisite to the establishment and development of the business.

Whenever the contract is of the class which is ordinarily specifically enforceable, equity will restrain its breach by injunction, if that is the only practical mode of enforcement permissible by its terms. But the injunctive remedy is not confined to stipulations negative in form; it ofttimes extends to those affirmative in character, where the affirmative stipulations imply or include a negative. And where the contract requires the doing of some personal act calling for special skill or artistry, such as singing in a concert hall and not elsewhere, or where in the particular circumstances a decree of specific perform-ance would not be enforceable or practicable because of the need for continuing superintendency of the manufacturing process, equity will enforce the negative stipulation by the injunctive remedy if thereby substantial justice will be done between the parties. [DECISION FOR COMPLAINANTS]

King Motors, Inc. v. Delfino   72 A.2d 233 (Conn. 1950). Action by The King Motors, Incorporated, plaintiff, against Angelo Delfino, defendant. The Plaintiff, an automobile dealer, sold and delivered to the defendant on July 13, 1948, a new 1948 Cadillac car for $3,935.48. At the time of the sale the defendant executed a "contract for repurchase" which provided that the defendant would not sell the Cadillac for a period of six months without first offering it to the plaintiff for purchase. The contract further provided:

It is further understood and agreed by and between the parties that if the said Purchaser shall violate any of the terms of this Contract, expressed above, then the said Purchaser shall owe the said Dealer the sum of Three Hundred Dollars ($300.00) in current money of the United States, as liquidated damages, which amount shall be immediately due and payable.

On July 19, 1948, the defendant sold the Cadillac to another person without first offering to sell it to the plaintiff. The plaintiff brought this action to recover damages for breach of the repurchase agreement.

Maltbie, Chief Justice: The question presented in this case is whether a provision in a contract for the payment of a certain sum of money constituted one for liquidated damages, as stated in it, or one for a penalty. . . .

As a general rule parties can contract to liquidate their damages, and courts have not interfered with such contracts where the proof of damages would be uncertain or difficult and the amount agreed upon is reasonably commensurate with the extent of the injury. The conditions for recovery on such a contract are . . . : (1) the damages to be anticipated as resulting from the breach must be uncertain in amount or difficult to prove; (2) there must have been an intent on the part of the parties to liquidate them in advance; and (3) the amount stipulated must be a reasonable one, that is to say, not greatly disproportioned to the presumable loss or injury.

If the agreement had contained no provision for liquidated damages, the plaintiff's damages on the breach of the defendant's agreement to offer the car to it for repurchase would have been properly measured by the profits it would probably have made on a resale of the car. But what that profit might be was not capable of anticipation, particularly as the provision covered a period of six months after the sale. . . . The words of the contract clearly express the intent of the parties that the sum is to be "liquidated damages"; and the factual situation is such that those words fairly meant that, and not merely a penalty designed to compel the defendant not to make default.

. . . The agreement was not an unreasonable restraint upon trade; the plaintiff is a dealer in cars and presumably if it repurchased the car it would be in order to resell it; the agreement would not take the car out of the market, for, if the plaintiff did not exercise the option, the sale or transfer by the defendant would become effective, and if the option was exercised the plaintiff would have the car for resale. [DECISION FOR PLAINTIFF]

Barron G. Collier, Inc. v. B. Deutser Furniture Co.,   256 S.W. 330 (Tex. 1923). Action by Barron G. Collier, Inc. (plaintiff below), appellant, against B. Deutser Furniture Company (defendant below), appellee. The appellant, which company through various contracts controlled all advertising space in streetcars in the city of Houston, Texas, entered into two contracts dated June 1, 1919, with appellee whereby the appellee agreed to rent a specified number of advertising spaces for a period of five years from the date of the contracts. On August 2, 1920, appellee requested appellant to cancel and rescind the contracts. After the last-mentioned date, appellee refused to use the advertising space called for in the contracts or to make any further payments. The appellant brought this action for a breach of the contracts and, sought to recover as damages the contract price of the advertising space for the remainder of the contract period.

Hightower, Chief Justice: The undisputed evidence in this case shows that on July 2, 1920, appellee duly notified appellant by letter that it would not use any of the space contracted for in any of the streetcars . . . after August 1, 1920, and appellant was directed by the letter to re-rent such space in said cars or make such disposition of same as it might wish. Having been thus notified by appellee that it would no longer comply with its written contracts to use the space in any of the cars after August 1, 1920, it was appellant's duty to use reasonable efforts and diligence to ward off or minimize such threatened damages as might flow from appellee's breach of contract, and if appellant failed to use reasonable efforts and diligence to minimize such threatened damages, as was found by the trial court it did, it was not entitled to recover for any such damages as it might have prevented by the use of such efforts and diligence. It seems to be the general rule in the American Union that one who is threatened with damages in consequences of a tort or breach of contract, with some few special exceptions, must use reasonable diligence and efforts to ward off or minimize such threatened damages.

. . . We think, from the testimony of appellant's manager, Mr. J. F. Smiley, as reflected by this record, that appellant could have re-rented or relet the Deutser space in the local cars for as much or more than it was to receive under the Deutser contracts during the entire period of time between the breach of the contract and the trial of the case. [DECISION FOR APPELLEE]

Grubb v. Rockey, 79 A.2d 255 (Pa. 1951). Action by Homer A. Grubb and wife, plaintiffs, against Charles S. Rockey and wife, defendants. The plaintiffs and the defendants entered into a written contract which recited, among other things not material here, that the defendants agreed to sell and the plaintiffs to buy a certain farm "for the sum of Ten Thousand ($10,000.00) Dollars . . . to be paid in cash to the parties of the first part on or before March 1, 1949." The plaintiffs performed their part of the contract. The defendants refused to perform, and this suit was brought for specific performance. At the trial of the case, Mr. Rockey, one of the defendants, testified over the vigorous objection of counsel for plaintiffs that an oral agreement was made for "the sale of said farm for $11,200 and a reservation to the defendants of the wheat crop" after March 1, 1949. The trial court rendered a decree refusing specific performance, and plaintiffs appealed.

Bell, Justice: The narrow but very important question raised on this appeal is whether evidence of an oral contemporaneous inducing agreement is admissible to vary and contradict (1) a comprehensive written agreement, and (2) the purported real consideration set forth therein. . . .

Defendants attempted to both vary and contradict the written contract by the aforesaid oral agreement which they alleged induced the written contract. Defendant Rockey admitted that on Friday, January 7, he had offered to sell his farm to Grubb for $10,000. On Monday, January 10, plaintiff, Grubb, and defendant, Rockey, met, without their wives, to conclude the sale. Defendant took Grubb to the office of defendants' lawyer. Rockey testified that at the time he demanded $12,500 for the farm and after some haggling, agreed to accept $11,200 and the reservation to himself of the wheat crop which was to be harvested after March 1st; that Grubb agreed to this, but wanted to pay $1,200 on the side so his family wouldn't know he was paying more than $10,000 which was the price everyone had agreed upon. Grubb denied this. . . .

Where parties, without any fraud or mistake, have deliberately put their engagements in writing, the law declares the writing to be not only the best, but the only evidence of their agreement. All preliminary negotiations, conversations and verbal agreements are merged in and superseded by the subsequent written contract . . . and unless fraud, accident or mistake be averred, the writing constitutes the agreement between the parties, and its terms cannot be added to nor substracted from by parol evidence. . . .

But defendants further contend, and the chancellor found, that "parol evidence may always be introduced to prove the true consideration or purchase price. . . ."

No logical or sound reason has been suggested why, in a case like this, the purchase price or consideration set forth in an executory written contract for sale of real estate should be treated differently from any other term or provision therein, or, more particularly, why it should be excluded from the Parol Evidence Rule. The old rule probably originated in connection with deeds which frequently recited a consideration of $1 or other nominal consideration, and which did not purport to show the true consideration or the real purchase price which the parties had actually agreed upon. . . .

We therefore hold that where the purchase price set forth in a written agreement purports to be not merely a nominal, but the real or actual amount agreed upon, then in the absence of fraud, accident or mistake, evidence of an alleged contemporaneous oral agreement (on the faith of which the written contract was allegedly executed), is inadmissible to add to or subtract from or contradict or vary the purchase price or consideration set forth in said written contract. [DECISION FOR PLAINTIFFS]

PROBLEMS

1 Defendant signed a written offer to purchase certain real property owned by the plaintiff for the sum of $15,000, at which time defendant paid plaintiff the sum of $50. The written offer, which was accepted in writing by plaintiff, provided that, in the event the purchaser fails to pay the balance of the purchase price, the amount "paid hereon shall be retained as liquidated or agreed damages." A few weeks thereafter, defendant told the plaintiff that he had decided not to purchase the property. Plaintiff thereupon sold the property to another person for the sum of $14,000 and brought an action against defendant for damages for breach of contract. What amount, if any, do you think plaintiff is entitled to recover?

2 Plaintiff, the owner of the ship *Minehaha,* insured it for $50,000 with The Insurance Company. The policy contained a clause which stated: "The risk to be suspended while the vessel is at Miller's Island loading." The ship was at Miller's Island for the purpose of loading, and was destroyed by a hurricane. The Insurance Company refused payment, claiming that the risk was suspended at the time the ship was destroyed. At the trial, plaintiff offered evidence to show that the clause meant "actually loading" and not "for the purpose of loading." Discuss whether this evidence is or is not admissible.

3 Brown, a wholesaler in furniture, entered into a contract with Jones, a retailer, whereby Brown agreed to sell, and Jones agreed to purchase, twenty-five chairs of a specific type. Jones then notified Brown that he repudiated the contract and would not accept the chairs. Brown ignored the notice, and shipped the chairs to Jones, who returned them to Brown. The cost of transporting the chairs to Jones and returning them to Brown was $150. Brown brought an action against Jones for breach of contract and included the $150 for transporting and returning the chairs as damages. Will he recover the $150?

4 Plaintiff's factory ceased operating because of a broken crankshaft. He delivered the broken crankshaft to a common carrier with instructions to deliver it to a certain person for repairs. He did not, however, disclose to the carrier that the factory could not resume operations until the crankshaft was returned and reinstalled. The carrier was guilty of unjustifiable delay in transporting the crankshaft to and from the person who made the repairs. The plaintiff now sues the carrier for damages, including the loss of profits which resulted from nonoperation of the factory during the time the crankshaft was in transit. Will the plaintiff recover such damages?

5 The seller agreed to sell, and the buyer agreed to purchase, five boxes of oranges at a price of $4 per box. The seller then breached the contract, and the buyer brought an action to recover ·damages for the breach. At the trial, the evidence revealed that the buyer could purchase the same type of orange in the open market for $3.50 per box. What damages, if any, do you think the buyer can recover?

6 Plaintiff, who was in the business of renting houses, entered into an agreement with defendant, a contractor, for the construction of a house for rental purposes for the sum of $15,000. Defendant agreed to have the house completed by September 1, 1965. He further agreed that he would pay the sum of $100 per day in liquidated damages for each day of delay in completing the house after September 1, 1965. Plaintiff had hoped to rent the house at $100 per month. Defendant was five days late in completing construction of the house, and plaintiff brought an action to recover the sum of $500 as damages. Do you think he should recover?

14
DISCHARGE OF CONTRACTS

This chapter concludes the discussion of the law of contracts and will be devoted to discharge of contracts by (1) payment, (2) breach, (3) release of the debtor, (4) substituted agreement and alteration, and (5) arbitration.

DISCHARGE BY PAYMENT

The normal method by which a contract is discharged is by performance. A contract may also be discharged by the delivery of a negotiable instrument calling for the payment of money. A negotiable instrument, however, will discharge a contract conditionally unless the person entitled to payment promises to discharge the other person from his existing liability. In the absence of an agreement to the contrary, a check or note is presumed to be accepted conditionally.

Application of Part Payment A debtor may desire to make part payment and the question then arises as to which debt is paid when the account consists of several different debts. The debtor has the right to say which debt he intends to pay, and the creditor is obligated to apply the money as directed by the debtor. If the debtor does not direct the application of the money, the creditor may apply it to any valid claim that he chooses. If neither the debtor nor the creditor makes a specific application of the payment, the law makes it. The courts usually say that the payment will be applied according to the justice of the particular case. This rule is indefinite. The courts have, however, crystallized a few general principles. If the debts are of equal dignity, the payment will be applied to a prior matured debt rather than to a later one; if the creditor holds both secured and unsecured debts, the payment will be applied to the unsecured debt; if the debt is interest bearing, the payment will be applied, first, to the discharge of interest, and, secondly, to the reduction of the principal.

Tender   A tender—an offer—by the debtor to pay the exact sum of money due does not discharge the debt. A rejection of a valid tender, however, works to the disadvantage of the creditor. Any lien that secures the debt is extinguished and interest no longer accrues from the date of the tender. If the creditor brings a suit to collect the debt, the courts attempt to place the debtor in as good a position as he was in at the time of the tender. The costs of court are accordingly assessed against the creditor. A tender to be valid must conform to the terms of the contract as to time, place, and mode of payment. It is not a valid tender, therefore, if it is made before maturity. A creditor is entitled to demand legal tender, but a tender of a check is sufficient unless it is objected to on the ground that it is not legal tender. A tender of a check, therefore, is deemed valid unless the creditor, at the time of the refusal to accept, objects to it because it is not legal tender. It is generally held that a tender is unnecessary if the creditor has clearly indicated that it will be refused. One additional thought: In order to keep the tender valid, the debtor must remain ready, willing, and able to pay the debt at any time.

BREACH OF CONTRACT

A breach of contract occurs when one of the contracting parties fails to perform an immediate duty under the contract. The contract is then broken, and a remedy is available against the party breaking it. The breach may be total or partial. A partial breach does not discharge the injured party from performing his promise, but he may bring an action for damages and recover for the partial breach. A total breach discharges the injured party from the duty of performing his promise; he may rescind the contract or maintain an action for damages for the breach. These rules are merely a reiteration of previously mentioned principles of law. At this point, it is essential, however, to make known two particular kinds of total breach that will operate to discharge the contract: material breach and anticipatory breach.

Material Breach   A contract which is so framed as to show clearly it was intended that the failure to perform a condition precedent would terminate the contract will have that effect. A contract which is so framed, however, that the intention of the parties must be implied from the language used leaves room for speculation. It is impossible to coin any precise definition of the words "material breach" that would not be so narrow in scope as to exclude many of the various factual situations that must obviously be considered in arriving at a speculative decision. Most courts would probably agree, however, that failure to perform a term in a contract so essential to the nature of the contract that the object of the contracting parties could not be accomplished would be a material breach. The courts, in determining the materiality of the breach, nevertheless, attempt to arrive at the most equitable adjustment. If it is unfair and harsh to permit rescission, the courts are inclined to allow damages as a remedy for the breach rather than rescission. If the breach cannot be remedied by the payment of damages, however, or if it is extremely difficult to measure the damages in money, the courts ordinarily allow rescission. In any event, the courts tend to treat a willful failure to perform as a material breach.

A typical illustration of an equitable adjustment is found in sales contracts when the effect produced by the breach is used as a criterion to determine the materiality of the breach. A seller who enters into a contract to sell, deliver, and install an air-conditioning unit and who breaches a part of the contract by failure to install the unit may or may not have committed a material breach. The breach will ordinarily be immaterial if the buyer can employ other mechanics to properly install the unit. In these circumstances the object of the contract can still be carried out, and the partial breach can be measured in damages. The breach will ordinarily be material, however, if the machine can only be installed by specialists in the employ of the seller. In this event the breach would be of such vital importance that the object of the contract would be defeated and the materiality of the breach would undoubtedly justify rescission.

Anticipatory Breach   An announcement by one of the contracting parties, before the time for performance arrives, that he will not perform constitutes an anticipatory breach. The refusal to perform must be definite and positive, but it may be implied from acts as well as expressed by words. It is an anticipatory breach when a seller who has contracted to sell specified goods to a prospective purchaser sells them to another person before the time for performance has arrived. This type of anticipatory breach arises because the contracting party has put it out of his power to perform or, as it is sometimes stated, has "incapacitated" himself.

The breach of a contract by anticipation gives the injured party an election of three remedies: (1) to rescind the contract and recover the value of any performance which has been rendered, (2) to treat the repudiation as an immediate breach and sue at once for any damages which have been sustained, (3) to treat the contract as binding, await the time for performance of the contract, and thereafter bring an action on the contract, for its breach.

The third choice of remedies, however, is qualified to the extent that the anticipatory breach may be retracted at any time before the injured party, in reliance upon the breach, has changed his position to his detriment. The renunciation could be retracted expressly or the seller, in the illustration given above, could retract his renunciation by repurchasing the goods before the time for preformance arrives. Should the prospective purchaser purchase the goods from some other source in the meantime, however, he would so have changed his position to his detriment that the seller could not retract the renunciation.

The principles of law respecting anticipatory breach would not give a creditor the right to recover *immediately* money contracted to be paid in the future. The debtor may clearly state that he will not pay the debt when it falls due, but this would not give the creditor the right to sue immediately upon the renunciation. The creditor would have to wait until the maturity date before instituting an action to collect the debt.

Section 2–610 of the Code pertains to anticipatory repudiation with respect to the sale of goods. The repudiation must be such as will substantially impair the value of the contract. The aggrieved party may then await performance by the repudiating party for a reasonable time, resort to his remedies for breach, or suspend his own performance while he negotiates with or awaits performance by the other party. The official comment explains that the anticipatory repudiation may be (1) an overt communication of intention, (2) an action which renders performance impossible, or (3) an action which demonstrates a clear determination not to continue with performance.

RELEASE OF DEBTOR

Some important classes of contracts may be discharged by operation of law, as those where a debtor is released from a contract for the payment of his debts by statutory enactment. A debtor may be released (1) by a discharge in bankruptcy or (2) by a statute of limitations. These statutes, however, do not declare that the contract is discharged, nor do they have the same effect as the payment of the debt. They permit the debtor to say that the obligation cannot be enforced. It is frequently said that the debt continues but the remedy is barred. To bar the remedy, for all practical purposes, has the effect of discharging the contract. The bankruptcy act and the statute of limitations are similar in that they have the effect of releasing the debtor, but some of the essential characteristics are distinguishable in view of the fact that each statute has for its object a different purpose.

Statute of Limitations   The purpose of the statute of limitations is usually said to be the suppression of stale claims which are difficult to prove because proper evidence is lost by the death or removal of witnesses, or has become obscure in a defective memory through lapse of time. These statutes, nevertheless, have the effect of compelling the exercise of a right within a reasonable time and of remedying the general inconvenience resulting from delay in asserting a legal right.

The statutory time allowed for bringing an action on a debt varies from state to state. In a few states, no distinction is made between the different kinds of debts. In the majority of states, however, the time limit varies from two to eight years on an open account and from five to twenty years on bonds, promissory notes, and written contracts. The individual state's statutes should be examined to determine the exact time limit for bringing an action on any particular type of debt. Section 2–725 of the Code provides that the statutory period of time is four years with respect to the sale of goods.

The statutory period of time begins to run as soon as the cause of action accrues, and, as a general rule, the cause of action accrues the moment the right to start an action comes into existence. It ordinarily would begin to run on a contract when the contract has been breached and on the day after maturity on a promissory note. Some condition or act, such as insanity or infancy, will prevent the statute from running. This is said to "toll" the running of the statute. A voluntary part payment will generally toll the statute. A payment which is not voluntarily made, however, will not toll the running of the statute. [*Nilsson v. Kielman,* p. 177.]

Bankruptcy The concept of bankruptcy necessarily embraces the discharge of an embarrassed debtor from paying his antecedent debts, but the law of bankruptcy operates to satisfy a desire for a remedy to place the property of the bankrupt under the control of the court for equal distribution among his creditors. A discharge in bankruptcy releases the debtor from all his debts which are provable in bankruptcy, and he is thereafter immune from suit on any of the provable claims made against him. The debt may, of course, be revived by a new promise. This subject is treated more exhaustively in Chapter 62, "Bankruptcy." It is mentioned at this point merely to show that bankruptcy is a method whereby a contract for the payment of a debt may be discharged by operation of law.

SUBSTITUTED AGREEMENT AND ALTERATION
Five important methods by which a contract may be discharged by substituted agreement are (1) merger, (2) account stated, (3) material alteration, (4) novation, and (5) release.

Merger A discharge of a contract by merger is accomplished when a contracting party acquires a remedy or accepts a security of a higher nature, in legal estimation, than the one which is discharged. The subject matter must be identical, and the parties must be the same, but the two securities must be different. A judgment recovered in an action for breach of contract discharges by merger the right of action arising because of the breach. Any future attempt to enforce the claim would have to be directed against the judgment and not the discharged contract.

Account Stated An account stated is an agreement between contracting parties who have had previous transactions of a money character that the net balance, after offsetting all credits and debits, is correct. Failure to object within a reasonable time after receipt of the account stated implies an agreement that the net balance is correct and operates to discharge the individual items. A monthly statement of a bank to its depositors is a familiar example of an account stated. The account stated becomes a liquidated debt binding on the parties in the absence of proof of fraud or mistake.

Material Alteration   A material alteration is one which makes the instrument speak a different language, in legal effect, from that which it originally spoke. An intentional material alteration will ordinarily discharge any contract in writing. An alteration by one party, however, does not destroy the innocent party's rights under the contract. The innocent party may elect to be discharged, or he may assert his rights on the original contract.

Novation   A novation is understood to mean a mutual agreement among all parties concerned for the discharge of a valid existing agreement and the creation of a new agreement. The new contract, in and of itself, effects the discharge. It may be accomplished by the substitution of a new obligation for the old obligation, the substitution of a new creditor for the old creditor, or the substitution of a new debtor for the old debtor.

Suppose Brown and Smith enter into a contract by the terms of which Brown agreed to purchase 100 pairs of gloves from Smith at $2.20 a pair. Suppose further that Brown and Smith thereafter enter into a new contract, canceling the old contract, by the terms of which Brown agreed to purchase 200 pairs of gloves at $3.20 a pair. This is a novation by the substitution of a new obligation between the same parties. Suppose Brown, a manufacturer, consigned certain radios to Smith, a local retailer, for the purpose of sale. Suppose further that Brown thereafter transferred his interest in the radios to Jones and that Smith agreed that he held the radios on consignment from Jones. This is a novation of the original contract which vests title to the radios in Jones. Smith thereby becomes liable to Jones, the new creditor. The most frequent form of novation is the substitution of a new debtor in place of the old one, with intent to release the old debtor. The methods of effecting a valid novation are fairly uniform throughout the United States, and in a few states, the methods have been enacted into statute. [*Tannhauser v. Shea*, p. 178.]

Release   A release, at early common law, was a gratuitous waiver of a right of action and was therefore required to be under seal. In a few jurisdictions a release under seal is still effective without consideration, but in the majority of jurisdictions a consideration must be given in order to terminate the obligation. The most common form of release is a written document which contains a recital stating that the obligation is discharged. A discharge of one of several joint obligors, as by a release, discharges also the other joint obligors. Suppose Brown and Jones are jointly liable on a debt for $1,000 to Smith. The contributive share of Brown is $500. Suppose further that Brown pays Smith $500 and procures a release from Smith. Jones is also released, and Smith cannot collect the remaining $500 from Brown and Jones. This rule has been changed by statute in many of the states. In these states, therefore, one joint debtor is permitted to discharge his liability without the other joint debtors being discharged.

A "covenant never to sue" by a creditor is effective as an agreement not to enforce an existing cause of action. If the covenantor should later bring an action on the debt, the sole obligor could plead the covenant as a bar in the action. A covenant never to sue on a joint obligation, however, will not release any of the joint obligors. The creditor, moreover, can sue the covenantee jointly with the other joint debtors. Suppose Smith covenants never to sue Brown in the above illustration but later brings an action against Brown and Jones. Brown could not plead the covenant as a defense. The remedy of Brown, the covenantee, would be to bring an action for damages for breach of the covenant.

ARBITRATION

Arbitration is a method by which differences may be settled voluntarily, the object being to determine disputes and controversies speedily. The formalities, the delay, and the expense of ordinary litigation are thereby avoided. Conceding the desirability of arbitration, however, does not solve the problem. This problem emanates from the common-law rule which holds that a submission to arbitrate is revocable by either party before the award is made. In many states, as well as Congress, arbitration has been the subject of legislation. But this has not settled the law due to variance in terms of the statutes. The statutes do, broadly speaking, ordinarily provide some means of enforcing the award. This means they generally attempt to make agreements to arbitrate existing disputes, as well as future disputes, irrevocable. It should be pointed out, however, that some statutes pertain to written agreements only. It would appear that an oral agreement to arbitrate under this type of statute would still be revocable. This would leave the injured party with the remedy of suing for a breach of the agreement. In view of this unsettled law, a businessman should never attempt to draft an arbitration agreement, nor should a businessman enter into an arbitration agreement without consulting his attorney.

In spite of this unsettled law, it is well settled that arbitration agreements fall into two general classes: first, an agreement known as "a submission agreement," which is an agreement to submit an existing dispute to arbitrators; and second, an agreement known as "an agreement to submit to arbitration," which is an agreement to submit to arbitration some future dispute. The latter type of agreement is usually made in connection with some contract between the parties.

It is also well settled that where parties to a contract enter into an arbitration agreement and an award has been made, the court will not set the award aside in the absence of bad faith or fraud. [*Brennan v. Brennan,* p. 179.]

CASES

Nilsson v. Kielman 17 N.W.2d 918 (S.D. 1945). Action by M. T. Nilsson, plaintiff, against L. T. Kielman, defendant, to recover the balance due on a promissory note.

The defendant executed and delivered to plaintiff a promissory note for $4,000 payable on August 1, 1926. Five payments were indorsed on the notes, but the payments of $1,121 on January 19, 1940, and $74 on February 20, 1943, are the only ones claimed to have been made within six years immediately preceding the commencement of this action on June 25, 1943. These two payments were not payments made voluntarily by defendant for the purpose of reducing the indebtedness, but were the result of the sale of a grocery store from defendant to plaintiff. Plaintiff allowed defendant $1,121 for his equity in the building, and the indorsement of $74 represents an account which plaintiff collected. Plaintiff testified that "these accounts were all to be turned over to me and as I collected them I should credit them on this note." Defendant contended that the six-year period of the statute of limitations bars this action. Plaintiff contended otherwise on the ground that the payments started the running of the statute anew from the date of each payment.

Roberts, Judge: It is the settled law of this state that a part payment to be effectual to interrupt the statute must have been voluntary and must have been made and accepted under circumstances consistent with an intent to pay the balance. The principle on which a part payment operates to take a debt without the statute is that the debtor by the payment intends to acknowledge the continued existence of the debt.

The agreement with reference to the amount of the credit on January 19, 1940, constituted neither a new promise in writing nor a part payment as of that date. It is the fact of voluntary payment made by the debtor and not entry of credit that interrupts the running of the statute. Nor did the collection of the account amounting to $74 give new life to the debt. Plaintiff was authorized to collect the accounts and apply the proceeds to payment of the debt, but this did not have the same effect as if made personally by defendant. There is no vital distinction between such a case and one where money received by the payee of a note from collateral security such as notes and mortgages of third persons pledged by the maker is credited on the principal note. Such payment does not interrupt the running of the statute. [DECISION FOR DEFENDANT]

Tannhauser v. Shea, 295 Pac. 268 (Mont. 1930). Action by Frank J. Tannhauser, plaintiff, against Dennis A. Shea, defendant.

The defendant was driving an automobile belonging to M. J. Walsh Company and because of an accident became involved in litigation. M. J. Walsh employed counsel for the defendant who, for some reason, appeared only for the corporation. A default judgment was entered against the defendant without his knowledge. Thereafter, the plaintiff, the defendant, and Walsh agreed that if defendant would forbear from any effort to have the judgment set aside Walsh would pay the judgment. The judgment was not paid, and plaintiff instituted this action to recover on the judgment.

Galen, Justice The court found:

that the plaintiff herein, the defendant herein, and M. J. Walsh entered into an oral agreement that Walsh, in consideration of the release of the defendant Shea from said judgment, would pay, and did agree to pay, to plaintiff the amount of his judgment against defendant Shea; that Shea, in consideration of his release from said judgment, would not take, and agreed not to take, any steps to have it set aside or to open the default in connection therewith; and that plaintiff, in consideration of the said promise of Walsh to pay said judgment and of the forbearance of said Shea to take steps to have set aside said judgment or to open the default in connection therewith, would accept and did agree to accept, and did accept, the promise of Walsh to pay said judgment, and would relieve, and did relieve, said Shea therefrom; that the defendant executed his part of said agreement, by forbearing to take steps or action in court to open said default or set aside said judgment.

. . . Although the evidence is in direct conflict, there is testimony in support of such findings of fact. "Novation is the substitution of a new obligation for an existing one." It is accomplished in three ways:

1. By the substitution of a new obligation between the same parties, with intent to extinguish the old obligation; 2. By substitution of a new debtor in place of the old one, with intent to release the latter; or, 3. By the substitution of a new creditor in place of the old one, with intent to transfer the rights of the latter to the former. . . . In every novation there are four essential prerequisites: (1) A previous valid obligation; (2) the agreement of all the parties to the new contract; (3) the extinguishment of the old contract; and (4) the validity of the new one. It constitutes a new contractual relation and is based upon a new contract by all parties interested.

. . . A legal duty rested upon the defendant Shea at the time of entering into the agreement with Walsh and Tannhauser to pay the judgment, and by reason of such agreement Shea was released of such obligation, Tannhauser agreeing to accept Walsh in substitution of Shea. It amounted to an agreement to substitute a new debtor (Walsh) in place of the old one (Shea), with intent to release the latter—a "novation" as defined by our statute. [DECISION FOR DEFENDANT]

Brennan v. Brennan, 128 N.E.2d 89 (Ohio 1955). Action by Ralph E. Brennan, plaintiff, against Arthur D. Brennan, defendant. Plaintiff and defendant, who were associated together in The Brennan Company for many years, agreed that plaintiff would sell his shares of stock in the company to defendant. They thereupon entered into an agreement to sell, which among other things, provided that Chandler, Murray & Chilton, certified public accountants, should be the arbitrators. The agreement also gave the accountants instructions with respect to ascertaining the value of the shares of stock. The agreement contained the following provision:

"8. Both buyer and seller agree that the determinations made by the certified public accountants aforesaid shall be final and conclusive and will direct that a copy thereof be furnished to the seller at the same time that the account is delivered to the corporation."

The accountants found the book value of the stock to be $238.19 per share. When defendant received his copy of the accountants' report he turned over his check to cover the amount due for the stock. Plaintiff disagreed with the methods the accountants used in placing the value on the stock and brought an action to recover an amount which he alleged was still due.

Stewart, Judge: We are of the opinion that there is no ambiguity in the contract; that the accountants abided by its terms; and that, since the contract provides that the determination made by the accountants shall be final and conclusive, both plaintiff and defendant are bound by such determination

As was said by Judge Zimmerman in the case of *Campbell et al., Trustees v. Automatic Products & Die Co.,* 123 N.E.2d 401:

"It is the policy of the law to favor and encourage arbitration and every reasonable intendment will be indulged to give effect to such proceedings and to favor the regularity and integrity of the arbitrator's acts."

As far back as 1835, this court, in the case of *Ormsby's Admrs. v. Bakewell & Johnson,* 7 Ohio 99, held that, where arbitrators are substituted by parties, the award of the arbitrators is final and cannot be impeached for error; and that nothing but fraud in the parties or in the arbitrators can be alleged to avoid the award. . . .

It seems to be the universal law that where a matter is submitted by parties to an arbitrator for decision, with an agreement that the arbitrator's decision shall be binding upon the parties, they are bound by such decision provided there is no fraud or bad faith upon the part of the arbitrator and he acts according to the instructions given him. . . .

Since, as we have said, where parties submit a disputed question to a skilled arbitrator, giving him directions as to making the determination entrusted to him, and he without bad faith or fraud, follows those directions, and the parties agree to abide by his decision, neither party can thereafter question that decision simply because some other skilled person might have arrived at a different decision.

We hold that, under the contract between plaintiff and defendant, the accountants, who were the arbitrators whose decision was to be final and conclusive, did follow the directions in the contract and did employ ordinary and usual methods of accounting . . . they acted only in accordance with the instructions given them, and, by their contract with each other, plaintiff and defendant are bound by such determination. [DECISION FOR DEFENDANT]

PROBLEMS

1 Baker sold Abbot a house and lot. An unpaid balance of $21,000 remained unpaid after Abbot paid the closing cost and a part payment. Abbot, prior to paying any of the monthly installments on the unpaid balance, sold the house and lot to Cabot. Cabot promised Abbot that he would pay the balance to Baker, and thereby assumed the indebtedness. Cabot also assured Abbot that the installments would be paid promptly and that Abbot would not have any further liability. None of the installments was paid, and Baker brought an action against Abbot. Abbot claims he has no liability. Decide.

2 Brown borrowed $400 from Smith and promised to repay the loan on July 1, 1962, with interest at the rate of 4 percent per annum. On July 1, 1962, Brown offered the exact amount of the debt, including interest, in legal tender to Smith. This tender was refused by Smith, because he mistakenly thought the sum was several dollars more than the amount offered. (a) Brown contends the debt is discharged. Is this contention correct? (b) If the debt had been secured by a mortgage encumbering an automobile, what effect would the offer made by Brown have on the mortgage?

3 Defendant borrowed $1,000 from plaintiff and promised to repay this loan with 4 percent interest on July 1, 1956. Defendant signed a promissory note for the loan and indorsed twenty shares of stock in the X Corporation and delivered them to plaintiff as security for the note. None of the payments due on the loan was made by defendant. Plaintiff thereupon sold the shares of stock, but realized only $500 from the sale. The statutory period of limitations pertaining to the loan had expired prior to the sale. In an action by plaintiff against the defendant for the unpaid balance, plaintiff alleged that the statute of limitations as a bar to the action had been removed or tolled. Is the plaintiff correct?

4 Brown borrowed $300 from the plaintiff and executed a mortgage encumbering his automobile as security for the loan. Brown thereafter bought merchandise on several occasions from the plaintiff. Brown paid various sums to the plaintiff, but on no occasion did he state which account should be credited with such payments. Plaintiff credited all the payments to the merchandise purchased by Brown. Jones purchased the automobile from Brown, and contends that the payments should have been credited to the earliest unpaid item on the debit side of the account, which was the loan secured by the mortgage on the automobile. Is this contention of Jones correct?

5 Brown and Jones entered into a written agreement by the terms of which Brown agreed to sell and Jones agreed to purchase Whiteacre. They also agreed to close the deal on January 1, 1966. On December 15, 1965, Brown sold Whiteacre to Smith, who knew nothing of the agreement between Brown and Jones. Jones learned from the public records that Brown had sold Whiteacre to Smith. Jones then brought an action against Brown for breach of contract on December 20, 1965. Do you think he will recover?

Part

3

SALES

15
SALES: INTRODUCTION

The basic principles of the law of simple contracts are applicable to the law of sales, but additional special rules have evolved which are peculiar to sales alone. These were developed by the common law over a long period of time and were, for the most part, codified by the Uniform Sales Act. These rules have been revised and modernized by Article 2 of the Uniform Commercial Code. This chapter will be devoted to (1) the nature of sales, (2) some standardized shipping terms, (3) sale on approval and sale or return, (4) the passing of title and good faith purchasers, (5) bulk sales, and (6) the formation of the contract.

NATURE OF SALES
The Code provides that a "contract for sale" of goods includes both a present sale and a contract to sell goods at a future time, and defines a "sale" as consisting in the passing of title from the seller to the buyer for a price.

The Goods Section 2–105 defines goods as "all things which are movable at the time of identification to the contract for sale." The goods, however, must be both existing and identified to the contract before any interest in them may pass to the buyer. "Future goods" are those which are neither existing nor identified, and an attempted present sale of future goods operates as a contract to sell. A part interest in goods, however, may be sold in existing and identified goods. For example, Adams could sell a one-half interest in his automobile to Baker.

The definition of "goods" clearly indicates that Article 2 is intended to deal with things which are identifiable as movables before the contract is performed. The definition specifically includes (1) the unborn young of animals; (2) growing crops, such as fruit, perennial hay, nursery stock, and other seasonal crops; (3) things attached to realty, such as trees, as explained in Chapter 10, "Contracts Required to Be in Writing"; (4) specially manufactured goods; and (5) money, where it is treated as a commodity, such as rare coins. Investment securities, such as certificates of stock, are expressly excluded from Article 2, "Sales."

Fungible Goods   Fungible goods consist of a bulk of units of such equivalent kind that they are, for all practical purposes, indistinguishable. Common examples are grains and liquids. It follows that fungible goods are sold by weight and measure: one hundred bushels of wheat, one hundred gallons of oil. Section 2–105 provides, in effect, that an undivided share in an identified bulk of fungible goods may be sold although the quantity of the bulk may be undetermined. An owner of a part of the bulk may therefore sell any agreed proportion or any quantity agreed upon by number, weight, or measure whereby the buyer becomes an owner in common with the other owners of the bulk. A sale of "one hundred bushels of wheat in a bulk of wheat stored in Elevator No. 10" is a common example of such a sale. If it were later determined that there were 1,000 bushels of wheat stored in Elevator No. 10, the buyer would be regarded as owning a one-tenth undivided share in the wheat. If the wheat is destroyed, the loss falls upon the several owners in proportion to the share owned by each owner.

The Price   Section 2–304 provides that the price may be payable in money, goods, realty, or otherwise. It is clear, however, that the provisions of the Code apply only to those aspects of the transaction which concern personal property. The transfer of realty is specifically left to be governed by local statutes dealing with realty.

STANDARDIZED SHIPPING TERMS

Shipment by carrier contemplates a "shipment" contract or a "destination" contract. In a shipment contract, the seller is required to put the goods in the hands of the carrier; a destination contract requires the seller to deliver the goods to a particular destination. Certain shipping terms, however, have become standardized through mercantile practice which are used in both the shipment and the destination contract. These terms are continued by sections 2–319 and 2–320, but certain areas of uncertainty have been clarified. The most common terms are c.o.d., f.o.b., f.a.s., and c.i.f.

C.O.D. Shipments   The object of the common practice of sending goods marked "c.o.d."—collect on delivery—is to instruct the carrier not to deliver the goods until the purchase price has been paid. The carrier acts for the seller in collecting the purchase price and in returning it to the seller. It is apparent, therefore, that shipping goods c.o.d. merely reserves to the seller control over the possession of the goods until payment.

F.O.B. The delivery term "f.o.b." means "free on board" at a named place. It is a "shipping" contract if the place named is the place of shipment, and a "destination" contract if the place named is the destination. Suppose the seller in San Francisco is under a duty to ship the goods f.o.b. San Francisco to a buyer in New York. The seller is under a duty to comply with the requirements of a shipping contract, which means he must bear the expense and risk of putting the goods into the possession of the carrier. It would be a destination contract, however, if the shipment was to be f.o.b. New York. The seller is then under a duty to comply with the requirements of a destination contract, which means that he is under a duty to transport the goods to New York and make a proper tender of delivery at his own expense and risk. The contract may provide for f.o.b. vessel, car, or other vehicle. The seller then must load the goods aboard the vessel or car in addition to bearing the risks and expenses.

F.A.S. Vessel The term "f.a.s. vessel" means free alongside at a named port. This delivery term means that the seller must bear the risk and expense in delivering the goods alongside the vessel in the usual manner in that port or on a dock selected by the buyer. The seller is also under a duty to obtain a receipt for the goods from the carrier, which will give rise to a duty on the part of the carrier to issue a bill of lading.

C.I.F. Shipping goods c.i.f.—cost, insurance, and freight—means that the contract stipulates a lump sum payable by the buyer which covers the cost of the goods, insurance, and freight to the destination point. The term "c. & f." or "c.f." means that the price includes "cost and freight" to the destination. The c. & f. symbol is occasionally written c.a.f. The "a" is intended to be construed as the word "and," but this is a dangerous thing to do. In some countries, such as France, it is the custom to construe the "a" as meaning insurance. If insurance is intended, the abbreviation "i" should be used.

Section 2–320 defines the duties of the seller in a c.i.f. contract in detail. These duties may be summarized: The seller is under a duty to deliver the goods to the carrier and obtain a negotiable bill of lading which will enable the buyer to sell the goods while they are still in transit if he desires to do so. The seller is under a duty to pay the freight, or obtain credit from the carrier. The seller is under a duty to obtain insurance to cover the goods covered by the bill of lading. This insurance must be the usual or customary insurance at the point of shipment, including war insurance. The tender duty of the seller may be explained as follows: The seller will attach the freight receipt, invoice, insurance policy, and a draft for the lump-sum price consisting of the cost of the goods, insurance, and freight to the bill of lading. These documents should be forwarded to the buyer with diligence so that the buyer may resell the goods, claim them from the carrier, or, in case of loss or damage, file a claim for indemnity with the insurance company. These documents will ordinarily be forwarded through bank collection channels, and, unless it is agreed otherwise, the buyer is under a duty to pay for the goods when the documents are tendered prior to an examination of the goods. A c.i.f. contract, however, is not a destination contract; it is a shipment contract. This means that the risk of loss passes to the buyer when the seller has performed his duties at the point of shipment.

SALE ON APPROVAL OR RETURN

Consignment contracts have been a fruitful source of much confusion. Such contracts have been called "a sale," have been said to be "a security," and have been treated as "an agency" or "a bailment." Sections 2–326 and 2–327 make a bold attempt to solve this dilemma.

Sale on Approval A transaction is a sale on approval where the goods are delivered to the buyer primarily for use with the understanding that the buyer may return the goods even though they conform to the contract. The objective is to give the ultimate consumer an opportunity to test the goods. The title and risk of loss remain with the seller, and the goods are free of claims of creditors of the buyer until there is an acceptance. The buyer may expressly or impliedly accept the goods. Acceptance will result from acts, such as encumbering the goods by means of a mortgage; selling the goods to a third person; treating the goods in any manner as his own; or a failure to notify the seller of a rejection within a reasonable time or at the end of the time period—say seven days—if such a time period is a part of the contract.

A use of the goods is not an acceptance, however, provided such use is consistent with the purpose of the trial. An acceptance of a part of the goods is an acceptance of all of the goods if they conform to the contract. Good faith is required of the buyer in rejecting the goods, and the expenses and risks of the return must be borne by the seller when the buyer rejects in good faith. [*Lane Farm Supply, Inc. v. Crosby*, p. 193.]

Sale or Return A transaction is a sale or return where the goods are delivered to the buyer primarily for a resale. The goods, even though they conform to the contract, may be returned to the seller if there is no resale. If there is no resale, it is understood by the parties that the buyer may return all or any commercial unit of the goods which is substantially in the original condition, provided the buyer acts reasonably. The expenses and risk of loss are on the buyer if the goods are returned, and the risk of loss is on the buyer while the goods are in his possession.

One of the troublesome features of a sale or return is this: The creditors of the buyer may reach the goods to satisfy pre-existing debts while the goods are in the possession of the buyer. The Code provides that the creditors of the buyer may treat the arrangement as being a sale or return when words such as "on consignment" or "on memorandum" are used. Suppose The X Company, the consignor, delivers goods to Brown, the consignee, on a sale or return transaction. How can The X Company perfect its interest and prevent the goods from becoming subject to the claims of creditors of Brown? The X Company could comply with (1) the filing requirements of the state statute with respect to secured transactions or (2) an applicable law providing for a consignor's interest to be evidenced by posting a sign. If The X Company fails to perform either of these methods of perfection, the goods are subject to the claims of creditors unless it can be established that Brown completely identifies the name of his business with that of The X Company, or that Brown is generally known by creditors to be substantially engaged in selling the goods of others. [*General Electric Co. v. Pettingell Supply Co.*, p. 194.]

TITLE AND GOOD FAITH PURCHASERS

Passing of Title The passing of title from the seller to the buyer is relatively unimportant in solving problems in the sale of goods. The location of title, however, is important in some noncommercial transactions; for example, the probate of an estate and for purposes of taxation. The Code, therefore, establishes rules for the passing of title in these and other instances.

Title to the goods passes from the seller to the buyer in any manner and on any condition explicitly agreed on by the parties. Section 2–401, however, provides rules for the passing of title if the parties have not entered into such an agreement. The goods must first be identified to the contract, and section 2–501 provides that identification occurs when the goods are shipped, marked, or otherwise designated by the seller as the goods to which the contract refers. But assuming that the goods have been identified to the contract, the location of title depends upon whether there is or is not to be a physical delivery of the goods and whether the buyer retains or rejects the goods.

(1) *Physical Delivery of the Goods* The title passes to the buyer at the time and place at which the seller completes his performance. Delivery of the goods may be accomplished by either a "shipment" contract or a "destination" contract if the seller is required to send the goods to the buyer. Title passes at the time and place of shipment in a shipment contract and on tender of delivery at destination in a destination contract.

(2) *Without Moving the Goods* The time when title passes without moving the goods depends on whether the seller is required to deliver a document of title. Title passes when the seller delivers the document if the seller is required to deliver a document. Title passes at the time and place of contracting if the seller is not required to deliver a document.

(3) *Revesting of Title* Title revests in the seller when the buyer rejects or refuses to accept the goods. This is true irrespective of whether such rejection is or is not justified.

Good Faith Purchasers   It has been a well-recognized rule of property law for a long time that one who has no title at all can transfer no title to a good faith purchaser for value. The Code likewise recognizes that if the title of the seller is void he can pass no title to a purchaser. Section 2–403 provides that a purchaser may acquire "all title which his transferor had or had power to transfer."

Voidable Title   A good faith purchaser for value obtains a good title from a seller who had a voidable title, which had not been avoided at the time of the sale. Assume that the buyer purchases a television set from the seller under such circumstances that the seller had a right to rescind the sale. This could be the situation where the buyer gave a worthless check in payment or misrepresented his identity. The seller had a right to rescind. Suppose, however, that the buyer sells and delivers the set to Jones, an innocent purchaser for value before the seller had an opportunity to rescind. The Code makes it clear that Jones obtains a valid title which cuts off the right of reclamation by the seller.

Let us pursue the above illustration one step further. Suppose the buyer had no title at all. This could be the situation if he obtained possession of the television set by theft. Jones would obtain no title. The seller, therefore, would be able to recover the television set from Jones. [*Avis Rent-A-Car System v. Harrison Motor Co.*, p. 195.]

Entrusting Goods to a Merchant   The innocent purchaser for value has a superior right when he purchases from a merchant as opposed to one who entrusted merchandise to the merchant. Section 2–403 provides in effect that any merchant who is entrusted with goods of the kind which he sells is clothed with the power to transfer all of the rights of the entruster-owner to a buyer in the ordinary course of business. This appears self-explanatory, but further explanation might be helpful.

(1)   *Buyer in the Ordinary Course of Business*   A buyer in the ordinary course of business is one who buys in ordinary course from a person in the business of selling goods of that kind and who buys in good faith and without knowledge that the sale to him is in violation of the ownership rights or security interest of a third person in the goods. The Code specifically provides that this does not apply to a pawnbroker. The purchase, however, may be for cash or exchange of property, or on secured or unsecured credit. It includes goods or documents received under a pre-existing contract for sale. It does not, however, include a transfer in bulk; nor does it include a security for a money debt, in part or for all the debt. One final thought should be mentioned: One who buys from a merchant whose inventory is being financed is a buyer in the ordinary course of business. This is true even though he knows of a security interest which is perfected. The buyer is not protected, however, if he knows the sale is in violation of the secured rights of the lender.

(2)   *Entrusting*   "Entrusting" is defined by section 2–402 as any delivery and any acquiescence in retention or possession regardless of any condition expressed by the parties and regardless of whether such is larcenous under the

criminal law of the state. Suppose Brown takes his watch to a jeweler for repair. Suppose further that the jeweler ordinarily sells new and used watches. Suppose still further that Smith, an innocent purchaser in the ordinary course of business, purchases the watch. Smith would obtain a valid title. The same would be true if Brown purchased a watch and left it with the jeweler for a short time. If the jeweler sold the watch, the purchaser would obtain a valid title.

(3) ***Retention of Possession and the Protection of Creditors***   Section 2–402 provides that a creditor of the seller may treat a sale as void if a retention of the goods is fraudulent as against creditors. The Code provides, however, that it is not fraudulent for a merchant-seller to retain possession of the goods in good faith for a commercially reasonable time. The interest of the buyer in the goods is protected against claims of creditors of the merchant for a reasonable time. If Brown purchased a watch and left it with the jeweler for a commercially reasonable time, creditors of the jeweler could not attach the watch. The sale, however, must be in good faith and in the current course of trade and not in satisfaction of a pre-existing debt.

A final word about fraudulent retention of goods. Some states follow the rule that retention of possession by the seller is conclusively fraudulent. This rule has been changed by the Code: A retention of possession in good faith and in the current course of trade by a merchant-seller for a commercially reasonable time is not fraudulent. Other states treat a retention of goods as "presumptively" fraudulent. This rule has not been changed by the Code.

BULK SALES

The last decade of the nineteenth century saw much commercial fraud in the United States. A common way in which dishonest merchants defrauded their unsecured creditors was by selling inventory in bulk. The seller would then squander the proceeds and frequently disappear. A wave of indignation swept across the nation which resulted in the passage of bulk sales statutes. These statutes differed greatly. They did, however, condition the validity of sales not in the ordinary course of business. It was required that prompt and sufficient notice of the transfer be given to creditors. Article 6 of the Code recognizes that unsecured creditors of the transferor have rights which are worthy of protection. The Code, therefore, makes a serious attempt to add uniformity to bulk sales laws and to restrict the coverage to those transactions which are susceptible to the peculiar risks involved.

Bulk Transfer Defined   A bulk transfer is any transfer in bulk which is not made in the ordinary course of business but which consists of a *major part* of the materials, supplies, merchandise, or other inventory. A transfer of a *substantial* part of the equipment is also a bulk sale provided it is made in connection with a bulk transfer of inventory. A "major part" and a "substantial part" are not subject to precise definition. It appears that "major" means more than 50 percent while "substantial" may very well mean less than 50 percent. A "major part" refers to value and not to volume, weight, or measure. A sale of 20 out of a total of 120 items having a value of $40,000 would be a bulk transfer, but a sale of 100 items with a value of $500 would not be a transfer in bulk.

Businesses Subject to Article 6   The businesses that are within the coverage of the bulk sales law are those "whose principal business is the sale of merchandise from stock, including those who manufacture what they sell." This definition excludes those who sell services rather than merchandise, such as barbers, doctors, lawyers, accountants, and restaurateurs. Businesses such as insurance, hotels, railroads, and others that are not selling merchandise from stock are likewise excluded. A manufacturer who sells from stock, such as a small bakery, is subject to this law. A manufacturer of component parts for electronic equipment on special order, however, is excluded. Some other specific exclusions are security transactions, such as bulk mortgages, general assignments for the benefit of all creditors of the transferor; transfers in settlement of liens; sales by fiduciaries such as executors and administrators; and a transfer to a new business to take over and continue the business with proper notice along with the assumption of the old debts.

Requirements to Validate a Bulk Sale   A bulk transfer is valid provided the following procedure is observed:

(1) The transferee must require the transferor to prepare and furnish a list sworn to by the transferor of his existing creditors. The responsibility for the accuracy and completeness of the list rests on the transferor unless the transferee is shown to have had knowledge of the inaccuracy or incompleteness. An erroneous omission will not invalidate the list.

(2) The parties must prepare a schedule of the property which is sufficiently definite to identify the property.

(3) The transferee must file a list of the creditors and a schedule of the property with a designated state official.

(4) The transferee must give notice in person, or by registered or certified mail, of the proposed sale to all the creditors listed and to all those who assert claims against the transferor. The notice must be given at least ten days prior to the transfer of the property or payment of the consideration, whichever is to occur first.

(5) In auction sales, the burden with respect to filing the list of creditors and giving notice of the proposed sale is on the auctioneer.

Rights of Transferees   A transfer is ineffective against any creditor of the transferor if the parties do not comply with the procedure stated above. A purchaser from the transferee, however, obtains a valid title despite the noncompliance if he pays value in good faith and without notice of the defect.

Rights of Creditors Creditors will ordinarily be unable to prevent the transfer provided the procedure stated above is properly observed. The creditors, as a general rule, must look to the proceeds of the transfer.

FORMATION OF THE CONTRACT

The sale or contract to sell need take no special form. It may be in writing; it may be oral; it may be partly in writing and partly oral; or it may be inferred from the conduct of the parties. The rules pertaining to the formation of the sales contract were discussed in Part 2, "Contracts." The more important rules may be summarized:

Contracts for the sale of goods that are required to be in writing and the alternative methods of satisfying the Statute of Frauds were discussed in Chapter 10. It will be remembered that the sale or the contract to sell any goods for a price of $500 or more is required to be in writing to be enforceable. They may, however, be enforceable by acceptance and receipt of a portion of the goods or by part payment. Goods to be specially manufactured and not suitable for sale to others are held to be without the Statute of Frauds.

Chapter 5, "Agreement," discussed requirement and output contracts, auction sales, the firm offer, additional terms in acceptance or confirmation of the contract, acceptance of ambiguous offers, and acceptance of an offer for a unilateral contract. Chapter 6, "Consideration," explained that modification, rescission, and waiver need no new consideration to be binding. Chapter 9, "Reality of Consent," explained that an "unconscionable" contract will not be enforced, and Chapter 4, "Introduction to Contracts," explained the statute of limitations. [*Rufo v. Bastian-Blessing Co.*, p. 195.]

CASES

Lane Farm Supply, Inc. v. Crosby, 243 N.Y.S.2d (1963). Action by the Lane Farm Supply, Inc., plaintiff, against Everett Crosby, defendant, to recover the purchase price of a tractor and plow.

Grady, Justice: The tractor and plow were sold to Crosby on trial and approval on November 7, 1960, for the agreed price of $3,000. Crosby used the tractor and plow for a period of fifty-three days, plowing and skidding logs covering land of approximately sixty acres (four fields) and [they] were used approximately one hundred and ten hours.

Mr. Crosby, upon being questioned by an agent of the seller about payment for the tractor and plow, stated that he did not have any money and that he had a big deal pending and when that broke, he would be able to pay for the tractor and plow. The tractor was burned in a barn on the defendant's property on January 1, 1961.

Section 100 of the Personal Property Law provides:

2. When goods are delivered to the buyer on approval or trial or on satisfaction, or other similar terms, the property therein passes to the buyer: (a) When he signifies his approval or acceptance to the seller or does any other act adopting the transaction; (b) If he does not signify his approval or acceptance to the seller, but retains the goods without giving notice of rejection, then if a time has been fixed for the return of the goods, on the expiration of such time, and, if no time has been fixed, on the expiration of a reasonable time. What is a reasonable time is a question of fact.

Certainly, on the evidence presented, the title to the tractor and plow passed to the defendant, as he did not reject the sale and used the articles longer than a reasonable time. [DECISION FOR PLAINTIFF]

General Electric Co. v. Pettingell Supply Co., 199 N.E.2d 326 (Mass. 1964). Action by General Electric Company, plaintiff, against Pettingell Supply Company and David S. Miller, defendants.

Pettingell was a wholesaler buying and selling electrical, hardware, and housewares merchandise, but had received certain large lamps from plaintiff on consignment as "agent to sell or distribute" the lamps. Pettingell could sell directly to certain customers who bought for their own use or who bought in small volume for resale. Some of the lamps were in the possession of David S. Miller, assignee for the benefit of creditors of Pettingell, and plaintiff replevied these lamps. The lower court ruled that plaintiff must return the lamps, and plaintiff appealed. The parties stipulated that if the decision on appeal was in favor of defendants, David S. Miller might have judgment against plaintiff in the sum of $5,727 with interest at 6 percent a year from the date of replevin and costs, and no further suit would be brought against Pettingell for the same cause of action.

Whittemore, Justice: The plaintiff contends that section 2–326 is applicable only to cases where the relationship between manufacturer and dealer is that of seller and buyer and that inasmuch as the contract in suit establishes only a principal-agent relationship between the plaintiff and Pettingell no part of section 2–326 is applicable.

We disagree with the contention that section 2–326(3) is inapplicable. That subsection is by its terms concerned with certain transactions which, although they may not be sales under the definition of section 2–106(1), are nonetheless "deemed to be on sale or return" "with respect to claims of creditors of the person conducting the business. . . ." The subsection specifically states that it is applicable even though the "agreement purports to reserve title to the person making delivery until payment on resale or uses such words as 'on consignment' or 'on memorandum.'" The agreement between plaintiff and Pettingell binds the former "to maintain on consignment in the custody of the agent, to be disposed of as herein provided, a stock of said General Electric large lamps."

The plaintiff relies on the wording of the second sentence of section 2–326(3) which states that the subsection applies even though there is a reservation of title "to the person making delivery until payment or *resale*" (emphasis supplied). From this the plaintiff argues that the subsection applies only where the manufacturer has sold the goods to the dealer because otherwise there could be no "resale."

Since Pettingell had authority to sell the lamps they were "delivered" to Pettingell "for sale." Section 2–326(1)(b) does not, we think, require a different result. That section defines a "sale or return" as a sale where "goods are delivered primarily for resale." [DECISION FOR DEFENDANTS]

Avis Rent-A-Car System, Inc. v. Harrison Motor Co., Inc., 151 So. 2d 855 (Fla. 1963). Action by Avis Rent-A-Car System, Inc., plaintiff, against Harrison Motor Company, defendant, to replevy a 1959 Ford automobile.

The plaintiff, on or about July 1, 1959, purchased and took title to the automobile in Vermont, and subsequently took it to Plattsburgh, New York, to be used in the regular course of its car rental business. The automobile was rented on May 10, 1960, to Pasco Ferrucci for one day under a written rental agreement. When the time provided for return of the automobile had elapsed and the plaintiff realized that the car was stolen, it notified the New York State Police, the F.B.I., and the Plattsburgh Police. The automobile was transported to Florida, where, in November, 1960, an application for a Florida certificate of title was submitted to the Florida Motor Vehicle Commissioner by Ferrucci. He also submitted the Vermont title registration which had been altered so that plaintiff's name was removed and Ferrucci's name was inserted in its place. As a result of the fraudulent alteration, the state of Florida issued a certificate of title to Ferrucci. While the transfer was pending, he traded the car to the defendant, after defendant was assured by the Motor Vehicle Commissioner that Ferrucci had title to the car. The defendant maintained that it was a bona fide purchaser for value, without notice of the rights of the plaintiff, if any.

Shannon, Chief Judge: Defendant takes the position that it had no notice that the vehicle was stolen, nor did it realize that the Vermont title registration had been altered. In fact, it had relied upon the agent of the Motor Vehicle Commissioner to the effect that Ferrucci had submitted a valid Vermont title registration. Notwithstanding, the fact still remains that Ferrucci had altered or forged the title registration and therefore had not acquired valid title; not having such, he could not, by fraudulent acts, pass a title which he himself did not have. To secure the certificate under which this automobile was transferred in Florida, Ferrucci had to violate the law. Keeping in mind that the plaintiff had no knowledge of any of the acts of Ferrucci, it would have to be the victim of a forgery, and in the next place, a victim of Ferrucci's obtaining title by false or fraudulent procedures.

The laws of Vermont and of New York require the automobile to have the title certificate with it. The automobile was leased out to Ferrucci and Ferrucci then did an unlawful act. The plaintiff had no knowledge of anything that would put it on notice that Ferrucci would commit a crime and likewise had no knowledge that in committing the crime he would take the car to Florida. Having no knowledge of any of the facts in this case, it cannot be estopped in seeking the return of its car. [DECISION FOR PLAINTIFF]

Rufo v. Bastian-Blessing Co., 207 A.2d 823 (Pa. 1965). Action by Clementino Rufo, et al., plaintiffs, against The Bastian-Blessing Company, defendant. During

March of 1956, plaintiff, Clementino Rufo, purchased a refilled, portable cylinder of liquefied gas for use in a torch in connection with his work. On December 8, 1957, gas escaped from the valve and caught fire, causing personal and property damage to plaintiffs, who, on July 12, 1960, brought an action for breach of warranty against defendant, the manufacturer of the valve, to recover damages for the injuries so sustained. The lower court held that the complaint filed on July 12, 1960, showed on its face that the action was barred by the statute of limitations, and this holding was affirmed by the appellate court.

Cohen, Justice: The complaint was properly dismissed because it is apparent on its face that it was originally filed beyond the period permitted by the applicable statute of limitations. The Code provides:

An action for breach of any contract for sale must be commenced within four years after the cause of action has accrued. . . . A cause of action accrues when the breach occurs regardless of the aggrieved party's lack of knowledge of the breach. A breach of warranty occurs when tender of delivery is made, except that where a warranty explicitly extends to future performance of the goods and discovery of the breach must await the time of such performance the cause of action accrues when the breach is or should have been discovered.

Notwithstanding the fact that plaintiffs are claiming personal injuries, the suit is based upon warranties; therefore, it must be brought within four years of the breach of warranty, as the statute provides, regardless of the time of the accident directly giving rise to the damages claimed. Applying the statute, the latest time that the alleged breach of implied warranty could have occurred and, therefore, the latest time that the cause could have accrued was when Rufo took delivery of the allegedly defective cylinder in March of 1956. [DECISION FOR DEFENDANT]

PROBLEMS

1 Plaintiff was a merchant dealing in watches, diamonds, and other jewelry in the city of Hot Springs, Arkansas. Defendant was a retailer engaged in the same business in Pine Bluff, Arkansas. Plaintiff delivered certain diamond rings valued at $372 to defendant "with the agreement and understanding that if defendant was pleased with the diamonds, she should keep them and account to the plaintiff at the above value, and if not pleased would, within a reasonable time, return them to plaintiff at said city of Hot Springs." Defendant did not return the rings, which were lost without any fault or negligence on her part. Must the plaintiff or the defendant bear the loss?

2 Mixon owned all of the wheat which was stored in a specific elevator, but the quantity was undetermined. He sold 1,000 bushels to Mason, who paid the purchase price in cash. The specific 1,000 bushels, however, were not placed in containers or set aside or marked in any manner. It was agreed that Mason would take delivery of his wheat within a day or two when his trucks became available for use. The subject of a warehouse receipt was not discussed. During the following night, this particular elevator was completely destroyed by fire without the fault of anyone concerned. Mason contended that Mixon was under a duty to deliver wheat from another of the many elevators owned by Mixon. Is this contention of Mason correct?

3 Brown visited the store of plaintiff, and plaintiff knew that Brown and his wife were interested in a refrigerator. The plaintiff asked Brown if he had decided to purchase a refrigerator, to which Brown replied, "No, we haven't reached a point where we will decide on it." Plaintiff then suggested sending one out on approval, to which Brown replied, "If you want to take a chance and send it out on approval with the understanding I don't have to purchase it unless I want it, all right." The plaintiff agreed, and the refrigerator was delivered to Brown. A short time thereafter Brown sold and delivered the refrigerator to defendant. Should plaintiff recover in an action against the defendant for possession of the refrigerator?

4 Plaintiff, an automobile dealer, sold an automobile to Brown, who gave plaintiff a check for $1,500 in payment of the purchase price. Brown then sold the automobile to defendant for the sum of $1,455. The check which Brown gave plaintiff in payment of the automobile was worthless, and plaintiff brought an action against defendant to replevy the car. The action is founded on the contention that, since Brown obtained the car from plaintiff on the false representation that the check was good, when in fact it was worthless, plaintiff did not part with title and can replevy the automobile. Decide.

5 Plaintiff purchased a typewriter from the Office Equipment Company and paid cash for it. The typewriter would not operate properly, and plaintiff returned the typewriter to the company for repairs. Plaintiff went to the repair department of the company the next day to get his typewriter and was told by the manager that a salesman thought the typewriter was a part of the inventory and had sold it to Dunn. The manager offered plaintiff another typewriter to replace the one that had been sold, but it was of a different model and not suitable for the needs of plaintiff. Can plaintiff recover the typewriter from Dunn?

6 Defendant, a jeweler, had in stock as his entire inventory 100 diamonds valued at $100,000 and 500 sapphire stones valued at $30,000. Defendant sold the 100 diamonds to another jeweler for $100,000 in cash. The creditors of defendant contend that the sale of the diamonds is ineffective because defendant did not comply with the bulk sales statute. Do you agree with this contention?

16

SALES: WARRANTIES

A warranty, as the word is used here, is some undertaking of the seller with respect to the goods he sells. The seller may never use the word "warranty" but nevertheless find himself answerable in damages to the buyer for a breach of warranty. But this has not always been the law. The courts, in the early history of the law of sales, rigidly applied the maxim caveat emptor—let the buyer beware. The duty, therefore, was imposed on the buyer to examine the article he was buying and act on his own judgment and at his own risk. The emphasis today is placed on the maxim caveat venditor—let the seller beware. This does not mean that the seller is liable merely because the buyer is disappointed with his bargain. It does mean the seller is liable for his express warranties and the warranties implied by law. It is well to keep in mind, however, that a warranty is a part of the contract. It now remains to discuss (1) the express warranties, (2) the implied warranties of quality, (3) the warranty of title and infringement, and (4) the exclusion or modification of warranties.

EXPRESS WARRANTIES

Affirmation or Promise An express warranty need not be in any special form nor is it necessary to use the word "warranty" or any word of similar import; any affirmation of fact or any promise by the seller relating to the goods is an express warranty if the natural tendency of such affirmation or promise is to induce the buyer to purchase the goods. Statements, however, which are the opinion or the belief only of the seller, commonly referred to as "sales talk" or "puffing," are permissible in the law of sales. The legal distinction between sales talk and a warranty is often said to be the distinction between a statement of opinion and a statement of fact. It is to be realized, however, that any false statement in regard to the basis of value, such as the book value of the goods or the past income of the property, may amount to a false representation. The distinction between a statement of opinion and a statement of fact and those statements which, amounting to false representations with intent to defraud, give rise to a remedy in tort for fraud and deceit, were discussed in Chapter 9, "Reality of Consent."

It will be remembered that statements of opinion include words of commendation or praise, such as "valuable" or "the best product on the market," which are in their nature dependent on individual opinion, but statements of fact generally include words that are capable of proof or disproof, such as "this dress is 100 percent wool." It should be pointed out that if the actual information of the buyer is by him known to be equal or superior to that of the seller, reliance on the statement of the seller is not justified. The factual situations of the particular case are decisive as to whether or not the seller has made an express warranty because, in the final analysis, it is the natural consequence of what the seller says and the reliance thereon of the buyer that are important in determining whether or not the seller has made an express warranty.

Sale by Sample, Model, or Description Section 2–313 provides that an express warranty may be created in a sale by sample, model, or description. A sale by sample is created when the seller actually draws a sample from the bulk of the goods; a sale by model is created when the seller offers a model for inspection when the goods are not readily available. The whole of the goods, however, must conform to the sample or model. A sale by description may be made by patent name, trade name, blueprints, or the like. The mere exhibition of a sample or model or the use of trade names does not of itself create a warranty. Any of these factors, however, will create an express warranty if made a part of the basis of the bargain. If the warranty is made after the sale—as where the buyer is taking delivery—the warranty need not be supported by consideration since it is a modification. Irrespective of the time when the warranty is made, it is always a question of fact whether the language, samples, or models are to be regarded as a part of the contract. If the facts of the particular case do not reveal an express warranty, it may be that recovery will be allowed on an implied warranty. [*Standard Stevedoring Co. v. Jaffe*, p. 204.]

IMPLIED WARRANTIES
The two implied warranties of quality are the warranties of merchantability and fitness for a particular purpose. These warranties, however, are not necessarily

the only implied warranties. Other implied warranties may arise from a course of dealing or usage of trade. An implied warranty from usage of trade could arise, for example, if there was an obligation on the part of the seller to furnish pedigree papers in the sale of a pedigreed dog. These warranties are implied rather than express and may be excluded.

Warranty of Merchantability   Section 2–314, which is restricted to merchants, defines the term "merchantability" in detail. The term, broadly stated, means that the goods are of fair average quality or that they will pass in the trade without objection. The Code expressly provides that the merchant-seller impliedly warrants that the goods are fit for the ordinary purpose for which they are used. This provision differs from the "fitness for particular purpose" warranty. For example, shoes are generally used for the purpose of walking upon ordinary ground. A seller, however, may or may not know that a particular pair was selected to be used for climbing mountains. The seller also warrants that the goods are adequately contained, packaged, and labeled if the nature of the goods and of the transaction require a certain type of container, package, or label and that the goods conform to the representations made on the label or container. As for the requirement that the container be adequate, suppose Brown purchases fruit juice contained in a glass bottle and is injured from drinking the juice because of chipped glass. He could recover for breach of warranty of merchantability even though the fruit juice itself is wholesome. It is expressly provided that the serving of food or drink to be consumed on the premises or elsewhere is a sale. The warranty of merchantability, therefore, includes the serving of food or drink. It is generally held, however, that such things as an occasional clam shell in clam chowder are not foreign to the product and are to be expected. [*Webster v. Blue Ship Tea Room*, p. 205.]

Warranty of Fitness for Particular Purpose   This warranty—commonly referred to as a warranty of suitability—is a warranty that the goods will prove fit for the purpose for which they are purchased. This warranty will be implied whether the seller is or is not a merchant if the buyer (1) expressly or impliedly makes known to the seller the particular purpose for which the goods are wanted and (2) relies upon the skill and judgment of the seller in the selection of the goods. Both of these requirements are essential. The first element may be satisfied where the seller is apprised of the purpose of the buyer from the very nature of the transaction. The seller obviously knows that a fur coat is bought to be worn as a garment. The buyer, however, must make a particular purpose known to the seller if a special or unusual purpose is intended. A buyer who wants to purchase a pair of shoes for the particular purpose of climbing mountains, therefore, must make that purpose known to the seller. The sale of goods today is accomplished to a great extent by the use of trade names. Designation of an article by its trade name, however, is only one of the facts to be considered. The implied warranty of fitness applies, therefore, where the seller recommends an article having a trade name as being suitable for the particular purpose stated by the buyer. But it must appear that the buyer did not order the article by its trade name. The buyer who insists on a particular brand or trade name would not be relying on the skill and judgment of the seller. The buyer would be relying on the reputation of the branded article rather than upon the judgment of the seller. The test, whether the goods are purchased by trade name or otherwise, is whether or not the necessary facts are proved by showing knowledge of the seller of the particular purpose of the buyer and the required reliance by the buyer on the superior skill and judgment of the seller. [*Catania v. Brown*, p. 206.]

WARRANTY OF TITLE AND INFRINGEMENT

The rules pertaining to warranties of title and infringement are found in section 2–312, and are not designated as either express or implied warranties. This means that these warranties are not within the "as is" exclusion of warranties mentioned below.

Warranty of Title   The warranty of title is not applicable to a person who sells not in his own right as owner but in the right of another. A sheriff, auctioneer, pledgee, mortgagee, executor, administrator, or any other person professing to sell property by virtue of authority in fact or in law does not warrant the title. All other sellers of goods warrant that the title conveyed shall be good and that the goods are free from any security interest or other lien or encumbrance. The warranty is applicable whether the seller is in or out of possession of the goods. The buyer, therefore, is protected against encumbrances of which he has no actual knowledge. The buyer is also assured that the seller is the title owner of the goods and that he will not be disturbed in his possession by any person having a superior or paramount title. It is to be remembered that a thief has no title, and a purchaser from a thief who later sells the stolen property likewise has no title. The breach of warranty of good title occurs when the tender of delivery is made and not when the possession is disturbed. This is important when it is remembered that the statute of limitations begins to run when a breach occurs. Suppose the seller sells an automobile to the buyer and the buyer is disturbed in his possession ten years after the date of the sale. An action against the seller would be barred by the four-year period of the statute of limitations, and the disturbing claim will also ordinarily be barred. Probably of more importance to the buyer, however, is the fact that he is assured that he will have recourse against the seller if the statutory period has not expired.

Warranty of Infringement   The warranty against infringement applies to all sellers who are merchants and means that the seller is under a duty to protect the buyer against any claim of infringement of a patent or trade-mark that might cloud his title. The infringement warranty, however, does not apply when the buyer orders goods to be assembled or manufactured by the seller to the specifications of the buyer. In these circumstances, the buyer is under an obligation to indemnify the seller for any loss suffered by the infringement.

EXCLUSION OF WARRANTIES

The parties may desire some particular kind of warranty or they may desire to eliminate the warranties provided for by the Code. This they may generally do. But it should be pointed out that if the parties desire any particular warranty or desire to exclude warranties, language should be used which clearly expresses their intention.

Express Warranty   An express warranty may be excluded, and an express warranty and a disclaimer will be construed as consistent with each other wherever reasonable. An agreement containing an express warranty and a clause disclaiming the express warranty, however, contains inconsistent clauses. Suppose the subject matter of the sales contract is "Grandmother's Brand Pork and Beans," and the contract includes a clause which disclaims "all express warranties." This language contains an express warranty that the goods will conform to the description and a clause disclaiming the express warranty. The seller should not be able to perform by delivering another brand of pork and beans. A decision must be made, therefore, as to which clause will predominate. Section 2–316 settles the inconsistency by providing that the warranty language will prevail over the disclaimer when the two cannot be reconciled. The purpose of this provision is to protect the buyer from unexpected language of disclaimer. The seller who wishes to disclaim an express warranty, therefore, should use language of disclaimer so specific that the buyer is apprised that he is assuming the risk that the goods may not conform to the description, sample, or model.

In explaining an exclusion or modification or an express warranty, it seems necessary to recall that the parol-evidence rule provides that the terms of a written agreement may not be contradicted by evidence of a prior or contemporaneous oral agreement. Section 2–202, however, provides that the written agreement may be supplemented or explained by a course of dealing or usage of trade or by evidence of additional consistent terms unless the court finds that the writing was intended by both parties as a complete statement of all the terms. A disclaimer, therefore, would not be effective as against oral express warranties unless it contained a clause stating that the contract contained all the terms agreed upon. This is sometimes referred to as an "entirety clause," which may not be contradicted by evidence of a prior or contemporaneous oral agreement.

Implied Warranties of Quality   A disclaimer of the implied warranty of merchantability and fitness is expressly provided for by section 2–316. The disclaimer of warranty of merchantability may be made either orally or in writing, but in either case the language must mention merchantability; if in writing, it must be conspicuous. A written disclaimer with regard to the warranty of fitness is required, irrespective of whether or not the other terms of the contract are in writing. It is expressly provided that "to exclude or modify any implied warranty of fitness, the exclusion must be by a writing and conspicuous."

Three exceptions to the above rule may be summarized:
(1) No implied warranty with regard to defects arises when the buyer has

examined the goods, or the sample, or the model as fully as he desired or has refused to examine the goods. It is not sufficient, however, that the goods are merely available for inspection. There must also be a demand by the seller that the buyer examine the goods fully.

(2) An implied warranty can be excluded or modified by a course of dealing or course of performance or usage of trade.

(3) General terms, such as "as is," "with all faults," and the like, may be used to exclude implied warranties if such expressions in common understanding call the attention of the buyer to the exclusion of warranties and make it plain that there is no implied warranty. [*First Nat'l Bank of Elgin v. Husted,* p. 206.]

Warranty of Title and Infringement   A seller may only disclaim the warranty of title by specific language. A seller who desires to disclaim the warranty of title, therefore, should make it clear that the buyer is assuming the risk of title failure.

The modification or exclusion of the warranty by infringement is not mentioned by the Code. The section pertaining to the infringement warranty, however, uses the words "unless otherwise agreed." The courts, therefore, would surely give effect to a clause in a contract whereby the seller does not warrant the goods against infringements upon the patent of third persons.

It should also be mentioned that the effect of not designating the title and infringement warranties as implied warranties means that these warranties are not subject to the "as is" exclusion of warranties mentioned above.

Privity of Contract   A problem which has troubled the courts is whether the ultimate consumer can recover from the manufacturer. The former general rule held that the ultimate consumer, except in some food cases, cannot recover from the manufacturer on a breach of warranty. This is, of course, due to the fact that no privity of contract exists between the consumer and the manufacturer. The consumer, however, can recover from the manufacturer in tort if the manufacturer is guilty of fraud, since privity of contract is not required in a tort action. The concealment of defects in an article with putty or paint—as in a rung of a stepladder—is an illustration of fraud. But this does not mean that the consumer can recover from the manufacturer for all tortious acts. Negligence of the manufacturer, for instance, does not generally make the manufacturer liable to the consumer. But three important situations where the manufacturer may be liable for negligence are worthy of mention. These are (1) where there is a statute which imposes a duty on the manufacturer for the benefit of the ultimate consumer, (2) where the goods are inherently dangerous, and (3) where the goods are imminently dangerous. A statute which imposes the duty of labeling the word "poison" on a container which contains poison is an illustration of a statutory duty on the manufacturer to protect the consumer. Explosives, unwholesome foodstuffs, oils for illuminating purposes, and poisons are illustrations of goods that are classed as being inherently dangerous. A defective automobile is an illustration of an article that is classed as being imminently dangerous. There is a tendency on the part of the courts to abandon the "privity of contract" rule. It should be mentioned, however, that the rules pertaining to privity of contract are not well settled and are constantly changing. The Code does not attempt to change this branch of developing law. [*Speed Fastners, Inc. v. Newsom* p. 207.]

Third-Party Beneficiaries of Warranties The Code gives the buyer's family, household, and guests the benefit of the same warranty—whether express or implied—which the buyer receives in the contract of sale. Suppose Mrs. Brown purchases defective food at her neighborhood grocery and she and the members of her family eat it and are injured. The members of the family who suffer such injury may recover from the grocer on a breach of warranty. The Code also provides that a seller "may not exclude or limit the operation of this section." This merely means that the seller cannot disclaim the warranty protection of the beneficiaries with respect to any warranties that are made by the seller. There would obviously be no warranty protection for the members of the household or guests in case no warranty is made. This could be accomplished if the seller disclaimed the warranties. In the absence of a disclaimer, however, section 2–318 provides that the warranty protection is extended to any natural person who is in the family or household of the buyer or who is a guest in his home.

CASES

Standard Stevedoring Co. v. Jaffe,   302 S.W.2d 829 (Pa. 1956). Action by Standard Stevedoring Company, Inc., complainant, against Sol I. Jaffe, doing business as United Steel Products Company, defendant.

The complainant purchased a crane as a result of an advertisement as follows: "Motor Crane: 15–20 ton P & H mechanical crane mounted on White 4 x 8 carrier." Soon after the crane was received, the complainant attempted to use it and found it did not have the necessary lifting capacity. He then brought an action to rescind the purchase and sale of the motor crane. The lower court found that the crane would not stand the stress and strain of "15–20 ton" operation of the normal and ordinary operation of a crane of the capacity as advertised, and entered a decree for complainant.

Carney, Judge: We concur in the Chancellor's finding that there was an express warranty on the part of the defendant that the crane had a 15–20 ton capacity and that the crane which was sold had a capacity of substantially less tonnage and that, therefore, the express warranty had been breached. We also concur in his finding, that the defendant was guilty of no fraud or intentional wrongdoing in warranting the said machine to have a 15 or 20 ton capacity. That fact does not relieve the defendant of liability.

Complainant relies upon the rule that where the seller of goods makes an affirmation of fact which has a tendency to induce and does induce the buyer to purchase, there is an express warranty, and if it is false the seller is liable irrespective of any fraud or knowledge on his part that the affirmation was untrue and irrespective of whether he intended to warrant the goods or not.

It follows that a decree will be entered in this court in favor of the complainant. [DECREE AFFIRMED]

Webster v. Blue Ship Tea Room, Inc.,   198 N.E.2d 309 (Mass. 1964). Action by Priscilla D. Webster, plaintiff, against Blue Ship Tea Room, Inc., defendant, to recover damages for personal injuries resulting from an alleged breach of an implied warranty of merchantability of food served by the defendant.

The plaintiff went to the Blue Ship Tea Room, located on the T Wharf overlooking the ocean in Boston, and ordered a cup of fish chowder, which was quickly served. It contained haddock, potatoes, milk, water, and seasoning which gave it a milky color. The haddock and potatoes were in chunks. After she ate three or four spoonfuls along with wafers, she was aware that something had lodged in her throat because she couldn't swallow and couldn't clear her throat by gulping, and she could feel it. Two esophagoscopies at the Massachusetts General Hospital were required, the second of which resulted in the finding and removal of a fish bone.

Reardon, Justice: We must decide whether a fish bone lurking in a fish chowder, about the ingredients of which there is no other complaint, constitutes a breach of implied warranty under applicable provisions of the Uniform Commercial Code.

The plaintiff has vigorously reminded us of the high standards imposed by this court where the sale of food is involved, and to certain other cases, here and elsewhere, serving to bolster her contention of breach of warranty.

The defendant asserts that here was a native New Englander eating fish chowder in a "quaint" Boston dining place where she had been before; that fish chowder, as it is served and enjoyed by New Englanders, is a hearty dish, originally designed to satisfy the appetites of our seamen and fishermen; that this court knows well that we are not talking of some insipid broth as is customarily served to convalescents. We are asked to rule in such fashion that no chef is forced "to reduce the pieces of fish in the chowder to miniscule size in an effort to ascertain if they contained any pieces of bone." In so ruling, we are told, "the court will not only uphold its reputation for legal knowledge and acumen, but will, as loyal sons of Massachusetts, save our world-renowned fish chowder from degenerating into an insipid broth containing a mere essence of its former stature as a culinary masterpiece."

It is not too much to say that a person sitting down in New England to consume a good New England fish chowder embarks on a gustatory adventure which may entail the removal of some fish bones from his bowl as he proceeds. We are not inclined to tamper with age old recipes by any amendment reflecting the plaintiff's view of the effect of the Uniform Commercial Code upon them. We are aware of the heavy body of case law involving foreign substances in food, but we sense a strong distinction between them and those relative to unwholesomeness of the food itself, e.g., tainted mackerel, and a fish bone in fish chowder. We consider that the joys of life in New England include the ready availability of fresh fish chowder. We should be prepared to cope with the hazards of fish bones, the occasional presence of which in chowders is, it seems to us, to be anticipated, and which, in the light of a hallowed tradition, do not impair their fitness or merchantability. We are most impressed by Allen v. Grafton, 164 N.E.2d 167, where in Ohio, the Midwest, in a case where the plaintiff was injured by a piece of oyster shell in an order of fried oysters, Mr. Justice Taft in a majority opinion held that "the possible presence of a piece of oyster shell in or attached to an oyster is so well known to everyone who eats oysters that we can say as a matter of law that one who eats oysters can reasonably anticipate and guard against eating such a piece of shell." [DECISION FOR DEFENDANT]

Catania v. Brown, 231 A.2d 668 (Conn. 1967). Action by Michael Catania, plaintiff, against Charles J. Brown, defendant, to recover for breach of warranty.

Plaintiff asked defendant, who was engaged in the retail paint business, to recommend a paint to cover the exterior stucco walls of the plaintiff's house. Plaintiff told defendant that the stucco was in a "chalky" and "powdery" condition, and defendant recommended a product known as Pierce's shingle and shake paint. Defendant advised plaintiff to "wirebrush" any loose particles which were "flaky" or "scaly" before applying the paint, to mix two or three gallons of the paint in a container, and to add a thinner. Plaintiff followed the instructions, but five months thereafter the walls of the house began to peel, flake, and blister. This was because the condition of the walls was such that thorough wirebrushing and sandblasting of the entire surface were required before applying the paint.

Jacobs, Judge: Under the statute governing implied warranty of fitness for a particular purpose (section 2–315), two requirements must be met: (a) the buyer relies on the seller's skill or judgment to select or furnish suitable goods; and (b) the seller at the time of contracting has reason to know the buyer's purpose and that the buyer is relying on the seller's skill and judgment. . . .

The raising of an implied warranty of fitness depends upon whether the buyer informed the seller of the circumstances and conditions which necessitated his purchase of a certain character of article or material and left it to the seller to select the particular kind and quality of article suitable for the buyer's use. . . . So when the buyer orders goods to be supplied and trusts to the judgment or skill of the seller to select goods or material for which they are ordered, there is an implied warranty that they shall be reasonably fit for that purpose. Green Mountain Mushroom Co. v. Brown, 117 Vt. 509, 95 A.2d 679. . . .

The finding, which may not be corrected, discloses that the buyer, being ignorant of the fitness of the article offered by the seller, justifiably relied on the superior information, skill and judgment of the seller and not on his own knowledge or judgment, and under such circumstances an implied warranty of fitness could properly be claimed by the purchaser. . . . As we have construed section 2–315, the facts of this case fall within its provisions. [DECISION FOR PLAINTIFF]

First Nat'l Bank of Elgin v. Husted, 205 N.E.2d 780 (Ill. 1965). Action by The First National Bank of Elgin, Illinois, plaintiff, against Richard Wayne Husted, Jr. and wife, defendants.

Defendants, as buyers, entered into a retail installment contract with Reed Motors, Inc., as sellers, for the purchase and sale of a 1958 Ford. The retail sales contract was assigned to plaintiff on August 30, 1963. Plaintiff was awarded a judgment against defendants in the sum of $672.18, and defendants appealed. Defendants alleged that they purchased the Ford upon an oral warranty that it was in good working condition; that the car did not operate properly; that it finally became inoperative. The defense was based on a breach of the oral express warranty and the implied warranties of quality.

Davis, Justice: The exclusion or modification of warranties is governed by Article 2 of the Uniform Commercial Code. It provides that "all implied warranties are excluded by expressions like 'as is,' 'with all faults' or other language which in common understanding calls the buyer's attention to the exclusion of warranties and makes plain that there is no implied warranty."

The contract in question, immediately beneath the names of the parties, in language printed in the size type of all of the words of the paragraphs of the contract, provided: "Buyer acknowledges delivery, examination and acceptance of said car in its present condition." The "Covenants and Conditions" of the contract contained the following language, printed in the same size type: "This agreement constitutes the entire contract and no waivers or modification shall be valid unless written upon or attached to this contract, and said car is accepted without any express or implied warranties, agreements, representations, promises or statements unless expressly set forth in this contract at the time of purchase." The contract contained no express warranties pertaining to the car.

We believe that the words "in its present condition" are similar to the words "as is" or "with all faults" and have the effect of excluding implied warranties. [DECISION FOR PLAINTIFF]

Speed Fastners, Inc. v. Newsom, 282 F.2d 395 (Okla. 1967). Action by Ray Newsom, plaintiff, a carpenter foreman, against Speed Fastners, Inc., defendant.

A fellow employee of plaintiff was using a power-loaded gun to drive studs through a steel beam for the purpose of attaching a piece of wood to a beam. Plaintiff, who had first adjusted the gun, gave it to the fellow employee for use. The employee had difficulty in getting the desired penetration. He therefore changed to a heavier power charge and a shorter plunger setting, which increased the driving force of the gun. The ricocheting shank of the stud separated and hit plaintiff in the abdomen and lodged in a nerve center of the pelvic region. According to medical testimony given at the trial, it cannot be removed safely. Plaintiff brought this action to recover damages for the injuries so sustained. The trial court awarded plaintiff a judgment, and defendant appealed.

Breitenstein, Circuit Judge: The first question is whether the manufacturer's liability extends to a person who is neither a purchaser nor a user. Under the Oklahoma law, the warranty extends "to any natural person who is in the family or household of his buyer or who is a guest in his home." The manufacturer argues that this clause has the effect of excluding all those not within the mentioned categories. We are convinced that this was not the legislative intent. In the comment following section 2–318 appears the following: "3. This section expressly includes as beneficiaries within its provisions the family, household, and guests of the purchaser. Beyond this, the section is neutral and is not intended to enlarge or restrict the developing case law on whether the seller's warranties, given to his buyer who resells, extend to other persons in the distributive chain."

The plaintiff was neither the buyer nor the user. The buyer was his employer and the user was a fellow workman. The plaintiff insists that in the situation presented the principle of strict liability applies and that even a bystander might recover. The manufacturer argues that, except in food and drink cases, Oklahoma has never applied the theory of strict liability in implied warranty cases. . . . No Oklahoma decision has considered the specific issue with which we are confronted.

The extension of a manufacturer's liability to anyone injured by a product not suitable for the use intended has been the subject of much discussion. In general, privity is not essential where an implied warranty is imposed by the law on the basis of public policy. We believe that the injured employee stands in the shoes of his employer and that his cause of action based on implied warranty is not barred by the shield of privity. The manufacturers know that most businesses are carried on through employees who will actually use the product purchased by their employers. In the absence of an Oklahoma decision to the contrary, we are satisfied that the employee may sue on the theory of implied warranty. . . .

We have here an inherently dangerous product. Although our concern is with a stud rather than with a gun or cartridge, the stud was designed, made, and sold for the use to which it was put. The possibility of separation and ricochet may not be disregarded. The stud is harmless in itself, but, when used for the purpose intended, it is a component of a lethal weapon. [DECISION FOR PLAINTIFF]

PROBLEMS

1 Craig visited a hardware store and told the clerk that he desired to purchase a lawn mower. The clerk recommended a rotary type lawn mower, which Craig purchased. Craig sustained injuries when he fell while mowing a small embankment on the front of his lawn and his foot slid under the mower. He thereupon brought an action against the hardware store to recover damages for breach of an implied warranty of fitness for a particular purpose. He contended that the hardware store was liable because he relied on the skill and judgment of the clerk. Decide.

2 The Canning Company is an independent reputable processor of canned goods and employs modern methods to prevent the presence of foreign substances in processing its products. The defendant, a chain grocery company, purchased a large quantity of sealed cans of baked beans from the canning company. To each can was attached: "Grandmother's Brand Pork & Beans." The defendant did not supervise the process of canning and had no knowledge, or means of knowledge, that any foreign substance was in the cans. The defendant sold to the plaintiff one of these sealed cans containing beans, among which was a small pebble. The plaintiff was ignorant of the presence of the pebble and, while eating the beans, broke his tooth on the pebble. Can plaintiff recover damages from the defendant?

3 The seller knew the particular purpose for which the buyer wanted to use a Fordson tractor, a two-wheel truck used as a trailer, a connecting hitch, and a hydraulic hoist for unloading. The buyer relied upon the seller's judgment that the equipment was suitable for the particular purpose. The machinery was not suitable for the needs of the buyer. The seller claims there was no implied warranty because it was orally agreed that no warranties had been made in reference to said motor vehicle. Has the implied warranty of fitness for a particular purpose been excluded?

4 Plaintiff purchased a secondhand automobile from defendant for the sum of $150. About a month thereafter, plaintiff learned that defendant had purchased two of the tires on the car from Brown on a conditional sales contract and that Brown still held the title to them and a debt of $28.50 against them. Plaintiff refused to pay the $28.50, and Brown replevied the two tires. Plaintiff thereupon delivered the car to defendant and demanded the return of the purchase price. Defendant refused. What warranty, if any, has been breached?

5 The seller and the buyer entered into a written contract for the sale of one motor. The writing contained no express warranties. It did, however, contain a provision that "this writing comprises the entire agreement." The motor was described as follows: "1 Each 3-/15 H.P. Induction Motor Crop Proof 3600/1800 RPM single winding, constant torque, 220 volt A.C., 60 cycle, 3 phase Frame 365. Shaft to be tapered and threaded as per sketch forwarded to factory, Gladstone, Mich." The buyer accepted the motor upon delivery, and has used it since that time. In an action for the price, the buyer alleged the breach of two warranties: (a) an oral warranty of quality and (b) a warranty of suitability for a particular purpose. How should the court decide both points?

6 Defendant, a retail hardware company, placed an advertisement in the newspaper directing attention to ladders it had for sale. The headlines were: "Sensational Factory Purchase of 'Safety First' Ladders." Plaintiff took the advertisement to the store and asked to see one of the ladders. Plaintiff then asked the salesman if the ladder would be good for cleaning wallpaper. The salesman said: "This ladder is exactly what you want." When asked about the strength, the salesman said: "As far as strength, they were tested to two hundred pounds or better." When asked about the wood, the salesman said: "It is very good wood." Plaintiff thereupon purchased the ladder. The next morning plaintiff, who weighed 170 pounds, was using the ladder, and when he stepped on about the seventh rung, the ladder broke through both rails and plaintiff fell to the floor. Plaintiff brought an action for breach of warranty. At the trial, according to expert testimony, the cause of the ladder's breaking was a defective side rail consisting of cross-grained wood in the side rail near the seventh rung. Should plaintiff recover?

7 Brown stole a TV set from Jones and sold it for value to Smith, an innocent purchaser who had no knowledge that the TV set had been stolen. Smith sold the same TV set for value to Davis, who was also an innocent purchaser with no knowledge that the TV set had been stolen. Jones learned that the TV set was in the possession of Davis and promptly repossessed it. Does Davis have a right to recover from Smith for breach of warranty?

17

SALES: PERFORMANCE

The seller is under a duty to transfer and deliver the goods, and the buyer is under a duty to accept and pay for the goods in accordance with the terms of the contract. These are concurrent conditions, but the duty of each party is conditioned upon tender of delivery or tender of payment. The parties are free to change this obligation, but, unless they do so, the Code provides further rules for clarification and implementation and relies heavily on modern commercial practice and the presumed intention of the parties. It is convenient to discuss performance by the parties from the viewpoint of (1) duties of the seller, (2) duties of the buyer, (3) risk of loss, (4) excuses for nonperformance, (5) insurable interest, and (6) cure and assurances.

DUTIES OF THE SELLER
The duties of the seller pertain to tender of delivery and delivery of the goods.

Tender of Delivery   The seller performs when he tenders delivery of conforming goods to the buyer. The seller's first duty is to deliver the goods or documents to the right place at the right time, and his second duty is to "tender" these goods or documents to the buyer. Section 2–503 sets forth the primary requirements of tender: The seller is required to "put and hold conforming goods at the buyer's disposition and give the buyer any notification reasonably necessary to enable him to take delivery." It should be mentioned that the buyer must furnish his own facilities reasonably suited to receive the goods unless the parties agree otherwise. [*Balthauser & Moyer, Inc. v. Hayden*, p. 221.]

The notice of delivery must be given so as to enable the buyer to take possession of the goods at a reasonable hour. A tender at one or two o'cock in the morning would not ordinarily suffice. The parties will frequently agree that the seller is to deliver documents. The seller is under a duty to tender such documents in correct form. The tender may be correctly made through customary banking channels, but the buyer rejects the goods if he dishonors a draft accompanying the documents.

The goods are sometimes in the possession of a bailee and are to be delivered without being moved. The seller is then required to tender a negotiable document of title covering the goods to the buyer, or the seller may obtain an acknowledgment by the bailee stating that the buyer has a right to possession of the goods. The tender of a nonnegotiable document of title or a written direction to the bailee to deliver is sufficient tender unless the buyer seasonably objects.

Delivery   The seller, in all contracts for sale, is under a duty to deliver the goods. The courts will respect their specifically expressed intent, although the parties frequently fail to have a clear understanding with respect to (1) the time for delivery, (2) the place of delivery, (3) delivery to the carrier, and (4) delivery in single or several lots.

(1)   *Time for Delivery*   The buyer and the seller may expressly agree upon a time for delivery or shipment. In the absence of such an agreement, section 2–309 provides that it shall be a reasonable time. If the parties belatedly realize that this "reasonable time" is not to their liking, they can only blame themselves for not setting a time for delivery. The contract may call for successive performances without limiting the duration. In this situation, the contract is valid for a reasonable time. Either party, however, may terminate the contract by giving reasonable notice to the other party. This enables the receiving party to make substitute arrangements during the remaining time. A provision in a contract to the effect that no notice of termination will be given is invalid; such a provision would very likely be unconscionable. If the termination is to occur on the happening of some event—such as the cessation of hostilities in South Vietnam—no notice from either party would be required. The happening of the event is sufficient notice.

(2)   *Place for Delivery*   Section 2–308 deals with contracts for sale when no place of delivery is agreed upon and the seller is not required to ship the goods by carrier. In the absence of usage of the trade to the contrary, the place of delivery is the seller's place of business if he has one. His residence is designated as the place of delivery if the seller has no place of business. If the goods are known to be in another place, however, the place of delivery is that other place. Suppose the goods are in the hands of a warehouseman or other bailee. The goods are deemed to be delivered when the seller notifies the bailee that he has

transferred title to the buyer and the bailee assents to hold the goods for the buyer. A delivery of documents of title may be anticipated rather than the delivery of the goods themselves, but a tender of documents would not be expected to be made at the place where the goods are located. Section 2–308 provides, therefore, "documents of title may be delivered through customary banking channels." A delivery of goods may occur by delivering a bill of sale. The bill of sale, however, must identify the goods to the contract in order for the risk of loss to pass to the buyer. [*Chatham v. Clark's Food Fair, Inc.*, p. 222.]

(3) *Delivery by Carrier*   Delivery by carrier contemplates a "shipment" contract unless the contract requires the seller to deliver the goods to a particular destination. The seller, therefore, is under a duty to effect a contract with the carrier which will protect the buyer. The seller should also make arrangements so that produce will be refrigerated, livestock will be watered, and liquids will not be frozen. The seller should set the value of the goods so that the buyer may adequately recover from the carrier. The seller should also make other arrangements which are reasonable under the circumstances.

The seller is under a duty to place the goods in the hands of the carrier, make a proper contract for transportation, obtain the necessary documents, deliver them to the buyer, and notify the buyer promptly of the shipment. The reason for prompt notification is to give the buyer an opportunity to secure insurance and to make preparations for the receipt of the goods. It might be wise if the seller gave notification by wire or cable or even by telephone. Suppose the seller defaults in one of his duties in making the shipping arrangements. The buyer may recover for any damages he has suffered, or he may reject the goods as a result of the seller's breach.

The duties of the seller to deliver the goods in a "destination" contract are not terminated upon delivery at the place of shipment. The seller is required to do whatever is necessary to deliver conforming goods to a particular destination. He is also under a duty to give notice to the buyer and tender any necessary documents so that he may take possession of the goods.

(4) *Delivery in Single or Several Lots*   The parties to the contract for sale should state whether delivery is to be in a single lot or several lots. In the absence of such a statement of intent, the Code presumes that the parties intended the customary or normal thing in the circumstances, that is to say, a delivery in a single lot. This may be illustrated by a contract for the sale of twenty-four boxes of citrus and the seller is entitled to payment upon a proper tender. Section 2–307 recognizes, however, that delivery cannot always be made in one lot—perhaps 100,000 bricks. The buyer in such circumstances is not justified in rejecting partial deliveries. The seller, moreover, is entitled to payment for each partial delivery if the price is apportionable.

DUTIES OF THE BUYER

Section 2–507 provides in effect that the buyer performs properly by accepting the goods and paying in accordance with the terms of the contract. It is convenient, therefore, to discuss acceptance and payment separately.

Acceptance   Acceptance of goods is usually signified by the receipt and retention of, and the payment for, the goods after an inspection reveals them to be conforming. A buyer, under section 2–606, accepts the goods: (1) When, after a reasonable opportunity to inspect the goods, he (a) signifies to the seller that the goods are conforming or that he will take them in spite of their nonconformity, or (b) fails to make an effective rejection.

The buyer has a right to accept only a part of the commercial units without incurring the risk of being liable for acceptance of all the units. Section 2–601 provides that the buyer may accept all of the goods, reject all of the goods, or he may accept any commercial unit and reject the rest provided the goods fail to conform to the contract in any respect. Suppose that the seller tenders a truck to the buyer but the engine is nonconforming. An acceptance would include all of the truck, engine and chassis, since the truck is one commercial unit. The buyer cannot accept the chassis and reject the engine. If the seller tenders radios or boxes of fruit, each being a commercial unit, the buyer may accept a part of the goods and reject the rest. The buyer may furthermore retain a part of the goods for use as evidence in the event of litigation concerning the quality or condition of the goods. It is believed that section 2–515 will be construed to indicate that such retention will not be an acceptance of all the goods.

The right of inspection is the very essence of determining whether the buyer is under a duty to accept and pay. The parties in the original agreement may provide for the place and method of inspection which will be controlling on both parties. Suppose, however, that inspection becomes impossible at the agreed place or by the agreed method. Is the sale to fail or will another place of inspection be substituted? The Code assumes, unless the contract provides otherwise, that the parties did not intend the sale to fail because the type of inspection agreed upon is not possible. The buyer—if no place or method of inspection was agreed upon—will be permitted to inspect the goods at the time and place of his receipt of the goods. The "shipment" contract merits particular mention. Suppose the buyer in New York orders produce from the seller in San Francisco. Section 2–513 provides that the buyer may inspect "at any reasonable place and time and in any reasonable manner." The expenses of inspection must be borne by the buyer, but such expenses may be recovered from the seller if the goods do not conform to the contract and are rejected by the buyer. It would appear, therefore, that the buyer may inspect the goods either in New York or in San Francisco.

A buyer who desires to reject the goods should act within reason. A failure to make an effective rejection will be construed as an acceptance. Sections 2–606 and 2–602 require the buyer to speak out and to notify the seller of the rejection within a reasonable time after tender or delivery. Is a merchant-buyer under an additional duty to effect a salvage sale for the seller if he rightfully rejects goods which are perishable or the value of which is likely to decline? If the seller has no local agent, the buyer is under a duty to follow any reasonable instructions of the seller with respect to the disposition of the goods. In the absence of in-structions, the merchant-buyer is under a duty to make a reasonable effort to sell such goods for the seller. If the merchant-buyer acts in good faith in selling the goods, such action is neither an acceptance nor a conversion for which he will be liable.

Payment   An acceptance of the goods by the buyer gives rise to a duty to pay in accordance with the terms of the contract. The Code attempts to bring the rules concerning the payment obligation in line with modern commercial practice with respect to (1) payment upon receipt of the goods, (2) manner of payment, and (3) documentary sales.

(1)   *Payment upon Receipt of Goods*   The parties may agree as to the time and place of payment. In the absence of such an agreement, however, section 2–310 provides that payment for the goods will be due at the time and place where the buyer receives the goods. It should be kept in mind that the buyer has a right to inspect the goods before payment or acceptance. A buyer, however, waives his right of inspection in a c.o.d. sale. [*Alpirn v. Williams*, p. 222.]

(2)   *Manner of Payment*   The parties are competent to agree on the manner of payment, and the contract for sale does ordinarily state the consideration in terms of dollars and cents payable at a certain time and place. The contract, however, rarely states the manner of payment. Our legal system down through the years has recognized "cash" as the proper manner of payment, but it is a general practice today to make payment by check. Section 2–511 provides that tender of payment is sufficient when it is made in any manner which is current in the ordinary course of business unless the seller demands cash and allows the buyer a reasonable time in which to procure the cash. The seller, therefore, can still demand cash unless there has been an agreement to the contrary.

(3)   *Documentary Sales*   Pre-Code law recognizes that, first, delivery of the goods and payment of the price are concurrent conditions, and second, the buyer is entitled to inspect the goods before he is deemed to have accepted them. These two propositions led to the following general rule: When goods are delivered to a carrier, the payment obligation does not arise until actual delivery in order to give the buyer an opportunity to inspect the goods. Section 2–310 continues this general rule and, further, provides for a documentary sale.

The buyer may contract to pay for the goods when the documents of title are tendered for payment although the goods are still in transit. This type of sale is referred to as a "documentary sale" and is understood to mean that the payment obligation matures at the time and place where the buyer is to receive the documents regardless of where the goods are to be received. The buyer, therefore, is deemed to have waived his right of inspection when the sale is a documentary sale.

This section of the Code, however, gives the buyer a right of inspection even though the sale is a documentary sale. This right is accomplished by shipping the goods "under reservation," which means the seller may obtain a bill of lading and attach to it a sight draft—a bill of exchange—for the purchase price. The bill of lading may be marked "hold until arrival; inspection allowed." A shipment under reservation, therefore, gives the buyer the right to inspect before payment "unless such inspection is inconsistent with the terms of the contract." It is thus clear that goods shipped under a c.o.d. or c.i.f. contract would not give the buyer a right of inspection before payment. The c.i.f. contract may, of course, be altered to allow an inspection by the buyer.

The credit period runs from the time of shipment where the seller is authorized to ship the goods on credit. Postdating the invoice or delaying its dispatch, however, will correspondingly delay the starting of the period.

RISK OF LOSS

The Code allows the parties substantial freedom of contract. They can, therefore, agree on the risk of loss. They can agree to divide it equally or on an unequal basis, or they can agree that the entire risk is to be on either the buyer or the seller. Parties to a sales contract should consider the problems of risk of loss. The Code, in the absence of an agreement allocating the risk of loss, makes provision for loss (1) in the absence of breach of contract and (2) coupled with a breach of contract.

Risk of Loss in Absence of Breach   Section 2–509 provides the rules for a risk of loss when the seller has not breached the contract.

(1)   *Shipment by Carrier*   Shipment by carrier may be by a "shipment" contract or by a "destination" contract. In a shipment contract, the risk of loss passes to the buyer at the place of shipment as soon as the seller completes his duties with respect to placing the goods in the hands of the carrier, arranges for transportation, delivers the necessary documents to the buyer, and notifies the buyer of the shipment. This is the usual situation with respect to a c.i.f. or a c. & f. contract, an f.o.b. place-of-shipment contract, and an f.a.s. contract. The risk of loss passes to the buyer even though the seller ships under reservation, as where the seller reserves the title to the goods for security reasons.

In a "destination" contract, the risk of loss passes to the buyer when the seller has made a proper tender of delivery of conforming goods at the place of destination. An f.o.b. destination contract is a good example of this rule. The risk of loss passes to and remains with the buyer although he refuses to accept conforming goods. The risk of loss would be on the buyer, therefore, if they should be destroyed on the return trip to the seller. This is because the seller has made a proper tender of goods to the buyer.

(2)   *Goods Held by Bailee*   Suppose the contract covers goods which are held by a warehouseman, carrier, or other bailee and that delivery is to be made to the buyer without moving the physical possession of the goods. The risk of loss passes to the buyer when he receives a negotiable document of title—a warehouse receipt or a bill of lading—covering the goods, or when the bailee acknowledges that the buyer has a right to the possession of the goods. The risk of loss, however, does not pass to the buyer immediately when he receives a nonnegotiable document of title. Suppose the seller gives the buyer a nonnegotiable document of title or a mere written direction to the bailee to deliver the goods. The risk of loss passes to the buyer after he has a reasonable time to present the document or direction to the bailee so that he may attorn to the buyer. Attorn means that the

bailee acknowledges the right of possession in the buyer. If the buyer makes no effort to obtain an attornment, the risk of loss passes to the buyer after a reasonable length of time. The risk of loss will pass back to the seller if the bailee fails to attorn.

(3) *Other Sales* In any other case—namely, other than a shipment or a destination contract and goods in the possession of a bailee—the important word to remember is "merchant." A distinction is made between a seller who is a merchant and a seller who is not a merchant. The risk of loss passes to the buyer upon his "receipt of the goods" if the seller is a merchant. This rule is based upon the assumption that the merchant is more likely to have insurance coverage. The risk of loss passes to the buyer upon a "tender of delivery," however, if the seller is not a merchant. Tender means, broadly speaking, that the seller puts and holds conforming goods at the buyer's disposition and gives reasonable notice to the buyer so that he may take possession.

Risk of Loss Coupled with a Breach   Section 2–510 makes provision for risk of loss when there has been a breach of contract, and, as a general rule, it will be on the party that breaches the contract. It is more accurate to say that the risk of an uninsured loss is on the breaching party. Stated otherwise, the injured or aggrieved party in control of the goods has the risk of loss to the extent that he has effective insurance available. Three situations deserve mention.

(1) *Buyer Has Right of Rejection* The buyer may reject the goods if they fail to conform to the contract. The risk of loss is on the seller since he is in breach of contract. It should be added, however, that the seller may cure the nonconformity, or the buyer may see fit to accept the goods despite the nonconformity.

(2) *Revocation of Acceptance* A buyer may revoke his acceptance of the goods if he had no reasonable way of knowing at the time of acceptance of a latent defect in the goods. Suppose the buyer had known of the nonconformity but he understood that the seller would cure the nonconformity. He may revoke his acceptance provided the seller does not cure the nonconformity. This may be done within a reasonable time, and the risk of loss will be on the seller who is in breach of contract. The novel aspect of insurance, however, provides that the risk to the seller will be to the extent of any deficiency in the buyer's insurance.

(3) *Conforming Goods Identified to the Contract* The third situation involves this situation: The seller identifies conforming goods to the contract for sale and the buyer later repudiates or breaches the contract before the risk of loss passes to him. The seller may treat the risk of loss to the extent of any deficiency in his effective insurance as being on the buyer for a commercially reasonable time. Any loss which is not covered by insurance, therefore, falls on the breaching buyer. [*Canyon State Canners v. Hooks,* p. 223.]

EXCUSES FOR NONPERFORMANCE
The rules excusing performance in the sale of goods pertain not only to impossibility, as explained in Chapter 12, "Performance," but also to im-

practicability. It should be mentioned at the outset that business risks which are ordinarily assumed by the seller and the buyer will not excuse performance, nor will such factors as increased costs or a rise or collapse in the market unless due to some unforeseen contingency which alters the essential nature of the performance.

Impossibility   Section 2–613 provides that the seller is excused from performance on the basis of impossibility where the goods are destroyed without the fault of either party before the risk of loss passes to the buyer. This section, however, applies (1) only to goods which have been identified to the contract at the time the parties entered into the contract and (2) only before the risk of loss passes to the buyer. Suppose the seller, having twenty like refrigerators, agreed to sell one refrigerator to the buyer without identifying the specific refrigerator. A total destruction of one refrigerator would not excuse the seller from performing, because he could tender another refrigerator. Suppose, however, that the seller and the buyer had agreed on one particular refrigerator as the subject matter of the contract. The total destruction of the particular refrigerator would render performance impossible, and the seller would be excused from performing. The seller would bear the risk of loss, but he would not be liable for breach of contract. Suppose the one particular refrigerator was only partially destroyed. The buyer could demand an inspection and treat the contract as avoided, or he might accept the refrigerator with a price adjustment.

Impracticability   It should be mentioned that goods "identified when the contract was entered into" are not involved in impracticability of performance. The goods, therefore, need not be one particular refrigerator. The rules excusing performance on the ground of impracticability are found in section 2–615, but the word "impracticability" is not defined. The rules are stated in broad terms, which leaves the courts free to interpret the section so as to arrive at fair results between the seller and the buyer. Broadly stated, the rules excuse the seller from delivery of the goods where his performance has become impracticable because of an unforeseen contingency not within the contemplation of the parties at the time they entered into the contract. The contract must have been entered into on the assumption that the contingency would not occur, such as an unexpected war or an unexpected embargo which causes a severe shortage of raw materials or supplies. Suppose the seller needed steel to perform his contract and the government took control of the sale of steel. The seller would be completely excused from performance if the government confiscated all steel, because it would be completely impracticable to obtain steel. Suppose, however, the seller is able to partially perform his contract by obtaining a certain amount of steel. His partial performance must take into account the needs of all his customers by making a fair allocation of the steel to them. The seller is given much latitude, however, and he may allocate the steel in any manner which is fair and reasonable. The buyer is not required to accept an allocated part of the steel, but the seller is not liable for breach of contract.

Method of Delivery and Payment   Section 2–614 provides that when the agreed method of transportation becomes impracticable the seller *must* tender and the buyer *must* accept substitute transportation where a commercially reasonable substitute is available. Suppose the seller and the buyer agree that ten refrigerators are to be shipped by railroad, but this method of transportation becomes unavailable because of a strike of railroad workers or the unavailability of box cars. The seller would be required to make delivery and the buyer to accept delivery by truck or other available substitute transportation.

 This section also covers the situation where the agreed manner of payment fails because of a governmental regulation. The seller is given the right to withhold or stop delivery of the goods unless the buyer provides a substantially equivalent manner of payment. The buyer is given the right, however, to discharge his payment obligation in the manner provided by the regulation where he has already accepted the goods. This is true even though the payment is not the equivalent, provided the regulation is not oppressive.

INSURABLE INTEREST

As a general rule, any person may become a party to a contract of insurance provided the person—among other things—possesses an insurable interest in the subject matter of the insurance. The insured may be an owner, a lienholder, or a person in possession. The rules defining an insurable interest in the seller and the buyer of goods, however, are found in section 2–501. These rules are designed to supplement and not replace existing statutes and rules governing an insurable interest. This is made clear by section 2–501(3): "Nothing in this section impairs any insurable interest recognized under any other statute or rule of law."

Insurable Interest of the Buyer   This section recognizes that the buyer in a sales transaction should have an insurable interest in the goods at an early stage. A contract to sell future goods is nothing more than a contract to sell. The buyer cannot have an interest in the goods until the goods are in existence and identified as the subject matter of the contract. To illustrate: A retailer, who owns no radios, agrees to sell a radio to Smith. This is merely a contract to sell a future good, and one in which Smith does not have an insurable interest since the radio is not in existence. Suppose the retailer obtains a radio; the buyer's insurable interest accrues at the time the seller identifies it as the subject matter of the contract. Suppose, however, the seller obtains ten radios. The identification of one specific radio as the subject matter of the contract would be necessary for an insurable interest of the buyer to arise.

 May a seller sell an undivided interest in a mass of goods? He may do so provided the mass exists and it is identified. Let us pursue the above illustration when the seller obtained ten radios. He may sell an undivided interest—say 10 percent—and the insurable interest of the buyer accrues immediately since the mass is in existence and it is identified.

A seller, in a sale of future goods, may identify the goods by shipping, marking, or otherwise designating the goods as those to which the contract refers provided there is no agreement to the contrary. The identification of crops would occur when they are planted or otherwise become growing crops provided it is a contract to sell crops to be harvested within twelve months thereafter or the next harvest season whichever is longer. The young of animals are identified when conceived provided it is a contract to sell unborn young to be born within twelve months after the contract is entered into.

Insurable Interest of the Seller   Section 2–501 provides that "the seller retains an insurable interest in goods so long as title to or any security interest in the goods remains in him." This appears self-explanatory. Some explanation, however, might be necessary. An insurable interest accrues to the buyer upon identification of existing goods to the contract of sale, but title does not ordinarily pass to the buyer at that time. The title remains with the seller, and so does an insurable interest. The seller's insurable interest terminates, however, when the goods are delivered to the buyer. This is understandable since the risk of loss passes to the buyer no later than the time of delivery. The risk of loss may possibly remain on the seller after delivery, however, if the contract so provides. An insurable interest, therefore, would likewise remain with the seller in this situation. This is either because he retained the title or because an insurable interest always accompanies a risk. One final thought: The destruction or loss of "any security interest" in the goods would mean a pecuniary loss to the seller. The seller, therefore, retains an insurable interest as long as he retains any security interest in the goods.

CURE AND ASSURANCES

The Code makes provision (1) for the seller to "cure" when the buyer rejects nonconforming goods, (2) for the buyer to "cure" when the seller rejects a check in payment of the goods, and (3) for either party to suspend performance when reasonable grounds arise with respect to performance of the other party.

Cure by the Seller   The basis for a cure by the seller is found in section 2–508. Suppose the seller delivers nonconforming goods which are rejected by the buyer. The seller may be allowed to cure provided reasonable notice is given to the buyer of his intention to cure. The seller must, however, make a conforming delivery within the contract time. The seller may likewise cure where the tender of a quantity is less than the contract quantity. Suppose the seller tenders twenty-four of thirty units under such circumstances that he reasonably thought the buyer would accept the twenty-four units and accept the remaining six units at a later date. This could be the case if it were current practice. Suppose, however, that the buyer refuses to accept the twenty-four units. The seller will have a further reasonable time in which to cure by substituting a conforming tender.

The seller is also given the right to cure in those instances in which there is a good faith insistence on strict adherence to the contractual terms. A buyer may honestly and ethically insist upon strict performance by a total delivery of the quantity when the seller knew or should have known that a lesser quantity would not suffice. The seller is not given an absolute right to cure. His right to cure is limited to those instances where he has reasonable grounds to believe that his "tender would be acceptable," such as a prior course of dealings or usage of trade. [*Zabriskie Chevrolet, Inc. v. Smith*, p. 224.]

Cure by the Buyer   The basis for a cure by the buyer is found in section 2–511. It is there provided that a tender of payment by the buyer is a condition to tender of the goods and complete delivery by the seller. The tender of payment is sufficient if it is made by any means or in any manner which is current in the ordinary course of business. Suppose, however, that the seller logically refuses to accept the buyer's check in payment for fear that it is worthless or that payment of the check will be stopped. The seller may demand legal tender, but he must allow the buyer a reasonable time in which to obtain the money if he does make such a demand. The seller must give the buyer a receipt for payment if the giving of receipts is customary when the buyer obtains the money and pays the seller.

Adequate Assurances of Performance   The discussion of "cure" indicates that when either the seller or the buyer is attempting to cure the other party may, and in many instances will, be uncertain of performance. The other party, therefore, has a right to assurances of performance.

Insecurity of the Seller or the Buyer   Section 2–609 deals with both the buyer and the seller and recognizes a situation where the willingness or the ability of either the buyer or the seller to perform declines materially between the time of contracting and the time for performance. Three measures are adopted to meet the needs in such a situation. First, the aggrieved party may suspend his own performance until the situation is clarified; second, the aggrieved party may make written demand for adequate assurances of performance; and third, the aggrieved party may treat the contract as broken if the other party fails to provide adequate assurances within a reasonable time—not to exceed thirty days—after receipt of a demand.

The grounds for insecurity depend upon the factual situations and do not necessarily need to be related to the contract in question. The official comment explains that a seller may have grounds for insecurity if the buyer falls behind in his account with the seller, even though the items relate to a separate contract. A buyer may have grounds for insecurity if he requires precision parts intended for use immediately upon delivery when he learns that his seller is making defective deliveries of such parts to other buyers. The acts which may constitute adequate assurances also depend on the factual situations. A known corner-cutter might have to post a guaranty to make adequate assurances of performances, but a mere promise to pay by a substantially solvent person of good repute might be sufficient.

CASES

Balthauser & Moyer, Inc. v. Hayden, 59 N.W.2d 828 (N.D. 1953). Action by Balthauser & Moyer, Incorporated, plaintiff, against Hayden, defendant. The plaintiff and the defendant entered into an agreement by the terms of which the plaintiff agreed to buy and the defendant agreed to sell 20 to 25 two-year-old steers. The defendant was to deliver the steers f.o.b. cars at Medora on September 15, 1950, or as soon thereafter as the plaintiff directed. On September 6, plaintiff wrote the defendant, "Please have strs. in the morning of September 15 as we load on the stock pick up due at 9:15 A.M. at Medora." Defendant did not deliver the steers as directed, nor did he notify the plaintiff of his reasons for nondelivery. On September 16, plaintiff again wrote the defendant directing that the steers be delivered on September 20. Defendant stated that he did not take the notice from the mailbox until September 19. The next day, September 20, defendant delivered the steers which arrived in Medora between 1:30 and 2 P.M. He was unable to find plaintiff's agent and drove back to his ranch. In the meantime, plaintiff's agent had arrived in Medora at 7 A.M., where he waited until 1:30 P.M. He then left Medora and returned at 4 P.M. to find the defendant had left town. The next day plaintiff's agent saw defendant at his ranch in an attempt to arrange a new delivery date. The defendant told him, "You ain't got anything more to do with those cattle, I delivered them and you weren't there." Two days later, the defendant sold the cattle to another buyer. This action was then brought for breach of contract.

    Burke, Judge: Defendant had agreed to deliver the cattle at a time to be fixed by the plaintiff. On two occasions he failed to make delivery in accordance with plaintiff's instructions. When he failed to deliver on September 15th, he did not inform plaintiff as to the reasons for his failure, nor did he make any attempt to notify plaintiff that delivery on September 20th would be late. Defendant offered testimony which tended to show that delivery in accordance with plaintiff's instructions was impossible, not because of any unreasonable demand on the part of the plaintiff, but because of the condition of the roads on September 15th, and because he didn't go to his mailbox on the 18th and thus failed to receive the notice to have the cattle in Medora on the morning of the 20th until late in the afternoon on the 19th, at which time it was too late to round up the cattle for morning delivery on the following day.

    Whatever may have been defendant's excuses for not making delivery in accordance with plaintiff's instructions and whether such excuses might justify his failure to deliver at the time specified, it is certainly clear that the transportation of the cattle to the place of delivery at a time other than that specified by the plaintiff, when plaintiff's agent was not present to receive them, was not a sufficient tender of delivery to put the plaintiff in default. It is only the neglect or refusal of a buyer to accept delivery of goods properly tendered that will place him in default in this respect. In this case there was neither refusal to accept delivery nor neglect on the part of the buyer's agent. He had no opportunity to refuse and there could be no neglect on his part because he was at the place specified ready to accept delivery during all of the time within which delivery was to be made and he had no notice that the delivery would be attempted at a later time.

When defendant thereafter refused to discuss the fixing of another time for delivery of the steers and sold them to another buyer, he clearly breached the contract. [DECISION FOR PLAINTIFF]

Chatham v. Clark's Food Fair, Inc., 127 S.E.2d 686 (Ga.1962). Action by R. P. Chatham, plaintiff-buyer, against Clark's Food Fair, Inc., defendant-seller, to recover the purchase price which had been paid for a boathouse.

The buyer purchased a boathouse from the seller and paid the purchase price in advance. The seller delivered a bill of sale to the buyer which recited: "For: One Model 924 boathouse." The buyer went to the location of several boathouses of the same particular model, but could not take possession due to adverse weather conditions. No markings were on any boathouse to indicate which one was the subject of the sale, and no particular one was identified in the bill of sale. The buyer returned at a later time, but was informed by an agent of the seller that his boathouse "had sunk." The seller, as a defense to this action for the return of the purchase price, alleged that he did not fail to deliver the boathouse inasmuch as he had delivered a bill of sale.

Carlisle, Presiding Judge: Three elements are essential to a contract of sale: 1. An identification of the thing sold; 2. An agreement as to the price to be paid; 3. Consent of the parties. A document which purports to be a bill of sale but which fails to identify the thing sold is not sufficient to convey title to anything, and the thing sold must be so identified by the contract, agreement, or bill of sale as to be capable of being separated from the mass of other similar articles and to be identified.

While actual delivery of the thing sold is not essential to the completion of the sale, unless the intention of the parties manifests otherwise, there must be at least a constructive delivery. But, whether the delivery be actual or constructive, it cannot be accomplished without the identification of the thing sold, and so, where there has been no identification there can be no delivery, and the sale is incomplete.

Applying the foregoing principles of law to the facts in this case, the plaintiff's evidence was sufficient to authorize the jury to find that there had been no delivery of any property which was the subject matter of the contract of sale, and that the plaintiff, having paid his money and having failed to get delivery of anything therefor, was entitled to recover it back. [DECISION FOR PLAINTIFF]

Alpirn v. Williams Steel & Supply Co., 199 F.2d 734 (1952). Action by Morton Alpirn, doing business as Western Smelting & Refining Company, plaintiff, against Herman Williams, doing business as Williams Steel & Supply Company, defendant, for breach of contract. Plaintiff was engaged in the business of selling metal products as a broker and wholesale dealer in Omaha, Nebraska, and ordered from the defendant, a dealer in Milwaukee, Wisconsin, "1/2 inch new galvanized hot dipped steel pipe 21 feet lengths as per sample recently submitted." It was agreed that the pipe was to be sent c.o.d.

Swain, Circuit Judge: When the shipment of this pipe arrived in Omaha it was sent to the warehouse of Morris Levey to whom the plaintiff had negotiated a sale of the pipe at 18³/₄¢ per foot. When Mr. Levey arrived at the warehouse the truckdriver had unloaded 40 or 50 pieces of pipe and had then been stopped by Levey's foreman who did not consider the pipe satisfactory. After Levey's arrival he examined the pipe that had been unloaded and then took a few pieces off of the truck "to see if it was probably some just on top, and we walked around the truck and looked as far as we could without unloading it all, and when we saw that it was all of that nature I [Levey] said, 'Let's call Morton Alpirn.'"

Mr. Alpirn said that when he arrived at Levey's warehouse about 50 pieces of the pipe had been removed from the truck and that Mr. Levey and his employee and the plaintiff's brother-in-law were inspecting them. The plaintiff testified that after the pipe had been inspected he notified the defendant that the pipe had arrived and was rejected because it was not in accordance with the contract.

The plaintiff thereafter brought an action for the alleged breach of the contract. . . .

The defendant contends that where, as here, a sale is for cash on delivery and the buyer fails to make such payment prior to delivery, the buyer does not have the right to inspect the goods and to reject the shipment for failure of the shipment to meet the specifications, and, further, that, under these circumstances, the buyer had no right to bring an action for a breach of the contract.

If we grant, arguendo, that under the terms of the contract the plaintiff was not given the right to inspect the shipment prior to his payment of the balance of the purchase price, the fact remains that such an inspection was made and that the inspection revealed that the shipment consisted of pipe substantially inferior to the pipe which the plaintiff had contracted to buy. The inspection was made by the plaintiff at the warehouse of Levey where the truckdriver had started to unload the pipe on Levey's shipping dock. There it was in plain sight of anyone who happened to be there and wanted to look at it. It is not apparent who, if anyone, told the truckdriver to start unloading the pipe. If the contract had been for the purchase of a horse and the attempted delivery had been of a cow which the plaintiff saw, surely the defendant would not contend that the plaintiff was under an obligation to pay the balance of the purchase price before rejecting delivery of the cow. Certainly, before there was any duty on the plaintiff to pay, there was the obligation of the defendant to deliver, or have ready for delivery, the pipe which the plaintiff had bought.

While the record contains some conflicting evidence as to the condition of the pipe and as to the methods used in testing it, there was an abundance of evidence, when we consider the record as a whole, to justify the court's finding that the pipe tendered neither met the written specifications of the contract of purchase nor corresponded to the sample furnished by the defendant. [DECISION FOR PLAINTIFF]

Canyon State Canners v. Hooks,   243 P.2d 1023 (Ariz. 1952). Action by Dan T. Hooks (plaintiff below), appellee, against Canyon State Canners (defendant below), appellant, to recover for the breach of an alleged contract to sell sweet potatoes to the defendant.

De Concini, Justice: Plaintiff at the time this action was commenced was a farmer engaged in growing various vegetable crops such as tomatoes, chili, sweet potatoes and corn in the Sulphur Springs valley near Douglas, Arizona. Defendant, an Arizona corporation, was engaged in the canning of various vegetables grown locally by the farmers. The cannery entered into contracts with the farmers of that area to buy their produce for canning. Plaintiff contends that he entered into a contract with defendant for the sale of sweet potatoes to be grown by him, through the defendant's plant manager, Mr. Kermit Day. The defendant failed to accept for delivery to it plaintiff's sweet potatoes; therefore plaintiff contends that since no timely notice of breach was given to him by the defendant the sweet potatoes were spoiled and rendered practically worthless. . . .

Defendant contends that delivery of the goods and payment are concurrent conditions and if no delivery is made there is no right of action for breach of contract. While that is a correct statement of the law, it is not applicable because of the evidence in this case. When the potatoes were ready to harvest, plaintiff notified the cannery and an agreement was made between the plaintiff and defendant, through its manager, Mr. Day, whereby plaintiff was to store the potatoes until notified by defendant to deliver them for canning. Defendant never at any time called or notified the plaintiff to bring the potatoes to be canned and when plaintiff realized the contract was breached, the potatoes were in a bad condition and unfit for use. There was evidence that there was no available market for this type of sweet potato at that time. Actual delivery here would have been an unnecessary condition since by defendant's agent's own acts, constructive delivery was had.

The potatoes were harvested and, when stored at plaintiff's farm with consent of defendant's agent, they became identified and applied irrevocably to the contract. [DECISION FOR PLAINTIFF]

Zabriskie Chevrolet, Inc. v. Smith, 240 A.2d 195 (N.J. 1968). Action by Zabriskie Chevrolet, Inc., plaintiff, against Alfred J. Smith, defendant, to recover the balance of the purchase price of a new automobile.

Defendant signed a purchase-order form for a new Chevrolet Biscayne sedan, which was represented to him to be a brand-new car that would operate perfectly. He paid $124 by way of deposit and later tendered his check for $2,069.50. The car was delivered to the wife of defendant the next day. After traveling about seven-tenths of a mile she had trouble, and the car stalled at a traffic light. The car stalled thereafter each time she was required to stop. She was fearful of completing the journey to her home and called her husband, who drove the car in "low-low" gear about seven blocks to his home. Defendant immediately called his bank, stopped payment on the check, and then called plaintiff and stated that he had stopped payment on the check and that the sale was canceled. Plaintiff sent a wrecker to defendant's home the next day and brought the car to defendant's repair shop. Defendant refused to take delivery of the car after it was repaired, and plaintiff brought this action to recover the balance of the purchase price. Defendant counter-claimed for a return of his deposit. Plaintiff's expert testified at the trial that the car would not move; that there was no power in the transmission; and that the car could not move in that condition.

Doan, Judge: It is clear that a buyer does not accept goods until he has had a "reasonable opportunity to inspect." Defendant sought to purchase a new car. He assumed what every new car buyer has a right to assume and, indeed, has been led to assume by the high powered advertising techniques of the auto industry—that his new car, with the exception of very minor adjustments, would be mechanically new and factory-furnished, operate perfectly, and be free of substantial defects. The vehicle delivered to defendant did not measure up to these representations. Plaintiff contends that defendant had "reasonable opportunity to inspect" by the privilege to take the car for a typical "spin around the block" before signing the purchase order. If by this contention plaintiff equates a spin around the block with "reasonable opportunity to inspect," the contention is illusory and unrealistic. . . .

Even if defendant had accepted the automobile tendered, he had a right to revoke under section 2–608:

"(1) The buyer may revoke his acceptance of a lot or commercial unit whose nonconformity *substantially impairs its value* to him if he has accepted it." . . .

Lastly, plaintiff urges that under the Code, section 2–508, it had a right to cure the nonconforming delivery. The Uniform Commercial Code Comment to section 2–508 reads:

"Subsection (2) seeks to avoid injustice to the seller by reason of a surprise rejection by the buyer. However, the seller is not protected unless he had 'reasonable grounds to believe' that the tender would be acceptable." . . .

Nor did the plaintiff have reasonable grounds to believe that a new automobile which could not even be driven a bare few miles to the buyer's residence would be acceptable. The dealer is in an entirely different position from the layman. The dealer with his staff of expert mechanics and modern equipment knows or should know of substantial defects in the new automobile which it sells. There was offered into evidence the dealer's inspection and adjustment schedule containing over seventy alleged items that plaintiff caused to be inspected, including the transmission. According to that schedule the automobile in question had been checked by the seller for the satisfaction of the buyer, and such inspection included a road test. The fact that the automobile underwent a tortured operation for about two and one-half miles from the showroom to defendant's residence demonstrates the inherent serious deficiencies in this vehicle which were present when the so-called inspection was made by plaintiff, and hence plaintiff was aware (or should have been) that the vehicle did not conform to the bargain the parties had made, and plaintiff had no reasonable right to expect that the vehicle in that condition would be accepted.

Accordingly, and pursuant to section 2–711, judgment is rendered on the main case in favor of defendant. On the counterclaim judgment is rendered in favor of defendant and against plaintiff in the sum of $124, being the amount of the deposit, there being no further proof of damages.

Defendant shall, as part of this judgment, execute for plaintiff, on demand, such documents as are necessary to again vest title to the vehicle in plaintiff. [DECISION FOR DEFENDANT]

PROBLEMS

1 Carter received and accepted an order from Farley for thirty-five pairs of shoes to be shipped by carrier. Conforming goods were properly packed and delivered to the carrier, and notification of the shipment was given to Farley. Some of the shoes, however, were badly damaged en route. Farley accepted only four pairs and mailed a check to Carter in payment of the invoice price of the four pairs of shoes. Carter refused to accept the check or the return of the thirty-one pairs which were rejected. Is Farley liable in an action by Carter for the contract price of thirty-five pairs of shoes?

2 Davis agreed to sell to Baker 200 steers weighing 450 to 600 pounds each at the agreed price of forty cents per pound. It was further agreed that delivery would be made on October 1, although no place of delivery was specified. Davis knew, at the time this contract was created, that Baker agreed to purchase these steers in order to perform a pre-existing contractual obligation to deliver 200 steers to the Acme Company on October 2. On October 1, Davis had confined in his corral and ready for delivery 200 steers, several cows, calves, and deformed cattle. He insisted that Baker would have to accept all the cattle and pay him forty cents per pound. Baker refused and insisted that Davis was under a contractual duty to deliver the 200 steers to the nearest railway which was ten miles away. (a) Has Davis made a proper tender of delivery? (b) Is Davis under a duty to deliver the steers to the railroad?

3 Brown purchased a harvester from Smith for use in harvesting his grain. It was agreed that payment would be made within thirty days. The harvester was delivered to the farm of Brown at the proper time, but it did not perform as warranted. Brown nevertheless used the machine in harvesting more than 200 acres, and to paraphrase him, "so I could gather more evidence of the breach of warranty." He now contends that he has a right to return the machine since he has not accepted it. Is this contention correct?

4 Kerson agreed to sell to Yon a piano at an agreed price of $800. The parties discussed the fact that the piano was stored in the "Security Warehouse," but there was no discussion with respect to delivery. Kerson later demanded payment, which was refused. Yon contended that Kerson should have delivered the piano to his fifth-floor apartment in the building in which he lived. Is the contention of Yon correct?

5 Plaintiff, doing business in St. Louis, Missouri, contracted to purchase from defendant, doing business in Wellington, Kansas, 1,600 sacks of bran, to be delivered in East St. Louis. Defendant shipped the bran in four cars and forwarded the bills of lading to plaintiff. After receipt of the bills, plaintiff remitted the full purchase price to defendant. Two of the cars were destroyed en route by a flood. Plaintiff therefore received only two of the carloads. Plaintiff thereupon brought an action to recover damages for failure to deliver the two cars of bran. Decide.

6 Defendant gave one of plaintiff's traveling salesmen a written order for a quantity of gloves, describing them by number, name, and size. The salesman sent the order to plaintiff together with a memorandum stating that the gloves were to be shipped over the Chicago &

Northwestern Railway. The order was accepted by plaintiff who notified the defendant of the acceptance. Plaintiff had the gloves in stock, selected those ordered, packed them for shipment, set them aside in plaintiff's warehouse, and attached shipping tags bearing the name and address of defendant. On June 30, defendant breached the contract and requested plaintiff to cancel it, but plaintiff refused. The gloves were later destroyed in plaintiff's warehouse. Did the risk of loss pass to defendant so that plaintiff can recover the purchase price?

7 The Wholesale Company, which owned certain furniture stored in a warehouse in the City of X, sold the furniture to Brown, also of the City of X. The Wholesale Company then delivered a negotiable warehouse receipt to Brown, who delayed taking delivery of the furniture for over three weeks. Brown then drove his truck to the warehouse for the purpose of taking delivery, but the furniture was on fire through no fault of the warehouseman. Brown and the warehouseman attempted to extinguish the fire, but the merchandise was destroyed. Should The Wholesale Company or Brown stand the loss?

18
SALES: REMEDIES

The key concept around which the Code remedies revolve is the acceptance of the goods by the buyer. It seems necessary, therefore, to first determine when an acceptance occurs. Acceptance of goods is usually signified by the receipt and retention of the goods after an inspection reveals them to be conforming. A buyer, under section 2–606, accepts the goods when, after a reasonable opportunity to inspect the goods, he (a) signifies to the seller that the goods are conforming or that he will take them in spite of their nonconformity or (b) fails to make an effective rejection. Acceptance is a factual situation, but a buyer who pays for the goods after delivery or uses the goods over a long period of time without a complaint would certainly tend to signify an acceptance. The Code expressly provides that the buyer accepts the goods when he does any act inconsistent with ownership in the seller. [*Lang v. Fleet*, p. 235.]

Section 2–719 allows the parties considerable contractual freedom so that they may create their own remedies within reasonable limitations. Reasonable liquidated damages clauses, for example, are enforceable. Any unreasonable limitation of remedies will probably be considered unconscionable and will not be enforceable in court, because to do so would unfairly surprise or oppress the victim. Such an unreasonable limitation would be subject to deletion, and the victim would have available the remedies provided by Article 2.

It now remains to consider the remedies available to the seller and the buyer prior to acceptance of the goods and subsequent to acceptance of the goods.

REMEDIES OF THE SELLER PRIOR TO ACCEPTANCE

The remedies available to the seller prior to acceptance may be summarized: (1) withhold delivery of the goods, (2) stop the goods in transit, (3) resell the goods, (4) recover damages for nonacceptance, (5) recover the price, and (6) cancel the contract.

Withhold Delivery of the Goods   The seller may withhold delivery of the goods on grounds of insolvency or on grounds of breach of contract.

(1)   *Insolvency of the Buyer*   A person is insolvent who has ceased to pay his debts in the ordinary course of business, cannot pay his debts as they become due, or is insolvent within the meaning of the federal bankruptcy act. It is thus clear that the word "insolvency" is interpreted to mean a buyer who is insolvent in the mercantile sense as well as a person who has been adjudicated a bankrupt.

Assuming that the buyer is insolvent, section 2–702 gives the seller the right to refuse to deliver the goods on credit. The seller may also refuse to deliver the goods to an insolvent buyer unless the buyer tenders cash for the goods in question and pays for all goods theretofore delivered. Suppose the seller enters into a contract to make five deliveries on credit at a price of $500 per delivery. Suppose further that the seller makes two deliveries before he learns of the insolvency of the buyer. The seller could not be compelled to make the three remaining deliveries unless the buyer was prepared to pay cash for the previous two deliveries as well as the three remaining deliveries.

(2)   *Grounds of Breach*   The seller may withhold delivery of the goods if the buyer wrongfully rejects or revokes acceptance of the goods or fails to make payment. This is the situation when the buyer demonstrates a clear intention not to continue with performance. This merely continues the rule that the seller should not be required to perform if it is reasonably certain that the buyer cannot or will not perform. It exemplifies the rule which permits a party to suspend performance upon an anticipatory breach.

Stoppage in Transit   The right to stop the goods in transit extends the withholding remedy by allowing it to be used during transit. The reason is obvious. The seller cannot withhold during the transportation period because he is not in possession. Under pre-Code law, the seller was permitted to stop the goods in transit only if the buyer was insolvent and only if the goods were in transit. This right has been expanded by section 2–705 to include cases where the buyer has breached the contract and where the goods are held by a warehouseman. This will usually—but not necessarily—be the case when the carrier has ended its duties as a carrier and stored the goods in its own warehouse. The right of stoppage has also been extended by section 2–707 to include a "person in the position of a seller," such as a bank that has financed the sale by discounting a draft when the goods have been shipped under a negotiable bill of lading. The right of stoppage ceases when the goods are no longer in the possession of the carrier.

(1) *Insolvency of the Buyer* The unpaid seller who has delivered the goods to the transportation agency for shipment to the buyer may stop the goods in transit by notifying the carrier not to deliver the goods to the buyer. The carrier must obey an order to stop provided the carrier is given enough time to carry out the order and is also given protection against misdelivery. The carrier is not under an obligation to carry out the order to stop the goods if there is an outstanding negotiable bill of lading unless the bill of lading is surrendered. The carrier is not obligated to stop the goods, in the case of a straight bill—a nonnegotiable bill—if the order comes from someone other than the consignor. The seller will ordinarily be the consignor, which would prevent a financing agency or other stranger to the contract from exercising the right of stoppage in the case of a straight bill. The person issuing the stop order is under a duty to pay the carrier any damages or charges resulting from the stoppage.

(2) *Grounds of Breach* The right to stop the goods in transit because of a breach of contract or fraud is limited to delivery of carload, truckload, planeload or larger shipments. The seller, therefore, may stop any shipment in transit where the buyer is insolvent, but only deliveries of carload, truckload, planeload, or larger shipments for breach of contract or fraud.

(3) *Duration of Right of Stoppage* The right of the seller to stop the goods in transit ends when the buyer has received the goods. The buyer has obviously received the goods when he has taken physical possession of them. The right to stop, however, also ends when a bailee—other than the carrier—acknowledges to the buyer that the goods are being held for the buyer.

The right of stoppage also ends when there is a reshipment of the goods. This happens when the seller ships the goods to the buyer, and the buyer ships them to a third person without taking actual possession of the goods. Suppose a seller in San Francisco is under a contract to ship goods to a buyer in Chicago but that the buyer in Chicago has already resold the goods to a buyer in Los Angeles. Must the goods travel from San Francisco to Chicago and then back to Los Angeles? This would not be good business practice. The goods, therefore, may be reshipped. A "reshipment" can be accomplished by having the carrier transport the goods from San Francisco to Los Angeles. The seller should not be able to stop the goods in transit from San Francisco to Los Angeles, because the general notion is that the goods are being shipped from Chicago to Los Angeles.

Resell the Goods A seller who is in possession of the goods as a result of withholding, stopping in transit, or because the goods have been rejected by the buyer, may resell the goods. The seller must, however, comply with the restrictions set out in section 2–706 on the manner of resale. The resale may be at private or public sale—an auction—but it must be made "in good faith and in a commercially reasonable manner." The seller must give the buyer reasonable notification of his intention to sell the goods at a private sale. [*Wood v. Downing*, p. 236.]

Special restrictions are imposed upon a seller who employs a public sale. These restrictions involve the place of sale, the type of notice that must be given, and the kinds of goods that may be resold.

(1)   *Place of Sale and Notice*   The sale must be made at a usual place for public sale, but, if such place is not available, the seller may hold the sale at another place where prospective bidders may reasonably be expected to attend. The notice must contain information as to the location of the goods and the times when the goods may be inspected. The seller, however, may resell goods which are perishable or threaten to decline in value speedily without notice to the buyer.

(2)   *Kinds of Goods*   Only identified goods may be resold except where there is a recognized market for a public sale for futures—raw material purchased for the manufacture of sweaters. This is for the reason that futures are not apt to command the best price at a public sale at which they are not ordinarily sold.

Assume this set of facts: The seller and the buyer have entered into a contract for the sale and purchase of 100 sweaters. The seller has invested $500 in raw material and completed manufacture of 50 of the sweaters. The buyer then repudiates the contract. What remedies are available to the seller? The seller is given the right by section 2–704 to cease manufacture, identify the 50 sweaters to the contract, and make a resale of the finished sweaters and the raw material. The seller, however, is given an alternative remedy. He may complete manufacture of the sweaters and identify the 100 sweaters to the contract. He may then resell the 100 sweaters and collect damages. He may also withhold the sweaters and bring an action for nonacceptance.

It may be well to mention that a good faith purchaser at a resale takes the goods free of any rights of the original buyer. This is true even though the seller fails to comply with one or more of the restrictions imposed by the Code on the manner of resale.

(3)   *Measure of Damages*   A seller who has complied with the restrictions on resale may recover from the buyer any deficiency between the resale price and the contract price, together with any incidental damages. The expenses for transporting the goods for resale, for instance, could be recovered as incidental damages. The seller may also retain any profit made on any resale.

Damages for Nonacceptance   The measure of damages under section 2–708 for nonacceptance is the difference between the contract price and the market price of the goods. The seller, however, may include in the damages any profit he would have made by performance if damages based on market price are inadequate to put the seller in as good a position as performance would have done.

Recovery of the Price   An action for the price of the goods is available to the seller who is in possession of the goods where the goods have been identified to the contract. An action for the price prior to acceptance by the buyer, however, is limited to those situations where the seller is unable to resell the goods or the circumstances indicate that an effort to resell would be unsuccessful. The seller who brings an action for the price must hold any goods in his possession for the buyer. He may, however, resell them at any time prior to the collection of the judgment against the buyer for the price.

Cancellation   Section 2–703 provides that the seller may cancel the contract if the buyer wrongfully rejects the goods, revokes acceptance of the goods, fails to make payment, or repudiates the contract. Section 2–106 provides that cancellation terminates all unperformed obligations on both sides, but also provides that the seller does not lose his right to bring an action for breach of contract. Section 2–720 makes it clear that the use of the words "cancellation" or "rescission" or the like is not a discharge of any claim for damages for breach of contract. Cancellation, therefore, is not to be regarded as a common-law rescission of the contract where the rescinding party loses his right to damages.

REMEDIES OF THE SELLER AFTER ACCEPTANCE

The remedies available to the seller after the buyer has accepted the goods are: (1) bring an action to recover the price, and (2) reclaim the goods from an insolvent buyer.

Recovery of the Price   An action for the price of the goods is available to the seller after acceptance of the goods by the buyer, or when conforming goods have been lost or damaged after the risk of loss has passed to the buyer. [*Park County Implement Co. v. Craig*, p. 236.]

Reclaim the Goods   The seller would obviously have no opportunity to withhold the goods or to stop them when the goods have been delivered to an insolvent buyer. Section 2–702, therefore, gives the seller the right to reclaim the goods upon discovery of the buyer's insolvency. As a condition of the right to reclaim, however, the seller must make his demand within ten days after the buyer has received the goods. A written misrepresentation of solvency is made an exception to this time limitation. The ten-day limitation does not apply, therefore, if the buyer has made a misrepresentation of solvency to the particular seller in writing within three months before delivery of the goods. This right of the seller to reclaim the goods is made subject to the rights of buyers in the ordinary course of business or other good faith purchasers or lien creditors. The seller, therefore, could not reclaim the goods if they have been resold to a buyer in the ordinary course of business or resold to other good faith purchasers; nor could the seller reclaim the goods if they have been attached by a lien creditor.

REMEDIES OF THE BUYER PRIOR TO ACCEPTANCE

The remedies available to the buyer prior to acceptance may be summarized: (1) recover the goods, (2) specific performance and replevin, (3) the "cover" remedy, (4) damages for nondelivery, (5) resell the goods, and (6) cancellation.

Recover the Goods The buyer is given the right to reach the goods on the insolvency of the seller by section 2–502. The buyer must, however, have an insurable interest in the goods; that is, the goods must have been identified to the contract. The insolvency must also have occurred within ten days after payment for the goods. If the goods have not been fully paid for, the insolvency must have occurred within ten days after the first installment payment and the buyer must make and keep good a tender of the balance due. One further point: It will be remembered that the buyer himself can identify the goods to the contract, even though they are nonconforming. The right of the buyer to reach the goods on the insolvency of the seller, however, is limited to conforming goods if the buyer makes the identification.

Specific Performance and Replevin The buyer who has not accepted the goods is given the right to reach the goods by means of specific performance. Section 2–716 gives the buyer this right where the goods are unique or in other proper circumstances. Output and requirements contracts which involve a particular source or market would present a typical specific performance situation as contrasted to heirlooms or priceless works of art in the earlier cases. The buyer is also given the right to replevy the goods which have been identified to the contract. This is true even though the title has not passed to the buyer. The buyer, however, is required to make a reasonable effort to procure substitute goods by his cover remedy prior to exercising his right of replevin.

"Cover" Remedy A buyer who has not accepted the goods or who has justifiably revoked his acceptance is given a cover remedy by section 2–712. This remedy is available when the seller fails to make delivery of the goods or has delivered nonconforming goods. This means that a buyer who needs the goods for himself or for the purpose of resale may purchase other goods as a substitute for those which the seller should have delivered. A buyer who takes advantage of this cover remedy may recover from the seller as damages the difference between the cost of cover and the contract price, but "less expenses saved in consequence of the seller's breach."

Suppose the buyer has contracted to purchase drapery material for $3.25 a yard and plans to make the material into draperies himself at a cost of ten cents a yard. Suppose further that the buyer has a customer who is anxious to purchase the finished draperies. The buyer may—if the materials for the draperies are not forthcoming from the seller—pursue his cover remedy and purchase the finished draperies for $3.50 a yard. The cover damages are fifteen cents a yard and not twenty-five cents a yard. The breach has saved the buyer ten cents a yard in finishing costs. Credit must be allowed the seller, therefore, for this savings.

Damages for Nondelivery The buyer is under no duty to pursue his cover remedy. He may prefer to recover damages for nondelivery under section 2–713. The measure of damages for nondelivery is the difference between the market price at the time the buyer learned of the breach and the contract price together with any incidental damages. The buyer must, however, deduct from his damages any expenses saved as a result of the breach. The market price is to be determined as of the place for tender or, in cases of rejection after arrival or revocation of acceptance, as of the place of arrival.

Resell the Goods   Section 2–711 provides that the buyer may, on rejection or justifiable revocation of acceptance, hold the goods in his possession and resell them in the same manner as an aggrieved seller. This right of resale is given the buyer when he has a security interest in the goods. The buyer would have a "security interest" when he has paid a part of the price or incurred expenses in inspection and handling of the goods. The buyer may retain out of the funds received from the resale the amount he paid on the price and other expenses. Any surplus funds must be transmitted to the seller.

Cancellation   Sections 2–106 and 2–720 are applicable to the buyer as well as the seller. The buyer, therefore, may cancel the contract and terminate all unperformed obligations on both sides. He does not, however, lose his right to damages. It will be remembered that the use of the words "cancellation" or "rescission" or the like is not a discharge of any claim for damages. Section 2–711 provides specifically that the buyer may cancel the contract (1) if the seller fails to make delivery, breaches the contract, or repudiates the contract, or (2) if the buyer rightfully rejects the goods or justifiably revokes his acceptance. The buyer is not required to cancel the contract. If he does or does not cancel, however, he may in addition to recovering so much of the price he has paid (a) use his "cover" remedy and recover damages or (b) recover damages for nondelivery.

REMEDIES OF THE BUYER AFTER ACCEPTANCE

The remedies available to the buyer after the goods have been accepted are (1) revocation of acceptance, (2) action for damages, and (3) recoupment.

Revocation of Acceptance   A buyer may revoke his acceptance of nonconforming goods under section 2–608. In order to revoke, however, the acceptance must have been made because the buyer had difficulty discovering the defects, or because of the assumption that the nonconformity would be cured and it has not been cured. The buyer must notify the seller of his revocation within a reasonable time after he discovers or should have discovered the nonconformity. The buyer loses his right of revocation if the goods have undergone any substantial change in condition not caused by their own defects. A revoking buyer has the same rights and duties with regard to the goods as if he had rejected them.

Damages for Nonconformity   Damages for nonconformity include not only a breach of warranty but also any failure of the seller to perform according to his obligation under the contract. Section 2–714 allows the buyer to recover for his loss "in any manner which is reasonable."

Damages for Breach of Warranty The measure of damages for breach of warranty is the difference between the value of the goods accepted and the value they would have had if they had been as warranted. This difference in "value" is calculated at the time and place of acceptance. Suppose the buyer purchases a refrigerator for $150. Suppose further that the refrigerator as warranted would be worth $400 at the time and place of acceptance. Suppose still further that the refrigerator is actually worth only $75 at the time and place of acceptance. The measure of damages for breach of warranty would be $325.

Recoupment Section 2–717 gives the buyer the right of recoupment for breach of contract. The buyer, however, is obligated to notify the seller of his right to recoup. Recoupment means that the buyer may deduct all or any part of the damages resulting from the breach from any part of the price still due under the same contract.

CASES

F. W. Lang Co. v. Fleet, 165 A.2d 258 (Pa. 1960). Action by F. W. Lang Company, plaintiff, against Bertram Fleet and Sidney Danowitz, defendants, to replevy goods sold on an installment sales contract.

On April 30, 1957, defendants purchased an ice cream freezer and a refrigeration compressor unit from the plaintiff for the sum of $2,160 on an installment sales contract. About one year after the equipment was installed, the defendants moved to a new location and took the equipment with them. Sometime thereafter, the defendants disconnected the compressor from the freezer and connected it to an air conditioner where it was used by the defendants to operate the air conditioner. Defendants paid the sum of $200 at the time of receiving the freezer and compressor but made no further payments. On July 30, 1959, plaintiff replevied the equipment. Plaintiff then sold the equipment for $500, the highest price then obtainable. The defendants were given credit for this sum, and judgment was entered for the unpaid balance. Defendants filed an action for rescission of the sales contract alleging that the equipment was defective, wholly unusable for the purpose intended, and demanded the return of the $200 and damages for the cost of maintenance of the equipment while it was in the possession of the defendants.

Boyle, Judge: The Uniform Commercial Code, section 2–602, provides: "(1) Rejection of goods must be within a reasonable time after their delivery or tender. It is ineffective unless the buyer seasonably notifies the seller. (2) . . . (a) after rejection any exercise of ownership by the buyer with respect to any commercial unit is wrongful as against the seller."

Section 2–606 provides: "(1) Acceptance of goods occurs when the buyer . . . (c) does any act inconsistent with the seller's ownership; but if such act is wrongful as against the seller it is an acceptance only if ratified by him."

In the instant case, the defendants exercised dominion over the compressor unit by using it to operate an air conditioner. This is completely inconsistent with the seller's ownership. The seller ratified the sale as represented by the installment sales contract. The seller never accepted or agreed to a rescission by the defendants. Therefore, under the cited provisions of the Uniform Commercial Code, the buyer is deemed to have accepted the goods and is precluded from unilaterally asserting a rescission of the sales contract.

A rescission based on breach of warranty must be made within a reasonable time and cannot be made if the buyer exercises an act of dominion over the goods or permits the goods to be altered or changed while in his exclusive possession. [DECISION FOR PLAINTIFF]

Wood v. Downing, 418 S.W.2d 800 (Ark. 1967). Action by Ned Downing, plaintiff-appellee, against Arnold Wood, doing business as Arnold Wood Radio and TV Service, defendant-appellant, to recover the down payment on a color television set which was sold to another person.

On January 5, appellee entered into an agreement at appellant's store with appellant, who is engaged in the business of retailing and servicing radio and TV sets, to purchase a specific color TV set for the price of $450. Appellee paid $100 on account of the purchase price and agreed to pay the balance within thirty days. Early in May, appellee went to the store to pay the balance and accept delivery of the set. He was informed by appellant, however, that the set had been sold to another person and that he had no other set of the same make. Appellee demanded the return of the $100, appellant refused, and appellee brought this action to collect the $100. The trial court rendered judgment against appellant, and he appealed.

Ward, Justice: It is our opinion that the decision of the trial court (sitting as a jury) is supported by substantial evidence. Also we point out that appellant, after the lapse of thirty days from January 5, was still holding the set in storage and that he did not give appellee notice that he intended to sell the same to another party. Under the situation here, we think appellee was entitled to a reasonable notice under section 2–706(3). [DECISION FOR APPELLEE]

Park County Implement Co. v. Craig 397 P.2d 800 (Wyo. 1964). Action by Park County Implement Company, plaintiff, against Dave Craig and Roger Holler, defendants, to recover the purchase price of a truck.

Defendants ordered a 1962 International A-162 chassis and cab from plaintiff for the agreed price of $3,150. Defendants put the vehicle in their shop, and were installing a hoist and dump bed when a fire occurred and destroyed the chassis and cab. Defendants contend that they are not liable for the price because (1) they had not accepted the vehicle, and (2) the Uniform Commercial Code does not apply since a motor vehicle cannot be classified as "goods."

Parker, Chief Justice: At the inception of the synthesis, we note that the Uniform Commercial Code—Sales had been adopted in Wyoming, January 1, 1962, and was in effect at the time of the transaction, and further that this Code has been held as applicable to motor vehicles. The buyers accepted the goods under the provisions of section 2–606, "Acceptance of goods occurs when the buyer does any act inconsistent with the seller's ownership," when they began installing a hoist and dump bed on the vehicle. At that time the buyer became liable under the provisions of section 2–607(1), "The buyer must pay at the contract rate for any goods accepted." Under the admitted facts, the defendants accepted the goods at an agreed price. [DECISION FOR PLAINTIFF]

PROBLEMS

1 Adams, as seller, contracted with Welch, as buyer, for the sale of 150 lawnmowers. The purchase order stated: "Ship direct to 30th and Harcum Way, Pitts., Pa." Welch accepted the lawnmowers on March 28. Adams, upon learning of the insolvency of Welch, made unsuccessful telephone and written demands for a return of the lawnmowers. The first of such demands was made on April 4. In the meantime, Welch sold 50 of the lawnmowers to third persons in the ordinary course of business. Discuss Adams' right to reclaim the 150 lawnmowers.

2 Lovell agreed to sell his trucking business to Mack. It was further agreed that Lovell would transfer to Mack the Interstate Commerce and Pennsylvania Public Utilities Commission certificates which he owned in connection with the trucking business. Mack brought an action for specific performance when Lovell refused to perform. Lovell contended that Mack had an adequate and complete remedy at law and that equity therefore had no jurisdiction. Is Mack entitled to a decree of specific performance?

3 Gordon and Hamilton entered into a written contract which provided in part: "This certifies that D. Gordon hereby sells and agrees to deliver to Hamilton, in his warehouse, on or before October 1st, all the grain harvested by me, on land described below, wheat sacked in good merchantable sacks, the same being that certain crop now harvested, or hereafter to be harvested during the current season." The contract, which was signed by both parties, also stated the acreage and the price. Gordon, except for 234 sacks, delivered all the harvested wheat to Hamilton . Hamilton brought an action to recover possession of the 234 sacks of wheat. Does Hamilton have a right to replevy the wheat?

4 Craig had purchased a quantity of farm machinery from a manufacturer, and the First Bank financed the sale. The machinery was shipped by carrier, and a nonnegotiable bill of lading was issued to Craig. Prior to the arrival of the machinery, Craig was adjudicated a bankrupt. The First Bank, therefore, notified the carrier not to deliver the machinery to Craig. Was the First Bank justified in attempting to stop the goods in transit?

5 The Appliance Company and Brown, a retail dealer, entered into a contract for the sale and purchase of ten refrigerators. Brown paid $500 on the purchase price and signed a conditional sales contract for the balance. The company then assigned the sales contract to the First Bank. The refrigerators were defective, and the company agreed to send a truck to return them to the company's warehouse. Brown made repeated requests to the company to send a truck for the refrigerators, but the company failed to do so. About a year later, Brown made repairs to the refrigerators and sold them at a reduced price after having given proper notice to the company. The First Bank, as assignee, then brought an action against Brown to recover the purchase price. Should the First Bank recover?

6 The Hardware Company and Jones entered into a written contract by the terms of which The Hardware Company agreed to sell and Jones agreed to purchase 100 motors at a price of $100 each. Just prior to the time that The Hardware Company was to deliver the motors, Jones notified the company that he would neither receive nor accept the motors. The Hardware Company thereupon sold the motors at public auction for $90 each. Was The Hardware Company obligated to give Jones notice of the sale?

7 The seller and the buyer entered into a written contract by the terms of which the seller agreed to sell and the buyer agreed to purchase 500 boxes of apples that were of a variety and quality readily available on the open market. The seller had a large quantity of such apples on hand, but he refused to deliver them to the buyer. The buyer thereupon attempted to recover the goods by means of specific performance. Will the buyer succeed?

8 Baker, the owner and operator of a grocery store, entered into a contract with Cabot whereby Cabot agreed to sell and Baker agreed to purchase 1,000 cartons of eggs for the sum of $1,000. Cabot breached the contract by a failure to deliver the eggs on the day specified in the contract for delivery. Baker, who needed the eggs for resale, purchased the eggs in the open market for $1,200. What action, if any, does Baker have against Cabot?

Part

4

COMMERCIAL PAPER

19
NATURE OF
COMMERCIAL PAPER

It cannot be definitely stated just when the use of negotiable instruments was first adopted. Commercial paper was used in the Middle Ages. The origin of our present-day law of commercial paper was the law merchant. This law was gradually assimilated by the English common law and consequently became a part of our law when the American states adopted the English common law. During the years that followed, various state legislatures enacted a variety of statutes pertaining to commercial paper. The result was a great lack of uniformity in the statutes as well as in court decisions. The National Conference of Commissioners on Uniform State Laws, therefore, drafted the Negotiable Instruments Law. Article 3 of the Code now covers the law of commercial paper, and is a revision and modernization of the Negotiable Instruments Law.

A negotiable instrument is a contractual obligation which calls for the payment of money, the primary function of which is to provide a medium of exchange that can be used in lieu of money. It should not be presumed, however, that this brief definition is all-inclusive. Certain formal requisites of negotiability—to which the next chapter is entirely devoted—must be satisfied before an instrument may be classed as a "negotiable instrument."

TYPES OF NEGOTIABLE INSTRUMENTS

Negotiable instruments are classified by the Code as promissory notes, drafts (bills of exchange), checks, and certificates of deposit. There are, to be sure, many various forms of negotiable instruments. An analysis of the many variations will reveal, however, that they belong to one or the other of the four titles mentioned. These four titles, as well as other special titles which are commonly used, will be continually recurring through the chapters that follow. It will be helpful at the outset, therefore, to have a working knowledge of these titles.

Promissory Notes   A promissory note, briefly stated, contains a promise to pay a sum of money. It embraces two persons: the maker and the payee. The person promising to pay is called the "maker"; the person to whom the promise is made is called the "payee." Promissory notes are sometimes payable on demand, sometimes in installments, and sometimes at a stated time in the future. The promise of the maker is frequently supported by a security contract, the terms of which may be set out in a separate agreement, to which reference is made in the note, or incorporated in the note itself. This latter arrangement often results in a quite elaborate note. There are five principal kinds of promissory notes; the simplest form is shown in the illustration.

(1)   *Mortgage Notes*   Two kinds of mortgage notes are the chattel mortgage note and the real estate mortgage note. As the name implies, a chattel mortgage note is secured by personal property; a real estate mortgage note is secured by real property. The security contract, known as a mortgage, most frequently provides that the mortgage can be foreclosed if the note is not paid when it is due.

(2)   *Title-retaining Note*   This type of note is secured by a conditional sales contract which ordinarily provides that title to the goods shall remain in the payee's name until the note is paid in full. It is used to secure the purchase price of goods.

(3)   *Bonds*   A bond is a sealed instrument ordinarily issed by corpora-

Promissory note

tions, public and private, by which the issuer promises to pay a designated sum of money to a person known as the bondholder. The two forms of bonds in common use are coupon bonds and registered bonds. Coupon bonds have promissory notes called "coupons," redeemable for each interest period, attached to them. The coupons may be clipped off by the holder of the bond as they become due. The usual procedure is to leave the coupon with a bank for collection. Bonds payable to a specified person whose name is registered in the books of the issuer are known as "registered bonds." These bonds are transferable only by registering the name of the transferee in the books of the issuer. Payments on a registered bond are ordinarily transmitted to the registered payee by check.

(4)   *Collateral Note*   This type is an ordinary note, and is used when the maker   pledges   securities   to   the   payee   to   secure   the   payment   of the amount of the note. Shares of stock, bonds, and other property are frequently pledged by the maker and placed with the holder as collateral security. Banks usually require a special form of collateral note which refers to the collateral and contains a provision giving the holder the right to sell the collateral in the event of a default.

(5)   *Judgment Notes*   This type is an ordinary promissory note to which is added a power of attorney enabling the payee to take judgment against the maker without the formality of a trial if the note is not paid on its due date. Judgment notes are used only in a limited number of states.

Drafts   A draft, briefly stated, is an order from one person to another person to pay a third person a sum of money. It embraces three persons: the drawer, the drawee, and the payee. The person ordering payment is called the "drawer"; the person to whom the order is addressed is called the "drawee"; and the person to whom the drawee is ordered to pay is called the "payee." A typical form of draft is shown in the illustration.

Drafts may be classified as to place. A draft, which appears on its face, to be drawn or payable outside of the states and territories of the United States and the District of Columbia is known as an international draft. If it is drawn and

Draft

payable in the same state or payable in another state, territory, or the District of Columbia, it is known as a domestic draft.

(1) **Sight Draft** Drafts may be further classified as to time. A draft payable at sight is known as a "sight draft." A draft payable at a stated time in the future is known as a "time draft." A time draft may be payable after date or after sight. If it is payable after date, as thirty days after date, it is payable thirty days after the date of the instrument. If it is payable after sight, as thirty days after sight, it is payable thirty days after the date of presentment.

(2) **Trade Acceptance** The trade acceptance is a popular form of draft used particularly by manufacturers and wholesalers. The usual form of trade acceptance is drawn by the seller-drawer on the buyer-drawee, payable to the seller at some future time, for the sale price of a shipment of goods. The seller then sends the draft to the buyer, who "accepts" it. The acceptance usually consists of the word "accepted," the date, and the name of the drawee written across the face of the instrument. The buyer then returns the accepted draft to the seller who, as payee, may deposit it as collateral for a loan or discount it with a bank. The buyer, by giving the trade acceptance, cannot later dispute the debt against the holder of the trade acceptance. The bank or other holder, therefore, can hold either or both the drawer and the acceptor in the event of a default. Consequently, the seller can more readily secure a loan on a trade acceptance than on an assignment of an open account. The trade acceptance is a convenient medium of trade which enables the seller to get his money immediately and at the same time to extend credit to his customer. A standard form of trade acceptance is shown in the illustration.

(3) **Banker's Acceptance** A banker's acceptance is used under circumstances similar to those under which the trade acceptance is used. The two are distinguishable, however, because the banker's acceptance is drawn on the buyer's bank rather than on the buyer himself. The buyer, before the date he

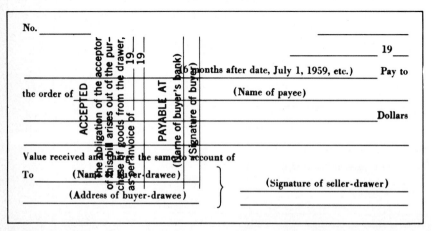

Trade acceptance

desires to purchase the goods, makes the necessary arrangements with his bank to accept the draft. He may be required to deposit collateral with the bank, or he may agree to keep a sufficient amount of money on deposit with the bank to cover the draft. The bank then accepts the draft in the same general manner as the buyer accepts the trade acceptance. The bank, however, is not making a loan; it is merely lending its credit to the buyer. The seller is, nevertheless, enabled to get his money immediately. The buyer is also enabled to buy on credit. A banker's acceptance is preferable to a trade acceptance because it is ordinarily more readily marketable.

Checks The Code defines a "check" as a draft drawn on a bank and payable on demand. This definition is satisfied by any written order drawn by the depositor-drawer, ordering the bank-drawee to pay on demand and unconditionally a definite sum of money to the payee. A check, however, is customarily made out on the printed form supplied by the bank. Checks may be distinguished from the other forms of drafts because they are always drawn on a bank or banker; they are payable on demand; and they are intended for immediate payment rather than for circulation. The check is used more than any other instrument of credit as a means of making payment.

(1) *Cashier's Check* A cashier's check is a check issued by the cashier of a bank and is commonly used for the same purpose as a bank draft. A cashier's check, however, is drawn by the bank on itself ordering itself to pay a stated sum of money. The drawee, therefore, is the bank that issues the check.

(2) *Traveler's Check* Traveler's checks are a particularly convenient and safe form in which to carry credit. The purchaser of the instrument signs his name on the instrument at the time of its issuance. The name of the payee is left blank. When he wishes to cash the check, he writes the name of the payee in the space provided and countersigns it in the presence of the person who is converting it into cash or accepting it in payment of a purchase.

(3) *Bank Draft* A bank draft is in the customary form of a personal check but is distinguishable because it is always drawn by one bank upon another bank. The drawer-bank would, of course, have funds on deposit in the drawee-bank. The bank draft is ordinarily used because the credit of the bank is more

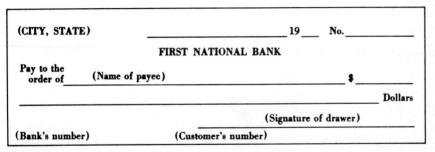

Check

acceptable than the credit of the individual. Let us assume that a buyer in one city desires to purchase merchandise in another city. Let us further assume that the buyer is unknown to the seller or for some other reason his personal check is not acceptable as payment. The buyer could purchase a bank draft from the drawer-bank in his city, drawn on the drawee-bank in the other city, payable to the order of the seller-payee.

Certificates of Deposit   A certificate of deposit is a written acknowledgment by a bank of receipt of money with an engagement to repay it. This writing will be a negotiable instrument provided it meets all the requirements for negotiability contained in section 3–104.

NEGOTIABLE INSTRUMENTS DISTINGUISHED

A negotiable instrument is one form of a contract. But there are many points of departure from contract law in the law of commercial paper. A few of the most prominent departures are noted at this point merely to indicate the nature of the problems with which the law of commercial paper deals. These departures will become more and more pronounced throughout the chapters that follow.

Presumption of Consideration   A creditor seeking to enforce the promise contained in a simple contract must prove a consideration. A negotiable instrument is presumed to have been issued for valuable consideration. The holder of the instrument, therefore, need not allege and prove consideration in order to establish a cause of action.

Transferability   A simple contract right to receive money may be assigned, in which case the assignee takes it subject to all the defenses between the parties, that is, all the defenses that may be set up against the assignor may be set up against the assignee. A negotiable instrument may be transferred by negotiation. This method of transfer makes it possible for the transferee to acquire a better right to it than the transferor had. This distinguishing characteristic goes to the very heart of the law of commercial paper. True, a negotiable instrument may be assigned, but that is not the usual procedure.

Letter of Credit   It should be mentioned at the outset that letters of credit are not classified as a negotiable instrument by the Code. They are governed by Article 5. They are, however, similar to commercial paper in that they have to do with issuing and honoring drafts.

A letter of credit, briefly stated, means an engagement by a bank or other person, on behalf of a buyer-customer, to make payments on the terms and conditions stated in the letter of credit. Letters of credit are ordinarily issued by banks. They are, however, occasionally written by financial institutions. This is particularly true if the drafts are accompanied by documents of title covering the goods involved in a sales contract. Section 5–102 makes the Code applicable to both the "clean" as well as the "documentary" letter of credit. Clean letters of credit require no document, and they are used by travelers. The traveler carries with him both the letter of credit and a signature identification card. The use of this device, however, may not be feasible unless the integrity of the customer is well established. The remainder of this discussion will be devoted to documentary letters of credit.

Suppose a United States seller has entered into a sales contract with a Brazilian buyer for the sale of certain machinery. The contract may or may not require the buyer to procure a letter of credit, but suppose the contract does require this type of credit. The buyer will go to his bank in Brazil and make the arrangements for the letter of credit. The letter is prepared in the form of a letter authorizing the seller to draw on the bank for account of the buyer up to the aggregate amount of a certain sum. The letter will contain a list of the documents which the seller will have to present with the draft in order to obtain payment. The bank will often cable the letter of credit to its correspondent bank in the country of the seller.

The seller, upon shipment of the goods, will present a sight draft and the necessary documents to the bank in the United States. The bank will immediately give the seller cash or credit. A draft secured by a letter of credit is almost as good as money.

Scope of Article 3   Article 3 does not purport to deal with any negotiable instruments other than commercial paper; it does not apply to money, documents of title, or investment securities. Money is, of course, negotiable at common law or under separate statutes, but the provisions of Article 3 are not applicable to money. Documents of title, such as bills of lading and warehouse receipts, are given characteristics of negotiability by Article 7. The order bill of lading and order warehouse receipt, however, call for the delivery of goods rather than the payment of money. Investment securities, such as certificates of stock, are dealt with in Article 8, "Investment Securities." Article 3, "Commercial Paper," therefore, is restricted to drafts, checks, certificates of deposit, and notes. Article 3, which is designed to describe fully the law of commercial paper, states precisely (1) the form of the instrument, (2) the manner in which the instrument may be negotiated, (3) the requirements necessary to become a holder in due course, (4) the defenses of the parties, (5) how the instrument must be presented for acceptance and payment, (6) the liabilities of the parties, and (7) the discharge of all parties and also of a single party. Article 4, "Bank Deposits and Collections," and Article 3 provide the rules for Chapter 27, "Relationship between Payor Bank and Its Customer."

PROBLEMS

1   Enumerate the four types of negotiable instruments as classified by Article 3 of the Uniform Commercial Code.

2   Explain whether a negotiable instrument is or is not a contract.

3 Explain the difference between a negotiable instrument and a negotiable document of title.

4 Explain some of the advantages of a trade acceptance.

5 As a general rule, the assignee of an ordinary contract right—the right to receive money—is subject to the same defenses that the debtor could have asserted against the creditor-assignor. Does this rule apply to a bona fide purchaser of a negotiable instrument in many instances?

6 Distinguish a domestic draft from an international draft.

7
                                                                    July 1, 1971
                                                                    American City, America
One year after date, I promise to pay to the order of Tom Brown One Hundred Dollars with interest. This instrument is given in payment of merchandise.

                                                                    (Signed) Bill Smith

    a Is the above instrument a note or a draft? Explain how you reached your decision.
    b Name the maker.
    c Name the drawer.
    d Name the payee.
    e Name the drawee.

8
                                                                    July 1, 1971
                                                                    American City, America
One year after date, pay to the order of Tom Brown One Hundred Dollars with interest. This instrument is given in payment of merchandise.

                                                                    (Signed) Bill Smith
To:
Bob Jones
123 Main Street
American City, America

    Tom Brown indorsed the above instrument and delivered it to Al Baker for Ninety-eight Dollars.

    a Is the above instrument a note, a check, or a draft? Explain how you reached your decision.
    b Name the maker.
    c Name the drawer.
    d Name the payee.
    e Name the drawee.
    f Name the transferee.

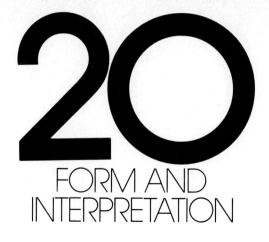

FORM AND INTERPRETATION

A negotiable instrument acquires its characteristics of negotiability because of its form. Section 3–104 provides that any writing to be a negotiable instrument must (1) be signed by the maker or drawer; (2) contain an unconditional promise or order to pay a sum certain in money; (3) be payable on demand, or at a definite time; and (4) be payable to order or to bearer. An instrument which does not comply with these requirements is nonnegotiable, and the law of contracts controls.

WRITING AND SIGNATURE

A negotiable instrument must be in writing. If it is a promissory note, it must be signed by the maker. If it is a draft, it must be signed by the drawer. There is no such thing as an oral negotiable instrument. No precise and exact form is required to render an instrument negotiable. Nevertheless, it should be so framed that it will pass freely from hand to hand in the business world.

Materials for Writing The instrument need not be on any particular kind of material. Any convenient substitute for paper will suffice. It is conceivable that the instrument may be written on parchment, cloth, leather, or wood. Such materials, however, are not used in the usual course of business, and the courts, therefore, might inquire into the reasons for so peculiar an instrument.

The Writing   The instrument need not be set down in words by any particular method. It may be written manually; it may be typewritten; it may be printed or engraved. Any device that makes a visible impression is sufficient. The writing, including the signature, may be in pencil. The use of a pencil, however, is undesirable because of the possibility of inviting a forgery.

The Signature   The usual method for signing an instrument is for a person to place his signature in his own handwriting and in pen and ink in the lower right-hand corner of the instrument. This usual method is desirable, but it is not entirely essential. The signature may be made by the use of a rubber stamp; it may be printed; it may be made by initials; or it may be made by a mark. Some state statutes, however, require that a signature made by a mark must be attested by a witness or witnesses. The signature may appear in the body of the instrument. The use of these unusual signatures, however, should be discouraged. It may be difficult to prove that the alleged maker or drawer used or authorized the use of a rubber stamp or that he had adopted the mark, the print, or the initials as his signature, or that he intended to sign the instrument. [*In re Donohoe's Estate*, p. 258.]

PROMISE OR ORDER TO PAY IN MONEY
The instrument must contain an unconditional promise or order to pay a sum certain in money. The elements to be stressed in this requirement of negotiability are as follows: (1) a note must contain a promise; (2) a draft must contain an order; (3) the promise or order must be unconditional; (4) the sum to be paid must be certain; and (5) the sum must be payable in money.

A Note Must Contain a Promise   An instrument to constitute a promissory note must contain an unconditional promise to pay. The safest way is to use the word "promise," but it is not essential that this exact word appear in the instrument. The words "I will pay" will suffice. It will also suffice if it can be fairly implied from the entire instrument that a promise to pay is intended. An implied promise to pay, however, should be distinguished from a mere acknowledgment that a debt exists. "I O U Brown the sum of $100," or "Due Brown the sum of $100" are illustrations of statements generally held to be acknowledgments of an indebtedness.

A Draft Must Contain an Order   To constitute a draft, an instrument must contain an order upon a third person to pay. The phrase "pay to the order of" is ordinarily used, but it should be explained that the words "order of" do not constitute the *order* contemplated by the requirement of an unconditional order. The words "order of" are used to direct the drawee to pay in accordance with the order or direction of the payee. The word "pay" is the order; it is a command to pay. It is quite clear, therefore, that the exact word "order" is not an essential requirement of an unconditional order. The order, nevertheless, must be expressed in the form of a demand upon the drawee, carrying with it the implication that the drawer has the right to command and the drawee has the duty to pay.

The Promise or Order Must Be Unconditional   The promise or order to pay must be unconditional. The reason for this rule is obvious. No one would buy paper or accept it for a debt if the right to recover were not absolute. A condition on the face of a note or a draft, therefore, would embarrass its free circulation as a means of exchange. In this connection it should be mentioned that the negotiability of instruments is favored in the law. The courts will construe the language so as to make the promise or order unconditional whenever that can be done without doing violence to the language used. Conditions preventing promises or orders from being absolute usually arise out of statements which (1) make payment out of a particular fund and (2) refer to a separate agreement.

(1)   *Instruments Payable out of a Particular Fund*   A statement on the face of the instrument that a particular fund is to be charged does not make the instrument conditional. A promise or order to pay out of a particular fund, however, is conditional. It is immaterial whether or not the fund is in actual existence or merely has a potential existence. The fund may prove inadequate to meet the demand in full, and, if the fund fails, the obligation likewise fails. If it were not for the rule, the maker or drawer would assume no personal responsibility. The test applied, therefore, is whether the general credit of the maker accompanies the instrument. If it does, the instrument is negotiable; if it does not, the instrument is nonnegotiable. The dividing line is, nevertheless, not always easy to draw. If the instrument clearly states that the amount is to be charged to a certain account, no difficulty arises. In these circumstances the statement is a direction of accounting procedure. There is a difference between "Pay Brown $100 out of my general account" and "Pay Brown $100 and charge to my share of the profits." It is generally held, however, that a promise or order to pay "out of the proceeds of" a contract is a conditional promise to pay out of a particular fund, but a promise or order to pay "on account of" a contract is not a promise to pay out of a particular fund.

Section 3–105 makes two exceptions to the "particular-fund" rule. First, municipal corporations or other governments or governmental agencies are permitted to draw checks or to issue short-term paper in which payment is limited to a particular fund or to the proceeds of particular taxes or other sources of revenue. Second, the Code adopts pre-Code decisions which hold that an instrument issued by a partnership, unincorporated association, trust, or other estate is negotiable even though payment is expressly limited to the assets of the partnership, association, trust, or other estate. The provision, however, affects only the negotiability of the instrument. It does not change the law of any state as to the liability of a partner, trustee, executor, administrator, or any other person who signs the instrument.

(2)   *Reference to a Separate Agreement*   Instruments frequently contain statements referring to a separate agreement. These statements may or may not render the promise or order conditional. Section 3–105 provides, in effect, that a

provision which requires one to refer to something outside the instrument for the purpose of determining his rights will render the promise or order conditional, but a mere reference in an instrument to a separate agreement does not destroy the negotiability of the instrument. [*Federal Factors, Inc. v. Wellbanke*, p. 259.]

Mere recitals in instruments, such as "This note is given to secure the payment of" a certain automobile, or "This note is given for payment as per contract for the purchase of" certain goods of even date, will not make the promise or order conditional. Such recitals are not intended to condition payment according to the terms of another agreement. Statements such as "Payment must be made according to the terms of" another agreement, or this instrument is "subject to all the terms and conditions" of another agreement would condition the promise in an instrument. A recital in a mortgage note, "This note is secured by a mortgage of even date," would not condition the promise, but the addition of the further words "and is subject to all the terms and conditions of said mortgage" would condition the promise. The general rule is that an *as per* recital does not make the promise or order conditional, but a *subject to* recital will condition the promise or order. [*D'Andrea v. Feinberg*, p. 260.]

The Sum to Be Paid Must Be Certain The points to be remembered here are that the amount due at maturity must be certain and the sum to be paid must be determined from the face of the instrument. A promise to pay "whatever sum is now due and owing me from Brown" is obviously uncertain. There would be no way to determine from the face of the instrument how much was due. Section 3–106 expressly provides that the sum payable is a sum certain, although it is to be paid with interest, by stated installments, with a stated discount, or with costs of collection or an attorney's fee.

The provision with respect to interest may be a promise to pay interest at a stated rate from date until paid, or it may be a promise to pay a different rate before and after maturity. A promise to "pay $500 with interest at 6 percent, but if not paid at maturity, interest to be at the rate of 8 percent for the total period," or a promise to "pay $500 with interest at the rate of 8 percent, but if the note is paid on or before maturity, interest shall be only 6 percent" does not render the instrument nonnegotiable. The amount due at maturity in either event is certain. If the amount of interest is left blank, the legal or judgment rate is payable.

A promise to pay, in addition to the principal sum, costs of collection in case payment shall not be made at maturity is a collateral obligation separate and apart from the primary promise to pay money. The sum is certain at maturity. An uncertain sum after maturity does not destroy negotiability.

A promise to pay "with exchange"—the charge for transferring money from one place to another—does not destroy negotiability. According to most authorities, however, a promise to pay taxes which may be assessed against the note, or the holder thereof, does destroy negotiability.

The Sum Must Be Payable in Money Section 1–201 defines "money" in terms of a "medium of exchange authorized or adopted by a domestic or foreign government as part of its currency." This definition coupled with the provision of section 3–107 makes it clear that governmental sanction is the test of "money." An instrument which expresses the amount to be paid in sterling, francs, lire, or any other recognized currency of a foreign government is negotiable even though payable in the United States. Payment is calculated by the number of dollars which the stated foreign currency will purchase at the buying sight rate for that currency on the date on which the instrument is payable. An instrument payable in gold dust, beaver pelts, or cigarettes is not payable in money even though the members of the particular community might treat gold dust, beaver pelts, or cigarettes as a medium of exchange. The Code expressly provides that an instrument payable in "currency" or "current funds" is payable in money. [*Moore v. Clines,* p. 260.]

TIME OF PAYMENT

The instrument must be payable on demand or at a definite time. The reason for this requirement is that the holder should know when he may legally demand payment. The persons liable on the instrument should know when they can be compelled to pay or when they will be privileged to pay the instrument. If this were not so, a businessman would be unable to arrange his affairs upon definite expectations. The element of this requirement to be remembered is that the time of payment is certain when the instrument is payable on demand, or at a definite time.

Payable on Demand   An instrument payable on demand, or at sight, or on presentation clearly is negotiable. The words "payable on demand" are ordinarily used in promissory notes; the words "payable at sight," in drafts. When no time of payment is specified, it is payable on demand. A check will suffice to illustrate such an instrument. The holder of overdue paper has an immediate right of action to sue for the money promised or ordered to be paid. Overdue paper, therefore, is necessarily demand paper.

Payable at a Definite Time   It is quite clear that an instrument is payable at a definite time when it is payable at a stated time, as January 1, 1971. It is equally clear that an instrument is payable at a definite time when it is payable at a stated time after date or sight, that is, thirty days after date or sight. An undated instrument payable "thirty days after date," however, is not payable at a definite time. Acceleration and extension clauses, instruments payable upon the happening of an event, and postdated, antedated, and undated instruments need further clarification.

    (1)   *Acceleration Clauses*   A clause which hastens the date of maturity of the instrument is called an "acceleration clause"; it can only apply to an instrument which, although it has a fixed date of maturity, may be made payable before the arrival of the fixed date. A common type of clause in a promissory note which permits the maker to hasten the date of maturity is the "on or before"

clause. An instrument which is made payable on or before a fixed date, that is, on or before thirty days *after* date, or on or before January 1, 1971, is payable at a definite time. Another common type of clause is a provision which gives the maker the option of paying the whole or any part of the principal on any interest-paying date. Promissory notes sometimes contain clauses giving the holder the option to accelerate payment "at any time he deems the note insecure." These clauses, which are known as "insecurity clauses," do not destroy negotiability under section 3–109. The option to accelerate, however, can only be exercised in the good faith belief that the prospect of payment is impaired.

(2) *Extension Clauses* Suppose a promissory note is payable on January 1, 1971, and the maker is given the right to extend the time of payment to January 1, 1972. This type of extension clause does not destroy negotiability; it is payable at a definite time. If the maker is given the right to extend the payment date indefinitely, the note is not negotiable; it is not payable at a definite time. A clause providing for extension at the option of the holder, even without a time limit, does not affect negotiability. The holder, however, is not free to refuse payment and keep interest running by extending it over the objection of a party who tenders full payment when the instrument is due.

(3) *Payable upon the Happening of an Event* An instrument payable "one year after the war," "when a ship shall return from sea," "when I reach my twenty-first birthday," "six months after the death of my uncle," and the like are not payable at a definite time and are not negotiable. [*Kelley v. Hemmingway*, p. 261.]

(4) *Postdated, Antedated, and Undated Instruments* Section 3–114 states that the negotiability of an instrument is not affected by the fact that it is postdated, antedated, or undated. The instrument is payable according to the stated date when it is postdated or antedated. The instrument is treated as payable on demand when it is undated. One situation exists, however, when an undated instrument could not be payable on demand. Suppose an undated instrument is made payable "thirty days after date." It is not payable on demand because of its own express language. It is uncertain as to time of payment. It is, therefore, not payable at a definite time. It is an incomplete instrument. The date may be inserted later. It is then payable thirty days after date.

WORDS OF NEGOTIABILITY
The words "order" and "bearer" are words of negotiability, and these precise words should be used if negotiability is intended. If these exact words are not used, some other word or words must be used which clearly indicate that the instrument was intended to be negotiable. The courts are not in agreement, however, as to what other words may be used. Therefore, the recognized words of negotiability should be used. It is imperative to distinguish between order paper and bearer paper because order paper is negotiated by indorsement and delivery, and bearer paper is negotiated by delivery alone.

Order Paper   An instrument is payable to order when it is drawn to the order of a specified person, or to a specified person or his order. An instrument payable "to the order of Brown" or "to Brown or order" is negotiable. An instrument "payable to Brown" is not negotiable. It may be helpful to remember that in the first two illustrations, the promise is to pay the payee or any other person whom the payee may designate. In the latter illustration, the promise is limited to paying one person.

The payee must be named or otherwise indicated with reasonable certainty in order paper. This is obvious because the instrument could not circulate by indorsement if no payee was named. It has been argued that the payee is not designated with reasonable certainty when the name of the payee is misspelled or when a corporation is designated in language slightly different from the name as it appears in the charter. If the name of the payee is misspelled, however, he may indorse the instrument as therein described, adding, if he thinks fit, his proper signature. The same is true of a corporation which is designated slightly differently. It is clear, therefore, that if the name of the payee is misspelled or designated in slightly different language the payee will be regarded as having been otherwise indicated therein with reasonable certainty. These slight variations, although not recommended practice, will not ordinarily prevent an instrument from being order paper.

Section 3–110 enumerates the persons to whose order an instrument may be drawn payable. These may be summarized: The maker, drawer, drawee, a payee who is not a maker, drawer or drawee, two or more payees, an estate, a trust or fund, an office or an officer, a partnership, or an unincorporated association.

(1)   *Instruments Payable to the Order of the Maker, Drawer, or Drawee* The typical payee is some person who is not the maker, drawer, or drawee. The instrument, however, may be drawn to the order of either of these persons. A note which reads, "I promise to pay to the order of Brown," and is signed by Brown is an order instrument. The indorsement of the maker-payee would be necessary to permit it to circulate as negotiable paper. The modern trade acceptance payable to the order of "ourselves" is typical of an instrument where the drawer is named as payee. An instrument payable to the order of the drawee may be illustrated by a situation in which a depositor in a bank draws and delivers his checks, payable to the order of his bank, in payment of notes held by the bank.

(2)   *Instruments Payable to Two or More Payees* The instrument may be drawn to the order of two or more payees together or in the alternative. Instruments payable to "A or B" are in the alternative, and such instruments are payable to either A or B. The instrument, therefore, may be negotiated, enforced, or discharged by either A or B. Instruments payable to "A and B" together are not in the alternative and may be negotiated, discharged, or enforced only by both of them. Both A and B, therefore, must indorse in order to negotiate the instrument. Instruments payable to "A and/or B" are payable in the alternative to A, or to B, or to A and B together and may be negotiated, enforced, or discharged accordingly.

(3) ***Instruments Payable to an Estate, a Trust, or a Fund***   An instrument payable to the order of an estate, trust, or fund is payable to the order of the representative of such estate, trust, or fund or his successors. An instrument payable to the order of the "Estate of Brown," the "Linder Trust," or the "Community Fund" is therefore payable to order. The instrument must be drawn so that the payee can be identified, and in each instance it is to be treated as payable to the order of the appropriate representative or his successor.

(4) ***Instruments Payable to an Office, a Partnership, or an Unincorporated Association***   An instrument may be made payable to the order of an office, an officer by his title, a partnership, or an unincorporated association. The purpose of this provision is to specify that instruments payable to various associations, such as "The XYZ Club," "Brown, Treasurer of XYZ Club," "Brown Brothers," and the like, are order paper. Any person having authority from the association to whose order the instrument is payable may indorse or otherwise deal with the instrument.

Bearer Paper   The payee, it will be remembered, must be named with reasonable certainty in order paper. The same exactness is not required of bearer paper. Section 3–111 provides that an instrument is payable to bearer when by its terms it is payable to bearer or the order of bearer, a specified person or bearer, or "cash" or the order of "cash" or any other indication which does not purport to designate a specific payee.

(1) ***Instruments Payable to Bearer***   The first two instances above enumerated may be illustrated: An instrument which states "Pay to Bearer," "Pay to the order of bearer," or "Pay Brown or bearer" is bearer paper. An instrument payable to "bearer" followed by the named payee, that is, "Pay to bearer Brown," is not a negotiable instrument. An instrument "Pay to the order of _____" is not bearer paper. It is an incomplete order instrument.

(2) ***Instruments Payable to a Specified Person or Bearer***   Instruments are sometimes found which state that an instrument is payable to the order of a named payee or bearer. This usually results from the use of printed forms. This section clarifies this situation by stating that "an instrument made payable to the order of a named payee or bearer is payable to order unless the bearer words are handwritten or typewritten." Suppose the printed form is in this style: "Pay to the order of _____ or bearer." The instrument filled in with the name of the payee would be order paper. The comment explains that the person who fills in such a printed form usually does not intend this ambiguity, since he does not notice the word "bearer." Such person, therefore, indicates an intent that the word "order" control when he writes in the name of the payee.

Suppose, however, the printed form is in this style: "Pay to the order of _____." The instrument, filled in with the name of the payee, coupled with the words "or bearer," would be bearer paper. In this instance, there is sufficient indication of an intent that the instrument should be bearer paper.

(3) ***Instruments Payable to Cash***   The instrument is payable to bearer when the name of the payee does not purport to be the name of any person. The most common illustration of this class of bearer paper is an instrument drawn

payable to the order of "cash." The same result is reached when the instrument is drawn payable to any impersonal payee, as to a number, or to "bills payable."

(4) *Instruments Indorsed in Blank* An instrument is payable to bearer when the only or last indorsement is an indorsement in blank, that is, the payee merely writes his name on the back of the instrument. This rule is explained more fully in Chapter 21, "Transfer and Negotiation." It seems wise, however, to give a word of caution. A check which is made payable to the order of a named payee and is indorsed in blank becomes bearer paper and can be negotiated by delivery alone. If the check is lost or stolen, the finder or thief could further negotiate the check by delivery. The disadvantage of following this procedure with a paycheck is obvious.

THE DRAWEE

When the instrument is addressed to a drawee he must be named or otherwise indicated therein with reasonable certainty. This element, of course, applies only to drafts. A note has no drawee. The reason for the rule is to enable the payee or holder to know upon whom he is to call for acceptance or payment. The facts of the particular case will determine whether or not this element of negotiability has been complied with. The name of the drawee, his street address, city or town, and state would ordinarily be sufficient. The name of the drawee, the city or town, and state would likewise be sufficient unless there should be two drawees by the same name in the particular city or town. The draft, as a general rule, must be addressed to some definite person or contain words by which the identity of the drawee can be sufficiently determined. The drawee may be a firm, corporation, association, or other legally recognized group or entity. Section 3–102 provides that the draft may be addressed to two or more drawees jointly; it may be addressed to two or more drawees in the alternative but not in succession. This is to enable the holder to make only one presentation for acceptance or payment.

MISCELLANEOUS PROVISIONS

Terms and Omissions Not Affecting Negotiability Sections 3–112 and 3–114 enumerate a number of terms and omissions that have no effect upon the negotiability of an instrument. The terms themselves may be invalid under some local law, and subsection 3–112(2) makes it clear that such local law remains unchanged. The negotiability of the instrument, however, is not affected. The more important of these terms and omissions are as follows:

(1) The omission of a statement of any consideration, or the omission of the place where the instrument is drawn or payable.

(2) A clause which states that collateral has been given, or authorizes the sale of such collateral upon "any default." This includes a default in payment of an installment or of interest.

(3) A promise or power to maintain or protect the collateral, or to post additional collateral.

(4) A "confession of judgment" clause. Negotiability is affected, however, unless the clause is limited to situations in which the instrument is not paid when due.

(5) A term purporting to waive the benefit of any law intended for the advantage or protection of any obligor. This "right of waiver" applies to the benefits under the Code, such as presentment and notice of dishonor or protest, and also to any other law, such as homestead exemption.

(6) The fact that the instrument is under seal.

(7) A satisfaction recital on an instrument, such as "payment of rent in full for the month of October, 1970."

Ambiguous Terms and Rules of Construction   Section 3–118 deals with rules of construction, the more important of which are as follows:

(1) A holder may treat the instrument as a note or draft when the instrument is so ambiguous that its identity is in doubt.

(2) A draft drawn on the drawer is effective as a note.

(3) Handwritten terms control typewritten and printed terms. Typewritten terms control printed terms.

(4) Words control figures, but figures control if the words are ambiguous.

(5) Unless the instrument provides differently, a provision for interest means interest at the judgment rate at the place of payment from the date of the instrument, or from the date of issue if the instrument is undated.

(6) Unless the instrument provides differently, two or more persons who sign as maker, acceptor, drawer, or indorser and as a part of the same transaction are jointly and severally liable, even though the instrument contains such words as "I promise to pay."

(7) Section 3–402 provides that a signature is an indorsement if the instrument does not clearly indicate the capacity in which the signature was made.

CASES

In re Donohoe's Estate, 115 Atl. 878 (Pa. 1922). Action by Richard Donohoe, claimant, against the estate of Donohoe. Cecelia Donohoe died in 1919, and the claimant presented the following note to the estate for payment:

$13070.86   August 30th, 1910

  I, Cecelia W. Donohoe, after date, August 30th, promise to pay to the order of Richard Donohoe, Thirteen Thousand and Seventy Dollars and 86/100 Dollars. . . . Witness my hand and seal.

                HESTER JOHNSON, (Seal)
                Notary Public

The note was on a printed form, and the words italicized were in the handwriting of Mrs Donohoe.

Walling, Justice: That Mrs. Donohoe's signature appears in the body of the note and not at the end is unimportant, so long as she intended thereby to obligate herself for its payment. There is no law requiring a note to be signed at the end thereof, as in the case of a will, hence, whenever it can be found that the signature, wherever it appears, was intended as an execution of the note, it is sufficient. For example, to write, "On demand, I, John Smith promise to pay Thomas Brown, one hundred dollars," is, in form, a good obligation, and that is essentially this case. . . . The fact that for greater solemnity Mrs. Donohoe called in a notary public, who was a stranger to the instrument and mistakenly wrote her name in the wrong place, is unimportant; the obligation remained that of Cecelia W. Donohoe and, being perfected by delivery, is unassailable. [DECISION FOR CLAIMANT]

Federal Factors, Inc. v. Wellbanke, 406 S.W.2d 712 (Ark. 1966). Action by Federal Factors, Inc., appellant, against Joe Wellbanke, appellee, to enforce three trade acceptances which were signed by appellee and Richard J. Martin, and which were sold by Chemical Products to appellant. Appellee contended that the trade acceptances were not negotiable and that "breach of contract" was therefore a defense to the action.

George Rose Smith, Justice: In October 1962 Wellbanke and Martin signed a contract by which they became exclusive local dealers for Chemical Products. In the contract they agreed to purchase a quantity of merchandise, which was to be shipped to them for resale. At the trial, Wellbanke testified that Chemical Products violated certain oral assurances that its agent had given, such as promises to prepay the freight on the shipment and a promise not to transfer or assign the Trade Acceptances to anyone else.

The three instruments, evidencing the unpaid purchase price, were alike except for serial numbers and dates of maturity. Apart from inessential matters such as the drawer's telephone number, the instruments were in this form:

Chemical Products Incorporated
Salt Lake City, Utah

No. 687   October 5, 1962.

On November 10, 1962 Pay to the order of Chemical Products Inc. Two Thousand Four Hundred Thirty-two and No/100 Dollars ($2,432.00). The transaction which gives rise to this instrument is the purchase of goods by the acceptor from the drawer.

Chemical Products Inc.
By Bob Chron

Accepted at Conway, Ark. on October 5, 1962.
Payable at First National Bank
Bank Location Conway, Ark.
Buyer's Signature Joe Wellbanke
     & Richard J. Martin

Neither the trial court nor the appellee's attorney has suggested any reason for holding the instruments to be nonnegotiable. To the contrary, they contain all the elements of negotiability specified in the Uniform Commercial Code, Section 3–104. The mere reference to the transaction giving rise to the instruments does not affect negotiability. In view of the undisputed proof that the plaintiff was a holder in due course it took the instruments free from the defenses relied upon by Wellbanke. Section 3–305. [DECISION FOR PLAINTIFF]

D'Andrea v. Feinberg, 256 N.Y.S.2d 504 (1965). Action by Vincent B. D'Andrea and Davis Levitt, plaintiffs, against Samuel Feinberg and Sain Builders, defendants, to recover on a promissory note.

The note in question was signed in behalf of Sain Builders by Samuel Feinberg, as president, and was indorsed by Samuel Feinberg, as president, and individually. The note was presented to the maker for payment, and was dishonored and protested.

John J. Dillon, Justice: On behalf of the individual defendant, it is urged that plaintiffs are not holders in due course because at the time they acquired the note they were aware of the existence of a contract between the corporate defendant and the payee of the note. This fact cannot be disputed because the note itself has indorsed thereon, in the lower left hand corner the legend "as per contract." It is argued that the indorser should not be held liable on the note until such time as the primary obligation between the maker and the payee has been resolved. The court is thus faced with two questions: (1) whether the note is a negotiable instrument; and (2) whether the plaintiffs are holders in due course.

The note meets all the requirements of section 3–104 of the U.C.C. with the possible exception that it does not contain an unconditional promise because of the legend "as per contract." Section 3–105(1)(c) expressly states that an unconditional promise "is not made conditional by the fact that the instrument . . . (c) refers to or states that it arises out of a separate agreement or refers to a separate agreement for rights as to prepayment or acceleration." . . . The Court is satisfied that the legend "as per contract" does not affect the negotiability of an instrument as would a statement that the instrument "is subject to or governed by any other agreement."

The court determines that the note being sued upon is a negotiable instrument and that the plaintiffs are holders in due course. Since a cause of action against "an indorser of any instrument accrues upon demand following dishonor of the instrument" [Uniform Commercial Code, section 3–122(3)], it is clear that the plaintiffs need not first recover judgment against the maker as the individual defendants urge. [DECISION FOR PLAINTIFFS]

Moore v. Clines, 57 S.W.2d (Ky. 1932). Action by C. P. Moore, plaintiff, against Thomas D. Clines, defendant. The instrument sued upon was in the following form:

$1100.00   Louisville, Ky., May 1, 1924

Four months after date, for value received I promise to pay to the order of C. P. Moore Eleven Hundred Dollars. Negotiable and payable at the Citizens Union National Bank, Louisville, Ky. It is agreed by the parties hereto that this note shall bear interest at the rate of — per cent per annum until paid.

It is agreed that this note is to be paid in Elks Club#8 Second Mortgage real estate bonds.

Thos. D. Clines

Perry, Justice: There is thus presented upon this appeal only the question as to whether a note, whereby its maker agrees and promises to pay a certain sum to the order of another at a certain time stated, with interest thereon, and where it is further stipulated upon the face of the note that the said amount thereof is to be paid through a medium or with something other than money, to wit, in mortgage bonds, is a negotiable instrument or an instrument upon which recovery may be had by suit thereon of the amount promised to be paid therein in money, rather than in the provided medium or in something other than money, to wit, in mortgage bonds.

The stipulation written on the face of the note at the time of its execution became a part of it and the instrument was thereby rendered unnegotiable. [DECISION FOR DEFENDANT]

Kelley v. Hemmingway,   13 Ill. 604 (1852). Action by Moses Hemmingway, plaintiff, against David Kelley, defendant. The instrument out of which the cause of action arose was in the following words: "Castleton, April 27, 1844. Due Henry D. Kelley $53, when he is twenty-one years old, with interest. David Kelley." Henry Kelley, the payee, attempted to negotiate the instrument to the plaintiff by an indorsement on the back. The payee became twenty-one years old in August, 1849, and plaintiff, the indorsee, brought this action against the maker. Plaintiff's recovery depended upon whether or not the instrument was negotiable.

Treat, Chief Justice: To constitute a promissory note, the money must be certainly payable, not dependent on any contingency, either as to event or the fund out of which payment is to be made, or the parties by or to whom payment is to be made. If the terms of an instrument leave it uncertain whether the money will ever become payable, it can not be considered as a promissory note. . . . Thus, a promise in writing to pay a sum of money when a particular person shall be married is not a promissory note, because it is not certain that he will ever be married. So of a promise to pay when a particular ship shall return from sea, for it is not certain that she will ever return. In all such cases, the promise is to pay on a contingency that may never happen.

In this case, the payment was to be made when the payee should attain his majority—an event that might or might not take place. The contingency might never happen, and therefore the money was not certainly and at all events payable. The instrument lacked one of the essential ingredients of a promissory note, and consequently was not negotiable under the statute. [DECISION FOR DEFENDANT]

PROBLEMS

1 The defendant purchased certain automobile accessories from the plaintiff in payment of which he executed a promissory note. The note appeared to be negotiable in form except that the following provision immediately preceded the signature of the maker: "This note is given in payment of merchandise and is to be liquidated by payments received on account of sale of such merchandise." Is the contention of the defendant that the note is nonnegotiable correct?

2 B. B. Brown signed a promissory note payable to the order of J. J. Jones. It was dated June 14, 1926, and contained a promise to pay the sum of $50,000 "in successive semiannual payments of not less than One Thousand Dollars each, for a period of eight years from date, and the balance then due to be payable on demand thereafter, with interest on the principal unpaid at the rate of six percent per annum, payable semiannually, together with all taxes assessed upon said sum against said payee or the holder of this note." Is this note a negotiable instrument?

3 Brown executed a promissory note which contained the following clause: "Six months after date, I promise to pay myself $2,500, for value received, with interest at 6 percent per annum," followed by the signature of Brown. Brown then indorsed the note in blank and delivered it to Smith. Brown contends the note is nonnegotiable because the maker and the payee are the same person. Smith contends the note should circulate as negotiable paper because it is indorsed in blank. Who is correct?

4 Defendant wrote the following words and figures on a slip of paper: "Pay to L. O'Rourke—$1,000." He then signed the paper and stated in the presence of witnesses: "I am giving her a thousand dollars, which I think she deserves, because she has been a very good, faithful saleslady." Does the writing constitute either a negotiable draft or check or a negotiable promissory note?

5 A note contained the following clause: "One year after my wife's death, I promise to pay B. B. Brown the sum of $10,000." Discuss the effect of this clause with respect to negotiability.

6 Rooke borrowed $500 from Smith and executed a promissory note for the sum of $500 payable to the order of Smith, payable on August 1, 1968, with interest at 6 percent. The note which was signed A.B.R., was not paid when it became due, and Smith brought an action against Rooke to recover the $500 and interest at 6 percent. Rooke contended that he was not liable because his signature did not appear on the note. Is this contention correct?

7 The Construction Company and R. M. Jones entered into a contract whereby the company agreed to construct a swimming pool for Jones at a contract price of $3,500. The company had completed a part of the pool and requested Jones to pay $1,000 to the First Bank in part payment of the pool. Jones asked for an order to do so, and the order read as follows:

"R. M. Jones, Dear Sir: Pay to the order of the First Bank $1,000 on account of contract between you and The Construction Company." (Signed) "The Construction Company, By R. M. Linder, President."

Is this writing a negotiable draft?

21

TRANSFER AND NEGOTIATION

An instrument which contains all the elements of negotiability may be negotiated. Negotiable instruments, however, may be transferred by assignment or by negotiation. "Negotiation" is the transfer of an instrument in such form that the transferee becomes a "holder." A person is a holder if he is in possession of bearer paper or if he is in possession of order paper which is properly indorsed. Transfers which are not "negotiations" are assignments. A mere surrender of an instrument to a drawee-bank, however, is not a transfer by assignment or by negotiation. A holder when presenting a check to the drawee-bank for payment is commonly requested to write his name on the back of the instrument before surrendering it. Such a signature merely serves as a receipt for the money. The bank is not a new holder. The bank is the drawee who had paid the check.

With this distinction in mind, inquiry can be made into the manner in which an instrument may be transferred so as to constitute the person in possession a holder. If the instrument is bearer paper, delivery is all that is necessary to pass the ownership from one person to another. If the instrument is order paper, ownership is transferred by the indorsement of the holder completed by delivery. These are the only two modes of negotiation. In order to understand "negotiation," however, it will be necessary to discuss (1) the delivery of the instrument, (2) the indorsement and delivery, and (3) the kinds of indorsements.

DELIVERY

Delivery, which is defined by section 1–201 to mean a voluntary transfer of possession, is an essential part of every negotiation. The rules with respect to delivery of bearer paper, therefore, are equally applicable to order paper. Delivery by the maker of a note to the payee is not a negotiation, but such a delivery is essential in those instances where the payee is attempting to collect from the maker. [*In re Martens' Estate,* p. 270.]

INDORSEMENT AND DELIVERY

An indorsement is the act of writing one's name on a draft or note. An instrument is usually indorsed for the purpose of transferring title. It may be indorsed, however, for the purpose of adding the obligations of the indorser to those of the maker, drawer, or drawee. An indorser becomes a party to the instrument, and, as you will learn, he may be liable for its payment without receiving any consideration. The indorsement is customarily and properly written on the back of the instrument, but this is not essential. It may appear anywhere on the instrument, or, in some circumstances, it may be written on a piece of paper annexed to the instrument.

The indorsement, unless it is made by the use of an allonge, must be written on the instrument itself. It is possible, however, for an indorser to sign in the place where the maker of a promissory note customarily signs and to indicate by appropriate words that he intends to be bound only as an indorser. The indorsement, quite clearly, may appear on the face of the instrument. But this is a dangerous thing to do. A person who intends to indorse a promissory note but who signs in the place where the maker customarily signs may be bound as a maker. The liability of the maker and the liability of an indorser are very different. A person who intends to indorse a note, therefore, should take care not to sign in the place where the maker customarily signs.

It will be remembered that when an instrument is payable to the order of two payees, such as to "A and B," both payees must indorse the instrument in order to negotiate the instrument. If the instrument is payable to the order of two payees in the alternative, such as to "A or B," the instrument may be indorsed and negotiated by either A or B.

Allonge   An allonge is a piece of paper annexed to the instrument for the purpose of writing indorsements when there is no room on the instrument itself. Section 3–202 recognizes that this is the one exception to the rule that the indorsement must be written on the instrument itself. The paper must be firmly attached to the instrument. An attempt to negotiate an instrument by writing on the back of another paper or document to which the instrument might be temporarily attached, as by pinning, especially when there is space available on the instrument itself for the indorsement, will not operate as a negotiation. Such an attempt is ordinarily held to be an assignment.

Incapacity It is expressly provided by section 3–207 that a negotiation is effective to transfer the instrument although the negotiation is (1) made by any person without capacity; (2) obtained by fraud, duress, or mistake; (3) a part of an illegal transaction; or (4) made in breach of duty. An infant, therefore, may negotiate the instrument so as to constitute his transferee a holder. The infant may be able to rescind the negotiation and recover the instrument. The indorsee, however, is a holder and may further negotiate the instrument to a holder in due course. An infant cannot then recover the instrument from the holder in due course. It is thus clear, therefore, that there is a difference between the power to negotiate an instrument and the power to incur liability on it.

Wrong or Misspelled Name Section 3–302 provides that a person whose name is misspelled may make an indorsement effective for negotiation in his own name only, the misspelled name only, or by using both names. The proper and desirable form of indorsement is to use both names. Any purchaser of the instrument or any person called upon to pay the instrument, moreover, may demand an indorsement in both names.

KINDS OF INDORSEMENT

The indorsement must be an indorsement of the entire instrument. An indorsement that conveys less than the entire amount of the instrument does not result in a negotiation. Neither Brown or Jones would become a holder if the instrument were indorsed "Pay Brown one-half," or "Pay Brown two-thirds and Jones one-third." Such an indorsement operates as a partial assignment. Indorsements may be either blank, special, or restrictive.

Blank Indorsement Section 3–204 provides that the signature of the indorser, without anything more, written upon the back of an instrument is a blank indorsement. Such an indorsement on an instrument originally payable to order causes the instrument to become payable to bearer. The instrument may then be

Blank indorsement

negotiated by delivery alone. Suppose an instrument is payable "to the order of Baker." Suppose further that Baker wishes to negotiate the instrument to Bender. This may be accomplished by Baker's writing his name on the back of the instrument "Baker," accompanied by delivery. It is important to remember that an instrument in this form may be further negotiated by the indorsee by delivery alone. A thief or a finder could likewise negotiate the instrument by delivery alone. Moreover, a thief or finder could present the instrument, if it were a promissory note, to the maker for payment on its due date, and if payment were made in good faith, the real owner would not be able to collect from the maker. The holder who receives an instrument indorsed in blank, however, may protect himself by changing the blank indorsement to a special indorsement. The last indorsement controls the further negotiation of the instrument.

Special Indorsement   Section 3–204 provides that a special indorsement specifies the person to whom, or to whose order, the instrument is to be payable. "Pay to the order of Bender" is a special indorsement. But it is not necessary, as in the case of the instrument itself, to use words of negotiability. "Pay to Bender" has the same effect as "Pay to the order of Bender." The indorsement of the special indorsee is necessary to further negotiate the instrument. This rule explains how a holder who receives an instrument indorsed in blank may protect himself by changing the blank indorsement to a special indorsement.

Special indorsement

Restrictive Indorsements   A restrictive indorsement restricts the right of the indorsee in some way. Section 3–205 defines indorsements as (1) conditional, (2) those which purport to prohibit transfer of the instrument, (3) those in the bank deposit or collection process, and (4) those to a fiduciary. The Code expressly provides that a restrictive indorsement does not prohibit the transfer or negotiation of the instrument.

(1)   *Conditional Indorsement*   A conditional indorsement is a special indorsement with words added which provide for payment on the occurrence of some condition. Suppose Baker indorses a note "Pay to the order of Robert

Conditional indorsement

Bender on completion of Building X." The use of this language on the face of the instrument would render the instrument nonnegotiable, because the promise to pay must be unconditional to satisfy the requisites of negotiability. Indorsers, however, are permitted to condition the rights of their indorsees without destroying negotiability. If Building X is not completed, Robert Bender will have no rights in the instrument, and the maker should refuse to pay the note on its date of maturity. Suppose the building is not completed and the maker, nevertheless, pays Robert Bender. The maker will also be required to pay Baker. Suppose still further that Bender negotiates the note before maturity to Cabot. Section 3–206 provides that any transferee, except an intermediary bank, must pay or apply any value given by him for the instrument consistently with the indorsement and to the extent that he does he becomes a holder in due course. If Building X is not completed, in our example, Cabot will be required to pay Baker—the conditional indorser—the amount which he paid Bender for the note. The note possibly may be negotiated many times, but any subsequent transferee is in the same position as Cabot.

Restrictive indorsement

(2) *Indorsements for Deposit or Collection* The most commonly used restrictive indorsement is the indorsement "for collection" or "for deposit." Suppose Brown wishes to deposit a check in the First Bank. He could indorse the check specially:

"Pay First Bank
For deposit in my account
Brown"

or in blank:

"For deposit
Brown"

These indorsements are restrictive; they specify a single use—deposit—for the check.

Restrictive indorsement

(3) *Indorsements Which Purport to Prohibit Negotiation* **Indorsements, such as "Pay Bender only," which purport to prohibit further transfer of the** instrument are without effect for that purpose. The indorsee becomes a holder, and may negotiate the instrument in the same manner as an instrument with an unrestricted indorsement.

Restrictive indorsement

(4) *Indorsements to a Fiduciary* Trust indorsements, such as "Pay Bender in trust for Drake," are treated similarly to those for deposit and collection. The duty to act consistently with the indorsement, however, is limited to the first taker. This is for the reason that trustees commonly sell trust assets. Suppose Bender sells and negotiates the instrument to Jones. Assuming that Jones bought the instrument in good faith, he could be a holder free and clear of Drake's equity. [*Hook v. Pratt*, p. 270.]

Qualified Indorsement A qualified indorsement, the effect of which is to disclaim the liability of the indorser, is recognized by section 3–202. It is thus clear that an indorser may disclaim his liability on the instrument. He is, nevertheless, liable for certain warranties. The liabilities and warranties are discussed in Chapter 25, "Liability of Parties." The customary manner of disclaiming the indorser's liability is to indorse the instrument with the words "without recourse." Such an indorsement, however, has no effect whatsoever on the negotiation of the instrument. [*Fay v. Witte*, p. 271.]

Qualified indorsement

Words Added to an Indorsement Section 3–202 provides that any signature with added words of assignment, condition, waiver, guaranty, limitation, disclaimer of liability, and the like, is an indorsement. Instruments with words such as "I hereby assign all my right, title, and interest," therefore, may be negotiated. Instruments with words such as "I guarantee payment," may affect the liability of the indorser. Such indorsements do not, however, affect the character of the indorsement as an indorsement.

Transfer: Right to Indorsement An order instrument may be transferred without an indorsement. The person to whom the instrument is transferred, however, is not an indorsee. He is a transferee. Section 3–201 provides that such transferee acquires the right to have the unqualified indorsement—blank or special—of the transferor when the instrument is payable to order or specially indorsed. The transferee also acquires whatever rights the transferor had. Negotiation takes place when the indorsement is made, and, prior to such time, there is no presumption that the transferee is the owner. This problem generally arises where the purchaser has paid in advance and the indorsement is omitted through an oversight.

CASES

In re Martens' Estate, 283 N.W. 885 (Iowa 1939). Action by Mabel Martens Bonk (claimant below), appellant, against the administrator of this estate, appellee, to recover on a note for $1,500, payable to her and signed by the decedent. On the back of the note were the following words: "This money is coming to her for teaching $1,000, and $500 is what the rest got also. Mother."

Miller, Justice: Appellant testified that, about March 11, 1936, in examining the contents of her mother's safe, she discovered an envelope on which, in her mother's handwriting, was the notation: "Please give this to S. Fisher in case of death. Mabel Martens from Mother"; she delivered the envelope to said Simon Fisher at his law office shortly after she discovered it; Fisher opened the envelope, which was sealed, in her presence and in the presence of the administrator; the note, Exhibit A, was found in the envelope; her mother had told her that, in case of death there was a letter for her, but she knew nothing of any note; she found the envelope after the administrator had made an examination of the contents of the safe and had not discovered it; she had loaned her parents $1,000 from time to time out of money earned teaching school; her brothers and sisters each had received $500 when they were married; she married subsequent to March 1, 1930, and did not recive her $500.

Obviously, the note here sued upon could not be made the basis of a valid claim against the estate unless there was a legal delivery of the same, during the lifetime of the decedent. . . . Appellant did not present to the trial court and does not present to this court the question involving what rights, if any, she might have had had she undertaken to file a claim based upon the alleged indebtedness of the decedent to her independent of the note. Her claim and her petition are based solely upon the note. [DECISION FOR APPELLEE]

Hook v. Pratt, 78 N.Y. 498 (1879). Action by the trustee of Charles H. Hook, plaintiff, against the executor of the will of Charles P. Haskin, deceased, defendant, to recover on a draft drawn by Charles P. Haskin and payable to his own order. It was indorsed by the drawer by a special indorsement, "Pay to the order of Mrs. Mary Hook, for the benefit of her son Charlie." The defendant claims that the indorsee cannot recover without proving a consideration, because this type of restrictive indorsement does not purport to be made for a consideration.

Rapallo, Judge: As a general rule an indorsement of a negotiable bill which purports to pass the title to the bill to the indorsee imports a consideration, and the burden of proving want of consideration rests upon the party alleging it. The restrictive indorsements which are held to negative the presumption of a consideration are such as indicate that they are not intended to pass the title, but merely to enable the indorsee to collect for the benefit of the indorser, such as indorsements "for collection," or others showing that the indorser is entitled to the proceeds. These create merely an agency, and negative the presumption of the transfer of the bill to the indorsee for a valuable consideration.

When a bill is indorsed, "Pay to A or order for the use of B," A cannot pass the bill off for his own debt, but he can by indorsing it transfer the title, and will hold the proceeds for the benefit of B, and be accountable to him for them. . . . In the present case the indorsement did not purport to restrain the indorsee from negotiating the draft, for it was "Pay to *the order* of Mrs. Mary Hook," for the benefit of her son Charlie. She was constituted trustee of her son and held the legal title. The indorsement gave notice of the trust, so that if she had passed it off for her own debt, or in any other manner indicating that the transfer was in violation of the trust, her transferee would take it subject to the trust, but there was nothing reserved to the drawer and indorser. [DECISION FOR PLAINTIFF]

Fay v. Witte,   186 N.E. 678 (N.Y. 1933). Action by Richard Fay, plaintiff, against Harry C. Witte, defendant, to recover on a promissory note payable to the order of Harry C. Witte, and indorsed by him as follows: "I hereby assign all my right and interest in this note to Richard Fay in full. Harry C. Witte." The question before the court is whether defendant, by the use of these words, has rendered himself liable as an unqualified indorser or is an indorser without recourse and therefore not liable.

Crane, Judge: The placing of this assignment and his name upon the note constituted Witte an indorser unless the words indicate a different intention. The signing on the back of the note has a different effect than would such signing under the same words on a separate paper not attached to the note. This would not be an indorsement at all. It would be a mere assignment transferring title. It is the writing on the back of the instrument itself which constitutes the indorsement. . . . The payee's name being upon the back of the note, he is presumed to be an unqualified indorser, unless there are words which express a different intention.

. . . The denial of recourse to a prior indorser must be found in the express words, "without recourse," or words of similar import. This indorsement contains no such words. Witte, the defendant, became an unqualified indorser liable as such upon nonpayment and notice of protest. This is the law as stated in most of the authorities, textbooks, and treatises. . . .

There are authorities the other way, but we are of the opinion that the law is as we have expressed it. [DECISION FOR PLAINTIFF]

PROBLEMS

1 Defendant, during the year 1935, executed four promissory notes in the sum of $2,500, payable to the order of Elliott. The payee wanted to collect the interest on these notes during her lifetime, but apparently she wanted Whitehurst to have the notes after her death. The payee, therefore, on July 10, 1937, indorsed each note with a pencil in the following manner: "Pay within note to Lydia Mae Whitehurst without recourse." The payee did, however, retain possession of these notes and did collect the interest on them during her lifetime. After the payee's death, both plaintiff, executor of the estate of the payee, and Whitehurst claimed ownership of the notes. Was the title to these notes transferred by the payee to Whitehurst?

2   Mills executed a negotiable promissory note, payable to the order of the payee, which was secured by a real estate mortgage. The payee, prior to the date of maturity, transferred and delivered the note and mortgage to Bailey. The payee—although there was ample space—did not indorse the note. The payee did, however, transfer the note and mortgage by a separate instrument of assignment. All three documents were fastened together with a gem clip when they were delivered to Bailey. Was this a negotiation?

3   The maker executed a promissory note payable to the order of William Brown. Brown indorsed the note to Jones as follows: "I hereby transfer my right to this note over to Jones. (Signed) William Brown." In an action against Brown to recover the proceeds of the note, Brown contended that he is not liable, for the reason that his indorsement was merely for the purpose of transferring the title and he and Jones had an oral understanding that the indorsement was without recourse. Do you agree with the contention of Brown?

4   Stevens, the maker, executed a promissory note for the sum of $1,500 payable to the order of Cox. Cox thereafter purchased a tract of land from James and in payment thereof executed a written instrument by which he transferred the note to James. Cox did not, however, indorse the note. James contends that he nevertheless has the rights of an indorsee. State the rule of law upon which this contention is founded and explain how it would be beneficial to James.

5   The XYZ Company issued a check for the amount of $750, payable to the order of John Doe and Mary Roe. The check was delivered to John Doe, who indorsed his own name in blank on the back of the check and cashed it at The Grocery Store. The Grocery Store then presented the check without further indorsement to the drawee-bank for payment, which was refused. The Grocery Store contends that the instrument may be negotiated by delivery alone, because it is indorsed in blank. Is this contention correct? Was the drawee-bank justified in refusing payment?

6   Abbott drew his check for $500 on the First Bank payable to the order of Drew. Drew, who had a checking account with the Second Bank, indorsed the check "Pay to the order of Second Bank." Drew then sent the check to the Second Bank accompanied by a letter which stated: "This is to instruct you to act as my agent in collecting the enclosed check and to deposit the proceeds in my checking account with your bank." The Second Bank, however, indorsed the check in blank and negotiated it to Potter, a good faith purchaser. Potter then presented the check to the First Bank for payment, and the First Bank dishonored the check because of insufficient funds in the account of Abbot. Potter then presented the check to Abbot for payment, and Abbot refused payment. Would Potter prevail in an action against Abbot for payment of the check?

7   Drake executed his promissory note for $1,000 payable to the order of Aaron. Aaron, who was a senior in college, needed the cash. Aaron therefore sold the note to Baxter, and indorsed it as follows: "Pay to the order of Baxter if I graduate from college in June." Baxter then sold the note to Jones and indorsed it in blank. Drake refused to pay the note when Aaron graduated from college in June, and Jones brought an action against Aaron and Baxter on their indorsements. Should Jones recover from Aaron?

8 Davis executed a demand promissory note payable to the order of Fox for the sum of $2,500. Fox indorsed the note in blank and sold and delivered it to Smith. Smith, without his indorsement, delivered the note as a gift to his son, Smith, Jr., from whom the note was stolen. The thief negotiated the note to a holder in due course, who presented the note for payment to Davis, who, not knowing the note was stolen, made payment in good faith. Smith, Jr., then brought an action against Davis to collect the $2,500. Should he recover?

22
HOLDERS IN DUE COURSE

A holder in due course occupies the protected position of holding the instrument free of personal defenses. This means that there may be a good defense against the payee. A holder in due course, notwithstanding such a defense, may recover from the drawer or maker. [*Shotts v. Pardi,* p. 280.]

These defenses have been reserved for the next chapter, however, because it seems best to understand first the conditions under which a holder must take the instrument in order to qualify as a holder in due course. These conditions, as enumerated by section 3–302, are as follows: A holder in due course is a holder who takes the instrument (1) for value, (2) without notice that it is overdue or has been dishonored or of any defense against or claim to it on the part of any person, and (3) in good faith.

THE REQUIREMENT OF VALUE
The requirement that the holder must take the instrument for value poses two major questions: What is value? When is a holder a holder for value?

The Meaning of Value It is quite clear that "value" and "consideration" are not identical. Consideration is important only on the question as to whether the obligation is enforceable. Value means the actual giving of the consideration, and a holder is a holder for value when the agreed consideration has in fact been performed.

Holder for Value   Section 3–303 enumerates the instances when a holder takes an instrument for value:

(1) A holder takes the instrument for value to the extent that the agreed consideration has been performed. Suppose Brown sells certain goods for $1,000 to Jones and accepts his note for $1,000. Suppose, however, Brown delivers only one-half of the goods. Brown would be a holder for value to the extent of $500.

(2) A holder takes the instrument for value to the extent that he acquires a security interest in or a lien on the instrument. Suppose the payee of a note for $1,000 borrows $500 from a bank and pledges the note as collateral security for the loan. The bank would be a holder for value to the extent of $500.

(3) A holder takes the instrument for value when he takes the instrument in payment of or as security for an antecedent claim against any person. A creditor who takes a negotiable instrument from his debtor in settlement of a past-due debt, therefore, has given value. This rule extends to any claim against any person. Suppose Brown owes Jones $1,000. Suppose further that Smith executes and delivers his note to Brown for $1,000. Suppose still further that Brown transfers the note to Jones in discharge of the original debt. Jones has met the requirements of a holder for value.

(4) A holder gives value when he gives a negotiable instrument in exchange for a negotiable instrument. This means that an exchange of negotiable notes constitutes each holder a payor of value for the instrument received by him. Suppose, however, that Brown transfers his nonnegotiable note to Jones in exchange for a transfer by Jones of his negotiable note. Brown is not a holder for value. The reason for the difference between the two cases is that the promise of the party to a negotiable instrument may get into the hands of a holder in due course, after which the party who gives it cannot ordinarily refuse to pay

(5) A holder gives value when he makes an irrevocable commitment to a third person. The issuer—for instance, a bank—may give an irrevocable letter of credit in exchange for a check. The letter of credit is irrevocable, but payment of the check could be stopped.

(6) Section 4–209 provides that a bank gives value to the extent that it has a security interest in the instrument. A bank, therefore, may be a holder in due course provided it meets all the requirements of a holder in due course.

OVERDUE OR DISHONORED INSTRUMENT
Section 3–302 provides that a person must take an instrument without notice that it is overdue or that it has been dishonored in order to qualify as a holder in due course. Businessmen customarily pay their debts when they are due. The reason for the rule, therefore, is apparent. A person who fails to pay an instrument when

it is due presumably has some valid reason for the nonpayment. A negotiable instrument, however, may be transferred even though it is overdue or has been dishonored. An instrument in circulation past its maturity date, nevertheless, presents a suspicious circumstance that the instrument may not have been paid because of a valid defense to such payment. It is apparent from the paper itself that the instrument is overdue if it is payable on a fixed date. It is not always so apparent, however, if the instrument is payable on demand, payable in installments, or subject to acceleration. It is likewise not always apparent if the instrument has been dishonored.

Instruments Payable on a Fixed Date An instrument with a fixed maturity designated by a calendar date is overdue at the beginning of the day after the fixed date. An instrument payable May 1, therefore, would not be overdue until May 2. An instrument dated May 1 and payable one day after date would not be overdue until May 3. If the date of payment falls on Sunday or on a holiday, the instrument is payable on the next succeeding business day.

Instruments Payable on Demand A purchaser cannot qualify as a holder in due course if he has reason to know that a demand for payment of the instrument has been made or if he takes the instrument more than a reasonable length of time after issue. A clear-cut dividing line between a "reasonable" and an "unreasonable" time is impossible to draw. The nature of the instrument, and the facts and circumstances of the particular case are factors to be taken into consideration in arriving at the maturity date of a demand instrument. Section 3–304(3)(c), however, provides that a "reasonable time for a check drawn and payable within the states and territories of the United States and the District of Columbia is presumed to be thirty days." [*Anderson v. Elem*, p. 281.]

Instruments Payable in Installments The principal of a promissory note is frequently made payable by installments. May a purchaser be a holder in due course if one or more installments are overdue and unpaid at the time the note is transferred? The purchaser would be a holder in due course if he had no reason to know that the past-due installments have not been paid. The same is true of notes issued in a series. He would have notice that the instrument was overdue, however, if he had reason to know that default had been made in the payment of one or more of a series of notes. Knowledge that there had been a default in the payment of interest, however, would not prevent the purchaser from taking as a holder in due course. Interest payments are frequently delayed.

Instruments Subject to Acceleration An instrument with a fixed date of maturity but subject to acceleration upon the happening of a recited event, either automatically or at the option of the holder, is not overdue until the fixed date. The holder, to be sure, may advance the maturity date by exercising the option to accelerate the instrument, or the maturity date may be automatically advanced by the happening of the recited event. The purchaser will nevertheless be a holder in due course if he takes without notice that the option to accelerate has been exercised or that the event has happened.

Dishonored Instruments   An instrument is dishonored when it has been presented for payment or acceptance and payment or acceptance, as the case may be, has been refused. If the purchaser, however, has no notice that the instrument has been dishonored he may take the instrument as a holder in due course.

GOOD FAITH
Good faith is a broad term. It implies honest intention. It is another one of those terms in the law that cannot be precisely and definitely defined. Good faith, nevertheless, permeates all the requirements that are essential for a person to qualify as a holder in due course. The term, viewed with respect to the rights of a holder, signifies a lack of knowledge of defenses against the instrument or claims to it on the part of any person. A person, therefore, who takes an instrument with knowledge that the instrument was procured by fraud does not take the instrument in good faith. Section 3–304 states certain facts that constitute "notice" to purchasers. This section, therefore, has an important bearing on the ascertainment of good faith. [*Wilson v. Gorden,* p. 281.]

NOTICE TO PURCHASERS
A holder is not a holder in due course if he has notice that the instrument is so incomplete or so irregular as to call into question its validity, that the obligation of any party is voidable, that all parties have been discharged, or that a fiduciary negotiated the instrument in payment of his own debt.

Complete and Incomplete Instrument   Illustrations of incomplete instruments are the omission of such matter as the sum payable, the name of the payee, the name of the drawee, or the time of payment, as "on or before one _____ after date." The instrument is not incomplete, however, if it is blank as to some unnecessary particular. The omission of the pronoun "we" or "I" in spaces left therefor on a printed note, as "_____ promise to pay," would not necessarily make the instrument incomplete.

Suppose an undated promissory note was issued on January 1, 1971, payable "thirty days after date." This is an incomplete order instrument, and the holder could fill in the date of issue. The note would then be negotiable. Suppose, however, the holder fraudulently dated the note December 15, 1970, in order to hasten the date of maturity. The purchaser of such a note, even though the note was completed in his presence, could be a holder in due course unless he had notice that the completion was improper.

Regular and Irregular Instrument   An instrument is not irregular if it is antedated or postdated. An instrument is irregular, however, if it is apparent that it has been materially altered. This does not mean that every apparent change on the face of the instrument is a material alteration within the meaning of the rule. A difference between the handwriting in the body of the instrument and the signature is not an irregularity; nor does the absence of revenue stamps, when such are required by statute, make the instrument irregular. Any apparent alterations, erasures, or discrepancies in the name of the payee, the amount, the due date, or the interest rate, however, constitute a material alteration. The purchaser, therefore, should be on the alert to detect any visible tamperings that might change the material terms of the instrument. [*Medeiros v. Fellsway Motors, Inc.,* p. 282.]

Voidable Obligation   The maker of a note may have a defense against the payee which entitles him to avoid the obligation. This could be the situation if the note was obtained by acts such as fraud, duress, or undue influence. Suppose the payee transfers the note to Brown. Would Brown take the note as a holder in due course? This would depend on whether Brown had notice of the defense at the time the note was transferred to him. He could not take the note in good faith if he had notice of the defense.

Discharge of Parties   A purchaser who takes an instrument with notice that one or more parties had been discharged, however, will not prevent the purchaser from taking as a holder in due course. The purchaser with such notice takes the instrument subject to the discharge. A purchaser, for instance, may take the instrument with notice that an indorser has been discharged and still be a holder in due course as to the maker. A purchaser who takes an instrument with notice that all parties have been discharged cannot be a holder in due course.

Fiduciary   A purchaser has notice of a claim against the instrument when he has knowledge that a fiduciary has negotiated the instrument in payment of, or as security for, his own debt or benefit. Suppose Brown executes a promissory note payable to the order of "Jones, Jr., executor of the estate of Jones, Sr." The instrument shows on its face that Jones, Jr., holds the instrument in a fiduciary capacity. Suppose Jones, Jr., transfers the note to Smith in payment of his own personal debt. Smith has knowledge that the note was transferred in a breach of duty. He is, therefore, deprived of being a good faith purchaser. He could not be a holder in due course. Mere knowledge of the fact that the person negotiated the instrument as a fiduciary does not, of itself, give the purchaser notice of a claim or defense. Fiduciaries are frequently given the right to transfer trust assets. If Jones, Jr., sold the note to Smith in the ordinary course of business, Smith would be a purchaser in good faith. It is only when the purchaser has knowledge that the fiduciary is acting in breach of his duty that he is deprived of his status of a holder in due course.

Actual Knowledge as Notice   The word "notice" as used here does not include constructive notice. A person is not required to search the public records for possible defenses before purchasing a negotiable instrument. The payee of a promissory note may have induced the maker to issue the note by means of fraud. The maker, upon learning of the fraud, may institute court proceedings to have the note canceled. The payee may thereafter negotiate the note to a purchaser. Such a purchaser, who qualifies in all other respects, is not precluded from taking the instrument as a holder in due course by the mere fact that a search of the court records would have revealed a defect in the title. A purchaser, however, before purchasing a negotiable instrument should examine the instrument for possible infirmities and defects. Actual knowledge is, in many instances, shown by the instrument itself. A person who has taken an instrument with an apparent material alteration has undeniably actual knowledge of the alteration. A purchaser of an instrument may become a holder in due course although he takes the instrument with knowledge that it is accompanied by a separate agreement. A purchaser, however, who has reason to know of a defense or claim arising from the terms of the agreement cannot be a holder in due course. [*General Motors Acceptance Corp. v. Daigle*, p. 283.]

MISCELLANEOUS HOLDERS

Payee as a Holder in Due Course   It might be thought that a payee cannot be a holder in due course, because a holder in due course will ordinarily be a person who takes an instrument by negotiation. A payee, however, who meets the requirements of value, good faith, and acquisition prior to maturity may be a holder in due course to the same extent and under the same circumstances as any other holder.

Successor in Interest   Section 3–302 provides that a holder does not become a holder in due course, regardless of his good faith at the time he acquires an instrument, if he takes the instrument as a successor in interest to a prior holder who was not himself a holder in due course. This rule applies, for example, to purchasers at a judicial sale, an attaching creditor, an executor who takes the instrument as a part of an estate, and the like. It also applies to bulk purchases lying outside of the ordinary course of business of the seller, such as a new partnership taking over all of the assets of an old partnership. If the prior holder was himself a holder in due course, the purchaser would succeed to the status of a holder through a holder in due course.

Holder through a Holder in Due Course   Section 3–201 sets out the rule of the "umbrella" or "shelter" protection by providing that a holder, although he may not satisfy the requirements of a holder in due course, who derives his title through a holder in due course and who is not himself a party to any fraud or illegality affecting the instrument has all the substantive rights of his former holder. To illustrate: The payee, by means of fraud, induces the maker to issue a promissory note. The payee negotiates the instrument to a first indorsee who qualifies as a holder in due course. Such first indorsee then makes a gift of the note to a second indorsee. Such second indorsee, although he gave no value for the note, has all the rights of a holder in due course and can enforce the note against the maker.

Reacquirer A reacquirer is a holder who negotiates an instrument and then reacquires it. A reacquirer, for the most part, is remitted to his former position. A holder who takes an instrument as a holder in due course and negotiates it to a holder other than one in due course and reacquires it will hold the instrument as a holder in due course. He is remitted to his former position.

CASES

Shotts v. Pardi, 483 S.W.2d 879 (Tex. 1972). Action by Mark Shotts, the holder of a check, plaintiff, against George J. Pardi, the drawer of the check, defendant, to recover on the check after payment had been stopped.

Plaintiff operated a business under the name of Mack Shotts Truck Stop, and defendant was engaged in the business of growing, packing, and selling fresh vegetables. Defendant contracted with one George Schnell, a driver of a truck, for the transportation of a shipment of cabbage and carrots from Texas to Ohio. Defendant issued his check drawn on the First State Bank of Uvalde, Texas, and made payable to George Schnell for the sum of $300. The check was for a down payment on the freight for transporting the produce. Schnell immediately indorsed the check unconditionally and cashed it with plaintiff as payment for goods, wares, and merchandise. Schnell failed to transport the produce, and defendant stopped payment on the check. Plaintiff cashed the check for George Schnell. However, the check was thereafter returned to plaintiff marked "payment stopped." Plaintiff then brought this action.

Nye, Chief Justice: A holder in due course is entitled to recover against the drawer or maker, notwithstanding there may be a good defense to the instrument against the payee. . . . In a case very similar to the one before us, *Full Gospel Assem. in Christ v. Montgomery Ward*, 237 S.W.2d 657, the appellant church hired one McMillan to paint the church for an agreed consideration of $260.00. After the job was apparently completed, McMillan demanded his pay. The church authorities executed and delivered to him a check for the full amount. On the same day, McMillan took the check to appellees' place of business (Montgomery Ward) and received cash and merchandise for it. On the following Monday the church discovered that McMillan had painted the church with inferior materials and so they stopped payment on the check. Montgomery Ward brought suit against the church to recover the amount of the check. The appellant church contended that Montgomery Ward had accepted the check subject to the right of the church to stop payment on it for fraud, failure of consideration or other good cause. Montgomery Ward contended that the check was a negotiable instrument and that since it was a holder in due course it was entitled to recover the amount of the check even though the consideration between the church and McMillan had entirely failed. The judgment for Montgomery Ward was affirmed. The court held that a check is a draft drawn on a bank and payable on demand. Where such a check is made payable to order or bearer it is a negotiable instrument. Every holder of a negotiable instrument, which at the time of its acquisition is complete and regular on its face, is deemed to be a holder in due course. A holder in due course holds the instrument free . . . from the defenses available to prior parties among themselves. [DECISION FOR PLAINTIFF]

Anderson v. Elem, 208 Pac. 573 (Kan. 1922). Action by J. Anderson, plaintiff, against J. H. Elem, defendant. The defendant drew a check dated October 20, 1919, payable to the order of W. B. Lynch and, for reasons immaterial to the rule of law involved, stopped payment on the check the next day. The check was negotiated to the plaintiff on November 14, 1919, and when payment was refused by the drawee-bank, the plaintiff brought this action as indorsee to recover from the drawer. The defendant contended that the check was not presented for payment within a reasonable time after issue.

 Burch, Justice: The payee, W. B. Lynch, was a patron of the plaintiff's hotel in Salina. The plaintiff was in the habit of cashing checks for his guests, and had cashed a $50 check for Lynch two weeks before he was asked to cash the check sued on. The plaintiff testified as follows:

On the afternoon of November 14, 1919, W. B. Lynch presented check marked Exhibit "A" to me at Planters' Hotel, asking me to cash same. I said to him I did not have $200 in cash at the hotel. Mr. W. B. Lynch asked me if I would cash same at the bank. I asked if check was good. Mr. J. R. Stanely was standing near at that time, and asked to look at the check, and said: "Mr. Elem, of Wichita, Kan., is O.K., and is known to me personally. He is a real estate man of Wichita, and is worth considerable money." He mentioned the sum, $50,000. So I told Mr. Lynch to sign the check, and I took it to the Planters' State Bank, Salina, the same afternoon of November 14, 1919, and received $200 currency, with which I returned to the hotel, and presented it to Mr. W. B. Lynch.

Did the lapse of 24 days from the date the check was issued, without more, necessarily give to it, in the eyes of the plaintiff, or in law, the same appearance as that of a dishonored draft, or of an overdue and unpaid promissory note? A check is not overdue, for purpose of negotiation, unless there has been unreasonable delay in presenting it, and unreasonable delay must be interpreted to mean such delay as to make the check obviously stale.

 The facts are all before the court. It is essential to uniformity that the court itself should determine questions of this character, and the court holds that the time elapsing between the issuing of the check and its negotiation did not deprive the plaintiff of the rights of a holder in due course. [DECISION FOR PLAINTIFF]

Wilson v. Gorden, 91 A.2d 329 (D.C. 1952). Action by Grover C. Wilson, plaintiff, against Charles D. Gorden, defendant. United Television, Inc., sold defendant a television set on February 8, 1951, in consideration of which defendant signed a conditional sales contract and a promissory note in the amount of $362.50. Plaintiff purchased the note from United Television, Inc., for $246.50 on the same day. About three weeks thereafter, because of some trouble which is immaterial here, the defendant returned the television set to the television firm. The note was not paid when it was due, and this action followed. Plaintiff testified that he had no connection with the television firm and that he bought the note in good faith for a valuable consideration and became a holder of the note before it was due. He admitted that he furnished the television firm with blank conditional sales contracts.

Quinn, Judge: Every holder of a negotiable instrument is deemed prima facie a holder in due course, but if it is shown that the title of any person who had negotiated the instrument was defective, the burden is on the holder to prove that he or some person under whom he claims acquired the title as a holder in due course. Accordingly, plaintiff first showed that he was a holder of the negotiable instrument and how he acquired it, thereby raising the presumption that he was a holder in due course. Defendant attacked this position by attempting to show that he acquired title to this negotiable instrument in breach of faith or under such circumstances as amount to fraud. Defendant claims that plaintiff was in reality a payee due to the close association between plaintiff and the television firm. . . . This close association was attempted to be shown by the fact that plaintiff acquired title on the same date as the date of the sale of the television unit to defendant along with the exceptionally large discount coupled with plaintiff's admission that he had furnished the television firm with blank conditional sales contracts. This evidence is not sufficient in law to defeat plaintiff's claim as a holder in due course. . . .

While breach of faith or such circumstances as amount to fraud or knowledge of an infirmity in a negotiable instrument may be established by circumstantial evidence, it has been well said that an indorsee's bad faith or fraud in acquiring a negotiable note can never be assumed but must be shown by clear and unequivocal testimony and mere suspicion is insufficient to upset the proof offered by a plaintiff that he was a holder in due course. It appears clear from defendants' evidence that they have a cause of action against the television firm, payee of the note. But we must hold that plaintiff established that it was a holder in due course of the note and hence that he took the instrument free from defenses available between the immediate parties. [DECISION FOR PLAINTIFF]

Medeiros v. Fellsway Motors, Inc., 96 N.E.2d 170 (Mass. 1951). Action by Manuel Medeiros, plaintiff, against Fellsway Motors, Inc., defendant. The defendant, a used-car dealer, purchased an automobile on October 23, 1946, from a person purporting to be one Therrien who, at the time of the sale, showed the defendant some papers identifying himself as Therrien, and a bill of sale for the automobile. The defendant gave Therrien a check for $1,200 which was dated ahead to October 25, 1946, in order that defendant would have an opportunity to investigate the title to the automobile. The next day the defendant discovered that the person from whom the automobile had been purchased was an imposter who had stolen the automobile and the identifying papers. The defendant stopped payment on the check. The impostor, in the meantime, drew a line through the numeral "5" in the date of the check to make it resemble the numeral "8," and, on October 29, 1946, purchased an automobile from the plaintiff, also a used-car dealer, for $764. He paid for the automobile with the $1,200 check and received the balance in cash. The plaintiff deposited the check on October 30, 1946, but received nothing because payment had been stopped by the defendant. The plaintiff, claiming to be a holder in due course, then brought this action against the defendant, the drawer of the check.

    Ronan, Justice: We have examined the check. The written portion of the body of the check is in very broad flowing lines. The alteration was made by a straight, narrow, diagonal line from the right hand top edge of the figure 5 to the lower left hand curved end of this figure. This line was made with different ink. We cannot say that the finding that this alteration was apparent on inspection is erroneous as a matter of law although the question is close.

    The check at the time it was taken for value by the plaintiff disclosed upon its face a change in its date which was a material alteration. . . . The judge found that this change was made by the impostor without the knowledge or assent of the defendant and after it had been delivered to him by the defendant. The check was not complete and regular on its face because of a patent alteration in its date, and the plaintiff, although he took it for value, did not become a holder in due course.

[DECISION FOR DEFENDANT]

General Motors Acceptance Corp. v. Daigle, 72 So. 2d 319 (La. 1954). Action by General Motors Acceptance Corporation, plaintiff, against John Daigle, defendant. The controversy in this case revolves around a Pontiac sedan. On February 18, 1953, the car was sold by the Louisiana Motors, Inc., to Blaine Cotter, for the sum of $3,089.99. Louisiana Motors handled the papers for financing, but the actual financing was assigned to plaintiff. The car was thereafter involved in a collision, and Blaine Cotter traded the car to Louisiana Motors and purchased another car. Louisiana Motors then paid plaintiff the amount remaining unpaid on the car. On August 8, 1953, defendant purchased the Pontiac from Louisiana Motors for the sum of $2,900. Louisiana Motors again handled the papers for financing, but the actual financing was assigned to plaintiff. Defendant refused to pay the second monthly installment due on the car, and this action followed.

    Moise, Justice: General Motors Acceptance Corporation had full knowledge and was informed that the car was a used car, having a previous title. It had only to compare the bill of sale and mortgage with the title papers. . . .

    The title under consideration had a definite defect, because General Motors Acceptance Corporation was the actor in the first transaction when the car was sold to Cotter. The car was represented in the bill of sale and mortgage to Daigle to be a new demonstrator, whereas, the papers in possession of the General Motors Acceptance Corporation showed this not to be correct. The title certificate to make the car marketable and merchantable showed on its face that it was a used car, having been sold to another. . . .

    We, therefore, conclude that plaintiff is not a holder in due course.

[DECISION FOR DEFENDANT]

PROBLEMS

1 Pope, who represented to Marion that he owned a one-acre tract of land in Florida that was located on the side of a lake, offered to sell the land to Marion for $1,000. Marion accepted the offer but stated that he did not have the $1,000. Marion also stated that he would give Pope a promissory note payable in six months in payment of the land. Pope agreed with the arrangement, and Marion thereupon executed the promissory note. Pope then borrowed $600 from the First Bank for six months, indorsed the note in blank, and delivered it to the First Bank. The loan was not paid when it became due, and the First Bank brought an action against Marion to recover the $600. At the trial, Marion proved that the land was covered with water and was worthless. Marion argued that the First Bank could not therefore be a holder in due course. Is this a good defense?

2 The maker executed and delivered a note for $5,000, payable on demand and bearing the date of September 9, 1960. Someone altered the note by erasing the date and writing in ink the words "November 17, 1960" over the erased date. This alteration was apparent by a visual examination of the note. Could a holder of the note who purchased it after the date was so changed qualify as a holder in due course?

3 Defendant and the seller entered into a contract by the terms of which the defendant purchased certain land and in payment thereof executed and delivered his note to the seller for $1,500. The note was made payable "on or before four — after date." About four months later, the parties mutually agreed to rescind the sale, and the seller agreed to return the note to the defendant. The note was not returned. The blank was not filled in. Plaintiff, who is the holder of the note, seeks to recover from the defendant the amount for which the note was given. Will the defendant be able to assert his defense against the plaintiff?

4 A representative of The Builders persuaded defendant to purchase an aluminum roof for his residence. Defendant was illiterate and unable to read but was capable of signing his name. At the time he purchased the roof, therefore, he was led to believe that he was signing a promissory note for $700. He signed, in fact, a note payable to the order of plaintiff, The Loan Association, for $1,000. In an action by plaintiff to recover on the note, defendant contended that plaintiff could not be a holder in due course on the ground that the payee of a negotiable instrument may not be a holder in due course. Do you agree with this contention?

5 The Appliance Company purchased a refrigerator from Brown on credit and sold it to Smith. Brown held the title to the refrigerator. Smith therefore gave The Appliance Company a check in payment of the refrigerator with the understanding that The Appliance Company would pay Brown and obtain title to the refrigerator. The Appliance Company, however, indorsed the check and delivered it to The Finance Company with directions to apply the proceeds toward payment of a previously owing debt. Smith contends The Finance Company did not take the check for value and is therefore not a holder in due course. Do you agree?

6 Tully, doing business as the Refrigeration Sales Company, sold to the defendant a beverage cooler, for which the defendant executed his promissory note payable to bearer for the sum of $700. Tully thereafter sold and delivered the note to plaintiff. The cooler proved to be defective and unfit for the purpose for which it was sold, and defendant rescinded the sale. Plaintiff brought an action against defendant to recover the $700 when the note became overdue. Defendant claimed he was not liable upon the note since he had returned the cooler to Tully. The court held in favor of plaintiff. Discuss the rules of law upon which this holding was founded.

7   Defendant executed a promissory note for the sum of $1,750, dated December 15, 1958, payable to Brown, one year after date. Brown sold the note to The Investment Company, who took it as a holder in due course. The Investment Company then sold the note to plaintiff, who demanded that the defendant pay the note. Defendant refused on the ground that the note was given in payment of stock in a certain corporation, that the stock was never delivered, that plaintiff knew the stock had never been delivered, and that plaintiff was not therefore a good faith purchaser. Do you think plaintiff could recover?

23
DEFENSES

A defense is that which may be offered by the defendant in an action as a reason why the plaintiff should not recover what he seeks. The plaintiff, in the usual action on an instrument, will be the holder; the defendant will be the maker, drawer, acceptor, or indorser, or possibly a combination of these parties.

Defenses are classified as personal and real defenses. Personal defenses may be used to defeat any action brought by any holder who neither qualifies in his own right as a holder in due course nor is a holder through a holder in due course. Stated otherwise, a holder in due course and a holder through a holder in due course take the instrument free of personal defenses. Real defenses may be used to defeat any action brought by any holder including a holder in due course. It will be worthwhile, therefore, to keep in mind the distinction between a holder and a holder in due course, as well as the distinction between real and personal defenses.

PERSONAL DEFENSES

Personal defenses include those which arise out of the relation of the parties to the contract. Some of the more important of these are nondelivery of a completed instrument, nondelivery of an incomplete instrument, delivery of an incomplete instrument, conditional delivery of a completed instrument, payment before maturity, absence or failure of consideration, fraud in the inducement, and discharge of the parties.

Nondelivery of Completed Instrument   Delivery of the instrument is indispensable to the acquisition of the legal title to the instrument. The drawer of a check may complete the instrument in all details and leave it on his desk. A thief could not enforce the check against the drawer. The same would be true if the check were secured by fraud, duress, or similar means. The defrauding party could not enforce the check against the drawer. Nondelivery of a completed instrument is not available as a defense against a holder in due course. [*Gimbel Bros. v. Hymowitz*, p. 291.]

Nondelivery of Incomplete Instrument   Sections 3–115 and 3–407 provide that the nondelivery of an incomplete instrument cannot be asserted against a holder in due course. This is, therefore, a personal defense. A holder in due course sees and takes the paper in good faith on the signature of the maker. A person may sign a note or check in blank and leave it on his desk or in a safe. A thief may in some way obtain possession of the blank instrument and complete it by filling in the blanks. The loss should fall upon the person whose conduct in signing a blank note or check made the fraud possible rather than upon an innocent holder in due course.

Delivery of Incomplete Instrument   A person may sign an instrument incomplete in some particular, deliver it to another person, and give such other person authority to fill in the blanks. If the blanks are filled in strictly in accordance with the authority given and within a reasonable time no difficulty arises. Suppose the drawer of a check completes the check in every particular except for the amount and delivers it to his agent with authority to complete it for $200. If the agent completes the instrument for $200, the drawer is liable for that amount. No problem arises in this illustration. To pursue the illustration a little further: Suppose the instrument completed for $2,000 gets into the possession of a holder in due course. Such holder in due course may enforce the instrument for $2,000 against the drawer even though it is not filled in strictly in accordance with the authority given or within a reasonable time. This could be disastrous.

Conditional Delivery of Completed Instrument   It sometimes happens that the drawer or maker will sign and deliver an instrument to the payee upon condition that it shall not be enforced except upon the happening of a certain contingency, or the instrument may be signed and delivered for a special purpose only. Such an instrument is not enforceable by the payee until the condition is fulfilled. Brown may place his signature on a completed promissory note payable to Henry with the understanding that it is not to become a binding obligation until it is signed by Smith. Henry cannot enforce the note against Brown if Smith for some reason refuses to sign the note. The delivery, in these circumstances, may be shown to have been conditional and not for the purpose of transferring the property in the instrument. A subsequent holder in due course, however, has the right to collect from Brown although Smith did not sign.

Payment before Maturity   Payment of an instrument prior to maturity or to the wrong person is only a personal defense. A person who takes overdue paper takes it with all its infirmities. A person who takes a negotiable instrument before its maturity date, however, is not required to determine if the instrument has been paid. Such a rule would clog the circulation of negotiable instruments. The maker of a note, therefore, who pays it before maturity and allows it to continue in circulation will have to pay it again if it come into the hands of a holder in due course. The rule may seem harsh, but the remedy is simple. The maker should not have paid it in the first instance without securing possession of the instrument. [*Silver Spring Title Co. v. Chadwick*, p. 292.]

Absence or Failure of Consideration   The common-law cases which draw a dividing line between the facts that do and the facts that do not constitute consideration are applicable to the law of commercial paper relative to the immediate parties; for example, the maker and the payee. Those facts, therefore, that will constitute consideration in the law of simple contracts—with the addition of the past-due debt—will constitute consideration between the immediate parties on a negotiable instrument. A holder in due course, however, takes the instrument free of the personal defense of absence or failure of consideration. The maker gratuitously delivers his promissory note to the payee. The payee cannot enforce the note against the maker. A holder in due course to whom the note has been negotiated, however, may enforce the note against the maker. The rule is equally applicable to an accommodation maker. A holder in due course could enforce the instrument against the accommodation maker. The accommodation maker may assert the same defense against any other person not a holder in due course. [*National City Bank v. Parr*, p. 293.]

Fraud in the Inducement   Fraud in the inducement, or consideration, is so called because the defrauded party was fraudulently induced to sign the instrument; it results when the defrauded party intended to create an instrument but would not have done so if he had known the true facts. A typical illustration of fraud in the inducement would result if the maker of a note was induced to sign a note for the price of a worthless clock which was fraudulently represented by the payee to be a valuable antique. The maker clearly intended to sign the note. He would not have done so, however, if he had known that the clock was worthless. As between the maker and the payee, the maker may assert the personal defense of fraud in the inducement. As between the maker and a holder in due course, however, the defense may not be asserted. The holder in due course takes the instrument free of this type of defense.

Discharge of Parties   It is provided by section 3–602 that no discharge of any party is effective against a subsequent holder in due course unless he has notice of the defense when he takes the instrument. Any discharge of a party, therefore, is only a personal defense. This rule applies only to discharge arising under Article 3 of the Code.

It is to be remembered that a person may take an instrument as a holder in due course even though he has notice that one or more parties have been discharged. Suppose one indorser's signature has been canceled and that the holder took the instrument with knowledge of the discharge. The holder in due course would be subject to the defense of discharge with respect to the discharged indorser, but could enforce the instrument against all other parties liable on the instrument.

REAL DEFENSES

Real defenses include those which arise out of the fact that no instrument or liability was created in the first instance, or, if such instrument or liability was created, it has been destroyed. Some of the more important of the real defenses are forgery, incapacity, material alteration, fraud in the execution and misrepresentation, illegality, duress, and discharge in insolvency proceedings.

Forgery   A holder in due course occupies a favored position in the law. But he is not so favored that a person who neither makes, draws, nor accepts an instrument can be held liable to pay such an instrument. It is quite clear that a party whose signature was forged or used without authorization has a real defense against a holder in due course.

Incapacity   The validity of every contract is dependent upon the capacity of the parties thereto to enter into legally binding contracts. The law of commercial paper provides no exception to this rule. The general rule, therefore, is that incapacitated persons may assert incapacity as a real defense against any holder. The Code, however, takes no position on whether infancy amounts to incapacity. This question is left to be dealt with under state law. This is made clear by section 3–305, which provides that infancy is a real defense "to the extent that it is a defense to a simple contract." Any other incapacity, such as mental incompetence, lack of corporate capacity to do business, and other incapacity apart from infancy, is also a real defense if such incapacity "renders the obligation of the party a nullity" under state law. This question, therefore, is also left to be dealt with under state law.

Material Alteration   An alteration is a *material alteration* when it changes the contract of a party to the instrument. The addition of a surety on a note would not ordinarily change the obligation of the maker and would not be material as to the maker. The addition of an alternative payee would be material, however, since it changes the obligation of the drawer or maker. For example: a note drawn "payable to the order of Brown" which is altered by Brown to read "payable to the order of Brown or Jones." The advance in the date of payment, or an addition to the amount payable, would also change the contract of the maker or drawer.

A holder in due course, not a party to the alteration, may enforce payment of a materially altered instrument according to its original tenor. A material alteration, however, is a real defense to the extent of the alteration. If the payee of a check raises a check from $10 to $110 and negotiates it to a holder in due course, the holder in due course may enforce the check against the drawer for $10. It should not be presumed, however, that the defense is limited to the sum payable; it is equally applicable to any material alteration. The rule in its broadest aspect permits a holder in due course to recover upon the instrument just as if it had not been altered. The cases involving a material alteration of the sum payable, nevertheless, do present a unique question of estoppel when the issuer is so careless in his draftsmanship that the alteration of the instrument is rendered comparatively simple. Is the issuer, in these circumstances, estopped from asserting the defense of material alteration? The answer is found in section 3–406. The defense is not available to any person who by his negligence substantially contributes to the material alteration. The question as to what acts will constitute negligence is left to the court or jury upon the circumstances of the particular case. Spaces left in the body of the instrument in which words or figures may be inserted might be considered negligence.

Misrepresentation of Character or Essential Terms of Instrument   Section 3–305 recognizes fraud in the execution, or inception. This is the situation where a person signs an instrument under such circumstances that he is deceived as to the character of the paper he signs. A clear illustration of fraud in the execution exists where the defrauding party cleverly substitutes one paper for another. The maker is tricked into signing a note when he thought it was a receipt. If the maker is "excusably ignorant," this defense may be asserted against a holder in due course. This is a real defense on the reasoning that the maker did not intend to sign a note. The defense extends to an instrument signed with knowledge that it is a negotiable instrument, but without knowledge of its essential terms. The test is in the definition of "excusable ignorance," but these words are not precisely defined. All the pertinent facts of the case must be considered in determining whether a person has a reasonable opportunity to ascertain the essential elements of the contract. Some of the facts to consider are as follows: his education and intelligence; his sex and age; his business experience; his ability to communicate in the English language; the representations made to him and why he relied upon them; availability of a third person to read and explain the essential terms of the contract; and why he did not postpone signing the contract. This defense may not be as formidable as it appears at first. If the person who signed was negligent, the defense of misrepresentation may not be used against a holder in due course. [*Burchett v. Allied Concord Financial Corp.*, p. 294.]

Illegality   Contracts which tend to corrupt public officers, contracts which encourage immorality, gambling contracts, usurious contracts, and many others are illegal either under the common law or by statutory provision. A negotiable instrument given in payment of an illegal transaction, as between the immediate parties, operates according to the law of contracts. Most types of illegality, therefore, may be asserted as a personal defense.

A different problem is presented, however, when a negotiable instrument which was issued in payment of an illegal transaction reaches the hands of a holder in due course. Illegality may or may not be a real defense. The solution to the problem is largely dependent upon statute. Some statutory provisions expressly, or by unavoidable implication, declare the instrument to be absolutely void. The effect of such a statutory provision will, as a general rule, permit a primary party to assert a real defense against a holder in due course. For example, the particular state statute may render obligations created by gambling a nullity. Under such a statute, illegality would be a real defense. If the state statute merely made the contract illegal but not null and void, the transaction would carry with it a personal defense only.

Duress   Duress, or force and fear, when used to make someone sign an instrument, may be a personal or a real defense. A person who signs an instrument under direct compulsion which seriously threatens him with actual physical harm—if, for example, his life is threatened with a gun—would be permitted to assert a real defense against a holder in due course. Duress is only a personal defense, however, when the force and pressure used consist only of threats.

Discharge in Insolvency Proceedings   Section 3–305 treats a discharge in bankruptcy or insolvency proceedings as a real defense to which a holder in due course is subject. This section is designed to make it clear that such a defense is not cut off when the instrument is negotiated to a holder in due course.

THE IMMEDIATE PARTIES
The distinction between personal and real defenses becomes unimportant as between the immediate parties. Either a personal or a real defense may be asserted against a person with whom the holder has dealt. [*Brotherton v. McWaters,* p. 296.]

CASES
Gimbel Bros. v. Hymowitz,   51 A.2d 389 (Pa. 1947). Action by Gimbel Brothers, Inc., plaintiff, against Herman T. Hymowitz, defendant, to recover on a dishonored check. The facts upon which the defendant based his defense were that Bruce K. Redding, the drawer of the check, came to the defendant's plumbing supply store to purchase certain supplies for which he gave a check naming the defendant as payee. The payee at this time indorsed the check. Redding asked for immediate delivery of the supplies. While defendant was telephoning the drawee-bank from a private office to inquire if the check was good, Redding left and took

the check with him. Redding indorsed the check bearing the prior indorsement of the defendant and took it to plaintiff, who cashed the check. This action, therefore, is brought by a holder of a check against a prior indorser.

Arnold, Judge: The defendant-indorser could not defend on the ground of his own nondelivery. The reason which precludes the prior indorser from defending on the ground of nondelivery is the maxim that as between two innocent parties (in this case the holder for value and prior indorser) liability should be borne by the one, i.e., the indorser, who made the loss possible.

The payee and prior indorser could easily have protected himself by making his indorsement "for deposit only" or with some similar notation. He could have protected himself by not allowing the indorsed check to go out of his possession. He could have protected himself by not indorsing the check until he was ready to receive it. Thus his act or acts enabled Redding to commit the fraud and induced the payment by the plaintiff of the check. To hold otherwise would require one proposing to become the purchaser of a check to inquire of each indorser whether his indorsement was intended, or in default thereof to release him. [DECISION FOR PLAINTIFF]

Silver Spring Title Co. v. Chadwick, 131 A.2d 489 (Md. 1957). Action by Silver Spring Title Company, appellant, against George A Chadwick, appellee.

The facts, insofar as they are important here, are as follows: The Title Company, as agent for two builders, prepared for the builders two notes so that the builders could procure two construction loans of $5,000 each. Each note was made payable to Moore & Hill Company. The notes were then negotiated to Chadwick. When construction was completed on one of the lots, the Title Company drew its check in the required amount payable to Moore & Hill Company. This payment was passed on to Chadwick, who surrendered possession of the note. The Title Company thereafter attempted to have the outstanding note canceled by again drawing its check payable to Moore & Hill Company. The same procedure, therefore, was followed. This check was deposited to the account of Moore & Hill Company, but the proceeds were never paid to Chadwick. The Title Company, upon learning that Moore & Hill Company did not have sufficient assets to refund the payment made by the Title Company, brought this action against Chadwick, to cancel the note.

Brune, Chief Justice: The question is, who should bear the loss when the agent of the borrower pays the debt to someone other than the holder of the note? The Title Company claims that Moore & Hill Company was acting as agent for Chadwick in receiving the money on these loans. This claim of agency is based upon the fact that the previous note had been paid off in an identical manner.

The notes used in these transactions were negotiable, and of such a character that they could and quite possibly would be negotiated and passed on into the hands of a third party. No effort was made by the Title Company to discover the actual holder thereof and payment was made to Moore & Hill Company in spite of the Title Company's knowledge that the previous note had been negotiated to a third party. While it is true that Chadwick did not object to the payment of the previous note to Moore & Hill Company, there is no evidence that he ever authorized Moore & Hill Company to accept payment for the same. Chadwick's conduct in this one instance would not be sufficient to lead a reasonably prudent and careful person to believe that Moore & Hill Company were authorized to receive payments on the notes.

It has long been recognized in this State that when a maker of a note pays the debt to someone who does not have possession of the note, such payment is no defense to an action by the holder of the note. [DECISION FOR APPELLEE]

National City Bank v. Parr, 185 N.E. 904 (Ind. 1933). Action by National City Bank (plaintiff below), appellant, against Modessa Bates Parr (defendant below), appellee, to recover on a promissory note. Modessa Bates Parr executed as an accommodation maker the promissory note for which payment is sought in this action. It was payable to her sister, Geneva Bates Myers, by whom it was indorsed to the appellant bank.

Treanor, Judge: In the instant case the accommodation maker Modessa Bates Parr was entitled to the defense of absence of consideration if appellant was not a holder in due course; but the burden was on her to prove the absence of consideration. This involved no difficulty, since it was not questioned that she was an accommodation maker.

Considering only the evidence most favorable to appellee, there was some evidence from which the jury could have found the following facts:

(1) The payee, Geneva Bates Myers, as a result of fraudulent representations of one Griffin, had purchased worthless oil company stocks and interests in certain leases. Also that one James, cashier of the appellant bank, had aided Griffin in his fraudulent activities.

(2) Geneva Bates Myers executed various promissory notes totaling $8,100 to pay for the stocks and leases, and these were purchased from Griffin by the National City Bank.

(3) The bank had notice of the fraud, since James, the cashier with knowledge of the fraud arranged with Griffin to have the notes discounted at the bank, actually knew of and participated in the discounting of the notes.

(4) The various notes were merged in one renewal note executed by Geneva Bates Myers, in the amount of $8,100.

(5) Later, at the insistence of the bank, Geneva Bates Myers took up the $8,100 note by her own note for $2,500 and a check for $5,706.27; the bank knowing at the time that there were no funds available to meet the check.

(6) Under threats of prosecution for issuing the check, Geneva Bates Myers, at the suggestion of the bank, procured the $6,000 note in suit which was signed by her sister, Modessa Bates Parr, as an accommodation maker, and payable to Geneva Bates Myers, payee, and upon receipt of this note the bank surrendered the unpaid check.

On the facts we must treat the note in suit as a renewal of the original notes executed by Geneva Bates Myers; and if the appellant bank was not a holder in due course of the original notes it is not a holder in due course of the note in suit. The jury's verdict was for appellee Modessa Bates Parr, and in answer to interrogatories the jury found that the original notes were obtained from Geneva Bates Myers by Griffin through fraud and that the National City Bank had knowledge of the defenses to these notes when it purchased them. The jury also found that Geneva Bates Myers was ignorant of the fraud practiced upon her until after the note in suit had been executed. There was no evidence to indicate that Modessa Bates Parr knew anything about her sister's transaction with Griffin or the National City Bank. Since the jury found that Geneva Bates Myers was induced to execute the original notes through fraud, the burden was upon the holder, the National City Bank, to prove by a preponderance of the evidence that it was a holder in due course.

We conclude that there was sufficient evidence to support the finding that the original notes were obtained by fraud and that the National City Bank, plaintiff below, took with knowledge of the fraud. Consequently, the plaintiff below was not a holder in due course either of the original notes or of the accommodation note in suit. Not being a holder in due course the plaintiff below (under the facts) was in no better position than an assignee of a chose in action. Since the plaintiff's assignor, the payee, could not enforce the accommodation maker's promise because of an absence of consideration, it follows that the plaintiff holder was subject to the same defense. [DECISION FOR APPELLEE]

Burchett v. Allied Concord Financial Corp., 396 P.2d 186 (N.M. 1964). Action by John Burchett and Tinnie Burchett, plaintiffs-appellees, against Allied Concord Financial Corporation, defendant-appellant, to have certain notes and mortgages held by the defendant-appellant canceled and declared void.

The evidence revealed that a man named Kelly represented himself as selling Kaiser aluminum siding for a firm named Consolidated Products; that Kelly talked to the appellees at their house offering to install the aluminum siding for a certain price in exchange for using the house as a "show house" in order to further other sales; that Kelly told appellees that they would receive $100 credit on each sale in a specified area, which was the cost on the installation of the aluminum siding on the house; that appellees were given a form to read; that while they were reading the form, Kelly was filling out blanks in other forms; that appellees then signed, without reading, the forms filled out by Kelly; that appellees in fact signed a note and mortgage encumbering their house to cover the cost of the installation which contained no mention of the credit for other sales; that appellees thereafter received a letter from appellant stating that appellant had purchased the note and mortgage and that appellees were delinquent in the first payment; and that appellees then discovered that the note and mortgage had been recorded. Appellees then brought this action, contending that the note and mortgage were fraudulently procured and that the defense of fraud was available against the appellant.

Carmody, Justice: The only real question in the case is whether, under these facts, appellees, by substantial evidence, satisfied the provisions of the statute relating to their claimed defense as against a holder in due course. . . .

The provision of the Code applicable to this case appears as section 3–305(2)(c), which, so far as material, is as follows:

To the extent that a holder is a holder in due course he takes the instrument free from . . .

(2)   All defenses of any party to the instrument with whom the holder has not dealt except

(c)   Such misrepresentation as has induced the party to sign the instrument with neither knowledge nor reasonable opportunity to obtain knowledge of its character or its essential terms.

Although fully realizing that the official comments appearing as a part of the Uniform Commercial Code are not direct authority for the construction to be placed upon a section of the Code, nevertheless they are persuasive and represent the opinion of the National Conference of Commissioners on Uniform State Laws and the American Law Institute. The purpose of the comments is to explain the provisions of the Code itself, in an effort to promote uniformity of interpretation. We believe that the official comments following section 3–305(2)(c) provide an excellent guideline for the disposition of the case before us. . . .

The test of the defense here stated is that of excusable ignorance of the contents of the writing signed. The party must not only have been in ignorance, but must also have had no reasonable opportunity to obtain knowledge. In determining what is a reasonable opportunity all relevant factors are to be taken into account, including the age and sex of the party, his intelligence, education and business experience; his ability to read or to understand English, the representations made to him and his reason to rely on them or to have confidence in the person making them; the presence or absence of any third person who might read or explain the instrument to him, or any other possibility of obtaining independent information; and the apparent necessity, or lack of it, for acting without delay.

Unless the misrepresentation meets this test, the defense is cut off by a holder in due course.

We recognize that the reasonable opportunity to obtain knowledge may be excused if the maker places reasonable reliance on the representations. The difficulty in the instant case is that the reliance upon the representations of a complete stranger (Kelly) was not reasonable, and all of the parties were of sufficient age, intelligence, education, and business experience to know better. In this connection, it is noted that the contracts clearly stated, on the same page which bore the signature of the various appellees, the following:

"No one is authorized on behalf of this company to represent this job to be 'A SAMPLE HOME OR A FREE JOB.'" . . .

We determine under these facts as a matter of law . . . appellant as a holder in due course took the instrument free from the defenses claimed by the appellees. [DECISION FOR APPELLANT]

Brotherton v. McWaters, 438 P.2d 1 (Okla. 1968). Action by C. D. Brotherton, R. L. Brotherton, and James R. Brotherton, a partnership, doing business as Brotherton's Automotive, plaintiffs, against Lloyd McWaters, defendant, to recover the amount of a check indorsed to them by defendant.

Plaintiffs made certain repairs to defendant's diesel truck, and in payment of a portion of the repair work, defendant indorsed and delivered to them a check in the amount of $690 payable to the order of defendant and drawn by a broker on a Colorado bank. The drawer thereafter stopped payment on the check, and defendant refused to pay the $690. Defendant contended, among other things, that the repair work was done in an unworkmanlike manner and that the truck experienced mechanical difficulty which required the truck to be repaired again. The case was submitted to the jury on the question of whether plaintiffs properly repaired the truck, and the jury returned a verdict in favor of defendant.

Williams, Justice: Plaintiffs apparently are contending that as the drawer of the check, rather than defendant, stopped payment thereof, defendant became absolutely liable to pay the check in accordance with section 3–414, which provides, in pertinent part:

"(1) unless the indorsement otherwise specifies (as by such words as 'without recourse') every indorser engages that upon dishonor and any necessary notice of dishonor and protest he will pay the instrument according to its tenor at the time of his endorsement to the holder."

Plaintiff continues by arguing this contention is valid regardless of whether they are holders or holders in due course. . . . We cannot agree with this contention. Section 3–408 provides, again in pertinent part:

"Want or failure of consideration is a defense *as against any person* not having the rights of a holder in due course (Section 3–305)." (Emphasis added.)

One of the requirements of being a holder in due course as defined in section 3–302(a) is that a holder take the instrument for value. As applicable herein, section 3–303(a) provides that a holder takes for value "to the extent that the agreed consideration has been performed." Of course, the contention of the defendant herein is that the agreed consideration, i.e., the workmanlike repair of his truck, has not been performed.

However, it is our opinion that whether plaintiffs herein are holders in due course or merely holders makes no difference. As noted above, section 3–408 provides that the defense or failure of consideration is applicable to any person not having the rights of a holder in due course. Section 3–305, which defines the rights of a holder in due course, provides, inter alia, that a holder in due course ". . . takes the instrument free from . . . (2) all defenses of any party to the instrument *with whom the holder has not dealt.*" (Emphasis added.) As plaintiffs herein dealt with defendant, it is our opinion that even assuming they were holders in due course, they are not immune to the defense of want or failure of consideration as set forth in section 3–408.

Further, we have found no provision of our Commercial Code, and plaintiffs have cited none, which restricts the defense of want or failure of consideration to the drawer of a check or requires that an indorser, to take advantages of such defense, stop payment of a check himself. In our opinion, the defense contained in section 3–408, except as restricted therein, is available to any person, i.e., drawer, payee, indorser, etc., in the chain of title. [DECISION FOR DEFENDANT]

PROBLEMS

1   Defendant was engaged in a poker game with Jones and others on the evening of December 19, 1960. At the close of the game, defendant executed and delivered to Jones his negotiable check in the sum of $2,902 to cover his losses. On the following morning, Jones transferred the check by delivery and indorsement to plaintiff, to whom Jones was indebted. Jones received in cash the difference between the amount of the check and the debt. Jones departed for California. Defendant stopped payment on the check, and the check was not paid. Plaintiff now seeks to recover from the defendant. Decide.

2   The plaintiff is a holder in due course of two promissory notes. The defendants are the makers. The trial court found the following facts: that defendants are husband and wife; that they are illiterate, being unable to read or write the English language; that the payee knew of that fact; that the payee gained the trust and confidence of defendants and secured their signature to the notes by false representations which induced the defendants to believe that they were signing a contract to repair dwelling houses and nothing else; that defendants were ignorant of the fact that they were signing notes; that defendants relied upon such false representations and were prevented thereby from seeking independent advice although they requested that they be permitted to obtain it; that defendants were not negligent in signing the notes; and that plaintiff had no notice of any infirmities in the notes at the time they were acquired. What defense, if any, is available to the defendants?

3   Defendant signed a check and locked it in his safe before locking his office and leaving at the close of the business day. An employee, after all the other employees had left for the day, unlocked the office and safe and removed the check. The employee thereafter inserted the date, filled in the amount as $1,000, and named himself as payee. The employee then indorsed the check, and negotiated it to plaintiff for $1,000.00, who took as a holder in due course. Defendant stopped payment on the check when he discovered that it had been stolen. Do you think plaintiff can recover from defendant?

4   On June 1, 1962, Brown executed and delivered to Jones a note in the amount of $300, payable twenty-four months after date, with interest at the rate of 6 percent per annum from maturity until paid. The following words appeared on the face of the note: "This note is for land." On August 30, 1962, Jones negotiated the note to Smith by the following indorsement: "For value received I transfer this note to Smith." Brown paid Jones $300 before the date of maturity. Will Brown be able to assert the defense of payment when Smith seeks to collect the amount of the note?

5   The defendant drew a check dated September 2, 1954, payable to Smith. The next day Smith represented to defendant that he had lost the check, whereupon payment thereof was stopped at the bank. The defendant five or six days later gave Smith another check for the same amount. On September 12, 1954, the original check of September 2 with a "1" inserted before the "2," making the date September "12," was indorsed over to the plaintiff by Smith, who took as a holder in due course. Is the defendant liable on the check?

6   Lozano and his wife executed two promissory notes, one for $45,000 and the other for $2,000, both payable to the order of The Construction Company. These notes were given under a contract whereby the payee, as contractor, agreed to secure a loan and finance the building of a house for Lozano and his wife. The Construction Company sold and negotiated the $2,000 note to Thompson, who purchased as a holder in due course. It was then learned that The Construction Company was unable to provide the necessary financing for the construction of the house, and the house was never built. Do you think Lozano and his wife would prevail in an action to have the two notes canceled?

7   Lyle found a promissory note payable to the order of Anthony Boone for the amount of $2,000. Lyle forged the indorsement of Boone and sold the note to Taylor. Taylor thereafter indorsed and delivered the note to Cabot, who took the note as a holder in due course. Cabot presented the note to Kelly, the maker, for payment on the maturity date of the note, and Kelly refused payment. Cabot then brought an action against Boone on the indorsement to collect the $2,000. Decide.

24

PRESENTMENT, NOTICE OF DISHONOR, PROTEST

Presentment, notice of dishonor, and sometimes protest are important conditions precedent to enforcing the liability of drawers of checks and drafts and all unqualified indorsers. The holder of an instrument who attempts to collect from drawers and indorsers must have exercised proper diligence in first making a presentment to the drawee or maker, followed promptly by notice of dishonor to the drawers and indorsers in case of a dishonor. If the holder fails to meet these conditions precedent, he can still seek to collect from the maker or acceptor during the applicable period of the statute of limitations, but he loses his right of collecting from the drawers of checks and drafts and all unqualified indorsers. As will be shown, however, these conditions are excused in some instances.

PRESENTMENT FOR ACCEPTANCE

The mere drawing of a draft and its delivery to the payee put the drawee under no obligation to the payee to pay the amount of the draft. This is for the reason that a draft or check does not operate as an assignment of funds in the hands of the drawee. How, then, may the drawee be bound? By acceptance. The acceptance is the signification by the drawee of his assent to the order of the drawer. He then becomes primarily liable.

Mode of Acceptance   The acceptance must be written on the draft and signed by the drawee. It need not be in any particular words. The most usual mode of acceptance, it will be remembered, is the writing of the word "accepted" across the face of the draft, followed by the date and the signature of the drawee. The acceptance, however, may consist of his signature alone. The rule applies to checks as well as drafts, because certification of a check is an acceptance. A drawee who fails to accept may be liable to the drawer or to the holder for breach of an agreement by which he is obligated to accept as provided in section 3–409. He may also be liable in tort for conversion under section 3–419 if he refuses to return the instrument on demand. The action, however, is not on the instrument. The action is in tort for conversion of the instrument. A draft presented for acceptance which is not accepted within the prescribed time must be treated as dishonored by the person presenting it, otherwise he will lose the right of recourse against the drawer and indorsers.

Is the draft dishonored if the drawee does not accept it immediately? No. This is for the reason that the drawee should have a period of time in which to decide whether to accept the draft. Section 3–506 provides that the drawee may, without dishonor, defer acceptance until the close of the business day following the day of presentment. The holder may, however, extend the time for another day. In the case of presentment for payment, the draft is dishonored unless the drawee pays it before the close of the business day of presentment. Section 5–112 provides a "three-day rule" only in the case of banks where a documentary draft drawn under a letter of credit is presented. This additional time is to enable the bank to examine carefully the accompanying documents.

Acceptance Varying Draft   Section 3–412 provides for the situation where the acceptance varies the draft in some respect. It may be varied where the drawee in his acceptance specifies a place of payment such as "accepted, payable at First Bank *only*." It may be varied as to the time of payment, as "accepted, payable January 1, 1967," which is not the maturity date of the draft. It may be partial, that is, an acceptance to pay only a part of the amount for which the draft is drawn. The acceptor may also attach a condition to the acceptance if he so desires. [*Lewis Hubbard & Co. v. Morton*, p. 305.]

If the holder assents to a varied acceptance, the drawer and indorsers are discharged unless they affirmatively agree to the varied acceptance. The holder, in the case of a varied acceptance, may take the qualified acceptance, or he can insist upon a general acceptance written on the draft itself. If this is refused, he may treat the draft as dishonored. Each drawer and indorser who does not affirmatively assent to the variance is discharged. This means that the assent of the drawer or indorser must be affirmatively expressed. Mere failure to object within a reasonable time is not assent which will prevent the discharge.

Drafts That Must Be Presented   Presentment for acceptance is not always necessary. A draft drawn payable at sight is payable on presentment and will not be presented for acceptance. It may be to the interest of the drawer and the holder, however, to present all time drafts for acceptance before maturity. It will then be possible to determine whether or not the draft will be honored. The holder may, nevertheless, await the maturity date of most drafts and then present them for payment. Section 3–501 provides that presentment for acceptance, unless excused, is a required proceeding before an action may be brought against the drawer or an indorser in the following three situations:

(1) Where the draft expressly stipulates that it shall be presented for acceptance.

(2) Where the draft is drawn payable elsewhere than at the residence or place of business of the drawee. Suppose Brown draws a draft payable to Smith; Jones is the drawee; the place of payment is 210 Market Street, which is neither the residence nor the place of business of Jones. The draft must be presented for acceptance; otherwise Jones will not know of his obligation to pay the draft at the place designated for payment.

(3) Where the draft is payable after sight or in any other case where presentment for acceptance is necessary in order to fix the maturity of the instrument. A draft payable ten days after sight means ten days after it is presented to the drawee. A draft payable at a stated time after sight, therefore, must be presented in order to fix the maturity date of the instrument.

PRESENTMENT FOR PAYMENT

The holder may treat a draft which has been presented for acceptance and has been dishonored as due immediately. He will not be required, in these circumstances, to present the draft for payment. He may, on the other hand, proceed at once to protest the draft—when that is required—and give the proper notice of its dishonor. Promissory notes and accepted drafts must be presented for payment in order to charge the person secondarily liable in case the instrument is not paid. The presentment must be made in a proper form by the holder to the person primarily liable, at a proper place and at a proper time.

Bank-domiciled Instruments   Instruments payable at a bank are known as bank-domiciled instruments. Two views prevailed under pre-Code law with respect to such instruments. The first is that an instrument so payable is an order on the bank to pay the instrument from the account of the primary party. This is the view of New York and the surrounding states. A maker of a note payable at a bank utilizing this view, therefore, should stop payment on a note if he does not intend to pay the note. The second view is that an instrument so payable is only a designation of the place of payment. This is the view of the West and South. Section 3–121 continues these two views and gives the states an alternative choice to adopt either view. The risk of the bank's insolvency after the maturity of the bank-domiciled instrument, under either alternative, is placed on the holder under the new provisions pertaining to bank-domiciled instruments.

Time of Presentment All the rules applicable to time of presentment are stated in section 3–503. Instruments payable at a stated date, or at a fixed period after a stated date, must be presented for acceptance on or before the date on which the instrument is payable; instruments payable at a stated date must be presented for payment on the stated date. These rules are obvious.

Instruments payable after sight must be presented for acceptance or negotiated within a reasonable time after date or issue, whichever is later. Accelerated instruments must be presented within a reasonable time after acceleration.

A reasonable time for presentment is determined by the nature of the instrument, any usage of banking and trade, and the facts of the particular case. The reasonable time within which the check must be presented is thirty days as to the drawer and seven days after his indorsement as to the indorser. [*Eastman v. Pelletier,* p. 306.]

Because of the increasing practice of closing banks and businesses on Saturday or other holidays, this section provides: Any presentment which is due on a day "which is not a full business day for either the person making presentment or the party to pay or accept, presentment is due on the next following day which is a full business day for both parties."

Presentment must be made at a reasonable hour and, if at a bank, during its banking hours.

Rights of Party to Whom Presentment Is Made Sections 3–504 and 3–505 make it clear that any demand upon the party to pay or accept is a presentment. The person to whom presentment is made, however, may require exhibition of the instrument; reasonable identification of the person making the presentment, if the person on whom demand is made does not know the person making the presentment; the production of the instrument at a proper place; a signed receipt on the instrument for any partial or full payment; or the surrender of the instrument upon full payment. The presentment is invalidated if the person making the presentment fails to comply with any of the requirements when he is requested to do so. But this does not mean that the instrument has been dishonored. The time for presentment is, however, extended to give the person presenting the instrument a reasonable opportunity to comply with the requirements.

PRESENTMENT FOR ACCEPTANCE OR PAYMENT

Section 3–501 makes it clear that a presentment is necessary in order to charge secondary parties. Such secondary parties are discharged of any liability unless there is a presentment.

Place of Presentment If the instrument is made payable at a bank in the United States, the instrument must be presented at the bank so designated. If no place is specified in the instrument, it may be presented at the place of business or residence of the party to accept or pay. Presentment is excused, however, if no person with authority to make an acceptance or refuse the acceptance or payment is accessible at such place to accept or pay. Presentment also may be made by mail or through a clearing house. In these circumstances, the presentment is made when it reaches the obligor. Presentment may be made at the place specified in the instrument when such a place is specified.

To Whom Presentment Should Be Made   Presentment for acceptance or payment may be made to the drawee or primary party or some person authorized to accept or refuse acceptance or payment. A personal representative, for instance, would ordinarily have authority to accept or pay the instrument if the drawee or primary party is dead. If there are two or more persons to whom presentment may be made, presentment may be made to any one of them.

DISHONOR AND PROTEST

Notice of Dishonor   The object of giving notice of dishonor is twofold: first, to inform the parties secondarily liable that the maker or acceptor, as the case may be, has failed to meet his obligation; and, second, to advise such parties that they will be required to make payment. A misdescription in the notice which does not mislead the party being notified does not invalidate the notice. Notice may be given in any reasonable manner. A bank will ordinarily return the instrument bearing a stamp, ticket, or a writing which states that acceptance or payment has been refused. Notice may be written; or it may be oral, but an oral notice may be difficult to prove; it may be given in any terms which are sufficiently clear to identify the instrument and to indicate that it has been dishonored. [*Chouteau v. Webster,* p. 306.]

The holder of the instrument will ordinarily give the notice, but section 3–508 makes it clear that any person who may be compelled to pay the instrument is permitted to give notice to any party who may be liable on the instrument. A prior indorser, therefore, may give notice to a subsequent indorser. It is also clear that such notice operates for the benefit of all parties who have rights on the instrument against the party so notified.

The notice must be given by a bank before its midnight deadline after dishonor or receipt of notice of dishonor. The notice must be given by any other person before midnight of the third business day after dishonor or receipt of notice of dishonor.

Notice is also permitted to be sent to the last known address of a person who is dead or incompetent. This will dispense with the necessity of ascertaining the name of, and sending the notice to, the representative before sending it to the address of the original party. Written notice is given when sent although it is not received. Mail addressed to the original party almost always will reach the representative. This provision, therefore, should save time and expense. With respect to insolvency proceedings, notice may be given to the bankrupt himself or to the representative of his estate. Notice given to one partner is notice to the other partners. This is true even though the firm has been dissolved.

Protest A protest is a written notice—a certificate of dishonor—that the instrument has been presented for acceptance or payment, as the case may be, and that it has been dishonored. Protest is not necessary, however, except on drafts drawn or payable outside of the United States. Section 3–509 provides that the protest must identify the instrument; certify that presentment has been made or the reason why it is excused; and that the instrument has been dishonored by nonacceptance or nonpayment. The protest may be made by a United States consul or vice-consul or a notary public. It may be annexed to the instrument or it may be forwarded separately.

Excused or Delayed Presentment, Notice of Dishonor, Protest The underlying reason for excusing presentment, notice of dishonor, and protest is that the law does not expect a person to do an impossible or a useless thing. Section 3–511 uses the terms "excused" and "entirely excused."

(1) *Excused or Delayed Presentment* Delay in presentment is excused when the party has acted with reasonable diligence and the delay is not his fault. A holder, for instance, could not be expected to make presentment if the instrument has been accelerated by a prior holder without his knowledge. The holder would, however, be required to make presentment when he learned of the acceleration.

(2) *Entirely Excused or Delayed Presentment* The conditions of presentment, protest, and notice are entirely excused where they have been waived. The conditions are for the protection of the drawer and indorsers. This protection, therefore, may be waived by the drawer or by any of the indorsers. The words "presentment, protest, and notice waived," or similar words written across the face of the instrument, are frequently used for this purpose. It is binding upon all parties when it is embodied in the instrument itself. It binds an indorser only when it is written above his signature.

The conditions are entirely excused where the party to be charged has no reason to expect or right to require that the instrument be accepted or paid, as where he has himself dishonored the instrument; or where by reasonable diligence the presentment or protest cannot be made or the notice given. Presentment is entirely excused where a holder might reasonably think that payment was an impossibility, as where the maker or acceptor is dead or is in insolvency proceedings. In these circumstances, the holder is permitted to have immediate recourse against the drawer or indorsers, who may file any necessary claim in probate or insolvency proceedings.

Unexcused Delay in Making Presentment Any drawer, acceptor, or maker of a *bank-domiciled* instrument may claim a complete discharge where the holder delays presentment for payment or notice of dishonor and the bank becomes insolvent. These factual situations will be involved: An instrument is made payable at a bank; the holder delays making presentment for payment; and the bank becomes insolvent during the time of delay. Who should stand the loss? Section 3–501 provides that presentment for payment and notice of dishonor are necessary to charge any drawer, the acceptor of a draft payable at a bank, and the maker of a note payable at a bank; and section 3–502 prescribes the circumstances and the extent to which such drawer, acceptor, or maker is discharged if the holder unnecessarily delays making the presentment and notice beyond the time such presentment and notice are due. The party claiming the discharge (maker, drawer, or acceptor) is discharged only (1) if he maintained with the drawee or payor bank sufficient funds to cover payment of the instrument, (2) if the bank becomes insolvent during the period of delay, and (3) if he makes a written assignment of his rights against the bank to the holder with respect to such funds. Compliance with these requirements, therefore, will shift the loss to the holder.

CASES

Lewis Hubbard & Co. v. Morton,   92 S.E. 252 (W. Va. 1917). Action by Lewis Hubbard *&* Company, plaintiff, against J. J. Morton *&* Company (and J. J. and L. L. Morton, partners), defendants.

Williams, Judge: Being indebted to Lewis Hubbard & Co., a corporation, defendants gave it the following order:

"West Virginia Timber Co., Charleston, W. Va.: $165.49. Please pay to the order of Lewis Hubbard & Co. one hundred sixty-five and 49/100 dollars and charge to our acct. J. J. Morton & Co., by J. J. Morton."

The West Virginia Timber Company conditionally accepted the order as follows:

"This order will be paid whenever the lumber is inspected and placed to the credit of J. J. Morton & Co. West Virginia Timber Co., G. E. Breece, President."

. . .

The West Virginia Timber Company never paid the order, and this action against the drawers is predicated upon their implied promise to pay it if the drawee did not. Defendants were not notified of the conditional acceptance of the order, nor of its nonpayment, until this action was instituted in the justice's court, more than seven years after acceptance. . . . The acceptance being qualified, the drawers were entitled to reasonable notice thereof, and there is no pretense that they were ever notified, nor that they ever either expressly or impliedly authorized such acceptance, or thereafter assented to it. They knew nothing of it, and, after the lapse of a reasonable time after the bill was issued, were justified in assuming it had been paid. . . . The payee had a right to treat the qualified acceptance as a dishonor. It did not do so, and left the bill in the possession of the acceptor after acceptance, together with the note, marked paid, for the discharge of which the bill had been issued, and apparently forgot all about the transaction, until shortly before the institution of this suit a discrepancy was discovered in the accounts between the payee and acceptor. This discrepancy was caused by the acceptor's failing to debit its account with the order, whereas the payee had charged it with it.

In endeavoring to ascertain the cause of the discrepancy, the West Virginia Timber Company discovered the order and the note, filed away among its papers, where, apparently, it had slumbered for nearly eight years. Under the facts and circumstances, disclosed by undisputed testimony, plaintiff was guilty of such negligence as discharges the drawers from liability.

Having failed to give defendants notice of the qualified acceptance, plaintiff has lost its right of recourse on the drawers. Its position is not different from what it would have been if the bill had been dishonored and defendants had received no notice of the dishonor. [DECISION FOR DEFENDANTS]

Eastman v. Pelletier, 47 A.2d 298 (Vt. 1946). Action by Dale Eastman, plaintiff, against Leo Pelletier, defendant, to recover the amount of a dishonored check indorsed by defendant.

Moulton, Chief Justice: In June, 1943, the plaintiff sold four cows to the defendant and the latter gave a lien note for $385 signed by himself and his wife. The note was duly recorded. Thereafter, and without the knowledge of the plaintiff, the defendant sold certain of the cows to Carlton Achilles, and received in payment a check for $250 signed by Achilles and payable to the plaintiff and the defendant jointly. The defendant went to see the plaintiff on July 10, indorsed and delivered the check to him and paid the balance on the lien note in cash. The plaintiff accepted the check and cash in full payment of the lien note, and indorsed a receipt thereon. The defendant then informed him of the sale to Achilles. The plaintiff held the check until July 30, before depositing it in the bank, although he lived at a distance approximately one mile from that institution. On August 5th he received notice from the bank that the check had been dishonored by a stop payment order from Achilles dated July 13. . . .

The only fact here reported that bears upon the issue of due presentation, other than the lapse of 20 days between the receipt of the check by the plaintiff and its deposit, is that the plaintiff's residence was approximately a mile distant from the bank. The transcript of evidence shows nothing more than this and no other reason or excuse for the delay appears. This circumstance cannot be said to have been an insuperable barrier to prompt presentation, and a cause of delay beyond the control of the plaintiff, and not imputable to his default or negligence. The fact that if presentation had been made with all diligence the stop order would have made it unavailing, did not absolve the plaintiff. We hold, therefore, that upon the record here presented, the delay was unreasonable as a matter of law and no sufficient excuse for it has been shown. [DECISION FOR DEFENDANT]

Chouteau v. Webster, 6 Met. (Mass.) 1 (1843). Action by Pierre Chouteau, plaintiff, against Daniel Webster, defendant, to recover from defendant, as indorser, the amount due on two promissory notes. The defense is based upon the contention that notice of the dishonor was not properly sent to the defendant.

Shaw, Chief Justice: It is admitted that these notes were duly made and indorsed; that they were seasonably presented for payment, at the bank in New York, where by their terms they were payable, and payment refused; that notice thereof, in due form, was seasonably prepared by the proper officer, and put into the post office; and the only question is, whether, under the circumstances stated, it was rightly addressed to the defendant, at Washington. . . .

The ground relied upon, to show that such notice was not sufficient, is, that the defendant's general domicil and place of business was in the city of Boston, where he had, at all times, an agent, who had the charge and management of his affairs. But it does not appear that he had made any request to have notices sent to him at Boston, or that any actual or constructive notice was had by the holder of these notes, that he had an agent at Boston. This fact, therefore, must be considered immaterial. The defendant, though his domicil was at Boston, was actually residing at Washington, in discharge of his public duties as a senator, at a session of Congress, called by public proclamation, and continued until after the time at which this notice was sent; so that the place, where he might be presumed to be actually residing, was fixed and well known by the nature of these duties. Under these circumstances, the court are of opinion, that notice to the defendant, by mail, addressed to him at Washington, was good and sufficient notice of the dishonor of these notes.

This decision is founded on the circumstances of the particular case, and may be varied by other facts. It is not like the case of a merchant stopping, for a day or two, at a hotel or watering place, or on a journey of business or pleasure; though we are not prepared to say that actual personal notice to an indorser, at such a place, would not be sufficient; but of this we give no opinion. [DECISION FOR PLAINTIFF]

PROBLEMS

1 Sanders drew a check on the First Bank in the amount of $100, payable to the order of Brewer. Brewer delayed presenting the check to the First Bank for payment for six months, at which time the First Bank became insolvent. Sanders had over $1,000 on deposit in the First Bank at the time the First Bank became insolvent, and he thereafter made a written assignment of his rights against the bank to Brewer with respect to the $100. The creditors were paid only 50 percent of their claims in insolvency proceedings. Brewer thereupon brought an action against Sanders to recover the remaining amount of the check. Do you think he will recover?

2 Plaintiff seeks to recover from defendant, an indorser, on a promissory note which was dishonored by the maker. Plaintiff offered evidence that he gave notice of the dishonor to the defendant "two or three days after it was due." Was this notice given too late?

3 Plaintiff brought an action against the defendant-indorser to recover $6,000, the balance due upon a promissory note, which the plaintiff acquired as a holder in due course. Prior to the maturity of the note, it was deposited with the American Trust Company of New York for collection. On the day it became due, during the business hours of that day, a notary public in the employ of the Trust Company delivered the note to an employee of the Trust Company who carried the note to the Bank of Manhattan Company, where the note was made payable, and demanded payment. Payment was refused because of insufficient funds. Has a sufficient presentation for payment been made upon the party primarily liable in view of the fact that the note was not presented personally to the maker by the notary public?

4 On January 14, 1960, Samuel Jacobson and his wife executed a promissory note, payable to the order of Frank Sarandrea, which was later purchased by the plaintiff. The note became due on January 14, 1964. In the meantime, it was indorsed by the plaintiff and deposited in his bank for collection. Plaintiff, although he had made inquiries of relatives and others, was unable to learn the address of the Jacobsons. The bank, therefore, caused a notary public—who had already called at several places in an effort to locate the Jacobsons—to present the note at the former address of the Jacobsons. The notary was told, "Samuel Jacobson and Annie Jacobson have moved from here and I do not know their present address." The defendant, Frank Sarandrea, received notice of dishonor either on the day the note was due or the following day. Was the presentment made at the last-known address of the Jacobsons sufficient to enable plaintiff to recover from defendant?

5 Plaintiff made a loan to Smith in the amount of $11,500. Smith then requested his employee, a person of no financial ability, to sign a note as maker payable to the order of plaintiff for $11,500. Smith did, however, indorse the note before delivery to plaintiff. The note was unpaid on its due date, and plaintiff brought an action against Smith and his employee to recover the amount due. No presentment for payment was made of the note, and no notice of dishonor was given to Smith. Smith claims, therefore, that his liability ended upon the failure to make presentment and to give notice. Do you agree with Smith?

6 Kerr, a resident of the City of X, was staying in a hotel in the City of Y for a few days. The hotel refused to accept his check in payment of his room when he attempted to check out of the hotel. Kerr then suggested that the manager of the hotel telephone his bank in the City of X and ascertain if the check was good. The manager telephoned as Kerr suggested, and the bank replied by telegram in approximately one hour as follows: "The check is good. Will honor when presented." The manager then accepted the check, and Kerr returned to the City of X. Kerr immediately withdrew all his funds except $1.00 in his bank, and the check was returned to the manager of the hotel by the bank marked "insufficient funds." Would the hotel prevail in an action against the bank for failure to pay the amount of the check?

7 Brown borrowed $100 from Jones, and then drew a draft in favor of Jones on Smith, as drawee, as security for the loan. Jones presented the draft to Smith for acceptance, but Smith did not like the idea of Brown's drawing the draft without first consulting him. Smith, therefore, tore the draft in small pieces and threw them away. What rights, if any, does Jones have against Smith?

25
LIABILITY OF PARTIES

Certain parties to a negotiable instrument incur liability by reason of their implied warranties, and all parties incur certain contractual liabilities unless they disclaim liability. Their contractual liability, however, will be either primary or secondary. Primary parties are makers of promissory notes and acceptors of drafts, and these parties incur a contractual primary liability. The maker and acceptor are primarily liable because no demand for payment or other conditions precedent is necessary to fix their liability. Secondary parties include drawers of drafts (and checks) and all indorsers.

PRIMARY PARTIES
The maker of a promissory note, by executing it, and the acceptor of a draft, by accepting it, unconditionally promise to pay the instrument according to its tenor at the time of the issuance or acceptance, or as subsequently completed. The drawee, however, is not liable to the payee or any other holder of the draft unless and until he accepts it. The acceptance, however, is final. An acceptor of a draft or check on which the signature of the drawer was forged will be required to pay the instrument.

He then becomes the party primarily liable to the holder for its payment and is therefore referred to as the acceptor. An indorser or drawer, as will be seen, may be required to pay the note. But such indorser or drawer is entitled to recover from the maker or acceptor. The maker and acceptor, therefore, remain the ultimate debtors. By putting the note in circulation, the maker and acceptor not only create an absolute obligation to pay the instrument, but under section 3–413, they also make two important admissions—that the payee exists and has the capacity to indorse the instrument. This rule of law operates to prevent the maker and acceptor from denying, as against a holder in due course, the existence of the payee or the capacity of the payee to indorse the instrument at the time it was issued. The payee may be a fictitious person or some incapacitated person against whom the instrument could not be enforced. The maker and acceptor, nevertheless, cannot escape payment by showing the nonexistence or incapacity of the payee.

The "subsequently completed" provision refers to an instrument which is issued as an incomplete instrument and subsequently completed. The maker and the acceptor will be liable on the instrument if the instrument is subsequently completed in accordance with the authority given. The completion of an instrument in a manner other than in accordance with the authority given is a material alteration. The maker and the acceptor will be liable on the instrument as altered, therefore, if their negligence substantially contributes to the alteration.

SECONDARY PARTIES

The Drawer   The drawer of a check or draft makes the same two admissions as does the maker of a promissory note and the acceptor of a draft—that the payee exists and has the capacity to indorse the instrument. The drawer, therefore, cannot escape payment of the instrument by showing the nonexistence or incapacity of the payee. The drawer also has a contractual obligation to pay the instrument if it has been dishonored upon presentment and he has received the necessary notice of dishonor. This liability may be disclaimed by drawing the instrument "without recourse."

The Indorser   The indorser has a contractual obligation to pay the instrument if it is dishonored upon presentment and if he is given the necessary notice of dishonor and protest. The liability of the indorser runs to any holder and to any indorser subsequent to him who has paid the instrument. An indorser may disclaim his liability on the contract of indorsement by writing the words "without recourse" on the instrument. Such an indorser, however, may be liable for breach of warranty.

Indorsers are presumed to be liable to one another in the order in which they indorse. This is presumed to be the order in which their signatures appear on the instrument. Parol evidence, however, is admissible to show that they have indorsed in another order or that they have otherwise agreed as to their liability to one another.

Liability of Accommodation Parties   Section 3–415 defines an accommodation party as "one who signs the instrument in any capacity for the purpose of lending his name to another party to it." This section also recognizes that the accommodation party is a surety. The rights and defenses given a surety by the law of suretyship, therefore, are available to the accommodation party. These rights and defenses are discussed in Chapter 26, "Discharge." The following provisions are also worthy of mention:

An accommodation indorser is liable only after presentment, notice of dishonor, and, when necessary, protest. The obligation of the accommodation party, however, is determined by the capacity in which he signs the instrument. An accommodation maker, therefore, is bound on the instrument, and it is not necessary for the creditor to proceed against the accommodated party first in order to hold the surety-maker liable. [*Wilbour v. Hawkins*, p. 316.]

If an accommodation party pays the instrument, he has a right of recourse against the accommodated party. The surety who signs a negotiable instrument, therefore, has the rights of exoneration, reimbursement, contribution, and subrogation.

Parol evidence is admissible, for the purpose of discharge, to prove that the party has signed for accommodation, except as against a holder in due course without notice of the accommodation. An indorsement, however, which is not in the regular chain of title—irregular indorsement—is notice to all persons of the accommodation character of the indorsement.

Contract of Guarantor   Section 3–416 deals with instruments when words, first, such as "payment guaranteed," and second, such as "collection guaranteed," are added to the signature.

An indorser who guarantees payment engages that, if the instrument is not paid when due, he will pay it without resort by the holder to any other party. An indorser who uses this type of indorsement, therefore, waives not only presentment, notice of dishonor, and protest, but also demand for payment upon the maker. The liability of the indorser who guarantees payment is thus the same as that of a comaker. [*Richmond Guano Co. v. Walston*, p. 316.]

A guarantor of collection likewise waives presentment, notice of dishonor, and protest. But a guaranty of collection, as distinguished from a guaranty of payment, requires that the holder first proceed against the maker or acceptor. The holder must also reduce his claim to a judgment and show that the maker or acceptor has no property out of which the judgment could be satisfied. However, proceeding first against the maker or acceptor is excused where the maker or acceptor is insolvent or where such proceeding would be useless.

Unauthorized Signature   An unauthorized agent who signs an instrument in the name of the principal and a forger are personally liable on the instrument. This rule seems to run head on with section 3–401, which provides that "no person is liable on an instrument unless his signature appears thereon." The rule, however, is a necessary one to prevent the unauthorized agent and forger from escaping liability on the ground that his name did not appear on the instrument.

Signature by Authorized Representative   The liability of authorized representatives is dealt with in section 3–403. The comment sets out and explains the liability of representatives who use an awkward form of signature by authorized representative. The liability of authorized representatives is dealt with in section 3–403, and a "representative" is defined by section 1–201 so as to include an agent, an officer of a corporation or association, a trustee, executor, or administrator of an estate, or any person empowered to act for another. Let us assume that Ben Brown is the secretary of the XYZ Corporation:

(1) "XYZ Corporation"
(2) "Ben Brown"
(3) "XYZ Corporation, Secretary"
(4) "XYZ Corporation
    Ben Brown"

The signature in form (1) does not bind Ben Brown if he was authorized. The signature in form (2) personally obligates Ben Brown, and parol evidence is not admissible to disestablish his obligation. A representative is permitted in both forms (3) and (4) to use parol evidence in litigation, but only between the immediate parties, to prove that he signed in a representative capacity. Ben Brown, therefore, could not exonerate himself from liability to a holder in due course.

An instrument signed in the name of a corporation should not be confused with an instrument which is signed in a trade name. An instrument may be signed in a trade or assumed name. An individual, therefore, who is the sole proprietor of a business which he operates under a trade name may sign in the trade name. He would be liable to the same extent as if he had signed in his own name.

A different problem arises when officers of a corporation purport to sign in their representative capacity but omit words descriptive of their office even though the name of the corporation appears upon the instrument. The use of a corporate form of promise in the body of the instrument with the signature of the principal followed by the words "by" or "per" and the name of the agent would eliminate litigation. For example, "The ABC Corporation, by John Doe, President." Suppose John Doe signed a promissory note in the following form:
    "The ABC Corporation
    John Doe"
It would be difficult to determine whether John Doe signed as a comaker or in a representative capacity. John Doe could not exonerate himself from liability to a holder in due course. [*Universal Lightning Rod, Inc. v. Rischall Electric Co.*, p. 317.]

Section 3–403, however, provides that the representative capacity may be shown to exonerate the representative from personal liability to an immediate party. Where the representative is exonerated by parol evidence, the corporation is liable on the instrument.

Impersonation Impersonation may arise in these circumstances: An impostor will appear before the person to be defrauded and represent himself to be some other person. This representation is commonly supported by the use of stolen credentials for identification. This enables the impostor to more readily maneuver some sort of fraudulent business transaction. The transaction results in the defrauded person's delivering to the impostor a check payable to the order of the person whom the impostor represents himself to be. The impostor will then start the check in circulation by indorsing the name of the payee on the back of the check. The indorsement, however, does not need to be made by the payee. It may be made by any person—the imposter himself, a second impostor, or a thief. The drawer has been defrauded. A holder in due course of the check is an innocent party. Who should stand the loss? Section 3–405 places the loss upon the maker or drawer. This is true irrespective of whether the impersonation is face-to-face imposture or imposture by mail. This section enumerates three situations in which "an indorsement by any person in the name of a named payee is effective" to transfer the instrument.

The first situation deals with impersonation, as where the impostor appears before the person to be defrauded and represents himself to be some other person. The loss will fall upon the drawer. [*Montgomery Garage Co. v. Manufacturers' Liability Ins. Co.*, p. 318.]

The second situation is not concerned with impersonation. Suppose that the treasurer of the XYZ Corporation draws a check naming Jones, who is not a fictitious person, as the payee with the intention that Jones should not receive the check; that the signature is made by the use of a rubber stamp; and that the treasurer thereafter indorses the name of Jones and cashes the check. The loss will fall upon the XYZ Corporation.

The named payee may or may not be a fictitious person, and the person signing as the drawer, or on behalf of the drawer, may or may not be an employee. The test is whether the signer intends that the named payee should have no interest in the instrument.

The third situation includes the "padded payroll" cases and other instances where an agent or employee prepares the checks for the signing officer of a corporation, or otherwise furnishes the signing officer with the name of the payee with the intent that the payee have no interest in the instrument. It is reasoned that the loss should fall upon the employer as a risk of business rather than upon a subsequent holder; that the employer is normally in a better position to prevent such forgeries by reasonable care in the selection of his employees; and that the employer is in a better position to cover the loss by fidelity insurance.

Suppose the bookkeeper of a corporation prepares a payroll for the treasurer to sign and pads the payroll by adding the name R. K. Adams; that R. K. Adams does not exist; that the bookkeeper knows this fact, but the treasurer does not; that the treasurer signs the check as drawer and names R. K. Adams as the payee; and that the bookkeeper indorses the check with the name of R. K. Adams, obtains the money, and absconds. The loss will fall upon the corporation.

WARRANTIES

Section 3–417(1) states a number of presentment warranties that run against a person who obtains payment or acceptance of an instrument, and section 3–417(2) states the transfer warranties that run against a person who transfers an instrument and receives consideration.

Warranties on Presentment A person presenting an instrument for payment or acceptance and any prior transferor warrants to the payor or acceptor (1) that he has good title to the instrument, (2) that the instrument has not been materially altered, and (3) that he has no knowledge that the signature of the maker or drawer is unauthorized. These warranties run against the person who obtains payment or acceptance and against any prior transferor, and they run in favor of any payor or acceptor who pays or accepts in good faith. The remedy of the payor or acceptor, therefore, is to recover from the person presenting the instrument on the breach of warranty.

The warranty of title permits the payor or acceptor to recover from the person presenting the instrument when an *indorsement* turns out to be forged, because the payor or acceptor does not ordinarily have an opportunity to verify the indorsement. The warranty against material alteration permits the payor who pays a materially altered instrument to recover from the person presenting the instrument for payment, and permits the acceptor to avoid the acceptance of such an instrument. The warranty against unauthorized signature permits the payor or acceptor to recover from the person presenting the instrument or from a prior transferor where the signature of the maker or drawer has been forged, provided the presenter or prior transferor had knowledge of the forgery at the time of presentment or transfer.

The warranty against material alteration is not imposed against a holder in due course who obtains payment or acceptance (1) in favor of a maker of a note or a drawer of a draft, because the maker and drawer should know the form and amount of the note or draft which he has signed; (2) in favor of the acceptor of a draft or a bank which certifies a check, because the acceptance of a draft or certification of a check is a definite obligation to honor a definite instrument; or (3) in favor of the acceptor of a draft or check where the draft or check was altered after acceptance or certification. Suppose the holder presents a draft for acceptance and the draft is accepted. The acceptor at the time of acceptance has an opportunity to ascertain the form of the draft. Suppose further that the draft is thereafter materially altered and is presented for payment. The acceptor should have the necessary information in his records to verify the draft. The warranty against material alteration, therefore, is not imposed on a holder in due course where the instrument was altered after acceptance.

The warranty against unauthorized signature is not imposed against a holder in due course (1) in favor of a maker with respect to the maker's own signature or to a drawer with respect to the drawer's own signature, because a maker or drawer should know his own signature and should not be permitted to recover payment from a holder in due course where he fails to detect that his signature has been forged; (2) in favor of the acceptor of a draft if the holder took the draft after acceptance, because the drawee of a draft is presumed to know the signature of the drawer; or (3) in favor of the acceptor of a draft if the holder obtained the acceptance without knowledge that the drawer's signature was forged even if he thereafter learns of the forgery, because the acceptance would be valueless if the holder became obligated to return the payment by reason of a breach of warranty.

Warranties on Transfer   Any person who transfers an instrument and receives consideration makes certain warranties. The warranty rules provide answers to three important questions: First, in whose favor do the warranties run; second, against what persons do they run; and third, what is the nature of the warranty?

(1) The warranties on transfer run in favor of the transferee and any subsequent holder who takes the instrument in good faith when the transfer is made by indorsement. The warranties run to the transferee only, however, when the transfer is made by delivery.

(2) The warranties run against any transferor who receives consideration, including a selling agent who does not disclose the fact that he is acting only as an agent. A selling agent warrants only as to his good faith and authority where he discloses his representative capacity on the instrument. The warranties do not run against an accommodation indorser.

(3) The transferor warrants:

    (a) That he has good title to the instrument; this warranty permits a transferee to recover from the transferor when an indorsement is forged. Suppose a thief forges the indorsement of the payee on an instrument and transfers the instrument to Brown. Brown would not have good title, but he would be liable to Jones for breach of warranty if he transferred the instrument to Jones.

    (b) That all signatures are genuine or authorized: this warranty permits a transferee to recover from the tranferor when a signature is forged or unauthorized.

    (c) That the instrument has not been materially altered. Suppose the payee raises the amount of the instrument from $500 to $5,000 and transfers the instrument to Brown, who knows nothing of the alteration, and Brown transfers to Jones. Suppose further that the maker refuses to pay the $5,000. Jones can recover the $5,000 from Brown on his breach of warranty.

    (d) That no defense is available against him. The transferor would breach this warranty if the maker or drawer could use the defense of things, such as infancy or adjudicated insanity. A transferor indorsing "without recourse" warrants only that he has no knowledge of any defense of any party that is good against him.

    (e) That he has no knowledge of any insolvency proceedings instituted with respect to the maker, acceptor, or drawer of an unaccepted instrument.

CASES

Wilbour v. Hawkins, 94 Atl. 856 (R.I. 1915). Action by Benjamin F. Wilbour, plaintiff, against Clarence M. Hawkins and Isabelle P. Hawkins, defendants, to recover on a promissory note.

Vincent, Justice: The plaintiff is a retail grocer. In the course of his business he delivered groceries from time to time at the house of the defendants as ordered by the wife, Isabelle P. Hawkins, but the defendants claimed at the trial that the liability for payment therefor rested solely upon the husband, Clarence M. Hawkins, which liability he admitted. . . .

It was agreed between the parties that the groceries were delivered by the plaintiff to the Hawkins house and that on or about December 18, 1912, there was owing to the plaintiff therefor the sum of $372.77, and that at that time the defendants executed a note to the plaintiff for that amount, whereupon the plaintiff receipted the bill for groceries as "paid in full by note."

. . . [At] the trial counsel further admitted the liability of Clarence M. Hawkins on the note, but denied the liability of Isabelle P. Hawkins.

The note in question is in words and figures as follows:

$372.77   December 18, 1912.
One year after date I promise to pay to the order of Benjamin F. Wilbour three hundred seventy-two 77/100 dollars. Value received.

Mrs. Isabelle P. Hawkins,
Clarence M. Hawkins.

. . . The defendants now claim that Isabelle P. Hawkins was an accommodation maker, so far as the plaintiff was concerned and that inasmuch as the note was never negotiated or passed to a third party for value, her relation to the plaintiff continued to be that of an accommodation maker, and that she had the right to have the question submitted to a jury as to whether or not there was any consideration for the note so far as she was concerned.

With this contention of the defendants we cannot agree. The defendants are jointly and severally liable upon the note. We think also that the plaintiff is a holder for value. An antecedent or pre-existing debt constitutes value; and is deemed such whether the instrument is payable on demand or at a future time.

The note was given for a debt due to the plaintiff and in consideration thereof he receipted the grocery bill, which amounted to the cancellation of an antecedent or pre-existing debt. The plaintiff being a holder for value it is immaterial whether the defendant Isabelle P. Hawkins be considered as an accommodation party or otherwise. [DECISION FOR PLAINTIFF]

Richmond Guano Co. v. Walston, 133 S.E. 196 (N.C. 1926). Action by Richmond Guano Company, plaintiff, against H. H. Walston, Jr., and Britton Harrell, defendants, on a promissory note. The plaintiff's evidence was to the effect that it purchased the note on March 15, 1921, for full value, before maturity, and without notice of any equities.

Defendants alleged that they stored certain cotton with Tomlinson Guano Company upon certain terms to be sold and applied on the note and that said company sold the cotton but the proceeds thereof were not applied on the note. They contend, therefore, they have a defense against the plaintiff because the plaintiff is not a holder in due course. The note is in the following form:

$6,000.00   Wilson, N.C., Feb. 23, 1921

Nov. 1, 1921, after date, we promise to pay to the order of Tominson Guano Company, six thousand dollars at 6% int. from Jan. 1, 1921. Value received.

H. H. Walston, Jr. (Seal)

Britton Harrell. (Seal)

No. 82

Demand, notice, and protest waived; payment guaranteed by the undersigned.

Tomlinson Guano Company,

N. L. Finsh, Partner

Clarkson, Justice: The note is negotiable in form. The language on the note being "demand, notice and protest waived; payment guaranteed by the undersigned," the plaintiff contends it is an indorsement with the enlarged liability. The defendants contend the language only showed a guaranty and nothing more, and does not constitute commercial negotiation in due course.

If the language makes plaintiff a holder in due course, it makes same free from equities and defenses which the maker has against the payee.

We can find no decision bearing on the question in this state. We must look elsewhere. The language, "Payment guaranteed by the undersigned," would indicate, as contended by defendants with much force, only a guaranty and not a commercial negotiation in due course. It is contended that especially is this true from the fact that the guarantor had cotton in its possession of defendants to sell, pledged to pay this note, which would further indicate that it would not, by the language, intend to make the note such a one, in due course, as to cut off the right of defendants to have the cotton, as agreed upon, applied on the note when sold according to the terms. . . .

We have given this case thorough consideration, appreciating the hardship on defendants but, we must hold that the writing on the negotiable note is an indorsement in due course, so far as to transfer to and vest title in the plaintiffs, and the guaranty is "an indorsement." [DECISION FOR PLAINTIFF]

Universal Lightning Rod, Inc. v. Rischall Electric Co.,   192 A.2d 50 (Conn. 1963). Action by Universal Lightning Rod, Inc., plaintiff, against Rischall Electric Company and Harold M. Rischall, defendants, to recover on a note. Rischall offered no evidence to prove nonliability.

This action was brought by plaintiff against Harold M. Rischall seeking to hold him personally liable on a note dated April 9, 1962, in the amount of $590, wherein plaintiff was the payee. Defendant contended that he was not personally liable on the note, which note was signed by defendant in the following form:

"Rischall Electric Co., Inc.

Harold M. Rischall"

Holden, Judge: The decision must be based upon the terms of section 3–403 of the General Statutes, which is part of the Commercial Code enacted into law effective October 1, 1961. A liberal construction must be given to the sections of this law so as to secure them a reasonable meaning and to effectuate the intention of its framers and to make it workable and serviceable to the important business to which it relates. Section 3–403 states in part: "(2) An authorized representative who signs his own name to an instrument . . . (b) except as otherwise established between the immediate parties, is personally obligated if the instrument names the person represented but does not show that the representative signed in a representative capacity." When the defendant executed the note in question, he did not indicate that he did so in any representative capacity. . . .

The Negotiable Instruments Act was no longer in operation when the defendant executed the note, and its provisions, however helpful, cannot apply to him.

For the reasons stated above, the issues are found for the plaintiff and the claim of the defendant that he is not personally liable is overruled. [DECISION FOR PLAINTIFF]

Montgomery Garage Co. v. Manufacturers' Liability Ins. Co., 109 Atl. 296 (N.J. 1920). Action by Montgomery Garage Company, plaintiff, against Manufacturers' Liability Insurance Company, defendant, to recover the amount of a check for $1,500 signed by the defendant. One Ennis, representing himself to be N. K. Turner, went to the defendant company and delivered to it a check for $5,000—which turned out to be worthless—and received from the company its check for $1,500, being the check in question. On the same day the $1,500 check was indorsed and delivered to the plaintiff by the person representing himself to be N. K. Turner. The check was promptly presented to the bank for payment, but payment had been stopped by the defendant.

Trenchard, Justice: We think that the rule is where, as here, the drawer of a check delivers it, for a consideration which turns out to be fraudulent, to an impostor under the belief that he is the person whose name he has assumed and to whose order the check is made payable, a bona fide holder for a valuable consideration, paid to the impostor upon his indorsement of the payee's name, is entitled to recover from the drawer; it appearing that the person to whom the check was delivered was the very person whom the drawer intended should indorse it and receive the money, and that the drawer made no inquiry before issuing the check concerning the identity or credit of the named payee who was unknown to the drawer.

Clearly, therefore, the plaintiff has simply paid the money to the person to whom the drawer intended it should be paid. Now either the plaintiff or the defendant must suffer the loss. Both were innocent parties, and the loss justly falls upon the defendant whose mistake in issuing the check facilitated the fraud and primarily made such loss possible. . . .

The plaintiff, being a holder of the check in due course, and having paid the full amount agreed to be paid therefor before receiving notice of any infirmity in it or defect in the title of the person negotiating it, "may enforce payment of the instrument for the full amount thereof against all parties liable thereon." [DECISION FOR PLAINTIFF]

PROBLEMS

1 Tilton, the maker, signed a promissory note, payable to the order of plaintiff, complete in every respect except the amount, which was left blank. Tilton presented the note to the defendant who, for the accommodation of Tilton, signed in blank on the back of the note with the express representation and agreement of Tilton that the signature of the defendant would not be operative and the note would not be delivered unless and until one Leonard Grant also signed the note on the back, and that the note would be filled out for $200 and no more. Leonard Grant did not sign the note, and the blank space in the note was filled in for $400. This was done without the knowledge or authority of the defendant and in violation of the agreement between defendant and Tilton. The note was then delivered complete in form to the plaintiff—the payee—who took it for value, in good faith, and without any knowledge of the agreement between the maker and the defendant. Is the defendant liable to the plaintiff?

2 Brown drew a check for $100, payable to his wife. This check was enclosed in an envelope and placed in a mailbox for outgoing mail. For some unexplainable reason, an impostor obtained possession of the check, forged the indorsement of the payee, and, using an assumed name, indorsed the check. The imposter then induced the defendant to cash the check. The defendant thereafter indorsed the check and received $100 from the drawee-bank. In the meantime, Brown learned that his wife did not receive the check. He therefore attempted to stop payment on the check, but it had already been paid by the drawee-bank, and the account of the drawer had already been debited for $100. The drawee-bank later credited Brown's account with $100. Will the bank be able to recover the $100 from the defendant?

3 The Acme Company drew a draft to the order of Brown against the Second Bank, as drawee. Jones, in some mysterious way, stole the draft, erased the name of Brown and inserted his own name so skillfully that the forgery could not be detected by an examination. Jones presented the draft to the Second Bank for acceptance, and the acceptance was written across the face of the draft. Jones then purchased a new automobile from Smith, indorsed the draft in blank, and gave the draft to Smith in payment of the automobile. The Second Bank refused to pay the draft when Smith presented it for payment. What is the liability of the Second Bank on the draft?

4 Brown executed a note payable to the order of Jones. Jones, who indorsed the note "payment guaranteed," negotiated it to the First Bank. The note was not paid at maturity. The First Bank, therefore, brought an action against Jones to recover the amount of the note. Discuss the liability of Jones.

5 Baxter, although he was not an agent of The Acme Sales Company, did execute a negotiable promissory note in a representative capacity. The note read in part: "The Acme Sales Company promises to pay to the order of Cash" and was signed "The Acme Sales Company, by Thomas Baxter, secretary-treasurer." Baxter then indorsed the note in blank and sold it to Davis. Two days later, Davis sold the note to Mills and indorsed it "without recourse." Mills presented the note for payment on the date of maturity to The Acme Sales Company, but payment was refused. Does Mills have a right to collect the amount of the note (a) from Davis, (b) from Baxter?

6 Davis, the drawer of a draft, drew the draft for $500 payable to the order of Pope, or bearer, and designated Loomis as the drawee. Jones, who knew that Pope had been judicially declared insane for more than one month, stole the draft and presented it to Loomis for acceptance. Loomis, who did not actually know of the insanity of Pope, wrote his acceptance across the face of the draft. Jones then sold the draft to the First Bank, which bank took the draft as a holder in due course. Jones then absconded. The First Bank presented the draft to Loomis on the date of maturity, and payment was refused. Should the First Bank prevail in an action against Loomis to recover on the draft?

7 Aaron, Bacon, and Crews signed and delivered a promissory note to the First Bank for a loan of $5,000. The money received from the First Bank was given to Aaron and Bacon, since Crews was an accommodation maker. The note was not paid when it became due, and the First Bank brought an action against Aaron, Bacon, and Crews to recover the $5,000. Crews contended that he is liable only after presentment and notice of dishonor since his liability is secondary to that of Aaron and Bacon. Do you agree with this contention?

26
DISCHARGE

The Code speaks of the parties being discharged from their liability on the instrument and distinguishes between the discharge of all parties and the discharge of a single party. Section 3–602 makes certain that no discharge "of any party provided by this Article" is effective against a subsequent holder in due course, unless he has notice of the discharge when he takes the instrument. This means, of course, that the discharge of any party is only a personal defense. The extent of the discharge of any party from liability on an instrument was discussed in Chapter 23, "Defenses," with respect to discharge of the parties, and in Chapter 24, "Presentment, Notice of Dishonor, Protest," with respect to unexcused delay in making presentment of the instrument and also with respect to an acceptance which varies the draft. The remaining methods of discharging parties are discussed in the sections that follow.

Discharge by Payment   Section 3–603 expressly provides that payment to the holder discharges the liability of the paying party, even though the payment is made with knowledge of a claim of another person. A party who has a claim against the instrument, however, may prevent the paying party from paying the instrument. This section provides that the adverse claimant may restrain payment by supplying an adequate indemnity, such as an indemnity bond or other security, or by procuring an order of a court restraining payment in which the adverse claimant and holders are parties. The reason for the rule is to prevent the paying party from incurring the inconvenience of a dispute between two other parties unless he is indemnified or served with appropriate process.

Two exceptions are made in the cases of bad faith and restrictive indorsements. First, payment does not result in discharge of liability of a person who in bad faith pays a holder who acquired the instrument by theft or who holds through a person who acquired the instrument by theft. Second, payment will not result in discharge of liability of a person who makes payment in a manner inconsistent with the terms of a restrictive indorsement.

Tender of Payment　The Code does not define the word "tender." The word, however, is generally thought to mean a readiness and willingness to pay the instrument when it is due at the place specified. Section 3–604 provides that "it is equivalent to tender" when the maker or acceptor is able and ready to pay at every place of payment specified in the instrument when it is due. The maker or acceptor must be able and ready to pay at each place, however, where the instrument is payable at any one of two or more specified places.

This section specifically provides that any party making the tender of full payment is discharged to the extent of all subsequent liability for interest, costs, and attorney's fees. Any party who has a "right of recourse against the party making the tender" is wholly discharged. To illustrate: The payee of a note which was made for his accommodation tenders payment to the holder who refuses the tender. The accommodation maker would be discharged, because he has a right of recourse against the payee—the accommodated party.

Cancellation and Renunciation　Section 3–605 states that a holder of an instrument may, even without consideration, discharge any party by cancellation or renunciation. Cancellation must be done "in any manner apparent on the face of the instrument," and renunciation may be accomplished by a "signed writing" delivered to the party to be discharged, or by "surrender of the instrument to the party to be discharged." [*Shaffer v. Akron Products Co.*, p. 324.]

Reacquisition　Section 3–208 provides that intervening parties are discharged where a prior holder reacquires the instrument. For example: Adams negotiates an instrument to Baker; Baker then negotiates the instrument to Cabot; and Cabot negotiates the instrument back to Adams, the reacquirer. Adams cannot hold Baker and Cabot liable. Adams may, however, further negotiate the instrument— namely, to Davis. Baker and Cabot would be liable to Davis provided he is a holder in due course.

The express purpose of reacquiring an instrument, however, is normally to discharge an intervening indorser from liability. In the above illustration, Adams could discharge Baker from liability by cancellation when he reacquired the instrument. This may be accomplished by striking the indorsement of Baker, but such action would not prevent Davis from becoming a holder in due course. The discharge of Baker would be effective against Davis, however, because Davis had notice of the cancelled indorsement.

Impairment of Recourse or of Collateral The following general principles of suretyship law with respect to discharge have been incorporated in section 3–606: (1) A release of the debtor by the creditor discharges the surety: (2) a surrender by the creditor of the security furnished by the debtor discharges the surety; and (3) a binding agreement by the creditor and the debtor to extend the time of payment discharges the surety. These rules are based on the notion that a creditor who releases the debtor or his collateral intends that the debtor should be discharged. It is necessary, therefore, to treat the discharge of the debtor as a release of the surety. These rules apply to any surety, including accommodation makers and acceptors, provided the holder had knowledge that the primary parties are sureties. To illustrate: Suppose the maker signs a note for the accommodation of the payee. The holder, knowing that the maker is a surety, releases the payee-indorser. The maker, having a right of recourse against the payee, is discharged. The maker would not be discharged, however, if the holder had no knowledge that the maker was a surety. The surety may or may not be discharged by an agreement extending the time of payment or discharging the primary party. This depends upon whether or not he reserved his rights against the surety. [*Faneuil Hall Nat'l Bank v. Meloon*, p. 325.] [*In re Paskett's Estate*, p. 325.]

A holder may release the debtor or extend the time of payment and expressly reserve his rights against the surety. Such a reservation of rights, in order to be effective, must be accompanied by notification to any party against whom rights are so reserved. The surety remains bound on the instrument, but his right of recourse against the debtor remains intact. He can pay the holder and proceed against the debtor. Any party who agrees to such a release or extension is not discharged. Consent may be embodied in the instrument, or it may be given later, and no consideration is required.

Any party who has a right of recourse will be discharged to the extent that the holder unjustifiably impairs the collateral. To illustrate: Suppose the holder in the above illustration unjustifiably impairs the collateral. The accommodation maker would be discharged to the extent that the collateral is impaired.

Fraudulent and Material Alteration It was shown in Chapter 23, "Defenses," that a material alteration is a personal defense of the entire obligation and a real defense to the extent of the alteration. As a personal defense, therefore, the alteration operates as a discharge. Section 3–407, however, provides that an alteration by a holder which is both material and fraudulent discharges any party when the contract of such party is changed. A discharge of such party, however, is not effective against a subsequent holder in due course who had no notice of the discharge when he took the instrument. Alteration by the holder of the amount payable which does not change the contract of any party and mere spoilation by an interfering stranger, therefore, will not discharge the liability of the parties. [*Bank of New Mexico v. Rice*, p. 326.]

Discharge of Simple Contract Section 3–601 provides that any party is discharged from his liability to another party by any act or agreement which would discharge his simple contract for the payment of money. The various methods of discharging a simple contract such as release, rescission, novation, and accord and satisfaction will, therefore, discharge the maker of a note as between the immediate parties. This does not necessarily mean, however, that all parties to the instrument are discharged. Section 3–602 provides that no discharge of any party is effective against a holder in due course unless he has notice of such discharge when he takes the instrument.

CASES

Shaffer v. Akron Products Co., 109 N.E.2d 24 (Ohio 1952). Action by Paul Shaffer, appellant, against Akron Products Co., appellee. The Akron Products Company executed a promissory note dated September 6, 1947, payable fifteen months after date, for the sum of $5,554.55, payable to the order of Paul Shaffer in payment for a portion of his salary as an officer and employee of the company. After the note was given, the company and Shaffer reached an arrangement whereby Shaffer was to release the company from any liability on the note for the unpaid salary claim, apparently for the purpose of bettering the financial condition of the company. The release was in the following form:

Release

I, Paul Shaffer, holding a note of Five Thousand Five Hundred Fifty-four and 55/100 ($5,554.55) dated September 6, 1947, signed by the Akron Products Company, do hereby by agreement destroy such evidence of liability of the Akron Products Company, and further agree that no liability or claim shall ever be made against said company by me.

Paul Shaffer.

C. J. Geigel
Witness.
Dated at Akron, Ohio, this 22nd day of December, 1947.

Shaffer did not surrender his note and, when his services with the company were terminated, brought suit on the note for the full amount with interest. The question presented to the court was: Did Shaffer, by executing the release, renounce his rights against the company?

Hunsicker, Judge: The "Release" which Shaffer signed was executed by him on December 22, 1947; and hence, if a renunciation by Shaffer (the holder of such note) did take place, such renunciation occurred before the maturity of the note and while Shaffer was still the holder of such note. . . .

The problem we have before us is one of "renunciation." . . . By "renunciation" is meant the gratuitous abandonment or giving up of a right; an express waiver without consideration. . . .

The transaction in the instant case upon which all of the parties agree is that Shaffer did execute the paper writing called a "release." By the terms of such "Release," Shaffer agreed to destroy the note, and further agreed "that no liability or claim shall ever be made against said company by me."

This written release by Shaffer, an officer, employee, and stockholder of the Company, was executed at the same time that similar releases were executed by two other principal stockholders and officers of the Company. Both of the releases were then given to the secretary of the Company, who was present at the signing of the releases and witnessed each signature.

We, therefore, find that Shaffer, by executing the written instrument dated December 22, 1947, and designated "Release," did make an absolute and unconditional renunciation of his rights against the Company. [DECISION FOR APPELLEE]

Faneuil Hall Nat'l Bank v. Meloon, 66 N.E. 410 (Mass. 1903). Action by Faneuil Hall National Bank, plaintiff, against Mary C. Meloon, William H. Wyeth, and Hopkins H. Meloon, defendants. The firm of Meloon & Wyeth signed a note payable to the order of plaintiff. The firm consisted of Mary C. Meloon and William H. Wyeth, and they, with one Hopkins H. Meloon, severally indorsed the note before it was delivered to plaintiff. Before the note became due, the firm notified plaintiff that they were unable to pay it. The plaintiff thereupon executed and delivered to the firm an agreement stating that, in consideration of the payment by the firm of 25 percent of the amount due on the note, it would never prosecute any legal proceedings against the firm to collect the note. The plaintiff, however, expressly reserved "all its rights to proceed against Mary C. Meloon, H. H. Meloon, and W. H. Wyeth, the indorsers upon said notes, individually, to collect the balance due upon said notes." The firm subsequently paid the plaintiff the percentage agreed upon. Plaintiff then brought this action against the indorsers to collect the balance remaining unpaid.

Morton, Justice: The defendants Wyeth and Mary C. Meloon were none the less indorsers and none the less liable as such because they were also liable as members of the firm which made the note. The effect of the covenant not to sue was to release the firm as the maker, not the individual members as indorsers. It is true that each partner is liable in solido for the debts of the firm; but his separate estate is liable in the first instance for his individual debts, and his individual indorsement of a firm note may, therefore, enhance the security afforded by it. For this reason the holder of a firm note indorsed by the individual members of the firm might be willing to compound his claim against the firm, if he could reserve his rights against the indorsers; and we see no objection to his doing so. [DECISION FOR PLAINTIFF]

In re Paskett's Estate, 273 N.Y. Supp. 84 (1934). Proceeding by Mount Vernon Trust Company, claimant, against George McCauslan, executor of the estate of Adeline R. T. Paskett, deceased. The decedent, on January 31, 1931, indorsed for accommodation a negotiable promissory note made by Sarah E. Updike payable to the order of the claimant. It was dishonored by nonpayment at maturity, and notice of the dishonor was given the decedent. The claimant then took a new negotiable promissory note from the maker and, upon default, brought this claim against the estate of the indorser. At the trial, the claimant's witness testified, among other things, that the decedent inquired about what happened to the old note and was told by the claimant that "a new note had been made which consolidated all of Mrs. Updike's notes of the bank into one new note."

Henderson, Surrogate: I find that the maker's time to pay the original debt was extended, and the holder's right to enforce the old note was postponed by agreement binding upon the payee-holder without expressly reserving the latter's right of recourse against the decedent, indorser and without the assent of such indorser. I therefore hold that the decedent was thereby discharged from her liability as indorser of the old note. [THE CLAIM OF THE MOUNT VERNON TRUST COMPANY WAS DISMISSED]

Bank of New Mexico v. Rice,   429 P.2d 368 (N.M. 1967). Action by Bank of New Mexico, plaintiff-appellant, against Earl B. Rice and Lahoma Rice, defendants-appellees, to recover on two promissory notes.

The evidence pertinent to the liability of defendants on the notes revealed that the notes were signed by Earl B. Rice, as maker, and by Lahoma Rice, his wife, as guarantor; that one of the notes was a renewal note; and that there was a material alteration on the other note. The defense of defendants as to liability, therefore, was based on a failure of consideration and material alteration.

Wood, Judge: Defendants assert that there is an issue of fact on the defense of consideration. They say there is a question of consideration because one of the notes had been renewed. This is answered by section 3–408, which provides in part:

". . . No consideration is necessary for an instrument or obligation thereon given in payment of or as security for an antecedent obligation of any kind."

There were two alterations of the larger note. (1) The note was in the amount of $77,905.00. This amount had been crossed out and the figure $54,255.00 had been penciled in. This lesser figure was the balance remaining after a payment was made. It is the amount sued for, and it is the amount of the judgment entered on the directed verdict. (2) A red line was drawn across the face of the note. The evidence is that this line was drawn by the Bank Examiner to indicate he had examined the note.

Defendants contend that these alterations raise a question of fact as to whether they were discharged from liability on the note. Section 3–407 pertains to alteration of commercial paper. It provides in part:

"(2) As against any person other than a subsequent holder in due course

"(a) alteration by the holder which is both fraudulent and material discharges any party whose contract is thereby changed unless that party assents or is precluded from asserting the defense."

The statute is not applicable unless the alteration made by the holder was fraudulent. There is no evidence from which an inference of fraud could be drawn, and thus no question of fact for the jury concerning discharge. [DECISION FOR PLAINTIFF]

PROBLEMS

1 The holder of a $100 note met the maker on the street on July 1, 1965, and stated that he was going to release the maker from his obligation to pay because of the maker's economic difficulties. The maker expressed his appreciation. The holder was killed in an automobile accident on December 18, 1965, and the executor of his estate found the note in the decedent's safe-deposit box. If the executor presents the note for payment on its maturity date, will the maker be required to pay it?

2 Tully executed a promissory note payable to the order of Linder for $1,000, and Brown signed the note as comaker as an accommodation party. Tully tendered payment of the note to Linder on the date of maturity of the note, and the tender was refused by Linder. Linder thereafter brought an action against both Tully and Brown to recover the $1,000 with interest, costs, and attorney's fees. What amount, if any, should Linder recover from (a) Tully, (b) Brown?

3 The Dredging Company, as principal, and defendant, as surety, executed a promissory note in favor of the First Bank for the sum of $10,000. The note was payable on January 1, 1962, and on that date the First Bank and The Dredging Company entered into an agreement whereby the time of payment of the note was extended to July 1, 1962. The note was not paid on July 1, 1962, and the First Bank brought an action against The Dredging Company and defendant to collect the amount due on the note. The defendant contends he is not liable because the First Bank extended the time of payment without his knowledge or consent. Do you think the defendant has been discharged from liability?

4 Aiken advanced to the defendant the sum of $1,000 for which the defendant executed a nonnegotiable promissory note for that amount, dated November 20, 1964, payable to Aiken, one year after date, with interest. Aiken sold the note to plaintiff. Defendant, who had no notice and had no reason to know that the note had been sold to plaintiff, paid Aiken from time to time the entire amount of the note. The trial court found that plaintiff knew, or was put upon inquiry and ought to have known, that Aiken was dealing with and collecting money on the note from defendant. Has the note been discharged by payment?

5 Abbott, as an accommodation for Linder, executed a promissory note for $500, payable to the order of Linder. Linder indorsed the note in blank and delivered it to Smith. Smith, with full knowledge that Abbott was an accommodation party, entered into a binding agreement with Linder whereby he released Linder from all liability on the note. The note became due, and Smith brought an action against Abbott to recover the $500. Will he recover?

27

RELATIONSHIP BETWEEN PAYOR BANK AND ITS CUSTOMER

A bank is a place of business where credit is established by the deposit or collection of money. Such credit is subject to be paid upon checks, drafts, and orders. A bank is also a place of business where money is loaned. The most obvious purpose and primary function of a bank are to provide a place for the deposit of money. A deposit in a bank is either a "special" or a "general" deposit. A special deposit, although not pertinent to this discussion, creates a situation in which the bank is merely the custodian of property without any right to use such property. The depositor-customer is entitled to a return of the identical money or property deposited since this is a bailor-bailee relationship. In the case of the general deposit, pertinent to this discussion, title to the money deposited passes to the bank. This creates a debtor-creditor relationship, the depositor being the creditor and the bank the debtor.

A deposit will be deemed a general deposit unless the customer and the bank agree that it is to be a special deposit. The customer, in the case of a general deposit, may draw checks against the account if the parties agree on the creation of a "checking" account. A depositor does not have the right to draw checks against a "savings" account, although it is a general deposit. It becomes apparent, therefore, that the duty of the bank to honor—pay—checks drawn against a checking account arises as a result of the contract created by the customer and the bank. It should be mentioned, however, that the Code does not provide rules governing "special" or "savings" accounts.

Article 4, "Bank Deposits and Collections," is intended to provide rules governing the deposit and collection by banks of a large volume of checks and rules governing the relationship between the bank and the customer. It should be pointed out that these rules may be, and frequently are, varied by agreement. Section 4–103, however, provides that the bank cannot by agreement disclaim its responsibility for its own lack of good faith or failure to exercise ordinary care. This chapter will be devoted to the rights and duties of the bank and the customer arising from (1) the deposit of checks, (2) the payment of checks, (3) stopping payment of checks, and (4) the duty of the customer to examine his statement of account.

DEPOSIT OF CHECKS

The depositor should deposit all checks promptly after they are received, but the general rule provides that uncertified checks drawn and payable in the United States should be deposited within a reasonable time. Section 3–503 provides specified time limits which are presumed to permit a reasonable time to initiate bank collections. The payee or holder must deposit the check with the bank within thirty days as to the drawer or seven days as to the indorser or assume the risk of the payor bank's insolvency.

Speeding Up Collections   Unless the check contains the words "payee's indorsement required," or the like, the depositor may speed up collections. He might gain one day in effecting the collection of a check by depositing the check before 2 P.M. Section 4–107 permits banks to fix that hour or later, as the cut-off hour, and any deposit received after the cut-off hour may be treated as being received at the opening of the next business day. Section 4–205 is also designed to speed up collections by permitting the bank to supply missing indorsements when the depositor fails to indorse his check. An indorsement stamp of the bank "credited to the account of the within named payee" is given the effect of the indorsement of the depositor.

Provisional Credit and Charge Back   The depositor does not have a right to withdraw against deposited checks immediately, because he is normally given a provisional credit when he deposits a check in the bank. This is for the protection of the bank due to the fact that the check may be dishonored by the drawee bank for such reasons as insufficient funds, stop order, or a forged signature of the drawer. The check will then be returned to the bank, which bank will revoke the provisional credit. The bank may then charge back the check to the depositor's account in accordance with section 4–212. This right of charge back is permitted even though the depositor may have drawn checks against the provisional credit, the nonpayment resulted from negligence of a collecting bank, or the check was improperly dishonored. [*Douglas v. Citizens Bank of Jonesboro*, p. 333.]

BANK'S DUTY TO PAY CHECKS

The bank is under a duty to pay checks drawn by the depositor as long as there are sufficient funds in the account of the depositor to cover the checks. The measure of damages for wrongful dishonor is stated in section 4–402 to be the actual damages sustained by reason of the wrongful dishonor. Damages may, however, include damages for arrest and prosecution of the customer. Of course, whether the dishonor was or was not the cause of the arrest and prosecution is a question to be determined by the facts of the particular case.

Time Allowed for Payment   A check which is presented to the bank on which it is drawn is known as an "on us" check. Section 3–506 provides that the bank must pay or dishonor the check before the close of business on the day of presentment where such check is presented over the counter for immediate payment. Section 4–213 provides that the bank has until the second banking day following receipt of the check to pay or dishonor the check where such check is presented for deposit. Suppose Brown and Jones are both customers of the same bank and Brown deposits a check drawn by Jones on the bank in his account on Monday. Brown would be entitled to payment or notice of dishonor on the opening of business on Wednesday. A bank can hold a check which has been presented for certification until the close of the next business day without dishonoring the check.

Stale Checks   A stale check—one that is presented for payment an unusually long time after the date of the check—puts the bank on notice that something is wrong, and the bank may not be allowed to charge the account of the drawer if a stale check is paid. A refusal by the bank to pay an apparently stale check is a wrongful dishonor, however, if the bank later learns that the check is not stale. This risk is greatly lessened by section 4–404, which provides that a bank is not obligated to pay a check presented for payment more than six months after the date of the check. This section also provides that the bank may pay a check more than six months after the date of the check if the payment is made in good faith. The bank may be in a position to know that the drawer wants the bank to pay the check. This option, therefore, is given the bank. Certified checks are expressly excluded because the account of the drawer is charged when the check is certified. [*Hartsook v. Owens*, p. 334.]

Certification of a Check   Section 3–411, which states that certification of a check is an acceptance of the check, provides the rules pertaining to certification. A check is a demand instrument calling for payment rather than acceptance. It is clear, therefore, that a bank is under no duty to certify a check. Does certification of a check discharge the drawer? The answer depends on whether the certification is procured by the holder or by the drawer. The drawer and all prior parties are discharged where the holder procures the certification, but the drawer is not discharged when he procures the certification. The drawer cannot stop payment on the check once it is certified, however, irrespective of who procures the certification.

Death or Incompetency of Customer   The Code has adopted the pre-Code decisions which permit a bank to charge a customer's account for payment of items drawn by an incompetent or deceased person prior to the time the bank has notice of an adjudication of incompetency or death of the drawer. Section 4–405, however, expressly gives the bank the right to pay checks for a period of ten days even though the bank has notice of death. The purpose of this provision is to give holders of checks drawn by a decedent shortly before death an opportunity to cash them. The useless formality of filing a claim in probate is therefore avoided. It is to be remembered, however, that a person claiming an interest in the account of the decedent may order the bank to stop payment of checks. The Code does not specify who such persons might be, but it would seem that such persons as surviving relatives and creditors would have a right to stop payment.

STOP PAYMENT OF CHECKS

Section 4–403 provides that the customer has a right to stop payment on a check unless the check is a certified check. The drawer of the check is expressly given this right, but the payee or indorsee has no right to stop payment. Section 4–405 makes an exception to the rule by giving any person the right to stop who claims an interest in the account of the drawer after the death of the drawer. May a member of a joint account against which a check is drawn stop payment if the check was drawn by the other member? The Code does not expressly answer this question. This section, however, would seem to indicate that any member of a joint account may stop payment on any check drawn on the account.

Method of Stopping Payment   A direction to stop payment may be given orally, and an oral stop order is binding for a period of fourteen days. This rule, however, makes it possible for persons other than the drawer to telephone a stop order to the bank. A bank, therefore, would obviously prefer to have a written stop order. The bank could enter into an agreement with its customer providing for recognition of only written stop orders. A written stop order is effective for six months, and may then be renewed in writing.

Bank's Right of Subrogation   Section 4–407 gives the bank the right of subrogation if the bank improperly pays a check over a stop order. The bank may be subrogated to the rights of (1) a holder in due course, (2) the payee or other holder, or (3) the drawer.

Let us assume this set of facts: The buyer issues his check in favor of the seller in payment of an order of goods; the seller negotiates the check to a holder in due course; the buyer then learns that the goods are nonconforming, revokes his acceptance, and issues a stop order to the bank; and the bank inadvertently pays the check over the stop order. The bank must recredit the account of the drawer, but section 4–403 places the burden on the drawer to establish the amount of the loss. The drawer-buyer could not sustain the burden of proving the loss because failure of consideration is a personal defense which is not available to the drawer against a holder in due course. The payor bank, therefore, is subrogated to the rights of the holder in due course. This means that the payor bank may bring an action against the drawer.

Suppose the buyer was fraudulently induced to issue his check in favor of a salesman in payment of a worthless grandfather's clock which had been represented by the salesman to be a valuable antique and the buyer stopped payment on the check. A bank which inadvertently paid over the stop order would be subrogated to the rights of the drawer-buyer against the fraudulent salesman—the payee. The right might prove to be worthless, but the loss should not be that of the drawer. [*Commercial Ins. Co. of Newark, N.J. v. Scalamandre*, p. 334.]

DUTY OF CUSTOMER TO EXAMINE STATEMENT OF ACCOUNT

A bank can debit the account of the drawer only to the extent of the original tenor of a check that has been fraudulently altered, and a bank that pays a check with a forged signature cannot debit the account of the drawer for any amount. A drawer, however, is precluded from asserting forgery or material alteration if he negligently contributes to the forgery or alteration. Suppose the drawer signs a check leaving the amount incomplete. The bank may charge the account of the drawer with the amount of the check as completed unless the bank knows that the completion was improper. The customer, therefore, must (1) exercise reasonable care and promptness to examine the bank statement and canceled checks to discover any forgeries or alterations, (2) notify the bank promptly if any forgeries or alterations are discovered, and (3) notify the bank promptly of any change in his address.

Forgeries and Alterations   The bank might prove that it suffered a loss because the customer failed to comply with these duties. The loss, therefore, would be that of the customer. For example, the bank might be able to prove that it could have recovered from the forger if the customer had reported the forgery promptly. A customer who fails to report forgeries and alteration, moreover, opens the door for future forgeries. This could easily be the situation if a bookkeeper used a company stamp for a signature and then cashed the checks for his own benefit. Section 4–406 provides, therefore, that the bank is not required to prove that it suffered a loss where forgeries and alterations are committed by the same wrongdoer and the customer failed to report earlier wrongdoing. A specific limit of fourteen days is placed on the customer for purposes of this rule. These rules assume that the bank has used ordinary care in paying the checks, and the bank will be found guilty of negligence if it pays an obviously altered check or a check with an obviously forged signature.

Statute of Limitations   The customer is limited by the statute of limitations to a period of one year in which to report any forgeries of his signature and alterations of checks whether the bank was or was not guilty of negligence. The period of the statute of limitations is three years in the case of forged indorsements. The distinction is made because there is little excuse for a customer not to detect a forgery of his own signature or an alteration of his own check. The customer, however, does not always know the signature of indorsers. He may, therefore, be delayed in learning that the indorsements are forged.

CASES

Douglas v. Citizens Bank of Jonesboro   424 S.W.2d 532 (Ark. 1968). Action by Weldon Douglas and Janie Chandler, plaintiffs-appellants, against The Citizens Bank of Jonesboro, defendant-appellee, for wrongful dishonor of checks. This litigation involves two separate causes of action which were similar and were, by agreement, disposed of at one hearing.

Weldon Douglas maintained a checking account in the defendant-bank. Another customer, who also had a checking account, issued and delivered a check in the amount of $1,000 to Douglas, who presented the check to the bank for deposit to his checking account. An employee at the teller's window prepared a deposit slip and gave Douglas a duplicate, and an employee thereafter stamped on the back of the check in red ink: "Pay to any bank—P.E.G., Citizens Bank of Jonesboro, Jonesboro, Arkansas." The bank thereafter dishonored the check for insufficient funds, and charged the amount back to the account of Douglas. The question presented to the court was whether the bank accepted the check for payment by stamping the indorsement upon the check deposited by plaintiff and by delivering to plaintiff the deposit slip. The answer of the court and the reasons therefor are stated in the opinion of the court.

Harris, Chief Justice: The answer is, "No," and it might be stated at the outset that cases decided prior to the passage of the Uniform Commercial Code are not controlling. This case is controlled by the following sections of the Code: Section 4–212(3) . . . and section 4–301(1). . . .

When we consider the statutes above referred to, it is clear that appellants cannot prevail. Clark, Bailey and Young, in their American Law Institute pamphlet on bank deposits and collections under the Uniform Commercial Code (January, 1959), p. 2, comment as follows:

If the buyer-drawer and the seller-payee have their accounts in the same bank, and if the seller-payee deposits the check to the credit of his account, his account will be credited provisionally with the amount of the check. In the absence of special arrangement with the bank, he may not draw against the credit until it becomes final, that is to say, until after the check has reached the bank's bookkeeper and, as a result of bookkeeping operations, has been charged to the account of the buyer-drawer. (The seller-payee could, of course, present the check at a teller's window and request immediate payment in cash, but that course is not usually followed.) If the buyer-drawer's account does not have a sufficient balance, or he has stopped payment on the check, or if for any other reason the bank does not pay the check, the provisional credit given in the account of the seller-payee is reversed. If the seller-payee has been permitted to draw against that provisional credit, the bank would recoup the amount of the drawing by debit to his account or by any other means. [DECISION FOR APPELLEE]

Hartsook v. Owens   370 S.W.2d 69 (Ark. 1963). This is an appeal by Ester Myrtle Hartsook, administratrix of the estate of Guy Hartsook, appellant, against S. C. Owens, appellee, from an order of the probate court allowing a claim against the estate.

Appellee filed a claim against the estate of Guy Hartsook, decedent, for $1,050 based upon a check which had been given by the decedent to the appellee. The controversy emanates from the fact that the check was more than six months past due at the time the claim was filed.

George Rose Smith, Justice: It is contended that the check became a nullity as a result of the appellee's failure to cash it within six months after its date. This contention is based upon the statutes that relieve a bank of the duty of cashing checks more than six months old. Ark. Stat. Ann. section 67–534; Uniform Commercial Code section 4–404. These statutes were adopted for the protection of the bank and plainly do not have the effect of extinguishing a valid obligation merely because it is more than six months past due. Such a holding would create an extremely short statute of limitations where none was intended. [DECISION FOR APPELLEE]

Commercial Ins. Co. of Newark, N.J. v. Scalamandre   289 N.Y.S.2d 489 (1967). Action by Commercial Insurance Company of Newark, as subrogee of the First National State Bank of Newark, plaintiff, against Gino Scalamandre, defendant, to recover the amount of certain checks which the bank had paid after the drawer had ordered stop payment of the checks.

David Zarin, who drew two checks on the First National Bank of Newark for $1,000 each, delivered both checks to defendant, who deposited the checks in his own bank. David Zarin thereafter telephoned a stop order to the bank requesting that payment be stopped on the two checks. The stop order, however, was not confirmed in writing. Substantially more than fourteen days after receiving the stop order, the bank made payment on both checks and debited the account of David Zarin. But when he protested payment of the checks in the face of his stop order, the bank recredited his account. Plaintiff made good the loss to the bank under an insurance policy insuring the bank for losses sustained by mistake. Plaintiff then brought this action to recover the amount of the checks together with attorney's fees.

Arnold L. Fein, Judge: The rights of the bank and plaintiff, as its subrogee, against defendant depend upon Uniform Commercial Code section 4–407(C), which provides in substance that the bank is "subrogated to the rights . . . of the drawer or maker against the payee or any other holder of the item with respect to the transaction out of which the item arose." As the various practice commentaries indicate, all this intends is that the bank stands in the shoes of the maker of the check. If the maker or drawer has a right to recover against the payee or holder or has a right to refuse payment, the bank has the same right. As U.C.C. section 4–407 states, if the payment was made "under circumstances giving a basis for objection by the drawer or maker" the bank is subrogated to the rights of the maker or drawer "to prevent unjust enrichment." Nowhere in the complaint in this action are any facts alleged showing that defendant was unjustly enriched or that Zarin, the maker of the check, has a right to refuse payment on the checks or a right to recover from the defendant once the checks were honored and paid. . . .

It is conceded that defendant was the holder of the checks at the time he deposited them in his bank and that he had received them from Zarin. The law is well settled that a presumption arises from the delivery of a check that it was delivered in payment of a debt. . . . The burden of proof is on plaintiff to establish that the payee was not entitled to the proceeds of the check. [DECISION FOR DEFENDANT]

PROBLEMS

1 Defendant employed McMillan to paint certain property for an agreed consideration of $260. When the work was apparently completed, McMillan demanded his pay. The defendant thereupon executed and delivered to McMillan a check for $260. On the same day, McMillan took the check to plaintiff's place of business and purchased certain merchandise. Plaintiff acquired the check in good faith and for value, in the ordinary course of business, and without notice of any defect in the title of McMillan. Two days thereafter, defendant discovered that McMillan had not used the type and kind of materials he had promised to use. Defendant immediately stopped payment on the check. In an action to recover the amount for which the check was drawn, the defendant contended that the plaintiff took the uncertified check subject to the right of the defendant to stop payment on it for fraud, failure of consideration, or other good cause. Is the defendant correct?

2 Plaintiffs brought an action against the defendant-bank to recover for money the defendant paid out on forged checks. Plaintiffs were general insurance agents in Chicago and were officers and stockholders in the Federal Union Insurance Company, which company's business was transacted in plaintiffs' office. Plaintiffs' books and those of the company were kept separately, and the bank accounts of each were kept separately. DeLisle was in the employ of plaintiffs from the fall of 1958 continuously until 1965. He was gradually advanced to head bookkeeper. He kept the books of the plaintiffs, as well as those of the company. He checked all monthly statements received from the bank showing balances of plaintiffs and the company. He forged indorsements to many checks over a period of years. The following is an example of the system he used: He drew a check for $49 on plaintiffs' checkbook, payable to Federal Union Insurance Company, had the same properly signed by an officer of the plaintiff-company, and then forged the indorsement of the insurance company. He received the money and converted it to his own use. Decide.

3 Brown was a customer who maintained a checking account in the First Bank. He drew a check for the sum of $200, but some subsequent holder fraudulently raised the amount of the check to $300. The check was later presented for payment, and the bank, in good faith, paid $300 and charged Brown's account $300. Does Brown have a cause of action against the bank?

4 Brown signed a blank check and left it on top of his office desk. A thief removed the blank check, completed it for $2,000, and sold it to Jones, a holder in due course. Jones presented the check for payment and received $2,000. Brown contends that the bank had no right to charge his account $2,000. Is Brown's contention correct?

5 Discuss what action, if any, a customer has against a bank in case the bank wrongfully dishonors a check.

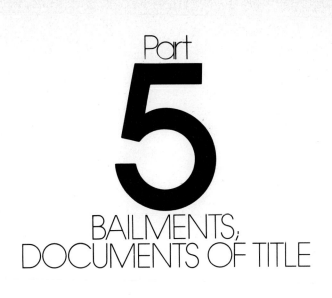

Part

5

BAILMENTS;
DOCUMENTS OF TITLE

BAILMENTS

The essence of a bailment is that one person called the "bailor" gives the possession and control of personal property to another person called the "bailee" with the understanding that the bailee is to hold the property in behalf of the bailor. The characteristic elements of a bailment lie in the transfer of possession of personal property from the bailor to the bailee, without a transfer of the title, for some temporary purpose, the possession to revert to the bailor or the property to be otherwise disposed of as directed by the bailor.

Delving into the law of bailments reveals that the undertakings of the bailor and the bailee vary with the classes and types of bailments. It seems, therefore, that an insight into the subject of bailments might best be grasped by (1) distinguishing bailments from similar transactions, (2) classifying bailments with respect to the degrees of care, (3) discussing the rights and duties of the parties in ordinary bailment situations, (4) mentioning some special bailment situations, and (5) explaining how the relationship may be terminated. This chapter, however, will be devoted to bailments other than those governed by Article 7, "Documents of Title."

BAILMENTS DISTINGUISHED

Distinguished from Custody The element of intent to possess and control is lacking in custody. The absence of this element of intent distinguishes a bailment from mere custody. The owner of goods may place them in the actual physical control of another. The possessor is a mere custodian, however, unless the owner intends to relinquish the right to their control. Property which has been lawfully taken by authority of legal process and is in the possession of a public officer is a clear illustration of custody as distinguished from a bailment. Another illustration of custody, probably not so clear but equally well settled, is where goods have been delivered to an employee by the employer to be used by the employee in the employer's business. An employee who is entrusted with his employer's truck to drive to a certain place in behalf of his employer is not a bailee. The truck, it is said, is in the legal possession of the employer. The distinction is purely technical. The courts generally hold, on the other hand, that a bailment arises when an agent has been entrusted with his principal's goods. These disputes, however, are ordinarily worked out on a basis of the law of agency rather than on the law of bailments.

Distinguished from Sale   The rule of law which distinguishes a bailment from a sale is quite simple. In a bailment, the title to the goods does not pass to the bailee; in a sale, the title does pass to the vendee. The rule is generally stated that a bailment results when the identical thing is to be returned in the same or in an altered form; but that a sale results where there is an agreement to pay money or its equivalent for the thing delivered and the receiving party is under no obligation to return the specific thing or to account for it.

Types of Bailments Distinguished   The distinction made between bailments and similar transactions might leave one with the impression that there is only one type of bailment. There are several types: The bailment may be for safekeeping, as where goods are stored in a warehouse, or where securities are deposited in a safe-deposit box, or where an automobile is left at a parking lot, or where baggage is checked; it may be for hire, as where an automobile is rented; it may be for work, as where a watch is left to be repaired; it may be a pledge, as where personal property is pledged as security for a loan; or it may be a consignment, as where the consignor ships goods to a consignee—most likely, a retailer—for the purpose of having the goods sold by the consignee.

CLASSIFICATION OF BAILMENTS

Bailments are broadly classified, with respect to the degree of care that should be exercised by the bailee, as "ordinary" and "extraordinary." This classification distinguishes bailees who have imposed upon them the usual duty of serving all comers, such as innkeepers, from other bailees. An inquiry into the degree of care that should be exercised by the bailee, however, directs attention to another classification of bailments: those for the sole benefit of the bailor, those for the sole benefit of the bailee, and those for the mutual benefit of the bailor and the bailee.

Bailments for the Sole Benefit of the Bailor   This type of bailment results when one person renders some service without compensation in respect to the bailed property. Such a bailment exists when one person is permitted to store some item of personal property on his neighbor's premises. It is said the bailee in a bailment for the sole benefit of the bailor is required to use slight care and is liable only for gross negligence.

Bailments for the Sole Benefit of the Bailee   This type of bailment results when some item of personal property is entrusted to another without compensation. Such a bailment exists when one person borrows some chattel from another person. It is said the bailee in a bailment for the benefit of the bailee is required to use great care and is liable even for slight negligence.

Bailments for the Mutual Benefit of the Parties   This is the most common type of bailment. It includes all commercial bailments. The mutual benefit feature of the bailment may be illustrated by the familiar case where the owner of some item of personal property stores it in a warehouse. The owner, the bailor, has the benefit of having his property cared for during the period of the storage, and the warehouseman, the bailee, is compensated for his services. It is said the mutual benefit bailee is required to use ordinary care and is liable for ordinary negligence.

Modern View   The courts have experienced unusual difficulty in trying to settle disputes on the basis of these three degrees of care and negligence. But they cannot be lightly discharged because they are still occasionally found in the decisions. The rule most generally applied today, however, is that the bailee should be required in all cases to exercise ordinary care, generally defined as that care which a person of ordinary prudence customarily takes of his own goods of a similar kind and under similar circumstances. The care required to be taken, of course, may vary with the circumstances of the particular case. The nature and value of the bailed property, for instance, would be an important factor. A bailor would have a right to expect a different care of a diamond ring than he would expect of a lawnmower. The place where the goods are stored would be important. A bailor would have a right to expect a different protection and care if he stored securities with a banker than he would have a right to expect if they were stored with the manager of a rooming house. All the circumstances of the particular case are taken into consideration. The fact that the bailee received no compensation for his services, moreover, is taken into consideration along with other factors in settling disputes arising out of gratuitous bailments.

RIGHTS AND DUTIES OF THE PARTIES

The important rights and duties of the bailor and bailee pertain to the right of the bailee to limit his liability, the duty of the bailor to notify the bailee of defects in the property, the duty of the bailee to return the property, the duty of the bailee not to deviate from the terms of the contract, the duty of the bailor or the bailee to pay the expenses in connection with the property, and the rights of the bailor and the bailee against third persons.

Contractual Limitations against Care   The bailor and the bailee may agree as to the extent of the liability of the bailee so long as it is not opposed to law or public policy. The practice is quite common for prospective bailees to attempt to limit their liability by the posting of public notices and the printing of conditions on the receipt or identification check given to the bailor upon the transfer of possession of the property. The words "property at the owner's risk" are frequently used for this purpose. A sharp conflict has developed in the law over the validity of these limitations. The unsettled question is: May a bailee contract to limit his liability for negligence? The question is sometimes answered in the affirmative on the ground that it is a valid right of the individual to contract without interference. The question is sometimes answered in the negative, and probably it is so answered in a slight majority of the times, on the ground that the bailee may not limit his liability for negligence because it is opposed to public policy. The courts, in many cases, have reached a decision without referring to the negligence on the ground that the bailor had not consented to the limitation. It seems quite clear, therefore, that unless the bailee expressly informs the bailor of the limitation, or at least takes reasonable steps to do so, the limitation is not effectual. [*Healy v. New York Cent. & H.R.R.,* p. 349.]

Duty to Inform of Defects in Chattel.   It is probably correct to say that in every case of bailment a minimum obligation rests upon the bailor to inform the bailee of hidden defects in the bailed chattel. The bailor's duty is clear where the bailment contemplates use of the chattel. It is a general rule that the lender of a chattel who knows of defects in it which would render it dangerous for the purpose for which it is ordinarily used is under a duty to inform the bailee of such defects. The bailor is liable for any injury caused by such defects of which the bailee is ignorant. A person who lends his automobile to his neighbor knowing that the brake is faulty is under a duty to inform the borrower of the defect. The gratuitous bailor, however, is not under a duty to take affirmative measures to see that the chattel is free from danger.

The rule with respect to a bailment for the mutual benefit of the parties is somewhat enlarged. The general rule in a mutual benefit bailment for hire is that there is imposed on the bailor an obligation to see that the chattel bailed for use shall be reasonably fit for the purposes intended. Statutes have been enacted in some states to the effect that a warranty is implied that the chattel is reasonably fit for the purpose for which it is leased or hired where a person hires or leases out a chattel which is to be used for a particular purpose. These statutes, however, do not seem to make any material change in the general rule. [*Aircraft Sales & Service v. Gantt,* p. 350.]

Duty of Bailee to Return Property   The bailee owes a duty to the bailor to return the bailed property to the bailor on demand when the purpose of the bailment has been accomplished or to dispose of the property as directed by the bailor. This duty is not excused even though the goods are those of the bailee. The bailee, by accepting the goods from the bailor, impliedly recognizes the right of the bailor to the goods. This implied recognition, therefore, prevents the bailee from keeping the goods even though they are his own. The bailee may have accepted the goods in ignorance of his own rights. He is, nevertheless, estopped from asserting his right until he has fulfilled his obligation by returning them to the bailor. The duty to return the goods, of course, may be excused where the property has been destroyed without negligence on the part of the bailee. It may be excused if the bailee can prove that he delivered the property to a third-person claimant who was the one rightfully entitled to the property. The bailee may have been compelled to deliver the property to a third person by compulsion of valid legal process. It is the duty of the bailee, however, to notify the bailor of any action that may be instituted by a third person for the possession of the property so that the bailor may intervene and assert his rights.

It is to be realized that a perplexing problem arises when a third person demands possession of the property. A bailee is liable to the bailor, irrespective of how free he may be of negligence, if he delivers the property to a third person who is not the rightful claimant to the property. The bailee, on the other hand, is liable to the third person if he refuses to deliver the property to the third-person claimant who is rightfully entitled to the bailed property. But the law is not unmindful of this predicament of the bailee on the appearance of adverse claims. The bailee is not required to act immediately; he is given a reasonable time to investigate. In a few instances the bailee may file a bill of interpleader. This is a suit in equity whereby the adverse claimants may be compelled to litigate their claims by themselves. But this remedy is available only in those instances where the third person is in privity with the bailor under a title derived from him. The inadequacy of this equitable remedy, therefore, has prompted many states to enact statutes for the express purpose of permitting the bailee on the appearance of adverse claims to seek the aid of a court. The bailee is sometimes permitted to deposit the property, or the title thereto, with the court; he is sometimes permitted to take a bond of indemnity from the third-person claimant; or he may, in some instances, require the claimant to prove his title. These statutes are not uniform. They do, however, protect the bailee from the embarrassment of conflicting claims. But it should not be presumed that these statutes in any way protect a bailee who delivers the bailed property to a third person who is not entitled to the possession of the property. [*Baer v. Slater,* p. 351.]

Duty Not to Deviate from the Terms of the Contract   It is a general rule that the bailee, in every bailment contract, is under a duty not to deviate from the terms of the bailment agreement. A deviation may arise because of an excessive use of the chattel. A bailee who has the right to use a horse for riding purposes has no right to use the horse for plowing. A deviation may arise because the bailee had no right to use the chattel in the first place. A garagekeeper has no right to use for his own purposes automobiles which are placed with him for storage. It may be stated as a general rule, therefore, that the bailee will be liable for any loss which results from using the bailed property for a different purpose, in a different manner, for a longer period, or in a different place from that which was intended. A number of cases have been litigated with respect to the liability of a bailee who deviates from the contract as to the place of storage. A few cases in which the loss results from the inherent nature of the goods have not held the bailee liable. A bailee is under a duty, however, to remove the goods to a safer place to protect them from such occurrences as an impending flood. A bailee is liable, therefore, where it is anticipated that damage will occur to the goods and he has a reasonable opportunity to remove them to a place of safety but fails to take advantage of the opportunity. The majority of the cases, however, have held the bailee liable when he moves the bailed property from the agreed place of storage to another place and a loss occurs which would not have occurred had the property been stored in the place agreed upon. This liability is apparently imposed even though the bailee is not negligent. [*McCurdy v. Wallblom Furniture & Carpet Co.*, p. 352.]

Expenses   Must the bailee or the bailor bear the ordinary, as well the extraordinary, expenses in connection with the bailed property? The answer to the question is not always easy. It depends upon the express or presumed intention of the parties, the nature and purpose of the bailment, the nature and amount of compensation, if any, the extent to which the bailee is to use the property, and the custom, usage, and character of the bailed goods. The bailee, in a bailment for the sole benefit of the bailor, is entitled to reimbursement for all necessary expenses if reasonably expended. The bailee, in a bailment for the sole benefit of the bailee, seemingly must bear any expenses incurred in using the bailed property. The bailor, in a bailment for hire, should provide an article in a condition sufficiently good that it will last during the period of the bailment. A bailor for hire, therefore, is not required to pay ordinary expenses. The bailee of a horse for hire would be required to pay the usual expenses of housing and feeding, but extraordinary expenses, such as veterinarian services due to an unexpected illness of the horse, should be borne by the bailor. The bailee of an automobile for three months would usually be required to pay the ordinary expenses. The bailee of an automobile for a short period of time for a short trip, on the other hand, probably would not be required to pay the ordinary expenses. It should be kept in mind, however, that the bailee is required to pay any expenses which are caused by his own neglect or fault.

Rights against Third Parties   The bailor and the bailee, both of whom have a property interest in the bailed goods, can recover damages from a wrongful third party for conversion or damage inflicted. If the bailee should recover the entire amount of the damages, however, whatever amount is in excess of his interest will be held for the bailor. It is also true that the bailee's rights are generally held, under the modern rule, to be broad enough to permit him to bring an action of replevin against the third party. The bailee may, in some cases, reach a voluntary settlement with the third party which will be binding on the bailor. But this rule is subject to serious criticism and has been rejected by some courts on the theory that an indifferent bailee may not arrive at an adequate settlement. The bailor, in those cases where the bailee has not recovered in behalf of both the bailor and the bailee, may recover his damages from the wrongful third party. The bailor, unless he is entitled to immediate possession, probably would not be permitted to bring an action for wrongful interference with the goods. But no one would deny that the bailor is entitled to recover damages to his reversionary interest in the bailed property. The bailee, however, apparently is not precluded from recovering his possessory damages if the bailor recovers his damages first. A recovery first by the bailee of his damages likewise does not prevent a subsequent recovery by the bailor for damages to his interest. But it should be mentioned that the third party will not be required to answer twice. It is a general rule, therefore, that a recovery by either party of the entire damages will preclude an action by the other party for the same tortious act of the third party.

SPECIAL BAILMENT SITUATIONS

It is to be remembered that, in order to constitute a bailment, the bailee must be placed in possession of the property concerned. Furthermore, in order to constitute possession, there must be a delivery and acceptance of the article. Few problems arise in this connection where the property is actually delivered and accepted. But no end of problems have arisen when it is contended that the property has been constructively delivered or impliedly accepted. All is not, however, chaotic. The legislatures of the various states, by enacting statutes, have solved some of the problems. The courts have likewise developed some fairly well-standardized rules that may be used as guides in settling disputes. These rules have found their most frequent application with respect to hotels and motels, restaurants and barbershops, safe-deposit boxes, parking lots, and involuntary bailments.

Hotels and Motels   At early common law, innkeepers were insurers against all loss sustained by guests unless the loss was caused by the negligence or fraud of the guest or by an act of God. The liability of proprietors of hotels and motels for loss sustained by guests is controlled today by statutes of the several states. These statutes are not uniform, but the purpose of all of them is to give the proprietor an opportunity to limit his common-law liability. They usually include all proprietors who hold themselves out to receive transients generally. The typical statute provides that *if* the proprietor of the hotel or motel shall provide an iron safe, or some similar place, for the keeping of valuable property and shall notify the guests of such depositary, the proprietor shall not be liable for the loss of any property which the guest may fail to deliver to him.

Restaurants and Barbershops   The problem of sufficiency of delivery is the great obstacle in holding a proprietor liable as bailee in those cases where a customer deposits articles of clothing in restaurants, barbershops, dance halls, and the like.

The courts are generally agreed that no bailment exists where the patron hangs his own coat or hat on a hook or some similar object. This conclusion is reached on the ground that there was no actual delivery of the article. Some courts go a step further and say that the proprietor does not have such a possession of the article as to exclude the possession of the patron. The courts are likewise generally agreed that a bailment does result in those cases where the proprietor furnishes facilities for the specific purpose of depositing hats, coats, and wraps with an attendant. The usual procedure is for the patron to deposit his coat or hat with the attendant, receiving in return therefor a claim check. In these cases, it is to be noted, the proprietor does have such possession of the article as to exclude the possession of the patron. A sharp question arises when the patron from outward appearances seems to deposit a hat and coat but deposits some additional article. A favorite illustration is the patron who deposited a coat with a fur piece wrapped up and concealed within it. The courts in deciding this class of cases hold that there was no legal delivery on the ground that the bailee did not intend to assume possession of the bailor's property—in this particular case, the fur piece.

Safe-Deposit Boxes   In the usual operation of a safe-deposit box two keys are necessary to gain access to the contents of the box. One is held by the safe-deposit company and the other is held by the customer. The safe-deposit company has control of the premises but its physical control of the contents of the box is clearly limited. It has been ably argued that the safe-deposit company is not a bailee because of an absence of control without which there can be no possession. The great majority of the courts have held, however, that the customer is a bailor and the safe-deposit company a bailee.

Parking-Lot Cases   The parking-lot cases have been a fruitful source for argument. The courts ordinarily decide the cases on a basis of whether possession has been delivered, but the decisions are not entirely uniform. The courts generally hold, however, that the proprietor is merely renting space, rather than a bailment, in that class of cases where the customer drives his own vehicle into the lot, parks it, retains the ignition key, and has the privilege, upon his return, to drive the vehicle away without consulting the proprietor. The courts are agreed that the proprietor is a bailee in that class of cases where the proprietor takes possession of the automobile at the entrance of the parking lot and gives the customer a claim check in exchange therefor. It should be pointed out, however, that in this class of cases the proprietor retains the ignition key to the automobile, drives it into the parking lot, parks it, and redelivers it to the customer at the entrance or exit of the parking lot upon presentation of the claim check.

Involuntary Bailments   A person may be forced into the possession of property of another in various ways: The possessor may be a finder; a storm may deposit property of one person on the land of another; animals may stray from their owners; or a third person through mistake may place the property of one person on the land of another. Can it be said that the possessor of these chattels is a bailee? The finder voluntarily assumes the role of quasi bailee. The courts, therefore, have little trouble in holding a finder a gratuitous bailee on the theory that the loser impliedly requests the finder to take possession of and care for the lost property. The finder, on this theory, is generally entitled to recover the value of his services. The courts have not applied the same line of reasoning to unwilling possessors. The unwilling possessor cannot convert the property to his own use or refuse to redeliver it to the true owner, but, aside from a moral duty to care for the property, his duties of care have not been defined. Some courts have held that the unwilling possessor is under no duty to take possession of property thrust upon him but that if he undertakes to do so, he becomes a bailee and is liable for negligence in caring for the property. A few states have statutes that might be interpreted as imposing a duty of care on the involuntary bailee. This is about all that may safely be said with respect to involuntary bailments.

TERMINATION

A bailment may be terminated by performance, by acts of the parties, and by operation of law.

Performance   The most obvious way in which a bailment is terminated is by complete performance of the bailment contract. The bailment may have been created for some particular purpose. When the objective has been fully realized, therefore, the bailment comes to an end. The bailment may have been created to exist for a definite time. When the time for which the bailment was created has expired, therefore, the bailment is terminated by the limitation placed on it when it was created.

By Acts of the Parties   The parties who created the bailment may likewise destroy it. It is obvious, therefore, that a bailment may be mutually terminated, and neither party is answerable in damages to the other party. It is also true that either one of the parties has the right to terminate some bailments without a corresponding duty to respond in damages. A bailment which is created for the sole benefit of either party may be terminated at any time by the party receiving the benefit. A bailment which is created for an indefinite time may be terminated at the will of either the bailor or the bailee. The right to terminate other bailments generally carries with it the right to recover damages, and some bailments may not be terminated. The bailor may terminate a bailment because of some wrong on the part of the bailee. The bailee, to be sure, will have to answer in damages. The bailment, nevertheless, may be terminated. A bailee who makes an unauthorized use of the property, disposes of the property contrary to the terms of the contract, or abandons the bailment gives the bailor the right to terminate the bailment. A bailment for a definite time or purpose cannot, as a general rule, be terminated at the will of either party. The bailment of an automobile for a stated period of time, for example, gives the bailee a property interest in the automobile that will be protected against everyone including the bailor. The bailor, therefore, cannot free himself of the bailment contract by the payment of damages.

By Operation of Law   A bailment may be terminated by operation of law if the property is lost or destroyed without the fault of the bailee. The same would be true if the bailee becomes the owner of the bailed property. A bailee for hire, for example, may purchase the bailed property.

LIENS ON PERSONAL PROPERTY

Various liens on personal property could be acquired at common law. Such liens were accorded persons engaged in a public calling. They sometimes attached by custom of the particular trade. The innkeeper, the public warehouseman, and the public carrier are prominent examples of persons engaged in business of public calling. The artisan's lien is a prominent example of a lien which attaches by custom of the particular trade.

The innkeeper had a lien on the goods of each guest as security for the payment of the cost of lodging. The public warehouseman had a lien on goods stored with him as security for the payment of storage charges. The common carrier had a similar lien on goods transported and stored in connection with such transportation. The statutes in the various states have expressly included many of the common-law liens and have in addition thereto created new liens. Those that merit particular mention are the factor's lien and the artisan's lien.

Factor's Lien   The common-law factor's lien arises out of a consignment transaction. It should be mentioned that a consignment exists when a manufacturer, called the "consignor," ships goods to a "factor," called the "consignee," for the purpose of having the goods sold by the factor. The consignee receives a commission for his services. He is, therefore, sometimes referred to as a "commission merchant." The consignee, in accordance with the general rule which gives the lienor in possession of property the right to hold the property for any unpaid amount which may be due him from the owner, may assert a lien against the goods in his possession. The lien may be asserted for any amount owed the consignee by the consignor as a result of the consignment. The lien, therefore, may be asserted for any amount which the consignee has paid for the benefit of the consignor, such as freight or insurance.

Artisan's Lien   An artisan, who is generally defined as a person skilled in some kind of mechanical craft or art, has a right to retain the chattel that has been enhanced by his work. This is a common-law lien, and it applies only where the chattel has been improved. It continues until the price of the work has been paid. The lien does not arise, however, where the artisan contracts for a period of credit. The early common law required the lienholder to continue in possession of the chattel. A lien holder who surrendered possession, therefore, lost his lien. The lien, moreover, did not survive if the same chattel was returned to the lien holder for further repairs. The same is true where the artisan makes repairs on two separate chattels. Suppose Brown delivers a chair to Smith for repairs and at a later date delivers a table for repairs. Smith has a lien on the chair for the repairs made to the chair and a separate lien on the table for the repairs made to the table. If Smith should deliver the chair to Brown without receiving payment, the lien is lost. Smith would not have a lien on the table for the repairs made to the chair. This is for the reason that the lien on the table is a specific lien, which is good only against the table. The parties could have agreed in advance, however, that Smith would have a lien on the table for any and all obligations owing to Smith. This would be a general lien, which would give Smith the right to retain possession of the table until the bills for the chair and table are paid. It would also give him a lien on the table for any other debts owned by Brown to Smith.

The only means available to an artisan for the enforcement of his lien at common law was to retain the property until the charges were paid. He had no right to sell the subject matter of the lien. The common-law artisan's lien, however, has been superseded by statute in practically all of the states. The statutes are generally declaratory of the common law, but the language of the statutes varies exceedingly. The repairman, in many of the states, may sell the chattel at a public or private sale after a specified time coupled with notice to the owner. Some of the statutes touch upon the question of priority between repairmen and other lienors. Several of the statutes specifically declare the artisan's lien to be superior to the liens of conditional sellers or chattel mortgagees. A few statutes, on the other hand, expressly subordinate the lien of the artisan to prior liens of record. Prior encumbrances not on record are, of course, inferior to the artisan's lien.

Section 9–310 of the Code provides that an artisan's lien takes priority over an earlier security interest—an interest in personal property which secures payment or performance of an obligation—where the services are furnished in the ordinary course of business and the goods are in the artisan's possession. Some state statutes, however, expressly make the artisan's lien subordinate to prior liens. This section does not repeal such statutory provisions.

CASES

Healy v. New York Cent. & H.R.R., 138 N.Y.S. 287 (1912). Action by William J. Healy, plaintiff, against New York Central & Hudson River Railroad Company, defendant. The plaintiff, on the afternoon of November 4, 1911, checked his handbag at the parcel room of the defendant at its station in the city of Albany, receiving therefor a cardboard coupon two by three inches in size. The following words were printed upon the back of the coupon in fine print, with the exception of the words "ten dollars":

Charged 10 cents for first 24 hours, and 5 cents for each additional 24 hours, or fraction thereof, and each piece of handbag, parcel, etc. Glass, china, etc., taken only at owner's risk of breakage. The depositor in accepting this duplicate coupon expressly agrees that the company shall not be liable to him or her for any loss or damage on any piece to an amount exceeding TEN DOLLARS.

The evidence showed that plaintiff, upon receiving the coupon, put it in his pocket without reading it and without his attention having been called to the limitation of liability printed thereon; that about ten o'clock in the evening of that day the plaintiff presented the coupon at the parcel room and demanded his handbag; that, through the mistake of the person in charge of the parcel room, coupons had been mismatched; that plaintiff's handbag had been delivered to another person; and that it has never been recovered. This action was brought to recover the sum of $70.10, the value of the handbag and its contents. The defendant claims that its liability is limited to $10.

Lyon, Justice: I think that the decision of this appeal should be placed upon the broader ground that under the circumstances disclosed by the record the unreasonable condition printed upon the coupon, attempting to limit the liability, of the defendant to not exceeding $10, was void. Had notice been given by the bailee to the bailor of the conditions limiting the liability of the former, and the latter then seen fit to enter into the bailment, a different question would be presented. But in the case at bar no notice whatever was given to the bailor of the existence of this condition; neither was there anything connected with the transaction, which was for the mutual benefit of both parties, which would tend in any way to suggest to a reasonably prudent man, or lead him to suspect, the existence of such a special contract, or tend to put him on guard or on inquiry relative thereto.

The coupon was presumptively intended as between the parties to serve the special purpose of affording a means of identifying the parcel left by the bailor. In the mind of the bailor the little piece of cardboard, which was undoubtedly hurriedly handed to him, and which he doubtless hurriedly slipped into his pocket, without any suggestion having been made upon the part of the parcel room clerk as to the statements in fine print thereon, did not arise to the dignity of a contract by which he agreed that in the event of the loss of the parcel, even through the negligence of the bailee itself, he would accept therefor a sum which, perhaps, would be but a small fraction of its actual value.

The plaintiff having had no knowledge of the existence of the special contract limiting the liability of the defendant to an amount not exceeding $10, and not being chargeable with such knowledge, the minds of the parties never met thereon, and the plaintiff cannot be deemed to have assented thereto, and is not bound thereby.

The judgment entered upon the decision of the County Court, awarding to the plaintiff the full value of the handbag and contents, together with the costs of the action, should be affirmed. [DECISION FOR PLAINTIFF]

Aircraft Sales & Service v. Gantt 52 So. 2d 388 (Ala. 1951). Action by Charles F. Gantt (plaintiff below), appellee, against Aircraft Sales & Service (defendant below), appellant. The evidence disclosed that appellant was conducting a flight school in which students were trained as airplane pilots, and that appellee was enrolled as a student in this school; that appellee, prior to being injured, had received about twelve or thirteen hours of instruction with an instructor in the airplane with him and about fifteen hours of solo time; that appellee, on the day he was injured, was on a practice flight; that when he was about 900 feet he went straight into a left bank and that when he tried to straighten up from this left bank his rudder stuck and the plane would hardly straighten up; that he finally got the wing up a little but he was still going down at an angle; that the plane continued down at about a 45-degree angle and struck the ground; that appellee was severely injured; and that when the plane was dismantled the next day, a screw driver about ten inches long was discovered in the area between the floor board and the bottom and the surface of the plane. This action was brought for personal injuries received in the crash.

Livingston, Chief Justice: Here the relationship between the parties was that of bailor and bailee for hire. Where there is a bailment for the mutual benefit of the parties, as for hire, there is imposed on the bailor, in the absence of a special contract or representation, an obligation that the thing or property bailed for use shall be reasonably fit for the purposes or capable of the use known or intended. And if the use of the instrumentality threatens serious danger to others unless it is in good condition, there is a duty to take reasonable care to ascertain its condition by inspection. The liability is not to be determined by the contract alone, but is rested on the bailor's duty beyond the contract. The duty of diligence of a bailor in such a bailment is an obligation imposed by law on one in his dealings with his fellows to refrain from acts of omission or commission which he may reasonably expect would result in injury to the bailee or others. . . .

Appellant argues that there is no evidence that the aircraft was not inspected periodically, and further, that there is no evidence that an inspection would have disclosed the presence of the screw driver beneath the floor board of the aircraft. But, be that as it may, there is evidence from which the jury could infer that the mechanics or employees of appellant left a screw driver beneath the floor board of the aircraft and that it jammed the controls of the aircraft to such an extent as to cause it to fall. Regardless of whether or not appellant inspected the aircraft, it was appellant's duty to exercise due care to furnish appellee with a plane reasonably fit for the purposes, or capable of the use known or intended. The furnishing of a plane with a screw driver under the floor board where it may come in contact, and interfere with, the controls of the plane may, on that theory, be a breach of that duty. [DECISION FOR APPELLEE]

Baer v. Slater   158 N.E. 328 (Mass. 1927). Action by Alvin H. Baer and others, plaintiffs, against H. B. Slater, defendant.

Braley, Justice: It was undisputed that the plaintiffs employed the defendant as a salesman on commission, to whom they shipped merchandise for sale which he received and kept in his place of business, and that the plaintiffs some time in January, 1924, directed the defendant to return the merchandise to them by express. In accordance with the order to reship, the defendant, whose place of business was in Boston, packed the merchandise in several bundles which he addressed to plaintiffs, who were located in New York, and on February 16, 1923, "a man came onto the floor in the building . . . and called out, 'American Express.'" The defendant called this man, who wore a cap, badge, and a blouse similar to those worn by drivers of the American Railway Express Company, into his office, and delivered to him the merchandise in question. A receipt book had been furnished the defendant by the express company, and he had used it for a number of years, and the man signed in it a receipt for the merchandise in the name of "O'Connor." The defendant had seen him similarly clad prior to the time when the shipment was made, and he "believed that he was delivering the packages in the usual way to an agent of the American Express Company." The defendant also sent the receipt to the plaintiffs and gave a copy to the express company. In connection with this testimony there was evidence tending to show, and it could be warrantly found, that the apparent driver was not at the time an employee of the express company, but an impostor who in the manner just described obtained possession of the merchandise, which he purloined. The trial judge on the evidence was justified in finding that the party, to whom the goods were delivered, was not the servant or agent of the American Railway Express Company, "and that said goods were not delivered to the said express company." The title was in the plaintiffs, who had the right to demand a return of the merchandise in accordance with their directions, and, if such directions were not complied with and the merchandise was thereby lost, the defendant would be liable for conversion. It is contended, however, by the defendant, that he was a gratuitous bailee, and in the absence of bad faith or of gross negligence, of which there is no evidence, the action cannot be maintained. . . .

A delivery to an unauthorized person is as much a conversion as would be a sale of the property, or an appropriation of it to the bailee's own use. In such cases neither a sincere and apparently well founded belief that the tortious act was right, nor the exercise of any degree of care, constitutes a defense even to a gratuitous bailee.

The defendant's request . . . that the defendant cannot be held liable if he used ordinary care, having been denied rightly, the order of the appellate division dismissing the report, is affirmed. [DECISION FOR PLAINTIFF]

McCurdy v. Wallblom Furniture & Carpet Co. 102 N.W. 873 (Minn. 1905). Action by W. S. McCurdy, plaintiff, against Wallblom Furniture & Carpet Company, defendant. The plaintiff took his goods to the retail furniture store of the defendant for storage. The defendant explained that his warehouse, in which the goods were to be stored, was situated in another part of the city. The storage charges were agreed upon, and it was also agreed that the bailor would take his goods to the warehouse. The bailor then took the goods in wagons hired by himself to the warehouse mentioned and saw them stored therein. The bailor was given a warehouse receipt in conventional form which provided for storage generally but did not specify where the goods were to be kept. The bailee subsequently transferred the goods to a new location where they were destroyed by fire. This action was then brought to recover the value of the goods so destroyed.

Jaggard, Justice: Where goods, which have been removed by the bailee from an agreed to another place of storage without notice to or consent of the bailor, are destroyed by fire, the bailee is liable in an action at law for the reasonable market value of the goods. Such a state of facts makes out "a case of the defendant having taken the plaintiff's goods to a place where he had no right to take them; therefore he must pay for the goods." The bailor is entitled to the safety, to the convenience, and to any and every advantage of the agreed location. He is entitled to unchanged hazards as to things priceless to him personally, as well as to things only merchantable, and to insure or not, according to his judgment with reference to the place agreed. The bailee may not, to suit his own whim or interest, change his place of business and move the goods to a new place, and if the goods be destroyed, refuse the bailor both his property and its value. If the rule were otherwise, how would the physical extent of the justifiable removal be determined? Would the bailee be allowed to remove the repository a mile—out of the city, out of the country? The conventional requirements of the law, as to a bailor's care, would not contain the limitations. If, as here, the bailee no longer conducts the place at which the goods were received, it would be unreasonable to require the bailor to institute search to find his belongings. The point at which the bailee would be required to deliver the goods on demand might then have to be fixed by construction. Any other rule than that here applied would serve no useful purpose, but would easily conduce to misappropriation and fraud, put a premium on craftiness, jeopardize the property of the ordinarily prudent man, and wholly fail to afford adequate protection to the community in general.

. . . We are of the opinion that in this case, upon its own peculiar facts, the learned trial court properly charged the jury, as a matter of law, that the bailee obligated himself to keep the goods stored in the building in which they were received, because the undisputed facts show a specific agreement to store in a designated place. That agreement was made before the issuance of the warehouse receipt, in form indefinite as to place of storage. The conversation between the bailor and the bailee, taken in connection with the delivery of the goods and all immediate subsequent transactions, prove a valid parol agreement, in which were specified, with sufficient definiteness, the parties, the consideration, the goods to be stored, and the place of storage. The name of the bailor was not expressly mentioned, but he was just as obviously a party to the contract. The place was expressly mentioned and involved in the execution of the contract, and is just as much a part of its terms as the consideration. [DECISION FOR PLAINTIFF]

PROBLEMS

1 Plaintiff left a suit of clothes with defendant, the Nuway Cleaners & Dyers Co., to be cleaned and pressed. Two days later the proprietor of the cleaning and dyeing company

advised plaintiff that, after the suit was cleaned and pressed, the shop used for cleaning and dyeing and its contents were destroyed by fire. Assume that no one concerned was negligent with respect to the fire. Is the defendant liable for the loss of plaintiff's suit of clothes?

2 Defendants are the owners and operators of a barbershop and a beauty shop which consists of three rooms, the back room being the barbershop, the middle room being the operating room of the beauty shop, and the room facing the outside being a reception room. No attendant is kept in the reception room, and the interior of it is visible to outsiders through a glass door. There was a sign in a conspicuous place which read: "Not responsible for hats, coats, and purses." The plaintiff, on the day in question, came into the shop and sat in the reception room until she was invited into the operating room. She then removed her fur coat and hung it on a hook provided for wraps in the reception room. Is the defendant liable as a bailee of the fur coat?

3 Plaintiff, who was engaged in the business of selling shirts, delivered certain silk to defendant, a manufacturer of shirts. Plaintiff and defendant then entered into an agreement whereby defendant agreed to manufacture the shirts from the silk so delivered. The price was fixed at $100 for a dozen shirts, against which price a credit of $2.50 per yard was to be given plaintiff for the silk. Defendant carelessly left his place of business unlocked one night. The place was burglarized, and the silk was stolen. Who should bear the loss?

4 Plaintiff, the owner and operator of an airplane, was on a business trip from Michigan to Pennsylvania. The weather was very cold, the oil in the pipes of the plane was congealing, and plaintiff decided it was not safe to continue his flight. He therefore landed at the Toledo airport of the defendant-company. Plaintiff inquired of the manager of the airport about leaving the plane there for a while. The manager said it would be agreeable, but that the regular storage rate was $1.50 per night. Plaintiff thereupon left his plane at the Toledo airport and continued his trip by train. The next morning there was a low-lying, heavy fog. The manager, therefore, assisted pilots looking for the field by going up and piloting them into the field. He used the plane of plaintiff for one such mission, and within a few minutes—although he was exercising great or extraordinary care—the plane took a nose dive into the field and was totally destroyed. Plaintiff thereafter brought an action against the defendant-company to recover the value of the plane. What defense, if any, is available to the defendant?

5 On February 7, 1951, plaintiff purchased and paid $535 for an air-conditioner unit from the defendant store. Plaintiff was about to build a new home, and it was agreed that the unit would be retained by the defendant until plaintiff sent for it. The construction of the new home was delayed until 1954, at which time plaintiff sent for the air conditioner. It was then learned that the unit had disappeared, and the store's employees had no knowledge of what had happened to it—whether it was stolen, sold by mistake to another customer, deteriorated and thrown away, or otherwise lost. Plaintiff brought an action to recover the $535. Defendant attempted to escape liability on the ground that a bailee, in a bailment for the sole benefit of the bailor, is liable only for gross negligence. Decide.

6 About 10 A.M., plaintiff drove her automobile to the entrance of the parking lot of the defendant and received in exchange a claim check, on which was printed: "We close at 6 P.M. Cars left later at owner's risk." She put the check into her purse without reading it. An employee of the defendant then drove the automobile out of the entrance area into a larger adjoining fenced lot. At 6 P.M. an employee of defendant moved the automobile from the large enclosed area, parked it near the sidewalk, and left the keys in the automobile. When plaintiff returned to the parking lot at 7 P.M., her automobile was not there and no employee of defendant was present. The automobile was stolen, and plaintiff contends she is entitled to recover damages for its loss. Decide.

7   Carson owned 100 logs, which he desired to have sawed into lumber of certain specific dimensions. He transported the logs to the sawmill of Benson, and Carson and Benson entered into an agreement whereby Benson agreed to deliver to Carson a certain quantity of specified pieces of lumber sawed from the logs of Carson or from the logs of other owners which had been brought to the sawmill. During the following night, the sawmill and all the logs and lumber were destroyed by fire through the fault of no one concerned. Carson and Benson both contended that the loss must fall on the other. Who must bear the loss?

8   Slater, who planned to take an extensive trip, delivered certain household goods to The Storage Company for safekeeping. The Storage Company agreed in writing to redeliver the household goods to Slater upon his demand. While Slater was on his trip, Pratt, a creditor of Slater, brought an action against Slater, obtained a judgment, and attached the household goods. The Storage Company notified Slater at his last known address of the attachment. Slater did not, however, defend the action. The household goods were, therefore, sold by the sheriff at public auction. When Slater returned, he demanded that The Storage Company redeliver the household goods. Does Slater have a cause of action against The Storage Company for (1) damages or (2) conversion?

29
DOCUMENTS OF TITLE, CARRIERS, WAREHOUSEMEN

Documents of title are important in the storage and shipment of goods; they are also bought and sold as symbols of the goods; and they are used as a means of obtaining credit. The rules with respect to documents of title are found in Article 7, "Documents of Title," which defines documents of title, makes requirements for the form and content of the document, provides for the duties and liabilities of the issuer, provides in detail for the negotiation and transfer of the document, and regulates the procedure for the enforcement of the lien of the carrier and warehouseman.

It should be pointed out that the Federal Bills of Lading Act governs shipments in interstate commerce and the United States Warehouse Act, the purpose of which is to establish standards for the safe storing of agricultural products in federally licensed warehouses while in storage for interstate commerce, governs warehousemen licensed under that act. The majority of the warehousemen have not applied for a license, and those who have applied have done so mostly for the storage of grain and cotton. State statutes and decisions, therefore, govern the majority of the warehousemen. But the majority of the shipments today are made in interstate commerce. This results in a lack of uniformity between interstate and intrastate rules governing storage and transportation of goods. The rules found in Article 7, however, are very similar to those found in the Federal Bills of Lading Act and the United States Warehouse Act.

This chapter will be devoted to (1) documents of title and (2) carriers and warehousemen.

DOCUMENTS OF TITLE

Documents Defined The two most common documents of title are the bill of lading and the warehouse receipt. The definition of a document of title in section 1–201, however, is broad enough to include "any other document which in the regular course of business or financing is treated as adequately evidencing that the person in possession of it is entitled to receive, hold and dispose of the document and the goods it covers. To be a document of title a document must purport to be issued by or addressed to a bailee and purport to cover goods in the bailee's possession which are either identified or are fungible portions of an identified mass." Section 7–102 defines a bailee as "the person who by a warehouse receipt, bill of lading or other document of title acknowledges possession of goods and contracts to deliver them."

Warehouse Receipt and Bill of Lading Defined Section 1–201 defines a "warehouse receipt" as a receipt issued by a person engaged in the business of storing goods for hire, and a "bill of lading" as a document evidencing the receipt of goods for shipment issued by a person engaged in the business of transporting and forwarding goods. The definition of a bill of lading includes airbills, air consignment notes, air waybills, and bills issued by contract carriers and freight forwarders. Freight forwarder bills, through bills, and destination bills deserve especial mention.

(1) *Freight Forwarder Bills* Freight forwarders are in the business of soliciting goods in less-than-carload lots, accumulating them into carload lots, and arranging with a carrier to transport the goods as carload shipments, indicating destinations where the shipments are broken up and ultimately delivered to the consignees. The freight forwarder does not generally transport the goods himself but relies for a profit on the difference between the less-than-carload rates and the carload rates. The Interstate Commerce Commission requires the freight forwarder to issue bills of lading to his shippers. The carrier who receives the shipment, in turn, issues a second bill of lading to the freight forwarder.

(2) *Through Bills of Lading* Goods are frequently delivered to an initial carrier for shipment including services of connecting carriers, and section 7–302 provides that the carrier *may* issue a through bill. This section is patterned after the Interstate Commerce Act, but does not impose any obligation on the carrier to issue through bills in intrastate shipments. An initial carrier is liable for wrongs committed by a connecting carrier where a through bill is issued, but the connecting carrier is then liable to the initial carrier. This rule relieves the shipper of the hardship of bringing an action in a jurisdiction other than his own.

(3) *Destination Bills* Section 7–305, with respect to the function of a document of title, provides that "a carrier may, at the request of the consignor,

procure the bill to be issued at destination or at any other place designated in the request." It is thus made possible for the consignor to obtain a "destination bill." This provision is necessary because the use of order bills in connection with shipments by air is not too satisfactory, since the goods may arrive at destination before the document. This means that no one would be ready to take delivery from the carrier. The destination bill is also useful for carriers by truck, when such carriers do not have terminal facilities where the goods can be held to await the appearance of the consignee. The provision is only permissive, and it is left to the carriers whether or not they will act as an issuing agent. The procedure may be explained by the following illustration:

Brown, the seller, in Jacksonville delivers goods to an airline with instructions to issue a bill of lading in Boston to the First Bank. Brown thereupon receives a receipt incorporating this undertaking to issue a destination bill. The airline wires its Boston freight agent to issue the bill of lading as instructed by Brown. Brown then wires the First Bank in Boston a draft on Jones, the buyer. The First Bank indorses the bill of lading to Jones when he honors the draft. Brown would ordinarily act through his bank in Jacksonville by receiving credit from the bank in reliance on the contract of the airline to deliver a bill of lading to the order of the buyer in Boston.

Form and Content   Documents of title may be negotiable or nonnegotiable, and the distinction is important. A bailee, as a general rule, is under a positive duty to deliver the goods only when the negotiable document of title is surrendered. In the case of a nonnegotiable document of title, however, a bailee may deliver the goods upon a separate written authority without a surrender of the document. Additional importance of negotiability is indicated by the fact that the rights of conflicting claimants will be resolved in many instances on the basis of negotiability and by the further fact that the Interstate Commerce Commission has issued a rule to the effect that order bills of lading will be printed on yellow paper and straight bills of lading will be printed on white paper.

Section 7–104 defines a negotiable document of title as one which is negotiable if the terms provide that the goods are to be delivered to bearer or to the order of a named person. In addition, a document is likewise negotiable if it runs to a named person or assigns provided it is recognized as being negotiable in overseas trade. All other documents are nonnegotiable.

(1)   *Bills of Lading*   The Code does not enumerate the essential terms of a bill of lading. This is perhaps explained by the fact that carriers are regulated by agencies, such as the Interstate Commerce Commission, and it was apparently felt that the form and terms should likewise be regulated by those agencies.

A document may qualify as a bill of lading provided it evidences "the receipt of goods for shipment." It cannot be stated affirmatively but some of the elements of a bill of lading will undoubtedly include (a) the date of its issue; (b) the name of the person from whom the goods have been received; (c) a statement whether the goods received will be delivered to the bearer, a specified person, or to a specified person or his order; (d) the place where the goods have been received; (e) the place to which the goods are to be transported; (f) a description of the goods; and (g) the signature of the carrier.

(2) *Warehouse Receipts* Section 7–202 provides that a warehouse receipt need not be in any particular form. The failure to include certain essential terms within the written or printed provisions of the bill, however, imposes liability on the warehouseman to a person injured by such omissions. Some of the essential terms are: (a) the location of the warehouse where the goods are stored; (b) the date of issue of the receipt; (c) the consecutive number of the receipt; (d) a statement whether the goods received will be delivered to the bearer, to a specified person, or to a specified person or his order; (e) the rate of storage charges; (f) a description of the goods; (g) the signature of the warehouseman; and (h) a statement of the charges for which the warehouseman claims a lien on the goods covered by the receipt.

Functions of Documents of Title   Documents perform three functions: (1) as a receipt for a bailment, (2) as a contract for storage or shipment, and (3) as a symbol which evidences ownership of the goods.

The negotiable document operates in such a manner that the owner of goods is enabled to retain control of them while they are in the possession of a carrier or warehouseman. A normal procedure may be illustrated by a shipment of a carload of oranges from a seller in Florida to a buyer in New York. The seller may desire to retain control over the oranges as security for credit, or it may be that he desires to get his money from a discounting bank at the time of shipment. The desires of the seller, in either event, may be accomplished by the issuance of a bill of lading to the order of the seller. The seller, therefore, is both the consignor and the consignee. The name of the buyer will appear on the document as the party to be notified. The seller will then draw a draft on the buyer, attach the draft to the bill of lading, take them both to a bank in his home city, and indorse the draft and the bill of lading. The bank will then discount the draft—thus enabling the seller to get his money—and forward the documents to its correspondent bank in New York. The bank in New York upon receipt of the documents will make formal presentation of the draft to the drawee-buyer who, upon paying the draft, is given possession of the bill of lading. The carrier, upon arrival of the oranges in New York, will notify the buyer who, upon surrendering the order bill of lading, is given possession of the oranges.

The seller, however, may find it unnecessary to use the order bill of lading. This is frequently the case when the credit rating of the buyer is high and well known to the seller. The seller, in these circumstances, will probably ship the carload of oranges under the nonnegotiable bill—commonly referred to as a "straight" bill of lading—and name the buyer as the consignee. The carrier, when the shipper uses the straight bill of lading, will deliver the oranges to the consignee without requiring the surrender of the bill of lading.

Documents of title may play an important function in financing as well as in the storage and shipment of goods. Documents are used extensively in the field of finance in that large sums of money are lent by using the documents as security. The usual methods are: (1) A negotiable document will be issued which stipulates that delivery is to bearer or to the order of the depositor, or (2) a nonnegotiable document is issued which stipulates that delivery is to be to the lender, usually a bank. In either case, the document will be delivered to the lender as security for a loan. Documents, as collateral, are discussed more fully in Article 9, "Secured Transactions."

Negotiation of Documents Delving into the problem of negotiation poses three questions: Who may negotiate a document? How may a document be negotiated? Is negotiation impaired by fraud, mistake, or duress?

(1) *Who May Negotiate a Document* Section 7–501 provides, in effect, that a negotiable document may be negotiated by any person in possession of the same. This is true irrespective of how such possession may have been acquired if, by the terms of the document, the bailee undertakes to deliver the goods to the order of such person, or if, at the time of negotiation, the document is in such form that it may be negotiated by delivery. A thief or a finder, therefore, could negotiate an order document which has been indorsed in blank. Interstate order bills which have been indorsed in blank are negotiable by such persons in all jurisdictions of the United States by virtue of the Federal Bills of Lading Act.

(2) *Manner of Negotiation* A warehouse receipt, it will be remembered, is sometimes issued to bearer. If this is the case, it may be negotiated by delivery alone. The same is true of an order bill of lading which has been indorsed in blank. But order bills of lading, as well as order warehouse receipts, are negotiated by indorsement and delivery. The two types of indorsements in common use are the special indorsement—"Deliver to Brown"—followed by the signature of the holder of the document, and the blank indorsement which consists only of the signature of the holder.

(3) *Negotiation without Authority to Transfer* The validity of the negotiation of a document is not impaired by the fact that such negotiation was a breach of duty on the part of the person making the negotiation or by the fact that the owner of the document was deprived of the possession of the same by fraud, accident, mistake, duress, or conversion if the person to whom the document was negotiated, or a person to whom the document was subsequently negotiated, gave value therefor, in good faith, without notice of the breach of duty, or fraud, accident, duress, mistake, or conversion.

Warranties of Indorsers and Transferors It will be remembered that the law of commercial paper imposes the duty on an indorser of a draft or note to pay the instrument if, on certain conditions, the primary party failed to do so. The same is not true of an indorser of a negotiable document. The indorser of a document does not guarantee performance. The indorser of a document of title, therefore, cannot be held liable if the bailee fails to perform. The only remedy which the holder of a negotiable document has for misappropriation of, or refusal to deliver, the goods by the bailee, therefore, is an action against the bailee. Section 7–507 provides that the indorser or transferor of a negotiable document, however, impliedly warrants (1) that the document is genuine, (2) that he has no knowledge of any fact which would impair its validity or worth, and (3) that his negotiation or transfer is rightful and fully effective with respect to the title to the document and the goods it represents. It should be mentioned, however, that the warranties run to the immediate purchaser only.

Is a discounting bank liable for these warranties? Section 7–508 provides that collecting banks and other intermediaries which transfer documents warrant only their good faith and authority. This rule also applies to the intermediary who has purchased or made advances against the draft or claim which is to be collected.

Rights Acquired by Due Negotiation A document is duly negotiated when the holder takes the document in good faith in the regular course of business and for value. The holder of a document by due negotiation has rights that are paramount to the previous owner in case the document was stolen, taken by means of fraud, lost, or mislaid. Section 7–502 provides that the holder acquires title to the document and to the goods, including all rights accruing under the law of agency or estoppel. The holder also acquires, as a general rule, the right to have the bailee who issued the document hold the goods according to the terms of the document.

A holder who claims under a forged indorsement cannot acquire rights that will be paramount to the rights of the previous owner since the forged indorsement precludes a "due negotiation." Suppose the original bailor was a thief. It is obvious that the purchaser could acquire no property rights in the goods for the reason that a thief cannot pass title to stolen goods by depositing them in a warehouse, procuring a document of title, and negotiating it to a holder. The situation in which the original bailor was a thief should be sharply distinguished from the situation in which a thief steals a document in bearer form. A good faith purchaser who pays value in the ordinary course of business obtains greater rights than the person from whom the document was stolen.

Section 7–205 provides that a buyer in the ordinary course of business of fungible goods sold and delivered by a warehouseman who is also in the business of buying and selling such goods takes free of any claim under a warehouse receipt even though it has been duly negotiated.

Rights Acquired in the Absence of Due Negotiation The "umbrella" protection is given to the transferee where a negotiable document has not been duly negotiated. Section 7–504 provides that the transferee acquires the title and rights which his transferor had or had actual authority to convey. The absence of a due negotiation of a document may be the result of a failure of the transferor to indorse the document before delivering it to the transferee. In this case, the transferee has been given the specifically enforceable right to have his transferor supply any necessary indorsement by section 7–506. The transfer becomes a negotiation, however, only as of the time when the indorsement is supplied.

Transferee of Nonnegotiable Document The transferee of a nonnegotiable document acquires all "the title and rights which his transferor had actual authority to convey." This is also the "umbrella" protection. The transferee, in order to protect his rights, however, should give notice to the bailee of the transfer of the document. If such notice is not given, the transferee incurs the risk that his rights will be defeated. For example, suppose that Arnold sells a nonnegotiable document to Baker who fails to notify the bailee of the transfer. Suppose still further that Arnold took delivery of the goods from the bailee—and he may do so without having to surrender the nonnegotiable document—and sells such goods to Cabot, a good faith purchaser. Cabot will be protected under the provisions of section 7–504.

Altered Warehouse Receipts   Section 7–208 provides that a bona fide purchaser may treat as authorized the filling in of a blank in a negotiable warehouse receipt. An absolute liability, therefore, is imposed on warehousemen for the unauthorized filling in of blanks in a negotiable warehouse receipt. This rule imposes a much higher standard on the warehouseman than is imposed on the carrier. The apparent reason for this rule—although not too impressive—is the fact that truck drivers and others away from the place of business of the issuer frequently must prepare bills of lading; this is not true of the warehouseman. A warehouseman, therefore, must avoid the execution of warehouse receipts in blank. An unauthorized alteration in the warehouse receipt, however, may be enforced according to its original tenor.

Altered Bills of Lading   Section 7–306 provides that the unauthorized alteration or filling in of blanks in bills of lading leaves the bill enforceable according to its original tenor. Alterations and filling in of blanks, therefore, do not change the obligation of the issuer.

Lost and Destroyed Document   A bailee is under a duty to require the surrender of a negotiable document when the goods are delivered. Difficult problems arise, however, when the document is lost, stolen, or destroyed. Section 7–601 provides that the court may authorize the delivery of the goods or the issuance of a substitute document when the evidence satisfactorily shows that the document is missing. The claimant must post security approved by the court if the document is negotiable, but the posting of security is discretionary with the court if the document is nonnegotiable. The bailee may issue a substitute document without a court order, and he is protected from personal liability if he acts in good faith and requires the claimant to post a bond.

CARRIERS AND WAREHOUSEMEN

Carriers may be classfied as (1) contract, or private, carriers and (2) common carriers. A contract carrier engages to transport goods or passengers in a particular instance, and does not offer to serve the public generally. His liability is that of an ordinary bailee. A common carrier engages to transport goods and passengers without unjust discrimination, and legal liability is incurred for a failure to do so.

Warehousemen are sometimes classified as public and private warehouse-men, but the distinction is unimportant for most purposes. A warehouse company ordinarily carries on a business which concerns only the warehouseman and the private parties for whom he stores. The United States Warehouse Act, however, provides that a warehouseman shall receive for storage agricultural products without "discrimination between persons desiring to avail themselves of ware-house facilities." A few state statutes, governing for the most part grain and cotton, also require the warehouseman to store for everyone soliciting his services.

Strict Liability of the Common Carrier The common-law rule says that the common carrier is an insurer of the goods entrusted to him by the shipper. This rule imposes a strict liability—that is, without proof of negligence—on the common carrier for loss or damage to the goods. The general rule, however, is not without its exceptions. These are acts of God, acts of the public enemy, acts of public authorities, acts of the shipper, and damage due to the inherent nature of the goods themselves. These rules and exceptions prevail today in both intrastate and interstate transportation.

(1) *Acts of God* This exception to the general rule excuses the carrier from liability when the loss or damage results from an act due to natural forces as distinguished from an act due to human agency. An unprecedented wind or storm, extreme temperature, an earthquake, or a stroke of lightning are all considered acts of God. It has been settled law for a long time, however, that any loss caused by fire due to human origin—other than the shipper himself—irrespective of whether it was started maliciously or innocently, is not an act of God. The carrier may be entirely free from negligence, but the rule is the same. The carrier would not be liable, on the other hand, if the fire was caused by lightning. This exception to the general rule is weakened when it is realized that the carrier owes a duty to the shipper to exercise reasonable care to protect the goods against loss from natural forces.

(2) *Acts of the Public Enemy* Acts of the public enemy refer to acts of a public enemy of the state. They do not include acts of robbers, rioting mobs, and similar acts. Acts of the armed forces of another nation that is at war with the state to which the carrier owes allegiance fall within the exception.

(3) *Acts of Public Authorities* Acts of the state refer to a taking of the goods by legal process. Such taking may be a seizure of stolen goods or narcotics by the state itself; it may be the result of an action instituted by a private party. The carrier, in either event, is under a duty to notify the owner of the goods of the taking so that he may have an opportunity to appear in the proceeding and make a defense.

(4) *Acts of the Shipper* Justice demands that the carrier should not be liable when the loss is caused by an act of the shipper. The carrier would not be liable for any loss caused by fire, whether maliciously or innocently, which was the result of an act of the shipper. The usual instances of acts of the shipper pertain to defective packing or negligence on the part of the shipper in loading the car. Is the carrier liable when the goods are damaged due to defective packing?

The answer to the question depends on whether the defective packing is latent or apparent. If the defective packing is latent, the carrier is generally not liable; if the defective packing is apparent and the carrier accepts the goods, the carrier is generally liable. As a general rule, the carrier is not liable for loss occasioned by improper loading on the part of the shipper where the defective loading was not apparent at the time the carrier accepted the goods. The carrier is liable to the "holder of an order bill" under the Federal Bills of Lading Act and the "holder to whom a negotiable bill has been duly negotiated" under section 7–301 of the Code. In the case of a nonnegotiable bill, the complaining party must be "the owner" of the goods under the Federal Bills of Lading Act and a "consignee" who has given value in good faith under the Code. [*G.A.C. Commercial Corp. v. Wilson,* p. 369.]

(5) *Inherent Nature of the Goods* The carrier, according to this exception, is not liable for any loss arising out of the inherent characteristics of the goods. This rule is uniformly applied to livestock in transit, as where unruly animals injure or destroy themselves or die from fright. Perishable fruit and vegetables have been a great source of litigation, and there is some conflict in the decisions. With respect to wholly intrastate shipments, the rule in some states is that a carrier is not liable upon proof that it exercised reasonable care and complied with the shipper's instructions, such as the use of refrigerated cars. With respect to interstate shipments, the burden of proof is on the carrier to show that it was free from negligence and also that the damage was due to one of the exceptions relieving the carrier from liability. [*Missouri Pac. R.R. v. Elmore & Stahl,* p. 371.]

Disclaimer of Liability of Carrier Section 7–301 places a duty on the carrier to deliver goods which conform to the description in the bill of lading or to answer in damages. An illustration of nonreceipt or misdescription occurs when the agent of the carrier issues a bill of lading for a radio when he receives a television set, or the agent gives a receipt for 900 units when he actually receives 600 units. The carrier, therefore, will not know in many instances the content or quality of goods that are to be shipped. This section makes it clear that the carrier may avoid liability by appropriate statements on the bill of lading that the issuer does not know whether any part or all of the goods were, in fact, received or conform to the description. A carrier may disclaim liability by the use of such words as "shipper's weight, load, and count." This notation indicates that the goods were loaded by the shipper. Words such as "said to contain" will free the carrier from responsibility for misdescription resulting from improper loading by the shipper. The carrier's disclaimer, unlike the disclaimer of the warehouseman, does not have to be conspicuous since carriers have not been held liable for losses caused by the acts of the shipper. The words of disclaimer of liability, must, however, be truthful.

Disclaimer of Liability of the Warehouseman Section 7–203 places a duty on the warehouseman to deliver goods which conform to the description in the warehouse receipt or to answer in damages. Frequently the warehouseman will not know the content or quality of goods that are to be stored. This could easily be the situation where the bailor delivers packaged goods to the warehouseman. The warehouseman may avoid liability, however, by an appropriate statement on the warehouse receipt that he does not know whether any part or all of the goods were received or conformed to the description. Words such as "said to contain" or "contents, condition and quality unknown" written *conspicuously* on the warehouse receipt will suffice. These words will serve to relieve the warehouseman from acts of the bailor. The words of disclaimer, must, however, be truthful.

Duty of Care of Carrier Section 7–309, which is a generalized version of the Interstate Commerce Act, provides that a carrier must exercise that degree of care which "a reasonably careful man would exercise under like circumstances." As mentioned earlier, most states follow the view that the common carrier has a strict liability. The Code does not change this strict liability of a common carrier in intrastate commerce. The burdens on the common carrier which result from the strict-liability rule have been diminished to some extent by the "agreed valuation clause." The agreed valuation clause will determine the extent to which the carrier is liable for loss or damage to the goods. Such clauses have never been a device for absolving the carrier from a duty to exercise due care, but it is a valid reason for permitting the carrier to charge a freight rate which is commensurate with the agreed value of the goods. The Code provides, however, that the shipper must have the opportunity to declare a higher value, but it does not change tariffs, classifications, and storage regulations. It seems well recognized that the shipper-consignor need not make a conscious choice between different rates. It is likewise well recognized that this limitation of liability, which is incorporated in the bill of lading, is binding upon the shipper irrespective of whether or not the shipper reads the document. [*Kaufman v. Penn. R.R.*, p. 372.]

A contract or private carrier is liable for damages for loss of the merchandise only when such damages are the result of the carrier's negligence. Neither the contract nor the common carrier is permitted to disclaim its duty to exercise reasonable care, but an agreement is permissible which defines the standard by which the performance will be measured. In addition, carriers are permitted to include as a part of the bill of lading procedural limitations concerning the time and manner in which the shipper may file claims for loss or damage against the carrier. No limitation will be effective, however, where the carrier converts to itself property which belongs to a shipper.

Duty of Care of Warehouseman Section 7–204 provides that warehousemen are under a duty to exercise that degree of care as "a reasonably careful man would exercise under like circumstances." Unlike the common carrier, the warehouseman has never been regarded as an insurer of the goods. Agreed valuation clauses are nevertheless commonly found in warehouse receipts. The Code provides that increased rates may be charged based on increased valuation and that the bailor may demand that the valuation be increased. The warehouseman, however, cannot use the agreed valuation clause to protect himself from liability for conversion to his own use.

Duty to Provide Facilities and Services Common carriers are under a legal duty to provide reasonably adequate facilities and services which are employed by the carrier with substantial impartiality and at reasonable rates. The Interstate Commerce Commission is authorized to require carriers by railroad to file with the Commission their rules and regulations regarding car service, and may direct that such rules and regulations be incorporated in their tariff schedules.

Duty to Deliver the Goods The carrier and the warehouseman, unless excused, must deliver the goods to the person entitled, that is, to (1) the holder of a negotiable document or (2) the person to whom delivery is to be made according to written instructions under a nonnegotiable document. Upon delivery of the goods, the bailee must take up the negotiable document or note partial deliveries conspicuously on the document or be liable to any person to whom the document is thereafter negotiated. If the goods are destroyed, the modern view places the burden on the warehouseman to show that the destruction was not caused by the bailee's negligence. [*Canty v. Wyatt Storage Corp.*, p. 373.]

The excuses for nondelivery are enumerated in section 7–403. They may be summarized:

(1) Delivery of the goods to a person whose receipt was rightful as against the claimant. Suppose a thief deposits stolen goods in a warehouse, receives a negotiable receipt, and negotiates the receipt to a good faith purchaser. The warehouseman is not liable if he delivers the goods to the true owner.

(2) Damage to or delay, loss, or destruction of the goods for which the bailee is not liable.

(3) Exercise by a seller of his right to stop the goods in transit under the law of sales.

(4) A diversion or reconsignment of the goods.

(5) Any other lawful excuse.

Diversion and Reconsignment Modern commercial practice recognizes that on occasions the consignor and the consignee will have valid reasons for instructing the carrier to divert or reconsign goods that are in the process of shipment to another destination. Suppose the seller in San Francisco ships goods consigned to the buyer in New York. The buyer, while the goods are still in transit, locates a sub-buyer in Chicago, and instructs the carrier to divert the goods to Chicago. Suppose still further that the consignor and the consignee give conflicting instructions to the carrier. The carrier's position is uncertain if the goods are shipped on a straight bill of lading. Section 7–303 attempts to resolve this dilemma by permitting the carrier to obey the instructions of the consignor. The carrier may obey the instructions of the consignee, however, and assume the risk of delivery to the wrong person. It appears safe to conclude that the carrier will not assume this risk. If the carrier has not received conflicting instructions, the instructions of the consignee may be safely obeyed provided the goods have arrived at the billed destination or the consignee has possession of the bill of lading.

A final comment is necessary. The holder of a negotiable bill of lading is the proper party to give instructions for a diversion and reconsignment of the goods. The carrier should, however, note such changes on the bill so that notice of such changes will be given to a subsequent purchaser of the bill. If the changes are not noted, a subsequent purchaser to whom the bill was duly negotiated can hold the carrier liable in accordance with the original terms of the bill.

Lien of the Carrier   Section 7–307 gives both the common carrier and the contract carrier a specific lien on the goods covered by the bill of lading. The lien covers all charges for storage and transportation from the date the carrier receives the goods, including (1) charges at the terminal point of transportation, (2) expenses necessary for preservation of the goods, and, if necessary, (3) expenses for a sale to satisfy the lien. The lien of the carrier is good against the consignor and against any person entitled to the goods. This rule assumes that the carrier had no notice that the consignor lacked authority to subject the goods to such charges. The lien is a possessory lien, and the carrier loses his lien if he voluntarily delivers the goods or if he unjustifiably refuses to deliver the goods.

Lien of the Warehouseman   Section 7–209 gives the warehouseman a specific lien and a general lien. Both liens are possessory, and the warehouseman loses his lien if he voluntarily delivers the goods or if he wrongfully refuses to deliver the goods. This rule prevents a wrongdoer from destroying the lien. Suppose the bailor wrongfully seized the goods from the warehouseman. The warehouseman would lose possession, but his lien would continue. The specific lien attaches automatically, without a notation on the warehouse receipt, to goods stored under a nonnegotiable receipt. However, the specific lien can be made a general lien by noting on the receipt that "a lien is claimed for charges and expenses in relation to other goods." Suppose the owner of goods stores them in a warehouse in January. The warehouseman has a specific lien on the goods and may retain possession of the goods until the charges are paid as discussed above. If the warehouseman surrenders the goods voluntarily without collecting the charges, the lien is terminated. Suppose further that the goods are delivered by the warehouseman to the bailor without collecting the charges, and the owner stores different goods in the same warehouse in June. The warehouseman may, in addition to the specific lien, claim a general lien on the goods presently stored for those charges which arose from the January storage. These rules are also applicable to a negotiable receipt, except that the lien is limited to the amount or rate specified on the receipt as against a holder by due negotiation of the receipt. If no amount or rate is noted on the receipt, the lien is limited to a reasonable charge for storage of the specific goods.

Commencement of Liability of Common Carrier   The extraordinary liability of the carrier commences when the goods are delivered to and accepted by the carrier for immediate transportation. The carrier sometimes receives the goods into its own warehouse, on platforms, or on partly loaded cars awaiting further instructions of the shipper. This frequently happens with respect to the destination of the goods. The liability of the carrier, in these circumstances, is that of a warehouseman. But if the goods are placed in the warehouse of the carrier as a mere accessory to the carriage, the extraordinary liability of the carrier commences upon receipt of the goods. The general rule, quite broadly stated, is that the extraordinary liability of the carrier does not commence so long as something remains to be done on the part of the shipper. This "remaining something" commonly pertains to things such as loading or the giving of shipping instructions.

Termination of Liability of Common Carrier   As a general rule, the liability of a common carrier as an insurer changes to that of a warehouseman after the carrier has fulfilled the carriage contract and is holding the goods for the consignee, but a definite rule cannot be stated as to the precise point of time when the liability changes to that of a warehouseman only. The bill of lading or a tariff frequently provides that goods not removed within a specified time after arrival at destination may be held by the carrier as a warehouseman. A delivery by the carrier may be sufficient which conforms to the custom of the place of destination where the mode of delivery is not specified in the contract of carriage. An express company will ordinarily make personal delivery of the goods to the consignee. Its liability as a common carrier, therefore, ordinarily ceases when it delivers the goods, or offers to deliver them, to the consignee at his place of business or residence.

Termination of Storage   The obligation of the warehouseman commences when he assumes control of the goods, and terminates when he delivers the goods to the proper person. Section 7–206, however, provides some specific rules for the termination of storage at the option of the warehouseman. If the goods are stored for a fixed period, the warehouseman may notify the bailor and other persons known to claim an interest in the goods that he intends to terminate the storage upon expiration of the fixed time. Most storage contracts, however, are for an indefinite time. This means that the warehouseman cannot terminate the storage immediately. He must give notice of the termination, which cannot take effect less than thirty days after notification of the termination. Charges for storage are usually computed on a monthly basis, and the framers of the Code felt that thirty days would be the appropriate time for terminating the indefinite storage contract. In addition, the person entitled to the goods will have ample opportunity for placing himself in a position to take delivery.

(1) *Perishable Goods*   If the goods are perishables, a thirty-day delay might conceivably make the warehouseman's lien valueless. The warehouseman may, therefore, terminate the lien by giving reasonably shorter notice than thirty days. It should be mentioned that the person entitled to the goods may redeem such goods at any time before the foreclosure sale. If the sale occurs and there is a deficiency, the warehouseman may collect it from the person who is liable for the storage charges under the contract. If there is a surplus, on the other hand, it belongs to the person entitled to the surplus.

(2) *Hazardous Goods* A similar situation occurs when the warehouse-man discovers that the goods are hazardous to the warehouse or other goods. This section provides that the warehouseman may terminate the storage by giving notice to all persons known to claim an interest in the goods. The period of time for giving notice must be reasonable under the circumstances, but undoubtedly it may actually be a very short period of time. If the warehouseman knew of the hazard at the time he accepted the goods for storage, he cannot take advantage of the emergency procedures in terminating the storage.

Enforcement of Warehouseman's Lien The warehouseman may sell the goods if they are not removed provided that the storage has been properly terminated. Section 7–210 provides the procedures when the warehouseman forecloses his lien. Goods that are hazardous may be sold at a public or a private sale without advertising provided that all interested persons have been notified. If a sale is not possible, the warehouseman may dispose of the goods in any reasonable manner without incurring any liability by reason of such disposal. A public sale is required, however, in the case of goods that are declining in value, and such a sale cannot occur in less than one week after a single advertisement or posting.

CASES

G.A.C. Commercial Corp. v. Wilson, 271 F. Supp. 242 (N.Y. 1967). Action by G.A.C. Commercial Corporation, plaintiff, against John D. Wilson, Dudley Luce, Burton C. Meighan, Abe Cooper, Sheru Lalvani, and Norwood & St. Lawrence Railroad Company, defendants. The individual defendants, with the exception of Sheru Lalvani, are described as officers and/or directors of St. Lawrence Pulp & Paper Company (St. Lawrence), but this motion for judgment on the pleadings is addressed solely against Norwood & St. Lawrence Railroad Company (Norwood).

St. Lawrence entered into an accounts receivable financing agreement with plaintiff by the terms of which St. Lawrence agreed to pledge, assign, and transfer to plaintiff all of the right, title, and interest of St. Lawrence in and to the accounts receivable owed to St. Lawrence. In accordance with the terms of this agreement, St. Lawrence forwarded to the plaintiff sixty-two invoices and accompanying straight bills of lading, sixty of which concerned interstate shipments. The other two concerned intrastate shipments. Plaintiff, upon receipt of the invoices and bills of lading, ultimately advanced $356,883.57 to St. Lawrence. This sum has not been repaid, and St. Lawrence is now bankrupt. The carrier is charged with failing to require any inspection of the quantity of paper shipped before verifying the bills of lading.

Frederick van Pelt Bryan, District Judge: The method by which the alleged fraudulent scheme was carried out appears for purposes of this motion to be as follows: The bankrupt St. Lawrence, as part of its facilities in Norfolk, New York, maintained a railroad siding connected with the lines of defendant carrier which had a freight office approximately one-eighth of a mile from the siding. St.

Lawrence was permitted to load freight at its spur track in preparation for shipments on defendant's line. The railroad cars were sealed by St. Lawrence with seals provided by the railroad. St. Lawrence also prepared the bills of lading on blanks furnished in quadruplicate by defendant Norwood. The bills thus prepared were then presented to Norwood's agent who signed the original and one copy without inspecting the contents of the cars. No notation such as "contents of packages unknown" or "shipper's weight, load and count" was written on the bills. The signed copies were returned to St. Lawrence and forwarded with the invoices to G.A.C. which made advances on the goods described, which, as it turned out, had not been shipped.

Since sixty of the bills of lading were issued by a common carrier for the transportation of goods in interstate commerce, the issues as to these bills are controlled by the provisions of the Federal Bills of Lading Act. . . .

Under section 22 of the Act . . . "the carrier shall be liable to . . . the holder of an order bill, who has given value in good faith, relying upon the description therein of the goods . . . for damages caused by the nonreceipt by the carrier of all or part of the goods upon or prior to the date therein shown." However, the liability of the carrier for nonreceipt extends only to "the owner of goods covered by a straight bill."

It is clear that a party in the position of Norwood is not included within the narrow category of those liable on a straight bill under the federal legislation. In the first place there is no question that the straight bills of lading here involved are nonnegotiable.

As a consequence plaintiff G.A.C., as apparent transferee of these bills and invoices representing accounts receivable under the agreement with St. Lawrence, upon notification to the carrier of the transfer, could only "Become the direct obligee of whatever obligations the carrier owed to the transferor of the bill immediately before notification." Norwood obviously owed St. Lawrence nothing because no goods in fact were received. There was therefore no outstanding obligation to G.A.C.

Plaintiff G.A.C. fares no better with respect to the two bills of lading representing intrastate shipments in New York. . . . Although the awkward term "owner" in 49 U.S.C. has been replaced by the word "consignee" in the Uniform Commercial Code, section 7-301, . . . which would govern the issues of liability on . . . the bills of lading representing an intrastate shipment, the change is immaterial for purposes of this case. Plaintiff, perhaps an assignee, transferee or pledgee of the nonnegotiable bills, though it claims not to be, is certainly not a "consignee," which is the only party protected. . . .

G.A.C., as a knowledgeable lender, is fully aware of the risks inherent in straight bills, and could well have required order bills to protect itself. It nevertheless chose to rely upon straight bills to lend money to the now bankrupt St. Lawrence at a profitable rate of interest. Wiser now, G.A.C. seeks to shift its loss to Norwood, an undoubtedly solvent defendant. The Federal Bills of Lading Act protects against this type of hindsight by requiring the lender to accept this kind of security subject to the defenses between the carrier and the shipper. [DECISION FOR THE DEFENDANT CARRIER]

Missouri Pac. R.R. v. Elmore & Stahl, 377 U.S. 134 (1964). Action by Elmore & Stahl, respondent, against Missouri Pacific Railroad Company, petitioner, to recover damages to honeydew melons shipped under a straight bill of lading. The Texas Supreme Court affirmed a decision by the Texas Court of Appeals in favor of the shipper, and the carrier brought this appeal.

Respondent, a fruit shipper, sought to recover from petitioner, a common carrier, for damage to 640 crates of honeydew melons in Car ART 35042 from Rio Grande City, Texas, to Chicago, Illinois. At the trial, the jury were instructed that "inherent vice" means "any existing defects, diseases, decay or the inherent nature of the commodity which will cause it to deteriorate with lapse of time." The jury were then asked specifically whether they found from the evidence that the condition of the melons on arrival was due solely to an inherent vice at the time the melons were received by the carrier for transportation. The jury found that the melons were in good condition when delivered to the carrier for transportation; that they were damaged upon arrival in Chicago; that the carrier was not negligent; and that the damage was not due to an "inherent vice."

Mr. Justice Stewart: The question presented in this case is whether a common carrier which has exercised reasonable care and has complied with the instructions of the shipper, is nonetheless liable to the shipper for spoilage in transit of an interstate shipment of perishable commodities, when the carrier fails to prove that the cause of the spoilage was the natural tendency of the commodities to deteriorate. . . .

The parties agree that the liability of a carrier for damage to an interstate shipment is a matter of federal law controlled by federal statutes and decisions. The Carmack Amendment of 1906, section 20 (11) of the Interstate Commerce Act, makes carriers liable "for the full actual loss, damage, or injury . . . caused by" them to property they transport, and declares unlawful and void any contract, regulation, tariff, or other attempted means of limiting this liability. It is settled that this statute has two undisputed effects crucial to the issue in this case: First, the statute codifies the common-law rule that a carrier, though not an absolute insurer, is liable for damage to goods transported by it unless it can show that the damage was caused by "(a) the act of God; (b) the public enemy; (c) the act of the shipper himself; (d) public authority; (e) or the inherent vice or nature of the goods." Second, the statute declares unlawful and void any "rule, regulation, or other limitation of any character whatsoever" purporting to limit this liability. Accordingly, under federal law, in an action to recover from a carrier for damage to a shipment, the shipper establishes his prima facie case when he shows delivery in good condition, arrival in damaged condition, and the amount of damages. Thereupon, the burden is upon the carrier to show both that it was free from negligence and that the damage to the cargo was due to one of the excepted causes relieving the carrier from liability. . . .

The petitioner appears to recogize that, except in the case of loss arising from injury to livestock in transit—a well-established exception to the general common-law rule based on the peculiar propensity of animals to injure themselves and each other—no distinction was made in the earlier federal cases between perishables and nonperishables. It is said, however, that the "large-scale development, in relatively recent years, of long distance transportation of fresh fruit and vegetables in interstate commerce has led to the evolution" of a new federal rule governing the carrier's liability for spoilage and decay of perishables, similar to the "livestock rule," which absolves the carrier from liability upon proof that the carrier has exercised reasonable care, and has complied with the shipper's instructions. We are aware of no such new rule of federal law. . . .

Finally, all else failing, it is argued that as a matter of public policy the burden ought not to be placed upon the carrier to explain the cause of spoilage, because where perishables are involved, the shipper is peculiarly knowledgeable about the commodity's condition at and prior to the time of shipment, and is therefore in the best position to explain the cause of the damage. Since this argument amounts to a suggestion that we now carve out an exception to an unquestioned rule of long standing upon which both shippers and carriers rely, and which is reflected in the freight rates set by the carrier, the petitioner must sustain a heavy burden of persuasion. The general rule of carrier liability is based upon the sound premise that the carrier has peculiarly with its knowledge "[a]ll the facts and circumstances upon which [it] may rely to relieve [it] of [its] duty. . . . In consequence, the law casts upon [it] the burden of the loss which [it] cannot explain or, explaining, bring within the exceptional case in which [it] is relieved from liability." We are not persuaded that the carrier lacks adequate means to inform itself of the conditions of goods at the time it receives them from the shipper, and it cannot be doubted that while the carrier has possession, it is the only one in a position to acquire the knowledge of what actually damaged a shipment entrusted to its care. [DECISION FOR RESPONDENT]

Kaufman v. Penn. R.R.,   47 N.Y.S.2d 639 (1944). Action by Albert Kaufman and others, plaintiffs, against Pennsylvania Railroad Company, defendant. The plaintiffs delivered to the defendant in the City of New York a suitcase to be transported by railroad to Jacksonville, Florida. The suitcase arrived at its destination with its contents pilfered, and this action was brought to recover damages for the actual value of its contents.

Genung, Justice: The plaintiffs accepted a bill of lading "Subject to the classifications and tariff in effect on the date of issue of this bill of lading."

The suitcase is described in the bill of lading as "personal effects." The plaintiffs prepaid the freight charges and such notation appears on the bill of lading signed by the plaintiffs and the defendant. The defendant relies on the tariff described as "Consolidated freight classification No. 411" duly filed and posted by it to limit its liability for the loss.

"Personal effects" under the aforesaid tariff are transported at released valuations and those values are set up in the classifications, under the general caption of "Household Goods," as the basis for graduated freight rates. The classification item "24215 et seq." gives the shipper the choce of different freight rates based on a limited or released value, the lowest of which covers articles released at values not exceeding ten cents per pound. Graduated rates are provided in the classification based on the ranges of the released values set up therein. The freight rate paid by the shipper, under which the shipment was transported, was the lowest of the available rates. Having selected and paid the lowest freight rate, the shipper seeks, nevertheless, to recover the actual value of the loss. . . .

Carriers are permitted to set up rates based on released valuations and thereby limit their liability. 49 U.S.C.A. sec.20(11). Classifications and tariffs duly filed by carriers with the Interstate Commerce Commission have the same force and effect of statute, of which the shippers are presumed to have knowledge, and are binding on the shippers, and the shippers are bound to know the relation between the values and the rates charged and provided for in the classifications, and the provisions of the published tariffs.

The bill of lading issued by the defendant for the shipment herein involved together with the classifications and schedules on file with the Commission constitute the contract of carriage.

The shippers agreed, accepted, and acted upon the freight rate and made a valid choice of the different values available to them for transportation of the shipment. The plaintiffs selected the lowest rate which attached the released value of ten cents per pound, which in this case, since the shipment weighed 100 pounds, releases the value of the shipment at $10. [DECISION FOR PLAINTIFFS FOR THE SUM OF $10]

Canty v. Wyatt Storage Corp., 56 S.E.2d 582 (Va. 1967). Action by Thomas Canty and Margaret Canty, husband and wife, plaintiffs, against Wyatt Storage Corporation, defendant, to recover for breach of contract to return household goods delivered to defendant for storage. The parties stipulated that the value of the goods involved was $600.

Plaintiffs proved an oral contract of bailment with defendant, the delivery of the goods to defendant, and the failure of defendant to return the goods because of a destruction of the bailed property when the warehouse of defendant containing the goods was consumed by fire. The plaintiffs then rested their case. They contend that defendant must go forward with the evidence and show that the fire was not caused by any lack of care on the part of defendant. Defendant contends that plaintiffs must go forward with the evidence again and show that the fire was caused by the negligence of the defendant.

Spratley, Justice: There is a conflict of judicial opinion as to the respective duties of the bailor and bailee in a case of this character. Some courts take the view that in such a situation, there is no presumption that the fire was caused by the negligence of the bailee, and the burden is on the bailor to prove such negligence by a preponderance of the evidence. Other courts have adopted the more modern view that where a bailor makes out a prima facie case, and the fact appears that the bailed goods were destroyed by fire, the burden of showing that the fire did not originate from the bailee's negligence is upon the latter. . . . In Virginia we have adopted the modern rule. . . .

The obligation of a warehouseman with reference to property entrusted to him is set out in section 7–403, as follows:

(1) The bailee must deliver the goods to a person entitled under the document . . . unless and to the extent that the bailee establishes any of the following:

(a) . . .

(b) damage to or delay, loss or destruction of the goods for which the bailee is not liable.

In the note of the Code Commission to that section, this is said:

The official text of the Uniform Commercial Code offers as optional language at the end of subsection (1)(b) of the section, the following: ["but the burden of establishing negligence in such cases is on the person entitled under the document."]

The optional language was omitted to accord with Virginia law as noted in the Virginia Comment to this section. . . .

The effect of our rule is not to shift the ultimate burden of proof from bailor to bailee, but merely to shift to the bailee the burden of going forward with the evidence to prove that the loss was not due to such failure to exercise due care. . . .

For the foregoing reasons, we hold that . . . Wyatt having failed to overcome the prima facie case made out against it, final judgment in the sum of $600 will be here entered for plaintiffs, with interest and costs. [DECISION FOR PLAINTIFF]

PROBLEMS

1 Twenty-four bales of cotton belonging to various planters were stolen by Carr. He carried the cotton to the defendant, a warehouse company, and received negotiable receipts in three fictitious names. He then took the receipts to nearby towns and sold them to plaintiffs and received checks in payment. He indorsed the checks in the names of the three fictitious payees and received cash. He then disappeared and his whereabouts are unknown. The warehouse company was not negligent in issuing the receipts. Plaintiffs claim they are entitled to the cotton. The various planters also claim that they are entitled to the cotton. Decide.

2 The seller, in San Francisco, shipped certain merchandise to the buyer, in Chicago, taking a bill of lading from the railway company for the delivery of the merchandise in Chicago, to the order of the seller, buyer to be notified. The seller then drew a draft on the buyer, attached the same to the bill of lading, took them both to his bank in San Francisco, indorsed the draft and bill of lading, and received his money for the merchandise. The bank in San Francisco then forwarded the documents to its correspondent bank in Chicago for collection, with instructions to surrender the bill of lading upon payment of the draft. When the merchandise arrived in Chicago, the buyer fraudulently procured its delivery without production of the bill of lading and at once deposited the merchandise in a public warehouse, taking negotiable warehouse receipts therefor, which he negotiated to a purchaser in good faith and for value. The good faith purchaser claims title to the merchandise by virtue of the warehouse receipts. The bank in Chicago claims title by virtue of the bill of lading and draft. Decide.

3 Plaintiff delivered to defendant, a common carrier, 29 bales of cotton with the understanding that the cotton would be shipped when plaintiff delivered 71 more bales, so as to constitute a shipment of 100 bales. The defendant placed the 29 bales on a certain platform used for shipping purposes. The first night the cotton was on the platform 23 bales were destroyed by fire without any negligence on the part of defendant. Is the defendant liable, if at all, as a carrier or a warehouseman?

4 Defendant shipped a carload of machinery from Massachusetts to Bridgeport, Connecticut. The carrier issued to the defendant a straight bill of lading and named the defendant both the consignor and the consignee. The defendant then arranged by telephone to sell the machinery to Brown, indorsed the bill with a special indorsement, and mailed it to Brown. Defendant then learned of the insolvency of Brown and notified the carrier to return the machinery to the defendant. In the meantime, Brown sold the machinery for cash to the plaintiff, a bona fide purchaser, and indorsed the bill with a blank indorsement, Plaintiff presented the bill to the carrier, and the carrier informed plaintiff that the machinery had been returned to defendant. Plaintiff thereupon brought an action to recover the machinery or its value. Decide.

5 Gray ordered an expensive machine from the manufacturer and paid the purchase price in advance. The manufacturer shipped the machine by carrier and received a bill of lading, which was mailed to Gray. On the day the machine arrived at destination, Gray sold the bill of lading to Parker. Gray went immediately thereafter to the office of the carrier and took delivery of the machine, which he sold to Drake. Both Parker and Drake claim a prior right in the machine. Explain the difference in the outcome of this controversy which would result from the bill of lading being negotiable or nonnegotiable.

6 Aaron stored a sealed box with the X Warehouse, and, at the time the box was stored, he stated that the box contained books. The X Warehouse, therefore, issued a negotiable warehouse receipt for "books." Aaron negotiated the warehouse receipt to Dixon, who bought in good faith and for value. Dixon thereafter surrendered the warehouse receipt to the X Warehouse, and the warehouseman delivered the sealed box to him. It was then discovered that the sealed box contained worthless pieces of wood, and the X Warehouse was required to respond in damages. Explain how the X Warehouse could have avoided this liability under the Code.

Part

6

SECURED TRANSACTIONS

30
SECURED TRANSACTIONS: INTRODUCTION

Secured transactions were handled rather haphazardly under pre-Code law. The security devices were known by various titles, such as conditional sales and chattel mortgages. A conditional sale is a contract for the sale of goods under which possession of the goods is delivered to the buyer but the seller reserves the title until the buyer has performed the conditions of the contract, which usually consists of payment of the purchase price. Section 2–401 provides that any retention or reservation of title by the seller of goods is limited in effect to a reservation of a security interest.

For those who are not familiar with pre-Code law of conditional sales, an illustration may be helpful: A farmer who wished to purchase a tractor but did not have the full purchase price would arrange to purchase the tractor from a dealer on time. The farmer would then sign a conditional sales contract setting forth the terms of the arrangement. The title would remain in the seller, but the buyer would have possession of the tractor. Under the Code: The farmer would sign a security agreement. The writing evidencing the security agreement, however, may be entitled "conditional sales contract." A chattel mortgage may be, but is not necessarily, given in a transaction for the sale of goods. It may be, and frequently is, given where the borrower gives the lender a lien on a chattel as security for the loan. It is a mortgage on personal property as distinguished from a mortgage on real property. The Code does not abolish previous security devices by prohibiting their use. It is permissible, therefore, to use the pre-Code forms. The Code, nevertheless, governs the transaction, and the security device is known as the "security agreement." The new forms of the security agreement are becoming more and more widespread in use.

The terminology in Article 9, "Secured Transactions," is not highly technical, but it is necessary that the meaning of certain words and phrases be clearly understood before undertaking to study the basic operation of secured transactions. This is concededly a tedious process, but it is essential. A "secured party" may obtain a "security interest" in "collateral" by entering into a "security agreement." To use a simple illustration: Suppose Brown borrows $500 from the First Bank and uses his television set as security for the loan. Brown, the debtor, and the First Bank, the secured party, have entered into a security agreement using the television set as collateral whereby the secured party obtains a security interest in the television set.

COLLATERAL CLASSIFIED
The collateral may be classified as tangible or intangible personal property.

Tangible Personal Property Some very common forms of tangible personal property that may be used as collateral are automobiles, jewelry, sterling silver, and the like. The Code calls tangible personal property "goods," and section 9–109 classifies goods into the following four categories: consumer goods, equipment, farm products, and inventory. It may be well to keep in mind that goods may fall into different categories at different times. The same property cannot, however, fall into two different categories at the same time as to the same person. The classification of goods is nevertheless important in determining the rights of persons who buy goods from a debtor subject to a security interest, in determining the priority of claims, in determining the place of filing the financing statement, and in working out the rights of the parties after default.

(1) *Consumer Goods* Goods are "consumer goods" if they are used or bought for use primarily for personal, family, or household purposes.

(2) *Equipment* Goods are "equipment" if they are used or are bought for use primarily in business, including farming, a profession, a nonprofit organization, or a governmental agency. The principal test is a negative one: Goods are classed as equipment if they are neither inventory, farm products, nor consumer goods. Some examples of equipment are machinery used in manufacturing; a tractor used in farming; trucks and automobiles used in business; and a television set used by a physician in the waiting room of his office. Would the television set be classified as consumer goods if the physician occasionally took it home on weekends? The set would undoubtedly be equipment, because the primary use of the goods is controlling in determining whether the goods are equipment or consumer goods.

(3) *Farm Products* Goods are "farm products" only if they are in the possession of a debtor engaged in raising, fattening, or grazing livestock, or other

farming operations. This includes crops, livestock, and supplies used or produced in farming; and products of crops or livestock in the unmanufactured state, such as ginned cotton, wool clip, maple syrup, milk, and eggs. Goods are neither equipment nor inventory if they are farm products.

The term "farming operations" is not defined by the Code. It seems clear, however, that farming operations include raising livestock as well as crops, and that fowl would also be "livestock" since eggs are products of livestock. How would the products of an amateur home grower be classified? They would be "consumer goods" if they were used primarily for family or household purposes.

(4) *Inventory*   Inventory includes goods held for sale or lease. Inventory also includes raw materials, work in process, or materials used or consumed in a business. Goods held for sale or lease include television sets, refrigerators, and the like held by a retailer, wholesaler, or distributor for the purpose of sale or lease. This would include motor vehicles held by a rental service for lease to customers. "Materials used or consumed in business" would include steel held by a manufacturer in producing an automobile; coal to be used by the manufacturer to power his machinery; fuel oil to be used to heat the building in which the business is conducted; and containers to be used to package the goods.

It is to be remembered, however, that goods are not to be classified by looking solely to the nature of the goods. To illustrate: A farmer raises sheep as a business; the sheep are farm products. The farmer shears the sheep and sells the wool to a manufacturer who processes the wool into woolen cloth; the cloth is inventory. If the cloth is manufactured into suits and one suit is sold to a customer, the suit would be consumer goods.

Intangible Personal Property   Intangible personal property has no physical existence as does tangible personal property—a television set—but is only a right to receive property, such as a patent right, an insurance policy, and a share of stock. The Code classifies intangible personal property as instruments, documents, chattel paper, accounts, and general intangibles.

(1) *Instruments*   Section 9-105 defines the word "instrument" as a negotiable instrument as that word is used in Article 3 on commercial paper, or an investment security as those words are used in Article 8 on investment securities. This definition would include drafts, promissory notes, checks, certificates of deposit, bonds, and shares of stock. In its broadest use, the term includes other writings which evidence a right to the payment of money which is transferred by delivery with any necessary indorsement. A writing which is itself a security agreement or lease with respect to specific goods, however, is not an instrument although it otherwise meets the term of the definition.

(2) *Documents*   The word "document" includes bills of lading, warehouse receipts, and the like. To be a document of title "a document must purport to be issued by or addressed to a bailee and purport to cover goods in the bailee's possession which are either identified or are fungible portions of an identified mass." The definition is broad enough to include documents which may develop in the future for use in transporting freight by air. It should be kept in mind,

however, that the document must purport to be issued by or addressed to a bailee. It must also purport to cover goods in the possession of the bailee.

Section 7–201 provides an important exception to the rule that a document must purport to be issued by or addressed to a bailee. This section provides that a receipt in the nature of a warehouse receipt issued for distilled spirits or agricultural commodities has the effect of a warehouse receipt. This is true where a bond is required by statute for the withdrawal of such goods or if a license is required for the issuance of such a receipt and even though the receipt is issued by the owner who is not a warehouseman.

(3) *Chattel Paper* The words "chattel paper" are defined in section 9–105 as a "writing or writings which evidence both a monetary obligation and a security in or lease of specific goods." When a transaction is evidenced both by a security agreement or a lease and by an instrument or a series of instruments, the group of writings taken together constitutes chattel paper. It may be well to mention that chattel paper is, in most instances by definition, a security agreement.

The chattel paper security agreement is sometimes the collateral. Suppose a dealer transfers a security agreement to the bank to secure a loan. The security agreement is now the type of collateral called "chattel paper," the bank is the secured party, the dealer is the debtor, and the farmer is the "account debtor," that is, he is the person who is obligated on an account or chattel paper. In the above illustration, there are two separate and distinct secured transactions.

(4) *Account* The definition of "account" includes a right to payment for goods sold or leased, or for services rendered, which right to payment is not evidenced by an instrument or chattel paper. The account may be earned or unearned by performance, but performance is not important with respect to the meaning of the word "account." It should be noted that a charter or other contract involving the use or hire of a vessel is an account.

Suppose a golfer purchased and charged a set of golf clubs from the Sports Shop for $300 on May 1 but the obligation of the golfer to pay the $300 would not be due until May 31. The obligation is nevertheless a present form of collateral which the Sports Shop could utilize as security. This is true irrespective of whether the golfer was permitted to take possession of the clubs or whether the Sports Shop retained possession of them. This same transaction, however, could be an "instrument" or "chattel paper." Suppose the golfer signed a promissory note as security for the clubs. The Sports Shop would then have an instrument, which could be used as collateral. Suppose the golfer signed a security agreement. The Sports Shop would have chattel paper, which could be used as collateral.

(5) *General Intangibles* The definition in section 9–106 of "general intangibles" includes intangibles which do not fall within the definition of the other five kinds of intangibles (account, chattel paper, documents, instruments, and money). The definition would also include personal property not within the definition of "goods." The inclusion of "general intangibles" as collateral looks more to the future than the present. Goodwill, literary rights, rights to performance, copyrights, trade-marks, and patents are examples of personal-property interests which would fall within the definition of general intangibles.

It should be pointed out that section 1–206 provides that a contract for the sale of personal property beyond $5,000 is not enforceable unless there is some writing which indicates that a contract for sale has been entered into between the parties at a stated price. The writing must reasonably identify the subject matter and be signed by the party against whom enforcement is sought. This provision will apply principally to general intangibles. It does not apply to contracts for the sale of goods, securities, or security agreements.

POLICY AND SUBJECT MATTER OF ARTICLE 9

Section 9–102 provides that this article, as a general rule, applies to any transaction, irrespective of its form, if it is intended to create a security interest in personal property or fixtures and to the sale of accounts or chattel paper. Security interests are governed by this article when created by contract, including pledge, assignment, chattel mortgage, chattel trust, trust deed, factor's lien, equipment trust, conditional sale, trust receipt, other lien or title retention contract, and lease or consignment intended as security. [*Witmer v. Kleppe,* p. 383.]

CASES

Witmer v. Kleppe, 469 F.2d 1245 (W.Va. 1972). Appeal by Kenneth Witmer, d.b.a. Witmer Foods, appellant, against Thomas S. Kleppe, Administrator of the Small Business Administration, appellee. The critical issue is whether Kenneth Witmer's contract with Wit-Mor Foods, Inc., created a security interest within the meaning of Article 9 of the Uniform Commercial Code. The district court held that it did.

Butzner, Circuit Judge: Witmer delivered a walk-in food freezer to Wit-Mor Foods. Witmer agreed to sell and Wit-Mor Foods to buy, the equipment for $6,000. The purchase price could be paid in any of three ways: first, the full amount could be paid immediately; second, Wit-Mor Foods could defer payment for six months and have its monthly "rent" of $30 credited against the purchase price; third, if payment were deferred for more than six months, no credits would be given. The agreement also provided that Witmer was to retain title to the equipment until the purchase price was paid in full.

Witmer did not file a financing statement covering the equipment. Although Wit-Mor Foods paid all monthly charges that came due, it never paid the purchase price.

Several months after delivery of the freezer, Wit-Mor Foods applied for an SBA Loan, listing the freezer among its assets. The SBA lent Wit-Mor Foods $25,000 and filed a financing statement covering all of the company's equipment and fixtures. About two and one-half years later, Wit-Mor Foods defaulted on the loan, and the SBA sold the assets securing the indebtedness. Before the sale Witmer claimed he owned the freezer, but the SBA insisted its security interest was superior. Witmer then purchased the freezer for $3,800 at the foreclosure sale and brought this action to obtain reimbursement.

Witmer contends that the agreement should be construed as a lease with an option to purchase. He relies on the undisputed proposition that a financing statement need not be filed for a true lease in order to protect leased property in possession of a tenant. Therefore, he concludes, the absence of a financing statement did not afford the SBA a superior right to the equipment.

The government contends that the transaction was a conditional sale. Alternatively, it asserts that even if the transaction were a lease, it was intended as security. Under either of these interpretations, the government claims Witmer's unperfected security interest was subordinate to the perfected security interest of the SBA.

Though Wit-Mor Foods, Inc., is owned by Witmer's brother, the SBA and Witmer concede that the transaction was conducted at arm's length. Neither party presented any evidence about a prior course of dealing. Consequently, the meaning of the agreement must be determined by the language the contracting parties used when read in the light of commercial practices. Applying this standard, we conclude that the parties did not intend a lease. Instead, as the following factors indicate, they intended a sale and delivery of the freezer with retention of title to secure the purchase price:

The paper itself is described as a "Contract of Sale and Agreement," not as a lease.

The parties termed themselves buyer and seller, not lessee and lessor.

They expressed a desire to consummate a sale of the freezer; there is no mention of any desire to lease it.

Witmer agreed to sell, and Wit-Mor Foods to buy, the freezer for a price of $6,000.

Although the contract uses the term "rent" to describe the monthly payments Wit-Mor Foods was to make if it deferred paying the purchase price, there is no evidence from which it can be inferred that, dealing at arm's length, the owner of a $6,000 piece of equipment would rent it for $30 a month—$360 a year; a more reasonable interpretation is that Wit-Mor Foods' monthly payments were in reality interest on the deferred purchase price at the rate of 6 per cent per annum.

The absence of any provision for the expiration or termination of the monthly payments, other than by purchase, buttresses the conclusion that the parties did not intend a lease of the equipment.

Payment of the "rent" did not expressly convert the agreement into a lease, nor did it discharge Wit-Mor Foods' unequivocal obligation to purchase the equipment.

Witmer's retention of title until he received the purchase price in full is a common commercial device typical of conditional sales.

Article 9 of the Uniform Commercial Code, dealing with secured transactions, applies "to any transaction (regardless of its form) which is intended to create a security interest in personal property or fixtures. . . ." The Code defines security interest as "an interest in personal property or fixtures which secures payment . . . of an obligation." Examination of Witmer's contract indicates that the parties intended that his retention of title would secure Wit-Mor Foods' payment of the purchase price. The district court, therefore, properly held the contract created a security interest. This interpretation accords with the policy of including all consensual secured transactions involving personal property within the scope of Article 9. Because Witmer never filed a financing statement to perfect his security interest, the perfected security interest of the SBA had priority. [DECISION FOR APPELLEE]

PROBLEMS

1 Mrs. Brown purchased a new refrigerator from The Appliance Store to be used in her cottage on the beach. Classify the refrigerator as collateral with respect to (a) The Appliance Store, (b) Mrs. Brown.

2 Jones owned 100 shares of stock, which he pledged with the First Bank as security for a loan. Classify the shares of stock as collateral with respect to the First Bank.

3 Linder purchased a new office desk from The Furniture Company for $600, payable in ninety days. (a) If Linder signed a security agreement as security for payment of the desk, how would the security agreement be classified as collateral? (b) If Linder signed a promissory note for the desk, how would the note be classified as collateral?

4 Tully, who was an amateur horticulturist, grew vegetables in his back yard for consumption by his family. Classify the vegetables as collateral.

5 Smith employed a contractor to construct a swimming pool in his back yard and signed a contract to pay the contractor when the pool was completed. Classify the building contract as collateral.

6 The Music Mart sold a portable radio to a dentist who used the radio in the waiting room of his office and occasionally took it home on weekends. Classify the radio with respect to (a) The Music Mart, (b) the dentist.

7 Brown, a farmer who raised fifty thoroughbred horses, sold twenty-five of the horses to The Marketing Agency for the purpose of resale and twenty-five to The Racing Company for the purpose of entering into the racing business. Classify the horses as collateral with respect to (a) Brown, (b) The Marketing Agency, (c) The Racing Company.

8 A dealer sold a tractor to a farmer on credit, and a security agreement was properly signed as security. The dealer transferred the security agreement to the First Bank to secure a loan. Classify the tractor and the security agreement as collateral.

9 Brown borrowed $500 from the First Bank and pledged a negotiable warehouse receipt as security for the loan. Classify the warehouse receipt as collateral.

10 A farmer, who grew cotton as a business, sold the cotton to the owner of a cotton gin, who removed the seeds and bound the cotton in bales. Classify the cotton in the hand of (a) the farmer, (b) the owner of the gin.

31

THE SECURITY INTEREST

A security interest means an interest in personal property which secures payment of money or performance of an obligation. The five things which should be discussed are (1) the agreement creating the security interest, (2) the attachment of the security interest, (3) the perfection of the security interest, (4) multiple state transactions, and (5) the rights and duties of the parties with respect to the collateral.

THE SECURITY AGREEMENT

A sharp distinction between the security agreement and the financing statement *must* be kept clearly in mind. A security agreement is the agreement which creates a security interest such as a "loan agreement," "credit agreement," or a "conditional sale" and which the debtor signs when he borrows money or makes a purchase of goods on credit. A financing statement, in contrast to the security agreement, is a form prepared and filed in a designated public office in order to notify third persons that the debtor and creditor are going to be engaged in financing. The financing statement in many instances will be prepared and filed long before a security agreement is executed.

The security agreement is not enforceable against the debtor or third parties (1) unless the collateral is in the possession of the secured party pursuant to an agreement or (2) unless the debtor has signed a security agreement. Section 9–203 further provides that the security agreement must contain a description of the collateral and a description of the land when the security interest covers crops growing or to be grown or from which timber is to be cut.

The security agreement will ordinarily contain many optional provisions. A clause pertaining to after-acquired property and future advances is very likely to be included, and such clause may secure all obligations covered by the security agreement. It should be pointed out that section 9–204 provides that no security interest attaches under an after-acquired property clause to consumer goods other than accessions unless the debtor acquires rights in them within ten days after the secured party gives value. An example of an accession is a new engine installed in an old automobile. The formal requisites of the security agreement are neverthe-less reduced to a minimum. [*In re Drane*, p. 399; *Piggott State Bank v. Pollard Gin Co.*, p. 399.]

ATTACHMENT OF THE SECURITY INTEREST

"Attachment," as the word pertains to secured transactions, is far removed from the definition as used in the attachment of property in satisfaction of a judgment. "Attach," loosely stated, means "create." Section 9–203 provides that three events must occur before a security interest attaches:

(1) The collateral is in the possession of the secured party pursuant to an agreement, or the debtor has signed a security agreement which describes the collateral including a description of the land on which crops are to be grown or from which timber is to be cut.

(2) Value has been given by the secured party.

(3) The debtor has rights in the collateral.

A security interest attaches as soon as all three of these events have taken place, unless the parties explicitly agree to the contrary. A security interest attaches when it becomes enforceable against the debtor with respect to the collateral.

The secured party to give "value" must give up something or legally commit himself to do so. The debtor has rights in the collateral when he has acquired some legal or equitable right in or to a specific or identified thing. Suppose Brown borrows $200 from the First Bank to purchase a television set. Suppose still further that the television set is in the possession of the Appliance Store. The security agreement does not attach until the Appliance Store marks or otherwise identifies one television set as belonging to Brown.

It may be helpful to make a distinction between "attachment" and "perfection." Attachment relates to the coming into existence of the security interest. Perfection relates to taking the security into possession or to filing a financing statement to make the security interest effective against third parties. It will be seen, however, that a security interest is effective against third parties by attachment alone in a few instances.

PERFECTION OF THE SECURITY INTEREST

The purpose of perfecting a security interest is to give the secured party a superior position over certain other lien creditors with respect to the collateral. The secured party may perfect his security interest in three ways: (1) by taking physical possession of the collateral; (2) by filing a financing statement; and (3) by attachment alone in some instances. The methods of perfection are set out in sections 9–304 and 9–305, and are determined by the classification of the collateral. It seems appropriate, therefore, to discuss the methods of perfection by class of collateral.

Account; General Intangibles Perfection of this class of collateral may be accomplished only by filing. The rule is obvious, because there is nothing which may be taken into possession.

Goods Perfection of this class of collateral—consumer goods, equipment, farm products, and inventory—may be accomplished by either taking actual possession of the goods or by filing a financing statement. The security interest may also be perfected when the goods are in the physical possession of a bailee. If the bailee has issued a negotiable document for the goods, a security interest may be perfected by perfecting a security interest in the document, and such security interest has priority over any other security interest perfected during the time such goods are in the possession of the issuer of a negotiable document. If the bailee has not issued a negotiable document of title, the secured party may perfect by (1) having a document of title issued in his name, (2) filing as to the goods, or (3) the bailee's receipt of notification of the secured party's interest in goods. Notice to the bailee of the secured party's interest in the goods is a perfection on the line of reasoning that the secured party is deemed to have possession of the goods from the time the bailee receives notice of the secured party's interest in the goods. No filing is necessary to perfect the security interest, however, where the secured party has possession of the collateral. [*In re Midas Coin Co.,* p. 400.]

Section 9–203 provides that the security agreement may be perfected by attachment alone with respect to a purchase-money security interest in consumer goods regardless of the price. Perfection by attachment alone may be illustrated by a purchase-money security interest in consumer goods. Suppose the Finance Company financed the purchase of a television set by Brown. The security interest of the Finance Company would be perfected the moment the security interest was created—attached. Could the Finance Company assert its security interest without filing a financing statement if Brown sold the television set to his neighbor? Not if the neighbor was without knowledge of the security interest, gave value, and used the television set for his own personal, family, or household purposes. Suppose Brown sold the television set to a dealer. The Finance Company would be protected. A secured party, therefore, can gain further protection by filing. The only thing gained by filing, however, would be protection against a consumer selling to another consumer.

The general rule which provides that perfection by filing is not required in order to perfect a security interest in consumer goods has two exceptions which should be mentioned at this point, namely (1) filing is required in order to perfect a purchase-money security interest in goods which are to become fixtures—the so-called fixture filing—and (2) motor vehicles are covered by special rules. The first of these exceptions is discussed later in this chapter, and the second is discussed in Chapter 32, "Priorities and Remedies."

Money, Instruments, Documents, Chattel Paper   A security interest in money and instruments, as a general rule, can be perfected only by the secured party's taking possession of the collateral. A security interest in negotiable documents and chattel paper may be perfected either by possession or by filing. It is important to mention, however, that a security interest in instruments and negotiable documents is perfected by attachment alone for a period of twenty-one days without filing or possession. An illustration of a share of stock should explain the twenty-one-day rule: Suppose Brown owned a share of stock which he wanted to use as collateral for a loan of $500 from the First Bank. Suppose further that the bank made the loan but left the share of stock in the possession of Brown so that he could have it registered in his name on the books of the corporation. What happens if Brown uses the share of stock to secure a loan from the Finance Company?

The bank would have a superior claim to the share of stock if it can show (1) that twenty-one days have not elapsed since it advanced the $500 to Brown and (2) that the Finance Company was not a bona fide purchaser of the share of stock. The First Bank, however, would have to show that the Finance Company was not a holder in due course if the collateral had been a negotiable promissory note, or the Finance Company was not a bona fide purchaser if the collateral had been a negotiable document of title. It is thus clear that the protection afforded the secured party under the twenty-one-day rule is limited to protection against third parties other than holders in due course and bona fide purchasers. This means that a secured party who surrenders possession of the collateral to the debtor must bear the risk of losing his security by an unauthorized negotiation of the collateral.

Proceeds   The word "proceeds" is defined by section 9–306 to include whatever is received when collateral or proceeds are sold, exchanged, collected, or otherwise disposed of. This definition is broad enough to include insurance on collateral which is payable as a result of loss of or damage to the collateral, unless the insurance contract designates a beneficiary who is not a party to the security agreement. Money, checks, deposit accounts, and the like are "cash proceeds." All other proceeds are "noncash proceeds." Section 9–105 defines a "deposit account" as "a demand, time, savings, passbook or like account maintained with a bank, savings and loan association, credit union, or like organization, other than an account evidenced by a certificate of deposit."

Section 9–306 provides in effect that if the secured party perfects his security interest in the collateral by filing a financing statement, permanent perfection in the proceeds will be automatic in most instances. In the following chapter where proceeds are discussed in the context of priorities, some instances will be discussed in which a claim to proceeds must be made if the security interest in the proceeds is to remain effective for more than ten days.

Perfection by Filing   The principal method of perfecting the security interest of the secured party is by filing a financing statement. The form of filing prescribed by section 9–402 is termed "notice filing." This means that the security agreement itself need not be filed, but simply a financing statement which indicates that the secured party claims a security interest in the described collateral. Notice filing offers great utility with respect to collateral that is constantly changing, such as inventory. It is true, however, that notice filing places a minimum of information on record which prevents third persons with no real interest in the transaction from learning too much about the details. Persons with a legitimate interest may learn more of the details by further inquiry of the secured party. Notice filing with respect to inventory collateral becomes effective prior to the signing of the security agreement. The secured party, therefore, is given maximum protection at an early date.

A carbon, photographic, or other reproduction of the financing statement or the security agreement may be filed as a financing statement provided the financing statement meets the requirements of this section and is signed by the debtor.

(1) *Formal Requisites*   The formal requirements of a financing statement are rather simple as shown by the suggested form in section 9–402. It must contain the name and address of both the debtor and the secured party and a description of the collateral by type or items, and it must be signed by the debtor. No claim to proceeds is required. A financing statement must also contain a description of the real estate when the collateral consists of crops growing or to be grown, timber to be cut, fixtures installed or to be installed, and minerals, oil, and gas to be removed. In connection with a description of the real estate, this section also provides that the financing statement must contain a recitation that it is to be filed in the real estate records if the collateral is timber to be cut, minerals, oil, gas, and accounts resulting from the sale of same at the wellhead or minehead, and goods to be installed as fixtures. It must be indexed, therefore, in the real estate search system where a mortgage encumbering real estate would be recorded or filed. In case of a fixture—for example, a furnace to be installed in a house—the debtor, as a general rule, must have an interest of record in the real estate.

The financing statement should contain the precise names of the debtor and the creditor. In case of a corporate debtor, the name of the corporation should be used. If the debtor is a partnership, the name of the partnership should be used. The names of the individual partners are not required, although they may be included. In case of a debtor who operates a business as a sole proprietor or under a trade name, the individual name of the debtor *must* be used even though the trade name may be included. [*In the Matter of Leichter*, p. 402.]

Suppose there is a change of name, identity, or corporate structure which results in a filed financing statement that is seriously misleading. In these circumstances, the filing is not effective to perfect a security interest in collateral acquired by a debtor more than four months after the change unless there is a perfection by filing a new financing statement before the expiration of the four months.

A signature by the secured party is not generally required, but his signature alone will suffice concerning (1) collateral brought into the state where a financing statement was filed in another state, (2) proceeds when the security interest of the secured party in the original collateral was perfected, (3) a change in the location of the debtor from one state to another, (4) the original financing statement which lapsed because no continuation statement was filed, and (5) a debtor who has acquired collateral after the debtor's name, identity, or corporate structure was changed. One situation exists in which both the debtor and the creditor must sign the financing statement. This situation pertains to an amended financing statement. It should be pointed out, however, that the amended financing statement does not extend the period of the effectiveness of the filing.

A financing statement which substantially complies with the requirements of this section is effective although it contains minor errors which are not seriously misleading. [*In re Excel Stores, Inc.,* p. 403.]

(2) ***Duration of Perfection*** Section 9–403 provides rules pertaining to the duration of perfection. The perfection is effective at an early point of time. The financing statement becomes effective at the time at which it is presented for filing along with a tender of the filing fee or when the filing officer accepts the statement. The duration of the perfection is effective for a period of five years after the date of filing, but it will lapse at the end of five years unless a continuation statement is filed by the secured party within six months prior to the expiration of the five years. Duration of perfection may be continued indefinitely, however, if continuation statements are properly filed. The continuation statement must be signed by the secured party, state the original file number, and state that the original statement is still effective. The continuation statement may possibly be filed by someone other than the secured party of record. In these circumstances, the continuation statement must be accompanied by a separate signed written assignment by the secured party of record. The assignment must also meet the requirements of section 9–504, which are basically a disclosure of the details along with the names of the assignor, assignee, and the signature of the assignor.

The duration of perfection will not terminate, although no continuation statement is filed, in three situations: (1) When a real estate mortgage is filed as a fixture filing, the perfection will remain effective until the mortgage is terminated by being released, satisfied of record, foreclosed, or the like; (2) when insolvency proceedings are commenced by or against the debtor, the perfection will remain effective until the expiration of the normal five years or until termination of the insolvency proceedings and thereafter for sixty days; and (3) when the debtor is a transmitting utility—such as a person who is engaged in the railroad, electric, pipeline, or water business—the duration of perfection will continue until a termination statement is filed.

(3) *Place of Filing* Three alternative systems of filing are stated in section 9–401. Filing of the financing statement, therefore, may be central, dual, or local filing. This makes it necessary to examine the Code as enacted in the particular state in order to determine the proper place to file the financing statement. If local filing is required, filing will be in the office of some named county or town official; if central filing is required, filing will be in the office of a named state office. Some states adopting the Code have selected the office of the county clerk and the office of the secretary of state as the designated places for filing.

Farm products deserve a brief mention. Suppose the collateral consists of growing crops or crops to be grown. In addition to a description of the land, the financing statement must be filed in the chattel records in the county where the crops are growing or to be grown and in the county where the farmer resides if the two places are located in different counties. This presents a difficult problem when the farming operations are conducted by a corporation, partnership, or other organization. If the collateral is farm products, farm equipment, or an account which arose from the sale of farm products, the proper place of filing is the county where the corporation, partnership, or other organization has its place of business or its chief executive office if it has more than one place of business.

Termination Statement Provision is made in section 9–404 for giving notice that a financing arrangement has been terminated. In the case of consumer goods, after there is no longer an outstanding obligation or commitment, the secured party must file a termination statement within one month or within ten days after a written demand is made by the debtor. In cases of other collateral, after there is no longer an outstanding obligation or commitment, the secured party must send to the debtor a termination statement for each filing officer within ten days after a written demand from the debtor. A secured party who fails to furnish such a termination statement as required by this section or within ten days after a proper demand is liable to the debtor for $100, together with any loss caused the debtor by such failure.

MULTIPLE STATE TRANSACTIONS

Section 1–105 provides that the parties may agree as to whether the law of this state or the law of the other state will govern the transaction where a transaction bears a reasonable relation to this state and also to another state or nation. Failing such agreement, the Code applies to transactions bearing an appropriate relation to this state.

Section 9–103 is devoted to multiple state transactions and is limited to perfection of the security interest. This law is not confined to motor vehicles, but cases involving motor vehicles alone would make inevitable an examination of some of the complex multiple state problems. The basic rule to remember is that the governing law of the perfection of a security interest in "ordinary goods" is the law of the jurisdiction where the collateral is located when the "last event" occurs for the perfection of the security interest. It is most important to remember, however, that (1) perfection is achieved after attachment of the security interest, (2) three events must occur before the security interest attaches, and (3) these three events may occur in different jurisdictions. The important controlling point to remember is that when the last step for perfection occurs—for example, filing—the filing should be in the jurisdiction where the collateral is located. The law of that particular jurisdiction will control. Perfection will only occur when all the events required for attachment and all the steps for perfection have been completed. It is quite clear, therefore, that filing before the security interest attaches will not constitute perfection. The giving of value should occur in the jurisdiction where the financing statement is filed if the giving of value is the last step in perfection.

Goods to Be Moved The above-mentioned "last event" rule is qualified by a number of exceptions. The first one to be discussed involves a purchase-money security interest in goods which arises in one jurisdiction but, at the time of attachment, the parties understand that the goods are to be kept in another jurisdiction. Perfection will be governed by the law of the other jurisdiction— where the goods are to be kept—from the time of attachment until thirty days after the debtor receives the goods. If the goods are taken to the other jurisdiction before the expiration of the thirty days, perfection will continue to be governed by the law of the other jurisdiction beyond the thirty days. Suppose the purchase-money security interest attaches to the goods in State A and the parties understood at the time that the goods would be moved to State B. The law of State B will govern perfection for thirty days after the debtor receives possession, and it will continue to govern thereafter if the goods are moved to State B. The secured party should, therefore, perfect by filing a financing statement in State B before expiration of the thirty days.

Without Agreement to Move Collateral Suppose that goods subject to a security interest are in State A, where the security interest is perfected, but there is no agreement that the collateral will be moved to another jurisdiction. Suppose further that the debtor does remove the goods to State B. Perfection will remain valid in State B without any action on the part of the secured party until the occurrence of one of two events, whichever occurs first: (1) Perfection lapses in State A, or (2) four months expire after the collateral was brought into State B. If action is required in State B for perfection to continue valid in State B, the secured party, prior to the occurrence of one of the two named events, must file a financing statement in State B. The security interest which was perfected in State A will lapse if the secured party does not file in State B. Consequently, a person who purchases the collateral or perfects a security interest in the collateral in State B after removal from State A will have a claim which is superior to the security interest perfected in State A.

An exception should be noted. In the case of consumer goods excluding motor vehicles and fixtures, section 9–302 provides that filing is not required in order to perfect a purchase-money security interest in consumer goods. Consumer goods brought into State B will be subject to the security interest perfected in State A, and such perfection will continue beyond the four-month period.

Documents and Instruments   Perfection of a security interest in documents and instruments is governed by the "last event" rule. This means that perfection of the security interest will be governed by law of the jurisdiction where the last event occurs for the perfection of the security interest. This is the same rule which was discussed above in connection with "ordinary goods." The secured party must perfect by filing in State B before the lapse of the perfection in State A or within four months after the documents are taken to State B, whichever occurs first if a security interest in documents is perfected in State A and the debtor in possession removes the documents to State B. A security interest in instruments must generally be perfected by possession, and the law of the jurisdiction where the secured party is in possession will govern the perfection.

Account; General Intangibles; Mobile Goods   Perfection will be governed by the law of the jurisdiction where the "debtor is located." The location of the debtor will be his place of business if he has one, at his chief executive office if he has more than one place of business, or at his residence if he has no place of business. Mobile goods refer to goods which are *not* covered by a certificate of title and are normally used in more than one jurisdiction, such as rental cars, trailers, road building, construction machinery, and the like. Mobile goods are usually mobile equipment and leased inventory.

Change of Debtor's Location   The debtor may move his place of business or chief executive office to another jurisdiction after the secured party perfects his security interest in accounts, general intangibles, chattel paper, or mobile goods. For example, the secured party properly perfects his security interest in State A, after which the debtor changes his location to State B. The perfection will remain valid in State B without any action on the part of the secured party until the occurrence of one of two events, namely (1) perfection lapses in State A or (2) four months expire after the debtor changes his location to State B. If action is required in State B on the part of the secured party for the perfection to be maintained permanently, such action must be taken before either one of the two above-named events occurs unless the collateral is consumer goods. If the secured party does not take such action in State B, a person who purchases the collateral or acquires a perfected security interest in the collateral after the debtor changes his location will have an interest in the collateral which will be prior to the security interest perfected in State A.

It should be mentioned that the law of the jurisdiction where the "debtor is located" will govern the perfection of a nonpossessory interest in chattel paper. This is where the debtor retains possession of the collateral. Suppose the secured party takes possession of the chattel paper. Perfection will then be controlled by the law of the state where the chattel paper is located.

Minerals, Oil, Gas   The law of the jurisdiction where the wellhead or minehead is located will govern the perfection of a security interest in the minerals, oil, or gas or in an account resulting from a sale of the minerals, oil, or gas.

Motor Vehicles and Other Property   Perfection of a security interest in passenger automobiles cannot be understood unless it is remembered that most states have a certificate of title law but that several states do not have such a law. The certificate of title statute generally covers automobiles and sometimes other property, such as mobile homes, trailers, farm tractors, and boats. Perfection of a security interest in motor vehicles must be accomplished in the usual manner by filing in those states which do not have a certificate of title statute. This is correct even though the security interest is a purchase-money interest and passenger automobiles are consumer goods. Special mention should be made of the perfection of a security interest in those states which have a certificate of title statute. Section 9–302 provides that filing is required for a motor vehicle for which registration is required. This section also provides that filing is not necessary or effective in order to perfect a security interest in property subject to a certificate of title statute. Compliance with the certificate of title statute is equivalent, however, to perfection of a security interest by filing. This compliance—filing— must also include, among other things, an indication of the security interest on the certificate of title as a condition of perfection. Compliance with the certificate of title law is in fact the only method of perfection except that (1) perfection by filing is still required to perfect a security interest in new and used motor vehicles constituting inventory for sale and (2) exceptions occur in multiple-state transactions, as noted in the paragraphs that follow.

The mobility of a passenger automobile makes the perfection of a security interest in the automobile troublesome. Legal problems may be exemplified by the fact that an automobile may be moved from a non-title state to another non-title state, from a non-title state to a title state, from a title state to a non-title state, or from a title state to another title state. For reasons of simplicity, assume that States A and B are non-title states and States X and Y are title states. Assume further that the automobile is moved from one state to another as indicated.

(1)   *Non-title State to a Non-title State*   Suppose the secured party perfected in State A and the debtor moved the automobile to State B. The security interest perfected in State A will continue perfected in State B (1) until perfection lapses in State A or (2) for four months after the automobile has been moved to State B, whichever occurs first. If the secured party perfects by filing a financing statement in State B before either of the two events occurs, perfection will continue beyond the four months or after it would have lapsed in State A. If the secured party does not perfect in State B before there is a lapse of the perfection in State A or within the four months, a purchaser of the automobile in State B before or after the lapse will have priority or be superior to the security interest which was perfected in State A.

(2)   *Non-title State to Title State*   Suppose the secured party perfected his security interest in State A, a non-title state, and the debtor moved the automobile

to State X, a title state. Suppose further that a certificate of title was issued by State X which does not show that the perfected security interest is in State A or that the automobile may be subject to a security interest not indicated on the title certificate. A purchaser who is not an automobile dealer and who receives the automobile after the certificate of title was issued in State X and without knowledge of the security interest which was perfected in State A will take the automobile free of the security interest to the extent that he pays value. It is felt that the purchaser should be protected when he buys the automobile under these circumstances since he relies on a clean certificate of title issued by State X. The rules discussed in a "Non-title State to Non-title State" above will apply, however, if State X does not issue a new certificate. The security interest perfected in State A will remain perfected in State X for four months or until it lapses in State A.

Let us suppose, however, that the automobile is sold to a dealer in State X. The security interest perfected in State A will remain valid in State X until it lapses in State A or for four months after the automobile was brought into State X, whichever occurs first. The dealer-purchaser is not protected despite the fact that a clean certificate of title was issued in State X. This is because a dealer-purchaser is sophisticated in the automobile business and should be required to check into the background of the title to the automobile for at least the four months. These same rules and line of reasoning are applied to financers. Levying creditors and trustees in bankruptcy also are not protected for the reason that they do not rely on the certificate of title.

(3) **Title State to Non-title State** Suppose the security interest was perfected in State X, a title state, and was properly indicated on the certificate of title as required by the statute of State X, and the debtor moved the automobile to State A, a non-title state. The perfection of State X will continue in State A for four months and thereafter until the automobile is registered in State A, but not beyond the time of the surrender of the certificate of title. It is apparent that the certificate of title cannot be surrendered in State A *if the secured party retains possession of the certificate of title.* The secured party, therefore, will have priority in State A over (1) any buyer of the automobile, (2) anyone who lends money to the debtor using the automobile as collateral, (3) a creditor of the debtor who levies on the automobile, or (4) a trustee in bankruptcy of the debtor. The period of perfection in State A will continue beyond the four months if there is no registration of the automobile in State A.

(4) **Title State to Title State** Suppose that with the security interest perfected in State X and properly noted on the certificate of title as required by the statute of State X the debtor moves the automobile to State Y. The security interest will continue perfected for at least four months if the secured party in State X retains possession of the certificate of title so that it cannot be surrendered. No new certificate of title will be issued in State Y if the vehicle is not registered in State Y. Until such time as a registration in State Y occurs, therefore, the perfection as noted on the certificate of title in State X will remain perfected after the expiration of the four months. Suppose a new certificate is issued in State Y and the security interest is not noted on the new certificate. The

security interest will be subordinate to a nondealer buyer who gives value, obtains delivery of the automobile after the certificate of title was issued, and does so without knowledge of the security interest.

The four situations discussed above indicate how important it is for the secured party to maintain the perfection of his security interest when the automobile is moved permanently from one state to another state. This can be done by filing in the second non-title state or by having the security interest noted on a new certificate of title issued in a second title state. The secured party may have difficulty locating the automobile if the debtor removes the automobile to another state. If the automobile is moved to a non-title state, perfection by filing within the four months rule would be the answer. If the automobile is moved to a title state, however, it would be difficult—if not impossible—to compel a purchaser who is not cooperative or the title authorities to note the security interest on the certificate of title. In some states, an applicant for a new certificate of title will be required to disclose the history of the title to the automobile and the applicant will be required to show that the certificate of title has been canceled or surrendered if the automobile came from a title state. Some other states will issue a clean certificate of title without making any inquiry into the history of the title. Still other states will issue a new certificate of title showing that the automobile may be subject to a security interest perfected in the other state, and a new clean certificate of title will be issued after four months. The framers of the Code made a sincere effort to improve this area of the law. These problems, however, can only be solved by making changes in the certificate of title statutes.

RIGHTS AND DUTIES OF THE PARTIES

The secured party and the debtor have substantial freedom of contract. They can, therefore, reach an understanding with respect to the nature of the secured obligation; they may decide whether the secured party or the debtor will have possession of the collateral; they may decide on the terms of repayment; and they may agree on the circumstances which will constitute a default by the debtor. Article 9 nevertheless establishes certain rules which may not be varied by the security agreement. Article 9 also provides certain rules which will govern the rights and duties of the parties in the absence of controlling provisions in the security agreement. The rules which should be discussed pertain to the rights and duties of the parties when the collateral is in the possession of the secured party and when it is in the possession of the debtor.

Secured Party in Possession of Collateral   The nature of the secured transaction and the agreement of the parties, in the absence of a default by the debtor, will determine which party will be in possession of the collateral. The parties may intend a secured transaction in the nature of a pledge. If this be the case, the secured party will retain possession of the collateral until there is satisfaction of the obligation, and, for all practical purposes, Article 9 does little more than to codify the common-law rules.

The common-law duty of the secured party to exercise reasonable care in preserving the collateral is codified in section 9–207 and is one duty which Article 9 will not permit the parties to disclaim or negate. The parties may, however, under section 1–102, agree on the standard which will be used in measuring reasonable care provided such standard is not obviously unreasonable. Chattel paper and instruments are given special treatment. The duty of reasonable care requires the secured party to take reasonable steps with respect to presentment and notice in order to preserve the rights of the holder against prior parties. This duty, however, may be changed by agreement. The duty of preserving the rights and remedies against prior parties, therefore, may be placed on the debtor by agreement in spite of the fact that he does not have physical possession of the collateral.

Additional familiar common-law rules which are applicable when the collateral is in the possession of the secured party are set out in detail in section 9–207. They may be summarized: Reasonable expenses, including costs of insurance and taxes, incurred in the custody, preservation, and operation of the collateral are to be paid by the debtor and are secured by the collateral; risk of accidental loss or damage is on the debtor to the extent not covered by insurance; any increase of the collateral may be held by the secured party, except money which shall be applied in reduction of the debt unless it is remitted to the debtor; the collateral must be kept identifiable, but fungibles may be commingled; and the collateral may be repledged by the secured party, but not in such a manner as to impair the right of the debtor to redeem the collateral. It should be mentioned that these common-law rules may be changed or varied by agreement between the parties. Liability is imposed on the secured party when he does not exercise reasonable care or for failure to meet the foregoing obligations, but this does not mean that the secured party loses his security interest.

Agreements frequently provide that the secured party may use or operate the collateral, such as a going business, in order to preserve the collateral or its value. In this case, the agreement may also provide that the risk of loss will be on the secured party, or that he has the duty of insuring the collateral.

Debtor in Possession of Collateral   Section 9–205 provides: "A security interest is not invalid or fraudulent against creditors by reason of liberty in the debtor to use, commingle or dispose of all or part of the collateral." This provision clearly rejects cases which hold such an arrangement void as a matter of law when the debtor is given complete control over the collateral. It is an attempt to provide workable rules to give adequate legal protection to the secured party when, because of the very nature of the circumstances, it is necessary for the debtor to retain possession of the collateral. Secured transactions involving inventory and accounts receivable have vastly increased in numbers and are good illustrations of collateral to which the rule may be applied.

The terms of the security agreement—not Article 9—will determine the duties of the debtor with respect to collateral in his possession. The debtor, therefore, will be governed by the agreement with respect to things, such as taxes, insurance, the use and maintenance of the collateral, and any other pertinent provisions.

CASES

In re Drane   202 F. Supp. 221 (Ky. 1962). In the Matter of Willard Lee Drane, bankrupt. The bankrupt executed a security agreement by which he mortgaged to Popular Finance Company the following described property:

1—2 pc. living room suite, wine
1—5 pc. chrome dinette set, yellow
1—3 pc. panel bedroom suite, lime oak, matt. & spgs.

The security agreement stated the address of the mortgagor, and provided that the property "will be kept at the debtor's address above and not moved without the written consent of the secured party."

Shelborne, District Judge: The sole question on review is whether the description of this property in the security agreement is a sufficient description under the law of Kentucky. The creditor relies on the Uniform Commercial Code, particularly section 9–110 which provides: "For the purposes of this article any description of personal property or real estate is sufficient whether or not it is specific if it reasonably identifies what is described."

The creditor insists that the description meets the test of the Uniform Commercial Code and also meets the test required by the Kentucky Court of Appeals before the adoption of the Code. The cases relied upon by the referee involved mortgages in which the address of the mortgagor was not stated. In the *Hauseman Motor Co. v. Napierella,* 3 S.W.2d 405, case, the court had character- ized as sufficient a description, assisted by external evidence that does not add to or contradict the terms of the contract, which will enable a third party to identify the property.

Guided by this rule, a third party would have had little difficulty in identifying the two-piece wine living room suite, whether comprised of a divan or davenport and a chair or two chairs. It would have been equally easy to identify the yellow dinette set, whether it consisted of a table and four chairs or a table, sideboard, and fewer chairs. The same "external evidence" would have identified the lime oak panel bedroom suite, mattress, and springs. The location of the property at the address of the mortgagor and in his possession furnished reference to "external evidence" of identification. [DECISION FOR THE CREDITOR]

Piggott State Bank v. Pollard Gin Co.,   419 S.W.2d 120 (Ark. 1967). Action by Piggott State Bank, plaintiff, against Pollard Gin Company, defendant.

Denzil Karnes borrowed $1,200 from the plaintiff-bank upon the security of crops to be grown by him during the ensuing year. The defendant purchased the cotton crop from Denzil Karnes, and the plaintiff-bank brought this action for conversion. The description used in the combined security agreement and financing statement was as follows:

CROPS. All of the following crops to be planted or growing within one year from the date hereof on the lands hereinafter described: 7 acres of cotton and 53 acres of soybeans to be produced on the lands of S. E. Karnes; 11.6 acres of cotton and 50 acres of soybeans to be produced on the lands of Mary Gilbee; 4 1/2 acres of cotton and 11 acres of soybeans to be produced on the lands of George Nixon; all of the above crops to be produced in Clay County, Arkansas during the year 1965.

The question presented to the court was whether the description of the crops was sufficient to put third persons on notice under the Uniform Commercial Code.

George Rose Smith, Justice: With respect to crops the Code requires, both as to the financing statement and as to the security agreement, that there be a description of the land that is involved. Sections 9–203 and 9–402. The description "is sufficient whether or not it is specific if it reasonably identifies what is described." Section 9–110. The Commissioner's Comment to the latter section states: "The test of sufficiency of the description laid down by this section is that the description do the job assigned to it—that it make possible the identification of the thing described."

Here the description referred merely to seven acres of cotton to be produced on the lands of S. E. Karnes (together with two other similar references). Neither the security agreement nor the proof adduced at the trial sheds any light whatever upon the question (a) whether Denzil grew exactly seven acres of cotton on the S. E. Karnes land in 1965 and (b) whether anyone else was also growing cotton upon the S. E. Karnes land. We need not speculate upon what might have been the posture of the case if both those possibilities had been explained, for that is not the situation before us.

Of course we do not cite as controlling authority decisions of this court that were handed down many years before the enactment of the Commercial Code. Yet we have no hesitancy in relying upon such decisions when they help us decide whether, in the language of the Code, a description "reasonably identifies what is described." We have said more than once that "a mortgage of a specified number of articles out of a larger number will not be allowed to prevail, unless it furnishes the data for separating the property intended to be mortgaged from the mass." . . . That principle is so reasonable and so plainly applicable to the case at hand that we see nothing to be accomplished by a more extended discussion of the matter. [DECISION FOR DEFENDANT]

In re Midas Coin Co.,   264 F. Supp. 193 (Mo. 1967). Petition in bankruptcy by St. John's Community Bank, petitioner, to foreclose a collateral note.

The bankrupt, who was engaged in the business of buying and selling coins and stamps for money, executed a collateral note in favor of St. John's Community Bank and pledged certain coins as security for the loan. A financing statement was not filed, but the bank took possession of the coins. The trustee in bankruptcy seeks to have the bank turn over to him the coins as assets of the estate of the bankrupt on the ground that the bank failed to perfect its security interest. The bank seeks authority to foreclose the collateral note by public sale of the pledged coins and apply the proceeds of the sale to the balance due on the collateral note.

Regan, District Judge: The coins in question and others had been purchased by the bankrupt either from other coin dealers or from collectors because of their numismatic value, and such coins are considered part of the bankrupt's inventory and stock in trade which it owned and intended to sell in its regular course of business. . . .

The trustee contends, and the referee held, that section 9–305 is not here applicable upon the theory that coins are money, and that since money is not one of the kinds of property enumerated in that section, the only method of perfecting a security interest therein is by filing a financing statement. Concededly, the pledged coins are not instruments, negotiable documents or chattel paper as these terms are defined by the Uniform Commercial Code or otherwise. Nor are they letters of credit or advices of credit. The only other class of property specifically referred to in section 9–305 is "goods."

The issue here argued by the parties is whether the pledged coins are "goods" as that term is used in section 9–305. Although not here directly pertinent, we note that goods are further classified by the Code into four classes: Consumer Goods, Equipment, Farm Products and Inventory, the definition of each relating to the use made of the goods rather than the nature of the goods itself. Section 9–109. Unquestionably, if the coins here involved are "goods," they would be inventory within the meaning of the Code, as they are in fact. . . .

The Referee, in sustaining the position of the trustee, held that since the coins here involved are United States Government coins like other such coins which circulate freely as a medium of exchange and could have been used as money, they are necessarily and for all purposes "money" as defined by the Code. And since "money" is excluded from the Article 9 definition of "goods," the Referee concluded that even though the pledged coins were treated as a commodity and not as a medium of exchange, the Bank could not perfect its security interest therein simply by taking possession, but was required to file a financing statement. In our judgment, this interpretation of the Code, as applied to the circumstances in this case, is unreasonable and unrealistic and not in accord with the legislative intention. . . .

That money is a thing, in the sense it is tangible, is indisputable, but insofar as the definition thereof is concerned, we believe that what is contemplated thereby is its *use*. The definition of "money," *as used in the Code,* to mean "a medium of exchange" etc., clearly has no reference to money *when treated as a commodity*. It is our view, therefore, that the exclusion of "money" in the definition of "goods" pertains solely to money when used as a medium of exchange and intended to be so used by the parties at the time of the transaction in question. When used or intended to be used and treated as a *commodity,* as were the coins here involved, they are considered "goods," just as are all other commodities.

The orders of the Referee are reversed, with directions to sustain the petition to foreclose the security agreement as prayed and to deny the petition of the trustee for a turnover order. [DECISION FOR PETITIONER]

In the Matter of Leichter, 471 F.2d 785 (N.Y. 1972). This is an appeal by Michael F. Friedman, trustee in bankruptcy, appellant, against Matthew R. Leichter, individually and doing business under the trade name and style of Landman Dry Cleaners, bankrupt, and Northern Commercial Corporation, appellees.

Kenston Corporation sold Leichter some dry cleaning equipment in 1967 under a conditional sales contract and filed with the Secretary of State and the Kings County Clerk a financing statement. Both the conditional sales contract and the financing statement were signed:

"Landman Dry Cleaners
By: Matthew R. Leichter"

Kenston Corporation filed and indexed the financing statement only under the name of Landman Dry Cleaners and not under Leichter's own name. Kenston Corporation subsequently assigned the conditional sales contract and security interest to Northern Commercial Corporation. The referee in bankruptcy held that Leichter and not Landman Dry Cleaners was the legal "debtor" and that omitting to file under Leichter's own name was not simply a "minor error." The district court reversed, and this appeal followed.

Per Curiam: The district court improperly relied upon our decision in *In re Excel Stores, Inc.,* 341 F.2d 961 (2d Cir. 1965). We think the rule of that case when applied to the plainly distinguishable facts here requires a different result. We, therefore, think that the Referee was correct.

Excel Stores presents entirely different critical facts since the financing statement there was filed under "Excel Department Stores" rather than "Excel Stores, Inc.," the real debtor. This court held, and we completely agree with its decision, that the filing gave "the minimum information necessary to put any searcher on inquiry," and was a "minor error" and not "seriously misleading." In our case, however, would a subsequent creditor looking under "Leichter" be led to find the security interest filed and indexed under "Landman"? We think not, even though Leichter apparently did his business under the trade name.

Recently the Ninth Circuit Court of Appeals added its weight to this construction of UCC Section 9–402, when it held that filing against a debtor named Thomas under his trade name of "West Coast Avionics" was ineffective. *In re Thomas,* 466 F.2d 51 (9th Cir. 1972). As the court there said, "If the debtor's name is not given, the purpose of the statutory scheme of requiring security interest to be perfected by filing a financing statement—to give notice to future creditors of the debtor—would be seriously undermined." In this regard, the trustee in bankruptcy must be deemed to stand in the shoes of the most favored creditor, not simply one who could by virtue of his dealings with the debtor acting under his trade name be held to a semblance of knowledge of the true facts; even such a creditor, knowing how UCC Section 9–402 reads, might never search the filings under the trade name. That is to say, the trustee is more than a subsequent creditor seeking to build up his own equities at the expense of good faith creditors.

Here the assignee of the filing creditor seeking to be secured over others, engaged in the financing business so that it should surely be familiar with the requirements of the Code, must be held to substantial compliance with the notice statute. Filing under the trade name only, we hold was insufficient. [DECISION FOR APPELLANT]

In re Excel Stores, Inc., 341 F.2d 961 (Conn. 1965). Petition in bankruptcy by National Cash Register Company, the secured party and petitioner, to reclaim six cash registers from the Trustee of Excel Stores, Inc., bankrupt.

A National Cash Register salesman negotiated with Andrew F. Machado, treasurer of Excel Stores, Inc., for the sale of six cash registers to Excel Stores. Andrew F. Machado, however, inadvertently made the mistake of writing "Excel Department Stores" instead of "Excel Stores, Inc.," when he filled out the security agreement, adding after the printed word "by" his signature, "Andrew F. Machado." The question presented to the court was whether this mistake was in the category of "minor errors which are not seriously misleading" within the meaning of section 9–402(5).

Medina, Circuit Judge: It is clear that the parties intended to execute a valid and binding contract. Section 1–201(39). Nor can it be doubted that any creditor of Excel or other interested person searching the record would come to the Excel Department Store at the Shopping Center of Pawcatuck, find Machado's name and be put on notice that a lien against Excel might be outstanding and that communication with Machado might be appropriate. This is precisely all that the Code requires. . . .

Subdivision (5) we think is dispositive of this case:

"A financing statement substantially complying with the requirements of this section is effective even though it contains minor errors which are not seriously misleading."

We hold the error made by Machado to be a "minor error" which is not "seriously misleading." [DECISION FOR PETITIONER]

PROBLEMS

1 Plaintiff and Henry entered into a security agreement whereby plaintiff sold to Henry one household Whirlpool dryer. The agreement provided that title would not pass to Henry until the entire purchase price was paid. Henry sold the dryer to defendant, a dealer in used household appliances, at which time $180 was still owing on the dryer. Plaintiff did not file a financing statement. Does plaintiff or defendant have a superior claim to the dryer?

2 Brown borrowed $5,000 from the First Bank and pledged as security for the loan a promissory note for $8,000 issued by Jones, as maker, in favor of Brown and indorsed by Smith. The note became due, but neither Brown nor the First Bank made presentment of the note to Jones for payment nor gave notice of dishonor to Smith. As a result of this inaction. Smith was discharged from liability. The First Bank contended that it was the duty of Brown to make presentment and give notice. Do you agree with this contention?

3 Brown, in order to finance the purchase of a farm tractor for $3,000, entered into a security agreement with plaintiff. The agreement was signed by Brown only, but there was no perfection by filing. Defendant thereafter received the tractor as a trade-in from Brown. Plaintiff contends that Brown had no authority to dispose of the tractor without plaintiff's consent. Plaintiff, therefore, brought an action against defendant to recover the value of the tractor. Defendant contends that the lien of plaintiff is invalid, because the security agreement was not signed by plaintiff as the secured party, and there was no perfection by filing. Do you agree with this contention?

4 Plaintiff and Smith entered into a conditional sales contract for the purchase by Smith of certain equipment. Smith thereafter filed a voluntary petition in bankruptcy and was adjudged a bankrupt. The trustee in bankruptcy took possession of the equipment, and plaintiff attempted to reclaim the equipment. A financing statement was filed, but it did not contain the mailing address of plaintiff and Smith. Is this financing statement sufficient to perfect the security interest?

5 Marcus owned 100 shares of stock in the XYZ Corporation. He borrowed $5,000 from the First Bank, and pledged the shares as collateral. During the year of 1965, the XYZ Corporation declared a 10 percent stock dividend. A dispute then arose over the possession of the share dividend. Is the First Bank correct in its contention that it is entitled to the possession of the share dividend?

6 Mary Jones, who desired to purchase a new living room suite, borrowed $600 from the First Bank to pay for the suite, which she had selected from the window display at the Furniture Company. She signed a security agreement and a financing statement covering "One 3-piece living room suite." The financing statement was properly filed. Mary Jones then went to The Furniture Store, and was told by a clerk that other living room suites would be arriving in a few days. She thereupon decided to postpone her purchase until the arrival of the new suites. She then changed her mind, and used the $600 for a vacation. Explain whether the First Bank does or does not have a security interest in any of the living room suites constituting the inventory of The Furniture Company.

7 Plaintiff, the secured party, and defendant, the debtor, entered into a contract whereby defendant borrowed $1,000 from plaintiff. As security for the loan, defendant executed a security agreement in the form of a chattel mortgage encumbering certain specifically described farm equipment. Defendant did not pay the loan when it became due, and plaintiff attempted to take possession of the collateral. Defendant contended that the mortgage was invalid because plaintiff did not sign the security agreement in accordance with the provisions of the Code, which requires the signatures of both the debtor and the secured party. Do you agree with this contention?

8 Johns, in the state of New York, purchased a crane on a conditional sale from the Acme Equipment Company. The Acme Equipment Company properly perfected by filing a financing statement on January 3, 1969, but no date of maturity was included. Johns moved the crane to one of his farms in New Jersey on December 21, 1973, although there was no agreement authorizing him to move the crane. The Acme Equipment Company filed a financing statement in New Jersey, as required by the law of New Jersey, on January 2, 1974. Johns sold the crane to Black in New Jersey on January 10, 1974. Does Black own the crane free of the security interest of the Acme Equipment Company?

32

PRIORITIES AND REMEDIES

This chapter concludes the discussion of secured transactions, and will be devoted to (1) priorities among conflicting security interests and (2) the remedies of the secured party and the debtor after default.

PRIORITIES

Section 9–312 contains an index to sections for determining priorities among conflicting security interests in the same collateral, and section 9–301 lists the classes of persons who take priority over an unperfected security interest. The various sections of Article 9 then prescribe some rather technical rules for determining priorities.

Filing The priority of perfected security interests will be determined by the time of filing or perfection. Priority dates from the time a filing is first made or the time the security interest is first perfected if there is no period thereafter when there is neither filing nor perfection. If the security interests are unperfected, however, the first to attach has priority. Suppose Brown perfects his security interest on April 1 by taking possession, Jones perfects his security interest on April 10 by filing, and the security interests have existed without interruption. Brown perfected first in time, and he has priority over the interest of Jones. Suppose, however, that Jones perfected on April 1 by filing and Brown perfected on April 2 by filing or taking possession of the collateral. Jones will obviously have priority since he was the first to file or perfect. [*Walker Bank & Trust Co. v. Burrows,* p. 417.]

Artisan's Lien Section 9–310 provides that a lien securing a claim arising from work which enhances or preserves the value of the collateral takes priority over a prior security interest. It is immaterial whether the prior security is or is not perfected. This lien is basically the common-law artisan's lien but includes all persons, such as mechanics, tradesmen, and laborers, who receive property for the purpose of mending, repairing, and improving the condition of the property. The artisan's lien today finds its most frequent application in the repair of automobiles. It should be emphasized, however, that some state statutes make liens securing claims arising from work subordinate to a prior security interest. The Code recognizes these statutes by providing that a prior security interest takes priority only when a statute *expressly* makes artisan's liens subordinate. Suppose Brown gives The Finance Company a security interest in his automobile, which The Finance Company perfects by filing. Suppose further that an automobile mechanic thereafter makes certain repairs on the automobile. Would the lien of The Finance Company or the lien of the mechanic be superior? The lien of the mechanic would be superior, unless a state statute expressly subordinated the lien of the mechanic to the lien of The Finance Company.

Lien Creditors The rights of a lien creditor are governed by section 9–301, which section provides that a lien creditor is one who acquires a lien on the property in question by attachment, levy, or the like. This definition includes an assignee for the benefit of creditors, a trustee in bankruptcy, or a receiver in equity, and each dates from the time of the assignment, the filing of the petition in bankruptcy, or the appointment of a receiver in equity, as the case may be. This section provides that an unperfected security interest is subordinate to the rights of a lien creditor who becomes such lien creditor before the security interest is perfected.

Purchase-Money Security Interest A purchase-money security interest, as defined in section 9–107, will arise (1) when a seller sells goods to the buyer and retains a security interest in the goods, (2) when a lender advances money to the seller and takes back an assignment of the chattel paper, and (3) when a lender advances money to the buyer—for instance, on a chattel mortgage—to enable him to buy the goods, and the buyer uses the money for that purpose. It is thus clear that a pre-existing claim or an antecedent debt are both excluded from the category of purchase-money security interests.

    The rules pertaining to the priority of a purchase-money security interest are found in section 9–312 and relate to "inventory collateral" and "collateral other than inventory." It will be seen that the effect of the rules is to give a purchase-money security interest priority over an after-acquired security interest. It may be well to remember that a secured party may have a "temporarily perfected security interest in goods" covered by documents for twenty-one days.

(1) *Inventory Collateral* Suppose Brown, who is engaged in the retail business, enters into a security agreement with Jones, a lender, whereby the security interest of Jones covers all present inventory and all inventory thereafter acquired by Brown. Suppose further that Jones perfects his security interest by filing. Suppose still further that Brown thereafter purchases inventory of the same type from Smith, who retains a security interest in the collateral. The security interest of Jones would take priority. This is because all subsequent purchases of inventory of the same type by Brown—whether for cash or on credit—would fall within the security interest of Jones, who had a perfected security interest in after-acquired inventory. Smith could have perfected his security interest in the inventory and identifiable cash proceeds, however, if his security interest had been perfected at the time Brown received possession of the collateral and if he, before delivering the inventory to Brown, had notified Jones that he had or expected to acquire a purchase-money security interest in the inventory of Brown, describing the inventory by item or type. The written notice to Jones, in order for Smith to have priority, must be given to Jones before Smith delivers the inventory to Brown and before Smith perfects by filing. The notice to Jones must be in writing since Jones perfected by filing. [*Evans Products Co. v. Jorgensen,* p. 418.]

Pursuing the above example one step further, suppose Smith released documents of title to Brown under a documentary draft or letter of credit without perfecting by filing. Section 9–304 would give Smith temporary perfection for twenty-one days. Smith could achieve permanent priority over Jones by, before releasing the documents to Brown, searching the records where he will find the financing statement filed by Jones. Smith should then file a financing statement and notify Jones of the pending financing before he releases any documents to Brown. Jones will have priority, however, if Smith does not follow this procedure.

A similar problem is presented where goods are consigned to a merchant-debtor whose inventory, for example, is being financed by a bank. A similar problem also exists with respect to a trustee in case of bankruptcy of the debtor and in the situation where creditors of the debtor are attempting to levy on the consigned goods to satisfy a debt owed by the debtor. The consignor will have priority over the bank, creditors of the debtor, and the trustee if the consignor will (1) file a financing statement and (2) send written notice to the bank of the pending consignment describing the goods by items or type. These two things must occur before the consignee receives the goods.

(2) *Collateral Other than Inventory* A purchase-money security interest in collateral other than inventory is given priority over a conflicting security interest by section 9–312 if the security interest is perfected at the time the debtor receives possession of the collateral or within ten days thereafter. The purchase-money security interest in collateral other than inventory takes priority even though the purchase-money-secured party knows of a prior security interest or the prior security interest has been perfected by filing.

Suppose The Country Club executed and delivered to The Finance Company a mortgage encumbering its real property and the mortgage contained an after-acquired property clause encumbering all the after-acquired fixtures, furniture, and furnishings attached to or used in or about the building. Suppose The Furniture Company thereafter sold certain furniture to The Country Club and retained a security interest in the furniture. The furniture would be equipment rather than inventory, and The Furniture Company would have priority over The Finance Company in the furniture provided The Furniture Company filed a financing statement at the time The Country Club received possession of the furniture or within ten days thereafter. This is true even though The Furniture Company knew of the prior security interest of The Finance Company or the mortgage had been perfected by filing.

Suppose in the above Country Club example that a creditor of the club obtained a judgment against the club and attempted to levy on the new furniture or the club had attempted to sell the new furniture to a purchaser in bulk. Section 9–301 provides that, as against bulk purchasers and lien creditors, the purchase-money security interest is given a grace period of ten days from the date the secured party advanced value. The purchase-money–secured party—The Furniture Company—would therefore have priority over levying creditors or bulk purchasers if the secured party had perfected by filing at the time the debtor received the collateral or within ten days thereafter.

It should be kept in mind that the ten-day grace period applies to a purchase-money security interest in collateral other than inventory but it does *not* apply to a purchase-money security interest in inventory.

Proceeds A secured party ordinarily has a permanently perfected security interest in proceeds automatically even though no specific reference is made to proceeds in the financing statement. In some instances, however, the perfection will be a temporary perfection for ten days only and will terminate unless the secured party claims a permanently perfected security interest by filing a financing statement or by taking possession of the proceeds. Some of the limitations on the permanent perfection in the proceeds, therefore, deserve mention.

Section 9–306 provides that a security interest in the proceeds will continue to be perfected if the proceeds are such that a security interest in the proceeds can be perfected by filing in the same office in which a filing was made with respect to the collateral. Suppose a furniture dealer sells a sofa on an installment sales contract. Prior to this event the First Bank took a non-purchase-money security interest in the dealer's inventory to secure a loan of $50,000 to the dealer which was perfected by filing. The First Bank will have a permanently perfected security interest in the chattel paper if the First Bank could have perfected a security interest in the chattel paper by filing in the same office in which the financing statement concerning the inventory was filed. Suppose the furniture dealer had sold the sofa for a diamond. The First Bank would have a permanently perfected security interest in the diamond. Suppose, however, that the sofa had been sold for cash and the dealer used the cash to purchase the diamond. The First Bank would have a permanently perfected security interest in the diamond only if the diamond is of the type of collateral described in the financing statement. In this example, it is unlikely that the diamond is the type of collateral described in the financing statement. The security interest in the diamond, therefore, will be temporarily perfected for ten days only unless the First Bank takes possession of the diamond or files a financing statement with respect to the diamond.

Let us suppose still further that the sofa was sold and the dealer received a negotiable note which constituted the proceeds. Perfection by filing is not possible with respect to the negotiable note, and the security interest of the First Bank in the note will terminate unless the First Bank takes possession of the note within ten days. If the sofa had been sold for cash, however, the First Bank would have a permanently perfected security interest in the identifiable cash proceeds until the debtor is involved in insolvency proceedings. This rule will be discussed later under "Debtor in Insolvency Proceedings."

This discussion of proceeds would not be complete without reference to section 9–312, which provides that a perfected *purchase-money* security interest in inventory carries over only to *identifiable cash proceeds.* But this is not true if the collateral is other than inventory. Suppose the First Bank filed a financing statement with respect to all the equipment of the debtor and the debtor later bought two additional tractors from the Acme Company, which company retained a perfected purchase-money security interest by filing. Suppose further that the debtor at a later date sold one of the tractors to Jones. The Acme Company will have priority over the First Bank in all the proceeds—money, chattel paper, and the like—as well as the tractor which was not sold by the debtor. If this example, however, had involved inventory and the Acme Company had retained a purchase-money security interest in the two tractors which became a part of the debtor's inventory, the priority of the Acme Company over the First Bank would extend only to the one unsold tractor and the identifiable cash proceeds from the sale of one tractor by the debtor to Jones. This conclusion is based on the assumption that the Acme Company properly perfected its security interest.

Future Advances   Sections 9–301, 9–307, and 9–312 provide priority rules for future advances. Suppose the secured party has perfected by filing a security interest in collateral to secure credit already extended to the debtor under an arrangement whereby the creditor is to extend additional credit in the future. The security interest for the future advances will have the same priority as the first advance. This is because the initial creditor should not have to perfect again in order to continue his perfected security interest since the filing or possession gives notice to third persons who might decide to intervene and advance credit to the debtor. In the case of temporary perfection for twenty-one days or the automatic perfection in consumer goods, third persons are not given notice. A future advance in either situation takes priority from the date of the advance and not from the date of the initial advance.

A purchaser of the collateral not in the regular course of business and a lien creditor deserve brief mention. The law pertaining to the two is not identical, but it is similar. Suppose the secured party makes his first advance and then a later advance to the debtor. Suppose still further that after the first advance, but before the later advance is made, there is a purchaser of the collateral not in the regular course of business or that a creditor of the debtor obtains a lien against the collateral. Unless the secured party has knowledge of the sale, he will have priority in making advances to the debtor for forty-five days. If the secured party has knowledge of the sale and makes a future advance to the debtor or if the advance is made more than forty-five days after the sale, such advances will not be secured by the collateral which has been sold.

The secured party will have priority in making a future advance to the debtor as opposed to a lien creditor if only one of the following occurs: (1) The advance is made within forty-five days after the existence of the lien creditor; (2) the advance is made without knowledge of the lien creditor; or (3) the advance is made pursuant to a commitment to make the advance which commitment was entered without knowledge of the lien creditor during the forty-five days. One could logically ask why the framers of the Code settled on the forty-five days mentioned above. The forty-five-day rule was adopted in order to correspond to the priority which is given to a secured party who makes an advance of credit to the debtor after a federal tax lien has been filed against the collateral.

Fixtures Section 9–313 provides that "goods are fixtures when they become so related to particular real estate that an interest in them arises under real estate law." This section further provides, however, that no security interest can arise under the Code in ordinary building materials. This means that the law of the various states will determine whether lumber, bricks, and the like incorporated in a building upon the land are or are not a fixture. The real estate law of the various states, moreover, may be used for the creation of a security interest in fixtures. For example, a real estate mortgage may include fixtures. If the real estate mortgage contains all the elements required of a financing statement, it will be effective as a fixture filing from the date of recording or filing.

The first task is to distinguish between an "ordinary filing" of a financing statement—often referred to as a regular filing—and a "fixture filing." An ordinary filing has been previously discussed. The fixture filing is more complex and is designed to give the fixture-secured party priority over real estate parties, such as real estate mortgagees, subsequent purchasers, financers, and the like. The fixture filing must (1) occur in the office where the records pertaining to real estate are recorded or filed, (2) indicate that it covers fixtures, (3) recite that it is required to be recorded or filed in the real estate records, and (4) contain a description of the real estate. If there is doubt as to whether the collateral is a fixture or personal property, the secured party should effect both an ordinary filing and a fixture filing. The general rule tells us that a secured party who complies with the requirements of a fixture filing will be prior to both existing and future real estate interests. This rule is qualified by the exceptions discussed later in this chapter under "Fixture Filing Not Required."

(1) *The Construction Mortgage* The construction mortgage is designed to secure an obligation incurred for the purpose of making improvements to land, including the cost of the land if the recorded writing so indicates. This mortgage,

therefore, should be so drafted that it indicates that it is security for construction financing. The construction mortgage will then have priority over a purchase-money seller or a financer of goods installed as a part of the original construction provided the mortgage is on record at the time the goods are installed. If there is a construction mortgage on record, however, a purchase-money seller or financer of goods to be installed would likely hesitate to sell or finance such goods since he would occupy a junior position to the construction mortgage.

The secured party—seller or financer of goods to be installed in the premises—in order to have priority over competing real estate parties should strictly observe the following:

(1) The debtor must have an interest in the real estate which is on the real estate records or be in possession of the real estate.

(2) The security interest must attach before the fixtures are installed.

(3) The secured party must have a purchase-money security interest by being the seller of the goods or the financer of the sale of the goods. A secured party can achieve priority over an existing mortgage or other encumbrance only by means of a purchase-money security interest unless the prior encumbrancer waives his interest in the fixture in writing. A purchase-money or a non-purchase-money security interest, perfected by a fixture filing, will have priority over a real estate interest which is created after the fixture filing.

(4) There must be no construction mortgage against the premises which is recorded or filed.

(5) A fixture filing must occur before the fixtures are installed or within ten days thereafter. The ten days of grace carry risks because subsequent mortgagees and buyers during the ten days after the installation of the collateral and before the filing will not be bound by a subsequent filing although it is within the ten days. The safest way is to file before the fixtures are installed and thereby achieve priority over existing and subsequent encumbrancers and owners.

(2) *Fixture Filing Not Required* Section 9–313 permits an ordinary filing—in the chattel records—in a few instances. Perfection of a security interest in *readily removable office and factory machines* in any manner allowed by Article 9 before the collateral becomes fixtures will have priority over conflicting interests of an encumbrancer or owner of the real estate including a construction mortgagee. A seller or financer of relatively inexpensive fixtures may also perfect by an ordinary filing. The secured party—seller of inexpensive fixtures—will achieve priority in case of judgments against the debtor and, it is believed, when the debtor becomes a bankrupt. Such secured party, however, will not have priority over real estate parties.

A purchase-money security interest in a *readily removable replacement of a domestic appliance which is consumer goods* will have priority over real estate parties and other security interests without a filing since a filing is not required for the perfection of a security interest in consumer goods. In the absence of a filing, however, the secured party will be subordinate to the rights of a buyer of such goods for value, without knowledge of the security interest and for his own personal, family, or household use.

Trade Fixtures Fixtures are very often "trade fixtures" if the purchaser is a tenant who has no interest recorded in the real estate records. The trade fixtures remain personal property, and an ordinary filing will be adequate for the protection of the secured party. If the right of removal of the fixtures terminates, the security interest will continue to have priority over the real estate parties for a reasonable length of time.

Removal of Fixtures The pre-Code law held that a fixture could not be removed by someone having an interest in it provided substantial damages would be inflicted on the premises, by such removal. The Code abandons this "material injury to the freehold" rule. Therefore, a secured party, who has priority over all owners and encumbrancers of the real estate may remove his goods or collateral. He must, however, be willing to pay for any damages inflicted to the whole. Such damages would not include the diminution of value of the whole caused by the absence of the goods.

Accessions Accessions and fixtures are similar, but an understanding of the rules in section 9–314 should explain the distinction between fixtures and accessions. A new engine installed in an old automobile is a good example of an accession. Suppose Brown, a retailer, sells an engine to Smith in a conditional sale with the understanding that the engine is to be installed in an old automobile—the "whole." The safest way for Brown to acquire a security interest which will be prior to all other interests in the whole is to make certain that his interest attaches to the goods—the engine—and is perfected before the affixation, that is, the engine is installed. If Brown's interest is not perfected and it attaches after the affixation, existing interests in the whole will be prior unless such claimants waive their interests in the goods or consent to the affixation. If Brown's interest is not perfected but it does attach before the affixation, it will be prior to all perfected or unperfected existing claims in the whole, but it will be subordinated to subsequently acquired interests unless such claimants had knowledge of Brown's interest when such claims were created.

A secured party who has priority over all claims of persons who have an interest in the whole may remove his goods or collateral. He must, however, be willing to pay for any damages inflicted to the whole. Such damages would not include the diminution of value of the whole caused by the absence of the goods—the engine.

Buyers of Goods in the Ordinary Course of Business Section 9–307 provides that a buyer in the ordinary course of business takes free of a security interest created by the seller even though the security interest is perfected and the buyer knows of its existence. This is because a lender knows or should know that the borrower ordinarily intends to sell the encumbered goods in order to raise money to repay the loan, and also because buyers would probably be reluctant to purchase the goods if they were required to take the goods subject to an inventory lien. A buyer in the ordinary course of business is defined by section 1–201 as one who buys in good faith and "without knowledge that the sale to him is in violation of the ownership rights or security interest of a third party" and who buys in the "ordinary course from a person in the business of selling goods of that kind." [*O. M. Scott Credit Corp. v. Apex Inc.*, p. 419.]

A person who buys minerals, oil, and gas at the wellhead or minehead is making a purchase from a person who is deemed to be in the business of selling goods of that kind. Such a purchaser, therefore, may be a buyer in the ordinary course of business.

The above-mentioned sections 9–307 and 1–201 taken together mean that a buyer takes free if he merely knows that a security interest covers the goods. He will take subject to the security interest, however, if he knows that the sale is in violation of some term in the security agreement.

Section 9–307 expressly excludes a purchaser who purchases farm products from a person engaged in farm operations. This exclusion was made because a purchaser from the farmer does not buy from inventory: the things a farmer sells are classified as farm products. Casual sales would be excluded by implication. The protection given buyers, therefore, will primarily be buyers of inventory.

Chattel Paper and Instruments   The rules governing (1) the inventory financer in chattel paper proceeds and (2) the receivables financer in chattel paper and instruments are found in section 9–308.

(1)   *Inventory Financer*   It is to be remembered that an inventory financer frequently claims chattel paper and instruments proceeds when he files his inventory-financing statement. It should also be remembered that a security interest in chattel paper may be perfected by filing. This method of perfection, however, leaves the inventory financer with a nonpossessory security interest. Suppose the inventory financer finances an automobile dealer and does claim the chattel paper proceeds in his financing statement. Suppose further that the automobile dealer sells an automobile to a consumer buyer under an installment sales agreement and the resulting chattel paper is assigned to a second financer. Does the inventory financer or the second financer have priority to the proceeds of the chattel paper? The second financer has priority provided he gives new value and takes possession of the chattel paper in the ordinary course of his business. This is true even though the second financer knew that the specific paper was subject to the security interest of the inventory financer. This rule governs the situation where the security interest in chattel paper or instruments is claimed merely as proceeds by the inventory financer, the chattel paper or instruments are left in the possession of the debtor, and the second financer gives new value and takes possession of the chattel paper or instruments.

(2)   *Receivables Financer*   The rules governing the receivables financer

pertain to the situation where a security interest in specific chattel paper or an instrument is based upon the value advanced against the chattel paper itself and not against inventory. Suppose a consumer buyer purchases furniture from a furniture dealer on a credit basis and executes chattel paper payable in installments in payment of all or a portion of the purchase price. Suppose further that the dealer refinances the transaction by assigning the chattel paper—which is itself collateral—to a receivables financer who perfects his security interest by filing. Suppose still further that the chattel paper is left in the possession of the dealer to facilitate collection from the consumer buyer and that the dealer thereafter assigns the collateral to a second receivables financer. Does the first financer or the second financer have priority? The second financer will have priority if he gives new value and takes possession in the ordinary course of his business *without knowledge* that the collateral is subject to a prior security interest. A secured party in possession of chattel paper, therefore, is given priority against the claims of a secured party with a nonpossessory security interest in the same collateral. It is thus important for the receivables financer to take possession of the chattel paper or instruments where possible, because his interest is subject to being cut off by a purchaser in the ordinary course of business who has no knowledge of the security interest. A secured party who wishes to leave the paper in the possession of the debtor should protect himself against purchasers by stamping or noting on the paper in such a way as to indicate the outstanding security interest.

Reacquisition of Goods by Seller Goods which have been sold are sometimes returned to or repossessed by the seller. The original security interest of the inventory financer will continue perfected without any further action on the part of the secured party if the original security interest was perfected by filing. The inventory financer—if he has not filed—must either take possession of the returned goods or file a financing statement in order to protect his interest. The rights of the inventory financer, however, will be cut off when the goods are resold to a buyer in the ordinary course of business.

Debtor in Insolvency Proceedings Two definitions should be repeated. Section 9–306 defines money, checks, deposit accounts, and the like as "cash proceeds" and all other proceeds as "noncash proceeds." Section 1–201 defines "insolvency proceedings" so as to include not only bankruptcy proceedings but any assignment for the benefit of creditors or other proceedings intended to rehabilitate the debtor.

A secured party who has a perfected security interest in proceeds will continue to have a perfected security interest in the proceeds whenever the debtor is involved in insolvency proceedings with respect to (1) identifiable noncash proceeds and in separate deposit accounts containing only proceeds, (2) identifiable cash proceeds in the form of money which is not commingled with other money nor deposited in a deposit account prior to the insolvency proceedings, and (3) identifiable cash proceeds in the form of checks which are deposited in a deposit account prior to the insolvency proceedings.

The secured party has a security interest in all cash and bank accounts of the debtor with respect to cash proceeds which are not identifiable and which have been commingled or deposited in a bank account. This security interest, however, is subject to any right of setoff. It is also limited to cash received by the debtor within ten days prior to the institution of the insolvency proceedings, less any amount the debtor may have paid the secured party during the ten-day period.

REMEDIES ON DEFAULT

The rights of the secured party in the collateral after the default of the debtor are the very essence of the secured transaction. These rights distinguish the secured lender from the unsecured lender. The secured party is given the right, unless the secured transaction is a possessory one in the nature of a pledge, to take possession of the collateral. He may proceed to take possession without judicial process if this can be done without a breach of the peace. The seller of a television set on a conditional sale to a consumer, for example, may repossess the set if the consumer defaults in his payments. This is the familiar situation which is a time-saver and is inexpensive. The secured party may, if he anticipates difficulty or a breach of the peace, obtain judicial process to aid him in effecting possession. After the secured party takes possession of the collateral, there is no longer any distinction between a nonpossessory and a possessory security interest.

The particular circumstances of the case will determine which alternative the secured party may pursue in order to satisfy his claim out of the collateral. He may be compelled to sell the collateral, but he may retain, sell, or otherwise dispose of the collateral in most situations.

Collection Rights   Section 9–502 recognizes that collateral may consist of claims held by the debtor against third persons. The secured party has the right after default to collect claims due the debtor from third persons. A secured party with respect to instruments which call for the payment of money, including earned or unearned accounts, general intangibles, and chattel paper is entitled to notify the account debtor or obligor on an instrument to make future payments to the secured party. This may be illustrated by the familiar situation where a retailer borrows money from a bank with the agreement that his accounts receivable will be collateral. If the retailer defaults, the bank may take over the accounts, notify the account debtors, and collect from them. The bank must proceed, however, in a commercially reasonable manner and it may deduct the reasonable expenses of collecting from the collections. It should be noted that this is a loan, and any surplus belongs to the retailer-borrower, and the retailer is liable for any deficiency. This is to say that if the bank is unable to collect the total amount of the debt, the retailer is liable for any deficiency. The surplus-deficiency rule obviously would not apply if this had been a sale of the accounts rather than a loan, unless it is contractually agreed that the surplus-deficiency rule will be applied.

Retention of Collateral   Section 9–505 provides that the secured party may, unless he is compelled to sell the collateral, propose in writing to retain the collateral in satisfaction of the obligation. If he chooses this alternative, he must notify the debtor only in case of consumer goods if the debtor has not signed a statement after default in which he renounced or modified his rights. In other cases, notice to other secured parties is required only if they have given written notice of their claim of an interest in the collateral to the secured party before the secured party has sent notice to the debtor or before the debtor renounced his rights. The secured party is under a duty to dispose of the collateral if he receives an objection in writing from a person entitled to receive notification within twenty-one days after the notice was sent. On the other hand, if the secured party does not receive such notice, he may retain the collateral in satisfaction of the debtor's obligation.

Disposition of Collateral   Section 9–505 compels the secured party to dispose of the collateral if the secured transaction involves consumer goods and the debtor has paid 60 percent of the purchase price on a purchase-money security interest or 60 percent of the loan in the case of another security interest. A secured party who fails to dispose of the collateral within ninety days after he takes possession may be compelled to respond to the debtor for conversion, or in damages for failure to comply with the provisions of Article 9.

The secured party, when disposal of the collateral is desired or required, may sell, lease, or otherwise dispose of the collateral. The sale may be by public or private proceedings. The secured party must give reasonable notice of the time and place of any intended public sale unless the collateral is perishable or is likely to decline speedily in value or is of a type usually sold on a recognized market. He must also give notice of any intended private sale, but the notice may merely state a date after which the disposition will be made. Such notice must be sent to the debtor if he has not signed a statement in which he renounced or modified his right to such notice. This is the only notice required in the case of consumer goods. In other cases, notice to other secured parties is required only if they give written notice to the secured party of their claim to an interest in the collateral before the secured party sent notice to the debtor or before the debtor renounced his rights. All aspects of the sale, however, must be commercially reasonable. [*Vic Hansen & Sons, Inc. v. Crowley*, p. 420.]

Proceeds of Sale   The secured party, as a result of a sale, must apply any funds coming into his hands, first, to the reasonable expenses pertaining to the sale, second, to the satisfaction of the indebtedness secured, and third, to the satisfaction of any subordinate security interest if a demand is made therefor. The secured party must then account to the debtor for any surplus, and the debtor is liable for any deficiency. The underlying transaction, however, may have been a sale of intangibles rather than a transfer for security. Section 9–504 provides, therefore, that the debtor is neither entitled to any surplus nor liable for any deficiency, unless the security agreement so provides, where the underlying transaction involved the sale of accounts, or chattel paper.

Section 9–506 gives the debtor the right to redeem the collateral at any time before it has been disposed of or a contract has been entered into for its disposition.

Liability of Secured Party for Failure to Comply   Section 9–507 provides a remedy for the debtor, or any other person adversely affected, when the secured party is proceeding in a contrary manner relating to default. The debtor may obtain an order of the court ordering the secured party to dispose of the collateral, or he may obtain an order to restrain disposition of the collateral. Damages representing the loss caused by a failure of the secured party to comply with the Code provisions may be recovered if the secured party has disposed of the collateral.

The secured party must act in a manner which is commercially reasonable in disposing of the collateral. He is said to have sold or disposed of the collateral in a commercially reasonable manner if he has sold or disposed of it (1) in the usual manner in any recognized market, (2) at a price current in any recognized market at the time of disposition, or (3) otherwise in conformity with reasonable commercial practices among dealers in the type of property in question. The fact that a better price could have been obtained by a sale at a different time or in a different method is not of itself sufficient to establish that the sale was not made in a commercially reasonable manner.

CASES

Walker Bank & Trust Co. v. Burrows,   507 P.2d 384 (Utah 1973). Action by Walker Bank and Trust Company, plaintiff, against Gale G. Bailey, McKay G. Bailey, LaFaye Bailey, Gloria Bailey, Terrill W. Bailey, and Colleen Bailey, defendants, to determine the priority of rights to certain cattle which had been sold to Wesley Burrows.

Tuckett, Justice   On or about June 28, 1966, the Baileys entered into an installment sales contract with one Wesley Burrows for the sale of Baileys' ranch including 311 cows and 12 bulls. Burrows took possession of the livestock on June 30, 1966, and retained possession until sometime in 1968 when the Baileys repossessed the ranch and cattle. On June 15, 1966, Walker Bank made a loan to Burrows in the sum of $80,000. The loan was secured by a chattel mortgage from Burrows to the bank covering 700 head of cattle which Burrows was purchasing. On June 21, 1966, Walker Bank filed a financing statement with the Secretary of State listing Burrows as debtor and the bank as creditor. On or about December 29, 1966, Burrows executed and delivered to Walker Bank a security agreement covering 700 head of cattle located in Washington, Kane, and Garfield counties. On February 8, 1967, Walker Bank filed a financing statement with the Secretary of State listing Burrows as debtor and the bank as creditor and described cattle bearing the "pitchfork" and "scissors" brands as security. Out of the proceeds of the loan the Baileys were paid the sum of $20,000 on the installment sale contract.

After a trial of the issues the court below made a finding to the effect that

311 cows and 12 bulls were delivered by the Baileys to Burrows on or about June 30, 1966, and remained in the possession of Burrows until sometime in 1968, when the Baileys repossessed the ranch and cattle. On May 26, 1967, the Baileys filed a financing statement with the Secretary of State covering the livestock in question.

It is quite clear that the Baileys did not perfect a security interest in the livestock in question by retaining possession and they did not perfect a security interest by filing a financing statement with the Secretary of State until after Walker Bank's filing. The record shows that Walker Bank perfected its security interest pursuant to the provisions of Section 70A–9-302, U.C.A. 1953, as amended, prior to the filing of the financial statement by the Baileys. We therefore conclude that the security interest of the bank is prior to that of the Baileys. [DECISION FOR PLAINTIFF]

Evans Products Co. v. Jorgensen, 421 P.2d 978 (Ore. 1966). Action by Evans Products Company, plaintiff, who had a security interest in the inventory of Coos Plywood, a manufacturer of plywood, against Karl Jorgensen and Richard Jorgensen, partners, doing business as Winter Lake Veneer Company, defendants, who sold veneer to Coos Plywood. This action involves a question of priority between a secured party and a supplier of raw materials to the debtor.

Plaintiff made loans to Coos Plywood which were secured by a security agreement, the provision of which gave plaintiff a security interest in the inventory of Coos Plywood as follows:

"All green and dry veneer, work in progress, and finished plywood now owned and all similar goods hereafter acquired, including their product, and proceeds."

Plaintiff had taken all the applicable steps required for the perfection of its security interest.

Defendants thereafter sold and delivered three truckloads of veneer, which is the basic raw material for the manufacture of plywood, to Coos Plywood. Coos Plywood had no funds to pay for the plywood when the invoice was presented, and defendants accepted plywood in payment of the veneer and had the plywood removed to defendant's plant. Plaintiff then brought this action to foreclose its lien against such plywood.

Denecke, Justice: In order for Evans to secure a security interest in the veneer delivered by defendants to Coos, there must be an agreement that it attach, that value be given, and "the debtor (Coos) has rights in the collateral." Section 9–204(1). The first two conditions are clearly satisfied. . . .

In the present case there was delivery to the buyer "Coos" and the only interest that could be retained by defendant was a "security interest." Coos had possession of the veneer which was delivered pursuant to the contract of sale. Under these circumstances Coos had "rights" in the collateral, the veneer; therefore Evans' security interest attached to the veneer when it was delivered to Coos. . . .

If defendants' intention was to retain title to the veneer after delivery and until cash was paid, and we will assume that was their intention, they could have reserved a "security interest" in the veneer and had priority over Evans. Section 9–312(3) gives one with a purchase-money security interest priority over an inventory financer when certain steps have been taken. Defendants could have had a "purchase-money security interest" as defined in section 9–107(1). To create such interest an agreement signed by Coos and describing the collateral is necessary to satisfy section 9–203. To perfect such interest a financing statement must be filed. Section 9–302. Evans must be notified before delivery that the sellers intend to have a purchase-money security interest in the veneer.

Defendants did not attempt to create nor perfect any purchase-money security interest in the veneer (that was the only interest they could reserve when delivery was made) and, therefore, Evans' security interest must prevail. . . .

We have held that Evans acquired a security interest in the veneer upon its delivery to Coos. It is admitted that Evans had a security interest in the plywood delivered by Coos to defendants and we have held that such security interest was not divested; therefore, under the UCC Evans is entitled to both the veneer and the plywood. If the defendants had refused to deliver the veneer except for cash upon delivery, not upon invoice, or if defendants had perfected a purchase-money security interest in the veneer, they would have had either the cash or a prior security interest in the veneer. They did not avail themselves of the protection afforded under the UCC while Evans did and, therefore, Evans is entitled to prevail. [DECISION FOR PLAINTIFF]

O. M. Scott Credit Corp. v. Apex Inc.,   198 A.2d 673 (R.I. 1964). Action by O. M. Scott Credit Corporation, plaintiff, a financing corporation, against Apex Incorporated, defendant, the operator of a discount house, to replevy 300 bags of fertilizer.

O. M. Scott & Sons Company, a manufacturer of garden supplies, distributes its products through authorized dealers who are expressly restricted to sales to ultimate consumers. Massachusetts Hardware & Supply Company, an authorized distributor of such products, held such products in its possession under a trust receipt which provided, among other things, that the dealer "agrees to hold said products in trust for the sole purpose of making sales to consumers functioning as a wholesaler." The defendant conducts a discount house, and operates the Old Colony Distributing Company for the purpose of purchasing merchandise. Jack Rabinowitz, an employee of defendant in a managerial capacity, discussed with Bernard J. Moran, an employee of Massachusetts Hardware, the sale to Old Colony of 300 bags of fertilizer manufactured by O. M. Scott & Sons Company. The sale was consummated, but Massachusetts Hardware failed to pay the purchase price thereof. Plaintiff, a financing corporation that had a perfected security interest in the fertilizer, contends that its security interest continued in the collateral notwithstanding the sale thereof to defendant. Defendant contends that, as a purchaser in the ordinary course of business, it took free of the security interest.

Roberts, Justice: The trial justice summarized the evidence and made findings of fact as follows:

Rabinowitz frankly testified that Moran told him that Massachusetts Hardware could not sell to Apex and accordingly Rabinowitz suggested that the sale be made to Old Colony Distributing Company, a subsidiary of Apex, with the indication some of it would go to a large user, perhaps a golf course, and that later Moran agreed to sell 300 bags in that manner. It thus appears that Rabinowitz knew that a sale to Apex would be contrary to the authority and intention of the seller and if with that knowledge he used a subterfuge to bring it about he could not be found to have acted in good faith. If it is thus clear that Moran made it known he could not sell to Apex it seems most likely, and is found by the Court, that he told Rabinowitz why, namely the restriction upon Massachusetts Hardware to sell only at retail and not to discount houses, together with the information as to the bags bearing serial numbers which would show their origin, which, once disclosed to Scott, would result in loss to Massachusetts Hardware of a valuable line. On these facts the Court must find that the buyer was not acting in good faith as that term has significance at this point.

We then turn to the questions of law raised by the parties. This is a situation, as we understand it, in which plaintiff had perfected a security interest in the merchandise by virtue of its recordation of its trust receipt under the pertinent provisions of the Uniform Commercial Code. . . .

The trial justice in his decision directed attention to the Code provisions holding that a buyer in the ordinary course of business is one who buys "in good faith and without knowledge that the sale to him is in violation of" the security rights of a third party. We agree that in such circumstance a buyer takes the goods free of the security interest even though he knows there is a security interest therein. It is only when in addition thereto he knows that the sale violates some term of the security agreement not waived by the secured party, either in express terms or by conduct, that he takes subject to the security interest. It is our opinion that the trial justice has correctly disclosed the nature of the good faith contemplated by the provisions of the Code relating to purchases in the ordinary course of business. . . .

We are of the opinion that the defendant took the merchandise in the instant transaction subject to the security interest of the plaintiff and that, therefore, the plaintiff had a right to possession of the goods superior to that of the defendant and that replevin lies for the recovery thereof. [DECISION FOR PLAINTIFF]

Vic Hansen & Sons, Inc., v. Crowley, 203 N.W.2d. 728 (Wis. 1973). Vic Hansen & Sons, Inc., plaintiff, brought this action against Joyce T. Crowley and Autry Smithson, defendants, to recover a deficiency which arose from the repossession and resale of an automobile. On August 15, 1970, the defendants purchased from the plaintiff a used 1965 Oldsmobile for the total time price of $2,253.52, which comprised a cash price of $1,595 subject to other charges, such as tax, insurance, and the like. The automobile was returned for repairs on several occasions within a few days. On August 24, 1970, the automobile was surrendered to plaintiff, who had the title re-entered in its name. After making a demand for payment and receiving none, plaintiff sent a notice to defendants on October 1, 1970, stating that after October 15, 1970, the automobile would be sold at a private sale. The automobile was "purchased" at a private sale by the plaintiff by means of an interoffice exchange of papers, and the defendants were credited with $700. A net balance of $939.63 remained after certain adjustments for insurance, and the like. This sum was later reduced to $859.19 as a result of the usurious rate of interest and the time-price differential which could not be collected. This action was then brought to recover the $859.19 as a deficiency. The trial court dismissed the complaint, and this appeal followed.

Connor T. Hansen, Justice: The dispositive issue raised on this appeal is whether, under the Uniform Commercial Code (UCC) as adopted in Wisconsin, defendants are liable to plaintiff for any deficiency arising out of their default on their contract for the sale of the automobile.

Section 409.504, Stats., in part provides: "The secured party may buy at any public sale if the collateral is of a type customarily sold in a recognized market or is of a type which is the subject of widely distributed standard price quotations he may buy at private sale."

The record indicates that the plaintiff "sold" the automobile to itself through an interoffice exchange of papers. There is no evidence of any bids sought or given, or any attempt to ascertain the value of the automobile other than from those within plaintiff's business organization. It is undisputed that it was a private sale. Much of counsel's arguments and discussion are concerned with the commercial reasonableness of this "sale" and the price obtained.

The trial court held that the sale of the automobile was not "commercially reasonable" as required by section 409.504 (3), Stats., in that while the defendants were indebted as to the "retail value" of the automobile, plaintiff unilaterally assigned a "wholesale value" upon sale. It was the opinion of the trial court that the application of different standards of valuation results in a sale that is not "commercially reasonable," and that the plaintiff failed to submit sufficient evidence to establish the amount of the deficiency, if any, to which it was entitled.

Although defendants plead as an affirmative defense the allegation that the "sale" and price obtained were not commercially reasonable, there is some conflict as to who has the burden of proof thereto.

One line of authority holds that the secured party must establish that every aspect of the sale was commercially reasonable.

Other authorities have held that a secured party makes out a case for a deficiency judgment by proving the debt and security agreement and that a credit of a stated amount has been allowed as the result of the sale of the collateral, and that the burden shifts to the debtor to show why the creditor should not recover the deficiency.

It is our opinion that those jurisdictions which hold that the secured party must establish that every aspect of the sale was commercially reasonable enunciate a rule that more appropriately recognizes the tenor of the Code. This will henceforth be the rule in this state in those instances where the property is sold at "private sale." The secured party has the duty under the Code to proceed in good faith and in a commercially reasonable manner. It follows that he who has the duty should also have the burden of proof.

Upon trial it was necessary for the plaintiff to establish that every aspect of the sale was commercially reasonable, including the adequacy of the price for which the collateral was sold.

The evidence submitted on the sufficiency of the sale is scant. When the vehicle was first traded to the plaintiff, prior to sale to the defendants, it was appraised at $800 and, with minor repairs amounting to $107.70, was thereafter resold to the defendants for a cash value of $1595. Approximately 60 days later, after its return, the car was sold back into inventory at an appraised "wholesale" value of $700. The original appraisal of $800 was also designated as "wholesale." Plaintiff's witnesses testified that the $700 was a "fair value," and close to what other dealers would have paid for it. The record is barren on the subject of the retail value of the car on October 15, 1970, the time of the private sale to the plaintiff. The vehicle resold for $995 in February, 1971, after having had repairs made in the amount of $210.12.

There is no evidence as to what the fair market value of the vehicle was upon deficiency sale; nor did plaintiff establish that the $700 was in fact the wholesale price, or what effect the repairs of the vehicle had upon the value of the automobile itself. There is some evidence of abuse to the vehicle but no evidence as to its effect upon the value. All that was submitted were self-serving assertions that the vehicle was worth $800 to $700 wholesale, and $1595 to $995 retail.

We, therefore, affirm the judgment of the trial court finding that the plaintiff's sale of defendants' collateral was not "commercially reasonable," and that the plaintiff failed to carry his burden of proof as to the amount, if any, of the deficiency. [DECISION FOR DEFENDANTS]

PROBLEMS

1 Benson purchased a used automobile from the Acme Auto Sales for $1,200 on a conditional sales contract. He made an initial payment of $200 and agreed to pay the balance in twenty-four installments. Benson drove the automobile for 10,000 miles in six months, after which time he delivered the automobile to Mason, a mechanic, for extensive repairs. The repair bill was $325, which Benson refused to pay. Benson also refused to make any additional installment payments to the Acme Auto Sales. A controversy then arose between Acme Auto Sales and Mason with respect to the right of possession of the automobile. Does Acme Auto Sales have a right to repossess the automobile from Mason?

2 Brown, who was a tenant of Smith, purchased a bathtub and kitchen sink from plaintiff on a conditional sales contract and installed them in the rented house. Smith thereafter sold the property to defendant, and Brown defaulted in his payment on the conditional sales contract. Plaintiff then attempted to repossess the bathtub and sink, but the court held that the bathtub and sink passed as realty to defendant when he purchased the property. How could plaintiff have protected his interest?

3 Plaintiff sold a refrigerator for $300 to defendant on a conditional sales contract, which provided for payment in twelve monthly installments. Defendant was to have possession at once, but title was not to pass until the final payment was made. The contract also provided that, in case of default by defendant, plaintiff might retake possession of the refrigerator at any time. Defendant defaulted after the first monthly installment was paid. Plaintiff retook possession of the refrigerator, and notified defendant by letter that the refrigerator would be retained by the plaintiff in satisfaction of the unpaid balance of $200. Defendant wrote plaintiff immediately and requested a resale. Plaintiff complied with the request, and notified defendant of the time and place of the resale. The proceeds of the sale amounted to $175 after the expenses were deducted. Is defendant correct in his contention that he has no further liability?

4 The security interest of a lender covered all present inventory and all inventory to be thereafter acquired by a retailer. The lender perfected his security interest by filing. A wholesaler thereafter sold certain goods which are classed as inventory to the retailer and retained a security interest in the goods. Discuss the procedure whereby the wholesaler may protect his security interest.

5 Morgan purchased a new automobile from Tropical Auto Sales. Tropical Auto Sales borrowed $3,000 from the Finance Company and used the conditional sales contract as collateral. The Finance Company, however, permitted Tropical Auto Sales to retain possession of the conditional sales contract in order to collect the monthly installments from Morgan. Tropical Auto Sales, in violation of the rights of the Finance Company, sold the conditional sales contract to the First Bank. The First Bank paid value and took possession of the conditional sales contract in the ordinary course of business and without knowledge that the conditional sales contract was subject to a security interest. What are the rights of the Finance Company in the conditional sales contract as opposed to those of the First Bank?

6 Kelley visited The Electric Shop for the purpose of purchasing a radio. He was aware of the fact that the First Bank was an inventory financer for The Electrical Shop and that the inventory was, therefore, subject to a security interest which was perfected. Kelley purchased a radio for $150 and paid for it in cash. Two weeks later, the First Bank attempted to recover the radio from Kelley, contending that it had a right to do so since The Electric Shop was in arrears in its payments and no accounting had been made for the radio. Is the First Bank correct in this contention?

7 Dyer owned a house in which a furnace was installed that ceased to function during the time in which the temperature reached a low of ten degrees. He purchased a new furnace from Strawn on a conditional sales contract for the consideration of $2,800. The furnace was installed, and it functioned properly. Strawn, for some unexplained reason, failed to file a financing statement. Dyer, three months after the purchase of the furnace, sold the house to Wills, who had no notice of the conditional sale. Dyer defaulted in the payments to Strawn, who attempted to remove the furnace. Strawn contends that the Code allows the removal of the furnace provided he is willing to pay for the damages to the premises. Is this contention of Strawn correct?

8 Brown, who carried on business in a state which required both local and central filing, purchased two tractors from the XYZ Company under a conditional sales contract. The tractors were to be used in the construction business. The company retained a security interest in the machinery, and filed a financing statement in the local office of the county in which the buyer had his sole office, but there was no filing with the Secretary of State. Brown was thereafter adjudicated a bankrupt, and the trustee in bankruptcy sold the machinery. Does the XYZ Company or the trustee have a superior claim to the proceeds of the sale?

Part

7

AGENCY

33

CREATION AND AUTHORITY

The word "agency" is broad enough to include all situations in which one person is employed to act for another person. Briefly stated, however, the law of agency deals with the rules of law when one person, called the "agent," agrees to act for the benefit of another person, called the "principal." This chapter will be devoted to (1) the distinction between agents and similar relationships, (2) the kinds of agents, (3) the capacity of parties, (4) the creation of the relation, (5) the authority of agents, and (6) ratification.

AGENCY DISTINGUISHED

Independent Contractor   An independent contractor is a person who contracts to do a piece of work according to his own judgment and methods. He has the right to employ and direct the action of the workmen independently of his employer. He is freed from any superior authority in his employer to say how the specified work shall be done, and he is not subject to his employer except as to the result of the work. The employer, more concisely stated, contracts for the result with no control over the means of accomplishment. An agent, on the other hand, is subject to control by his principal. The distinction between an independent contractor and an agent is most important because, as a general rule, the employer is not liable for the business commitments made by the contractor, torts that might be inflicted upon third persons by the contractor, or the acts of the employees of such a contractor. This exemption from liability, no doubt, has influenced many employers to employ independent contractors to do whatever work can be accomplished on that basis.

It should not be presumed, however, that the general rule which exempts an employer from liability for the conduct of the independent contractor is all-inclusive. Some important exceptions to the rule cannot go unnoticed. The employer is not relieved from liability if the injury is caused by his own negligence. This rule is broad enough to prevent the employer from escaping liability if he either knew, or by the exercise of reasonable care might have ascertained, that the contractor was not properly qualified to undertake the work. The employer is liable for the results of his interference in, or control of, the work. In such cases, however, the liability of the employer might be grounded upon the theory that the contractor was not independent. The employer is liable where the act contracted for is illegal or wrongful. There is also a growing number of cases which hold the employer liable when the work consists of such extrahazardous duties as dynamiting and excavating. In the absence of unusual circumstances, however, the employer is not liable for acts of an independent contractor. [*Newman v. Sears, Roebuck & Co.,* p. 435.]

Employer and Employee   The vital point of distinction between an agent and an employee is that an agent is the business representative of the principal. It is absolutely essential that there shall be a third person with whom the agent may create, modify, or terminate contractual obligations in behalf of the principal. An agent acts in the place of and instead of his principal. An employee, on the other hand, is employed to render service for the employer, and has no power to create contractual relations with third persons. In a principal and agent relationship three persons are involved; in an employer and employee relationship only two persons are involved. A person who is employed, however, may have duties of both types to perform. A common illustration is a janitor who is authorized to purchase janitorial supplies; in this respect, he is acting as an agent. When his services are restricted to the care of a building, he is acting as an employee.

Many of the rules of agency, however, are as applicable to an employee as they are to an agent. Some are obviously inapplicable. A rule pertaining to the authority of the agent, for instance, is inapplicable to an employee because the employee has no authority. The rules of agency that follow are applicable to an employee except when a particular rule applies to the agent alone because of the nature of his relationship to the principal.

KINDS OF AGENTS
A principal and agent may, practically speaking, create almost any kind of an agency they desire. References to agents as general, special, professional, or gratuitous agents are found frequently in cases.

General and Special Agents   The distinction between these two agents is more accurately a difference in degree rather than in kind. A general agent usually has wide general authority to act for his principal. A manager of a store is an illustration of a general agent. A special agent is one employed to conduct a single transaction or perhaps a limited series of transactions. An agent with authority to sell a house—a real estate broker—is an illustration of a special agent. The reason for the distinction seems to be founded on a difference in the extent of the authority of the two agents. A general agent ordinarily has considerable authority, apparent or otherwise, over and above his actual authority. A special agent ordinarily has little or no apparent authority beyond the single transaction he is authorized to conduct. The reason, however, is not very convincing. The cases, as will be seen, are not decided upon the distinction between a general and a special agent but rather upon whether the agent in the particular case was within or without his authority. Agents are, nevertheless, frequently classified as general and special agents.

Professional Agents   Professional agents are usually employed to conduct a single transaction. They are, therefore, special agents. It is true that professional agents exercise great discretion in the manner of performing their work and consequently closely resemble independent contractors. They have the authority, however, to enter into contractual relations with third persons in behalf of their principal. They cannot, for this reason, be independent contractors. A few of the more common illustrations of professional agents are factors, brokers, and auctioneers.

(1) *Factors*   A factor, frequently referred to as a "commission merchant," is an agent employed to sell merchandise consigned to him for that purpose. He has possession of the merchandise and usually sells in his own name for and in behalf of his principal. A factor who sells merchandise on credit for an additional commission and guarantees the solvency of the purchaser and his performance of the contract is known as a "del credere agent." If the purchaser makes default, the del credere agent is liable to his principal.

(2) *Brokers*   The primary function of a broker is to act as an intermediary between two other parties. A broker ordinarily does not have possession of the property involved in the transaction, nor does he have authority to bind his principal contractually. Familiar examples are insurance brokers and real estate brokers.

(3) *Auctioneers*   An auctioneer is a person authorized or licensed by law to sell property at a public sale. His authority to conduct a particular sale is derived from the person whose property he undertakes to sell. Upon the acceptance of a bid, he becomes the agent of the purchaser as well as the agent of the seller. This dual agency, however, is solely for the purpose of signing the memorandum of the sale.

Gratuitous Agents   An agency relationship, unlike a contract, may be created by an agreement unsupported by consideration. This relationship arises when the agent acts gratuitously for the principal. The promise of the gratuitous agent to perform is not enforceable, but where the gratuitous agent enters upon the performance of the promised act, he is then under a duty to perform properly and completely in accordance with his promise.

CAPACITY OF PARTIES

Capacity to Act as Agent   The agent normally binds not himself but his principal when he makes a contract with third persons. As a general rule, therefore, anyone can act as an agent who has the capacity to carry out instructions. This rule is broad enough to permit a person with limited contractual capacity to act as an agent. It should not be presumed, however, that the rule is broad enough to include an infant who is so young or an insane person who is so devoid of reason as to be completely incapable of comprehending the task he is attempting to perform. The court, no doubt, would disregard the attempt of such a person to act.

Capacity to Act as Principal   The general rule with regard to capacity to act as principal is that a person may do through his agent whatever he may do in person. The question then arises: May persons with limited contractual capacity act through an agent? This question, for the most part, may be answered by an application of the rule of the law of contracts relative to capacity of parties. A few states still follow the older cases which held that the attempt of an infant to appoint an agent was void. But this is not the majority rule. The majority of the cases today hold that the acts of the agent are subject to ratification or rescission by the infant-principal. As a general rule, therefore, the acts of the agent are voidable at the election of the infant-principal. Corporations and other business organizations which have power to contract have the capacity to appoint agents. Most of the business of these organizations is, in fact, transacted through its agents.

MODES OF CREATION

The most common method by which an agency may be created is by appointment. An agency is sometimes created, however, by necessity, operation of law, and estoppel.

Appointment of the Agent   The appointment of the agent, with few exceptions, need not comply with any formalities. The common law required that authority to execute an instrument under seal must be evidenced by an instrument of equal dignity. The common-law distinction between the sealed and the unsealed instrument, however, has been abolished in many of the states. Thus the importance of the rule has been greatly diminished. The appointment of the agent is, nevertheless, sometimes required to be in writing. The authority of the agent to sign a deed, mortgage, or lease is sometimes required by statute to be in writing. In a few states the agent is required to have written authority where the contract to be made by the agent comes within the Statute of Frauds. The written authorization may ordinarily be in the form of a letter, contract, or a power of attorney. The person holding a power of attorney is known as an "attorney in fact" and should not be confused with an attorney at law.

An agent is appointed for the purpose of altering legal relations between the principal and a third person. An act of the agent which is done in accordance with the manifestations of consent of the principal to the agent is effective in altering such legal relations. Such an act of the agent within the scope of such consent, or authority conferred, is binding on the principal to the same extent as if the principal had performed the act himself. In legal contemplation, it is the act of the principal accomplished by means of another person.

Agency by Necessity, Operation of Law, Estoppel An agency relationship, as between the principal and agent, is created by mutual consent. A so-called agency relationship may be created in a few instances, however, when there is no contractual relation between the so-called principal and the so-called agent. This relationship may arise from necessity, from operation of law, or by estoppel. A good illustration of an agency by necessity is when an emergency or disaster occurs during an ocean voyage. The disaster constitutes the master of the vessel the agent by necessity of owners, insurers, and all other persons having an interest in the vessel and the cargo. An agency by operation of law arises when a state statute provides that a service of process may be made upon the secretary of state in lieu of a nonresident motorist. An agency by estoppel may be created when one person voluntarily or negligently permits another person to conduct himself in such a manner that a third person is led to believe that an agency relationship has been created. Some authorities attempt to distinguish estoppel from apparent authority, but most authorities say that apparent authority is more accurately "estoppel." The distinction is scarcely more than a choice in terminology. For all practical purposes, the result is the same. The general rule is that an agency arises by estoppel whenever there is a holding out with the knowledge of the so-called principal and the third person acts in justifiable reliance thereon to his damage. [*Kanelles v. Locke,* p. 437.]

AUTHORITY OF AGENTS
The authority of an agent may be either actual or apparent.

Actual Authority Actual authority is the authority which the principal intentionally delegates to the agent. It may be delegated to the agent expressly or impliedly.

(1) *Express Authority* Express authority is directly and specifically delegated to the agent orally or in writing. For example, Brown, the principal, may authorize Smith, as agent, to sell certain furniture to Mrs. Jones for $500 and to deliver the furniture by truck. The agent has been expressly authorized to sell and deliver the furniture. The agent may, at the same time, be clothed with certain "implied authority."

(2) *Implied Authority* Implied—or incidental—authority is actual authority which arises from the words or acts of the principal and from the facts and circumstances of the case. An agent will be impliedly authorized to do those things that are incidental, or reasonably necessary, in order to perform the express authority which has been delegated. Smith, in the above example, would be impliedly authorized to contract in the principal's name for repairs to the truck if it should cease to function in a remote area while he was attempting to deliver the furniture. Suppose the principal instructs his agent to cash a check. Suppose, however, the principal neglects to indorse the check prior to his departure on an extended business trip. The agent would probably be impliedly authorized to indorse the check on behalf of the principal in order to cash it. Implied authority may also arise in case of an emergency. The agent is impliedly authorized to protect the interest of the principal when it is not reasonably possible to communicate with the principal. This expanded authority is limited, however, to the necessity and it terminates when the necessity ceases.

A custom of the business will frequently mean that an agent is clothed with implied authority. This is sometimes referred to as "customary authority," and means that the principal is deemed to have delegated authority to the agent to act in conformity with the general custom of the business. Suppose Brown, a used automobile dealer, as principal, authorizes Smith, as agent, to sell a used automobile. Suppose still further that it is the custom for the seller to warrant that the automobile is in excellent mechanical condition. Brown would be bound by such a warranty made by Smith, and the third person may recover from Brown if the warranty is breached.

The agent will *not* be impliedly authorized to perform acts which are *not* reasonably necessary, essential, usual, and proper for carrying out the express authority. An agent would not, therefore, be impliedly authorized to commit an illegal act.

Apparent Authority Apparent—or ostensible—authority is that authority which the principal permits the agent to exercise or which he holds the agent out as having although such authority has not been delegated to the agent. The principal may clothe the agent with such authority by statements, a lack of care on his part, past or present conduct, or any other manifestation which leads third persons to reasonably believe that the agent is so authorized. Such manifestation may include those instances in which the principal has ratified or failed to repudiate acts of the agent in the past. Third persons may safely assume that the agent possesses the authority which is usually delegated to similar agents of that character. Suppose agents for used automobile dealers in the community are authorized to make warranties as to the mechanical condition of automobiles for sale. Suppose still further that Brown, the principal, instructs his agent Smith to effect a sale but not to make any warranty as to mechanical condition. The principal did actually negate the customary—implied—authority to make the warranty. The agent, however, viewed by reasonable third persons would possess apparent authority on the basis that an agent of this character usually has authority to warrant the mechanical condition. It may be well to keep in mind a corollary rule to the effect that secret instructions to an agent are not binding on third persons. The important point to remember is that the apparent authority of an agent depends on the manifestations of the principal with respect to the agent's authority.

In order to establish that an agent has apparent authority, the following must be shown: (1) The principal, in some way, manifested his consent to such authority or, with knowledge, permitted the agent to exercise such authority; (2) the third person who acted in good faith knew the facts and did in fact believe that the agent was authorized; and (3) the third person in reliance on such belief changed his position and will suffer loss unless the act is binding on the principal. [*R. H. Kyle Furniture Co. v. Russell Dry Goods Co.,* p. 438.]

RATIFICATION

Agency by Ratification   Ratification is the subsequent acceptance or approval by one person of an unauthorized act of another person. It may be helpful to distinguish ratification from estoppel: Ratification is approval after conduct, while estoppel is inducement to another to act to his detriment; liability resulting from ratification arises from intention, while liability resulting from estoppel arises despite intention. The distinction in many cases is unimportant. It perhaps makes little difference, so far as the rights of third persons are concerned, whether the acts of the principal constitute ratification or whether they constitute estoppel. The principal is bound by the acts of the agent in either situation. Ratification of the contract by the principal, however, gives rise to rights of the principal against the third person. This is not true of estoppel.

Ratification may be express or implied. It is express when the principal makes a statement to the effect that he will carry out the contract made in his name by the agent. In a few instances, the authorization must be given in some particular form. If the law requires a sealed authorization, the ratification must be under seal; if the law requires a written authorization, the ratification must be by a written instrument. Ratification is frequently implied from any conduct on the part of the principal which reasonably tends to show an intention to ratify the unauthorized act. The conduct may be shown by some affirmative act or it may be shown by silence. The same formalities, as a general rule, must be observed in ratifying the act as would be necessary initially to authorize it. If the authorization must be in writing, therefore, the ratification must likewise be in writing.

(1)   *Ratification by Affirmative Conduct*   Ratification by conduct is established when the principal brings an action based on the validity of the act. The rule, of course, would not apply to actions brought for the purpose of repudiating the act or preventing loss by it. One of the most common methods of ratification implied from conduct is the acceptance of the benefits of the transaction.

(2)   *Ratification by Silence or Acquiescence*   It is the duty of a person, after learning that an act has been done without authority by one purporting to act as

his agent, to elect within a reasonable time to reject or ratify such an act. No precise rule can be stated as to what constitutes a reasonable time. A failure to repudiate the act promptly, therefore, may be considered as some evidence in establishing ratification. But delay alone is not sufficient; silence alone is not sufficient. Silence is, nevertheless, always to be considered as some evidence from which ratification may be inferred. Such evidence is usually given more weight in the case of an agent who has exceeded his authority than in the case of a stranger who has volunteered to act in behalf of another. Whether there has been a ratification by silence is, consequently, a question of fact. It is quite apparent that the principal should repudiate the unauthorized act promptly after receiving information of the transaction in order to avoid liability resulting from the unauthorized act. The significance of this assertion is supported by the fact that silence may operate to subject the principal to liability toward the third person because of the doctrine of estoppel. Estoppel is clearly applicable where the third person has acted to his prejudice. The principal is estopped from denying the authority of the agent, as a general rule, if the third person, in reliance on the principal's silence or failure to repudiate the act of the agent, changes his position for the worse.

Conditions for Ratification   In addition to an intent to ratify, the following conditions must be fulfilled for ratification to be effective: (1) The principal must have the capacity to ratify; (2) he must have knowledge of all the material facts; (3) he must ratify the act in its entirety; (4) the act must be capable of ratification, and (5) the act must be done in behalf of the principal.

(1)   *Capacity to Ratify*   There is no essential difference between the capacity to appoint an agent and the capacity to ratify an act. As a general rule, therefore, anyone capable of being a principal may become so by ratification. The principal, however, must have capacity at the time the act is performed as well as at the time of ratification. This question frequently arises: May a corporation, after organization, ratify contracts made by its promoters before it had an existence? No, there can be no ratification. The subsequently formed corporation may, however, adopt the contract. This means, for one thing, that the effective date of the contract is the date of its adoption. The effective date of a ratified contract relates back to the date it was originally made by the unauthorized agent. The adoption of the contract is discussed in later chapters under "Corporations."

(2)   *Knowledge of Material Facts*   Ratification will not be implied unless the principal acts with full knowledge of all the material facts. A principal will be bound by ratification, however, if he deliberately and expressly ratifies the act knowing that his information is incomplete, disregards whatever the facts may be, or does not make any effort to learn the facts.

(3)   *Ratification Must Be Entire*   The act must be ratified in its entirety or not at all. A person cannot ratify that portion which is beneficial and repudiate that portion which is burdensome. The acceptance of the result of the act, moreover, ratifies the whole transaction including the means whereby that result was

achieved. This rule is constantly applied to promises, misrepresentations, and even fraud upon which the contract was based. A principal, therefore, who ratifies with knowledge is ordinarily liable for any wrong flowing from such promises, misrepresentations, or fraud. At the time of accepting the benefits of the act, the person may be ignorant of the practices resorted to. Even so, he is liable unless he attempts to undo the wrong within a reasonable time after he is advised of it. The rule, however, is not broad enough to constitute ratification of another act which, though closely related to the ratified act, is not a part of it. [*Fritsch v. National City Bank*, p. 439.]

(4) *Acts That May Be Ratified* Usually, those acts that may be authorized may be ratified. It follows that acts which are absolutely void cannot be ratified, but acts which are merely voidable may be ratified. The general rule is subject to qualification in one important particular. A substantial number of cases hold that one whose name has been forged can ratify the act. A slight majority of the cases, however, hold that since forgery involves a crime and public wrong, and is also opposed to public policy, it cannot be ratified. This is another instance where ratification should not be confused with estoppel. All would probably agree that a person who expressly or impliedly represents that his forged signature is genuine, would be estopped from denying its genuineness against one who has changed his position for the worse.

(5) *Act Must Be Done as Agent* An act, to be capable of ratification, must be done by one party as agent for someone else. Stated another way, a principal cannot ratify the unauthorized act of another person unless that person purported to act as agent for, and in the name of, the principal. The rule operates to prevent one person from acquiring the rights of another. One person may enter into a fruitful contract with another person; a stranger cannot acquire the rights in the contract by attempting to ratify it.

Effect of Ratification The general effect of ratification is to place the principal, the agent, and the person with whom the agent dealt in substantially the same position they would have been in if the act had been authorized initially. In most states, however, the person with whom the agent dealt may withdraw from the transaction at any time before ratification. But ratification once made is irrevocable. The authority, moreover, relates back and becomes effective as of the date the act was performed by the agent except for intervening rights of third persons.

CASES

Newman v. Sears, Roebuck & Co., 43 N.W.2d 411 (N.D. 1950). Action by Claude Newman (plaintiff below), appellant, against Sears, Roebuck & Company and Alfred S. Dale (defendants below), respondents. Alfred S. Dale was the owner of an apartment house in Bismarck, North Dakota. He ordered three folding beds from Sears, Roebuck & Company, and had Christ Nelson install one of them in one of his furnished apartments. Plaintiff rented the apartment. About ten o'clock on the evening of February 28, 1948, after plaintiff had gone to bed, the bed collapsed. Plaintiff was seriously injured. The evidence showed that the collapse of the bed was due to the fact that Nelson used ordinary wood screws instead of the lag screws designated to hold the bed in place. The District Court found that Christ Nelson was an independent contractor.

Grimson, Judge: The appellant, however, argues that even if Nelson is held to have been an independent contractor the nature of the work done was such as to render Dale, the employer, liable. He cites the case of Ruehl v. Lidgerwood Telephone Company . . . which holds: "Where, in the making of an improvement, it is manifest that injury is likely to result unless due precautions are taken, a duty rests upon him who causes the work to be done to see that such necessary precautions are taken." In that case the telephone company hired a man to dig holes for telephone poles at so much per hole. He dug the hole in the yard of a man for whom the company had contracted to install a telephone and left it unguarded. A 3 1/2 year old boy fell into the hole and was either drowned or smothered in the mud. The court held that even if the man who dug the hole was an independent contractor the telephone company employer was liable. The principle laid down in that case was further discussed in Taute v. J. I. Case Threshing Machine Company. . . . In that case, one Kerr contracted to bring into the town of Tolley from a distance of 12 miles, a steam engine. On the way a fire started nearby and the suit was brought for damages on the theory that the fire was started from the engine because of the negligence of Kerr. The court says:

It is no doubt the law that an owner of property can be held liable in damages in certain cases even where the work is intrusted to an independent contractor, and where the work ordered to be done or the structure ordered to be erected is, in itself, intrinsically dangerous or a nuisance. The origin and reason of this rule is the duty of due consideration which one in a civilized community owes to his fellows and to the public, and that such a duty precludes the ordering of that which, if done, will be inherently dangerous. These considerations are hardly applicable to the case at bar. It can hardly be said, as a matter of law, that the machine was a nuisance, or that, the moving of it was an essentially dangerous transaction.

The distinction between the cases in which the owner is held liable for work which he engaged an independent contractor to perform and that for which he is not held liable is thus made clear. In the first classification is the work which even if carried out according to the orders of the owner is inherently dangerous to people, such as the open hole dug in the Ruehl case. In the second classification is such work which when accomplished is not in itself dangerous to people such as the moving of the engine in the Taute case. Applying that distinction to the case at bar the folding bed itself when properly installed is not inherently dangerous and does not constitute a nuisance per se. It was, we shall assume, the use of the wood screws, not the bed itself or the ordinary installation of it that was dangerous. The use of the wood screws was not ordered by Dale and not known by him. Clearly the evidence here shows that the work delegated by Dale to Nelson comes within the second classification for which Dale cannot be held responsible. [DECISION FOR RESPONDENTS]

Kanelles v. Locke, 12 Ohio App. 210 (Ohio 1919). Action by D. Kanelles, plaintiff, against Ida J. Locke, defendant.

On December 23, 1918, at one o'clock in the morning, plaintiff was received by J. C. Clemens as a guest in the Hotel Ohio, Cleveland, which was operated by defendant. Plaintiff told J. C. Clemens, who appeared to be in charge, that he desired to leave his money and valuables with the hotel proprietor for the night, whereupon Clemens accepted the money and valuables and gave plaintiff the following receipt:

Mr. D. Kanelles, Man in Room 111 Gave me 1 Diamond pin and $484.00 in bills and two $5.00 checks.

Mrs. Locke
Hotel Ohio
J. C. Clemens

The next morning plaintiff presented the receipt to Mrs. Locke and requested the return of his money and valuables. He then learned that Clemens was a roomer in the hotel and was not in the employ of Mrs. Locke at all. Mrs. Locke then went to his room and found he had absconded, taking the money and valuables with him. She refused to make good the loss to her guest. This action was then brought to recover the sum of $744, the amount of the money and valuables so deposited.

The evidence showed that J. C. Clemens was and had been for some time a roomer in the hotel; that the hotel was open to receive visitors at this time in the morning, or night; that no one, except this person Clemens, was in the office to take charge of guests who might arrive; and that when plaintiff entered and asked for a room, Clemens, who appeared to be in charge, got up and went behind the counter, had him register, got the key from its proper place, assigned him to a room, and took him to his room.

Vickery, Judge: It is claimed by the defendant that this man was not her agent and had no authority to receive valuables or do anything around the hotel, and that therefore she was not responsible for any money or valuables that might be deposited with him. We cannot acquiesce in this doctrine. An agency may be created by estoppel, and that estoppel may be allowed on the ground of negligence or fault on the part of the principal, upon the principle that when one of two innocent parties must suffer loss, the loss will fall on him whose conduct brought about the situation. . . .

Here the proprietress of this hotel left this man in the office either designedly or negligently, clothed with apparent authority to do what hotel clerks usually do, and one who came for the purpose of becoming a guest, and did become a guest, might reasonably conclude that he had apparent authority to do what clerks under similar circumstances would have a right to do.

. . . Where an innkeeper has permitted one to occupy a position which would tend to mislead the public, he cannot divest himself of the liability; for the agency of the person presuming to act under such circumstances is created by estoppel, and cases of estoppel are limited to those in which there is no real, but only apparent agency, and here was an apparent agency. Accordingly we think the principle alluded to above, namely, that where one of two innocent persons must suffer loss, the loss will fall on him whose conduct brought about the situation, is applicable here.

We think that she by her voluntary act, or by her negligent act, had placed someone in a position where it would appear to anyone coming in to become a guest at the hotel that he was properly in charge, and that therefore she made herself by her conduct responsible for his acts, acting within the apparent scope of a clerk or employee in a hotel, to receive property of her guest. [DECISION FOR PLAINTIFF]

R. H. Kyle Furniture Co. v. Russell Dry Goods Co.,   340 S.W.2d 220 (Ky. 1960). Action by R. H. Kyle Furniture Company, plaintiff, against Russell Dry Goods Company, Inc., defendant.

Plaintiff was a wholesale dealer in furniture. Defendant conducted a general dry goods store, and Clyde Thomas was in charge as general manager. The inventory of the store was primarily textile fabrics, but it did at times contain certain items which would ordinarily be listed for sale in a furniture business. Items of furniture had been ordered from the plaintiff on several occasions by the manager of the defendant, and such items were paid for by the defendant. On April 28, 1956, another order was given by the manager for an assortment of rugs, carpeting, dishes, lawnmowers, electric fans, and furniture. The order was sent as having been sold to the defendant, and its account was charged. When the truck arrived, the store was on fire or had already burned down. At the request of Thomas, the goods were taken to his garage and unloaded there. Defendant refused to pay for the goods so delivered, and plaintiff brought an action to recover the price. It was contended that the manager had been positively denied authority to make any purchase of stock.

Stanley, Commissioner: Though it was competent for the principal to limit the authority of an agent, the restriction on the authority of Thomas to buy merchandise for the store is not binding on the plaintiff, for there was no evidence that it had notice or knowledge thereof; and the directive was ineffective to limit the agent's apparent authority in this transaction or relieve the company of an obligation to pay for the merchandise. Therefore, the defendant is bound on this contract of purchase if it was made by Thomas within the implied or ostensible scope of his authority as manager of the store, unless plaintiff's salesman knew or had reason to know that he was exceeding his authority in ordering the goods on the credit of the company. There are many cases holding that a general manager of a store is presumed to have authority to buy merchandise. As stated in some of the cases, it would be impossible for persons to deal safely with corporations if in each case they were required at their peril to determine the exact scope of the authority of such agents as managers and superintendents; hence, they are justified in relying upon the apparent or implied authority of such agents. We think that is sound law. The term "apparent or implied authority" could not likely apply to the purchase of goods wholly outside the character or line of merchandise carried, e.g., the manager of a men's clothing store buying a large quantity of drugs. In the instant case, the stock of the defendant's country store was not limited to "dry goods," which is generally defined as textile fabrics. [DECISION FOR PLAINTIFF]

Fritsch v. National City Bank, 24 S.W.2d 1066 (Mo. 1930). Action by Mary Fritsch, plaintiff, against National City Bank of St. Louis, Missouri, defendant.

Plaintiff obtained a judgment of $1000 against Charles W. Fricke. Sometime thereafter, one Dean S. Rogers, who was wholly unknown to plaintiff, called her on the telephone and informed her that he was in charge of a collection agency, his purpose being to obtain authority from her to collect the amount of the judgment. She advised him that she was not interested in his proposition. Rogers, nevertheless, through the course of events, settled the judgment for $425.25. A check payable to the order of plaintiff for that amount was then given to Rogers who cashed the check at the defendant-bank by indorsing thereon the name of plaintiff and his own as her attorney-in-fact. About four months thereafter, plaintiff's attorney learned of the settlement and immediately wrote the plaintiff so advising her. The information so obtained was the first that plaintiff had received, either as to the settlement of the judgment or as to the act of Rogers in indorsing her name upon the check and cashing it at the defendant-bank. This action was brought to recover the proceeds of the check which the defendant-bank paid upon the unauthorized indorsement.

Bennick, Commissioner: It is quite true, as counsel suggests, that one who ratifies an act done in his name without previous authority must ratify it as done, and he cannot accept in part, and reject in part. In other words, he must take the bitter along with the sweet, and he cannot affirm that portion of the act done which suits his fancy, and reject the balance which serves to impose a burden upon him. Consequently, if he sees fit to adopt an unauthorized act at all, he must adopt it as a whole, and in its entirety.

So in this case, since plaintiff elected to adopt Rogers' act in settling her claim with the judgment debt, she must be held to have adopted each and every part of that act; and the judgment now stands satisfied, not alone as to Fricke, but also as to the world. The settlement of the judgment, however, was one transaction, and the cashing of the check at defendant-bank was another. The parties were different, and the two transactions were wholly independent, separable, and disassociated; and while it is incidentally true that the check cashed was the one given in satisfaction of the judgment, yet so far as concerns the rights and obligations of the parties to this appeal, it might as well have been obtained by Rogers from any other source. . . .

If a way can be imagined in which defendant would be affected by the existence of plaintiff's judgment against Fricke, the judgment stands satisfied of record beyond the power of plaintiff now to question such satisfaction, either as to Fricke, or as to defendant. But whatever plaintiff did by way of ratifying Rogers' settlement of the judgment could not extend to and cover a further unauthorized act of Rogers in an entirely separate and independent transaction. [DECISION FOR PLAINTIFF]

PROBLEMS

1 Mrs. Brown, the owner of a dwelling house, telephoned The Janitorial Service and inquired about the price for washing windows in her house. The manager of The Janitorial Service then came to her house and said the price would be $75, and it was agreed that the work would be done that afternoon for that price. The manager sent an employee to do the work, and the employee brought all the materials for doing the work with him. The employee was placing a ladder near a window and struck a boy, and the boy was injured. The boy, who was not a trespasser, was seen by the employee. May the boy recover for his injuries from (a) Mrs. Brown, (b) The Janitorial Service?

2 Cramer, the owner of a certain tract of land, listed the land with Rogers, a real estate broker, for sale at a cash price of $5,000. Rogers, in an attempt to sell the land to Jason, represented to Jason that the land was fertile and was ideal for growing vegetables. Such representations were not true, and Rogers had no authority from Cramer to make them. Jason signed a contract to purchase the land for $5,000. Rogers took the contract to Cramer and told him that he had made the representations to Jason, and Cramer signed the contract. Rogers took the signed contract to Jason, received the $5,000, and delivered the $5,000 to Cramer. Jason learned thereafter that the land was not fertile and would not grow vegetables. Jason brought an action against Cramer to recover damages for deceit, and the defense offered by Cramer was that Rogers had no authority to make such representations. Is this a good defense?

3 Brown, who was employed as cashier of the First Bank, entered into a conspiracy with Smith whereby it was agreed that Brown would fraudulently issue a cashier's check drawn on the First Bank payable to Smith; that Smith would cash the check; and that the two would divide the proceeds. Brown thereupon issued the check for $2,000, and Smith presented it to the teller at the Second Bank for payment. The teller telephoned the First Bank, and Brown answered the call. The teller inquired about the check, and Brown stated that the check was properly issued. The teller then cashed the check. Brown and Smith divided the proceeds and absconded. The First Bank refused to pay this check when it was presented for payment. Is the First Bank liable on this check?

4 Acme Auto Sales employed Mills as a salesman to sell used automobiles. It was customary in the community in which Acme Auto Sales transacted its business for dealers to make certain warranties as to the mechanical condition of the automobiles that were sold. Acme Auto Sales instructed Mills to sell a certain used automobile. He was, however, instructed to make no warranty as to the condition of the automobile. Mills learned that Wertz was definitely interested in this particular automobile, and Mills, in his enthusiasm to sell the automobile, stated to Wertz that the automobile was covered with a ninety-day warranty or 15,000 miles against all mechanical defects. In reliance on this warranty, Wertz purchased the automobile. Mechanical defects became apparent the next day. Wertz thereupon brought an action against Acme Auto Sales for damages for breach of warranty. Should he recover?

5 Brown was employed by the X Company as a driver of a truck, and Smith was employed by the same company as Brown's assistant. They were acting within the scope of their employment and were miles from the X Company when Brown was seriously injured in a collision with another truck. Smith, being the only other employee present and unable to contact the home office, directed a doctor to give medical aid to Brown. Will the doctor be able to collect for his services from the X Company?

6 Defendant employed Brown to contact certain debtors of defendant and persuade the debtors to come to the office of defendant and make arrangements for payment of the debts. Defendant instructed Brown to contact the debtors privately. Brown contacted plaintiff, one of the debtors, and a dispute arose over the method of collection. Plaintiff ordered Brown to leave. Brown became angered and assaulted plaintiff. In an action to recover damages for the assault, defendant contended that Brown was an independent contractor. Do you agree with this contention?

7 Plaintiff brought an action against Brown and Jones to recover on an open account for tires allegedly sold to Jones. Brown leased a filling station and paid the rent, but Jones, who was eighteen years of age, was operating the station as agent for Brown. Jones attempted to disaffirm the contract for the purchase of the tires on the ground that he was a minor at the time the purchase was made. Decide.

8 Plaintiff, a real estate broker, and the son of defendant entered into an agreement whereby plaintiff agreed to find a tenant for a dwelling owned by the defendant. It was agreed that the rental should be $3,000 a year and that plaintiff's commission for finding the tenant would be $300. Plaintiff, a few days later, found a tenant who was willing to rent the dwelling for a year. He thereupon prepared a lease in accordance with the agreement which was signed by the son in the name of the defendant. Defendant thereafter enclosed a check for $50 in a letter stating that the check was in part payment for services in finding the tenant. Defendant refused to pay the balance, however, on the ground that the son had no authority to rent the dwelling or to sign a lease. Decide.

34
PRINCIPAL
AND THIRD PERSON

The controversies between the principal and the third person revolve around those acts that are within and those that are without the course and scope of the authority of the agent. Generally speaking, however, a purported principal will have no liability if the person who pretended to act as his agent had no authority to represent the principal. This is the basis for the common statement that "one who deals with an agent does so at his own risk." The significance of the relation between the principal and the third person is, indeed, that the principal is bound by, and liable for, those acts which the agent does within the course and scope of his authority. For this reason it seems best to approach the rights and liabilities of the principal and the third person from the viewpoint of the authority of the agent. For purposes of clarity only, these rights and liabilities have been divided into (1) the disclosed principal, (2) the undisclosed principal, and (3) the tort liability of the principal.

DISCLOSED PRINCIPAL
A disclosed principal is, as the name implies, one whose existence and identity are known to the third person. This is the usual type of agency.

Authority to Sell Land The employment of a real estate agent to find a purchaser for land does not impliedly authorize him to execute a contract of sale. The professional broker or real estate agent, as a general rule, has performed his duty when he has found a purchaser who is ready, willing, and able to purchase upon the terms specified; if no terms are specified, then upon terms acceptable to the principal. The authority to conclude the sale, of course, may be expressly given. Such authority must be clearly conferred and in most states must be by written instrument. [*Halsey v. Monteiro,* p. 448.]

Authority to Sell Personal Property The problem pertaining to implied authority to sell personal property is twofold: first, the circumstances from which the authority may be implied and, secondly, the extent of the authority.

(1) *Circumstances Implying Authority* Possession alone will not confer authority upon the possessor to sell. Possession of the property must be coupled with some other acts of the principal which clothe the agent with apparent authority to sell. A traveling salesman authorized only to exhibit samples and solicit orders has no authority to sell his samples. Possession of the property coupled with written evidence of the title thereto, however, would ordinarily be sufficient. Implied authority to sell personal property may exist when such authority is in conformity with the usual trade or business custom. An agent behind the counter who sells goods quite clearly has authority to sell the goods. Statutes have been enacted in most states for the protection of innocent buyers who, relying upon apparent ownership, purchase property. These statutes—commonly known as Factors' Acts—are, however, usually restricted to a particular class of agents, or "factors."

(2) *Extent of the Authority* Authority to sell personal property does not ordinarily carry with it the implied authority to make any unusual contract. The agent, therefore, would not ordinarily have the implied authority to exchange the property for other property, to give credit, unless that was in accordance with business custom, or to make any warranties that are not implied in law.

Authority of Purchasing Agent Authority to purchase will be implied if the principal has put the agent in a situation where authority to buy is usually exercised, if he has held the agent out as possessing such authority, or if it is practically essential to accomplish the authorized act. An agent having full and discretionary authority to buy has implied authority to agree upon the terms of purchase, provided they are usual, and to fix the price, provided the price is reasonable. Mere authority to buy does not imply authority to buy on credit, but the agent has implied authority to buy on credit if his principal has not supplied him with funds. The principal may instruct the agent to purchase for cash only. If this is the case, the principal is not liable for the value of the goods purchased by the agent on the credit of the principal, provided the principal has furnished the agent with money to make payment for the goods and the seller has not relied upon apparent authority in ignorance of such instructions.

Authority to Collect or Receive Payment The authority of a selling agent to receive payment for the goods so sold has been a fruitful source of litigation. The usual employment of a clerk in a retail store is to sell goods to customers. It is implied from such authority that he has authority to receive payment for them at the time of the sale unless custom requires that the customer make payment to the cashier. It is not implied for such employment, however, that the clerk has authority to present bills later and collect for them when the goods are sold on credit and taken from the store. It is clear that care should be taken in making payment to an agent; the courts are hesitant to imply authority to collect. Assuming the authority to receive payment, however, does not give the agent the implied authority to accept anything other than money in payment. He does not have the implied authority to accept promissory notes or other property in settlement of the indebtedness. Checks are customarily accepted as conditional payment. The debt is not paid, however, until the check has been honored. The principal, therefore, has the option of bringing an action on the contract which gave rise to the indebtedness or to sue on the check should it be dishonored.

Most of the troublesome litigation pertaining to the authority of a selling agent to receive payment has been with reference to traveling salesmen. It is nevertheless quite clear that a traveling salesman authorized to solicit orders to be transmitted to his principal for acceptance has no implied authority to collect or receive payment therefor. The purchaser in paying the price to such agent does so at his peril, and payments to such agents may again be collected from the purchaser. [*Fairbanks Morse & Co. v. Dale & Co.,* p. 449.]

Authority to Appoint Subagents   A general rule has developed in the law that an agent, in the absence of the express or implied consent of his principal, cannot delegate his authority to a subagent. This rule is based upon the presumption that the principal selected the particular person because he relied upon the judgment, discretion, skill, or experience of that particular person. That this is so does not mean that the agent may not employ other persons, such as bookkeepers, stenographers, and messengers, to assist him in the purely ministerial or mechanical details of his duty. Such persons, however, are not agents of the principal and are not entitled to look to the principal for their compensation.

The principal may, of course, give express authority to his agent to delegate the authority conferred upon the agent. An authority to delegate the agent's authority, moreover, may be implied from the nature of the agency. In these circumstances, the subagent represents the principal and is entitled to be compensated by the principal. In some instances, the authority conferred upon the agent cannot be exercised without the aid of subagents. It is, therefore, generally held that authority to appoint a subagent may exist where the nature of the business is such that it must be contemplated by the principal that the authority conferred on the agent will be exercised through subagents.

UNDISCLOSED PRINCIPAL

An undisclosed principal is one who is represented by an agent who does not reveal the fact that he is acting in a representative capacity. A third person who does not know that the agent is acting in a representative capacity, therefore, finds himself under a contract with a person whom he did not contemplate. This may be surprising or even shocking. The doctrine of the undisclosed principal certainly does run counter to the fundamental notion that a contractual relationship is the result of a voluntary agreement between the parties. It is convenient, however, to the principal who desires to secrete his identity. It ordinarily imposes no hardship upon the third person. Such a result is prevented by the rules that have been formulated to govern the rights and liabilities of the parties to the undisclosed agency.

Rights and Liabilities of the Third Person   The third person who contracts with an agent acting in behalf of an undisclosed principal in the belief that he is contracting with the agent individually can obviously enforce the contract against the agent. The third person also has the right, when he learns of the existence of the agency, to elect to hold the agent or to hold the principal liable. It should be kept in mind, however, that it is only after discovery of the principal that the third person is in a position to make a choice. No conduct of the third person before he learns of the existence of the agency, therefore, could constitute an election. After the discovery of the relation of agency, however, the third person may hold either the agent or the undisclosed principal. This may be accomplished, of course, by an express election. But an election may be gathered from conduct and the surrounding circumstances. The fact that the third person merely looks to the agent for performance or refuses to take any action against the principal or takes a promissory note from the agent does not constitute an election. More definite action is essential. The mere commencement of an action against the agent is not conclusive. The majority of the courts hold that a final election is made when the third person, after learning of the identity of the principal, reduces his claim to a judgment.

It might be supposed that an agent of an undisclosed principal can have no apparent authority. But this is not true. The third person may, when the identity of the principal is established, hold the principal liable in the same manner as if his identity had been known. The principal, therefore, is liable for all contracts entered into within the scope of the agent's authority. An undisclosed principal cannot, however, be held liable upon a negotiable instrument signed or indorsed by his agent alone. The third person may have relief. He may, in some instances, sue upon the agreement which furnished the consideration for the instrument. But one whose name does not appear on the instrument cannot be held liable on the instrument. This rule does not apply to written contracts. It is well established that a principal may be liable upon a written contract entered into by his agent in his own name. This is true even though the name of the principal does not appear on the instrument, was not disclosed, and the third person supposed the agent was acting for himself.

Rights and Liabilities of the Undisclosed Principal   The undisclosed principal may appear at any time in his true character and claim all the benefits of the contract from the third person so far as he can do so without prejudice to the third person. The principal could not enforce a contract which involves elements of personal trust and confidence or personal services. The undisclosed principal obviously could not enforce performance of a contract entered into by his agent and a third person by the terms of which the third person had agreed to serve as chauffeur for the agent. The principal could not enforce a contract to lend money to the agent. The reason for the rule is that the credit of a stranger could not be thrust upon the lender.

It sometimes happens that the undisclosed principal, as purchaser, settles with the agent. Where the disclosed principal has bought goods from a third person through his agent, the principal remains liable for the purchase price until the third person is paid. Should the same rule apply to an undisclosed principal? Apparently it does not. Suppose the agent purchases goods on his own credit and the undisclosed principal has furnished him the funds with which to make the purchase, or suppose the agent purchases on his own credit and the undisclosed principal thereafter settles with the agent. Suppose further that the agent, in either event, fails to pay the third person and the third person then learns of the undisclosed principal. The few cases that have considered the problem hold that the third person cannot recover from the principal. It is apparently felt that it would be more equitable to require the third person to seek recovery from the agent whose credit was originally trusted rather than require the principal to pay for the same goods twice.

The broad rule which governs the rights of an undisclosed principal permits the undisclosed principal to sue in his own name and take any benefit or advantage derived by the agent from the contract. [*Kelly Asphalt Block Co. v. Barber Asphalt Paving Co.*, p. 450.]

Rights and Liabilities of the Agent It is the duty of the agent to disclose his principal if he would avoid personal liability. It is well settled that a person acting as agent for an undisclosed principal is individually liable if, at the time of making the contract, he fails to disclose his agency. The agent, without such disclosure, is subject to all the liabilities created by the contract in the same manner as if he were the principal. The third person, however, may acquire knowledge of the identity of the principal from the facts and circumstances surrounding the transaction.

Partially Disclosed or Unnamed Principal The partially disclosed principal is one represented by an agent who discloses the fact that he is acting as an agent but does not reveal the identity of his principal. In the absence of a contrary intention, the partially disclosed principal can enforce the contract the same as any other principal, and the third person can enforce the contract against either the principal or the agent. For all practical purposes, the rules applicable to an undisclosed principal are also applicable to a partially disclosed principal.

LIABILITY FOR TORTS OF AGENT

A general rule of agency is that the principal is civilly liable for the torts committed by his agent which are committed within the course and scope of the employment of the agent. The rule is well settled; it is equally applicable to employer and employee. The chief problem is to distinguish at the time of the commission of the tort those acts which may be said to lie within the course and scope of the employment of the agent from those that may be said to lie outside. The problem can only be solved by a consideration of all the facts and circumstances of the particular case. Any phrase or short form of expression says too little. In determining whether or not a particular act is within the course and scope of employment, however, two requirements must ordinarily be met: first, the tort must be committed in the interest of the principal to further his business, and secondly, it must not be an extreme deviation from the normal conduct of such agents. The meaning of these requirements will become more apparent by applying them to some specific acts of the agent.

Liability for Negligent Acts of Agent   The principal is not liable for a tort committed by his agent during the agent's own time. This is true even though the principal may have entrusted the agent with the physical object with which the tort is committed. It is thus quite clear that the principal is not liable when the agent negligently injures a third person while driving his principal's car for his own purpose on a Sunday or other holiday. It is not so clear, however, when the agent is driving the principal's car in the course and scope of his employment on a regular working day and temporarily departs from the business of the principal. The principal cannot escape liability by showing that the act which caused the tort was unknown to him. The principal, moreover, may have expressly forbidden the agent to do the act. The agent may have injured a third person while driving his principal's car at a rate of speed of thirty miles an hour. The principal cannot escape liability by showing that he instructed the agent to drive no more than twenty-five miles an hour. The "dual enterprise" cases provide much of the litigation concerning negligence of the agent when the principal attempts to show that the agent was not acting within the scope of his employment. These cases involve situations where the agent combines his own with his principal's business. This fact alone will not relieve the principal. The relative extent of the departure is usually the most important factor to be considered.

Liability for Willful Torts of Agent   The principal cannot escape liability merely because the act causing the tort was done by the agent willfully. The principal is not liable, however, if the willful misconduct was motivated entirely because of a personal grudge. Suppose the agent is on an errand for his principal during the course of which he meets a person who has been owing him a personal debt for some time. The principal will not be liable for any tort committed by the agent in attempting to collect the debt. The rule does not hold, however, where the facts and circumstances reveal that the agent committed the tort in furtherance of his principal's business. [*Son v. Hartford Ice Cream Co.,* p. 451.]

Liability for Fraud and Misrepresentations   The older cases held that the principal was not liable for his agent's misrepresentations unless such misrepresentations were authorized or ratified. This rule is still followed in a few states. The prevailing rule today, however, is that the principal is liable for the misrepresentations of his agent which are committed in the course and scope of his employment. This rule, moreover, has been extended to include fraudulent misrepresentations which are committed by the agent for his own benefit. This rule has been difficult to justify because it is not in agreement with the requirement that, in order to hold the principal liable, the tort must be committed in the interest of the principal to further the business of the principal. Many theories have been advanced to justify the rule. Be that as it may, most courts now hold that, even though the agent is committing the fraud for his own benefit, the principal is liable therefor if it is within the actual or apparent scope of the agent's employment. It is also true that attempted fraud on the part of the agent generally binds the principal. This rule, however, has found its most frequent application to insurance cases pertaining to proof of loss. [*Bockser v. Dorchester Mut. Fire Ins. Co.*, p. 452.]

Liability for Crimes   The principal will not ordinarily be held liable for the crimes of the agent unless he participates in, counsels, aids or abets, or approves of the crime, or directs the agent in committing the crime. Some state statutes, however, provide that certain acts will fix liability on the employer or principal. Suppose the owner of a supermarket never instructed his employees to give short weight and had no knowledge that his employees were giving short weight in violation of a statute. The owner would very likely be convicted of the crime. An act committed by an agent outside the scope of the agent's authority will not ordinarily impose liability on the principal.

CASES

Halsey v. Monteiro,   24 S.E. 258 (Va. 1896). Action by A. Monteiro, plaintiff, against J. M. Halsey, defendant. The defendant wrote the following letter to M. C. Staples & Company, real estate agents:

Mitchell's Sta., Feby. 12, 1891. Messrs. Manning C. Staples & Co., Richmond, Va.—Gents: Your favor of the 5th inst. received; contents noted. In reply, will say I must decline the offer to trade my farm for the houses with a mortgage of $4,000. Real estate is advancing, and I have offered my farm through you at extremely low rates for a year, hoping to make a sale. You may list it for twelve months next on the following terms: 732-1/3 acres, at $16.00 per acre, payable as follows: 1/3 cash; balance in 1, 2, and 3 years; or I will take $10,000 cash. I will allow you a liberal commission if you can place the farm. Most truly yours, &c., J. Morton Halsey.

The agents thereafter purported to enter into a contract for the sale of the land to plaintiff. Defendant refused to sell the land, and this action was brought for specific performance of the contract.

Reilly, Judge: A real estate broker or agent is defined to be one who negotiates the sale of real property. His business generally is only to find a purchaser who is willing to buy the land upon the terms fixed by the owner. He has no authority to bind his principal by signing a contract of sale. A sale of real estate involves the adjustment of many matters besides fixing the price. The delivery of the possession has to be settled; generally, the title to be examined; and the conveyance, with its covenants, to be agreed upon and executed by the owner— all of which require conference and time for their completion. They are for the determination of the owner, and do not pertain to the duties, and are not within the authority, of a real estate agent. For obvious reasons, therefore, the law wisely withholds from him any implied authority to sign a contract of sale in behalf of his principal. . . .

A real estate agent is not a general agent, but a special agent, acting under a limited power. He must pursue his instructions and act within the scope of his limited power; not exceed nor deviate from it. He who deals with him, if the agent exceeds or deviates from his authority, deals with him at his peril. He cannot in such case hold the principal bound, unless there has been an intelligent ratification of the unauthorized act of the agent, free from mistake or fraud. [DECISION FOR DEFENDANT]

Fairbanks Morse & Co. v. Dale & Co.,   159 So. 859 (Miss. 1935). Action by Dale & Company (plaintiff below), appellee, against Fairbanks Morse & Company (defendant below), appellant.

Appellee was engaged in the mercantile business in Prentiss. Dewees Fixture Company was engaged in business in Jackson. Appellant had its office for the territory in New Orleans. One Steel was a traveling salesman for the Dewees Fixture Company; he solicited and received an order for a pair of scales from appellee. The scales were to be shipped c.o.d.; draft was to be drawn through the Capital National Bank at Jackson by the appellant on the Dewees Fixture Company for the price, with shipper's order bill attached. At the time the order was taken appellee gave Steel a check on its bank for the price of the scales payable to the Dewees Fixture Company. This check was later cashed by the Dewees Fixture Company and no part thereof has been paid to the Fairbanks Company.

Anderson, Justice: The case turns on whether or not Dewees Fixture Company, through its agent Steel, was the agent of the Fairbanks Company with authority to take the order for the scales and collect the price. . . .

The evidence relied on, which for the purpose of this decision will be taken as true, as constituting the Dewees Fixture Company and its agent Steel the agents of the Fairbanks Company with authority to not only take orders but collect, was substantially as follows: Some months before Steel took this order he was in Prentiss; he had a business interview with appellee; he had with him a Fairbanks Company catalogue, and claimed to be representing that company. At that time he took no order from appellee. When the order for the scales was taken, Steel had with him the Fairbanks catalogue, the scales were selected by appellee therefrom, and the price fixed from the catalogue price. In other words, let this be the case: Dewees Fixture Company was the agent of the Fairbanks Company to solicit orders and send them in for the approval of the latter. The evidence certainly went no further; there was nothing to show either directly or indirectly that the Fairbanks Company had given the Dewees Fixture Company the additional authority to collect for the scales. The draft with the shipper's order bill attached is conclusive proof that all the parties concerned knew that no one had authority to collect except the bank that held it.

Where an agent has not the possession of the goods and no other indicia of authority, and he is authorized to solicit orders or make contracts to submit to the principal for approval, there is no implied authority to collect, and the purchaser makes payment to him at his own peril. Under this principle, brokers and traveling salesmen who have not the possession of the goods, and who sell for future delivery to be paid for on delivery or at a future time, are without authority to collect payment for the goods. If payment is made to a person occupying that relation, the purchaser makes him his agent to pay the seller, and, if he fails, it is the purchaser's loss and not the seller's. . . .

It was not shown either directly or by reasonable inference that either the Dewees Fixture Company or Steel had any authority to go beyond merely soliciting and forwarding orders subject to the acceptance and approval of the Fairbanks Company. It follows that the payment by appellee to the Dewees Fixture Company was not a payment to the Fairbanks Company, and the loss must therefore fall on appellee and not on the Fairbanks Company. [DECISION FOR APPELLANT]

Kelly Asphalt Block Co. v. Barber Asphalt Paving Co., 105 N.E. 88 (N.Y. 1914). Action by Kelly Asphalt Block Company, plaintiff, against Barber Asphalt Paving Company, defendant.

Cardozo, Judge: The plaintiff sues to recover damages for breach of an implied warranty. The contract was made between the defendant and one Booth. The plaintiff says that Booth was in truth its agent, and it sues as undisclosed principal. The question is whether it has the right to do so.

The general rule is not disputed. A contract not under seal, made in the name of an agent as ostensible principal, may be sued on by the real principal at the latter's election. The defendant says that we should establish an exception to that rule, where the identity of the principal has been concealed because of the belief that, if it were disclosed, the contract would not be made. We are asked to say that the reality of the defendant's consent is thereby destroyed, and the contract vitiated for mistake.

The plaintiff and the defendant were competitors in business. The plaintiff's president suspected that the defendant might refuse to name him a price. The suspicion was not based upon any previous refusal, for there had been none; it had no other origin than their relation as competitors. Because of this doubt the plaintiff availed itself of the services of Booth, who, though interested to the defendant's knowledge in the plaintiff's business, was also engaged in a like business for another corporation. Booth asked the defendant for a price and received a quotation, and the asphalt blocks required for the plaintiff's pavement were ordered in his name. The order was accepted by the defendant, the blocks were delivered, and payment was made by Booth with money furnished by the plaintiff. The paving blocks were unmerchantable, and the defendant retaining the price, contests its liability for damages on the ground that if it had known that the plaintiff was the principal it would have refused to make the sale.

We are satisfied that upon the facts before us the defense cannot prevail.

. . . Booth made no misrepresentation to the defendant. He was not asked anything, nor did he say anything, about the plaintiff's interest in the transaction. Indeed, neither he nor the plaintiff's officers knew whether the defendant would refuse to deal with the plaintiff directly. They suspected hostility, but none had been expressed. The validity of the contract turns thus, according to the defendant, not on any overt act of either the plaintiff or its agent, but on the presence or absence of a mental state. We are asked to hold that a contract complete in form becomes a nullity in fact because of a secret belief in the mind of the undisclosed principal that the disclosure of his name would be prejudicial to the completion of the bargain. We cannot go so far. [DECISION FOR PLAINTIFF]

Son v. Hartford Ice Cream Co.,   129 Atl. 778 (Conn. 1925). Action by Louis Son, plaintiff, against Hartford Ice Cream Company, defendant.

The defendant is a manufacturer of ice cream. Plaintiff is a shopkeeper. Plaintiff had for some time been receiving ice cream delivered by defendant's truck driver whose instructions were to collect the price on delivery. On the date in question, plaintiff claimed that the ice cream was not properly iced and refused to receive it. The driver insisted on leaving it. Plaintiff refused to pay for it. The driver then undertook to take the price out of plaintiff's cash register. Plaintiff succeeded in locking the cash drawer of the register. The driver then attempted to carry away the cash register bodily. This led to a struggle for its possession in the course of which the plaintiff was kicked and severely beaten by the driver and his helper. This action was then brought to recover damages for the act of the driver in assaulting and beating the plaintiff. Defendant claims that his instructions to this driver, as well as to other drivers, were to use no force in making collections but in case of dispute to call defendant's office. His contention, therefore, is that, especially in view of the driver's disobedience of his order, the assault was not an act done in the execution of the defendant's business nor within the scope of the driver's employment.

Beach, Justice: The earlier cases including our own, held that a master was not liable for the willful torts of his servants without proof of the master's assent or approval, on the ground that it would not be presumed without such proof that the commission of a willful tort was an act done within the scope of the servant's employment.

On the other hand, it now seems plain enough that the liability of a master for his servant's torts is quite independent of the master's assent to or approval of the tortious act; and also that the rule respondeat superior is not applicable upon any theory which does not make it applicable to a willful as well as to a negligent tort. It may be more difficult for a plaintiff to sustain the burden of proving that a willful, as distinguished from a negligent, injury was inflicted while the servant was upon the master's business, and acting within the scope of his employment; but when these conditions are shown to exist there is no satisfactory reason for holding a master, who is himself free from fault, liable for his servant's lapses of judgment and attention, which does not also apply to the servant's lapses of temper and self-control. . . .

The defendant does not deny that a master may be liable for the willful torts of his servant, but insists that in the case at bar the circumstances show that the defendant's servant was not, at the time of the assault, engaged in the defendant's business, and was not acting within the scope of his employment.

. . . When the servant is doing or attempting to do the very thing which he was directed to do, the master is liable, though the servant's method of doing it be wholly unauthorized or forbidden. . . .

Here the defendant's servant was instructed to collect for goods delivered, and the assault complained of grew out of his attempt to enforce payment by helping himself out of the plaintiff's cash register. What followed was a direct consequence of the servant's tortious method of performing the duty delegated to him. . . .

So in the case at bar the truck driver's attempt to collect out of the plaintiff's cash register precipitated a series of acts constituting one continuous transaction, and the beating occurred in the course of the servant's attempt to perform the business of the master. [DECISION FOR PLAINTIFF]

Bockser v. Dorchester Mut. Fire Ins. Co., 99 N.E.2d 640 (Mass. 1951). Action by Bennie Bockser, plaintiff, against Dorchester Mutual Fire Insurance Company, defendant, to recover on certain policies for a fire loss.

The evidence showed that plaintiff hired a public adjuster to adjust the loss and to do whatever was necessary to adjust the loss. The defendant contended that the adjuster attempted to defraud the defendant, and that the plaintiff was bound by the acts of the adjuster.

The fraud allegedly attempted by the adjuster concerned two bills, which were in evidence. (1) A receipted bill of a carpenter and builder for $17,519.90, which the defendant contended had been increased from $5,200. (2) A receipted bill of an electrician totaling $2,498.17 for labor and materials, which the defendants contended had been marked up from $400.

There was no evidence of personal fraud on the part of plaintiff. The question, therefore, was the effect of such conduct of the agent upon his principal, the plaintiff. The policies provided that they "shall be void if the insured shall make any attempt to defraud the company either before or after the loss."

Wilkins, Justice: In general, the fraud of an agent acting in the course of his employment is binding upon his principal. The precise question is whether an agent's attempt to defraud, which was wholly unsuccessful, should be treated the same as similar conduct on the part of the principal and should result in forfeiture of the principal's rights under the policies. This is a matter upon which there is a difference of opinion in other jurisdictions. The majority, and we think the better reasoned, view is that the attempted fraud of the agent acting in the scope of his employment binds the principal. Any other result would tend to circumvent the public policy which calls for the enforcement of the clause in the standard policy now before us. [DECISION FOR DEFENDANT]

PROBLEMS

1 W. E. Terrell, as agent for defendant, entered into a contract in his own name to purchase a tract of land from the plaintiff. Defendant was a wealthy property owner, holding many lots in a new suburban addition to the city of Richmond, and it was thought that plaintiff might demand a higher price for his land if he discovered during the negotiation that defendant was desirous of buying this property. Terrell declined to go through with the negotiations, and disclosed his principal to plaintiff. The defense is made that defendant is not named in the contract and he is not therefore bound by it. Is plaintiff entitled to specific performance?

2 Louis Jordan had been driving for defendant, Mrs. S. R. Cockrill, for some time; whenever she needed the car she instructed him to bring the car from the garage to the front of the house. The customary route followed did not necessitate crossing the street at any point. On this occasion, however, the driver, instead of obeying the directions of his employer and without her knowledge, went on a trip to a drugstore to buy cigarettes. In order to make the trip, it was necessary for him to travel the distance of six blocks in order to get back to the front of his employer's residence. When he was returning from the drugstore, he ran into the car occupied by plaintiff. Is the plaintiff entitled to recover for personal injuries which were inflicted upon the occupants of plaintiff's car as well as for damage to the car itself?

3 Defendant, a building contractor, visited the office of plaintiff, a lumber company, for the purpose of establishing credit for the purchase of materials to be used in a construction project. As a result of this visit, an account was set up in the name of defendant, who agreed to pay the bills by the 10th of each month following delivery. From October, 1954, to April, 1955, the plaintiff made 162 deliveries to the project. An invoice made out to the defendant accompanied each order, and monthly statements made out to the defendant were mailed to him at his home address. Payment for a portion of the materials so delivered was made by corporate checks in the name of "Crute and Associates, Inc." and signed by defendant as treasurer. Plaintiff brought an action against defendant to recover the unpaid balance. Defendant contends that the payment by corporate checks was notice to the plaintiff that the materials were purchased in behalf of the corporation and that the defendant is not therefore personally liable. Do you agree with defendant?

4 The defendant-company, which company was engaged in the business of manufacturing machinery including tractors, was a member of a golf league organized by the Y.M.C.A. The defendant-company furnished shirts with the name of the company on the shirts to the players, paid the green fees, gave a banquet at the end of the year with a distribution of trophies for athletic prowess, and received publicity from its participation in the golf league. An employee of the defendant-company, known as the athletic supervisor, asked Brown, also an employee of the defendant-company, whether he cared to play on the team. Brown voluntarily and without coercion consented. Brown was playing golf under this arrangement, after his working hours, without compensation, when he hooked a golf ball to the left, thereby injuring the plaintiff. Assume plaintiff brought an action for damages for the injuries so sustained against the defendant-company and proved that Brown had

committed a tort. Decide. Discuss the rules of law which could be advanced in favor of both plaintiff and defendant-company.

5 Lindquist and Dickson entered into a contract by the terms of which Lindquist decorated and repaired a house which, unknown to Lindquist, belonged to the wife of Dickson. The amount owing for the decoration and repair work remained unpaid for several months. Lindquist learned that Mrs. Dickson owned the house. He, nevertheless, brought an action and recovered a judgment against Mr. Dickson for the amount so owing. The judgment likewise remained unpaid. Lindquist then brought an action against Mrs. Dickson. What defense, if any, is available to Mrs. Dickson?

6 Brown instructed Jones to purchase certain described bricks from The Masonry Company for $1,000 and to charge the bricks to the account of Brown. Jones purchased the bricks, but had the bricks charged to his own personal account. Jones then delivered the bricks to Brown and told Brown that he had charged the bricks to his own personal account rather than to the personal account of Brown. Brown then paid Jones the $1,000 to pay for the bricks, and then proceeded to use the bricks in the construction of a house for Abel. The Masonry Company, however, had no knowledge that Jones was acting as the agent of Brown or that Brown had paid Jones. Jones absconded, and The Masonry Company learned the true facts. Would The Masonry Company recover in an action against Brown to recover the price of the bricks?

7 The Automobile Agency sold certain automobiles to its customers and accepted promissory notes in payment therefor. The agency authorized Black to sell some of the notes at a discount to other customers. Black was instructed to inform the prospective customers about the financial condition of the makers of the notes, but not to make any false or untrue statements. Black, who was negotiating with White for the sale of a note signed by Hall as maker, represented that Hall was a man of wealth with a large account in a local bank. The Automobile Agency and Black both knew at the time the representations were made that Hall was on the verge of bankruptcy. White purchased the note, and it turned out to be worthless. White thereupon brought an action against The Automobile Agency for deceit. Decide.

35
AGENT AND THIRD PERSON

Some of the situations where the agent and the third person may be liable to each other have already been mentioned. It is not surprising then to learn that the agent may very well find himself liable to the third person and that the third person may find himself liable to the agent. This is true because certain duties and liabilities emanate from the nature of the relationship of agent and third person. These duties and liabilities may arise out of (1) contract or (2) tort.

LIABILITY OF AGENT ARISING OUT OF CONTRACT
The agent may be acting for an undisclosed principal. The personal liability of an agent of an undisclosed principal has already been mentioned. Some of the other important situations where the agent may be personally liable to the third person are when he voluntarily assumes liability, when he carelessly signs a written contract, when he acts for an incompetent or nonexistent principal, when he has money in his possession which the third person may recover, or when he is liable on an implied warranty of authority.

Assumption of Liability The agent may voluntarily make himself liable to third persons. His liability will depend on the promises which he has made to such persons. He may bind himself to perform the obligations of the principal or he may guarantee such performance by the principal. The more common way in which the agent may voluntarily make himself liable is where the contract is entered into on the strength of the credit of the agent. In order to hold the agent liable, however, it must appear clearly that it was the intention of the agent to assume the obligation as a personal liability and that he knew that credit was extended to him alone. The agent may, however, find himself personally liable even though he had no intention of being so. This is frequently the plight of an agent who carelessly executes a written agreement.

Liability on Contracts in Writing A word of caution needs to be emphasized at the start. The liability of an agent who signs a negotiable instrument is treated under that subject. The following rules are limited to simple contracts.

An agent who signs a writing within the course and scope of his authority has no personal liability on the instrument if he names his principal and expresses by appropriate words that the writing is that of the principal. The agent, however, does not always do this. Judging from reported cases, he often is quite careless in placing his signature to a writing. The liability of the agent, therefore, frequently turns on the form of signature made by the agent. The name of the agent is sometimes followed by such words as "agent," "agt.," or "trustee." The older cases practically all held that such words were descriptio personae—descriptive of the person—and held the agent personally liable. Many of the cases today, probably most of them, follow this same line of reasoning. A number of cases, however, hold that the addition of such words renders the contract ambiguous and will permit extrinsic evidence to show that it was the intent to bind the principal. The cases are not in harmony. This is not the only instance where an agent is careless in placing his signature to a writing. It is sometimes shown as "The XYZ Company," followed by "John Doe," which gives the appearance that the company and John Doe both intended to be bound. Again the cases are not in harmony. Any definite statement, therefore, would be reckless. All courts would no doubt hold that an agent has no personal liability when the body of the writing names the principal and the signature is in this form: "The XYZ Company, by John Doe, Secretary."

Liability of Agent for Incompetent or Nonexistent Principal An incompetent person is one who lacks the legal capacity to manage his own affairs by reason of causes, such as insanity or infancy. It is a general rule that an agent who assumes to contract in the name of an incompetent or nonexistent principal renders himself liable to third persons. The liability, if any, of an agent who contracts in the name of a person with limited contractual capacity is not clear. The few cases in which this problem has been discussed seem to indicate that the third person has a right to assume that the agent undertakes to act for a principal having normal legal capacity. The agent clearly would be liable if he intentionally misrepresents or conceals his principal's incapacity. The agent, on the other hand, would not be liable where both parties are equally informed. Beyond this it is not so clear.

The general rule stated above has found its most frequent application to the nonexistent principal. The promoter of a proposed corporation, for instance, would be personally liable unless the third party agreed to look to the subsequently formed corporation or the corporation, on being subsequently incorporated, adopts the contract. It is likewise true that one who purports to act as agent of an unincorporated club or organization assumes the risk of incurring personal liability. An unincorporated body has no status or existence as a legal person. Only those members who vote in favor of the contract or later adopt it, or actively promote the project, would be liable. [*Cousin v. Taylor,* p. 459.]

Liability of Agent for Money Paid to Him It is the duty of the agent to turn the money over to his principal, and it is of no concern to the third person if the agent does not perform his duty. Money which has been properly paid to an authorized agent and which the principal has a right to receive and retain, therefore, cannot be recovered from the agent by the third person. This is true even though the agent fails to pay it over to his principal. The rule is different when the principal is not entitled to the money. The agent would be liable if he knows that the principal is not entitled to the money; the agent would also be liable where he fraudulently or otherwise wrongfully induces the third person to pay money over to him for his principal. This is true even though the agent may have paid the money over to his principal. The third person may recover from an agent of an undisclosed principal any money so paid through mistake, even though the agent has paid the money over to the principal. But an agent to whom money has been paid through mistake, such as an overpayment, is not liable where he turns the money over to his principal before he has notice that the principal is not entitled to it. An agent would be liable to the third person for money paid through mistake, however, so long as the money remains in his hands.

Liability of Agent on Implied Warranty of Authority The general rule now prevailing is that an agent who so exceeds his authority that the principal is not bound becomes liable himself to the third person for whatever damages the third person has suffered. An agent who expressly represents that he is authorized to enter into a contract for a principal knowing full well that he has no such authority is liable in tort in an action of deceit. An agent who acts in good faith and honestly believes that he has the authority which he assumes to exercise, but who has no such authority, is liable upon an implied warranty of authority. The third person, however, may rely upon his own judgment rather than upon the representations of the agent. If this is the case, the agent would not be liable. [*Robinson v. Pattee,* p. 460.]

LIABILITY OF THIRD PERSON ARISING OUT OF CONTRACTS
The agent may, as has been shown, intentionally or inadvertently make himself a party to the contract. The third person, therefore, becomes liable to the agent on the contract. The agent of an undisclosed principal always binds himself and has

the right to sue the third person in his own name in the event of nonperformance. It should be pointed out, however, that either the principal or the agent may bring suit. The right of the agent to sue is secondary to that of the undisclosed principal, therefore, if the principal asserts his rights under the contract. Another quite important situation where the third person may be answerable to the agent is when the agent possesses a beneficial interest in the subject matter of the agency. He may then sue in his own name. A factor selling under a del credere commission, or an auctioneer by virtue of his lien, may sue for the purchase price in the event of default by the buyer. In these circumstances, however, the agent will hold the proceeds in a fiduciary or trust capacity for his principal in the event the agent sues the third person, recovers a judgment, and payment is made to the agent.

LIABILITY OF AGENT FOR TORTS

The agent is liable to third persons for his torts. The agent is liable even though the tort is committed in the course and within the scope of his employment. The principal, to be sure, is liable. But this does not relieve the agent. The principal and the agent are jointly and severally liable for the torts of the agent committed in the course and within the scope of the employment. The third person may choose which one he will hold. One further point should be mentioned.

It is commonly stated as a general proposition of law that an agent is not liable to third persons for a breach of duty owing to the principal. The agent, it is said, has agreed with no one except the principal to perform such duties and no one has a right to complain when the agent fails to perform them. This does not mean, however, that the agent can find shelter behind his principal in all cases. The agent will be liable to the third person if his failure to perform a duty owing to his principal results in an injury to the third person. Various illustrations could be given. An agent owes a duty to his principal to obey instructions. Suppose the principal instructs his agent, the driver of his automobile, to drive carefully. Suppose further that the agent recklessly drives the automobile and injures a third person. The agent, to be sure, would be liable.

LIABILITY OF THIRD PERSON FOR TORTS

The agent may bring an action to recover damages for his personal injuries caused by the tortious acts of a third person. The rule extends beyond physical injuries inflicted upon the agent. It is interesting to note, however, that the tort liability is only connected with the agency in a few instances. The liability of third persons to the agent for torts in connection with the agency sometimes arises because of interference with the agent's possession of chattels. A factor or other agent who is in possession of goods of his principal may sue for injuries affecting his possession. It is also true that a third person who induces a principal to discharge his agent without justification is liable in damages to the agent so discharged.

CASES

Cousin v. Taylor,   239 Pac. 96 (Ore. 1925). Action by Edward M. Cousin, plaintiff, against Walter K. Taylor and others, defendants. The evidence showed that a group of telephone users in and around the county of Benton, Oregon, organized themselves into what was known as the "Oregon Telephone Federation"; that they had several mass meetings, at one of which some of the members authorized Walter K. Taylor to engage a rate expert to represent them and said Federation at a hearing in regard to telephone rates to be held before the Public Service Commission of the State of Oregon; that pursuant to this authority Walter K. Taylor employed the plaintiff to represent the Federation at the hearing; that others among the members ratified and approved the contract made by Walter K. Taylor with plaintiff; and that plaintiff performed the services contracted for. This action was brought for his services.

    Rand, Judge: Since this association was not a legal entity and there is no statute in this state authorizing such an organization, or defining the duties, powers, and liability of the members of such an association when voluntarily formed, the association could neither sue nor be sued, and as such it had no capacity to enter into a contract, or to appoint an agent for any purpose. Therefore a contract entered into in the name of the association, or in its behalf, by any of the officers or members of the association would not be binding upon the association or enforceable against it. But no such a limitation exists upon the powers and liabilities of the individual members who compose such an association. As individuals they are free to contract, and to appoint agents or committees to enter contracts for them, and any such contract, when thus entered into by such agent or committee, if within the scope of the authority conferred, is binding upon them as principals. It is true that no person can be charged upon a contract alleged to have been made upon his responsibility unless it can be shown that to the making of the contract he had given his express or implied consent. While under this principle no member of the association would be directly responsible as principal upon a contract made by Taylor, unless it was first shown that to the making of the contract by Taylor, such member gave his assent, expressly or impliedly, but when it was shown that any member of the association present at the meeting assented to the appointment of Taylor for the purpose of employing plaintiff, or assented to the making of the contract by Taylor, or ratified and approved the contract after it was made, then under this principle such person would be directly responsible as principal. . . .

    It has always been a familiar principle of the law of agency that one professing to act as agent, unless he binds his principal, is ordinarily held to bind himself. Since the contract entered into by Taylor could not be enforced against the association, Taylor, in acting as agent for the association of which he was an officer and member, in entering into a contract which has been performed by the other contracting party, is personally liable under the contract, and the same is true as to those who either assented to his appointment or assented to the contract which he entered into. [DECISION FOR PLAINTIFF]

Robinson v. Pattee, 222 S.W.2d 786 (Mo. 1949). Action by William M. Robinson, plaintiff, against Eula D. Pattee and Eula D. Pattee and Walter J. Pattee, Jr., as coexecutors of the estate of Walter J. Pattee, deceased, defendants.

Walter J. Pattee was physically and mentally ill prior to his death, and his wife, Eula D. Pattee, acted in his behalf by authority of his power of attorney. In such capacity, she signed for herself and for her husband, as his attorney in fact, a contract for the sale of certain land which they owned as tenants by the entirety. The power of attorney, however, did not authorize her to enter into a contract for the sale of land. Plaintiff was ready, able, and willing to perform, but the wife, upon learning that the power of attorney was insufficient, announced that she was "not going through with the deal." Plaintiff then brought an action for damages for breach of contract for the sale of the land.

Van Osdol, Commissioner: It is a well-recognized principle of law that where one undertakes to bind a principal without being authorized or empowered so to do, he thereby renders himself personally responsible even though he, in so undertaking, acted in the utmost good faith and honestly believed he was authorized.

The basis of the purported agent's liability is not the contract but an express or implied covenant of authority. The personal responsibility does not obtain if the absence of authority or the incompetency of the principal is known to the plaintiff. In the instant action, the wife's belief of her authority should not constitute a defense in view of an express or implied warranty of her authority and of the competency of her principal, save and except the plaintiff knew of her want of authority, or of her husband's mental incompetency, if so. [REMANDED FOR NEW TRIAL]

PROBLEMS

1 Plaintiff and Hagan entered into a contract by the terms of which plaintiff leased to Food Shops, Inc., certain premises. During the negotiations leading up to the execution of the lease, Hagan represented that he was entering into the contract for, and in behalf of, a corporation known as Food Shops, Inc., of which he was president. As proof of said representation, he showed plaintiff a copy of a resolution purporting to have been passed by the directors of said corporation which expressly authorized Hagan to execute the contract in behalf of the corporation. At the time the contract was executed no such corporation as Food Shops, Inc., was in existence, but this fact was unknown to plaintiff. Hagan refused to pay the rent for the first month when it became due. Plaintiff claims that defendant Hagan is personally liable. Is plaintiff's claim correct?

2 Defendant, acting as agent for her husband, sold certain land to the plaintiff. During the course of the negotiations, defendant falsely stated that the land was free of encumbrances. Plaintiff relied upon these statements in making the purchase. The entire premises were thereafter sold as the result of a foreclosure of a mortgage which encumbered the property at the time defendant sold it to plaintiff. The defendant argues by way of defense that plaintiff has failed to show that she had any interest in the property. Does the liability of defendant for making this intentionally false statement depend upon her having an interest in the property?

3   Plaintiff became the tenant of certain dwelling property in December, 1941, under a lease which provided for a monthly rental of $85 and which was signed by defendant J. Wesley Brown as "Agent for the Owner only." It was later revealed that the property should have been rented at $65 a month under the Rent Act. Plaintiff brought an action to recover the overpayment of rent, and defendant disclaimed liability on the ground that his status was that of a mere agent as disclosed by his signature. Decide.

4   The defendant as treasurer of the Little League Club, an unincorporated club, entered into a written contract with plaintiff whereby plaintiff agreed to build a club house for the Little League Club for the sum of $2,000. Plaintiff built the club house, but the Little League Club refused to pay for the construction. Plaintiff then brought an action against defendant individually to recover the $2,000. Defendant offered the following rule as a defense: An agent who signs a writing within the course and scope of his authority has no personal liability on the instrument if he names his principal and expresses by appropriate words that the writing is that of the principal. Do you think plaintiff will recover?

5   Plaintiff, while riding in an automobile across the street crossing of The Railroad Company, sustained serious injuries when the automobile was struck by a backing locomotive because of the negligence of the engineer. Plaintiff brought an action against The Railroad Company and the engineer. The Railroad Company contends it is not liable because the engineer was not authorized to operate the locomotive in a negligent manner. The engineer contends he is not liable because he was operating the locomotive in the service of The Railroad Company. Who is correct?

6   Linder, who was a building contractor, employed plaintiff as a carpenter. Plaintiff accidentally fell from the roof of a building under construction and seriously injured his back. The Casualty Company had previously insured Linder against damages for personal injuries to his employees. The adjuster for the company offered to settle with plaintiff for $300, and plaintiff refused the offer. The adjuster for the company then told Linder that the company would no longer insure Linder unless plaintiff was discharged. Linder regretfully explained the situation to plaintiff and reluctantly discharged plaintiff. Would plaintiff prevail in an action against the company to recover damages because the company had him discharged from his job?

7   A. B. Robert, a farmer, authorized Taylor to sell corn to The Milling Company. Taylor visited the president of the company and entered into a contract for the sale of the corn at a specified price. The body of the contract contained the name A. B. Robert, and the contract was signed "A. B. Robert, by Tim Taylor, Agent." The corn was delivered, and the company paid the price to Robert. It was then learned by the company that the corn was not the quality represented because it contained weevils. The company brought an action against Taylor for breach of contract. Should the company recover?

8   Mason, an agent of the Fine Foods Corporation, was authorized to deliver food to various customers who had previously submitted orders. He was also authorized to collect when such food was delivered. On June 1, Mason delivered certain food to Jackson and collected $1,200, which represented an overpayment of $300 as a result of a mistake in addition. This overpayment was detected on June 3 after Mason had already accounted to the Fine Food Corporation. Jackson is now demanding a refund of the $300 from Mason. Mason contends that he has no liability and that Jackson should try to recover from the Fine Food Corporation. Is the contention of Mason correct?

PRINCIPAL AND AGENT

The principal and agent may, and very often do, enter into a contract of employment defining the terms of their relationship. It may contain terms describing such things as compensation, duties, and the duration of the relationship itself. This practice is commendable. Certain duties and liabilities arise impliedly and incidentally from the relationship. This chapter, therefore, logically divides itself into (1) the duties and liabilities of the agent, (2) the duties and liabilities of the principal, and (3) termination of the relationship.

DUTIES AND LIABILITIES OF THE AGENT
The chief duties of the agent to the principal are to be loyal, to give notice of material facts, to obey instructions, and to account.

Duty to Be Loyal   The duty of good faith and loyalty is broad enough to include all the duties which the agent owes his principal. There are, nevertheless, certain duties which are more closely allied to the duty to be loyal than any of the other duties. The most important of these require the agent to act for only one principal, not to act for himself, and not to divulge secret information.

   (1)   *Duty to Act for Only One Principal*   The agent is subject to the duty to refrain from acting for a party whose interests are adverse to those of his principal. As a general rule the agent will not be permitted to act as agent for both

parties to the transaction. An agent who acts for both parties, without the knowledge and consent of both, is not entitled to compensation. If only one of the parties knows of and consents to the agent's acting for both, such party is bound but the other party may have the transaction set aside. It is recognized, however, that an agent may act in a dual capacity provided both principals have been fully informed of the dual role of the agent and have consented to it. In these circumstances the duties of the agent to each principal do not conflict. Such an agent is commonly referred to as a "middleman" whose function is to bring the parties together. The parties then bargain for themselves.

(2) *Duty Not to Act for Himself* An agent cannot, unless the principal with full knowledge of all the facts consents, have an interest in the subject matter of the agency. He may not make any profit out of the agency beyond his stipulated compensation. An agent, therefore, will be required to account to his principal for any secret profit which he may have received or for any gift or bribe received by him in violation of his duty. A principal may instruct his agent that he is willing to pay a certain price for property. The agent may purchase the property for a smaller price. The agent, however, cannot charge the principal with the larger price and thereby make a profit for himself. An agent authorized to buy cannot buy from himself; an agent authorized to sell, cannot sell to himself. This he may not do either directly or indirectly. He cannot buy for or sell to himself in the name of another.

(3) *Duty Not to Divulge Secret Information* An agent owes a duty to his principal not to use confidential information obtained in the course of his agency for his own benefit to the detriment of his principal. This duty continues after the employment is terminated. The agent, may, however, go into business for himself or work for a competitor unless there is an agreement to the contrary. An agent who has made the acquaintance of customers during the course of his employment may communicate later with those whom he can remember. His acquaintance is generally said to be acquired as part of the general knowledge of the business of the principal. The agent will naturally acquire such general knowledge and information. He will become more efficient and skilled in the particular type of business. The agent is privileged, after his agency is terminated, to engage in similar employment and to use whatever knowledge he has acquired pertaining to general usages of the business. The use of this privilege may be prevented by including a clause in the contract of employment that the employee will not compete or work for a competitor for a specified period of time after his agency is terminated. A restriction created by such a clause may be set aside by the court unless the restriction is limited to a reasonable time and a reasonable area.

General information and ordinary experience, however, are quite distinct from secret information. Code price lists and similar confidential matter are generally treated as secret information. Formulas and processes are clearly trade secrets. [*A. Hollander & Son v. Imperial Fur Blending Corp.*, p. 471.]

Duty to Give Notice of Material Facts The agent is under a duty to give prompt notice to his principal of all facts coming to his knowledge which may materially affect the subject matter of the agency. The importance of this duty becomes apparent when viewed in the light of the general rule that knowledge of the agent is imputed and held to be knowledge of the principal even though the agent never communicates such knowledge to the principal. The rule includes knowledge of all material facts relating to the subject matter of the agency which the agent acquires during his agency and within the scope of his authority. A typical illustration is where an agent is purchasing property for his principal and learns that there is an outstanding but unrecorded mortgage against the property. The knowledge of the agent will be imputed to the principal who will acquire the property subject to the mortgage.

Many courts go a step further and hold that knowledge of an agent acquired prior to the agency is notice to the principal, provided the agent may be considered as having remembered such knowledge and had it in his mind when acting in behalf of the principal. This proviso is a question of fact, and it may be difficult to prove that knowledge was present in the agent's mind. The information, of course, might have been acquired so recently as to make it incredible that he had forgotten it. Knowledge is not imputed where it appears that the agent was acting for his own secret gain or the third person and the agent were acting in collusion to defraud the principal. In the above illustration, suppose the agent had received knowledge of the unrecorded mortgage from the third person with the request that it be kept a secret from the principal. This knowledge would not be imputed to the principal who would acquire the property free of the mortgage.

The general rule, of course, would not apply to privileged communications. The law will not impute knowledge to the principal, therefore, where an attorney acquires information from a privileged source so that it would constitute a breach of professional confidence to disclose such information to another. This is an example of a duty of nondisclosure.

In the vast majority of agency relationships, however, it is the duty of the agent to keep his principal informed of all facts affecting the principal's business which may come to his knowledge. An agent who fails to do so may be liable in damages for any resulting loss. [*Mason Produce Co. v. Harry C. Gilbert Co.*, p. 472.]

Duty to Obey Instructions   The agent has the duty to obey all lawful instruction given by his principal. The instructions may depart from the usual procedure; they may appear impractical, or even capricious, to the agent. The agent may act in good faith or intend to benefit the principal but the disobedience of clear and precise instructions will not be excused. The agent has, with few exceptions, no discretion in the observance of instructions. He must, therefore, answer to the principal for any loss which results from the disobedience of all lawful instructions. Typical illustrations are where the instructions are given an agent to sell goods at a certain specified price, or on a certain day only, or for cash only. The agent renders himself liable to his principal for any loss which results from selling at a different price, or at a different time, or from taking a check which proves to be worthless.

A departure from instructions may be justified by a sudden emergency. Where some unexpected emergency or unforeseen event occurs which will admit no delay for communication with the principal, the agent is justified in adopting the course which seems best to him under the circumstances. A company foreman may be instructed to call a certain physician in case of accident. Surely the foreman is justified in calling another physician if a serious accident occurs and he is unable to communicate with either the named physician or his principal. The rule is applicable only where the principal cannot be consulted and where the circumstances will not admit delay. Ambiguous instructions are another instance which may justify an agent in not following instructions; the agent will not be liable if he chooses reasonably one of two possible interpretations. Custom and usage may aid in the interpretation of ambiguous instructions but not to the extent of overruling positive instructions to the contrary. Nor will the agent be justified in following ideas of his own which are not within any interpretation of the instructions. [*Washington v. Mechanics & Traders Ins. Co.*, p. 473.]

Agent's Duty to Account   The duty of an agent to account to his principal for any money or property entrusted to the agent is well settled. An agent who is engaged in a transaction which requires or involves collections is under a duty to keep and be prepared to render a true and correct account at any time the principal may demand it. The agent is under a duty not to commingle the property of the principal with his own property. This rule is all-important when money is involved. The agent should never commingle funds of the principal with those of his own. The principal may follow and recover any funds misappropriated by the agent so long as they have not come into the hands of an innocent purchaser for value without notice. Money belonging to the principal which is deposited in a bank should be deposited under some designation which clearly indicates that the money is that of the principal and not that of the agent. If the agent fails to do this, it is possible that the money may be attached as the personal assets of the agent. The agent then would have to bear the loss. The agent would also have to bear any loss resulting from insolvency of the depository.

DUTIES AND LIABILITIES OF THE PRINCIPAL
The chief duties of the principal to the agent are (1) to pay him compensation for services rendered, (2) to reimburse him for money expended in the execution of the agency, and (3) to indemnify him against losses and liabilities.

Duty to Compensate Agent   The contract creating the agency relationship will ordinarily stipulate the compensation which the agent is to receive for his services. It is the duty of the principal, in these circumstances, to pay the agent the agreed compensation. In the absence of any agreement, the law implies a promise on the part of the principal to pay what the services are reasonably worth. If the services are rendered in a business or profession in which there is established by custom a rate for such services, it is generally inferred that the principal intended to pay that rate. This is particularly true where both parties knew or had reason to know of such rate. The law will not imply a promise to pay when the circumstances indicate that it was the intention of the parties that the services should be rendered gratuitously. The law ordinarily implies a promise to pay, however, if the services are of such a character that compensation is usually expected. If the services are rendered by one member of the family to another and are such as are usually performed by persons in that relation, no promise to pay will be implied.

The agent who is paid on a commission basis is not to be overlooked. The traveling salesman, the broker, and the agent who has an exclusive agency are worthy of mention.

(1) *Compensation of Traveling Salesman* A traveling salesman is commonly employed to solicit orders which are to be transmitted to and approved by the principal. Such an agent, in the absence of an agreement to the contrary, is certainly entitled to his commission on all orders accepted by his principal. This is true although the customer thereafter refuses to receive the goods. It is especially true if the refusal to accept is due to some fault of the principal, as, for example, where the goods do not comply with the terms of the order taken by the agent or are not shipped within the time specified in the order.

Some contracts expressly provide that acceptance is to be made at the discretion of the principal. A right reserved to reject orders, where the agent's commission is dependent upon approval, must nevertheless be exercised honestly and in good faith. Honest dissatisfaction with the credit of the customer would ordinarily justify the principal in disapproving the order. The contract of employment sometimes stipulates that payment is contingent upon delivery of the goods to the purchaser; it sometimes stipulates that payment is contingent upon receipt of the purchase price. In either event the salesman is not entitled to his compensation until the contingency has been fulfilled. This does not mean, however, that the principal can terminate the agency prior to delivery of the goods or receipt of the purchase price and thereby escape paying the agent his commission.

An agent is frequently permitted a weekly or monthly advance, commonly referred to as a "drawing account." These advances may represent a loan to the agent which he repays by commissions that he earns in the future. They sometimes represent a minimum salary to which the agent is entitled. Practice varies. The court, in the absence of a specific agreement, treats such advances as a minimum salary.

(2) *Compensation of Agent Having Exclusive Territory* The increasing litigation which involves agents of manufacturers deserves special attention. These agents are commonly given a specified territory in which to sell. The agent clearly is entitled to a commission on all sales which he solicits and consummates. The question often arises, however, whether the agent is entitled to a commission on sales made within his territory by another agent or by his principal. Practically all states permit an agent having an exclusive territory to recover a commission on sales made by another agent. Some conflict prevails, however, with respect to sales made by the principal.

A distinction is made in many states between an "exclusive right to sell" and an "exclusive agency." In these states an agent having an exclusive right to sell is entitled to a commission on all sales made within his territory regardless of whether the sale was made by the principal or by someone else. An agent having an exclusive agency, on the other hand, is not entitled to a commission on sales made by his principal. The principal, therefore, could invade the territory of an agent having an exclusive agency and make sales without obligating himself to pay a commission to his agent. But the rule is not broad enough to deny a commission to the agent who has spent time and money in procuring the sale. An agent, therefore, who solicits and induces a sale is generally entitled to a commission even though the sale is finally consummated by the principal. A few states do not observe the distinction. These states generally permit an agent to recover a commission on all sales made within his territory regardless of who made the sale and regardless of whether the agent solicited the sale. This is the same as an "exclusive right to sell" in those states which observe the distinction. The agent could protect himself by insisting upon an express provision in his contract of employment which would entitle him to a commission on all sales made by anyone within his territory.

(3) *Compensation of Brokers* Brokers may be authorized to effect contracts, or they may be authorized to secure customers for their principals with the resulting contracts being made between the principal and the customer. The broker, as a general rule, is entitled to his commission upon the completion of whichever type of service he has undertaken to perform. The real estate broker's commission has been the subject of much of the litigation pertaining to compensation of brokers. A real estate broker employed to secure a purchaser is, in accordance with the general rule, entitled to his commission when he has produced a purchaser ready, able, and willing to perform upon the terms fixed, leaving to the seller the actual closing of the sale; a broker employed to effect the sale is not entitled to his commission until he has actually effected the sale or secured from the prospective purchaser a binding contract of purchase. This second type of employment contract is subject to one important qualification: where the broker in good faith and in reliance upon the contract secures a purchaser ready, able, and willing to purchase the property and the seller defeats his transaction, not for any fault of the broker or purchaser, but solely because the seller will not or cannot complete the transaction, then and in such case the broker is entitled to his commission. [*Buhrmester v. Independent Plumbing & Heating Supply Co.,* p. 474.]

Duty to Reimburse and Indemnify the Agent. Two well-recognized rights which the agent possesses against the principal are reimbursement and indemnity. Reimbursement as here used refers to repayment of money expended or expenses incurred by the agent for the benefit of the principal upon the express or implied request of the latter. Indemnity refers to any loss or liability which the agent may sustain as the result of performing, without knowledge that it was illegal or wrong, an act directed by the principal. The agent, as a consequence of these two rights, is entitled to recover for any expenses, losses, or liabilities which he incurs in behalf of the principal while acting within the scope of his authority, provided the detriment was caused by reason of the agency and cannot be attributed to the agent's own fault. The agent could not recover from his principal, however, if while driving his principal's car on the principal's business he should negligently run into and damage a third person's car. The agent may be compelled to pay for the damage, but he would not be entitled to indemnity because the loss was due to his own wrongdoing. The agent is entitled to be indemnified, however, if the act is not manifestly illegal and he does not know that it is wrongful.

TERMINATION OF THE RELATION

The legal consequences which flow from the termination of the relation of principal and agent are particularly important because third persons are so often involved. Attention is therefore directed to termination (1) by act of the parties, (2) by operation of law, (3) by agency coupled with an interest, and (4) by notice of termination.

Act of the Parties The principal and agent, of course, may put an end to the relation by mutual consent at any time. The relation, however, may terminate by force of the original agreement. If the contract calls for the accomplishment of a particular object, the relation terminates when the object has been accomplished. The agency authorizing a real estate broker to sell a particular piece of property, for instance, would terminate when the sale is consummated. If the contract is for a definite period of time, as a month or a year, the relation terminates upon the expiration of the time specified. If the agent continues in the employment of the principal after the expiration of the original term, a renewal of the employment for another equivalent term will—in the absence of anything to indicate a different intention—be presumed. If it is an agency at will, it may be terminated at any time by either party. The contract of employment is known as "an agency at will" when it contains no provision for its duration nor anything to indicate that it is to continue for a certain period of time.

(1) *Revocation or Renunciation* The principal has the power to revoke the agency, and the agent has the power to renounce the agency. This is true even though the contract is for a definite duration. To do so in violation of the terms of the contract, however, would be a breach of contract. The distinction between the power and the right to terminate the agency, therefore, should be kept in mind. The principal, although he has the power to do so, could not wrongfully discharge the agent without subjecting himself to liability to the agent. The measure of damages is controlled by the general rules governing an action for damages for breach of contract. The agent, therefore, is ordinarily permitted to recover compensation for services rendered before his dismissal plus a sum for damages. The action for damages is ordinarily the only remedy for breach of the agency contract. Courts will not undertake to enforce the specific performance of a contract for personal services.

The principal who can show good cause has the right to discharge the agent without being subject to damages. A failure to follow instructions would ordinarily be good cause. The principal, however, could not terminate an agency at will without subjecting himself to liability to the agent if the agent has partly executed his authority. A principal, therefore, has no right to dismiss an agent who is working on a commission basis when the agent is actively negotiating for a sale and has a reasonable chance of effecting the sale and earning his commission. Such a dismissal would be an exercise of bad faith.

Operation of Law   It is a well-established rule that the agency relationship may be terminated by operation of law upon the happening of some event which makes the existence of the relationship impracticable or impossible. Among the more important of these events are death, insanity, and bankruptcy.

(1)   *Death of the Principal or Agent*   The general rule is that the death of the principal or of the agent operates to terminate the agency. This rule sometimes works a hardship on third persons who, in ignorance of the death of the principal, continue to do business with the agent. An agent authorized to collect rents may fail to account for rents collected after the death of the principal. The tenant, nevertheless, could be held liable to the estate of the principal for the amount so paid to the agent. A few states have enacted statutes to the effect that the authority continues until the third person has notice of the death of the principal. The general rule prevails, however, in the vast majority of states.

(2)   *Insanity of the Principal or Agent*   The general rule is that insanity of the principal or of the agent terminates the agency. Termination by insanity, however, differs from termination by death in at least one important particular. Third persons who deal with an agent in good faith, unaware of the insanity of the principal, are generally protected. The third person, however, could not claim to be unaware of the insanity when the principal has been judicially declared insane.

(3)   *Bankruptcy of the Principal or Agent*   An adjudication in bankruptcy of either party normally terminates the agency if it affects the subject matter of the agency. The assets of a bankrupt are placed in the hands of a referee in bankruptcy, and the owner ceases to have any control over the property. An agent, therefore, who had previously been authorized to enter into contracts with third persons obviously would no longer have any authority to do so. The bankruptcy of the agent may appear to have no effect upon the subject matter of the agency. It is recognized, however, that bankruptcy of an agent terminates his authority to receive money and to perform acts of a like nature.

Agency Coupled with an Interest   The general rule tells us that an agency coupled with an interest is not revocable by the principal before the expiration of the interest. But, the general rule continues, the interest must be in the subject matter of the agency in order to render the agency irrevocable. Precisely what shall be deemed an "interest in the subject matter" is not easy to define. The idea involved may be clarified by distinguishing an agency coupled with an interest from an agency given as security.

The agent makes a loan to the principal. The principal thereupon delivers to the agent a mortgage containing a clause authorizing the agent, in case of default, to sell the mortgaged property. The principal, in these circumstances, gives to the agent an immediate legal or equitable interest in the subject matter of the agency. This cannot be taken away. The principal cannot terminate the agency during his lifetime, nor will the agency be terminated by the principal's death. This is a true agency coupled with an interest.

The agent makes a loan to the principal. The principal thereupon authorizes the agent, in case of default, to sell certain property belonging to the principal and apply the proceeds toward the debt. The principal, in these circumstances, gives the agent an interest in the proceeds of the property when the property is sold. The principal cannot terminate the agency during his lifetime; the agency will be terminated, however, by the principal's death. This is an agency given as security.

It may be helpful to mention the reason for the rule. The agent in a true agency coupled with an interest may proceed against the property in his own name. But an agent in an agency given as security would have to exercise the authority in the name of the principal; the principal being dead, this could not be done.

A few modern cases make no distinction between "interest" and "security." These cases treat both of these agencies as essentially similar and hold them both irrevocable by any means until they have served the purpose for which they were created. These modern cases may represent a tendency among the courts. They do not, however, represent the weight of authority.

Notice of Termination Notice of the termination of the agency relationship generally need not be given third persons where the termination results from operation of law. The rule is different where the agency is terminated by act of the parties. A prudent principal, therefore, will exercise caution and communicate notice to all persons who will be affected by the termination. This includes (1) those persons who have previously dealt with the agent in reliance upon his former authority; (2) those who, in common with the public at large—although they never dealt with the agent prior to the revocation of the agency—are justified in believing the agency continues to exist; and (3) the agent himself. It follows that notice ordinarily need not be given to third persons when the authority of a special agent is revoked, but notice should be given when the authority given the agent is general, that is, apparently continuing. The importance of this assertion becomes apparent when it is realized that acts of a former general agent will, revocation notwithstanding, continue to bind the former principal to third persons unless proper notice is given.

Constructive notice, or notice in some newspaper of general circulation in the place in which the business is carried on, is sufficient to persons who have never dealt with the agent. The principal is required, however, to give actual notice to all persons who have had dealings with the agent. Actual notice does not have to be in any particular form so long as the necessary knowledge is conveyed to those persons entitled to be notified. It may be oral or written. But to be sure of avoiding litigation and possible liability, the principal should see to it that all persons who have previously dealt with the agent, as well as the agent himself, actually receive written notice of the revocation of the agency. [*Baum v. Rice-Stix Dry Goods Co.*, p. 475.]

CASES

A. Hollander & Son v. Imperial Fur Blending Corp., 66 A.2d 319 (N.J. 1949). Suit by A. Hollander & Son, Inc. (plaintiff below), appellant, against Imperial Fur Blending Corporation, Philip A. Singer, Richard Villani, and Robert Caruba (defendants below), respondents. The Hollander corporation, operating many plants, was engaged in the business of processing, dyeing, and blending raw furs and skins. The respondent Philip A. Singer was employed as a dresser and dyer of furs and as manager of the Long Branch plant. The employment contract was dated February 10, 1940, for a term ending December 31, 1944. Singer covenanted, in paragraph 2, that he would faithfully perform his duties and would not divulge to any person any of the trade secrets or processes and not use them for profit to himself or another. The Hollander corporation was to be the sole owner of all discoveries by Singer of any shades of color, new formulas, and processes used in the dressing and dyeing of fur skins. Such discoveries were to be turned over to the Hollander corporation and not otherwise disclosed by Singer. He further covenanted, in paragraph 3, to serve the Hollander corporation exclusively and not to engage directly or indirectly in any other business during the term of his employment. In December, 1942, Singer organized a competing company, the Imperial Fur Blending Corporation. Stock in the corporation was distributed as follows: 25 percent to Sol Hordoff, 25 percent to Richard Villani, and 50 percent to Robert Caruba. Singer retained control over the Hordoff stock through an option to purchase. Officers of the Hollander corporation became suspicious of Singer's relation with the newly formed corporation and suspended him under the terms of the contract. Charles Russell was placed in charge of the plant. It was then learned that Singer had developed a new shade of dyed fur which he did not disclose to the Hollander corporation but which he diverted to the Imperial corporation. Russell asked Singer for the formula books which he had removed from the plant, but they were never returned. This action was brought for injunctive relief and for an accounting of the profits made by respondents.

 Wachenfeld, Justice: The covenants in Paragraph 2 and 3 in the employment contract to perform faithfully the assigned duties, not to divulge trade secrets or processes or use them for personal profit, to turn over to the employer all new discoveries made by Singer and not to engage in other businesses during the term of employment, are clearly reasonable demands which the employer may exact from his employee. The validity of these covenants cannot be and is not disputed but it is claimed breaches thereof have not been established. The record fully supports the conclusion that each restriction has been violated by Singer and through participation in the conspiratorial plan, by each of the other respondents.

. . . Although previous to the association with Hollander Singer admittedly was highly skilled, during the employment he was placed in a special position to learn the various secret formulas and processing methods of Hollander. Through possession of the formula books and supervision of the dye house, he became intimately acquainted with and fully cognizant of the very core of Hollander's successful operations. This information was of substantial value and of such vital importance as to warrant the company in taking the greatest precautions in attempting to fashion a cloak of ample protection. In addition, Singer's discovery of a new dye formula, which under the employment agreement became the property of Hollander, was clearly in the category of a business secret. It was that formula which was extensively used by Imperial in competing with Hollander. . . .

The validity of the covenants and the breaches being established, it necessarily follows that Imperial Corporation, Caruba and Villani, by participation in the undercover activities, were properly joined in these proceedings. The protection afforded an employer through the enforcement of the covenants not to compete nor to divulge trade methods or secrets extends against third persons who, knowing of the employee's obligation, may profit from his disclosure. This is true although the third party might have reached the same result independently by his own experiments or efforts. A stranger and its employees may be enjoined where, with knowledge of the employee's covenant and in violation thereof, the stranger applies to his own use the property of the complainant. [DECISION FOR APPELLANT]

Mason Produce Co. v. Harry C. Gilbert Co., 141 N.E. 613 (Ind. 1924). Action by Mason Produce Company, plaintiff, against Harry C. Gilbert Company, defendant. Plaintiff is a corporation in Colorado engaged in selling food products at wholesale. Defendant is a corporation in Indiana engaged in selling such food products as a broker. A company in Kentucky telegraphed defendant for an order of pinto beans. The defendant then telegraphed plaintiff for authority to accept the offer and received from plaintiff the authority to do so. The defendant thereafter wired the Lexington company to the effect that the carload of beans had been shipped. After receiving the telegram, the Lexington company telegraphed defendant: "Cancel offer Colorado Pinto. Bought elsewhere. Delayed too long." Defendant insisted it was too late to cancel the order, and the Lexington company answered saying, "You delayed too long," and suggested that the car be diverted to some other point. The defendant waited more than three weeks before communicating these facts to plaintiff. The carload of beans had already traveled to Lexington. The plaintiff, therefore, was compelled to incur expense for unloading, storage, insurance, and another broker's commission in order to sell the beans in Lexington. When they were sold the price obtained was much lower than the market price on the date they were shipped. Plaintiff sued for damages alleging that defendant was negligent in failing to give plaintiff notice that the order had been canceled.

Ewbank, Chief Justice: The evidence shows . . . that much of the loss resulting from the refusal of the purchaser to perform such contract resulted from its failure to do what the law required of it. A broker owes to his principal the duty to act with the utmost good faith in all their dealings with each other, and is under the legal obligation to disclose to a person by whom he is employed as broker all facts within his knowledge or which he may learn in the course of a transaction in behalf of such person that are or may be material to the matter in which he is employed, or which might influence the action of his principal in relation thereto. And, where the broker, at a time when its employer's property was still in his warehouse in Colorado, where it was of the full market value for which a sale had been negotiated, learned that the purchaser to whom it was to be shipped had repudiated his order and bought elsewhere, and denied liability on the order given to such broker, claiming that it was not accepted in time, and without communicating those facts to the employer permitted such employer, at an expense of more than $500, to ship the beans 1,000 miles away to a customer in a small city who had fully supplied his needs by purchasing from others, where they arrived more than three weeks later, when there was little demand for them, he is liable in damages for any resulting loss sustained by the employer. If the facts known to the broker had been communicated to the employer he might have sold the beans to others at the place where they were, or diverted the car, while in transit, to some other city where the demand for beans had not been met by purchases from others, or kept the beans in the warehouse, and thus have minimized if not wholly prevented the alleged loss. [DECISION FOR PLAINTIFF]

Washington v. Mechanics & Traders Ins. Co., 50 P.2d 621 (Okla. 1935). Action by Mechanics & Traders Insurance Company, plaintiff, against J. Wilson Washington, Virgil D. Carlile, and Joe E. Edmondson, defendants. Joe E. Edmondson was the local policy-writing agent of the plaintiff. The other two defendants were sureties on his bond. Edmondson delivered to Sallie Young a policy of insurance upon her property which the plaintiff instructed him to cancel. This he neglected to do. The insured property was destroyed by fire. Plaintiff was compelled to pay for the loss, and this action followed.

Per Curiam: The undisputed testimony in the record shows that the plaintiff instructed the said Edmondson on October 21, 1927, to cancel the policy issued to Sallie Young and said instruction was repeated on November 1, 1927, November 15, 1927, and November 29, 1927; yet, in view of these instructions, the agent, Edmondson, failed, neglected, or refused to cancel said policy. The further fact was undisputed that the house of the assured was destroyed by fire and that the husband of the assured, John Young, was in the agent's office the day before the fire, and that the cancellation of this policy was discussed and the agent, Edmondson, at that time did not cancel the policy when he had sufficient funds on hand to return the premiums, but instead of this he continued the policy in effect in direct conflict with his instructions and refused to talk the matter over with the general agent, Kline, of the insurance company when he came to his office the next week, and the property was destroyed the next night and the plaintiff company had to pay the loss.

Where an agent, whose powers extend to the cancellation of policies, is directed by the company to cancel a policy, and he neglects to do so within a reasonable time, and in the meantime there has been a loss, he is liable to the company for the amount which the latter is compelled to pay on such loss, unless he can show some valid reason for his failure to follow the company's direction. His delay or failure to cancel the policy will not be excused by the fact that he believed that the company was mistaken as to the safety or danger of the risk, or as to the wisdom of retaining it, or by the fact that he gave notice of the cancellation to the broker who negotiated the insurance and directed him to cancel it. 32 C.J. 1073, §151. . . .

The neglect and failure of the agent, Edmondson, to carry out the instructions of plaintiff company, to cancel the Sallie Young policy, for more than five weeks, was not the exercise of good faith and reasonable diligence, as to which reasonable men could differ, and the fact that the plaintiff company had the same authority to cancel the policy would not excuse or justify the agent, Edmondson, in failing or refusing to follow its instructions. [DECISION FOR PLAINTIFF]

Buhrmester v. Independent Plumbing & Heating Supply Co.,   151 S.W.2d 509 (Mo. 1941). Action by C. F. Buhrmester, plaintiff, against Independent Plumbing & Heating Supply Company, defendant. Plaintiff was the agent of defendant in Flat River, Missouri, and other nearby towns to sell heating, plumbing, and sprinkler supplies and systems. He claims that he earned commissions as an agent in the sale of certain supplies for which he has not been paid. Defendant claims the plaintiff did not earn the commissions. This action followed. The agreement pertaining to the commissions to be paid was stated in a letter from defendant to plaintiff dated April 10, 1936: "Wish to advise that any of the jobs that you secure, we will allow you 5 percent commission on the regular price of the material or unless you desire a certain amount added in for you."

At the trial the evidence showed that plaintiff contacted Mr. McGraw, secretary and treasurer of the Industrial Corporation of Flat River, in an effort to interest him in a heating system; that plaintiff left with him some of defendant's business cards with plaintiff's name thereon; that later plaintiff made an appointment with Mr. McGraw for defendant's manager in connection with the proposed sale; and that thereafter defendant signed a contract with the Industrial Corporation for a $6,740 heating system. The evidence further showed that plaintiff contacted the superintendent of the Dillard, Missouri, public schools in an effort to interest the school board in a heating system; that he also left with the superintendent some business cards; that he later wrote a letter to the superintendent with respect to the proposed sale; and that thereafter the superintendent wrote plaintiff that the contract for the heating plant had been given to the defendant.

McCullen, Judge: With respect to the heating plant sold by defendant to the Industrial Corporation of Flat River, defendant concedes that the evidence is conflicting as to whether or not it received its first information of that job from plaintiff, but it contends nevertheless that it secured the Flat River job without any aid or assistance from plaintiff. It is argued by defendant that plaintiff's only activity in connection with the Dillard job was to write a letter or two to the superintendent of schools at Dillard, Missouri; that plaintiff's only activity with respect to the Flat River job was to call on W. A. McGraw, secretary of the Industrial Corporation of Flat River; and that plaintiff did not see the members of the board of the Flat River Industrial Corporation; that plaintiff wholly failed to adduce any testimony showing that he was the procuring cause of the sale in either the Flat River or the Dillard job.

We are unable to agree with defendant's contentions. There is nothing in the record to indicate that there was a revocation by defendant of plaintiff's agency prior to the time the two contracts for the supplies in question were made. The contract of agency was broad, general, and sweeping. By its terms defendant agreed to allow plaintiff five percent commission on the regular price of material on "any of the jobs that you secure." There is nothing in the contract requiring plaintiff to do any particular thing, or to go any particular place, or to see any particular parties with respect to any particular job. . . .

The real test in the case is whether or not plaintiff was the "procuring cause" of the sales in question, and under the rule heretofore mentioned, we must take as true plaintiff's evidence showing his various activities in his effort to procure for defendant the orders for the sales in question. If defendant wished to limit plaintiff in his agency for procuring "jobs" so that he would be entitled to commissions only for sales concluded and completed by him alone, it should have made that kind of a contract with plaintiff. Having made a contract containing no such restrictions, it cannot now be heard to complain that plaintiff did not make a case for the jury because he did not do things which the contract did not require him to do. To make a case for the jury under the contract involved herein, plaintiff was required to adduce evidence to show that he was the "procuring cause" of the sales to be entitled to the commissions promised by defendant, and it was not necessary that the evidence should show that he was the sole cause thereof. [DECISION FOR PLAINTIFF]

Baum v. Rice-Stix Dry Goods Co.,   157 S.W.2d 767 (Ark. 1942). Action by Rice-Stix Dry Goods Company (plaintiff below), appellee, against Robert Baum (defendant below), appellant. The appellant owned the New York Sales Company store, of which Jack Fine was manager. As manager of the store, Fine purchased merchandise from appellee on appellant's account. This merchandise was always paid for by the appellant. On June 10, 1939, appellant sold the store to Jack Fine, who continued thereafter as owner and manager. He also continued to purchase merchandise from appellee. This action was brought to recover for the merchandise so sold after June 10, 1939. Appellee's salesman testified that no notice was given him of the sale of the store to Fine and that there was no difference in the operation of the store before and after June 10. The appellant contends that he is not liable for any merchandise purchased for the New York Sales Company store after the sale of the store to Fine.

Holt, Justice: Appellee contends, on the other hand, that appellant having placed Jack Fine in charge of the New York Sales Company as manager, and having bought merchandise through Fine from appellee prior to the sale, supra, and having established a line of credit with appellee for this store, appellant remained liable for any merchandise purchased by Fine for the New York Sales Company store subsequent to said sale, or until appellant notified appellee to the contrary.

No rule of law is better settled than that one who recognizes another as his agent cannot escape liability for the agent's acts unless he notifies third persons of the termination of the relationship. Appellant admitted that Jack Fine was manager of the New York Sales Company store prior to June 10, 1939. . . . [*The court then quoted from Courtney v. G. A. Linaker.*]

In a note to 41 L.R.A. (n.s.) at page 664, it is said that it is settled that the acts of an agent, after his authority has been revoked, bind a principal as against third persons, who, in the absence of notice of the revocation of the agent's authority, rely upon its continued existence. It is also said that the cases are practically unanimous on this general rule, and most of them summarily state it as if it were an axiom. Many cases are cited in support of the rule. . . .

Under the authorities cited above, after a principal has appointed an agent in a particular business, parties dealing with him in that business have a right to rely upon the continuance of his authority until in some way informed of its revocation. [DECISION FOR APPELLEE]

PROBLEMS

1 Plaintiff, as agent of defendant and at the request of defendant, purchased and held title in his own name to certain land. Plaintiff, also at the request of defendant, sold the land and executed his warranty deed therefor. The purchaser thereafter sued plaintiff for breach of warranty. The plaintiff notified the defendant of the pending suit, but defendant declined to defend plaintiff. The plaintiff-agent now sues the defendant-principal for the amount of the judgment and expenses of litigation which he was obligated to pay as a result of the suit. Plaintiff claims that he paid the money for defendant. Was the defendant-principal under a duty to defend the plaintiff-agent when he was sued for breach of warranty?

2 Brown entered into a written contract of employment with The Broadcasting Company by the terms of which the company employed Brown as its general manager of a radio broadcasting station for a period of one year. The contract stated that the "duties to be performed by the general manager are those which usually appertain to such employment." During the first six months that the contract was in effect, the net income from the station decreased considerably. The company thereupon instructed Brown to appoint Mary Smith as assistant manager "immediately, and until further notice issue all orders through her and contract for no expenditures without her approval." Brown was also directed to post notice of her appointment and authority on the bulletin board forthwith. Brown refused to continue with his employment as long as the order was in effect. Was he justified in so doing?

3 Brown, who was employed by Jones as manager of the farm of Jones, was a stockholder in the Farmers' Co-operative Exchange. He made purchases of farm supplies to be used on the farm from this Exchange. By reason of these purchases, he received seven shares of stock as a bonus from the Exchange, for which he did not account to Jones. Both Brown and Jones claim ownership of these shares of stock. Does Brown or Jones have a better claim to the shares of stock?

4   Plaintiff, who was interested in purchasing a certain parcel of land, contacted defendant, a licensed real estate broker. Plaintiff stated that $36,000 was the maximum price he would pay for the land, which price included the real estate commission of 10 percent. Defendant, at that time, did not know who owned the land, and it was not listed with him for sale, but he told plaintiff: "I will find out how you can buy it." Defendant thereupon located the owner of the land, negotiated a sale for a price of $26,000, and took title to the land in his own name. About two weeks thereafter, plaintiff took title to the land from defendant and paid him a total price of $36,000. Plaintiff then learned that defendant had purchased the land for $26,000. The court held plaintiff was entitled to recover from the defendant the $10,000 profit so made by defendant. Discuss the rules of law upon which this decision was founded.

5   Mack appointed Reese his agent to sell a horse. Reese, thinking Mathews might be interested in purchasing the horse, went to the Mathews residence to discuss the possibility of selling the horse to him. Mathews, however, authorized Reese to act as agent for him in the purchase of the horse. This authorization was given before Reese had an opportunity to say anything to Mathews about the sale. Reese then arranged for the sale and purchase between Mack and Mathews, but he did not advise either that he was acting as agent for the other. Reese was paid a commission by both Mack and Mathews, who contend that they are entitled to a return of the commissions so paid to Reese. Do you agree with this contention?

6   Brown, the owner and manager of a department store, owed $2,000 to Jones, which he was unable to pay. He thereupon entered into a contract with Jones whereby Jones, as agent of Brown, was to collect certain accounts of the store and retain a 25 percent interest in any money which might be recovered. Brown died soon thereafter, and his son became manager of the store. The son notified Jones to discontinue with the collection of the accounts. Jones contended that the contract with Brown created an agency coupled with an interest and was irrevocable. Do you agree with this contention?

7   An attorney, who brought an action and recovered a judgment for Wangsness, deposited the money in his personal account in the First Bank. He then sent his personal check made payable to Wangsness for the amount so collected. The First Bank, however, became bankrupt before the check cleared. Wangsness thereupon brought an action against the attorney to recover the amount of the judgment which had been collected by the attorney. The attorney defended the action on the ground that he was, as a special agent, entitled to exercise great discretion in the manner of performing his work; that the loss resulted solely from the failure of the bank and not from the negligence of the attorney; and that he exercised reasonable care in discharging his duty. Do you think this is a good defense?

8   The First Bank made an application to The Surety Company for a surety bond to cover loss by embezzlement by any of its employees or agents. The application contained a statement that the First Bank had suffered no loss through embezzlement by any of its employees or agents within a period of ten years and that the First Bank knew of nothing which would indicate that any of its employees or agents were dishonest. The application was signed by Gordon as cashier. At the time the bond was signed, Gordon knew that some employee had been embezzling small amounts of money from the First Bank from time to time over a period of five years, but this fact was not known to any of the directors or officers of the First Bank. Gregory, one of the tellers, thereafter embezzled $200. The First Bank upon discovery of the embezzlement of $200 demanded indemnity from The Surety Company. Should the First Bank recover?

Part

8

BUSINESS
ORGANIZATIONS

37
PARTNERSHIP: NATURE, CREATION, PROPERTY

The different modes of carrying on business range from the individual proprietorship to the giant corporation. The individual proprietorship is the simplest form of business enterprise. The individual proprietor, to be sure, is within the purview of the licensing statutes and regulations of business. He is, however, otherwise unhampered in the conduct of his business. He furnishes all the capital, assumes all the risks, and takes all the profits. The partnership and the corporation are the most widely used forms of business organization having two or more owners. This part of the book, therefore, is devoted almost entirely to partnership and corporation law. The first four chapters discuss partnership, the next chapter discusses the limited partnership, and the remaining six chapters discuss corporations.

INTRODUCTION TO PARTNERSHIP
The law of partnership embraces rules which had their origin in the civil law, the law merchant, the common law, and equity. One should not be surprised to learn, therefore, that the development of the law of partnership, in England as well as in the United States, was accompanied with so much confusion and uncertainty that demands for statutory uniformity arose. The result in England was the Partnership Act of 1890. In the United States a draft of an act known as the Uniform

Partnership Act was completed by the Commissioners on Uniform State Laws in 1914. This Act, which will be referred to hereafter as the Partnership Act, has been adopted by over four-fifths of the states, the Virgin Islands, the District of Columbia, and Guam. Its provisions, which are mostly a codification of the rules prevailing at the time it was drafted, are also quite generally followed in the remaining states. The Partnership Act, therefore, is used as a basis for the material presented on this topic. The common-law rules which are still observed in some of the states will also be considered. This chapter will be devoted to (1) classifications of partnerships and partners, (2) the formalities required in the formation of a partnership, (3) the nature of a partnership, and (4) partnership property.

CLASSIFICATIONS

Kinds of Partnerships   Partnerships may be broadly classified as the general and limited partnership and the trading and nontrading partnership. The classification of partnerships as "general" and "limited" is used to distinguish the ordinary partnership from the statutory limited partnership. The present discussion pertains to the ordinary partnership. The limited partnership is reserved for Chapter 41. The classification of partnerships as "trading" and "nontrading" is used to distinguish the so-called commercial partnership from the professional partnership. The characteristic feature of a trading partnership, as originally defined, was that of buying and selling. The courts have, however, expanded the category of trading partnerships to include building and plumbing contractors, manufacturers, and similar commercial businesses. The professional partnerships, such as lawyers, accountants, and physicians, are the nontrading partnerships.

It may be well at this point to mention the joint adventure which is for all practical purposes a form of partnership. The generally accepted distinction between the two forms of organizations lies in the extent of the business undertaken. A partnership is ordinarily formed for the transaction of a general business of a particular kind while a joint adventure relates to a single transaction of a particular kind. The relation of the parties to a joint adventure and the nature of the organization, however, are so similar that it is commonly held that the rights, duties, and liabilities of the associates are to be tested by rules which are generally substantially the same as those which govern partnerships. A common purpose for which a joint adventure is created is to buy specific real estate with the expectation of reselling it at a profit. [*Rehnberg v. Minnesota Homes,* p. 489.]

Kinds of Partners   Partners are classified as "general" and "limited" partners in connection with the statutory limited partnership. They are referred to variously in the ordinary partnership. The terms "ostensible," "dormant," "retiring," "incoming," "surviving," and "continuing" partners frequently appear in legal writings. Ostensible partners are not actually partners but are persons who appear to the public as such. They are subject to liability by the doctrine of estoppel. Dormant partners are those who are not known to the public as such and who take no active part in the management of the business. They are nonetheless partners and are subject to liability for all partnership obligations. The remaining terms are self-explanatory. The duties and liabilities of these various kinds of partners will be explained in the appropriate places throughout the discussion that follows. They are merely grouped here for convenience.

FORMALITIES OF FORMATION

An agreement, express or implied, is essential to the formation of every partnership. But it is not essential that any particular formalities be complied with. The vast majority of agreements to form a partnership, furthermore, are equally valid whether oral or written.

The Oral Agreement Let it be assumed that Brown and Smith agree orally to purchase "Bill's Garage"; that they agree on the share of capital to be contributed by each, on their respective duties, on a division of the profits, and that they enter upon the performance of their agreement. They are partners. It should be clearly understood, however, that this method of forming a partnership is very unwise. There is, for instance, the problem presented by the Statute of Frauds. The two clauses that merit mention pertain to contracts that cannot be performed within the space of one year and contracts to transfer an interest in land.

(1) *The Year Clause* The courts are not entirely agreed as to whether or not an agreement to form a partnership which contemplates the continuance of the partnership for a definite time beyond a period of one year is within the Statute of Frauds. The majority of the courts take the view that such a contract must be in writing to be enforceable. A few courts have reached a different result on the ground that such a contract is subject to the implied condition that the death of one of the partners terminates it. The courts are fairly well agreed on this proposition: The parties have formed a partnership at will if, in pursuance of an oral agreement, the partnership business is carried on. This means the partnership will continue for no fixed period of time.

(2) *An Interest in Land* It will be remembered that any agreement to transfer an interest in land must be in writing to be enforceable. Must an agreement to form a partnership for the purpose of dealing in real estate be in writing? Suppose Brown has the opportunity to purchase a tract of land which could be subdivided into lots and resold at a profit, but he needs working capital. He therefore enters into an oral agreement with Smith by the terms of which Smith agrees to invest a certain amount of money for a share of the profits. The majority of the courts hold that the Statute of Frauds does not require such an agreement to be in writing. A few courts have held otherwise. At any rate, oral evidence may be used to show that the land constitutes a part of the partnership assets if the partnership business, in pursuance of the oral agreement, is actually carried on.

The Written Agreement A properly drafted partnership agreement will contain numerous carefully thought-out provisions which will save the partners many pitfalls. It would not be safe to attempt to enumerate all these provisions. Those which are common to most partnership agreements, however, embrace the date of the agreement, the names and addresses of the partners, the nature of the business, the name of the partnership, the duration of the partnership, the place where the business is to be carried on, the amount of the capital to be contributed by each partner, the respective duties of the partners, a method for settling disputes, the amount of money each partner may withdraw from the partnership funds, and the manner in which the profits are to be divided. It is to be realized, however, that the provisions will vary with the nature of the business. There may also be statutory requirements of the particular state that must be satisfied. Two such requirements common to most states pertain to the partnership name and fictitious names.

(1) *Partnership Name* It is not essential to the existence of a partnership that a firm name be adopted. Such a practice, however, is customary as a matter of convenience in the transaction of business. The name selected is frequently a combination of the surnames of the partners. It is sometimes a fictitious name. In the absence of statutory regulation, the partners may adopt any name they choose to use. The various state legislatures, however, have enacted a variety of statutes regulating the use of a partnership name. A common illustration is a statute prohibiting the use of terminology that would indicate that the organization was a corporation. The use of the words "and Company" therefore is sometimes prohibited unless it is followed by the words "not incorporated" or similar words. It is sometimes provided that if words such as "and Company" or "and Co." are used, such words must represent an actual partner or partners. A partnership, of course, cannot adopt a name so nearly like a name already in use as to mislead the public.

(2) *Fictitious Name Statutes* Most of the states today have "fictitious name statutes" which prohibit the use of any fictitious name unless a certificate stating the name under which the business is to be conducted, as well as the true names and residences of the members of the partnership, is published in a local newspaper and filed with designated public officials. The rights of a nonregistered partnership to enforce contracts made by it have been the source of much litigation. The earlier view that such contracts are invalid and unenforceable has generally disappeared. The prevailing view today is that contracts entered into by noncomplying individuals or partnerships are not for that reason invalid and are enforceable by such parties. This is certainly the prevailing view where no harm or injury has resulted to the other party because of noncompliance with the statute. It should be pointed out, however, that noncompliance with the statute is a misdemeanor in some states; the liability imposed in other states is in the way of a fine.

NATURE OF A PARTNERSHIP
Coming now to that type of partnership which businessmen create without any certain predetermined arrangement, one may be surprised to learn—but it

certainly is true—that businessmen quite commonly purport to form a partnership when their arrangement is something very different, or, as more frequently happens, they enter into the relationship without realizing it. They then take a serious view of the position in which they find themselves. How then is one to determine beforehand the kind of an arrangement he is entering into? The answer to the question is found in an analysis of the essential elements of a partnership. Section 6 of the Partnership Act defines a partnership as (1) an association, (2) of two or more persons, (3) to carry on a business, (4) as co-owners, (5) for profit.

An Association   An association, as the word is understood in the law of partnership, implies a voluntary act. Persons cannot, therefore, be forced into becoming partners without their consent. This rule eliminates the possibility of persons having a partnership thrust upon them when they become co-owners of property by gift, devise, or descent. It also eliminates the possibility of a stranger's being thrust upon the members of the partnership. No person can become a member of a partnership association without the consent of all the other associates.

Two or More Persons   The usual partnership is composed of individual human beings, but it is well recognized that the membership may be composed of a combination of individuals, a corporation, another partnership, or other associations. The test is the capacity to contract, and the rules of contract law pertaining to persons with limited contractual capacity are, as a general rule, applicable to partnership agreements. A few rules are peculiar to partnerships.

(1) *Infants*   It is well settled that an infant may become a member of a partnership with all the rights and powers of a partner. An infant's contract of partnership, however, is voidable. The infant partner, therefore, has the right to disaffirm the contract. This means he may withdraw from the partnership without being answerable in damages for breach of contract. The courts are divided, however, as to whether or not the infant may recover his capital investment when there are claims of copartners or of unpaid creditors. Some courts hold that the infant will have to bear his proportionate share of the losses up to, but not in excess of, the amount of his capital investment by reason of losses incurred in the partnership business or by reason of unpaid claims of creditors. Other courts go the full way in protecting the infant and hold that he may recover his capital investment without deduction for losses. The general rule permits an infant to disaffirm his individual liability on partnership contracts.

(2) *Insane Persons*   Whether an insane person can enter into a partnership relation depends upon his capacity to enter into contracts generally. It should be pointed out, however, that insanity is a ground for dissolution of the partnership. This does not mean that insanity alone dissolves the partnership. It does mean that the court, on petition of any partner, will decree a dissolution of the partnership. In these circumstances, the rules pertaining to dissolution generally are applicable. The above presupposes that those who dealt with the insane partner did so in ignorance of the insanity.

(3) *Corporations* The Partnership Act says nothing to prevent a corporation from becoming a partner. Section 2 of the Partnership Act, on the other hand, defines the word "person" as individuals, partnerships, corporations, and other associations. But the general rule provides that, in the absence of express authority conferred by its charter or an enabling statute, a corporation lacks the capacity to become a partner. But the general rule loses much of its significance through the fact that many corporate charters do confer such powers.

Carrying On a Business This phrase is the most difficult one of all the elements to define. But it is quite clear that the nature of the business is not controlling. Section 2 of the Partnership Act expressly states that the word "business" includes every trade, occupation, or profession. The meaning of the phrase is found in the extent of the undertaking. An agreement to find a lost dog and divide the reward offered would not fall within the meaning of the phrase. An agreement to perform a particular piece of work and immediately divide the profits would also indicate that the parties did not intend to carry on a business. It should not be assumed, however, from these illustrations that a single transaction might not constitute a partnership. The phrase is commonly understood to mean the carrying on of a general and continuing business of some particular kind and not merely the carrying on of some single transaction.

Co-owners The word "co-owners" means that the members of the association must be joint owners of the business. Co-ownership in either real or personal property does not of itself prove anything. The Partnership Act expressly declares that a joint tenancy, tenancy in common, tenancy by the entireties, joint property, common property, or part ownership does not of itself establish a partnership. This is true even though such co-owners share in the profits made incident to the joint ownership. This is for the reason that the profits are derived from property ownership rather than from the operation of a business. The word "co-owners" means that the members of the association must be co-owners of the business.

Profits The purpose of the business must be for a profit, and the associates must share in the profits. It is quite clear, therefore, that purported articles of partnership for the purpose of carrying on a nonprofit association would not result in a partnership. The sharing of profits is not so clear. This is for the reason that a partnership does not result if a share of the profits is received for some purpose other than compensation of a partner as a partner. Section 6 of the Partnership Act, after declaring that the receipt by a person of a share in the profits of the business is prima-facie evidence that he is a partner in the business, proceeds to enumerate certain instances where such an inference shall not be drawn. These are in payment of (1) a debt, (2) wages to an employee or rent to a landlord, (3) an annuity to a widow or representative of a deceased partner, (4) interest on a loan, and (5) a consideration for the sale of the goodwill of a business or other property by installments or otherwise. The sharing of profits, therefore, does not of itself prove the existence of a partnership. But it is considered as such strong evidence that a partnership is presumed unless something to the contrary is shown. The courts, nevertheless, consider all the essential elements of a partnership in the light of the facts of the particular case before deciding whether or not a partnership exists. [*Rizzo v. Rizzo,* p. 490.]

PARTNERSHIP PROPERTY

The significance of the term "partnership property" is more pronounced in the process of the dissolution and winding up of a partnership than it is in the creation of a partnership. An insight to the meaning of the term, however, is essential to a clear understanding of the nature of the partnership. Attention is therefore directed to (1) a definition of partnership property, (2) partnership capital, (3) goodwill, and (4) title to partnership property.

Partnership Property Defined   Section 8 of the Partnership Act says that all property originally brought into the partnership stock or subsequently acquired by purchase or otherwise on account of the partnership is partnership property, and, unless a contrary intention appears, property acquired with partnership funds is partnership property. It is thus clear that the term "partnership property" is broad enough to embrace everything that the partnership owns, including partnership capital, partnership name, and the goodwill of the partnership.

Partnership Capital   A partnership usually commences business with contributions derived from the partners. Such contributions are commonly in the form of money, but they may consist of anything which the partners agree to consider as capital. It is not unusual to find contributions which, although stated in terms of money, consist of real estate, the use of real estate, or any kind of tangible or intangible personal property. The capital of the partnership, more concisely stated, is a monetary figure representing the aggregate of the sums contributed by the members as permanent investments. No partner can of himself increase or diminish his proportion. The members as a whole must agree. The partnership property, as the term is used in its broadest sense, fluctuates according to the fortunes or misfortunes of the business. But the agreed capital remains fixed and represents the amount the partners are entitled to have returned to them upon dissolution.

It is sometimes thought that loans which the individual members make to the partnership constitute partnership capital, but this is not true. Nor are undivided profits which individual members sometimes permit to accumulate in the business a part of the capital. Loans and accumulated undivided profits are individual property. Even more serious are misunderstandings with respect to the use of property.

Property originally dedicated to use in the operation of a partnership may be partnership capital or it may remain individual property. The distinction is exceedingly important if the partnership, as well as the partners, becomes insolvent. The creditors of the partnership have first claim on partnership property, and the creditors of the individual partners have first claim on individual property. The distinction is equally important when an attempt is made to adjust the accounts between the partners. Whether or not property is dedicated to the partnership or is to remain individual property is governed by the agreement of the partners. The partnership agreement, therefore, should clearly define the intent of the partners. But such is not always the case. The courts then have the burden of trying to determine the intention of the partners. [*Cyrus v. Cyrus*, p. 491.]

Goodwill Notwithstanding the importance of "goodwill" in the business world, the word has not yet received a definition which is acceptable to all. The word is quite generally said to mean the "expectation of continued public patronage." But whatever goodwill may be today, it is well settled that goodwill is an intangible element of value which may be sold and transferred. It is likewise well settled that it requires the unanimous consent of all the partners to dispose of the goodwill. The courts are not agreed, however, as to the respective rights of the seller and the purchaser of goodwill of a business with respect to the use of the old name of the firm. In some states, the purchaser of goodwill acquires the right to use the firm name, and even trade-marks and trade names used in the conduct of the business. In other states, the purchaser does not acquire the right to use the old firm name, and its use may be enjoined by showing a possible injury to the seller by the use of such name. It is generally agreed that the purchaser gets the right to advertise to the public that he is the successor to the business of his seller and that he is taking on that business.

   Another problem with respect to goodwill pertains to the extent to which the seller may compete with the old firm. In a few states, the sale of a going business carries with it an implied promise not to compete. The majority of the courts, however, permit the seller to compete but do not permit him to advertise that he is carrying on the old business, or to solicit directly the continued patronage of old customers, or to use the old firm name, or even his own name, if its use is for the purpose of leading the public into believing that he is continuing the old business.

   Goodwill is unquestionably partnership property. The representative of a deceased partner, therefore, is entitled to have an accounting of the value of goodwill. [*Richter v. Richter*, p. 493.]

Title to Partnership Property It is well settled that the title to all kinds of personal property may be acquired and disposed of in the partnership name by any partner for the purpose of carrying on the partnership business. The common law, however, required that the title to real property be held by a person, either natural or artificial. This common-law rule means that all of the members of the partnership are required to join in the conveyance of real property. Sections 8 and 10 of the Partnership Act, however, provide that any estate in real property may be acquired in the partnership name, that any title so acquired can be conveyed only in the partnership name, and that any partner may convey title to such property by a conveyance executed in the partnership name. It is thus clear that real property may be acquired and disposed of in the firm name in those states which have adopted the Partnership Act or have a similar enabling statute. A conveyance to one or more members of the partnership is generally held to vest the legal title in those persons whose names appear in conveyance, either as tenants in common or as joint tenants, depending upon the interpretation of the terms of the conveyance. A court of equity, however, will regard and protect the realty as partnership property and will direct the holder of the legal title to make such disposition of the realty as may be necessary to protect the equitable rights of the partnership creditors or of the partners. [*McCormick v. McCormick*, p. 494.]

The restrictions which the common law places on the partnership with respect to holding title to real property have never been applied to personal property. The title to all kinds of personal property, therefore, may be acquired and disposed of in the partnership name in all states.

CASES

Rehnberg v. Minnesota Homes, 52 N.W.2d 454 (Minn. 1952). Action by Arthur E. Rehnberg, plaintiff, against Minnesota Homes, Inc., and Gilbert C. Hamm, defendants. The plaintiff alleged that he discovered a tract of land and conceived the idea of subdividing it and erecting homes thereon for sale to the public; that he interested the defendant, Gilbert C. Hamm, and other persons in the project; that as a result of his activities the defendant corporation was formed; that after the corporation was organized, it entered into a contract with plaintiff whereby it employed plaintiff to sell said houses for a fee of $150 per house plus 25 percent of the net profit to the corporation from the sale of said houses; that the first twenty-six homes were completed and sold, but that plaintiff has received no part of the money due him under the contract; and that the agreement established a joint adventure for the mutual benefit of the contracting parties, and that the legal title to the premises is therefore held by the corporation in trust for the benefit of the joint adventure, inclusive of himself. Plaintiff also alleged that it has become impossible for the corporation to make a profit. Plaintiff asks, therefore, that he be given judgment for the amount due him under the contract and that his agreement be declared to constitute a joint adventure. If the arrangement is a joint adventure, plaintiff's claim could be protected in the form of a specific lien against the properties.

Matson, Justice: We come to the basic issue of whether we have a joint adventure. Generally speaking, a joint adventure is created—assuming that a corporation has not been organized and the circumstances do not establish a technical partnership—where two or more persons combine their money, property, time, or skill in a particular business enterprise and agree to share jointly, or in proportion to their respective contributions, in the resulting profits and usually in the losses. In a qualified sense, a joint adventure is a limited partnership, not limited in a statutory sense as to liability but as to scope and duration.

Although a joint adventure is not, in a strict legal sense, a copartnership, the rules and principles applicable to a partnership relation, with few if any material exceptions, govern and control the rights, duties, and obligations of the parties. No definite rule has been formulated for identifying the joint adventure relationship in all cases. Each case depends on it own peculiar facts. It is recognized, however, that an enterprise does not constitute a joint adventure unless each of the following four elements are present, namely:

(a) Contribution—the parties must combine their money, property, time, or skill in some common undertaking, but the contribution of each need not be equal or of the same nature.

(b) Joint proprietorship and control—there must be a proprietary interest and right of mutual control over the subject matter of the property engaged therein.

(c) Sharing of profits but not necessarily of losses—there must be an express or implied agreement for the sharing of profits (aside from profits received in payment of wages as an employee) but not necessarily of the losses.

(d) Contract—there must be a contract, whether express or implied, showing that a joint adventure was in fact entered into.

The first element of contribution is here present, in that plaintiff contributed his time, knowledge, and skills to the undertaking in discovering and promoting the enterprise, as well as in the subsequent sale of the houses. The essential element of joint proprietorship and control is, however, lacking. There is no showing that plaintiff had any control over the manner in which the enterprise was carried on or that he even had any voice in the management of the corporation. In fact, the contract by its express terms identifies plaintiff's status as simply that of an employee.

Likewise, the third element of sharing in the profits in a manner consistent with a status of a joint adventure is absent. It is true, plaintiff was to share in the profits, but only for the specific purpose of compensating him as an employee. . . . Furthermore, the indispensable element of a contract for the formation of a joint adventure is also absent.

We have a contract, but it is one that expressly creates an employment relation and thereby negatives any intent to create a joint adventure. There is no merit in plaintiff's contention that the corporation by its organization thereby became a partner or a member of a joint enterprise. [DECISION FOR DEFENDANT]

Rizzo v. Rizzo, 120 N.E.2d 546 (Ill. 1954). Action by Miglore Rizzo, administratrix of the estate of Rocco Rizzo, Jr., deceased, plaintiff, against Michael, Joseph, and John Rizzo, defendants. From the evidence it appears that in 1910 Rocco Rizzo, Sr., operated a wastepaper business at 612 West Taylor Street, Chicago, Illinois; that Michael, the oldest son, went to work for his father in 1910, Joseph in 1913, Rocco, Jr., in 1916, and John in 1920; that Michael was the general manager, Joseph the receiving clerk, and John and Rocco, Jr., were truck drivers; that the name of the business was originally "Rocco Rizzo & Co.," later it was "Rocco

Rizzo Son & Co.," and still later "Rocco Rizzo Sons & Co."; and that Michael, Joseph, and John admitted on examination that they all worked in the business, shared equally in the profits, and went without pay if there were no profits.

In 1929 the father, who had retired from active participation in the business, deeded the business property to Michael. On June 27, 1931, Rocco Rizzo, Jr., died. The plaintiff thereafter brought this action against the three brothers as surviving partners of Rocco Rizzo Sons & Co., claiming that the estate of the decedent should be awarded a one-quarter share in the partnership as of the date of his death. The defendants claim that the business is a sole proprietorship with Michael as the sole proprietor. They contend that the business was turned over to Michael when his father retired, that Michael was regarded as the boss by persons dealing with the firm, and that the profits were merely the measure of compensation for the brothers.

Bristow, Justice: The fact that Michael, as the oldest son, had more authority in the management than the other brothers does not of itself preclude the existence of a partnership, particularly in view of the custom in such closely-knit immigrant families. In fact, Michael stated that the business was turned over to him because he was the oldest son. Furthermore, it is an accepted partnership practice that one partner may be charged with greater managerial responsibilities.

The fact that the brothers admitted that they all worked in the business, sharing equally in the profits and going without pay if there were none, tends to comply with the essential requirement for a partnership. . . .

Furthermore, the fact that the firm name, originally Rocco Rizzo & Co. had been changed to Rocco Rizzo Son & Co. when Michael entered the business, and was again changed to Rocco Rizzo Sons & Co., and was so listed in the telephone book and on the truck during the lifetime of Rocco, Jr., is further evidence of the existence of a partnership between the brothers as of 1931. . . .

In the instant case, Michael Rizzo was under a duty as a partner, and as the oldest brother on whom the other children relied, not to take advantage of his fiduciary position. The business property, originally at 612 West Taylor Street, was conveyed to him by his father in 1929. No consideration was paid for the deed, nor did the deed recite that it was given in consideration of love and affection; nor was there a disclosure to the partners or the grantor that the deed would give Michael alone ownership of the property to the exclusion of the other partners, for Michael merely gave the deed to his father to sign with his mark. Under those circumstances, even though the deed was absolute on its face, it is clear that the understanding of the parties, and from the nature of Michael Rizzo's fiduciary obligation, that this property should be deemed to be held for the benefit of the firm. [DECISION FOR PLAINTIFF]

Cyrus v. Cyrus, 64 N.W.2d 538 (Minn. 1954). Action by Edna Cyrus, administratrix of the estate of Cecil Cyrus, deceased, plaintiff, against Curtis Cyrus, defendant. The evidence discloses that Cecil and Edna Cyrus and their children were living on a farm in North Dakota; that they received letters from the defendant urging them to move to Minnesota and enter into a partnership for the purpose of building and operating a tourist camp and resort; that they, in response to such requests, moved to Minnesota and erected a cabin on a sixty-acre tract of land which defendant had purchased in his own name; that this cabin as well as all the other improvements were paid for out of earnings derived from the operations of the resort; that an additional forty-acre tract was acquired in the name of the defendant which was also paid for out of resort earnings; that out of the resort earnings Cecil was allowed the living expenses for his family; that he contributed his labor, and his wife did the washing and ironing and cleaning of the cabins; that Cecil's three children helped with the resort work; that defendant was regularly employed in Minneapolis; that the earnings were accounted for and defendant was given his one-half share every fall when he visited the resort; that this continued until Cecil died in December of 1944; that after Cecil's death, defendant sent two letters to the plaintiff offering to deed one-half of the resort to her, and in one of these letters he stated that "it's yours as much as mine and I'll make the deed over that way when I have the opportunity" and that defendant himself, or others renting from him, have operated the resort since the death of Cecil.

This action was brought for a division of the partnership assets. The trial court found that a partnership had been formed, that the value of the resort was estimated to be $10,000, and that Cecil's interest therein at the date of his death was of the value of $5,000. The defendant appealed.

Matson, Justice: The trial court was justified in finding that the forty-acre tract was partnership property. The evidence supports a finding that it was purchased with earnings from the resort, a fact which in the absence of other circumstances denotes that the property belonged to the partnership.

It is uncontradicted that the original sixty-acre tract was purchased by the defendant with his own money and that the title was taken in his own name. As already noted it was acquired prior to the creation of the partnership. If the sixty-acre tract constitutes partnership property, it must be on the theory that it was contributed to the partnership by the defendant. Whether real property acquired by a partner individually prior to the formation of a partnership belongs to or had been appropriated to the partnership is a question of intent. The fact that such realty is used for partnership purposes is not of itself, when standing alone, sufficient to establish an intent to contribute it to the partnership assets. In addition to the element of partnership use, we have, however, certain other evidentiary factors. Cabins, docks, and other improvements were built upon this land for the use of the partnership and were paid for out of partnership earnings. Improvements so made at partnership expense, although not of controlling significance, tend to show an intent that the land should be partnership property. As with the forty-acre tract, we have the salient fact that the evidence sustains a finding that the taxes were ultimately paid for out of partnership earnings. In the light of these factors, the court could reasonably attach considerable significance to the statements which defendant made to plaintiff by letter and otherwise after Cecil died. These statements clearly recognized plaintiff's legal right to one-half of the property, a right which could exist only if the parties believed the property belonged to the partnership. Under the circumstances we can only conclude that the evidence sustains the trial court's conclusion that the entire realty was partnership property. [DECISION FOR PLAINTIFF]

Richter v. Richter, 43 S.E.2d 635 (Ga. 1947). Suit by Mary Bell Richter, as administratrix of the estate of F. A. Richter, and others, plaintiffs, against W. H. Richter and others, defendants. The petition of the plaintiffs alleged substantially as follows: For a great number of years two brothers, F. A. Richter and W. H. Richter, carried on a business under the firm name of "Richter Bros.," the business being that of buying and selling at wholesale and retail, the processing of pecans, selling farm produce and products, fertilizer and seeds; that the name "Richter Bros." constituted an asset of the partnership; that F. A. Richter died in 1945 and the firm was dissolved by his death; that in May, 1946, W. H. Richter and others were granted a corporate charter in the name of "Richter Brothers Company, Inc."; that the defendants had advertised in a newspaper under the name "Richter Brothers Company, Inc.," to the effect that it had been in the active produce business for nearly seventy years; that there had been no division of all the partnership assets, including the trade name; and that the defendants should be restrained from using the name "Richter Brothers" as a part of the corporate name.

Almand, Judge: The firm name is a firm asset subject to sale as any other firm property. It is inseparable from the goodwill of the firm and in the absence of contract, will, or estoppel, the estate of the deceased partner is entitled to a distribution with other assets of the firm.

Where there has been no final sale or distribution of the partnership business, the surviving partner cannot organize a corporation which he virtually controls by stock ownership, and carry on a similar line of business to that of the partnership, at the same location as the partnership, and represent to the former customers of the partnership, and to the public generally, that the corporation is a continuation of the partnership business. . . .

It is true that in the absence of fraud, contract, or estoppel, every man has the right to use his own name in any legitimate way, either as the whole or part of the corporate name, and courts of equity will not interfere with such use where confusion only results from the similarity of the names. But if the name is used to deceive or mislead the public so as to palm off the goods of one on the representation, by the use of the name, as the goods of another *or to deprive another of his rights,* equity will interfere upon the showing of such unfair competition. . . .

The value of the property interest of the estate in the trade name is vitally affected in its use by the corporation when it represents that the corporation is but a continuation of the partnership business.

Counsel for the plaintiffs in their brief concede that the defendants in the use of the corporate name have the right to use the name of "Richter" and that they have no objection to the corporation's trade name as long as it does not contain the descriptive word "Brothers." We, therefore, hold that the petition states a cause of action for equitable relief against the defendants using the word "Brothers" as a part of the corporate name. [DECISION FOR PLAINTIFFS]

McCormick v. McCormick, 70 N.W.2d 706 (Mich. 1955). Suit by Clarence Louis McCormick, plaintiff, against Jesse William McCormick, defendant. The plaintiff and the defendant are brothers. In 1921 they purchased certain real estate in Allegan County, Michigan, each contributing approximately one-half the purchase price. Shortly thereafter they conveyed an undivided one-third interest in the property to their mother. The brothers then built a gas station on the property, which was destroyed by fire. The brothers and their mother were also engaged in operating a restaurant in South Haven, apparently as partners. The profits from this business and the proceeds of insurance collected on the loss of the gas station were used in erecting a small cottage and a restaurant known as the "Dixie Inn" on the land in Allegan County. The brothers, some time during the process of the construction, conveyed their remaining interest in the property to their mother. The mother then conveyed the property to the defendant and reserved a "life lease and full control for herself and Clarence Louis McCormick." The common use of the property was not changed in any way. Such situation continued after the death of the mother in 1940. But disagreements arose in later years. Finally, in 1950, defendant advanced the claim that he was the sole owner of the property. The plaintiff then brought this suit to obtain a determination as to his rights in the property.

Carr, Chief Justice: We are in accord with the finding of the trial judge that plaintiff, defendant, and the mother were copartners in conducting their business operations, including those involving the use of the land here in question. They worked together in the furtherance of their objectives, and shared the profits. The defendant in his testimony referred to the manner in which the property was used as a "cooperative living proposition." He stated further that the gas station was his idea, that his mother and brother were running the restaurant, and that "it all supposedly went in the family pot." He testified also that he felt free to take money out of the till. Apparently the actual situation was that each of the parties took from the businesses conducted such portion of the profits as he or she deemed proper, and without objection from the others. Under the testimony of plaintiff and defendant the conclusion is fully justified that the parties were carrying on lawful businesses together as co-owners for profit, and that they were sharing in the profits from each operation.

. . . The fact that the legal title to the property in question here first stood in the names of plaintiff and defendant, then in the names of the three partners, and subsequently by her to defendant, did not deprive it of its character as a partnership asset. The parties obviously so regarded it. The conveyance by Mrs. McCormick to defendant in 1934 clearly recognized, in the proviso above quoted, that both she and plaintiff had rights in the property. It is in evidence also that the mother stated to defendant at the time of such transaction, or shortly thereafter, that she knew that he and plaintiff would get along together all right. . . . Further discussion of the testimony would serve no useful purpose. The trial judge correctly held that the land in question here belonged in equity to the partnership. [DECISION FOR PLAINTIFF]

PROBLEMS

1 Fenwick employed Chesire as a reception clerk and cashier in his beauty shop. Chesire demanded higher wages. Fenwick agreed to the demand provided the income from the business warranted a raise. Fenwick and Chesire thereupon entered into a written agreement which provided that they associate themselves into a partnership under the name of United Beauty Shoppe. The agreement further provided that Chesire make no capital investment; that Fenwick have control and management of the business at a weekly salary of $50 and 80 percent of the profits; that Chesire act as reception clerk and cashier at a weekly salary of $15 and a bonus at the end of the year of 20 percent of the profits, if the business warranted it; that Fenwick alone should be liable for the partnership debts; and that each should have the right to inspect the partnership books. Does this agreement create a partnership?

2 Brown and Jones, an insolvent partnership, entered into an agreement with the creditors of the partnership by the terms of which it was agreed that the partnership business should be continued under the supervision of a managing committee. The creditors were given the privilege of designating the persons who were to be members of the committee, and the committee was to function until the claims of creditors were fully paid out of the profits of the partnership business. The partnership business, operating under this new arrangement, acquired a new set of creditors. Are the old creditors liable as partners to the new creditors?

3 Defendants, building contractors, were, and for a number of years had been, engaged in the business of developing various suburbs. They approached plaintiff with respect to joining their partnership. An agreement was thereupon reached by the terms of which plaintiff was to be a "junior partner" at a salary of $1,000 a month and 25 percent of the profits derived from the partnership. The agreement also provided that "plaintiff was to have no other financial interest in the firm and no authority to participate in the management of the firm." A dispute arose, and defendants refused to permit plaintiff to inspect the partnership books. Plaintiff contends he is entitled to do so, and in support of this contention quotes the Partnership Act which provides that "every partner shall at all times have access to and may inspect the partnership books." Decide.

4 Brown, a minor, and Smith, an adult, formed a partnership for the purpose of purchasing and operating a foundry. They purchased the foundry from plaintiff, and each contributed $5,000 toward the purchase price and gave plaintiff four notes for $2,500 for the balance. The foundry was not successful, and the partnership became insolvent. Plaintiff thereupon brought an action against the partnership and Brown and Smith individually to recover $10,000, the amount due on the unpaid notes. Discuss the rights and liabilities of Brown.

5 Philip Brown and Joseph Brown owned and operated a retail clothing business under the partnership name of "Brown Company." Joseph Brown sold his share in the partnership to Philip Brown, and the sale included the "goodwill of said business." Joseph Brown would like to operate a retail clothing business two blocks from the location of the former partnership under the name of "Brown's." Discuss the reasons why he should or should not be permitted to do so.

6 For several years prior to March 1, 1925, Robert and Franklin were engaged in the business of farming. On that date Franklin, who was the individual owner of the farm, entered into an agreement with Robert and Lisle, forming a partnership for the purpose of carrying on a greenhouse business. The agreement provided that Franklin would allow the use of his farm by the partnership; that each partner would devote his time, labor, and energy to carrying on the partnership business; and that each would share equally the profits and the losses. The partners then proceeded to construct four greenhouses on the farm. These greenhouses were constructed by the labor of the three partners and were paid for with partnership funds and partnership credit. Discuss whether or not the farm upon which these greenhouses were constructed should be treated as the individual property of Franklin or as partnership property.

38
PARTNERSHIP: RELATION TO THIRD PERSONS

The courts agree that the relation of partners to third persons is founded on the doctrine of mutual agency, but they differ in describing the representative capacity of a partner. One line of decisions regards each partner as an agent of his copartners when he is acting and as a principal of his copartners when they are acting. Each partner, therefore, is regarded as both a principal and an agent. Another line of decisions regards each partner as an agent of the partnership. Section 9 of the Partnership Act states that "every partner is an agent of the partnership for the purpose of its business." Whichever view one may choose, the problem pertaining to the relation of the partners to third persons remains, for all practical purposes, the same. It remains to determine (1) the extent to which a partner has the authority to bind the partnership, (2) the liabilities of the partnership—and incidentally of the partners individually—which result from an exercise of authority, and (3) the liabilities which result from ratification, estoppel, and admissions.

AUTHORITY OF PARTNERS

The rights, duties, and functions of partners embody those of agents. It is understandable, therefore, that a study of the law of partnership is, to a remarkable degree, a continuation of the study of the law of agency. It has been stated that the law of partnership is a branch of the law of agency. The liability of a partner or of the partnership for an act of a partner will be determined, therefore, by the law of agency. It should be kept in mind, however, that an act of an agent, in order to bind the principal, must be committed within the course and scope of the agent's authority. It is usually stated that an act of a partner, in order to bind another partner or the partnership, must be committed "within the scope of the partnership business."

A partner has authority to act as an agent only within the scope of the partnership business. An unauthorized act of a partner which is not within the scope of the partnership business is neither binding on the partnership nor another partner. A partner who commits an act which is not within the scope of the partnership business is personally liable. It should be understood, however, that an act of the partner which is beyond the scope of the partnership business may bind the partnership or another partner providing the acting partner is expressly or impliedly authorized to so act. This principle is stated in the Partnership Act as follows: An act of a partner which is not apparently for the carrying on of the business of the partnership in the usual way does not bind the partnership unless authorized by the other partners. An act of a partner for apparently carrying on in the usual way the business of the partnership, however, is binding on the partnership and the other partners, unless the acting agent is in fact not authorized and the third person with whom he deals has knowledge of such lack of authority. A clearer understanding of the authority of partners may be acquired by a brief review of the authority of agents. The authority of agents was discussed in detail in Chapter 33, "Creation and Authority."

Actual Authority   Actual authority is the authority which the principal delegates to the agent. It may be delegated expressly or impliedly. Express authority is directly and specifically delegated to the agent orally or in writing. The agent may, however, be impliedly authorized. Implied—or incidental authority—is actual authority which arises from the words or acts of the principal and from the facts and circumstances of the case. An agent will be impliedly authorized to do those things that are incidental, or reasonably necessary, in order to perform the express authority which has been delegated.

A custom of the business will frequently mean that an agent is clothed with implied authority. This is sometimes referred to as "customary authority," and means that the principal is deemed to have delegated authority to the agent to act in conformity with the general customs of business. The agent will not be impliedly authorized to perform acts which are not reasonably necessary, essential, usual, and proper for carrying out the express authority. An agent would not, therefore, be impliedly authorized to commit an illegal act. Attention is now directed to the implied authority (1) to borrow money and execute negotiable instruments, (2) to transfer partnership property, (3) to insure partnership property, (4) to settle controversies, and (5) of the majority-decision rule.

Authority to Borrow Money and Execute Negotiable Instruments   The courts, for the purpose of determining whether a partner has the implied authority to borrow money and execute negotiable instruments, make a distinction between trading and nontrading partnerships. The general rule says a partner in a trading partnership has such authority but a partner in a nontrading partnership does not have such authority. The rule, however, is not inflexibly fixed. The authority may be expressly conferred. A partner in a nontrading partnership, moreover, may bind the firm where it is shown that borrowing money and issuing negotiable instruments are within the usual course of the partnership business. A farming partnership, for example, is clearly not in the business of buying and selling. But it is frequently the custom of such partnerships to borrow money from time to time in making and gathering their crops. A third person, before parting with his money, would nevertheless be wise if he determined the authority of a partner in a nontrading firm to borrow the money. The authority to borrow, when it exists, carries with it the power to mortgage or pledge firm property to secure the payment of the debt. [*Gordon v. Aumiller,* p. 503.]

Implied Authority to Transfer Property The rules for transferring personal property differ in many respects from those for transferring real property. It is necessary, therefore, to treat the two sets of rules separately.

(1) *Personal Property* A partner, in a partnership whose business consists of buying and selling, has the implied authority to sell any part of the partnership personal property which is held for the purpose of sale. This authority carries with it the authority to execute whatever documents are necessary to transfer the title and to make the customary warranties with respect to the property. A partner does not have the implied authority to sell property, such as office furniture and other equipment used in the business. The transaction, according to the general rule, is voidable by the other partners. A prospective purchaser of such property, therefore, would be well advised to look for express authority before making such a purchase. This authority, like any implied authority, is limited to acts for the purpose of carrying on the partnership business in the usual way. [*Bole v. Lyle,* p. 505.]

(2) *Real Property* The implied authority of a partner to sell real property, like the authority to sell personal property, is limited to property acquired for resale. The conveyance of real property, however, poses two important questions which are not present in the transfer of personal property: How may the title be conveyed? What is the effect of an unauthorized conveyance?

If the record title is in the name of one or more of the partners, the deed should be signed by those partners in whose name the title stands. Suppose the title is in the name of Bill Smith and Duke Brown. The deed should be signed by both partners. If the record title is in the name of the partnership, as it probably will be in those states that have adopted the Partnership Act, any partner has the power to convey the title by executing a deed in the name of the partnership. Suppose the record title is in the name of "Smith and Brown." The deed may be signed "Smith and Brown, by Duke Brown." If the conveyance is made in the name of one other than the title holder, the conveyance passes the equitable interest. This means that if the deed in either illustration was executed in the name of Duke Brown only, the grantee would be entitled to obtain a deed from Bill Smith.

An unauthorized transfer sometimes results in a hardship to the other partners by virtue of the operation of the recording statutes. To further pursue the above firm of Smith and Brown: If the record title is in the name of Duke Brown only, an unauthorized conveyance by Duke Brown passes good title. The same would be true if the record title was in the name of the firm and the deed was signed "Smith and Brown, by Duke Brown." The harshness of the rule is considerably lessened by the further rule which gives the other partners the right to have the conveyance set aside if the purchaser knew or should have known that the title was held for the partnership. The decisions generally say, in this connection, that a prospective purchaser is not justified in assuming that a partner is authorized to sell the site on which the partnership activities are conducted, nor is he justified in assuming that a partner was authorized to sell realty unless the partnership was in the business of buying and selling real property.

The real hardship that results from the rule, however, is founded on one further rule: A conveyance by the first purchaser to a second purchaser for value without knowledge passes good title. It is to be realized, furthermore, that a second purchaser probably would not know of the circumstances surrounding the first sale. There is certainly nothing in the record title to put him on notice.

Authority to Insure A partner as co-owner has an insurable interest in the partnership property. He may, therefore, take fire and other indemnity insurance on the specific partnership property, the proceeds of which are payable to him personally in case of loss. The firm may also carry its own indemnity insurance. A life insurance program poses several questions. It is generally conceded that a partner has an insurable interest in the life of his copartners because of the benefits which may be expected to flow from the continuance of the partnership relation. Suppose partner Brown pays the premiums on his life insurance with partner Smith as the beneficiary, and that partner Smith reciprocates. Would the proceeds of such a policy belong to the surviving partner personally, or would they be part of the partnership property? If the partners name their respective estates as the beneficiary but pay the premiums with partnership funds, a dispute between the surviving partners and the estate of the deceased member would probably be resolved in favor of the surviving partner. This is for the reason that property purchased with partnership funds is presumed to be partnership property. Assuming the proceeds are partnership property, are they to be used in purchasing the share of the deceased partner? This could have been the purpose because businessmen frequently put most of their resources in their business. Such a plan, therefore, would aid the surviving partner should he find himself financially unable to purchase the share of the deceased partner. Would the proceeds increase the share of the deceased partner? There are no definite rules for determining the answers to these questions. This is just another instance, therefore, which should be taken care of in the partnership agreement.

Authority to Settle Controversies   A partner has the implied authority to compromise claims for or against the partnership. Such authority, however, cannot be delegated to third persons. One partner, therefore, cannot bind his copartners by the submission of a firm controversy to arbitration.

A partner has the implied authority to institute legal proceedings in behalf of the partnership and to defend actions brought against the partnership. He does not have the implied authority to confess a judgment. The reason for the rule is generally predicated on the duty of a partner to proceed with diligence in the defense of actions brought against the firm. To confess a judgment, it is said, is to abandon defenses.

Implied Authority of a Majority   Section 18 of the Partnership Act provides that in case of diversity of opinion among the partners with respect to ordinary matters connected with the partnership business the decision of the majority of the members binds the partnership. The rule prevails even though a dissenting member gives notice of his dissent to the person with whom the majority are dealing in behalf of the partnership. The rule presupposes that the majority is acting in good faith and within the scope of the partnership business. What happens if there is an even division of partners and they are equally divided in opinion? No rule has been formulated for answering this question. It appears that the partners are powerless to act with respect to the disagreement so long as the deadlock continues. About the only thing the partners can do, if the disagreement is hopelessly deadlocked, is to dissolve the partnership. This is another situation that could be avoided by providing for such a contingency in the articles of partnership.

The majority-decision rule is not unyielding. Some acts, indeed, require unanimous consent of all the partners. Section 9 of the Partnership Act states the rule: No act in contravention of any agreement between the partners may be done rightfully without the consent of all the partners. The majority, therefore, could not alter the partnership agreement by performing such acts as reducing or increasing the capital investment of the partners, changing the essential nature of the business, or admitting new members into the partnership. Section 9 also, in addition to imposing the above general prohibition of the authority of the majority, expressly enumerates certain acts which, unless authorized by the other partners or unless they have abandoned the business, require unanimous consent of all the partners. These are substantially as follows: assigning the partnership property for the benefit of creditors; disposing of the goodwill of the business; performing any other act that would make it impossible to carry on the ordinary business of the partnership; confessing a judgment; and submitting a partnership claim to arbitration.

LIABILITIES OF PARTNERS
The rules for determining the liabilities of partners do not differ materially from the rules found in the law of principal and agent. It is only necessary, therefore, to mention briefly (1) contractual obligations, (2) torts, and (3) crimes.

Contractual Obligations   The law with respect to the contractual obligations of the members of a partnership is well settled. All partners are liable for the debts and obligations of the firm. A debt is, in substance, a debt of each individual member of the firm, as well as the debt of the firm. The property of each individual member, as well as the property of the firm, is liable for the debt. This is true even though the acting partner enters into the contract in his own name. The only thing that needs to be shown is that the partner acted within the scope of his authority.

Liability for Torts   All the members of the firm are liable for the torts committed by one of the members acting within the scope of the firm's business. This is true even though they do not participate in, ratify, or have knowledge of the tort. Nonacting partners are liable if one partner receives money or property from a third person and misapplies it, or if one partner misapplies it while it is in the custody of the partnership. [*Philips v. United States,* p. 506.]

Liability for Crimes   A nonacting partner, in a lawful enterprise, is not criminally liable for the acts of another partner. All partners who participate in the criminal act, of course, are criminally liable. Partners who are engaged in a criminal business are liable for acts committed within the scope of that business. A nonacting partner in a partnership engaged in the business of illegal sales of liquor, therefore, would be liable.

RATIFICATION, ESTOPPEL, ADMISSIONS

Borrowed from the law of agency, like the other liabilities, is the manner in which a partnership may be bound by (1) ratification, (2) estoppel, and (3) admissions.

Ratification of Unauthorized Acts   A subsequent ratification of an unauthorized act of a partner is equivalent to antecedent authority. A partner who does an act which is not within the scope of his express or implied powers, therefore, may impose a liability on the partnership by subsequent ratification. It is a question of fact for the jury as to whether or not there has been a ratification in any particular case, and the general rules of agency governing ratification are applicable to partnerships. These agency rules were discussed more fully in Chapter 33, "Creation and Authority."

Liability by Estoppel   It is a well-settled rule that a person who is in fact not a partner may be and frequently has been held liable to third persons just as if he were a partner. A partnership, however, is not created by estoppel. It is only the duties and liabilities appertaining to the relationship that are created by estoppel. Section 16 of the Partnership Act follows the majority view at common law by imposing liability only when there is consent in fact to the representations. But it may not always be safe to rely on the majority view because a strong minority says that a person who knows he is being claimed as a partner is under a duty to make reasonable efforts to assert his denial. A person who knows his name is being falsely advertised as a partner, therefore, would be wise in notifying the partnership to cease such advertising. A person who openly permits himself to be named as a partner is clearly under a duty to speak. A person who permits his name to form part of the partnership name or to appear on letterheads or advertisements may also find himself liable as a partner.

Section 15 of the Partnership Act provides for a partnership liability and for an individual liability. Suppose Brown and Jones are partners doing business as The Redfront Grocery. Suppose further that Brown and Jones represent that Smith is also a member of the partnership and that Smith consents to the representation. A partnership liability would result, and Smith would be liable as though he were an actual member of the partnership. No partnership liability would result, however, if Brown, the sole proprietor of The Redfront Grocery, held Smith out with his consent as a partner. Brown and Smith would be liable jointly. The creditors who thought there was a partnership of Brown and Smith would have no priority on the assets of The Redfront Grocery, as opposed to the creditors of Brown, because there was in fact no partnership fund.

The third person, in all situations, must show that the purported partner represented himself, or permitted others to represent him, as a partner; the third person must also show that he, in justifiable reliance on such representations, dealt with the partnership to his injury. [*Boone v. General Shoe Corp.,* p. 506.]

Partnership Bound by Admissions   Section 11 of the Partnership Act provides that an admission or representation made by any partner concerning partnership affairs within the scope of his authority is evidence against the partnership. Statements which are not within the scope of the authority of the partner are not admissible as evidence. Statements which are made after dissolution of a partnership, unless made as a part of the winding-up process, and statements made to prove the existence of a partnership are also not admissible as evidence. Smith could not, for example, impose a liability on Jones simply by walking into the Farm Supply Store and saying: "Jones is my partner; we would like to purchase our supplies for this month on credit." But once the existence of the partnership relation has been proven by other independent evidence, statements made by a partner speaking for the partnership concerning partnership affairs, while acting within the scope of his authority, are admissible as evidence against the partnership. [*Boise Payette Lumber Co. v. Sarret,* p. 507.]

CASES

Gordon v. Aumiller,   187 Pac. 354 (Wash. 1920). Action by J. H. Gordon, plaintiff, against W. C. Marburger, defendant, wherein W. J. Aumiller intervened. On April 10, 1917, plaintiff and defendant entered into a partnership agreement looking to the raising of potatoes on a tract of land owned by Henry Pagel. Marburger was to supervise the farming, and Gordon was to furnish the money. On April 30, Gordon having furnished the money, Marburger paid Pagel $170 for the rent of the land. The receipt for the payment stated that it was for rent and that it was made by W. C. Marburger and J. H. Gordon. It was in typewriting and was written by Aumiller at the request of Marburger. Gordon furnished other money from time to time. On June 12, 1917, Marburger, individually and in his own name, borrowed from Aumiller $150 for which he executed and delivered his promissory note. He executed and delivered, at the same time, a chattel mortgage upon the growing crop of potatoes to secure the payment of the note. Marburger thereafter borrowed from Aumiller $50 at one time and $100 at another time. Marburger, after the potatoes were harvested, failed to account to Gordon. Gordon then brought this action for an accounting of their partnership affairs. Aumiller intervened seeking to have his claim amounting to $300 established as a claim against the proceeds of the sale of the potatoes. The claim of Gordon against Marburger is not presented on this appeal.

Parker, Justice: In the doing of acts ordinarily necessary to be done by one partner in the performance of partnership duties assigned to such partner, he can bind the other partners and their interest in the partnership property. It is plain, however, that in this partnership Marburger had no duties to perform in the partnership business rendering it at all necessary for him to borrow money to further the partnership interests, nor was there any custom of dealing by either of the partners touching the partnership business in the least suggesting that Marburger was authorized to borrow money for the partnership or encumber its property. The contentions of counsel are rested upon the theory that Gordon was a silent or dormant partner, and that Aumiller was warranted in dealing with Marburger upon the assumption that he was the sole owner of the potatoes. It is true that Aumiller testified in substance that he had no notice of Gordon's interest in the potatoes until after he had made all of the three loans to Marburger. It is hard to believe that Aumiller was wholly ignorant of Gordon's interest in the potatoes, in view of the fact that Aumiller prepared the rent receipt evidencing the leasing of the land to both Marburger and Gordon for the raising of these potatoes. The chattel mortgage given by Marburger to Aumiller to secure the first loan of $150 described the crop of potatoes as being then growing upon the same land, describing it, and referring to it as belonging to Henry Pagel, which mortgage was executed on June 12th, only 1 month and 12 days after Aumiller had prepared the rent receipt for Marburger. Surely this ought to be held to be sufficient to at least put Aumiller upon inquiry as to the probability of Gordon being interested in the potatoes. This significant fact, together with the fact that Gordon made no effort to conceal, and did no act tending to conceal, the existence of the partnership relation between him and Marburger, and the fact that this was purely a nontrading partnership, we think, compels the conclusion that in no event can Aumiller at this time be heard to say, as against the rights of Gordon, that he was led to believe that Marburger was the sole owner of the potatoes, with absolute right to borrow money and secure the payment of the same by encumbering them.

[DECISION FOR PLAINTIFF]

Bole v. Lyle, 287 S.W.2d 931 (Tenn. 1956). Action by John Bole, Jr., plaintiff, against B. Frank Lyle, Homer S. Peters, and W. J. Barton, Jr., defendants, partners formerly operating under the name of "Cherokee Box and Handle Company." The partnership operated a manufacturing business in Johnson City, Tennessee, where it made packing crates and other products from wood. To supply the needs for lumber, the partnership had purchased a boundary of timber which it was in the process of cutting and manufacturing into lumber. W. J. Barton, Jr., as the managing partner, entered into an agreement for the sale of specified types and amounts of lumber to the Lakeview Lumber Company of Lakewood, Michigan, which company was owned and operated by the plaintiff. Barton received a check for $1,500 and shipped a part of the lumber. The partnership dissolved. This action was then brought to recover $738.60 alleged to have been advanced to defendants for the purchase of lumber which was never delivered.

McAmis, Presiding Judge: After indorsing the check "Cherokee Box and Handle Co. by Wm. J. Barton, Jr., Gen. Mgr.," Barton opened a bank account in the name of "Wm. J. Barton, Jr., Agent," indorsing the check in his name as agent. He explained to the bank official that he was trading in his individual name and for that reason desired a separate account from that of Cherokee Box and Handle Company. The partnership received no part of the proceeds of the check and the other partners knew nothing of the transaction until claim was made after the dissolution of the partnership.

While the record is not clear, it is perhaps inferable that that part of the lumber which was shipped by Barton came from the tract of timber owned by the partnership. No other lumber was ever sold in this manner by Barton or by the partnership and the undisputed proof shows that neither this timber nor any other was ever bought for sale. The partnership was not a trading partnership but solely engaged in the business of manufacturing. . . .

Section 9 of the Uniform Partnership Act, provides in part as follows:

"(2) An act of a partner which is not apparently for the carrying on of the business of the partnership in the *usual way* does not bind the partnership unless authorized by the other partners." [Italics ours.]

The act of Barton was not done "for apparently carrying on in the usual way the business of the partnership." On the contrary, the act was entirely outside the only business ever conducted by the partnership and there is no showing that his act "apparently" had a connection with the manufacturing business. This was not surplus or defective lumber such as a business engaged in the manufacture of wood products might find it desirable to sell from time to time, in which case the sale might conceivably have the appearance of being incident to the business of the partnership. Sub-section (2) above quoted exonerates the partnership for such an act in the absence of ratification or a prior course of conduct upon which third parties are entitled to rely. . . .

We think the case here presented is simply that of a nonresident unfamiliar with the partnership operations, being defrauded by one of the partners acting in a matter beyond both the real and apparent scope of the business and beyond the real or apparent scope of the agency. [DECISION FOR DEFENDANTS]

Philips v. United States, 59 F.2d 881 (1932). Suit by the United States, plaintiff, against John L. Philips, John Stevens, and others. At the close of World War I there was an accumulation of surplus lumber scattered at various points throughout the country. The government, in order to avoid dumping this vast quantity of materials upon the market at once, adopted a policy of disposing of it upon a graduated scale. John L. Philips and John Stevens entered into a partnership agreement providing for a joint interest in the undertaking. Philips was the directing head, in charge of the field work. Stevens was in charge of the office and clerical part of the organization. It was agreed that any profit and loss should be divided equally between them. The partners, according to their agreement with the government, were required to sell the lumber and account to the United States for the proceeds of the sale. George M. Chambers was appointed as the agent for the government to inspect the lumber and fix the base price. It appears from the finding of the lower court that, in making sales of the lumber, invoices were sent to the government for each sale but that the price shown by the invoices was not the price at which the lumber was sold but merely the base price fixed by Chambers and Philips. The court further found that "Philips, the active contractor with the government, and Chambers, the direct representative of the government, fixed the base prices of all the lumber disposed of, and that they made large profits on the lumber sold." Judgment was rendered in favor of the United States in the sum of $1,381,447.00. There was no evidence to show that Stevens participated in the secret profits with Philips or that he had any knowledge of the fraudulent transactions. Stevens contends, therefore, that he should be relieved from liability.

Van Orsdel, Justice: The liability of both Philips and Stevens is based upon the contract, and the suit is for a violation of the Government's rights under that contract. Indeed, the suit is for a breach of the contract, and the fraud alleged and proved is material as showing and establishing that fact. In the last analysis the question is whether Stevens is liable for Philips' breach, which in law is the breach of both.

The agreement between Stevens and Philips was in the nature of a partnership agreement. It provided for an apportionment of the work, a division of the profits, and a common undertaking. These constitute the elements of a partnership. Each of the partners was not only an agent for the partnership but an agent for the other partner. They were, therefore, liable for the default or fraud of each within the scope of the common undertaking.

It follows, therefore, that, Philips having been held liable to the United States for the profits realized under this contract which accrued to him in fraud of the rights of the United States, Stevens' liability as a partner follows as a matter of law by reason of the joint responsibility which he assumed with Philips under the contract. [DECISION FOR PLAINTIFF]

Boone v. General Shoe Corp., 242 S.W.2d 138 (Ark. 1951). Action by General Shoe Corporation (plaintiff below), appellee, against Mrs. Pearl Boone, J. E. Jones, and The Jacqueline Shop (defendants below). The lower court rendered judgment against Mrs. Boone and J. E. Jones, jointly and severally, for $1,989.90.

Mrs. Boone, appellant, appealed, contending that J. E. Jones was the sole owner of the shoe department.

The appellee alleged substantially that it sold to The Jacqueline Shop certain shoes for which a balance remains unpaid in the sum of $1,989.90; that said shoes were sold through J. E. Jones in the belief that he was a partner or agent of The Jacqueline Shop; that the shoes were shipped to and accepted in the name of The Jacqueline Shop; that the acts of appellant caused appellee to extend credit which was based upon her credit rating and not upon that of Jones; that appellant held Jones out to the public as her partner or agent and allowed him to hold himself out to the public as such; and that appellant is now estopped from denying it as against appellee. Judgment was rendered in favor of appellee in the sum of $1,989.90. Appellant contends that Jones was sole owner of the shoe department.

Ward, Justice: It is our opinion that there is an abundance of testimony to support the verdict of the jury on the ground that the action or lack of action on the part of Mrs. Boone, together with the manner in which the business was conducted and the apparent relationship between Mrs. Boone and Jones, led appellee to believe that Jones had authority to purchase merchandise for "The Jacqueline Shop." They were doing business together in the same room which had only one entrance, and the only name by which the business was known was "The Jacqueline Shop." Appellee had shipped merchandise to "The Jacqueline Shop" over a period of months and had on each occasion sent an invoice showing that the merchandise was charged to "The Jacqueline Shop" and mailed to that address. The evidence shows clearly that Mrs. Boone had access to the mail and could not but have known these facts. The evidence also shows that over this period of time 150 or 200 invoices were mailed to "The Jacqueline Shop." All of these facts were known to appellee's employees who went to the place of business and solicited orders for merchandise. Although appellant contends that she sold only ladies ready to wear and that Jones alone was interested in the sale of shoes, yet the newspaper advertisements offered both classes of merchandise under the name of "The Jacqueline Shop." Jones himself at unguarded moments on the witness stand spoke of the business as "our business." [DECISION FOR APPELLEE]

Boise Payette Lumber Co. v. Sarret, 221 Pac. 130 (Idaho 1923). Action by Boise Payette Lumber Company (plaintiff below), respondent, against Jules Sarret and J. M. Stevens, doing business under the firm name of "Sarret & Stevens" (defendants below). J. M. Stevens is the appellant. It appears from the record that certain lumber, fence posts, barbed wire, nails, etc., were sold by respondent to the firm of Sarret & Stevens. It does not appear that appellant was informed that the purchases had been made until respondent requested payment. Appellant refused to pay for the merchandise, and respondent instituted this action to recover the purchase price. Appellant admitted the existence of the copartnership but contended the purchases were not within the scope of the business conducted by the partners.

Lee, Justice: The evidence showed that Sarret went to respondent's place of business at Blackfoot and told its local manager that he wanted to purchase some materials for Sarret & Stevens; that they were in partnership in the sheep business, and that they needed the materials for building sheds, fences, etc., on a ranch operated by the partnership. Respondent thereupon sold and delivered the materials, for the payment for which this action was instituted.

Appellant insists that the fact of partnership could not be proved by testimony of conversations with Sarret in appellant's absence. Appellant is correct in his contention, but it has no application here, inasmuch as appellant admitted in his answer that he and Sarret were partners in the sheep business. . . . Were it not for the admission of the partnership in the answer, the testimony of conversations with Sarret, in the absence of appellant, as to the existence of the partnership, would not have been admissible. The fact of the partnership being admitted, however, the statements of Sarret that he wanted the merchandise for use by the partnership in its sheep business were admissible.

Another point raised by appellant is that, since the partnership was limited to the sheep business, Sarret could not bind him by any contract not relating to that particular business, and that respondent was deemed to have knowledge of the limited nature of the partnership and the fact that its operations were restricted to the single business of raising and selling sheep.

. . . The witness who testified in this connection said that he had, for the past 15 years, sold merchandise to people engaged in the business of raising and selling sheep, and was familiar with the nature and character of the articles purchased by such people for use in their business. The burden was on respondent to prove that the purchases made by Sarret were made within the scope and course of the particular business which appellant admitted was conducted by the partnership, and to do this we see no reason why it was not proper to prove that sheepmen generally purchase and use such materials in carrying on their business. . . .

It appearing, therefore, that the materials were such as are ordinarily purchased by men engaged in the business in which appellant admitted the partnership was engaged, the partnership was liable for the purchase price of such materials. [DECISION FOR RESPONDENT]

PROBLEMS

1 Wells and Sanders, partners, whose sole business was that of storage and trucking, operated under the name of "Security Storage & Transfer Company." Wells purchased a quantity of roofing material in the name of the partnership for the purpose of resale. Sanders, as soon as he discovered the transaction, repudiated it and so notified the seller. In an action by the seller to recover the purchase price, the court found that Wells, having been induced to make the purchase by false and fraudulent representations, was not liable. Is either the partnership or Sanders liable?

2 Wilson and Hansen, partners doing business as the "Barbara Fishing Company," owned the fishing vessel "Barbara." Wilson, as the managing partner, employed certain fishermen with the understanding that they were to go halibut fishing on the vessel, and that they were to be compensated for their work—both in preparing the vessel and her gear for the fishing season and for their services as fishermen during the season—by sharing in the proceeds of

the season's catch. After the fishermen had completed the preparation of the vessel and her gear for the fishing season, Wilson took the "Barbara" on a fishing expedition leaving the fishermen behind. Hansen had no dealings with any of the fishermen. Is he personally liable to the fishermen for the time they worked on the "Barbara"?

3 Loomis and Blackburn formed a partnership for the purpose of building residences for sale; Loomis and Davis formed a partnership for the purpose of building and selling residences in the same city; Loomis, the common partner, was the overall supervisor of all construction for both partnerships; Sanders, under the impression that there was only one partnership composed of Loomis, Blackburn, and Davis, sold lumber to Loomis that went into the construction of the buildings; the accounts of the two partnerships were so commingled that it was impossible to determine on whose separate project the materials were used; and neither partnership had assets with which to pay for the lumber. Who is liable for the lumber?

4 Brown, Smith, and Jones formed a partnership for the purpose of operating a gasoline service station and buying and selling used cars. The partnership agreement provided that the initial capital of the partnership should consist of $25,800 to be contributed in equal amounts by the partners. The agreement further provided that Brown should receive $100 a week for operating the business and that his capital contribution would be paid "from his share of the profits over and above his salary." The business did not prosper, and it became necessary to borrow money from time to time. Brown borrowed $8,600 from plaintiff, for which amount he signed a promissory note in the name of the partnership. In an action by plaintiff to recover the $8,600, Smith and Jones contend they are not individually liable because the money so borrowed was used by Brown as his contribution to capital. Do you agree with this contention?

5 Chase and Carson, who were the members of a partnership engaged in the retail business of buying and selling jewelry, retailed both sterling silver and silver-plated merchandise. Chase sold Brown a silver-plated coffee service by fraudulently representing that the coffee service was sterling silver. Carson was unaware of the fraudulent representation made by Chase until Brown brought an action against the partnership and Chase and Carson individually to recover damages which resulted from the representation. Carson contended that he was not liable because he had no knowledge of the representation and did not ratify the act. Will Brown recover?

6 Beggs, Harvey, and Clark formed a partnership for the purpose of buying and selling office supplies and books. The partnership was prosperous, but Beggs and Harvey wanted to add a snack bar. They reasoned that a snack bar near the entrance of their place of business would attract customers who would purchase office supplies and books. They proposed selling such items as coffee, cold drinks, and sandwiches. Clark objected. He reasoned that it would be to the advantage of the partnership to upgrade the office supplies and books. Beggs and Harvey, nevertheless, invoking the implied authority of a majority rule, entered into a contract with a skilled carpenter to add the snack bar. Clark disclaimed any liability on the contract. Decide.

7 John Brown, his wife Mary, and his son James were partners engaged in the operation of a restaurant known as the "Dutch Treat." James, who conceived the idea of also operating a cocktail lounge, entered into a contract with a building contractor for the construction of the lounge. The contract provided that any disagreements which might arise with respect to the construction work would be submitted to arbitration. John and Mary read the contract but did not express an opinion as to their approval or disapproval. During the process of construction, a dispute arose over the lighting fixtures. Do you think the arbitration provision is binding on the partnership?

39
PARTNERS: RELATION TO ONE ANOTHER

As a general proposition, the law demands that the partners exercise the utmost good faith and integrity toward one another. An inquiry into some of the specific rules for governing the relation of the partners to one another, however, reveals that the relationship is governed by rules which logically divide themselves into (1) the rights and duties of the partners to one another and (2) the property rights of a partner.

RIGHTS AND DUTIES

The most obvious right which each partner has against his copartners, and the most obvious duty which each partner owes his copartners, is the reciprocal right and duty of each partner to conform strictly to the stipulations contained in the partnership agreement. In the absence of an agreement defining the rights and duties of the partners, however, certain rules have been formulated for that purpose. These rules pertain to (1) the fiduciary relation, (2) rendering information, (3) the partnership books, (4) actions by partners against the partnership, (5) formal accountings, (6) compensation for services, (7) indemnity and contribution, (8) interest, and (9) profits and losses.

Duty to Account as a Fiduciary   The duty to account as a fiduciary operates to prevent a partner from competing with his firm. The rule is generally stated: A partner cannot, without the consent of his copartners, carry on a business in competition with the business of his firm. A partner who violates this rule may be enjoined from so competing, and he may also be required to account to his copartners for the profits derived from the competing business. The rule does not operate so as to prevent a partner from investing his own funds. A partner may engage in an enterprise in his own behalf so long as he neither competes with the business of his firm nor violates his agreement with his copartners with respect to devoting his time and energies to outside matters.

The duty to account as a fiduciary also operates to prevent a partner from making a secret profit. It includes any transaction connected with the formation, conduct, or liquidation of the partnership. It includes any use by a partner of partnership property. Section 21 of the Partnership Act states that every partner must account to the partnership for any benefit and hold as trustee for it any profits derived by him without the consent of the other partners. A partner, therefore, who makes a secret profit out of the operation of the partnership, or who accepts a secret commission from a third person dealing with the partnership, must account to, and share such profit or commission with, his copartners. [*Van Hooser v. Keenon,* p. 515.]

Duty to Render Information   Section 20 of the Partnership Act declares that partners shall render to any partner, on demand, true and full information of all things affecting the partnership. But the use of the words "on demand" does not mean that a partner is under no duty to disclose voluntarily information affecting the partnership. A partner who has exclusive information of the discovery of a valuable mine on partnership property would therefore be under a duty to disclose such information before purchasing the interest of another partner.

The general rule requires each partner to make a full disclosure of all material facts within his knowledge relating to partnership affairs. The rule operates to make it unnecessary for third persons who desire to give notice to the partnership to give such notice to all the partners. A notice delivered to one partner is an effective communication to the partnership. The rule also operates to impute knowledge obtained by one partner, while acting within his authority and within the scope of the partnership business, to all the partners. Knowledge of one, it is said, is knowledge of all. Knowledge of a guilty partner, however, is not knowledge of all. Suppose Smith, a member of a partnership in the business of buying and selling diamonds, wrongfully appropriates diamonds from his firm and passes them along to Jones, who sells the diamonds and divides the proceeds of the sale with Smith. Jones certainly could not defend an action brought against him for the fraud on the theory that "knowledge of one is knowledge of all."

Right to Inspect and Duty to Keep Books   The duty to render information does not ordinarily arise with respect to facts appearing on the partnership books. This is for the reason that each partner has the right to inspect the books. He is, therefore, presumed to have knowledge of their contents. Section 19 of the Partnership Act states that partnership books shall be kept at the principal place of business of the partnership, and every partner shall at all times have access to and may inspect and copy any of the partnership books. The information gathered, to be sure, must be used for a partnership purpose. A partner would not be permitted to copy a list of the customers of the firm and give them to a competing firm for individual gain. But the general rule regarding partnership books is that they should be kept open to the inspection of any partner at all reasonable times, even after dissolution.

Right of Partner to Sue Partnership　It is generally conceded that an action may be maintained for the breach of an agreement to enter into a partnership, or an agreement to furnish capital, or to do some other act antecedent to the formation of the partnership. The courts, however, make a distinction between an agreement to form a partnership and a partnership already entered into. The result is a well-settled general rule: No action at law may be maintained between partners, or between a partner and the partnership, for breach of a contract arising out of the partnership relation. The reason generally assigned for the rule is that it cannot be determined what portion of such claims belongs to one or the other until the partnership accounts are settled. What then may an aggrieved partner do? His only remedy, in the majority of the situations, is to bring a suit in a court of equity, or a court with equity powers, for an accounting and dissolution of the partnership.

Right to a Formal Accounting　A formal accounting is a necessary incident to the dissolution of a partnership. A court of equity, however, is quite reluctant to entertain a suit for a formal accounting except as incident to a decree of dissolution. The courts say partners should dissolve their firm if they cannot carry on their business amicably. But a forced accounting without dissolution is not impossible. Section 22 of the Partnership Act gives any partner a right to a formal accounting if the right exists under the terms of any agreement, if a partner is accountable as a fiduciary, if a partner is wrongfully excluded from the partnership business or possession of its property, or whenever the circumstances render it just and reasonable. A partner who does not have access to the partnership books because he is traveling for a long period of time on partnership business would have the right to a formal accounting. The same would be true of a seasonable business coupled with an agreement to divide the profits at the close of the season. A good illustration of such an arrangement is a partnership composed of farmers.

Right to Compensation for Services　The general rule at common law provides that no partner is entitled to remuneration for acting in the partnership business. This rule has been incorporated by section 18 in the Partnership Act. The rule is qualified, however, to the extent that a surviving partner is entitled to reasonable compensation for his services in winding up the partnership affairs. The partners may, to be sure, enter into an agreement to pay a salary to one or more of the partners for services rendered. Such an agreement is frequently entered into when some of the partners do not desire to participate actively in the management of the business. Such an agreement, moreover, may be implied in a few rare instances.

Suppose one partner gives his entire time to the management of the business while another partner gives no time to the partnership business. Such an arrangement, coupled with a custom and usage in the community for such active partners to receive compensation for their services, may very well lead the courts to decide that the facts and circumstances were such as to show a mutual intention to pay a salary to the active partner in addition to his share in the profits. In the absence of unusual circumstances, however, each partner is impliedly bound to devote his time, attention, and skill to the management of the affairs of the firm, and his only compensation for this service is a share in the profits. [*Boyer v. Bowles*, p. 516.]

Indemnity and Contribution   A partner who, by his wrongful act or negligence, creates an unnecessary loss to the partnership is under a duty to indemnify the partnership. It has been held that a partner was under a duty to indemnify the partnership where he made and sold goods of an inferior quality which resulted in the partnership's becoming liable in damages to the buyer. A partner, on the other hand, who pays more than his share of the partnership obligations is entitled to contribution from his copartners. Section 18 of the Partnership Act states that the partnership must indemnify every partner with respect to payments made and personal liabilities reasonably incurred by him in the ordinary and proper conduct of its business or for the preservation of its business or property. A partner who properly expends his own money as traveling expenses would be entitled to be reimbursed and indemnified out of the partnership funds.

Right to Interest   A distinction is made between advances and capital for the purpose of determining the right of a partner to interest. A partner who makes a loan—commonly referred to as an "advance"—beyond the amount of the capital which he has agreed to contribute is entitled to be paid interest from the date of the advance. A partner, as a general rule, is not entitled to interest on capital. Section 18 of the Partnership Act says that a partner shall receive interest on the capital contributed by him only from the date when repayment should be made. Suppose Brown, upon dissolution of the partnership of Brown and Jones, is in charge of the winding-up process. Suppose further that Brown unreasonably delays to settle the accounts or unjustifiably refuses to account. Jones would be entitled to receive interest on his capital investment from the time when Brown should have accounted. The facts of the particular case are controlling.

Profits and Losses   An essential feature of a partnership is the right to share in the profits. This right carries with it the duty to contribute to the losses. Disputes with respect to profits and losses, however, rarely require settlement prior to dissolution. The rules for sharing profits and losses are therefore reserved for Chapter 40, "Partnership: Dissolution, Winding Up, Termination."

PROPERTY RIGHTS OF A PARTNER
Section 24 of the Partnership Act enumerates the property rights of a partner as (1) his rights in specific partnership property, (2) his interest in the partnership, and (3) his right to participate in the management.

Rights in Specific Partnership Property   The nature of partnership property was defined and explained in Chapter 37, "Partnership: Nature, Creation, Property," but it remains to explain a partner's right in the specific partnership property.

The courts at common law agree that a partner is a co-owner with his partners in specific partnership property, but they disagree as to the type of co-ownership. Section 25 of the Partnership Act simplifies the common law by declaring that a partner holds the specific partnership property as a tenant in partnership. This type of tenancy (1) prohibits a partner's right in the specific partnership property from being subject to dower, curtesy, or allowances to widows, heirs, or next of kin, (2) prohibits the assignment of a partner's right in the specific property unless all the other partners join in the assignment, and (3) prohibits the attachment of a partner's right in specific property except on a claim against the partnership. This type of tenancy gives each partner the right to possess the property for partnership purposes during his lifetime and vests such right in the surviving partner or partners upon the death of any partner.

(1)   *Possession of Specific Partnership Property*   Each partner has a right to possess in common with his copartners the partnership property for partnership purposes. But no partner has the right to possess partnership property for his own individual purposes without the consent of the other partners. The wrongful exclusive possession of partnership property by one or more partners is grounds for dissolution of the partnership, and any partner who wrongfully deprives his partners of possession of the property will be held accountable for any profits derived therefrom.

(2)   *Survivorship Rights*   The common-law decisions hold that the title to a deceased partner's share in specific partnership personal property passes to the surviving partner for the purpose of liquidation but that his share in the real property descends to his heirs. Courts of equity, however, protect the creditors of the partnership by applying the so-called equitable-conversion doctrine. This means that the courts treat the real property as if it were personal property for the purpose of liquidation. Unless the real property is needed for partnership purposes, however, the share of the deceased partner descends to his heirs at common law. Section 25 of the Partnership Act has simplified these rules by declaring that on the death of a partner his rights in specific partnership property vest in the surviving partner or partners for partnership purposes. This means that it is possible for the surviving partner as a part of the process of winding up the partnership business to dispose of the real property without the heirs or devisees joining in the conveyance.

Partner's Interest in the Partnership   Section 26 of the Partnership Act draws a clear-cut dividing line between the specific partnership property and a partner's interest in the partnership. This is accomplished by defining a partner's interest as his share in the profits and surplus and declaring the same to be personal property. [*Windom Nat'l Bank v. Klein*, p. 517.]

(1)   *Assignment of Interest*   A partner may assign his interest in the partnership, but such an assignment merely entitles the assignee to receive the

profits which the assigning partner would otherwise be entitled to receive. Section 27 of the Partnership Act specifically provides that the assignment does not of itself dissolve the partnership nor entitle the assignee to interfere in the management of the partnership business. The assignee is not entitled to inspect the partnership books or require any other information on the partnership transactions. It is thus clear that the assignee has no rights in specific partnership property but is only entitled to receive his assignor's profits during the continuance of the business of the partnership and the assignor's interest in case of dissolution of the partnership.

(2) *Interest Subject to Charging Order*   Legislation has been enacted in most states to enable a separate creditor of a partner to reach the interest of a partner with the least possible disturbance to the carrying on of the partnership business. A bill in equity is sometimes used, but section 28 of the Partnership Act provides a device known as a "charging order." The court, by the use of this device, will charge the interest of the debtor-partner with an unsatisfied judgment. The charge may be enforced by the appointment of a receiver to accept the debtor-partner's share of the profits until the debt is paid. It follows that, although the separate creditors of an individual partner may reach the interest of a partner, they cannot reach the specific partnership property. The other partners may purchase the interest of the debtor-partner with or without dissolving the partnership.

Participation in Management   The members of a firm often perform different functions. One member may be the purchasing agent; another may be in charge of personnel; and still another may devote his energies to sales. But all partners, in the absence of an agreement to the contrary, have equal rights in the conduct and management of all the firm's business. In this connection, the rules with respect to the implied powers of the majority should be kept in mind.

CASES

Van Hooser v. Keenon   271 S.W.2d 270 (Ky. 1954). Action by R. W. Keenon and Eloise Keenon, plaintiffs, against James D. Van Hooser, Harold J. Utter, and three others, defendants below. James D. Van Hooser and Harold J. Utter are the defendants on appeal. The plaintiffs and the defendants below were partners operating a bus line under the name of "Western Kentucky Stages." Van Hooser and Utter, after negotiations, entered into an agreement with Greyhound, Inc., by the terms of which Greyhound, Inc., agreed to pay $37,500 for an option to buy 60 percent of Western's stock in the event Western would alter its status from a partnership to that of a corporation. Van Hooser and Utter thereafter sought out plaintiffs and requested that the partnership be changed to a corporation. The reason offered for this change, among other things, was that they desired to be relieved of the personal liability imposed by the partnership setup. Plaintiffs testified they opposed substituting a corporation for the partnership for some time but that they finally yielded to the plan. After the partnership became a corporation, the option money was forfeited by the refusal of Greyhound, Inc., to complete its deal. The $37,500 was divided among the five defendants below. Plaintiff R. W. Keenon received information that some sort of transaction had taken place with Greyhound, Inc., but he was unable to induce Van Hooser and Utter to disclose the nature of the transaction. The plaintiffs then instituted this action, claiming 25 percent of the $37,500. The lower court rendered judgment solely against the defendants on appeal on the theory that they should be treated as trustees for the partnership.

Stewart, Justice: We should state, at the outset, that there is no relation or trust or confidence known to the law that requires of the parties a higher degree of good faith than that of partnership. Nothing less than absolute fairness will suffice. Each partner is the confidential agent of all the others and each has a right to know all that the others know. Nor will one partner be permitted to benefit at the expense of the firm. . . .

Applying the foregoing basic rules of the common law to the admitted facts of this case. . . . We conclude as did the lower court, and the evidence abundantly supports our conclusion, that the five defendants were and are under a legal obligation as partners to share proportionately with plaintiffs the option money which was obtained by the optioners by virtue of the partnership relationship. The important factor is that these defendants received money which should have gone into the partnership treasury and then should have been divided proportionately among all of the partners. The excuse advanced by them that they were compelled to keep the Keenons in the dark, in order for their plan to work, certainly furnishes no legal basis under the circumstances for their retention of all the money.

Furthermore, we believe it was proper to render judgment against the two appealing defendants alone for the full amount due plaintiffs. They initiated and consummated the option deal with Greyhound, Inc., and they collected and divided up among the five optioners the cash benefits from the transaction. When they received the money under the conditions recited they became in effect trustees of this fund for the benefit of the other partners for the share of each one in the proceeds. [DECISION FOR PLAINTIFFS]

Boyer v. Bowles, 37 N.E.2d 489 (Mass. 1941). Action by Walton T. Boyer, plaintiff against Sherman H. Bowles, defendant. The plaintiff and the defendant entered into a partnership under the name of "New England Neon Sign Company" for the purpose of manufacturing and selling neon signs. The defendant agreed to furnish all the necessary financial backing, and the plaintiff was to receive $60 a week, which was termed as a "drawing account." The plaintiff, who had received over $15,000, instituted this action for an accounting of the partnership affairs. He contends that the money was received as compensation for services. The defendant contends that the money was received as a partial distribution of profits.

Cox, Justice: The master found that the parties agreed "to go 50–50," and, in answer to the question to the plaintiff as to whether it was his understanding of the agreement that he was to be paid and Bowles was not to be paid for services, he replied: "We were to go 50–50." When he answered this question, he knew that he had received over $15,000 by way of a drawing account, and that Bowles had never received anything by way of distribution of earnings. . . .

We construe this expression, "to go 50–50," to mean that the parties in question agreed that they were to be equally interested in the partnership business.

The plaintiff was a glass blower, and was recommended to Bowles as one who was familar with, and had the ability to build, neon signs. The purpose of the partnership was to manufacture and sell such signs. Bowles was to furnish the "necessary financial backing," and it is a reasonable inference that the plaintiff, in turn, was to devote himself to the manufacture, at least, of the signs. Under such an arrangement, and the specific agreement "to go 50–50," neither partner would be entitled to compensation for services in the absence of an express or implied agreement. It is to be observed that there is no specific agreement that the plaintiff should receive any salary, as such. It has been said that a drawing account is a well recognized modern business method of furnishing the employee with means of maintenance while engaged in a service from which wages and commissions are to accrue. ∴ . . . In any event, he did not stipulate, in terms, for the payment of any salary. He was merely to receive a weekly amount, termed a "drawing account," from a partnership that was upon a "50–50" basis. Upon all the findings, we are of opinion that his drawing account was against possible profits, and not by way of payment for his services. [DECISION FOR DEFENDANT]

Windom Nat'l Bank v. Klein, 254 N.W. 602 (Minn. 1934). Action by Windom National Bank and another, plaintiffs, against Charles H. Klein, defendant, to annul certain mortgages encumbering livestock, farm equipment, and other specific chattels executed in favor of defendant not by or for the firm of Bender Bros. but by Gottlob Bender and Howard G. Bender, individually.

Stone, Justice: During the period here determinative and for many years before, Gottlob, Howard G., Gustave, and Mathias Bender, as partners, have owned and operated a dairy farm, the firm name being Bender Bros. Windom National Bank has an unsatisfied judgment against Howard G. and Gottlob for upwards of $1,500. Proceeding under section 28 of the Uniform Partnership Law, it procured the appointment of its coplaintiff, Gillam, as receiver of all right and interest of Gottlob and Howard G. Bender in and to the partnership, and also got an order charging their interest in the firm with payment of the judgment debt.

It is claimed for plaintiffs that the mortgages in question are void. The principal argument for defendants in support of the demurrer is that, whatever the status of the mortgages, neither plaintiff can question them. Decision depends upon construction of the Uniform Partnership Act.

. . . It appears that tenancy in partnership is a restricted adaptation of the common-law joint tenancy to the practical needs of the partnership relation. One of those needs arose from the formerly conflicting claims to specific partnership property of (1) separate creditors of a partner, and (2) assignees of a partner's share in an aliquot part of the firm assets. To meet that need, two simple "incidents" have been attached to the tenancy in partnership: (1) Expressly, the interest of each tenant or partner in specific partnership property is put beyond reach of his separate creditors; and (2) it has been made nonassignable. That means simply that the partner owner is deprived of all power of separate disposition even by will.

All a partner has now, subject to his power of individual disposition, and all that is subject to the claims of his separate creditors, is his interest, not in specific partnership property, but in the partnership itself. Plain is the purpose that all partnership property is to be kept intact for partnership purposes and creditors. . . .

It follows that a receiver, such as plaintiff Gillam, of a partner's "share of the profits," acting under a charging order and section 28, has the right in a proper action to have adjudicated the nullity of any mortgage or other assignment by some but not all of the partners of their interest in specific property of the partnership less than the whole. Such a receiver is entitled to any relief under the language of the statute "which the circumstances of the case may require" to accomplish justice under the law. Obviously, a part of such relief is the avoidance of any unauthorized attempt to dispose of partnership property. Such a receiver is entitled to the "share of profits and surplus" of the partner who happens to be the judgment debtor. While he is not entitled to share in the management of the firm as a partner, the receiver would be of little use if he could not protect "profits and surplus" by preventing such unauthorized and illegal dissipations of firm assets as the complaint alleges in this case. [DECISION FOR PLAINTIFF]

PROBLEMS

1 Brown, Cooper, Jones, and Smith entered into a partnership for the purpose of developing certain real estate. Brown, who was the owner of the land in question, conveyed an undivided three-fourths interest in the property to his partners. Cooper, Jones, and Smith, in return, executed in favor of Brown, a promissory note bearing interest at the rate of 6 percent, secured by mortgage, in payment for their interest in the land. Brown and Cooper, sometime thereafter, bought the interest of Jones and Smith in the partnership. Cooper thereby became liable for two-thirds of the mortgage indebtedness owed to Brown. An action was brought for an accounting. Is Cooper liable for interest on the mortgage debt owed to Brown?

2 Brown, Smith, and Jones formed a partnership whose articles provided that any partner who made advances to the partnership out of his private funds should be allowed interest at the rate of 6 percent until he was reimbursed. Brown advanced $12,000 for a period of one year for partnership purposes. The debt was overdue. Brown thereupon brought an action against Smith for $4,000. Decide.

3 Abbot and Cabot formed a partnership for the purpose of buying and selling small appliances such as refrigerators, ranges, washers, and dryers. Abbot thereafter individually purchased and operated a dairy farm, and made a considerable profit therefrom. Cabot contended that Abbot had breached his duty of loyalty and good faith to Cabot. Do you agree with this contention?

4   Jim and John were partners engaged in the business of operating the Manor Motel. Jim was on his vacation in Europe, and John moved a substantial number of pieces of furniture and other furnishings from the motel to his individual cottage on the lake without the consent of Jim. When Jim returned, he requested John to return the furniture and furnishings. John refused. Jim then brought a suit in equity for an accounting and dissolution of the partnership. Will he succeed?

5   Plaintiff and defendant were partners in the operation of a sanitarium. Defendant, in anticipation of acquiring the one-half interest of plaintiff, entered into an agreement with Brown by the terms of which Brown and defendant would become partners in the operation of the sanitarium. Shortly thereafter, Brown paid defendant $2,500 for a one-half interest in the business. Defendant thereupon acquired the one-half interest of plaintiff for $900. Defendant and Brown then became partners and entered upon the business of continuing the operation of the sanitarium. About seven months thereafter, plaintiff learned for the first time of these transfers. Plaintiff then brought an action against defendant to recover $1,600. Do you think he should recover?

6   Brown, one of two members of a partnership engaged in the business of farming and livestock production, borrowed $5,000 from the First Bank for the purpose of making improvements to his residence. In order to secure the loan, he gave the First Bank a mortgage covering his undivided one-half interest in the partnership property. The loan was not paid when it became due, and First Bank brought an action against Brown to foreclose the mortgage and requested the sheriff to seize and sell one-half of the partnership property to satisfy the loan. Explain whether or not the First Bank is pursuing the proper remedy to recover the $5,000.

7   Black and Decker operated a business of selling used automobiles. They sold a certain automobile to Cabot, who became disillusioned with it. Cabot called the partnership by telephone and stated to Decker that he was abandoning the automobile in a certain vacant lot in the city. The excuse for the abandonment was to the effect that the automobile ceased to operate and that it was not as it was represented by the seller. The wrecking truck of Black and Decker was being repaired. Decker therefore hired Davis to tow the car in to the lot for the consideration of $15. Decker paid Davis out of his personal funds since the safe had already been locked for the night. The next day Black objected to Decker being reimbursed out of partnership funds. Does Decker have a right of reimbursement?

40

PARTNERSHIP: DISSOLUTION, WINDING UP, TERMINATION

The dividing line between the terms "dissolution," "winding up," and "termination" is not always clearly drawn. It should prove helpful, therefore, to distinguish the terms from one another at the outset. As they are used in the Partnership Act, and as they are used here, "dissolution" designates the time when the partners cease to carry on the business together; "winding up" means the process of settling the partnership affairs; "termination" automatically takes place when the winding up is completed and is the end of the firm's life. It should be clearly understood, however, that winding up does not necessarily always follow dissolution. The business of a partnership is frequently carried on after dissolution—certainly in so far as the general public is concerned—in the same manner as if the partnership had not been dissolved. For purposes of clarity, therefore, it seems best to discuss (1) the causes of and grounds for dissolution, (2) the rights, duties, and liabilities of the partners when the business is continued after dissolution, and (3) the process of winding up the partnership and distributing the assets.

CAUSES OF, AND GROUNDS FOR, DISSOLUTION

The causes of, and grounds for, dissolution of a partnership are found in section 31 of the Partnership Act, and logically divide themselves into those that may bring about dissolution (1) without violation of the partnership agreement and (2) in contravention of the agreement.

Without Violation of the Agreement A partnership may be dissolved without violating the partnership agreement in four specific instances:

(1) When consent to dissolution is agreed upon in advance by the terms of the agreement which creates the partnership relation; a provision that the relation is to end at a specified future time will operate to dissolve the partnership when that date arrives. The same is true of a provision that the relation is to continue until some particular undertaking is accomplished.

(2) When the partnership is one at will; such a partnership has no definite duration, and may be dissolved by the will of any partner at any time. Some cases have held, however, that a partner who exercises the power to dissolve a partnership at will with unfair design must answer in damages.

(3) By mutual agreement of all the partners; this method of dissolution is nothing more than an application of the well-established general rule of the law of contracts which permits a mutual release to discharge a contract. The Partnership Act qualifies the general rule with one exception: The consent of any partner who assigns his interest, or permits a judgment to be taken against him and execution placed in the hands of the sheriff, is not necessary. The remaining partners may dissolve the partnership.

(4) By the expulsion of a partner when the partnership agreement so provides; the power must be exercised in good faith. Section 31 of the Partnership Act states the rule: "By the expulsion of any partner from the business bona fide in accordance with such a power conferred by the agreement between the partners."

Contravention of the Agreement The partnership may be dissolved in contravention of the partnership agreement by (1) the express will of any partner, (2) decree of court, and (3) operation of law.

(1) *Express Will of Any Partner* The majority of the cases at common law hold that a partner has the power to dissolve the partnership even though it is to exist for a definite period of time or for the accomplishment of a particular purpose. Section 31 of the Partnership Act has adopted this view by declaring that dissolution may be caused in contravention of the partnership agreement by the express will of any partner at any time. A partner who dissolves the partnership in contravention of his agreement, however, breaches his contract. He is therefore subject to liability for the harm he has caused, and the remaining partners may recover damages.

(2) *Decree of Court* There are many events that may be a valid reason for a partner to apply to the court for a dissolution of the partnership but which are so uncertain and subject to dispute as to make a judicial dissolution necessary. Section 32 of the Partnership Act provides that a partner may apply for a dissolution because of (1) insanity, (2) incapacity, (3) misconduct, (4) willful or

persistent breach of the partnership agreement, and (5) failure of the business. It is also provided that a purchaser of a partner's interest may apply for a dissolution (1) after the termination of the specified term or particular undertaking of the partnership or (2) when the interest was assigned or the charging order was issued if the partnership is a partnership at will.

A few cases have held that the adjudicated insanity of a partner automatically dissolves the partnership. The majority of the cases, however, hold that insanity is only a ground for applying to the court for a dissolution decree. Neither temporary insanity nor past insanity from which there has been a recovery is a proper ground for a judicial dissolution. It must be shown that a partner is so far disordered in his mind as to be incapable of carrying out the terms of the partnership agreement.

It is generally stated that the sickness of a partner is one of the risks incidental to the partnership relation. Any illness or other physical incapacity which is of a temporary nature, therefore, is not a sufficient ground for a dissolution decree. A court will decree a dissolution, however, where the infirmities of a partner are of such a nature as to render him incapable of discharging the partnership duties incumbent upon him.

Courts are cautious to dissolve a partnership for misconduct or failure of the business because it is impossible to draw a clear-cut dividing line between those acts that will and those acts that will not justify a dissolution. The facts and circumstances of the particular case are always controlling. It is quite clear, however, that temporary grievances, differences of opinion, errors in judgment, and similar trifling causes are not sufficient grounds for a dissolution decree. Among the acts which are generally held to be sufficient are fraudulent conduct, habitual drunkenness, the wrongful exclusion of one partner from participation in the management of the business, irreconcilable dissensions so as to endanger the partnership's goodwill and property, and impossibility or impracticability of carrying out the partnership enterprise without loss to the partners. In this connection, the distinction between the power, as opposed to the right, of dissolution in contravention of the partnership agreement should be kept in mind. [*Collins v. Lewis,* p. 527.]

(3) *Operation of Law* Section 31 of the Partnership Act provides that a partnership is dissolved by operation of law by illegality, bankruptcy of any partner, bankruptcy of the partnership, and death of any partner.

Illegality will cause dissolution automatically, first, by any event which makes the business of the partnership itself unlawful or, secondly, by any event which makes it unlawful for the members to carry on the business together. A common illustration of the first of these situations is where a partnership is conducting a liquor business at the time prohibition goes into effect. The second situation may be illustrated by a member of a law firm who incapacitates himself in the practice of law by becoming a judge.

The adjudication of bankruptcy of any partner, or of the partnership, operates to dissolve the partnership. The same is true of the death of any partner. This is a well-established rule, yet a few cases have said that partners may postpone dissolution by providing in the articles of partnership that death shall not work a dissolution. The majority of the cases hold, however, that a dissolution is effected by the death of a partner in spite of such an agreement.

CONTINUANCE OF BUSINESS

Any change in the membership of a partnership produces, technically, the immediate dissolution of the existing partnership and the formation of a new one. Turning then to the newly formed partnership which continues to carry on the same business as the dissolved partnership, it is appropriate to observe (1) the necessity of giving notice of dissolution, (2) the rights of the continuing partners, (3) the effect of dissolution on existing liabilities, and (4) the liability of an incoming partner.

Necessity of Giving Notice   The necessity of giving notice at common law is not as emphatic as under the Partnership Act. Section 35 of the Partnership Act demands that notice be given (1) to third persons and (2) to the nonacting partners.

(1)   *Third Persons*   The Partnership Act, in respect to the kind of notice that must be given, makes a distinction between third persons who have extended credit to the partnership prior to dissolution and those who have not extended credit but nevertheless knew of the partnership. The partners must give actual notice to third persons who have extended credit, and may give notice by publication to third persons who have not extended credit but who knew of the partnership. "Actual notice" requires actual delivery of the communication. It may be made by delivery through the mails or by other means of communication, but a letter that never arrives will not constitute actual notice. Notice by publication is satisfied when it is advertised in a newspaper of general circulation at the place or places where the partnership business was regularly carried on.

The causes of dissolution, with two exceptions, are immaterial under the Partnership Act. It is not necessary to give notice where the partnership is dissolved because it is unlawful to carry on the business. Nor is it necessary to give notice where the third person deals with the bankrupt partner himself. This is said to be for the reason that a person is supposed to know with whom he deals.

(2)   *The Partners*   Section 34 of the Partnership Act imposes a liability upon each partner for any contracts entered into by one of the partners after dissolution, first, if the acting partner had no knowledge of the dissolution where it is caused by an act of any partner, and, secondly, if the acting partner had no knowledge or notice of the dissolution where it is caused by death or bankruptcy.

In the first situation, A, B, and C are partners. A withdraws from the partnership; B, in ignorance of the dissolution, enters into a contract for the purchase of merchandise. B has a right to call upon A and C to share the price of the merchandise. If A wishes to escape liability, he must be able to prove that B had knowledge of the dissolution of the partnership at the time he entered into the contract.

In the second situation A, B, and C are partners. The partnership is dissolved by the death of A. B entered into a contract for the purchase of merchandise. B may call upon C and the representative of the estate of A to contribute toward the purchase price of the merchandise, if B acted in ignorance of the death of A. The representative of the estate of a deceased partner should give notice of the death of a partner. The same is true of bankruptcy.

Rights of Continuing Partners It was previously pointed out that a partner who exercises his power to dissolve a partnership in contravention of the partnership agreement must respond in damages to the remaining partners. To have a business brought to a premature end, however, is frequently a hardship on the remaining partners. They are, therefore, protected. Section 38 of the Partnership Act provides that the partners who have not caused the dissolution wrongfully may continue the business in the same name until the agreed term has expired or the undertaking has been completed, provided they pay the withdrawing partner the value of his interest in the partnership. The capital contribution of the withdrawing partner and any undivided profits, less any damages caused by the breach of the contract, are to be taken into consideration in ascertaining the value of the interest of the withdrawing partner. Goodwill is not to be taken into consideration. The remaining partners may accomplish the same result by securing payment at the later date by bond approved by the court. But they must, if they elect this alternative, indemnify the withdrawing partner against all present and future partnership liabilities.

Effect of Dissolution on Existing Liabilities Section 36 of the Partnership Act provides that the dissolution of a partnership does not of itself discharge the existing liability of any partner. This embraces all situations where the business of the old partnership is continued by any one partner or a combination of the partners without a liquidation of the partnership affairs. Suppose that Brown, Smith, and Jones are partners and that Brown retires and assigns his right in the partnership to Smith and Jones, who continue the business without any agreement to pay the partnership debts. This creates two sets of creditors: one set of creditors of the old partnership of Brown, Smith, and Jones and another set of creditors of the new partnership of Brown and Smith. Section 36 of the Partnership Act places the two sets of creditors on an equal basis.

The remedy against the partners personally remains. It is possible for the retiring partner and the continuing partners to agree as to who, among themselves, shall assume the existing liabilities. Such an arrangement, however, would not be binding on existing creditors. The same would be true even if notice of the agreement were given to the creditors. In order for the retiring partner to be discharged from his existing liabilities, an agreement to that effect must be entered into between the retiring partner, the continuing partners, and the creditor. Such an agreement, however, must satisfy all the requirements of a novation. [*Shunk v. Shunk Mfg. Co.,* p. 527.]

Liability of Incoming Partner The admittance of Jones as a new member into the existing partnership of Brown and Smith also creates two sets of creditors: one set of creditors of the old partnership of Brown and Smith and another set of creditors of the new partnership of Brown, Smith, and Jones. Section 17 of the

Partnership Act places the two sets of creditors on an equal basis so far as the partnership property is concerned. The new member's liability to the old creditors, therefore, is limited to his share in the partnership property. The result is that the old and new creditors have equal rights against the partnership property and the individual property of the previously existing members of the partnership, and only the new creditors have rights against the individual property of the new member. The incoming partner, to be sure, may expressly assume the old debts. The incoming partner may also find himself liable under general rules of some other branch of law. [*Ellingson v. Walsh, O'Connor & Barneson*, p. 528.]

THE WINDING-UP PROCESS

The process of winding up brings the life of the partnership to an end. Three questions are posed: Who has the right to wind up the partnership affairs? What are the powers of the person who has charge of the winding-up process? What are the rules for distribution?

Persons Who Have the Right to Wind Up The right to wind up the partnership affairs is vested in all the partners where the partnership is dissolved by agreement or by operation of its agreed term; the right is vested in the nonacting partner where dissolution is caused by the wrongful act of a partner; the right is vested in the nonbankrupt partner where the dissolution is caused by the bankruptcy of one of the partners; the right is vested in the surviving partners where dissolution is caused by death or, if such be the case, the representative of the last surviving partner. The court may, in its discretion, appoint a receiver to wind up the partnership affairs where it is shown to be to the best interests of all persons concerned.

Duties in Winding Up The person in charge of the winding-up process not only has the power but the duty to proceed promptly with the performance of those acts which are necessary to wind up the affairs. These acts include transactions, such as the completion of acts begun but left unfinished on dissolution, auditing the partnership accounts, selling the partnership property, collecting moneys due, and such other acts as the nature of the business and the circumstances of the particular case demand in order to liquidate and distribute the partnership assets. In this connection, two propositions deserve particular mention. The first is that in the absence of an agreement to the contrary the distribution will be in cash and not in kind. A partner who wishes the return of specific property should make sure that the partnership agreement includes a stipulation that he is entitled to its return. The second is that after payment of the partnership debts, the interest of the deceased partner in the real property descends to his heirs at common law. In those states that have not adopted the Partnership Act the surviving partner is authorized to sell only that portion of the real estate that is required to pay partnership debts. Real property, under sections 8 and 10 of the Partnership Act, passes on the death of a partner as personalty. [*Wharf v. Wharf*, p. 529.]

Rules of Distribution All of the partners, unless there is an express or implied agreement to the contrary, are entitled to share equally in the profits although the partners may have made unequal contributions to capital or services. The partners may agree on the basis on which the losses will be apportioned. In the absence of such an agreement, however, the partners will share in the losses in the same manner in which they share in the profits. It remains, therefore, to observe the rules for (1) the sharing of profits where the partnership is solvent, (2) the sharing of profits and losses where the partnership is insolvent, and (3) the sharing of losses where the partners, as well as the partnership, are insolvent.

(1) *Solvent Partnership* The assets of the solvent partnership will be distributed in the following order: (a) payment of partnership debts; (b) payment of claims of partners other than capital contributions and profits, such as advances; (c) payment of claims of partners in respect to capital contributions; and (d) distribution of whatever remains as profits.

(2) *Insolvent Partnership* In the firm of Brown, Smith, and Jones, suppose Brown contributed $6,000 capital. Smith contributed $4,000, and Jones contributed his services, and that liabilities to creditors exceed partnership assets by $8,000—an aggregate loss of $18,000. The partners bear this loss equally. Brown's capital contribution equalizes his one-third of the loss, but Smith must pay $2,000, and Jones must pay $6,000.

(3) *Insolvent Partnership and Insolvent Partners* The doctrine of marshaling assets is applicable where the individual partners, as well as the partnership, are insolvent. This doctrine gives partnership creditors priority over the individual creditors in the partnership assets and gives individual creditors priority over partnership creditors in the individual assets of the partners. The rule is sometimes succinctly stated: "Firm creditors in firm assets and individual creditors in individual assets." The firm creditors, however, are protected. The firm of Brown, Smith, and Jones is insolvent, and the individual creditors of Smith and Jones have exhausted all their individual assets. Brown, in the supposed firm above, would be required to pay the $8,000 loss, but, having done so, he would have a right to contribution against Smith for $2,000 and against Jones for $6,000.

The rule of marshaling assets is qualified by three well-recognized exceptions. The first exception pertains to dormant partners. If Brown deals with the public as the sole owner of the business, the partnership creditors and his individual creditors would share equally in whatever assets may be available. Firm creditors, in all likelihood, would not be paid in full. Smith and Jones, therefore, would be personally liable to the unpaid firm creditors. The second exception is where there are no firm assets and no living solvent partners. In these circumstances, the firm creditors and the individual creditors share equally in the distribution of the assets of the individual estate. The partnership of Brown, Smith, and Jones has no assets; Brown and Smith have no individual assets; Jones is deceased. Partnership creditors would share equally with the individual creditors of Jones. The third exception is where a partner has fraudulently converted the partnership assets to his own use. Firm creditors and individual creditors share equally in the individual assets of such partner.

CASES

Collins v. Lewis,   283 S.W.2d 258 (Tex. 1955). Action by Carr P. Collins, plaintiff, against John L. Lewis, defendant. The plaintiff and the defendant formed a partnership known as the "L-C Cafeteria" to exist for a term of thirty years. As a part of the undertaking, Collins agreed to furnish all of the funds necessary to build, equip, and open the cafeteria for business; Lewis agreed to plan and supervise such construction and to manage the operation of the cafeteria after it was opened for business. Disputes arose between the partners, and Collins brought this action for a judicial dissolution of the partnership. The jury found:

Lewis was competent to manage the business of the L-C cafeteria; that there is not a reasonable expectation of profit under the continued management of Lewis; that but for the conduct of Collins there would be a reasonable expectation of profit under the continued management of Lewis.

> **Hamblen, Chief Justice:**   We agree . . . that there is no such thing as an indissoluble partnership only in the sense that there always exists the power, as opposed to the right, of dissolution. But legal right to dissolution rests in equity, as does the right to relief from the provisions of any legal contract. The jury finding that there is not a reasonable expectation of profit from the L-C Cafeteria under the continued management of Lewis, must be read in connection with their findings that Lewis is competent to manage the business of L-C Cafeteria, and that but for the conduct of Collins there would be a reasonable expectation of profit therefrom. In our view those are the controlling findings upon the issue of dissolution. It was Collins' obligation to furnish the money; Lewis' to furnish the management, guaranteeing a stated minimum repayment of the money. The jury has found that he was competent, and could reasonably have performed his obligation but for the conduct of Collins. We know of no rule which grants Collins, under such circumstances, the right to dissolution of the partnership.
> . . . We have already pointed out the ever present inherent power, as opposed to the legal right, of any partner to terminate the relationship. Pursuit of that course presents the problem of possible liability for such damages as flow from the breach of contract. [DECISION FOR DEFENDANT]

Shunk v. Shunk Mfg. Co.,   93 N.E.2d 321 (Ohio 1949). Action by Shunk, plaintiff, against Shunk Manufacturing Company, defendant. Three partnerships are involved all of which operated under the name of Shunk Manufacturing Company. The first will be referred to as the "old partnership," the second as the "McGraw partnership," and the third as the "successor partnership." The old partnership, of which plaintiff was a member, sold its business to the McGraw partnership. The plaintiff and the McGraw partnership thereafter entered into an employment contract dated September 1, 1943, by the terms of which plaintiff was employed as general manager of the business from August 1, 1943, to July 31, 1945, for the sum of $50,000 payable in monthly installments. On September 2, 1943, an announcement was posted on the stationery of Shunk Manufacturing Company carrying the name of plaintiff as general manager. The announcement was also to the effect that Arthur E. Socin had been appointed general superintendent with full authority and responsibility for the management of all shop operations and that Arno W. McGraw had been appointed treasurer and office manager with full responsibility of treasurer and accounting and office procedure. The announcement stated that the entire shop personnel would receive all orders directly from Socin and the entire office personnel would receive orders from McGraw. Plaintiff construed the announcement as depriving him of authority and responsibility over the shop and office.

The contract also provided that if the company should discharge him without good and just legal cause, the company would, within thirty days from such event, pay the plaintiff the unpaid balance of the $50,000. On March 31, 1944, the McGraw partnership was sold to the successor partnership without notice or knowledge on the part of plaintiff, which sale was a voluntary dissolution of the partnership and which therefore terminated plaintiff's employment without fault on his part. From September, 1943, to April, 1944, plaintiff spent a limited number of hours at the plant, following the same schedule he had observed prior to the sale, but after April 1, 1944, he reported at the plant with less frequency and remained for shorter periods of time. Plaintiff says he had no authority to do anything and was ignored by the personnel. On December 31, 1944, plaintiff, still without notice or knowledge of the successor partnership, was notified that his employment contract was terminated. Plaintiff, having received no compensation since December 31, 1944, brought this action against the McGraw partnership to recover the unpaid balance due under the employment contract.

Fess, Judge: A retiring partner remains liable for all the existing debts of the firm, to the same extent as if he had not retired. . . .

As between the members, the new partnership could continue the business of Shunk Manufacturing Company, but as to strangers, the legal status of the McGraw partnership ceased to exist except for the purpose of winding up its affairs. Plaintiff's employment contract could not be assigned to the new partnership without his consent, and the evidence does not indicate it was so assigned or that plaintiff ever agreed to work for the new partnership. Nor was plaintiff obligated to work for the defendant incident to the winding up of its affairs. Under such circumstances, the payment by the successor partnership of plaintiff's salary from April 1 to December 31, 1944, did not create a novation or relieve the defendant of its obligation to plaintiff under its contract. . . .

In the instant case the employment contract provided that should the plaintiff be discharged "without good and just legal cause, then the company shall, within thirty days from the happening of any of said events, pay the party of the second part, or to his estate," etc. It therefore follows that, since plaintiff was discharged without good and just legal cause on March 31, 1944, as a matter of law the defendant became obligated to pay plaintiff within 30 days the unpaid balance due upon his contract. [DECISION FOR PLAINTIFF]

Ellingson v. Walsh, O'Connor & Barneson, 104 P.2d 507 (Cal. 1940). Action by Ellingson, receiver of the First National Bank of Beverly Hills, plaintiff, against

Walsh, O'Connor & Barneson, a copartnership, and others, defendants. Lionel T. Barneson is the appellant. The First National Bank of Beverly Hills became the holder of a lease of which the partnership of Walsh, O'Connor & Company was the lessee. On April 28, 1931, appellant Lionel T. Barneson was taken in as a partner, and the new partnership paid the rent up to March, 1932. This action was brought to recover the rent claimed to be due for the period commencing March 1, 1932, and ending January 25, 1933. The lower court rendered a judgment against the partnership and all of its members, and Lionel T. Barneson has appealed. He claims that, as an incoming partner, his personal assets cannot be reached in satisfaction of the judgment.

Gibson, Chief Justice: The issue in this case is not the liability of the partnership as such, nor the liability of its assets. There is no doubt whatever that the plaintiff may satisfy his claim against the partnership out of any of its properties. The sole question is whether the appellant's liability as an incoming partner may be satisfied by resort to his personal assets. . . . Appellant contends that since the lease was executed before he became a partner, the obligation of the lease arose before his admission, and therefore his liability can only be satisfied out of partnership property.

This contention would be sound if the only obligation of the partnership in this transaction was one which arose prior to appellants' admission to the firm. . . . When appellant became a member, the first partnership was, in legal theory, dissolved and a new partnership came into being composed of the old members and appellant. This second partnership did not expressly assume the obligations of the lease, but it occupied the premises. Whether it was liable contractually on the lease is immaterial; it became liable for rent as a tenant. Strangers coming in with consent and occupying the premises would be liable; tenants would be liable even if there were no lease at all; and this second partnership and all its members were liable regardless of any lack of assumption of the obligations of the lease.

. . . Appellant's theory is that he, as a member of the second partnership, may receive the benefits of years of occupancy under the lease, but that his personal assets cannot be reached in satisfaction of liability therefor if the lease was executed before he became a member of the partnership. . . . Under the general law the obligation of a tenant arising from occupation of the premises is a continuing one; that is, it arises and binds him continually throughout the period of his occupation. This obligation on the part of appellant first arose when the new partnership, of which he was a member, occupied the premises as a tenant. It follows that his obligation as a tenant arose after his admission to the partnership. [DECISION FOR PLAINTIFF]

Wharf v. Wharf, 137 N.E. 446 (Ill. 1922). Action by Eugene C. Wharf, plaintiff, against Edith Stone Wharf, administratrix of the estate of James E. Wharf, and others, defendants. Plaintiff and his father, James E. Wharf, formed a partnership for the purchase of real estate to be improved and sold for their mutual benefit. The title to the land was taken in the names of both partners individually. James E. Wharf died on October 25, 1921. Plaintiff brought this action asking that he, as surviving partner, be authorized to complete the unfinished business of the partnership by carrying out the contracts of sale, executing deeds, and releasing mortgages as the debts were paid. He further asked the court to decree that he was vested, free from all dower rights, with an undivided half of fifty-eight lots which had not been sold and which would not be needed for the settlement of the partnership, and that the remaining half was vested in the heirs of decedent. The disputed question is whether a one-half interest in the fifty-eight lots is vested in plaintiff and the remainder in the heirs of the decedent or whether the lots pass as personal property. The heirs of decedent claimed that the real estate passed as personal property.

Cartwright, Justice: The rule of nearly all courts in the United States is that real estate is to be regarded as personal property only for the business of the partnership and the settlement of its affairs, and, when no longer needed for that purpose, the ordinary incidents and quality of real estate revive and the property goes according to the statute of descent. . . .

That being the state of the law, the Legislature in 1917 passed an act entitled "An Act relating to partnerships and to promote uniformity in the law with reference thereto." [The Uniform Partnership Act] . . . The Act made material changes in the law of this state relating to partnerships.

. . . The provision that a partner's interest in the partnership is his share of the profits and surplus, and the same is personal property, and that, when dissolution is caused by death, each partner, as against his copartner and all persons claiming through them; in respect to their interest in the partnership, unless otherwise agreed, may have the partnership property applied to discharge its liabilities and the surplus applied to pay in cash the net amount owing to the respective partners, is inconsistant with the doctrine heretofore held that upon the settlement of the partnership affairs real estate resumes its original character and descends to heirs. It seems that the legislative intention was to adopt the English rule that real estate which becomes personal property for the purposes of a partnership remains personal property for the purpose of distribution.

. . . The title of his partner in the specific partnership property having vested in him, plaintiff has a right to convey to purchasers, release mortgages, sell and convey the property, and distribute the proceeds. [DECISION FOR DEFENDANTS]

PROBLEMS

1 Clark retired from the partnership of Clark, Wood & Hall. Wood and Hall assumed the outstanding debts of the partnership and paid Clark the value of his interest. Freeman was then admitted to the partnership, and the business was continued under the partnership name of "Wood, Hall & Freeman." What are the rights of unpaid creditors of the partnership of Clark, Wood & Hall?

2 Plaintiff and defendant are partners. Plaintiff brought an action for the dissolution of the partnership. The evidence revealed that the partners disagreed on matters of policy relating to the operation of the business; that constant dissension over money affairs culminated in defendant's appropriating small sums of money from the partnership funds to his own use and in so doing set aside a like amount for plaintiff; that defendant declined to do any substantial amount of the work required for the successful operation of the business; and that defendant informed plaintiff that he, the defendant, "had not worked yet in forty-seven years and did not intend to start now." The defendant invokes the general rule that trifling and minor differences will not authorize a court to decree a dissolution of the partnership. Decide.

3 Plaintiff sold and delivered certain merchandise on credit to defendants, Fiedler & Sullivan, individually and as partners trading as "Fied-Sul Paper Mills." The defendants thereafter organized a corporation which took over the partnership business. The plaintiff, unaware that a corporation had been organized, continued to extend credit and deliver merchandise as had been done prior to the formation of the corporation. Plaintiff brought an action against Fiedler and Sullivan as individuals to recover for the merchandise so sold. Decide.

4 Plaintiff and defendant entered into a partnership agreement on December 2, 1940, for the purpose of manufacturing machinists' tools. Plaintiff was to be in charge of the shop, and defendant was to be in charge of the office and the partnership books of account. In December, 1941, plaintiff sustained a physical injury and was unable to supervise the work in the shop until the following February. When plaintiff returned to work, he found defendant had hired a new crew of men in the shop. Defendant had built a partition through the building occupied by the partnership and began to conduct an individual enterprise in the south side of the building. The building was then so arranged that it had but one entrance door, and defendant changed the lock on the door so that plaintiff could not enter. Plaintiff was told by defendant that he did not want plaintiff interfering with the work in the shop or seeing "what they were doing." Defendant thereafter took over the entire management and control of the partnership business, and plaintiff was excluded from any participation therein. What remedy, if any, is available to plaintiff?

5 The partnership of Brown, Jones, and Smith and all three members individually, were adjudged bankrupts. No assets remained in the estates of Brown and Jones after the necessary expenses of administration had been paid. As to the estate of Smith and the partnership, however, there remained the sums of $1,600 and $2,000, respectively. Are the creditors of the partnership entitled to share in the assets remaining in the estate of Smith with Smith's personal creditors?

6 Brown, Jones, and Smith were equal partners in a partnership at will engaged in the business of buying and selling air conditioners. Smith was personally indebted to Linder in the amount of $2,000, and the court had granted Linder a judgment for that amount. The judgment was unsatisfied, and the court awarded Linder a charging order as a means of satisfying the judgment. Smith was unsatisfied with this arrangement and applied to the court for a decree dissolving the partnership so as to determine what interest he had in the partnership. Should the court grant the decree?

7 Daniel and Downing, the members of a partnership in the business of buying and selling farm supplies, agreed to dissolve the partnership. Daniel and Downing each had contributed $5,000 to the capital of the partnership when the partnership was formed, and Daniel had advanced $2,000 to the partnership at a later date. The assets of the partnership amounted to $20,000 at the time of dissolution, and the partnership was indebted to creditors in the amount of $1,000. Discuss the order in which the $20,000 should be distributed.

41
LIMITED PARTNERSHIP

The limited partnership, which is a modified form of partnership, has been recognized by most of the states by the enactment of limited partnership statutes. These statutes are not entirely uniform. A Uniform Limited Partnership Act, however, has been adopted in over three-fourths of the states. This Limited Partnership Act serves as a convenient source for the material presented in this chapter.

Nature of Limited Partnership A limited partnership is a form of business organization which consists of one or more persons, known as "limited partners," who do not participate in the management of the business and are not personally liable to creditors and one or more persons, known as "general partners," who conduct the business and are personally liable to creditors. A limited partnership, in the absence of statute to the contrary, may carry on any business which could be carried on by a general partnership. Some state statutes, however, expressly exclude certain types of business such as banking and insurance.

Formation of Limited Partnership A limited partnership, as contrasted to a general partnership, may not be created by a mere informal agreement. It is strictly a creature of statute, and the statutory formal proceedings must be followed. The Limited Partnership Act provides that two or more persons desiring to form a limited partnership must sign and swear to a certificate, which shall state the partnership name; the character and location of the business; the names and places of residence of the general and limited partners; the term for which the partnership is to exist; the amount of cash and a description, with the agreed value, of other property contributed or agreed to be contributed by each limited partner; the time, if agreed upon, when the contributions of each limited partner are to be returned; the share of profits or other compensation which each limited partner shall receive; the right, if given, of a limited partner to substitute an assignee as contributor in his place; the right, if given, of the partners to admit additional limited partners; the right, if given, of one or more of the limited partners to priority over other limited partners as to contributions or compensation; the right, if given, of the remaining general partners to continue the business on the death, retirement, or insanity of a general partner; and the right, if given, of a limited partner to demand and receive property other than cash in return for his contribution.

Filing or Recording Certificate   The words of the statutes vary in details with respect to the place where the certificate must be filed. As a general proposition, however, the certificate must be filed in the office of some public official of the county in which the principal place of business of the partnership is located. If the partnership maintains offices in other counties, however, certified copies of the certificate must be filed in each such county. The Act does not require publication of the certificate in a newspaper. Many of the states have, nevertheless, added the requirement of publication. The purpose of requiring filing of the certificate is to give persons dealing with the partnership actual or constructive notice of the limited liability of the limited partners.

Partnership Name   The Act disallows the use of the surname of a limited partner in the partnership name. It may be done, however, if the surname of the limited partner is also the surname of a general partner, or if the surname was already used in the partnership name prior to the time the limited partner became a partner. The limited partner who allows the use of his surname in the partnership name is liable, as a general partner, to creditors of the partnership who had no actual knowledge that he was not a general partner.

Rights and Liabilities of General Partner   A general partner has all the rights and is subject to all the restrictions and liabilities of a partner in a partnership without limited partners. The Act, however, enumerates certain specific things which a general partner, without the written consent of all the limited partners, has no authority to do. He may not do the following: perform any act in contravention of the certificate; perform any act which would make it impossible to carry on the ordinary business of the partnership; confess a judgment against the partnership; possess partnership property for other than partnership purposes; admit a person as a general or a limited partner; continue the business with partnership property on the death, retirement, or insanity of a general partner.

Rights and Liabilities of Limited Partner   The Limited Partnership Act expressly authorizes the limited partner to inspect and copy the partnership books; to have, on demand, true and full information of all things affecting the partnership; to have the partnership dissolved by decree of court; to receive a share of the profits; to receive the return of his contribution; to lend money to and transact other business with the partnership; to receive on account of resulting claims against the partnership, with general creditors, on a pro rata basis; and to receive partnership property as collateral security. The Act also authorizes a limited partner to make his capital contribution in cash or in property. A contribution in services, however, is specifically disallowed.

The Act expressly provides that a limited partner shall not become liable as a general partner unless, in addition to the exercise of his rights and powers as a limited partner, he takes part in the control of the business. The law with respect to those acts that may and those that may not constitute an exercise of "control" over the partnership affairs, however, has not been fully developed.

Dissolution   The Limited Partnership Act contains no extensive provisions furnishing grounds which would justify dissolution of the partnership. It has been held, however, that a limited partner was entitled to dissolution when the partnership business was carried on at a loss. The Act expressly provides for priority in the distribution of the assets after dissolution. General creditors are entitled to first distribution, and limited partners take priority over general partners.

PROBLEMS

1 Plaintiff brought an action against the copartners of a limited partnership to recover damages for fraud. One partner denied liability on the ground that he was a limited partner. The evidence revealed that the general partner made false representations to plaintiff concerning the business and assets of the partnership, thereby inducing plaintiff to invest $10,000 in the partnership, and that the limited partner authorized the general partner to proceed with the negotiations. Is the limited partner liable?

2 The certificate of a limited partnership recited that the capital contribution of the defendant, a limited partner, was of the agreed value of $25,000. The property which the defendant contributed to the partnership was, in fact, less than one-half that amount. Plaintiff, after obtaining legal advice that the limited partner would be liable to the extent of the $25,000, extended credit to the partnership. Would the defendant be liable as a general partner under a statute which provided that a limited partner shall be liable as a general partner for false statements in the certificate if he knew the statement was false and that the claimant suffered loss by reliance on such false statement?

3 Davis, Mayer, and Sterling entered into an oral agreement to form a limited partnership whereby Davis and Mayer would be the general partners and Sterling would be a limited partner. Sterling refused to enter into such an agreement unless it was agreed and understood that he was unwilling to assume the unlimited liability of a general partner. Each partner contributed $10,000, and the business was operated successfully for two years. Economic difficulties, however, began to develop until $45,000 was owed to various creditors, who brought an action to recover from all three partners. Sterling contends that he has no liability. Is his contention correct?

4 Brown and Jones entered into an agreement to create a limited partnership, Brown being the general partner and Jones being the limited partner. The partnership became indebted to Smith, which indebtedness was not paid when it became due. Smith thereupon brought an action against Brown and Jones as general partners. Jones pleaded as a defense that the certificate of partnership disclosed that he was a limited partner. Smith then proved that the certificate had not been filed. Should Smith recover from Jones?

42

CORPORATIONS: INTRODUCTION; PROMOTERS

Each corporation in the early days of the United States was chartered by a special legislative act. This made it necessary to obtain a special act of the legislature each time businessmen entered into the corporate form of business organization. This procedure was wholly inadequate to take care of American business opportunities. Corporations needed to be more expeditiously chartered. The problem was solved by the enactment of corporation statutes which would permit incorporation without resort to the favor of the legislature. The legislatures in all the states today have enacted a variety of corporation statutes. A common plan of legislation is the enactment of general corporation statutes with broad provisions under which corporations may be incorporated for most businesses and, in addition, one or more special statutes for the incorporation of some specialized type of business or some special type of organization.

The American Bar Association has proposed a Model Business Corporation Act, which has been the basis for the corporation statutes in several of the states and has been enacted into law in some of the states. There is no uniform act, but the statutes do follow a general pattern. The corporation statutes, therefore, provide a convenient framework for the material presented on this subject. This chapter will be devoted to (1) a brief observation of the general nature of corporations, (2) the relation of the corporation to the state, (3) the distinguishing characteristics of the different kinds of corporations, (4) the promoters and their expenses, (5) the formalities prescribed by statute for incorporation, and (6) liability on preincorporation contracts.

NATURE OF A CORPORATION

The courts, in developing the law of corporations, advanced many theories in an effort to explain the "true nature" of a corporation. A reading of the reported decisions, however, reveals that the corporate entity theory is the one most used by the courts today in solving legal problems. This theory conceives a corporation as being a legal entity, separate and distinct from its stockholders. Suppose A, B, and C own all the shares of stock in the ABC Corporation. The corporation is an entirely distinct legal entity from A, B, and C. If D lends money to the corporation, he must look to the corporation for repayment. He cannot look to A, B, or C individually. The corporation, moreover, may enter into contracts with its own shareholders and may sue and be sued by them as a separate and distinct legal entity. The legal consequences which result from the conception of a corporation as a legal entity provide fruitful sources of litigation throughout the law of corporations. This theory, therefore, should be kept in mind.

The very nature of a corporation, as well as the statutes of the several states, prohibits a corporation from practicing a learned profession, for the reason that a learned profession can be practiced only by natural persons who have received a license to do so after an examination as to their knowledge of the subject. A corporation, therefore, cannot engage in the practice of law, medicine, surgery, or dentistry. It is also true that a corporation cannot engage in the practice of the learned professions through employees or other persons who are licensed. It has frequently been said that the practice of medicine by a corporation for profit through the employment of licensed practitioners has a tendency to debase the profession and is, therefore, contrary to public policy. In recent years, however, federal legislation has been enacted to give the members of the learned professions and other self-employed groups equality of the tax treatment given to employees covered by employer-financed pension plans. As a result of this federal legislation, several states have authorized the learned professions to incorporate as professional service corporations. The individual practitioner, however, must still comply with all the rules and canons of professional ethics.

It should also be mentioned that a corporation is held to be a person under some provisions of the United States Constitution, but a corporation does not have the status of a citizen for all purposes. A corporation is not a citizen within the meaning of Article IV, section 2, which provides that "the citizens of each state shall be entitled to all the privileges and immunities of citizens in the several states." A corporation is likewise not a citizen within the meaning of the Fourteenth Amendment, which provides that "no state shall make or enforce any law which shall abridge the privileges or immunities of citizens of the United States." A natural person, for example, has the privilege of going into any state in the United States and of there conducting a business on the same terms and conditions as any citizen of that state. A corporation does not have this privilege.

A corporation, however, is treated as a person under the Fourteenth Amendment, which provides "nor shall any state deprive any person of life, liberty, or property without due process of law; nor deny to any person within its jurisdiction the equal protection of the laws." It is likewise true that a corporation, for purposes of jurisdiction, is "a citizen of any state by which it has been incorporated and of the state where it has its principal place of business." The rule whereby a citizen may bring an action at law or a suit in equity in the federal courts provided the plaintiff and defendant are citizens of different states and the controversy exceeds $10,000, exclusive of interest and costs, is therefore applicable to corporations.

RELATION TO THE STATE

The relation between the corporation and the state permeates the entire field of the law of corporations. It begins with the promotion of the corporation and continues until the corporation is terminated. The United States Supreme Court in 1819, in the celebrated case of *Dartmouth College v. Woodward*, 4 Wheat. (U.S.) 518, held that the charter of the corporation was a contract between the state and the college and, as such, was entitled to the protection of the United States Constitutional provision prohibiting any state from enacting any law which would impair the obligations of a contract. A charter granted by the state to a corporation, therefore, is a contract between the state and the corporation. But it is appropriate to observe that the states, when granting a charter, frequently reserve the right to amend or modify the charter whenever the state may deem it necessary. The state may not amend or modify the charter, however, in the absence of this reservation.

KINDS OF CORPORATIONS

Corporations have been classified in many ways depending upon the element in them which is emphasized. One classification, however, frequently cuts across the lines of another classification. Rather than attempt a classification of corporations, therefore, it seems more appropriate to merely describe the various kinds of corporations.

Government Corporations   Government, or public, corporations are created for public purposes. They are generally considered to be an agency or instrumentality of the government and are used by the United States and by the states. They include various lines of governmental activity. They are sometimes used in the administration of the government. An incorporated county, city, or town—generally referred to as a municipal corporation—are illustrations of corporations used in the administration of the government. They are sometimes used to operate and conduct a public business, such as the Reconstruction Finance Corporation or the Tennessee Valley Authority.

Corporations for Profit   A corporation for profit is the ordinary business corporation created and operated for the purpose of making a profit which may be distributed to the shareholders in dividends. A corporation for profit may be a "close corporation" or a "public-issue corporation." The close corporation, or family corporation, is a corporation whose shares are held by a few shareholders or by a single individual. The associates might all be members of the same family or members of two or more families. Most close corporations are small business enterprises, but the shares in some large corporations also are held by a closely knit group of shareholders. The shareholders are generally active in the management of the business of a close corporation, and there are no voting shares in the hands of the public. The close corporation and the corporation with public shareholders are basically different, but both are generally incorporated in pursuance of and governed by the general corporation statutes. Many of the state legislatures have, however, enacted statutes which provide especially for the incorporation of some particular class of business, such as banks, railroads, insurance companies, and building and loan associations.

Corporations Not for Profit   Most of the state legislatures have enacted statutes which provide especially for the formation of corporations not for profit. These statutes provide a convenient method of holding property. They embrace charitable, educational, recreational, social, and similar organizations. These organizations do not contemplate the distribution of dividends to their members on invested capital. They are sometimes referred to as nonstock or membership corporations. Many cooperative associations are formed in pursuance of these corporations-not-for-profit statutes. This kind of corporation, however, should not be confused with a nonprofit association.

Nonprofit Association   Nonprofit unincorporated associations embrace a large variety of charitable, social, political, and trade associations. These associations are formed to advance the interest of their members, and being unincorporated, lack the capacity to hold title to property. The title to the property of the association, therefore, is generally held by trustees.

De Jure and De Facto Corporations   Corporations are generally classified, with respect to the extent of their compliance with the incorporation statutes, as corporations de jure and corporations de facto.

   (1) *De Jure Corporations*   A corporation de jure is said to be one so perfectly formed that the validity of its organization cannot be successfully attacked in a direct proceeding by the state. A corporation de facto, on the other hand, is said to be one whose organization is defective to the extent that it may be successfully attacked by the state. This means that the state may bring a proceeding, called a "quo warranto" proceeding, for the particular purpose of testing the existence of the corporation de facto and, if the circumstances so justify, oust the corporation from the unauthorized exercise of corporate powers. To say then that there is a corporation de facto is merely to say that a corporation

has been formed which the courts will recognize as a corporation for all purposes except the state of incorporation.

The general rule says "substantial" compliance is all that is required to defeat a quo warranto proceeding. It would indeed be hazardous, however, to attempt to draw the dividing line between those defects in incorporation that will or will not satisfy the substantial compliance rule. It has been held that where notice of the first meeting of the shareholders was given but not in the precise manner set forth in the statute there was not a sufficient basis to support a quo warranto proceeding. The same holding has been reached when the corporation failed to comply with a statute which required that the statement of incorporation be under seal. The failure of one of the incorporators to acknowledge his signature has been held to be a sufficient basis to support a quo warranto proceeding.

(2) *De Facto Corporations* A de facto corporation, insofar as third persons are concerned, possesses all the powers of a de jure corporation. It may enter into contracts, sue and be sued, and do all other things necessary to corporate existence. The chief problem pertaining to the relation between a defectively formed corporation and third persons arises when persons presume to do business as a corporation without having gone far enough in their organization attempt to create even a corporation de facto. The problem commonly arises in suits by creditors, the issue being whether the shareholders of the alleged corporation are liable on the corporate debts. The attribute of limited liability of shareholders, therefore, is challenged.

The essential elements of de facto corporate existence are the existence of a valid statute under which the corporation can be formed, an actual exercise or use of corporate powers, and colorable substantial compliance in good faith with the statutory requirements. The first of these elements is rarely litigated today. The second element is not likely to be seriously litigated if the associates have tried to incorporate and, after so trying, have engaged in any business activity. The decisions are in conflict with respect to the third element. The courts are not agreed over such defects as the execution of the articles of incorporation, failure to file the certificate of incorporation, failure to pay in capital, and many other miscellaneous defects. A few generalizations may be deduced from the decided cases by approaching the problem from the standpoint of whether the associates have dealt with third persons on a corporate basis or on an individual basis. One line of decisions holds that regardless of the nature of the defect, the associates are personally liable if the dealings were on an individual basis. Another line of decisions holds that if the articles are filed with the proper state official, the shareholders have limited liability if the dealings were on a corporate basis. Still another line of decisions holds that if no attempt has been made to incorporate, the associates are personally liable irrespective of whether or not the dealings were on a corporate basis.

This does not mean that all is chaotic. Modern incorporation statutes have eliminated much of the confusion. Many of the state statutes make the issuance of a certificate of incorporation by the secretary of state conclusive evidence of corporate existence except against the state. The general rule, moreover, is well established that third persons may not collaterally challenge de facto existence. [*Adler Slope Ditch Co. v. Moonshine Ditch Co.*, p. 546.]

Corporations by Estoppel   Sometimes a third class of corporations is recognized, namely, corporations by estoppel. This class of corporations, however, is not based upon the same principles as are corporations de facto and de jure. Corporations by estoppel are based upon the principal that one who deals with an apparent corporation in such manner as to recognize its corporate existence is thereby estopped from denying the fact thus admitted. The maker of a promissory note may give the note to an apparent corporation. The maker would be estopped from contending that the apparent corporation was not a corporation. It is obvious that an organization which has not complied with the conditions precedent to even de facto existence is not a corporation for any purpose. The expression "corporation by estoppel" merely means that the incidents of corporate existence may exist between the parties by virtue of estoppel.

Foreign Corporations   Corporations are classified with respect to the state of their incorporation as domestic and foreign. To the state of its incorporation, a corporation is a domestic corporation; to all other states and countries, it is a foreign corporation. A corporation which has been incorporated in one state is subject to the legislative and judicial jurisdiction of another state when it carries on business in that other state.

(1)   *Legislative Jurisdiction*   The states have enacted statutes which must be complied with before a corporation is permitted to do business within the state. The words "doing business" mean intrastate business. The foreign corporation is frequently required to file its charter and bylaws with some state official, pay certain fees and taxes, and designate some person in the state to act as agent for service of process upon the foreign corporation. The statutes of most states impose some kind of penalty on foreign corporations which do business within the state without complying with the foreign-corporation laws. A foreign corporation may, however, engage in interstate commerce without the consent of the state; at the same time it may be subject to local taxation. A foreign corporation owning property within the state would be required to pay the property tax levied by the state. Some state statutes have attempted to define "doing business," but the words are more often subject to judicial interpretation.

(2)   *Judicial Jurisdiction*   The court decisions are not uniform with respect to the extent of a state's judicial jurisdiction over a foreign corporation which has not formally qualified to "do business," or "transact business," in the state. An agent of a foreign corporation who goes into a state and performs a series of transactions is frequently said to be "doing business" within the state. The problem, however, remains: What constitutes doing business? The solution to the problem depends primarily upon the facts of each particular case, considered in the light of the pertinent state statute and the commerce clause and the due process clause of the United States Constitution. It is, therefore, impossible to state any general rule as to what constitutes doing business in a state by a foreign

corporation. The problem of doing business finds its most frequent application when a resident of the state attempts to subject the corporation to due process by bringing an action against the corporation. Almost any activity within a state by a foreign corporation can subject the corporation to the state's personal jurisdiction over the cause of action arising from such activity. A proper service of process frequently presents a further problem. In the states that do not have statutes providing for it, service of process can only be made if some corporate officer, director, or managing agent can be found and served in the state. Most of the states, however, have statutes designating the secretary of state or some other official as the agent of foreign corporations for the purpose of service of process. [*Boney v. Trans-State Dredging Co.*, p. 547.]

PROMOTERS AND EXPENSES

A corporation, before it can become a legal entity, must have someone to plan its organization, to solicit subscriptions to its shares of stock, to acquire property for its use, to negotiate contracts for its operation, to complete the actual incorporation process, and to perform all other activities necessary to establish the corporation for the prosecution of its business. This is the function of the promoter. The relation between the corporation and the promoter begins before the corporation comes into existence and ordinarily ends when the business is turned over to the board of directors for operation as a going business. The promoter must (1) make some kind of an arrangement for compensation for his services and for reimbursement for any money he expends in the promotion of the corporation, but (2) the general rule says, in doing so, he must not make a secret profit.

Compensation and Repayment The courts, apparently prompted by the desire to compel the corporation to pay the necessary expenses of its creation, have advanced several views in an effort to accomplish this result. A few courts take the view that a promise by the corporation to pay after its organization and acceptance of benefits will be implied when promoters render services and incur expenses with the understanding that they are to be paid conpensation for such services and reimbursed for such expenses. A few cases have suggested that the corporation, when it comes into existence, ought to pay for the reasonable value of the promoter's services on the theory of quasi contract. This suggestion, however, is generally rejected on the practical ground of policy against imposition upon innocent investors. But investors cannot say they are innocent when they are faced with a statutory or charter provision. Some state statutes, therefore, expressly provide that the corporation when it comes into existence shall be liable for the necessary expenses of its promotion. The charter of the proposed corporation likewise sometimes contains a similar provision. One further source of recovery is an express promise to pay on the part of the fully organized corporation. In developing this phase of the law, the courts had difficulty in finding consideration to support such a promise. Lack of consideration today, however, is generally held to be no defense. An express promise on the part of the management of the corporation after it has been fully organized, therefore, is enforced in most states today. But the corporation, according to the general rule, is not liable for the services and expenses of its promoters in the absence of a statutory or charter provision or an express promise.

Fiduciary Relationship   During the promotion of a corporation, the promoters owe a fiduciary duty to one another. The fiduciary relation does not prevent the promoter from making a profit, but he may not make a secret profit. His dealings must be open and fair, and he must disclose fully all material facts and must advise those with whom he deals of any interest that he may have in the proposed corporation. After the corporation is organized, the promoter is under the duty of good faith and full disclosure to the board of directors and to all other persons interested in the corporation. Innocent shareholders and creditors who have been defrauded by the promoter could assert a direct action against the promoter. A full disclosure to an independent board of directors will suffice insofar as the corporation is concerned. Frequently, however, an independent board of directors is not elected. [*Frick v. Howard*, p. 548.]

The duties and liabilities of promoters are not ordinarily governed by statute, but the state "blue sky laws" and the Federal Securities Act of 1933 require full disclosure by promoters when public offerings are made. This legislation, coupled with administrative regulation, minimizes unfair dealings by promoters. These state blue sky laws, the Federal Securities Act of 1933, and the Securities Exchange Act of 1934 are discussed in Chapter 48, "Securities Regulation."

STATUTORY FORMALITIES
The formation of a corporation requires compliance with the formalities prescribed by the statute authorizing its formation. The procedure, therefore, varies from state to state. The following survey of the steps will serve as an illustration of the pattern quite generally followed. These steps conveniently divide themselves into (1) those that are necessary to obtain a certificate of incorporation and (2) those that are necessary to organize the corporation.

Certificate of Incorporation   The steps necessary to obtain a certificate of incorporation may be briefly summarized:

(1) A document variously known as the "certificate of incorporation," "articles of incorporation," or "charter" is drafted. The typical certificate will contain lengthy and thoroughly thought-out provisions. The usual requirements are the name of the corporation; the county and city in which the principal place of business is to be located; the name and address of the resident agent of the corporation; the purpose, objects, or general nature of the business; the capital structure, that is,

the total number of shares which the corporation is to be authorized to issue and, if such shares are to be with par value, the par value of each of such shares or a statement that such shares are to be without par value; the amount of subscriptions for shares and of capital to be paid in for the commencement of business; the names and places of residence of each of the incorporators; and whether the corporation is to have perpetual existence or is to exist for only a specified number of years.

(2) The certificate of incorporation, properly signed by those persons designated as the "incorporators"—who may or may not also be promoters—is then sent to some state officer, usually the secretary of state, together with the necessary filing fees and the organization tax. In some states, the state officer examines the certificate and, if it complies with the statutory requirements, files it; in some states, he returns a copy of the certificate to the incorporators stamped "approved"; in other states, he issues some kind of document to the effect that the corporation is authorized to do business.

(3) Many states require that the articles be filed in the county in which the principal place of business of the corporation is to be located. If this is the case, the certificate is left for recording in the office designated by the general incorporation statute.

(4) The copy of the certificate, after recordation has been completed, is returned to the incorporators officially stamped as recorded.

(5) The persons so associating themselves then become a body corporate. Organization, however, remains to be perfected.

Organization of the Corporation The organization of the corporation can ordinarily be accomplished by holding two meetings.

(1) The first formal meeting is held by the incorporators or by the subscribers to shares. At this meeting, directors are elected, and bylaws are adopted. It should be pointed out that the power of making bylaws is primarily vested in the shareholders, but the power as to the original bylaws is sometimes conferred by statute upon the incorporators. Some state statutes expressly require the bylaws to contain certain provisions. The purpose of bylaws, however, is to provide for the internal management of the corporation. Bylaws commonly deal with such matters as the time and place of holding and the method of conducting meetings of directors and shareholders; the qualifications, election, removal, and compensation of directors, executive committees of directors, and officers of the corporation; formalities as to voting; reports and audits; execution of corporate papers; and other internal matters. Bylaws are subordinate to both the statutes of incorporation and the articles of incorporation.

(2) The board of directors then holds its first formal meeting to prepare for the commencement of the business. At this meeting, officers are generally elected, the form of share certificate and the corporate seal are adopted, subscriptions to shares of stock are accepted, and such other acts are performed as are necessary to the actual beginning of the business.

LIABILITY ON PROMOTER'S CONTRACTS

Coming now to the fully organized corporation, it is interesting to observe that liability on preincorporation contracts may be imposed either (1) upon the corporation or (2) upon the promoter.

Liability of Corporation   A few state statutes impose liability on the corporation for preincorporation contracts made by its promoters with third persons. In the vast majority of the states, however, the corporation is not liable on such contracts unless it does something after its incorporation to bind itself. That the corporation may bind itself is clear, but the courts have had difficulty in finding some rational basis upon which the liability may be supported. Suppose a promoter, in behalf of a prospective corporation, enters into a contract with Brown by the terms of which Brown is employed to work for the corporation as bookkeeper for one year beginning January 1. Suppose further that the corporation does not come into existence until February 1 but that Brown enters upon the performance of the contract on January 1 and continues in the employment of the corporation until he is unjustifiably discharged on July 1. Upon what theory may Brown recover from the corporation for breach of contract?

A few courts have advanced the theory of "continuing offer accepted." This theory proceeds upon the assumption that the negotiations between the promoter and the third person are an offer to contract with the prospective corporation when it comes into existence and that the corporation makes itself liable by accepting the offer when it is chartered. This theory overlooks the fact that a contract exists between the promoter and the third person. The theory, nevertheless, has been used in a few cases by the courts to enforce subscription agreements made before the organization of the corporation is complete. A few courts have said the corporation may bind itself by ratification. This view runs into conflict with the rule that ratification, as applied in the law of agency, presupposes an existing principal at the time the contract is entered into. The majority of the courts today, in answering the posed question, apply the "adoption" of the contract theory.

What procedure is necessary to adopt the contract? It seems to require nothing more than would be required for a principal to ratify an unauthorized act of an agent. The words "ratification" and "adoption" are indeed frequently used synonymously. A promoter's contract may be expressly adopted by formal resolution of the board of directors. It may be impliedly adopted if the board of directors, or other officers who have authority to bind the corporation, recognize the contract as binding upon the corporation. Such recognition may be expressed in writing, it may be expressed orally, or it may be implied from conduct. To go back to Brown's employment contract, Brown should recover from the corporation on this reasoning: the contract between Brown and the promoter was impliedly adopted by the fully organized corporation because it continued to accept the services of Brown up to July 1. The corporation, in the absence of an express or implied adoption, is not bound. [*Air Traffic & Serv. Corp. v. Fay,* p. 549.]

Liability of Promoter It should not be presumed that the mere adoption of the promoter's contract by the corporation relieves the promoter from personal liability. Adoption of the contract usually gives the other contracting party a cause of action against the corporation. The promoter, nevertheless, continues to be personally liable. The courts, in holding the promoter liable, have done nothing more than apply a basic principle of contract law: a person cannot relieve himself of his liability on a contract unless the other contracting party expressly or impliedly consents thereto. It may be expressly agreed between the promoter and the other contracting party, at the time the contract is entered into, that the promoter is not to be personally liable. An express novation between the other contracting party, the corporation, and the promoter will also relieve the promoter from personal liability. A novation may sometimes be implied. To pursue Brown's employment contract once more, the promoter should escape personal liability on this reasoning: the novation took place after the corporation came into existence, whereby, through an implied agreement on the part of Brown, the promoter, and the corporation, a new contract was entered into between Brown and the corporation. This new contract released the promoter from further liability with respect to the original agreement and bound the corporation to Brown. In the absence of an express agreement not to be liable, or a novation, the promoter is personally liable on preincorporation contracts. [*King Features Syndicate v. Courrier*, p. 550.]

CASES

Adler Slope Ditch Co. v. Moonshine Ditch Co.,   176 Pac. 593 (Ore. 1918). Action by Adler Slope Ditch Company, plaintiff, against Moonshine Ditch Company, defendant, to contest the water rights in connection with the adjudication of the waters of Hurricane Creek. On November 28, 1901, three persons met for the purpose of organizing the defendant as a corporation. They signed articles of incorporation, established their main office, and appointed G. L. Cole as secretary and agent of the company. On November 29, 1901, they filed a copy of the articles with the county clerk of Wallowa County and forwarded another copy to the secretary of state. On November 30,1901, at 8 A.M., G. L. Cole caused a notice to be posted on Hurricane Creek for and in behalf of the defendant-company for the purpose of initiating an appropriation of the water from the creek. On December 4, 1901, the articles of incorporation were officially filed with the secretary of state, at which time the defendant was fully organized. On May 5, 1902, the defendant-company commenced the construction of a ditch and diverted the water of Hurricane Creek. On November 30, 1901, at 4 P.M., the plaintiff-company posted a notice on Hurricane Creek to initiate a water right and during the spring of 1902 constructed a ditch and made a beneficial use of the water of Hurricane Creek. The plaintiff contends that the defendant was not sufficiently organized at 8 o'clock on November 30, 1901, to initiate a water right.

Olson, Judge: As to ability to transact business, corporations may be divided into three classes: First, de jure corporations, or those where the organization is entirely and legally perfected. Second, de facto corporations, where there has been a bona fide attempt to organize a corporation and a user of corporate powers, but the organization is defective. Third, corporations not sufficiently organized to come within the latter class.

. . . We have clearly in this case a law under which the corporation could be organized, a bona fide attempt to organize a corporation, and an actual use of corporate powers. It was an act of using corporate powers to appoint G. W. Cole as secretary and agent of the corporation. The filing of a notice to initiate a water right, which was made in the name of the corporation, is a user of corporate powers. The act of G. W. Cole as secretary and agent in the making and filing of the notice in the name of the corporation, even if considered as the act of a promoter, was ratified by the corporation by following up said notice by the construction of an irrigation system and user of water therein, and their claim before the water board on the water rights so initiated. The act has been plainly ratified. Having established the Moonshine Ditch Company as a corporation de facto, it is a settled law of this state that the legality of its existence cannot be inquired into collaterally. A direct attack may be made by the state . . . but no collateral attack as attempted in this case will lie. [DECISION FOR DEFENDANT]

Boney v. Trans-State Dredging Co., 115 S.E.2d 508 (S.C. 1960). Action by John D. Boney, plaintiff, against Trans-State Dredging Company, defendant.

Plaintiff, a resident of South Carolina, was traveling downstream on the Savannah River, and defendant, a Florida corporation not domesticated in South Carolina, was engaged in dredging operations on the South Carolina side of the river. Plaintiff signaled for permission to pass defendant's dredge and was signaled to proceed. Plaintiff then attempted to pass between the dredge and the South Carolina bank of the river, and the dredge shifted its position, causing a cable running from the dredge under the surface of the water to the South Carolina bank to rise up and overturn the boat. Plaintiff brought an action to recover damages for the injury sustained as a result of the accident. Pursuant to statute, the secretary of state of South Carolina was served a substituted service of summons, and the defendant moved to set aside the service as ineffectual to bring defendant within the jurisdiction of the court.

Legge, Justice: The crucial issue here is: Was the defendant doing business in this state at the time of the accident? No universal formula has been, or is likely to be, devised for determining what constitutes "doing business" by a foreign corporation within a state in such sense as to subject it to the jurisdiction of the courts of that state. The question must be resolved upon the facts of the particular case. Recent decisions of both federal and state courts have tended to discard older concepts whereby jurisdiction was accorded on the fictional premise of the corporation's implied consent or on the theory that the corporation is "present" wherever its activities are carried on, and to substitute therefor, as the jurisdictional test, the requirement that the corporation have such contact with the state of the forum "that the maintenance of the suit does not offend 'traditional notions of fair play and substantial justice.'" International Shoe Co. v. State of Washington, 326 U.S. 310.

In the case at bar the defendant's operations extended over a continuous period of more than ten months and over an area of one hundred forty-two miles of the Savannah River, the middle of which . . . is the boundary between South Carolina and Georgia. Those operations were such as were normally incident to the defendant's business; they were conducted, of necessity, sometimes in Georgia and sometimes in South Carolina; they required dredging on both sides of the boundary; they required cutting banks on both sides of the river to make a new channel. In the present state of the record it appears uncontroverted that the accident from which this action resulted occurred in the course of those operations and when defendant's dredge was moored to the South Carolina bank by a cable, the sudden lifting of which overturned the plaintiff's boat. We are of opinion that the defendant's said operations, although not continuously performed in South Carolina, constituted corporate activity within that state sufficient to meet the test before referred to and therefore to render the defendant subject to the jurisdiction of the courts. [DECISION FOR PLAINTIFF]

Frick v. Howard, 126 N.W.2d 619 (Wis. 1964). Action by C. Frederick Frick, plaintiff, against Daniel W. Howard, Receiver under Voluntary Assignment of Pan American Motel, Inc., defendant.

Michael D. Preston, the promoter of the Pan American Motel Corporation, entered into a contract to purchase land for $240,000. He agreed to pay $5,000 as a down payment and $65,000 on the date of closing, and the seller agreed to take a purchase-money mortgage for $170,000. Michael D. Preston organized the corporation on April 1, 1958, and the land was conveyed to him on August 29, 1958. He paid the $5,000, withdrew at least $61,000 from the corporation to pay the closing payment, and gave the mortgage for $170,000. On September 1, 1958, the corporation offered him $350,000 for the land. The offer was accepted, and the corporation paid him $70,000 on closing, assumed the outstanding mortgage of $170,000, and executed a note and mortgage for $110,000 to make up the balance of the purchase price. The board of directors consisted of Michael D. Preston and two others, and the note and mortgage were signed by Michael D. Preston as president of the corporation and by Frank J. Mack as secretary. On February 28, 1961, a replacement nonnegotiable note for $145,000 was executed by the corporation in favor of Michael D. Preston and was signed by Henry R. Marohl as president. On December 8, 1961, the replacement note and the mortgage dated April 1, 1959, were assigned by Michael D. Preston to the plaintiff. On January 10, 1962, the defendant was appointed receiver of the corporation under an assignment for the benefit of creditors. Plaintiff then brought this action to recover $141,000 on the note of February 28, 1961, and asked for foreclosure of the 1959 mortgage. The trial court found that Michael D. Preston committed a fraud upon the corporation but that the transaction was not secret.

Beilfuss, Justice: The fact that the transaction was not secret does not in all instances relieve a promoter of his fiduciary obligation to the corporation.

It is clear that at the time of the sale of the land to the corporation, and the execution of the note and mortgage, that the corporation had no independent board of directors. The actions of the corporation were completely dominated by

Preston. The transaction to sell the land held for a very short period of time was controlled by Preston both as buyer and seller. This was not an agreement between an independent buyer and seller dealing at arm's length. Preston as an individual selling the property had a personal financial interest to obtain the highest price available; Preston as the alter ego of Pan American Motel, Inc., had a financial interest to purchase the property at the lowest price available. For Preston to obtain a profit of $110,000 for himself under the circumstances herein is unconscionable and a violation of his fiduciary obligation and as such a fraud upon the corporation.

The plaintiff, Frick, received an assignment of the mortgage which upon its face provided it was secured by a note described in the mortgage. The mortgage provided it was secured by a note of even date. The note that he did receive was not of even date and was by terms upon its face nonnegotiable. He paid $72,500 for a note of $145,000. Under the facts, Frick had the constructive notice of the infirmities of the original note of 1959. He was not a bona fide holder for value of the note which the mortgage secured. [DECISION FOR DEFENDANT]

Air Traffic & Serv. Corp. v. Fay, 196 F.2d 20 (1952). Action by Edward A. J. Fay, plaintiff, against Air Traffic & Service Corporation, defendant.

Washington, Circuit Judge: This litigation arises from a falling out between the promoters of a new corporation.

On October 20, 1947, Edward A. J. Fay and Max Tendler signed a promoters' agreement looking to the formation of a company to be called Fay Traffic and Service Corporation, which would render services to the transportation industry. One portion of the agreement recited:

Edward A. J. Fay will contract with the corporation to act as General Manager and tariff consultant for a period of not less than one (1) year at an annual salary of Ten Thousand Dollars ($10,000), renewable from year to year at the option of the corporation.

Shortly thereafter the company was incorporated in Delaware. Stock in the new company was first subscribed for, and the first directors' meeting was held, in April, 1948. Both Fay and Tendler were present at the meeting, but the subject of compensation for the executives apparently was not raised. The directors next met on July 10, 1948, Fay and Tendler again being in attendance. The following resolution was there adopted:

Resolved, That Edward A. J. Fay as President of the Fay Traffic and Service Corporation and Max Tendler as Treasurer of the Fay Traffic and Service Corporation shall each be paid an annual salary of $10,000.00, commencing July 16, 1948.

Up to this time, Fay had been in the employ of an airline agency in New York. On July 16, 1948, he left that job, moved to Washington, and began to devote full time to the new company. Disagreements thereafter arose between Fay and Tendler, and on October 31, 1948, Fay resigned from the company's employ. Some months later, he sued the corporation, alleging that it had agreed to pay him a salary of $10,000.00 as General Manager, and that there was due him for the period October 31, 1947, to October 31, 1948, the net sum of $7,100 (i.e. $10,000 less $2,900 which had been paid him as President for the period from July 16, to October 31, 1948). . . .

In the instant case, Fay seeks to recover from the company a fixed salary for a fixed term, relying squarely on the promoters' agreement of October 20, 1947. The corporation never expressly or formally ratified and adopted that contract. . . .

In some situations, it may no doubt be properly held that a promoters' contract has been ratified and adopted by implication or estoppel. This is particularly true where an obligation running to the corporation is carried out, and the corporation accepts performance under circumstances making it inequitable to allow the company thereafter to escape the provisions of the promoters' contract. The situation before us, however, in no way fits this description. Fay did not begin his active service with the company until July 16, 1948. Prior to that time he was still working in New York for another concern. His visits to Washington were on occasional week-ends, rather than on business days. He was consequently unavailable to act as "General Manager and tariff consultant" for the company, as provided by the agreement.

. . . Under the law of Delaware, which we apply in this case, much more must be shown in the way of ratification and adoption than the plaintiff here is able to show. Not only was the promoters' agreement not adopted by the company; it was in fact modified and superseded by the resolution of July 10, 1948. Fay voted in favor of this resolution in his capacity as a director, and he cannot now disavow it as an individual. The resolution provided for payments only after July 16, 1948, and these were made. We must conclude that the judgment against the corporation cannot be rested on the provisions of the promoters' contract. [DECISION FOR DEFENDANT]

King Features Syndicate v. Courrier, 43 N.W.2d 718 (Iowa 1950). Action by King Features Syndicate, plaintiff, against John F. Courrier, Billy M. Barron, and Willis L. Ashby, copartners doing business under the firm name of "Hawkeye Broadcasting Company," a partnership, defendants. The petition alleged that plaintiff was engaged in the business of gathering news and furnishing news reports over leased wires to newspapers and radio broadcasting stations throughout the country; that defendant John F. Courrier contacted plaintiff's agent relative to obtaining news-report service on behalf of a proposed corporation which he and the other defendants proposed to form under the name of "Mississippi Valley Broadcasting Corporation"; that a contract to furnish such news service was thereafter signed in behalf of the broadcaster, "Mississippi Valley Broadcasting Corp. by John F. Courrier, Manager"; that the corporation was never organized but that the defendants, in lieu of the corporation, entered into a partnership; that the defendant John F. Courrier notified the plaintiff of the formation of the partnership and said he would have the partnership sign a new contract, but that no new contract was ever signed. This action was brought for damages for breach of contract.

Mulroney, Justice: It is settled by the authorities that a promoter, though he may assume to act on behalf of the projected corporation and not for himself, will be personally liable on his contract unless the other party agreed to look to some other person or fund for payment. . . .

Applying the law set forth in the foregoing authorities to the facts in this case we find the individual defendants were promoters. They were "prospective incorporators." . . . All of the evidence points to a joint enterprise on the part of the individual defendants. The contract was well within the scope of the adventure. The representation that their association was soon to merge into a corporate entity was honestly made but their subsequent decision to substitute a partnership for the proposed corporation would not end their liability. As pointed out, the authorities generally are to the effect that their individual liability would not have ended if they had formed the corporation. Why then should it be said their individual liability ceased when they abandoned the plan to incorporate? We hold the individual defendants jointly and severally liable under the contract. . . . Their individual liability as partners is not because they entered into a partnership but because they were promoters of a corporation. [DECISION FOR PLAINTIFF]

PROBLEMS

1 Davis and four others associated themselves as a corporation under the name of "Cotton & Milling Company." From June to December they carried on business and entered into contracts in the name of the corporation. In December they filed articles of incorporation with the secretary of state but failed to state in the articles the number of shares that had been subscribed, as required by statute. They also failed to file a duplicate of the articles with the clerk of the county of the principal place of business of the corporation, as required by statute. Are Davis and his associates liable as partners?

2 Plaintiff, a Pennsylvania corporation, conducts a correspondence school from its offices in Scranton, Pennsylvania. Instruction papers are published and sent from Scranton to students throughout the United States. Local as well as traveling agents are employed to secure and forward applications for admittance to the school. These agents also collect and send to the plaintiff payments made by students. An agent of the corporation in Kansas maintains his own office at his own expense. The agent is, however, paid a salary by the company and a commission on applications secured. The defendant subscribed for a course in Kansas but failed to pay. The plaintiff—although not qualified to do business in Kansas—brought an action against the defendant in Kansas. Is the plaintiff entitled to a remedy on its claim?

3 Jones, who owned a chain of retail lumber yards, was elected treasurer of The Construction Company in 1918. The corporation, however, was completely terminated by judicial proceedings in 1919, and all the books of the corporation were turned over to Jones. In 1925, two officers of the First Bank and Jones decided to enter the business of operating a lath mill. They employed one Smith to manage the mill. Jones, Smith, and the two officers then agreed that the mill should be operated as a corporation. These four, therefore, purported to have a meeting of shareholders and elected themselves as the directors and officers of The Construction Company. No attempt was made to secure a formal transfer of the corporate charter from the original incorporators, and no attempt was made to secure a new charter from the state. The business of the mill was nevertheless carried on in the name of The Construction Company. The stock book, the seal, and the other books of the terminated corporation were likewise used in operating the lath mill. The lath mill was a losing proposition from the outset. The Construction Company was therefore placed in bankruptcy. Discuss whether or not you think Jones, Smith, and the two officers of the bank are individually liable for the debts of the corporation.

4 The statute under which the XYZ Corporation was organized was declared unconstitutional. Zale, a stockholder in the corporation with knowledge of this fact, continued thereafter to treat the corporation as an existing corporation. He received dividend checks, which he cashed and voted as a stockholder at the regular meetings. The corporation was thereafter adjudicated a bankrupt, and a receiver was appointed by the court. The receiver, pursuant to statute, called upon all the stockholders to contribute the par value of the stock they held in the corporation. Zale refused to contribute. He contended that the shares of stock of the corporation were void and that he was not a stockholder. Should Zale be held liable?

5 The promoter of the Wentworth Lumber Company borrowed $7,500 from the plaintiff bank for which he executed a note in favor of the bank. The note was signed by the promoter as president of the lumber company. The corporation, after it was organized, paid the interest on the note. In an action by the bank against the promoter to recover on the note, the promoter contended that he was not liable since the corporation had impliedly adopted the contract. Do you agree with this contention?

6 Plaintiff and two others were promoting a corporation to be engaged in the business of selling and servicing foreign cars. The three promoters agreed orally that plaintiff should receive a salary of $750 a month plus an expense allowance of $100 for his services as general manager of the corporation. After complying with the statutory formalities, an organization meeting of the stockholders was held. Plaintiff was elected president, and the other two promoters were elected the vice-president and secretary-treasurer. The minutes of the meeting expressly provided that these officers, as such, would serve without salary. The minutes were silent as to the employment of plaintiff in any capacity. Plaintiff worked for several months as general manager but the corporation refused to pay the promised salary on the ground that the preincorporation contract had not been adopted by the corporation after organization. Discuss the theory which plaintiff could invoke in order to recover this salary from the corporation.

7 Defendants, the promoters of a corporation for the purpose of publishing a newspaper, discussed with plaintiff the possibility of accepting a position as woman's editor. The corporation came into legal existence on January 12, 1946, and the defendants became the incorporators and the sole and only directors and officers thereof. On January 27, 1946, the general manager of the corporation wrote the plaintiff making a formal offer of the position for a period of three years. Plaintiff accepted and entered the discharge of her duties and continued to do so until February 9, 1946, when she was discharged without any fault on her part. Are the defendants liable for breach of contract?

8 Brown, who had patents for an improved refrigerator and other kitchen appliances, and Jones, who was experienced in the sale of appliances, discussed the possibility of forming a corporation for the purpose of manufacturing the appliances. Brown promised Jones that Jones would be the superintendent of the new factory and that he would be paid for his time and money spent in securing stock subscriptions. After the corporation was fully organized, the directors refused to pay Jones for his services in securing the stock subscriptions and also refused to employ him as superintendent of the new factory. What remedy, if any, is available to Jones against the corporations?

43
CORPORATIONS: CORPORATE FINANCIAL STRUCTURE

It may be well to mention at the outset that the words "capital stock" may mean one thing to an economist and another thing to an accountant. It is mostly a problem of statutory construction today to determine the meaning of the words as used in the law of corporations. The misuse of the words accounts for much of the conflict in corporation law. The words "capital stock" sometimes are used to indicate the amount or number of shares of stock that the corporation is authorized to issue. This use has reference to the "authorized capital stock." The words are more often used to indicate the shares of stock that have actually been issued. This use has reference to "issued capital stock" as distinguished from "unissued capital stock." A few modern corporation statues have attempted to minimize the confusion by using, and defining in detail, the words "stated capital." But these statutes have not settled the confusion because the different statutes give the words different definitions. Words more specific than "capital stock" will be used in this book.

The word "capital" is also used variously. The word is generally used to include the consideration received for issued capital stock plus any gains or profits from the use and investment of such consideration or, if losses have resulted, whatever remains after such losses have been deducted. A corporation, therefore, may have $500,000 authorized capital stock, $200,000 issued capital stock, and $300,000 unissued capital stock. The capital may be any amount, depending upon the success or failure of the business of the corporation.

Turning now to the corporate-stock structure, it is appropriate to observe (1) the methods of financing the corporation, (2) stock subscriptions, (3) the kinds of shares, and (4) share-selling schemes.

FINANCING THE CORPORATION

It is not the purpose of this book to encompass the field of corporation finance. No inquiry, therefore, will be made into the various combinations of corporate-finance methods. In order to understand the corporate-stock structure, however, it is essential to distinguish between (1) bonds and (2) shares of stock.

Bonds. The issuance and sale of bonds is known as creditor or debt financing. This is the most common method of long-term borrowing utilized by large corporations. It is more often used by the corporation after it has been in operation for a time. There are various types of bonds, and it is sometimes difficult to determine whether the agreement entered into has resulted in a bond or a share of stock. It has been held that a document which gives the holder a right to share in the profits of the corporation–although labeled a bond–is a share of stock. The document expressing the agreement in each particular case determines the identity of the document as well as the rights and liabilities of the persons who enter into the agreement. A usual type of corporate bond, however, is a written promise to pay a specified sum of money at a specified date with interest at a specified rate. It is usually one of a series of bonds, secured by a deed of trust or mortgage, in which the property of the corporation is mortgaged to a trustee for the benefit of all the bondholders. The deed of trust has grown to be a highly complicated legal document. The corporation almost invariably reserves the right to redeem the bonds on any interest-paying date prior to their maturity. Bondholders in the usual type of bond are secured creditors who have lent money to the corporation. The corporation that employs creditor or debt financing is doing nothing very different from the individual who borrows money.

Shares of Stock. The most common method of financing the beginning corporation is through the issuance and sale of shares of stock. This is known as owner or equity financing and differs materially from creditor or debt financing. The corporation, in the ordinary use of the word "debtor," is not a debtor to the shareholders. The shareholders are not creditors of the corporation. They are the owners of the business. A share of stock, in the hands of the individual shareholder, is intangible personal property. The share of stock is evidenced by a certificate. The certificate, however, is merely written evidence that the person named in the certificate is the owner of the number of shares of stock specified in the certificate. The shares–not the certificates–are the property.

STOCK SUBSCRIPTIONS

A stock subscription is an agreement to purchase a stated number and kind of shares of stock in the corporation when the shares are issued. The agreement, in the absence of statute, need not be in any particular form. It may pertain to (1) preincorporation subscriptions, (2) postincorporation subscriptions, and (3) in either event, conditions may be attached.

Preincorporation Subscriptions.   Preincorporation agreements are primarily entered into for the purpose of assuring the promoters that the money needed to finance the corporation will be forthcoming. They are sometimes necessary to satisfy a statute which requires that a certain amount of the authorized capital stock be subscribed for and paid in as a prerequisite to the filing of the articles of incorporation. The chief problem with respect to preincorporation agreements is to determine when the subscribers become bound. The courts, as between the subscribers themselves, generally hold that the subscribers did not intend to contract with one another where subscriptions are solicited from the public generally. An agreement among a number of persons to form a corporation and to subscribe to its authorized capital stock, however, is generally held to constitute a contract between the subscribers themselves. This holding prevents a subscriber from withdrawing his subscription without the acquiescence of the other subscribers.

Some courts hold, as between the subscribers and the corporation, that incorporation itself automatically constitutes an acceptance of preincorporation subscriptions. Most courts hold that there must be an express acceptance after incorporation or some act from which acceptance can be implied: demanding payment, entering the subscriber's name on the books of the corporation, or bringing suit would suffice. The subscription of each subscriber is said to be a continuing offer to the proposed corporation which may be revoked at any time prior to acceptance by the corporation. A few state statutes have settled the problem by providing that preincorporation subscriptions shall be irrevocable for a stated period of time.

Postincorporation Subscriptions.   The courts in some states have drawn a distinction between preincorporation subscriptions and postincorporation subscriptions. These courts hold a subscription for shares of stock to a corporation already in existence to be a contract of purchase and sale. The distinction, for the most part, has been applied where the subscription price is payable in installments and the issuance of the shares was conditioned upon full payment of the purchase price. The distinction is an important one. The purchaser, in the case of a purchase and sale, does not assume the position of a shareholder until the corporation delivers the certificate to him. The consequences are that tender of the certificate, or the ability and willingness to deliver the certificate, is a condition to the right of the corporation to bring an action for damages. Payment of the purchase price, on the other hand, is a condition to the right of the purchaser to become a member of the corporation. In those states that follow the purchase-and-sale view, bankruptcy of the corporation will excuse the purchaser for the unpaid balance even against the claims of the creditors. This result is reached on the reasoning that a bankrupt corporation cannot perform the condition by delivering the certificate. The courts in other states refuse to recognize this distinction and hold that any agreement for the issue of shares of stock is a subscription. Bankruptcy of the corporation, in these states, will not excuse the purchaser against creditors. A few states have settled the problem by enacting statutes to the effect that contracts to purchase shares have the same status as accepted subscriptions.

Conditions. A few state statutes authorize only absolute subscriptions. The courts, moreover, have not encouraged conditional subscriptions. In the absence of statute, however, share-subscription contracts–like other contracts–may be made upon conditions precedent or conditions subsequent in the same manner as any other conditional contract. An illustration of this is a subscription to shares made on the condition precedent that the check given in payment is not to be used until all the shares have been subscribed for and paid for in cash. The subscriber, in the case of conditions precedent, does not become a shareholder until the conditions have been performed. Failure to perform the condition precedent will release the subscriber from his subscription. The subscriber, however, may be estopped or he may waive his right to withdraw. To illustrate: A subscriber who attends shareholders' meetings and votes on motions with knowledge of the nonperformance of the condition precedent will not be permitted to set up the nonperformance in order to escape the liabilities of a shareholder.

The subscriber, on the other hand, becomes a shareholder at the time the subscription contract is entered into if the condition is a condition subsequent. Coupled with the subscription contract upon a condition subsequent is a collateral agreement that the corporation will perform a certain act. To illustrate: The corporation agrees to maintain its factory in a certain city for a fixed period. The shareholder, as a general rule, is liable for the amount of his subscription even though the corporation fails to perform the condition subsequent. The only remedy ordinarily available to the shareholder is an action against the corporation for any damages he may have sustained. Subscriptions with a condition subsequent attached, therefore, are generally sustained unless the condition amounts to fraud on other shareholders or corporate creditors.

A subscriber is not liable if the subsequently organized corporation does not correspond to the kind of corporation contemplated in the subscription agreement. Minor changes or additions, however, which are not prejudicial will not constitute a defense. [*Menominee Bldg. Co. v. Rueckert,* p. 560.]

KINDS OF SHARES

The statutes of the various states generally authorize the corporation to issue two or more kinds of shares of stock. The prevailing practice is to divide shares into classes with reference to voting rights, dividend rights, and rights on dissolution of the corporation. The kinds of shares that merit discussion are (1) par-value and no-par-value, (2) voting and nonvoting, (3) common and preferred, and (4) watered stock.

Par-Value and No-Par-Value Shares. The division of shares into par-value and no-par-value shares aids the corporation in marketing its issues of shares. The articles of incorporation, as required by statute, will state the authorized number and the par value of par-value shares as well as the authorized number of no-par-value shares. A charter amendment is required to increase the authorized number of shares, to change the par value of the shares, to change par-value shares into shares without par value, or to change shares without par value into par-value shares.

The par value of par-value shares will be stated upon the face of the certificate, and some state statutes provide that such shares cannot be issued at less than par at any time. As a general rule, however, this limitation is restricted to the time the corporation begins business.

No-par-value shares merely represent the proportionate interests of the shareholder in the total assets of the corporation, unexpressed in terms of money. No one will be injured by the issuance of no-par-value shares because the face of the certificate will show that such shares are issued without par value. The holders of the same class of shares, moreover, will be entitled to share equally in the distribution of dividends and assets. The shares are generally issued from time to time at different prices which will be determined by the directors or the shareholders in the light of current market conditions. Although no-par-value shares have no designated money value, it should not be presumed that the consideration received for them does not have to be valued or that they can be issued for no consideration.

Voting and Nonvoting Shares. This type of shares of stock, as the name implies, gives the owner of the shares either the right to vote or denies him such right. A few state statutes require that all shares have voting rights, and other statutes impose limitations on the issue of nonvoting shares. But in the absence of such a statute, nonvoting shares may usually be authorized and issued. Nonvoting shares, however, may have mandatory voting rights with respect to certain matters. A few statutes provide for voting rights with respect to amendments to the articles of incorporation, merger, or consolidation, sale or mortgage of assets not in the regular course of business, and voluntary dissolution. A few state statutes also permit voting rights to be conferred on holders of debt securities, such as bonds. This means, however, that shareholders' control is diluted to the extent that voting rights are conferred.

Common and Preferred Shares. The common shares are generally issued without extraordinary rights or privileges. The owners of the common shares have traditionally been given voting privileges. They are likewise entitled to share in the profits of the corporation and in its assets upon dissolution. Many small corporations issue only common shares. It frequently happens, however, that corporations cannot finance their organization by issuing only common shares. The result is the issuance of additional shares which take certain preferential rights.

Preferred shareholders are rarely given voting privileges. They are, however, entitled to certain preferences over the owners of the common shares. The authority and the extent of the preferences can only be determined by the terms of the share contract itself, by the articles of incorporation, sometimes by the bylaws of the corporation, and by the provisions of the statute from which the corporation derives the power to issue shares of stock. Preferred shareholders are almost invariably given a preference in the payment of dividends at some stated rate before any dividends are paid to the holders of common shares. Preferred shares are also frequently given priority in the distribution of corporate assets on the dissolution of the corporation. It is not unusual to find that the preferred shareholders are (1) entitled to cumulative dividends or (2) entitled to participate in dividend distributions.

(1) *Cumulative and Noncumulative.* A "cumulative dividend" means that if the preferred share dividend is not paid in any given year, the dividend is not necessarily lost. The holders of the shares will be entitled to payment of all arrears before any payments are made to holders of the common shares. The passed dividends are lost, however, if the shares are noncumulative. This means that only the current dividends must be paid before the common share dividends are paid. To illustrate: The XYZ Corporation made no profits for three years. No dividends, therefore, were declared. The corporation then earned a large profit during the fourth year. The arrears for the three years on the cumulative preferred shares, as well as the dividends for the fourth year, must be paid before the common shareholders receive a dividend.

The articles of incorporation and the share certificate may, in some instances, state that the corporation guarantees the dividends. This is not an absolute guaranty. It means that the dividends are cumulative. One further point should be noted: Dividends are held to be impliedly cumulative unless a contrary intention appears.

(2) *Participating and Nonparticipating.* The owner of the preferred shares of stock may or may not participate with another class of stock beyond the stipulated dividend. If the shares participate, they are said to be participating shares; if the shares do not participate, they are said to be nonparticipating. The articles of incorporation, the bylaws of the corporation, the share certificate, or a statute may provide that the holder of the preferred shares is to receive no more than the stipulated dividend. Sometimes, however, provision is made for participation. The manner of participation varies greatly, but a common method of participation may be illustrated by continuing with the XYZ Corporation: Suppose that the preferred shares are regular 7 percent for which dividends are paid for the fourth year. Suppose further that the common shareholders received a certain specified annual payment—say a 7 percent dividend—in the same year. Suppose still further that there is then a surplus remaining for dividends. The preferred shareholders will participate proportionately with the common shareholders in the remaining surplus.

Watered Stock. Shares of stock which have been issued as fully paid when the subscriber has not paid or agreed to pay their full value are known as "watered stock." The shares are said to be "diluted" or "watered" to the extent of such deficiency. Watered stock is ordinarily the result of shares of stock being issued in exchange for property or services at an overvaluation. This is a misrepresentation and, when participated in by the subscriber, constitutes a fraud upon creditors. The creditor who relies on such representation may recover the difference between the par value of the shares and the amount actually paid therefor from the subscriber or his transferee if his transferee has notice of the misrepresentation. Some courts, however, have adopted the "true value" rule. These courts hold that the holder of watered shares is liable to creditors and that the element of fraud or good faith is not essential. Other courts have adopted the "good faith" rule, and the shareholder or promoter is protected as against creditors if both parties believed that the consideration given is the equal of the par value of the stock taken in exchange for it. A creditor cannot, however, recover against a holder of watered stock until he has actually been injured. Future shareholders who have no knowledge that the stock has been watered would not be liable. An innocent shareholder who owns a share of stock, therefore, can sell it to anyone who will buy it for any price the purchaser is willing to pay.

SHARE-SELLING SCHEMES
There are many schemes employed for selling shares. The issuance of preferred shares is a scheme to entice purchasers. The same may be said with respect to (1) share warrants, (2) compulsory redemptions, and (3) a split-up of shares.

Share Warrants.   A share warrant is an option to purchase shares. The warrant ordinarily gives the purchaser the right to purchase a fixed number of shares of stock at a fixed cash price at some future time. Unless a statute prohibits, the warrant may be issued as a separate instrument. More frequently, however, warrants are attached to bonds or preferred shares as an additional attraction to prospective purchasers. They may be detachable or nondetachable when they are attached to the security. The detachable warrant may pass from hand to hand in much the same manner as shares of stock. The desirability of purchasing share warrants is a matter of business judgment. The warrant has a speculative value based on the possibility of a rise in the market price of the stock called for in the warrant. Any attempt to generalize the legal significance of share warrants would be guesswork. There is a dearth of decided cases on the subject.

Compulsory Redemptions.   Compulsory redemptions are frequently included in preferred share contracts to entice purchasers. Compulsory redemptions, however, should not be confused with voluntary redemptions. A voluntary redemption is not a preference for the benefit of the shareholder; it is a safeguard to be exercised by the directors to enable the corporation to retire a claim on the earnings. The corporation, by exercising the option, will be in a position to refinance at a lower rate of return on new securities and retire the old securities which call for a higher dividend. The usual compulsory-redemption provision requires the corporation to redeem its shares at a fixed date. The shareholder, therefore, is assured of the return on his investment. [*Sutton v. Globe Knitting Works,* p. 560.]

Split-up of Shares.   A share split-up is merely a dividing of the outstanding shares into a greater number of share units. A share split-up is a convenient method of reducing the market value of shares which are too high for convenience in trading. [*Lake Superior Dist. Power Co. v. Public Serv. Comm'n,* p. 562.]

CASES

Menominee Bldg. Co. v. Rueckert,   222 N.W. 162 (Mich. 1928). Action by Menominee Building Company, plaintiff, against August Rueckert, defendant. The action is brought to compel payment by defendant of the amount due on his subscription agreement. The defendant contends that he is not liable because of the variation between the purposes as expressed in the subscription agreement and the articles of incorporation.

Sharpe, Justice: Defendant, in response to a "community drive" in the city of Menominee, signed a document, dated December 5, 1924, wherein he agreed to subscribe for the purchase of 10 shares of the capital stock of the par value of $100 each in a corporation to be organized under the laws of this State, the object of which was stated therein to be—"to buy and hold a parcel of real estate in the city of Menominee and erect thereon and own a building to be occupied or leased for a department store, moving picture theater, office and other business and recreational purposes."

. . . The purposes of the corporation were stated in the charter to be:

"To purchase, hold, sell, improve and lease real estate, and mortgage and encumber the same, and to erect, manage, care for, and maintain, extend and alter buildings thereon."

. . . The incorporation was, of course, a condition precedent to defendant's liability.

"A material change in the character of the enterprise, the capital stock, or purpose of the proposed company releases those who do not assent thereto." 1 Cook on Corporations (8th Ed.) § 62.

The corporation when organized "must, as to its purposes, powers, and otherwise, be the same corporation as that contemplated by the subscription agreement." 14 C.J. p. 518.

. . . While the purpose as expressed in the articles is somewhat broader than that stated in the agreement, the organization was in effect the one contemplated therein. The main purpose—that of erecting a community building—was not departed from. [DECISION FOR PLAINTIFF]

Sutton v. Globe Knitting Works,   267 N.W. 815 (Mich. 1936). Action by R. E. Sutton, plaintiff, against Globe Knitting Works, defendant. Plaintiff, sometime prior to 1931, purchased 100 shares of preferred stock of the par value of $10 per share in the defendant company. At the time of his purchase the articles of association of the company contained the following provision: "The preferred stock shall be subject to redemption and shall be redeemed at par on January 25,

1932." The certificate issued for the shares contained a similar provision: "This stock is subject to redemption and shall be redeemed at par on January 25, 1932." Plaintiff tendered his shares and demanded payment of $1,000 on the redemption date. The defendant company refused to redeem in compliance with the demand. This action followed.

North, Chief Justice: The defense is based upon an amendment to defendant's articles of association in consequence of which the corporation claims the redemption date of plaintiff's stock has been extended to January 25, 1957. The amendment was made subsequent to plaintiff's becoming the owner of his 100 shares of preferred stock but prior to the date (January 25, 1932) it was tendered for redemption; and the amendment is asserted to have been made under the authority of and in accordance with Act No. 327 . . . The portions of Act 327 pertinent to decision are as follows:

Sec. 43. Any corporation formed or existing under this act may at a meeting of the shareholders duly called and held amend its articles without limitation so long as the articles as amended would have been authorized by this act as original articles, by the vote of the holders of the majority of its shares entitled to vote: Provided, that if any such amendment shall change the rights, privileges or preferences of the holders of shares of any class, such amendment shall be approved by the vote of the holders of a majority of the shares of each class of shares entitled to vote and a majority of shares of each class whose rights, privileges or preferences are so changed. . . .

It is conceded by plaintiff that the amendment to defendant's articles of association by which the redemption date of its preferred stock was changed from January 25, 1932, to January 25, 1957, was adopted by more than a majority of the holders of such stock. It is admitted by the pleadings that plaintiff's shares of stock were not voted in favor of this amendment to defendant's articles of association. It is plaintiff's contention that since he became the owner of this 100 shares of preferred stock prior to the effective date of Act No. 327, Pub. Acts 1931, it was not within the power of the corporation or of the other holders of preferred stock to vote to postpone the redemption date of the stock held by plaintiff, he having withheld consent to such postponement. Plaintiff asserts that postponement of the redemption date of his stock is an impairment of his contract right and deprives him of his property without due process of law.

. . . By virtue of the quoted provision contained in the certificate of stock held by plaintiff, he certainly had, immediately upon receiving it from defendant, a vested or accruing right to have it redeemed at par on the 25th day of January, 1932. This was a liability that the corporation assumed incident to issuing this stock. Section 59 of the act expressly provides that "the liability of any corporation . . . shall not in any way be lessened or impaired by . . . any change or amendment in the articles of any such corporations." It is not possible to give effect to this provision of the statute and at the same time deny plaintiff the right to recover.

. . . The redemption provision was a definite undertaking on the part of the defendant corporation to redeem at a given time and on given terms the stock plaintiff agreed to purchase. Assuming, as we fairly may, that in the absence of the redemption provision plaintiff would not have purchased his stock, or that defendant's undertaking to redeem was an inducing cause in consequence of which plaintiff did purchase, the provision for redemption was something more than a mere incident to corporate relationship, it was a definite contractual undertaking, the proposal for which antedated and consummation of which coincided with the purchase of the stock by plaintiff, who prior to that time was not identified with the corporation. [DECISION FOR PLAINTIFF]

Lake Superior Dist. Power Co. v. Public Serv. Comm'n, 26 N.W.2d 278 (Wis. 1947). Action by Lake Superior District Power Company, plaintiff (referred to as the "utility"), against the Public Service Commission, defendant (referred to as the "commission"). The utility reclassified its shares of common stock by having its shareholders exchange their 35,600 shares of common stock of $75 par value (amounting in the aggregate to $2,670,000) for 133,500 shares of $20 par value (likewise amounting in the aggregate to $2,670,000). The commission demanded a fee of $2,670 under the following statute:

Sec. 184.10(1), Stats: Each public-service corporation on filing an application for authority to issue any securities to which this chapter is applicable shall pay with such application, prior to the issuance of a certificate, a fee of one dollar per thousand for each thousand dollars par value of each authorized issue of securities, but in no case less than ten dollars for any issue.

The utility contends that the fee is not payable on a reclassification—as in this case—of its shares of common stock.

Fritz, Justice: The exchange of stock certificates by the utility is not in and of itself an issuance of securities. Such an exchange can constitute an issuance of securities only if in the process of the exchange some class of the corporation's stock is actually increased in consideration of its actually receiving additional money, property, or services equal to the par value of the issue of stock. As in the case at bar no such consideration is to be received by the utility and there is to be no increase, or anything to be added to its capital stock, there is and legally can be no issuance of securities. The proposed new certificates only evidence the division of the then outstanding capital stock into units of smaller size. The capital stock itself amounting in the aggregate to $2,670,000 had all been previously issued pursuant to authority of the commission. The transaction involved in the split-up of the shares of common stock aggregating $2,670,000 in no way changed the stockholders' proportionate interest therein and in the corporation. Each stockholder owned exactly as much stock after the division as prior thereto, and no new stockholders were added thereby. Consequently, as upon the split-up there was no issuance of any additional common stock or any change in the utility's existing capitalization, there was no additional original "issue of securities" within the meaning of that term as used in sec. 184.10(1), Stats. [DECISION FOR PLAINTIFF]

PROBLEMS

1 The articles of incorporation of the defendant-corporation gave the common shareholders the right to vote and denied such right to the preferred shareholders. The articles further provided, however, that the preferred shareholders should have the sole voting power until payment of all accumulated dividends, should the stipulated dividend on the preferred shares not be paid for two semiannual periods. The corporation paid the semiannual dividend on January 1, 1933, but the dividend was illegal. The corporation defaulted in the July 1, 1933, dividend. The common shareholders elected a board of directors on July 17, 1933. A preferred shareholder brought a suit in equity to test the right of the common shareholders to elect the board of directors. He alleged that the default on July 1 was the second default because the January 1 dividend was illegal. Decide.

2 Jones subscribed for twenty shares of stock in the Acme Corporation at $50 per share. He executed his demand promissory note for $1,000 payable to the corporation as payment for the shares. He was promised, at the time of the execution of the note, that the corporation would purchase the shares from him if he decided he wanted to sell the shares. The corporation thereafter became insolvent and was in the hands of a receiver, who brought an action against Jones to recover the $1,000. Jones contended, in defense of the action, that he desired to sell the shares and that the corporation had promised to purchase the shares. Do you think this is a good defense?

3 Brown, at the time of his death, was the owner of 100 shares of stock in the Brown Realty Company. The principal holdings of the company consisted of real estate. He left a widow and two sons. The statute provided that the widow was entitled to one-third of any real estate for life and one-third of any personal estate in absolute ownership. The sons contended that the shares of stock were to be considered as real estate and that the widow should have only a life estate therein. Decide.

4 Defendant and thirty-six other persons signed a stock-subscription agreement which contained the following objects clause: "For the purpose of forming a corporation to have for its object the furnishing of the incandescent system of electric lighting to those who may desire the same." A portion of the subscribers had a meeting—which meeting defendant did not attend—and organized the corporation. The articles of incorporation defined the objects of the corporation as follows: "That the purposes for which it is formed are producing electricity for light and power." Defendant refused to pay his stock subscription, and the fully organized corporation brought an action to recover the amount of his stock subscription. Do you think the corporation should recover?

5 Plaintiff paid $1,000 to the XYZ Corporation and received a receipt for ten shares of stock to be issued at once. On August 4, 1942, a few weeks thereafter, the attorney of the corporation wrote plaintiff a letter in which he stated that the stock certificate was in his possession and requested plaintiff to call for it. Plaintiff neglected, however, to call for the certificate. In a proceeding to liquidate the corporation, which was instituted on September 1, 1942, plaintiff claimed he was entitled to have the $1,000 refunded to him on the ground that he is not a shareholder because the certificate was never delivered to him. Do you agree with plaintiff?

6 The Power Company, in order to raise funds for expansion purposes, issued and sold $80,000 of preferred stock, bearing 7 percent dividends, payable semiannually. The dividends were paid the shareholders, and The Power Company deducted these dividends from its tax return as interest by reason of the following provision of the Revenue Act: To determine the net income of a corporation there may be deducted from the gross income all interest paid on indebtedness. The court held that these dividends were not deductible as interest. Explain the rules of law upon which this holding was founded.

7 Morgan, the promoter of a corporation who was soliciting subscriptions from the general public, entered into a subscription agreement with Collins whereby Collins agreed to take $25,000 in stock in the proposed corporation. A few days thereafter, Collins met Morgan and orally withdrew his subscription. The corporation was then organized, and Morgan was made president. He reported to the board of directors that he had secured certain subscription agreements, including that of Collins. The board of directors accepted the subscriptions, and those persons who had subscribed for shares of stock were requested to pay for their shares. Collins refused to do so. Decide.

8 The certificate of incorporation of the XYZ Company provided: "The holders of the Five Percent Profit Sharing Preferred Stock A of the Company shall be entitled to receive preferential dividends in each fiscal year up to the amount of Five Percent before any dividends shall be paid upon any other stock of the Company, but such preferential dividends shall be noncumulative." The company was organized in 1915, but from 1915 to 1926 less than 5 percent was paid on Class A. The net earnings during these years were used for the payment of improvements and additions to the property and equipment of the company. In 1926, the company announced a proposed payment of dividends of 5 percent on Class A, as well as payment of dividends on the common stock. The holders of Class A contend they are entitled to receive dividends up to 5 percent for prior years before any dividends are paid to the common stock. Do you agree with this contention?

9 The shares of stock in the Acme Corporation were divided into 5 percent preferred shares and common shares. The corporation made no profits during 1962, 1963, and 1964, and no dividends were paid to the shareholders during that period. The corporation did, however, make a profit during the year 1965. The directors of the corporation thereupon declared a 5 percent dividend for the preferred shareholders and a 5 percent dividend for the common shareholders. Plaintiff, a preferred shareholder, contends that the corporation should have paid the preferred shareholders a 5 percent dividend for the years 1962, 1963, 1964, and 1965 before paying a dividend to the common shareholders. Do you agree with this contention?

44

CORPORATIONS: POWERS

The subject matter of this chapter will be viewed from the standpoint of (1) the power of the corporation to enter into binding contracts with third persons, (2) limitations on corporate powers, and (3) the liability of the corporation for torts and crimes.

POWERS OF THE CORPORATION

The three classes of powers are inherent, express, and implied powers. The powers of a corporation, however, commonly cut across lines of this classification. The terms (1) "inherent powers," (2) "express powers," and (3) "implied powers" will therefore be defined first, and (4) the major legal problems pertaining to some of the particular powers will then be discussed.

Inherent Powers. The inherent, or incidental, powers of a corporation are those which are necessary to corporate existence. These include the power to have a corporate name and to contract, own, convey real and personal property for the purposes authorized by its charter in its corporate name; to sue and be sued in its corporate name; to have continued existence for the period for which it was created and if no such time limit is specified, then perpetually; to have a corporate seal; and to make and alter bylaws for the regulation of the affairs of the corporation.

Express Powers. The express powers of a corporation are ascertained by reference to the articles of incorporation and the statutes of the state under which the corporation was organized. The general incorporation statutes declare that certain enumerated powers—which are usually quite detailed—shall be granted to all corporations created pursuant to the statute. The purpose clause of the charter likewise enumerates certain powers—frequently a dozen or more paragraphs—covering the purposes and objects of the corporation. Practically all of the general incorporation statutes and practically all of the articles of incorporation contain provisions confirming the inherent powers of a corporation.

Implied Powers. The implied powers of a corporation are those which are necessary for the purpose of carrying out its express powers and the objects of its incorporation. These powers might be quite extensive under modern business conditions. To illustrate: A corporation chartered for the manufacture and supply of gas for light and heat has been held to have the power to buy and resell appliances which would increase the consumption of gas; a corporation chartered to manufacture and sell tile has been held to have the power to construct low-cost housing projects. It is largely a question of fact rather than law, and each case is decided on its own particular facts. A corporation chartered to maintain a hotel might be found to have the implied power to maintain a golf course if the hotel was located in the suburbs of a city and catered to weekly or monthly guests. The same probably would not be true if the hotel was located in the commercial area of the city and catered to overnight guests. The test generally applied is whether the transaction is in furtherance of the objects and purposes for which the corporation was incorporated.

Particular Powers. Most of the controversy has revolved around the powers (1) to make corporate gifts and donations, (2) to enter into partnership agreements, (3) to make loans of the assets or credit of the corporation, (4) to reacquire the stock of the corporation, (5) to acquire stock in other corporations, (6) to organize holding companies, and (7) to organize subsidiary corporations.

(1) *Corporate Gifts.* A corporation, as a general rule, has no implied power to expend money for purely philanthropic causes at the expense of the shareholders, unless the disbursement promotes the purpose for which the corporation was formed. The courts have been liberal, however, in finding as a responsibility of business the comfort, health, and well-being of its employees. It has been repeatedly held that a bonus to employees as a reward for work is within the implied powers of a corporation. The implied power to build houses, schools, churches, and libraries for the use of employees has also been sustained. The same is true with respect to contributions to colleges and universities engaged in developing possible employees who would be useful in the business of the corporation. Donations to political organizations are held to be unauthorized. Many of the states have enacted statutes authorizing corporate donations. Most of these statutes place restrictions on the amount which may be contributed.

(2) ***Partnership Agreements.*** A corporation has no implied power to enter into a contract of partnership. The reason for the rule is that the management of a corporation is exercised by the board of directors while the management of a partnership is exercised equally by each member of the firm. To permit a corporation to become a partner, therefore, would be to yield partial management to an outsider. An agreement to share profits and losses in a joint adventure, however, is usually sustained so long as the corporation retains exclusive control of its own corporate business. The corporation, of course, may enter into a contract of partnership if the statute or the corporate charter expressly so provides.

(3) ***Loan of Assets or Credit.*** A corporation, as a general rule, may not lend money unless it is authorized to do so by a statutory provision or by its charter. In many instances, however, such power may be implied from the authority to make such contracts as are reasonably necessary for the transaction of the business for which the corporation was organized. The courts, therefore, generally sustain loans which are to promote the business of the corporation. A good illustration is where the corporation was authorized to operate a public warehouse for storing tobacco and to buy, sell, and rehandle the tobacco on commission. It was held that the corporation had authority to lend money to a customer on his growing crop of tobacco. It is settled beyond dispute, however, that a manufacturing or mercantile corporation incorporated under general corporation statutes may not engage in the general business of lending money. The power, when it is implied, must be necessary to carry out the express powers of the corporation or the objects of its incorporation.

The problems involved in contracts to lend money are not dissimilar from those involved in contracts to lend credit. A corporation is said to have the power to act as a guarantor when it is an appropriate and effective means of promoting the corporate business. Some state statutes expressly extend to the corporation the power to act as a guarantor; others expressly forbid it. It is quite clear that a corporation does not have the implied power to lend its credit or pledge its assets purely as an accommodation. [*Brinson v. Mill Supply Co.,* p. 570.]

(4) ***Power to Reacquire Its Own Shares.*** Shares of stock that have been reacquired by the corporation that issued them are commonly referred to as "treasury shares." The state statutes of some states specifically grant corporations the right to purchase their own shares. These statutes, however, ordinarily enumerate the conditions under which such purchases may be made. Some states, in the absence of an enabling statute, hold that a corporation may not purchase its own shares. These states, however, have held that a corporation may reacquire its own shares by gift, in payment of a debt due the corporation, as security for a debt, or to effect a compromise in a disputed claim against a shareholder. The majority of the courts have held that in the absence of a statutory or charter provision prohibiting the corporation from acquiring its own shares, the corporation may purchase its own shares provided no harm is done. The corporation, therefore, is generally permitted to purchase its own shares provided the rights of creditors or shareholders are not prejudiced by the transaction; the corporation is

not insolvent or in the process of dissolution; the corporation does not by the transaction become insolvent or turn its surplus into a deficit; the transaction is made in good faith and is free from fraud. The general rule, however, provides that the purchase must be made from accumulated profits and surplus.

(5) *Power to Acquire Shares in Other Corporations.* A corporation, as a general rule, may acquire shares of stock of another corporation. The acquisition of the shares, however, must be in furtherance of the authorized business of the corporation. This rule has been enacted into statute in most of the states. A corporation may take stock in payment of a debt or in settlement of a claim. But a corporation would not be permitted to speculate in the market with the shareholders' money, nor would a corporation be permitted to purchase shares if the acquisition was for the purpose of gaining control of management in order to suppress competition.

(6) *Power to Organize Holding Companies.* The phrase "holding companies" as used here is limited to corporations which are organized for the particular purpose of acquiring and holding stocks of other corporations. Holding companies exist by virtue of statutes in almost all of the states. They are prohibited in a few states and may not be formed in any state for an unlawful purpose. They may not, for instance, be formed for the purpose of creating a monopoly. In most of the states today, however, the mere fact that a corporation is a holding company does not make it, or its purposes, unlawful. [*Baum v. Baum Holding Co.,* p. 571.]

(7) *Power to Organize Subsidiary Corporations.* It is not uncommon for corporations to carry on departments or geographical branches of a business through subsidiary corporations. The parent corporation and the subsidiary are separate entities. There are no objections to a corporation's forming a subsidiary in order to accomplish a legitimate business purpose.

LIMITATIONS ON CORPORATE POWERS

Two important limitations on the powers of a corporation are found (1) in that class of cases where the courts place limitations upon the separate corporate-entity privilege and (2) in the doctrine of ultra vires.

Disregarding the Corporate Entity. If the corporate form of organization is used for purposes detrimental to society, the courts will not recognize separate corporate existence. Such nonrecognition is usually expressed in terms of "disregarding the corporate entity" or "piercing the corporate veil." The question of separateness sometimes arises in connection with parent and subsidiary corporations. The courts have frequently held the parent corporation liable for torts and contracts of the subsidiary. Creditors of the subsidiary have been permitted to recover from the parent corporation when there was a failure to keep separate accounts. The parent corporation has been held liable where there was a public representation that the two organizations were one. The parent corporation has been held liable where it so completely dominated the activities of the subsidiary that the transactions of each corporation could not be distinguished.

There is no general rule of law to govern the various factual situations present in this class of cases. It is generally accepted as essential to separateness, however, that each corporation keep separate accounts, that the formalities of separate meetings be observed, and that the subsidiary be provided with sufficient assets to meet its liabilities.

Disregarding the corporate entity is not limited to parent and subsidiary corporations. The members of a partnership, for instance, could not defeat creditors by incorporating the business. The organization of a corporation for the sole purpose of avoiding individual liability will not justify disregard of the corporate entity. The owner of a business who incorporates his business, with the aid of the members of his family, does not thereby lose the limited-liability attribute of the corporate form of organization. The owner, of course, must not confuse corporate affairs or assets with his own. He must not use the corporate form of organization to promote fraud or defeat justice. [*Telis v. Telis*, p. 572.]

The Doctrine of Ultra Vires.   Transactions which are outside the purposes and business of the corporation are said to be ultra vires, or "beyond the powers" of the corporation. Transactions which are inside the purposes and business of the corporation are said to be intra vires, or "within the powers" of the corporation. The older decisions pertaining to the doctrine of ultra vires have lost most of their significance. Some of the older decisions held an ultra vires contract to be void or illegal, and some held the doctrine of ultra vires to be a perfect defense. All would agree today that a contract of a corporation may be both ultra vires and illegal, but that the contract is not necessarily illegal merely because it is ultra vires. The doctrine of ultra vires is rarely available as a defense today. Several factors have contributed to the decline of the doctrine of ultra vires: the practice of incorporation for almost any purpose rather than for a single purpose; the practice of including lengthy purpose and object clauses in the articles of incorporation; the development of the doctrine of implied powers; and the enactment of statutes by a majority of the states. These statutes are not uniform, but the general effect of all of these statutes is as follows: Shareholders are permitted to bring injunction proceedings against the corporation; the state may bring proceedings against the corporation; the corporation may bring actions against its officers and directors; and the doctrine of ultra vires has sometimes been abolished as a defense.

In the absence of statute, the majority of the courts will not interfere with an ultra vires contract which has been fully executed by both parties, and will not permit any party to maintain an action on a purely executory ultra vires contract; a shareholder may prevent an anticipated ultra vires act by seeking an injunction in a court of equity; and an ultra vires contract which interferes with the rights of creditors is voidable at the suit of creditors. A conflict of opinion prevails when the ultra vires contract has been performed on one side only. The majority of the courts, however, will enforce the contract. A minority of the courts declare the contract to be void but allow recovery in quasi contract for the reasonable value of the benefit conferred.

AND CRIMES

Liability for Torts. The courts, in the earlier cases, held that a corporation was not liable for the torts of its employees while acting in ultra vires transactions. The great majority of the cases today, however, make no distinction between intra vires and ultra vires transactions. The determining factor in all cases is whether the agent acted within the scope of his employment. The general rule is that a corporation is liable for the torts of its officers, agents, or employees acting within the scope of their authority or in the course of their employment. The liability is based on general principles of agency law.

Liability for Crimes. The courts, in some of the earlier cases, took the view that a corporation was not indictable. The general rule is now well established, however, that a corporation may be criminally liable. It is likewise well settled that it is no defense that the act constituting the offense was ultra vires. A corporation cannot be made criminally liable where the only punishment for the offense is death, imprisonment, or some similar punishment inapplicable to a corporation. A corporation likewise cannot be made criminally liable under a statute when it is obvious that the legislature intended to exclude corporations; murder, which is generally defined as the killing of one human being by another human being, is a good illustration of such a statute. The courts have had no difficulty, however, in finding the statute applicable to corporations where the penalty imposed is a fine and not imprisonment, or where the penalty imposed is a fine or imprisonment. [*State v. Willard*, p. 573.]

CASES

Brinson v. Mill Supply Co., 14 S.E.2d 505 (N.C. 1941). Action by W. T. Brinson, in behalf of himself and all other shareholders and creditors of the Mill Supply Company, plaintiff, against the Mill Supply Company, Incorporated, defendant. A claim which arose out of the following circumstances was filed: A. F. Patterson, president, and the secretary of the defendant-corporation executed in the name of the corporation a contract of guaranty of a promissory note signed by Albert F. Patterson, in his individual capacity, in the sum of $5,000, payable to Harriet L. Hyman, which note contained the following provision: "The payment of this note is guaranteed by The Mill Supply Company in accordance with a separate contract of guaranty of even date herewith executed by The Mill Supply Company." E. F. Smallwood, as a result of this action which was brought for the appointment of a receiver and liquidation of the company, was appointed receiver. He denied the claim, and the claimant appealed.

    Barnhall, Justice: For a contract executed by the officer of a corporation to be binding on the corporation it must appear that (1) it was incidental to the business of the corporation; or (2) it was expressly authorized; and (3) it was properly executed.

    The charter of the defendant corporation vests it with general authority to acquire, own, mortgage, sell and otherwise deal in real estate, chattels and chattels real without limit as to amount; to deal in mortgages, notes, shares of capital stock and other securities; to acquire the good will, rights, property and assets of all kinds and to undertake the whole or any part of the liabilities of any person, firm, association or corporation, and to pay for the same in cash, stock, bonds, debentures, notes or other securities of this corporation or otherwise; to purchase or acquire its own capital stock from time to time to such an extent and in such manner and upon such terms as its board of directors shall determine; to borrow or raise money for any purpose of its incorporation, and to issue its bonds, notes or other obligations for money so borrowed, or in payment of or in exchange for, any real or personal property or rights of franchises acquired or other value received by the corporation and to secure such obligations by pledge or mortgage; and

to do all and everything necessary, suitable, convenient or proper for the accomplishment of any of the purposes, or the attainment of any one or more of the objects herein enumerated, or incident to the power herein named, or which shall at any time appear conducive or expedient for the protection or benefit of the corporation, either as holders of or interest in, any property, or otherwise; with all the powers now or hereafter conferred by the laws of North Carolina upon corporations.

There are other powers granted which are in nowise pertinent to the question here presented.

The powers thus granted do not expressly authorize the corporation to issue accommodation paper or to guarantee the obligations of a third party. . . .

The contract of guaranty was executed for the benefit of an individual. No part of the consideration moved to the defendant corporation. It was not either expressly or impliedly authorized by its charter to enter into contracts for the accommodation of a third party. To permit the payment of the claim would clearly result in an invasion of the assets of the defendant corporation in the hands of the receiver as a trust fund for the payment of legitimate creditors. [DECISION FOR THE RECEIVER]

Baum v. Baum Holding Co., 62 N.W.2d 864 (Neb. 1954). Action by James E. Baum and others, plaintiffs, against Baum Holding Company and others, defendants. The Baum Realty Company was organized for the purpose of placing the ownership of properties owned by members of the Baum family in the hands of a corporation as a matter of convenience. Stock was issued in the amount of 1,237 shares to the members of the family in proportion to their interests. Shortly after the organization of the Baum Realty Company, David A. Baum, Daniel Baum, Charles L. Baum, and Margaret Greer Baum, who owned 620 shares of the realty company, organized the Baum Holding Company. Each assigned his shares of stock in the realty company to the holding company and received in exchange therefor an equal number of shares of holding-company stock. The articles of incorporation of the holding company stated that the purpose of its organizaton was "to acquire, own and hold 620 shares of the par value of $100 per share of Baum Realty Company." The plaintiffs, as minority shareholders of the realty company, brought this action seeking, among other things, an injunction to restrain the holding company from operating as a company.

Carter, Justice: The plaintiffs as minority stockholders question the right of the holding company to vote the 620 shares of realty company stock owned by it as a unit as directed by the majority stockholders of the holding company. The answer to this contention is found in section 21–1, 141 R.S. 1943, wherein it is stated that

any corporation operating or organized under this act may guarantee, purchase, hold . . . the shares of the capital stock of . . . any other corporation or corporations of this state . . . while owner of said stock may exercise all the rights, powers, and privileges of ownership including the right to vote thereon.

It is clear that the holding company has statutory authority to vote the stock owned by it as a unit. There is no merit to this contention of the plaintiffs. . . .

It is asserted in the petition that David A. Baum induced his two brothers, Daniel Baum and Charles L. Baum, to join with him in organizing the holding company for the express purpose of gaining personal control of the company. This is not an unlawful object. Contracts between stockholders whereby they agree or combine for the election of directors or other officers, so as to secure or retain control of the corporation where the object is to carry out a particular policy with a view to promote the best interests of stockholders, have been generally upheld. We can see no reason why the same object may not be obtained by the organization of a holding company as by a contract between the parties. In one sense of the word the organization of the holding company is by virtue of an agreement. David A. Baum, Daniel Baum, Charles L. Baum, and Margaret Greer Baum entered into the agreement to organize the holding company. They knew the contents of the articles of incorporation and affixed their signatures thereto. It is not claimed that any wrong was perpetrated in so doing, other than the claim that David A. Baum was seeking to control the corporation, an object that we have held to be entirely proper. [DECISION FOR DEFENDANTS]

Telis v. Telis, 132 N.J. Eq. 25 (1942). Action by Sophie Telis (complainant below), appellant, against Jacob Telis and Telise's Bargain Store (defendants below), respondents. The facts show that the respondent Jacob Telis and the appellant are husband and wife; that Jacob Telis, who was operating a store in Atlantic City, purported to form a corporation, called Telise's Bargain Store, for the purpose of operating the business; that 100 shares of stock were purportedly issued, 98 to Jacob Telis, 1 to his son, and 1 to Sarah Steinmetz; that approximately eight months later the purported corporation purchased certain real property located at 223 South Connecticut Avenue, Atlantic City; and that the purported corporation is about to sell this property. This action was brought, predicated upon the allegation that the property was purchased in the name of the corporation "solely for the purpose of defrauding his wife of her dower right in and to that real estate."

Perskie, Justice: The right of our courts, in a proper case, to pierce the corporate veil cannot be gainsaid. The common exercise of that right does not trench upon the general principle that a "corporation is not an individual even if the individual owned all the stock of the corporation." Nor does it trench upon the established principle that the legality of the existence of a de facto corporation may be attacked only by the state in a direct proceeding, by information in the nature of quo warranto proceedings. Rather is the common exercise of the right to pierce the corporate veil deeply and firmly rooted in the principle that our courts do not permit the doctrine of corporate entity to be used for the purpose of defeating justice.

The proofs in the case at bar clearly satisfy us that the respondent and not Telise's Bargain Store, the corporation, owns the real estate. The corporation was never perfected; respondent held all of the stock notwithstanding that the two shares were in the name of others; there never was a formal meeting; no bylaws were ever adopted and corporate funds were intermingled with respondent's funds and used in payment of respondent's personal obligations. Form and not substance was affected. These and all other circumstances in the case entirely convince us that the corporate creation was, and its existence is, a mere sham, a mere subterfuge, a mere instrumentality employed for concealing the truth and, therefore, in the equitable sense, fraudulent. [DECISION FOR APPELLANT]

State v. Willard, 54 So. 2d 183 (Fla. 1951). This is a proceeding brought by Howard Losey and Rolfe Armored Truck Service, Inc., relators, against Ben C. Willard as Judge of the Criminal Court of Record of Dade County, Florida, respondent. The relators are two of several defendants informed against on an information brought by the state of Florida based exclusively upon an indictment returned by the grand jury of Dade County. The relators are seeking a writ of prohibition on the contention that the Criminal Court of Record should be prohibited from trying this case because Rolfe Armored Truck Service, Inc., being a corporation and not a natural person, was not subject to prosecution under the gambling laws of the state.

Sebring, Chief Justice: It is the rule that, except where the only punishment for an offense is death or imprisonment, a corporation may be held criminally liable for acts of misfeasance, malfeasance or nonfeasance, even though the act constituting the offense may be ultra vires, or one as to which a specific intent is essential. And the fact that the punishment for an offense is either fine or imprisonment, or both, will not ordinarily render the offense inapplicable to a corporation. In recognition of this rule the courts have held a corporation subject to prosecution for obstructing a highway; for obtaining money by false pretenses; for criminal libel; for selling beer to a known intoxicant in violation of statute; for criminal conspiracy; for grand larceny; for usury; for selling butter under the statutory weight. And though a corporation is generally immune from prosecution for offenses involving personal violence, at least one court has held that a corporation is indictable for involuntary manslaughter.

The statute under which the criminal charge against the relators was brought provides:

Whoever by himself, his servant, clerk or agent, or in any other manner has, keeps, exercises or maintains a gaming table or room, or gaming implements or apparatus, or house, booth, tent, shelter or other place for the purpose of gaming or gambling or in any place of which he may directly or indirectly have charge, control or management, either exclusively or with others, procures, suffers or permits any person to play for money or other valuable thing at any game whatever, whether heretofore prohibited or not, shall be punished by imprisonment in the state prison not exceeding three years, or by fine not exceeding five thousand dollars.

See section 849.01, Florida Statutes 1941, F.S.A. We find no indication in the broad language used in this statute of a legislative intent to restrict its application to "natural" persons only, and we conclude that the statute was meant, also, to apply to corporations. [DECISION FOR RESPONDENT]

PROBLEMS

1 The defendant-company agreed to furnish costumes to the Continental Company, a producer and manufacturer of motion-picture films. The plaintiff-company agreed to furnish lumber and materials to the Continental Company, which company defaulted in its payments. The defendant thereupon undertook to guarantee payments of the Continental Company for such materials as were necessary to the production of the films. The defendant had no express power to enter into contracts of guaranty as an independent business. Plaintiff brought an action to recover on the contract of guaranty. Decide.

2 The defendant, a brewing corporation, was authorized by its articles of incorporation to engage in the manufacture and sale of beer. The plaintiff, owner of certain store premises, leased said premises to the defendant for a term of five years. The defendant used the premises, not only for the manufacture and sale of beer, but also for the sale of whiskey, cigars, soda water, and such other things as are ordinarily sold in a general saloon. The defendant, prior to the expiration of the lease, vacated the premises. The plaintiff thereupon instituted an action for the balance of the unpaid rent. The defendant offered as a defense that the lease was ultra vires. Decide.

3 The defendant-corporation and the plaintiff-corporation were rivals in the business of manufacturing ice machines. Wilson, who was in charge of one of the branch offices of the defendant-corporation, entered into competitive bidding with the plaintiff-company to install an ice machine desired by the North Lake Company. The plaintiff-corporation was the successful bidder. Wilson, upon learning of this fact, wrote a libelous letter to the North Lake Company. The letter was written on the letterhead of the defendant-corporation, and it was signed by Wilson as manager of the branch office. Is this a wrongful act of an employee for which the defendant-corporation is not responsible?

4 Brown, who had been president of the XYZ Corporation for thirty years, died March 23, 1949. The directors thereafter met and adopted a resolution to pay the widow of Brown the sum of $2,000 per month in recognition of the long and valued services rendered to the corporation by her deceased husband for many years. A shareholder, contending that the payment was ultra vires, sought an injunction in a court of equity to prevent the payment. Should the injunction be granted?

5 The X Corporation was engaged in the business of developing real estate, and White was engaged in the business of constructing paved roads. The corporation was in the process of developing a new subdivision and needed a contractor to pave the streets. The corporation, therefore, entered into an agreement with White whereby White agreed to pave the streets and the corporation and White agreed to share in the profits and losses from the sale of the houses and lots in payment to White for the construction of the pavement. The stockholders sought to enjoin White from proceeding with the construction. Should they succeed?

6 The Acme Lumber Corporation was organized under the general corporation laws of the State of X, which provided that the state may alter, amend, or repeal corporate charters. At the time the corporation was organized, however, there was no statute permitting corporations for profit to make contributions, including contributions to educational institutions, and the charter of the corporation did not contain such a provision. But several years subsequent to the incorporation of the corporation, the state did enact a statute authorizing corporations to make certain contributions, including contributions to educational institutions. The board of directors of the corporation thereupon approved a motion to make a contribution of $800 to State University. At a stockholders' meeting, a stockholder vigorously opposed such a contribution. The stockholder stated that the corporation did not have the legal right to make such a contribution and that the objective of the corporation was to make profits and distribute them to the stockholders and not to make donations to charity. Discuss whether the arguments of the stockholder are correct.

7 Jones purchased certain real property for the purpose of mining coal from the land. He organized the "Coal Company, Inc.," which was a de jure corporation. Jones was the owner of all the shares of stock except one which was owned by his wife. Neither Jones nor his wife paid the corporation any money for such shares. No directors were elected, no meetings of stockholders ever occurred, no corporate books were ever prepared, and no corporate control was ever exercised. Jones operated the mine as if it had been his personal property. All the expenses of the mine were paid by Jones, and all the income therefrom was deposited in the bank account of Jones. The mining operations were conducted negligently and Jason, an employee, was killed. Jason's executor sued both Jones and the Coal Company for this wrongful death. The trial court entered a judgment against both Jones and the Coal Company. Jones contends that he should not be liable because the Coal Company operated the mine. Does Jones have any personal liability?

8 The Lumber Corporation was properly organized, and its entire authorized capital stock of 200 shares at $500 par value per share had been issued. Aaron was the holder of eight shares. Brown was the holder of fourteen shares. Cabot was the holder of eighty shares. Donald was the holder of ninety-eight shares. Donald attempted to purchase the eight shares belonging to Aaron, but Aaron refused to sell. Aaron thereafter offered to sell his shares to the corporation. The directors thereupon passed a resolution authorizing the treasurer of the corporation to purchase the eight shares at par value, which was $4,000, out of accumulated profits and surplus. Brown and Cabot, minority shareholders, brought an action to enjoin the corporation from purchasing its own shares. Will they succeed?

9 The Aluminum Company, which was in the business of manufacturing aluminum products, decided to manufacture aluminum patio frames. The company, in order to carry out this objective, decided to purchase all the assets of the XYZ Corporation, which was already engaged in the manufacture of aluminum patio frames. The XYZ Corporation refused to sell its assets, but all the shareholders in the corporation agreed to sell all of the shares of stock in the corporation to the Aluminum Company. One of the shareholders in the Aluminum Company contended that the Company had no authority to purchase the shares. Do you agree with this contention?

45

CORPORATIONS: RELATION TO DIRECTORS AND OFFICERS

The relationship between a corporation and its directors and officers pertains to problems involving the management of the regular business affairs of the corporation. It is convenient to approach this relationship from the viewpoint of (1) the directors, (2) the dividends, and (3) the officers.

THE DIRECTORS

Directors are sometimes classified as "agents"; at other times, they are classified as "trustees." They are governed by rules similar to those found in both the law of principal and agent and the law of trusts. They are sometimes referred to as "representatives of the incorporated body of shareholders." To pursue the arguments which attempt to define directors further would serve no useful purpose because directors constitute a distinct class. Attention is therefore directed to the (1) qualifications, (2) fiduciary relationship, (3) standard of care, (4) compensation, (5) management functions, and (6) meetings of directors.

Qualifications of Directors. In the absence of any provision to the contrary, any person who is legally competent to contract may be a director. Many statutes require that a director be a shareholder, but unless there is such a provision, a director is not under an obligation to be a shareholder.

Fiduciary Relationship. It is a fundamental principle that directors of a corporation occupy a fiduciary relationship to the corporation. They must act in the utmost good faith. They must not make a secret profit. A director who violates these rules may very well become involved in legal entanglements (1) when he purchases shares of stock of the corporation of which he is a director, (2) when he is a member of the boards of corporations having common directors, and (3) when he is personally interested in a matter being considered by the board.

(1) *Fiduciary Relation to Shareholders.* May a director or officer take advantage of his intimate knowledge of corporate affairs when he purchases shares from innocent shareholders? A director or officer, according to the old common-law majority rule, was not obligated to disclose any information relating to corporate business to individual shareholders before purchasing their shares so long as he avoided fraud or misrepresentation. It cannot be stated emphatically, however, that this rule represents the majority view today. The rule has certainly been weakened by the special-circumstances doctrine. The courts, by the use of this doctrine, have had no difficulty in finding directors under a duty to volunteer their information with respect to impending declarations of unusual dividends, prospective mergers, and similar important transactions. A minority rule provides that directors and officers are under a fiduciary duty to shareholders with respect to insider stock trading. Under this rule and the special-circumstances doctrine, the nondisclosure of information must be of a fact, as distinguished from an opinion, and there must be reliance thereon by the shareholder. The Securities Exchange Act of 1934 contains a provision designed to protect "outsider" shareholders against trading by "insiders" with advance information. This provision is discussed in Chapter 48, "Securities Regulation."

(2) *Interlocking Directorates.* Closely allied to the problem of interested directors is the problem pertaining to contracts entered into between corporations having directors in common. The courts, therefore, scrutinize transactions entered into between corporations having common directors with the same care as they do those entered into between an interested director and the corporation. The early view that held all contracts in which any common director participated voidable at the option of either corporation has quite generally been repudiated. The prevailing view today is a showing of fairness, and contracts entered into between corporations having even a majority of directors in common are voidable only when they are unfair.

The Clayton Act of 1914 prohibits a person from being a director of two or more corporations at the same time if either corporation has capital, surplus, and undivided profits aggregating more than $1,000,000 where elimination of competition by agreement between such corporations would amount to a violation of any of the antitrust laws. The purpose of this provision is to remove the temptation to violate the antitrust laws through interlocking directorates.

(3) *Interested Directors.* A director who is personally interested in a matter that is being considered by the board of directors is known as an "interested director." The courts have not formulated an all-embracing rule with respect to contracts entered into between the corporation and an interested

director. The majority of the cases hold: (1) The contract is voidable at the option of the corporation when a director—in order to make up a quorum or a majority—votes on a contract affecting his own private interest, regardless of whether the contract is fair or beneficial; or (2) the contract is voidable only upon a showing of unfairness, unreasonableness, or fraud when a disinterested majority of the directors authorize the contract. A few courts have held that contracts entered into between the corporation and the director are not voidable even if it took the vote of the interested director to form a majority of the approving directors. These courts, however, are careful to point out that such transactions will be scrutinized with extraordinary care. The problems pertaining to interested directors are very pronounced when directors attempt to fix their own compensation.

Standard of Care Required of Directors. There may have been a time when it could be stated that a director, so long as he acted in good faith, was not liable for consequences of his reckless and absurd mistakes of judgment. This is not true today. Many statements of the required standard of care are found in the decisions. It is sometimes said that directors are held to the ordinary care, skill, and business judgment with respect to management of the affairs of the corporation. Other times it is said that a director is under a duty to give the affairs of the corporation that same degree of care and judgment that a man would exercise in connection with his own affairs. These abstract statements, however, are not susceptible of precise definition. Decisions are not wanting, moreover, in which directors have found themselves subject to criminal proceedings under the revenue or antitrust laws in spite of the degree of care exercised. The directors must not act contrary to the bylaws, the charter, the statutes, or properly adopted resolutions. [*Emmert v. Drake,* p. 583.]

Compensation of Directors. Directors, as a general rule, are not entitled to compensation for performing the ordinary duties pertaining to their office unless compensation is authorized. They have no inherent authority to vote a salary to any director. They are, nevertheless, frequently authorized by the articles of incorporation, the bylaws, or by a vote of the shareholders to do so. Directors, therefore, do commonly receive fees or salaries for attendance at meetings of directors. It is also true that in the majority of the states, the law will imply a contract to pay for services rendered by a director clearly outside his ordinary duties if the services were rendered under circumstances tending to show an understanding that payment was to be made therefor.

The question as to how directors can exercise their authority—when such authority has been given them—to fix the salaries of corporate officers when the directors themselves are the officers arises when the board of directors consists of three members. The directors are confronted with the general rule that a director may not vote on his own compensation. Suppose the president and the secretary are two of the three directors constituting the board. The board could not fix the salaries of the president and secretary by one resolution because there is not a sufficient number of disinterested directors to constitute a majority. Director-officers clearly may have their salaries fixed by a vote of the shareholders or by ratification of the action of the board by the shareholders. Some courts have held that the director-officers could fix their own salaries by a separate resolution, provided each officer refrains from voting on the resolution fixing his own salary. Most courts, however, refuse to recognize such a procedure. [*Stoiber v. Miller Brewing Co.*, p. 584.]

Management Function of Directors.   The board of directors has the authority to transact any business that is within the scope of the inherent, express, or implied powers of the corporation. The management of the regular business affairs of the corporation is indeed entrusted to the board of directors. It is to be emphasized, however, that the authority of the directors does not extend to fundamental changes in the corporate organization. The consent of the shareholders is generally required to perform such acts as electing and removing directors, accepting and amending the corporate charter, adopting and amending the bylaws, merging or consolidating the corporation with another corporation, altering the authorized stock structure, transferring all of the property of the corporation, and voluntarily dissolving the corporation. It should also be emphasized that the statute, charter, or bylaws may enumerate other acts which require the consent of all or a certain proportion of the shareholders. The general rule gives the board of directors exclusive authority to manage the corporation in all those matters within the power of the corporation which do not require the consent of the shareholders.

Meetings of Directors.   The directors, in the absence of a statute to the contrary, can bind the corporation only when they are assembled, acting as a body at a meeting of the board. This rule is qualified by three well-recognized exceptions. The shareholders, being the source of the powers of the directors, may waive the necessity of board meetings. A few courts, in order to protect third persons who rely on custom or usage, have said the corporation and its shareholders are bound where they have by long practice, with knowledge of the facts, acquiesced in informal action. The courts have also said that action taken without a meeting of directors—in those instances where the directors were the only shareholders—was corporate action. A growing number of statutes also permit corporate action to be taken without a meeting of the board of directors. These statutes are not uniform, but it is generally provided that directors may act without a meeting if they unanimously consent in writing and the consent is filed with the corporate minutes.

The bylaws generally provide for the method of calling a regular or special meeting of the directors. Notice of a regular meeting ordinarily need not be given if the bylaws or charter specify the time of the regular meeting, but notice of special meetings must generally be given to each director. The presence of a quorum at meetings is necessary to transact business; a majority of the required number of directors is the minimum requirement for a quorum; a director may not vote by proxy; and a majority vote of the directors present at a meeting, as distinguished from a majority of the full board, is sufficient to authorize action.

DIVIDENDS

A dividend may be broadly defined as a payment to the shareholder as a return on his investment, and the usual practice is for the board of directors to declare a dividend payable to shareholders of record as of some future date, frequently ten or twenty days. With respect to revocation of a declared dividend, the courts make a distinction between a cash, or property, dividend and a stock dividend. The prevailing rule is that the declaration of a cash, or property, dividend creates a debt from the corporation to the shareholders, which dividend may not be revoked without the consent of the shareholders. It now remains to discuss (1) the mode of declaring a dividend, (2) the discretion of the directors in declaring a dividend, (3) the necessity of a surplus or profits before dividends can be declared, (4) the result of declaring unlawful dividends, and (5) the medium of payment.

Mode of Declaring a Dividend. A dividend is properly declared by a formal resolution of the board of directors. The resolution should specify the amount of the dividend, the date when the dividend will be paid, the medium of payment, the classes of shareholders to whom the dividend is payable, and the record date to determine the time when the shareholders of record shall be ascertained. This mode of declaring a dividend, however, is not entirely essential. An informal division of profits made with the consent of all the shareholders and directors is equivalent to a dividend. Such a dividend is said to be paid by "common consent."

Discretion of Directors in Declaring a Dividend. It is a well-settled general rule that whether or not dividends shall be declared and the amount of the distribution are left to the honest discretion of the directors unless such discretion is lawfully limited. An unusual type of noncumulative preferred-share contract which imposes a positive duty on the directors to the extent earned in that year leaves the directors no discretion to withhold dividends. Shareholders, however, have no right to declare dividends. This is said to be for the reason that the directors are the judges of how and when to spend the corporate funds. The courts will not, therefore, interfere with the discretion of the directors if the latter have acted in good faith and in a manner that is not unjust or oppressive to the shareholders. The shareholders, on the other hand, may compel the declaration of a dividend if they can convince a court of equity that the directors have acted fraudulently, oppressively, or unreasonably in refusing to declare a dividend. This question frequently arises: May the shareholders compel the declaration of dividends when the corporation has a large surplus and the directors are on the verge of directing the flow of income in expanding the corporate business? The answer to the question depends on the facts of the particular case. The courts, however, generally take the view that the shareholders expect to obtain profits on their investment in the form of dividends and to withhold the entire profits merely to expand the business of the corporation would defeat their expectation. [*Dodge v. Ford Motor Co.,* p. 585.]

Necessity of Surplus or Profits before Declaring a Dividend.   The statutes governing the declaration of dividends vary in their terminology. Some of the statutes provide that directors shall not declare dividends except from "surplus profits" arising from the business. Some statutes use the words "net profits or actual surplus." It is generally conceded that dividends cannot be declared unless the corporation has a surplus. The meaning of the word "surplus," however, can only be determined by an examination of the statutes of the particular state. The surplus is generally calculated as the amount of the corporate assets in excess of all outstanding liabilities and outstanding shares of stock of the corporation. It is quite clear the dividends cannot lawfully be declared until the corporation pays or provides for the payment of its debts.

It is now expressly recognized by many modern statutory provisions that a corporation which owns wasting assets; such as mining property, oil and gas wells, patents, and leaseholds, may distribute the net proceeds derived from their holdings without allowance for depletion. This rule, however, is generally subject to the limitation of making provision for creditors and holders of preferred shares entitled to priority upon dissolution.

Unlawful Dividends.   Practically every state, by statutory provision, imposes a personal liability upon directors for the wrongful declaration and payment of dividends. The statutes vary. The directors are sometimes made absolutely liable. They are, according to other statutes, not liable if they act in good faith. This is particularly true where they rely upon corporation records showing funds available for dividends.

The creditors are the ones who generally complain when unlawful dividends are paid to shareholders. As a general rule, however, dividends which are paid to shareholders while the corporation is insolvent, or rendered insolvent, are recoverable from the shareholders. This is true even though the dividends were received in good faith. The federal courts and about one-half of the state courts take the view that unlawful dividends received in good faith by the shareholders are not recoverable if the corporation is solvent. Many states have passed statutes regulating the liability of shareholders in connection with the receipt of unlawful dividends.

Medium of Payment.   A cash dividend is the most common means of paying dividends. The directors, however, may declare dividends payable in shares of stock of the corporation, property, scrip, or bonds. Dividends payable in money require no comment. This leaves for consideration dividends payable in the form of (1) the so-called "share dividend," (2) property, and (3) scrip and bonds.

(1)   *Share Dividend.*   A share dividend, or stock dividend, is said to be a dividend payable in shares of the corporation. The declaration of such a dividend involves the issuance of new shares to be distributed pro rata to the shareholders. This is evidenced by a contemporaneous transfer of an equivalent amount of the surplus or profits to the capital fund of the corporation. A share dividend takes nothing from the corporation and adds nothing to the interest of the shareholder. A share dividend, therefore, is in essence not a dividend at all in the usual sense of

the word. A share dividend is not income to the recipient for federal income tax purposes. It becomes property of the shareholder from the date of its declaration and not from the date of its payment.

(2) *Dividends Payable in Property.* A corporation which holds shares of stock in another corporation, or any other kind of real or personal property not necessary for its corporate purposes, may distribute such shares or property to the extent of the surplus in the same manner as cash. Such a dividend is called a property dividend. The courts reason that the shareholder can take the property and sell it and realize the cash. The share contract, however, sometimes specifies that the dividend is payable in cash. It has been held, in interpreting such a contract, that a shareholder cannot be compelled to take a property dividend in settlement of accumulated arrears of dividends on cumulative preferred shares which were payable in cash.

(3) *Scrip and Bond Dividends.* A distribution to the shareholder in the form of notes or promises to pay the amount of the dividend at a certain future time is known as a scrip dividend. The notes are called "dividend certificates," and they usually bear interest. This type of dividend is generally declared when the corporation has a surplus but not sufficient cash to pay a cash dividend. A distribution in the form of bonds is called a "bond dividend." These are sometimes used when the corporation has the cash to pay the dividend but wishes to reserve it for corporate purposes.

OFFICERS

Officers in General. The officers of a corporation are merely its agents. Their authority to bind the corporation may be conferred by statute, the articles of incorporation, the bylaws of the corporation, or by resolution of the directors. Authority may also be derived by an application of the general rules of the law of principal and agent. It is a well-recognized general rule of agency that every delegation of authority carries with it the authority to do acts which are reasonably necessary to carry into effect the express powers conferred. There may be a holding out or clothing of an officer with apparent authority. The general rules of estoppel and ratification are frequently applied to acts of corporate officers. Custom and usage may determine their authority. It is also to be realized that the authority of a particular officer will necessarily vary according to the nature of the business in which the corporation is engaged. The fact should not go unnoticed that an officer, as well as a director, may be held personally liable for a proper cause. [*Bogardus v. Kentucky State Bank,* p. 587.]

Authority of Officer by Virtue of Office. The following sections will be limited to those few powers of a corporate officer which are derived by virtue of the nature of the particular office.

President. The courts have expressed different views as to the authority of the president to contract as representative of the corporation. Many cases support the view that in the absence of express authority, the president is a mere figurehead whose only right is to preside at the meetings of the directors. The modern tendency, however, is to recognize a presumption of authority. According to the modern view, therefore, contracts made or acts done by the president in the course of the ordinary business of the corporation will be presumed to have been done within his authority unless the contrary appears. It may be well, in view of this conflict, to verify the authority of the president.

Vice-President.   It is the duty of the vice-president in the event of absence or incapacity of the president to assume the duties of the president. He has no authority by virtue of his office alone to enter into contracts in behalf of the corporation.

Secretary.   The secretary of the corporation is a ministerial officer who keeps the books and minutes of the meetings of the shareholders and directors. He has no authority by virtue of his office alone to enter into contracts in behalf of the corporation.

Treasurer.   The treasurer is the custodian of the funds of the corporation and its disbursing officer. He has authority to receive and give receipt for money due the corporation and to make such disbursements as he may be authorized to make. He has no authority by virtue of his office alone to enter into contracts in behalf of the corporation.

Controller.   The office of controller is relatively new in the United States. An increasing number of statutes, however, recognize the controller as a corporate officer. The Securities Act of 1933 provides that the registration statement to be filed with the Securities and Exchange Commission must be signed by the controller or other principal accounting officer of the corporation in addition to certain other principal officers. His authority may be limited to the supervision of accounts and accounting procedure. He is, nevertheless, frequently given an official title and the privilege of ranking with other corporate officers.

General Manager.   The general manager has the implied authority to make any contract and do any other act appropriate in the ordinary business of the corporation. No formal resolution is necessary to confer such authority.

CASES

Emmert v. Drake,   224 F.2d 299 (1955). Action by Lawrence Drake and Hugh F. Walsh, plaintiffs, against H. R. Alrich, Jr., Roy C. Coffee, C. A. Mohrle, H. M. Oster, and D. U. Emmert, defendants. The defendants, directors of the Metals & Chemical Corporation, passed the following resolution on May 2, 1952:

Resolved: That the President of the corporation is hereby empowered and directed to borrow $100,000.00 for and on behalf of the corporation and to issue and execute therefor proper notes of the corporation with payments on or before six months from date, to bear five (5) percent interest per annum and to provide for payment thereof out of the first proceeds of any funds received by the corporation as a result of the public offer of its stock.

The corporation, in pursuance of the resolution, thereafter borrowed certain sums of money. The promissory notes given in payment of the sums so borrowed contained the following provision: "It is expressly understood and agreed that this note will be payable out of the proceeds of the first public financing through the public sale of the corporation stock." The corporation received a total of $221,044.20 as the result of the public sale of its shares of stock. The corporation, however, used such money for corporate purposes other than the payment of the notes. The plaintiffs, payees of two of the promissory notes containing the proviso mentioned above, brought this action against the directors of the corporation individually and jointly.

De Vane, District Judge: Here we have a case where the Directors of a corporation passed a resolution empowering and directing its President to borrow $100,000.00 for and on behalf of the corporation and to issue and execute therefor proper notes of the corporation and provided further in said resolution for the payment of these notes "out of the first proceeds of any funds received by the corporation as the result of a public offer of its stock." The record in this case shows that the money so borrowed was authorized and borrowed for the express purpose of enabling the corporation to make a public offering of its stock.

When the corporation note was delivered to Drake it contained a provision heretofore quoted that the note was payable out of the proceeds of the first public financing through the public sale of the stock of the corporation and plaintiff Drake was furnished with a copy of the resolution of the Board authorizing the President to borrow the money. The terms of the promissory note here sued upon and the resolution authorizing the corporation to borrow this money operated to create an equitable lien upon the first proceeds of any funds received by the corporation as the result of the public offering of its stock and it became the duty of the Directors of the corporation to see to it that this money was used for that purpose. They cannot excuse themselves by saying that in no way they misappropriated or dissipated any of the funds of the corporation or were in other respects derelict in their duty as Directors. [DECISION FOR PLAINTIFFS]

Stoiber v. Miller Brewing Co.,   42 N.W.2d 144 (Wis. 1950). Action by Michael T. Stoiber, plaintiff, against the Miller Brewing Company, defendant. On July 1, 1947, the plaintiff, Frederick C. Miller, and Lorraine J. Mulberger constituted the board of three directors of the defendant-corporation. At a meeting of the board on July 22, 1947, the following business was transacted: By the votes of directors Stoiber and Mulberger a resolution was adopted authorizing the defendant to enter into a contract with director Miller for his employment by defendant as one of its two executive managers for ten years at a salary of $12,000 per year, but Miller did not vote on this resolution; by the votes of directors Miller and Mulberger, a resolution was adopted authorizing the defendant to enter into a contract with director Stoiber for his employment by defendant as its coexecutive manager for ten years at a salary of $12,000, but Stoiber did not vote on this resolution. At a meeting of the board on February 22, 1949—which plaintiff failed to attend—the board adopted a resolution for the discharge of plaintiff as coexecutive manager of the defendant-company. At a meeting of the board on May 9, 1949, which Miller and Mulberger attended, the discharge was confirmed as an avoidance of the employment contract for causes, including the invalidity of the reciprocal resolutions and votes of July 22, 1947, to authorize said employment contract. This action was then brought to recover damages for breach of the employment contract. The defendant-company contends that the resolution purporting to authorize the employment contract was illegal and void and that defendant by its board of directors has avoided said contract.

    Fritz, Chief Justice: From the undisputed corporate record it appears that neither the resolution to authorize Stoiber's contract, nor the resolution to authorize Miller's contract was supported by a disinterested majority of the defendant's board of three directors. Instead it is obvious that their attempted adoption was by reciprocal votes. . . .

As stated in 175 A.L.R. 592–593. The rule which forbids a director of a corporation from casting the vote essential to the adoption of a resolution fixing his own salary is applicable to the situation in which the salaries of two or more directors are to be fixed and, in voting, the interested directors act in co-operation, each voting for the resolution fixing the salary of another. . . . The reasoning behind the rule seems to be that each director would, as a rational human being, vote in favor of salaries for the others in the expectation that they would in turn vote for him and that therefore they would be casting their votes in their own interests and not in the interest of the corporation.

And in Ballantine, Corporations (1946 Ed.) sec. 74, p. 190, it is stated:

A corporation is not liable, as a general rule, for services rendered by directors on special contracts authorized by the votes of interested directors. It has generally been held that where various directors are interested in the common object of procuring a salary or a salary increase for each of them as officers, the device of passing several resolutions for each instead of one joint resolution for all will not be effective. The mutual back-scratching or reciprocal voting invalidates the action as to each.

    The rules thus stated are applicable and controlling in the case at bar. Therefore the adoption of the resolutions in question by the reciprocal votes of the directors was void and ineffectual to authorize the making of the contracts in question. [DECISION FOR DEFENDANT]

Dodge v. Ford Motor Co.,   170 N.W. 668 (Mich. 1919). Suit by John F. Dodge and Horace E. Dodge, plaintiffs, against Ford Motor Company and others, defendants. The plaintiffs, who are two minority shareholders holding one-tenth of the issued shares, sued to compel the distribution of an extra dividend of not less than three-fourths of the available cash balance. At the time this suit was instituted the corporation had assets of more than $132,000,000, a surplus of almost $112,000,000, and its cash on hand and municipal bonds were nearly $54,000,000. Its total liabilities were a little over $20,000,000. The trial court decreed that the directors of the Ford Motor Company declare a dividend upon all of the shares of stock in an amount equivalent to one-half of the accumulated cash surplus, less the aggregate amount of the special dividends declared and paid after the filing of this suit.

    Ostrander, Chief Justice: When plaintiffs made their complaint and demand for further dividends the Ford Motor Company had concluded its most prosperous year of business. The demand for its cars at the price of the preceding year continued. It could make and could market in the year beginning August 1, 1916, more than 500,000 cars. Sales of parts and repairs would necessarily increase. The cost of materials was likely to advance, and perhaps the price of labor, but it reasonably might have expected a profit for the year of upwards of $60,000,000. . . . It had declared no special dividend during the business year except the October, 1915, dividend. It had been the practice, under similar circumstances, to declare larger dividends. Considering only these facts, a refusal to declare and pay further dividends appears to be not an exercise of discretion on the part of the directors, but an arbitrary refusal to do what the circumstances required to be done. These facts and others call upon the directors to justify their action, or failure or refusal to act. In justification, the defendants have offered testimony tending to prove, and which does prove, the following facts. It had been the policy of the corporation for a considerable time to annually reduce the selling price of cars, while keeping up, or improving, their quality. As early as in June, 1915, a general plan for the expansion of the productive capacity of the concern by a practical duplication of its plant had been talked over by the executive officers and directors and agreed upon, not all of the details having been settled and no formal action of directors having been taken. The erection of a smelter was considered, and engineering and other data in connection therewith secured. In consequence, it was determined not to reduce the selling price of cars for the year beginning August 1, 1915, but to maintain the price and to accumulate a large surplus to pay for the proposed expansion of plant and equipment, and perhaps to build a plant for smelting ore. It is hoped, by Mr. Ford, that eventually 1,000,000 cars will be annually produced. . . .

    "My ambition," said Mr. Ford, "is to employ still more men, to spread the benefits of this industrial system to the greatest possible number, to help them build up their lives and their homes. To do this we are putting the greatest share of our profits back in the business."

    . . . The difference between an incidental humanitarian expenditure of corporate funds for the benefit of the employees, like the building of a hospital for their use and the employment of agencies for the betterment of their conditions, and a general purpose and plan to benefit mankind at the expense of others, is obvious. There should be no confusion (of which there is evidence) of the duties which Mr. Ford conceives that he and the stockholders owe to the general public and the duties which in law he and his codirectors owe to protesting, minority stockholders. A business corporation is organized and carried on primarily for the profit of the stockholders. The powers of the directors are to be employed for that end. The discretion of the directors is to be exercised in the choice of means to attain that end and does not extend to a change in the end itself, to the reduction of profits or to the nondistribution of profits among stockholders in order to devote them to other purposes.

. . . It is obvious that an annual dividend of sixty percent upon $2,000,000, or $1,200,000, is the equivalent of a very small dividend upon $1,000,000,000, or more.

The decree of the court below fixing and determining the specific amount to be distributed to stockholders is affirmed. [DECISION FOR PLAINTIFFS]

Bogardus v. Kentucky State Bank, 281 S.W. 2d 904 (Ky. 1955). Action by Kentucky State Bank (plaintiff below), appellee, against O. A. Bogardus, Jr. (defendant below), appellant. R. M. Jones borrowed $3,500 from the plaintiff-bank and pledged as security 750 shares of stock in the Wellner Construction Company, a corporation. All the shareholders agreed sometime thereafter to liquidate the corporation. The assets of the corporation were thereupon sold and the shareholders were paid in cash, but the shareholders were not required to surrender their share certificates. This action was then brought against defendant, the officer of the corporation who had charge of its liquidation, to recover the loss resulting from the distribution of a part of the assets of the corporation to the shareholder who was indebted to the plaintiff-bank.

Clay, Commissioner: The legal theory upon which the claim is based is that the corporation and its officers had no right to distribute the assets of the corporation without the surrender of stock certificates, and that in so doing they violated the rights of the plaintiff as pledgee and transferee of the certificate.

Under the common-law rule the plaintiff would have no valid claim against the corporation or its officers, since they owed no duty in liquidation to unregistered transferees of the corporate stock. . . .

However, on facts very similar to those here presented, the Michigan Supreme Court has held that a pledgee of stock has rights which will be protected in liquidation.

The Michigan Supreme Court held that a corporation could recognize the exclusive right of the holder of registered stock to the payment of *ordinary dividends,* but that in paying liquidating dividends the corporation must have due regard for the rights of unregistered transferees of the stock.

Since it would impair the free negotiability of stock certificates if the rights of an unregistered transferee or pledgee were dependent on notice of the transfer or pledge given the corporation, we are of the opinion that the defendant at his own risk distributed liquidating dividends to Jones, the registered owner, without requiring the surrender of the stock. [DECISION FOR PLAINTIFF]

PROBLEMS

1 Brown was the president and a director of the Concrete Corporation. Smith was a director of the same corporation. The total number of the board of directors was four members. Brown and Smith, at a meeting at which one director was absent, presented their claims against the corporation for special services rendered by them. Brown and Smith voted in favor of paying the claims. The only other director present voted against the claims. The next year a new board of directors was elected, and the corporation brought an action to recover the amount of money so paid to Brown and Smith. The court found that the services were not of an unusual nature. Decide.

2 Plaintiff was employed as a sales manager of the Rocky Mountain Power Corporation in May, 1942, at which time it became necessary to suspend all operations. An officer and director of the corporation approached plaintiff and asked him to safeguard the assets of the corporation until new financing could be obtained. Plaintiff did safeguard the assets of the corporation by personal attention for the next twelve years, at which time he caused its reactivation. Plaintiff was thereafter elected to the board of directors at a special meeting of shareholders, and that board, at a meeting at which plaintiff was present but refrained from voting, adopted a resolution directing the president and secretary to execute in favor of plaintiff a promissory note of the corporation for $11,625 in payment of his services in safeguarding the assets of the corporation. Is the corporation liable on the note?

3 Defendant was the director and manager of a large corporation, the shares of which corporation were registered on a national exchange. Plaintiff was the owner of five shares of the common stock of the corporation, which defendant purchased for $300 a share. Defendant knew at the time he purchased these shares that the directors of the corporation had already decided to declare a 100 percent dividend within the next two months. Discuss the duty of defendant under the special-circumstances doctrine. Discuss the duty of defendant under the Securities Exchange Act of 1934.

4 Defendant is a business corporation, and three persons own all its capital stock and are also its directors. The corporation became indebted to plaintiff in the sum of $4,500. The three directors met at the place of business of plaintiff, discussed the indebtedness owing to plaintiff, and agreed that a note should be executed by the corporation to secure the indebtedness. The note was then executed in the name of the corporation by its treasurer. The corporation made payments on account of the note amounting to $2,150, and refused to pay the balance. The corporation contends that the note was not authorized at any meeting of its board of directors and its treasurer was not authorized by its board of directors to execute the note. Do you agree with this contention?

5 The board of directors of the Land Company accepted an offer to purchase all the property of the Valley Company. A special meeting of the stockholders of the Land Company was called for the purpose of ratifying the proposed purchase. The meeting was held as scheduled, and the proposed purchase was ratified by an affirmative vote of 1,550 shares out of a total of 1,950 shares and opposed by 400 shares represented by plaintiff. Plaintiff, a minority shareholder in the Land Company, seeks to avoid the sale on the ground that the two corporations have identical directors. Do you think he will succeed?

6 Brown, Smith, Jones, Taylor, and Blake are the directors of the Hauling Company, Inc., a contract carrier. Blake is the owner and operator of an automobile agency. The Hauling Company has been purchasing all of its new trucks from Blake since he was elected a director. Blake has never voted, during the directors' meetings, on the motion to purchase trucks from him. He has in no way tried to influence the decision of the other directors. The Hauling Company needs twenty-five new trucks and the board of directors, except Blake, who did not vote, voted unanimously to purchase all the new trucks from Blake. The contract price for the new trucks is the usual price charged for twenty-five such trucks. Clark, a stockholder in the Hauling Corporation, brought an action on behalf of the corporation to have the contract of purchase canceled. How should the court decide this case?

7 The Y Corporation was fully organized as a de jure corporation, and a board of directors was elected and bylaws were adopted at a meeting of all of the stockholders. Thereafter at a regular meeting of the board of directors, the board passed by a majority vote an amendment to the bylaws adding the following provision: "Any officer of the corporation may be removed by a majority vote of the board of directors." The board of directors then removed Davis as vice-president of the corporation. Would Davis succeed in a suit asking the court to declare void the act of the board of directors in removing him from office?

46

CORPORATIONS: RELATION TO SHAREHOLDERS

This chapter will be devoted to (1) the rights and liabilities of the shareholder in general, (2) devices used for gaining and maintaining control of the corporation, (3) the remedial rights of the shareholder, (4) meetings of the shareholders, and (5) the transfer of shares of stock.

RIGHTS AND LIABILITIES IN GENERAL

It may prove helpful for purposes of clarity to (1) summarize the rights of the shareholder before considering (2) the liabilities of the shareholder.

Summary of Rights　The rights of a shareholder may be summarized as the right to share in the profits of the corporation by way of dividends, the right to share in the assets upon dissolution, the right to vote—which carries with it the right to share in the control and management of the corporation—and the remedial rights. The rules pertaining to these rights are scattered throughout these chapters on corporations. They are merely grouped here for convenience.

Liabilities of the Shareholders　The personal liability of the shareholder with respect to watered shares, the de facto doctrine, the separate entity privilege, and the distribution of unlawful dividends have already been considered. It remains, therefore, to consider the liability of the shareholder to pay for his shares of stock.

The liability of the shareholder to the corporation for nonpayment of his agreed subscription price is quite clear and simple. There is a positive legal contractual liability on the part of the shareholder to pay his subscription agreement. The corporation, therefore, may recover from the shareholder the amount remaining unpaid on his subscription agreement irrespective of whether such amount is necessary to pay the debts of the corporation.

The liability of the shareholder to creditors for the amount remaining unpaid on his subscription agreement is equally clear. It is not, however, quite so simple as is his liability to the corporation. The courts proceed on the theory that the positive legal liability is transferred into an equitable liability and have established—in the absence of receivership or bankruptcy—a creditor's bill in equity as the normal device for collecting unpaid subscriptions. This theory presupposes that the creditor has first exhausted his remedy against the corporation. A creditor who has an unsatisfied judgment against the corporation, therefore, may proceed against the shareholders for the unpaid balance of their subscriptions. In some states a creditor's bill may be brought by an individual creditor, but in most states the bill must be brought in behalf of all the creditors. This is to prevent any one creditor from going into equity and appropriating the balance due on unpaid shares to himself exclusively. The shareholder, in either event, is not liable beyond the amount of his agreed subscription price unless some statute expressly so provides. Such statutes are rarely found today. It should be mentioned, however, that there was a time when constitutional and statutory provisions imposed an additional or superadded liability upon shareholders. Superadded liability provisions as to state banks still survive in a few states, and occasionally a statute is found which imposes superadded liability upon shareholders for wages of employees. As a general rule, however, the shareholder has a limited liability. This means, of course, that the shareholder is liable only to the extent that his shares have not been fully paid.

CORPORATE CONTROL DEVICES

An attempt will be made to point out some of the legal incidents which attend (1) the solicitation and exercise of proxies, (2) the voting trust, (3) cumulative voting, and (4) the pre-emptive right of the shareholder.

Proxy Absent shareholders are given the right to vote at a meeting by written proxy which is a special form of agency whereby the shareholder, as principal, delegates authority to another person, as agent, to vote his shares at a meeting of the shareholders. If the delegation of authority is general, the proxy authority ordinarily has the authority to vote the shares in any manner he pleases. The authority, however, may be limited in such a way that the proxy holder must vote the shares as directed by the shareholder. The proxy form of agency, unless coupled with an interest, is revocable.

It is unquestionably true that the proxy system may be used to take control out of the hands of the many and place it in the hands of a few. Proxy solicitation today, however, is fairly well regulated. It was declared unlawful by the Securities Exchange Act of 1934 to solicit any proxy from the holder of any security registered on any national exchange or registered as a public utility holding company except in accordance with rules and regulations prescribed by the Securities and Exchange Commission. This Commission, pursuant to this authorization, has issued a series of rules and regulations governing the solicitation of proxies. The general purpose of the rules is accomplished by requiring those who solicit proxies to furnish the shareholder with a proxy statement containing sufficient information so that they may know what they are authorizing.

The Securities and Exchange Commission promulgated in 1956 new rules regulating contested proxy solicitation. A proxy contest arises when there is a dispute between groups attempting to gain or to retain control of the board of directors. The new rules require all nominees for directors and other participants in a proxy contest to file with the commission a schedule making a full disclosure of interest. The information contained in the schedule, as under the old rules, must be included in the proxy statement that is required to be sent to the shareholders.

Voting Trusts and Agreements   A voting trust is accomplished when several or all of the shareholders vest the legal title to their respective shares of corporate stock in specified trustees for the purpose of voting the shares. The trustees, in turn, issue "voting trust certificates" to the shareholders. Legal title to the shares and the right to vote are then in the trustees as owners who distribute to the shareholders their proportionate share of the dividends received from the corporation. A voting trust, unlike a proxy, is not revocable. In many states specific statutory provision controls the method of creating voting trusts and the length of time for which they may exist. It is commonly ten years.

The holder of a voting trust does not have the rights of a shareholder. He has only the rights given him by the voting-trust certificate. He cannot, for instance, inspect the books of the corporation unless the right is specifically given to him. A voting trust, nevertheless, performs a useful purpose. It is a convenient device that may be used when a corporation finds it necessary to borrow money and needs a speedy vote to carry out the corporate plan for raising the money. But the voting trust is also subject to abuse. A voting trust will not be continued merely to enable the trustees to earn their compensation. Nor will it be permitted to continue if its sole object is to secure permanency of management for a scheming group. Voting trusts are "securities" as defined by the Securities Act of 1933. They are, therefore, subject to regulation.

A participant in a voting agreement, as distinguished from a voting trust, may retain the possession and title to his shares of stock. The participant does, however, bargain away his right to vote his shares in any manner other than as provided in the agreement. Voting agreements have been held to be invalid by a very small number of cases, but the modern view is that such agreements are not by their nature invalid. Public policy requires, however, that a voting agreement be given no effect when it is inspired by fraud or when it bargains away the duties of directors. Participants in a valid voting agreement cannot withdraw from the agreement unilaterally, and one of the participants may petition the court for the enforcement of a valid voting agreement. [*Weil v. Beresth*, p. 599.]

Cumulative Voting   Statutory authority is now found in practically all of the states for cumulative voting, the aim of which is to enable minority shareholders to secure representation on the board of directors. This aim is accomplished by permitting each shareholder to multiply the number of votes to which he is entitled by the number of directors to be elected. He may cast all these votes for one candidate or he may distribute them among the various candidates. The statutes in a few states require advance notice of the intention of shareholders to cumulate their vote. This requirement is intended to prevent the minority from defeating the purpose of cumulative voting which is to give the minority representation rather than control.

Pre-emptive Right   The common-law pre-emptive right of a shareholder is his right to purchase a pro rata share of newly authorized issues of shares before the shares are offered to others. Suppose a corporation has 1,000 shares of issued capital stock and that Smith owns 200, or one-fifth, of these shares. If the corporation should issue ten additional shares, Smith would have the right to purchase two of these shares. This rule has the effect of permitting a shareholder to maintain his same pro rata interest in the corporation. The pre-emptive-right rule, however, is so qualified by exceptions today that it has lost much of its significance. The right, as a general rule, does not exist in shares issued for services or for property instead of for cash; nor in shares used to effect a consolidation or merger; nor in shares issued under employees' stock-purchase plans; nor in treasury shares. There is a conflict in the law as to whether or not the right exists to authorized but unissued shares as distinguished from newly authorized shares. It is probable, in most states, that the right does not extend to a new issue of previously authorized shares. The extent to which the holder of one class of shares has a pre-emptive right to the issue of another class is very uncertain. Many modern corporation statutes permit charter provisions to limit or deny the pre-emptive right.

REMEDIAL RIGHTS
The remedial rights of a shareholder include (1) the right to information and inspection of the corporate books and records and (2) the right to bring shareholder suits.

Right to Inspect the Books   A right to inspect corporate books and records, either personally or by agent, for a proper purpose and at reasonable times is given to shareholders by the common law. It has been held that the purpose was proper where the shareholder desired to ascertain the financial condition of the corporation for the purpose of determining the value of his shares or the possibility of dividends. The copying of the names of other shareholders in preparation for a meeting of the shareholders, as well as gathering information to be used in an action against the directors for mismanagement, has been held to be a proper purpose. The shareholder, however, had to show that he was a shareholder of record. The right of inspection is now governed by statute in practically all of the states. The type of statute which broadly provides that books and records shall be open to the inspection of every shareholder enlarges the common-law right of inspection because the shareholder is relieved of showing a satisfactory reason or proper purpose. Some courts have refused to inquire into the purpose of the shareholder seeking an inspection under this type of statute on the reasoning that the statutory right is absolute. Other courts have refused to order an inspection when it was proved that the shareholder made the demand for an improper purpose. Some of the other statutes require that the demanding shareholder be a record holder of a certain minimum number of shares or that he be a shareholder of record for a certain period of time. Many of the modern statutory provisions have returned to the common-law rule which limits the right of inspection upon the appropriateness of the purpose of the shareholder.

Shareholder Suits   Suits by shareholders may be divided into three general categories: individual suits, representative suits, and derivative suits. A shareholder who has business dealings with the corporation—as where he lends money to the corporation—may bring an action in his individual capacity if the corporation fails to repay the loan when it becomes due. A shareholder may bring an individual suit to compel the corporation to recognize his status as a shareholder, or to protect his pre-emptive right. A representative suit and a derivative suit are both class suits, and the use of the word "representative" to refer to both direct representative suits and derivative suits has caused some confusion in the reported decisions. The distinction between the two types of suits is nevertheless important.

(1)   *Representative Suit*   A representative suit is a direct suit against the corporation brought by a shareholder as representative of a class of shareholders similarly situated. The class may be minority shareholders or perhaps the holders of a class of shares of stock. This is the type of suit which is usually used to enjoin an ultra vires act or other threatened wrong by the corporation before it is consummated. Two or three of the preferred shareholders, for instance, could bring a representative suit to compel the corporation to pay the dividends on all of the outstanding preferred shares of stock before paying the dividends on the common stock.

(2)   *Derivative Suit*   A derivative suit is one brought by one or more shareholders as a representative of the corporation and a class of shareholders. This type of suit is brought when a cause of action accrues in favor of the corporation. The corporation, to be sure, could bring a direct action against the wrongdoers. A derivative suit may be brought, however, when the corporation for some reason fails to bring a direct action. The wrongdoers may be persons either within or without the corporation. A derivative suit is usually brought against persons outside the corporation for breach of contract, or against the corporation

for things such as mismanagement by the board of directors. [*Taormina v. Taormina Corp.*, p. 600.]

MEETINGS OF SHAREHOLDERS

The statutes of the various states, as a general rule, provide that the time and place of holding meetings and the manner of calling them may be regulated by the bylaws. The statutes are not uniform. It is essential, therefore, that the governing statute, charter, or bylaws provision be examined carefully in order to accord the shareholders their right of participation in corporate action. In practically all states, however, provision is made for two kinds of meetings of shareholders: the regular annual meeting and the special, or called, meeting. Most state statutes require that a regular meeting for the election of directors shall be held annually. Any transaction within the ordinary course of business, however, may generally be considered at a regular meeting. It should be pointed out that statutes sometimes provide that certain transactions can be consummated only at a "special meeting of shareholders called for that purpose."

Notice of the time and place of holding regular meetings, as a general rule, is not required when the time and place are fixed by the bylaws. Notice of all special meetings must be given each shareholder. The notice must specify the time and place of the meeting and the business to be transacted at the meeting. The words "call" and "notice" of meetings are sometimes used synonymously. The two words are easily distinguished. The "call" for a meeting is exercised by the persons who have the power to call the meeting. It may consist of a direction to the secretary to notify the shareholders of the special meeting. The "notice" of the meeting is the writing apprising the shareholders of the meeting. Some modern statutory provisions declare that notice shall be given in writing to shareholders entitled to vote. Typical expressions are "notice of meetings," "notice of all meetings," and "notices of meetings, annual and special." Formal notice may be waived by the shareholder either in writing or by participating in the meeting. This principle is expressly recognized in many statutory provisions.

A quorum of shareholders must be present at the meeting, and, in the absence of any contrary statute, charter, or bylaw provision fixing the vote for corporate action, the holders of a majority of the voting shares must be represented in person or by proxy in order to constitute a quorum. Otherwise no action can be taken, except to adjourn. If a quorum assembles, however, a minority group cannot prevent corporate action by walking out.

INVESTMENT SECURITIES

Article 8, "Investment Securities," covers certificates of stock, bearer bonds, registered bonds, and other instruments which the securities markets are likely to regard as suitable for trading or which are commonly recognized as a medium of investment. Securities are negotiable instruments, but they are not governed by

Article 3, "Commercial Paper." There are, nevertheless, many similarities in the Code between the articles on commercial paper and investment securities.

Section 8–302 provides that a purchaser of a security acquires the rights in the security which his transferor has. This is similar to the "shelter or umbrella provision" in commercial paper which gives a holder through a holder in due course the rights of a holder in due course. Section 8–302 defines a "bona fide purchaser" as a purchaser for value in good faith and without notice of any adverse claim. A bona fide purchaser, therefore, is likened to a holder in due course. This is as it should be, because the investor must have confidence in the genuineness of the security in order for the security to move freely in the marketplace. The following discussion is intended to create an awareness that the Code provides a set of rules for the negotiation and transfer of stock and bonds, and will be limited to (1) the issuance of shares, (2) restrictions on transfer, (3) transfer and registration of shares, (4) lost, destroyed, and stolen certificates, and (5) the Statute of Frauds.

Issuance of Shares   The word "issuer" as used in section 8–201 includes a person whose name is placed on a security to evidence that it represents a share in an enterprise. The issuer, in most instances, will be a private corporation. Often, however, it will be a corporation chartered as an agency of a governmental unit. The definition is broad enough to include a partnership, a sole proprietor, or a joint adventure.

Most state statutes provide that certificates of stock shall be signed by the president or vice-president and the secretary or assistant secretary of the corporation. The signatures are sometimes facsimiles, and the certificate is then signed by the transfer agent. The transfer agent, however, is not the issuer. The shares are ready for sale to the general public when the shares are issued and the certificate properly signed, unless the shares are to be retained by a few persons—as frequently is the case in a close corporation—or there are restrictions on transfer.

Restrictions on Transfer   Section 8–204 impliedly permits restrictions on transfer by providing that the restriction must be noted conspicuously on the certificate. Unless the restriction is noted on the certificate, it is ineffective against a purchaser without actual knowledge of the restriction. This section, however, deals only with restrictions imposed by the issuer. Restrictions imposed by statute and private agreements between shareholders are not affected. Most jurisdictions permit restrictions, and restrictions which have been held to be valid include a restriction which limits the power of the shareholder to transfer his shares when he is indebted to the corporation; a restriction which takes the form of an agreement among the shareholders giving the corporation an option to purchase their shares before they are purchased by outsiders; and a restriction which requires the employees to resell their shares to the corporation on the termination of their employment.

Transfer and Registration of Shares   The owner of the shares of stock represented by the certificate can transfer title to the certificate indorsed either in blank or to a specified person. A convenient method of transferring the certificate is through utilization of the printed form of transfer which is commonly placed on the back of the share certificate. The transfer is then completed by delivery of the certificate.

It is then the duty of the transfer agent to record the transfer, cancel the surrendered certificate, and issue a new certificate in the name of the transferee. The stock exchanges, however, might require the appointment of a bank or trust company—someone other than an employee of the issuer—as a "registrar" when the stock is listed on a stock exchange. The principal duty of the registrar is to guard against the issuance of shares in excess of the authorized capital stock and to countersign the certificate.

Lost, Destroyed, or Stolen Certificate   The owner of a certificate which has been stolen and has been transferred by a forged indorsement to a bona fide purchaser may reclaim his security from the bona fide purchaser. The remedy of the purchaser is against the seller on his warranties as provided in section 8–306. The selling shareholder warrants to his purchaser for value that (1) his transfer is effective and rightful, (2) the security is genuine and has not been materially altered, and (3) he knows of no fact which might impair the validity of the security.

If the owner is unable to reclaim his security from the purchaser, he may protect himself by giving written notice to the issuer within a reasonable length of time after he has notice of the loss or has reason to know of the loss or theft of his security. The issuer must then issue a replacement certificate to the true owner. The owner, however, must comply with all reasonable requirements of the issuer. This may include the giving of an indemnity bond to protect the issuer.

Although the owner may reclaim a stolen certificate transferred by a forged indorsement while it is still in the hands of a bona fide purchaser, he may not reclaim a new reissued and reregistered certificate from a bona fide purchaser. Section 8–306 provides that a purchaser for value without notice of an adverse claim who receives a new reissued and reregistered security warrants to the issuer that he has no knowledge of any unauthorized signature in an indorsement. The bona fide purchaser who presents a security and receives a new security is therefore protected against a claim based on the forgery of an indorsement.

The rights and duties of the issuer, the original owner, and the bona fide purchaser will ordinarily arise in the following four situations:

(1) Where the owner fails to notify the issuer as required by section 8–405 within a reasonable period of time after he knows of the loss or theft of the certificate, and the certificate is presented for registration and transfer by a bona fide purchaser: The owner is not entitled to a replacement certificate, and he is estopped from asserting any claim against the issuer for the registration of the transfer. This is true even though the certificate was transferred to the bona fide purchaser by a

forged indorsement. The reason for this rule is that the registered owner was in the best position to prevent the loss, destruction, or theft of the certificate.

(2) Where the issuer issues a replacement certificate, and the lost certificate is thereafter presented for registration and transfer by a bona fide purchaser: For example, the owner borrows money from the First Bank, indorses his certificate in blank, and delivers it to the First Bank as security. He thereafter repays the loan, and the First Bank returns the certificate. The owner then leaves the indorsed certificate—which is now negotiable by delivery alone—in his desk drawer. The certificate is thereafter stolen, and the thief sells it to a bona fide purchaser. The issuer must register the transfer, and the issuer may recover the replacement certificate from the original owner. If the replacement certificate has reached the hands of a bona fide purchaser, the issuer is required to honor both certificates unless an overissue would result. This is the situation where the number of outstanding shares exceeds the number of shares authorized by the corporate charter. If an overissue would result, the issuer will be required to purchase a certificate in the open market. If the security is not available in the open market, the bona fide purchaser is relegated to an action against the issuer for damages measured by the price he or the last purchaser for value paid for the certificate with interest from the date of his demand. The issuer may then recover from the original owner on his indemnity bond.

(3) Where the issuer makes a wrongful transfer: An issuer who has received notice that a certificate is lost or stolen but who nevertheless registers a transfer of the certificate wrongfully—as where the indorsement on the certificate is a forgery—is required by section 8–404 to issue a replacement certificate to the original owner unless the replacement certificate would result in an overissue. In case of an overissue, the remedy of the original owner would be an action against the issuer for damages. The issuer generally requires the signature of the indorser to be guaranteed by a member of a local stock exchange, a local bank, or some other person of responsibility who is familiar with the signature of the transferor. The issuer, therefore, would ordinarily have a remedy against the guarantor of the signature. Section 8–312 provides that a person who guarantees a signature of an indorser of a security warrants to the issuer that (a) the signature was genuine, (b) the signer was the appropriate person to indorse, and (c) the signer had legal capacity to sign.

(4) Where a certificate in bearer form or a certificate indorsed in blank is stolen and comes into possession of a bona fide purchaser: The bona fide purchaser will have a claim to the security superior to the claim of the prior owner from whom the certificate was stolen.

Statute of Frauds   The provisions of the Statute of Frauds pertaining to investment securities are quite similar to those pertaining to the sale of goods. Section 8–319, therefore, similarly provides that an oral contract for the sale of securities is not enforceable by way of action or defense. This section, however, applies to any contract for the sale of securities irrespective of the amount involved. The writing must indicate that a contract has been entered into for the sale of a stated quantity of described securities at a defined or stated price. The contract is enforceable, however, if delivery of the security has been accepted or if payment has been made, but the contract is only enforceable to the extent of such delivery and acceptance. The contract is also enforceable if a written confirmation of the contract is received within a reasonable time, unless written notice of objection is given to the sender within ten days after it is received.

CASES

Weil v. Beresth, 220 A.2d 456 (Conn. 1966). Action by Nathan Weil, plaintiff, against Edward Beresth and Gershon Weil, defendants, for the enforcement of a voting agreement.

On August 27, 1954, Nathan Weil, Edward Beresth, Gershon Weil, and Raymond S. Harrison, the holders of a majority of the stock in the Self Service Sales Corporation, entered into a written voting agreement. By the terms of paragraphs 2 and 3 of the agreement, each stockholder agreed that he would vote for election as directors the other stockholders who signed the agreement; that he would vote in this manner at every meeting held for the purpose of electing directors as long as he remained a stockholder of the corporation; that he would vote to amend the bylaws to reduce the number of directors from five to four and to provide that three directors should constitute a quorum; and that he would not vote to amend "the bylaws so adopted" without the consent of all the other individual parties to the agreement. The bylaws were adopted in accordance with the agreement, and the terms of the agreement were carried out for over ten years. On April 19, 1965, however, Edward Beresth, Gershon Weil, and Raymond S. Harrison voted to repeal the existing bylaws and adopt new bylaws which increased the number of directors from four to five and provided for amendment to the bylaws by a vote of a majority of the board of directors. Plaintiff then instituted this suit in equity seeking the rescission of the new bylaws and the restoration of the old bylaws. Raymond S. Harrison, who voted by proxy, was not made a party defendant.

King, Chief Justice: The defendants correctly concede that a voting agreement is not, per se, invalid under the general, common-law rule. Nor do they claim that the agreement here was entered into for any fraudulent or illegal purpose, even though not apparent on its face, which would deprive it of validity. Thus, the defendants do not claim that this agreement works a fraud on minority stockholders, that it confers any benefit on the plaintiff at the expense of the corporation, or that it contravenes public policy in any similar fashion. They do not claim that it is anything but a voting agreement. . . . Their sole claim of invalidity is predicated upon an alleged lack of a limit as to the duration of the agreement, which they claim is contrary to public policy. . . .

The voting agreement under consideration here is not unlimited in duration. The obligation of each stockholder to vote for the other signatories as directors expressly exists only "so long as he is a stockholder of Sales." Thus, even if there were a public policy forbidding voting agreements of unlimited duration, it cannot be said that that policy has been violated in the instant case. . . .

The plaintiff is entitled to a decree ordering the defendants to join with him in taking the appropriate steps promptly to call and hold a stockholders' meeting for the following purposes, and at that meeting to vote their stock to carry out those purposes: (1) to reenact the two bylaws which were originally enacted pursuant to paragraphs two and three of the agreement; (2) to repeal all bylaws or parts of bylaws conflicting or inconsistent therewith; and (3) to withdraw from the board of directors the power to amend those two provisions of the bylaws either directly or indirectly by the adoption of conflicting or inconsistent bylaws. [DECISION FOR PLAINTIFF]

Taormina v. Taormina Corp., 78 A.2d 473 (Del. 1965). Action by Rosa Maggie Taormina, widow and executrix of the estate of Calogero Taormina, and Samuel Miles Fink, ancillary administrator of said estate, plaintiffs, against the Taormina Corporation and individual shareholders, defendants.

The Taormina Corporation carried on the business of canning goods. Calogero Taormina owned 498 shares of stock of the corporation at the time of his death, and the individual defendants owned the remaining shares. The individual defendants, being the officers and directors of the corporation, formed a partnership under the name of Taormina Company and caused the assets and goodwill of the corporation except certain real estate to be transferred to the partnership. The same canning business developed by the corporation was thereafter conducted by the partnership.

The evidence revealed that the individual defendants caused the assets of the corporation to be transferred to the partnership for inadequate consideration and caused the real estate and machinery of the corporation to be leased to the partnership for a wholly inadequate yearly rental; and that they entered into a conspiracy to appropriate the going successful business of the corporation and to deprive it of further profits from the operation of the business for their personal profit.

Plaintiffs alleged that the individual defendants unjustly profited themselves at the expense of the corporation and asked the court that the individual defendants be directed to account for all profits made by the partnership and for all sums of money misappropriated by them, and that the shares of stock of the individual shareholders be confiscated. The individual defendants contend that the injury was to Calogero Taormina individually and that the remedy is a direct suit against the corporation to recover a share of the profits obtained from the business conducted by the partnership.

Wolcott, Chancellor: It is true that Calogero Taormina as a minority stockholder suffered financial loss by being deprived of his rightful share as a stockholder of corporate profits, but this is true of most derivative actions. If the argument of the defendants is to be accepted, it would mean that no derivative action could be maintained by a stockholder to redress corporate wrongs if those wrongs had resulted in loss to the value of his stockholdings. The defendants argue that the only stockholder who can have been injured as a result of the action of the individual defendants is Calogero Taormina for the reason that he is the only stockholder of the corporation who did not participate in the course of action instigated by the individual defendants. They argue that the injury was to him individually and that he must bring suit in his own name for the redress of these wrongs.

The argument ignores the fundamental basis of a derivative stockholder's action which is to enforce a corporate right. To make this argument, the defendants impliedly recognize that a wrong has been done the corporation. . . . The relief to be obtained in a derivative action is relief to the corporation in which all stockholders, whether guilty or innocent of the wrongs complained of, shall share indirectly. Indeed, it is doubtful whether the result would be different even if the suing stockholder owned all of the stock of the wronged corporation. I conclude, therefore, that the pending action is a derivative action brought by the plaintiffs to enforce a cause of action owned by the corporation. [DECISION FOR PLAINTIFFS]

PROBLEMS

1 Plaintiff, owner of 200 shares of stock in the defendant-corporation, went to the seashore for the summer. He left his office and business affairs in charge of his private secretary to whom he gave a power of attorney to draw and indorse checks and drafts on his bank. He also directed his secretary to pay the last installment on his shares of stock and to receive and keep the same. These instructions were followed by the secretary, and the shares were delivered to the secretary. The secretary thereupon forged the name of the plaintiff to the blank form of transfer, sold the shares, and absconded. The corporation had, in the meantime, canceled the old certificates and issued new certificates in the name of the purchaser. Four months thereafter, the plaintiff attempted to compel the defendant-corporation to issue to him 200 shares in lieu of the 200 shares so canceled by the corporation. Decide.

2 Plaintiff, a newspaper publisher, acquired 40 percent of the stock of the defendant-corporation, a competing newspaper in the same city. Plaintiff thereafter demanded that he be permitted to inspect the books of the defendant-corporation; the demand was complied with insofar as books showing the financial condition and the value of the capital stock of the corporation were concerned. Plaintiff insists that he is entitled to see all the books of the corporation. Is he correct?

3 Marshall was the owner of 100 shares of the XYZ Corporation, which was evidenced by a stock certificate in his possession. For some reason apparently known only to Marshall, he indorsed the certificate in blank and placed it in his private safe in his home. Marshall and his wife were the only people who knew the combination to the safe. One night while Marshall and his wife were at the theater a burglar succeeded in opening the safe and removed the certificate. The theft was discovered when Marshall and his wife returned from the theater. Marshall reported this to the police and, within a few hours, widespread publicity concerning the theft was given over radio, television, and the newspapers. Two days later Andrews, by means of a due negotiation, purchased the certificate of stock from an acquaintance and thereby became a bona fide purchaser. Andrews immediately notified

the corporation that he desired a new certificate in his name. Marshall objected to the issuance of the new certificate and claimed that his rights as a stockholder must be protected. Will Andrews or Marshall prevail in this controversy?

4 Plaintiffs are stockbrokers and dealers in securities and in the course of their business deliver securities to other brokers within the City of New York. On the day in question, the plaintiffs telephoned a messenger service to send a messenger to the office of plaintiff for the purpose of delivering securities to certain other brokers. The messenger was handed certificates which were indorsed in blank and transferable by delivery. The messenger stole the certificates, and they eventually came into the possession of the defendant, a bona fide purchaser. As between the plaintiff and the defendant, who has a better claim to the certificates?

5 The ABC Corporation called a special meeting of its shareholders for the purpose of electing a new board of directors. The corporation had 400 shares of stock outstanding, of which Brown was the owner of 205 shares. The president of the corporation, in hope of keeping the same directors, induced Brown the day before the meeting to give him a proxy to vote Brown's shares at the meeting. Brown thereafter decided it would be to the best interest of the corporation to elect new directors and therefore attended the meeting. The meeting was called to order by the president in his office, and the owners of all the 400 shares were present. Brown then revoked his proxy, but the president, who was presiding, would not recognize the revocation. The president and his faction then proceeded to re-elect the same directors by virtue of the Brown proxy. The meeting was then adjourned by the president, and he and his faction locked the office door and left the building. Brown and his faction thereupon continued the meeting in the hall just outside the office of the president and elected a new board of directors. Who are the duly and lawfully elected directors of the corporation?

6 Jones, the owner of a large builders' supply business, decided to incorporate the business. Smith, who had been in the employ of Jones for some time, was issued 100 shares in the newly formed corporation with the understanding that he would not sell or assign the shares to any one without the written consent of the corporation. It was also agreed that the certificates representing the shares would remain in the safety vault of the corporation. Smith received dividends for approximately ten years, at which time he was discharged from his employment for inattention to his duties. The corporation thereupon offered to pay Smith the par value of the 100 shares and requested him to resell them to the corporation. Smith refused to resell his shares to the corporation on the ground that a corporation cannot restrict the transfer of its shares of stock unless the restriction is stated upon the face of the certificate. Is Smith entitled to compel the corporation to deliver the certificates of stock to him?

7 The Land Corporation, which had entered into a contract with twenty-five individuals to construct twenty-five houses in a new suburb, entered into a contract with a builder whereby the builder agreed to construct the houses. The builder then repudiated the contract. The directors of the corporation, acting as a body at a meeting of the board, acted in the utmost good faith in deciding that it would be unwise to bring an action against the builder. A shareholder then brought an action in his individual capacity to compel the corporation to bring an action against the builder for breach of contract. Will the shareholder succeed?

8 Plaintiff purchased ten shares of stock in the XYZ Corporation. The certificates representing the shares were prepared by the corporation in the name of plaintiff. The certificates, however, were wrongfully delivered by an employee of the corporation to a third person. This third person transferred the shares to Smith by means of a forged indorsement. What are the rights, if any, of plaintiff? What are the rights, if any, of Smith?

9 The Dredging Corporation and the First Bank entered into an agreement whereby two-thirds of the shareholders transferred their shares to the First Bank for voting purposes and the First Bank made a substantial loan to the Dredging Corporation. The First Bank then issued voting trust certificates to the shareholders. At the next meeting of shareholders, the First Bank voted the two-thirds shares for an entirely new board of directors. The owners of the remaining shares voted in favor of the old board. The members of the old board refused to permit the new directors to take office. The new board then brought an action to have it determined that the new board was the duly elected board of directors of the Dredging Corporation. Do you think they will succeed?

47

CORPORATIONS: TERMINATION

Coming now to the termination of a corporation, it is only necessary to observe briefly (1) how corporations may be unified by consolidation and merger, (2) how the corporate existence may be brought to an end, and (3) the effect of bringing the corporate existence to an end.

CONSOLIDATION AND MERGER

Consolidation and merger are both statutory proceedings whereby two or more corporations are unified. The distinction between the two procedures is that in a consolidation two or more existing corporations are dissolved and a single new corporation is created, while in a merger one of the corporations—the surviving corporation—remains in existence and absorbs the other corporations which are dissolved. A merger, therefore, might be preferable to a consolidation if the surviving corporation has nonassignable leases or employment contracts which may not pass by a consolidation. It may likewise be preferable where the surviving corporation is qualified to do business as a foreign corporation.

Both procedures involve a transfer of the assets of the constituent corporations in exchange for securities in the new or surviving corporation; both involve an assumption of the debts and liabilities of the constituent corporations;

both involve the dissolution of the constituent corporations; but neither consolidation nor merger involves the liquidation and winding up of the affairs to the
extent that the assets are distributed to the shareholders. This question is
sometimes posed: Is the right of preferred shareholders to arrears of cumulative
dividends a vested right in the nature of a debt which cannot be abrogated? The
courts, as a general rule, hold that the right is nothing more than a contractual
preference subject to change by consolidation or merger. Some statutes expressly
so provide. [*Anderson v. Cleveland-Cliffs Iron Co.*, p. 607.]

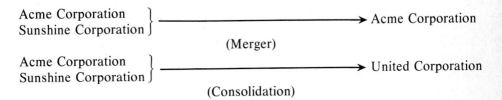

END OF THE CORPORATE EXISTENCE

How may the corporate existence be brought to an end? By dissolution. This
involves two steps: the termination of the corporate existence and the winding up
of the affairs of the corporation. Dissolution may be (1) voluntary or (2)
involuntary.

Voluntary Dissolution   Voluntary dissolution may be brought about by (1)
expiration of the charter of the corporation and (2) consent of the shareholders.

(1)   *Expiration of the Charter*   A corporation may be granted perpetual
existence. It·may, on the other hand, have been organized to exist for a definite
period of years; the corporation, in these circumstances, automatically terminates
at the expiration of the stated period. It is not necessary to seek the aid of a court
to terminate the corporation. Some state statutes permit an extension of the term
of existence. This ordinarily may be done by an amendment of the charter or by
filing a certificate of renewal with designated public officials.

(2)   *Consent of the Shareholders*   Practically all of the states have enacted
statutes providing for the voluntary dissolution of a corporation. The most
common method is by a majority vote of the shareholders at a meeting duly called
and held. The procedure varies. The following steps, however, will serve to
illustrate how voluntary dissolution by the shareholders may be brought about:
The board of directors will adopt a resolution recommending that the corporation
be dissolved voluntarily; notice of a meeting to consider the resolution will be
given to the. shareholders; the resolution to dissolve will be adopted by the
majority vote of the shareholders at the properly called meeting; a certificate
evidencing the action taken by the shareholders will be filed with some designated
public official; and notice of the dissolution will be given to the creditors of the
corporation either by publication or by mailing a copy of the certificate directly to
the creditors.

Involuntary Dissolution Involuntary dissolution may be brought about by (1) a suit for dissolution maintained by the shareholders or (2) forfeiture of the corporate charter by the state.

(1) *Dissolution by Shareholders* Many of the states have enacted statutes pertaining to the right of shareholders to maintain a suit for dissolution. These statutes vary considerably. They provide generally, however, that the corporation may be dissolved for reasons such as the impossibility of performing the corporate objectives, incurable dissensions which make continuance of the corporation unprofitable, abandonment of the corporate business, and fraud or serious mismanagement on the part of the persons in control. The early cases established the general rule that in the absence of statutory authority, the courts were without jurisdiction to wind up the affairs of a solvent corporation or to appoint a receiver with that end in view at the suit of a minority shareholder or creditor. Receivership is still recognized as a radical remedy. The general rule has, nevertheless, been abandoned in an increasing number of decisions. Courts of equity have afforded relief to minority shareholders where there was such dissension among the shareholders as to render it impossible to continue the business of the corporation, where fraud was shown on the part of the majority shareholders, and where serious mismanagement was shown on the part of the directors and officers. It is now generally agreed that, in the absence of any statutory provision to the contrary, the dissolution of a corporation may be brought about through a suit in equity when the facts of the particular case reveal that such action is necessary to protect the interests of creditors or shareholders. [*Goodwin v. Milwaukee Lithographing Co.,* p. 608.]

(2) *Forfeiture of Corporate Charter* The state of incorporation has the right, through its attorney general, to institute a quo warranto proceeding requesting the court to dissolve the corporation. The grounds upon which forfeiture may be declared by the state are generally enumerated in the statute. These include such things as failure to file annual reports, failure to pay franchise taxes, fraud practiced on the state in securing the charter, misuser and nonuser, and the like. "Misuser" and "nonuser" mean that the corporation has abused, or has failed to exercise, the powers given to it. The courts, however, are reluctant to decree a forfeiture of the corporate charter and will refuse to do so if some other adequate remedy is available. [*State v. Zale Jewelry Co.,* p. 609.]

EFFECT OF DISSOLUTION

A dissolved corporation, in the absence of a statute to the contrary, ceases to exist. It no longer has the power to sue or be sued, to enter into contracts, to hold or convey property, or to exercise any other powers granted by its charter. Most of the state statutes today, however, provide that a dissolved corporation shall have a qualified existence for a limited time. These statutes generally give the directors the power to use the corporate name for the purpose of prosecuting and defending suits by or against the corporation, disposing of and conveying its property, settling and closing its affairs, paying the corporate debts, and distributing the assets to the shareholders.

The assets of the dissolved corporation clearly belong to the shareholders. A shareholder who has not paid for his shares of stock in full, however, will participate in the assets only in proportion to the amount actually paid. If the liabilities exceed the assets, the shareholder will be liable to creditors to the extent of the balance unpaid upon his shares. If distribution is made prior to the payment of the debts, unpaid creditors may proceed against the shareholders who have received the assets as well as against the directors who made the improper distribution.

CASES

Anderson v. Cleveland-Cliffs Iron Co.,   87 N.E.2d 384 (Ohio 1948). Action by Leander Anderson and others, plaintiffs, against Cleveland-Cliffs Iron Company and others, defendants. An "agreement of consolidation" was properly entered into by the terms of which it was proposed to consolidate the assets and liabilities of the defendant-corporation with the assets and liabilities of the Cliffs Corporation in a new corporation to be known as "The Cleveland-Cliffs Iron Company." The plaintiffs, whose dividends on the cumulative preferred shares are in arrears, claim that they are entitled to receive the liquidation value of their shares including the dividend arrearages. This claim is based on the following provision in the preferred share contracts:

Upon the dissolution, liquidation or winding up of the Corporation the holders of record of preferred shares shall be entitled to receive out of the assets of the Corporation, if such dissolution, liquidation or winding up be voluntary, an amount equal to $102.50 per share . . . with all dividends accrued or in arrears, for each of their preferred shares, before any distribution of the assets shall be made to the holders of common shares.

McNamee, Judge: A consolidated corporation comes into being as a result of and at the time of the Consolidation Agreement. By operation of law all of the property of the constituent corporations is transferred to the new corporation and the debts and liabilities of the constituent companies are assumed by the consolidated company. The rights and interests of consenting shareholders of constituent corporations, in the consolidated corporation, are fixed by the Agreement of Consolidation which may provide for the issuance of shares in the consolidated company or the distribution of cash, notes, bonds, or property in lieu thereof. If there are existing dividend arrearages on the preferred stock of one of the constituent companies, the consolidation agreement must give effect to the value of the preferred shareholders' rights to such accumulated dividends in determining a fair basis of conversion of shares or distribution of property in lieu of shares in the consolidated corporation. Assuming the plan to be fair, a preferred shareholder's interest in a constituent company, including his right to cumulative dividend arrearages, is fully protected by its conversion into shares or other considerations of the consolidated corporation. In the absence of an abuse of discretion by the directors, in failing to pay dividend arrearages, a shareholder in a constituent corporation has no immediate assertable right to collect the full amount of such arrearages. The consolidation of his corporation with another does not confer such right.

. . . It is clear that the term "dissolution" as used in the preferred shareholders' contract means statutory dissolution. . . . Upon consolidation of a corporation there is no complete distribution of assets to all of the shareholders of the constituent companies. [DECISION FOR DEFENDANTS]

Goodwin v. Milwaukee Lithographing Co.,   177 N.W. 618 (Wis. 1920). Action by H. W. Goodwin and others, minority shareholders of the defendant-company, plaintiffs, against the Milwaukee Lithographing Company and Alfred Von Cotzhausen, its president, general manager, and treasurer, and other officers of the corporation, defendants. The purpose of this action is to procure the appointment of a receiver, to wind up the affairs, to distribute the assets, and to decree a dissolution of the defendant-corporation. The question presented to the court is whether or not the facts of this case present a proper situation for the exercise of the power of a court to dissolve a corporation.

Owen, Justice: The tabulations set forth in the statement of facts showing the course of business of the company from the year 1913 down to the appointment of the receiver March 9, 1916, shows that up to the year 1913, the year during which the defendant Von Cotzhausen acceded to the presidency and general manager thereof, the company did a thriving business, earned handsome profits, and paid gratifying dividends. In the year 1912 the company made profits of $45,465.50. In 1913 they dwindled to $11,617.64. In 1914 there were losses of $21,260.85. The losses during 1915, up to November 12th, were $29,592.08, and from November 12, 1915, to March 9, 1916, there were further losses of $22,772.92. The amount of sales in 1912 were $310,697.23. In 1914 the first full year of management by Von Cotzhausen, the sales were $164,508.45, a dropping off of nearly 50 percent. The first six months of 1915 the sales were only $25,783.27, and from July 12th to November 12th of the same year the amount of sales were $15,086.94. This shows an amazing decrease in the business and indicates that in but a short time the business would be practically nil. One marvels at the possibility of such a slump in such a short time, but the record furnishes ample evidence for the reason thereof.

When Von Cotzhausen assumed management of the company there was a well-organized sales force. There was a general sales agent on the Pacific Coast, one in New York, one in New Orleans, and two in Chicago. These sales agents were procuring the business for the company. Good business judgment would plainly require a continuance of cordial relations between these sales agents and the company and a retention of their services. The evidence discloses, however, that Von Cotzhausen immediately proceeded to get into a row with all these men and made it so disagreeable for them that they quit the service of the company. The services of one Frank W. Wentworth, of Chicago, appears to have been particularly valuable to the company. . . .

Instead of maintaining satisfactory arrangements with the said Frank W. Wentworth, Von Cotzhausen started an action against him to recover for the company $36,000 which he claimed Wentworth owed to it for overcharges, which the referee finds to have been unfounded, resulting in the loss of Wentworth's services and the business which he secured for the company.

This furnishes but a glimpse of the real character, attitude and diplomacy of the said Von Cotzhausen and is but a small part of the evidence which justifies the finding of the referee—

. . . that the defendant Alfred Von Cotzhausen for many years past had, and still has, the reputation among the trade and business in which the Milwaukee Lithographing Company is engaged as being unreasonable, unreliable, dishonest, and litigious, and as being a dangerous man to deal with.

We cannot escape the conclusion that this company can be no longer operated under Von Cotzhausen's domination and control except to its own ruin and the loss by the stockholders of their entire investment. The purposes for which the company was organized are no longer possible of accomplishment, and the only rational thing to do is to wind up its affairs and save the stockholders from further loss. [DECISION FOR PLAINTIFFS]

State v. Zale Jewelry Co.,   298 P.2d 283 (Kan. 1956). Action by state of Kansas, on the relation of Harold R. Fatzer, Attorney General, plaintiff, against Zale Jewelry Company of Wichita, Inc., a corporation, defendant.

Smith, Chief Justice: This is an original action in quo warranto brought by the state on the relation of the attorney general wherein the state asks that the defendant corporation be ousted from engaging in the practice of optometry. Plaintiff also asks that the charter of the corporation be forfeited and a receiver appointed. . . .

What are the facts and circumstances we must consider? The defendant is a domestic corporation with its stock all owned by a Texas corporation. It is engaged in the main in the retail jewelry business. In Wichita it operates a jewelry store in a two-story store building. Its jewelry business is transacted on the ground floor. The second story is used for storage purposes. In the rear of the first floor is a balcony reached by stairs from the floor. On this balcony Dr. Marks and The Douglas Optical Company carried on their activities. Each had a lease with defendant, both leases executed on April 1, 1952. Dr. Marks rented a room about 8 by 20 feet for a refracting room and a room adjoining for a waiting room. The rent was $100 a month. Defendant agreed to service and handle the accounts receivable of Marks, including his collections, bookkeeping and clerical work. Marks agreed not to engage in any business in competition with defendant. Douglas Optical leased the entire balcony except what was leased to Marks. It agreed to pay defendant 20% of its gross sales to be paid on the 10th of every month. Defendant agreed to service and handle at its own expense the accounts receivable of Douglas, including collections, bookkeeping and clerical work. It should be pointed out here that the business of Marks, the optometrist, was to test eyes and to ascertain what glasses, if any, the patient needed. That of the optical company was to grind the lenses according to the optometrist's prescription and to furnish frames for the lenses. The lenses were all ground in Dallas, Texas.

In the early stages of the case there was in the rear corner of defendant's store near the stairway to the balcony a neon sign reading "Optical Dept." After this action was commenced this was changed to "Douglas Optical."

There is no dispute about how business was carried on. When a customer entered the store a clerk would ask what he wanted. When he answered he had come to get some glasses he was directed to the stairs at the back of the optical department. On arriving at the balcony he would be met by a young lady who would ask him some questions. Dr. Marks then proceeded to examine his eyes. A prescription by Marks was then handed to the optical company. He was shown frames, informed of the price of glasses and made arrangements how he wanted to pay, whether cash or in payments. The fact is the glasses could be paid for in payments. The customer would be taken downstairs then to defendant's cashier, where credit arrangements on payments were made. Payments were made to defendant's cashier and correspondence as to delinquent accounts was on defendant's stationery.

In the front of defendant's store are display windows. One is devoted exclusively to the display and advertising of eye glasses. Above the front of the store is a large projecting neon sign bearing the words "Zale's Jewelers." Below these words appear the replica of a pair of glasses and the words "Glasses Fitted." . . .

Defendant carried on an extensive advertising campaign in the local newspapers. These were usually rather large display ads. They would devote considerable space to the jewelry business of defendant but always a portion would be devoted to the optical business.

. . . We find as a matter of fact that the relationship between defendant and Dr. Marks is that of employer and employee. Dr. Marks is practicing optometry. He is employed to do so by defendant—hence defendant is practicing optometry, which it cannot do.

Judgment is in favor of plaintiff ousting defendant from the practice of optometry in the state. Plaintiff asks us to order the dissolution of defendant and the appointment of a receiver to wind it up. We find the record does not warrant such a drastic measure. [DECISION IN PART FOR PLAINTIFF AND IN PART FOR DEFENDANT]

PROBLEMS

1 A contract which provided for the purchase of linseed oil by the buyer-corporation was assigned by the seller to the plaintiff. The buyer-corporation was thereafter merged into and become a part of the defendant-corporation. The defendant refused to purchase the linseed oil. Does the plaintiff have a cause of action against the defendant-corporation for breach of contract?

2 A statutory provision relating to forfeiture provided that upon the declaration of any forfeiture "it shall be the duty of the attorney general to apply to the district court of the

proper county for the appointment of a receiver to close out the business of such corporation." The charter of the plaintiff-corporation was forfeited by the proper state charter board. The plaintiff thereafter brought an action against the defendant for the conversion of property that belonged to the corporation. The defendant offered as a defense that the corporation was without authority to maintain the action because it had ceased to exist as a corporation. Is this a good defense?

3 Dissension arose between two factions of shareholders soon after the XYZ Corporation was organized, as a result of which no meeting of shareholders or directors constituting a quorum was held for approximately six years and no dividends were paid for six years. Both factions admitted that the corporation's business—that of owning and operating a hotel—was poorly managed and that its property was run down and in need of repairs. Plaintiffs, one faction of shareholders, brought a suit in equity for dissolution of the corporation. Defendants, the other faction of shareholders, contend that dissolution is unwarranted because there is no claim of fraud or misappropriation of assets. Decide.

4 The bylaws of the Central Leather Company provided that the holders of the preferred stock were entitled to cash for par value and accrued dividends in case of the liquidation and winding up of the affairs of the company. The Central Leather Company and the United States Leather Company were consolidated. The preferred shareholders of the Central Leather Company petitioned the court asking for a decree ordering the company "to pay to each shareholder the par value of his respective shares of such stock, together with arrears of dividends, amounting to $42 for each share." Do you think the court will issue the decree ordering the company to do so?

5 The Sportswear Corporation was chartered for the purpose of making ladies' sportswear. The corporation leased a building from defendant as a place to conduct its business, which lease contained a clause giving the corporation an option to purchase the building for $75,000 at any time during the life of the lease. The lease was for a period of five years, beginning July 1, 1943, and ending June 30, 1948. On May 28, 1945, the corporation was dissolved by the consent of all its shareholders, and the board of directors entered upon the process of closing its affairs. The board of directors, on December 17, 1945, sought to exercise the option to purchase the building. The defendant rejected the offer to purchase, and the corporation brought a suit for specific performance. Decide.

6 The majority of the shareholders of The Railway Corporation reasonably believed that a dissolution and winding up of the business of the corporation was in the best interest of everyone concerned. A meeting of the shareholders was therefore called, and a motion to dissolve the corporation was approved by a majority vote. Notice of such action was then sent to the creditors of the corporation. The minority of the shareholders vigorously objected to the dissolution. What remedy, if any, is available to the minority shareholders?

Part

9

SECURITIES REGULATION; ANTITRUST; LABOR RELATIONS

48
SECURITIES REGULATION

The first significant legislation to be enacted in the area of the issuance of and transactions in securities was the Securities Act of 1933. The Federal Trade Commission administered the Securities Act for the first year of its existence, but Congress created the Securities and Exchange Commission—hereinafter referred to as the Commission—when the Securities Exchange Act (hereinafter the Exchange Act) was enacted in 1934. Federal securities legislation consists of several statutes, all of which are based on the federal power over interstate and foreign commerce and the mails. The Securities Act and the Exchange Act, however, are the two principal federal statutes relating to securities. The Securities Act relates primarily to the issuance and distribution—also referred to as a public offering—of securities. The Exchange Act relates primarily to the regulation of trading in securities.

The Securities Act, the Exchange Act, and the rules and regulations promulgated by the Commission are numerous and complex. It is impossible to cover all the provisions of these two acts in this chapter, but it is hoped that the materials presented will give some indication of their importance. This chapter, after giving some definitions of important words and terms, will be devoted to those areas of securities regulation pertaining to (1) the exempted securities and transactions, (2) the preparation and filing of a registration statement, (3) the waiting period, (4) the preparation and filing of regulation A, (5) the registration of securities, (6) the antifraud provisions, (7) beneficial owners of securities, (8) reports by directors, officers, and principal shareholders, (9) corporate control contests, (10) persons deemed not to be underwriters, (11) the Securities and Exchange Commission, and (12) the state blue sky laws.

DEFINITIONS

An understanding of the following words and terms which are used in the Securities Act, the Exchange Act, and the rules and regulations promulgated by the Commission may be helpful before a study of the principles of law and rules regulating securities is undertaken.

Affiliate   The term "affiliate of," or a "person affiliated with a specified person," may be broadly defined as indicating a person who controls, is controlled by, or is under common control with the person specified.

Certified   The term "certified," when used in regard to financial statements, means certified by an independent public accountant or an independent certified public accountant.

Control   The term "control" means the power to direct the management and policies of a person, whether through the ownership of voting securities, by contract, or otherwise.

Dealer   The term "dealer" means any person who engages as agent, broker, or principal in the business of offering, buying, selling, or otherwise dealing in securities issued by another person.

Equity Security   The term "equity security" means any stock or similar security, any security convertible into such a security, or any right to subscribe to purchase such a security.

Issuer   The term "issuer" means the person who issues or proposes to issue a security.

Offer   The term "offer" includes every attempt or offer to dispose of, or an offer to purchase, a security for value.

Person   The term "person" means an individual, corporation, or other business organization, a trust, or a government or political subdivision thereof.

Prospectus   The term "prospectus" means any prospectus, notice, circular, advertisement, letter, or communication which offers any security for sale or confirms the sale of any security.

Restricted Securities   The term "restricted securities" means securities acquired directly or indirectly from the issuer, or an affiliate of such issuer, in a transaction or chain of transactions not involving any public offering.

Security   The term "security" includes not only the more commonly recognized securities, such as shares of stock and bonds, but also unusual plans and schemes based upon prospective profits through the efforts of others. [*SEC v. Payne*, p. 636.]

Underwriter   The term "underwriter" means any person who has purchased securities from an *issuer* with a view to distribution, or who offers or sells securities for an issuer in connection with a distribution, but not a person whose interest is limited to a commission from an underwriter or dealer not in excess of the customary commission paid to sellers. The term "issuer" as used in this definition also includes an affiliate.

EXEMPTIONS

The use of a prospectus and the filing of a registration statement with respect to the offer and sale of certain classes of securities and with respect to certain transactions are not necessary.

Exempted Securities   The following is a general indication of the classes of securities that are exempted from the coverage of the Securities Act.

(1) Any security issued by the federal government, the states, or subdivisions of the states, and securities issued by banks which are supervised by the states or the federal government; any security issued by or representing an interest in any trust fund maintained by a bank for investment by such bank in its capacity as trustee, executor, administrator, or guardian; and any interest maintained by a bank or an insurance company with respect to bonus, pension, and profit sharing plans.

(2) Any note, draft, bill of exchange, or bankers' acceptance having a maturity date at the time of issuance not exceeding nine months.

(3) Any security issued by religious, educational, benevolent, fraternal, charitable, or reformatory organization and not for pecuniary profit.

(4) Any security issued by building and loan associations, farmers' cooperative associations, or similar institutions, substantially all the business of which is confined to making loans to members.

(5) Any security issued by a common or contract carrier, the issuance of which is governed by the Interstate Commerce Act.

(6) Any certificate issued by a receiver or by a trustee in bankruptcy with the approval of the court.

(7) Any insurance or endowment policy, or annuity contract, issued by a

corporation subject to the supervision of the insurance commissioner or other agency or officer performing like functions.

(8) Any security exchanged by the issuer with its existing security holders exclusively where no commission or other remuneration is paid or given directly or indirectly for soliciting the exchange. Since this exemption pertains to existing security holders exclusively, it would not be available (a) where an issuer issued common shares to a large group of existing shareholders in exchange for their preferred shares with the intention of offering the common shares to the public or (b) where shareholders making the exchange acquired a substantial number of new securities with the intention of redistributing them and do, in fact, redistribute them to a substantial number of persons. A small number of resales by a few small shareholders following an exchange would, however, probably fall within the exemption.

(9) Any security which is issued in exchange for one or more outstanding securities under the supervision of the courts or governmental agencies.

(10) Any security which is a part of an exclusively intrastate issue. This exemption is available only to local financing, by local industries and local investment, and depends upon the situation as it exists at the time of completion of ultimate distribution. The exemption, including that portion sold to residents of the state in which the issuer was incorporated and doing business, would therefore be lost if one or more of the offerees resided in some other state. The exemption would also be lost if a corporation incorporated and doing business in State A sold its securities to residents of State A and one of those residents purchased the securities intending to resell all or a part of them and did resell them to a resident of State B. This is because the *ultimate distribution* would not have been completed prior to the purchase by the residents of State B.

(11) Securities issued in small offerings where the aggregate offering price does not exceed $500,000 in a period of one year. Pursuant to this provision, the Commission has promulgated several regulations, the most important of which is regulation A. This regulation will be discussed later in this chapter.

(12) Regulation B exempts fractional undivided interests in oil or gas rights. This exemption refers to the conveyance of a stated percentage of royalty rights with respect to the production of such oil or gas. It is provided, however, that no issue or offering is exempt where the aggregate issue or offering exceeds $250,000.

(13) Regulation E exempts certain small business investment companies. This regulation exempts registered securities issued by small business investment companies for offerings not exceeding $500,000 in a period of one year.

The procedure to be followed in regulation B and regulation E is similar to, but not identical with, the procedure to be followed in regulation A.

Exempted Transactions   The following is a summary of the transactions that are exempted from the coverage of the Securities Act.

    (1)   *The Nonprofessional Exemption*   This is the exemption which ordi-

narily permits investors to make casual sales of their securities without registration. This exemption, however, extends only to routine trading.

(2) *The Private-Placement Exemption* This exemption pertains to transactions by an issuer not involving any public offering. This exemption, which has been implemented by rule 144, "Persons Deemed Not to Be Underwriters," is discussed later in this chapter.

(3) *The Dealer Exemption* Transactions by dealers are generally exempted from the registration provisions. A few exceptions exist, as where the transactions occur within forty days after the securities are offered to the public.

(4) *The Broker Exemption* Transactions by brokers executed upon orders of customers on any exchange or in the over-the-counter market are exempt. The solicitation of such orders, however, is not exempt. And, as you will observe later in this chapter, there are certain over-the-counter securities that are not exempt.

REGISTRATION STATEMENT

Section 5(a) of the Securities Act provides that it shall be unlawful for any person to sell any security in interstate commerce or through the use of the mails, or to deliver a security by such means after sale, unless a registration statement is in effect as to such security. The Commission has established forms which are required to be used as guides and has promulgated rules and regulations for particular securities or issuers where disclosure problems differ from the typical security. Regulation C and form S-1 govern every registration of securities under the Securities Act where no other special regulation or form is prescribed.

Regulation C Instructions are given in regulation C as to the type and size of paper to be used and the printing or typing of the registration statement. Rule 402 provides that copies of the complete registration statement shall be filed with the Commission and states the procedure for binding the registration statement. It is also provided that additional copies of the registration statement, similarly bound, shall be furnished for use in the examination of the registration statement, public inspection, copying, and other purposes. A registration on form S-1 consists of (1) a facing sheet, (2) the prospectus, (3) certain information not required to be included in the prospectus, (4) financial statements, and (5) exhibits.

(1) *Facing Sheet* The facing sheet consists of the name of the registrant, the address of the principal executive offices, the name and address of the agent for service, the approximate date of commencement of the proposed sale to the public, and certain information that is required for the calculation of the registration fee. The "agent for service" is the person to whom the Commission will send communications regarding the registration statement.

(2) *The Prospectus* The prospectus, the purpose of which is to inform investors, must be given to all persons to whom the securities are offered. It should be pointed out, however, that neither the filing nor the becoming effective of the registration statement constitutes approval by the Commission. Rule 425

makes this clear by requiring the following statement to appear in prominent type on the outside cover page of every prospectus:

THESE SECURITIES HAVE NOT BEEN APPROVED OR DISAPPROVED BY THE SECURITIES AND EXCHANGE COMMISSION NOR HAS THE COMMISSION PASSED UPON THE ACCURACY OR ADEQUACY OF THIS PROSPECTUS. ANY REPRESENTATION TO THE CONTRARY IS A CRIMINAL OFFENSE.

The disclosure requirements consist of twenty-one items and pertain to matters such as (1) the offering price to the public, (2) the names of all directors and officers, (3) the plan of distribution and whether or not the securities are to be offered through underwriters, (4) the principal purpose for which the net proceeds to the registrant are to be used, (5) a description of the business done and intended to be done by the registrant, (6) the capital structure of the registrant, and (7) a summary of earnings of the registrant for the last five fiscal years, for any period between the end of the latest of such fiscal years and the date of the latest balance sheet furnished, and for the corresponding period of the preceding fiscal year.

(3) *Information Not Required in Prospectus* This information pertains to such matters as (a) the arrangements made for the marketing of the securities; (b) the expenses in connection with the issuance and distribution of the securities; (c) the names of persons, other than underwriters or dealers, to whom securities have been sold, or are to be sold, at a price different from the price at which the securities are to be offered to the general public; and (d) if capital stock is being registered and any portion of the consideration received therefor is to be credited to an account other than the appropriate capital stock account, to what other account such portion is to be credited.

(4) *Financial Statement* The Securities Act and the rules and regulations promulgated by the Commission require the registrant to file many financial statements as a part of the registration statement. A few of such statements pertain to the following:

(1) A balance sheet of the issuer as of a date within ninety days prior to the date of filing the registration statement, including any loan in excess of specified amounts to any officer, director, shareholder, or affiliate and any surplus of the issuer and the source of such surplus. The registration statement must be certified or, in the alternative, must be accompanied by a certified balance sheet as of a date not more than one year prior to the filing of the registration statement.

(2) A certified profit and loss statement of the issuer showing such matters as earnings and income, the nature and source thereof, and the expenses and fixed charges in such form as the Commission shall prescribe for the latest fiscal year for which such statement is available and for the two preceding years, year by year; if the issuer has been in business for less than three years, then for such time as the issuer has been in business, year by year.

(3) A certified balance sheet and a profit and loss statement for the three preceding

years where the proceeds, or any part of the proceeds, of the security are to be applied to the purchase of any business.

(4) A certified consolidated balance sheet of the registrant and its subsidiaries, reorganization of the registrant, and certain historical financial information.

(5) *Exhibits* The exhibits that are to be filed as a part of the registration statement pertain to such matters as (a) copies of each underwriting contract between the registrant and the underwriters, (b) copies of the charter and bylaws of the registrant, (c) specimens of the securities being registered, (d) an opinion of counsel as to the legality of the securities being registered, (e) copies of any voting trust agreement, (f) copies of all pension and retirement plans, and (g) copies of every material contract not made in the ordinary course of business.

THE WAITING PERIOD

Section 8(a) of the Securities Act provides that a registration statement will become effective on the twentieth day after it is filed. The registration statement, however, normally omits such matters as the offering price or commission to paid underwriters. These omissions are usually supplied by an amendment to the registration statement. The effective date of the registration statement, therefore, may be delayed for a period of six or seven weeks. During this waiting period, oral offers may be made. It is most important, however, that no material omissions or untrue statements of a material fact be made.

Rule 134 also permits the making of written offers by a preliminary or summary prospectus. This rule permits the publication of notices, circulars, or advertisements and the transmission of letters after a registration statement has been filed but before it has become effective. The contents of such offer, however, are limited to specified statements. Some of the statements are optional, but others are mandatory.

The optional information includes such matters as the name of the issuer, the title of the security, an indication of the general type of business of the issuer, the price of the security, and any statement required by any state securities blue sky law. Where the communication is accompanied by a prospectus, it is also optional to include in the communication a solicitation of an offer.

It is mandatory that the communication contain (1) a clause making it clear that an offer to purchase the security may be withdrawn at any time prior to the effective date of the registration statement, (2) a statement as to whether the offering is made by the issuer or by a security holder and whether the issue represents new financing, and (3) the name and address of the person from whom a prospectus may be obtained.

The above-described mandatory information need not be contained in a communication (1) which does no more than state from whom a prospectus may be obtained, identify the security, state the price, and state by whom orders will be executed, or (2) which is accompanied or preceded by a prospectus or summary prospectus.

OFFERINGS EXEMPTED FROM REGULATION C

Regulations A, B, and E were previously mentioned. However, only the conditions the Commission says must be met to comply with regulation A will be explained since the procedure required to take advantage of these three exemptions are similar.

Regulation A   This is a general regulation which permits a public offering not exceeding $500,000 of securities without complying with the requirements of regulation C provided certain conditions are satisfied. Among these conditions are (1) that a notification be filed with the Commission and (2) that, except for certain securities involving not more than $50,000 of securities, the offering may be made by an offering circular. The information contained in the notification is similar to that contained in regulation C, and the offering circular is similar to the prospectus. Regulation A, therefore, might be regarded as a simplified procedure for small offerings rather than as an exemption from the registration requirements of the Securities Act.

   (1)   *Amount of Securities Exempted*   Rule 254 promulgated by the Commission provides that the aggregate offering price of all securities of the issuer offered or sold within a one-year period shall not exceed $500,000 if the securities are offered or sold (a) by the issuer, (b) by the estate of a decedent if the securities are offered or sold within two years after the death of the decedent, or (c) by affiliates of the issuer. The aggregate offering price offered or sold within a one-year period (a) by any one affiliate is limited to $100,000, (b) by or on behalf of an estate is limited to $500,000, and (c) by any person other than the issuer and its affiliates is limited to $100,000, with a limitation of $300,000 for all such other persons.

   (2)   *Offering Circular*   Rule 256 provides that no written offer of securities shall be made under regulation A—except for certain offerings not exceeding $50,000 mentioned below—unless an offering circular is concurrently given or has previously been given to the person to whom the offer is made. The information to be given in the circular is described in schedule 1 and form 1-A and requires the following statement to be set forth on the outside front cover page of the offering circular in capital letters:

THESE SECURITIES ARE OFFERED PURSUANT TO AN EXEMPTION FROM REGISTRATION WITH THE UNITED STATES SECURITIES AND EXCHANGE COMMISSION. THE COMMISSION DOES NOT PASS UPON THE MERITS OF ANY SECURITIES NOR DOES IT PASS UPON THE ACCURACY OR COMPLETENESS OF ANY OFFERING CIRCULAR OR OTHER SELLING LITERATURE.

   Information also required to be on the front cover, in tabular form, is the offering price to the public, underwriting discounts or commissions, and contemplated proceeds to be received by the issuer or other persons. The other required information includes such items as a brief description of the securities being offered, the business and properties of the issuer, information regarding directors and officers and their remuneration, and a specified financial statement of the issuer to be certified by an independent public accountant or a certified public accountant.

(3) *Filing of Notification* The filing procedure prescribed by this regulation requires that copies of a notification on form 1-A be filed with the regional office of the Commission for the region in which the principal business operations of the issuer are conducted or proposed to be conducted. This notification must be filed at least ten days—Saturdays, Sundays, and holidays excluded—prior to the date on which the initial offering of any securities is to be made. The notification must be signed by the issuer and each person for whose account any of the securities are to be offered.

(4) *Form 1-A* This form is precise, but the information that must be given pertains to such persons as the issuer, his predecessors, and his affiliates and the directors, officers, and promoters of the issuer. Information is also required to be given concerning the jurisdiction in which the securities are to be offered, any unregistered securities sold within the previous year, and any other present or proposed offerings.

(5) *Exhibits* Specified documents must also be filed as exhibits to the notification. The pertinent provisions of these documents include (a) an instrument defining the rights of the holders of the securities, (b) all underwriting contracts and a written consent signed by each underwriter, and (c) the written consent of each accountant, engineer, geologist, appraiser, or any other expert whose name is used in connection with the offering.

(6) *Sales Material to Be Filed* Copies of certain specified sales material prepared or authorized for use with the offering of any securities must be filed at least five days—exclusive of Saturdays, Sundays, and holidays—prior to the use thereof. This material includes such communications as advertisements proposed to be published in newspapers, magazines, or other periodicals, scripts of radio or television broadcasts, and letters and other written correspondence.

(7) *Offerings Not in Excess of $50,000* The offering circular need not be filed or *used* if the aggregate offering price of all securities of the issuer, its predecessors, or its affiliates does not exceed $50,000, provided that the notification filed with the regional office shall contain an exhibit containing the information which otherwise would be contained in the offering circular. This rule also provides that no advertisement published in any newspaper or other periodical, and no radio or television broadcast regarding the offering, shall contain more than the name of the issuer, the title of the security, the amount offered, the offering price to the public, the identity of the general type of business of the issuer, the general character and location of the issuer's property, and information as to where further information may be obtained.

(8) *Special Requirements for Certain Offerings* Regulation A establishes more stringent requirements with respect to offerings of securities of any issuer without a meaningful earnings history, because such securities involve a greater risk to the investor than do issues of well-established issuers. Special requirements, therefore, are made for issuers which were (a) incorporated or organized

within one year prior to the date of filing the notification and have not had a net income or (b) incorporated or organized more than one year prior to such date and have not had a net income for at least one of the last two years. The pertinent provisions are that (a) the securities shall be offered *only* by the issuer and (b) an offering circular must be used even though the amount of the offering is less than $50,000.

REGISTRATION OF SECURITIES

Section 12(a) of the Exchange Act makes it unlawful for any member, broker, or dealer to effect any transaction in any security on a national exchange without compliance with the registration procedure, except for certain exemptions. The major portion of the exempted securities are those representing governmental obligations, such as securities issued for cooperatives by the Farm Credit Act and those issued by the National Mortgage Association under authority of the National Housing Act.

Procedure for Registration Section 12(b) of the Exchange Act provides that a security may be registered and listed on a national securities exchange by the issuer filing an application for such registration and listing with the exchange and with the Commission. The Exchange Act requires registration, but the exchanges generally require that a separate listing application be filed.

The application for registration is lengthy and detailed. Information is required to be furnished pertaining to the registrant and its directors, officers, properties, and principal security holders. Briefly stated, this information pertains to such matters as (1) the nature of the registrant's business, (2) a summary of operations for the registrant for the last five years, (3) the location of the physical properties of the registrant, (4) identification of the principal security holders and the security holdings of management, and (5) identification of all directors with a listing of the remuneration paid to directors and officers.

Financial statements, exhibits, and other information must be furnished. The procedure to be followed is similar to that made on form S-1 under the Securities Act, and the information given in form S-1 may be used as the major portion of the application.

The registration of the securities becomes effective thirty days after the exchanges certify to the Commission that the securities have been approved for listing and registration. A clear distinction, however, must be kept in mind between a registration statement under the Securities Act for the purpose of making a distribution and a registration statement under the Exchange Act for the purpose of trading on the national exchanges.

Over-the-Counter Securities A failure to register securities does not ordinarily prevent trading in the over-the-counter market, but section 12(g) of the Exchange Act requires that certain over-the-counter securities be registered with the Commission. The test is whether (1) the issuer has total assets exceeding $1,000,000 and a class of equity securities "held of record by 500 or more but less than 750 persons" and (2) the securities are to be traded by the use of the mails or by any means or instrumentalities of interstate commerce. Such registration is required to be effected within 120 days after the first fiscal year on which the total assets and number of shareholders tests are met.

Current and Other Reports   Registration in connection with a listing upon a national exchange and registration in connection with an over-the-counter issuer subject the issuer to certain reporting requirements. The Commission, therefore, has prepared certain forms which are to be used as guides in the preparation of the reports. The forms to be used for listed and registered over-the-counter securities require all issuers of such securities to file (1) current reports and (2) annual and quarterly reports.

(1)   *Current Reports*   A current report must be filed within ten days after the close of any month during which certain specified changes occur. These changes include (a) changes in the management of the registrant, (b) acquisition or disposition of a significant amount of assets, (c) any material legal proceedings to which the registrant has become a party, (d) any changes in securities, such as defaults in payments of principal or interest and increases or decreases in outstanding securities, and (e) changes in any other materially important event.

The registrant is also required to file, as a part of this report, (a) balance sheets and profit and loss statements with respect to the acquisition or disposition of a significant amount of assets and (b) certain documents as exhibits concerning such changes as those in the registrant's charter or plans for reorganization, consolidation, or merger.

(2)   *Annual and Quarterly Reports*   The rules promulgated by the Commission require that certified annual reports be filed ninety days after the end of the year covered by the report. The information required to be contained in the report closely parallels the information for the registration of the securities.

The quarterly reports pertain primarily to the (a) financial information concerning the registrant, (b) capitalization of the registrant, (c) shareholder's equity, and (d) title and amount of unregistered securities sold during the fiscal year.

ANTIFRAUD PROVISIONS, LIABILITIES, PENALTIES

The Securities Act and the Exchange Act both (1) contain antifraud provisions, (2) impose civil liabilities, and (3) impose criminal penalties.

Antifraud Provisions   Section 17(a), which is the principal antifraud provision of the Securities Act, applies only to the offer and sale of securities; it does not apply to their purchase. This section makes it unlawful for any person, with respect to such offer and sale, (1) to employ any device, scheme, or artifice to defraud, (2) to obtain money or property by means of any untrue statement or any omission to state a material fact, or (3) to engage in any transaction, practice, or course of business which operates or would operate as a fraud or deceit upon the purchaser.

Section 10(b) of the Exchange Act and rule 10b promulgated by the

Commission are the principal antifraud provisions of the Exchange Act. These provisions apply not only to the sale and purchase of securities but to any transaction in connection with the sale and purchase of securities. These provisions also apply to securities which are or which are not registered on a national securities exchange. Rule 10b specifically provides that it shall be unlawful for any person (1) to use or employ any device, scheme, or artifice to defraud, (2) to make any untrue statement of a material fact or omit to state a material fact, or (3) to engage in any act, practice, or course of business which operates or would operate as a fraud or deceit upon any person. The facts of the particular case will determine whether there has been a violation of the antifraud provisions, but much of the litigation has involved an untrue statement of a material fact or an omission to state a material fact. [*List v. Fashion Park, Inc.*, p. 637.]

The definition of an "insider" has also caused much of the litigation. Directors, officers, corporate executives, and controlling shareholders have traditionally been subject to the disclosure requirements. This is so because of their access to inside information about the affairs of the corporation. The rules promulgated by the Commission and the court decisions, however, define insiders so as to include employees of the corporation, close friends and relatives of directors and corporate executives, brokers, dealers, and underwriters. Insiders are ordinarily required to wait, as a minimum, until the inside information can be expected to appear over the media of widest circulation before entering into a transaction concerning inside information.

Civil Liability   The Securities Act imposes a civil liability upon various designated persons where a registration statement contains an untrue statement of a material fact or omits to state a material fact required to be stated therein. The injured person may bring an action against such persons to recover damages sustained by reason of such untrue statements or omissions. The persons designated include (1) persons who signed the registration statement, (2) directors of the issuer, and (3) any accountant, engineer, appraiser, or any other professional person who has prepared the registration statement or any report in connection with the statement. Civil liabilities are also imposed upon any person who offers or sells a security for making untrue statements or omissions in connection with prospectuses or other communications. Similar provisions are contained in the Exchange Act for untrue statements and omissions in connection with an application, report, or document filed pursuant to the Exchange Act or any rule or regulation prescribed pursuant to the act.

Criminal Penalties   The Securities Act and the Exchange Act both provide for the imposition of criminal penalties for *willful* violations of *any* provision of the two acts or of any rule or regulation promulgated by the Commission pursuant to the acts. The penalties which may be imposed are a fine, imprisonment, or both. The maximum fine varies from $5,000 to $500,000, and the length of imprisonment varies from two years to five years. The Exchange Act also provides a penalty for the failure of the issuer to file any information, document, or report required to be filed under the Exchange Act or the rules and regulations thereunder. The penalty requires the issuer to forfeit $100 per day for each day that such failure shall continue.

BENEFICIAL OWNERS OF SECURITIES

A precise definition of the term "beneficial owner" is not found in the Securities Act, the Exchange Act, or in the rules promulgated by the Commission. It is a question of fact, therefore, to be determined in the light of all the circumstances involved. The commission has published Releases 1965 and 7824, however, and these releases are helpful in determining what persons are to be regarded as beneficial owners for the purpose of filing reports. A partnership would be the beneficial owner where the partnership holds the securities for its own account, and a trustee would be the beneficial owner of an irrevocable trust. A person who possesses the power to revoke a revocable trust, however, would appear to be the beneficial owner.

The so-called benefits test and the so-called power to vest and reinvest title in himself have been adopted in determining the beneficial ownership of securities held by family members. A person is regarded as the beneficial owner of securities held in the name of his or her spouse, their minor children, or other relatives sharing the same house. This is because the beneficial owner obtains substantially the equivalent of ownership, including the right to use the income from the securities to maintain a common home or meet expenses such beneficial owner otherwise would meet from other sources and the ability to exercise a controlling influence over the purchase, the sale, or the voting of such securities. The release states, however, that *a person* may also be regarded as the beneficial owner of securities held in the name of another person if by reason of any contract or other arrangement he obtains benefits equivalent to ownership. The "benefits test" and the "power to vest and reinvest title in himself," therefore, will obviously apply regardless of the family relationship between the parties.

Reports by Beneficial Owners Rule 13 provides that any person, within ten days after acquiring directly or indirectly the beneficial ownership of more than 5 percent of a class of any registered equity security, shall file with the Commission the information contained in schedule 13D and shall also send a copy thereof to the issuer and to any exchange on which the securities are traded. The required information may be summarized: (1) the title and class of securities and the name and address of the issuer; (2) the name and address of the person filing the statement, his present occupation, the material occupations held by him during the past ten years, and whether or not such person has been convicted in a criminal proceeding during the last ten years; (3) the source and amount of funds used in acquiring the securities; (4) the purpose of the purchase and, if the purchaser is to acquire control of the issuer, a description of any plans the purchasers may have to liquidate the issuer, such as by a merger or any other major change; (5) the number of shares which are beneficially owned and the number of shares concerning which there is a right to acquire; (6) information as to any contracts or understanding with any person with respect to the securities, such as a division of profits or losses or the giving or withholding of proxies; (7) the identity of all persons employed or to be compensated in making the solicitations for tenders to security holders and a brief description of the terms of such employment; and (8) the filing as exhibits of copies of all invitations for tenders, advertisements making the tender, and recommendations to the holders of the securities to accept or reject a tender offer.

The information required in (7) and (8) is applicable only to a "tender offer," discussed later in this chapter under "Corporate Control Contests."

DIRECTORS, OFFICERS, PRINCIPAL SHAREHOLDERS

Beneficial ownership is of significance in connection with the reporting requirements of various sections of the securities acts. Beneficial ownership, however, is of special significance to section 16 of the Exchange Act. This section regulates the activities by certain specified insiders in equity securities. The insiders regulated are (1) any person who is, directly or indirectly, the beneficial owner of more than 10 percent of any class of any registered equity security and (2) any director or officer of the issuer of such security.

Short-Swing Profits   The provisions of the Exchange Act regulating short-swing profits apply to such a beneficial owner, director, or officer. It is provided that any profit realized by such beneficial owner, director, or officer from any purchase and sale, or any sale and purchase, within any period of less than six months may be recovered by the issuer. The owner of any security may also bring an action to recover the short-swing profit if the issuer fails to bring an action within sixty days after being requested to do so. This procedure is known as the "recapture of short-swing profits." This provision does not apply to any security which was acquired in good faith in connection with a debt previously contracted. It should be pointed out that the provisions of section 16 do not prohibit short-swing profits. All the insider is required to do is wait one day more than the six-month period to buy or sell.

Arbitrage Transactions   Rule 16 makes it unlawful for any *director* or *officer* to effect any *foreign* or *domestic* transaction unless he includes such transaction in his initial report and accounts to such issuer for the profits realized by the transaction. An "arbitrage" transaction may be briefly defined as securities bought in one market and sold in another for purposes of profit arising in the differences in price in the two markets.

Reporting Requirements   The Commission has published specified forms to be used as guides by beneficial owners, directors, or officers in reporting their holdings. Such persons are required to (1) file at the time of the registration under the Exchange Act, or the effective date of the registration, or within ten days after becoming the beneficial owner, an initial report on form 3 with the Commission stating the amount of each equity security of which he or she is the beneficial owner, and (2) a statement of changes on form 4 within ten days after the close of each month thereafter if there has been any change in such ownership.

A reporting person, however, may disclaim any beneficial ownership in the securities for the purpose of this section 16 reporting. This may be done by expressly declaring in the statement that the filing of such statement shall not be construed as an admission that such person is the beneficial owner of any security covered by the statement.

Exemptions The Commission has promulgated a number of exemptions from the provisions of section 16. Some are directed at the reporting requirements and the short-swing provisions, but others are directed at short-swing profits only.

(1) *Administration of Estates* An important exemption provides that such a beneficial owner, director, or officer who is authorized by law to administer the estate or assets of other persons is exempted from the reporting requirements and from the short-swing provisions during the twelve months following appointment. This exemption includes executors, administrators, guardians, receivers and trustees in bankruptcy, and other similar persons. These persons, however, are required to file reports and are liable for short-swing profits after the twelve-month period.

(2) *Exemptions from Short-Swing Profits* A number of lengthy and explicit transactions are exempt from the provisions pertaining to short-swing profits. A summary of the pertinent exemptions, however, should give an indication as to their nature. These exemptions include (a) certain transactions by registered investment companies, (b) transactions which are effected in connection with a distribution of a substantial block of securities, (c) acquisitions of shares of stock pursuant to a stock bonus, profit sharing, retirement, savings, or similar plan, (d) transactions by public utility holding companies, (e) acquisitions of equity securities by a director or officer of the issuer by way of redemption of another security, (f) any transaction involving the purchase and sale of any equity security pursuant to certain options and employment contracts, (g) acquisitions and dispositions of securities pursuant to mergers and consolidations, (h) acquisitions or dispositions involved in the deposit or withdrawal of securities under a voting trust, (i) acquisitions or dispositions of an equity security involved in the conversion of an equity security, (j) certain transactions by railroads, and (k) certain transactions involving the sale of subscription rights.

CORPORATE CONTROL CONTESTS

A corporate control contest arises when an aggressor group attempts to take control of the corporate affairs from the controlling group by (1) soliciting proxies from the shareholders for the purpose of election contests or (2) purchasing shares from the shareholders, commonly referred to as the "cash tender offer."

Election Contests The Commission has promulgated special and detailed disclosure requirements that must be filed with the Commission and made available to the shareholders by those soliciting proxies. Additional disclosures are required, however, when there arises a proxy contest between participants with respect to the election or removal of directors. The term "participant" includes any person or committee who solicits proxies, any nominee for whose election proxies are solicited, and those persons who finance the solicitation.

The additional information to be filed with the Commission and included in the soliciting material relates—other than the identification of the issuer—to disclosures relating to activities of the participant. A summary of the pertinent information which the participant is required to furnish includes such items as (1) a ten-year history of his occupations and employments, activities in proxy contests involving any issuer, and his criminal convictions, if any; (2) a description of his holdings of the issuer's securities; (3) his purchases and sales of securities of the issuer within the past two years, and the source of the funds if any such purchases were represented by borrowed funds; and (4) whether he was a party to any contract or other arrangement with any person with respect to any securities of the issuer, such as guarantees against loss, guarantees of profit, division of profits or losses, or the giving or withholding of proxies.

Cash Tender Offer A means of acquiring control of a corporation, other than by winning a proxy contest, is through a device known as a "cash tender offer," sometimes referred to as a "takeover bid." Such an offer may be broadly defined as an offer to the shareholders of the target corporation to tender a certain class of their shares to an aggressor group for the purchase, during a fixed period of time, of all or a portion of the securities of the target corporation at a price considerably above the current market price. Prior to 1968, the cash tender offeror was required to disclose little information. In 1968, however, the Williams Act was enacted by Congress as an amendment to the Exchange Act. This amendment made it unlawful for any person to make a tender offer of any class of any registered equity security if, after consummation thereof, such person would be the beneficial owner of more than 5 percent of such class unless such person files such information as the Commission may require. The information to be filed with the Commission is the information and exhibits required by schedule 13D, previously summarized under "Beneficial Owners of Securities."

(1) *Solicitations of Tenders* The tender invitation advising shareholders of the tender offer is the means employed in the solicitation of tenders, and should contain all the terms and conditions of the offer as is necessary to enable the shareholders to evaluate the offer. The offeror, in order to reach the maximum number of security holders, will usually publish the tender offer in general and financial newspapers of national daily circulation. The offeror will also probably transmit copies of the invitation to shareholders if a list of the shareholders can be obtained. Rule 14 requires that all tender offers sent to the shareholders shall include certain additional information. This information pertains to such items as the name of the person making the tender; the dates prior to which, and after

which, security holders depositing their securities in escrow will have a right to withdraw their securities; and if the offeror is not obligated to purchase all of the securities tendered, the date when the securities will be purchased on a pro rata basis.

(2)   *Purchase of Securities by Issuer*   The issuer may not, during the pendency of a tender offer by another person, purchase its own equity securities unless the issuer has filed with the Commission a statement containing certain information and has given to its equity security holders within the past six months the substance of the information contained in the statement. The statement must set forth such information as the amount of securities to be purchased; the names of the persons from whom the securities are to be purchased; the purpose for which the purchase is to be made; whether the securities are to be retired, held as treasury stock, or otherwise disposed of, indicating such disposition; and the source and amount of funds to be used in making the purchase.

(3)   *Change in Majority of Directors*   Provision is made for the situation where persons are to be elected or designated as directors other than at a meeting of security holders, and the persons so elected or designated will constitute a majority of the directors. It is provided that the issuer, not less than ten days prior to the date any such persons take office as directors, shall file certain information with the Commission and transmit such information to all holders of securities who would be entitled to vote at a meeting for directors. This information pertains to such points as the number of shares outstanding in each class of voting securities; the persons who own more than 10 percent of the outstanding voting shares; changes in control of the issuer occurring since the beginning of its last fiscal year; any contractual arrangements which may result in a change in control of the issuer; certain information with respect to each person nominated as a director and other directors whose term will continue after the meeting; and certain information in instances where nominees own more than 10 percent of any class of securities.

PERSONS DEEMED NOT TO BE UNDERWRITERS

An examination of the law prior to rule 144 reveals that it was possible to purchase unregistered securities from an issuer in a private-placement transaction and then make a distribution of those securities. The purchasers thought they were entitled to a nonprofessional exemption when they resold those securities, but their opponents thought that the purchasers were underwriters as the term "underwriter" is defined by the Securities Act. This led to confusion, and the question most often posed was: When can a purchaser of securities in a private-placement transaction make a distribution and resell those securities without filing a registration statement as required by the Securities Act? Rule 144 purports to answer this question by excluding from the term "underwriter" any person who complies with all the conditions of the rule and who (1) sells restricted securities of an issuer for his own account and (2) sells restricted or other securities on behalf of an affiliate of the issuer of those securities.

The term "person" when used with reference to a person for whose account securities are to be sold includes, in addition to that person, the following:

(1) Any relative or spouse of such person or any relative of such spouse, any one of whom has the same home as such person, frequently referred to as "related person."

(2) Any trust or estate in which such person or related persons collectively own 10 percent or more of the total beneficial interest, or of which such persons serve as trustee, executor, or in any similar capacity; and

(3) Any corporation or other organization—other than the issuer—in which such person or related persons are the *beneficial owners* collectively of 10 percent or more of any class of equity securities or 10 percent or more of the equity interest.

The six basic conditions that must be complied with in order to satisfy the provisions of rule 144 may be summarized:

Current Public Information Adequate current public information must be available with respect to the issuer. This information includes, among other things, the exact name of the issuer, the address of its principal executive offices, the exact title and class of the security, the number of shares or total amount of the security outstanding, the nature and extent of the facilities of the issuer and the product or service offered, and financial information concerning the issuer including its most recent balance sheet and profit and loss statement, which shall be reasonably current.

Holding Period of Restricted Securities If restricted securities are to be sold, the seller must have been the beneficial owner of the securities for at least two years prior to the sale, and the full purchase price or other consideration must have been paid at least two years prior to the sale. Special provisions are made for such matters as promissory notes given in payment of the purchase price; securities acquired as a gift; securities held by the estate of a deceased person; and securities acquired by the settlor of a trust.

Limitations on Amount of Securities Sold If the securities are to be sold for the account of an *affiliate*, the amount of securities sold, together with all sales of restricted or unrestricted securities of the same class for the account of the same person within the preceding six months, may not exceed the following:

(1) If the securities are traded on a national securities exchange, the lesser of 1 percent of the class outstanding as shown by the most recent report or statement published by the issuer, or the average weekly reported volume of trading on all such exchanges during the four weeks preceding the filing of the notice of the proposed sale.

(2) If the securities are not traded on a national securities exchange, 1 percent of the class outstanding as shown by the most recent report or statement published

by the issuer. The quantity limitations apply only to *restricted securities* where the securities are to be sold for the account of a person other than an affiliate.

Manner of Sale   The securities must be sold in "broker's transactions" within the meaning of the "broker exemption" mentioned earlier in this chapter, and the seller shall *not* solicit or arrange for the solicitation of orders to buy the securities, or make any payment to anyone other than the broker who executes the order to sell the securities.

The term "broker's transaction" for the purpose of this rule means that the broker (1) does no more than act as agent for the seller and receives no more than the usual and customary broker's commission, (2) must make reasonable inquiry to determine that the seller is not an underwriter with respect to the securities and that the transaction is not a part of a distribution, and (3) must not solicit or arrange for the solicitation of orders to buy the securities, except that the broker may make inquiries of other brokers or dealers who have indicated an interest in the securities within the preceding sixty days.

Notice of Proposed Sale   Copies of a notice of the proposed sale, which must be signed by the seller, must be transmitted to the Commission concurrently with the placing of the order to sell with the broker. The notice need not be filed, however, if the amount of the securities sold during any six-month period does not exceed 500 shares and the aggregate sale price of those shares does not exceed $10,000.

Bona Fide Intention to Sell   The person filing the notice shall have a bona fide intention to sell the securities within a reasonable time after filing the notice.

SECURITIES AND EXCHANGE COMMISSION

The Commission is composed of five commissioners to be appointed by the President with the advice and consent of the Senate, and not more than three of such commissioners shall be of the same political party. The Commission is given the power to make such rules and regulations as may be necessary for the execution of the duties vested in the Commission, to make investigations, and to determine whether any person has violated or is about to violate any provision of the Securities Act, the Exchange Act, or the rules and regulations prescribed by the Commission, and to bring actions in the United States district courts. The rules and regulations referred to in this chapter are those promulgated by the Commission in pursuance of this power given to the Commission.

The Securities and Exchange Commission also administers the Public Utility Holding Company Act of 1935, the Trust Indenture Act of 1939, the Investment Company Act of 1940, the Investment Advisors Act of 1940, and the Securities Investor Protection Act of 1970.

The purpose of the Public Utility Holding Company Act was to correct abuses in the use of the holding company device in the nation's electric and gas utility industries. The Trust Indenture Act is designed to protect investors by requiring trust indentures under which securities are issued so as to assure investors the services of a qualified trustee. The trust indenture is the instrument stating the terms and conditions of the trust created by way of a security for a bond issue. The purpose of the Investment Company Act is the regulation of companies engaged primarily in the business of investing, reinvesting, or trading in securities. The purpose of the Investment Advisors Act is to protect the public and investors against malpractice by persons paid for advising other persons about securities. The purpose of the Securities Investor Protection Act is to protect investors in securities against losses due to financial failure of brokers or dealers.

BLUE SKY LAWS
The state securities statutes, more frequently referred to as the "blue sky laws," are said to be aimed at protecting the investor against "speculative schemes which have no more basis than as many feet of blue sky." The blue sky laws differ greatly, but the Conference of Commissioners on Uniform State Laws approved a Uniform Securities Act in 1956. This act—in part at least—has been incorporated into the blue sky laws by over one-half of the states, and nearly all of the other states have enacted blue sky laws of one type or another. These statutes, therefore, provide a convenient framework for the material presented on this subject. No attempt is made to delve into the details of these statutes, but it is hoped that an awareness will be created as to the importance of these blue sky laws. Consideration will be given to (1) the types of blue sky laws, (2) procedures to effect registration, and (3) the classes of securities and transactions that are exempted from the blue sky laws.

Types of Blue Sky Laws The blue sky laws divide themselves into three broad types: (1) the disclosure type, (2) the antifraud type, and (3) the broker-dealer type. Nearly all of the states have enacted one of these types or a combination of these three types.

The disclosure type or, as it is frequently referred to, "registration-of-securities" type, is used by a majority of the states. It is provided that any circular, prospectus, or other advertising material must disclose all the essential facts with respect to the security offered, and such advertising material is sometimes required to be sent or given to each person to whom an offer is made. Provision is also sometimes made for filing a registration statement and a prospectus with some state official, usually an administrator. This type is frequently combined with the antifraud type or the broker-dealer type, or both types.

The antifraud type generally prohibits fraud in the sale of securities, provides remedies to defrauded persons, and imposes criminal penalties. The Attorney General is also authorized to investigate questionable practices by security salesmen and, if the investigation so justifies, to apply to the court for an injunction restraining the fraudulent sale of securities. It is also made unlawful for any person in connection with any offer, sale, or purchase of any security to employ any device, scheme, or artifice to defraud; to make any untrue statement of a material fact or omit to state a material fact; or to engage in any act, practice, or course of business which would operate as a fraud upon any person.

The broker-dealer type, as a condition to engage in the business of buying and selling securities, requires brokers and dealers to procure a license. An examination into the character and trustworthiness of the applicant is usually made before the license is granted. This type, therefore, regulates persons, namely, brokers, dealers, agents, and the like, who are engaged in the securities business. Many of the states also require registration of investment advisers.

Procedures to Effect Registration   The blue sky laws provide for three different procedures to effect registration: (1) registration by "notification," or by "description"; (2) registration by "co-ordination"; and (3) registration by "qualification."

Registration by "notification" is a simplified procedure. It is available to certain issuers with demonstrated performance and stability, and the procedure is similar to the registration under regulation A of the Federal Securities Act of 1933. Registration by "co-ordination" is available where a registration statement has been filed with the Securities and Exchange Commission. Registration by "qualification" requires substantially more extensive information than is required under the other two simplified procedures, and is patterned after regulation C under the Federal Securities Act of 1933. The registration statement filed must be accompanied by writings, such as a consent to service of process, a copy of the security that is being registered, and a copy of an opinion of counsel as to the legality of the security.

Exemptions   The blue sky laws exempt certain classes of securities and certain transactions from the registration requirements. The following is a summary of the frequently exempted securities and transactions.

(1)   *Exempted Securities*   The securities exempted include (a) securities, such as those issued or guaranteed by the United States and by the states and the political subdivisions and agencies thereof; (b) securities issued or guaranteed by any bank organized under the laws of the United States, or any bank, savings institution, or trust company organized and supervised by the state; (c) certain insurance companies; (d) securities issued by or guaranteed by any common carrier, public utility, or holding company under the jurisdiction of the Interstate Commerce Commission; (e) securities listed or approved for listing on certain national exchanges; (f) securities issued by nonprofit associations, and (g) certain investment contracts, such as pension, profit sharing, or similar benefit plan.

(2)   *Exempted Transactions*   The exempted transactions include (a) an offer by the offeror to sell securities to not more than ten persons in the state during any period of twelve consecutive months; (b) sales or offers to broker-dealers; (c) instances where registration statements have been filed but have not become effective—offers of the securities may be made but no sales may be consummated prior to the effective date of the statement; (d) transactions by persons who sell not in their own right or in some fiduciary capacity, such as

executors, sheriffs, guardians, and trustees in bankruptcy; (e) transactions in bonds or other evidences of indebtedness by a mortgage or deed of trust; and (f) certain nonissuer transactions, as where an owner sells his own securities in an isolated sale and not in the course of repeated and successive transactions. This provision is exempted from the licensing requirements as well as the registration requirements.

CASES

SEC v. Payne, 35 F. Supp. 573 (1940). Action by the Securities and Exchange Commission, plaintiff, against Louis Payne, defendant. The defendant entered into "purchase and ranching agreements" with various purchasers by the terms of which he agreed to sell live silver foxes for breeding purposes at a price of $970 a pair for full silver foxes and $770 a pair for three-quarter silvers. The agreements provided that the foxes purchased from him should be ranched at "Louis Payne Associate Ranch" at Lynxville, Wisconsin, at an annual cost of $50 per pair. The defendant agreed substantially that he would provide tattoo identification for the foxes so purchased; that he would furnish the serial number of the pen in which the purchaser's foxes were to be kept; that he would sell the offspring or the pelts thereof produced by the purchaser's foxes and would transmit the proceeds of such sale to the purchaser; that he would replace all losses of breeding foxes due to death, theft, or escape; and that the purchaser might have actual delivery of his foxes upon the payment of accrued charges. The defendant guaranteed a minimum of three pups a pair during the year following the date of the agreement. Pursuant to these agreements, the defendant purported to sell the foxes to the public and evidenced the sale by a "bill of sale." This action was brought to enjoin the violations of the Securities Act of 1933. The sole question presented is whether the transactions are investments or sales.

Conger, District Judge: In the Act [Securities Act of 1933], a "security" is defined as follows:

(1) The term "security" means any note, stock, treasury stock, bond, debenture, evidence of indebtedness, certificate of interest or participation in any profit-sharing agreement, collateral-trust certificate, preorganization certificate or subscription, transferable share, investment contract, voting-trust certificate, certificate of deposit for a security, fractional undivided interest in oil, gas, or other mineral rights, or, in general, any interest or instrument commonly known as a "security," or any certificate of interest or participation in, temporary or interim certificate for, receipt for, guarantee of, or warrant or right to subscribe to or purchase, any of the foregoing. . . .

True the said documents on their face, and judged according to form, appear to be contracts of sale; true the purchaser is given title and the right to possession of the animal or animals mentioned in the contracts; true there are other indicia of ownership, such as marking of the animals for each individual "purchaser," the recording in the proper office of the "bill of sale" in the name of the purchaser and the payment of personal tax on each animal; nevertheless, viewing the various transactions by and large and all the surrounding circumstances one can conclude only that these transactions were investments and not actual and bona fide sales. . . .

Let me quote from one of the letters defendant sent to prospective customers:

Making money in fur farming is simplicity itself. You buy breeding stock of proven capacity. We place the animals in spacious pens, feed and care for them in a most scientific manner, and when they have bred and puppies are mature we pelt the off-spring and send the furs to markets. In a short time you receive a substantial check for your pelts and the proceeds are usually larger than expected.

Again, I quote from another letter:

The purpose of selling breeders to investors is similar to that of any other well established producing company which employs stock certificates as a means of raising capital for expansion purposes. Also it further enables investors for income to share to a measurable extent in the substantial pelt profits enjoyed by a well managed fur farm. . . .

I am satisfied from the picture as presented to me by the pleadings, affidavits and exhibits that these purchasers of foxes, while they may have owned the foxes, yet took no part and intended to take no part in their breeding, raising or marketing; that they were not buying animals, but the right to profits to be realized through no effort of their own, through an enterprise run by the defendant, part of which earnings they received before there were any earnings, by way of anticipated profits. Such an arrangement involves an investment contract, a security within the meaning of Section 2(1) of the Securities Act of 1933. [DECISION FOR PLAINTIFF]

List v. Fashion Park, 340 F.2d 457 (N.Y. 1965). Action by Albert A. List, plaintiff, against Fashion Park and others, defendants, to recover damages for the sum of $160,293 for violation of the antifraud provisions of the Exchange Act.

Fashion Park, a manufacturer and distributor of men's clothing, had not been prospering for several years. The president, therefore, called a director's meeting. Defendant Lerner, a minority shareholder, was among the directors who attended the meeting. The possibility of selling Fashion Park was discussed at this meeting. Negotiations to sell Fashion Park to Hat Corporation began about ten days later, and a formal contract of sale was signed on February 3, 1961.

Plaintiff, an experienced and successful investor who had purchased 5,100 shares of Fashion Park at $13.50 per share, authorized his broker to sell his shares at a net price to him of not less than $18.00 per share. After intensive negotiations between plaintiff's broker and Lerner and several other persons, the sale of the 5,100 shares owned by plaintiff was consummated at $18.50 per share. Lerner purchased 4,300 shares, and the other persons purchased the remaining 800 shares. Lerner, within two weeks after this transaction, disposed of a part or all of his interest in 3,137 shares at a profit of about $1.00 per share. Plaintiff then brought this action alleging that defendants had conspired to buy his stock and then to sell it at a substantial profit, and that they had failed to disclose to him material facts in their possession which would have affected his decision to sell his stock. The undisclosed facts, alleged to be material and upon which plaintiff relied to support his allegations, were that one of the buyers of his stock was a director of Fashion Park, and that with a potential purchaser on the horizon, the Fashion Park board had resolved to sell or merge the company.

Waterman, Circuit Judge: Because there is much disagreement and confusion among the parties concerning the meaning and applicability of "reliance" and "materiality" under Rule 10b-5, we think it advisable first to set forth the well known and well understood common law definitions of these terms and the reasons for the rules in which the terms are incorporated. Insofar as is pertinent here, the test of "reliance" is whether "the misrepresentation is a substantial factor in determining the course of conduct which results in [the recipient's] loss." The reason for this requirement, as explained by the authorities cited, is to certify that the conduct of the defendant actually caused the plaintiff's injury. The basic test of "materiality," on the other hand, is whether "a reasonable man would attach importance [to the fact misrepresented] in determining his choice of action in the transaction in question." Thus, to the requirement that the *individual plaintiff* must have acted upon the fact misrepresented, is added the parallel requirement that a *reasonable man* would also have acted upon the fact misrepresented.

The proper test is whether the plaintiff would have been influenced to act differently than he did act if the defendant had disclosed to him the undisclosed fact. To put the matter conversely, insiders "are not required to search out details that presumably would not influence the person's judgment with whom they are dealing." This test preserves the common law parallel between "reliance" and "materiality," differing as it does from the definition of "materiality" under Rule 10b-5 solely by substituting the individual plaintiff for the reasonable man. Of course this test is not utterly dissimilar from the one hinted at by the trial court. That the outsider did not have in mind the negative of the fact undisclosed to him, or that he did not put his trust in the advice of the insider, would tend to prove that he would not have been influenced by the undisclosed fact even if the insider had disclosed it to him.

The trial court concluded that plaintiff would have sold his stock even if he had known that defendant Lerner, an insider, was one of the buyers. The trial court based this result upon its findings that plaintiff is an experienced and successful investor in securities; that he actively solicited the sale to defendants; that he did not ask his broker whether any insiders were bidding for stock in the corporation; that his broker knew two directors were bidding but did not think it necessary to inform plaintiff of this; that the only restriction plaintiff placed on his broker related to price; and that his broker suggested that five points would be a nice profit, to which plaintiff agreed. From these facts, the trial court presumably inferred that plaintiff was so desirous of "the potential five point profit he would make" and so reliant on knowledge acquired through "his many dealings in the securities field" that the identity of the buyer would have been of little or no concern to him. [DECISION FOR DEFENDANT]

PROBLEMS

1 A promoter and four other persons were promoting a corporation to be engaged in the wholesale business of importing and selling rare jewels. They completed the organization of the corporation, and filed all the necessary documents with proper state officials. They had also properly prepared and, on November 30, 1974, filed a registration statement with the Securities and Exchange Commission. On December 4, 1974, the promoter began making oral offers to the general public over the radio and television to sell the securities. He stated the securities had been "approved by the Securities and Exchange Commission." Was the promoter acting within his rights when he made the oral offers prior to the effective date of the registration statement? What offense, if any, has he committed?

2 Wilcox, who was a director of the XYZ Corporation, attended a meeting of the board of directors. At this meeting, a resolution was passed authorizing a split-up of shares of the corporation. Wilcox related this information to Williams, a close friend of Wilcox. Williams, knowing that all of the securities of the corporation were registered on the national securities exchanges, purchased 200 shares of stock of the corporation for $52 per share. After the split-up of shares had been consummated, Williams sold his shares for $65 per share. In an action by a minority shareholder against Williams for violation of the antifraud provisions of the Exchange Act, the defense of Williams was that he was neither a director, an officer, nor a controlling shareholder of the corporation. Do you think this is a good defense?

3 Mason, who was the beneficial owner of 12 percent of a class of a registered equity security of the ABC Corporation, purchased 150 additional shares of securities for $20 per share on October 1, 1973. He then sold the 200 shares for $25 per share on January 10, 1974. Mason was not, however, a director, officer, or a corporate executive of the corporation. May the profit so made by Mason be recovered by (1) the issuer, or (2) any other shareholder of the corporation?

4 Lewis, who was promoting a membership club, mailed numerous letters to prospective members inviting them to join the club. The letter solicited $20,000 from each member but stated, among other things, that there would be no membership fees or dues; that the money received from the members would be used to purchase and expand the facilities of the Oceanfront Tourist Resort; that the resort was prosperous; that the members would receive checks on the last day of June and December of each year representing their share of the profits; and that the membership would be limited to the first 300 persons who applied for membership. Lewis received over $600,000 in response to his letter during the first six months that he solicited members. Do you think Lewis is subject to the provisions of the Securities Act of 1933?

5 Defendant claimed to have invented an electrical device which would extract gold from the waters of Mono Lake. In order to promote the scheme, certain "units of interest" were offered to the public at the rate of $100 per unit. Several persons purchased two units each and entered into a written agreement with the defendant which stated that such persons had paid unto the defendant "the sum of two hundred dollars, the receipt of which is hereby acknowledged, and shall receive two units of interest" in the venture for the development of said project. The blue sky statute of the particular state was of the "dealer" type of statute. Do you think defendant, who failed to procure the license, has violated this blue sky statute?

6 Carson, the promoter of a large corporation, had complied with all the provisions of regulation C. The registration statement had been filed with the Securities and Exchange Commission and had become effective. Carson then delivered the prospectus to several prospective investors, and said to them: "This is a good investment; these securities have been approved by the Securities and Exchange Commission; and the Commission has verified the accuracy of the prospectus." What offense, if any, has been committed by Carson?

7 The treasurer of the XYZ Corporation was preparing a registration statement in anticipation of registering the securities of the corporation with the Securities and Exchange Commission in accordance with regulation C. A profit and loss statement had been prepared, and the treasurer had the statement certified by a notary public. Explain whether the treasurer acted correctly in having the statement certified by the notary public.

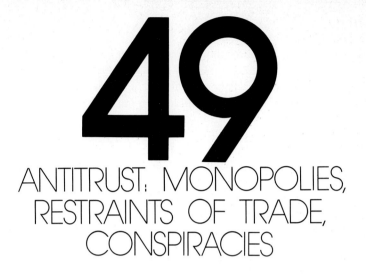

49

ANTITRUST: MONOPOLIES, RESTRAINTS OF TRADE, CONSPIRACIES

Business in the United States went through a period of widespread trust formation around the turn of the century. Corporations engaged in the same type of business, through the use of a trust agreement, could transfer the stock in each company to a board of trustees consisting of important management personnel of the corporations by common agreement of the shareholders involved. The shareholders were then given trust certificates naming them the beneficiaries of the trust and entitling them to dividends on the shares they had transferred. A merger of the corporations was not necessary under this arrangement, and the corporations could remain as separate corporations. The board of trustees under this trust arrangement could control the management of all the corporations. They could monopolize trade and conspire in restraint of trade.

Some of the first statutes aimed at controlling monopolies were enacted during the period these trusts were flourishing. These laws, therefore, came to be known as "antitrust" laws. The word "antitrust" today, however, is generally applied to any monopolistic combination. The antitrust laws obviously were not aimed at trusts, such as charitable and spendthrift trusts, that serve a legitimate and desirable purpose.

The areas of antitrust laws that will be considered in this chapter include (1) the Sherman Act, (2) the Clayton Act, (3) the Robinson-Patman Act, (4) the Federal Trade Commission Act, and (5) state antitrust laws.

SHERMAN ANTITRUST ACT, 1890

The Sherman Act was the first major antitrust law enacted by Congress, and its purpose is to protect trade and commerce against unlawful restraint and monopolies. The most important provisions are found in the first two sections. Section 1 declares unlawful "every contract, combination in the form of trust or otherwise, or conspiracy, in restraint of trade or commerce among the several states." Section 2 deems every person guilty of a misdemeanor "who shall monopolize, or attempt to monopolize, or combine or conspire with any other person or persons, to monopolize any part of the trade or commerce among the several states."

Price-Fixing   Resale price maintenance contracts are exempted from the coverage of the antitrust laws, and should not be confused with price-fixing under the Sherman Act. The resale price maintenance contracts are permitted under the fair trade laws and are discussed later in this chapter. Price-fixing by joint activities whether it is horizontal—between competitors—or vertical—between suppliers and distributors or retailers—is per se an illegal restraint of trade because it eliminates competition. This assertion is true regardless of whether the effect on prices is direct or indirect.

Group Boycotts   Group boycotts, sometimes referred to as trade boycotts, are per se violations of the Sherman Act. A manufacturer, retailer, or any person has the right to exercise his own independent discretion as to whom he will have business dealings with. A concerted refusal to have business dealings, however, is illegal per se. In *Klor's, Inc. v. Broadway-Hale Stores, Inc.,* 359 U.S. 207 (1959), Klor's operated a retail store in San Francisco next door to Broadway-Hale, and the two stores competed in the sale of household appliances. Klor's brought an action against Broadway-Hale and the manufacturers and distributors of such well-known brands as General Electric, RCA, Admiral, Zenith, and others alleging that they had conspired among themselves and with Broadway-Hale either not to sell to Klor's or to sell to Klor's only at discriminatory prices. The court agreed with Klor's that these activities had taken place and showed a type of trade restraint and public harm prohibited by the Sherman Act.

Remedies   Congress attempted to enforce the provisions of the Sherman Act by furnishing legal remedies for violations thereof. The remedies most often used may be summarized:

(1) Persons found guilty in accordance with either of these sections are subject to criminal prosecution, and, on conviction thereof, may be punished by fine of up to $50,000, or by imprisonment not exceeding one year, or by both fine and imprisonment.

(2) The federal government is given the power to obtain injunctions to restrain violations of the provisions of the Sherman Act.

(3) Persons who have been injured by another person who violates this act are

given the right to bring a civil action for treble damages against the violator, plus court costs and reasonable attorney's fees.

The Sherman Act deals primarily with practices which have already become established. Conduct which produced monopolies, therefore, could not be effectively curtailed. This act also proved to be too broad in its intention and too general in its purpose. The Sherman Act, therefore, was amended by the Clayton Act in 1914.

CLAYTON ACT, 1914

The purpose of the Clayton Act was to supplement and strengthen the Sherman Act by enumerating certain practices and making it possible to attack such practices in their incipiency. These practices were not themselves contracts, combinations, or conspiracies in restraint of trade. The Clayton Act makes it unlawful for any person engaged in commerce to sell commodities on condition that the purchaser shall not use other commodities of a competitor where the effect of such sale may be to substantially lessen competition or *tend* to create a monopoly. Tying sales, exclusive dealing agreements, and acquisitions of stock in other corporations were specifically prohibited where they would have this effect.

Tying Sales or Leases   Section 3 of the Clayton Act made it unlawful for a person to sell or lease commodities, whether patented or not, with tying restrictions. These restrictions occur where the purchaser or lessee agrees that he will use with the sold or leased article only such other articles as are sold or leased by the seller even when some other named brand of equal quality is available. The rule pertaining to tying restrictions, however, does not prevent a seller from discriminating in price in order to meet competition in good faith.

International Salt Co. v. U.S.,   332 U.S. 392 (1947), explains the type of business activity that is prohibited. In this case, the company had leased its patented machines for dispensing salt in industrial processing, such as fish canning and meat packing, to customers only on condition that the lessee would purchase salt from the company. The court held that this condition was an unreasonable restraint which might lessen competition.

Exclusive-dealing Contracts   Contracts whereby a retailer agrees to refrain from dealing in the goods of a competitor of a seller-manufacturer in consideration of the retailer's being supplied with the products of the manufacturer are known as exclusive-dealing contracts. Such contracts are unlawful where the effect may be to substantially lessen competition or tend to create a monopoly. Contracts are generally held to be in violation of the Clayton Act where a manufacturer has achieved a dominant position in his industry and seeks to maintain such a position through the aid of exclusive-dealing agreements. [*Standard Oil Co. of California v. United States,* p. 647.]

Acquisition of Stocks and Mergers   The Clayton Act was designed to arrest in its incipiency the acquisition by one corporation of the whole or any part of the *stock* of a direct competing corporation. Almost all authorities held the view, however, that this section referred only to horizontal mergers and acquisition of stock. Corporations, therefore, expanded their control over rival corporations by the acquisition of the *assets* of such corporations. This action prompted Congress to amend the Clayton Act by enacting the Celler-Kefauver Antimerger Act of 1950.

This Antimerger Act prohibits the acquisition of "the whole or any part of the stock . . . or assets of another corporation engaged also in commerce where in any line of commerce in any section of the country the effect of such acquisition may be to substantially lessen competition, or tend to create a monopoly." Acquisitions of assets, as well as stock, were therefore prohibited. [*FTC v. Procter & Gamble Co.,* p. 649.]

This act did not restrain mergers of small companies whereby they could compete more effectively with larger corporations; nor did it restrain the merger of a financially healthy corporation with a failing corporation. The Antimerger Act did prohibit all acquisitions where the effect might have been to lessen competition substantially in any line of commerce in any section of the country. This includes vertical and conglomerate mergers as well as horizontal mergers.

It may be well to mention that a horizontal merger combines two businesses directly competing with each other in a particular line of commerce. A vertical merger combines two businesses, one of which is a supplier-seller and the other a buyer-customer. A conglomerate merger applies to acquisitions engaged in diverse and unrelated businesses, which businesses neither compete nor are related as customer and buyer. Diversification could be the purpose of a conglomerate merger.

ROBINSON-PATMAN ACT, 1936

No major federal legislation in the field of antitrust was enacted from 1914 until Congress enacted the Robinson-Patman Act as an amendment to the Clayton Act. Under the Clayton Act, the large chain stores were able to obtain large discounts from their suppliers on their purchases because they purchased larger quantities of goods. These discounts made it possible for the chain stores to cut their prices to their retail customers, thereby eliminating the small competitors. The complaint, therefore, came from the small independent stores and the wholesalers who supplied them. It was contended not only that the suppliers discriminated in prices between different customers but that the chain stores were also able to obtain indirect benefits, such as advertising and promotional allowances and other inducements to buy not available to their competitors. The Robinson-Patman Act is aimed at these practices used by the chain stores and is therefore often referred to as the "Chain Store Act."

The Robinson-Patman Act provides in substance that it shall be unlawful for any person engaged in commerce to discriminate in prices between different purchasers of commodities of like grade and quality where the effect of such discrimination may be to substantially lessen competition or tend to create a monopoly, or to injure competition with any person who either grants or knowingly receives a benefit from such discrimination, or with customers of them. A seller, however, is permitted to make the following differences in prices:

(1) Differences based on the difference in cost to the seller in manufacture, sale, or delivery where the differences are caused by differences in methods or quantities.

(2) Differences made in good faith to meet the price of a competitor.

(3) Differences in response to changing conditions, such as deterioration of perishable goods, obsolescence of seasonal goods, or sales in good faith in the discontinuance of business of the goods concerned.

Indirect Methods of Price Discrimination The Robinson-Patman Act makes illegal the following indirect methods of price discrimination, and it is not necessary to show that competition has been lessened in order to prove a violation:

(1) Section 2(c) makes it illegal to pay or receive a commission, brokerage fee, or other discounts on sales or purchases. This provision is aimed at former practices, such as where some chain stores purchased directly from the manufacturer and demanded that the brokerage fee ordinarily paid to the broker be allowed as a deduction, which fee was paid by other buyers using brokers.

(2) Sections 2(d) and 2(e) make it illegal to pay for or furnish a customer with services or facilities for promotional and advertising purposes, such as advertising, displays of goods, demonstrations, and distribution of services unless such payments and services are made available on a proportionately equal basis to all purchasers—small as well as large purchasers.

Buyer Inducement Section 2(f) makes it illegal for a buyer to knowingly induce or receive a discrimination in price which is prohibited by section 2(a). The buyer need not be aware that the discrimination substantially lessens competition, but it is a violation where the buyer knows that the price he receives is lower than the price received by other customers.

Exemptions The antitrust laws have a limited application to certain industries and activities regulated by specific statutes. This does not mean the complete withdrawal of these industries and activities but rather that certain parts of the antitrust laws are superseded by specific statutes relating to certain industries and activities. These include transportation (railways and airlines); communication (radio, television, telephone and telegraph services); exporters operating in international activities; securities exchanges; and banking. Labor, agricultural, and horticultural organizations, instituted for the purpose of mutual help, are specifically exempt from the Clayton Act. This merely means that the cooperative associations of farmers and labor organizations may carry out the legitimate objectives of their organizations without being held to be illegal combinations or conspiracies in restraint of trade. This does not mean, however, that they may engage in predatory trade practices at will.

FEDERAL TRADE COMMISSION ACT, 1914

The Federal Trade Commission Act established the Federal Trade Commission and gave the Commission investigating, prosecuting, legislative, and judicial powers. The Commission was empowered to issue cease and desist orders upon a finding that a violation did in fact exist, but subject to review by the Circuit Courts of Appeals of the United States. The Clayton Act gave the Commission jurisdiction over the antitrust provisions of that act. The Federal Trade Commission Act, as amended in 1938, made unlawful unfair methods of competition in commerce and unfair or deceptive acts or practices in commerce. This amendment gave the Commission broad powers to determine what methods, acts, and practices fell within the meaning of the amendment.

STATE ANTITRUST LAWS

A few state constitutions have provisions prohibiting monopolies and combinations in restraint of trade, and most of the state legislatures have enacted antitrust legislation. Proceedings under these constitutional provisions and statutes have been relatively rare. This is probably because of the broad authority given Congress by the United States Constitution to regulate commerce among the several states. More important are the fair trade laws which have been enacted by most of the states.

Fair Trade Laws   The purpose of the fair trade laws is to permit fair trade pricing contracts for certain products for retail sale. Such a contract is created when a manufacturer, or a distributor, of a brand name product enters into a contract with a retailer and the retailer agrees to sell the product at no less than a specified price. These contracts, frequently referred to as "resale price maintenance contracts," were held to be in violation of the antitrust laws. In 1937, however, Congress exempted resale price maintenance contracts from the coverage of the antitrust laws by enacting the Miller-Tydings Act. Such contracts are valid in interstate commerce, therefore, provided the law of the state where the resale is to be made permits this type of contract and the product bears a trade-mark, trade name, or trade brand.

Many states have enacted statutes permitting resale price maintenance contracts, and some state statutes contain a so-called nonsigner clause. This clause binds retailers to the terms of the resale price maintenance contract irrespective of whether they did or did not enter into the contract. In 1952, Congress enacted the McGuire Fair Trade Act to permit fair trade pricing for articles for retail sale including the nonsigner provisions in those states that have fair trade laws. The state statutes containing a nonsigner clause, therefore, do not violate the federal antitrust laws. Some state courts, however, have held such clauses to be invalid. The fair trade laws, therefore, are not uniform throughout the several states.

CASES

Standard Oil Co. of California v. United States, 337 U.S. 293 (1949). Action by United States, plaintiff, against Standard Oil Company and its wholly owned subsidiary Standard Stations, Inc., defendants, for an injunction to prevent the defendants from enforcing or entering into exclusive supply contracts with any independent dealer. It was alleged that these contracts violated section 3 of the Clayton Act.

Standard Oil Company entered into, as of March 12, 1947, exclusive supply contracts with the operators of 16 percent of the retail gasoline outlets in the Western area, which operators purchased from Standard $57,646,233 worth of gasoline and $4,200,089.21 worth of other products in 1947. Some outlets are covered by more than one contract so that in all about 8,000 exclusive supply contracts are here in issue. These are of several types, but a feature common to each is the undertaking by the dealer to purchase from Standard all his requirements of one or more products. Two types, covering 2,777 outlets, bind the dealer to purchase of Standard all his requirements of gasoline and other petroleum products as well as tires, tubes, and batteries. The remaining written agreements—4,368 in number—bind the dealer to purchase of Standard all his requirements of petroleum products only. Independent dealers had also entered into 742 oral contracts by which they agreed to sell only Standard's gasoline. In some instances, dealers who contracted to purchase from Standard all their requirements of tires, tubes, and batteries, had also orally agreed to purchase of Standard their requirements of other automobile accessories. Of the written agreements, 2,712 were for varying specified terms; the rest were effective from year to year but terminable "at the end of the first six months of any contract year, or at the end of any such year, by giving to the other at least thirty days prior thereto written notice." The District Court granted the injunction, and Standard appealed.

Frankfurter, Justice: The District Court held that the requirement of showing an actual or potential lessening of competition or a tendency to establish monopoly was adequately met by proof that the contracts covered "a substantial number of outlets and a substantial amount of products, whether considered comparatively or not." The issue before us, therefore, is whether the requirement of showing that the effect of the agreements "may be to substantially lessen competition" may be met simply by proof that a substantial portion of commerce is affected or whether it must also be demonstrated that competitive activity has actually diminished or probably will diminish.

International Salt Co. v. United States, 332 U.S. 392, at least as to contracts tying the sale of a nonpatented to a patented product, rejected the necessity of demonstrating economic consequences once it has been established that "the volume of business affected" is not "insignificant or insubstantial" and that the effect of the contracts is to "foreclose competitors from [a] substantial market." Upon that basis we affirmed a summary judgment granting an injunction against the leasing of machines for the utilization of salt products on the condition that the lessee use in them only salt supplied by defendant. It was not established that equivalent machines were unobtainable, it was not indicated what proportion of the business of supplying such machines was controlled by defendant, and it was deemed irrelevant that there was no evidence as to the actual effect of the tying clauses upon competition. It is clear, therefore, that unless a distinction is to be drawn for purposes of the applicability of section 3 between requirements contracts and contracts tying the sale of a nonpatented to a patented product, the showing that Standard's requirements contracts affected a gross business of $58,000,000 comprising 6.7% of the total in the area goes far toward supporting the inference that competition has been or probably will be substantially lessened.

We may assume, as did the court below, that no improvement of Standard's competitive position has coincided with the period during which the requirements-contract system of distribution has been in effect. We may assume further that the duration of the contracts is not excessive and that Standard does not by itself dominate the market. But Standard was a major competitor when the present system was adopted, and it is possible that its position would have deteriorated but for the adoption of that system. When it is remembered that all the other major suppliers have also been using requirements contracts, and when it is noted that the relative share of the business which fell to each has remained about the same during the period of their use, it would not be farfetched to infer that their effect has been to enable the established suppliers individually to maintain their own standing and at the same time collectively, even though not collusively, to prevent a late arrival from wresting away more than an insignificant portion of the market. If, indeed, this were a result of the system, it would seem unimportant that a short-run by-product of stability may have been greater efficiency and lower costs, for it is the theory of the antitrust laws that the long-run advantage of the community depends upon the removal of restraints upon competition.

We conclude, therefore, that the qualifying clause of section 3 is satisfied by proof that competition has been foreclosed in a substantial share of the line of commerce affected. It cannot be gainsaid that observance by a dealer of his requirements contract with Standard does effectively foreclose whatever opportunity there might be for competing suppliers to attract his patronage, and it is clear that the affected proportion of retail sales of petroleum products is substantial. In view of the widespread adoption of such contracts by Standard's competitors and the availability of alternative ways of obtaining an assured market, evidence that competitive activity has not actually declined is inconclusive. Standard's use of the contracts creates just such a potential clog on competition as it was the purpose of section 3 to remove wherever, were it to become actual, it would impede a substantial amount of competitive activity. The judgment is affirmed. [DECISION FOR PLAINTIFF]

FTC v. Procter & Gamble Co.,   386 U.S. 568 (1967). Proceeding by the Federal Trade Commission, petitioner, against Procter & Gamble Company, respondent. The Commission charged that Procter & Gamble Company had acquired the assets of Clorox Chemical Company in violation of section 7 of the Clayton Act, and that such acquisition may substantially lessen competition or tend to create a monopoly in the production and sale of household liquid bleaches. The Commission ordered a divestiture, the Court of Appeals reversed and dismissed the action, and this appeal followed.

Douglas, Justice: As indicated by the Commission in its painstaking and illuminating report, it does not particularly aid analysis to talk of this merger in conventional terms, namely, horizontal or vertical or conglomerate. This merger may most appropriately be described as a "product-extension merger," as the Commission stated. The facts are not disputed, and a summary will demonstrate the correctness of the Commission's decision.

At the time of the acquisition, Clorox was the leading manufacturer of household liquid bleach, with 48.8% of the national sales—annual sales of slightly less than $40,000,000. Its market share had been steadily increasing for the five years prior to the merger. Its nearest rival was Purex, which manufactures a number of products other than household liquid bleaches, including abrasive cleaners, toilet soap, and detergents. Purex accounted for 15.7% of the household liquid bleach market. The industry is highly concentrated; in 1957 Clorox and Purex accounted for almost 65% of the Nation's household liquid bleach sales, and, together with four other firms, for almost 80%. The remaining 20% was divided among over 200 small producers. Clorox had total assets of $12,000,000; only eight producers had assets in excess of $1,000,000 and very few had assets of more than $75,000.

In light of the territorial limitations on distribution, national figures do not give an accurate picture of Clorox's dominance in the various regions. Thus, Clorox's seven principal competitors did no business in New England, the mid-Atlantic States, or metropolitan New York. Clorox's share of the sales in those areas was 56%, 72% and 64% respectively. Even in regions where its principal competitors were active, Clorox maintained a dominant position. Except in metropolitan Chicago and the west-central states Clorox accounted for at least 29%, and often a much higher percentage, of liquid bleach sales.

Since all liquid bleach is chemically identical, advertising and sales promotion is vital. In 1957 Clorox spent almost $3,700,000 on advertising, imprinting the value of its bleach in the mind of the consumer. In addition, it spent $1,700,000 for other promotional activities. The Commission found that these heavy expenditures went far to explain why Clorox maintained so high a market share despite the fact that its brand, though chemically indistinguishable from rival brands, retailed for a price equal to or, in many instances, higher than its competitors.

Procter is a large, diversified manufacturer of low-price, high-turnover household products sold through grocery, drug, and department stores. Prior to its acquisition of Clorox, it did not produce household liquid bleach. Its 1957 sales were in excess of $1,100,000,000 from which it realized profits of more than

$67,000,000; its assets were over $500,000,000. Procter has been marked by rapid growth and diversification. It has successfully developed and introduced a number of new products. Its primary activity is in the general area of soaps, detergents, and cleansers; in 1957, of total domestic sales, more than one-half (over $500,000,000) were in this field. Procter was the dominant factor in this area. It accounted for 54.4% of all packaged detergent sales. The industry is heavily concentrated—Procter and its nearest competitors, Colgate-Palmolive and Lever Brothers, account for 80% of the market.

The Commission found that the acquisition might substantially lessen competition. The findings and reasoning of the Commission need be only briefly summarized. The Commission found that the substitution of Procter with its huge assets and advertising advantages for the already dominant Clorox would dissuade new entrants and discourage active competition from the firms already in the industry due to fear of retaliation by Procter. The Commission thought it relevant that retailers might be induced to give Clorox preferred shelf space since it would be manufactured by Procter, which also produced a number of other products marketed by the retailers. There was also the danger that Procter might underprice Clorox in order to drive out competition, and subsidize the underpricing with revenue from other products. The Commission carefully reviewed the effect of the acquisition on the structure of the industry, noting that "the practical tendency of the . . . merger . . . is to transform the liquid bleach industry into an arena of big business competition only, with the few small firms falling by the wayside, unable to compete with their giant rivals." Further, the merger would seriously diminish potential competition by eliminating Procter as a potential entrant into the industry. Prior to the merger, the Commission found that Procter was the most likely prospective entrant, and absent the merger would have remained on the periphery, restraining Clorox from exercising its market power. If Procter had actually entered, Clorox's dominant position would have been eroded and the concentration of the industry reduced. The Commission stated that it had not placed reliance on postacquisition evidence in holding the merger unlawful.

The judgment of the Court of Appeals is reversed and remanded with instructions to affirm and enforce the Commission's order. [DECISION FOR COMPLAINANT]

PROBLEMS

1 Plaintiffs brought this action against the Realty Association, defendants, seeking an injunction to restrain defendants from conspiring to fix the price level of rental apartments in violation of the Sherman Act. Plaintiffs alleged that they are students at Community College, Boone County, Florida; that they lived in apartments owned and managed by defendants; that defendants control the apartment market available to plaintiffs; that defendants have restricted construction of new apartments; and that defendants have fixed unreasonably high rentals on the available apartments. Should the court grant the injunction?

2 The Typewriter Company, a manufacturer, sold its patented typewriters to various dealers throughout the United States, but only on the condition that the dealers would purchase their supplies of typewriter ribbons, type cleaner, and typewriter brushes from the company. The general manager of the company also wrote letters to all the salesmen telling them to sell typewriters only to those customers who agreed to purchase the additional products. Discuss whether you think this condition does or does not violate the antitrust laws?

3 The XYZ Company sold its canned vegetables and fruits in the Southeast to independent grocery stores and also to the large chain stores. The company allowed discounts of up to 10 percent based on the volume of purchases made by each customer. The result was that the large chain stores received much larger discounts than did the independent stores. The independent stores contended that they were being injured, because they had to pay more than the chain stores. They also contended that such action prevented them from competing with the large chain stores. Do you think this action on the part of the company violated the antitrust laws?

4 The Brown Company and the Smith Company were both manufacturers of glass patio doors, which they sold throughout the United States at their company-owned retail stores. The Brown Company, which sold doors under the patented name of "Brown Patio Doors," was the third largest retail seller of the doors. The Smith Company, which sold doors under the patented name of "Smith Patio Doors," was the fifth largest seller. The Brown Company acquired all of the assets of the Smith Company, the Smith Company was dissolved, and the new Brown Company was created. The result was that in many cities and towns the new Brown Company was the only seller of glass patio doors. Discuss whether you think this merger is or is not a violation of the antitrust laws.

5 The XYZ Company was the manufacturer of certain cosmetics patented under the name of "Clear Skin." The company entered into resale price maintenance contracts with retailers in many parts of the United States, and the contracts contained "nonsigner clauses." Discuss whether these contracts do or do not violate the federal antitrust laws.

6 The A Corporation, the B Corporation, and the C Corporation were the three major distributors of prefabricated windows for mobile homes in the states of Alabama, Georgia, and Florida. These three corporations experienced competition from other sources. The managers of the three corporations thereupon held a series of meetings to discuss this problem. At these meetings, the three managers unanimously agreed to reduce their prices by 15 percent. An agreement to this effect was then drafted and signed by the three managers. The attorney for the United States district court contended that these three managers violated the Sherman Act by means of their participation in a price-fixing conspiracy. Do you agree with this contention?

7 Brown, the owner and operator of a large department store in Honolulu, Hawaii, contended that Smith, the designer and distributor of "Her Majesty" clothes for women and whose place of business was in Los Angeles, California, was discriminating in prices. Brown contended that "Her Majesty" clothes could be purchased by retail stores in San Francisco, California, at substantially lower prices than the identical clothes could be purchased in Honolulu. Discuss whether you do or do not agree with this contention.

50
LABOR RELATIONS

The word "labor" appearing in some statutes, such as the mechanic's lien statutes, may have a meaning different from that accorded the word in another statute. The word "labor" as used in the labor laws, however, comprises intellectual labor as well as manual labor.

Labor organizations—as was mentioned in Chapter 49—were exempted from the provisions of the Clayton Act, and this exemption permitted the labor organizations to carry out their legitimate objectives without being held to be illegal combinations. The exemption did not, however, provide the protection labor needed. Labor union growth, moreover, was impeded in the courts by the use of injunctions. These injunctions were used by employers to prevent all sorts of organized labor activity, such as picketing, striking, and organizing unions. Congress, therefore, attempted to promote freedom in bargaining between labor and management by limiting the use of strikebreaking union-organization injunctions in the federal courts by enacting the Norris-La Guardia Act in 1932. This act also provided that the yellow dog contract—a clause in the contract of employment whereby the employee stipulates that he is not and will not become a member of a union—"shall not be enforceable in any court in the United States." But the Norris-La Guardia Act also failed to supply the necessary impetus for union growth.

Since 1932, Congress has continued to enact labor legislation. This legislation is administered by a number of federal administrative agencies, of which the National Labor Relations Board is the most important in the area of labor-management relations. The two basic functions of the Board are (1) to hold elections among the workers to determine which labor organizations shall be certified as the collective bargaining agent of the workers and (2) to investigate, hear, and reach decisions concerning complaints alleging unfair labor practices.

The Railway Labor Act of 1926 was the first federal statute to promote prompt and orderly settlement of labor disputes between interstate carriers and their employees by collective bargaining. This act does not require the parties to a dispute to reach an agreement. It does, however, encourage the parties to reach a voluntary agreement with respect to rates of pay, rules of work, or working conditions in order to prevent labor disputes from interrupting transportation. In 1936, the act was extended to air transportation.

The remainder of this chapter will be devoted to (1) the Wagner Act, (2) the Taft-Hartley Act, (3) the Landrum-Griffin Act, (4) the Civil Rights Act, (5) the Fair Labor Standards Act, (6) public works and contracts, (7) the Occupational Safety and Health Act, (8) the Social Security Act, (9) unemployment compensation, and (10) state labor laws.

THE WAGNER ACT, 1935

Labor received its greatest motivation from the enactment of the National Labor Relations Act, better known as the Wagner Act. By encouraging the labor movement and collective bargaining, this act sought to diminish the causes of labor disputes which burdened and obstructed commerce. The act also specifically enumerated five labor practices defined to be unfair to employees. These five practices may be summarized as follows:

(1) To interfere with, restrain, or coerce employees in the exercise of their rights (a) to bargain collectively through representation of their own choosing, (b) to engage in concerted activities for the purpose of collective bargaining or other mutual aid or protection, or (c) to self-organization. [*NLRB v. Northwestern Mut. Fire Ass'n,* p. 665.]

(2) To dominate or interfere with the formation of any labor organization. This provision outlawed the company-dominated union emanating from such practices as the employer's providing the union with bulletin boards, a company automobile, or stenographic services.

(3) To discriminate in regard to hire or tenure of employment on any term or condition. This provision was directed against the discharge of employees who were union members or those who would promote the formation of unions.

(4) To discharge or otherwise discriminate against an employee because he has filed charges or given testimony under the Wagner Act.

(5) To refuse to bargain collectively with the designated representative of the employees.

TAFT-HARTLEY ACT, 1947

National labor problems were governed by the Wagner Act from 1935 to 1947. The Wagner Act, however, was heavily weighted in favor of labor. This fact, coupled with a series of crippling strikes by labor unions under the protection of the Wagner Act, led Congress to amend the Wagner Act by enacting the Labor-Management Relations Act, commonly known as the Taft-Hartley Act, in 1947. This act retained all the provisions of the Wagner Act that were needed to protect the labor unions, but it eliminated certain improper union practices and protected the rights of individual employees, employers, and the general public. The outstanding provisions of this act pertain to (1) the closed shop, (2) the right-to-work laws, (3) unfair union practices, and (4) the so-called eighty-day cooling-off period.

The Closed Shop The Taft-Hartley Act outlawed the closed shop, which provides that a worker must be a member of a union before obtaining work. It did not, however, outlaw the union shop, which requires union membership within a certain number of days after the worker is employed. An "agency shop" arrangement requires a nonunion employee to pay an initial service fee and monthly dues to the union as a condition of employment. Instead, the Taft-Hartley Act left to the states the right to outlaw or restrict the union shop and related union-security agreements that would be applicable to interstate commerce. Thus the federal government invited the states to enact legislation in an area reserved by the Constitution of the United States to the federal government. As a result, the types of union security available to labor organizations today are those found in the state right-to-work laws discussed later in this chapter.

Unfair Labor Practices The Taft-Hartley Act declares six specific practices by unions to be unfair labor practices. These practices may be summarized as follows:

(1) Restraining or coercing employees to join a union, which also entails coercion of employees who refrain from joining a union.

(2) Causing or attempting to cause the employer to discriminate in any way against an employee or to encourage or discourage union membership.

(3) Refusing to bargain collectively with the employer.

(4) Engaging in secondary strikes and boycotts for illegal purposes. Primary boycotts are legal, but this section makes all secondary strikes and secondary boycotts illegal. A strike by employees against their own employer to gain their own objectives is a primary strike. The former union practice of striking, picketing, or otherwise boycotting one employer in order to exert pressure on another employer is a secondary strike or boycott.

(5) Requiring new members covered by union shop agreements to pay excessive and discriminatory initiation fees or dues.

(6) "Featherbedding," the requirement of payment by an employer for work not performed.

The Landrum-Griffin Act added the following two practices as unfair union practices:

(1) Picketing for recognition where the employer has lawfully recognized another union or where the correct procedure for becoming the certified bargaining agents has not been followed.

(2) Executing "hot-cargo" agreements. Hot-cargo agreements refer to those by an employer and a union whereby it is agreed that goods declared unfair by the labor organization will not be handled by the employer. Goods declared unfair usually refer to those produced by nonunion members.

Eighty-Day Cooling-Off Period   The Taft-Hartley Act provides that the President of the United States may ask the court for an injunction ordering the union to suspend a strike for eighty days where the strike, threatened or actual, affects the national defense or key industries, or has a substantial effect on the economy. During this eighty-day period, the Federal Mediation Service will work with the two parties to try to achieve an agreement. If an agreement is not reached during the eighty-day period, the strike may continue until the disagreement is resolved by collective bargaining or unless there is legislation by Congress to solve the problem. This procedure is referred to as the "eighty-day cooling-off period."

LANDRUM-GRIFFIN ACT, 1959

The Labor-Management Reporting and Disclosure Act, commonly known as the Landrum-Griffin Act, was enacted as a direct outgrowth of Senate investigations revealing that there had "been a number of instances of breach of trust, corruption, disregard of the rights of individual workers, and other failure to observe high standards of responsibility" on the part of some labor organizations. This act, building on the previously mentioned unfair labor practices by labor unions, (1) provides a bill of rights for union members, (2) requires certain reports to be filed with the Secretary of Labor, (3) provides certain financial safeguards for labor organizations, and (4) enumerates election procedures.

Bill of Rights   The bill of rights for union members is widesweeping. It gives union members many rights, such as the right (1) to nominate candidates; (2) to vote in elections and on an increase of dues or fees; (3) to attend meetings and have a voice in business transactions; (4) to have free expression in union meetings, business discussions, and conventions; (5) to sue and testify against the union; (6) to be given full and fair hearing before any disciplinary action is taken against them by the union; and (7) upon request, to be given a copy of the collective bargaining agreement that they work under.

The above rights are in addition to any other rights given to union members by the union constitution and bylaws. The union members are also given the right to bring civil actions against the union for a violation of the above rights.

The Initial Report Every labor organization is required to adopt and file a copy of its constitution and bylaws with the Secretary of Labor together with an initial report giving (1) the names and titles of union officers and the name and address of the union office and the place where the records are kept and (2) a detailed statement of procedures for such matters as membership qualifications, calling meetings, imposition of fines, suspensions and expulsion of members, and authorization of strikes.

Annual Financial Reports A labor organization is required to file such information as will disclose its financial condition for the preceding year. The report must indicate: (1) its assets and liabilities; (2) its receipts and the sources thereof; (3) salaries and allowances paid to each officer and also to each employee who received more than $10,000; (4) loans to any officer, employee, or member aggregating more than $250; (5) loans to any business enterprise; and (6) other disbursements made by it and the purpose thereof.

Annual Conflict-of-Interest Reports Every union officer or employee, other than those performing clerical or custodial services exclusively, is required to file annual reports if he or his family had any financial transactions that might constitute a conflict of interest. This provision pertains to such matters as holding shares of stock in companies with which the union has had dealings and payments received from employees.

Trusteeship Reports A trusteeship is normally used to prevent or eliminate malpractices, such as mismanagement of union funds, violation of collective-bargaining agreements, and corruption in subordinate organizations. A trusteeship arises when a national union suspends the charter of a subordinate organization—intermediate bodies and local unions—and designates some person to be in complete charge of all the affairs of the local union. The Landrum-Griffin Act provides that the national union must file reports on each trusteeship giving information, such as the names and addresses of subordinate organizations, the date the trusteeship was established, and the reasons for the establishment of the trusteeship.

Employer Reports An employer must file annual reports (1) showing arrangements and payments made to a consultant whom he engages to deal with the union and (2) giving information with respect to payments made to unions or union officials. The same duty is imposed on the consultant with respect to the arrangements and payments.

Financial Safeguards for Labor Organizations The Landrum-Griffin Act, after declaring that union officers and representatives occupy positions of trust in relation to the union and its members, provides (1) that union officers and representatives handling union funds must be bonded by a surety company authorized by the Secretary of the Treasury and (2) that the amount of loans the unions can make to officers and employees cannot exceed $2,000. The penalty for violation of these two provisions is imprisonment for one year or a fine up to $10,000, or both. It is also provided that employers and unions cannot pay the fines of any officer or employee convicted of violating this act.

Embezzlement of union funds by those handling such funds is made a federal crime. The penalty imposed is imprisonment for up to five years or a fine of up to $10,000, or both.

Elections   The Landrum-Griffin Act provides for an elaborate system of regulating election procedures. A few of the provisions may be summarized: Elections must be made by secret ballot; national unions must hold elections every five years, intermediate bodies every four years, and locals every three years; unions are obligated to provide adequate safeguards for fair elections; and every candidate for union office must have access to membership lists.

CIVIL RIGHTS ACT, 1964

One of the goals of the Civil Rights Act of 1964 which affects labor is the elimination of job discrimination because of "race, color, religion, sex, or national origin." The act declares and describes certain things to be "an unlawful employer practice" in fairly complicated language. The essence of this provision may be summarized: An employer commits an unlawful employment practice when he takes into consideration in any way an individual's race, color, religion, sex, or national origin in any matter that is connected in any way with, or that might have any effect upon, his employment.

The coverage of the act is widespread, but the most difficult cases are those alleging discrimination on the basis of sex. The act permits discrimination in those certain instances where sex is a *bona fide occupational qualification* reasonably necessary to the normal operation of a particular enterprise. Jobs where a particular sex is a bona fide occupational qualification are nevertheless extremely rare.

FAIR LABOR STANDARDS ACT, 1938

The Fair Labor Standards Act, commonly known as the Wage and Hour Law, is administered by the Wage and Hour Division in the Department of Labor. The purpose of the act is to regulate hours and wages of employees in commerce or in the production of goods for commerce, and to prohibit oppressive child labor. The act provides that employers, with certain exceptions, must pay a minimum hourly wage as established by Congress for a forty-hour workweek and for overtime compensation for employment at a rate not less than $1\frac{1}{2}$ times the regular rate the employee is earning.

The coverage of the act has been constantly broadened, and the minimum wage has been steadily increased. A businessman, therefore, would be well advised to examine his operations from time to time to determine if his particular business is covered by the Fair Labor Standards Act.

Oppressive Child Labor The term "oppressive child labor" as used in the Fair Labor Standards Act means a condition of employment under which an employee under the age of sixteen years is employed in any occupation, except where the employment is by his parent or guardian in an occupation other than manufacturing or mining. With respect to children between the ages of sixteen and eighteen years, the term means an occupation found by the Secretary of Labor to be particularly hazardous or detrimental to the health of the employee. The following is a general indication of some of the occupations which the Secretary of Labor has declared to be hazardous employment: manufacturing and storing of explosives; motor vehicle driving; coal mining; logging and sawmill activities; power-driven woodworking, hoisting apparatus, metal forming, and saws and shears; exposure to radioactive substances; and wrecking and demolition.

Exemptions The minimum-wage and overtime compensation provisions of the Fair Labor Standards Act do not apply to employees in certain industries. The pertinent exemptions may be summarized as follows:

(1) Employees employed in a bona fide executive, administrative, or professional capacity.

(2) An outside salesman whose hours of nonselling do not exceed 20 percent of the hours worked by nonexempt employees.

(3) Employees employed by a retail and service establishment, 75 percent of whose annual dollar volume of sales of goods or services, or both, is not for resale in the particular industry (a) if more than one-half of the establishment's sales or services is within the state and (b) if the establishment is not engaged in commerce or if it has an annual volume sales amounting to less than $250,000.

(4) Employees employed in farming, including employment such as horticulture and the raising of livestock. Employees engaged in the processing of farm products grown by others, such as packing and shipping farm products, are not exempt.

(5) The overtime compensation provisions of the Fair Labor Standards Act do not apply to a person employed in an industry of a seasonal nature, such as the processing of seasonal fresh fruits; nor to various other industries, such as railroad, pipeline, motor or air carriers; nor to drivers making local deliveries.

Employers may also obtain certificates from the Wage and Hour Administrator for the exemption of certain classes of employees from the minimum wage provisions of the Act. These exemptions include (1) learners, apprentices, and messengers employed primarily in delivering letters and messages; (2) full-time students who are employed on a part-time basis or full-time during the summer; and (3) employees whose earning or productive capacity is impaired.

Equal Pay Act, 1964 The Fair Labor Standards Act, as amended by the Equal Pay Act, prohibits discrimination in wages between employees on the basis of sex. The requirement is that the same wages be paid "for equal work on jobs the performance of which requires equal skill, effort, and responsibility and which are performed under similar working conditions." This language leaves unanswered many questions which will have to be answered by the courts.

PUBLIC WORKS AND CONTRACTS

The Contract Work Hours Standards Act, 1962, prescribes, with certain exceptions, that no contractor on any federal work shall require or permit any laborer or mechanic to work more than eight hours in any calendar day or more than forty hours in any workweek.

Davis-Bacon Act, 1964 This act pertains to construction contracts for federal public works in excess of $2,000. The wage provision requires that the contractor must agree in his construction contract to pay laborers and mechanics a minimum wage based upon the wages that will be determined by the Secretary of Labor to be prevailing for laborers and mechanics in the locality for similar work.

Walsh-Healy Act, 1942 This act pertains to suppliers who agree to manufacture or furnish materials, supplies, or equipment for the United States in excess of $10,000. The wage provision requires that the contract contain a stipulation for payment of the prevailing wages in the locality for similar work, as determined by the Secretary of Labor.

Federal Kickback Act, 1948 This act pertains to persons employed in the construction, completion, or repair of any public building or work financed by the United States. It is provided that whoever by any means whatsoever induces any person so employed to give up any part of the compensation to which he is entitled shall be fined $5,000 or imprisoned for not more than five years, or both. [*United States v. Alsup,* p. 666.]

OCCUPATIONAL SAFETY AND HEALTH ACT, 1970

The stated purpose of this act, frequently known as the Williams-Steiger Act, is to assure, so far as possible, every man and woman in the nation safe and healthful working conditions. Prior to the enactment of this act, a piecemeal approach to occupational safety and health problems left the bulk of the nation's employees unevenly covered. The general duty clause of the act provides that employers shall furnish to their employees a place of employment which is free from recognized hazards that are likely to cause the employees serious physical harm.

The Secretary of Labor, pursuant to the authority of this act, has promulgated regulations for health and safety standards. These standards are set forth in great detail and pertain to such occupational and industrial equipment as walking platforms, manlifts, vehicle-mounted platforms, hazardous materials, and equipment for personal protection and fire protection. Procedures are also set for activities, such as handling and storage of material, machines and machine guarding, and hand and portable power tools. These regulations also contain specifications as to environmental control, ventilation, noise exposure, radiation, and air contaminants.

This act also provides that any state which desires to assume responsibility for the development and enforcement of occupational safety and health standards shall submit a state plan to the Secretary of Labor for approval. The Secretary of Labor is also empowered to make grants to the states and to assist them in areas of occupational safety and health.

SOCIAL SECURITY ACT, 1935

The first federal social security legislation, which is a type of insurance, was the Social Security Act of 1935. This act covered only the employee when he or she retired and applied only to employees in industry and commerce.

The coverage of social security, however, has been constantly expanding. Those persons covered by social security today include self-employed persons, most state and local employees, household employees, farm employees, clergymen, and members of the armed forces. Most workers in the United States today, therefore, are covered by social security. It logically follows that social security benefits and the social security taxes have also been constantly increasing. The businessmen would be well advised, therefore, to stay abreast of the latest amendments. The social security programs relating to the employer-employee relations may be divided into those relating to (1) retirement and survivorship, (2) health and disability, and (3) unemployment.

Retirement and Survivors Programs A special tax is imposed equally on the employer and the employee for the purpose of providing monthly checks to the employee when he or she retires. An employee receives a social security card from the Social Security Board showing his name and number, and the employer uses the social security number in filing quarterly reports with the Collector of Internal Revenue stating the wages paid to the employee. The salary credited to the employee is then used to compute the amount of retirement benefit the employee is entitled to when he or she files a claim for retirement benefits. The same procedure is used in computing benefits for survivors of the deceased employee. These survivors include certain unmarried children and a widow or dependent widower.

Health and Disability An employee who becomes severely disabled before reaching the age of retirement is entitled to monthly disability benefits. Certain disabled unmarried children are also entitled to disability benefits when a parent receives social security retirement or disability benefits. Disabled widows and dependent widowers are also entitled to these benefits. A program of health insurance is also available to retired and severely disabled employees.

UNEMPLOYMENT COMPENSATION

Unemployment compensation, frequently referred to as unemployment insurance, is a program authorized by the federal government and administered by the states. Prior to 1972, the major federal statutes were the Social Security Act of 1964 and the Federal Employment Tax Act of 1954. The Social Security Act authorized the Secretary of Labor to grant funds to the states to pay for all necessary costs in administering the program and required the states to provide reports to the Secretary of Labor. The Federal Employment Tax Act imposes a federal payroll tax on the employer but allows the employer to deduct a credit for the unemployment tax so paid in filling out his tax returns. The employee is not required to pay any part of the tax.

All of the states have a program of unemployment insurance which provides temporary income payments to employees who are thrown out of work through no fault of their own and who are available for work. The state statutes are not uniform, but they provide the details for determining such matters as the amount, duration, and conditions for eligibility of benefits and the rate and amount of contributions that must be paid by the employer. Employers who are not otherwise liable may apply for voluntary coverage for their employees, and many employers have complied with this provision. The states have also created agencies, frequently a bureau or board of unemployment compensation, to administer the details of the state statutes.

Employment Security Amendments Act, 1970   This federal act made significant changes in the unemployment compensation program. The following paragraphs are not exhaustive, but some of the pertinent provisions are discussed briefly.

The federal statutes prior to January 1, 1972, defined the term "employer" to be any person who had four or more employees in each of twenty weeks during a calendar year. A new definition of the term "employer," which became effective on January 1, 1972, and is applicable to employers after that date, is defined to be a person who meets either of two conditions: (1) If he or she employs one or more employees on each of some twenty days during the calendar year, or (2) if he or she pays wages of $1,500 or more during a calendar quarter. This provision covers employees employed by small businesses who were not previously covered. Other major provisions of the act pertain to (1) an expanded coverage of employees and (2) extended benefits.

(1) *Employees Covered*   A person is defined to be an "employee" if he or she (1) is employed as an officer of a corporation, (2) has the status of an employee under the common-law definition of employer-employee, (3) is an agent-driver or commission-driver engaged in distributing products, such as vegetables, fruits, and beverages—other than milk—or is engaged in laundry or dry-cleaning services, (4) is a full-time life insurance salesman, (5) a home worker performing

work on materials furnished by the employer to be returned to the employer, such as an embroidery-machine operator, (6) a traveling or city salesman, (7) an employee processing agricultural products, (8) a person under the age of twenty-two and enrolled as a student regularly attending classes in a public or nonprofit institution. A spouse of a student employed by the institution is not covered, but the spouse must be informed upon beginning employment that the employment is designed to furnish financial aid to the student and that the employment is not covered by the unemployment compensation program. The new act also requires states to cover nonprofit organizations. The organization must employ four or more workers in each of twenty weeks in a year. Religious organizations and services by a minister or a member of a religious organization are not covered.

(2) *Extended Benefits* The extended-benefit program is an important provision and is designed to operate in periods of high unemployment. Provision is made for additional weeks of benefits for employees who have exhausted their regular benefits. Such employees are entitled to receive extended benefits amounting to 50 percent of their regular benefits up to a maximum of thirteen weeks.

STATE LABOR LAWS

The state statutes which regulate the employer-employee relationship are varied. They regulate such matters as maximum hours of employment and minimum wages for men, women, and children; inspection of factories and other places of employment; safety appliances and conditions of work; and health and sanitation in places of employment. Particular mention is now made of the laws pertaining to (1) right-to-work laws and (2) workmen's compensation.

Right-to-Work Laws Right-to-work laws is a term normally referring to state constitutional and statutory laws prohibiting the requirement of union membership as a condition of employment. Prior to 1947, these laws applied only to intrastate commerce. It will be remembered, however, that the Taft-Hartley Act left it to the states to determine the type of union-security laws that should be enacted.

A substantial number of states prohibit all forms of union-security agreements, and various forms of security agreements are often permitted in the other states. The law with respect to union security, therefore, is not uniform. This is not true, however, in the railroad and airline industries. Congress, by an amendment to the Railway Labor Act in 1951, nullified the right-to-work laws as they apply to these two industries. This amendment permits union shop agreements by the railroad and airline industries and a labor union notwithstanding the law of any state.

Workmen's Compensation Laws The workmen's compensation laws provide a system of compensation for employees who become disabled because of injuries or occupational diseases in the course of their employment and for the dependents of these employees. These laws are not uniform, but the National Commission on State Workmen's Compensation Laws has been working diligently toward uniformity. This Commission, which was established by Congress in 1970, submitted its report to the President and Congress on July 31, 1972. The Commission made recommendations for improvements in the state workmen's compensation laws, and, among these recommendations, nineteen were specified as "essential elements" of a modern workmen's compensation program. The Commission also recommended that Congress guarantee compliance if the states have not complied with the essential elements as of July 1, 1975.

The state legislatures have made significant progress in complying with the recommendations, and the changes have been wide-sweeping. Most states, however, will have to enact additional legislation to voluntarily comply with the essential elements as of July 1, 1975. Thus it is clear that the statute of the particular state will have to be consulted from time to time to determine the law of that particular state.

The nineteen "essential elements" recommended are enumerated as follows:

(1) That coverage be compulsory rather than elective and that no waivers be permitted. Coverage cannot therefore be avoided by any action on the part of an employer or by an employee, or by an agreement between them.

(2) That employers not be exempted from workmen's compensation coverage because of the number of their employees. This recommendation would require employers with only one employee to comply with the workmen's compensation laws.

(3) That agricultural employers who have an annual payroll of $1,000 or more provide coverage to all their employees as of July 1, 1973, and that all agricultural employees be covered on the same basis as other employees as of July 1, 1975.

(4) That household employees and all casual employees be covered at least to the extent that they are covered by social security by July 1, 1975. This means that an employee who earns $50 or more in any calendar quarter from a single household must be covered.

(5) That workmen's compensation be mandatory for all government employees.

(6) That there be no exemptions for any class of employees, such as professional athletes or employees of charitable organizations.

(7) That all states provide coverage for work-related diseases. Many states have provided workmen's compensation for occupational diseases, such as poisoning from lead, mercury, and the like. This is usually accomplished by listing compensable diseases in a schedule. The Commission used the words "work-related diseases" and recommended that the test used by the courts in determining whether an *injured* employee was or was not covered by workmen's compensation be used to determine the coverage of work-related diseases. This test is: "Did the injury arise out of and in the course of the employment?"

(8) That there be no statutory limits of time or dollar amount for medical care or physical rehabilitation services for any work-related impairment. This recommendation supersedes statutes authorizing payments for "all reasonable and necessary medical, surgical, and hospital care." This recommendation requires coverage for such benefits as rehabilitation centers, health home programs, and the like, until the employee's rehabilitation is complete.

(9) That the right to medical and physical benefits not terminate by the mere passage of time. This means that once an employee receives medical benefits, a claim for further medical care can be filed at any time.

(10) That an employee or his survivor be given the choice of filing a workmen's compensation claim in the state (a) where the injury or death occurred, (b) where the employment was principally localized, or (c) where the employee was hired. This recommendation is for the benefit of employees with multistate contracts, such as truck drivers or airline stewardesses; for example, an airline stewardess injured in State A, with corporate headquarters in State B, but who was hired in State C.

(11) That, subject to the state's maximum weekly benefit, temporary total disability benefits be at least 66-2/3 percent of the employee's gross weekly wage. Some recent statutes define "temporary total disability" as a disability total in character but temporary in quality.

(12) That (a) as of July 1, 1973, the maximum weekly benefit for temporary total disability be at least 66-2/3 percent of the state's average weekly wage and (b) as of July 1, 1975, the maximum be at least 100 percent of the state's average weekly wage.

(13) That the definition of "permanent total disability" used in most states be retained. This definition is interpreted to mean an employee who experiences a work-related injury or disease which leads to a permanent impairment that makes it impossible for him to engage in any substantial gainful activity for a prolonged period.

(14) That, subject to the state's maximum weekly benefit, permanent total disability benefits be at least 66-2/3 percent of the employee's gross weekly wage.

(15) That as of July 1, 1973, the maximum weekly benefit for permanent total disability be at least 66-2/3 percent of the state's average weekly wage, and that as of July 1, 1975, the maximum be at least 100 percent of the state's average weekly wage.

(16) That, subject to the state's maximum weekly benefit, death benefits be at least 66-2/3 percent of the employee's gross weekly wage.

(17) That as of July 1, 1973, the maximum weekly death benefits be at least 66-2/3 percent of the state's average weekly wage, and that as of July 1, 1975, the maximum be at least 100 percent of the state's average weekly wage.

(18) That total disability benefits be paid for the duration of the employee's disability, or for life, without any limitation as to dollar amount or time.

(19) That (a) death benefits be paid to a widow or widower for life or until remarriage,

and, in the event of remarriage, that two years' benefits be paid in a lump sum to the widow or widower, (b) that benefits for a dependent child be continued at least until the child reaches eighteen, or beyond such age if actually dependent, or at least until age twenty-five if enrolled as a full-time student in any accredited educational institution.

CASES

NLRB v. Northwestern Mut. Fire Ass'n, 192 F.2d 886 (Wash. 1944). Petition by National Labor Relations Board, petitioner, against Northwestern Mutual Fire Association and others, respondents, to enforce an order entered upon the Board's finding that respondents had engaged in an unfair labor practice.

One Sylvester, a salesman of the respondents insurance companies, undertook to organize a union of the home office employees as an affiliate of the American Federation of Labor. Plans were announced for holding a meeting of all employees at a local hotel for the purpose of perfecting the organization. Two supervisory employees attended the meeting, but left when they were requested to do so. A number of employees thereafter signed membership cards. Pressure, by threats and otherwise, was then brought upon Sylvester by the secretary of the respondent companies and other superiors of Sylvester to dissuade him from further participation in the union movement. Sylvester thereupon destroyed all but a few of the application cards. The unionization movement then subsided, and a drive immediately followed to set up an independent association, or company union, among the employees. After the establishment of an independent association, an employee named O'Connell became chairman of a small remnant still adhering to the AFL group. O'Connell was discharged, but the reasons given for his discharge were inconsistent. The Board ordered the disestablishment of the independent association, a cease and desist order, and the reinstatement of O'Connell. This appeal followed.

Healy, Circuit Judge: The Board found that the establishment of the latter association was aided by the respondents' demonstrated antagonism toward the AFL union and its leader and by their active assistance in soliciting members for the association; also that the administration of the so-called independent union was completely dominated and controlled by representatives of the respondents. We will not stop to discuss this phase of the case in detail. Enough to say that the Board's finding has substantial support in the record. The management's attitude toward these two essays in the field of self-organization was markedly different, the first movement receiving the treatment already described whereas the second was given every encouragement. The propriety of the order requiring the disestablishment of the association, as well as the propriety of the cease and desist order, is not open to serious doubt.

We have felt some hesitation as to a third provision of the order. This relates to the reinstatement of an employee named O'Connell. O'Connell had been in the employ of respondents since 1934, and for more than four years had been assistant cashier of the companies. He was one of the leaders—second only to Sylvester—in the abortive AFL movement.

The Board found that in any event "the unexplained inconsistency of the respondents' reasons for discharging O'Connell negatives the claim that he was discharged for either of these reasons," and that his employment was terminated because the companies had learned from his testimony that he "was taking an active part in the (AFL) Union's attempt to revive interest among their employees." Respondents were ordered to reinstate O'Connell upon request and to make him whole for any loss of pay he might have suffered by reason of his discharge.

On the whole record we are not able to say that the finding is unsupported or the order improper. It is the province of the board, not of the courts, to determine what affirmative action will effectuate the policies of the Act. [DECISION FOR PETITIONER]

United States v. Alsup,   219 F.2d 72 (Miss. 1955). Action by United States, appellant, against Scottie Alton Alsup, appellee, for violation of the Kickback Act.

The indictment charged the appellee knowingly, willfully, unlawfully, feloniously and fraudulently induced Joe Hancock and three other employees, by means of intimidation of procuring dismissal from employment, to give up and pay over to appellee the sum of $2.00 per day for a period of forty working days, or more, which sum was a part of their compensation to which they were entitled as employees of Ewin Engineering Company, at Keesler Air Force Base in the Southern District of Mississippi, said Joe Hancock being employed in the construction of a public work by the United States. The indictment also charged that said Ewin Engineering Company agreed previously with appellee that it would employ only members of International Association of Structural Bridge and Ornamental Iron Workers Union, Local 600, American Federation of Labor, of Mobile, Alabama, and such other employees as the Union or appellee might approve.

Dawkins, District Judge: The trial court dismissed the indictment on the authority of *United States v. Carbone,* 327 U.S. 633, saying "that the law was not intended to affect legitimate union activity." In the Carbone case the indictment charged in detail that the accused union officials were collecting from the employees weekly contributions toward initiation fees in the union, pursuant to union rules, and in furtherance of an agreement between the union and employer whereby the latter agreed to employ only those persons who were members of or approved by the union. According to the majority of the Supreme Court, the trial judge in that case construed the indictment to set up a factual situation which only described a legitimate union device for collecting lawful dues or fees.

In the instant case, however, no such facts appear in the indictment. It is shown that there was an agreement between the employer and the union whereby the former would employ only those persons who were members of or approved by the union or its representative (appellee); but the indictment does not disclose that the appellee was collecting the money from the employees pursuant to any instructions from his union or in furtherance of any union rules. For aught that appears in the indictment, appellee may very well have been using his union position and the agreement with the employer to extort money from employees for his own private gain in no way connected with the union or its "legitimate activities". It affirmatively appears in the indictment that his position was such that he had control over the employees' jobs. [DECISION FOR APPELLANT]

PROBLEMS

1 A national union organization advised The Industrial Company that the union was conducting an organizational campaign. The general manager of the company thereupon sent a letter to the employees and, after reminding them of the benefits they had received in the past, stated: "The union can't put any of those benefits in your pay envelope, and it won't take a union to get additional benefits in the future." The letter then spoke of additional new benefits that were being planned for the future. Do you think the general manager acted within his rights in writing the letter?

2 Brown, who was engaged in the business of constructing apartments, purchased all of his building materials from The Construction Company. The employees of Brown were members of a union, but the employees of The Construction Company were not union members. The union called a strike against Brown in an attempt to force him to cease doing business with The Construction Company. Do you think the union committed an unfair labor practice when it called the strike?

3 The X Corporation, a manufacturer of decorations used during the Christmas season, received more orders for decorations than had been anticipated. The manager of the corporation, in order to have the merchandise packaged and shipped to various customers throughout the United States before November 15, required all of the employees to work overtime for a period of ten days without additional compensation for the overtime. Several of the employees contended that they were entitled to overtime compensation for these ten days. Do you agree with this contention?

4 Albert, a competent mechanic employed by the XYZ Company, was negligent in repairing a tractor. The tractor, therefore, was repaired improperly. Scott, also an employee of the company, was driving the tractor during the course of his employment. Scott, while so driving the tractor, was seriously injured due to the negligence of Albert. Scott contended that he was entitled to the benefits provided by the workmen's compensation laws, but the corporation contended that it was not liable for the negligence of a fellow employee. Decide.

5 The manager of the X Company, which was engaged in the business of manufacturing and storing explosives for shipment in interstate commerce, was accepting applications for employment. Ben Brown, who had just reached his sixteenth birthday, applied for work storing explosives in the company warehouse. Explain whether you think the manager should employ Ben Brown.

6 Jim Jones, a competent and experienced plumber, filed an application with The Plumbing Company, which was engaged in the business of repairing household and commercial plumbing fixtures, for employment repairing such fixtures. The employees of The Plumbing Company, however, were all members of a union. The manager of The Plumbing Company, therefore, said to Jim Jones: "I will give you employment, but you will have to join the union as a condition of employment." Discuss whether you think the manager of The Plumbing Company was within his rights when he set this condition of employment for Jim Jones.

7 Mary Miles, who had been previously employed as a waitress in a renowned restaurant, filed an application for employment as a waitress with the XYZ Company, which is a corporation organized under the laws of the United States and is the owner of a large seagoing vessel. The manager of the company explained to Mary Miles that meals would be served in the dining room throughout the day, but that the practice of the company was to employ only male waiters in the dining room. The manager, therefore, refused to employ Mary Miles. Do you think the reason given by the manager for refusing Mary Miles employment was justifiable?

Part

10

PROPERTY

51
INTRODUCTION TO PROPERTY

The word "property" has many meanings. It is commonly used to denote a thing or object. The word is used in this sense when a person says, "This is my automobile." The word is used in most law cases, however, to indicate ownership of the object. The essence of the word is the right to possess, to use, and to dispose of the object in every legal manner.

CLASSES OF PROPERTY

Property may be divided into several major and a number of minor classes. It is here classified with regard to its movable or immovable nature and character, as real and personal; with regard to its existence, as tangible and intangible; and with regard to its ownership, as public and private.

Real and Personal The broadest, and no doubt the most important, classification of property is that of real and personal. It is frequently said that real property consists of things which are immovable, and personal property of things which are movable. This distinction used in a broad sense is useful, but it will be seen that many kinds of property classed as personal property are not, strictly speaking, movable. It will suffice for the present to define real property as land and those things firmly attached to the land and personal property as all other objects and rights capable of being owned.

Tangible and Intangible Property classified as tangible and intangible—sometimes termed corporeal or incorporeal—is based upon its physical existence. Property which has a physical existence, such as land, buildings, furniture, and animals, is tangible. Property which has no physical existence but is only a right to receive property, such as patent rights, insurance policies, and a share of stock, is intangible.

Public and Private Property which is owned by the government, or a political subdivision thereof, is classed as public property. It follows that property which is owned by an individual, a private corporation, or some other private organization is classed as private property. The fact that private property serves a quasi-public service—for example, a college or university founded by private individuals, supported by private funds, or privately endowed—does not alter its character as private property. Colleges, universities, and similar organizations which are founded and supported by the state, on the other hand, are public property.

Restrictions on Ownership The underlying structure of private property is that individuals may acquire private ownership of property and use, enjoy, and dispose of it to the exclusion of all others. But private ownership of property is restricted in a number of ways. To mention a few: All property is subject to restriction by the government through the exercise of its police power. The government, therefore, may pass reasonable rules and regulations restricting the use and enjoyment of property in order to protect the safety, health, morals, and general welfare of the community. Private ownership is subject to the rights of creditors. Private property, therefore, cannot always be disposed of to the exclusion of all others. Property is subject to taxation. A most important restriction on absolute ownership is the power of eminent domain.

The right of eminent domain is that inherent power in the government to take private property for a public use. The right may be exercised by governmental agencies or by corporations and other organizations created to perform public functions, such as public utilities. In no event, however, can private property be taken without the payment of compensation. The Constitution of the United States provides that private property shall not be taken for a public use without just compensation. The various state constitutions have similar provisions with similar restrictions. This does not mean that private property can be taken arbitrarily simply by the payment of compensation. There are statutes, both federal and state, which prescribe the procedure to be used in appropriating property under this power. The use for which the property is to be taken must in fact be a public use. It must, moreover, be established that the compensation is in fact a fair and just compensation.

FORMS OF OWNERSHIP

An estate which is held by a person in his own right, without any other person's being joined with him, is known as an estate in severalty. But co-ownership in property is well recognized. The forms of co-ownership that are generally recognized throughout the United States, although no one state may recognize them all, are joint tenancy, tenancy in common, tenancy by the entirety, and community property.

Joint Tenancy   A joint tenancy is an estate held by two or more persons jointly with equal rights to share in its enjoyment during their lives. While it appears that joint tenancies were originally confined to interests in real property, it is generally recognized today that there can be a joint tenancy in almost any kind of personal property. But a joint tenancy will not be presumed. The prevailing rule is that a conveyance to two or more persons will create a tenancy in common unless the intent to create a joint tenancy is clearly expressed. Some states go a step further and require the conveying instrument to state specifically that the title is to be held by the grantees "as joint tenants with the right of survivorship, and not as tenants in common," or other words to that effect.

The general requisites necessary to constitute a joint tenancy are a unity of interest, a unity of title, a unity of time, and a unity of possession. This means that the joint tenancy must be acquired simultaneously, the title must be derived from one conveying instrument, the interest must be coextensive, and the right to possession must be coequal. It should be pointed out that a few states have enacted statutes which provide that a joint tenancy may be created by a conveyance which names as grantees the grantor and another as joint tenants. It could be argued, therefore, that the unities of time and title are lacking since a grantor cannot convey to himself. These statutes, however, have met with no difficulty. The essential elements necessary to create a joint tenancy are, on the other hand, still recognized.

The distinguishing feature of a joint tenancy is the right of survivorship by virtue of which the entire estate goes to the survivors upon the death of any one of the joint tenants. The entire property passes to the last survivor. It is to be realized, however, that a joint tenancy may be severed by a conveyance of the interest of any joint tenant, or it may be severed by an execution sale of any interest. The mere docketing of a judgment, even though a lien results therefrom, would not result in a severance. When such severance does take place, the joint tenancy terminates and right to survivorship is destroyed.

Tenancy in Common   A tenancy in common is an estate of such a character that two or more persons have, or are entitled to have, an undivided possession of the common property. This tenancy, unlike a joint tenancy, is characterized by the single essential unity—that of possession—and is not endowed with the attribute of survivorship. Upon the death of a tenant, therefore, his undivided interest passes to his heirs or devisees. This tenancy is created variously. It may be created as the result of a statutory declaration that a grant to two or more persons is to be regarded as a tenancy in common unless it expressly appears that the intention was otherwise; it may be created by the voluntary act of the parties; or it may be the product of a mistake in an attempt to create a joint tenancy. It may exist with respect to every species of property, real or personal.

Tenancy by the Entirety The distinguishing characteristic of an estate by the entirety is that it can only be held by husband and wife. It is dependent upon the marital relation of the cotenants. This tenancy is endowed with the attribute of survivorship. The entire property goes to the surviving spouse upon the death of one spouse. Neither of the parties, however, can defeat the right of survivorship in the other by conveying to a third person, as may be done in a joint tenancy. They may, however, terminate the estate by a joint conveyance of the property. Estates by the entirety are more generally recognized in real property than in personal property. But the decided weight of authority is that such an estate may exist in personal property as well as in real property. It should also be mentioned that the majority of the courts hold that a tenancy by the entirety becomes a tenancy in common upon the divorce of the husband and wife.

Community Property The community property system, which prevails in several of the Western and Southwestern states, is a product of statute. The underlying theory of community ownership is that the husband and wife make equal contributions in the acquisition of property after marriage, and consequently each spouse is entitled to share equally with the other. The statutes are not uniform. They provide generally that all property acquired after marriage, unless it is acquired by gift, devise, bequest, descent, or as the proceeds of noncommunity property, becomes the joint property of the husband and wife. Some of the statutes provide for the right of survivorship; others provide that the half of the property belonging to the deceased spouse shall descend to the heirs of the decedent.

PROBLEMS

1 By the terms of his will, Hubbard devised 100 acres of a large tract of land to Moore, the residue of which he devised to Mosely. The 100-acre tract had not been surveyed and made specific. The will of Hubbard, however, indicated that a future division of the tract would be made. Are Moore and Mosely tenants in common or joint tenants?

2 Plaintiff brought an action against Brown and was awarded a judgment by the court in the sum of $10,000. Brown was unable to pay the judgment, and the plaintiff attached the interest of Brown in a large parcel of land which Brown and his brother owned as joint tenants. The interest of Brown was thereafter sold to Smith by the sheriff at an execution sale for the sum of $10,000 to satisfy the judgment. About two weeks thereafter, Brown and his brother were both killed in an automobile accident. Explain whether or not Smith is correct when he claims that he is the owner of the entire parcel of land.

3 Brown and Smith, who owned a 320-acre farm as tenants in common, became involved in a dispute concerning their arrangement in farming the land. Brown therefore conveyed the north half of the farm to Jones, who immediately conveyed the land to Brown's son. Brown and his son then constructed a fence around the north half of the farm, thereby restricting Smith to the south half of the farm. Was Brown within his rights in dividing the land in this manner?

52
THE NATURE
OF PERSONAL PROPERTY

Coming now to a closer view of personal property, it is appropriate to observe (1) the kinds of personal property and (2) the various ways by which personal property may be acquired.

KINDS OF PERSONAL PROPERTY
Personal property may be divided into two classes: chattels real and chattels personal.

Chattels Real A clearer understanding of the nature of chattels real may be grasped by distinguishing between freehold and nonfreehold estates. Those that endure for the life of the holder, or longer, are termed "freehold estates." Those that endure for a term of years, or at the will of the parties, are termed "nonfreehold estates." Chattels real include these latter interests in land; stated otherwise, they may be defined as any interest in land less than a freehold. A lease is a good illustration of a chattel real.

Chattels Personal Chattels personal are divided into chattels personal in possession, or choses in possession, and chattels personal in action, or choses in action. Chattels personal in possession include definite tangible and movable things, such as furniture and garments, of which possession may be taken. It is to be noticed that chattels personal in possession may be transferred from hand to hand. Chattels personal in action include rights of property which can only be claimed or enforced by action. It is to be noted that chattels personal in action are intangible things which generally include all rights of action. A right of action arising out of a breach of contract is clearly a chose in action. Right of action arising out of an infliction of a tort was formerly included. The courts have said, however, that the term "chose in action" as used in some of the state statutes does not include rights arising out of torts. A common illustration of a chose in action is a negotiable instrument. It evidences a right to money, but it may require an action at law to reduce the money to possession.

ACQUISITION OF TITLE

The title to personal property may be acquired and transferred in a variety of ways. Three common methods of accomplishing this result—purchase and sale, wills, intestate succession—are commented on in other chapters. This chapter is devoted to acquisition by occupancy, finding lost or mislaid property, accession, confusion, gift, and creation.

Title by Occupation The title to some ownerless things may be acquired by taking and holding possession. Wildlife and abandoned property to which no one has the title are the most conspicuous of such things.

   (1) *Wildlife* Title to wildlife, such as animals, birds, and fish, may be acquired by taking possession and control. The common-law right to take wildlife, however, is subject to control and regulation by the state. Game laws for the conservation and protection of wildlife have been enacted in all the states, and severe penalties are frequently imposed for such offenses as hunting for wildlife during a closed season. It should also be mentioned that a trespasser who captures the wildlife on the land of another does not acquire title. The title is in the landowner. Reducing wildlife to possession and control, therefore, must not be wrongful.

   (2) *Abandoned Property* Property is said to be abandoned when the owner voluntarily relinquishes possession of it with the intention of terminating his ownership but without vesting the ownership in any other person. The title to abandoned property, therefore, may be acquired by the first person who reduces it to his control and possession with the intent to take dominion over the article. Suppose the owner of a bicycle considers it worthless and throws it away with no intention of ever retaking it. The first person who finds the bicycle and, with the intent to take it as his own, reduces it to his control and possession acquires the title. The only problem is to determine when property is in fact abandoned because there can be no abandonment without an intent to abandon. A person who throws an article away stating that it was of no value to him would certainly be strong evidence of an intent to abandon. A person, on the other hand, who casts an article aside but who evidences some exercise of control over the article—as where the owner of the castaway bicycle continues to make an effort

to find new parts for it—would be strong evidence of an intent not to abandon. It is a question of fact for the jury.

Lost or Mislaid Property   The courts draw a distinction between lost and mislaid property when a dispute arises between the finder and the proprietor of the premises on which it was found. Lost property is that which the owner has parted with accidentally and of which he does not at any time know the location. Mislaid property is that which is voluntarily placed and is forgotten by the owner. The fact that the article was in a place where it is highly improbable that a person would voluntarily place it—such as on the floor of a shop or under a table—is evidence to show that the property is lost property. The fact that the article was in a place where it is probable that a person would voluntarily place it—such as on a table—is evidence to show that the property is mislaid property.

It is to be realized, however, that the title to lost or mislaid property remains with the true owner. But the true owner may never become known. Who then is entitled to the possession of the property? The question cannot be answered in a few pithy words. It is generally conceded that, as between the proprietor and the finder, the proprietor of the premises upon which mislaid property is found is entitled to its possession until the true owner becomes known. The rule with respect to lost property, however, is generally stated to be that the finder is entitled to its possession as against everyone but the true owner. The rule would be simple enough were it not for the public-private test. According to this test, the custody is awarded to the proprietor of the premises on which the property was found if it is determined that the article is found in a private place, but the custody is awarded to the finder if it is determined that the article was found in a public place. But it is impossible to draw a clear dividing line between a private and a semipublic place. The courts are not agreed. A private dwelling is clearly a private place. A public park is a public place. It has been said that the entrance to a safe-deposit vault is semipublic but that a private room in a safe-deposit company is a private place. The lost-mislaid, as well as the public-private, test leaves much unsaid. This has resulted in a conflict in the law. The most that can safely be said is that the finder would surely be entitled to the possession of property which is legally lost in a public place and that the proprietor would be entitled to the possession of the property mislaid in a private place. [*Dolitsky v. Dollar Sav. Bank,* p. 681.]

Accession   An accession, literally speaking, means that something has been added. Sometimes raw materials of one person are so changed by the labor of another person as to form a new chattel; sometimes a chattel of one person is so united to the chattel of another as to become a constituent part thereof. It is convenient to refer to the first of these as "accession by specification," and to the second as "accession by adjunction." The problem at hand in either event is to determine the rights and liabilities of the parties when the improvement is made by common consent, when it is made by an innocent trespasser, and when it is made by a willful trespasser.

(1)   *Accession by Specification*   In accession by specification a new chattel

is created from the material of one person and the labor—sometimes labor and materials—of another. Few problems arise when the accession is made with the consent of the owner. Suppose Smith, the owner of the raw materials, employs Brown to build a yacht from the foundation. Smith was the owner of the raw materials, and he would likewise be the owner of the yacht manufactured from it, in all the stages of its progress up to the time of its completion. The title to the resulting product, therefore, goes to the owner of the raw materials.

The problem is not so readily solved when an innocent trespasser takes the materials of another without the consent of the latter and makes them into a valuable article. The early cases attempted to establish a test by which the title to the finished product would pass to the innocent trespasser if by his labor he produced a new and distinct thing of an entirely different species, such as bricks from clay. These cases, however, did not apply the rule where there was no change of species, such as carving a work of art out of the stone of another person. The test, although still referred to in the cases, proved unsatisfactory. Most of the courts today, therefore, have resorted to the relative, or comparative, value theory. This theory takes into consideration the proportion in which the labor of one and the materials of another contribute to the value of the resulting product. This theory permits the title to the raw materials to pass from the original owner to an innocent improver who, through the use of skill and labor, greatly increases the relative value of the materials taken. Suppose Brown, innocently using timber belonging to Smith, builds a chair worth $100; suppose further that the value of the timber used was $10. A ratio of ten to one. The title to the chair, other factors being equal, would very likely pass to Brown. Smith would be able to recover from Brown the value of the timber at the time and place of his taking it. The amount of the increase required to vest title to the finished product in the innocent improver has never been precisely stated. The idea seems to be that it must be sufficiently great to make an award of title to the owner of the raw materials very unjust.

The prevailing rule with respect to a willful trespasser is different: The title to the finished product, irrespective of the increase in value made by a willful trespasser, passes to the owner of the raw materials. The owner of the raw materials may reduce the finished product to his possession, or he may recover the value of the finished product without reduction for the expenditure of labor expended by the wrongdoer. [*Sligo Furnace Co. v. Hobart-Lee Tie Co.,* p. 682.]

(2) *Accession by Adjunction* In accession by adjunction, the chattel of one person who is the owner of the smaller unit is joined to the chattel of another person who is the owner of the larger unit. The first obstacle to be overcome is to determine whether accession by adjunction has in fact resulted. The test most frequently used is that accession by adjunction results when the added article cannot be separated and removed from the principal unit without damage to the latter. The title to the finished product thereupon passes to the owner of the principal chattel. Suppose Smith employs Brown to repair his yacht and Brown uses his own materials in making the repairs. The title to the yacht, together with the added materials, belongs to Smith.

The rule applies irrespective of whether the improvement was made with or without the consent of the owner of the smaller unit. A familiar illustration is the case where the owner of the larger unit of a chain incorporated into his iron chain two or three links belonging to another person without the consent of the latter. The chain remained the property of the owner of the larger unit. The owner of the smaller unit was left to his remedy of damages. The usual rule, in the case of innocent conversion, is to assess as damages the value of the chattel as of the time and place of the taking. The majority of the courts, however, assess as damages the value of the finished product against a person who wantonly and willfully incorporates a smaller unit into his own larger unit.

One further rule is worthy of mention: An innocent purchaser of the principal chattel who greatly increases its value will be required to pay the original owner only the former value of the property. [*Ochoa v. Rogers,* p. 683.]

Confusion   The distinction between accession and confusion is this: In accession the property of one is either changed by the labor of another or so united to the property of another as to become a constituent part thereof. In confusion the property of different owners is merely intermingled. The intermingling may be done with the consent of all the owners of the different parcels. The owners, in these circumstances, have equal equities and are entitled to their proportionate share. This most commonly occurs in connection with fungible goods—such as grains or oils—which are customarily sold by weight and measure.

Confusion may occur, however, with respect to such things as cattle, timber, and packages of merchandise, as well as with respect to fungible goods. It may result from accident, mistake, or willful act, as well as by agreement of the parties. Few, if any, problems arise where the goods, intermingled with or without the consent of the different owners, can be identified, separated, and returned to their respective owners. Suppose cattle with different brands are mixed in one lot. The only task is the mechanical one of separating them because each owner retains his title to his separate goods.

Problems do arise, however, where the confusion results from intermixing goods owned by different persons in such a manner that the goods of each owner can no longer be distinguished. If the confusion results from an innocent act or inevitable accident and the goods are of the same kind, quality, and value, the courts hold that each person is an owner of a proportionate share of the common mass. The only problem is the one of proving the share that each contributed to the mass.

Confusion which results from the deliberate commingling by one of the parties presents a serious problem. Some of the courts punish the wrongdoer by depriving him of his goods and awarding them to the innocent party. The majority of the modern cases, however, permit the innocent party to temporarily claim the entire mass. The wrongdoer, in order to reclaim his share of the mass, must show that the per unit value of the commingled mass is equal to, or greater than, the per unit value of that of the innocent party. To illustrate: Suppose Brown wrongfully intermingles his wheat with that of Smith; the per unit value of the commingled mass is $2 or more per bushel and that of the wheat belonging to Smith is worth $2 per bushel. Brown could retrieve the number of bushels that he had contributed to the mass. The burden of proving the respective shares of each party and the value of the wheat, together with all the difficulty and doubt of proof, rests upon the wrongdoer. The wrongdoer, moreover, can claim nothing if the per unit value of the mass is less than the per unit value of the innocent party. Suppose the commingled mass is worth only $1 per bushel and the grain belonging to Smith was worth $2 per bushel. Smith would be entitled to keep the entire mass; Brown could retrieve nothing.

Transfer by Gift   A gift is a voluntary transfer by the owner of his property to another person without any consideration being given for the transfer. Gifts of personal property may be gifts inter vivos, gifts causa mortis, and testamentary gifts. The first two of these types are discussed here; the third, in Chapter 56, "Wills and Estates of Decedents."

A gift inter vivos may be distinguished from a gift causa mortis in that the former is a gift among the living, and the latter a gift in contemplation of death. The two gifts may be further distinguished: A gift inter vivos, once executed, is irrevocable. A gift causa mortis is a conditional gift. It is made with the understanding that the donee will return the property to the donor if the donor survives the crisis and lives. The donor, in either event, must presently *deliver* the chattel to the donee, or to some third person who holds the property in behalf of the donee, with the *intent* of vesting ownership in the donee. The donee must *accept* if the gift is to be effective.

The acceptance by the donee presents little trouble. The acceptance is clearly shown when the donee receives the possession of the property from the donor. The donee, however, may not be aware of the intent to make the gift. This could easily be the situation if the property were delivered to a third person. It is generally said that the acceptance is presumed if the gift appears to be beneficial from the viewpoint of the donee. This presumption seems to mean nothing more than that the gift takes effect immediately upon its execution by the donor but subject to later repudiation by the donee. Delivery and intent are more troublesome.

Delivery may be accomplished by actually handing the specific chattel over to the donee. It may be accomplished by symbolic delivery, that is, delivery of a symbol of the gift accompanied by language indicating a desire to make a gift. This is commonly done by delivering the means of control of the property: a key to a locked box in which the subject matter of the gift is kept, a bill of lading, or a warehouse receipt. The donee may be in possession of the thing given. The gift is complete, if this be the case, when the donor declares that he gives the property to the donee.

Turning now to the problems which may arise when the property is delivered to a third person. The courts, for the most part, solve these problems by a resort to the law of agency. It is said that if the third person is the agent of the donor, the gift must fail for lack of delivery. The donor, in such cases, retains control over the property by means of his control over the agent. If the third person is the agent of the donee, however, the delivery is complete. [*In re Gorden's Will,* p. 684.]

Title by Creation   The creative producer acquires title to the results of his intellectual labor and production. This right is given by the common law. The creative producer, at common law, had an absolute property right in his production so long as it remained unpublished. This right is expressly protected by statute. The United States Constitution provides that Congress shall have the power to promote the progress of science and useful arts by securing for limited times to authors and inventors the exclusive rights to their respective writings and discoveries. The Congress, under this authority, has enacted copyright statutes which give to authors and artists the exclusive right to publish and sell their intellectual and artistic productions for a period of twenty-eight years. The copyright may be renewed for like periods. The Congress has also enacted patent statutes which give to inventors the exclusive right to sell their inventions for a period of seventeen years. A patent cannot be renewed. The procedure necessary to acquire a copyright or a patent is exacting and must be followed carefully.

CASES

Dolitsky v. Dollar Sav. Bank,   118 N.Y.S.2d 65 (1952). Action by Betty Dolitsky, plaintiff, against Dollar Savings Bank of the City of New York, defendant, to recover the sum of $100 allegedly found by plaintiff.

   Plaintiff, a renter of a box in the safe-deposit vault maintained by defendant, requested access to her safe-deposit box. The vault attendant gave her an access slip, and she placed her box number and signature on the slip. She was then directed to the opening to the right of metal grill door in the wall of a restricted area which permits access to the safe-deposit vault. Another vault attendant checked the access slip against the vault records and was satisfied as to her identity. The metal grill door was then opened, and she was permitted to enter the restricted area. Another attendant took her inside the vault, she produced her key, and the attendant removed her box in her presence. She was then escorted to Booth No. 2 in the restricted area. She completed her business in the booth and informed the booth attendant that she had found a $100 bill in a folder advertising Bank Life Insurance, which she had removed from a rack attached to the wall above the table in the booth. The vault attendant turned over the bill to his superior. Approximately one year thereafter, plaintiff contended that she was entitled to the $100 as a finder of property since the rightful owner had not appeared to claim the bill. Defendant contended that the bill was mislaid and that the duty of defendant was to retain possession of the bill until a claim for the bill is made by the rightful owner.

   Trimarco, Justice: At common law property was lost when possession had been casually and involuntarily parted with, so that the mind had no impress of and could have no knowledge of the parting. Mislaid property was that which the owner had voluntarily and intentionally placed and then forgotten. . . . In the case of mislaid property discovered on the premises of another, the common-law rule is that the proprietor of the premises is held to have the better right to hold the same for the owner, or the proprietor has custody for the benefit of the owner. . . . The bank is a gratuitous bailee of mislaid property once it has knowledge of the property. As such the bank has the duty to exercise ordinary care in the custody of the articles with a duty to redeliver to the owner.

No authority has been discovered as to how long a gratuitous bailee in the bank's position is expected to hold mislaid property for the owner. The broad statement of the cases that the holder of mislaid property is a gratuitous bailee for the owner seems to indicate that the bank would have to hold the property indefinitely.

The recent case of *Manufacturers Saving Deposit Co. v. Cohen,* 1950, 101 N.Y.S.2d 820, which held that the property found on the floor of a booth located in an outer room used by a safe deposit company in conjunction with a bank access thereto not being limited to box holders or officials of the safe deposit company was lost property and as such should have been turned over to the property clerk of the Police Department, can be distinguished from the present case. In the Cohen case the court found that the booth on the floor of which the money was found was not located within the safe deposit vault but rather in an outer room adjoining said vault and in a part of the bank which was accessible to the ordinary customer of the bank for the purchase of bonds and the opening of new accounts; as such the court considers the room in which the booth was located a public place not restricted to safe deposit officials and persons having safe deposit boxes in the vault. The case is further distinguished from the present case since its facts disclose that the money was found on the floor of the booth which indicated to the court that the money was not mislaid. The court points out that the testimony shows the money to have been found on the floor of the booth and not on any table or other normal resting place. [DECISION FOR DEFENDANT]

Sligo Furnace Co. v. Hobart-Lee Tie Co.,   134 S.W. 585 Mo. (1911). Action by Sligo Furnace Company, plaintiff, against Hobart-Lee Tie Company, defendant, to recover as damages the value of timber in its improved condition. The court found from the evidence that the plaintiff was the owner of certain timberland, that the defendant trespassed thereon, and that the defendant willfully cut the timber from the land belonging to plaintiff and made the timber into railroad crossties.

Cox, Judge: In our judgment the true rule for fixing the measure of damages is that if the timber was taken by honest mistake, then the value of the timber before being cut is the measure of damages, but if the party taking the timber knew he had no right to it, and thus became a willful trespasser in the first instance, then in a suit against him the measure of damages is the value of the timber in its improved condition without reduction for labor bestowed, or expense incurred by the wrongdoer.

The law is not only careful to compensate the owner for the loss of his property, but it is also careful to see that a willful wrongdoer shall not profit by his own wrong, and by requiring him to respond in damages for the value of the property in its improved state both these purposes are accomplished. To fix the measure of damages at the value of the property in its improved condition when the party had taken it by honest mistake would be as harsh as to fix it at the value in the tree when taken by a willful trespasser would be unjust. In the former case the owner would be profiting by the labor of an honest man mistakenly bestowed upon his property, and in the latter case a willful trespasser would be profiting by his own wrong. [DECISION FOR PLAINTIFF]

Ochoa v. Rogers,   234 S.W. 693 (Tex. 1921). Action by Miguel Ochoa, plaintiff, against Henry A. Rogers, defendant.

Smith, Justice: On Christmas Eve, 1918, a 6-cylinder Studebaker passenger automobile was stolen from its owner, Miguel Ochoa, in San Antonio. In some unaccountable way it got into the possession of the United States government, and on November 12, 1919, the government sold it to Henry A. Rogers, at an auction sale at Camp Travis, at which a large number of dismantled cars called "junk" were likewise disposed of. At the time it was so purchased by Rogers no part of the car was intact. It had no top except a part of the frame thereof; its steering rod was without a wheel; it had no tires, no rims, no cushions, no battery; the motor was out of the car, but included in the junk, as was also the radiator; one headlight was entirely gone, the other was useless; part of the gears were out and one wheel was gone, as was one axle; the fenders were partly gone, and had to be entirely replaced; the differential was beyond repair, and the frame, or chassis, was there, but broken. It was no longer an automobile, but a pile of broken and dismantled parts of what was once Ochoa's car. It was "junk." Rogers paid the government $85 for this junk at the auction sale, which was its market value at the time. Having purchased these parts, Rogers used them in the construction of a delivery truck, at an expense of approximately $800. When the truck was completed, he put it in use in his furniture business. This was late in 1919. On August 7, 1920, Ochoa, passing Rogers' place of business recognized the machine from a mark on the hood and another on the radiator, and completed the identification by checking the serial and engine numbers, which tallied accurately with similar numbers on the car he had owned. The identification being complete and satisfactory to himself and other witnesses, Ochoa demanded the property of Rogers, who refused to surrender it, whereupon Ochoa brought this suit to recover possession of the property, or, in the alternative, for the value thereof at the time of the suit, which he alleged to be $1,000, and for the value of the use of the car at the rate of $5 per day from the time Rogers purchased it from the government.

The case was tried before the court without a jury, and from a judgment in his favor for $85 Ochoa has appealed. . . .

It is of course settled that, if Ochoa had found his property in the hands of the one who stole it, he would have been entitled to at once reclaim it in the condition it was then in. In such case the thief would not be entitled to consideration for any money he had expended in enhancing its value, and this would have been true as well of one who had obtained possession of the property knowing, or failing to exercise care to ascertain that the car was stolen property. . . . If the one in wrongful possession be an innocent or unintentional trespasser, and in good faith improves and enhances the value of the property, and such improvements and additions exceed, or even substantially approach, the value of the article in its raw state when found, the property in dispute becomes merely accessory to the resulting product, and title thereto passes to the purchaser, who is liable to the original owner only for the market value of the lost article at the time it is found. [DECISION FOR DEFENDANT]

In re Gorden's Will, 27 N.W.2d 900 (Iowa 1947). Proceeding by Westfall, executor under the will of Jessie Gorden, plaintiff, against Joseph Henry Bryan and others, defendants.

Oliver, Chief Justice: In 1944 defendant Joseph Henry Bryan held money totaling $5,000 which his aunt, Jessie Gorden, had sent him for safekeeping at various times between 1935 and 1940. In May, 1944, he received by mail a letter dated May 8, 1944, addressed to him and signed by her, stating, ". . . and at my death the money I have down there you take it and divide it among your sisters your brother and yourself." The record indicates she then had no thought of impending death from a present illness or impending peril.

Jessie Gorden died July 17, 1944, aged eighty-four years. She was a widow and apparently left no direct heirs. The residuary clause of her will, made in 1930, divided the bulk of her estate (about $26,000) equally between various collateral heirs, among whom were Bryan, his six sisters and his brother, defendants herein.

The executor of her will instituted this proceeding, praying that said $5,000 be adjudicated to be part of her estate and be charged against the residuary shares of the defendants. Upon trial the application was denied and the $5,000 adjudicated to be no part of testatrix' estate. The executor appeals.

We are satisfied the record clearly shows a valid gift inter vivos to defendants. Jessie Gorden's letter of May 8, 1944, evidenced her intention to make such gift. The letter also consummated the gift. Prior thereto Bryan had possession of the money for Jessie Gorden. The letter directed him to divide it between the donees, when Jessie Gorden should die. Implicit in this direction was the requirement that, until such time, he hold it for said donees. Jessie Gorden thereby relinquished all right to and dominion over the money and transferred the same to Bryan as trustee for the use and benefit of the donees. She reserved no right of revocation and had none.

That a gift may be executed in this manner is well settled. Delivery directly to the donees is not essential. It may be made to some person as agent or trustee for the use of the donees. If such person already has possession of the property for the donor it is not essential to the validity of the gift that the property be returned to the donor and redelivered to said person. [DECISION FOR DEFENDANTS]

PROBLEMS

1 Defendant operated the Arthur Hotel, Portland, Oregon, and plaintiff was employed as a chambermaid. It was the duty of plaintiff to change the linen, dust and clean the rooms,

etc. She was instructed by the defendant—her employer—to deliver to him any items left by departing guests. She found, while she was cleaning one of the rooms, eight $100 bills concealed under the paper lining of a dresser drawer. She removed the money and delivered it to the defendant in order that he might restore the money to the true owner. Defendant was unable to find the true owner. Plaintiff demanded the money, which demand was refused by the defendant. Decide.

2 On September 29, 1946, Brown, who had borrowed money from his uncle for the purpose of attending college, executed a promissory note in the sum of $6,000 payable to the order of his uncle to secure the loan. On January 7, 1947, the uncle executed a release of the note, which was in approved form. The uncle thereafter placed the release in a secret drawer in a bookcase in his home. After the death of the uncle, the executor of his estate found the release in the secret drawer among various other papers of the uncle, including the note above mentioned. Do you think this note should constitute a part of the estate of the uncle?

3 The mother of Mary, an unmarried daughter living with her mother, designated a trunk as a hope chest for Mary. The mother and Mary from time to time had placed linens, blankets, and similar articles in this trunk. The mother explicitly stated that these articles belonged to Mary, and handed Mary the key to the trunk. The mother died in 1946, and the trunk came into the possession of Mary. When the trunk was opened, Mary found three bags containing $950 sewed in a blanket which was in the trunk. The administrator of the mother's estate contends that the $950 belongs to the estate of the decedent. Do you agree?

4 Robert and Rogers, the owners of adjoining forest land, each owned ten stacks of logs. Each stack contained five logs which had recently been cut from pine trees growing on their respective tracts of land. The logs were of the same kind, quality, and size. A violent tornado destroyed the fence between the two tracts of land, carrying the logs from the land of Robert and depositing the logs on the land of Rogers. Explain the manner in which the logs should be divided.

5 Plaintiff, who had a number of beehives on his farm, sold the honey therefrom to a local store. There was, however, a swarm of bees which had made their hive in a hollow tree on the land of plaintiff near the beehives. Defendant, a neighbor farmer, captured the bees in the hollow tree and located them in a beehive on his land. Plaintiff demanded the possession of the bees, but defendant refused to surrender possession. Defendant contended that the bees were wild and that he was the owner since he was the first possessor to take possession and control. Do you agree with this contention?

6 Brown and Jones were owners of adjacent tracts of land on which stood growing oak trees. Brown, thinking he was on his own land, cut down one of the trees which was growing on the land of Jones. The tree had a value of approximately $25. He fashioned the tree into a desk, which sold at public auction for $800. Jones then brought an action against Brown to recover $800. Should he recover?

THE NATURE
OF REAL PROPERTY

Peculiar to the nature of real property are (1) the system of land registration, (2) abstracts and title insurance, (3) the types of estates, (4) the manner in which the title to real property may be acquired, (5) the rights which one landowner may have in the land of another, (6) the transformation of personal property into real property by means of the law of fixtures, and (7) mechanic's liens.

LAND REGISTRATION

It is essential to the security of ownership in real property that there exist some method by which the title can be made clear of record. This has been accomplished by the enactment of recording statutes in all of the states and the enactment of the Torrens System in a few of the states.

Recording Statutes The recording statutes are not uniform, but they do follow a general pattern. All transactions which affect the title to real property are generally required to be recorded in the county in which the land is situated. The most important of these transactions are deeds, mortgages, contracts to sell, liens, judgments, and estate proceedings. These statutes do not, however, ordinarily make recording essential to the transfer of a title as between the grantor and the grantee. They generally provide that as against certain persons the transfer is void unless the deed is recorded. An unrecorded deed, the statutes often say, is void as against subsequent purchasers without notice. It is needless to say, therefore, that a new owner of real property should see to it that his deed of conveyance is recorded promptly. The failure on the part of the grantee to do so makes it possible for his grantor to pass title to a second grantee. But were it not for the recording laws, a prospective purchaser would have no way of determining whether or not the title to the property which he is seeking to purchase is encumbered with outstanding claims.

Torrens System The Torrens System of land registration, so called because it was developed by Sir Robert Torrens in Australia in 1858, is in use in a few of the states. The precise procedure which must be followed in order to bring land under this system of registration is specifically set out by statute. The result is to furnish a purchaser with a certificate of title on which all outstanding claims and interests are noted. This system of land registration has met with little success in the United States, and the recording statutes are not superseded in the states that have adopted the system. The Torrens System, however, is an alternative system of land registration.

ABSTRACTS AND TITLE INSURANCE

Abstracts of Title An abstract of title is a summary of the history of the title to, and all outstanding claims against, a specific parcel of land. The summary will include all conveyances, wills, and judicial proceedings which affect the title to the property. An abstractor does not, however, ordinarily give an opinion as to the legal effect of the title to the property, nor does he give an opinion as to the legal effect of any of the instruments shown in the abstract. An attorney is ordinarily employed to examine the abstract and advise the purchaser with respect to any outstanding interests which may affect the title.

Title Insurance Title insurance is a policy of insurance whereby the insurer agrees to indemnify the insured in a specified amount against loss through a defect in the title to real property. The policy also generally insures against things outside the scope of the abstract, such as matters of forgery and incompetence of the grantor and unknown and hidden hazards. Numerous claims and interests, such as unknown heirs, fall within the hidden-hazard category. The two types of policies generally issued are the owner's policy and the mortgagee policy. This type of insurance is not available everywhere in the United States, but most of the sizable cities have title insurance companies. Many companies have extended their operations statewide, and a few companies operate nationally.

TYPES OF ESTATES

It is to be emphasized at the outset that the law of real property is highly complicated. A layman, therefore, should never attempt to be his own conveyancer. This is particularly true when future interests are involved. Only a lawyer well versed in the law of real property is qualified to do this type of work. No attempt is made here to give even a complete outline of the various estates. An attempt is made, however, to discuss briefly the major ones. The leasehold estate is treated in Chapter 54, "Landlord and Tenant." This leaves for present treatment the fee simple, the fee simple determinable, the fee simple subject to a condition subsequent, the life estate, and future interests.

Fee Simple or Fee Simple Absolute   This estate is the highest interest one can possess in land. Some of the authorities, in an attempt at exactitude, have made a distinction between the words "fee simple" and "fee simple absolute." The words, however, are used interchangeably by the courts. They are so used here. The fee-simple estate is an estate of inheritance. This means that, upon the death of the owner, it descends to his heirs if it has not been transferred by will. It may be alienated. This means that it may be transferred by the owner by sale or by gift. The basic characteristic of the fee-simple estate, therefore, is that it is an estate of inheritance and it may be alienated.

Fee Simple Determinable   The word "determinable" is used interchangeably with the words "base" or "qualified" to describe a fee. This estate is one created to subsist only until the happening of some event. A conveyance to the XYZ Church for so long as the church shall exist gives the church a determinable fee. The interest left in the grantor is a possibility of reverter. The estate may last forever; it is, therefore, a fee. It may end upon the happening of an event; it is, therefore, a determinable fee. No particular formal language is necessary to convey a fee simple determinable. The words commonly used are "so long as" or "until" coupled with a provision that the estate is to revert to the grantor upon the happening of the event. Some courts have held that a fee simple absolute was created when words of reverter were omitted. This is particularly true when the land is conveyed for a stated purpose. Most courts take the view that a purpose clause, standing alone, will not create a fee simple determinable. A conveyance to the XYZ Church to be used as a parsonage, according to this view, creates a fee simple absolute. The distinguishing characteristic of the fee simple determinable is that it automatically ceases upon the happening of the event, and the fee returns to the grantor or his heirs.

Fee Simple Subject to a Condition Subsequent   This type of estate is subject to termination upon the happening of a named event. A conveyance to Brown upon the express condition that the buildings are to be kept in repair gives Brown a fee simple subject to a condition subsequent. The interest left in the grantor is a right of entry for condition broken. The words commonly used to create this estate are "provided that" or "upon the express condition that" coupled with a provision reserving to the grantor the power of termination. The courts look with disfavor upon a power of termination and are likely, in the absence of very clear language, to construe the condition as a restrictive convenant. This is particularly true when the condition is a purpose clause. The distinguishing characteristic of this type of estate is that it will continue in the grantee unless and until the power of termination is exercised.

Life Estates   Life estates are classified as those which come into existence by operation of law and the conventional life estates. Those that come into existence by operation of law are known as "dower" and "curtesy" and arise out of a marital relationship. The conventional life estates are created by the voluntary act of the owner of the land.

(1)   *Dower and Curtesy*   A wife, at common law, was the holder of an inchoate or incomplete right of dower in the real property of her husband. This right became complete upon the death of the husband with the wife surviving and consisted of an estate for life in one-third of the real property of the husband. The corresponding right of the husband was a life estate in all of the estates of inheritance of the wife. This right, which was known as "curtesy," existed only when a live child had been born to the marriage. Modern statutes have almost completely superseded the common law with respect to dower and curtesy. These statutes, however, have quite generally made some provision for the surviving wife or husband. A few states give the surviving spouse a one-third interest in the estate of the other. In those states which recognize community property, the surviving spouse is entitled to one-half of the community property.

It may be well to remember that, unless the statute provides otherwise, neither the husband nor the wife can defeat the other by conveying his or her separate real property prior to the death of the other. They both must ordinarily join in the conveyance.

(2)   *Conventional Life Estates*   A life estate, or a tenancy for life, is an interest which begins with its creation and, unless it is terminated sooner, continues for the duration of the life by which it is measured. It is commonly measured by the life of the tenant, but it may be measured by the life of some other person. A life estate is not an estate of inheritance. Upon the death of the life tenant, therefore, no interest remains to pass to his heirs. The life estate may be sold, but the purchaser must realize that the estate may be terminated at any time by the death of the person by whose life the estate is measured. The problems which arise most frequently pertain to the rights and duties of the life tenant. The general rule gives the life tenant the right to receive the rents and profits and a correlative duty to the reversioner or remainderman to expend them in payment of current charges. The holder of a life estate, therefore, is required to pay the taxes, the interest on any outstanding mortgage, the interest on any tax assessments for permanent improvements, and other current charges. He is not under a duty to pay special improvement taxes and the principal on any mortgage indebtedness which may have been outstanding at the time the life estate was created. Nor is he under a duty to make permanent improvements. He is required, however, to use reasonable care to maintain the property in the condition in which it was received. He is not permitted to commit acts which constitute waste. The meaning of the word "waste" will vary with the purpose for which the land is

used. It is generally recognized that the life tenant may work opened mines and cut a moderate amount of timber but that to strip the land of timber or open new mines would constitute waste. [*Beliveau v. Beliveau,* p. 699.]

Future Interests A future interest is, broadly stated, an estate which is to commence in possession at some future time. The possibility of reverter which a grantor has in a fee-simple-determinable estate and the right of entry for condition broken which the grantor has in a fee-simple estate subject to a condition subsequent are both classed as future interests. Executory limitations, remainders, and reversions are the three other types of future interests.

(1) *Executory Limitation* This type of estate passes the title to the fee to some third person upon the happening of some event. The executory interest is subject to a condition precedent and does not vest until the condition is performed. Take the example of a conveyance to Brown, which is subject to the condition that if Smith pays Brown $500 within two months, it shall then go to Jones. This is an illustration of a fee-simple estate subject to an executory limitation in Brown and to an executory future interest in Jones.

(2) *Remainder* A remainder differs from an executory interest in that the estate preceding the remainder—frequently called the "particular estate"—may not be a fee simple. The particular estate, however, may be a life estate or a term of years. A good illustration of a remainder is a conveyance to Brown for life, remainder to Smith.

(3) *Reversion* A reversion may be distinguished from a remainder in that a remainder is always in some person other than the conveyor. A reversion is a future estate left in the conveyor. If Brown conveys to Smith for life, there is a reversion in Brown.

ACQUISITION OF TITLE

Private ownership of land in the United States had its beginning by means of the early land grants. Some of the land within the original thirteen states was granted by the King of England to certain individuals. The Spanish grant is the source of title of much of the land in the Southwest. Except for those portions of land which were derived from other sovereigns, however, private ownership of land in the United States was originally acquired by patent from the federal government. Private individuals who fulfilled certain requisites as to settlement, improvement, residence, and cultivation were thus enabled to acquire title to land by original entry. This method of acquiring ownership is quite commonly referred to as "title by occupancy." The common methods by which title to real property may be acquired today—leaving for later chapters the transfer of title by will and intestate succession—are by deed of conveyance, adverse possession, sale by public officer, and accretion.

Deed of Conveyance The most common of all methods by which the title to real property may be acquired is by deed of conveyance by the terms of which the owner of real property, known as the "grantor," conveys the title thereto to another person known as the "grantee." The deed is used whether the title is acquired by purchase or by gift, and, in either event, it must be in the form prescribed by the law of the particular state in which the property is located. The two types of deeds which are in use generally throughout the United States are the warranty deed and the quitclaim deed.

(1) ***The Warranty Deed*** Many of the states have statutes which set out the form of deed that may be used in those states. The courts have said, however, that a deed which does not follow the statutory form is not void provided it satisfies the essential requirements of a deed. The requirements of a warranty deed ordinarily embrace the names and descriptions of the parties, the consideration expressed for the deed, words of conveyance, a description of the property sought to be conveyed, the covenant of warranty and other covenants, the date, and the signature of the grantor. Most state statutes require that the deed be acknowledged before a notary public. Some go a step futher and require that the deed be executed in the presence of two or more witnesses. Delivery is essential to the validity of every deed. Delivery is most frequently accomplished by a manual transfer of possession of the deed from the grantor to the grantee. The question of delivery, in cases of dispute, is a question of fact to be decided by the jury. The fact that a deed is recorded is prima-facie evidence of delivery. But delivery is not presumed from the mere fact that the grantor has signed the instrument. It takes some further circumstances which indicate an intent to pass title by delivery.

No particular words of conveyance are required, but the phrase "give, grant, bargain, sell, and convey unto the grantee, his heirs and assigns, in fee simple forever" is quite commonly used. The warranty and other covenants commonly made by the grantor are to the effect that he covenants and warrants that he has good right and lawful authority to sell the premises, that they are free of encumbrances, and that he will defend the same against the lawful claims of all persons whomsoever. Restrictive covenants as to the use of the land or the location or character of buildings or other structures thereon are likewise frequently incorporated in deeds. These restrictions are known as "equitable servitudes" and are mutually enforceable as between all the owners within the area. [*Arlt v. King,* p. 701.]

(2) ***The Quitclaim Deed*** This type of deed is commonly used to clear the title to real property. In a quitclaim deed, therefore, the grantor conveys whatever title he has to the grantee. He does not claim to have a good title or, in fact, any title at all. Suppose the abstract of title reveals that the title to a particular parcel of land is in Brown but that somewhere in the chain of title it appears that Smith may possibly have an interest in the land. Smith, by executing a quitclaim deed, parts with whatever title he had, thereby clearing the title for Brown.

Adverse Possession A person, under the doctrine of adverse possession, may take possession of land which, with the aid of statutory law, will ripen into a legal title. The possession must be (1) actual and exclusive, (2) open and notorious, (3) hostile to the superior title of another, and (4) continuously for the statutory period. In some states, the claimant is required to pay the taxes as they accrue.

(1) *Actual and Exclusive Possession* The claimant, to satisfy the requirement of actual and exclusive possession, must actually occupy the land. This he may do by exercising that degree of control over the land which is commensurate with the character of the land and the ordinary use to which it is adapted. Pasturing cattle on land which is ordinarily used for grazing purposes generally satisfies the requirement of actual possession. But a word of warning: Most state statutes—where actual occupancy is attempted in this manner—require that the land must be fenced by the claimant in order to give the owner notice that the possessor is asserting an adverse claim. One further word of warning: The rule does not mean that a person may claim actual occupancy by cutting timber on land which is ordinarily used for growing timber. This would be a trespass.

A claimant may, under the doctrine of constructive possession, acquire title without taking actual possession of all the land involved. This is accomplished when a claimant takes actual possession of a part of the land under a color of title to the entire area and in good faith asserts a claim to the entire area which bears a reasonable relationship in its size and use to that occupied. Color of title is essential to constructive possession. An occupant who asserts as evidence of his title some writing describing the total area claimed, which is believed by the occupant to constitute a valid conveyance, is in possession under a color of title.

(2) *Open and Notorious Possession* The requirement that possession must be open and notorious is founded upon the theory that no owner of land should be deprived of his title unless he knows, or has the means of knowing, that another is asserting an adverse claim to his land. The general rule requires that the acts of the possession be sufficiently open and notorious to be known by members of the community.

(3) *Hostile Possession* Possession is said to be hostile when it is not in subordination to the rights of the true owner. This means that possession must not be that of a tenant or by any other means that has the permission of the owner. A person who claims to be in possession as a tenant, or by any means that has the owner's permission, cannot be said to be in hostile possession.

(4) *Continuous Possession* The possession must be continuous for the statutory period which varies in the several states from five to twenty years. Two or more unconnected possessions by the claimant, therefore, cannot be tacked to one another for the purpose of computing the statutory period. But the possession of one occupant may be tacked to the possession of another if a privity of estate, such as grantor and grantee or devisor and devisee, exists between the adverse claimants. Suppose Brown is in possession as the adverse claimant for two years, at which time he sells his interest to Smith. If Smith takes possession immediately and remains in possession for the remainder of the statutory period, the period of time during which Brown was in possession may be tacked to the period of time during which Smith was in possession for the purpose of computing the statutory period.

Sale by Public Officer   Title to real property may be transferred by a judicial sale. This occurs when it is necessary to obtain money to satisfy a judgment of a successful plaintiff or to obtain money to satisfy the obligation of an unpaid mortgage. The sale is commonly made by a sheriff or other public officer who is directed by the court to sell the property at public sale. The proceeds are then paid into court to be applied toward the debt. Land is sometimes sold as a means of collecting unpaid taxes. The purchaser at such a sale ordinarily acquires a tax title, but the procedure is by no means uniform throughout the several states.

Accretion   It is a general rule that a riparian owner—one whose land is bounded or traversed by a natural stream—acquires title to the addition to his land caused by accretion. A distinction, however, must be made between accretion and avulsion. Accretion means an increase by the gradual deposit by water of solid material so as to cause land which was covered by water to become dry land. A sudden addition to land by the action of water, such as a flood, is known as avulsion. A riparian owner does not acquire title where the increase is caused by avulsion. Nor does a riparian owner acquire title where he himself creates an artificial condition for the purpose of effecting such an increase.

RIGHTS IN THE LAND OF ANOTHER

The rights which one landowner may have in the land of another that merit mention pertain to water, light, air, and, view, lateral support, easements, party walls, profits, and licenses.

Water Rights   Many of the common-law water rights have been superseded by statute. The power of the United States to regulate commerce, for instance, includes the power to control the use of bodies of water that are capable of use as interstate highways. Rights in running waters, for another instance, have largely been superseded by local usages and by statute in some of the semiarid sections of the United States where agriculture is so dependent upon irrigation. The various states have enacted statutes for the control and regulation of bodies of water. The law is by no means uniform. A few rules are, nevertheless, mentioned even though they may amount to nothing more than a brief introduction to the subject.

(1)   *Riparian Rights*   The rights of a riparian owner, as a general rule, are such as are necessary for the use and enjoyment of his property, qualified by the correlative rights of other riparian owners. Each riparian owner may take from the stream whatever water he needs for the natural domestic uses of riparian land. He may, in some jurisdictions, take sufficient water for reasonably necessary domestic uses and for watering livestock, even though it may exhaust the supply. Ordinarily, however, he may not take water for secondary uses, such as mining and manufacturing, if it would unreasonably diminish the flow of the stream to the prejudice of the lower riparian owner.

(2)   *Surface Water*   Surface water is that which is diffused over the surface of the ground. It is generally derived from falling rain and melted snow. A

person may use all the surface water which gathers upon his land. Under the common-law rule followed in some states, a person may erect barriers to prevent surface water from flowing upon his land. Under the civil-law rule which has been adopted in some states, all land is subject to a servitude to receive the natural flow of surface water. In other states, liability for obstruction of surface water depends upon reasonableness of conduct.

(3) **Percolating Water** Percolating water is water beneath the surface of the earth not following a well-defined or known channel. If it is in a well-defined or known channel, it is an underground stream or lake, Percolating water, under the common-law rule, is at the absolute disposal of the owner of the land. But many states today apply the reasonable-use rule. This rule suggests that a landowner may use percolating water if such use is reasonably necessary for the beneficial enjoyment of his land. The reasonable-use rule will also allow an owner to divert or obstruct the flow of percolating water if such obstruction is necessary to the reasonable enjoyment of the land.

Light, Air, View The doctrine of ancient lights gave the owner of land, by an uninterrupted enjoyment for twenty years, a cause of action against an adjoining landowner who erected any structure on his land which interfered with his light and air. This doctrine has been almost unanimously repudiated in the United States. As a general rule, therefore, the owner of land has no legal right to the light, air, and view from the adjoining land. It can only be acquired by an express grant. A few states have enacted statutes to the effect that a landowner shall not erect any structure on his land, although otherwise lawful, if he does it maliciously and with the intent to injure his neighbor. In the absence of statute or an express grant, however, a landowner is not liable to his adjoining landowner for the maintenance or erection of structures on his own land even though they result in cutting off the light and air coming laterally from the land on which they are erected.

Lateral Support Lateral support is the support which land receives from the adjoining land, including artificial supports which have been substituted for the supporting soil which has been removed. The right of lateral support entitles the owner of land to have it supported and protected in its natural condition by the land of his adjoining proprietor. This right applies only to land in its natural condition; it does not extend to land on which have been erected the added burdens of buildings. Excavations have been the chief source of the litigation pertaining to lateral support. An owner of land, it is said, must exercise due care in excavating near buildings on adjoining land. It is impossible to state what constitutes due care in terms of a general rule. The excavator, to be sure, is not a guarantor of the safety of the adjoining property. The owner of land, however, is under a duty to notify the adjoining landowner of his intention to make excavations. The excavator is also under a duty to perform the work in a workmanlike manner. Recovery may be allowed if the work is done in a careless and reckless manner. Recovery is not allowed, however, unless it can be shown that the subsidence was due to some act of the excavator. [*Carrig v. Andrews,* p. 701.]

Easement   An easement is a right to use in some way the land of another. It may be acquired by a conveyance, or it may be acquired by prescription. Acquisition by prescription is similar to acquiring title to real property by adverse possession. Easements may be for the benefit of the possessor of the land, or they may be for the benefit of someone other than the possessor of the land.

(1) *Appurtenant Easement*   An easement is appurtenant when it is created to benefit the possessor of adjoining land. The land benefited is known as the "dominant tenement"; the land subject to the burden is known as the "servient tenement." An easement may be affirmative or negative. An easement which gives the dominant tenement a right of way across the land of the servient tenement is a good illustration of an affirmative easement. An easement which gives the dominant tenement the right to prevent the servient tenement from erecting a structure which would cut off light, air, or view of the dominant tenement is a good illustration of a negative easement.

(2) *Easement in Gross*   An easement in gross is one which is not created to benefit the possessor of adjoining land. It is personal to the grantee, and for this reason it is held by the majority of the cases not assignable or inheritable. An easement of a commercial character, however, such as an easement for a pipeline or one to run telephone wires across land, is frequently made assignable by the terms of the instrument creating the easement. Some courts, moreover, have held that an easement in gross is assignable unless it is expressly made personal to a particular person. It has been said that a right of way in gross is not an easement since it is not supported by a dominant estate. It is well settled today, however, that there is a class of rights which may be impressed upon the land of one person in favor of another person and not in favor of a tract of land. The existence of easements in gross, therefore, is well recognized in the law.

Party Walls   A party wall may be defined, quite generally, as a dividing wall located upon or at the division line between adjoining landowners which is used by both for their common benefit. A distinctive feature of a party wall is that it is located so as to support structures that may be erected upon the respective adjoining parcels of land. Each part owner ordinarily has the right to the full use of the wall for whatever purposes he chooses so long as such use does not impair the value of the wall or infringe upon the right of the adjoining owner in the enjoyment of the wall. The view has been taken that where the wall is acquired by long use and where the actual division line of the adjoining land is not known, such long use will make the adjoining tenants tenants in common of the wall. The weight of authority, however, is to the effect that each landowner owns in severalty the part of the wall which rests upon his side of the land, with an easement of support from the other side of the land.

Profit a Prendre   A profit a prendre is a nonpossessory interest in land. It consists of a right to take soil or the substance of the soil, such as coal or minerals, from the land of another. This clearly distinguishes a profit a prendre from an easement.

License   A license in real property, as a broad general rule, is a privilege to go upon or temporarily use the land of another in a limited manner. A license in fact merely gives one the privilege to enter the land of another without committing a trespass. A landowner may give his neighbor permission to cut across his land for the purpose of going back and forth to work. The neighbor has nothing but a license, revocable at any time. It is in some respects similar to an easement. A license, however, is not an interest in land, and it is not assignable. A license is frequently distinguished from an easement in that a license is revocable. In some situations, however, a license is not revocable. Suppose upon the basis of a license the licensee has expended money to exercise the right. The courts may hold the license irrevocable on the theory that not to do so would result in undue hardship upon the licensee. In such cases, however, the license is practically indistinguishable from an easement.

FIXTURES

The provisions of the Code giving a secured party the right to remove fixtures were discussed in Chapter 32, "Priorities and Remedies," and the right given a tenant to remove trade fixtures has been reserved for Chapter 54, "Landlord and Tenant." This leaves, for present discussion, the rules pertaining to chattels which have been annexed by the owner of the real property.

The word "fixture" is generally used in reference to some originally personal chattel which has become a part of the real property by affixation to the soil itself or to some structure legally a part of the soil. It is thus seen that a fixture is a species of property which lies along the dividing line between real and personal property. The real question, therefore, in settling disputes between parties is to determine on which side of the line the particular item of property belongs. The answer to the question is not an easy one. The controlling criterion in practically all of the cases, however, is the intention of the person causing the chattel to be annexed. The test applied by the courts in determining this intention is the objective and presumed intention of that hypothetical, ordinary reasonable person. This test, though stated somewhat variously, is substantially: Would the ordinary reasonable person be justified in assuming that the person attaching the chattel intended it to become a part of the real estate? The assumption is, for the most part, reached by a consideration of the mode of annexation, the adaptation to the use or purpose of the premises, and the custom of the time and place.

Mode of Annexation   There must, of course, be annexation. But actual annexation to the soil or some appurtenant thereto is no longer—if ever it was—the determining criterion of a fixture. The tendency is to accord less and less significance to actual annexation. It is customary today to say that a chattel is "constructively annexed" when the other requirements of a fixture are present and physical annexation is lacking. Although physical attachment is entirely lacking in some instances, the intention of the landowner to make the particular chattels a part of the realty is so pronounced that they may be considered real property. Any specially designed chattel, such as a door or window, placed on the premises for the purpose of completing a partially built house may very well pass with a conveyance of the realty. It would certainly be strong evidence of an intention to make the chattel a permanent part of the realty. It is quite clear that the mode and degree of annexation may be relevant evidence in the particular case. Annexation alone, however, is not controlling. Probably the most that can be said for annexation is that a chattel is, as a general rule, regarded as a fixture when it is so affixed as to be incapable of severance without material injury to the freehold.

Adaptation to the Use or Purpose   The appropriateness to the use or purpose of that part of the realty with which the article is connected is important as evidence of an intention. The article, therefore, is usually regarded as a fixture when it is so necessary or convenient to the use of the realty that it is commonly accepted as a part of the realty. The decisions in the machinery cases, however, are rather divided. Machinery placed in a special-purpose building which has been constructed expressly to contain it—such as ice machinery erected in a building for that particular purpose—would probably be considered a fixture. Machinery which is incidental merely to the particular business—such as woodworking machinery—attached only so that it may be used advantageously, would probably be considered personal property. Machines which are attached for the sole purpose of operating them, and which are usable in any other building and can be removed without damage to them or to the building, are strong evidence of an intention not to make them a permanent annexation to the freehold.

Custom of Time and Place   Whether or not a particular article is or is not a fixture may vary according to the place, time, and custom. In the final analysis, the intention of the annexer is controlling. This intention, moreover, is gathered from the circumstances of the particular case. [*Strain v. Green,* p. 702.]

MECHANIC'S LIEN
A mechanic's lien is a lien upon real property to secure the payment of debts owing those persons who contribute labor or materials to the improvement of the property. Liens of this kind were unknown at common law. All the state legislatures, however, have enacted statutes providing for such a lien. The statutes vary in the protection accorded as well as in the procedure for perfecting and enforcing the lien. The chief differences will be indicated in the sections that follow.

Property Subject to Lien   A mechanic's lien may be enforced against any interest in real estate that is transferable, assignable, or conveyable. A fee simple, a life estate, or a lease for years are all interests which may be subject to a lien. Under modern statutes, a lien may attach to the interest of a vendee under an executory contract of sale which extends to the legal title when acquired. Such a lien terminates if the vendee loses all rights under his contract. As a general rule, therefore, a mechanic's lien may attach to any interest in real estate of the person at whose instance the improvement was made. The lien ordinarily covers both the land improved and the improvement. The lien, however, would not attach against the interest of the person who did not authorize or knowingly permit the improvement to be made. To illustrate: Brown is the lessee of certain real estate and, unknown to the owner, contracts for the construction of valuable improvements. The mechanic's lien would not attach to the interest of the owner.

Persons Entitled to Lien   The statutes of the several states specify the class or classes of persons who are entitled to protection. The word "mechanic," however, has come to have a very broad meaning when used in connection with liens upon real property. It is broad enough to include all contractors, subcontractors, mechanics, materialmen, artisans, and laborers. Those persons who contract directly with the owner are ordinarily thought of as contractors, irrespective of the nature of the improvement which may be to construct a building, attach a fixture, or landscape a garden. Those persons who contract not with the owner but with the contractor are thought of as "subcontractors." Contractors and subcontractors are both entitled to a lien.

Materialmen—those persons who merely furnish materials to be used in making the improvement—merit special mention. Their right to assert a lien for materials, whether furnished to the owner, contractor, or subcontractor, will be denied if it is found that the materials were furnished upon the general credit of the purchaser. To illustrate: Jones, who has entered into a contract to make certain improvements on the property of Smith, purchases a large quantity of bricks from Brown. Jones thereafter stores the bricks in his own warehouse and subsequently uses some of the bricks in making the improvement. Jones, in these circumstances, is his own materialman. No lien, therefore, will arise in favor of Brown. Some state statutes specifically define a materialman as a person who furnishes the materials on the site of the improvement or for direct delivery to the site of the improvement. But even in the absence of statute, the general rule requires a materialman to show that the materials were furnished for the improvement of a particular project in order to establish a lien.

Priority of Conflicting Claimants   A properly recorded lien existing on the property before the mechanic's lien attaches is quite clearly protected. The statutes quite generally provide, however, that a mechanic's lien is to be preferred to any encumbrance attaching subsequent to the time when the improvement was commenced. A mechanic's lien, therefore, attaches prior to the time it is filed for record. For this reason, a prospective purchaser or mortgagee would be well advised to inquire into the possibility that unrecorded mechanic's liens resulting from recent or present improvements may encumber the property.

Perfecting the Lien All of the statutes require filing or recording a claim of lien within a stated period in order to preserve the lien. A typical statute requires every original contractor to file his claim within a stated period of time—usually three months—after the completion of the improvement. Other common provisions for computing the time within which the claim must be filed are from the time the materials or the last items thereof are furnished, or the last labor performed, or after the debt becomes due. The claim must be filed in some public office in the county in which the property is situated and must ordinarily contain a description of the property to be charged with the lien, the name of the owner, a statement of the terms of the contract, and a statement of the lienor's demand.

The statutes giving a lien to subcontractors, materialmen, and laborers are not uniform. However, most of the statutes are of two general types. Some give a derivative lien and others give a direct lien to subcontractors, materialmen, and laborers. The lien is limited to the amount fixed in the contract between the owner and the contractor when a derivative lien is given. The property is subject to the full extent of the lien claims, however, when a direct lien is given.

Protection of Owner The owner should proceed cautiously in making payment to the contractor. Instances are common in which the owner paid the contractor, who did not pay subcontractors, laborers, and materialmen, which persons, generally speaking, are entitled to a lien against the premises. To avoid the possibility of having to pay twice, the owner is usually required to obtain a sworn statement from the contractor which sets out in detail the claims of subcontractors and materialmen with respect to the particular job. The owner should ascertain the amount of claims that are due or to become due, including any liens already filed or recorded in the county records, and deduct such claims from the sum of money to be paid to the contractor. Any excess may then be paid to the contractor. The owner will be protected, although the sworn statement may not be complete or accurate. The subcontractors and materialmen, whose claims are not listed, would have a right to proceed against the contractor. An owner who pays the contractor without the sworn statement is making payment at his own risk.

It is well to mention that an owner could require the contractor to provide a bond to indemnify the owner against claims that should have been paid by the contractor. It is likewise possible for the owner and the lien claimants to enter into an agreement that all liens will be waived. Such an agreement with the contractor alone, however, would not preclude subcontractors, laborers, and materialmen from claiming liens that had already attached. The waiver would not preclude the liens if the claimants had no knowledge of the waiver at the time the labor and materials were furnished. Their rights would likewise not be prejudiced if the state statute provides for each claimant a lien separately and independently.

CASES

Beliveau v. Beliveau, 14 N.W.2d 360 (Minn. 1914). Action by Extras Raymond Beliveau and others, plaintiffs, against Josephine Beliveau, defendant. The defendant was given, under the will of her husband, a life estate in all of his property, coupled with a power to sell and the right to use the proceeds of any sale for her comfort and support, with remainder to his brothers and sister. The property consisted of about 320 acres of farm land in Sibley County on which there were farm buildings and a dwelling house, some personal property consisting of household goods and furnishings, some tools, chickens, a cow, and other items. Defendant remained in possession of the property for about eight years, at which time plaintiffs, the remaindermen named in the will, brought this suit. The evidence showed that the defendant at the time of trial was sixty-six years old and was unable and unwilling to care for and successfully operate the property; that the buildings and fences were in a condition of serious disrepair; that quack grass, thistle, and other foul weeds were permitted to infest, and depreciate the value of, the farm; and that the defendant became involved in serious and expensive lawsuits over rental contracts and other matters pertaining to the management and operation of the property. The plaintiffs asked the court to appoint a receiver to manage the estate.

Peterson, Justice: The life tenant's rights included those of possessing, using, managing, and selling the land and using the proceeds thereof. But these rights were qualified and were limited to her necessary comfort and support. Where the life tenant acts in good faith and not for the purpose of defrauding the remaindermen, he may in such cases encroach on and use the entire estate. He cannot, however, in the exercise of his powers of sale and encroachment use the corpus for other purposes such as giving it away, granting, or devising it; nor waste or squander it in profligate living. Under a general power to sell and encroach, as here, the determination of the necessity for a sale and the amount to be used for the life tenant for his comfort and needs rests entirely in his honest judgment and discretion, uncontrolled and unlimited by the courts, in the absence of bad faith or fraud. The life tenant's discretion is not, however, without limits. . . .

There is a community of interest between a life tenant and a remainderman which gives rise to obligations and duties as between them. By implication, a life tenant is a quasi trustee of the property in the sense that he cannot injure or dispose of it to the injury of the remainderman, even though a power of disposition and encroachment is annexed to the life estate.

It was the duty of appellant as a life tenant not to permit waste, to make necessary and reasonable repairs, to pay current taxes, to pay the interest on the mortgage, and not to permit noxious weeds to infest the lands to the injury of the freehold. . . . Her failure to pay the taxes and make necessary and reasonable repairs of the building and fences constituted waste. While there is some conflict among the authorities, we think the better rule is that a life tenant commits waste by permitting farm lands to become infested with noxious weeds which do injury to the freehold. Such acts not only constitute ill husbandry but also injury to the land itself. . . .

The exigencies brought to pass by appellant's conduct with respect to the property justified the intervention of equity to preserve the property not only for the remaindermen but also for the appellant as the life tenant and to protect the interest of all. [DECISION FOR PLAINTIFFS]

Arlt v. King,   44 N.W.2d 195 (Mich. 1950). Suit by Erwin A. Arlt and others, plaintiffs, against James Pearl King and Nina King, defendants. The parties in this case are owners of lots in Huron Pine Beach, resort property on Lake Huron. The lots involved are in Block A. Defendants are owners of Lots 15, 16, 17, and 18. The plaintiffs are several of the owners of the other lots in the block. In each conveyance to the plaintiffs and to the defendants a restriction was included, among other things, to the effect that the property was restricted to residence purposes only. Most of the conveyances contained, as apparently did the conveyance to the defendants, a provision that there should not be more than one residence on each lot. The defendants divided their lots into six smaller lots, and erected a cottage on each. These cottages were used as rental property. This suit was brought for an injunction to prevent defendants from using their lots for commercial purposes.

   Boyles, Chief Justice: The defendants used their residence on their property as an office from which to rent and operate their cabins and cottages as a tourist court business, renting them by the week, for week ends, or overnight. Defendant King admitted:

At the present time, I am renting such cottages to people who come to me. I have a sign at the road, "Cottages for rent. . . ." I rent the cottages near the road for $45 a week. I get $55 a week for the cottages nearer the lake. The longest period of time I have had any of these cottages rented to one person was 2 weeks. . . .

The decree as entered enjoins the defendants from using their lots for business or commercial purposes or renting the same. . . . The provision against having more than one cottage upon any one lot is proper. [DECISION FOR PLAINTIFFS]

Carrig v. Andrews,   17 A.2d 520 (Conn. 1941). Action by Nellie F. Carrig, plaintiff, against Alfred A. Andrews, defendant, to require defendant to fill a depression in his land to afford lateral support for the adjacent land of the plaintiff.

   Ells, Judge: This appeal presents a new question in the law of lateral support, in that the excavation on the defendant's land was made by force of wind and water generated by an unprecedented hurricane, and not by the hand of man. The parties to the action are owners of adjoining premises fronting on Long Island Sound at Shore Beach. During the unforgettable hurricane of 1938 the tidewaters washed out a sizable portion of the defendant's seawall and the land back of it, close to but not immediately at the plaintiff's boundary line. There was left a 3-foot strip of wall and soil, which continued to furnish lateral support to plaintiff's land in its natural condition. The plaintiff promptly notified the defendant that the supporting wall and soil would subside and deprive her land of support and demanded that he take preventative measures. The supporting land subsided, erosion caused a small portion of plaintiff's land to crumble away, and she brought this action based on deprivation of lateral support.

. . . We have said of the nature of the so-called right of lateral support that it is regarded as an incident to the ownership of land. It is a right of property necessarily and naturally attached to the soil, and passes with it. 1 Am. Jur., sec. 21, p. 519. There is no right of ownership in a neighbor's soil, for the latter may excavate his land up to the very boundary line, and use the soil as he chooses, provided he refurnishes by artificial means the support thus removed. It is not a property right in the use of the adjoining proprietor's land. That right is in the latter, but is limited by an obligation of lateral support. He must not excavate so near the line that his neighbor's soil, by reason of its own weight or the action of the elements, is liable to give away. . . .

These considerations and citations are sufficient to enable us to say that, as applied to the facts of this case, the so-called right of lateral support is in essence not an insurance that nothing will happen to adjoining land that will cause an interference with the owner's or possessor's right of lateral support, but rather that the adjoining owner or possessor will do no act which will cause such interference. The wrong complained of here is that the defendant, after notice, failed and refused to refurnish lateral support removed, not by his own act, but by an unprecedented act of nature. He was under no such duty. [DECISION FOR DEFENDANT]

Strain v. Green, 172 P.2d 216 (Wash. 1946). Action by William Strain and his wife, plaintiffs, against Jacob Green and his wife, defendants. The defendants sold their home to the plaintiffs. It appeared from the evidence that the following articles were in the house at the time of the agreement to purchase but had been removed by the defendants when they vacated the premises: (1) a large and beautiful crystal chandelier in the center of the dining room ceiling and five other matching fixtures in that room and adjoining rooms; the distinctive feature of these articles was their ornamentation by a great number of pendants of imported crystal. The defendants installed in place of these fixtures some inferior plastic imitations; (2) a large plate-glass mirror on one of the dining room walls which had been installed in the following manner: A large piece of three-eighths-inch plywood was firmly nailed to the plastered wall, and the mirror was attached to this backing by screws. The mirror itself was readily removed. When it was removed a large square of plywood was left in the middle of the plastered wall. The plaintiffs removed the plywood, and when it was pried from the wall, each nail brought some of the plaster with it. It was introduced in evidence and had twenty-six nails in it; (3) a mirror in the powder room which also had a plywood backing but which did not appear to be nailed or attached to the wall; it apparently rested upon a table and was held in place by a wire which ran to a hook above it in the way pictures are hung; (4) the Venetian blinds from the windows, of odd sizes cut and built especially for the windows in the house; (5) a hotwater heater and enclosed electric heater from the basement. It appeared that when defendants purchased the home, they found the hot-water system inadequate. They therefore put in a large, modern insulated tank with an automatic electric control. When they removed this, they reconnected the much smaller tank which was serving the house when they bought it.

This action was brought to compel defendants to return or pay the value of these articles. The trial court held the automatic hot-water tank and the Venetian blinds to be fixtures. No appeal was taken from this holding. The court, however, held that the light fixtures and mirrors were personal property which the defendants had a right to remove. The plaintiffs have appealed from this judgment.

Robinson, Justice: Both Mr. and Mrs. Green categorically testified that they never had any intention that the chandelier, sidelights, and mirrors should ever become fixtures, and that they had removed them, as personal property, from the former houses in which they had lived. Furthermore, their testimony was in no way rebutted. . . .

It has never been the law in this jurisdiction, nor, we think, of any other, that the secret intention of the owner who affixed the disputed article, of itself, determines whether or not it was a fixture or a mere personal chattel. . . .

The chandelier and sidelights were actually annexed to the realty, and, clearly, for the use or purpose of that part of the realty (the house) with which they were connected. Their purpose, of course, was to make it livable. The fact that such articles are universally called "light fixtures" is, though not determinative, some evidence that they are fixtures. The fact that, after removing the chandelier and sidelights, the respondents replaced them with others, amounts to an implied admission on their part that a house without light fixtures would not be a complete house. In our opinion, the chandelier and sidelights were fixtures in the law and in fact.

The mirrors—at least two of them—present a much closer question. We are satisfied that there is no adequate proof that the powder room mirror was physically annexed to the realty, and as to that mirror, which seems to have been the most valuable of the three, we need not inquire further. It was not a fixture. The others present a unique situation. Each of them could be taken down from the respective walls by removing a few screws, but in each case that would leave on the wall a large square of plywood which could not be removed, in the one case without damaging the plaster, and, in the other, without leaving some damage by nail holes, and a portion of the wall of a different shade. We have arrived at the opinion that each of these mirrors and its plywood backing should be regarded as one article, and that in each case that article should be regarded as having been a portion of the house walls, and that, as such, they went with the house to the purchasers by the warranty deed which contained no reservations whatsoever. [DECISION FOR DEFENDANTS AS TO THE POWDER ROOM MIRROR; DECISION FOR PLAINTIFFS AS TO THE OTHER ARTICLES]

PROBLEMS

1 The grantor, Smith, for and in consideration of the sum of $10,000, conveyed and quitclaimed to Brown all of his interest in a house and lot situated in Suncrest Subdivision, as shown on the recorded map thereof as Lot 6, Block 10. A short time thereafter it was

learned that Jones was the true owner of the real property. Brown then sued Smith for breach of warranty of title. Decide.

2 Plaintiff and defendant were owners of adjoining land. The opening to a subterranean cavity was located on the land of plaintiff. The cave extended under the land owned by defendant. Plaintiff maintained exclusive possession of the cave for the statutory period and thus claimed that he had acquired title to defendant's part of the cave by adverse possession. Decide.

3 The state of Iowa was admitted into the Union in 1846, and its western boundary was the middle of the main channel of the Missouri River. The state of Nebraska was admitted in 1867, and its eastern boundary was likewise the middle of the channel of the Missouri River. Between the years 1851 and 1877, in the vicinity of Omaha, there were marked changes in the course of the channel so that in 1877 the channel occupied a very different bed from that through which it flowed in the former year. This change resulted when the Missouri River above Omaha, which had pursued a course in the nature of an oxbow, suddenly cut through the neck of the bow and made for itself a new channel. Does this change affect the boundary lines between the two states?

4 Plaintiff and defendant were sisters. Plaintiff owned a one-third undivided interest in certain real property, and defendant owned the other two-thirds interest in the property. They executed deeds of conveyance whereby each party conveyed to the other the real property which they respectively owned, with the purpose and intention that the deed executed by the sister who died first should be, upon such decease, then delivered to the survivor, and thereafter recorded. The deeds were then placed in a cabinet in plaintiff's home. Defendant, who caused the deed conveying to her a one-third interest to be recorded, contends she is the owner in fee simple of the entire property. Is she correct?

5 In 1908, Waller's mother took possession of certain real property and continued in adverse possession of the land until her death in 1931. Waller then inherited the property, made certain improvements, and continued in adverse possession until 1944. Parsley claims title to the property by deed dated 1944. He further contends Waller cannot be the owner of the property because he has not been in continuous possession of the property for the statutory period of twenty years. What defense, if any, has Waller?

6 Wiley, who was the owner of a large tract of farmland, conveyed the land to Linder for the remainder of the life of Linder. Linder thereafter leased the land to Cabot for a period of fifty years. Cabot took possession of the land and used it as a vegetable farm for approximately five years, at which time Linder died. Wiley, Cabot, and the heirs of Linder all contend that they are entitled to the possession and use of the land. Who is correct?

7 Andrews was the owner of two acres of land with a large building thereon. The building and the land were desirable for use as a courthouse by the City of Y. Andrews thereupon conveyed the premises to the City of Y "for so long as the City of Y used the land for a courthouse and when it is no longer used as a courthouse" it should revert to Andrews or his heirs. The City of Y accepted the deed of conveyance and commenced to use the premises as a courthouse. Andrews then conveyed by quitclaim deed "all my interest" in the premises to Cabot. The City of Y ceased to use the courthouse after ten years, and Cabot took possession of the premises. Does the City of Y have a right to eject Cabot from the premises?

8 Brown purchased a certain building lot from Jones in July and received a properly executed warranty deed therefor. Brown then executed and delivered a mortgage for the entire purchase price. The deed was recorded on October 1, and the mortgage was recorded on November 3. Brown began the construction of a house upon the lot in September, and plaintiff commenced to furnish materials for the construction at the request of Brown on September 29. Plaintiff filed a mechanic's lien, and brought an action to foreclose the lien. Jones contended that he had priority over the mechanic's lien because his mortgage was a purchase-money mortgage. Do you agree with this contention?

54
LANDLORD AND TENANT

The common law relating to landlord and tenant has been superseded by statute in many respects. But the rules which are an outgrowth of the fundamental concept of the law of landlord and tenant—the fact that one person is able to occupy the real property of another—are still generally recognized by all states. It is to these rules that this chapter is devoted. They are found in (1) the creation of the relationship, (2) the kinds of tenancies, (3) the rights and duties of the landlord and of the tenant, (4) the effect of assigning and subleasing, and (5) the termination of the relationship.

CREATION OF THE RELATION

The relation of landlord and tenant is created by an agreement whereby one person, known as the "landlord" or "lessor," gives the possession and use of real property to another person, known as the "tenant" or "lessee." The agreement is known as a "lease." The leasehold interest conveyed to the tenant is an estate less than a freehold. The estate of the landlord is called the "reversion." The landlord, therefore, is entitled to retake possession of the demised premises upon the expiration of the lease.

Form of the Lease The various state legislatures have enacted statutes which provide that leases for a stated period of time must be in writing to be enforceable.

The period of time is not uniform throughout the United States. In most of the states, however, leases for a period of more than one year—sometimes three years—must be in writing. Leases for more than a specified period are sometimes not only required to be written but also to be witnessed, acknowledged, and recorded. But assuming the lease does not fall within the period specified by statute, no particular form is required to create the tenancy. The agreement may be express; it may be implied; or it may be oral.

CLASSIFICATION OF TENANCIES

Tenancies classified as to the duration of the leasehold interest of the tenant are tenancy for years, periodic tenancy, tenancy at will, and tenancy by sufferance.

Tenancy for Years   The expression "tenancy for years" is applied to all tenancies less than a freehold for a fixed period. It must be certain as to the commencement as well as the duration of its term. But it may be—except when regulated by statute—for any specific period. It may be for 1 month, 1 year, 99 years, or even 999 years. A lease, the duration of which depends upon the happening of a contingency which is not certain to happen, is not a lease for a fixed period. A lease to continue until all the gravel on the land is removed, therefore, does not create a tenancy for years. A lease for ten years after the life of a person in being, however, would create a tenancy for years. The beginning of the tenancy could be reduced to a certain fixed term by the death of the person referred to.

Periodic Tenancy   The expression "periodic tenancy" is used to designate tenancies that will continue for another period equal to the one that has expired and which will continue for successive periods of the same length of time until terminated by notice given by the landlord to the tenant or by the tenant to the landlord. A common type of periodic tenancy is from year to year. Such tenancies, however, may be from quarter to quarter, from month to month, from week to week, or for any other period of time. Periodic tenancies may be expressly created by agreement between the landlord and the tenant. They frequently arise, however, by implication. A periodic tenancy arises where no definite time is agreed upon and the rent is fixed at so much a year or so much a month. A periodic tenancy arises where the tenant enters under a parol lease, void under the Statute of Frauds, followed by any unequivocal act on the part of the landlord by which he recognizes the tenant as holding under the void lease. The acceptance of rent by the landlord would suffice. A periodic tenancy arises where the tenant holds over after a lease for a definite duration has expired.

The question frequently arises as to the length of the recurring periods of the tenancy. The reservation of the rent is generally the controlling factor in answering this question. A lease at an annual rental payable in monthly installments for a term of one year is generally deemed to be from year to year. A lease for a term of one year at a monthly rental is generally deemed to be from month to month.

Tenancy at Will   A tenancy which is held at the will of either the landlord or the tenant is known as a tenancy at will. Such a tenancy may be expressly created. These tenancies, however, will arise by implication when a person occupies the premises by permission of the owner for an indefinite period and without any reservation of rent. A prospective tenant who moves in and occupies the premises of the landlord while the parties are negotiating to fix the terms of the lease would be a tenant at will. Tenancies at will are rather uncommon; they should not be confused with a holding over under a tenancy for years.

Tenancy at Sufferance   A tenant at sufferance is one who wrongfully continues in possession after coming into possession rightfully. A very usual instance of a tenancy at sufferance is where a tenant for a definite period holds over after the expiration of the term. This type of hold over tenancy should not be confused with a periodic tenancy which arises by holding over. The difference between the two is that a tenancy at sufferance arises where the landlord performs no act which recognizes the continued tenancy. A tenant at sufferance has no election to regard himself as a tenant; such an election is with the landlord. If the landlord elects to exercise his right to hold the tenant for another term, he cannot thereafter rescind such election.

DUTIES AND LIABILITIES OF THE PARTIES

Written leases frequently contain clauses, usually referred to as covenants, which specifically enumerate the respective obligations of the landlord and tenant. This practice is commendable. It eliminates doubt with respect to the liabilities and duties of the parties. Some liabilities and duties, in the absence of an express covenant, arise out of the nature of the relation of landlord and tenant. These are sometimes referred to as "implied covenants" or "implied warranties." In either event, they spell out the liabilities and duties of the parties. Some of the important liabilities and duties pertain to the possession of the premises, fitness of the premises for use, repair of the premises, personal injuries caused by defects, waste, the trade-fixture doctrine, and rent.

Possession of the Premises   The essence of a tenancy is that the tenant shall have the undisturbed possession of the premises during the term of the lease. Possession includes both the right to acquire possession at the beginning of the lease and the right to quiet enjoyment during the term.

   (1) *Right to Acquire Possession*   The right of the tenant to acquire possession of the premises at the beginning of the term may seem so obvious as to be unworthy of mention. Questions frequently arise, however, when the premises are occupied. The landlord quite clearly is under a duty personally to vacate the premises in favor of the tenant. If he refuses to do so, the tenant may treat the lease as at an end, or he may take possession at a later date, or he may bring an action to obtain possession. In any event, he is entitled to whatever damages may

result from such refusal. A different problem arises, however, when the landlord is not directly responsible for the tenant's deprivation.

A previous tenant may be holding over without the consent of the landlord, or a stranger may have taken possession wrongfully. The question, therefore, is whether or not the landlord is also under a duty to see that third persons do not prevent the tenant from taking possession. The law is not uniform on this question. Some states hold that the landlord is under a duty to deliver possession of the premises to the tenant. These states give the tenant the right to sue the landlord directly. Other states, and probably a majority, hold that the landlord is not obliged to oust a stranger who may be in possession wrongfully or a tenant who holds over wrongfully. These states, therefore, hold that the tenant must sue the person who is in wrongful possession. The landlord and the tenant may each protect themselves against any doubts by appropriate express covenants with respect to a tenant then in possession or with respect to any other person who wrongfully withholds possession from the tenant.

(2) *Quiet Enjoyment of the Premises* A covenant of quiet enjoyment protects the tenant against disturbances of his possession of the premises. The landlord may expressly agree that the tenant shall have "quiet enjoyment of the premises" during the term. The modern rule prevailing in nearly all of the states, however, is that the covenant will be implied from the mere relation of landlord and tenant. A landlord who wrongfully disturbs or interferes with the possession or enjoyment of the premises by the tenant may constitute a constructive eviction of the tenant. This is one method of terminating a lease. A tenant, even if he is not constructively evicted, has a right of action in tort against the landlord for wrongful disturbances or interferences with his possession and enjoyment even though he remains in possession of the premises.

Fitness for Use The law gives rise to no implied covenant that the premises are reasonably fit for the use for which they are rented. It is a familiar principle of the law of landlord and tenant that the tenant takes the premises as he finds them. The tenant, therefore, assumes all the risk with respect to the fitness of the premises for his purpose in the absence of an express warranty as to their condition. A landlord who conceals hidden defects of which he has knowledge, or ought to have knowledge, of course will be liable to the tenant in tort for fraud. The landlord, therefore, is under a duty to disclose hidden defects that are likely to endanger the life or health of the tenant and which the tenant could not discover upon a reasonable inspection. The landlord, for instance, who leases a house knowing, or under such circumstances that he should have known, that it is infected with a contagious disease is answerable to the tenant who becomes a victim of the disease.

Repair of Premises The common law has always thrown the duty upon the tenant to make repairs to the demised premises. This duty requires the tenant to make such repairs as will preserve the property substantially in the same condition it was in at the time the tenancy arose, depreciation from ordinary wear and tear during the term being excepted. The tenant, therefore, is required to repair such things as leaking roofs, broken windows, or doors. He is not required to make repairs which are permanent in nature, such as restoring the roof by a new covering of shingles, boards, or the like. Nor is he required to rebuild or restore buildings destroyed by fire or storm, or a building which has become so ruinous from ordinary wear and tear that it must be rebuilt.

The tenant may, however, covenant to keep the premises in repair, or to surrender the premises in good repair, or to return the premises in as good a condition as they were in when he received them. The precise meaning of these and similar covenants is not clear. Some states hold that the tenant, under covenants to repair, must rebuild a building on the premises which has been destroyed by fire, storm, or in any other way. Other states hold that such covenants require the tenant to rebuild only if the destruction is brought about by his fault. It is obvious, therefore, that the tenant should take care in signing a lease to make sure that his responsibility to make repairs is clearly defined.

The landlord is under no duty at common law to repair the demised premises. He may, however, covenant to keep the premises in repair in the same general manner as the tenant. The landlord's liability, in these circumstances, is subject to the condition precedent that he have knowledge of, or that the tenant give him notice of, the need of repairs. This is due to the fact that the tenant is in possession and is in a position to discover the need of repairs. Public health and safety laws, in some states, provide that the premises must be kept in good repair by the owner. These laws deal largely with tenement houses.

Public authorities in a number of states have the prerogative to order changes in the demised premises which go beyond ordinary repairs. The landlord will have the obligation to pay for them if there is no provision in the lease to the contrary. A conflict exists, however, if the repairs are ordinary. Some of the cases take the position that, in the absence of an agreement, the duty to make the repairs is on the landlord; other cases take the position that the duty is on the tenant. The significance of the duty of the landlord to repair the premises, however, is more pronounced in the personal injury cases.

Personal Injuries Caused by Defects   The logical conclusion from the rule that the landlord is under no duty to repair the premises, in the absence of statute or a covenant to do so, is: he is not responsible to the tenant, members of his family, or his invitees for injuries caused by defects in the premises. The majority of the cases, moreover, hold that the tenant cannot recover for personal injuries arising from the defective condition of the premises even though the landlord has covenanted to keep the premises in repair. These cases exempt the landlord from liability on the theory that the tenant may make the necessary repairs and recover for the expenditure if the landlord fails to do so within a reasonable time after receiving notice of the defective condition of the premises. If the landlord undertakes to repair the premises, however, he is liable for injuries caused by his negligence or unskillfulness in making them or in leaving the premises in an unsafe condition.

The landlord is under a duty without notice from the tenant to keep in repair entry ways, stairways, walks, courts, vestibules, and other parts of the premises over which he retains possession and control. A few states go a step further and hold the owner of business property under a duty to keep in repair property which is leased for a public purpose. [*Reiman v. Moore,* p. 716.]

Waste   Closely allied to the duty of the parties to keep the premises in repair is the subject of waste. Waste may be defined very generally as the destruction, misuse, alteration, or neglect of the premises by the tenant to the prejudice of the reversionary estate of the landlord. Such acts as the alteration or removal of buildings are voluntary waste. The failure of the tenant to exercise the ordinary care of a prudent man for the preservation of the estate is permissive waste. The tenant, however, may be given an estate unimpeachable for waste. The phrase "without impeachment for waste" is sometimes used in leases for such purpose. The intention of the phrase is to enable the tenant to do many things, such as cutting wood, which would otherwise constitute waste. This does not mean, however, that the tenant may commit acts which are unjust or malicious. The clause, therefore, would not operate to permit the tenant to cut down fruit-bearing trees, or trees which serve for shade or ornament. The landlord may petition a court of equity for an injunction to prevent the tenant from committing waste. If the tenant has committed waste, however, the landlord may bring an action at law to recover damages. The damages are measured by the injury actually sustained to the leased property.

Fixtures   The trade-fixture doctrine gives the tenant for years the right to remove those fixtures which he has attached for the purpose of his trade or business. The doctrine is usually justified on the ground that the tenant intended to make such additions for his own benefit. Not everything that the tenant attaches to the realty, however, may be removed by him. The dividing line between those chattels that may be removed and those that may not is determined by whether they were annexed for purposes of trade or not. The right of removal has been extended to tenants engaged in agriculture as well as to tenants engaged in trade or manufacture. The courts are liberal in permitting the tenant to remove trade fixtures. Even substantial buildings may be removed if they were constructed for the purpose of trade. The tenant, however, probably would not be permitted to damage the freehold materially. A tenant is permitted to remove domestic and ornamental fixtures which are annexed for the tenant's own convenience. The courts, however, tend to restrict the right to remove domestic fixtures to such things as may be easily severed. Shrubs planted by a nurseryman for sale could ordinarily be removed; ornamental shrubbery, however, would ordinarily become a part of the realty. It may be well to mention that the right of a tenant to remove his fixtures is forfeited if he does not remove them at the expiration of a lease for a fixed period. The right to remove fixtures is clearly forfeited when, at the expiration of a lease for a fixed period, the tenant removes from the premises, and leaves the fixtures behind. The tenant for an indeterminate period—a tenant at will—has a reasonable time in which to remove his fixtures after the expiration of the lease. [*Becwar v. Bear,* p. 717.]

Rent The word "rent" is commonly defined as the consideration agreed to be paid by the tenant for the use and enjoyment of the land. In modern leasing agreements which include both land and chattels, however, the consideration to be paid for the use of the chattels is not ordinarily segregated from that to be paid for the use of the land. The entire consideration, in these circumstances, is treated as rent. Rent is ordinarily, but not necessarily, payable in money. The landlord and the tenant, for instance, may agree that the rent is to be paid from profits to be derived from the use of the land. If no agreement has been reached with respect to rent, a promise will be implied on the part of the tenant to pay a reasonable rent for the use and enjoyment of the premises. This implied promise presupposes the existence of the relationship of landlord and tenant. A person who occupies land without the express or implied consent of the owner, therefore, may be held liable for the mesne profits. This, in effect, gives the owner the right to recover profits, as well as any loss due to waste and dilapidations, during the time the occupier was in possession of the premises. One additional thought should be mentioned: Rent does not accrue from day to day. This means that rent is not apportionable unless there is an agreement for such apportionment. A tenant who pays rent in advance, therefore, cannot recover a portion of the rent so paid if the tenancy is terminated between rent days. The tenant could recover the portion of the rent so paid, however, if he were wrongfully evicted.

(1) *Remedies of the Landlord* The device used by the landlord for the collection of rent at common law was known as "distress." This device gave the landlord the power, when the tenant was in arrears for rent, to seize chattels located on the leased land whether they belonged to the tenant or to a third person. At first, the landlord could only hold the property as security; later, he was given the power to sell it. Statutes have been enacted in some states abolishing distress for rent; in some states, the remedy has been retained, but the former harshness has been lessened; in still other states, courts have held that the creation of new remedies for the collection of rent has abolished distress for rent by implication. Many statutes today give the landlord a lien on the chattels of his tenant. These statutes are, to some extent, the outgrowth of the common-law right of distress. The law is by no means uniform throughout the United States.

(2) *Defenses of the Tenant* The tenant may be able to successfully defend an action brought by the landlord to recover rent. He is not obligated to pay rent if he has been actually evicted by the landlord or by a person having a title paramount to that of the landlord. If he is evicted by a third person claiming no paramount title, however, he is not relieved of his obligation to pay rent. The tenant may also be able to recover any damages he has suffered by a breach of covenant on the part of the landlord. If the landlord has covenanted to keep the premises in repair, for instance, the tenant may counterclaim for breach of this covenant, or the tenant may, in most states, repair the premises and set off the amount of the expenditures against the claim of the landlord for rent.

ASSIGNING AND SUBLEASING

A lessee, in the absence of a covenant or statute to the contrary, may generally assign his interest in the term or he may sublease the premises. A lessee, however, might be wise if he secured the consent of the lessor before assigning or subleasing. Leasing agreements frequently contain clauses against assigning or subleasing without the consent of the lessor. Statutes to the same effect have been enacted in some states. A few court decisions, moreover, have held leases to be nonassignable on the ground that the lessor placed personal confidence and trust in the lessee. But assuming the lease may be assigned or subleased, exceedingly complex problems arise as to the effect of such an assignment or sublease. A few of the rules are mentioned in the following two paragraphs. These will at least distinguish between an assignment and a sublease and possibly stimulate an awareness of the fact that great care should be exercised in assigning or subleasing the leasehold estate.

Sublease   A sublease consists of a transfer of a period less than the entire term; a reversionary interest remains in the sublessor. Suppose a lease of premises known as Lots 1 and 2 is to run for a term of one year. A transfer of the lease for one month would be a sublease. A sublease creates a new tenancy between the original tenant and the sublessee. The sublessee, however, can acquire no greater rights in the use and enjoyment of the premises than were held by the original lessee. As between the sublessee and the original lessor there is no privity of contract. The sublessee, therefore, incurs no liability directly to the original lessor because of the subletting. But this does not mean that the sublessee is not bound by the express restrictions contained in the original lease with regard to the use of the demised premises. The express restrictions are binding upon the sublessee, and the original lessor may maintain an action against the sublessee if they are breached.

Assignment   An assignment consists of a transfer by the lessee of his entire interest in the demised premises, or a part thereof, to a third person. In the above illustration, if the lessee had transferred his interest in the entire premises, or his interest in only one of the lots, for the entire term or the remainder thereof it would have been an assignment. The distinction between an assignment and a sublease, therefore, depends upon the quantity of interest transferred rather than upon the extent of the premises. A privity of estate is created between the assignee and the original lessor. The original lessor, therefore, has a right of action against the assignee on the covenants that run with the land. The difficulty with this rule is in determining those covenants that do and those that do not run with the land. There seems to be no one test which is accepted by all. It may be said, as a general rule, that a covenant to keep the premises in repair and similar covenants run with the land. A covenant which is personal, as a covenant to pay money to a third person, does not run with the land.

TERMINATION OF THE RELATION

A lease ordinarily terminates upon the expiration of its term. A lease may be terminated, however, before its expiration by an acceptance by the landlord of a surrender by the tenant, enforcement of a forfeiture, destruction of the building, and by eviction of the tenant.

Surrender   A surrender, as understood in the law of landlord and tenant, means the giving up of a lease before the expiration of its term. The surrender may be by mutual agreement or by operation of law. A surrender may be accomplished, therefore, by an agreement between the landlord and tenant whereby the tenant retransfers the estate to the landlord in the same manner in which it was originally created. It is said the old estate is surrendered by "operation of law" when the landlord and tenant, who have created a leasehold estate, create another estate inconsistent therewith. Suppose the landlord, with the consent of the tenant, makes a new lease of the same premises to a third person. The second leasehold is obviously inconsistent with the first. The first leasehold, therefore, is surrendered by operation of law. Much has been said with respect to whether or not the surrender must be in writing. Surrender by operation of law, generally speaking, is not affected by the Statute of Frauds. The broad rule that will serve as a guide in most of the other situations is that a surrender need not be in writing if the unexpired portion of the lease would not require a writing for its creation.

  The decisions are not completely uniform when the tenant abandons the premises. A few courts take the view that the landlord should make reasonable efforts to mitigate the damages by reletting the premises to a new tenant. However, the majority of the courts hold that the landlord is under no obligation to attempt to relet the premises but that he may let the premises lie idle when the tenant unjustifiably abandons the premises. A landlord may re-enter the premises for the purpose of protecting the premises without incurring any liability to the tenant as a trespasser, but the landlord must make it clear that he is not consenting to the abandonment by the tenant. A few cases hold that the lease is terminated when the landlord takes possession and relets the premises, but the decisions are generally governed by the facts of the particular case. [*Diatz v. Washington Technical School,* p. 718.]

Forfeiture   Leases sometimes contain stipulations which give the lessor the right to forfeit the leasehold estate upon a breach by the tenant of one or more of the covenants in the lease. It is not uncommon to find a stipulation authorizing the landlord to forfeit the lease if the lessee uses the premises for an illegal purpose, or if he fails to pay the rent after a specified number of days. Stipulations for forfeiture are not looked upon with favor by the courts, but they certainly will give effect to such provisions when they are clearly provided for in the lease. The landlord, in some states, is given the authority to forfeit the lease by virtue of a statutory provision.

Destruction   The general rule declares that destruction of the building upon the demised premises does not of itself terminate the lease where the lease includes both the buildings and the land. The tenant, therefore, remains liable for the rent notwithstanding the destruction of the building. The parties often make provision in the lease for its termination in the event the premises are destroyed. In many jurisdictions provision is made by statute for the relief of the tenant in case of destruction of the building. The lease is not terminated by destruction, however, in the absence of statutory provision or a stipulation to that effect in the lease. The rule is otherwise with respect to a lease of rooms or an apartment in the building. The destruction of the building by fire or other casualty terminates the lease.

Eviction   The word "eviction," in a popular sense, denotes turning a tenant of land out of possession by legal proceedings. The tenant may be evicted by an actual ouster as the result of an ejectment suit by the landlord or by one having a title paramount to that of the landlord. The tenant, however, may be constructively evicted. Any misconduct of the landlord, or one claiming under him, which amounts to a constructive eviction will give the tenant the right to abandon the premises and bring an action for breach of the covenant of quiet enjoyment. The tenant, however, must be substantially and materially deprived of the use and enjoyment of the premises, and possession must be given up by the tenant in consequence of such deprivation. [*Giddings v. Williams,* p. 718.]

Termination at the Expiration of the Term   The time at which a lease terminates upon the expiration of the term varies with the type of tenancy.
    (1)   *Tenancy for Years*   A lease for a fixed term and the right of possession thereunder terminate at the expiration of the term specified in the lease. No notice is required to accomplish this result. The lease does not terminate upon the death of the lessee or the lessor before the expiration of the term. The leasehold estate, being personal property, passes to the personal representative of the lessee. The reversion of the estate, being real property, passes to the heirs of the lessor subject to the terms of the lease. The lease may terminate, if the parties so stipulate, upon the happening of some contingency. It is not unusual for a lease to stipulate that it is to run for "a period of twenty years, or during the life of the lessee." Such a stipulation is interpreted to mean that the lease is to continue for twenty years if the lessee lives that long. The lease expires, however, if the death of the lessee occurs before the expiration of the twenty years. In a few instances, a lease may be terminated by death where its terms are so personal as to apply to the lessee only.
    (2)   *Periodic Tenancy*   A periodic tenancy may be terminated at the end of the period by a prior notice given by the landlord to the tenant or by the tenant to the landlord. The common-law rule required that the notice be given six months before the end of any year of a year-to-year tenancy; a month's notice for a month-to-month tenancy; and a week's notice for a week-to-week tenancy. The state statutes of the various states today specify the time when notice must be given. Some follow the common-law rule. Some require the notice to be in writing. In the absence of statute, however, oral notice is ordinarily sufficient.
    (3)   *Tenancy at Will*   These tenancies are terminated by the death of either the landlord or the tenant. No notice was required to terminate the tenancy

at common law. Some state statutes today require that notice be given. Some modern decisions, in the absence of statute, require that reasonable notice be given.

(4) *Tenancy at Sufferance* A tenancy at sufferance terminates when the landlord ejects the tenant or recognizes him as a tenant. No notice is ordinarily required to terminate this type of tenancy. In some instances of undue hardship, however, the tenant may be allowed a reasonable time to vacate the premises.

CASES

Reiman v. Moore, 108 P.2d 452 (Cal. 1940). Action by Betty Reiman (plaintiff below), appellee, against Lutie Hineline Moore and Stockton Realty Company (defendants below), appellants. The Stockton Realty Company has appealed from a judgment rendered in favor of plaintiff.

Parker, Justice, pro tem: The appellant Stockton Realty Company is the owner of a certain building in the city of Stockton, being a building three stories in height. The lower or street floor is used for business purposes. The second and third floors constitute an apartment house, having a separate street entrance and individual street number. The upper floors are leased to one Moore, codefendant, against whom no judgment was rendered and who is not before the court on this appeal. . . .

On the roof of the building was located a wash room, with an entrance out on the roof, which entrance was a doorway on which was hung a screen door opening out. On the roof immediately in front of the screen door and approximately five feet therefrom was a skylight. This skylight appears to have been the ordinary roof type, three feet wide and four feet long. There was a twelve-inch baseboard and above this were four panes of glass, each placed on a slope. The area on the roof immediately adjacent to the wash house was used by all occupants of apartments on the floors below as a place of hanging out laundry, and the clothes lines were maintained thereon for that purpose.

One of the tenants or occupants of a rented apartment was a Mrs. Green. This lady had become ill and had been confined to a hospital. As she was planning to return to her apartment she had requested certain members of her family to clean up her apartment and have it in readiness for her. Incident to this was the cleaning of the linen and other effects of Mrs. Green. The minor plaintiff herein was a relative of Mrs. Green and she was of the age of fourteen years. Accompanied by her cousin she took part in the preparations attending the homecoming of Mrs. Green. The clothes had been washed and hung out on the line and the plaintiff and her cousin, Leah Wyatt, a girl of sixteen years, went on to the roof to take the wash from the line. The Wyatt girl took the clothes off the line, placing them in plaintiff's arms as they stripped the line. When the clothes were thus gathered the plan was to take them downstairs. Accordingly, Miss Wyatt went ahead to open the doors and the plaintiff followed with the clothes. As the door of the wash room opened out it was necessary for plaintiff to step back to permit the door to swing and in so doing her heel struck against some object which tripped her and she fell backward against the skylight. The skylight glass was not strong enough to sustain or break the weight and plaintiff fell through to the floor below, sustaining the injuries complained of.

The first point under this statement of fact is whether or not, under the lease, or otherwise, the landlord had control over the premises whereon the accident occurred, and if so, what were his duties to the plaintiff, an invitee.

There can be no question but that the roof of a building is common to the entire building and where that building is leased to various tenants between whom there is no privity of contract or interest the control of the roof must remain with the landlord. [DECISION FOR APPELLEE]

Becwar v. Bear,   246 P.2d 1110 (Wash. 1952). Action by L. M. Becwar, plaintiff, against C. E. Bear, defendant, to recover the value of certain fixtures which plaintiff alleged the defendant converted to his own use. Judgment was entered in favor of plaintiff in the sum of $974, the market value of the fixtures. The defendant appealed.

Olson, Justice: The material facts established by the findings are: That plaintiff was a tenant of a building under a lease from defendant's grantor; that there was no heating equipment in the building; that the lease provided that the lessee would furnish his own heat; that it was necessary for plaintiff, in the conduct of his business, to heat a portion of the building, and that, with the consent of his lessor, he installed a boiler, an oil burner, and other equipment, in the basement beneath the leased premises; that, when defendant purchased the premises, he assumed the lease and knew that those installations had been made by the plaintiff to carry on his trade and business; that prior to the expiration of the lease, when plaintiff was about to vacate the premises, defendant notified him not to remove the equipment; that none of the heating equipment was attached to the building except by ordinary bolts and couplings, and it could have been removed without any damage whatsoever to the building; that plaintiff did not intend to make this equipment a part of the building, and placed it on the premises for the sole purpose of carrying on his trade.

. . . The fact is that plaintiff did not intend that the heating installations made while he was a tenant were to enrich the freehold by becoming a part of the building, but placed them there solely for the purpose of his trade. The intent of the party making the annexation is the cardinal inquiry in determining whether a chattel annexed to the freehold is a trade fixture or part of the realty. Being trade fixtures, it follows that defendant should have permitted plaintiff to remove them when his lease expired. . . .

Defendant contends that the court erred in "failing to hold" that it was the duty of plaintiff, as tenant, to disclose his claims to defendant, an innocent purchaser for value, before his purchase. This conclusion would not have been justified in view of the fact that, when defendant purchased the premises, he knew that plaintiff had made the heating installations to carry on his business. The facts known to defendant were naturally and reasonably connected with, and furnished a clue to, plaintiff's intention to remove this equipment. With such knowledge, defendant is deemed to have had notice of all facts which reasonable inquiry would disclose. [DECISION FOR PLAINTIFF]

Diatz v. Washington Technical School,   73 A.2d 718 (D.C. 1950). Action by Philip and Sonia Diatz (plaintiffs below), appellants, against Washington Technical School, Inc., and Eugene Sobel (defendants below). Eugene Sobel is the appellee.

Appellants leased the premises involved to J. A. Junsch and Washington Technical School for a term of two years beginning on November 1, 1946. J. A. Junsch thereafter sold and assigned his interest in the school to Eugene Sobel, who assumed the lease. Appellants consented to the assignment. The premises were abandoned on March 1, 1947, and no further rent was paid. The evidence revealed that appellants asked appellee for the keys to the premises; that appellee said he would turn over the keys provided appellants would give him a release from any obligation on the assignment of the lease; that appellants refused to give the release; and that appellee refused to surrender the keys. Appellants thereafter relet the premises, and brought this action to recover rent due on the unexpired term of the lease. The jury returned a verdict for appellants, against Eugene Sobel only.

Hood, Judge: Appellee has moved for a rehearing. His principal point is based on the contention that when he abandoned the premises and appellants took possession and relet, the privity of estate existing between them and him was terminated, and that without privity of estate there was no obligation on his part to pay rent. For this contention he relies on *Lincoln Fireproof Warehouse Co. v. Greusel,* 199 Wis. 428, 224 N.W. 6. That authority lends support to appellee's contention, but in our opinion it is contrary to the law of this jurisdiction.

It is well settled here that an entry and reletting by a landlord does not in and of itself amount to a surrender by operation of law. Whether it does or does not depends upon whether resumption of possession by the landlord is to the exclusion of the tenant with intent to release him from liability. In the present case, after appellee had abandoned possession he refused to deliver the key to appellants unless they would give him a release from liability. He was told he would be released only to the extent of the rent that would be obtained from a future tenant. He was given no release and he did not surrender the key. When a lessor refuses to release a tenant and notifies him that he looks to him for payment of rent the tenant remains liable. This principle does not change and the result is not different because the relationship is that of lessor and assignee. The abandonment or surrender by the assignee without consent of the lessor does not relieve the assignee of liability for rent due for the remainder of the term. The entry of the landlord and the reletting are regarded as done on account of the former tenant. [DECISION FOR APPELLANTS]

Giddings v. Williams,   168 N.E. 514 (Ill. 1929). Action by Charles C. and Mary E. Giddings (plaintiffs below), defendants in error, against Donald S. Williams and wife (defendants below), plaintiffs in error, to recover for rent claimed to be due and unpaid. On October 13, 1925, plaintiffs in error, as lessees, entered into a written lease with the defendants in error, as lessors, for a front and rear room in a building at 669 North Michigan Avenue, in Chicago, to be used as a salesroom and workroom for the sale of linen merchandise. The lease was to expire on April 30, 1930, but on March 6, 1927, plaintiffs in error vacated the premises claiming that they had been constructively evicted due, among other things, to a failure of the lessor to furnish heat in accordance with the terms of the lease.

Partlow, Commissioner: The question for determination is whether the alleged failure to furnish heat, together with the alleged acts of misconduct of defendants in error, constitute such a constructive eviction of plaintiffs in error as justified them in moving from the premises, canceling the lease, and refusing to pay further rent. . . .

The uncontradicted evidence shows that from November 6 defendants in error failed to furnish a reasonable amount of heat; that they were out of coal a part of the time; that during February very little heat was furnished; that the employees of plaintiffs in error had to fire the furnace, and had to work with their coats on; that the thermometer was as low as 55 and 60 degrees; that complaints were made to the landlord, and he promised to furnish heat, but did not do so.

. . . The written lease is not before this court, and we are unable to determine from it whether it did or did not provide that heat should be furnished by defendants in error. But regardless of the provisions of the written lease, the uncontradicted evidence shows that heat was to be furnished; that this duty was recognized by defendants in error; that heat was not furnished in sufficient quantity; and that defendants in error repeatedly promised to furnish it, but did not keep their promise. [DECISION FOR PLAINTIFF IN ERROR]

PROBLEMS

1 Plaintiff rented an apartment from defendant who bought and carried to the apartment in his car a wooden cabinet weighing about fifteen pounds. Defendant left the cabinet there and told the plumber he would get somebody to put it up. The plumber, however, on his own initiative attached the cabinet to the wall above the sink. When defendant came back and found the cabinet installed, he took hold of it, shook it and, as it seemed to be all right, thanked the plumber for his good work. About a year after the cabinet had been installed, the cabinet full of dishes fell and struck plaintiff. Is the defendant liable for the injuries sustained as a result of the accident?

2 The plaintiff and the defendant entered into an agreement by the terms of which the plaintiff rented to the defendant a house, with the furniture therein, for a term of five months, beginning June 1, for the rent of $325. The defendant took possession and after ten days abandoned the premises. He justified his abandonment by stating that the cellar was in a damp and unhealthful condition by reason of water which was admitted into the cellar through a hole in the cement on the cellar floor. The plaintiff, who had no knowledge of the condition of the cellar when the lease was entered into, brought an action to recover the payment of the rent. Is he entitled to recover?

3 Defendant leased a store building from plaintiff, and vacated the premises nine months before the expiration of the lease. Subsequently the plaintiff, in an attempt to lessen the damages, put a sign in the window of the premises that the property was for rent, and it was rented from time to time. Defendant was credited with the rent to the date of the expiration of the lease. Plaintiff brought an action to recover the balance of the rent claimed to be due. Defendant attempted to escape liability on the ground that a re-entry and reletting of the premises created a surrender by operation of law. Plaintiff contends he only attempted to lessen the damages. Decide.

4 Plaintiffs, husband and wife and their three-year-old daughter, lived in a house which they had leased from the defendant. The house was new and had been built by the defendant. The daughter stood on a chair to reach for a toy on the stone mantel in the living room and the mantel fell away from the wall to the floor, thereby injuring the daughter. The mantel was not attached to the wall in any way, but rested upon a brick fireplace. The defendant contends he is not liable for the injuries because of the familiar principle of law of landlord and tenant that the tenant takes the premises as he finds them. Do you agree with defendant?

5 Plaintiff, as lessor, and defendant, as lessee, entered into a written lease whereby plaintiff leased certain premises to the defendant for a term commencing January 1, 1952, and ending December 31, 1956, at a rental of $95 a month. Sometime in October, 1956, plaintiff and defendant engaged in certain oral negotiations relative to the execution of a new lease of the premises. The new lease, however, was never signed. Defendant continued to occupy the premises until April 30, 1957, at which time he gave plaintiff thirty days' written notice of termination of the tenancy, as required by statute. Defendant vacated the premises sometime during May, 1957. Plaintiff contends that a holding over by the lessee constitutes an election by the lessee to lease the premises for another term of five years. Do you think this contention is correct?

6 Plaintiff, as lessor, and Smith, as lessee, entered into a written lease by the terms of which plaintiff leased to Smith an apartment building for a term of ten years. The lease agreement provided that Smith would make all necessary repairs to the building during the term of the lease. Smith thereafter assigned the lease to defendant. The entrance door to the building later became dilapidated. Defendant contends he is under no obligation to repair the door because he was not a party to the original lease. Do you agree?

7 On August 1, 1968, defendant rented an apartment on a monthly basis from plaintiff at a monthly rental of $150 payable on the first day of each and every month in advance. On December 15, 1968, defendant, not having paid the rent for the month of December, found another apartment which was more desirable for his purposes. He therefore notified plaintiff in writing that he was vacating the apartment on that day. Defendant paid plaintiff $75 for rent for one-half month but refused to pay rent for the remaining one-half of the month of December. Would plaintiff recover in an action to recover rent for the remaining one-half month?

8 Plaintiff owned a large tract of land which was productive of crops and had been used for agricultural purposes for years. An abundance of valuable coal and oil was beneath the surface but had never been mined. Plaintiff conveyed the land to defendant for the period of defendant's life. Defendant farmed the land for three years, and then started opening mines and selling the coal and oil. Plaintiff petitioned the court asking for an injunction to enjoin defendant from mining the land. Do you think the court will grant the injunction?

55

REAL ESTATE MORTGAGES

The purpose of a mortgage is to enable the creditor to subject specifically described property of the debtor to a foreclosure sale if the debtor does not pay. The creditor is known as the "mortgagee," and the debtor is known as the "mortgagor." A mortgage of real property is known as a "real estate mortgage," and a mortgage of personal property is known as a "chattel mortgage." The rules of law pertaining to the two types of mortgages, however, differ substantially in many respects. This chapter, therefore, will discuss the real estate mortgage with emphasis on (1) the nature of the mortgage, (2) the form of the mortgage, (3) the nature of the obligation, (4) the transfer of the mortgaged property, and (5) mortgage foreclosures.

NATURE OF THE REAL ESTATE MORTGAGE

The nature of a mortgage can perhaps best be explained by observing some of the distinguishing characteristics between the title theory, the lien theory, the equitable mortgage, the deed of trust in the nature of a mortgage, and installment land contracts.

Title Theory It will require a glance into the past to explain this theory. In the beginning, the legal effect of a mortgage was to pass the legal title from the mortgagor to the mortgagee. The early mortgage was indeed an outright conveyance by the debtor-mortgagor to the creditor-mortgagee, coupled with a condition that the mortgagor might have his property back upon the payment of the debt. This meant the mortgagee had the right to take possession of the mortgaged property to the exclusion of the mortgagor. The title of the mortgagee, moreover, became absolute upon default of the mortgagor. The loan may have been small, the land of much value. The early law courts, nevertheless, rigidly adhered to the rule. But courts of equity, recognizing the harshness of the rule, intervened by advancing the notion that a defaulting mortgagor had an equity of redemption in the property. This meant that upon default by the mortgagor the court would then fix a specified time within which the mortgagor might redeem his land. The title, therefore, did not become absolute in the mortgagee unless the mortgagor failed to redeem within the time so fixed. This concept of a mortgage which passes the title to the mortgagee is still followed in some of the states. The time in which the mortgagor may redeem his land, however, is now generally fixed by statute. It is equally significant to observe that the mortgagor, coincident with the development of the equity of redemption, was recognized as having the right to continue in possession of the land.

Lien Theory The courts, after denying the mortgagee the right of possession, realized he had an interest in the land which had to be called something, so they called it a "lien." Thus emanated the lien theory of mortgages. This theory, which recognizes the mortgagor as the owner but gives the mortgagee a lien against the property as security for the loan, now prevails in most of the states.

Equitable Mortgages Creditors did not like this intervention of the courts of equity. They soon resorted to various devices to avoid the equitable doctrine. The equity courts retaliated. Thus the maxim "once a mortgage, always a mortgage" was formulated. This maxim still survives. The earliest form of an equitable mortgage is found where a deed absolute on its face was made in fact to secure a loan but was unenforceable at law as a mortgage because of the absence of a defeasance clause. Parol evidence, in spite of the general parol-evidence rule, may be admitted to establish the true nature of the transaction. An ordinary deed may be shown to be a mortgage by the use of parol evidence. [*Murley v. Murley,* p. 728.]

Deed of Trust A device called a "deed of trust" is in common use in many of the states. It consists of a conveyance not to the lender but to a third person in trust to hold the property as security for the payment of the debt. There are, therefore, three parties to a deed-of-trust transaction: the trustor, or mortgagor, who borrows the money; the lender, or mortgagee, who is the beneficiary; and the trustee, who holds the legal title. The purpose of the transaction, nevertheless, is the same as a mortgage. The practical difference between a mortgage and a trust deed lies in the method of foreclosure. A mortgage is ordinarily foreclosed by judicial sale; a trust deed, in effect, by virtue of a sale by the trustee. The trustee, of course, is under a fiduciary obligation to act fairly and impartially toward both parties. His chief duties are to sell the land upon default at public auction to the highest bidder and, after satisfying the mortgage debt and expenses of sale, to account to the trustor as to any remaining surplus.

Installment Land Contracts The installment land contract, which is a serious rival of the real estate mortgage, is ordinarily drawn scrupulously in favor of the vendor. The advantages of the land contract to the vendor are apparent. The contract is often used when a sale of land is made for a small initial payment, and it generally provides for a forfeiture upon default of the vendee. It also generally provides, among other things, that time is of the essence of the contract, that the vendee must keep the premises insured, and that the vendee must also pay all taxes and assessments. The vendor retains title to the land. The vendee, although he is usually given possession of the land, does not acquire title until he has paid the last installment. Probably one of the outstanding advantages of this type of contract to the vendor is the fact that, upon default, it is less troublesome to summarily declare a forfeiture and keep the land and the vendee's payments than it is to foreclose a mortgage.

The many jurisdictions that allow the forfeiture of the vendee's equity do so primarily on the theory that the parties have "freedom of contract." Some other jurisdictions, recognizing the analogy between the land contract and a mortgage, disallow such forfeiture by statutory enactment or by intervention of a court of equity. These jurisdictions seem to follow the view that freedom of contract is not sufficient reason to uphold a forfeiture since there is such an economic disparity between a vendor and a vendee of small means. These jurisdictions treat the vendee as a mortgagor, thereby protecting his equity of redemption.

FORM OF REAL ESTATE MORTGAGE

Printed statutory forms of real estate mortgages are now available in most states. The forms, however, vary considerably. It is not unusual to find, in both the title-theory and the lien-theory states, that the mortgage continues to employ words of conveyance coupled with a defeasance clause. Mortgages of this type usually state that the mortgagor does hereby "grant, bargain, sell, and convey" unto the mortgagee certain real property particularly described subject to certain conditions—usually the payment of a debt—upon the fulfillment of which the conveyance "shall be null and void." A much simpler form, however, has been developed in many states where the mortgage merely states that the mortgagor "mortgages" or "mortgages and warrants" the property described. The safest and simplest procedure, of course, is to adhere to the use of local mortgage forms. In spite of the fact that printed forms are available in most states, businessmen would nevertheless be well advised to seek the aid of a lawyer before entering into mortgage transactions. Not only is it imperative that the property be described accurately, the nature of the obligation may demand legal advice.

NATURE OF THE OBLIGATION
OF THE REAL ESTATE MORTGAGE

It is essential that there be some sort of an obligation for which the mortgage is given as security. The obligation ordinarily consists of the repayment of money lent to the mortgagor by the mortgagee. As a general rule, however, any obligation capable of being reduced to a money value—such as an open-book account—may be secured by a mortgage. Mortgages given to secure future advances, those given for a part or the whole of the purchase price of the land, and those which contain after-acquired property clauses merit particular mention.

Future Advances   A mortgage to secure future advances is frequently used for, although by no means limited to, construction and improvement loans. Such a mortgage may be drafted in one of two forms. The first will state a certain total sum as a present loan, which sum includes advances to be made at a later time. The second will state that the mortgage secures advances to be made in the future but will leave the amounts indefinite. This type of security needs to be discussed from the viewpoint of junior liens. It is quite clear that a mortgage for future advances has priority as to any advances made before a junior lien attaches. The problem is this: Suppose the mortgagee makes one advance, a junior lien in the nature of a judgment attaches, and the mortgagee is contemplating a further advance. Will the new advance have priority over the intervening junior encumbrance? The courts present two conflicting views. The rule which represents the majority takes the view that, since the mortgagee is not bound by constructive notice of junior liens, he is protected as to all advances he makes while ignorant of such liens. According to this rule, the mortgagee is not bound to search the record before making a second advance. This is due to the further rule that recording acts do not afford statutory notice to prior lienors. The other rule takes the view that since the mortgagee is not bound to make the later advances he is required to search the records for intervening liens. According to this rule, liens of record will prevail over the new advance. This rule seems to have gained strength in later years.

One further point should be observed: The courts make a distinction between obligatory advances and optional advances. The mortgagee who is bound by his contract with the mortgagor to make the advances whether he wants to or not may perform regardless of intervening encumbrances. This is true irrespective of whether he has constructive notice or actual knowledge of junior encumbrances. In these circumstances, it is for the junior lienor, when faced with a mortgage which shows that it is for future advances, to inquire whether such a contract is outstanding.

Purchase-Money Mortgage   The most usual type of purchase-money mortgage is a transaction whereby the seller conveys title to the purchaser and receives, as a part of the same transaction, a part of the purchase money and a mortgage given by the purchaser upon the property to secure the balance of the purchase price. Such a mortgage, as a general rule, takes precedence over any other claim or lien attaching to the property of the purchaser-mortgagor. The courts are uniform in holding that the lien of a purchase-money mortgage is superior to that of a judgment against the grantee-mortgagor even though the judgment is rendered before the purchase of the property. The priority of the purchase-money mortgage is subject to the operation of the recording acts. A mortgagee who fails to record his mortgage, therefore, will be postponed to subsequent liens that qualify as members of protected classes under the recording statutes. Most of the litigation arises from controversies as to whether the mortgage is in fact a purchase-money mortgage.

After-acquired Property   One of the presently, as well as historically, significant controversies pertaining to the nature of the obligation is that having to do with an after-acquired property clause. The early rule prohibited the mortgaging of such property on the reasoning that one cannot mortgage property which one does not own. If one accepts the concept of a mortgage as a present transfer of title, the rule and the reasoning are consistent. Such clauses, however, are recognized by equity. It is not unusual, therefore, for a mortgagor, in addition to mortgaging specifically described property, to include in the mortgage an after-acquired property clause. The clause may be stated quite broadly as "also all the property, real, personal, or mixed, wherever the same is situated, which is now owned by the mortgagor or shall be owned by the mortgagor during the continuance of" the mortgage. The prevailing rule today is that the after-acquired property clause creates an equitable lien as soon as the mortgagor acquires the property. Such a lien, moreover, will be good against all third persons except bona fide purchasers without notice of the mortgage and prior lienors.

TRANSFER OF THE MORTGAGED PROPERTY

Transfer of the Mortgagor's Interest   The mortgagor may transfer his interest in the mortgaged property. He may sell it, or he may give it away. These things he may do without the consent of the mortgagee. The mortgage, moreover, will follow the property into the hands of the person to whom it comes. The mortgagee is therefore fully protected unless he forgets to record his mortgage and it is cut off under an applicable recording statute and the mortgagor becomes insolvent. This question then arises: Does the purchaser of the mortgaged property acquire a personal obligation to pay the mortgage? The answer to the question depends upon whether the purchaser takes the property *subject* to the mortgage or *assumes* the mortgage.

A purchaser who takes the property subject to the mortgage does not, as a general rule, personally agree to pay the mortgage debt. To illustrate: Brown, as grantor, sells his property, which is encumbered by a $5,000 mortgage, to Smith, as grantee. Smith takes the property subject to the mortgage. The property is sold for $4,000 at a foreclosure sale. Smith cannot be held personally for the $1,000 deficit. The mortgagee, however, may recover the deficit from Brown.

A purchaser who takes the property and assumes the mortgage, on the other hand, personally agrees to pay the mortgage debt. This is the more common type of transfer. The mortgagee, in these circumstances, may recover the deficit from Smith. The effect of the assumption is to make Smith primarily liable as between himself and Brown. The mortgagee, however, may still hold Brown personally liable. These rules are well settled. It is, nevertheless, frequently difficult to determine the intent of the parties from the language used. [*Perkins v. Brown,* p. 729.]

Transfer of the Mortgagee's Interest   Troublesome questions sometimes arise when the mortgagee attempts to transfer his interest in the mortgaged property because the mortgagee has two things: the debt and the interest in the real property securing the debt. The manner in which the mortgagee may transfer his interest, moreover, differs in those states following the title theory from those following the lien theory. In all states the transfer of the debt carries with it the mortgage security. This may be accomplished—if the note evidencing the debt is negotiable—by negotiation of the note in accordance with the law of commercial paper. In the lien-theory states the negotiation of the note coupled with an assignment of the mortgage properly completes the transfer. A few of the title-theory states hold that the mortgage can only be transferred by a formal conveyance. An attempt to assign the mortgage without the debt in the lien-theory states is ordinarily treated as a nullity. This is based on the reasoning that the mortgage is merely security for the debt. The title-theory states, however, generally permit the mortgagee to pass the legal title without transferring the debt, but the transferee holds the title in trust as security for the debt.

FORECLOSURES OF REAL ESTATE MORTGAGES
The mortgagee may resort to several modes of foreclosure. The more common of these are considered briefly.

Foreclosure by Judicial Sale   This type of foreclosure is used in a majority of the states. It is the most efficient method of determining the rights of all interested parties. It is, nevertheless, a time-consuming procedure. Three stages are ordinarily involved: the procedure leading up to and including the decree of sale; the sale itself and the disposition of the property and the proceeds; and, if the property does not sell for enough to pay the mortgage indebtedness, a decree for the deficiency.

The first stage involves a petition by the mortgagee, or holder of the debt, asking a court of equity to settle matters between him and the mortgagor. The court will then determine the validity of the mortgage, ascertain the amount of the debt and the extent of the mortgagor's ownership, and decree a sale of the mortgagor's ownership.

The second stage is largely regulated by statutes in the different states. The following steps are quite generally followed: Notice of the sale—which must contain reasonably accurate information concerning the time, place, and manner of the sale and the property to be sold—is published sufficiently in advance of the sale so that all interested persons may be present. The court ordinarily names the sheriff or another officer to conduct the sale which is commonly held at the office of the sheriff of the county in which the property is located. The person appointed to conduct the sale will, after having completed it, turn over the proceeds of the sale to the court. The court will then confirm the sale, which authorizes the officer conducting the sale to give the purchaser a deed conveying the interest of the mortgagor in the property. The court, if the proceeds of the sale are more than sufficient to discharge the debt and expenses of sale, will return the surplus to the mortgagor.

The third stage will only arise if the proceeds are insufficient to discharge the debt. In these circumstances, however, the court will order payment of the proceeds to the mortgagee and may enter a deficiency decree against the mortgagor for the balance.

Statutes have been enacted in practically all of the states which provide that the mortgagor may within a specified time after the sale—usually six months or a year—redeem the property by paying to the purchaser the amount for which the property was sold.

Strict Foreclosure The strict foreclosure was the first type to be used by the English courts after the development of the right of the mortgagor to redeem his property. The mortgagee would ask the equity court to fix a date by which time the mortgagor must pay or lose his rights. The court, in response to the request, would decree that if the mortgagor did not pay the debt within a specified time he should "forever be foreclosed" of all his interest in the property. If the mortgagee was in possession of the property, he retained it; if not in possession, he could eject the mortgagor. The effect of the strict foreclosure, therefore, was merely to postpone the absolute title of the mortgagee for the period of redemption. This type of foreclosure has been used sparingly in the United States. It is permitted in some states but only under certain circumstances. The courts ordinarily must be convinced that it is not unfair or unjust, as where the value of the property exceeds the debt.

Power of Sale A provision in a mortgage reserving the power unto the mortgagee to sell the mortgaged property within a designated time after default by the mortgagor is recognized in a number of states. The sale is ordinarily made by public auction, preceded by notice by advertisement specifying the time, place, description of the property, and other terms of the sale. A question frequently arises, however, whether the surplus should go to the mortgagor or to the junior lienors. There is authority that an action may be maintained by junior lienors to recover their share in a surplus. It is not clear, however, whether the mortgagee should search the records to discover subsequent interests. A mortgagee would be well advised to seek the aid of his lawyer rather than proceed on his own. This method of foreclosure, moreover, is expressly prohibited in a number of states.

Entry and Possession Foreclosure by entry and continued possession is permitted in only a few states. Where it is used, however, the mortgagee is permitted to take possession of the mortgaged property upon default by the mortgagor. The mortgagee in some states may foreclose by entry and continued possession under certain specified conditions—such as publication of notice and advertising—without court help. In other states he must bring a writ of entry. The mortgagee, by remaining in undisputed possession of the premises for a specified period—usually one to three years—will get an absolute title. It should be pointed out, however, that the entry without court help must be peaceful.

CASES

Murley v. Murley, 37 N.E.2d 909 (Mass. 1956). Action by Joseph J. Murley and another, plaintiffs, against Timothy E. Murley, defendant. Mrs. Ellen Murley, a widow of about eighty years of age, was the owner of a house which consisted of two apartments, the lower of which she occupied. She became unable to run a coal furnace and decided to convert the heating system to oil heat. She did not, however, have the estimated $2,000 which the conversion would cost. The defendant-son agreed to pay for the conversion in full if "his name was to be put on the deed." After a family conference attended by plaintiffs—a daughter and another son—it was agreed that defendant would pay the $2,000 and a deed would be given by Mrs. Murley naming the defendant as grantee. It was also agreed that the defendant and his wife would move into the upper apartment of the house; that Mrs. Murley would live with them; and that the ground-floor apartment would be rented to provide for part of Mrs. Murley's support. A quitclaim deed, naming Mrs. Murley and her defendant-son as joint tenants, was executed and recorded on September 11, 1953. The arrangement was carried out for a time. Mrs. Murley soon tired of it, however, and moved back downstairs. The defendant thereafter paid rent at the rate of $40 a month. Mrs. Murley continued to make monthly payments of $46.28 on a bank mortgage on the house.

Mrs. Murley, about two months after the execution of the deed, executed a will in which she directed that the apartment house should go to her son Joseph, one of the plaintiffs. Mrs. Murley, in 1954, executed another will in which she directed that the residue of her estate should go to the plaintiffs. At this time, she was informed that the deed to the apartment house would vest the whole property in the survivor of herself and the defendant. There was evidence to show that Mrs. Murley indicated that she wanted the defendant to get the house upon her death. There was also evidence that she subsequently made efforts to persuade the defendant "to take his name off the deed." There was still further evidence that on the night the deed was executed the defendant kept urging his mother to sign and not to "be holding it up"; that she was then told, "Mrs. Murley, you will still own the house and you are the boss"; and that defendant said he "wanted security, he wasn't going to give the money away for nothing." After Mrs. Murley's death, plaintiffs brought a bill in equity to have a determination that plaintiffs were the beneficial owners of the house.

Cutter, Justice: The important thing is the intention of the parties when the deed was signed in 1953. The statements that the property would continue to be hers made to Mrs. Murley at the time of the execution of the deed, the references in the testimony to the defendant's desire for security for the $2,000, the continued payments of mortgage interest and taxes by Mrs. Murley (rather than the defendant) after the giving of the deed, and the fact that the defendant paid rent to her monthly for the upstairs apartment, all point to a security transaction instead of an absolute conveyance. Although there was some testimony which would lead to a different conclusion, there is sufficient testimony to support the findings of the trial judge, who saw the witnesses and was in a better position than we are to appraise their oral testimony. Giving to all the oral testimony all the weight the judge could justifiably give it we think his finding that the deed was given only by way of security was justified. [DECISION FOR PLAINTIFFS]

Perkins v. Brown, 38 P.2d 253 (Wash. 1934). Action by William D. Perkins, plaintiff, against Edwin J. Brown and others, defendants, to recover upon a promissory note and to foreclose a real estate mortgage given as security for the note. Plaintiff obtained a decree of foreclosure and a deficiency judgment in the trial court, and the defendant Netherlands American Mortgage Bank appealed. The question presented by the appeal relates to the liability of Netherlands American Mortgage Bank, appellant, for the deficiency judgment. The precise question presented on appeal is whether a purchaser personally agrees to pay the mortgage debt when he purchases real estate subject to a mortgage and agrees to "reimburse" the seller.

Steinert, Justice: We now come to the vital phase of the case. When the contract is read in its entirety and in connection with the deed that accompanied it, it becomes apparent, we think, that the word "reimburse" has an equivocal implication. The word itself, considered alone, is rather broad in its signification. According to Funk and Wagnall's Standard Dictionary, it is defined as follows:

"1. To pay back as an equivalent for what has been abstracted, expended, or lost; refund; repay; as, to reimburse one's expenses;

"2. To make return of an equivalent to; indemnify."

These definitions connote two ideas: (1) That of indemnifying one for that which he has paid for or lost, and (2) that of supplying one with the equivalent of that which he should have otherwise received. . . .

The rule undoubtedly is that the obligation of a grantee to assume and pay a mortgage debt must be established by evidence that is clear and conclusive, and cannot be established by inference. While the obligation need not be expressed in any particular language, yet the expression upon which reliance is placed must unequivocally show that the grantee has undertaken to pay the debt. . . .

We are of the view that the language of the deed and contract does not show a clear and unequivocal assumption by appellant of the mortgage, and that the trial court was, therefore, in error in holding as a matter of law, that it did. [DECISION FOR APPELLANT]

PROBLEMS

1 The Delta Land and Timber Company executed a mortgage to Taylor for the purpose of securing bonds issued by it. This mortgage, which encumbered properties then owned by the company, contained an after-acquired property clause. The instrument was properly recorded in the counties in which the properties were located. About three years later, the Delta Company entered into a contract with the Southwestern Company by the terms of which Delta was to acquire options on timberland and Southwestern was to provide the money with which to make the purchases. Delta departed from the contract terms by purchasing timber tracts with its own funds. Delta received reimbursement from Southwestern, however, and conveyed the tracts to Southwestern. Sometime thereafter receivers were appointed to take over the properties of the Delta Company. The receivers took possession of the tracts which Delta had conveyed to Southwestern. It was then that the Southwestern Company learned of the Delta Company's mortgage to Taylor with the after-acquired property clause. It was agreed that the receivers would sell the tracts and hold the proceeds of such sales pending a decision by the court as to whether the trustees under the Delta Company's mortgage or the Southwestern Company should be entitled to the proceeds. Who is entitled to the proceeds?

2 Plaintiff and defendant entered into an agreement whereby plaintiff, in consideration of the sum of $7,500, executed a deed of his land to defendant. The parties, at the same time, entered into a sales-purchase contract covering the same land which provided that plaintiff was to remain in possession of the property; that he was to take out and pay the premiums on insurance on the buildings; and that he was to pay the taxes. The contract stated that "the sum of $7,500 is to be considered the purchase price to be paid" by plaintiff for the property, payable over a twenty-year period in annual payments. Plaintiff petitioned the court to decree that the deed and contract constitute a mortgage. Defendant contends evidence is not admissible to change the terms of the deed. Decide.

3 George and Virginia, husband and wife, purchased a large tract of land and took title thereto as tenants by the entirety. The property was purchased with the aid of a temporary loan from Roy in the amount of $10,000, and George and Virginia executed and delivered a warranty deed conveying the land to Roy. When the loan was repaid, Roy reconveyed the property by warranty deed to George, individually. George thereafter died intestate. What are the rights, if any, of his surviving children in the land? What are the rights, if any, of Virginia in the land?

4 Brown, Smith, and Jones owned certain real property as tenants in common prior to the death of Jones. Brown and Smith, after the death of Jones, encumbered the property with a mortgage in favor of the XYZ Finance Company in the sum of $30,000. Brown and Smith thereafter sold the property to Black, subject to the mortgage. The entire mortgage indebtedness remained unpaid at its due date, and the XYZ Finance Company foreclosed the mortgage. The property was sold to Hawkins at the judicial sale for the sum of $20,000. Jim Jones, a minor son, was the only heir of Jones at the time of death. The XYZ Finance Company now seeks to recover the $10,000 deficiency. Who is liable for this deficiency? What is the interest, if any, of Jim Jones in the property?

5 Plaintiff's 1,200 acres of land was sold during a mortgage foreclosure proceeding. Prior to the time the redemption period expired, defendant agreed to and did pay to the sheriff the sum of $3,853.80. This was the sum needed to redeem the land. Plaintiff and defendant also signed a written agreement by the terms of which defendant agreed to hold the land in trust for plaintiff for four months, during which time plaintiff could sell the land or any part thereof in order to pay the debt. The agreement also provided that defendant could lease the land if the land was not sold in two weeks, and that title to the land belonged to defendant absolutely if the land was not sold or the debt repaid in four months. Discuss the rights of plaintiff.

6   Brown executed a mortgage encumbering a tract of land on which he was constructing a dwelling house to the First Bank to secure the sum of $10,000 and to secure a future advance of $10,000 to be advanced thirty days later. Brown then mortgaged the tract of land to Smith to secure the sum of $5,000. The First Bank thereafter advanced $10,000 to Brown so that Brown could complete the construction work. Discuss the priorities as to (a) the first loan made by the First Bank, (b) the loan made by Smith, and (c) the advance made by the First Bank.

7   Baker, who desired to purchase Blackacre, borrowed $20,000 from the First Bank in order to make the purchase. He executed a purchase-money mortgage in favor of the First Bank to secure the loan, and the mortgage was properly recorded. James, who had a judgment lien against Baker, learned that Baker had purchased Blackacre. James thereupon attempted to have Blackacre sold at public auction so that he could satisfy his judgment lien out of the proceeds of the sale. Will he succeed?

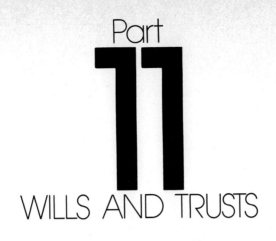

Part

11

WILLS AND TRUSTS

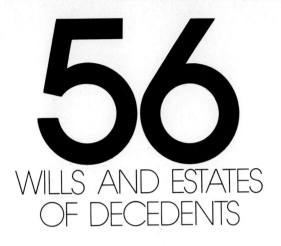

56
WILLS AND ESTATES
OF DECEDENTS

The law of each state lays down certain rules under which the owner of property may provide for the disposition of his property after his death. This is done by making a "last will and testament." The property of the decedent who has not made a will, however, will be distributed according to the laws of descent and distribution. It should be mentioned at the outset, however, that the law varies from state to state. It is by no means uniform. This fact should be kept in mind while reading the following general survey of (1) the manner in which property may be disposed of by will, (2) the manner in which a will may be revoked, (3) some special types of wills, (4) abatement and ademption, (5) the manner in which property may be disposed of by the statutes of descent and distribution, and (6) the provisions for the administration of estates by decedents.

THE WILL

A will is an expression of the wishes of a person called the testator, if a male, or the testatrix, if a female, concerning the distribution of his or her property after his or her death. The state statutes generally make provision for the kinds of property or interests in property that may be disposed of by will, and some estates are prohibited from being disposed of by will. For example, neither a husband nor a wife who owns property as a tenant by the entirety could defeat the right of survivorship in the other by devising his or her share to a third person. As a general rule, however, any estate that the owner may transfer may be disposed of by will. First, the formal will will be discussed and, secondly, some special types of wills.

The Formal Will   Every state legislature has enacted statutes prescribing required formalities that must be observed in the execution of a written will. A simple statement of the wishes of the testator properly signed and witnessed is sufficient in some states. A simple will commonly contains a statement of the testator that he is of sound and disposing mind and memory, coupled with a revocation of all prior wills; a direction with respect to the desires of the testator as to his burial; certain specific gifts; a residuary clause, giving to designated persons the residue of the estate; a clause appointing someone to administer the estate; and an attestation clause.

(1)   *Execution of the Will*   The minimum requisites generally necessary for the execution of the will are that the testator must sign the will; that he must sign the will in the presence of two, or perhaps three, witnesses; and that he must declare the will to be his last will and testament at the time of affixing his signature. Many states require an attestation clause, reciting that the will was signed, sealed, published, and declared by the testator as and for his last will and testament, and that the witnesses thereupon, at the request of the testator and in his presence, all being present at the same time, subscribe their names as attesting witnesses. Many of the statutes require that the will be signed at the end. The purpose of these statutes is to minimize the opportunity of subsequent additions to the will. These statutes are strictly construed, and it is not sufficient if the signature appears in the margin or at the beginning of the will, such as "I, John Doe, hereby make this my last will." [*Barnes v. Viering,* p. 743.]

(2)   *Testamentary Capacity*   Testamentary age is fixed by statute in all of the states. The age is most often fixed at twenty-one years, but in some states the age qualification is lowered to eighteen years, and in still others females are permitted to make a will at a lower age than males. Some wills, irrespective of age, may be refused probate or set aside if it can be shown that a proper testamentary intent has not been expressed. A will may be set aside if it is obtained through undue influence. The reason assigned for the rule is that the will speaks not the wishes of the testator but those of the person exercising the undue influence. A will may be set aside if it is obtained by fraud. The cases pertaining to fraud usually involve situations where the testator was willfully deceived by the beneficiary as to the character or content of the will. A will may be set aside if the testator did not have the mental capacity to make the will. The precise meaning of "mental capacity" is probably one of the most controversial subjects in the law of wills. The generally accepted formula for determining mental capacity is that a person need not possess superior or even average mentality, but that he must be capable of understanding and carrying on in his mind in a general way (a) the nature and extent of his property, (b) the persons who are the natural objects of his bounty, (c) the disposition he is making of his property, (d) an appreciation of

these elements in relation to each other, so that he may (e) form an orderly desire as to the disposition of his property.

Modification of Will   The testator, if he wishes to modify his will, may do so by executing a codicil, which is a separate writing executed by the testator subsequent to the will which alters the provisions of the will. A codicil, however, must be executed with the same formalities as a will. A will may sometimes be modified by a physical alteration of a part of a will, such as erasing an entire paragraph. The applicable statute, however, is controlling. Statutes providing for alteration of a will are generally construed to mean revocation of the entire will or none of it; statutes providing for alteration of a will "or a part thereof" are generally construed to mean a revocation of that portion only which is altered. The testator may, in most states, alter his will by interlineations or revise a revoked will by republication of the will. There is not sufficient republication of the altered will, however, if the witnesses merely attest to the alterations. The statutes generally provide that re-execution of the will must be done in the manner required for the original execution of wills. [*In re Shifflet's Estate,* p. 743.]

REVOCATION OF WILL

The exclusive methods of revocation of a will are (1) a subsequent instrument, (2) physical acts to the will, and (3) operation of law.

Subsequent Instrument   A few statutes provide that a will may only be revoked by a will or codicil. These statutes have been interpreted to mean that the will or codicil must make a disposition of the property of the testator. The majority of the statutes, however, provide that a will may be revoked by a subsequent instrument when the instrument is executed with the formalities required for a will. These statutes are interpreted to mean that any instrument which is executed with the required formalities is sufficient even though it merely declares a revocation and makes no testamentary provision. A will, therefore, may be revoked by the testator by the execution of a subsequent will which expressly revokes all prior wills. But does a subsequent will revoke a prior will in the absence of express revocation? The courts generally hold that the prior will is revoked by implied revocation if the testator disposes of his entire estate. The courts also generally hold that a subsequent will revokes any prior will insofar as it is inconsistent with the prior will. Suppose the first will disposes of certain shares of stock to Brown, certain real property to Jones, and the residue to the wife of the testator and the second instrument disposes of the shares of stock to Smith and the residue to his wife. The gift to Brown would be revoked because the gift is inconsistent with the gift to Smith. Is the gift to Jones also revoked? There is no explicit answer. It is mostly a matter of ascertaining the intention of the testator, and this frequently involves time-consuming litigation. This could be avoided. All the states have enacted statutes setting forth specific requirements which must be complied with in order to revoke a will. Revocation of a will, therefore, is simply a matter of complying with the statutory requirements.

Physical Acts   A will may be revoked by the deliberate and intentional destruction, cancellation, or mutilation of the will. Destruction of the will which is done accidentally does not operate as a revocation. The burning of a will, therefore, will not amount to revocation if the burning was done by mistake, A testator frequently executes a will in duplicate and leaves one will with his attorney and retains the other in his possession. The purpose of this procedure is to lessen the chance of accidental destruction since if either will can be produced it can be probated. The courts are agreed, as a matter of substantive law, that the testator could revoke the will by the deliberate and intentional destruction of the will in his possession. Suppose the testator's only heirs were A and B and that his will left all his property to A. Suppose further that B, upon learning that he had been omitted from the will, destroyed the will without the knowledge of the testator. A search for the will after the death of the testator would obviously be futile, and a presumption would then arise that the testator destroyed the will. In the absence of proof to the contrary, the property of the testator would descend and devolve according to the laws of descent and distribution. A testor would be well advised, therefore, to keep his will out of reach of disgruntled heirs. [*In re Riner's Estate,* p. 745.]

Operation of Law   The doctrine of revocation by operation of law recognizes that a will may be revoked by implication from certain changes in the family relations of the testator such as marriage or the birth or adoption of a child. The doctrine is not recognized in all states and it has been abrogated by statute in other states. Total revocation rarely arises today in view of the modern statutes which provide for the pretermitted child and for the surviving spouse. The statutes are not uniform, but they generally provide that a child born after the execution of the will is entitled to his intestate share unless it appears that the child was intentionally omitted from the will or that the child is otherwise provided for. The statutes also frequently provide that the surviving spouse takes under the law of descent if no testamentary provision has been made for the spouse. A subsequent divorce is sometimes held to impliedly revoke a testamentary provision for a spouse. This is particularly true when the divorce is coupled with a property settlement. A recommended method of eliminating uncertainties is to review periodically one's status with respect to the will. The frequency of the review will be determined by changes in the economic condition of the testator, birth, death, and marriage of children and grandchildren and other circumstances peculiar to the testator.

SPECIAL TYPES OF WILLS
Holographic wills, nuncupative wills, and wills of soldiers and sailors are permitted under certain unusual circumstances.

Holographic Wills   This type of will is written entirely in the handwriting of the testator. The holographic will is not recognized by all of the states, but those states that do recognize the holographic will prescribe the formalities which must be followed. Some states require each word to be in the handwriting of the testator, including the date. An instrument is not entitled to probate as a holographic will unless it complies with the statutes which prescribe the requisites of such a will.

Nuncupative Wills   This is an oral will and can be made only when the testator is in his last illness. The form of the statute which permits the making of a will by nuncupation determines the extent of the privilege. The privilege is denied absolutely in some states. Those states that do acknowledge this type of will, however, generally limit the privilege to personal property. Real property, therefore, cannot pass by nuncupation. No particular language is required. The testator must make some statement which shows that he intends to make a bequest. He must require the witnesses to act as witnesses to his will. Such wills are not favored because of the possibility of mistake or fraud. They are often difficult to prove.

Soldiers' and Sailors' Wills   Statutes in most of the states acknowledge privileged military and maritime wills. These statutes are, in general, to the effect that any soldier being in actual military service or any seaman being at sea may dispose of his personal estate without complying with the formalities required of other wills. Soldiers' and sailors' wills may be oral or written, but they are ordinarily limited to personal property. The written will may be in the form of a letter and need not be witnessed. The oral will would have to be proved by at least one witness. The privilege was originally limited to soldiers in actual military service and to sailors at sea. But the concept of "actual military service" and "sailors at sea" has changed considerably. It is not certain, therefore, whether a soldier in service but not in the actual theater of operations, or a sailor at shore, may take advantage of the privileged military and maritime will. This privilege accorded soldiers and sailors, however, is truly a doubtful privilege. It is conceivable that the words of a soldier in a faraway land might dispose of a large estate. Ex-service personnel might do well to make formal wills. This would, at least, avoid the consequences of a claim of an unscrupulous barroom companion based on an unrevoked informal will.

ABATEMENT AND ADEMPTION
"Abatement" is the process of determining the distribution of assets left by a testator at his death when such assets are insufficient to satisfy the provisions of his will. "Ademption" occurs when changed circumstances render impossible the performance of a provision in a will. Suppose Brown devises and bequeaths $10,000 to his good friend Smith, $10,000 to his good friend Jones, and his farm Whiteacre to his son. Suppose further that, at the time of Brown's death, only $10,000 and a farm Greenacre remain in his estate after the payment of debts,

Whiteacre having been sold. Jones and Smith would each receive $5,000, and the son, as a general rule, would not receive Greenacre. The gifts to Smith and Jones are said to have abated, and the gift to the son is said to have adeemed.

It is also important to note that residuary gifts are the first to abate. Suppose Brown, at the time he executes his will, has assets worth $50,000. Suppose further that he bequeaths $10,000 to his good friend Smith, $10,000 to his good friend Jones, and the residue of his estate to his son. Brown obviously intended that his son should inherit $30,000. Suppose, however, that Brown's estate, after the payment of debts and expenses, was worth only $25,000 at the time of his death. Smith would receive $10,000; Jones would receive $10,000; and Brown's son would receive only $5,000. Brown could have avoided this situation by bequeathing a percentage of his net estate to Smith and Jones. [*In re Gerlach's Estate,* p. 745.]

STATUTES OF DESCENT AND DISTRIBUTION

A person who dies without leaving a will dies intestate. The state will then decide the manner in which the real and personal property of the decedent will be inherited according to a fixed statutory formula. This means that the law of the state where the real property of the decedent is located will designate the heirs to whom the property will descend, and the law of the state where the decedent was domiciled will designate the distributees of the personal property. This rigid formula not only prescribes the persons but also the order in which they will inherit. The importance of leaving a will becomes apparent when it is realized that no statutory formula of a state makes an exception with respect to those heirs or relatives in unusual need, as shown by the following broad general survey of the statutes.

The Surviving Spouse   The lawful surviving spouse at common law was entitled to a life estate of dower, or curtesy, in the land of the deceased spouse. But the surviving spouse was never treated as an heir of the decedent. The surviving wife today is entitled to a one-third or a one-half interest of both the personal and the real property of the decedent. In a few states, however, the surviving spouse is treated as an heir. But the share to which the surviving spouse is entitled varies if there are children of the intestate. The surviving spouse will take an enlarged part, if there are no children of the intestate, and in some states will take the entire estate. A divorced spouse, of course, is completely excluded.

The Surviving Descendants   A surviving descendant is one who is in line of descent from the decedent. The expression includes children, grandchildren, and other descendants. Two common ways in which surviving descendants inherit are known as "per stirpes" and "per capita." Suppose Brown was survived by three children, A, B, and C. Each child would inherit a one-third interest of the estate of Brown. Suppose, however, that A, B, and C predeceased Brown; that A was survived by two children; that B was survived by three children; and C was survived by four children. How should the grandchildren inherit? If they inherit per capita—or by head—each grandchild would inherit a one-ninth share of the estate. If they inherit per stirpes, the two children of A would take A's share, and each would therefore take a one-sixth share; the three children of B would take B's share divided equally among them; and the four children of C would take C's share divided equally among them. Some states will permit the grandchildren to take per capita while other states will permit them to take per stirpes. It should be mentioned in this connection that a child of the intestate which is born after the death of the intestate is considered in being for the purpose of inheritance and will share in the estate in the same manner as if the child had been born during the lifetime of the intestate. An adopted child, in many states, inherits in the same manner as the other surviving descendants.

The Surviving Ascendants and Collaterals   Surviving ascendants include persons to whom one is related in an ascending line, such as parents and grandparents. Collaterals include those belonging to the same ancestral stock but not in a direct line of descent, such as brothers, cousins, uncles, and nephews. If there are no descendants, most states allow parents, subject to the interest of the surviving spouse, to share in the estate of the intestate. Brothers and sisters generally share if there is no surviving parent. In some states, however, brothers and sisters share equally with the parents. The law is not uniform. Two points, however, are generally applicable: First, relatives by marriage, excepting the surviving spouse, cannot share in the estate of the intestate. Secondly, if the intestate is not survived by a spouse, descendants, ascendants, or collaterals the estate will escheat to the state after a specified period of time. This is rather unusual.

ADMINISTRATION OF ESTATES

The purpose of the administration of any estate is to provide an efficient and impartial method to protect the creditors of the decedent and to distribute the assets of the estate to those persons who are entitled thereto. The rules for accomplishing this result are found in the various state statutes. These statutes, frequently referred to as the "probate law," provide that the administration of the estate shall be under the supervision of the court. The court is commonly designated as the "probate court" or the "surrogate's court." The administration of an estate is often burdened with highly complicated problems. These problems can only be solved, however, by a consideration of the facts of the particular case as controlled by the law of the particular state. It is the purpose here to mention a few rules that are applicable in general to administration of estates.

Personal Representative   The term "personal representative," in its commonly accepted sense, means the executor, executrix, administrator, or administratrix. A person who dies testate will ordinarily designate in the will some person who is to administer the estate. If the person so designated is a male, he is referred to as the "executor"; if a female, she is referred to as the "executrix." The court will appoint someone to administer the estate of a person who dies intestate. If the person so appointed is a male, he will be referred to as the "administrator"; if a female, she will be referred to as the "administratrix." Any person competent to make a will is, generally speaking, competent to act as a personal representative. Statutes usually prohibit certain classes of persons, such as illiterates, adjudged incompetents, and persons under the age of twenty-one years, from acting as a personal representative.

The functions of administration are mostly applicable alike to cases of testacy and intestacy. The overall duties of the personal representative in either event are to discover and collect the assets of the decedent, pay the lawful claims against the estate, and distribute the balance to the persons entitled thereto. A general insight into the administration of an estate might be best grasped by outlining some of the major steps required by a typical statute to probate a will.

Probate of Will　It is the duty of the executor to file the will in the proper court and petition the court that it be admitted to record and probated. This petition will ordinarily consist of a statement of the approximate value of the estate, and the name, age, residence, and relationship of the heirs of the decedent. It will then be necessary to prove the will by the witnesses. This is commonly done by a statement of the witnesses, under oath, that the instrument offered for probate is the same instrument to which they subscribed their names as witnesses. After the will is admitted of record, the executor will file an oath that he will faithfully administer the estate, pay the debts of the decedent, make distribution of the estate, and render accounts of the administration. It is sometimes necessary to file a bond. The court will then, by an instrument known as "letters testamentary," declare the executor to be duly qualified to act as executor. This is the executor's authority to administer the estate. He will ordinarily be required to publish notice in some newspaper to all creditors to file any claims they have against the estate within a stated period of time—probably eight or ten months, perhaps a year. The court will then, upon a petition of the executor, appoint appraisors who will appraise the value of the assets of the decedent and file their appraisal with the court. After collecting the assets of the estate, the executor will pay the debts of the estate in accordance to their statutory priority, distribute the assets to the persons entitled thereto, and finally petition the court for an order of discharge.

Administration Unnecessary　The administration of estates may be dispensed with in a few instances. It may be dispensed with if the property of the decedent is jointly owned property so that the interest of the decedent passes by survivorship to the surviving owner. This is the usual situation of property owned by a husband and wife as tenants by the entirety. But it should be mentioned that joint ownership does not always dispense with an inheritance tax. The present Federal Estate Tax Statute and some state statutes patterned after the federal law treat property which the decedent owns in joint tenancy with another as a part of the estate of the decedent for estate-tax purposes. The survivor of jointly owned property, therefore, might avoid litigation by determining the status of the inheritance-tax law with respect to jointly owned property. It often happens that a properly filed tax report will dispense with the necessity of a tax proceeding.

The administration of an estate may also be dispensed with in those states which have a simplified proceeding for the administration of small estates which do not exceed a specified amount, varying from $500 to $5,000. These statutes commonly provide that upon the application of some proper person the court may enter an order directing the applicant to collect the assets of the estate; pay the debts of the decedent, the funeral expenses, and expenses of administration; and distribute the balance to the persons entitled to share in the proceeds of the estate.

CASES

Barnes v. Viering, 206 A.2d 112 (Conn. 1964). Proceeding by Robert E. Barnes, plaintiff, against Victor V. Viering, executor of the Estate of Carrie T. B. Purinton, defendant, to have a certain letter admitted to probate as a will. The letter is in the following form:

Dear Robert:
You know this house and the furnishings that have been in the family for a good many years really belong to you. It was Grandfather Brown's wishes to keep it in the family to the last living relative and you Robert are the last one left. There is nothing I can do now but you can take it to court and file your claim if you have to.
I appoint Mrs. Lillian Bedore to write this letter for me and she has promised she will give you this letter after my death.

s/ CARRIE B. PURINTON
in the presence of
s/ LILLIAN BEDORE
s/ GEORGE DIETZ
s/ RUTH M. DIETZ

Witnessed,
March 16, 1963.

Comley, Associate Justice: A will is more than a document executed in compliance with the statutory formalities required for testamentary disposition. A will is the legal declaration of intention as to the disposition of one's property after death. "Will" as here used means the bequests and devises made by the testatrix and expressed in writing and made known through the writing in the manner prescribed by law. This letter makes no disposition; on the contrary it states that no disposition is intended. The will must contain language which in and of itself expressed the testamentary gift intended. The letter, as the trial court concluded, is not a will. [DECISION FOR DEFENDANT]

In re Shifflet's Estate, 170 So. 2d 96 (Fla. 1965). Proceeding by Ruth C. Jones, appellant, against Leroy J. Shifflet, Woodrow D. Shifflet, and David L. Klein, appellees, to revoke the probate of a will.

Florence I. Shifflet executed her last will and testament by the terms of which she provided, among other things, for certain bequests to her brothers-in-law Leroy J. Shifflet and Woodrow D. Shifflet. She also executed a codicil, by the terms of which she provided for a bequest of $1,000 to David Kline, Jr. She thereafter attempted to modify the will by drawing a line through the words "brothers-in-law Leroy J. Shifflet and Woodrow D. Shifflet" and writing above the same "Matthew C. Caldwell, sister Mary M. Mayo and nephew Donald C. Jones and niece Patricia Jones." She also crossed out the body of the codicil. On the margin of the pages, she placed the initials "F.I.S." opposite each of the stricken and interlineated portions of the page, which was witnessed by two witnesses. The will was admitted to probate. The appellees, however, contend that the obliterating and mutilating of the will and codicil had no legal effect.

Hendry, Judge: It is our opinion that the attempted partial revocation of the will by the testatrix was inoperable because she failed to comply with the statutory requirements.

It is uncontested that the will in its original form was validly executed and would be entitled to probate, but for the attempted partial revocation. Before going further, it might be helpful to restate a valid generalization; the statute providing for revocation of will must be strictly complied with, partial or substantial compliance is insufficient.

The statute dealing with this proposition provides:

A will or any part thereof may be revoked or altered by a subsequent written will, codicil or other writing, declaring such revocation or alteration; provided, that the same formalities required for the execution of wills under this law are observed in the execution of such will, codicil or other writing.

It is obvious that this was the statute that the testatrix attempted to follow by her actions because partial revocation of a will may only be accomplished by strict compliance with the above statute and no other.

The remaining question necessary for resolution of the instant case is whether the attempted partial revocation of the will was accomplished with the same formality as the execution of the will. The statute providing for the execution of wills is §731.07 Fla. Stat., which provides in relevant part:

Every will, other than a nuncupative will, must be in writing and must be executed as follows:
(1)The testator must sign his will at the end thereof, or some other person in his presence and by his direction must subscribe the name of the testator thereto.

It is readily apparent that the testatrix did not strictly adhere to the statutory requirements above stated, in her attempt to partially revoke her will. Our statute requires that the will be signed at the end, and accordingly any partial revocation must similarly be so signed. Assuming for the purpose of this discussion but specifically not deciding, that the initialling by the testatrix was sufficient to constitute a signature, the revocation was signed at three separate places, none of which constituted the end of the will. Accordingly, the attempted partial revocation was ineffective and the will as originally written was entitled to probate. [DECISION FOR APPELLEES]

In re Riner's Estate, 207 N.E.2d 486 (Ill. 1965). Proceeding by Alice Ann Taylor, and others, appellants, against Lenora Cummings, administratrix of the estate of Charles P. Riner, appellee, for the probate of an alleged will. The appellants, proponents of the will, are nieces and nephews of the predeceased wife of the decedent, Charles P. Riner. The appellee is the sole heir-at-law of the decedent.

Coryn, Justice: All parties hereto admit, and the court so found, that this document was torn lengthwise through the middle from the top to within two inches from the bottom, with a second tear extending from the bottom upwards two inches to within approximately three-fourths of an inch to the left of the first tear, leaving the two pieces connected. The upper left hand corner of the instrument was also torn off, and this corner remained attached to a blue cover bearing the legend "Last Will and Testament of Charles P. Riner."

The Probate Act provides that a will may be revoked by tearing by the testator himself, or by some other person in the presence of and by the direction of the testator. Where a torn will is found among the testator's papers, the presumption is that the tearing of the will was done by the testator with the intention to revoke. In such cases, the proponent of the will has the burden of proving not only due execution of the will, but also must rebut the presumption of revocation by proof that the will was in existence and unrevoked at the time of the testator's death.

The only evidence adduced in this case shows that two or three years before his death, the testator picked up the will from his lawyer's office. During the years that followed, testator broke his hip and was compelled to sleep and work in a first floor room of his home in Galva. The decedent conducted the operation of his farms and other businesses from this room and kept his business documents in a bureau drawer in this room. After the decedent's death, Miss Cummings, in the presence of Mrs. Johnson, opened this bureau drawer and removed therefrom the torn will. Mrs. Johnson testified that the condition of the will on the night of decedent's death was the same as when presented to the court for probate.

In this case the proposed will was presented to the court in a mutilated and torn condition. The only evidence presented indicates that the will was in this condition on the night of decedent's death, and that this will was removed from a drawer in which decedent normally kept his business papers. With this evidence it was incumbent upon the proponents of this will to rebut the presumption of revocation by establishing by competent evidence that the will was in existence and unrevoked at the time of the testator's death. This the proponents failed to do. [DECISION FOR APPELLEE]

In re Gerlach's Estate, 72 A.2d 271 (Pa. 1950). This is an appeal by Amanda Gerlach, appellant, against the specific legatees under the will of Charles L.

Gerlach, deceased, appellees. The Allentown Supply Company, a corporation, was owned by Charles L. Gerlach, John W. Pratt, and Morris A. Bitting. In 1937, the corporation was converted into a partnership, and Gerlach purchased the interest of Bitting. Gerlach executed his will on August 1, 1945, which provided in part as follows: "I give, devise, and bequeath all my right, title, and interest in my business, known as the Allentown Supply Company, to the following in equal shares absolutely." Thirteen persons were then named as the beneficiaries of the gift, most of whom were employees of the business. On November 16, 1946, the business was again changed to a corporation under the name of Allentown Supply Corporation, and Gerlach and Pratt owned all the shares of stock. Gerlach died on May 1, 1947. This appeal is brought by the testator's mother, and the question presented is whether the bequest of the testator's interest "in my business, known as Allentown Supply Company," was adeemed by conversion of the partnership to a corporation named the Allentown Supply Corporation.

Horace Stern, Justice: The bequest of testator's interest in his business was, of course, a specific one and therefore subject to ademption if the business was extinguished before his death. There seems to be some difference of opinion in the authorities as to whether weight should be given to the assumed intention of the testator in determining whether, if the subject of the specific gift has been sold or destroyed and the testator acquires another thing which possesses the same qualities as the original, such subsequently acquired property passes under his will, but *all* the authorities agree that if property which is specifically devised or bequeathed remains in existence, and belongs to the testator at his death, slight and immaterial changes in its form do not operate as an ademption. . . . The change in the subject of the bequest in the present case was obviously not like the one where real estate devised in a will was sold by the testator and what he owned at his death was a purchase money mortgage on the property; or where shares of stock were sold and a bond taken by the testator in payment; . . . or where certain life insurance policies bequeathed by the testator matured and were paid to him and he invested the proceeds in bonds; or where a farm devised in a will was sold by the testator who subsequently reacquired the underlying coal on which he had held a purchase money mortgage. It is obvious in all those cases the property bequeathed or devised was either wholly extinguished or changed into property of a distinctly different nature. . . . What the testator bequeathed in the present case was not an interest in a partnership as such, nor in a corporation as such, but an interest in *his business* as it existed at the time of his death—in his business *enterprise,* whatever its form. Since his interest in the corporation remained the same as his interest in the partnership, and since no change of any kind took place in the operation of the business, no ademption of the legacy resulted. [DECISION FOR APPELLEES]

PROBLEMS

1   The decedent undertook to make and execute her last will and testament. She used two sheets of paper, partly printed and partly written, which she fastened together. The testamentary provisions, with the exception of a residuary clause, were all written upon the first sheet. The second sheet contained the residuary clause, the nomination of executors, the signature of the decedent, and the signatures and attestation of two witnesses. The decedent, sometime thereafter, undertook to alter the will. She accordingly separated the two sheets from one another, totally discarded the first sheet, and in its place substituted another and different sheet which she fastened together with the original second sheet. The contents of the second sheet were unchanged. Is this instrument entitled to be probated as the last will and testament of the decedent?

2 Lewis, a widower with one son, prepared a will leaving most of his property to an old friend, Thomas. Lewis was suddenly taken ill. He asked his son to hurry and bring certain persons to attest the will. The son, intending to prevent the execution of the will and so take as heir, deliberately delayed and returned with only one witness and thereby made the will invalid. Lewis had relied on his son, had not secured other witnesses, so the will was never perfected. Is this will entitled to be probated as the last will and testament of the decedent?

3 The decedent made and delivered to Hall an instrument in the form of an ordinary deed which purported to convey to Hall "all real property, I may possibly own at my death." Could such an instrument take effect as a will?

4 The decedent executed a will. Subsequently thereto he executed a second will which contained a clause expressly revoking all previous wills. He did not, however, destroy the first will. Neither the first nor the second will contained any provision for his only son from whom he was estranged. The decedent and his son were later reconciled. Just before his death he said to witnesses that he wanted his son to have everything, and mutilated the second will. Are the beneficiaries under the first will entitled to have it probated or did the decedent die intestate?

5 Brown called at the office of a public stenographer and carried with him a six-page document in the form of a will written by himself in pencil. He asked the stenographer if she would copy the will, and she replied that she would. She further stated: "Would you like to sign this will in case anything should happen?" He thereupon signed the will in the presence of the stenographer and two other persons, who, at his request, subscribed their names as attesting witnesses. The stenographer subsequently made a typewritten copy of the will, but Brown became ill and died before he had an opportunity to sign it. Which of these wills, if either, should be admitted to probate?

6 Jones bequeathed the sum of $20,000 to each of his two sisters and his stock-in-trade and restaurant business now conducted at No. 10 Main Street to his brother. Jones was not actually engaged in the restaurant business at the time of his death due to a new zoning ordinance, and the stock-in-trade was stored in a public warehouse. After the payment of debts and expenses of administration, there was only $15,000 remaining in the estate of Jones. The two sisters contend that the bequest to the brother had adeemed and that they alone are entitled to inherit the assets of the estate. How do you think the estate should be distributed?

7 Decedent properly executed his will. It was dated January 1, 1954, and a first cousin was named as the sole beneficiary. Another first cousin contests the will, contending that the will had been revoked. This contention is based upon the testimony of several witnesses to the effect that the decedent had said he was going to make another will and gave indications as to what he might do with his land; that the testimony of another witness was to the effect that decedent had said he was revoking an old will and making a new one; that decedent had told the contestant that he had revoked his will; that contestant saw a certain "blueblack manuscript cover" on which decedent had written in his own handwriting "last will and testament"; and a letter written by decedent dated February 6, 1955, in which he stated: "I have changed my mind about my will. I am making a new one." Do you think this evidence is sufficient to prove that the will dated January 1, 1954, had been revoked? Explain how decedent, if he desired to modify or revoke his will, could have avoided this litigation.

8 Decedent, prior to her death, telephoned Mrs. Carrie to inquire whether she and her daughter would sign a paper as witnesses. At the time the witnesses signed their names to the paper it was so folded that they could see nothing except the places where they signed. Neither of the witnesses, therefore, saw the decedent's signature on the paper. After decedent's death, the paper writing was found in decedent's safety deposit box. It was typed, obviously professionally drawn, and on its face in the form of a will, and appeared to be properly signed by the decedent and by the witnesses. What, if anything, will prevent this paper writing from being admitted to probate as the last will and testament of decedent?

57

TRUSTS

A trust, which may be concerned with real or personal property, is a legal relationship by virtue of which one person owns the legal title to property and another person owns the beneficial interest. It is thus seen that the basic characteristic of a trust is the separation of the legal title to the trust property from the benefits emanating therefrom. The state legislatures have enacted statutes with respect to trusts, but the great bulk of the law of trusts is found in the reported decisions. This law is deep and complicated. It should not be presumed, therefore, that the principles of law which follow are final and exhaustive. This chapter, however, does present a general description of the trust and its parts. The principles of law are primarily based on the reported decisions and pertain to (1) express trusts, (2) implied trusts, and (3) trust administration.

EXPRESS TRUST

The minimum requirements necessary to create an express trust are (1) an intent on the part of the settlor, sometimes called the "trustor," to create the relationship, (2) satisfaction of certain formalities, (3) a trustee or trustees, (4) a beneficiary or beneficiaries, (5) a *res,* and (6) a proper trust purpose.

Intent to Create the Trust   A trust will not result unless the settlor intends to create a trust. The intent, moreover, must be something more than a mere subjective intent. It must be coupled with some positive action. An intent reduced to writing or communicated to others will suffice. Although no particular words or phrases are necessary to create the trust, the use of ambiguous and uncertain language in defining the trust elements indicates that no trust was intended. The use of the words "trust" or "trustee" is not conclusive. Some positive and unequivocal language is required. Precatory expressions alone are not positive and unequivocal. These expressions may be found in language which gives the donee an option to use the property for the benefit of another. The settlor must have intended to impose duties on the trustee. An expression which gives the trustee an option to serve or not to serve cannot be said to impose a duty. To illustrate: Brown devises an office building to Smith requesting that he "care for Jones from the income from the building." This is a precatory expression—a wish, a desire, or an entreaty—which is not decisive. It is questionable whether or not a trust was intended. Precatory expressions alone, therefore, are not generally enforceable. They will be enforced, however, if the necessary intent is found in other portions of the instrument or from the surrounding facts and circumstances.

(1) *Modification or Revocation* May the settlor modify or revoke the trust? The general rule tells us that he may not do so unless the trust instrument makes provision for such modification or revocation or unless the settlor makes himself the sole beneficiary of the trust. The doctrine of "worthier title" allows the settlor to change his mind as to how he may enjoy his property. He may, therefore, demand a return of the property from the trustee when he is the sole beneficiary. Suppose, however, that Brown, a very wealthy person, creates a trust for his children. Suppose further that Brown later suffers financial reverses and needs the money for his own use. He could not, in the absence of a power of revocation in the trust instrument, retake the property. There may be a moral obligation on the part of the children to return the property, but no implied power of revocation exists. The courts are also without power to return the property. The courts have no power to change the subject matter of the trust, add new beneficiaries, or alter the shares of the beneficiaries. It is thus quite clear that a settlor who may desire to modify or revoke a trust should include such power of modification or revocation in the trust instrument.

A power peculiar to charitable trusts, however, and which is confined to charitable trusts only, is the cy pres power of a court of equity. A gift which cannot be carried out in the precise manner prescribed by the donor will be transferred to another purpose which seems to be as near to the intention of the donor as existing conditions permit. A favorite illustration is where the trust was for the founding of a home for deaf children to be located on land belonging to the testator. The exact intent of the testator could not be carried out due to the inadequacy of the sum dedicated to the trust. The court allowed the fund to be applied to a similar home already established a few miles distant from the residence of the testator.

(2) *Rule against Perpetuities* The owners of land in feudal England attempted to arrange a succession of estates so that the property would not escheat to or be forfeited to the king, and the king's judges attempted to protect

the interests of the king. The Rule against Perpetuities emerged out of this 200-year struggle. The purpose of the modern rule against perpetuities is to limit the time during which a dead person may control property and to facilitate the marketability of property. The rule, broadly stated, prohibits the creation of future interests which may not become vested—become fixed—within a life or lives in being at the time of the death of the testator or the date of the instrument creating the future interest and twenty-one years thereafter. Nine months—the period of gestation—may be added to the twenty-one years provided gestation actually exists. A last will and testament becomes effective upon the death of the testator, and a deed is effective upon its delivery. The life or lives in being must exist upon the effective date. The life in being must be a human, not a dog or a horse.

The rule has been modified by statute in many of the states, but whether common law or statutory, the rule is a positive mandate of law which must be observed irrespective of any question of the intent of the testator. The rule is uncompromisingly lethal, and a future interest is invalid from the beginning if it violates the period of time established by the rule. Two simple illustrations may help to explain the rule: Suppose Brown, in his last will and testament, devises his estate to the children of his son, Brown, Jr., who reach the age of twenty-one. This is valid because the property will certainly vest no later than twenty-one years after the death of Brown, Jr. The devise would, however, be invalid if it is to the children of Brown, Jr., who reach the age of twenty-two. The vesting might possibly be more than twenty-one years after the death of Brown, Jr. This does not mean that all future interests are invalidated. A vested remainder, for instance, is not subject to the rule. Suppose Brown conveys to Smith for 999 years, and then to Jones. The interest of Jones is valid even though it will not be possessory and absolute for 999 years.

This meager explanation of the Rule against Perpetuities is only intended to demonstrate the scrupulously exacting nature of the rule. It cannot be emphasized too strongly that the rule is exceedingly perplexing and technical. Competent counsel is the only person qualified to draft a trust instrument. It is important, however, that one should be conscious that such a rule does exist.

Recent statutes also exempt trusts for the establishment of pension funds, profit-sharing trusts by corporations for the benefit of their employees from the operation of the Rule against Perpetuities.

(3) *Rule against Accumulations* Is a settlor permitted to direct the trustee to use the income from the trust property for the purpose of increasing the capital of the trust instead of paying the income to the beneficiaries? The common law does not limit the period of accumulations so long as ownership of the accumulated sum is sure to vest within the period of the Rule against Perpetuities. Some of the state statutes vary from the common-law rule, but some statutes allow accumulations for the life of the testator; some allow accumulations for twenty-one years from the date of the trust, some allow accumulations for twenty-one years from the death of the settlor; some pertain to real property only; and some permit accumulations for the benefit of an infant during the period of his minority.

The modern tendency of the statutes, however, is to allow accumulations if the accumulations are limited to the period of the Rule against Perpetuities. Recent statutes also exempt trusts for the establishment of pension funds, profit-sharing trusts by corporations for the benefit of their employees from the operation of the rule against accumulations. It should also be mentioned that the rule is not ordinarily applied to charitable trusts.

Formalities   The statutory requirements necessary to create a trust are not uniform. Some statutes provide that a trust of real property must be created or declared in writing. These statutes have sometimes been interpreted by the courts to mean that the creation of the trust must be contemporaneous with the writing. But other courts have said that a writing made after the trust arose satisfied the statute. The writing, in these circumstances, merely proves the trust. A few states recognize oral trusts in land. But evidence that is clear and convincing is necessary to prove such a trust. It may be stated as a general proposition, therefore, that most states either require that the trust be created in writing or proved by a writing. An informal writing is ordinarily sufficient if it identifies the beneficiary, specifies the trust property, and states the trust purpose. Many trusts are created by will. An instrument which is relied upon as a will to pass the title to the property to a trustee and beneficiary at the death of the testator must be executed in accordance with the formalities of the statutes pertaining to wills.

The Trustee   It is impossible for a trust to operate without a trustee. Equity will not, however, allow a trust to fail for want of a trustee. A court of equity, therefore, will appoint a trustee if the settlor does not name a trustee, if the named trustee dies, or if he declines the position of trust. But there is one instance in which equity will not supply a trustee: equity will respect the intention of the settlor and refuse to appoint a trustee if the settlor designates a trustee whom he thinks is the only person in the world qualified to so act and he states that no one else is to act as trustee.

Almost anyone is capable of being a trustee. The rule may be stated simply: Any person who is capable of taking title to property is capable of being a trustee. This rule embraces natural as well as artificial persons. But it should be pointed out that although infants and mentally incompetent persons are capable of taking title to property, their contracts are voidable. Equity, therefore, will replace them with competent trustees. Artificial persons—corporations—may qualify as trustees provided it is not in contravention of the charter authority. All trust companies, as well as many state and national banks, are authorized to act as trustees. The rule is generally stated that since a nonincorporated association is not an entity and cannot hold title to property, it cannot qualify as a trustee. A few modern decisions, however, recognize a nonincorporated association as a de facto trustee. All the cases acknowledge that the incapacity of the association will not prevent the trust from beginning. This means, therefore, that the trust will not fail. The court will appoint a trustee. The settlor may appoint himself as trustee. He may appoint himself as the sole trustee or one of several trustees. The trustee may be one of several beneficiaries. May the sole trustee be the sole beneficiary? This cannot be. Such a relationship would cause a merger of the equitable and legal titles. The trustee, therefore, would hold the legal title free of the trust.

A person who has been appointed a trustee may accept or reject the position of trust; a person cannot be forced to act as a trustee against his will. But if he does accept or reject the trusteeship, he must accept or reject it in its entirety. He cannot accept the benefits and reject the detriments. A trustee who has once accepted the trust cannot resign at will. The rule is generally stated to be that a trustee may be discharged from the trust by virtue of the trust instrument creating the trust, by an order of a court of equity, or by the general consent of all persons interested in the execution of the trust. The usual method of resignation, however, is by application to the court.

The Beneficiary   A trust without a beneficiary is obviously impossible. But any natural or legal person capable of holding title to property may be a beneficiary. A specific person, commonly referred to by name and address, is the usual type of beneficiary. An infant or an insane person may be designated as a beneficiary. A municipality, the state, or the federal government may be a beneficiary. A private corporation may be a beneficiary. This assumes, however, that the trust property is of a type to which the corporation is authorized by its charter to hold title. It is apparent that neither a cat nor a dog can be a beneficiary for the reason that neither a cat nor a dog can hold title to property. A trust for a cat or a dog, therefore, would generally be invalid in the United States. A familiar way of achieving essentially the same result, however, is to give the cat or dog, coupled with a sum of money, to a friend subject to a reverter for lack of care. This type of gift should not be confused with a charitable trust for animals in general.

The beneficiary must be definitely specified. This does not mean, however, that the beneficiary must be definitely named. A class—my brothers and sisters—is definitely specified. The trust will fail, however, if the trustee has the absolute discretion in selecting a beneficiary. But if his discretion is to select the most worthy from a class—for example, "the most worthy of my grandchildren"—the trust will not fail.

A trust may be created by the settlor without notice to or an acceptance by the beneficiary. But property cannot be thrust upon one without his assent. The beneficiary, therefore, has a choice of accepting or rejecting the trust. In some instances—although it is rather unusual—the beneficiary will elect to reject the trust. The beneficiary may dislike the settlor, or it may be that the trust property is attached with undesirable burdens and liabilities. If he does reject the trust, however, the trust property will revert to the settlor or his heirs. The beneficiary, if he desires the equitable ownership, must accept the trust. But this presents little difficulty because there is a presumption of acceptance until a rejection is made by the beneficiary. A beneficiary who accepts the trust may, unless he is prevented from doing so by a restraining statute or by a provision in the trust instrument, alienate his interest. The interest of the beneficiary may likewise be taken to satisfy his debts.

The *Res* The subject matter of the trust, which is sometimes referred to as the trust property or the trust corpus, is known in legal parlance as the *res*. The *res* may consist of any kind of property of value. It may, therefore, include an interest in land, a mortgage, claims against debtors, money, or shares of stock. But it must be definite and ascertainable. The rule seems simple enough. Reported decisions are nevertheless found in which efforts have been made to prove that a trust existed when the trustor had not dedicated a proper *res*. This difficulty is due to a failure to distinguish, first, a trustee-beneficiary relationship from a debtor-creditor relationship and, secondly, a mere expectancy from ownership.

A definite subject matter signals the distinction between a trustee-beneficiary relationship and a debtor-creditor relationship. The trust property is specific and definite. A debtor, on the contrary, does not ordinarily owe a creditor any specific money. If Brown is trustee for Smith, he owns specific property. It may be a certain farm or a certain number of shares of stock. But it is definite. If Brown borrows $10,000 from Smith, he may repay him with any money. He need not return the identical money that he borrowed. The distinction may seem simple, but it does have important consequences in business affairs. A bankrupt obligor will illustrate this assertion. If Brown owes Smith $10,000 and becomes bankrupt, Smith will be obliged to share pro rata with his fellow creditors the property of Brown. A beneficiary, on the other hand, may take the specific trust property from the bankrupt trustee. This assumes, of course, that the beneficiary can identify the specific trust property.

The rule which declares that the settlor must own the property at the time he creates the trust dispenses with the possibility that a mere expectancy may be the subject matter of the trust. A person who expects to receive property in the future by will or by intestacy has only an expectancy. A purported transfer of the expectancy to a trustee, therefore, imposes no obligation on the expectant heir to transfer the after-acquired property to the trustee. An attempt to create a present trust of property to be acquired in the future, therefore, amounts to no more than an unenforceable promise.

The Trust Purpose Trusts are classified with respect to their purpose as private or charitable and active or passive.

(1) *Private Trusts* A trust which has for its purpose the benefit of described and identified persons is known as a "private trust." A quite common purpose of a private trust is the distribution of the settlor's property among the members of his family and his friends. The provisions of the trust instrument, therefore, ordinarily direct that the income of certain property be paid to certain temporary beneficiaries, that the capital be preserved, and that the trust ultimately be distributed among certain relatives and friends. If the trust is created by the will of the settlor, it is known as a "testamentary trust." If it is created to exist during the life of the settlor, it is known as a "living trust," or "inter vivos trust." This latter type of trust is generally created by a person who wishes to free himself from the burdens of management. The spendthrift trust and the savings-bank trust should be mentioned.

A spendthrift trust is created when the purpose of the settlor is to protect a beneficiary who is incompetent, inexperienced, or immature. This does not mean, however, that the beneficiary must be of subnormal ability. The settlor may desire to protect a person who does not have sufficient business discretion. Suppose Brown transfers to the trustee certain stocks and bonds to hold in trust for his wife. Suppose further that the trust agreement contains a provision that the Trust Company shall pay to the wife the net income of the stocks and bonds, but that the wife shall not have the power to sell or mortgage her right to receive the income, and that the creditors of his wife shall not have the power to reach the income in the hands of the Trust Company. The object of the spendthrift trust is to prevent creditors from reaching the income as it accumulates in the hands of the trustee. The settlor, therefore, cannot name himself as a beneficiary of a spendthrift trust on the theory that to do so would offer too large a possibility for defrauding creditors. The trend today, however, is to limit or qualify the spendthrift trust in favor of creditors. Some statutes provide in substance that the surplus of the income, beyond the sum necessary for education and support of the beneficiary, shall be liable to the claims of creditors of the beneficiary. Some statutes also place a limit on the income that may be received by the beneficiary, or that only a certain amount of the income can be protected by the spendthrift clause.

The savings bank trust, or as it is sometimes called, the "Totten trust" or "poor-man's trust" operates this way: Suppose Brown, Sr., deposits $3,000 in a savings bank to his own credit in trust for his son, Brown, Jr., and states to an officer of the bank that the money remaining in the account is to be delivered to Brown, Jr., upon the death of Brown, Sr. The depositor, Brown, Sr., is the trustee of specific trust property, the beneficiary is clearly named, and Brown, Sr., has communicated his intention to a third person. The principles of law pertaining to the creation of a trust, therefore, lead to the conclusion that a valid trust has been created. The courts, however, have sometimes held that the arrangement does not create a trust. A married man, in a few cases, has created a savings bank trust in favor of others than his wife. The courts have found the trust to be illusory on the reasoning that it was the intent of the husband to deprive his wife of property to which she was entitled. This question sometimes arises: May the settlor withdraw the funds from the deposit in view of the general rule that a trust is irrevocable? The courts have generally held that there is an implied power of revocation of a savings bank trust. The modern prevailing rule is that the trust is a tentative trust, revocable at will, unless the testator completes the gift in his lifetime by some unequivocal act or declaration. The delivery of the passbook to the beneficiary has been held to create an irrevocable trust. The courts, however, will ordinarily sustain the validity of the savings bank trust where the evidence reveals that it was the intent of the testator to create a trust.

A few cases have held the arrangement to be invalid because it was testamentary and did not comply with the statutes pertaining to the execution of wills. The general rule, however, is that the person named as beneficiary is entitled to the balance of the account in existence upon the death of the depositor if the trust has not been revoked. [*In re Petralia's Estate*, p. 759.]

(2) *Charitable Trusts* A trust which has for its purpose the accomplishment of advantages to society is known as a "charitable trust." The purpose of a charitable trust is to bring social benefits to the public at large or to a reasonable segment of the public. Charitable trusts are traditionally extended tax exemptions. The courts, therefore, are careful to scrutinize an alleged charity to ascertain whether it in truth will advance the public interest in a spiritual, mental, or physical manner. The settlor must not embrace within the trust any notion that he intends to further a money-making enterprise. The operation of a hospital unquestionably aids the sick. But a trust to a private hospital which benefits the shareholders is not charitable within the meaning of a charitable trust.

Charitable trusts are created and administered in the same manner as private trusts. A few rules, however, are applicable only to charitable trusts. Some of the state legislatures have enacted statutes which provide that charitable trusts are invalid unless the trust instrument was executed a stated period of time prior to the death of the testator. The period varies from 30 days to one year. The purpose of the statutes is to prevent anxious representatives of charitable organizations from prevailing upon prospective donors during their last days to make bequests to charity when the donors do not have sufficient time to deliberate regarding the needs of their families. It is to be remembered that the rule against accumulations is not ordinarily applied to charitable trusts. Another unique rule is that charitable trusts, unlike private trusts, may be perpetual and of indefinite duration. The Rule against Perpetuities, therefore, is not applicable to charitable trusts. A somewhat similar situation is this: May a settlor of a charitable trust forbid the trustee from alienating the trust *res?* The prevalent view is that he may do so. [*Ohio Soc'y for Crippled Children & Adults, Inc. v. McElroy,* p. 760.]

IMPLIED TRUSTS

The two classes of implied trusts which are generally recognized are resulting and constructive trusts. The distinction between these two classes of trusts is this: A resulting trust arises where the parties have presumably expressed an intent to have a trust exist. A constructive trust arises where the parties have expressed no intent to have a trust exist, but is a creation of the courts to prevent injustice.

Resulting Trusts Resulting trusts, which arise for the purpose of carrying out a presumed intention of the parties, are of two main types: the so-called "purchase-money resulting trust," and those which arise because of a failure of an express trust. The purchase-money resulting trust arises where one person pays the consideration for the conveyance or transfer of real or personal property but has the legal title taken in the name of another person. A common illustration of a purchase-money resulting trust is where Jones, the payor, purchases a farm from Brown and has Smith, who is not a member of Jones's family, named as grantee in the conveyance. The courts presume that Smith is to hold the farm as trustee for

Jones because of the improbability that Brown intended to make a gift of the farm to a stranger. A resulting trust is also presumed where the payor is an uncle or aunt, a brother or sister, a child, or other relative of the grantee. A gift is presumed, however, where the payor is the husband or parent of the grantee. These presumptions may be overcome by oral proof that no gift was intended. The courts refuse to enforce a resulting trust for the payor if the transaction arose out of an illegal bargain, such as an attempt to defraud creditors. Suppose Jones, who is heavily in debt, wishes to purchase a tract of land but is fearful that his creditors might take the land from him if he takes title in his own name. He thereupon purchases the land but has a friend or relative named as grantee in the deed. The creditors, upon proper evidence, would be able to reach the land in the hands of the friend or relative. Purchase-money resulting trusts—although they are apparently quite common—are not recommended. The time and expense involved in litigation when it becomes necessary to prove this type of trust are often tremendous. [*Markert v. Bosley*, p. 761.]

The second type of resulting trust arises where an express private trust has been created gratuitously and it fails for some reason. Suppose the settlor transfers certain stocks and bonds to named trustees for the support and care of his elderly father. The trust would be impossible to carry out on the death of the father. The trust property, therefore, results to the settlor if living, or for his successors if he is dead. The same result would be reached in the case of a charitable trust if the cy pres rule could not be exercised.

Constructive Trusts   A constructive trust arises independently of any actual or presumed intention of the parties. The most obvious example of a constructive trust is where one person acquires by fraud property which rightfully belongs to another person. A clear illustration of a constructive trust is where Brown conveys the title to a certain tract of land to Jones, and Smith fraudulently deletes the name of Jones from the conveying instrument so that the record shows the title to be in Smith. Smith will be deemed to hold the land in trust for Jones who could institute an action for the purpose of conveying the land. A situation which has given rise to much litigation is this: Suppose Brown, the owner of a tract of land, executes a will devising the land absolutely to Jones, but informs Jones that he is expected to hold the land for the benefit of Brown, Jr., and Jones agrees that he will so hold the land. This type of arrangement runs head-on with the statutes prescribing the required formalities that must be observed in the execution of a written will, namely—that property cannot pass at the death of the owner to another without a written instrument, signed by the testator in the presence of witnesses. The courts are, nevertheless, almost unanimous in holding that Jones is a constructive trustee for Brown, Jr. Constructive trusts, however, are not limited to fraud and oral promises. A constructive trust is said to include all those instances when any person acquires property under any circumstances which would make it unjust or inequitable for him to retain it. The courts will deem such person to hold the property in trust for the person who is equitably entitled to it.

TRUST ADMINISTRATION

The administration of a trust estate logically divides itself into the powers and duties of the trustees, the remedies of the beneficiaries for mismanagement, and the termination of the trust.

Powers of the Trustee   The powers of the trustee may be express or implied. The trust instrument creating the trust ordinarily enumerates certain express powers. Although these powers vary considerably with the purpose of the trust, common illustrations are the power to collect the income from the trust property and distribute it to the beneficiaries, and the power to sell the original trust property and to invest the proceeds of the sale in securities. The express power of the trustee may also be derived from a court order. A court of equity, for instance, has the inherent power to direct a sale of any of the trust property whenever it is for the best interests of the beneficiaries to do so. The implied powers of the trustee commonly embrace the power to incur reasonable expenses in connection with the trust estate and the power to compromise and settle claims. The trustee, broadly stated, has those implied powers that are reasonably necessary in order for him to carry out the purpose of the trust.

Duties of the Trustee   The extent of the duties of the trustee depends upon whether the trust is an active trust or a passive trust. An active trust, as distinguished from a passive trust, imposes upon the trustee the duty of taking active measures in the execution of the trust. Property conveyed to a trustee with directions to sell and distribute the property among certain named beneficiaries is an active trust. Active trusts constitute the larger and more important part of the law of trusts.

A passive trust is referred to variously as a "simple," "dry," or "naked" trust. A passive trust requires no action on the part of the trustee beyond turning over money or property to the beneficiary. A trust which makes the trustee a mere depositary of the legal title is a passive trust. A conveyance to one person in trust for another person without anything more being said as to the trust, therefore, results in a passive trust. In a passive trust, the beneficiary is entitled to the *res*.

The duty of the trustee, as a general rule, is to use such care, skill, and prudence as prudent men of discretion and intelligence in like matters employ in their own affairs. But the general rule does not demand that a trustee use extraordinary ability or care. A more specific duty of the trustee is to take possession of the trust property and preserve it from damage. He is also under a duty to make the property productive. This is particularly true when the trust document directs the trustee to pay the income from the trust property to certain beneficiaries for a stated period of time and then to pay the principal to certain other beneficiaries free of the trust. A very important duty of the trustee is that of loyalty to the beneficiaries. The reason for the rule is obvious. Trustees are not only in a position of great confidence and trust but they also have a great degree of control over the property of others. The trustee, therefore, must not use his position for his own personal advantage or for the advantage of a third person.

Illustrations of disloyalty embrace acts such as purchasing the trust property for himself, selling his own property to the trust, granting to himself a lease of the property, and purchasing outstanding claims against the trust property.

Remedies   A beneficiary may, when the trustee is preparing to commit a breach of trust, obtain an injunction against the wrongful act. This is the unusual situation, however, because the beneficiary ordinarily is not aware of the impending wrongful act. A breach of trust is the usual situation. The seriousness of the wrong, therefore, demands that a few of the common remedies be mentioned. A beneficiary in a private trust may, upon the failure of the trustee to carry out the terms of the trust, seek the aid of a court of equity and obtain a decree directing the trustee to do so. A corresponding suit may ordinarily be brought by the attorney general of the state to compel performance of a charitable trust. A beneficiary may bring an action for damages for any injuries caused by a breach of trust. The trustee, therefore, may be compelled to pay into the trust fund the amount of any damages suffered due to his failure to perform any of the duties placed upon him. A beneficiary may bring a suit in equity by virtue of the "tracing the trust fund" doctrine. Suppose Brown is trustee for Smith, and the original trust property is land; suppose further that Brown breaches the trust by selling the land to Jones who knows of the breach; suppose still further that Brown deposits the proceeds of the sale in a bank. Smith may elect to recover the property from Jones, or he may follow the proceeds of the sale into the bank account. This remedy loses its prominence, however, when it is realized that the bona fide purchaser rule may block its application. A beneficiary cannot trace the trust fund into the hands of a bona fide purchaser who purchases the property in good faith and for value. The property may be reached, however, if it is in the hands of a donee.

Termination   The time when a trust terminates ordinarily involves little difficulty because the term is normally fixed by the trust instrument. The term is frequently fixed to last during minority, until the marriage of a stated person, for life, for a period of years, or for some similar standard. If the trust is created for a particular purpose, it will terminate when the purpose has been accomplished. But the death of the settlor, the trustee, or the beneficiary will not cause the trust to terminate unless the trust has been measured by the life of one or the other of these persons.

CASES

In re Petralia's Estate,   204 N.E.2d 1 (Ill. 1965). Action by Dominica Di Maggio, plaintiff, against Leo Petralia, administrator of the estate of Antonio Petralia, defendant. On November 8, 1948, Antonio Petralia opened a savings account in the First National Bank of Chicago, naming himself as "trustee" for the benefit of his daughter, Dominica Di Maggio. There was $17,189.15 in the account at the time of the death of Antonio Petralia, and plaintiff claimed title to the account.

Defendant contended that the form of trust attempted to be executed by the savings account trust is an attempt at a testamentary disposition and not operative due to the failure to conform with the Statute of Wills.

Hershey, Justice: Since the trust agreement was not executed in accordance with the formalities required by the Statute of Wills, the determinative issue becomes whether a valid inter vivos trust was created in that the beneficiary acquired a present interest during the lifetime of the settlor. The defendant argues that since the settlor alone retained the power to withdraw interest and principal from the account during his lifetime, the trust was illusory and testamentary in that the beneficiary never obtained any present interest during the settlor's lifetime.

We conclude that the instrument executed by Antonio Petralia on November 8, 1948, was sufficient to create a valid and enforceable inter vivos savings account trust. In so holding we accept the position adopted by the American Law Institute in sec. 58 of the Restatement (Second) of Trusts:

Where a person makes a deposit in a savings account in a bank or other savings organization in his own name as trustee for another person intending to reserve a power to withdraw the whole or any part of the deposit at any time during his lifetime and to use as his own whatever he may withdraw, or otherwise to revoke the trust, the intended trust is enforceable by the beneficiary upon the death of the depositor as to any part remaining on deposit on his death if he has not revoked the trust. [DECISION FOR PLAINTIFF]

Ohio Soc'y for Crippled Children & Adults, Inc. v. McElroy, 191 N.E.2d 543 (Ohio 1963). Action by The Ohio Society for Crippled Children and Adults (successor to The Ohio Society for Crippled Children, Inc.), plaintiff, against Mark McElroy, attorney general, defendant, requesting the construction of the last will and testament of John E. Harper, which provided in part as follows: "I give my said home farm to The Ohio Society for Crippled Children, Inc., whose address is now 5 W. Broad St., Columbus 15, Ohio, for use as a home for crippled children. This farm is not to be sold or leased but shall be used, operated and farmed by the said Society."

Taft, Justice: We must determine whether the testator not only expressed a desire that the Society would use the farm as a home for crippled children but also expressed an intention to impose a legal obligation upon the Society to so use it.

The words "for use as a home for crippled children," standing alone, would probably be considered as merely precatory and as not imposing any enforceable obligation. However, the following words prohibiting sale or lease are clearly mandatory, state what the testator intended *should not* be done with the farm, add strength to the immediately preceding words and thus tend to indicate his intention as to what *should* be done with the farm. This analysis leads to the conclusion that the testator intended to impose a legal duty upon the Society (1) to use the farm as a home for crippled children and (2) not to sell or lease this farm but to operate it. This conclusion is reinforced by other language in the will:

"In case the said The Ohio Society for Crippled Children, Inc. shall ever be dissolved, then I request that said farm be conveyed by said Society to its successors, if any, and if there be no successors that said farm be conveyed by said Society to some suitable organization for use as a Boys' Home."

Although these words are precatory in nature, they presuppose the existence of an enforceable obligation upon the Society to keep the property until the Society's dissolution and indicate the testator's belief that he had imposed a legal duty upon the Society to use the property as a home for crippled children.

This court has held that, where land is devised upon condition that the devisee shall not sell it, such a restraint is void as repugnant to the devise and contrary to public policy. However, such a restraint on alienation of property conveyed to a trustee to be held for charitable or other public uses will usually be given effect. There are two reasons for this: (1) the interest of the public in encouraging the creation and the continuation of trusts for charitable or public purposes and (2) the power of a court of equity to authorize a prohibited sale where necessary for the proper accomplishment of the charitable or public purposes of the trust, thereby preventing the trust property from being completely inalienable.

Our conclusion is that unless and until a court of equity in appropriate proceedings gives authority to do otherwise, the Society must hold the farm subject to obligations to use it as a home for crippled children, to operate it, and not to sell or lease it. [DECISION FOR DEFENDANT]

Markert v. Bosley,   207 N.E.2d 414 (Ohio 1965). Action by James M. Markert, executor of the estate of Francine M. Markert, to determine the ownership of 200 shares of stock. Fred S. Markert, father of Dorothy and James, and husband of the testatrix, purchased 300 shares of Fundamental Investors, Inc., and 300 shares of Massachusetts Investors Trust. Fifty of the shares of Fundamental and 50 of the shares of Massachusetts were purchased for Dorothy (now Mrs. Bosley) and were paid for out of her own money. Similarly, 50 of the shares of each stock were purchased for James and paid for out of his own money. In each instance, the money was drawn from the child's savings account. The shares were issued to and registered in the name of the mother. A memorandum signed by the testatrix was attached to the certificates stating that the shares belonged to Dorothy and James.

Andrews, Chief Referee: In the present case, Mrs. Dorothy Bosley and James Markert, daughter and son of the testatrix, want the court to declare that they own stock which is registered in the name of the testatrix. From the stipulation, including the exhibits, it is clear that the following determinative facts are "judicially admitted." Fifty shares of each stock were bought with Dorothy's money and for her account, and this stock was her property. Fifty shares of each stock were bought with James's money and for his account, and this stock was his property. All the shares were issued to and registered in the name of Francine M. Markert, the testatrix, for convenience, inasmuch as the children were minors at the time of purchase.

Whether or not the judicially admitted facts, including the exhibits, are sufficient to constitute an express trust need not be decided, for, in their brief, counsel for Mrs. Bosley and James Markert do not claim that an express trust was created. They stress the fact that although the stock in question was issued in the name of the testatrix, it was purchased with the moneys of Dorothy and James. Because of this, they argue, a purchase money resulting trust arose by operation of law, with the mother taking title as trustee for her minor children. Counsel's contention is correct; in fact, the situation here involved is one of the classic examples of a resulting trust. There is nothing in the record to rebut the inference of a resulting trust. [DECISION FOR THE EXECUTOR]

PROBLEMS

1 The decedent, brother of the defendant, by his will gave to his trustees the sum of $75,000 in trust to invest and to pay the net income thereof semiannually to the defendant. The will expressly provided that the payments should be made to the defendant himself personally, "free from the interference or control of his creditors, my intention being that the use of said income shall not be anticipated by assignment." Would the creditors of the defendant be entitled to reach the income of the trust fund by attachment before it is paid to defendant?

2 The decedent died at the age of eighty, leaving a will by which she gave the residue of her property to certain trustees "in trust for the person who makes a home and cares for me in my last days, the principal to be paid over by my trustees to such person within a year after my death." A good friend who had cared for the decedent for many years and who was the only person who had been of any material assistance or comfort to the decedent during that time claims she is entitled to the payment mentioned in the will. The heirs and next of kin claim a resulting trust for their benefit. Decide.

3 Plaintiff and defendant, husband and wife, owned a one-half interest in a motel. Domestic difficulties developed between plaintiff and defendant, and they agreed that plaintiff would find work in a distant town and defendant would continue to conduct the business until it was decided what disposition should be made of the motel. Plaintiff thereupon gave defendant his power of attorney for this purpose. The defendant then sold the one-half interest in the motel to a corporation and received 200 shares of stock in the corporation in payment therefor, taking the title to the shares in her own name. The court held that plaintiff was entitled to 100 shares of the stock. Explain the theory of law upon which this holding was founded.

4 Plaintiff alleged and proved the following facts: Plaintiff purchased a tract of land for $1,000; he borrowed $135 from defendant to make a down payment on the purchase price; as collateral for the loan, he had the seller include defendant's name as a grantee in the deed; defendant's name was to be removed from the deed upon payment of the loan; and the amount due on the loan has been tendered to the defendant which tender has been refused. Plaintiff seeks a reformation of the deed. Defendant contends that he is an owner of one-half of the land. Decide.

5 Mary executed and delivered a deed to an unincorporated charitable organization seeking to convey to the organization a sixty-acre farm. The deed contained a provision that the organization should cultivate the farm and pay to Charles out of the proceeds thereof the sum of $50 per month, beginning one month after Mary's death, for and during the life of Charles. After Mary's death, the organization recorded the deed and commenced cultivating the farm. In a dispute over title to the farm, the court held the deed was invalid because an unincorporated organization is incapable of taking title by deed. The court also refused to admit the deed to probate as a will because it failed to satisfy the statutory requirements of a will. The farm, therefore, descended to the heirs of Mary. Do the heirs take the farm free of any claim on the part of Charles? How could Mary have avoided this litigation?

6 Aaron bequeathed $25,000 to Jim to hold in trust for Mary, the daughter of Aaron. Jim deposited the money in the First Bank in the name of "Jim, in trust for Mary." Jim was quite anxious to open a savings account for his son, James, and he therefore withdrew $5,000 from the account of the trust estate and deposited the money in The Savings and Loan Association in the name of James. Jim fully intended to repay the trust when he received the money from the sale of some property which he intended to sell in a few weeks. What are the rights, if any, of Mary?

7 John Brown and Mary Brown, husband and wife, were the owners of Blackacre as tenants by the entirety. John Brown executed his will by the terms of which he devised and bequeathed all of his interest in Blackacre to Hunt to hold in trust for James, his son by a former marriage. John Brown died, and James brought a suit in equity asking the court to determine his rights under the will. How would you decide the case?

8 Mary Jones and John Jones were husband and wife. John Jones purchased a 120-acre farm from Wells for $25,000, and he requested Wells to name Mary Jones as grantee in the deed conveying the farm. Wells thereupon prepared the deed naming Mary Jones the grantee, and the deed was properly recorded. The creditors of John Jones attempted to attach the land to satisfy their judgment liens. The creditors contend that there is a purchase-money resulting trust in favor of John Jones. Do you agree with this contention?

Part

12

INSURANCE, SURETYSHIP, GUARANTY, BANKRUPTCY

58

THE INSURANCE CONTRACT

Insurance in the United States was at first influenced to a great extent by the decisions of the English courts. At the present time, however, insurance is regulated by the various states. Regulation by the federal government is only incidental. All of the states have established insurance departments under the jurisdiction of an official generally known as the "insurance commissioner," and all of the states have enacted statutes for the regulation of the insurance business. These statutes and the judicial interpretations of the statutes vary greatly. This leads to the inevitable conclusion that the law of insurance is not uniform. The statutes and the court decisions are numerous—indeed so numerous that it is impossible, because of space limitations, to do little more than present some of the fundamental principles of the law of insurance. Particular attention will be given in this chapter to (1) the types of insurance, risks, and policies, (2) agents, brokers, and representatives, (3) the formation of the contract, (4) representations and warranties, (5) assignment, (6) duration and termination, and (7) subrogation.

TYPES OF INSURANCE, RISKS, AND POLICIES

A contract of insurance is fundamentally a risk-bearing contract. The types of insurance, the risks embraced, and the kinds of policies are numerous. No attempt will be made, therefore, to do anything more than mention the most important and usual ones.

Types of Insurance The older forms of insurance are called marine, fire, life, and accident policies. Distinctive names that indicate the nature of the risk involved, however, have been given to the vast number of different types of insurance, such as hail insurance, automobile insurance, burglary insurance, theft insurance, and the like. The nature of accident and marine insurance merits particular mention.

(1) **Accident Insurance** Accident policies not only provide for payment of a principal sum as payment for loss of life, they also frequently provide payment of a percentage of the principal sum for loss of a limb, such as a hand, foot, or eye. These policies as well as life policies with double indemnity benefits, however, cover only specified types of accidents and exclude specified hazards. The provisions in the policies abound in conditions, exceptions, and exclusions. They quite generally exclude death resulting from suicide, injury and death resulting from disease and bodily infirmity, intentionally self-inflicted injuries, and declared or undeclared war. The courts have gone to great lengths in an effort to interpret these policies. A few factors to be considered by the courts in determining whether recovery will or will not be allowed, however, are the physical condition of the insured at the time of the injury or death, the medical testimony as to the nature and cause of the injury or death, the rules of law in the particular jurisdiction, and the language of the policy. [*Kukuchka v. Imperial Cas. & Indem. Co.*, p. 780.]

(2) **Marine Insurance** Marine insurance, as a general rule, insures against loss or damage to ship, cargo, or freight. The loss or damage covered is a matter of interpreting the language of the policy. War risks, for instance, may or may not be covered. Considerable weight, however, is given to usage. Coverage will ordinarily include capture and seizure, theft, barratry, jettison, and perils of the sea. Barratry is the willful misconduct of the master or crew which is prejudicial to the owner, such as mutiny of the crew. Jettison is the intentional act of throwing goods overboard to lighten a vessel in danger of being lost or wrecked. Perils of the sea are those things which are unusual and fortuitous, such as collision with another vessel. Coverage does not include ordinary wear and tear of the hull, rigging, and machinery. The insurer also is not liable if the vessel was not seaworthy at the beginning of the voyage, if there is a voluntary deviation from the agreed voyage, or if the vessel engages in an illegal venture.

Types of Risks Insurance classified in terms of what it protects will serve to indicate the many and varied risks for which insurance is obtainable today:

(1) **Loss of Property Interests** Some of the most common kinds of insurance which offer protection to property are those which insure the property against direct loss or impairment due to fire, lightning, tornado, hail, earthquake, strikes and riots, theft, and aviation risks.

(2) **Loss of Earning Power** The major types of insurance which offer protection against loss of earning power are those which insure the individual against accidental injury, ill health, old age, business interruption, and unemployment. Life insurance likewise is a protection against loss of earning power caused by death.

(3) ***Liability for Loss***   Liability insurance embraces all policies whereby the insurer assumes the risk of liability for damage to the person or property of a third person. This definition is broad enough to include indemnity contracts for money paid, under which an action does not ordinarily lie against the insurer until the insured has paid the injured party. Particular kinds of liability insurance include aviation liability insurance, whereby the owner of an aircraft is insured against loss on account of having to pay damages for injuries to persons or property inflicted by such aircraft, and contractor's liability insurance, whereby contractors are insured against liability for injuries in connection with the performance of their contracts.

Kinds of Life Insurance Policies   The most usual kinds of life insurance policies are as follows:

(1) Ordinary life insurance is sometimes referred to as "whole life" or "regular life." The terms of this type of policy require the insured, or someone in behalf of the insured, to pay a fixed premium at regular intervals throughout the life of the insured. The beneficiary is entitled to receive a stipulated sum only upon the death of the insured.

(2) A "limited-payment" life policy is similar to the ordinary life policy in that a stipulated sum is payable to the beneficiary upon the death of the insured. The difference between the two types of policies is that the premiums are payable only during a limited period, such as ten, fifteen, or twenty years.

(3) An "endowment" policy is similar to the limited-payment policy in that premiums are payable only during a limited period. It differs from the limited-payment policy in that a stipulated sum is payable to the insured when he reaches a given age or to the named beneficiary upon the decease of the insured if that occurs earlier.

(4) "Term" insurance means that a stipulated sum is payable only in the event of the death of the insured during a specified term, such as two, five, or ten years.

Kinds of Property Insurance Policies   The most usual kinds of property insurance policies are:

(1) A "valued" policy is one in which a definite valuation is placed upon the subject matter of the insurance. Such a valuation, in the absence of fraud or mistake, will be paid in case of total loss of property.

(2) An "unvalued" policy is one in which a certain fixed sum is written on the face of the policy, the sum being the maximum limit of recovery in case of destruction. The insurer, however, only pays the actual cash value of the property as determined at the time of the loss.

(3) A "floater" policy covers property without regard to its location at the time of the loss. This kind of policy is issued to cover property subject to frequent change in location or quantity.

(4) A "time" policy grants insurance from one specified time to another, for instance upon a house for the period from January 1, 1963, to January 1, 1964.

AGENTS AND BROKERS

The general rules of the law of agency are applicable to the law of insurance. Peculiar to the law of insurance, however, is the distinction between (1) brokers and agents and (2) general and special agents.

Brokers and Agents Distinguished A broker solicits business from the public generally, and is not under employment from one particular insurance company. He is a middleman between the insured and the insurer. He procures insurance for those persons who apply to him by selecting some particular company. He is, therefore, considered the agent of the insured although he receives a commission from the insurer with whom the insurance is placed. He is an agent of the insured in procuring the insurance, but he may be the agent of the insurer for the purpose of delivering the policy and collecting the premium. It is generally held that the broker ceases to be an agent of the insured when the contract is completed. An agent is under employment from the particular insurance company that he represents. It is clear, therefore, that every broker is also an insurance agent, but every insurance agent is not also a broker.

General and Special Agents Distinguished An agent who acts under general instructions and who has authority to conduct the business of his company within a state or district is properly referred to as a "general agent." Such an agent has broad apparent authority: He has authority to pass upon and accept risks, and execute and deliver policies of property insurance; he has authority to change the terms of a policy; and he has authority to waive a nonwaiver provision in the policy. A general agent is sometimes given authority to accept applications and issue and deliver accident policies covering the life of the insured. As a general rule, however, a life insurance agent is not authorized to accept risks for the insurer. The underwriting powers are ordinarily reserved for the home office. But a general life insurance agent may appoint subagents, submit applications for insurance, and collect premiums in a specific locality.

A special agent is a representative of the insurer who has been given authority to do some special act for the insurer. The title "special agent" means an agent who has limited power to contract, and such power is usually to be exercised in a limited geographical area. The special agent is ordinarily authorized to induce persons to make applications for insurance, forward the applications to the home office, deliver the policies, and collect the first premium. He may not ordinarily collect anything in payment of the premium except cash, and he may not ordinarily extend the time of payment of the premiums or modify the terms of the contract.

FORMATION OF THE CONTRACT

The formation of the contract of insurance differs very little from any other contract. The contract must contain all the essential elements of a contract. The offer in life insurance contracts is ordinarily made in the form of an application by the insured. The offer in contracts of insurance other than life is frequently made by the insurer. The terminology used in the law of insurance differs from that used in the traditional contract. The contract itself is described as a "policy"; the consideration moving from the insured is called a "premium"; and the parties to the contract are called the "insurer" and the "insured." Peculiar to the formation of insurance contracts is (1) the consideration, (2) the parties to the contract, (3) an insurable interest, and (4) the completion of the contract.

Consideration   Life insurance is essentially a cash transaction. The insured is almost invariably required to pay the first premium before the insurance takes effect. The prepayment of premiums in insurance contracts other than life, however, is not always required as a condition to the validity of the contract. The risk attaches immediately in most fire, casualty, and marine insurance coverages.

Parties to the Contract   The insurer is the underwriter or insurance company who undertakes to indemnify another by a contract of insurance. The insured is the person whose life or property is insured.

(1) *The Insurer*   Although the insurance business today is carried on mostly by corporations, the government as well as some fraternal organizations afford some insurance protection. The following are usual types of insurers:

(a) *Stock Company*   This type of insurance company issues shares of stock owned by shareholders. The holders of the shares receive the profits of the business in the form of dividends. The stock company writes most of the fire and casualty insurance in the United States.

(b) *Mutual Company*   The mutual company is made up of all the policy holders of the corporation in much the same manner as the stock company is made up of its shareholders. The members are both the insurers and the persons insured. These companies require that fixed premiums be paid for the purpose of accumulating a fund to assure the performance of their insurance contracts. The larger part of life insurance policies is now written by the mutual companies.

(c) *Mutual Benefit Associations*   Some fraternal associations, clubs, and benevolent organizations issue benefit insurance to their members. These associations are very similar to the mutual company but are ordinarily governed by different statutory regulations.

(d) *Government Insurance*   Both the federal and the state governments have enacted statutes providing for some particular kinds of insurance. Social security is a form of insurance. The federal government also now issues life insurance to members of the Armed Forces and to veterans; crop insurance to farmers; mortgage insurance to protect those who lend money on mortgages for the construction, purchase, and repair of houses and buildings; deposit insurance to protect depositors in banks and subscribers in building and loan associations.

The role of the state government as an insurer varies from state to state. A few states have a life insurance plan; some have nonoccupational benefits; and many have unemployment systems.

(2) **The Insured**   Any person, as a general rule, may become a party to a contract of insurance provided the person (a) is competent to enter into a contract and (b) possesses an insurable interest in the subject of the insurance. The decisions, however, are not entirely in agreement in regard to an infant. The vast majority of the decisions hold that a contract of insurance is not a contract for necessaries and that the policy is voidable. In most states, therefore, the infant may disaffirm the policy and recover the premiums paid. A few courts allow a deduction for the insurance protection received in the meantime. Many state statutes have, in effect, removed the disabilities of minority as to life insurance contracts. These statutes specifically authorize infants over a certain age, say fifteen or sixteen, to take out insurance payable to a limited class of beneficiaries, such as a mother or father.

Insurable Interest   It is a well-settled rule of insurance law that the insured must have an insurable interest in the subject matter of the insurance contract. This rule of law not only eliminates the possibility of an insurance contract's being classified as a mere wager, but it also removes the temptation to destroy the life or property of others inherent in a wager. What is an insurable interest? It is, broadly and simply stated, that interest which the law demands a person have in the thing or person insured. A more specific answer to the question necessitates distinguishing between property insurance and life insurance.

(1) **Property Insurance**   Any person who has such an interest in property that its destruction will cause him a pecuniary loss has an insurable interest therein. The title may be legal or it may be equitable. The insured may be an owner of the property; the insured may be a person who is responsible for the care and custody of the property of another, such as a trustee or bailee; or the insured may be a lienholder, such as a mortgagee or the holder of a mechanic's lien. A general creditor, however, would not have an insurable interest in the property of his debtor.

A few cases have held that the insurance company is liable for the loss when the policy was issued to a person who did not have a present insurable interest, but a reading of these cases reveals that the insured had a reasonable prospect of becoming the owner and did become the owner before the loss occurred. The vast majority of the cases hold that the insurable interest must exist at the time the policy is issued and at the time the loss occurs.

(2) **Life Insurance**   It is quite clear that every person has an insurable interest in his own life, and it is generally agreed that the insured may name anyone he desires as his beneficiary. Precisely what constitutes an insurable interest in the life of another person, however, is not quite as clear. There are two lines of cases which define such an interest. One line of cases places the insurable interest on a relationship basis. It seems unquestioned today that a husband has an insurable interest in the life of his wife, and that the wife has an insurable interest

in the life of her husband. But relationship by marriage alone, except that of husband and wife, is not sufficient. It has been held in a few cases that close blood relationship, such as brother and sister, was sufficient. As a general rule, however, the relationship must be coupled with some pecuniary interest. The other line of cases provides in substance that any reasonable expectation of benefit or advantage from the continued life of another creates an insurable interest in such life. According to this line of cases, a creditor may insure the life of his debtor, and a corporation may insure the life of its officers.

(3) *Marine Insurance* The insured must possess an insurable interest when the contract is created, or the insurable interest must arise thereafter, in order for the contract to be valid. A marine policy is never binding if the ship insured was already lost at the inception of the policy. If the insurer had expressly agreed to be bound "lost or not lost," the policy would be valid and retroactive.

The Binding Slip A binder is sometimes referred to as an "interim receipt"; it is sometimes referred to as a "memorandum of an agreement" for insurance; and it is sometimes referred to as a "binding slip." A binder, irrespective of the terminology used, is a temporary contract of insurance looking toward the actual, subsequent issuance of the policy. A binder will not express all the elements of the insurance contract. It does, however, carry with it those terms and conditions of the policy ordinarily used by the company to cover similar risks. The legal effect of a binder—unless and until it is revoked—is to protect the insured if the loss insured against occurs before the policy is written. Life insurance companies are generally not willing to grant temporary coverage to the applicant. One type of binding receipt prevailing today is the one which affords immediate coverage provided the applicant has paid the first premium, or a part of it, and is insurable at the time the receipt is delivered. Another type of binding receipt is the one which becomes effective when the application is acted upon favorably. This type, when it is acted upon favorably, dates back to the time of the application.

Completion of the Contract It seems more appropriate to treat separately the rules with respect to contracts for (1) life insurance and (2) property insurance.

(1) *Life Insurance* The parties may clearly express an intent to be bound prior to delivery of the policy, but, in the absence of such an agreement, the delivery of the policy by the insurer to the insured ordinarily completes the formation of the contract. Conceding the rule, however, does not mean that there must be an actual manual transfer of the policy. The courts have had no hesitancy in applying the doctrine of constructive delivery—which may be shown by acts or words—to contracts of insurance. All courts would probably hold that the placing of an unconditional policy in the possession of the agent of the insured, or some person for the benefit of the insured, is an act showing an intent to deliver the policy to the insured. The courts, by an application of this reasoning, are almost consistent in holding that an unconditional policy is delivered when the insurer executes and mails the policy to the insured.

Difficult problems arise, however, when the insurer puts the policy in the possession of the local agent of the insurer to be delivered to the insured. The problem is rather easily solved when nothing remains to be done except the simple ministerial duty of delivery. The courts say, in these circumstances, that the agent of the insurer holds the policy for the insured. The policy, therefore, is said to be delivered and the insurance operative when the insurer mails the policy to its local agent. Most life insurance policies and applications, however, contain a clause prescribing three conditions that must occur before the contract of insurance is consummated: Delivery of the policy, payment of the first premium, and good health of the applicant. Most of the cases which have denied liability, therefore, have been for reasons other than nondelivery of the policy. [*Locke v. Prudence Mut. Cas. Co.,* p. 781.]

(2) *Property Insurance* It is not essential that a policy of property insurance be delivered to the insured before the contract is complete. It is also not essential that the contract be in writing. An oral contract insuring against loss or damage to property may be valid unless a statute or the charter or bylaws of the insurance company prohibit oral contracts of insurance. It is to be remembered, however, that oral contracts are sometimes difficult to prove. The problem is frequently solved by the use of a binder giving temporary insurance until it is superseded by the issuance of the policy or until the risk is rejected by the insurer.

REPRESENTATIONS AND WARRANTIES

Representations are statements made by the applicant to the prospective insurer concerning facts and conditions on the basis of which the insurance policy is written. The statements may be made orally or in writing; they are frequently made in response to questions asked by the insurer as a part of the application for insurance. Warranties are a part of the contract of insurance, and are statements concerning facts the truth of which is made a condition precedent which must be fulfilled before the insurer is liable.

A reading of the decisions reveals that, as a general rule, a false representation will avoid a contract of insurance when it is material. This is generally true irrespective of the intent with which the representation was made. An applicant who states that a dwelling is constructed of concrete block when it is constructed of lumber would have made a material misrepresentation. The insurer undoubtedly would rely on this statement in entering into the contract. An applicant who states, however, that a dwelling is painted cream color when it is painted white would not have made a material misrepresentation. The insurer undoubtedly would have entered into the contract irrespective of the color of the paint.

The chief distinction between representations and warranties is that representations are inducements to inter into the contract; warranties are a part of the contract. The insurer must prove representations to be material; warranties are conclusively presumed to be material.

Affirmative and Promissory Warranties Warranties are affirmative if they represent facts that exist at the time they are made. They are promissory—sometimes referred to as continuing—if they represent that certain things must be complied with in the future. Are the statements "watchman on premises at night" and dwelling "occupied by family" affirmative or promissory warranties? Most courts have held such statements to be affirmative warranties. This means that the insurer would be liable even though there was no watchman on the premises at night or the dwelling was unoccupied at the time of a loss subsequent to the issuance of the policy. Modern policies, however, use language to require continuing compliance. Burglary policies usually have a provision that a "watchman will make hourly rounds." Such a provision is obviously worded as a promissory warranty.

Statutory Enactments   Statutes have been enacted in most states which moderate the harshness of the common-law rules of warranty. This does not mean that the common-law rules have been entirely abolished. The statutes themselves are sometimes limited to life or fire policies, and the judicial interpretations reveal that the common-law rules have not always been abolished. The statutes vary greatly, but they may be grouped under two broad general headings.

(1)   *Statements Made Representations*   The most widely enacted statute provides in substance that all statements by the insured are to be deemed representations and not warranties. The judicial interpretations of this type of statute generally hold that false statements in the nature of warranties which are innocently made will avoid the policy only if they are material. Statements in the nature of warranties which are fraudulently made, however, will avoid the policy irrespective of their materiality.

(2)   *Materiality of Statements*   Some statutes provide in substance that no misstatement, if made in good faith and without fraud, shall avoid the policy unless it relates to a matter material to the risk. This does not change the common-law rule with respect to representations.

Waiver and Estoppel   The words "waiver"—the voluntary relinquishment of a known right—and "estoppel"—an impediment raised by the law which prevents a person from alleging or denying certain facts in consequence of his own previous allegations or acts—are essentially used synonymously by the majority of the courts in insurance cases. The insurer, were it not for waiver and estoppel, would normally be entitled to escape payment under a policy because of the defense of misrepresentation or breach of a warranty condition on the part of the insured. The facts of the particular case, however, may reveal that the agent of the insurer has waived the defense. The insurer is then held to be estopped from taking advantage of the defense.

Suppose a life policy contained a condition that the policy shall not take effect until the policy is delivered and the first premium is paid in cash. The insurer could set up this condition as a defense to an action to recover on the policy if the policy were not delivered and the first premium were not paid in cash. Suppose further that Brown secures a policy containing such a condition but offers to execute a promissory note payable in one month in payment of the first premium.

Suppose still further that an authorized agent of the insurer accepts the note and delivers the policy. The court would undoubtedly hold that the defense had been waived. [*Fidelity & Guar. Ins. Underwriters v. Gregory*, p. 782.]

(1) *Nonwaiver Clause* The insurer frequently attempts to limit instances of waiver by including in the policy or the application a nonwaiver clause. The effect of these clauses is frequently decided on the authority of the agent. A common nonwaiver clause provides, in effect, that no representative of the insurer shall have authority to waive any condition of the policy, except in writing, written on the policy. The courts generally hold that these clauses have no effect in restricting the authority of a general agent who has full power to contract for insurance on behalf of the insurer during the time the contract is being entered into.

(2) *Entire-Contract Clause* Many applications for life insurance contain an agreement that the applicant has read the statements in the application and that they are correct. Many contracts for insurance also contain an entire-contract provision, and some states have enacted entire-contract statutes. These statutes provide in substance that the policy and the application attached thereto constitute the entire contract between the parties. In interpreting these provisions, the courts generally hold that the insured is under a duty to read his policy and the copy of the attached application.

(3) *Parol-Evidence Rule* The parol-evidence rule which excludes prior or contemporaneous evidence which would vary or contradict a completely written contract has not been applied rigidly by the courts with respect to contracts of insurance. The custom of the insured to rely on the skill and good faith of the agent of the insurer to fill out the application has undoubtedly influenced the courts in reaching a decision. Many courts, therefore, permit the insured to introduce evidence to support an estoppel against the insurer. The courts will not, however, permit the insured to show by parol evidence that the agent of the insurer was told one thing and that the agent placed a different or false answer in the application if the entire-contract provision is applicable or if the application contains an agreement that the applicant has read the statements and that they are correct. The courts will, however, permit parol evidence in support of an equitable estoppel in a proper case. Many of the cases involve not only a failure on the part of the insured to read the policy but also fraudulent conduct on the part of the agent of the insurer.

Concealment The general rule of the law of contracts is that, in the absence of a duty to speak, a person is not required to disclose his superior information. An exception to the rule prevails when applied to contracts of insurance. In marine insurance, concealment exists unless the insured discloses to the insurer every material fact that is known or ought to be known by the insured. This is true even though the nondisclosure happened through mistake, forgetfulness, or inadvertence. It is also true even though the insured was unaware that the fact was material. In contracts of insurance other than marine, concealment exists only when the insured knew the fact concealed was material and he concealed the fact with an intent to defraud the insurer. The prospective purchaser who knows that there is a valuable mine on the land of another is not under a duty to disclose his superior knowledge. The rule is otherwise with insurance. A prospective insured who knows that his dwelling is on fire is under a duty to disclose his superior knowledge to the insurer when applying for a policy of fire insurance over the telephone. This illustration is so obvious it is bordering on the ridiculous. In other situations not so obvious, the test of materiality is this: Would the insurer with knowledge of the concealed fact have rejected the risk? The concealed fact is material, therefore, if the insurer would not have entered into the contract knowing the concealed fact. The fact need not increase the risk nor contribute to the loss. The test of fraud is this: Did the insured believe the fact to be material? The validity of the policy is not affected if the insured did not conceal any fact that, in his own mind, was material.

ASSIGNMENT

A contract of insurance is essentially a personal contract between the insured and the insurer. The assignment of an insurance policy, therefore, is subject to the rules pertaining to the assignment of ordinary contracts. Some rules have developed, however, which are peculiar to the assignment of an insurance policy.

Life Insurance   Policies of industrial and group life insurance ordinarily expressly prohibit the assignment of the policy without the consent of the insurer. It is also true in those states which have community property laws that the premiums are most often paid with community funds. The insured, therefore, may not be able to divest the wife of all interest in the proceeds. The wife, as between a new beneficiary or an assignee, can ordinarily claim a share of the proceeds. In the absence of some prohibition against assignment, however, a life policy being a contingent chose in action may be assigned by the insured without the consent of the insurer.

The assignment of the life policy probably more often takes the form of a conditional assignment by way of a pledge to secure a loan or to secure a debt already existing. The assignee, as between the insurer and the assignee, is entitled to the whole of the proceeds. An absolute assignment in good faith to purchasers for value, or by way of gift, is now also generally accepted in the majority of the states. An insured who has procured a policy and finds himself unable to pay the premiums, therefore, may assign the policy to a stranger who has no insurable interest in the insured. The assignee, upon the death of the insured, is entitled to the face value of the policy.

May the insured assign the policy without the consent of the beneficiary? He may not under the vested interest rule. This rule, which formerly prevailed, placed the ownership of the policy in the beneficiary. The rule has been superseded by modern life insurance policies which ordinarily reserve to the insured the power to change the named beneficiary without the consent of the beneficiary. The beneficiary, under such policies, takes a mere expectancy rather than a vested right.

The standard life policies usually recognize that an assignment of the policy may be made, but does not contain any provision as to whether the revocable beneficiary should join in the assignment. Is the claim of the assignee superior to that of the named beneficiary? The majority of the cases hold in favor of the assignee. This is just another one of those situations where litigation could be avoided by revoking the named beneficiary and making the policy payable to the insured and his personal representatives and assigning the policy to the creditor. The assignment of an insurance policy may not be used under any circumstances as a cloak to hide an unlawful transaction. [*Albrent v. Spencer*, p. 782.]

Marine Insurance   Marine policies, by the custom of merchants, are ordinarily assignable. The policy, however, does not run with the vessel without the consent of the insurer. The seller of a vessel is required to assign the policy to the buyer at the time of the sale.

Property Insurance   Policies, other than marine, which grant compensation for loss or damage to property cannot be assigned before loss without the consent of the insurer. This rule is based on the reasoning that the risk varies with the person protected. It follows that the insurer cannot be forced to accept a new hazard which may be greater than the old one. The insured may, however, assign a fire policy as collateral security. In these circumstances, the insured retains an interest in the property insured. An insured, for example, may assign his policy to a person who has acquired a mortgage on the property. The insured, in case of loss, is entitled to any surplus of the proceeds of the insurance remaining after the payment of the mortgage debt. The proceeds of the policy which have become a fixed claim by the occurrence of a loss may be assigned in the same manner as any other chose in action. The general law of contracts as modified by statute is applicable to such assignments.

DURATION AND TERMINATION

Peculiar to the duration and termination of insurance contracts are the nonforfeiture, reinstatement, and cancellation provisions, and the "at and from" clause in marine insurance.

Nonforfeiture Provisions   A policy of life insurance is said to have lapsed if the payment of the premiums is discontinued. Practically all life insurance policies have provisions, either voluntarily on the part of the insurer or in accordance with a statutory mandate, which are designed to protect the equity of the insured if the policy lapses. These provisions are referred to as "nonforfeiture provisions." Ordinarily they are not included in a term policy. The statutory provisions now prevailing in a number of states provide that a lapsed policy with a reserve—fund set aside to meet policy obligations when they mature—entitles the insured to one or all of the following options: (1) to claim the cash surrender value of the policy, that is, the reserve value which is ordinarily fixed at a lower figure; (2) to have extended insurance, that is, to have the policy continue in force for a stated period of time or for a time equal to that which the reserve, as a single premium, would purchase; or (3) to have a paid-up policy equal to the amount of paid-up insurance which the reserve would purchase.

Reinstatement Clause   Life insurance policies, as a general rule, contain a provision which permits the insured to reinstate his policy after lapse for nonpayment of premiums. The insured, as a condition of reinstatement, is ordinarily required to furnish evidence of "good" or "sound" health satisfactory to the insurer. Policy provisions sometimes state definitely that the reinstatement will not be effective until approved by the insurer. The provisions of many policies as well as statute provisions are vague as to the date when the reinstatement policy shall become effective. Many courts, in interpreting this provision, have held that the reinstatement is effective as soon as the insured has met the policy requirements as to reinstatement. Many courts, however, have held that the reinstatement is not effective until the application for reinstatement has been approved by the insurer or until after a reasonable time for approval. May the insurer defend an action on the basis of fraud or misrepresentation if the reinstatement application is not attached to the policy? The courts are divided, but most of the courts have held that the insurer may do so. A few courts have held otherwise. A reinstatement clause is also found in policies other than life, but it is not of such great importance as in the life policy.

Cancellation   Life insurance policies do not contain a provision giving the insurer the option to cancel the policy, because the insurer selected the risk when the contract was entered into. Policies other than life, however, frequently give the insurer the option to cancel the policy upon giving notice to the insured. This option operates so as to give the insurer control over the risk. Suppose the risk was a dwelling with adequate fire protection. Suppose further that all fire protection was removed so as to leave the building unprotected. The insurer would no doubt feel that such removal increased the risk. Most fire policies give the insurer the right to cancel the policy by giving five days' notice to the insured. Such cancellation entitles the insured to the unearned portion of the premium. The insured may likewise terminate the policy at any time by surrendering the policy. Such surrender, however, entitles the insured to the return of the premiums paid on the customary short-rate basis. This merely means that the premiums are computed on a slightly higher basis than they are for the full term of the policy.

"At and From" Clause   A marine policy which uses the words "at and from" a stated port to another port attaches and becomes effective while the vessel is still in the harbor. A policy which reads "from" becomes effective at the moment of sailing. A voyage policy protects the vessel and cargo from the beginning of and until the destination although there may be delays. It is usually agreed, however, that the policy shall terminate after the vessel moors in the destination harbor for twenty-four hours in good safety.

SUBROGATION

Property Insurance The right of subrogation is the right of the insurer, upon paying for a loss, to recover from the third person who caused the loss. To illustrate: Suppose damage is done to the automobile of the insured. The insurer, upon paying the loss, may collect the amount paid to the insured under the policy from the person who caused the loss. The right of subrogation is applicable to all cases in which the loss for which the insurer is liable was caused by the tortious conduct of some third person. Property destroyed by fire and stolen property are pronounced illustrations. A word of warning: The insured who, prior to payment of the loss by the insurer, releases the tort-feasor will extinguish his claim against the insurer. The insured who, after payment of the loss, releases the tort-feasor will also lose his right to retain the insurance money. This is for the reason that such release extinguishes the right of subrogation of the insurer.

Life Insurance The right of subrogation has no application to life or health insurance, personal injury, or death by accidental means. Workmen's compensation acts, however, ordinarily provide that the insurer-carrier, upon paying the employee the compensation provided under the act, shall be subrogated to the claim of the employee against any third person liable for the injury suffered.

CASES

Kukuchka v. Imperial Cas. & Indem. Co., 237 F. Supp. 117 (Wyo. 1965). Action by Pearl Kukuchka, plaintiff, against Imperial Casualty & Indemnity Company, defendant, to recover the sum of $25,000 allegedly due and owing as a result of the death of the insured.

The insured, deceased husband of the plaintiff, was killed while he was driving his 1961 Chevrolet truck equipped with a cab chassis and stock rail; he was returning home after having used the truck to haul his cattle to the Sales Ring.

The defendant agreed to pay indemnity to the insured provided that the injury was sustained "while in, operating, entering or alighting from any private passenger automobile licensed as such by the State or County of its registry." Defendant denies liability on the ground that the insured was not killed while he was driving a private passenger automobile licensed as such.

Kerr, District Judge: As sympathetic as one is to the obvious desire of the insured to protect his beneficiary, this court is still obligated to respect the express terms and conditions of the insurance contract. It is not enough to bring the insured's truck within the definition of "Automobile," but it must also come within the further condition prescribed by the policy that it be a "private passenger automobile licensed as such." There is no ambiguity here; both conditions of the contract must exist before the defendant is obligated to indemnify the loss sustained by the insured. Where the terms of a policy are clear and unambiguous they must be enforced according to the plain ordinary meaning of the terms agreed upon by the parties just the same as are terms of other contracts.

In the light of the undisputed facts and circumstances in this case, and in accordance with the explicit terms of the insurance policy, I am constrained to find that the plaintiff is not entitled to recover the proceeds of the insurance policy for the reasons that the policy did not cover the insured's truck, which was not a private passenger automobile licensed as such by Sheridan County or the State of Wyoming. [DECISION FOR DEFENDANT]

Locke v. Prudence Mut. Cas. Co.,   172 So. 2d 351 (La. 1965). Action by Louise P. Locke, administratrix of the estate of her deceased husband, plaintiff, against Prudence Mutual Casualty Company, defendant, to recover on a policy of health and accident insurance.

Decedent applied for a policy of health and accident insurance with the defendant on January 8, 1963. At that time, the decedent also issued a check for $97.50 for the first annual premium. The decedent was confined to the hospital five days after applying for the policy, and his death occurred at the hospital on March 10, 1963. The defendant refunded the premium on March 27, 1963. The application contained the following provision: "No obligation is incurred by the Company unless said application is approved by the Company at its Home Office and a contract is issued and delivered during the lifetime and good health of the applicant."

Regan, Judge: The allegations of the petition reflect that five days after the decedent applied for the health and accident policy he became ill and was required to enter a hospital. After the onset of his illness, the condition in the application providing that no coverage was afforded until the policy was issued and delivered during the lifetime and *good health* of the applicant, supplied an ample excuse for the non-delivery thereof by the defendant.

In any event, the fundamental question which the facts hereof have posed for our consideration is whether the defendant was guilty of negligence in failing to issue and deliver the policy within five days after the application therefor was executed.

According to the allegations of the petition, the home office of the defendant company is in Chicago, Illinois. Since the application form for the insurance provided for the approval by the home office before issuance of the policy, it is clear that the application executed by the decedent had to be mailed from New Orleans to Chicago, where it was to be processed, and then the policy would be returned to New Orleans for delivery to the decedent. Under these circumstances, it would be virtually impossible for the policy to be delivered to the decedent within five days after he applied therefor.

Moreover, the petition does not reveal the existence of a cause of action against the defendant *ex delicto*. The defendant was not obligated to deliver the policy when the decedent was in ill health. Consequently, in order to establish as a fact a negligent delay in issuing the policy, the plaintiff would be required to prove that the defendant delayed an unreasonable length of time during the good health of the decedent. This could not be proved in view of the fact that the decedent became ill five days after he applied for the insurance. Under the particular facts hereof, a five day delay in issuing a health and accident policy could not be construed by us as negligence on the part of the defendant. [DECISION FOR DEFENDANT]

Fidelity & Guar. Ins. Underwriters, Inc. v. Gregory, 387 S.W.2d 287 (Ky. 1965). Action by Voris Gregory, plaintiff-appellee, against Fidelity & Guaranty Insurance Underwriters, Inc., defendant-appellant, to recover under a policy of insurance for a loss sustained by fire.

Appellee, whose dwelling was totally destroyed by fire on August 2, 1962, reported the loss to the agent from whom he had obtained the policy. The agent transmitted the information to appellant, who referred the loss to the General Adjustment Bureau. An adjuster, Wedding, was then sent to investigate the matter. The policy contained a clause which provided that the proof of loss must be filed within sixty days after the loss, and this action was begun on October 25, 1962.

Davis, Commissioner: Our cases recognize the validity of provisions of insurance policies requiring proof of loss. In some instances the cases have dealt with such clauses which incorporate a provision for forfeiture of the insurance claim; in others, as in the present case, the provision does not impose forfeiture but makes the proper filing a condition precedent to maintenance of a suit upon the policy.

We believe the insurance company is estopped here to rely on failure to file proof of loss. As noted, the company specifically directed General Adjustment to "Forward completed loss papers to this office." Adjuster Wedding did ask appellee to furnish a photograph of the residence, and this was done. Wedding told appellee, during the sixty-day period, that since the matter had been taken under consideration by the Fire Marshal, there was nothing more he could do pending that investigation. The inference is clear, we think, from Wedding's conversation with appellee, that after the Fire Marshal's investigation had been finished, Wedding would resume action looking toward adjustment of the claim. Wedding did not ask for proof of loss, although the company asked him to forward it.

It is our view that Wedding's conduct, without respect to what he may or may not have said to attorney Dycus, was of that nature as "would naturally induce delay or lead an ordinarily prudent person to believe that the requirement of the policy respecting proof was waived by the company." [DECISION FOR PLAINTIFF]

Albrent v. Spencer, 81 N.W.2d 555 (Wis. 1957). Action by Estelle Albrent, administratrix of the estate of E. A. Albrent, deceased, plaintiff, against William L. Spencer, and others, defendants. The plaintiff alleged substantially in her complaint that prior to March 29, 1954, E. A. Albrent owed William L. Spencer approximately the sum of $140,000; that, as security for said debt, Albrent pledged to Spencer stock valued at $119,268.28; that several policies of insurance having a face value of $85,000, which named Albrent's estate as beneficiary, were assigned by Albrent to Spencer to further collateralize the obligation; that the policies had a cash surrender value of $15,792; that Albrent became ill, and on March 29, 1954, Albrent and Spencer executed a written contract providing for the settlement of the debtor-creditor relationship which resulted in Albrent's making an absolute assignment of the policies of insurance to Spencer; that Spencer's only right under the assignment was to take the cash surrender value of the policies but that the other defendants prevailed upon Spencer and conspired with him to breach the agreement, to keep the policies alive for six months or a year, and to gamble that Albrent would die within that time; that the arrangement was a gambling contract which is forbidden as a matter of public policy; and that parol evidence would be admissible to show such conspiracy. The insurance company, upon the death of Albrent, paid the proceeds of the policy to Spencer who retained approximately $30,000 and distributed the balance to the other defendants who now claim no right thereto except as a gift from Spencer. The plaintiff contends that the estate of E. A. Albrent is entitled to the proceeds of the insurance, less the cash surrender value thereof. The defendants demurred to the complaint which was sustained by the lower court. Plaintiff appealed.

Steinle, Justice: We consider that the case presents the issue of whether it is against public policy for a creditor of the insured to avail himself of an absolute assignment of a previously pledged life insurance policy issued upon the life of the debtor, which assignment is intended to end the creditor-debtor relationship, for any other purpose than enabling the creditor to realize the cash surrender value of the policy. . . .

It offends one's sense of justice that a creditor should realize more out of the proceeds of the policy than the principal and interest due on the loan for which the policy was pledged plus any expenditure of the creditor for premiums necessary to protect his security. To uphold the result reached below in the instant case would be to encourage creditors to bring pressure upon necessitous debtors to convert the rights of the creditor from that of pledgee to that of owner in order that he might gamble upon the life of the insured in the hope of realizing the difference between the amount due on the loan and the face of the policy. In the instant case it is alleged that such difference amounted to the huge sum of approximately $90,000.

While it must be conceded that the majority rule is that, where an owner of a life insurance policy has an insurable interest therein he may make a valid assignment of the policy to a third party having no such insurable interest, it clearly is in the interest of public policy to engraft an exception on to such rule to cover situations such as that which confronts us here. A desirable exception and one that we are compelled to adopt is that any purported absolute assignment by a debtor to a creditor of a policy, which had previously been pledged as security to the creditor is only valid between the immediate parties to the extent of enabling the creditor to realize the cash surrender value of the policy. If the creditor after receiving such absolute assignment and the creditor-debtor relationship is terminated, continues to hold the policy for the purpose of gambling upon the life of the insured, he becomes a constructive trustee for the benefit of the estate of the deceased of any proceeds received upon the death of the insured, to the extent that such proceeds exceed the amount that would have been due such assignee if the creditor-debtor relationship had not been extinguished. . . .

If the facts relating to the assignment of the policies as to such cause of action are established at the trial, the court will be obliged to hold as a matter of law that Spencer and the other defendants who are his assignees are constructive trustees for the benefit of Albrent's estate of that portion of the life insurance proceeds which exceeds the amount which would have been owing on Albrent's indebtedness to Spencer if the absolute assignment of the policies had not been taken. [DECISION FOR PLAINTIFF]

PROBLEMS

1 Plaintiff brought an action to recover the proceeds of a fire insurance policy covering certain household furniture. At the time plaintiff made the application for the insurance, defendant's agent viewed the furniture at the residence of plaintiff and his wife. Both plaintiff and his wife, at that time, told the agent that they were going to move the furniture into a building nearby where they were operating a cafe. The agent agreed to insure the furniture for $1,000 and stated it would be all right to move the furniture. Plaintiff moved the furniture into the cafe building, and the furniture was destroyed by fire. The policy as issued stated that the furniture was located on premises described by metes and bounds, which was the description of the residence property. The policy also contained a provision which limited the liability of the defendant to 10 percent of the full coverage in the event the insured property was elsewhere than on the premises described in the policy. Do you think this limitation is binding on plaintiff?

2 The Insurance Company issued a policy of insurance to Brown insuring his home against loss by fire to the extent of $5,000. The home burned and was a total loss. Brown thereafter assigned the proceeds of the policy to the First Bank, to whom he was indebted in the sum of $5,000. The assignment was made "subject to the consent of" The Insurance Company. Certain other creditors of Brown attacked the validity of the assignment on the ground that The Insurance Company had not consented to the agreement. Do you think the assignment is valid without the consent of The Insurance Company?

3 Lewis, who purchased an automobile from The Automobile Company on a conditional sales contract, paid $1,000 on account of the purchase price and executed a promissory note for the balance of the purchase price. He insured the automobile against theft with the X Insurance Company. In the application for the insurance, which was made a part of the policy, he answered a question by stating that he was the sole and unconditional owner of the automobile although he knew that he owed $1,500 on the purchase price. This statement was made in order to secure the insurance, because the policy provided that he must be the sole owner of the automobile; otherwise, the policy would be void. The automobile was thereafter stolen by some unknown person. Lewis owed $500 on the automobile at the time of the theft, and the company refused to pay Lewis. Lewis then brought an action against the company to recover for the loss of the automobile. Should he recover?

4 Linder, who had an option to purchase a certain warehouse for which he paid $5,000, insured the warehouse against loss by fire. The warehouse was thereafter completely destroyed by fire. Linder therefore gave notice and proof of loss to the insurance company and demanded that he be paid $5,000, which was the amount for which Linder had insured the building. The insurance company refused to pay the $5,000, contending that Linder had no insurable interest in the warehouse. Is this contention correct?

5 Mills completed an application for a policy of life insurance on his life with the Y Insurance Company. His wife was named the beneficiary, and the application contained the following provision: "The proposed policy shall not take effect unless and until the first premium in the amount of $60 shall have been paid, during my continuance in good health, and the policy is delivered." The policy was issued by the insurance company, and was delivered to Mills by the agent of the insurance company. Mills, who was the owner and operator of a laundry, at that time entered into an agreement with the agent whereby Mills agreed to pay the first premium by furnishing the agent laundry services in the amount of $60. Mills died soon thereafter, but the insurance company had not been paid the amount of the first premium. Should the wife of Mills recover on the policy?

6 An agent of the XYZ Insurance Company, who was authorized to do so, entered into an oral contract with plaintiff whereby the agent agreed to insure plaintiff's grocery store against fire for $20,000 for an annual premium of $40. The agent promised plaintiff that the insurance would start at once, but there was no agreement as to when the first premium was to be paid. The written policy was to be prepared and delivered to plaintiff as soon as possible. On April 1, 1966, three days after the contract was entered into, the grocery store was destroyed by fire. The next day, April 2, 1966, the agent delivered the policy to plaintiff. The policy provided that the policy was not to take effect until the first premium was paid. Plaintiff brought an action against the insurance company to recover on the oral contract. Do you think he will recover?

7 The Insurance Company issued to plaintiff a policy of insurance in which plaintiff was insured against any loss or damage to his automobile. Plaintiff was attempting to cross a railroad track when a fast train ran into and completely demolished the automobile. Plaintiff thereafter executed to the railway company a full release of any claim he had against the company for damages to his automobile arising out of the collision. In an action by plaintiff against The Insurance Company to recover for the loss or damage to his automobile, the court decided in favor of The Insurance Company. Discuss the rule of law upon which this decision was founded.

59
STANDARD POLICIES AND PROVISIONS

The provisions in modern insurance policies are of almost an infinite variety. The nonwaiver clause, which is sometimes included in both life and property policies, and the "at and from" clause which is included in marine policies, were mentioned in the last chapter. Most of the standard provisions are included in the printed policies of insurance. There are, however, other standard provisions which are frequently attached to the policies as riders. A rider is a small printed form containing a desired change in the policy. A rider, therefore, may be used to modify or waive an existing provision as well as to add a new provision. The following sections—although by no means exhaustive—will explain some of the standard provisions that are in common use.

PROPERTY INSURANCE

The National Association of Insurance Commissioners drafted a standard form of fire insurance policy which was adopted by New York in 1943. This policy has now been adopted by almost all of the states. There are, however, many standard provisions other than those pertaining to a fire insurance policy.

Direct-Loss-by-Fire Clause The 1943 standard policy insures against all direct loss by fire and lightning. This clause covers every loss or damage to the insured property necessarily flowing from the occurrence of the fire or lightning. This covers damage, such as heat, soot, smoke, breakage, or water in an attempt to save the property. The insured is under a duty to mitigate the damage by removing goods from the path of the fire whenever this is possible, but the policy covers damage due to hasty efforts to remove the goods to a place of safety.

Fire insurance policies frequently contain a provision to the effect that the insurer will not be liable for loss caused by explosion. The courts, in interpreting this provision, hold that the insurer is liable for the total amount of the damage if the explosion was caused by a preceding fire. This is the situation where the explosion follows the fire. The insurer, however, is liable for the damage caused by fire only when the explosion was not caused by a preceding fire. This is the situation where the fire follows the explosion.

It is important to point out that the courts make a distinction between a "friendly" and a "hostile" fire. Damage or loss caused by a friendly fire is not ordinarily covered by fire insurance policies. A fire burning in a place where it is intended to burn, such as a stove, furnace, or fireplace, is a friendly fire. A friendly fire, however, may become a hostile fire. This is the situation where a fire escapes from the place it ought to be to some place where it ought not to be. A fire on a lighted cigarette is a friendly fire, but a fire on a rug caused by a lighted cigarette is a hostile fire. A fire in a fireplace is a friendly fire, but is a hostile fire should it escape to the roof of the house. The insured may recover even though the fire originates through the carelessness of the insured and members of his family. Articles which are carelessly or negligently placed in a friendly fire, however, are not ordinarily covered by a fire insurance policy. [*Youse v. Employers Fire Ins. Co.*, p. 794.]

Vacancy Clause Insurance policies commonly contain a clause to the effect that the insurer shall not be liable while the insured premises are vacant or unoccupied for a stated number of days. The period of vacancy varies, but it is ordinarily from ten to sixty days. The period of time is sixty days in the 1943 standard policy. The courts in construing these clauses make a distinction between "vacant" and "unoccupied." A building is said to be "vacant" when it is deserted by the former occupant including the removal of all furnishings therefrom, but is said to be "unoccupied" when the occupant leaves temporarily leaving the furnishings therein. It is obvious, however, that a building designed for a church or schoolhouse cannot be occupied in the same manner as a dwelling. The courts, therefore, in determining what constitutes occupancy of buildings consider the nature and character of the building, the purposes for which they are designed, and the uses contemplated. The earlier forms of policies used the words "vacant and unoccupied." The decisions construing these words held the policy to be valid unless the building was both vacant and unoccupied. The 1943 standard fire policy defeats these decisions by the use of the words "vacant or unoccupied." The courts generally hold, irrespective of the vacancy clause, that the policy covers only the premises which are identified in the policy. [*Allstate Ins. Co. v. Walker*, p. 794.]

Increase-of-Hazard Clause   The standard fire policies provide in substance that no misrepresentation made by the insured shall avoid the policy unless it is made with an intent to deceive, or unless it increases the risk of loss, or contributes to the loss for which the insured seeks to be indemnified. This type of provision is obviously intended to prevent the avoidance of a policy because of immaterial misstatements made in good faith. The general effect of this type of statute is to place the burden on the insurer to prove that the breach increased the risk of loss or contributed to the loss. Suppose a policy provides that the insured shall maintain a certain type of water sprinkler in his building for use in case of fire. Suppose further that the insured did not maintain the sprinkler and the building was damaged by fire. Should the insured recover? The question would undoubtedly be left to the jury as to whether or not the absence of the sprinkler contributed to the loss. [*Standard Marine Ins. Co. v. Peck*, p. 795.]

The Iron-Safe Clause   This clause is designed to protect the insurer against fraudulent claims of loss when the property insured is a stock of goods which is constantly changing. It is commonly found in fire and burglary policies. Under the terms of the clause, the insured agrees to take a complete itemized inventory at least once a year, or within one month after the policy is issued if an inventory has not been taken within the past year; to keep a set of books showing all sales; to keep such books securely locked in a fireproof safe at night and at all other times when the building mentioned in the policy is not open for business; and to produce the books for inspection of the insurer if a loss occurs. No special system of bookkeeping is required to be used. The amount and value of the goods, however, must be ascertained from the inventory and records. In the absence of extenuating circumstances, such as waiver or estoppel on the part of the insured, it is uniformly held that parol evidence is not admissible to establish the loss.

Coinsurance   A coinsurance clause provides that if the insured fails to carry insurance in an amount equal to a stated percentage of the value of the property insured—80 percent is common—the insured is a coinsurer for the uninsured excess. Suppose the property has a value of $10,000. Suppose further that the policy has no coinsurance clause and the amount of insurance is $4,000 and the loss is $4,000. The insured will recover $4,000. Let us assume, however, that the policy contained an 80 percent coinsurance clause. The insured would recover only $2,000 calculated on the following formula:

$$\frac{\text{Amount of insurance (\$4,000)}}{\text{\$8,000 (80 percent of value)}} \times \text{the loss} = \text{the amount of recovery}$$

The insured should make certain that he has the proper amount of insurance— $8,000 in our example—and if he does, he would be indemnified to the extent of $8,000 in case of a total loss. The probabilities are against a total loss, however, when the buildings are separated and if a fire fighting unit is located within the vicinity.

Coinsurance is prohibited in some states. Some other states permit it provided the insured asks for it or if there is a reduction in the premium.

Mortgage Clauses The usual manner of insuring mortgaged property is for the mortgagor to take out insurance for the benefit of the mortgagee. The older form of insurance obtainable for this purpose is a policy issued to the mortgagor with a "loss payable" clause. This clause provides that the loss shall be payable to the mortgagor and to the mortgagee "as his interest may appear." The courts, in interpreting this clause, have been unanimous in holding that the right of the mortgagee to recover is dependent upon the right of the mortgagor to recover. A breach of any of the conditions by the mortgagor which would bar a recovery by him, therefore, would likewise bar recovery by the mortgagee. The New York standard mortgage clause provides that "this insurance, as to the interest of the mortgagee only therein, shall not be invalidated by any act or neglect of the mortgagor." This provision insures the interest of the mortgagee as fully and to the same extent as if he had taken out a policy direct from the insurer. The right of the mortgagee to recover, therefore, will not be defeated by a default of the mortgagor. Payment to the mortgagee under either of these clauses discharges, so far as it goes, the mortgage debt.

It is to be remembered, however, that both the mortgagor and the mortgagee have a separate and distinct insurable interest in mortgaged property. A mortgagor, therefore, who independently insures his interest in the mortgaged property is entitled to the proceeds free of any claim by the mortgagee. The mortgagee may likewise insure his interest in the property.

Valued Policy Statutes Statutes have been enacted in almost one-half of the states which provide that the amount of insurance written on the face of the policy shall be taken conclusively to be the true value of the property insured and the true amount of loss and measure of damages. These statutory provisions cannot be altered or waived and all provisions of the fire insurance policy are subject to the statutes. These statutes, however, are ordinarily applicable only with respect to real property and only in case of total loss. A few statutes provide that the amount in the policy is not conclusive as to the amount if the insured has fraudulently overvalued his property. The courts, moreover, will apply such a limitation to a person who fraudulently overvalues his property.

Overinsurance Clause Insurance policies usually provide against the existence or the procuring of other or additional insurance upon the property insured without the consent of the insurer. The purpose of this provision is to prevent overin-surance. The effect of the provision, as a general rule, is to prevent recovery from either insurer. Suppose Brown, without the knowledge or consent of either company, applies for and receives a policy of insurance for $10,000 on his $10,000 residence from the A Insurance Company and a similar policy from the B Insurance Company. Suppose further that both policies contained a provision prohibiting other insurance and that a fire destroyed the residence. Brown, in the absence of extenuating circumstances—such as waiver or estoppel—would not be permitted to recover from either insurance company. The double insurance must cover the same interest and the same risk at the same time. The provision does not prevent persons, such as a mortgagor and mortgagee or bailor and bailee, holding separate interests in the same property from procuring insurance on their separate interests. The policy may, however, contain a pro rata provision. It is also true that many states have passed pro rata laws.

Pro Rata Clause   This clause applies to property insurance when the insured has insurance with more than one company. The effect of the clause is to place liability on each insurance company for its proportionate share of the loss. Statutes in some states make the clause applicable even though the policy provides that the "insuring company shall not be liable for loss occurring while the insured shall have any other contract of insurance." These statutes have been interpreted this way: Assume a building valued at $30,000 was totally destroyed by fire. Assume further that each of two insurance companies insured the building for $30,000. The insured could recover $15,000 from each company.

Notice and Proof of Loss   All kinds of property insurance policies require that the insurer be given notice and proof of loss within a specified period. Fire insurance policies describe the steps that must be taken by the insured when he has suffered a loss. The standard policy requires the insured to give immediate written notice to the insurer; to protect the property from further damage; to separate the damaged from the undamaged personal property; to furnish an inventory of the destroyed, damaged, and undamaged property; and to furnish the insurer, within sixty days, a proof of loss. Some life and accident policies include a provision requiring that a certificate of the attending physician of the insured be furnished as a part of the proof of death.

LIFE INSURANCE
Standard policy laws of life insurance have not met with success. There are, nevertheless, some provisions which are quite generally required to be included in life insurance policies. The nonforfeiture, reinstatement, and entire-contract clauses were mentioned in the last chapter, and the following sections explain some of the other standard provisions.

Incontestable Clause   The statutes of many states require life insurance policies to include an incontestable clause which provides that after a stated period of time—commonly two years—the policy is incontestable except for certain specified defenses. In the absence of statute, however, it is usual to include such clauses in life insurance policies. The theory of the incontestable clause is based upon the reasoning that the beneficiary, after the premiums have been paid for a number of years, should not be met with a contest to determine whether the insurance ever had any validity.

The insurer may contest the validity of the policy during the contestable time. What is a "contest"? A denial of liability under the policy and an offer to return the premiums would not be a contest in most states. A "contest" of the policy, according to the view followed by most of the states, requires court action in which the defendant is served with process. The insurer either brings the suit in an attempt to have the policy canceled or the insurer offers a plea or answer when suit is brought on the policy. It should be mentioned, however, that there is a view in some states that a return of the premiums accompanied by an explicit denial of liability on the policy is a contest although no suit is instituted.

The fact that the insurer cannot contest the validity of the policy as it is written provided the contestable period has expired should not operate to deprive the insurer of the right to resist payment in some well-recognized instances. A vicious type of fraud, such as the substitution of another for the physical examination by the insured or the procurement of a policy with the intention of murdering the insured, should be available to the insurer as a defense. The insurer may likewise resist payment of the policy on the ground that the action was not brought within the time specified; that proof of death was not properly made; or that the person who procured the policy had no insurable interest in the insured.

A familiar rule of construction of contracts is to the effect that an ambiguity will be most strongly construed against the person who prepared the contract. Ambiguities will, therefore, be construed in favor of the insured or beneficiary. The statutes and the incontestable clauses prepared in accordance with such statutes will almost invariably refer to the "date of issue." A question arises, therefore, when does the contestable period begin to run when the date on the policy, the premium date, and the date on which the policy actually became effective are different? Suppose the policy provides that it will become incontestable two years after the "date of issue" and the date of the policy is earlier than the actual date of issue. The court, in construing this, will hold that the date on the policy is the date of issue. If the policy contains a specific date as the "date of issue," the courts will attempt to respect such a stated intention. Suppose still further that the risk was assumed by the insurer earlier than the date on the policy. The court will hold that the "date of issue" is the date when the coverage became effective.

Misstatement of Age Reduced recovery is ordinarily allowed when the insured misstates his or her age in the application for insurance. By a clause in the policy, the amount of insurance is reduced to that sum which the premiums paid would have purchased at the true age of the insured. Statutes in many states require the insertion of such a provision in the policy. This merely means that the insured is moved to another age group. His premiums, therefore, are applied to the purchase of a policy at that age.

Grace Period Life policies ordinarily grant a grace period of a month or thirty-one days during which the premium may be paid. The best practice, however, is to pay the premium on or before the due date. If it is sent by mail, it must be sent early enough so that it will be received by the insurer on or before the due date or the expiration of the grace period.

Good Health Clause   Life policies almost invariably contain a condition as to the health of the insured, and the language of the clause varies greatly. The usual form is that the policy shall not take effect unless the insured is in "good" or "sound" health when the policy is delivered. The cases which deal with these clauses make a distinction between policies which require a medical examination of the insured by a physician appointed by the insurer and those that do not require such an examination. There is, however, a conflict in the cases.

When a medical examination is required: Some courts construe the clause literally and require that the insured be in good health at the time the policy is issued or delivered. The beneficiary, according to this view, could not recover if the insured died from lung cancer after the policy was delivered and he had an undetected lung cancer at the time of the examination. The majority of the cases, however, take the view that the good health provision relates only to changes in health occurring between the date of the examination and the date of delivery of the policy. The reason seems to be that the insurer required the examination and by doing so waived all future contentions as to the health of the insured at or prior to the examination.

When a medical examination is not required: A few courts take the view that the good health clause refers only to changes in health occurring between the date of the application and the date of delivery of the policy. The majority of the cases construe the clause literally and require good health of the insured at the time the policy is issued or delivered.

The courts agree that the determining factor is the state of health of the insured and not his knowledge or belief as to his health. The courts also agree that the words "good health" should be given a reasonable interpretation and that they do not necessarily mean perfect health. Temporary and trivial ailments, such as a common cold, do not represent a departure from good health.

Accidental Means Clause   The accident policies frequently provide for benefits in the event of injury or death arising from external, violent, and accidental means. This clause has led to an abundance of decisions where the courts have attempted to draw a distinction between "accidental result" and "accidental means." The distinctions drawn abound in figurative locutions and are frequently conflicting. It would seem, however, that "accidental result" is said to mean that which happens by chance and which is unforeseen; and that the "accidental means" is said to mean an act performed voluntarily by the insured to produce one result and which produced another result unexpectedly. To illustrate: Suppose Brown was cranking his power lawn mower and was injured when he slipped on the wet grass. The injury could be said to be due to accidental means. He was doing an intended act—cranking the lawn mower—but he produced the injury unexpectedly. But suppose Brown proceeded to crank the mower in this manner and was injured from overexertion, the injury could be said to be an "accidental result." He was doing an intended act, but the result was unforeseen. This is chaotic. It is heartening, therefore, to realize that most of the recent cases deny that there is any distinction between "accidental result" and "accidental means." [*Scott v. New Empire Ins. Co.*, p. 796.]

External and Visible Signs of Injury Accident policies frequently contain a provision to the general effect that the insurer shall not be liable for any bodily injuries suffered by the insured unless some external and visible signs of such injuries are found. Some courts have denied recovery in the absence of such "signs." The courts have, however, mostly abandoned the restrictive effect of this provision. The trend of the courts is to hold that visible signs include any signs of the injury, such as a pale face, provided the pale face is a direct result of the injury. External and visible signs, therefore, are not at the present time generally confined to injuries such as broken bones and bruises.

Violation of Law Clause A few policies contain a provision to the effect that the insurer shall not be liable for injuries sustained by the insured while violating the law. This provision is broad enough to include traffic accidents. This clause, however, is limited to felonies or illegal occupations in several states. Many policies do not contain such a provision, but some courts nevertheless hold that the insurer is not liable where the insured meets his death at the hand of the law. The insurer would not be relieved of liability if the officer of the law was not justified in killing the insured. The courts have used language to the effect that injury to or death of the insured is not recoverable where the injury or death is the natural and probable consequence of an assault committed by the insured. It is quite clear that injury to or death sustained by an insured in an encounter brought about by him upon another with a deadly weapon is not recoverable. [*Di Paoli v. The Prudential Ins. Co.*, p. 797.]

Diminished Liability Clause The classification of risks used by insurers is arrived at upon the basis of the employment in which the applicant is engaged at the time the policy is issued for the purpose of ascertaining what premium will be exacted for a given amount of indemnity. It is common practice, however, for the insured to change occupations. The diminished liability clause provides for a reduction in benefits if the insured engages in certain occupations which are classified by the insurer as more hazardous. The purpose of the clause, therefore, is to avoid forfeiture of the policy and permit the insured to recover indemnity proportionate to the hazard of the new employment. The term "occupation" has been frequently and variously defined by the courts, but generally the term is said to refer to the principal vocation or pursuit of the insured.

Notice and Proof of Loss Policies of life insurance require that the insurer be given proof of death within a specified period, usually thirty or ninety days. Some life and accident policies include a provision requiring that a certificate of the attending physician of the insured be furnished as a part of the proof of death. Some life and accident policies also give the insurer the right and opportunity to make an autopsy in case of death. The courts have held this to be a valid provision on the ground that it gives the insurer protection against invalid and fraudulent claims.

CASES

Youse v. Employers Fire Ins. Co., 238 P.2d 472 (Kan. 1941). Action by C. E. Youse, plaintiff, against Employers Fire Insurance Company, defendant, to recover for damage to a ring.

Price, Justice: The facts, which are not in dispute, are as follows:

On an occasion while the policy in question was in force the wife of insured was carrying her ring wrapped in a handkerchief in her purse. Upon arriving at her home she placed the handkerchief, together with some paper cleansing tissues (Kleenex), on the dresser in her bedroom. Later her maid, in cleaning the room inadvertently picked up the handkerchief containing the ring, together with the cleansing tissues, and threw them into a wastebasket. Still later, another servant emptied the contents of the wastebasket, along with other trash, into a trash burner at the rear of the premises and proceeded to burn the trash so deposited. The trash burner was intended for that purpose, the fire was intentionally lighted by the servant, and was confined to the trash burner. About a week later the ring was found in the trash burner. It had been damaged to the extent of $900.

The policy, a standard form, insured household goods and personal property, usual or incidental to the occupancy of the premises as a dwelling, belonging to insured or a member of his family while contained on the premises, ". . . against all direct loss or damage by fire."

. . . The very great weight of authority appears to be that "fires," within the meaning of standard insuring clauses in fire insurance policies, are classified as friendly or hostile in nature, notwithstanding that such distinction is not made in the language of the policy itself.

A friendly fire is defined as being a fire lighted and contained in a usual place for fire, such as a furnace, stove, incinerator, and the like, and used for the purposes of heating, cooking, manufacturing, or other common and usual everyday purposes.

A hostile fire is defined as being a fire unexpected, unintended, not anticipated, in a place not intended for it to be and where fire is not ordinarily maintained, or as one which has escaped in the usual and ordinary sense of the word. A fire originally friendly, by escaping, becomes hostile, and ordinarily recovery may be had for loss or damage resulting thereby. . . .

In our opinion there can be no question but that the fire which damaged or destroyed the sapphire ring was what in law is known as a "friendly" fire. It was intentionally lighted, was for the usual and ordinary purpose of burning trash, and was at all times confined to the place where it was intended, and did not escape. [DECISION FOR DEFENDANT]

Allstate Ins. Co. v. Walker, 140 S.E.2d 910 (Ga. 1965). Action by Robert L. Walker, Jr., plaintiff, against Allstate Insurance Company, defendant, to recover for loss of personal property by theft.

The insurance contract was a homeowner's policy covering loss from theft of unscheduled personal property. The premises are identified as being at "652

Park Lane, Decatur, Georgia." The insured, however, also owned a "house trailer" located on his lot at Lake Lanier in Forsyth County, Georgia, which he used primarily as a recreational facility. He seeks to recover for the loss of property which was stolen from the house trailer.

Bell, Presiding Judge: It is evident that the insurance coverage extended only (1) to the unscheduled personal property which was usual or incidental to the occupancy of the Park Lane premises as a dwelling or owned, worn or used by an insured while on the premises, and (2) to that property owned, worn or used by an insured in a manner usual or incidental to the occupancy of the Park Lane residence. If the property stolen meets those criteria, the loss is covered wherever it might have occurred. On the other hand the quoted exclusionary provision makes it clear that no coverage exists for other property the use of which is usual or incidental to the occupancy of a dwelling separate from the Park Lane property "except while an insured is residing therein."

Was the house trailer a "dwelling" separate and distinct from the Park Lane address to the extent that property kept there would be property the use of which would be usual or incidental to occupancy of the trailer? If so, the clear exclusionary provisions of the policy precluded coverage of the property stolen from the trailer since the property would have been stolen while in a dwelling owned by the insured while no insured was temporarily residing there.

When viewed in the light of the homeowner's policy in this case, the house trailer belonging to the insured but located outside the curtilage of the property identified in the policy is a dwelling not included in the coverage of the insurance contract. [DECISION FOR DEFENDANT]

Standard Marine Ins. Co. v. Peck, 342 P.2d 661 (Colo. 1959). Action by Robert B. N. Peck and Miriam N. Peck, plaintiffs, against Standard Marine Insurance Company, defendant.

Plaintiffs were the owners of the Lawn and Garden Supply and Equipment Company, and the defendant was the insurer of the building and its contents. The merchandise in the building was destroyed or damaged, and plaintiffs brought an action to recover for the loss. The policy contained the following provision: "This Company shall not be liable for loss occurring while the hazard is increased by any means within the control or knowledge of the insured."

Day, Justice: The defendant insurance company proved that plaintiff, the Lawn and Garden Supply and Equipment Company, stocked a display of fireworks openly on tables in its store. Three boys came into the store on a Sunday afternoon about 2 o'clock and from one of the display tables picked a toy gun which emitted sparks when the trigger was pulled. The boy said he was playing "rockets" which he explained as aiming the sparks at various of the fuses protruding from the fireworks to see if they would orbit. The boy succeeded in igniting a pyrotechnic device called a "fountain," whereupon the display, like some politicians, went off in all directions, and the ensuing fire destroyed the store and contents.

Regardless of the academic question as to where the burden of proof lies, the defendant did establish by the evidence, uncontradicted, that the fireworks in fact did increase the hazard. The evidence disclosed that the fire originated as the result of such increase of hazard and from the very merchandise which was added to the stock. The ordinary merchandise carried by the establishment was of the hardware variety consisting of garden and lawn tools, mowers, etc. The fireworks by demonstration to the court were conclusively shown to be highly inflammable and explosive in character. That they have a particular appeal to children is a matter of common knowledge, explicitly demonstrated in this case. If the offering and display of a stock of fireworks was not an increase in the ordinary hazards of a hardware store, it is difficult to conceive what would be. [DECISION FOR DEFENDANT]

Scott v. New Empire Ins. Co., 400 P.2d 953 (N.M. 1965). Action by Burk Scott, Jr., and others, plaintiffs, against New Empire Insurance Company, defendant, to recover on an accident policy for death of insured.

The decedent, who was insured under an accident policy issued by the defendant which provided for "indemnity for loss of life by accidental means," was killed while he was driving his car at night on a mountain road and failed to make a curve.

Carmody, Chief Justice: The defendant claims that there were no "accidental means" present in the case, because the deceased was speeding over a relatively unknown, dangerous road at night and should have foreseen the consequences of his intentional acts. Plaintiff, on the contrary, maintains that under this particular policy there really is not any difference between "accidental means" and "accident," and that the minds of reasonable men could not differ in the conclusion that the deceased came to his death by accident.

Although this court has not heretofore had occasion to consider this exact problem, we are cognizant of a distinct split of authority among the various appellate courts throughout the country. The view expressed by some courts, and as is contended here by the defendant, is that when the policy specifies "accidental means," the immediate or proximate cause of the death must be accidental, and if death results as the natural and probable consequence of the voluntary acts of the insured, death does not occur by accidental means. Prior to 1934, this view was generally followed by the courts which passed upon the question. In that year, the Supreme Court of the United States decided Landress v. Phoenix Mutual Life Insurance Co., 291 U.S. 491, and the majority of the court adopted the then prevailing view. However, the late Justice Cardozo dissented from the majority opinion and a part of his language bears repeating because of what has subsequently occurred. He said:

The attempted distinction between accidental results and accidental means will plunge this branch of the law into a Serbonian Bog. "Probably it is true to say that in the strictest sense and dealing with the region of physical nature there is no such thing as an accident." . . . On the other hand, the average man is convinced that there is, and so certainly is the man who takes out a policy of accident insurance. It is his reading of the policy that is to be accepted as our guide, with the help of the established rule that ambiguities and uncertainties are to be resolved against the company. . . .

When a man has died in such a way that his death is spoken of as an accident, he has died because of an accident, and hence by accidental means. . . .

. . . If there was no accident in the means, there was none in the result, for the two were inseparable. . . . There was an accident throughout, or there was no accident at all.

During the some thirty years since this dissent, increasing numbers of courts of last resort have followed the rationale expressed by Justice Cardozo.

There is no testimony that the misfortune which occurred to the decedent was intentional—heedless, perhaps, but certainly not voluntarily self-inflicted, nor does the defendant so contend. In light of our holding that the terms "accidental means" and "accident" are one and the same under this policy, the minds of reasonable men could not differ in concluding that the deceased died as a result of an accident. [DECISION FOR PLAINTIFF]

Di Paoli v. Prudential Ins. Co., 384 S.W.2d 861 (Mo. 1964). Action by Frances Di Paoli, plaintiff, against Prudential Insurance Company, defendant, to recover on an insurance policy. The face amount of the policy was $1,000, and the policy contained a provision for double indemnity in the event of "death by accidental means." Defendant paid plaintiff the sum of $1,000 but refused to pay for the accidental death benefit. This action, therefore, is brought to recover the accidental death benefits.

Anderson, Judge: Dr. Glaser testified the insured died of a fractured skull which had caused profuse hemorrhage within the membrane that covered the brain. John S. Farmer, defendant's witness, testified that during the evening of September 22, 1959, he was the bartender at 2350 North Market. At about 10:15 or 10:20 p.m., while he was talking to a customer, John Lindner, a stranger (later identified as the insured Luigi Di Paoli) entered the bar room, walked beyond Lindner, then turned around and without prior conversation pulled out a gun, cocked it and pointed it at Farmer, and threatened to kill him, saying "I'll kill you" several times. He further testified that Lindner then began talking to Di Paoli in an effort to persuade him from using the gun, whereupon Di Paoli turned and pointed the gun toward Lindner. When this occurred, he (Farmer) came from behind the bar to a position behind Di Paoli intending to relieve the latter of the gun, but just as Farmer got in back of him Di Paoli turned on Farmer with the gun. Farmer then struck Di Paoli with his left fist around the temple. Di Paoli fell to the floor and in the process of falling struck his head either on the bar rail or a rung of a bar stool. As he was falling, Farmer relieved him of the gun.

Where an insured as the aggressor voluntarily engages in an affray with another person, or assaults or threatens another with a deadly weapon which takes on the aspect of a threatened deadly encounter, he must be deemed to have invited resistance of such force as likely to put him in danger of death or bodily harm. Such resistance will be regarded as the natural and probable result of voluntary exposure to danger which ought to have been foreseen, and if it results in death or bodily harm, such injury or death cannot be regarded as resulting from accident within the provisions of a policy insuring against death or injury by "accidental means."

Considering the fact that the lives of the two men were threatened and that the action taken by Farmer to relieve them of their peril had to be and was a rapid process involving considerable danger and excitement, it is not strange to find the record disclosing some minor discrepancies in their testimony. If it did not, there would be more reason for doubting their veracity. On all matters of consequence, defendant's evidence stood unimpeached, with no room for reasonable controversy in regard to the circumstances under which insured received the injuries which caused the death. Those circumstances show no liability under the policy. [DECISION FOR DEFENDANT]

PROBLEMS

1 Brown mortgaged his farm to The Mortgage Company for $3,000. He then insured the building on the farm with The Insurance Company for $5,000. The policy of insurance provided that any loss shall be payable to the mortgagor and the mortgagee "as his interest may appear." The building was damaged by fire to the extent of $4,000. To whom should The Insurance Company pay the $4,000?

2 The Insurance Company issued a life policy to Powell which carried the following notation: "Effective date is October 27, 1959." The Insurance Company, about one and one-half years later, learned that Powell had given some false answers to questions which became a part of the application. The Insurance Company thereupon notified Powell that the policy was being canceled. The premiums were tendered to Powell, who refused the tender. The policy contained a two-year incontestable clause. Powell died on October 26, 1961. The Insurance Company refused to pay the beneficiary the proceeds of the policy. Is The Insurance Company liable?

3 Brown, in his application for a policy of insurance on his life, stated that he was fifty-six years old. The policy was delivered to Brown while he was in good health, but he died about one year thereafter as the result of an automobile accident. His widow, the beneficiary, then filed a proof of death and applied for the proceeds of the policy. The Insurance Company then learned that Brown was in fact sixty years old. The company, therefore, denied liability under the policy on the ground of false representation. The widow then brought an action against the company to recover the proceeds of the policy. What amount, if any, should she recover?

4 Wells, who resided at 1124 47th Street, applied for and received a policy of insurance for $20,000 on his residence, which was valued at $20,000, from the Z Insurance Company. Wells also applied for and received a policy of insurance for the same amount on the same residence from the Y Insurance Company. Neither the Z Insurance Company nor the Y Insurance Company had knowledge of or consented to the insuring by Wells of his residence with another insurance company. The residence was destroyed by fire. What are the rights of Wells?

5 Mrs. Brown had a standard fire insurance policy covering her home and all items of furniture in the home with the Z Insurance Company. Mrs. Brown, who had two kerosene hurricane lamps burning on the dining room table, negligently turned the wicks in the two lamps too high. This caused a great amount of soot and smoke to be emitted from the chimneys of the lamps. The soot and smoke completely ruined the wallpaper on the walls in the dining room. Will Mrs. Brown recover from the Z Insurance Company for the damage?

60

NATURE OF SURETYSHIP AND GUARANTY

The businessman, irrespective of how prudent he may be, will occasionally sustain a loss because of the dishonesty of an employee or because a debtor cannot pay his debts when they become due. The purpose of suretyship and guaranty, therefore, is to greatly reduce the risk of such loss. This is accomplished by the promise of the surety or guarantor to answer for the debt or default of the principal debtor, hereinafter referred to as the "debtor." The businessman will, therefore, have recourse against two persons. It is not to be presumed, however, that suretyship and guaranty are limited to the businessman. Contracts of suretyship are often required by law to secure the public against defalcations of public officers or to protect parties in connection with judicial proceedings.

A suretyship contract, broadly stated, is a contractual relation whereby one person engages to be answerable for the debt or default of another person. This broad definition includes contracts of guarantors, indorsers, indemnitors, accommodation parties on commercial paper, and all other persons who engage to be answerable for the debt or default of another person. The word "surety," in a narrow sense, indicates a primary obligation. The undertaking, to be sure, is secondary as between the surety and the debtor because the debtor must eventually pay the debt. The liability of the surety is nevertheless primary to the creditor. Three persons are always involved: the debtor, or obligor, who becomes obligated to the creditor, or obligee, and the surety who promises the creditor to answer for the default of the debtor. An insight into the subjects of suretyship and guaranty might best be grasped by (1) distinguishing suretyship contracts from similar transactions, (2) classifying the different kinds of guaranties, (3) discussing the formation of the contract, (4) discussing the rights of the creditor, and (5) observing the various kinds of surety bonds. The rights and defenses of the surety will be discussed in the next chapter.

SURETYSHIP CONTRACTS DISTINGUISHED

Surety and Indorser Distinguished An indorsement, in which the indorser of a negotiable instrument obligates himself to a subsequent holder of the instrument to pay if the party of primary liability refuses to pay, is clearly a form of suretyship. The contract of an indorser, however, may readily be distinguished from that of a surety. The liability of an indorser is conditional and secondary because he agrees to pay only where demand is made on the maker and notice of the dishonor is given to him; the undertaking of the surety is primary. The liability of an indorser in this respect is similar to that of a guarantor. It is to be remembered, however, that an indorser is liable for the warranties which he makes to subsequent holders. It is thus clear that the contract of an indorser is governed by the law pertaining to commercial paper and not by the law of suretyship.

Surety and Indemnitor Distinguished Indemnity and suretyship are easily distinguished. An indemnitor contracts to save another party harmless from some legal consequence; a surety undertakes to pay or perform if the principal debtor does not. The contract of indemnity is an original one; the contract of suretyship is collateral to some other original undertaking. The relationship of surety requires three persons; indemnity requires only two. The indemnitor ordinarily has no right of reimbursement from the debtor; the surety has such a right.

The idea of indemnity underlies all policies of insurance—whether fire, fidelity, or others—except life insurance, which is a contract to pay a beneficiary a certain sum of money in the event of death of the insured. This does not mean, however, that all contracts of indemnity are insurance contracts. Suppose Brown, the indemnitor, says to Smith, a dealer in secondhand automobiles, "Buy this automobile from Jones and if you lose money on a resale, I will indemnify you for the loss." This is a true indemnity contract; it is an original undertaking independent of any collateral contract. Should Brown be forced to make good a loss, he would have no right of reimbursement from Smith unless Smith had agreed to reimburse him.

Surety and Guarantor Distinguished The words "surety" and "guarantor" are often used as synonymous words, and the contract of suretyship and the contract of guaranty are not distinguishable in some situations. This is particularly true where the contract of guaranty is absolute or unconditional. The authorities, however, frequently distinguish between the contract of a surety and the contract of a guarantor.

The contract of the surety is generally created concurrently with that of the debtor; the contract of the guarantor is generally separate and distinct from that of the debtor and is founded on a separate consideration. The contract of the guarantor is also quite commonly entered into at a separate time. The promise of the surety is to do the same thing that the debtor undertakes to do; the promise of the guarantor is to perform if the debtor cannot perform. The surety, in effect, says, "I will pay if the debtor does not pay." The guarantor says, in effect, "I will pay if the debtor cannot pay." The surety, therefore, is primarily liable to the creditor without any demand of payment from the debtor. The secondary liability of a guarantor does not ordinarily become fixed until demand has been made upon the debtor and notice of default of the debtor has been given to the guarantor.

FORM AND CLASSIFICATION OF GUARANTIES

Form of Guaranty   A guaranty need not be in any special form nor is it necessary to use the word "guarantee" or any word of similar import. A mere recommendation, such as "I recommend Brown as a safe credit risk," or an expression "Brown is reliable," or an assurance "Brown will comply with his contracts" is not a promise to answer for the debt or default of Brown.

General and Special   A letter of guaranty addressed "to whom it may concern" or to all persons generally is known as a general guaranty. Any creditor who has knowledge of the guaranty and extends credit in reliance thereon may enforce the guaranty. A letter of guaranty addressed to a particular person, partnership, or corporation is special and may be enforced only by the person to whom the letter is addressed.

Temporary and Continuing   A temporary guaranty is limited by its terms to a single transaction or to a specified period of time. Suppose Brown, for a sufficient consideration, writes the following letter of guaranty to Jones, a merchant: "I guarantee to pay for all the merchandise that Smith may purchase from you." This is a continuing guaranty. A continuing guaranty contemplates a future course of dealing during an indefinite time. It may cover a succession of credits or give the debtor a standing credit to be used by him from time to time. Suppose Brown guarantees payment for sales made by Jones, a merchant, to Smith up to $1,500. This is a typical limited guaranty; it is limited as to the amount of indebtedness to be charged against the guarantor, but it is unlimited as to time. The courts, in construing this type of guaranty, generally agree that Jones could extend credit to Smith so long as at a given moment Smith does not owe more than $1,500. It is to be emphasized, therefore, that if a guarantor wishes to limit the guaranty as to time or if he intends that his guaranty be extinguished when the credit of the principal has reached $1,500, he should use language which unmistakably indicates his intention.

Absolute and Conditional Guaranty Distinguished Common forms of absolute and conditional guaranty are those indorsed upon promissory notes. The rules pertaining to "guaranty of payment" and "guaranty of collection" have been expressly incorporated in the Code with respect to commercial paper by section 3–416. Commercial paper, however, is not the only type of paper to which absolute and conditional guaranties are applicable. The words "payment of a debt" are often seen in contrast to the words "collection of a debt." A person guaranteeing payment of a debt undertakes to pay the debt upon default of the debtor. A person guaranteeing the collection of a debt undertakes to pay the debt on the condition that the creditor first make use of the ordinary legal means to collect it from the debtor.

(1) *Absolute Guaranty* An absolute guaranty binds the guarantor unconditionally to perform the obligation. The liability of an absolute guarantor, therefore, becomes fixed upon default of the debtor; no other event or condition, including notice to the guarantor, is required. Suppose Brown owes the grocer $50, and the grocer will not extend further credit to Brown. Suppose further that Jones and the grocer enter into an agreement whereby Jones, in consideration of the promise of the grocer not to bring an action against Brown to recover the $50, agrees to pay the $50 to the grocer and that Jones then writes upon the account: "If Brown does not pay this bill for $50 before January 31, 1971, I will pay the $50 at that time." This is an absolute guaranty. Jones, upon default of Brown, would be liable for the $50 on January 31, 1971, without notice from the grocer.

(2) *Conditional Guaranty* A conditional guaranty contemplates, as a condition to liability on the part of the guarantor, the happening of some contingent event or the performance of some act on the part of the creditor. It is usually conditioned upon (a) an unsuccessful attempt to collect from the debtor, (b) an unpaid judgment, or (c) a showing that it would be futile to proceed to a judgment against the debtor. The liability of the guarantor may depend upon whether or not the creditor has given the guarantor notice of default of the debtor. It may be that the guarantor would elect to pay the debt and proceed at once against the principal. The decisions are conflicting, but many cases have held that the creditor not only should give notice of default but also notice of acceptance of the guaranty. This is particularly true if the guaranty is a continuing guaranty.

FORMATION OF THE CONTRACT

The contract of suretyship and guaranty, like other contracts, must contain an offer and acceptance, supported by consideration, entered into by parties having capacity to contract, the object of which is legal, and it must be in writing. The suretyship contract, as a general rule, is created by express agreement of the parties. In some instances, however, the contract will arise by operation of law. Suppose mortgagor-Brown sells his house and lot to purchaser-Smith, who promises Brown, as a part of the consideration, to pay the outstanding indebtedness to mortgagee-Jones. Smith, as between Brown and Smith, becomes the principal debtor; Brown becomes the surety.

The important attributes of the contract which need to be discussed are (1) the Statute of Frauds, (2) offer and acceptance, and (3) consideration.

Statute of Frauds   The general rule says that contracts of suretyship and guaranty are collateral and within the Statute of Frauds and that contracts of indemnity are original and not within the Statute of Frauds. A few decisions have held otherwise, but a reading of the cases reveals that the promises were in fact original promises. The distinction is frequently made with respect to promises which may or may not be made to subserve the interest of the indemnitor or guarantor. Suppose that the president of the First Bank promised Brown, a depositor, that he would indemnify Brown for any loss occasioned by Brown's refraining from withdrawing his funds from the bank. Such a promise would ordinarily be construed as a promise to subserve the interest of the president. This then would be an original undertaking and not required to be in writing to be enforceable. Suppose, however, that Jones, who had no interest in the bank and no interest of his own to subserve but merely believed that the bank was not in financial difficulty, made the same promise to Brown. Such a promise would ordinarily be construed as a collateral promise and would be required to be in writing to be enforceable.

Offer and Acceptance   A contract of suretyship or guaranty, like other contracts, must contain an offer and acceptance. The nature of the circumstances will ordinarily fully inform the surety of the acceptance. As a general rule, therefore, the offeree-creditor is not required to notify the offeror-surety of the acceptance. It is also generally true that the creditor is not required to give notice of acceptance of the offer when the guaranty is an absolute guaranty. There is, however, a lack of harmony in the decisions as to what constitutes acceptance of a continuing offer or a continuing guaranty.

Suppose Brown, a merchant, goes to the city to purchase goods from a wholesale house. Suppose further that Brown carries with him a letter of guaranty from his local bank addressed to the wholesaler to guarantee payment of such goods as Brown may purchase. The bank has no way of knowing whether Brown will have any business dealings with the wholesale house, or, if he does, whether the wholesale house regards the security of the bank sufficient. Would it not be unjust for the wholesale house, some years later, to notify the bank that they were seeking payment from the bank on the strength of the letter of guaranty? If the bank had been notified of the acceptance, the bank could have taken steps to see that the debt was paid. The courts generally hold, therefore, that notice of acceptance of a continuing guaranty must be given the guarantor. The courts taking the view that no notice is necessary do so on the reasoning that if the guarantor desired notice and did not receive notice from the debtor, he should have inquired as to what had been done.

Even in those jurisdictions which require notice of acceptance, certain exceptions to the rule prevail: Express notice is not necessary if the circumstances are such that the very nature of the transaction sufficiently informs the guarantor of the acceptance; the guarantor, in the letter of guaranty, may expressly waive notice; notice is not required when the letter of guaranty recites a consideration paid by the creditor to the guarantor; and notice is not required when the guaranty is made in exchange for an extension of time to the principal on a pre-existing debt or a forbearance to resort to litigation by the creditor. [*Electric Storage Battery Co. v. Black,* p. 806.]

Consideration The promise of the surety is usually made at the same time as that of the debtor, as where Brown signs a promissory note as accommodation maker with Jones. The consideration which supports the promise of Jones, the debtor, also supports the promise of Brown, the surety. The promise of the guarantor is generally made independently of the promise of the debtor, and must have a separate consideration to support the promise. Suppose Smith, the creditor, promises Brown, the guarantor, to forbear suit against Jones, the principal, for six months. Smith has suffered a detriment, and Jones has been benefited. Consideration exists, therefore, for the promise of the guarantor to pay if Jones does not pay.

RIGHTS OF THE CREDITOR

Rights against the Debtor and Surety The creditor, as a general rule, has the right to proceed immediately against the debtor or the surety as soon as performance is due, and it is generally not necessary for the creditor to notify the surety that the debtor had defaulted on his promise. It is to be remembered, however, that notice of default is frequently required in the case of a guarantor.

Rights against the Security The creditor, according to the general rule, can subject to the payment of his debt any property given to the surety by the principal as security for the debt. One line of cases says the basis for the rule is founded on the theory of subrogation; another line of cases says there is an implied trust in favor of the creditor. There is, in fact, no satisfactory basis for the rule. For purposes of business law, it is enough to say that the general rule represents the weight of authority. The creditor, moreover, may follow the property in the hands of the principal. This he may do either before or after maturity of the debt. [*Fields v. Letcher State Bank,* p. 807.]

SURETY BONDS

A surety bond, broadly speaking, is an obligation in writing which binds the surety to pay a certain sum to the obligee because of some act or default of a third person. Surety bonds usually contain a clause to the effect that upon performance of a certain condition the obligation shall be void and of no effect.

Surety bonds have been classified in many ways, and one classification frequently cuts along lines of another. They may, however, be classified as common-law bonds and statutory bonds. A person who builds a house may require the contractor to furnish a bond; such a bond is a common-law bond. Statutory bonds are those required by statute; they include judicial and official bonds. There are also various types of bonds, but, as a general rule they are either (1) construction bonds, (2) fidelity bonds, (3) official bonds, or (4) judicial bonds.

Construction Bonds   All bonded private construction work involves common-law bonds, and the provisions of such bonds vary greatly. They most certainly cover the performance of the work. The bond provisions and the court decisions, however, are in conflict as to whether or not a performance bond covers unpaid bills of the persons performing labor for and furnishing materials to the principal contractor. The problem sometimes presented to the court is whether laborers and materialmen may bring an action against the surety as third-party beneficiaries. This problem sometimes arises: Suppose the condition in the bond, in additon to requiring the performance of the work—completion of the work in accordance with the plans and specifications—recites that the debtor (the contractor) shall pay all laborers for labor performed and indemnify the creditor (the home owner) from all claims for labor performed. Could the unpaid laborers bring an action against the surety? Some courts have held that the laborers could not do so on the reasoning that the surety and the contractor had not contracted for the benefit of any third parties. The courts have indicated, however, that if the laborers had filed liens against the property of the home owner then the surety would be liable for the amount thereof.

Some construction bonds today expressly provide that unpaid laborers and materialmen shall have a direct right of action against the surety. Surety companies also frequently furnish two bonds: a "performance bond," which is primarily for the performance of the work, and a "payment bond," which is primarily for the payment of laborers and materialmen. The Miller Act, which covers bonds on federal projects, requires both a performance bond and a payment bond for all contracts for United States work over $2,000. Laborers and materialmen working for and supplying material to the general contractor, the subcontractors, and sub-subcontractors are given a direct right of action on the payment bond. The provisions of the Miller Act, however, do not cover work which is merely financed by an agency of the United States government, such as the Federal Housing Administration. This type of work falls under the classification of private work.

Fidelity Bonds   Fidelity bonds are frequently written in the same manner as an insurance policy. They are ordinarily entered into by companies to indemnify an employer—the obligee—against loss from the dishonesty or default of an officer, agent, or employee—the debtor. The employer, therefore, secures the bond so that any loss due to the infidelity of an employee will be covered by insurance. The surety has a right of subrogation against a defaulting employee if the employee commits an act contrary to the conditions of the bond. The right may be worthless, but it still exists.

Official Bonds   Many public officers are required by statute to give a bond as a condition of entering upon the duties of their office. These bonds—known as official bonds—ordinarily include all officers who have custody of public funds. The official, to be sure, would be individually liable for any loss. The official, however, is not always in a position to make good the loss. The requirement of an official bond, therefore, is to protect public funds.

Judicial Bonds   Judicial bonds are those which are required in connection with judicial proceedings. Some of the most common kinds are injunction bonds, attachment bonds, replevin bonds, bail bonds, and appeal bonds. The purpose of requiring a litigant to furnish a judicial bond is to indemnify the adverse party against damages resulting from the proceeding.

CASES

Electric Storage Battery Co. v. Black,   134 N.W.2d 481 (Wis. 1965). Action by The Electric Storage Battery Company, plaintiff, against Milo Black, defendant, to recover on the contract of guaranty. The defense of defendant was that he did not receive an acceptance of the guaranty.

Gerald Black, one of the defendants, entered into the rebuilt battery business and had the defendant's aid in gaining credit. Defendant sent plaintiff a letter which contained the following: "In regard to credit rating for Gerald Black, I will guarantee payment of material purchased." The plaintiff did not send any acknowledgment of this letter to defendant. Gerald Black purchased materials from the plaintiff, the first invoice being dated August 29, 1960, and the last invoice being dated December 29, 1961. The plaintiff wrote to the defendant in April and May, 1962, stating that it had learned that Gerald Black had discontinued his business and reminding the defendant of his guaranty. The defendant refused to make payment.

Gordon, Justice: All courts agree that if the contract of guaranty affirmatively calls for notice, it is a condition which must be met in order to bind the guarantor on his promise. Mr. Milo Black's letter of guaranty, dated July 30, 1960, does not expressly cover the question whether he expected to be notified by the creditor that the latter accepted the guaranty and intended to make deliveries of merchandise in reliance thereon. Courts have not been uniform in their decisions on the issue whether notice of intention to accept such a guaranty is necessary in order to hold the guarantor liable.

Some courts have held that if there is any fair reason for the guarantor to be uncertain that the creditor will accept the proposed guaranty, a notice of the intention to accept is a constructive condition to the liability of the guarantor.

When the guaranty contract is executed contemporaneously with the signing of the primary contract, it would be unsound to require formal notice. In addition, the guarantor may, by his conduct, waive the necessity of notice of acceptance.

The plaintiff has referred the court to several cases which hold that notice of acceptance is not necessary when the guaranties are continuing in nature, as they are considered to be offers which become effective as soon as they are relied on by the creditor. However, in each of the foregoing cases (unlike the case at bar) the giving of the guaranty was contemporaneous with the execution of the primary contract; under such circumstances, notice of acceptance would indeed be a formality.

We conclude that Mr. Milo Black was entitled to receive from the plaintiff notice of acceptance of his guaranty contract and, since such notice was not given, the guarantor cannot be held liable. [DECISION FOR DEFENDANT]

Fields v. Letcher State Bank, 76 S.W.2d 908 (Ky. 1934). Action by Letcher State Bank, plaintiff, against Kelley Fields, W. E. Cook, and R. Monroe Fields, defendants. The facts of this case were not in dispute: Kelley Fields borrowed $750 from the Letcher State Bank and executed a note therefor with W. E. Cook and R. Monroe Fields as sureties. Kelley Fields and his wife executed a note and mortgage for the same amount in favor of the sureties for the purpose of indemnifying them against loss. The bank sued Kelley Fields and the sureties on the note which they had executed to it and asked to be subrogated to the rights of the sureties and sought a judgment enforcing the mortgage lien. W. E. Cook and R. Monroe Fields filed an answer seeking a recovery on the note executed to them and the enforcement of their mortgage. The lower court held the bank was entitled to be subrogated to the rights of the sureties under the mortgage, but that the sureties were not entitled to recover because they had not satisfied the debts sued on. Judgment was rendered ordering a sale of the land covered by the mortgage. The defendants appealed. Their contention is that, inasmuch as the sureties were not entitled to enforce the mortgage lien for the reason that they had not satisfied the debt, neither was the bank entitled to enforce the mortgage.

Clay, Justice: The argument is that the bank could not obtain by substitution greater rights than those possessed by the sureties to whose rights they were subrogated. We need not dwell at length on this contention. It is sufficient to say that a security given by the principal to his surety is a security for the debt, as well as for the ultimate protection of the surety, and operates eo instanti for the benefit of the creditor; and that in such case the creditor may be subrogated to the rights of the surety either on his own application or on the application of the surety after the debt matures in an action against his principal to compel payment. [DECISION FOR PLAINTIFF]

PROBLEMS

1 Brown and Jones, the members of a partnership, dissolved the partnership. Jones, who owed Brown $1,000 upon dissolution of the partnership, executed a promissory note for that amount payable in six months. At the same time and in consideration of an extension of time to pay the debt, the father of Jones wrote a letter to Brown stating that if his son could not pay the note when it became due he, the father, would guarantee collection of the amount of the note. Jones defaulted in the note, and Brown immediately brought an action against the father of Jones to collect the amount due. Should he recover?

2 Wallace, in consideration for goods purchased from the plaintiff, made and delivered to plaintiff four trade acceptances. The defendant, at the same time, guaranteed the collection of the debt. On the due date of the trade acceptances, Wallace had been adjudicated a bankrupt, and the receivership records indicated that no disbursement of any kind would be made to unsecured creditors. Plaintiff instituted an action against the defendant to recover the amount due on the trade acceptances. Does the defendant have a defense?

3 Defendant wrote the following letter to plaintiff: "Jones is operating a rather small restaurant in this town. He desires to buy supplies from you to the extent of about $3,000. He is good for all the supplies he may buy. I recommend him to you, and hope that you will be able to let him have the supplies on credit." Plaintiff thereupon sold the supplies to Jones, but Jones was unable to pay for the supplies so furnished. Do you think plaintiff can recover from defendant for the supplies furnished to Jones?

4 Abel signed a note for $500, and delivered it to Baker, the payee. Baker assigned the note to Carter for $475. Baker orally guaranteed that the note would be paid by Abel on the date of maturity. Abel was unable to pay on the date of maturity. Will Carter be able to recover from Baker on the guaranty?

5 Black borrowed $1,000 from the First Bank, and signed a note for that amount. Davis signed the note as an accommodation maker for Black. When the note matured, the First Bank made no attempt to collect the amount of the note from Black. The First Bank, however, attempted to collect from Davis. Davis offered two defenses: First, a lack of consideration, and second, the First Bank must proceed against Black prior to proceeding against Davis. Are these valid defenses?

6 Tully, who was in the business of designing ladies' handbags from alligator hides, was unknown to Jones, who was in the business of selling alligator hides. Smith therefore wrote a letter to Jones as follows: "Tully is coming to your place today to purchase some hides. Let him have the hides and charge them to himself. I will see that you are paid within a reasonable time." Jones thereafter sold the alligator hides to Tully on several different occasions, and the hides were charged to the account of Tully. Tully was unable to pay for any of the hides. What is the liability of Smith?

7 Mary wanted to purchase a mink stole from the Fine Furs Shop, but the proprietor would not sell the stole to her on credit. Andrews, who had accompanied Mary to the shop, told the proprietor to open a joint account in the names of Mary and Andrews and charge the stole to that account. The proprietor opened the account, and Mary signed a charge slip acknowledging the receipt of the stole. Mary failed to pay for the stole, and the proprietor attempted to collect the purchase price of the stole from Andrews. Andrews contended that he was not liable due to the fact that he had not signed anything. Is this a good defense?

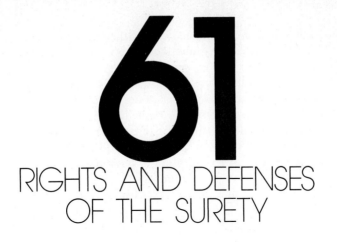

61
RIGHTS AND DEFENSES
OF THE SURETY

The material in this chapter will embrace (1) the rights of the surety before payment, (2) the rights of the surety after payment, and (3) the defenses of the surety.

RIGHTS OF THE SURETY BEFORE PAYMENT

The rights of the surety before the creditor has been paid are the right to request the creditor to proceed against the debtor and the right of exoneration.

Proceed against the Debtor   A few decisions have laid down the rule that a surety has the right to request the creditor to proceed against the debtor at maturity. The effect of these decisions is to discharge the surety to the extent that the surety can show damage by noncompliance with the request. Many of the states, moreover, have adopted this rule by statute. The decisions under the statute sometimes hold that a failure to sue the debtor upon request discharges the surety. This is sometimes true even though the failure to bring an action against the debtor has caused no loss to the surety. The decisions and statutes, therefore, have led to a conflict in the law.

Exoneration   The surety has the equitable right of exoneration against the debtor and his cosureties. The surety may, therefore, bring a suit in equity against the debtor and obtain a decree that the debtor pay the creditor. The remedy arises as soon as the claim of the creditor is due. The surety may assert this right before, or at the same time as, the creditor seeks recovery against the surety. It is not necessary that the surety allege any special reasons for fearing a loss, but the right is frequently asserted when the debtor is about to remove his property from the jurisdiction to avoid his creditors. The right, however, is in no way dependent upon a showing of a fraudulent disposition of property. As soon as the debt is due, the surety may bring a suit in equity and obtain a decree compelling the debtor to pay the debt. The remedy of exoneration is obviously of little value where the debtor is financially unable to pay the debt.

The surety has the same right against his cosureties. The right is obvious: Suppose Brown and three other persons were sureties for $20,000. It might be an undue hardship if Brown were compelled to raise the whole $20,000 at once. Brown could, therefore, bring a suit in equity and compel his cosureties to pay their pro rata share.

RIGHTS OF THE SURETY AFTER PAYMENT
The rights of the surety after payment are reimbursement, subrogation, and contribution.

Reimbursement It is eminently fair that when the surety has to pay the debt of the principal he should have recourse against the principal. In these circumstances, therefore, the surety has the right of reimbursement. The following has been settled law for a long time: A surety who has made payment is entitled to demand reimbursement from the principal for the amount which he has paid. The surety, moreover, is not required to pay the whole debt as a condition to enforce reimbursement; he is entitled to be reimbursed for any part of the matured debt which he has paid.

Two further rules should not be overlooked: Payment before maturity does not entitle the surety to proceed immediately against the principal as this would force the principal to pay the debt before he contracted to do so; and the right of reimbursement does not arise until the surety has paid the debt or a part of it.

It is sometimes thought that the discharge of the principal in a proceeding in bankruptcy will discharge the obligation of the surety to the creditor. This is not true. Payment by the surety, however, entitles him to file a claim for reimbursement. A surety who has a right of reimbursement at the time the principal is adjudicated a bankrupt, however, must present his claim as a creditor against the bankrupt estate. Do not confuse bankruptcy with a voluntary composition agreement. A creditor who enters into a voluntary composition agreement, as distinguished from bankruptcy, will discharge the surety.

The statute of limitations presents some interesting questions. What happens if a surety pays a debt which is barred as to both the debtor and the surety? The payment is said to be voluntary, and the surety is not entitled to reimbursement. May a surety be compelled to pay a debt which the creditor could not have forced against the debtor? He may be compelled to do so. Suppose the right of the creditor to sue the debtor is barred by the statute, but the surety has been out of the jurisdiction. The statute would not have run against the surety, and the creditor could compel the surety to pay but not the debtor. When the surety pays the debt, however, he is entitled to reimbursement from the debtor. The statute of limitations does not begin to run on the right of reimbursement until a payment has been made. [*Keyes v. Dyer*, p. 814.]

Subrogation The surety, after paying the debt of the debtor, steps into the place of the creditor and may recover from the debtor to the same extent and in the same manner that the creditor could have recovered. The surety is subrogated to the creditor's interest in property held as security for performance of the obligation; to the creditor's right against third persons who are also liable to the creditor on the obligation of the debtor; and to the creditor's right against cosureties and any security held by them. The surety, therefore, has the right to enforce any lien, pledge, or mortgage which secured the debt. The right of subrogation does not arise until the surety has wholly satisfied the debt, but as a general rule, a surety is not denied subrogation even though he could have successfully pleaded the statute of limitations.

Contribution The surety, in addition to the right of subrogation of all of the rights of the creditor against the cosureties, has a direct right of contribution against the cosureties. It is well settled that the right of contribution exists even though the sureties are not aware of the undertaking of each other. The right, however, does not arise until one of the sureties has paid more than his share of the debt. This is true whether the debt is fully satisfied or not. What happens when a surety compromises a claim? He may exact contribution from his cosureties to the extent that the creditor accepts satisfaction of the original debt. The creditor lends the debtor $10,000. A, B, C, and D are the sureties. D induces the creditor to accept $4,000 in payment of the debt. Each surety would be liable for $1,000. If D pays $2,000 in settlement, he will be entitled to exact $500 from A, B, and C provided all of the sureties are solvent. The amount of contribution that a surety can compel from each of his cosureties is ordinarily determined not by the number of the sureties but by the number of solvent sureties within the jurisdiction. A few states hold otherwise.

A surety who pays a debt when neither he nor his cosureties are legally obligated to pay it makes a voluntary payment and he is not entitled to contribution. It is not necessary, however, to wait until the creditor has started a suit to collect the debt. A payment by the surety, therefore, is not voluntary if a suit might be maintained on the debt by the creditor. As a general rule, however, a payment of a debt by one cosurety after the statute of limitations has run in his favor, or in favor of his cosureties, is voluntary and does not entitle him to enforce contribution from his cosureties. The courts are not agreed, however, as to the right of contribution where one surety pays a debt which he is legally obligated to pay, but which is barred as to his cosureties. Suppose the death of a cosurety makes applicable a shorter period of the statute of limitations against his estate; suppose the period of the statute of limitations has been kept alive as to the paying surety by a judgment in favor of the creditor. In such circumstances, most of the authorities support the rule that the paying surety would have the right of contribution.

DEFENSES OF THE SURETY

The defenses of the surety include (1) certain of the defenses which are available to the debtor, (2) the defenses that are personal to the surety, and (3) certain acts of the creditor which operate to discharge the surety.

Defenses of the Debtor   The defenses of the debtor—other than those that are entirely personal to the debtor—are, as a general rule, also available to the surety. A surety clearly cannot be held liable upon a contract that is void because of illegality. The same is true of a lack or failure of consideration. The courts, however, have been troubled with the defense of fraud. This is because the debtor, upon discovering the fraud of the creditor, can elect either to rescind the contract or to affirm it. These rules, however, are fairly well settled: If the debtor rescinds, the surety may avail himself of the defense of fraud. If the debtor affirms, the surety remains bound. What about duress? The same rules are applicable to duress except that duress upon the debtor is also considered duress upon the surety where the debtor and the surety are close relatives. Incapacity of the debtor to contract is, as a general rule, no defense of the surety. The reason sometimes given for the rule is that the creditor exacted the promise of the surety because of the incapacity of the debtor. Suppose an infant debtor disaffirms the contract and returns the consideration to the creditor? The courts agree that the surety is discharged. The recent cases hold, however, that he is discharged only to the extent of the value of the consideration at the time it is returned. The statute of limitations and bankruptcy have already been mentioned.

Defenses Personal to the Surety   The surety has available all defenses that are personal to him. The defense of concealment, nondisclosure, and misrepresentation have frequently been litigated. It is quite clear that failure on the part of the creditor to disclose facts material to the surety is a defense. It is, nevertheless, difficult to determine under just what circumstances the creditor has a duty to speak. The creditor clearly must answer fully and truthfully any inquiry of the surety. An employer, in accepting a bond for faithful performance, is under a duty to disclose facts to the surety pertaining to the honesty and integrity of an employee. It is quite clear that fraud practiced by the creditor on the surety is available as a defense. Fraud practiced by the debtor on the surety, however, does not relieve the surety. This presupposes that the creditor has no knowledge of, and that there is no reason why he should have knowledge of, such fraud practiced by the debtor on the surety. [*J. R. Watkins Co. v. Lankford*, p. 815.]

Acts of the Creditor   The following acts are generally held to be defenses of the surety:

(1)   ***Release of the Principal Debtor***   It is a well-settled rule of law that a release of the principal debtor by the creditor, without the consent of the surety, will release the surety. A release of a part of the debt will also release the surety to the extent of the released debt. The rule, however, has no application where the creditor releases the debtor but reserves his rights against the surety. This result is reached on the reasoning that the principal, by accepting a release containing such a provision, impliedly consents that the rights of the surety shall not be impaired. The agreement which releases the debtor with a reservation of rights against the surety is construed as a covenant not to sue. It is then, in effect, an agreement between the creditor and the debtor that the creditor may proceed against the surety, who, in turn, may then proceed against the debtor. The surety, therefore, is not prejudiced by the release. This rule may be illustrated: Brown executes a mortgage encumbering his house and lot in favor of Abel to secure a loan. Brown then sells the house and lot to Cabot, who assumes the mortgage indebtedness. Abel agrees to release Cabot from the indebtedness. Abel, however, reserves his rights against Brown. Brown may proceed against Cabot for reimbursement if Brown is required by Abel to pay the debt.

It is also held in the few cases that have been litigated that a release of the debtor does not discharge the surety if he is indemnified. Suppose Brown, the surety on a $1,000 debt, receives collateral in that amount from the debtor as security for the debt. Suppose further that the creditor releases the debtor. Could Brown plead the release of the debtor in an action against him by the creditor? He could not. The courts, in deciding the cases, have advanced several theories. It would appear, however, that the real reason for the rule is that the surety has not been injured because he may recover whatever is due him from the sale of the collateral.

(2)   ***Release of the Security***   The release of the security by a creditor will likewise release a surety to the extent of the value of the security released. The release, however, must constitute a material injury to the right of subrogation of the surety. A surety, therefore, is not discharged where a part of the security is released if that part which he retains is ample security for the debt. The burden of showing that no actual injury has resulted is upon the creditor.

Is the surety discharged when the security held by the creditor is lost or dissipated by inactivity of the creditor? There is no clear-cut answer to the question. The majority of the cases seem to hold that a surety is not thereby discharged. The reason given for the rule is that the surety has the right to pay the debt and then proceed against the debtor himself, or he may exercise his right of subrogation. Some courts, however, have said that the creditor has a duty to use reasonable care in preserving the security and that the surety will be discharged to the extent of the loss suffered by him in the absence of such care.

(3)   ***Alteration in the Contract***   The surety, according to the general rule, will be discharged by any material change in the contract existing between the debtor and the creditor. The change may be in the physical document which has been signed by the surety. The problem, however, is to determine when an alteration is material enough to discharge the surety. Any alteration in the amount, the date of maturity, and the place of payment would be material. The change may

also be with respect to the duty of performance of the debtor. The surety would ordinarily be discharged if the debtor were a clerk in a store and his duties were changed to that of cashier. The rule is otherwise with respect to official bonds. The liability of a surety for default in the performance of duties of the public officer imposed by law extends to duties which may from time to time be added to the office by amendment to the law.

The modern trend in the cases is to make a distinction between a gratuitous surety and a compensated surety. These cases generally hold that a change does not discharge a compensated surety unless the change is injurious to the surety. It is sometimes said that it would be unjust to permit a compensated surety to collect premiums for his services and then repudiate his obligation on a slight pretext. The modern-day surety company, therefore, must ordinarily show some injury in order to be exonerated. The surety, whether gratuitous or compensated, will not be discharged if he consents to the change.

(4) *Extension of Time*   An extension of time of payment or performance given by the creditor to the debtor is one of the most common methods by which a surety is discharged. This rule has been enacted into statute in a few of the states. There are, however, quite a few exceptions to the rule. A gratuitous promise to the debtor would not be binding; the extension must be based upon consideration. An extension given for an indefinite time, such as "a while longer," would not be binding: a promise to extend the time "for thirty days" would be binding and operate to discharge the surety. The surety is not discharged unless the creditor was aware of the existence of the suretyship relation when he gave the extension. The surety is not discharged if he consents to the extension. The surety is not discharged if he is fully indemnified against loss, that is, the surety has in his possession property of the debtor, or some lien upon property of the debtor, sufficient to pay the loss. The surety is not discharged if the creditor expressly reserves his rights against the surety. The rule is well settled, but the reason for the rule is somewhat clouded. The reason most often offered is that the surety is left unprejudiced because the surety may protect himself: He may pay the debt and proceed forthwith against the debtor for reimbursement.

(5) *Tender of Payment*   It is a general rule that a tender of payment, to be effective, must be kept good. The rule, however, does not apply to a contract of suretyship. A valid tender of payment by the debtor or by the surety, which is refused by the creditor, will discharge the surety at once from all liability. The reason generally assigned for the rule is that the refusal of a valid tender takes away the immediate right of the surety to proceed against the debtor for reimbursement. The tender, to be sure, must be legal and unconditional. Such acts as a tender of a part of the debt, a mere offer to pay, or a tender of property would not be sufficient.

CASES

Keyes v. Dyer,   243 P.2d 710 (Okla. 1952). Action by R. W. Dyer (plaintiff below), appellee, against M. W. Keyes (defendant below), appellant. It appears that plaintiff joined as a surety in executing a promissory note dated November 28, 1933, in favor of J. D. Laney, which was payable on December 1, 1934; that the plaintiff, on January 19, 1946, was compelled to pay a judgment which the payee, J. D. Laney, recovered upon said note; and that the plaintiff on November 5, 1948, brought this action for reimbursement. Defendant contends the action is barred by the three-year statute of limitations.

Per Curiam: According to the prevailing view, the remedy at law of the surety who has paid a note or satisfied a judgment for his principal is an action on the obligation, implied by law, of the principal to reimburse his surety.

. . . We observe that the obligation of a principal to reimburse his surety, implied in law, finds express recognition in a companion statute.

"If a surety satisfies the principal obligation, or any part thereof, whether with or without legal proceedings, the principal is bound to reimburse what he has disbursed, including necessary costs and expenses . . ." 15 O.S. 1951, § 381 . . .

The statute of limitations, supra, permits the bringing of the action within the applicable period of limitations "after the cause of action shall have accrued." Defendant urges that if the judgment herein was based upon the note, plaintiff's cause of action accrued upon the maturity of said note, nearly 14 years before the commencement of this action. We would recognize the merits of that contention were this an action brought upon the note by the payee thereof, but here we are considering the liability of the principal maker of the note for reimbursement of the amount paid by an accommodation maker in satisfaction of the principal obligation. The right to reimbursement under the statute, supra, 15 O.S. 1951, § 381, could not arise until payment is made. The principal obligation in the case at bar was due and owing at the time it was paid by the plaintiff surety, and when said payment was made the plaintiff surety was then, and not until then, entitled to maintain the cause of action for reimbursement under said statute.

Therefore, plaintiff's cause of action accrued on January 19, 1946. This action, having been commenced on November 5, 1948, was not barred by the applicable three-year statute of limitations. [DECISION FOR PLAINTIFF]

J. R. Watkins Co. v. Lankford, 256 S.W.2d 788 (Mo. 1953). Action by J. R. Watkins Company, plaintiff, against John T. Baker, T. J. Sanders, Louis Wilkerson, and J. L. Lankford, defendants, to recover for merchandise sold to the defendant John T. Baker under the terms of a dealer's contract, payment of which was guaranteed by the other defendants as his sureties. The pertinent facts pertain to the contest of defendant T. J. Sander. He contends that his signature as surety was obtained by fraud by Baker and a Mr. Paul Corbin who had a similar dealer's contract. His evidence shows:

Baker and Corbin drove out to his home and found him in the driveway. Baker got out first and asked Sanders to sign (saying it was a recommendation) while Corbin remained in the car. (Baker said he had never read the document but took Corbin's word for what was in it.) Sanders said, after he had talked with Baker, "he [Corbin] got out and said that he wanted me to sign this recommendation for Mr. Baker to sell Watkins' products and I said that I didn't have my glasses and couldn't read without them and I said that I didn't want to sign anything that would hurt me in any way and he said there was nothing there that would hurt me and that it was just a recommendation for Mr. Baker." Sanders then signed without going into the house for his glasses. Baker's contract and the suretyship agreement were both printed on one long (legal size) sheet of paper.

Hyde, Judge: The first question is whether the fact that the suretyship agreement was fraudulently misrepresented to Sanders by the principal Baker, and also by Corbin as only a recommendation, is any defense to plaintiff's action on the agreement. . . . The rule is thus stated in Restatement of Security, Sec. 119:

Where the surety by fraud or duress of the principal has been induced to become bound to the creditor, the fraud or duress is not a defense against the creditor, if, without knowledge of the fraud, he has extended credit to the principal on the security of the surety's promise or, relying on the promise, has changed his position in respect of the principal.

The following illustration is given:

P induced S to sign an instrument guaranteeing an extension of credit by C to P. S had an opportunity to read the instrument but did not do so and relied upon P's representation that it was a letter of recommendation. P exhibited the instrument to C, who extended the credit without knowledge of P's fraud. S is liable to C.

That illustration fits this case completely. Sanders could have gone into his house, got his glasses and read the agreement before he signed it, or he could have had it read to him. There is no evidence that plaintiff had any knowledge of the alleged misrepresentations. Thus there are no facts in evidence to show that the general rule should not apply in this case. [DECISION FOR PLAINTIFF]

PROBLEMS

1 Chase, an employee of the plaintiff, was authorized to solicit applications for insurance and deliver receipts for all monies received. Plaintiff, sometime thereafter, found that Chase had collected but had not accounted for premiums amounting to between $1,000 and $1,200. Plaintiff thereupon agreed with Chase that he might continue in his employment upon condition that he pay the shortage and furnish a bond. The amount of his arrearage was paid, and a bond was signed by Ellis and Marvin as sureties in the presence of plaintiff who made no disclosure of the facts relative to the shortage. Sometime thereafter Chase left the employ of plaintiff, at which time he failed to pay over to the plaintiff an amount of $1,029.04 which he had converted to his own use. The plaintiff thereupon instituted an action against the sureties for $1,029.04. Is the plaintiff entitled to recover?
2 Plaintiff, who had a contract for the construction of a building, entered into a contract with a subcontractor to commence and complete the erection of all structural steel for the building. Defendant, a surety company, executed to plaintiff a bond for the faithful performance of the contract by the subcontractor. The subcontractor was not proceeding with the work to the satisfaction of plaintiff. Plaintiff thereupon paid the subcontractor for the work he had performed and wrote him a letter in which he stated that "your contract is now terminated and canceled." Plaintiff then brought an action against the defendant as surety of the subcontractor. Is plaintiff entitled to recover?

3 Brown and Smith signed a promissory note as accommodation makers for Jones, the maker. The note was for the sum of $1,400 and was payable to the order of Brewer. The note was not paid on its due date, and Brewer brought an action against Brown to recover the $1,400. Brown answered and acknowledged that he signed the note as accommodation maker, that it was due and unpaid, and that Brewer was entitled to a judgment recovering the $1,400. He contends, however, that he is entitled to have included in the judgment an adjudication of his rights of subrogation and contribution. Do you agree with this contention?

4 Martin borrowed $5,000 from Brown, and Jones promised to pay the debt if Martin did not pay it when the debt became due provided Martin transferred ten shares of stock valued at $3,000 to Brown as security for the loan. Brown thereafter returned the shares of stock to Martin, and Jones refused to pay the debt when Martin did not pay. What amount, if any, will Brown be able to recover from Jones?

5 Langford purchased an automobile from The Automobile Agency for $3,500, and promised to pay therefor in six months. Watkins signed the purchase agreement as surety. The account became due. Langford, who desired to protect Watkins on the contract, offered to convey certain real estate he owned valued at $4,000 in payment of the automobile. The offer was refused, and The Automobile Agency brought an action against Watkins to recover the $3,500. Watkins contended that he was discharged because Langford had made a valid tender of payment which was refused. Do you agree with this contention?

6 Brown borrowed $5,000 from the First Bank and he, as maker, and Jones, as surety, signed the note for the loan. The First Bank thereafter requested Brown to furnish another surety. Smith thereupon, at the request of Brown, also signed for sufficient consideration the note as surety. Brown was unable to pay the note when it became due, and Jones was obligated to pay the $5,000. The First Bank surrendered the note to Jones, who then learned for the first time that Smith was also a surety on the note. What are the rights, if any, of Jones against Smith?

62
BANKRUPTCY

The Congress of the United States, in pursuance of its constitutional power, has enacted the Bankruptcy Act to establish a uniform system of bankruptcy throughout the United States. This act supersedes any state insolvency laws, and is the recognized medium for giving a distressed debtor a fresh start in life by means of a liquidation or some plan of rehabilitation.

Ten chapters of the act have a sufficiently important impact upon the business community to warrant their discussion. The first seven chapters cover ordinary or straight bankruptcy. This is the type of proceeding used when a debtor reaches "the end of the road," figuratively speaking, and a liquidation of his assets appears desirable. The creditors will usually receive small dividends; the debts will be discharged; and the debtor will be out of business with no assets. Debtor rehabilitation became increasingly desirable, more particularly since 1933, and new chapters embracing new concepts have been added to the act. Congress, in adding the new chapters, had as an objective the rehabilitation of the business of the debtor, thereby avoiding a liquidation of the assets. Three chapters will be discussed. Chapter X provides the machinery for the reorganization of a corporation without an interruption of its operations, Chapter XI provides that a debtor may work out a plan with unsecured creditors, and Chapter XIII is designed for the wage-earner-debtor who desires to pay his debts over a period of time and retain his assets. Straight or ordinary bankruptcy and these three chapters will be discussed in this order.

STRAIGHT BANKRUPTCY

Straight or ordinary bankruptcy is a means of liquidation for a debtor hopelessly in debt or for one who desires a liquidation for some reason. A person may file a petition with the federal district court and be adjudicated a voluntary bankrupt, or under certain circumstances, to be discussed later, a creditor or creditors may file the petition and literally force a debtor into involuntary bankruptcy.

Commencement of the Proceedings   The commencement of the proceedings poses four questions: How are bankruptcy proceedings instituted? What are the acts of bankruptcy? Who may file a petition? What happens after the petition is filed?

The answer to the first question depends upon whether the debtor himself or the creditor or creditors are instituting the proceedings.

(1) *Voluntary Bankrupts*   Any sane adult debtor may be adjudged—that is, pronounced by the court—a bankrupt on his own petition. The filing of a petition operates automatically as an adjudication except when less than all the partners file a petition on behalf of a partnership. The solvency of the petitioner is immaterial; the liabilities are likewise immaterial. The petitioner must owe debts, or more accurately, he must owe one debt. Substantially any individual, partnership, or corporation may become a voluntary bankrupt. A wage earner or a farmer may file a voluntary petition although they are not subject to involuntary bankruptcy. Some organizations, however, may not become voluntary bankrupts. They are municipal, railroad, insurance, and banking corporations, as well as building and loan associations. These organizations are regulated by other statutes.

(2) *Involuntary Bankrupts*   A debtor who is subjected to bankruptcy on the petition of his creditors is known as an "involuntary bankrupt." Almost any natural person, moneyed, business, or commercial corporation may be made an involuntary bankrupt. Municipal, railroad, insurance, and banking corporations, as well as building and loan associations, are again separately regulated and may not become involuntary bankrupts. In addition, nonprofit corporations, farmers, and wage earners are excluded from the act. A person who is personally engaged in farming or tillage of the soil and whose principal income is derived from the farm is a farmer within the meaning of the Bankruptcy Act. The definition of a "farmer" has been extended to include one who personally produces products of the soil or whose principal income is derived from such farming operations. All persons engaged in the tillage of the soil, in dairy farming, and in the production of poultry, livestock, and their products are farmers; a person growing garden products upon his own premises for the use of his table is not. A corporation engaged in farming is, however, subject to involuntary bankruptcy. It is not certain whether a partnership engaged in farming may be made an involuntary bankrupt. All persons earning over $1,500 a year are not wage earners within the meaning of straight bankruptcy. It should be kept in mind that professional men, traveling salesmen, independent contractors, and corporate officers who receive compensation in addition to their salaries are not wage earners within the meaning of the bankruptcy act.

ACTS OF BANKRUPTCY

The petitioning creditors are required to allege in their petition that the debtor, within the immediate four months prior to filing of the petition, has committed one or more of the following six acts of bankruptcy:

(1) The debtor has concealed, removed, or permitted to be concealed or removed any part of his property, with intent to hinder, delay, or defraud his creditors or any of them or made or suffered a transfer of any of his property, which is fraudulent under certain specified provisions of the act. It should be noted that insolvency on the part of the debtor is not an essential element. If the debtor is able to prove that he was solvent at the time the petition was filed; the proceeding will be dismissed, and the debtor will not be adjudicated a bankrupt.

(2) The debtor, while insolvent, made or suffered a preferential transfer of a portion of his property to a creditor on account of or for an antecedent debt, the effect of which will be to enable such creditor to obtain a greater percentage of his debt than some other creditor of the same class. It should be kept in mind that an intent to prefer such a creditor is no longer required as a part of this act of bankruptcy.

(3) The debtor has suffered or permitted, while insolvent, any creditor to obtain a lien upon any of his property through legal proceedings or distraint, such as by a seizure. The debtor could have the lien vacated or discharged within thirty days from the date of the lien or at least five days before the date set for any sale or other disposition of the property encumbered by the lien. He then could not be forced into bankruptcy under the third act of bankruptcy. If the debtor does pay the debt and discharge the lien, however, he will probably have committed the second act of bankruptcy. He could then be forced into bankruptcy under the second act of bankruptcy.

(4) The debtor has made a general assignment for the benefit of his creditors. The assignment must be to a trustee, not to the creditors, in order to make a distribution.

(5) The debtor, while insolvent or unable to pay his debts as they mature, has procured, permitted, or suffered voluntarily or involuntarily the appointment of a receiver or trustee to take charge of his property.

(6) The debtor has admitted in writing his inability to pay his debts and his willingness to be adjudged a bankrupt. One might wonder why the debtor does not go into voluntary bankruptcy instead. The answer might lie in the fact that some persons feel that the stigma of involuntary bankruptcy is less than that of voluntary bankruptcy. At any rate, it may well be that the sixth act of bankruptcy is used against those debtors who are negligent in drafting their correspondence. It should be mentioned that the bankruptcy test of insolvency is the "balance sheet" test. A debtor is considered insolvent, therefore, when there is an excess of liabilities over assets at a fair evaluation. This test of insolvency is entirely different from the "equity" test of insolvency, which is the inability of a debtor to pay his debts as they mature. [*Levy v. Carter Rice & Co.,* p. 832.]

The test of insolvency for the second and third acts is the "balance sheet" test, but the test for insolvency in the fifth act is either the "balance sheet" test or the "equity" test. The debtor, with respect to the sixth act, admits his insolvency in an "equity" sense.

It is important to remember that the petition must be filed within four months after the commission of the act of bankruptcy. When do the four months begin to run? The period of time begins to run with respect to the third act of bankruptcy at the time the lien was obtained. It is settled, however, that the creditor has only three months in which to file the petition since it cannot be filed until the expiration of thirty days after the lien was obtained. The time element is slightly more involved with respect to the first and fourth acts of bankruptcy. The four months begin at the time the fraudulent conveyance or the assignment is so far perfected that no bona fide purchaser from the debtor could obtain rights superior to the transferee. This means that the petition must be filed before the expiration of the four months following the filing or recording of the fraudulent conveyance or the assignment. With respect to an assignment, some states protect the assignee as of the time of the assignment and prior to the filing or recording of the assignment. In these states, the four months will be measured from the date of the assignment and not from the date of filing or recording.

The Petition The petition will be properly filed in the district court where the debtor had his principal place of business or where he resided or had his domicil for the preceding six months. The debtor himself will sign the petition in voluntary bankruptcy proceedings. The privilege of filing an involuntary proceeding, however, is regulated as follows: The liabilities of the debtor must amount to $1,000 or more; there must be at least three petitioning creditors if the debtor has twelve or more creditors; one petitioning creditor is sufficient if the debtor has less than twelve creditors; the petitioning creditor or creditors must hold claims which are provable, fixed as to liability and amount, and which aggregate $500 over and above the value of any security held by the creditor. Secured creditors may be petitioners only to the extent that their claims are unsecured. To illustrate: A creditor with a claim of $5,000 secured for $3,000 is an unsecured creditor to the extent of $2,000. A final statement with respect to a dispute as to whether there are less than twelve creditors: The Bankruptcy Act requires the omission of relatives, employees, stockholders, directors, officers, fully secured creditors, and any person who has received a preference or lien which is voidable under the provisions of the act.

The Adjudication The adjudication is the decree of the court which declares the debtor to be a bankrupt. The filing of a voluntary petition in straight bankruptcy, other than a petition filed in behalf of a partnership by less than all the partners, operates as an adjudication with the same force and effect as a decree of adjudication. The procedure is more complicated when an involuntary petition is filed. A subpoena and a copy of the petition will be served on the debtor. The service of the summons is accomplished in much the same manner as it is accomplished in the commencement of a civil action in the federal courts. The ordinary rules of pleading are proper. The rules of pleading, however, are the responsibility of the lawyer. Suffice it to say, the debtor will have an opportunity to answer the petition. He may deny insolvency, dispute the stated number of creditors, or offer any other defense that is available to him. If the debtor does not answer the petition within the prescribed time, the court—this is, the referee or judge—will adjudicate the debtor a bankrupt or dismiss the petition. If the debtor does answer the petition, the court will determine the issues and adjudicate the debtor a bankrupt or dismiss the petition. It should be mentioned that the debtor may demand a jury trial with respect to insolvency or the commission of an act of bankruptcy. All other issues, however, will be determined by the court.

A word of warning: A creditor or creditors should exercise extreme caution before forcing a debtor into bankruptcy proceedings. If the debtor contests the proceedings and is successful in having the petition dismissed, the petitioning creditors may be required to respond in damages for an action of malicious prosecution. This could be serious when a debtor is deprived of his business and other damages and expenses accrue.

ADMINISTRATION OF THE ESTATE

The administration of the estate of the bankrupt sometimes becomes highly complicated. An overall view of the administration, however, may be gained by briefly discussing the officers of the court, the first meeting of creditors, claims that are provable, transactions in which the trustee may be able to augment the estate of the bankrupt, and reclamation petitions.

Officers of the Court   The bankruptcy proceedings will, of course, be under the control of some district judge. The chief officers of the administration of the estate of the bankrupt, however, are the referee, the trustee, the receiver, and the appraiser.

(1)   *The Referee*   The referee in bankruptcy is generally in almost complete charge of the proceedings. He exercises most of the powers of a judge during the course of the administration of the estate. He is appointed by the judges of the several courts of bankruptcy on a salary basis for a period of six years. He must be competent; be a resident within the territorial limits of the bankruptcy court and maintain an office there; and be a member in good standing at the bar of the federal district court in which he is appointed. He must not hold a public office for profit; must not be related to judges of the bankruptcy courts or federal appellate courts; must not act in cases in which he is directly or indirectly interested; must not purchase, directly or indirectly, any property of an estate in bankruptcy. The referee sends out notices to all creditors advising them of the time and place of the first meeting of creditors.

(2)   *The Trustee*   The trustee, as soon as he has qualified, takes possession of the property of the bankrupt. He is charged with the actual physical administration of the estate. It is his duty to collect and reduce to money the

property of the estate and to close up the estate as expeditiously as is compatible with the best interests of the parties in interest; deposit all moneys received in designated depositories; keep records and accounts showing all amounts and items of property received and from what source, and all amounts expended and for what purpose; examine all proofs of claim and object to the allowance of such claims as may be improper; report to the court the condition of the estate, the amounts of money on hand, and such other details as may be required by the court; make final reports and file final accounts with the court; lay before the final meetings of the creditors detailed statements of the administration of the estate; and set apart the exemptions of the bankrupt, if claimed, and report the items and estimated value thereof to the court. It seems appropriate to mention at this point that the debtor is given an opportunity to file a schedule showing his exempt property. The Bankruptcy Act permits the debtor to hold, free from claims of his creditors, whatever property is exempt under state law. The state exemption statutes are not uniform. Most exemption statutes, however, exempt the home of the bankrupt and some miscellaneous personal property.

(3)   *The Receiver*   It is customary, in some situations where it is necessary to conserve the assets of the estate or dispose of perishable property, to have a receiver appointed by the bankruptcy court. The receiver is a temporary officer whose duty it is to preserve the estate for the creditors until a trustee is elected and qualified. He may be a mere custodian or he may be given broader powers, such as continuing the operation of the business for a limited period.

(4)   *The Appraiser*   The appraiser, who is appointed by the court, will appraise the property of the bankrupt and file a report thereon. In some instances, three appraisers will be appointed. The major objective in appointing an appraiser is to establish some reasonable standard in determining whether the bids are adequate in the sale of property of the bankrupt estate.

"Call" of First Meeting   The referee is under a duty to "call" by written notice to all creditors the first meeting of the creditors not less than ten and not more than thirty days after the debtor was adjudicated a bankrupt.

First Meeting of Creditors   The referee—sometimes the judge—presides at the first meeting of creditors. The following business is commonly transacted: Proofs of claims are filed and allowed. A trustee is elected by a vote of the claims that have been allowed. The person who receives a majority of the votes in number and amount is elected. Claims of less than $50 are counted as to amount but not as to number.

After the trustee has been elected, the bankrupt is examined. The debtor, once a petition in bankruptcy is filed, is required to file a "statement of affairs and schedules" showing a schedule of his property, and a list of all his creditors. This statement is usually used as a basis for the examination. In some jurisdictions, the referee conducts the examination and subsequently permits the creditors to examine the bankrupt. The entire examination, however, is sometimes conducted by counsel for the trustee. The bankrupt will be examined as to all his business affairs. The purpose of the examination is a complete disclosure of all the facts relating to his bankruptcy. The bankrupt, therefore, will be examined as to whether he has issued false financial statements, as to possible voidable transactions, as to his income tax returns, the causes of insolvency, concealed assets, excessive expenses (salaries, rent, etc.).

Property Acquired after Bankruptcy   Certain property which vests in the bankrupt by bequest, devise, or inheritance within six months after the filing of the petition passes to the trustee. This is to prevent an expectant heir from incurring debts and resorting to bankruptcy shortly prior to the death of someone from whom the inheritance is expected. This rule covers property which the bankrupt held by the entirety at the time of the filing of the petition and which becomes transferable by him solely, in whole or in part within six months thereafter. It too passes to the trustee.

Provable Claims   A provable claim is one that may be asserted and allowed against a bankrupt estate. The provability of a claim will be determined as of the time when the petition in bankruptcy was filed. The provability is important for two important reasons: First, if the claim is provable, the claim is entitled to share pro rata in the distribution of dividends, and second, a claim that is provable is discharged as a general rule.

A creditor, before he can participate in a bankruptcy proceeding, must prove his claim. The claim, moreover, must be allowed. It is, therefore, very important that the forms used for the various types of proofs of claim be properly filled out and verified. The original invoices should be attached to a claim based on an open account. The originals of promissory notes or written contracts should likewise be attached to the claim. Permission is usually given to substitute photostatic copies thereafter.

Proofs of claims must be filed within six months after the first date set for the first meeting of creditors. The notice which the creditors receive of the first meeting of creditors serves as a warning that creditors have six months after the date set for such meeting in which to file their proofs of claim.

Some of the important provable claims are as follows:

(1) A fixed liability which is evidenced by a judgment or an instrument in writing. The debt must be absolutely owing, but it does not have to be due at the time the petition is filed. It should be mentioned that a negotiable instrument is provable since it is in writing. Any debt evidenced by a judgment which was obtained prior to the filing of the petition is provable, including a claim based on a tort.

(2) Costs which are incurred prior to filing of the petition in actions by or against the bankrupt. This includes costs incurred by a creditor in good faith who brought an action on a debt which is provable.

(3) An open account, or a contract express or implied. It should be noted, however, that the debt must be due and owing at the time the petition is filed.

(4) A judgment recovered on a provable claim after the petition was filed and

before the bankrupt's application for a discharge is considered. The claim will be reduced, however, by the costs to accrue after the petition was filed.

(5) Workmen's compensation award for an injury that occurred prior to the adjudication.

(6) Tort claims are not provable as a general rule. A tort claim based upon negligence is provable provided that the action was instituted prior to the filing of the petition and provided further that it was still pending at the time the petition was filed. It is important to note, however, that this tort claim is unliquidated and it will be allowed only if it is liquidated in the time and manner as indicated by the court.

(7) Contingent debts and contingent contractual liabilities. Some examples are claims against bankrupt guarantors, sureties, and indorsers. The claims too must be liquidated without undue delay or they will not be allowed.

(8) Claims of accommodation parties when the principal debtor becomes bankrupt. The accommodation party may file a claim in his own name if he pays the debt prior to bankruptcy. If he has not paid the debt, however, he is a contingent claimant and must file a claim in the name of the creditor.

(9) Claims for anticipatory breach of executory contracts are provable. An executory contract is breached when the bankrupt is adjudicated a bankrupt since bankruptcy itself is an anticipatory breach. A sum in the amount of rent for one year is allowed for future rent under a lease. Any rent which has accrued and is due and owing at the time the petition was filed is provable in full.

Augmenting the Bankrupt's Estate   Consideration is now given to transactions in which the trustee may be able to augment the estate of the bankrupt for the benefit of the creditors. These transactions are in the nature of voidable transactions. The rules with respect to voidable transactions govern the following:

(1) *Preferential Transfers*   A preferential transfer which enables the recipient to obtain a greater percentage of his debt than other creditors may be recovered by the trustee if the transfer was made by an insolvent debtor within four months prior to the filing of the petition in bankruptcy, and if the recipient of the preference at the time he received it had reasonable cause to believe that the debtor was insolvent.

(2) *Preferential Liens*   A lien obtained by a creditor within four months of the filing of the petition, while the debtor was insolvent, to secure an existing debt may be set aside by the trustee.

(3) *Fraudulent Conveyances*   The Bankruptcy Act provides that if the bankrupt, within twelve months prior to the filing of the petition in bankruptcy, has committed a fraudulent conveyance, the trustee may have the fraudulent conveyance set aside and the proceeds returned to the trustee for the benefit of the creditors.

(4) *Unperfected Transfers*   The trustee succeeds to the right of a creditor with a provable claim who, under state law, could set aside a transaction of the debtor. To illustrate: The debtor, prior to bankruptcy, executed a mortgage on real

or personal property to Brown who did not record the mortgage until after Smith had obtained a judgment which became a lien on the land of the debtor before the mortgage was recorded. The lien, therefore, is superior to the mortgage. The trustee succeeds to the rights of Smith, the creditor, and can completely set the mortgage aside.

It should be remembered, however, that the object of prohibiting these voidable transactions is to prevent favoritism among the creditors of the debtor. A preferential transfer depletes the estate of the debtor. Such a transfer, therefore, makes it impossible for the creditors to stand on the same footing—a major objective of the bankruptcy law. No depletion of the debtor's estate occurs, however, when the debtor gives a creditor a mortgage to secure a loan, an advance of money, or property. Certain other transfers are likewise not considered voidable. To name a few: Labor performed by a debtor for the creditor, payment of current wages and rent, a transfer of the debtor's property for present consideration, and a bank deposit made in the regular course of the business and not made for the purpose of enabling the bank to have a setoff. [*Bank of Commerce & Trusts v. Hatcher,* p. 833.]

Reclamation Petitions A debtor, at the time he becomes a bankrupt, frequently has in his possession property in which third persons claim a superior interest. A conditional seller, for example, may wish to repossess under his conditional sales contract. A reclamation petition is filed for this purpose.

DISCHARGE

It remains to consider the order of payment of provable claims, the objections to the discharge, and the effect of a discharge.

Order of Payment Any valid secured lien against the property of the bankrupt continues after he is adjudicated a bankrupt. The trustee, therefore, must pay these claims prior to other claims in order to dispose of the property free of the lien. The priorities of payment, other than secured liens, are enumerated in the Bankruptcy Act:

(1) The actual and necessary costs and expenses of preserving and administering the estate of the bankrupt. These include filing fees paid by someone other than the bankrupt in voluntary proceedings.

(2) Claims of wage earners, not to exceed $600 to each claimant, which have been earned within three months before the date of the commencement of the proceeding. Claimants include workmen, servants, clerks, traveling or city salesmen on salary or commission basis, whole or part time, whether or not selling exclusively for the bankrupt. The courts have been rather liberal in construing the word "wages." Vacation and severance pay as provided in union contracts are generally included.

(3) Reasonable costs and expenses of creditors in opposing confirmation of compositions where the confirmation is refused or set aside.

(4) Claims for taxes which are legally due and owing by the bankrupt to the United States or to any state or any subdivision.

(5) Debts owing to any person, including the United States, who by the laws of the United States are entitled to priority, and rent owing to a landlord who is entitled to priority by applicable state law. It should be added that the amount allowed for rent as a priority claim is restricted to that which accrued within three months before the date of bankruptcy and which is legally due and owing for the actual use and occupancy of the premises affected.

(6) Claims of general creditors. The general creditors will share in the residue of the assets on a pro rata basis after the lien and priority claims have been paid in full.

Objections to Discharge of Bankrupt A discharge in bankruptcy is the most important part of the proceedings insofar as the bankrupt is concerned. He is entitled to a discharge unless an objection is made and verified by proof. Most of his obligations are thereby discharged. A denial of a discharge, however, does not relieve the bankrupt of such obligations. The denial is, moreover, res judicata with respect to all debts which are proved. The creditors retain claims in full which may not be discharged in a subsequent proceeding after the expiration of the six-year period, except in those instances when the six-year period was the reason for denying the discharge.

The adjudication of any person is treated as an application for a discharge. A corporation, however, must file an application for a discharge within six months after the adjudication or else the right is lost.

A creditor, the trustee, or such other attorney as the attorney general may designate, may file an objection within the time fixed by the court to a discharge for the bankrupt. The grounds for objecting to a discharge of the bankrupt are as follows:

(1) The bankrupt has committed a criminal offense as specified in the United States Criminal Code, Title 18, Section 152. Concealment and false oath are two common examples. A conviction is not necessary, but it is necessary to show by a fair preponderance of the evidence that the act was committed. A nonbankruptcy crime, such as larceny, is not a crime which may bar a discharge.

(2) He has destroyed, mutilated, falsified, concealed, or failed to keep or preserve adequate books of account or records from which the financial condition and business transactions might be ascertained, unless the court deems such acts or failure to have been justified under all the circumstances of the case.

(3) He has obtained money, property, or credit, or obtained an extension or renewal of credit, by making, publishing, or causing to be made or published, a materially false financial statement in writing.

(4) He has committed a fraudulent conveyance within twelve months prior to the

filing of the petition in bankruptcy. It should be noted that first, it is an act of bankruptcy; second, it can be avoided by the trustee; third, it is a valid reason for denying the bankrupt a discharge.

(5) The bankrupt has received a discharge under the Bankruptcy Act within six years prior to the filing of the petition.

(6) The bankrupt, in a proceeding under the Bankruptcy Act, has refused to obey any lawful order of the court or to answer any material question approved by the court.

(7) He has failed to explain satisfactorily any losses of assets or deficiency of assets.

Effect of Discharge   A discharge in bankruptcy does not relieve the bankrupt of all his obligations. Certain claims are not discharged because of public policy while others are not discharged due to the moral turpitude on the part of the bankrupt. It is well to keep in mind that certain claims which are not provable are not discharged. Certain tort claims, fines, and penalties are examples. Some of the most important debts that are not affected by a discharge in bankruptcy are as follows:

(1) Tax claims which became due and owing by the bankrupt to the United States or to any state or subdivision thereof within three years preceding bankruptcy. Tax claims which accrued prior to three years preceding bankruptcy are discharged unless the bankrupt failed to make a return as required by law or if the bankrupt made a false or fraudulent return. A discharge in bankruptcy does not release or affect any tax lien.

(2) Liabilities for obtaining money or property by false pretenses or false representations. This type of fraud is the same type of fraud that is discussed in contracts in Chapter 9, "Reality of Consent." If a judgment is obtained because of the fraud of the defendant prior to the bankruptcy of the defendant, the judgment is provable and is not discharged.

(3) Willful and malicious injuries to the person or property of another.

(4) Alimony due or to become due.

(5) Maintenance or support of wife and child.

(6) Debts not scheduled in time for proof and allowance, with the name of the creditor, if known to the bankrupt, unless such creditor had notice or actual knowledge of the proceedings in bankruptcy.

(7) Debts created by the fraud, embezzlement, misappropriation or defalcation while acting as an officer or in any fiduciary capacity. [*Airo Supply Co. v. Page,* p. 834.]

(8) Wages earned within three months before the beginning of bankruptcy by workmen, servants, clerks, or traveling or city salesmen, on salary or commission basis, whole or part time, whether or not selling exclusively for the bankrupt.

(9) Claims for money of an employee received or retained by his employer to

secure the faithful performance by such employee of the terms of a contract of employment.

CORPORATE REORGANIZATION, ARRANGEMENTS, WAGE EARNERS' PLANS

Corporate reorganization, arrangements, and wage earners' plans have a number of rules and procedure in common. It appears appropriate, therefore, to state some of the most important of the common rules before proceeding to a discussion of each proceeding separately. First, it should be kept in mind that each of these plans involves bankruptcy processes without a liquidation of assets. The provisions of the first seven chapters of the Bankruptcy Act apply to corporate reorganization, arrangements, and wage earners' plans unless such provisions conflict with the provisions of Chapters X, XI, and XIII. Chapter X deals with corporate reorganizations, Chapter XI deals with arrangements, and Chapter XIII deals with wage earners' plans.

The petition for a corporate reorganization, an arrangement, or a wage earners' plan may be filed as an original petition if no straight bankruptcy proceedings are pending. If such proceedings are pending, the petition may still be filed. The petition must be filed in the federal district court, and it must state that the debtor is insolvent or is unable to pay his debts as they mature. A plan must be proposed, and it must be approved and confirmed. The creditors' claims, generally speaking, must be filed and proved, or scheduled by the debtor in an arrangement, and allowed or disallowed by the court. If everything proceeds properly and no violation of bankruptcy law is committed, the plan will be consummated, the debtor will receive a discharge, and the proceedings will be dismissed.

Corporate Reorganization   Chapter X provides for corporate reorganization, which is designed primarily for large corporations with a complicated debt structure and whose securities are widely distributed. It might be mentioned that every corporation in seeking an adjustment would not necessarily seek a Chapter X way out. A Chapter XI proceeding might be desirable. This will be discussed later. A Chapter X proceeding is proper in subjecting security holders and stockholders to a plan.

Some of the important Chapter X rules on corporate reorganization are as follows:

(1) An involuntary petition may be filed upon the happening of one of certain enumerated technical events including the commission of an act of bankruptcy within the four months prior to the filing of the petition. Three creditors who have liquidated and noncontingent claims of $5,000 or more may file the petition. An indenture trustee may do likewise.

(2) Voluntary and involuntary proceedings are available.

(3) Any corporation that can become an ordinary bankruptcy may petition for a proceeding under Chapter X.

(4) A disinterested trustee or trustees must be appointed in all cases where the liquidated and noncontingent liabilities of the corporation are $250,000 or more. The debtor may remain in possession of its property only if the indebtedness is less than $250,000.

(5) The trustee is charged with the duty of drawing up a proposed plan of reorganization. A creditor, the debtor, or an indenture trustee may prepare the plan if the debtor remains in possession of its property. In addition, any shareholder may prepare a plan if the corporation is not found to be insolvent.

(6) The court must hear and approve a proposed plan before the security holders vote upon the plan. Solicitation of the creditors and shareholders for an acceptance is not permitted until after such court approval unless the court grants permission otherwise.

(7) The plan must be fair, equitable, and feasible. Fair and equitable means that the plan must provide that each class of creditors and shareholders, beginning with the class that has priority over all others, will receive securities or other consideration equal in value to their pre-existing rights or claims before the next junior class receives anything. Feasible means that there are reasonable prospects that the plan will work.

(8) The creditors and shareholders may accept the plan after court approval. The plan is not final, however, until it is later confirmed by the court.

(9) Acceptance is necessary by two-thirds in amount of each class of creditors. A majority in each class of shareholders is required provided the corporation is solvent. Shareholder approval is not required if the corporation is insolvent.

(10) The judge prescribes the manner and time during which claims must be filed and proved. All tort claims are provable unless the plan or a court order provides otherwise. A lessor may file a claim for rent for three years which would accrue in that time without acceleration.

(11) The judge will enter a final decree discharging the debtor, the trustee or trustees, and close the proceedings when the plan is consummated. This discharges all debts of the debtor and terminates the rights of the shareholders except as provided otherwise in the plan.

Arrangements   An arrangement under Chapter XI is designed primarily for individuals and small corporations. Such an arrangement is an outgrowth of the common-law composition which was discussed in Chapter 6, "Consideration." It will be recalled that a composition of creditors is strictly voluntary. It is binding on those creditors who agree and join in the composition. The creditors are entitled to no more than the amount for which they bargained. The composition is not binding, however, on any creditor who does not join in the agreement. This is where the most serious trouble often arises. The creditors may not agree to any out-of-court settlement of the debts, and they may resort to some general assignment for the benefit of creditors under state law. In resorting to some general assignment for the benefit of creditors under state law, the creditors will unwittingly raise a legal danger signal. It should be kept in mind that when state law takes on the nature of insolvency acts by providing for a discharge and involuntary proceedings, the Bankruptcy Act supersedes the state law.

Some of the most important rules of an arrangement are as follows:

(1) Any debtor who could become a bankrupt, voluntary or involuntary, may petition for an arrangement. This includes any natural person, any partnership, and any corporation except the ones excluded in ordinary bankruptcy. The creditors cannot file an involuntary petition since Chapter XI has no provision for such a petition.

(2) Only unsecured debts may be affected by an arrangement. Secured claims survive an arrangement.

(3) The debtor proposes his own plan to pay his debts. The proposal may provide for payment to the extent of 35 percent, 45 percent, or some other amount. The creditors may be divided into various classes. The plan must, however, appeal to the different classes of creditors, otherwise they will vote against the plan. Circumstances will determine the other provisions of the plan.

(4) The court is required to send notice of the first meeting of the creditors to all the creditors within ten days after the filing of the petition. Proofs of claims may be filed before or during the first meeting of the creditors. The debtor is usually examined by the referee, creditors, and other interested parties during the first meeting of the creditors.

(5) A lessor may file a claim for rent for three years. Claims for rent due and owing at the time the petition was filed, however, are provable in full.

(6) The proposed plan must be approved by a majority in number and amount by those creditors whose claims have been proved and allowed. If the creditors are divided into different groups, a majority in number and amount is required in each class. The court will take into consideration a number of things, but the plan will be approved by the court if it is feasible.

Wage Earners' Plans   Chapter XIII provides for a wage earners' plan and is probably the most important part of the Bankruptcy Act from a social point of view. The major objective is to rehabilitate the wage earner financially and in peace of mind. It is directed primarily at the low-income wage earner to assist him in keeping his job, in paying his debts, and in maintaining his family. A plan under Chapter XIII is designed to "keep the bill collector from the front door of the debtor," and to assist the creditors by providing them with a relatively simple and reasonably certain method of collection of the debts from the debtor.

Some of the most important rules are as follows:

(1) The wage earner, by definition, is an individual whose principal income is derived from wages, salary, or commissions. There is no limitation on the amount of the income in Chapter XIII.

(2) The petition which is filed by the wage earner must state that the debtor desires to effect a composition or extension, or both, out of his future wages or earnings.

(3) The wage earner is not adjudicated a bankrupt. He is known as the debtor.

(4) The judge or referee must promptly call a meeting of the creditors by sending notice by mail to the debtor and the creditors. Chapter XIII provides for ten days' notice.

(5) Claims will be allowed or disallowed at the first meeting of the creditors.

(6) The court will confirm the plan if all the creditors agree. A wage earners' plan may deal with secured as well as unsecured debts. All secured creditors must, however, agree to the plan, but only a majority in number and amount of the unsecured creditors must agree. Liens on real property, may not be adjusted.

(7) All unsecured debts must be treated equally, they cannot be divided into classes.

(8) The proceedings will remain under the jurisdiction of the court so that the plan, if necessary, may be adjusted. For example, the court may increase or decrease the amount of the installments being paid by the debtor, as well as altering the frequency of the installments, as the circumstances make necessary. A loss of job or other circumstances beyond the control of the debtor would be considered by the court in making adjustments.

(9) The court will grant a discharge to the debtor provided the plan has been properly performed. If, however, after three years, the debtor has been unable to pay his debts due to circumstances beyond his control, the court may nevertheless grant the debtor a discharge.

CASES

Levy v. Carter Rice & Co.,   70 A.2d 147 (Conn. 1949). Suit by Lawrence E. Levy, trustee in bankruptcy of Bochan Brothers, Inc., plaintiff, against Carter Rice and Company, defendant, to recover the value of merchandise alleged to have been transferred to the defendant within four months of the bankruptcy of the transferor.

Jennings, Judge: The trustee in bankruptcy of Bochan Brothers, Inc., brought suit to recover the value of a quantity of paper which Bochan had returned to the defendant for credit, claiming that the transaction amounted to a voidable preference under the Bankruptcy Act. Under the Act, a preference is voidable if the creditor who receives property of the bankrupt has, at the time of the transfer, "reasonable cause to believe that the debtor is insolvent." The trial court rendered, judgment for the defendant and the plaintiff appeals.

The following facts were undisputed: About thirty tons of paper were shipped to Bochan by the defendant in March, 1947, on thirty days' credit. On April 23 the defendant secured a confidential report from Dun and Bradstreet which showed Bochan to be in good condition. No payments were made until the latter part of April, when the defendant received $1,000. In May the defendant sent its representatives to call on Bochan. The prospects were discussed and an extension of time granted. No payments were made before the period of extension expired and, after several communications by letter and telephone, representatives of the defendant called on Bochan on June 10. The president informed them that the debt could not be discharged in full and that the best he could say was that the company's prospects for business would perhaps improve. It was finally decided that the March shipment would be returned for credit and that Bochan would give the defendant two checks for $500 each to apply on shipments received prior to March. This was done. One check, dated June 10, the day of the conference, was deposited in Boston when the representatives returned there and was paid. The other check was postdated two weeks, was deposited after six weeks and was not paid because payment had been stopped.

Bochan was insolvent on June 10 and the transfer preferred the defendant as a creditor. Bochan continued to operate until July 1, but on July 11 it sent notice to all of its creditors, including the defendant, of a proposed dissolution. It was declared bankrupt on August 6.

The court found as a subordinate fact that the defendant did not know or have reasonable cause to believe that Bochan was insolvent at the time the transfer was made. . . .

"A person shall be deemed insolvent within the provisions of [the Bankruptcy Act] whenever the aggregate of his property . . . shall not at a fair valuation be sufficient in amount to pay his debts." 52 Stat. 841, 11 U.S.C. sec. 1(19). Under this definition, the fact that a debtor is unable to pay current bills at the time of the transfer does not of itself establish insolvency as of that time. . . . In determining whether a creditor has reasonable cause to believe that a debtor is insolvent, the former is bound not only by what he knows but also by such facts as reasonable inquiry would disclose, if the known facts were such as to induce an ordinary prudent businessman to inquire further into the debtor's financial situation. . . . The court's conclusion, that the defendant did not have reasonable cause to believe Bochan insolvent, was one of fact. It must stand. [DECISION FOR DEFENDANT]

Bank of Commerce & Trusts v. Hatcher, 50 F.2d 719 (1931). Suit by Robert V. Hatcher, trustee in bankruptcy of the Allport Construction Corporation, plaintiff, against the Bank of Commerce & Trusts, defendant. The construction company was adjudged a bankrupt on December 17, 1927. It had been insolvent for some time prior thereto, and the fact of its insolvency was known to the defendant. The bankrupt, as a part of its agreement as subcontractor of C. S. Luck & Sons, agreed that the moneys received by the bankrupt were to be deposited in the defendant-bank and were to be paid out only on checks approved by the vice-president of the bank. The bankrupt was indebted to the bank in a considerable amount, and on the day in question, the bankrupt's bookkeeper handed checks to the vice-president aggregating $8,797.60 drawn in favor of certain of the creditors of the bankrupt with the request that the vice-president approve them. At the same time, the bookkeeper also handed the vice-president a certified check for the same amount drawn by C. S. Luck & Sons in favor of the bankrupt and indorsed for deposit. The vice-president refused to approve the checks drawn in favor of the creditors. He did, however, credit the bankrupt's account with the check of Luck & Sons, thus reducing the bankrupt's indebtedness to the bank. The trustee contends that the transaction constituted an unlawful preference within the meaning of the Bankruptcy Act.

Parker, Circuit Judge: The question in this case as stated by the judge below, is whether there was a deposit in regular course, whereby the relationship of debtor and creditor was created between the bank and bankrupt, or whether there was an attempt at deposit which the bank by its action converted into a payment on pre-existing indebtedness. . . .

It is perfectly clear that the transaction here involved did not constitute a deposit in regular course of business. The distinguishing characteristic of such a deposit is that it creates a balance in favor of the depositor which is subject to withdrawal at his will. Here the deposit lacked absolutely this characteristic. It was intended by the bankrupt to provide for the payment of certain checks which were presented for approval, not to create a balance in the bank subject to its control. It was received by the bank, not for the purpose of creating such balance, but for the purpose of being applied on the pre-existing indebtedness of the bankrupt. The balance created was at no time subject to the withdrawal of the bankrupt and was promptly applied by the bank upon the bankrupt's indebtedness. The net result of what took place was the transfer of the certified check of Luck & Sons to the bank as payment upon pre-existing indebtedness, not the creation of a deposit balance subject to withdrawal by the bankrupt in ordinary course.

. . . Here the deposit was made at the time that checks were presented for approval. The bank's vice president refused to approve them and he did this solely because he desired that the proceeds of the check deposited be applied on the indebtedness due the bank. [DECISION FOR PLAINTIFF]

Airo Supply Co. v. Page, 119 N.E.2d 400 (Ill. 1954). Proceedings by Airo Supply Company, plaintiff, against Thomas Page, defendant. The defendant had been employed by plaintiff as its only bookkeeper from 1944 to 1947 during which time he misappropriated $14,775.77 of plaintiff's money to his own use. The plaintiff thereafter secured a judgment against the defendant for the amount so misappropriated, and defendant filed his voluntary petition in bankruptcy. He obtained his discharge in bankruptcy on February 10, 1953, and the following month was employed by the Automatic Electric Company. Plaintiff thereupon instituted proceedings for garnishment of wages. Defendant offers the defense that plaintiff's judgment was discharged in bankruptcy.

Friend, Justice: Upon this state of the record the question presented is whether plaintiff's claim for the recovery of funds which defendant, its former employee, admittedly embezzled or misappropriated, is released by defendant's discharge in bankruptcy. Section 35, title 11, U.S.C.A. reads as follows: "A discharge in bankruptcy shall release a bankrupt from all of his provable debts, whether allowable in full or in part, except such as . . . (4) were created by his fraud, embezzlement, misappropriation or defalcation while acting as an officer or in any fiduciary capacity." There can be no doubt that the debt, which was reduced to judgment by agreement of the parties, was created by defendant's fraud, embezzlement, misappropriation or defalcation; this charge is not denied. It is conceded that defendant was not acting as an officer of the corporation; the inquiry is thus narrowed to whether he was acting in any fiduciary capacity. He argues that the phrase "in any fiduciary capacity," as used in the Bankruptcy Act, embraces only technical trusts and not trusts which are implied in a contract. . . .

All the circumstances of record clearly indicate that defendant occupied a position of trust. He handled plaintiff's funds and admits that he embezzled and wrongfully "converted" them while he was occupying this position. As plaintiff's counsel points out, defendant was not the "honest debtor" whom the Bankruptcy Act was intended to aid; both the letter of the law and every consideration of justice and public policy require that he be compelled to repay the money he misappropriated. [DECISION FOR PLAINTIFF]

PROBLEMS

1   An involuntary petition alleged that the debtor, while insolvent, had made a fraudulent transfer of property. It was shown that the debtor had conveyed certain real estate to his brother-in-law, without consideration, for the purpose of preventing Brown, a judgment creditor, from levying on the property. Does this transaction constitute an act of bankruptcy?

2   The debtor, within four months prior to filing a petition in bankruptcy, assigned certain accounts receivable to Brown to secure a present loan. The debtor, at the time of the assignment, was in fact insolvent. Brown did not know or have reason to know of the insolvency. Is the lien of Brown good as against the trustee in bankruptcy?

3   An involuntary petition was filed against Jones. He resisted on the ground that he was a farmer. It was shown that he had several occupations. He sold fertilizers in a small way. He had a general store which—although at one time a large business—had suffered greatly by increased competition. He operated a 240-acre farm employing two men. Is Jones exempt?

4   What is the distinction between the words "wage earner" with respect to straight bankruptcy and a wage earner's plan under Chapter XIII?

5   Are the following debts completely discharged by a discharge in bankruptcy?
   (a) Unpaid property taxes to the extent of $450.
   (b) A judgment for $600 for breach of contract.
   (c) Past due alimony in an amount of $1,000.
   (d) A claim of $500 for wages earned within three months of the filing of the petition in bankruptcy.
   (e) A judgment for $4,000 for malicious injury to the property of a creditor.

6   Is a lessor limited to a claim for rent in the same amount with respect to straight bankruptcy, corporate reorganization, and arrangements?

7   Brock committed an act of bankruptcy, and certain of his creditors filed an involuntary petition in bankruptcy on June 1. Brock was adjudicated a bankrupt. On the following

December 5, Brock inherited $65,000 from his deceased uncle. Is this money so inherited available for distribution in the bankruptcy proceedings?

8 The X Company, which was indebted to Jones in the amount of $2,300, failed to pay any part of the indebtedness for a period of over ten months. The company was also similarly indebted to six other creditors for various smaller amounts, and the liabilities of the company exceeded its assets by $3,000. Jones learned through certain records filed in court that the company had transferred a large portion of its assets to Smith, one of the creditors, in payment of an indebtedness. Jones then requested two of the creditors to join him in filing an involuntary petition in bankruptcy to have the company adjudicated a bankrupt, but the creditors refused to join in signing the petition. Would Jones, as the only petitioning creditor, be able to have the company adjudicated a bankrupt?

APPENDIXES

APPENDIX 1
UNIFORM COMMERCIAL CODE*

ARTICLE 1: GENERAL PROVISIONS

Part 1

Short Title, Construction, Application and Subject Matter of the Act

§1–101. Short Title. This Act shall be known and may be cited as Uniform Commercial Code.

§1–102. Purposes; Rules of Construction; Variation by Agreement. (1) This Act shall be liberally construed and applied to promote its underlying purposes and policies.

    (2) Underlying purposes and policies of this Act are

    (a) to simplify, clarify and modernize the law governing commercial transactions;

    (b) to permit the continued expansion of commercial practices through custom, usage and agreement of the parties;

    (c) to make uniform the law among the various jurisdictions.

    (3) The effect of provisions of this Act may be varied by agreement, except as otherwise provided in this Act and except that the obligations of good faith, diligence, reasonableness and care prescribed by this Act may not be disclaimed by agreement but the

parties may by agreement determine the standards by which the performance of such obligations is to be measured if such standards are not manifestly unreasonable.

(4) The presence in certain provisions of this Act of the words "unless otherwise agreed" or words of similar import does not imply that the effect of other provisions may not be varied by agreement under subsection (3).

(5) In this Act unless the context otherwise requires

(a) words in the singular number include the plural, and in the plural include the singular;

(b) words of the masculine gender include the feminine and the neuter, and when the sense so indicates words of the neuter gender may refer to any gender.

§1–103. Supplementary General Principles of Law Applicable. Unless displaced by the particular provisions of this Act, the principles of law and equity, including the law merchant and the law relative to capacity to contract, principal and agent, estoppel, fraud, misrepresentation, duress, coercion, mistake, bankruptcy, or other validating or invalidating cause shall supplement its provisions.

§1–104. Construction Against Implicit Repeal. This Act being a general act intended as a unified coverage of its subject matter, no part of it shall be deemed to be impliedly repealed by subsequent legislation if such construction can reasonably be avoided.

§1–105. Territorial Application of the Act; Parties' Power to Choose Applicable Law. (1) Except as provided hereafter in this section, when a transaction bears a reasonable relation to this state and also to another state or nation the parties may agree that the law either of this state or of such other state or nation shall govern their rights and duties. Failing such agreement this Act applies to transactions bearing an appropriate relation to this state.

(2) Where one of the following provisions of this Act specifies the applicable law, that provision governs and a contrary agreement is effective only to the extent permitted by the law (including the conflict of laws rules) so specified:

Rights of creditors against sold goods. Section 2–402. Applicability of the Article on Bank Deposits and Collections. Section 4–102.

Bulk transfers subject to the Article on Bulk Transfers. Section 6–102.

Applicability of the Article on Investment Securities. Section 8–106.

Perfection provisions of the Article on Secured Transactions. Section 9–103.

As amended 1972.

§1–106. Remedies to Be Liberally Administered. (1) The remedies provided by this Act shall be liberally administered to the end that the aggrieved party may be put in as good a position as if the other party had fully performed but neither consequential or special nor penal damages may be had except as specifically provided in this Act or by other rule of law.

(2) Any right or obligation declared by this Act is enforceable by action unless the provision declaring it specifies a different and limited effect.

§1–107. Waiver or Renunciation of Claim or Right After Breach. Any claim or right arising out of an alleged breach can be discharged in whole or in part without consideration by a written waiver or renunciation signed and delivered by the aggrieved party.

§1–108. Severability. If any provision or clause of this Act or application thereof to any person or circumstances is held invalid; such invalidity shall not affect other provisions or applications of the Act which can be given effect without the invalid provision or application, and to this end the provisions of this Act are declared to be severable.

§1–109. Section Captions. Section captions are parts of this Act.

Part 2

General Definitions and Principles of Interpretation

§1–201. General Definitions. Subject to additional definitions contained in the subsequent Articles of this Act which are applicable to specific Articles or Parts thereof, and unless the context otherwise requires, in this Act:

(1) "Action" in the sense of a judicial proceeding includes recoupment, counter-claim, set-off, suit in equity and any other proceedings in which rights are determined.

(2) "Aggrieved party" means a party entitled to resort to a remedy.

(3) "Agreement" means the bargain of the parties in fact as found in their language or by implication from other circumstances including course of dealing or usage of trade or course of performance as provided in this Act (Sections 1–205 and 2–208). Whether an agreement has legal consequences is determined by the provisions of this Act, if applicable; otherwise by the law of contracts (Section 1–103). (Compare "Contract".)

(4) "Bank" means any person engaged in the business of banking.

(5) "Bearer" means the person in possession of an instrument, document of title, or security payable to bearer or indorsed in blank.

(6) "Bill of lading" means a document evidencing the receipt of goods for shipment issued by a person engaged in the business of transporting or forwarding goods, and includes an airbill. "Airbill" means a document serving for air transportation as a bill of lading does for marine or rail transportation, and includes an air consignment note or air waybill.

(7) "Branch" includes a separately incorporated foreign branch of a bank.

(8) "Burden of establishing" a fact means the burden of persuading the triers of fact that the existence of the fact is more probable than its non-existence.

(9) "Buyer in ordinary course of business" means a person who in good faith and without knowledge that the sale to him is in violation of the ownership rights or security interest of a third party in the goods buys in ordinary course from a person in the business of selling goods of that kind but does not include a pawnbroker. All persons who sell minerals or the like (including oil and gas) at wellhead or minehead shall be deemed to be persons in the business of selling goods of that kind. "Buying" may be for cash or by exchange of other property or on secured or unsecured credit and includes receiving goods or documents of title under a pre-existing contract for sale but does not include a transfer in bulk or as security for or in total or partial satisfaction of a money debt.

(10) "Conspicuous": A term or clause is conspicuous when it is so written that a reasonable person against whom it is to operate ought to have noticed it. A printed heading in capitals (as: NON-NEGOTIABLE BILL OF LADING) is conspicuous. Language in the body of a form is "conspicuous" if it is in larger or other contrasting type or color. But in a telegram any stated term is "conspicuous". Whether a term or clause is "conspicuous" or not is for decision by the court.

(11) "Contract" means the total legal obligation which results from the parties' agreement as affected by this Act and any other applicable rules of law. (Compare "Agreement".)

(12) "Creditor" includes a general creditor, a secured creditor, a lien creditor and any representative of creditors, including an assignee for the benefit of creditors, a trustee in bankruptcy, a receiver in equity and an executor or administrator of an insolvent debtor's or assignor's estate.

(13) "Defendant" includes a person in the position of defendent in a cross-action or counterclaim.

(14) "Delivery" with respect to instruments, documents of title, chattel paper or securities means voluntary transfer of possession.

(15) "Document of title" includes bill of lading, dock warrant, dock receipt, warehouse receipt or order for the delivery of goods, and also any other document which in the regular course of business or financing is treated as adequately evidencing that the person in possession of it is entitled to receive, hold and dispose of the document and the goods it covers. To be a document of title a document must purport to be issued by or addressed to a bailee and purport to cover goods in the bailee's possession which are either identified or are fungible portions of an identified mass.

(16) "Fault" means wrongful act, omission or breach.

(17) "Fungible" with respect to goods or securities means goods or securities of which any unit is, by nature or usage of trade, the equivalent of any other like unit. Goods which are not fungible shall be deemed fungible for the purposes of this Act to the extent that under a particular agreement or document unlike units are treated as equivalents.

(18) "Genuine" means free of forgery or counterfeiting.

(19) "Good faith" means honesty in fact in the conduct or transaction concerned.

(20) "Holder" means a person who is in possession of a document of title or an instrument or an investment security drawn, issued or indorsed to him or to his order or to bearer or in blank.

(21) To "honor" is to pay or to accept and pay, or where a credit so engages to purchase or discount a draft complying with the terms of the credit.

(22) "Insolvency proceedings" includes any assignment for the benefit of creditors or other proceedings intended to liquidate or rehabilitate the estate of the person involved.

(23) A person is "insolvent" who either has ceased to pay his debts in the ordinary course of business or cannot pay his debts as they become due or is insolvent within the meaning of the federal bankruptcy law.

(24) "Money" means a medium of exchange authorized or adopted by a domestic or foreign government as a part of its currency.

(25) A person has "notice" of a fact when

(a) he has actual knowledge of it; or

(b) he has received a notice or notification of it; or

(c) from all the facts and circumstances known to him at the time in question he has reason to know that it exists.

A person "knows" or has "knowledge" of a fact when he has actual knowledge of it. "Discover" or "learn" or a word or phrase of similar import refers to knowledge rather than to reason to know. The time and circumstances under which a notice or notification may cease to be effective are not determined by this Act.

(26) A person "notifies" or "gives" a notice or notification to another by taking such steps as may be reasonably required to inform the other in ordinary course whether or not such other actually comes to know of it. A person "receives" a notice or notification when

(a) it comes to his attention; or

(b) it is duly delivered at the place of business through which the contract was made or at any other place held out by him as the place for receipt of such communications.

(27) Notice, knowledge or a notice or notification received by an organization is effective for a particular transaction from the time when it is brought to the attention of the individual conducting that transaction, and in any event from the time when it would have been brought to his attention if the organization had exercised due diligence. An

organization exercises due diligence if it maintains reasonable routines for communicating significant information to the person conducting the transaction and there is reasonable compliance with the routines. Due diligence does not require an individual acting for the organization to communicate information unless such communication is part of his regular duties or unless he has reason to know of the transaction and that the transaction would be materially affected by the information.

(28) "Organization" includes a corporation, government or governmental subdivision or agency, business trust, estate, trust, partnership or association, two or more persons having a joint or common interest, or any other legal or commercial entity.

(29) "Party", as distinct from "third party", means a person who has engaged in a transaction or made an agreement within this Act.

(30) "Person" includes an individual or an organization (See Section 1–102).

(31) "Presumption" or "presumed" means that the trier of fact must find the existence of the fact presumed unless and until evidence is introduced which would support a finding of its non-existence.

(32) "Purchase" includes taking by sale, discount, negotiation, mortgage, pledge, lien, issue or re-issue, gift or any other voluntary transaction creating an interest in property.

(33) "Purchaser" means a person who takes by purchase.

(34) "Remedy" means any remedial right to which an aggrieved party is entitled with or without resort to a tribunal.

(35) "Representative" includes an agent, an officer of a corporation or association, and a trustee, executor or administrator of an estate, or any other person empowered to act for another.

(36) "Rights" includes remedies.

(37) "Security interest" means an interest in personal property or fixtures which secures payment or performance of an obligation. The retention or reservation of title by a seller of goods notwithstanding shipment or delivery to the buyer (Section 2–401) is limited in effect to a reservation of a "security interest". The term also includes any interest of a buyer of accounts or chattel paper which is subject to Article 9. The special property interest of a buyer of goods on identification of such goods to a contract for sale under Section 2–401 is not a "security interest", but a buyer may also acquire a "security interest" by complying with Article 9. Unless a lease or consignment is intended as security, reservation of title thereunder is not a "security interest" but a consignment is in any event subject to the provisions on consignment sales (Section 2–326). Whether a lease is intended as security is to be determined by the facts of each case; however, (a) the inclusion of an option to purchase does not of itself make the lease one intended for security, and (b) an agreement that upon compliance with the terms of the lease the lessee shall become or has the option to become the owner of the property for no additional consideration or for a nominal consideration does make the lease one intended for security.

(38) "Send" in connection with any writing or notice means to deposit in the mail or deliver for transmission by any other usual means of communication with postage or cost of transmission provided for and properly addressed and in the case of an instrument to an address specified thereon or otherwise agreed, or if there be none to any address reasonable under the circumstances. The receipt of any writing or notice within the time at which it would have arrived if properly sent has the effect of a proper sending.

(39) "Signed" includes any symbol executed or adopted by a party with present intention to authenticate a writing.

(40) "Surety" includes guarantor.

(41) "Telegram" includes a message transmitted by radio, teletype, cable, any mechanical method of transmission, or the like.

(42) "Term" means that portion of an agreement which relates to a particular matter.

(43) "Unauthorized" signature or indorsement means one made without actual, implied or apparent authority and includes a forgery.

(44) "Value". Except as otherwise provided with respect to negotiable instruments and bank collections (Sections 3–303, 4–208 and 4–209) a person gives "value" for rights if he acquires them

(a) in return for a binding commitment to extend credit or for the extension of immediately available credit whether or not drawn upon and whether or not a chargeback is provided for in the event of difficulties in collection; or

(b) as security for or in total or partial satisfaction of a pre-existing claim; or

(c) by accepting delivery pursuant to a pre-existing contract for purchase; or

(d) generally, in return for any consideration sufficient to support a simple contract.

(45) "Warehouse receipt" means a receipt issued by a person engaged in the business of storing goods for hire.

(46) "Written" or "writing" includes printing, typewriting or any other intentional reduction to tangible form. As amended 1962 and 1972.

§1–202. Prima Facie Evidence by Third Party Documents. A document in due form purporting to be a bill of lading, policy or certificate of insurance, official weigher's or inspector's certificate, consular invoice, or any other document authorized or required by the contract to be issued by a third party shall be prima facie evidence of its own authenticity and genuineness and of the facts stated in the document by the third party.

§1–203. Obligation of Good Faith. Every contract or duty within this Act imposes an obligation of good faith in its performance or enforcement.

§1–204. Time; Reasonable Time; "Seasonably". (1) Whenever this Act requires any action to be taken within a reasonable time, any time which is not manifestly unreasonable may be fixed by agreement.

(2) What is a reasonable time for taking any action depends on the nature, purpose and circumstances of such action.

(3) An action is taken "seasonably" when it is taken at or within the time agreed or if no time is agreed at or within a reasonable time.

§1–205. Course of Dealing and Usage of Trade. (1) A course of dealing is a sequence of previous conduct between the parties to a particular transaction which is fairly to be regarded as establishing a common basis of understanding for interpreting their expressions and other conduct.

(2) A usage of trade is any practice or method of dealing having such regularity of observance in a place, vocation or trade as to justify an expectation that it will be observed with respect to the transaction in question. The existence and scope of such a usage are to be proved as facts. If it is established that such a usage is embodied in a written trade code or similar writing the interpretation of the writing is for the court.

(3) A course of dealing between parties and any usage of trade in the vocation or trade in which they are engaged or of which they are or should be aware give particular meaning to and supplement or qualify terms of an agreement.

(4) The express terms of an agreement and an applicable course of dealing or usage of trade shall be construed wherever reasonable as consistent with each other; but when such construction is unreasonable express terms control both course of dealing and usage of trade and course of dealing controls usage of trade.

(5) An applicable usage of trade in the place where any part of performance is to occur shall be used in interpreting the agreement as to that part of the performance.

(6) Evidence of a relevant usage of trade offered by one party is not admissible unless and until he has given the other party such notice as the court finds sufficient to prevent unfair surprise to the latter.

§1–206. Statute of Frauds for Kinds of Personal Property Not Otherwise Covered. (1) Except in the cases described in subsection (2) of this section a contract for the sale of personal property is not enforceable by way of action or defense beyond five thousand dollars in amount or value of remedy unless there is some writing which indicates that a contract for sale has been made between the parties at a defined or stated price, reasonably identifies the subject matter, and is signed by the party against whom enforcement is sought or by his authorized agent.

(2) Subject (1) of this section does not apply to contracts for the sale of goods (Section 2–201) nor of securities (Section 8–319) nor to security agreements (Section 9–203).

§1–207. Performance or Acceptance under Reservation of Rights. A party who with explicit reservation of rights performs or promises performance or assents to performance in a manner demanded or offered by the other party does not thereby prejudice the rights reserved. Such words as "without prejudice", "under protest" or the like are sufficient.

§1–208. Option to Accelerate at Will. A term providing that one party or his successor in interest may accelerate payment or performance or require collateral or additional collateral "at will" or "when he deems himself insecure" or in words of similar import shall be construed to mean that he shall have power to do so only if he in good faith believes that the prospect of payment or performance is impaired. The burden of establishing lack of good faith is on the party against whom the power has been exercised.

§1–209. Subordinated Obligations. An obligation may be issued as subordinated to payment of another obligation of the person obligated, or a creditor may subordinate his right to payment of an obligation by agreement with either the person obligated or another creditor of the person obligated. Such a subordination does not create a security interest as against either the common debtor or a subordinated creditor. This section shall be construed as declaring the law as it existed prior to the enactment of this section and not as modifying it. Added 1966.

Note: *This new section is proposed as an optional provision to make it clear that a subordination agreement does not create a security interest unless so intended.*

ARTICLE 2: SALES

Part 1

Short Title, General Construction and Subject Matter

§2–101. Short Title. This Article shall be known and may be cited as Uniform Commercial Code—Sales.

§2–102. Scope; Certain Security and Other Transactions Excluded from this Article. Unless the context otherwise requires this Article applies to transactions in goods; it does not apply to any transaction which although in the form of an unconditional contract to sell or present sale is intended to operate only as a security transaction nor does this Article impair or repeal any statute regulating sales to consumers, farmers or other specified classes of buyers.

§2–103. Definitions and Index of Definitions. (1) In this Article unless the context otherwise requires

(a) "Buyer" means a person who buys or contracts to buy goods.

(b) "Good faith" in the case of a merchant means honesty in fact and the observance of reasonable commercial standards of fair dealing in the trade.

(c) "Receipt" of goods means taking physical possession of them.

(d) "Seller" means a person who sells or contracts to sell goods.

(2) Other definitions applying to this Article or to specified Parts thereof, and the sections in which they appear are:

"Acceptance". Section 2–606.
"Banker's credit". Section 2–325.
"Between merchants". Section 2–104.
"Cancellation". Section 2–106(4).
"Commercial unit". Section 2–105.
"Confirmed credit". Section 2–325.
"Conforming to contract". Section 2–106.
"Contract for sale". Section 2–106.
"Cover". Section 2–712.
"Entrusting". Section 2–403.
"Financing agency". Section 2–104.
"Future goods". Section 2–105.
"Goods". Section 2–105.
"Identification". Section 2–501.
"Installment contract". Section 2–612.
"Letter of Credit". Section 2–325.
"Lot". Section 2–105.
"Merchant". Section 2–104.
"Overseas". Section 2–323.
"Person in position of seller". Section 2–707.
"Present sale". Section 2–106.
"Sale". Section 2–106.
"Sale on approval". Section 2–326
"Sale or return". Section 2–326.
"Termination". Section 2–106.

(3) The following definitions in other Articles apply to this Article:

"Check". Section 3–104.
"Consignee". Section 7–102.
"Consignor". Section 7–102.
"Consumer goods". Section 9–109.
"Dishonor". Section 3–507.
"Draft". Section 3–104.

(4) In addition Article 1 contains general definitions and principles of construction and interpretation applicable throughout this Article.

§2–104. Definitions: "Merchant"; "Between Merchants"; "Financing Agency". (1) "Merchant" means a person who deals in goods of the kind or otherwise by his occupation holds himself out as having knowledge or skill peculiar to the practices or goods involved in the transaction or to whom such knowledge or skill may be attributed by his employment of an agent or broker or other intermediary who by his occupation holds himself out as having such knowledge or skill.

(2) "Financing agency" means a bank, finance company or other person who in the ordinary course of business makes advances against goods or documents of title or who by arrangement with either the seller or the buyer intervenes in ordinary course to make or collect payment due or claimed under the contract for sale, as by purchasing or paying the seller's draft or making advances against it or by merely taking it for collection whether or not documents of title accompany the draft. "Financing agency" includes also a bank or other person who similarly intervenes between persons who are in the position of seller and buyer in respect to the goods (Section 2–707).

(3) "Between merchants" means in any transaction with respect to which both parties are chargeable with the knowledge or skill of merchants.

§2–105. Definitions: Transferability; "Goods"; "Future" Goods; "Lot"; "Commercial Unit". (1) "Goods" means all things (including specially manufactured goods) which are movable at the time of identification to the contract for sale other than the money in which the price is to be paid, investment securities (Article 8) and things in action. "Goods" also includes the unborn young of animals and growing crops and other identified things attached to realty as described in the section on goods to be served from realty (Section 2–107).

(2) Goods must be both existing and identified before any interest in them can pass. Goods which are not both existing and identified are "future" goods. A purported present sale of future goods or of any interest therein operates as a contract to sell.

(3) There may be a sale of a part interest in existing identified goods.

(4) An undivided share in an identified bulk of fungible goods is sufficiently identified to be sold although the quantity of the bulk is not determined. Any agreed proportion of such a bulk or any quantity thereof agreed upon by number, weight or other measure may to the extent of the seller's interest in the bulk be sold to the buyer who then becomes an owner in common.

(5) "Lot" means a parcel or a single article which is the subject matter of a separate sale or delivery, whether or not it is sufficient to perform the contract.

(6) "Commercial unit" means such a unit of goods as by commercial usage is a single whole for purposes of sale and division of which materially impairs its character or value on the market or in use. A commercial unit may be a single article (as a machine) or a set of articles (as a suite of furniture or an assortment of sizes) or a quantity (as a bale, gross, or carload) or any other unit treated in use or in the relevant market as a single whole.

§2–106. Definitions: "Contract"; "Agreement"; "Contract for Sale"; "Sale"; "Present Sale"; "Conforming" to Contract; "Termination"; "Cancellation". (1) In this Article unless the context otherwise requires "contract" and "agreement" are limited to those relating to the present or future sale of goods. "Contract for sale" includes both a present sale of goods and a contract to sell goods at a future time. A "sale" consists in the passing of title from the seller to the buyer for a price (Section 2–401). A "present sale" means a sale which is accomplished by the making of the contract.

(2) Goods or conduct including any part of a performance are "conforming" or conform to the contract when they are in accordance with the obligations under the contract.

(3) "Termination" occurs when either party pursuant to a power created by agreement or law puts an end to the contract otherwise than for its breach. On "termination" all obligations which are still executory on both sides are discharged but any right based on prior breach or performance survives.

(4) "Cancellation" occurs when either party puts an end to the contract for breach by the other and its effect is the same as that of "termination" except that the cancelling party also retains any remedy for breach of the whole contract or any unperformed balance.

§2–107. Goods to Be Served from Realty: Recording. (1) A contract for the sale of minerals or the like (including oil and gas) or a structure or its materials to be removed from realty is a contract for the sale of goods within this Article if they are to be severed by the seller but until severance a purported present sale thereof which is not effective as a transfer of an interest in land is effective only as a contract to sell.

(2) A contract for the sale apart from the land of growing crops or other things attached to realty and capable of severance without material harm thereto but not described in subsection (1) or of timber to be cut is a contract for the sale of goods within this Article whether the subject matter is to be severed by the buyer or by the seller even though it forms part of the realty at the time of contracting, and the parties can by identification effect a present sale before severance.

(3) The provisions of this section are subject to any third party rights provided by the law relating to realty records, and the contract for sale may be executed and recorded as a document transferring an interest in land and shall then constitute notice to third parties of the buyer's rights under the contract for sale. As amended 1972.

Part 2

Form, Formation and Readjustment of Contract

§2–201. Formal Requirements; Statute of Frauds. (1) Except as otherwise provided in this section a contract for the sale of goods for the price of $500 or more is not enforceable by way of action or defense unless there is some writing sufficient to indicate that a contract for sale has been made between the parties and signed by the party against whom enforcement is sought or by his authorized agent or broker. A writing is not insufficient because it omits or incorrectly states a term agreed upon but the contract is not enforceable under this paragraph beyond the quantity of goods shown in such writing.

(2) Between merchants if within a reasonable time a writing in confirmation of the contract and sufficient against the sender is received and the party receiving it has reason to know its contents, it satisfies the requirements of subsection (1) against such party unless written notice of objection to its contents is given within 10 days after it is received.

(3) A contract which does not satisfy the requirements of subsection (1) but which is valid in other respects is enforceable

(a) if the goods are to be specially manufactured for the buyer and are not suitable for sale to others in the ordinary course of the seller's business and the seller, before notice of repudiation is received and under circumstances which reasonably indicate that the goods are for the buyer, has made either a substantial beginning of their manufacture or commitments for their procurement; or

(b) if the party against whom enforcement is sought admits in his' pleading, testimony or otherwise in court that a contract for sale was made, but the contract is not enforceable under this provision beyond the quantity of goods admitted; or

(c) with respect to goods for which payment has been made and accepted or which have been received and accepted (Sec. 2–606).

§2–202. Final Written Expression: Parol or Extrinsic Evidence. Terms with respect to which the confirmatory memoranda of the parties agree or which are otherwise set forth in a writing intended by the parties as a final expression of their agreement with respect to such terms as are included therein may not be contradicted by evidence of any prior agreement or of a contemporaneous oral agreement but may be explained or supplemented

(a) by course of dealing or usage of trade (Section 1–205) or by course of performance (Section 2–208); and

(b) by evidence of consistent additional terms <u>unless</u> the court finds the writing to have been intended also as a complete and exclusive statement of the terms of the agreement.

§2–203. Seals Inoperative. The affixing of a seal to a writing evidencing a contract for sale or an offer to buy or sell goods does not constitute the writing a sealed instrument and the law with respect to sealed instruments does not apply to such a contract or offer.

§2–204. Formation in General. (1) A contract for sale of goods may be made in any manner sufficient to show agreement, including conduct by both parties which recognizes the existence of such a contract.

(2) An agreement sufficient to constitute a contract for sale may be found even though the moment of its making is undetermined.

(3) Even though one or more terms are left open a contract for sale does not fail for indefiniteness if the parties have intended to make a <u>contract and there is a reasonably</u> certain basis for giving an appropriate remedy.   *NO CONSIDERATION   TO MERCHANT*

§2–205. Firm Offers. An offer by a merchant to buy or sell goods in a signed writing which by its terms gives assurance that it will be held open is not revocable, for lack of consideration, during the time stated or if no time is stated for a reasonable time, but in no event may such period of irrevocability exceed three months; but any such term of assurance on a form supplied by the offeree must be separately signed by the offeror.

§2–206. Offer and Acceptance in Formation of Contract. (1) Unless otherwise unambiguous-ly indicated by the language or circumstances

(a) an offer to make a contract shall be construed as inviting acceptance in any manner and by any medium reasonable in the circumstances;

(b) an order or other offer to buy goods for prompt or current shipment shall be construed as inviting acceptance either by a prompt promise to ship or by the prompt or current shipment of conforming or non-conforming goods, but such a shipment of non-conforming goods does not constitute an acceptance if the seller seasonably notifies the buyer that the shipment is offered only as an accommodation to the buyer.

(2) Where the beginning of a requested performance is a reasonable mode of acceptance an offeror who is not notified of acceptance within a reasonable time may treat the offer as having lapsed before acceptance.   *NOT beTweeN MeRcHANTS*

§2–207. Additional Terms in Acceptance or Confirmation. (1) A definite and seasonable expression of acceptance or a written confirmation which is sent within a reasonable time operates as an acceptance even though it states terms additional to or different from those offered or agreed upon, unless acceptance is expressly made conditional on assent to the ~~additional or different terms~~.

(2) The additional terms are to be construed as proposals for addition to the contract. Between <u>merchants</u> such terms become part of the contract unless:

(a) the offer expressly limits acceptance to the terms of the offer;

(b) they materially alter it; or

(c) notification of objection to them has already been given or is given within a reasonable time after notice of them is received.

(3) Conduct by both parties which recognizes the existence of a contract is sufficient to establish a contract for sale although the writings of the parties do not otherwise establish a contract. In such case the terms of the particular contract consist of

those terms on which the writings of the parties agree, together with any supplementary terms incorporated under any other provisions of this Act.

§2–208. Course of Performance or Practical Construction. (1) Where the contract for sale involves repeated occasions for performance by either party with knowledge of the nature of the performance and opportunity for objection to it by the other, any course of performance accepted or acquiesced in without objection shall be relevant to determine the meaning of the agreement.

(2) The express terms of the agreement and any such course of performance, as well as any course of dealing and usage of trade, shall be construed whenever reasonable as consistent with each other; but when such construction is unreasonable, express terms shall control course of performance and course of performance shall control both course of dealing and usage of trade (Section 1–205).

(3) Subject to the provisions of the next section on modification and waiver, such course of performance shall be relevant to show a waiver or modification of any term inconsistent with such course of performance.

§2–209. Modification, Rescission and Waiver. (1) An agreement modifying a contract within this Article needs no consideration to be binding. *(NOT BeTWeeN MeRCHANTS oNLy)*

(2) A signed agreement which excludes modification or rescission except by a signed writing cannot be otherwise modified or rescinded, but except as between merchants such a requirement on a form supplied by the merchant must be separately signed by the other party.

(3) The requirements of the statute of frauds section of this Article (Section 2–201) must be satisfied if the contract as modified is within its provisions.

(4) Although an attempt at modification or rescission does not satisfy the requirements of subsection (2) or (3) it can operate as a waiver.

(5) A party who has made a waiver affecting an executory portion of the contract may retract the waiver by reasonable notification received by the other party that strict performance will be required of any term waived, unless the retraction would be unjust in view of a material change of position in reliance on the waiver.

§2–210. Delegation of Performance; Assignment of Rights. (1) A party may perform his duty through a delegate unless otherwise agreed or unless the other party has a substantial interest in having his original promisor perform or control the acts required by the contract. No delegation of performance relieves the party delegating of any duty to perform or any liability for breach.

(2) Unless otherwise agreed all rights of either seller or buyer can be assigned except where the assignment would materially change the duty of the other party, or increase materially the burden or risk imposed on him by his contract, or impair materially his chance of obtaining return performance. A right to damages for breach of the whole contract or a right arising out of the assignor's due performance of his entire obligation can be assigned despite agreement otherwise.

(3) Unless the circumstances indicate the contrary a prohibition of assignment of "the contract" is to be construed as barring only the delegation to the assignee of the assignor's performance.

(4) An assignment of "the contract" or of "all my rights under the contract" or an assignment in similar general terms is an assignment of rights and unless the language or the circumstances (as in an assignment for security) indicate the contrary, it is a delegation of performance of the duties of the assignor and its acceptance by the assignee constitutes a promise by him to perform those duties. This promise is enforceable by either the assignor or the other party to the original contract.

(5) The other party may treat any assignment which delegates performance as

creating reasonable grounds for insecurity and may without prejudice to his rights against the assignor demand assurances from the assignee (Section 2–609).

Part 3

General Obligation and Construction of Contract

§2–301. General Obligations of Parties. The obligation of the seller is to transfer and deliver and that of the buyer is to accept and pay in accordance with the contract.

§2–302. Unconscionable Contract or Clause. (1) If the court as a matter of law finds the contract or any clause of the contract to have been unconscionable at the time it was made the court may refuse to enforce the contract, or it may enforce the remainder of the contract without the unconscionable clause, or it may so limit the application of any unconscionable clause as to avoid any unconscionable result.

(2) When it is claimed or appears to the court that the contract or any clause thereof may be unconscionable the parties shall be afforded a reasonable opportunity to present evidence as to its commercial setting, purpose and effect to aid the court in making the determination.

§2–303. Allocation or Division of Risks. Where this Article allocates a risk or a burden as between the parties "unless otherwise agreed", the agreement may not only shift the allocation but may also divide the risk or burden.

§2–304. Price Payable in Money, Goods, Realty, or Otherwise. (1) The price can be made payable in money or otherwise. If it is payable in whole or in part in goods each party is a seller of the goods which he is to transfer.

(2) Even though all or part of the price is payable in an interest in realty the transfer of the goods and the seller's obligations with reference to them are subject to this Article, but not the transfer of the interest in realty or the transferor's obligations in connection therewith.

§2–305. Open Price Term. (1) The parties if they so intend can conclude a contract for sale even though the price is not settled. In such a case the price is a reasonable price at the time for delivery if

(a) nothing is said as to price; or

(b) the price is left to be agreed by the parties and they fail to agree; or

(c) the price is to be fixed in terms of some agreed market or other standard as set or recorded by a third person or agency and it is not so set or recorded.

(2) A price to be fixed by the seller or by the buyer means a price for him to fix in good faith.

(3) When a price left to be fixed otherwise than by agreement of the parties fails to be fixed through fault of one party the other may at his option treat the contract as cancelled or himself fix a reasonable price.

(4) Where, however, the parties intend not to be bound unless the price be fixed or agreed and it is not fixed or agreed there is no contract. In such a case the buyer must return any goods already received or if unable so to do must pay their reasonable value at the time of delivery and the seller must return any portion of the price paid on account.

§2–306. Output, Requirements and Exclusive Dealings. (1) A term which measures the quantity by the output of the seller or the requirements of the buyer means such actual output or requirements as may occur in good faith, except that no quantity unreasonably disproportionate to any stated estimate or in the absence of a stated estimate to any normal or otherwise comparable prior output or requirements may be tendered or demanded.

(2) A lawful agreement by either the seller or the buyer for exclusive dealing in the kind of goods concerned imposes unless otherwise agreed an obligation by the seller to use best efforts to supply the goods and by the buyer to use best efforts to promote their sale.

§2–307. Delivery in Single Lot or Several Lots. Unless otherwise agreed all goods called for by a contract for sale must be tendered in a single delivery and payment is due only on such tender but where the circumstances give either party the right to make or demand delivery in lots the price if it can be apportioned may be demanded for each lot.

§2–308. Absence of Specified Place for Delivery. Unless otherwise agreed

(a) the place for delivery of goods is the seller's place of business or if he has none his residence; but

(b) in a contract for sale of identified goods which to the knowledge of the parties at the time of contracting are in some other place, that place is the place for their delivery; and

(c) documents of title may be delivered through customary banking channels.

§2–309. Absence of Specific Time Provisions; Notice of Termination. (1) The time for shipment or delivery or any other action under a contract if not provided in this Article or agreed upon shall be a reasonable time.

(2) Where the contract provides for successive performances but is indefinite in duration it is valid for a reasonable time but unless otherwise agreed may be terminated at any time by either party.

(3) Termination of a contract by one party except on the happening of an agreed event requires that reasonable notification be received by the other party and an agreement dispensing with notification is invalid if its operation would be unconscionable.

§2–310. Open Time for Payment or Running of Credit; Authority to Ship under Reservation. Unless otherwise agreed

(a) payment is due at the time and place at which the buyer is to receive the goods even though the place of shipment is the place of delivery; and

(b) if the seller is authorized to send the goods he may ship them under reservation, and may tender the documents of title, but the buyer may inspect the goods after their arrival before payment is due unless such inspection is inconsistent with the terms of the contract (Section 2–513); and

(c) if delivery is authorized and made by way of documents of title otherwise than by subsection (b) then payment is due at the time and place at which the buyer is to receive the documents regardless of where the goods are to be received; and

(d) where the seller is required or authorized to ship the goods on credit the credit period runs from the time of shipment but post-dating the invoice or delaying its dispatch will correspondingly delay the starting of the credit period.

§2–311. Options and Cooperation Respecting Performance. (1) An agreement for sale which is otherwise sufficiently definite (subsection (3) of Section 2–204) to be a contract is not made invalid by the fact that it leaves particulars of performance to be specified by one of the parties. Any such specification must be made in good faith and within limits set by commercial reasonableness.

(2) Unless otherwise agreed specifications relating to assortment of the goods are at the buyer's option and except as otherwise provided in subsections (1) (c) and (3) of Section 2–319 specifications or arrangements relating to shipment are at the seller's option.

(3) Where such specification would materially affect the other party's performance but is not seasonally made or where one party's cooperation is necessary to the agreed performance of the other but is not seasonally forthcoming, the other party in addition to all other remedies

(a) is excused for any resulting delay in his own performance; and

(b) may also either proceed to perform in any reasonable manner or after the time for a material part of his own performance treat the failure to specify or to cooperate as a breach by failure to deliver or accept the goods.

§2–312. Warranty of Title and Against Infringement; Buyer's Obligation against Infringement. (1) Subject to subsection (2) there is in a contract for sale a warranty by the seller that

(a) the title conveyed shall be good, and its transfer rightful; and

(b) the goods shall be delivered free from any security interest or other lien or encumbrance of which the buyer at the time of contracting has no knowledge.

(2) A warranty under subsection (1) will be excluded or modified only by specific language or by circumstances which give the buyer reason to know that the person selling does not claim title in himself or that he is purporting to sell only such right or title as he or a third person may have.

(3) Unless otherwise agreed a seller who is a merchant regularly dealing in goods of the kind warrants that the goods shall be delivered free of the rightful claim of any third person by way of infringement or the like but a buyer who furnishes specifications to the seller must hold the seller harmless against any such claim which arises out of compliance with the specifications.

§2–313. Express Warranties by Affirmation, Promise, Description, Sample. (1) Express warranties by the seller are created as follows:

(a) Any affirmation of fact or promise made by the seller to the buyer which relates to the goods and becomes part of the basis of the bargain creates an express warranty that the goods shall conform to the affirmation or promise.

(b) Any description of the goods which is made part of the basis of the bargain creates an express warranty that the goods shall conform to the description.

(c) Any sample or model which is made part of the basis of the bargain creates an express warranty that the whole of the goods shall conform to the sample or model.

(2) It is not necessary to the creation of an express warranty that the seller use formal words such as "warrant" or "guarantee" or that he have a specific intention to make a warranty, but an affirmation merely of the value of the goods or a statement purporting to be merely the seller's opinion or commendation of the goods does not create a warranty.

§2–314. Implied Warranty: Merchantability; Usage of Trade. (1) Unless excluded or modified (Section 2–316), a warranty that the goods shall be merchantable is implied in a contract for their sale if the seller is a merchant with respect to goods of that kind. Under this section the serving for value of food or drink to be consumed either on the premises or elsewhere is a sale.

(2) Goods to be merchantable must be at least such as

(a) pass without objection in the trade under the contract description; and

(b) in the case of fungible goods, are of fair average quality within the description; and

(c) are fit for the ordinary purposes for which such goods are used; and

(d) run, within the variations permitted by the agreement, of even kind, quality and quantity within each unit and among all units involved; and

(e) are adequately contained, packaged, and labeled as the agreement may require; and

(f) conform to the promises or affirmations of fact made on the container or label if any.

(3) Unless excluded or modified (Section 2–316) other implied warranties may arise from course of dealing or usage of trade.

§2–315. Implied Warranty: Fitness for Particular Purpose. Where the seller at the time of contracting has reason to know any particular purpose for which the goods are required and that the buyer is relying on the seller's skill or judgment to select or furnish suitable goods, there is unless excluded or modified under the next section an implied warranty that the goods shall be fit for such purpose.

§2–316. Exclusion or Modification of Warranties. (1) Words or conduct relevant to the creation of an express warranty and words or conduct tending to negate or limit warranty shall be construed wherever reasonable as consistent with each other; but subject to the provisions of this Article on parol or extrinsic evidence (Section 2–202) negation or limitation is inoperative to the extent that such construction is unreasonable.

(2) Subject to subsection (3), to exclude or modify the implied warranty of merchantability or any part of it the language must mention merchantability and in case of a writing must be conspicuous, and to exclude or modify any implied warranty of fitness the exclusion must be by a writing and conspicuous. Language to exclude all implied warranties of fitness is sufficient if it states, for example, that "There are no warranties which extend beyond the description on the face hereof."

(3) Notwithstanding subsection (2)

(a) unless the circumstances indicate otherwise, all implied warranties are excluded by expressions like "as is", "with all faults" or other language which in common understanding calls the buyer's attention to the exclusion of warranties and makes plain that there is no implied warranty; and

(b) when the buyer before entering into the contract has examined the goods or the sample or model as fully as he desired or has refused to examine the goods there is no implied warranty with regard to defects which an examination ought in the circumstances to have revealed to him; and

(c) an implied warranty can also be excluded or modified by course of dealing or course of performance or usage of trade.

(4) Remedies for breach of warranty can be limited in accordance with the provisions of this Article on liquidation or limitation of damages and on contractual modification of remedy (Sections 2–718 and 2–719).

§2–317. Cumulation and Conflict of Warranties Express or Implied. Warranties whether express or implied shall be construed as consistent with each other and as cumulative, but if such construction is unreasonable the intention of the parties shall determine which warranty is dominant. In ascertaining that intention the following rules apply:

(a) Exact or technical specifications displace an inconsistent sample or model or general language of description.

(b) A sample from an existing bulk displaces inconsistent general language of description.

(c) Express warranties displace inconsistent implied warranties other than an implied warranty of fitness for a particular purpose.

§2–318. Third Party Beneficiaries of Warranties Express or Implied. Note: *If this Act is introduced in the Congress of the United States this section should be omitted. (States to select one alternative.)*

Alternative A—

A seller's warranty whether express or implied extends to any natural person who is in the family or household of his buyer or who is a guest in his home if it is reasonable to expect that such person may use, consume or be affected by the goods and who is injured in person by breach of the warranty. A seller may not exclude or limit the operation of this section.

Alternative B—

A seller's warranty whether express or implied extends to any natural person who may reasonably be expected to use, consume or be affected by the goods and who is injured in person by breach of the warranty. A seller may not exclude or limit the operation of this section.

Alternative C—

A seller's warranty whether express or implied extends to any person who may reasonably be expected to use, consume or be affected by the goods and who is injured by breach of the warranty. A seller may not exclude or limit the operation of this section with respect to injury to the person of an individual to whom the warranty extends. As amended 1966.

§2–319. F.O.B. and F.A.S. Terms. (1) Unless otherwise agreed the term F.O.B. (which means "free on board") at a named place, even though used only in connection with the stated price, is a delivery term under which

(a) when the term is F.O.B. the place of shipment, the seller must at that place ship the goods in the manner provided in this Article (Section 2–504) and bear the expense and risk of putting them into the possession of the carrier; or

(b) when the term is F.O.B. the place of destination, the seller must at his own expense and risk transport the goods to that place and there tender delivery of them in the manner provided in this Article (Section 2–503);

(c) when under either (a) or (b) the term is also F.O.B. vessel, car or other vehicle, the seller must in addition at his own expense and risk load the goods on board. If the term is F.O.B. vessel the buyer must name the vessel and in an appropriate case the seller must comply with the provisions of this Article on the form of bill of lading (Section 2–323).

(2) Unless otherwise agreed the term F.A.S. vessel (which means "free alongside") at a named port, even though used only in connection with the stated price, is a delivery term under which the seller must

(a) at his own expense and risk deliver the goods alongside the vessel in the manner usual in that port or on a dock designated and provided by the buyer; and

(b) obtain and tender a receipt for the goods in exchange for which the carrier is under a duty to issue a bill of lading.

(3) Unless otherwise agreed in any case falling within subsection (1) (a) or (c) or subsection (2) the buyer must seasonably give any needed instructions for making delivery, including when the term is F.A.S. or F.O.B. the loading berth of the vessel and in an appropriate case its name and sailing date. The seller may treat the failure of needed instructions as a failure of cooperation under this Article (Section 2–311). He may also at his option move the goods in any reasonable manner preparatory to delivery or shipment.

(4) Under the term F.O.B. vessel or F.A.S. unless otherwise agreed the buyer must make payment against tender of the required documents and the seller may not tender nor the buyer demand delivery of the goods in substitution for the documents.

§2–320. C.I.F. and C. & F. Terms. (1) The term C.I.F. means that the price includes in a lump sum the cost of the goods and the insurance and freight to the named destination. The term C. & F. or C.F. means that the price so includes cost and freight to the named destination.

(2) Unless otherwise agreed and even though used only in connection with the stated price and destination, the term C.I.F. destination or its equivalent requires the seller at his own expense and risk to

(a) put the goods into the possession of a carrier at the port for shipment and obtain a negotiable bill or bills of lading covering the entire transportation to the named destination; and

(b) load the goods and obtain a receipt from the carrier (which may be contained in the bill of lading) showing that the freight has been paid or provided for; and

(c) obtain a policy or certificate of insurance, including any war risk insurance, of a kind and on terms then current at the port of shipment in the usual amount, in the currency of the contract, shown to cover the same goods covered by the bill of lading and providing for payment of loss to the order of the buyer or for the account of whom it may concern; but the seller may add to the price the amount of the premium for any such war risk insurance; and

(d) prepare an invoice of the goods and procure any other documents required to effect shipment or to comply with the contract; and

(e) forward and tender with commercial promptness all the documents in due form and with any indorsement necessary to perfect the buyer's rights.

(3) Unless otherwise agreed the term C. & F. or its equivalent has the same effect and imposes upon the seller the same obligations and risks as a C.I.F. term except the obligation as to insurance.

(4) Under the term C.I.F. or C. & F. unless otherwise agreed the buyer must make payment against tender of the required documents and the seller may not tender nor the buyer demand delivery of the goods in substitution for the documents.

§2–321. C.I.F. or C. & F.: "Net Landed Weights"; "Payment on Arrival"; Warranty of Condition on Arrival. Under a contract containing a term C.I.F. or C. & F.

(1) Where the price is based on or is to be adjusted according to "net landed weights", "delivered weights", "out turn" quantity or quality or the like, unless otherwise agreed the seller must reasonably estimate the price. The payment due on tender of the documents called for by the contract is the amount so estimated, but after final adjustment of the price a settlement must be made with commercial promptness.

(2) An agreement described in subsection (1) or any warranty of quality or condition of the goods on arrival places upon the seller the risk of ordinary deterioration, shrinkage and the like in transportation but has no effect on the place or time of identification to the contract for sale or delivery or on the passing of the risk of loss.

(3) Unless otherwise agreed where the contract provides for payment on or after arrival of the goods the seller must before payment allow such preliminary inspection as is feasible; but if the goods are lost delivery of the documents and payment are due when the goods should have arrived.

§2–322. Delivery "Ex-Ship." (1) Unless otherwise agreed a term for delivery of goods "ex-ship" (which means from the carrying vessel) or in equivalent language is not restricted to a particular ship and requires delivery from a ship which has reached a place at the named port of destination where goods of the kind are usually discharged.

(2) Under such a term unless otherwise agreed

(a) the seller must discharge all liens arising out of the carriage and furnish the buyer with a direction which puts the carrier under a duty to deliver the goods; and

(b) the risk of loss does not pass to the buyer until the goods leave the ship's tackle or are otherwise properly unloaded.

§2–323. Form of Bill of Lading Required in Overseas Shipment; "Overseas." (1) Where the contract contemplates overseas shipment and contains a term C.I.F. or C. & F. or F.O.B. vessel, the seller unless otherwise agreed must obtain a negotiable bill of lading stating that the goods have been loaded on board or, in the case of a term C.I.F. or C. & F., received for shipment.

(2) Where in a case within subsection (1) a bill of lading has been issued in a set of parts, unless otherwise agreed if the documents are not to be sent from abroad the buyer may demand tender of the full set; otherwise only one part of the bill of lading need be tendered. Even if the agreement expressly requires a full set

(a) due tender of a single part is acceptable within the provisions of this Article on cure of improper delivery (subsection (1) of Section 2–508); and

(b) even though the full set is demanded, if the documents are sent from abroad the person tendering an incomplete set may nevertheless require payment upon furnishing an indemnity which the buyer in good faith deems adequate.

(3) A shipment by water or by air or a contract contemplating such shipment is "overseas" insofar as by usage of trade or agreement it is subject to the commercial, financing or shipping practices characteristic of international deep water commerce.

§2–324. "No Arrival, No Sale" Term. Under a term "no arrival, no sale" or terms of like meaning, unless otherwise agreed,

(a) the seller must properly ship conforming goods and if they arrive by any means he must tender them on arrival but he assumes no obligation that the goods will arrive unless he has caused the non-arrival; and

(b) where without fault of the seller the goods are in part lost or have so deteriorated as no longer to conform to the contract or arrive after the contract time, the buyer may proceed as if there had been casualty to identified goods (Section 2–613).

§2–325. "Letter of Credit" Term; "Confirmed Credit." (1) Failure of the buyer seasonably to furnish an agreed letter of credit is a breach of the contract for sale.

(2) The delivery to seller of a proper letter of credit suspends the buyer's obligation to pay. If the letter of credit is dishonored, the seller may on seasonable notification to the buyer require payment directly from him.

(3) Unless otherwise agreed the term "letter of credit" or "banker's credit" in a contract for sale means an irrevocable credit issued by a financing agency of good repute and, where the shipment is overseas, of good international repute. The term "confirmed credit" means that the credit must also carry the direct obligation of such an agency which does business in the seller's financial market.

§2–326. Sale on Approval and Sale or Return; Consignment Sales and Rights of Creditors. (1) Unless otherwise agreed, if delivered goods may be returned by the buyer even though they conform to the contract, the transaction is

(a) a "sale on approval" if the goods are delivered primarily for use, and

(b) a "sale or return" if the goods are delivered primarily for resale.

(2) Except as provided in subsection (3), goods held on approval are not subject to the claims of the buyer's creditors until acceptance; goods held on sale or return are subject to such claims while in the buyer's possession.

(3) Where goods are delivered to a person for sale and such person maintains a place of business at which he deals in goods of the kind involved, under a name other than the name of the person making delivery, then with respect to claims of creditors of the person conducting the business the goods are deemed to be on sale or return. The provisions of this subsection are applicable even though an agreement purports to reserve title to the person making delivery until payment or resale or uses such words as "on consignment" or "on memorandum". However, this subsection is not applicable if the person making delivery

(a) complies with an applicable law providing for a consignor's interest or the like to be evidenced by a sign, or

(b) establishes that the person conducting the business is generally known by his creditors to be substantially engaged in selling the goods of others, or

(c) complies with the filing provisions of the Article on Secured Transactions (Article 9).

(4) Any "or return" term of a contract for sale is to be treated as a separate contract

for sale within the statute of frauds section of this Article (Section 2–201) and as contradicting the sale aspect of the contract within the provisions of this Article on parol or extrinsic evidence (Section 2–202).

§2–327. Special Incidents of Sale on Approval and Sale or Return. (1) Under a sale on approval unless otherwise agreed

(a) although the goods are identified to the contract the risk of loss and the title do not pass to the buyer until acceptance; and

(b) use of the goods consistent with the purpose of trial is not acceptance but failure seasonably to notify the seller of election to return the goods is acceptance, and if the goods conform to the contract acceptance of any part is acceptance of the whole; and

(c) after due notification of election to return, the return is at the seller's risk and expense but a merchant buyer must follow any reasonable instructions.

(2) Under a sale or return unless otherwise agreed

(a) the option to return extends to the whole or any commercial unit of the goods while in substantially their original condition, but must be exercised seasonably; and

(b) the return is at the buyer's risk and expense.

§2–328. Sale by Auction. (1) In a sale by auction if goods are put up in lots each lot is the subject of a separate sale.

(2) A sale by auction is complete when the auctioneer so announces by the fall of the hammer or in other customary manner. Where a bid is made while the hammer is falling in acceptance of a prior bid the auctioneer may in his discretion reopen the bidding or declare the goods sold under the bid on which the hammer was falling.

(3) Such a sale is with reserve unless the goods are in explicit terms put up without reserve. In an auction with reserve the auctioneer may withdraw the goods at any time until he announces completion of the sale. In an auction without reserve, after the auctioneer calls for bids on an article or lot, that article or lot cannot be withdrawn unless no bid is made within a reasonable time. In either case a bidder may retract his bid until the auctioneer's announcement of completion of the sale, but a bidder's retraction does not revive any previous bid.

(4) If the auctioneer knowingly receives a bid on the seller's behalf or the seller makes or procures such a bid, and notice has not been given that liberty for such bidding is reserved, the buyer may at his option avoid the sale or take the goods at the price of the last good faith bid prior to the completion of the sale. This subsection shall not apply to any bid at a forced sale.

Part 4

Title, Creditors and Good Faith Purchasers

§2–401. Passing of Title; Reservation for Security; Limited Application of This Section. Each provision of this Article with regard to the rights, obligations and remedies of the seller, the buyer, purchasers or other third parties applies irrespective of title to the goods except where the provision refers to such title. Insofar as situations are not covered by the other provisions of this Article and matters concerning title become material the following rules apply:

(1) Title to goods cannot pass under a contract for sale prior to their identification to the contract (Section 2–501), and unless otherwise explicitly agreed the buyer acquires by their identification a special property as limited by this Act. Any retention or reservation by the seller of the title (property) in goods shipped or delivered to the buyer is limited in

effect to a reservation of a security interest. Subject to these provisions and to the provisions of the Article on Secured Transactions (Article 9), title to goods passes from the seller to the buyer in any manner and on any conditions explicitly agreed on by the parties.

(2) Unless otherwise explicitly agreed title passes to the buyer at the time and place at which the seller completes his performance with reference to the physical delivery of the goods, despite any reservation of a security interest and even though a document of title is to be delivered at a different time or place; and in particular and despite any reservation of a security interest by the bill of lading

(a) if the contract requires or authorizes the seller to send the goods to the buyer but does not require him to deliver them at destination, title passes to the buyer at the time and place of shipment; but

(b) if the contract requires delivery at destination, title passes on tender there.

(3) Unless otherwise explicitly agreed where delivery is to be made without moving the goods,

(a) if the seller is to deliver a document of title, title passes at the time when and the place where he delivers such documents; or

(b) if the goods are at the time of contracting already identified and no documents are to be delivered, title passes at the time and place of contracting.

(4) A rejection or other refusal by the buyer to receive or retain the goods, whether or not justified, or a justified revocation of acceptance revests title to the goods in the seller. Such revesting occurs by operation of law and is not a "sale".

§2–402. Rights of Seller's Creditors against Sold Goods. (1) Except as provided in subsections (2) and (3), rights of unsecured creditors of the seller with respect to goods which have been identified to a contract for sale are subject to the buyer's rights to recover the goods under this Article (Sections 2–502 and 2–716).

(2) A creditor of the seller may treat a sale or an identification of goods to a contract for sale as void if as against him a retention of possession by the seller is fraudulent under any rule of law of the state where the goods are situated, except that retention of possession in good faith and current course of trade by a merchant-seller for a commercially reasonable time after a sale or identification is not fraudulent.

(3) Nothing in this Article shall be deemed to impair the rights of creditors of the seller

(a) under the provisions of the Article on Secured Transactions (Article 9); or

(b) where identification to the contract or delivery is made not in current course of trade but in satisfaction of or as security for a pre-existing claim for money, security or the like and is made under circumstances which under any rule of law of the state where the goods are situated would apart from this Article constitute the transaction a fraudulent transfer or voidable preference.

§2–403. Power to Transfer; Good Faith Purchase of Goods; "Entrusting". (1) A purchaser of goods acquires all title which his transferor had or had power to transfer except that a purchaser of a limited interest acquires rights only to the extent of the interest purchased. A person with voidable title has power to transfer a good title to a good faith purchaser for value. When goods have been delivered under a transaction of purchase the purchaser has such power even though

(a) the transferor was deceived as to the identity of the purchaser, or

(b) the delivery was in exchange for a check which is later dishonored, or

(c) it was agreed that the transaction was to be a "cash sale", or

(d) the delivery was procured through fraud punishable as larcenous under the criminal law.

(2) Any entrusting of possession of goods to a merchant who deals in goods of that kind gives him power to transfer all rights of the entruster to a buyer in ordinary course of business.

(3) "Entrusting" includes any delivery and any acquiescence in retention of possession regardless of any condition expressed between the parties to the delivery or acquiescence and regardless of whether the procurement of the entrusting or the possessor's disposition of the goods have been such as to be larcenous under the criminal law.

(4) The rights of other purchasers of goods and of lien creditors are governed by the Articles on Secured Transactions (Article 9), Bulk Transfers (Article 6) and Documents of Title (Article 7).

Part 5

Performance

§2–501. Insurable Interest in Goods; Manner of Identification of Goods. (1) The buyer obtains a special property and an insurable interest in goods by identification of existing goods as goods to which the contract refers even though the goods so identified are non-conforming and he has an option to return or reject them. Such identification can be made at any time and in any manner explicitly agreed to by the parties. In the absence of explicit agreement identification occurs

(a) when the contract is made if it is for the sale of goods already existing and identified;

(b) if the contract is for the sale of future goods other than those described in paragraph (c), when goods are shipped, marked or otherwise designated by the seller as goods to which the contract refers;

(c) when the crops are planted or otherwise become growing crops or the young are conceived if the contract is for the sale of unborn young to be born within twelve months after contracting or for the sale of crops to be harvested within twelve months or the next normal harvest season after contracting whichever is longer.

(2) The seller retains an insurable interest in goods so long as title to or any security interest in the goods remains in him and where the identification is by the seller alone he may until default or insolvency or notification to the buyer that the identification is final substitute other goods for those identified.

(3) Nothing in this section impairs any insurable interest recognized under any other statute or rule of law.

§2–502. Buyer's Right to Goods on Seller's Insolvency. (1) Subject to subsection (2) and even though the goods have not been shipped a buyer who has paid a part or all of the price of goods in which he has a special property under the provisions of the immediately preceding section may on making and keeping good a tender of any unpaid portion of their price recover them from the seller if the seller becomes insolvent within ten days after receipt of the first installment on their price.

(2) If the identification creating his special property has been made by the buyer he acquires the right to recover the goods only if they conform to the contract for sale.

§2–503. Manner of Seller's Tender of Delivery. (1) Tender of delivery requires that the seller put and hold conforming goods at the buyer's disposition and give the buyer any notification reasonably necessary to enable him to take delivery. The manner, time and place for tender are determined by the agreement and this Article, and in particular

(a) tender must be at a reasonable hour, and if it is of goods they must be kept available for the period reasonably necessary to enable the buyer to take possession; but

(b) unless otherwise agreed the buyer must furnish facilities reasonably suited to the receipt of the goods.

(2) Where the case is within the next section respecting shipment tender requires that the seller comply with its provisions.

(3) Where the seller is required to deliver at a particular destination tender requires that he comply with subsection (1) and also in any appropriate case tender documents as described in subsections (4) and (5) of this section.

(4) Where goods are in the possession of a bailee and are to be delivered without being moved

(a) tender requires that the seller either tender a negotiable document of title covering such goods or procure acknowledgment by the bailee of the buyer's right to possession of the goods; but

(b) tender to the buyer of a non-negotiable document of title or of a written direction to the bailee to deliver is sufficient tender unless the buyer seasonably objects, and receipt by the bailee of notification of the buyer's rights fixes those rights as against the bailee and all third persons; but risk of loss of the goods and of any failure by the bailee to honor the non-negotiable document of title or to obey the direction remains on the seller until the buyer has had a reasonable time to present the document or direction, and a refusal by the bailee to honor the document or to obey the direction defeats the tender.

(5) Where the contract requires the seller to deliver documents

(a) he must tender all such documents in correct form, except as provided in this Article with respect to bills of lading in a set (subsection (2) of Section 2–323); and

(b) tender through customary banking channels is sufficient and dishonor of a draft accompanying the documents constitutes non-acceptance or rejection.

§2–504. Shipment by Seller. Where the seller is required or authorized to send the goods to the buyer and the contract does not require him to deliver them at a particular destination, then unless otherwise agreed he must

(a) put the goods in the possession of such a carrier and make such a contract for their transportation as may be reasonable having regard to the nature of the goods and other circumstances of the case; and

(b) obtain and promptly deliver or tender in due form any document necessary to enable the buyer to obtain possession of the goods or otherwise required by the agreement or by usage of trade; and

(c) promptly notify the buyer of the shipment.

Failure to notify the buyer under paragraph (c) or to make a proper contract under paragraph (a) is a ground for rejection only if material delay or loss ensues.

§2–505. Seller's Shipment under Reservation. (1) Where the seller has identified goods to the contract by or before shipment:

(a) his procurement of a negotiable bill of lading to his own order or otherwise reserves in him a security interest in the goods. His procurement of the bill to the order of a financing agency or of the buyer indicates in addition only the seller's expectation of transferring that interest to the person named.

(b) a non-negotiable bill of lading to himself or his nominee reserves possession of the goods as security but except in a case of conditional delivery (subsection (2) of Section 2–507) a non-negotiable bill of lading naming the buyer as consignee reserves no security interest even though the seller retains possession of the bill of lading.

(2) When shipment by the seller with reservation of a security interest is in violation of the contract for sale it constitutes an improper contract for transportation within the preceding section but impairs neither the rights given to the buyer by shipment and identification of the goods to the contract nor the seller's powers as a holder of a negotiable document.

§2–506. Rights of Financing Agency. (1) A financing agency by paying or purchasing for value a draft which relates to a shipment of goods acquires to the extent of the payment or purchase and in addition to its own rights under the draft and any document of title securing it any rights of the shipper in the goods including the right to stop delivery and the shipper's right to have the draft honored by the buyer.

(2) The right to reimbursement of a financing agency which has in good faith honored or purchased the draft under commitment to or authority from the buyer is not impaired by subsequent discovery of defects with reference to any relevant document which was apparently regular on its face.

§2–507. Effect of Seller's Tender; Delivery on Condition. (1) tender of delivery is a condition to the buyer's duty to accept the goods and, unless otherwise agreed, to his duty to pay for them. Tender entitles the seller to acceptance of the goods and to payment according to the contract.

(2) Where payment is due and demanded on the delivery to the buyer of goods or documents of title, his right as against the seller to retain or dispose of them is conditional upon his making the payment due.

§2–508. Cure by Seller of Improper Tender or Delivery; Replacement. (1) Where any tender or delivery by the seller is rejected because non-conforming and the time for performance has not yet expired, the seller may seasonably notify the buyer of his intention to cure and may then within the contract time make a conforming delivery.

(2) Where the buyer rejects a non-conforming tender which the seller had reasonable grounds to believe would be acceptable with or without money allowance the seller may if he seasonably notifies the buyer have a further reasonable time to substitute a conforming tender.

§2–509. Risk of Loss in the Absence of Breach. (1) Where the contract requires or authorizes the seller to ship the goods by carrier

(a) if it does not require him to deliver them at a particular destination, the risk of loss passes to the buyer when the goods are duly delivered to the carrier even though the shipment is under reservation (Section 2–505); but

(b) if it does require him to deliver them at a particular destination and the goods are there duly tendered while in the possession of the carrier, the risk of loss passes to the buyer when the goods are there duly so tendered as to enable the buyer to take delivery.

(2) Where the goods are held by a bailee to be delivered without being moved, the risk of loss passes to the buyer

(a) on his receipt of a negotiable document of title covering the goods; or

(b) on acknowledgment by the bailee of the buyer's right to possession of the goods; or

(c) after his receipt of a non-negotiable document of title or other written direction to deliver, as provided in subsection (4) (b) of Section 2–503.

(3) In any case not within subsection (1) or (2), the risk of loss passes to the buyer on his receipt of the goods if the seller is a merchant; otherwise the risk passes to the buyer on tender of delivery.

(4) The provisions of this section are subject to contrary agreement of the parties and to the provisions of this Article on sale on approval (Section 2–327) and on effect of breach on risk of loss (Section 2–510).

§2–510. Effect of Breach on Risk of Loss. (1) Where a tender or delivery of goods so fails to conform to the contract as to give a right of rejection the risk of their loss remains on the seller until cure or acceptance.

(2) Where the buyer rightfully revokes acceptance he may to the extent of any deficiency in his effective insurance coverage treat the risk of loss as having rested on the seller from the beginning.

(3) Where the buyer as to conforming goods already identified to the contract for sale repudiates or is otherwise in breach before risk of their loss has passed to him, the seller may to the extent of any deficiency in his effective insurance coverage treat the risk of loss as resting on the buyer for a commercially reasonable time.

§2–511. Tender of Payment by Buyer; Payment by Check. (1) Unless otherwise agreed tender of payment is a condition to the seller's duty to tender and complete any delivery.

(2) Tender of payment is sufficient when made by any means or in any manner current in the ordinary course of business unless the seller demands payment in legal tender and gives any extension of time reasonably necessary to procure it.

(3) Subject to the provisions of this Act on the effect of an instrument on an obligation (Section 3–802), payment by check is conditional and is defeated as between the parties by dishonor of the check on due presentment.

§2–512. Payment by Buyer before Inspection. (1) Where the contract requires payment before inspection non-conformity of the goods does not excuse the buyer from so making payment unless

(a) the non-conformity appears without inspection; or

(b) despite tender of the required documents the circumstances would justify injunction against honor under the provisions of this Act (Section 5–114).

(2) Payment pursuant to subsection (1) does not constitute an acceptance of goods or impair the buyer's right to inspect or any of his remedies.

§2–513. Buyer's Right to Inspection of Goods. (1) Unless otherwise agreed and subject to subsection (3), where goods are tendered or delivered or identified to the contract for sale, the buyer has a right before payment or acceptance to inspect them at any reasonable place and time and in any reasonable manner. When the seller is required or authorized to send the goods to the buyer, the inspection may be after their arrival.

(2) Expenses of inspection must be borne by the buyer but may be recovered from the seller if the goods do not conform and are rejected.

(3) Unless otherwise agreed and subject to the provisions of this Article on C.I.F. contracts (subsection (3) of Section 2–321), the buyer is not entitled to inspect the goods before payment of the price when the contract provides

(a) for delivery "C.O.D." or on other like terms; or

(b) for payment against documents of title, except where such payment is due only after the goods are to become available for inspection.

(4) A place or method of inspection fixed by the parties is presumed to be exclusive but unless otherwise expressly agreed it does not postpone identification or shift the place for delivery or for passing the risk of loss. If compliance becomes impossible, inspection shall be as provided in this section unless the place or method fixed was clearly intended as an indispensable condition failure of which avoids the contract.

§2–514. When Documents Deliverable on Acceptance; When on Payment. Unless otherwise agreed documents against which a draft is drawn are to be delivered to the drawee on acceptance of the draft if it is payable more than three days after presentment; otherwise, only on payment.

§2–515. Preserving Evidence of Goods in Dispute. In furtherance of the adjustment of any claim or dispute

(a) either party on reasonable notification to the other and for the purpose of ascertaining the facts and preserving evidence has the right to inspect, test and sample the goods including such of them as may be in the possession or control of the other; and

(b) the parties may agree to a third party inspection or survey to determine the conformity or condition of the goods and may agree that the findings shall be binding upon them in any subsequent litigation or adjustment.

Part 6

Breach, Repudiation and Excuse

§2–601. Buyer's Rights on Improper Delivery. Subject to the provisions of this Article on breach in installment contracts (Section 2–612) and unless otherwise agreed under the sections on contractual limitations of remedy (Sections 2–718 and 2–719), if the goods or the tender of delivery fail in any respect to conform to the contract, the buyer may

(a) reject the whole; or

(b) accept the whole; or

(c) accept any commercial unit or units and reject the rest.

§2–602. Manner and Effect of Rightful Rejection. (1) Rejection of goods must be within a reasonable time after their delivery or tender. It is ineffective unless the buyer seasonably notifies the seller.

(2) Subject to the provisions of the two following sections on rejected goods (Sections 2–603 and 2–604),

(a) after rejection any exercise of ownership by the buyer with respect to any commercial unit is wrongful as against the seller; and

(b) if the buyer has before rejection taken physical possession of goods in which he does not have a security interest under the provisions of this Article (subsection (3) of Section 2–711), he is under a duty after rejection to hold them with reasonable care at the seller's disposition for a time sufficient to permit the seller to remove them; but

(c) the buyer has no further obligations with regard to goods rightfully rejected.

(3) The seller's rights with respect to goods wrongfully rejected are governed by the provisions of this Article on Seller's remedies in general (Section 2–703).

§2–603. Merchant Buyer's Duties as to Rightfully Rejected Goods. (1) Subject to any security interest in the buyer (subsection (3) of Section 2–711), when the seller has no agent or place of business at the market of rejection a merchant buyer is under a duty after rejection of goods in his possession or control to follow any reasonable instructions received from the seller with respect to the goods and in the absence of such instructions to make reasonable efforts to sell them for the seller's account if they are perishable or threaten to decline in value speedily. Instructions are not reasonable if on demand indemnity for expenses is not forthcoming.

(2) When the buyer sells goods under subsection (1), he is entitled to reimbursement from the seller or out of the proceeds for reasonable expenses of caring for and selling them, and if the expenses include no selling commission then to such commission as is usual in the trade or if there is none to a reasonable sum not exceeding ten per cent on the gross proceeds.

(3) In complying with this section the buyer is held only to good faith and good faith conduct hereunder is neither acceptance nor conversion nor the basis of an action for damages.

§2–604. Buyer's Options as to Salvage of Rightfully Rejected Goods. Subject to the provisions of the immediately preceding section on perishables if the seller gives no instructions within a reasonable time after notification of rejection the buyer may store the rejected goods for the seller's account or reship them to him or resell them for the seller's account with reimbursement as provided in the preceding section. Such action is not acceptance or conversion.

§2–605. Waiver of Buyer's Objections by Failure to Particularize. (1) The buyer's failure to state in connection with rejection a particular defect which is ascertainable by reasonable inspection precludes him from relying on the unstated defect to justify rejection or to establish breach

    (a) where the seller could have cured it if stated seasonably; or

    (b) between merchants when the seller has after rejection made a request in writing for a full and final written statement of all defects on which the buyer proposes to rely.

    (2) Payment against documents made without reservation of rights precludes recovery of the payment for defects apparent on the face of the documents.

§2–606. What Constitutes Acceptance of Goods. (1) Acceptance of goods occurs when the buyer

    (a) after a reasonable opportunity to inspect the goods signifies to the seller that the goods are conforming or that he will take or retain them in spite of their nonconformity; or

    (b) fails to make an effective rejection (subsection (1) of Section 2–602), but such acceptance does not occur until the buyer has had a reasonable opportunity to inspect them; or

    (c) does any act inconsistent with the seller's ownership; but if such act is wrongful as against the seller it is an acceptance only if ratified by him.

    (2) Acceptance of a part of any commercial unit is acceptance of that entire unit.

§2–607. Effect of Acceptance; Notice of Breach; Burden of Establishing Breach after Acceptance; Notice of Claim or Litigation to Person Answerable Over. (1) The buyer must pay at the contract rate for any goods accepted.

    (2) Acceptance of goods by the buyer precludes rejection of the goods accepted and if made with knowledge of a non-conformity cannot be revoked because of it unless the acceptance was on the reasonable assumption that the non-conformity would be seasonably cured but acceptance does not of itself impair any other remedy provided by this Article for non-conformity.

    (3) Where a tender has been accepted

    (a) the buyer must within a reasonable time after he discovers or should have discovered any breach notify the seller of breach or be barred from any remedy; and

    (b) if the claim is one for infringement or the like (subsection (3) of Section 2–312) and the buyer is sued as a result of such a breach he must so notify the seller within a reasonable time after he receives notice of the litigation or be barred from any remedy over for liability established by the litigation.

    (4) The burden is on the buyer to establish any breach with respect to the goods accepted.

    (5) Where the buyer is sued for breach of a warranty or other obligation for which his seller is answerable over

    (a) he may give his seller written notice of the litigation. If the notice states that the seller may come in and defend and that if the seller does not do so he will be bound in any action against him by his buyer by any determination of fact common to the two litigations, then unless the seller after seasonable receipt of the notice does come in and defend he is so bound.

(b) if the claim is one for infringement or the like (subsection (3) of Section 2–312) the original seller may demand in writing that his buyer turn over to him control of the litigation including settlement or else be barred from any remedy over and if he also agrees to bear all expense and to satisfy any adverse judgment, then unless the buyer after seasonable receipt of the demand does turn over control the buyer is so barred.

(6) The provisions of subsections (3), (4) and (5) apply to any obligation of a buyer to hold the seller harmless against infringement or the like (subsection (3) of Section 2–312).

§2–608. Revocation of Acceptance in Whole or in Part. (1) The buyer may revoke his acceptance of a lot or commercial unit whose non-conformity substantially impairs its value to him if he has accepted it

(a) on the reasonable assumption that its non-conformity would be cured and it has not been seasonably cured; or

(b) without discovery of such non-conformity if his acceptance was reasonably induced either by the difficulty of discovery before acceptance or by the seller's assurances.

(2) Revocation of acceptance must occur within a reasonable time after the buyer discovers or should have discovered the ground for it and before any substantial change in condition of the goods which is not caused by their own defects. It is not effective until the buyer notifies the seller of it.

(3) A buyer who so revokes has the same rights and duties with regard to the goods involved as if he had rejected them.

§2–609. Right to Adequate Assurance of Performance. (1) A contract for sale imposes an obligation on each party that the other's expectation of receiving due performance will not be impaired. When reasonable grounds for insecurity arise with respect to the performance of either party the other may in writing demand adequate assurance of due performance and until he receives such assurance may if commercially reasonable suspend any performance for which he has not already received the agreed return.

(2) Between merchants the reasonableness of grounds for insecurity and the adequacy of any assurance offered shall be determined according to commercial standards.

(3) Acceptance of any improper delivery or payment does not prejudice the aggrieved party's right to demand adequate assurance of future performance.

(4) After receipt of a justified demand failure to provide within a reasonable time not exceeding thirty days such assurance of due performance as is adequate under the circumstances of the particular case is a repudiation of the contract.

§2–610. Anticipatory Repudiation. When either party repudiates the contract with respect to a performance not yet due the loss of which will substantially impair the value of the contract to the other, the aggrieved party may

(a) for a commercially reasonable time await performance by the repudiating party; or

(b) resort to any remedy for breach (Section 2–703 or Section 2–711), even though he has notified the repudiating party that he would await the latter's performance and has urged retraction; and

(c) in either case suspend his own performance or proceed in accordance with the provisions of this Article on the seller's right to identify goods to the contract notwithstanding breach or to salvage unfinished goods (Section 2–704).

§2–611. Retraction of Anticipatory Repudiation. (1) Until the repudiating party's next performance is due he can retract his repudiation unless the aggrieved party has since the repudiation cancelled or materially changed his position or otherwise indicated that he considers the repudiation final.

(2) Retraction may be by any method which clearly indicates to the aggrieved party that the repudiating party intends to perform, but must include any assurance justifiably demanded under the provisions of this Article (Section 2–609).

(3) Retraction reinstates the repudiating party's rights under the contract with due excuse and allowance to the aggrieved party for any delay occasioned by the repudiation.

§2–612. "Installment Contract"; Breach. (1) An "installment contract" is one which requires or authorizes the delivery of goods in separate lots to be separately accepted, even though the contract contains a clause "each delivery is a separate contract" or its equivalent.

(2) The buyer may reject any installment which is non-conforming if the non-conformity substantially impairs the value of that installment and cannot be cured or if the non-conformity is a defect in the required documents; but if the non-conformity does not fall within subsection (3) and the seller gives adequate assurance of its cure the buyer must accept that installment.

(3) Whenever non-conformity or default with respect to one or more installments substantially impairs the value of the whole contract there is a breach of the whole. But the aggrieved party reinstates the contract if he accepts a non-conforming installment without seasonably notifying of cancellation or if he brings an action with respect only to past installments or demands performance as to future installments.

§2–613. Casualty to Identified Goods. Where the contract requires for its performance goods identified when the contract is made, and the goods suffer casualty without fault of either party before the risk of loss passes to the buyer, or in a proper case under a "no arrival, no sale" term (Section 2–324) then

(a) if the loss is total the contract is avoided; and

(b) if the loss is partial or the goods have so deteriorated as no longer to conform to the contract the buyer may nevertheless demand inspection and at his option either treat the contract as avoided or accept the goods with due allowance from the contract price for the deterioration or the deficiency in quantity but without further right against the seller.

§2–614. Substituted Performance. (1) Where without fault of either party the agreed berthing, loading, or unloading facilities fail or an agreed type of carrier becomes unavailable or the agreed manner of delivery otherwise becomes commercially impracticable but a commercially reasonable substitute is available, such substitute performance must be tendered and accepted.

(2) If the agreed means or manner of payment fails because of domestic or foreign governmental regulation, the seller may withhold or stop delivery unless the buyer provides a means or manner of payment which is commercially a substantial equivalent. If delivery has already been taken, payment by the means or in the manner provided by the regulation discharges the buyer's obligation unless the regulation is discriminatory, oppressive or predatory.

§2–615. Excuse by Failure of Presupposed Conditions. Except so far as a seller may have assumed a greater obligation and subject to the preceding section on substituted performance:

(a) Delay in delivery or non-delivery in whole or in part by a seller who complies with paragraphs (b) and (c) is not a breach of his duty under a contract for sale if performance as agreed has been made impracticable by the occurrence of a contingency the non-occurrence of which was a basic assumption on which the contract was made or by compliance in good faith with any applicable foreign or domestic governmental regulation or order whether or not it later proves to be invalid.

(b) Where the causes mentioned in paragraph (a) affect only a part of the seller's capacity to perform, he must allocate production and deliveries among his customers but may at his option include regular customers not then under contract as well as his own requirements for further manufacture. He may so allocate in any manner which is fair and reasonable.

    (c) The seller must notify the buyer seasonably that there will be delay or non-delivery and, when allocation is required under paragraph (b), of the estimated quota thus made available for the buyer.

§2–616. Procedure on Notice Claiming Excuse. (1) Where the buyer receives notification of a material or indefinite delay or an allocation justified under the preceding section he may by written notification to the seller as to any delivery concerned, and where the prospective deficiency substantially impairs the value of the whole contract under the provisions of this Article relating to breach of installment contracts (Section 2–612), then also as to the whole,

    (a) terminate and thereby discharge any unexecuted portion of the contract; or

    (b) modify the contract by agreeing to take his available quota in substitution.

    (2) If after receipt of such notification from the seller the buyer fails so to modify the contract within a reasonable time not exceeding thirty days the contract lapses with respect to any deliveries affected.

    (3) The provisions of this section may not be negated by agreement except in so far as the seller has assumed a greater obligation under the preceding section.

Part 7

Remedies

§2–701. Remedies for Breach of Collateral Contracts Not Impaired. Remedies for breach of any obligation or promise collateral or ancillary to a contract for sale are not impaired by the provisions of this Article.

§2–702. Seller's Remedies on Discovery of Buyer's Insolvency. (1) Where the seller discovers the buyer to be insolvent he may refuse delivery except for cash including payment for all goods theretofore delivered under the contract, and stop delivery under this Article (Section 2–705).

    (2) Where the seller discovers that the buyer has received goods on credit while insolvent he may reclaim the goods upon demand made within ten days after the receipt, but if misrepresentation of solvency has been made to the particular seller in writing within three months before delivery the ten day limitation does not apply. Except as provided in this subsection the seller may not base a right to reclaim goods on the buyer's fraudulent or innocent misrepresentation of solvency or of intent to pay.

    (3) The seller's right to reclaim under subsection (2) is subject to the rights of a buyer in ordinary course or other good faith purchaser under this Article (Section 2–403). Successful reclamation of goods excludes all other remedies with respect to them. As amended 1966.

§2–703. Seller's Remedies in General. Where the buyer wrongfully rejects or revokes acceptance of goods or fails to make a payment due on or before delivery or repudiates with respect to a part or the whole, then with respect to any goods directly affected and, if the breach is of the whole contract (Section 2–612), then also with respect to the whole undelivered balance, the aggrieved seller may

    (a) withhold delivery of such goods;

    (b) stop delivery by any bailee as hereafter provided (Section 2–705);

(c) proceed under the next section respecting goods still unidentified to the contract;

(d) resell and recover damages as hereafter provided (Section 2–706);

(e) recover damages for non-acceptance (Section 2–708) or in a proper case the price (Section 2–709);

(f) cancel.

§2–704. Seller's Right to Identify Goods to the Contract Notwithstanding Breach or to Salvage Unfinished Goods. (1) An aggrieved seller under the preceding section may

(a) identify to the contract conforming goods not already identified if at the time he learned of the breach they are in his possession or control;

(b) treat as the subject of resale goods which have demonstrably been intended for the particular contract even though those goods are unfinished.

(2) Where the goods are unfinished an aggrieved seller may in the exercise of reasonable commercial judgment for the purposes of avoiding loss and of effective realization either complete the manufacture and wholly identify the goods to the contract or cease manufacture and resell for scrap or salvage value or proceed in any other reasonable manner.

§2–705. Seller's Stoppage of Delivery in Transit or Otherwise. (1) The seller may stop delivery of goods in the possession of a carrier or other bailee when he discovers the buyer to be insolvent (Section 2–702) and may stop delivery of carload, truckload, planeload or larger shipments of express or freight when the buyer repudiates or fails to make a payment due before delivery or if for any other reason the seller has a right to withhold or reclaim the goods.

(2) As against such buyer the seller may stop delivery until

(a) receipt of the goods by the buyer; or

(b) acknowledgment to the buyer by any bailee of the goods except a carrier that the bailee holds the goods for the buyer; or

(c) such acknowledgment to the buyer by a carrier by reshipment or as warehouse-man; or

(d) negotiation to the buyer of any negotiable document of title covering the goods.

(3) (a) To stop delivery the seller must so notify as to enable the bailee by reasonable diligence to prevent delivery of the goods.

(b) After such notification the bailee must hold and deliver the goods according to the directions of the seller but the seller is liable to the bailee for any ensuing charges or damages.

(c) If a negotiable document of title has been issued for goods the bailee is not obliged to obey a notification to stop until surrender of the document.

(d) A carrier who has issued a non-negotiable bill of lading is not obliged to obey a notification to stop received from a person other than the consignor.

§2–706. Seller's Resale Including Contract for Resale. (1) Under the conditions stated in Section 2–703 on seller's remedies, the seller may resell the goods concerned or the undelivered balance thereof. Where the resale is made in good faith and in a commercially reasonable manner the seller may recover the difference between the resale price and the contract price together with any incidental damages allowed under the provisions of this Article (Section 2–710), but less expenses saved in consequence of the buyer's breach.

(2) Except as otherwise provided in subsection (3) or unless otherwise agreed resale may be at public or private sale including sale by way of one or more contracts to sell or of identification to an existing contract of the seller. Sale may be as a unit or in parcels and at any time and place and on any terms but every aspect of the sale including the method,

manner, time, place and terms must be commercially reasonable. The resale must be reasonably identified as referring to the broken contract, but it is not necessary that the goods be in existence or that any or all of them have been identified to the contract before the breach.

(3) Where the resale is at private sale the seller must give the buyer reasonable notification of his intention to resell.

(4) Where the resale is at public sale

(a) only identified goods can be sold except where there is a recognized market for a public sale of futures in goods of the kind; and

(b) it must be made at a usual place or market for public sale if one is reasonably available and except in the case of goods which are perishable or threaten to decline in value speedily the seller must give the buyer reasonable notice of the time and place of the resale; and

(c) if the goods are not to be within the view of those attending the sale the notification of sale must state the place where the goods are located and provide for their reasonable inspection by prospective bidders; and

(d) the seller may buy.

(5) A purchaser who buys in good faith at a resale takes the goods free of any rights of the original buyer even though the seller fails to comply with one or more of the requirements of this section.

(6) The seller is not accountable to the buyer for any profit made on any resale. A person in the position of a seller (Section 2–707) or a buyer who has rightfully rejected or justifiably revoked acceptance must account for any excess over the amount of his security interest, as hereinafter defined (subsection (3) of Section 2–711).

§2–707. "Person in the Position of a Seller." (1) A "person in the position of a seller" includes as against a principal an agent who has paid or become responsible for the price of goods on behalf of his principal or anyone who otherwise holds a security interest or other right in goods similar to that of a seller.

(2) A person in the position of a seller may as provided in this Article withhold or stop delivery (Section 2–705) and resell (Section 2–706) and recover incidental damages (Section 2–710).

§2–708. Seller's Damages for Non-acceptance or Repudiation. (1) Subject to subsection (2) and to the provisions of this Article with respect to proof of market price (Section 2–723), the measure of damages for non-acceptance or repudiation by the buyer is the difference between the market price at the time and place for tender and the unpaid contract price together with any incidental damages provided in this Article (Section 2–710), but less expenses saved in consequence of the buyer's breach.

(2) If the measure of damages provided in subsection (1) is inadequate to put the seller in as good a position as performance would have done then the measure of damages is the profit (including reasonable overhead) which the seller would have made from full performance by the buyer, together with any incidental damages provided in this Article (Section 2–710), due allowance for costs reasonably incurred and due credit for payments or proceeds of resale.

§2–709. Action for the Price. (1) When the buyer fails to pay the price as it becomes due the seller may recover, together with any incidental damages under the next section, the price

(a) of goods accepted or of conforming goods lost or damaged within a commercially reasonable time after risk of their loss has passed to the buyer; and

(b) of goods identified to the contract if the seller is unable after reasonable effort to resell them at a reasonable price or the circumstances reasonably indicate that such effort will be unavailing.

(2) Where the seller sues for the price he must hold for the buyer any goods which have been identified to the contract and are still in his control except that if resale becomes possible he may resell them at any time prior to the collection of the judgment. The net proceeds of any such resale must be credited to the buyer and payment of the judgment entitles him to any goods not resold.

(3) After the buyer has wrongfully rejected or revoked acceptance of the goods or has failed to make a payment due or has repudiated (Section 2–610), a seller who is held not entitled to the price under this section shall nevertheless be awarded damages for non-acceptance under the preceding section.

§2–710. Seller's Incidental Damages. Incidental damages to an aggrieved seller include any commercially reasonable charges, expenses or commissions incurred in stopping delivery, in the transportation, care and custody of goods after the buyer's breach, in connection with return or resale of the goods or otherwise resulting from the breach.

§2–711. Buyer's Remedies in General; Buyer's Security Interest in Rejected Goods. (1) Where the seller fails to make delivery or repudiates or the buyer rightfully rejects or justifiably revokes acceptance then with respect to any goods involved, and with respect to the whole if the breach goes to the whole contract (Section 2–612), the buyer may cancel and whether or not he has done so may in addition to recovering so much of the price as has been paid

(a) "cover" and have damages under the next section as to all the goods affected whether or not they have been identified to the contract; or

(b) recover damages for non-delivery as provided in this Article (Section 2–713).

(2) Where the seller fails to deliver or repudiates the buyer may also

(a) if the goods have been identified recover them as provided in this Article (Section 2–502); or

(b) in a proper case obtain specific performance or replevy the goods as provided in this Article (Section 2–716).

(3) On rightful rejection or justifiable revocation of acceptance a buyer has a security interest in goods in his possession or control for any payments made on their price and any expenses reasonably incurred in their inspection, receipt, transportation, care and custody and may hold such goods and resell them in like manner as an aggrieved seller (Section 2–706).

§2–712. "Cover"; Buyer's Procurement of Substitute Goods. (1) After a breach within the preceding section the buyer may "cover" by making in good faith and without unreasonable delay any reasonable purchase of or contract to purchase goods in substitution for those due from the seller.

(2) The buyer may recover from the seller as damages the difference between the cost of cover and the contract price together with any incidental or consequential damages as hereinafter defined (Section 2–715), but less expenses saved in consequence of the seller's breach.

(3) Failure of the buyer to effect cover within this section does not bar him from any other remedy.

§2–713. Buyer's Damages for Non-Delivery or Repudiation. (1) Subject to the provisions of this Article with respect to proof of market price (Section 2–723), the measure of damages for non-delivery or repudiation by the seller is the difference between the market price at the time when the buyer learned of the breach and the contract price together with any incidental and consequential damages provided in this Article (Section 2–715), but less expenses saved in consequence of the seller's breach.

(2) Market price is to be determined as of the place for tender or, in cases of rejection after arrival or revocation of acceptance, as of the place of arrival.

§2–714. Buyer's Damages for Breach in Regard to Accepted Goods. (1) Where the buyer has accepted goods and given notification (subsection (3) of Section 2–607) he may recover as damages for any non-conformity of tender the loss resulting in the ordinary course of events from the seller's breach as determined in any manner which is reasonable.

(2) The measure of damages for breach of warranty is the difference at the time and place of acceptance between the value of the goods accepted and the value they would have had if they had been as warranted, unless special circumstances show proximate damages of a different amount.

(3) In a proper case any incidental and consequential damages under the next section may also be recovered.

§2–715. Buyer's Incidental and Consequential Damages. (1) Incidental damages resulting from the seller's breach include expenses reasonably incurred in inspection, receipt, transportation and care and custody of goods rightfully rejected, any commercially reasonable charges, expenses or commissions in connection with effecting cover and any other reasonable expense incident to the delay or other breach.

(2) Consequential damages resulting from the seller's breach include

(a) any loss resulting from general or particular requirements and needs of which the seller at the time of contracting had reason to know and which could not reasonably be prevented by cover or otherwise; and

(b) injury to person or property proximately resulting from any breach of warranty.

§2–716. Buyer's Right to Specific Performance or Replevin. (1) Specific performance may be decreed where the goods are unique or in other proper circumstances.

(2) The decree for specific performance may include such terms and conditions as to payment of the price, damages, or other relief as the court may deem just.

(3) The buyer has a right of replevin for goods identified to the contract if after reasonable effort he is unable to effect cover for such goods or the circumstances reasonably indicate that such effort will be unavailing or if the goods have been shipped under reservation and satisfaction of the security interest in them has been made or tendered.

§2–717. Deduction of Damages from the Price. The buyer on notifying the seller of his intention to do so may deduct all or any part of the damages resulting from any breach of the contract from any part of the price still due under the same contract.

§2–718. Liquidation or Limitation of Damages; Deposits. (1) Damages for breach by either party may be liquidated in the agreement but only at an amount which is reasonable in the light of the anticipated or actual harm caused by the breach, the difficulties of proof of loss, and the inconvenience or nonfeasibility of otherwise obtaining an adequate remedy. A term fixing unreasonably large liquidated damages is void as a penalty.

(2) Where the seller justifiably withholds delivery of goods because of the buyer's breach, the buyer is entitled to restitution of any amount by which the sum of his payments exceeds

(a) the amount to which the seller is entitled by virtue of terms liquidating the seller's damages in accordance with subsection (1), or

(b) in the absence of such terms, twenty per cent of the value of the total performance for which the buyer is obligated under the contract or $500, whichever is smaller.

(3) The buyer's right to restitution under subsection (2) is subject to offset to the extent that the seller establishes

(a) a right to recover damages under the provisions of this Article other than subsection (1), and

(b) the amount or value of any benefits received by the buyer directly or indirectly by reason of the contract.

(4) Where a seller has received payment in goods their reasonable value or the proceeds of their resale shall be treated as payments for the purposes of subsection (2); but if the seller has notice of the buyer's breach before reselling goods received in part performance, his resale is subject to the conditions laid down in this Article on resale by an aggrieved seller (Section 2–706).

§2–719. Contractual Modification or Limitation of Remedy. (1) Subject to the provisions of subsections (2) and (3) of this section and of the preceding section on liquidation and limitation of damages,

(a) the agreement may provide for remedies in addition to or in substitution for those provided in this Article and may limit or alter the measure of damages recoverable under this Article, as by limiting the buyer's remedies to return of the goods and repayment of the price or to repair and replacement of non-conforming goods or parts; and

(b) resort to a remedy as provided is optional unless the remedy is expressly agreed to be exclusive, in which case it is the sole remedy.

(2) Where circumstances cause an exclusive or limited remedy to fail of its essential purpose, remedy may be had as provided in this Act.

(3) Consequential damages may be limited or excluded unless the limitation or exclusion is unconscionable. Limitation of consequential damages for injury to the person in the case of consumer goods is prima facie unconscionable but limitation of damages where the loss is commercial is not.

§2–720. Effect of "Cancellation" or "Rescission" on Claims for Antecedent Breach. Unless the contrary intention clearly appears, expressions of "cancellation" or "rescission" of the contract or the like shall not be construed as a renunciation or discharge of any claim in damages for an antecedent breach.

§2–721. Remedies for Fraud. Remedies for material misrepresentation or fraud include all remedies available under this Article for non-fraudulent breach. Neither rescission or a claim for rescission of the contract for sale nor rejection or return of the goods shall bar or be deemed inconsistent with a claim for damages or other remedy.

§2–722. Who Can Sue Third Parties for Injury to Goods. Where a third party so deals with goods which have been identified to a contract for sale as to cause actionable injury to a party to that contract

(a) a right of action against the third party is in either party to the contract for sale who has title to or a security interest or a special property or an insurable interest in the goods; and if the goods have been destroyed or converted a right of action is also in the party who either bore the risk of loss under the contract for sale or has since the injury assumed that risk as against the other:

(b) if at the time of the injury the party plaintiff did not bear the risk of loss as against the other party to the contract for sale and there is no arrangement between them for disposition of the recovery, his suit or settlement is, subject to his own interest, as a fiduciary for the other party to the contract;

(c) either party may with the consent of the other sue for the benefit of whom it may concern.

§2–723. Proof of Market Price: Time and Place. (1) If an action based on anticipatory repudiation comes to trial before the time for performance with respect to some or all of the goods, any damages based on market price (Section 2–708 or Section 2–713) shall be determined according to the price of such goods prevailing at the time when the aggrieved party learned of the repudiation.

(2) If evidence of a price prevailing at the times or places described in this Article is not readily available the price prevailing within any reasonable time before or after the time described or at any other place which in commercial judgment or under usage of trade

would serve as a reasonable substitute for the one described may be used, making any proper allowance for the cost of transporting the goods to or from such other place.

(3) Evidence of a relevant price prevailing at a time or place other than the one described in this Article offered by one party is not admissible unless and until he has given the other party such notice as the court finds sufficient to prevent unfair surprise.

§2–724. Admissibility of Market Quotations. Whenever the prevailing price or value of any goods regularly bought and sold in any established commodity market is in issue, reports in official publications or trade journals or in newspapers or periodicals of general circulation published as the reports of such market shall be admissible in evidence. The circumstances of the preparation of such a report may be shown to affect its weight but not its admissibility.

§2–725. Statute of Limitations in Contracts for Sale. (1) An action for breach of any contract for sale must be commenced within four years after the cause of action has accrued. By the original agreement the parties may reduce the period of limitation to not less than one year but may not extend it.

(2) A cause of action accrues when the breach occurs, regardless of the aggrieved party's lack of knowledge of the breach. A breach of warranty occurs when tender of delivery is made, except that where a warranty explicitly extends to future performance of the goods and discovery of the breach must await the time of such performance the cause of action accrues when the breach is or should have been discovered.

(3) Where an action commenced within the time limited by subsection (1) is so terminated as to leave available a remedy by another action for the same breach such other action may be commenced after the expiration of the time limited and within six months after the termination of the first action unless the termination resulted from voluntary discontinuance or from dismissal for failure or neglect to prosecute.

(4) This section does not alter the law on tolling of the statute of limitations nor does it apply to causes of action which have accrued before this Act becomes effective.

ARTICLE 3: COMMERCIAL PAPER

Part 1

Short Title, Form and Interpretation

§3–101. Short Title. This Article shall be known and may be cited as Uniform Commercial Code—Commercial Paper.

§3–102. Definitions and Index of Definitions. (1) In this Article unless the context otherwise requires

(a) "Issue" means the first delivery of an instrument to a holder or a remitter.

(b) An "order" is a direction to pay and must be more than an authorization or request. It must identify the person to pay with reasonable certainty. It may be addressed to one or more such persons jointly or in the alternative but not in succession.

(c) A "promise" is an undertaking to pay and must be more than an acknowledgment of an obligation.

(d) "Secondary party" means a drawer or endorser.

(e) "Instrument" means a negotiable instrument.

(2) Other definitions applying to this Article and the sections in which they appear are:

"Acceptance". Section 3–410.
"Accommodation party". Section 3–415.
"Alteration". Section 3–407.
"Certificate of deposit". Section 3–104.
"Certification". Section 3–411.
"Check". Section 3–104.
"Definite time". Section 3–109.
"Dishonor". Section 3–507.
"Draft". Section 3–104.
"Holder in due course". Section 3–302.
"Negotiation". Section 3–202.
"Note". Section 3–104.
"Notice of dishonor". Section 3–508.
"On demand". Section 3–108.
"Presentment". Section 3–504.
"Protest". Section 3–509.
"Restrictive Indorsement". Section 3–205.
"Signature". Section 3–401.
(3) The following definitions in other Articles apply to this Article:
"Account". Section 4–104.
"Banking Day". Section 4–104.
"Clearing house". Section 4–104.
"Collecting bank". Section 4–105.
"Customer". Section 4–104.
"Depositary Bank". Section 4–105.
"Documentary Draft". Section 4–104.
"Intermediary Bank". Section 4–105.
"Item". Section 4–104.
"Midnight deadline". Section 4–104.
"Payor bank". Section 4–105.
(4) In addition Article 1 contains general definitions and principles of construction and interpretation applicable throughout this Article.

§**3–103. Limitations on Scope of Article.** (1) This Article does not apply to money, documents of title or investment securities.

(2) The provisions of this Article are subject to the provisions of the Article on Bank Deposits and Collections (Article 4) and Secured Transactions (Article 9).

§**3–104. Form of Negotiable Instruments; "Draft"; "Check"; "Certificate of Deposit"; "Note."** (1) Any writing to be a negotiable instrument within this Article must

    (a) be signed by the maker or drawer; and

    (b) contain an unconditional promise or order to pay a sum certain in money and no other promise, order, obligation or power given by the maker or drawer except as authorized by this Article; and

    (c) be payable on demand or at a definite time; and

    (d) be payable to order or to bearer.

(2) A writing which complies with the requirements of this section is

    (a) a "draft" ("bill of exchange") if it is an order;

    (b) a "check" if it is a draft drawn on a bank and payable on demand;

    (c) a "certificate of deposit" if it is an acknowledgment by a bank of receipt of money with an engagement to repay it;

    (d) a "note" if it is a promise other than a certificate of deposit.

(3) As used in other Articles of this Act, and as the context may require, the terms "draft", "check", "certificate of deposit" and "note" may refer to instruments which are not negotiable within this Article as well as to instruments which are so negotiable.

§3–105. When Promise or Order Unconditional. (1) A promise or order otherwise unconditional is not made conditional by the fact that the instrument

(a) is subject to implied or constructive conditions; or

(b) states its consideration, whether performed or promised, or the transaction which gave rise to the instrument, or that the promise or order is made or the instrument matures in accordance with or "as per" such transaction; or

(c) refers to or states that it arises out of a separate agreement or refers to a separate agreement for rights as to prepayment or acceleration; or

(d) states that it is drawn under a letter of credit; or

(e) states that it is secured, whether by mortgage, reservation of title or otherwise; or

(f) indicates a particular account to be debited or any other fund or source from which reimbursement is expected; or

(g) is limited to payment out of a particular fund or the proceeds of a particular source, if the instrument is issued by a government or governmental agency or unit; or

(h) is limited to payment out of the entire assets of a partnership, unincorporated association, trust or estate by or on behalf of which the instrument is issued.

(2) A promise or order is not unconditional if the instrument

(a) states that it is subject to or governed by any other agreement; or

(b) states that it is to be paid only out of a particular fund or source except as provided in this section. As amended 1962.

§3–106. Sum Certain. (1) The sum payable is a sum certain even though it is to be paid

(a) with stated interest or by stated installments; or

(b) with stated different rates of interest before and after default or a specified date; or

(c) with a stated discount or addition if paid before or after the date fixed for payment; or

(d) with exchange or less exchange, whether at a fixed rate or at the current rate; or

(e) with costs of collection or an attorney's fee or both upon default.

(2) Nothing in this section shall validate any term which is otherwise illegal.

§3–107. Money. (1) An instrument is payable in money if the medium of exchange in which it is payable is money at the time the instrument is made. An instrument payable in "currency" or "current funds" is payable in money.

(2) A promise or order to pay a sum stated in a foreign currency is for a sum certain in money and, unless a different medium of payment is specified in the instrument, may be satisfied by payment of that number of dollars which the stated foreign currency will purchase at the buying sight rate for that currency on the day on which the instrument is payable or, if payable on demand, on the day of demand. If such an instrument specifies a foreign currency as the medium of payment the instrument is payable in that currency.

§3–108. Payable on Demand. Instruments payable on demand include those payable at sight or on presentation and those in which no time for payment is stated.

§3–109. Definite Time. (1) An instrument is payable at a definite time if by its terms it is payable

(a) on or before a stated date or at a fixed period after a stated date; or

(b) at a fixed period after sight; or

(c) at a definite time subject to any acceleration; or

(d) at a definite time subject to extension at the option of the holder, or to extension to a further definite time at the option of the maker or acceptor or automatically upon or after a specified act or event.

(2) An instrument which by its terms is otherwise payable only upon an act or event uncertain as to time of occurrence is not payable at a definite time even though the act or event has occurred.

§3–110. Payable to Order. (1) An instrument is payable to order when by its terms it is payable to the order or assigns of any person therein specified with reasonable certainty, or to him or his order, or when it is conspicuously designated on its face as "exchange" or the like and names a payee. It may be payable to the order of

(a) the maker or drawer; or

(b) the drawee; or

(c) a payee who is not maker, drawer or drawee; or

(d) two or more payees together or in the alternative; or

(e) an estate, trust or fund, in which case it is payable to the order of the representative of such estate, trust or fund or his successors; or

(f) an office, or an officer by his title as such in which case it is payable to the principal but the incumbent of the office or his successors may act as if he or they were the holder; or

(g) a partnership or unincorporated association, in which case it is payable to the partnership or association and may be indorsed or transferred by any person thereto authorized.

(2) An instrument not payable to order is not made so payable by such words as "payable upon return of this instrument properly indorsed."

(3) An instrument made payable both to order and to bearer is payable to order unless the bearer words are handwritten or typewritten.

§3–111. Payable to Bearer. An instrument is payable to bearer when by its terms it is payable to

(a) bearer or the order of bearer; or

(b) a specified person or bearer; or

(c) "cash" or the order of "cash", or any other indication which does not purport to designate a specific payee.

§3–112. Terms and Omissions Not Affecting Negotiability. (1) The negotiability of an instrument is not affected by

(a) the omission of a statement of any consideration or of the place where the instrument is drawn or payable; or

(b) a statement that collateral has been given to secure obligations either on the instrument or otherwise of an obligor on the instrument or that in case of default on those obligations the holder may realize on or dispose of the collateral; or

(c) a promise or power to maintain or protect collateral or to give additional collateral; or

(d) a term authorizing a confession of judgment on the instrument if it is not paid when due; or

(e) a term purporting to waive the benefit of any law intended for the advantage or protection of any obligor; or

(f) a term in a draft providing that the payee by indorsing or cashing it acknowledges full satisfaction of an obligation of the drawer; or

(g) A statement in a draft drawn in a set of parts (Section 3–801) to the effect that the order is effective only if no other part has been honored.

(2) Nothing in this section shall validate any term which is otherwise illegal. As amended 1962.

§3–113. Seal. An instrument otherwise negotiable is within this Article even though it is under a seal.

§3–114. Date, Antedating, Postdating. (1) The negotiability of an instrument is not affected by the fact that it is undated, antedated or postdated.

(2) Where an instrument is antedated or postdated the time when it is payable is determined by the stated date if the instrument is payable on demand or at a fixed period after date.

(3) Where the instrument or any signature thereon is dated, the date is presumed to be correct.

§3–115. Incomplete Instruments. (1) When a paper whose contents at the time of signing show that it is intended to become an instrument is signed while still incomplete in any necessary respect it cannot be enforced until completed, but when it is completed in accordance with authority given it is effective as completed.

(2) If the completion is unauthorized the rules as to material alteration apply (Section 3–407), even though the paper was not delivered by the maker or drawer; but the burden of establishing that any completion is unauthorized is on the party so asserting.

§3–116. Instruments Payable to Two or More Persons. An instrument payable to the order of two or more persons

(a) if in the alternative is payable to any one of them and may be negotiated, discharged or enforced by any of them who has possession of it;

(b) if not in the alternative is payable to all of them and may be negotiated, discharged or enforced only by all of them.

§3–117. Instruments Payable with Words of Description. An instrument made payable to a named person with the addition of words describing him

(a) as agent or officer of a specified person is payable to his principal but the agent or officer may act as if he were the holder;

(b) as any other fiduciary for a specified person or purpose is payable to the payee and may be negotiated, discharged or enforced by him;

(c) in any other manner is payable to the payee unconditionally and the additional words are without effect on subsequent parties.

§3–118. Ambiguous Terms and Rules of Construction. The following rules apply to every instrument:

(a) Where there is doubt whether the instrument is a draft or a note the holder may treat it as either. A draft drawn on the drawer is effective as a note.

(b) Handwritten terms control typewritten and printed terms, and typewritten control printed.

(c) Words control figures except that if the words are ambiguous figures control.

(d) Unless otherwise specified a provision for interest means interest at the judgment rate at the place of payment from the date of the instrument, or if it is undated from the date of issue.

(e) Unless the instrument otherwise specifies two or more persons who sign as maker, acceptor or drawer or indorser and as a part of the same transaction are jointly and severally liable even though the instrument contains such words as "I promise to pay."

(f) Unless otherwise specified consent to extension authorizes a single extension for not longer than the original period. A consent to extension, expressed in the instrument, is binding on secondary parties and accommodation makers. A holder may not exercise his option to extend an instrument over the objection of a maker or acceptor or other party who in accordance with Section 3–604 tenders full payment when the instrument is due.

§3–119. Other Writings Affecting Instrument. (1) As between the obligor and his immediate obligee or any transferee the terms of an instrument may be modified or affected by any other written agreement executed as a part of the same transaction, except that a holder in due course is not affected by any limitation of his rights arising out of the separate written agreement if he had no notice of the limitation when he took the instrument.

(2) A separate agreement does not affect the negotiability of an instrument.

§3–120. Instruments "Payable Through" Bank. An instrument which states that it is "payable through" a bank or the like designates that bank as a collecting bank to make presentment but does not of itself authorize the bank to pay the instrument.

§3–121. Instruments Payable at Bank. Note: *If this Act is introduced in the Congress of the United States this section should be omitted. (States to select either alternative.)*

Alternative A—

A note or acceptance which states that it is payable at a bank is the equivalent of a draft drawn on the bank payable when it falls due out of any funds of the maker or acceptor in current account or otherwise available for such payment.

Alternative B—

A note or acceptance which states that it is payable at a bank is not of itself an order or authorization to the bank to pay it.

§3–122. Accrual of Cause of Action. (1) A cause of action against a maker or an acceptor accrues

(a) in the case of a time instrument on the day after maturity;

(b) in the case of a demand instrument upon its date, or, if no date is stated, on the date of issue.

(2) A cause of action against the obligor of a demand or time certificate of deposit accrues upon demand, but demand on a time certificate may not be made until on or after the date of maturity.

(3) A cause of action against a drawer of a draft or an indorser of any instrument accrues upon demand following dishonor of the instrument. Notice of dishonor is a demand.

(4) Unless an instrument provides otherwise, interest runs at the rate provided by law for a judgment

(a) in the case of a maker, acceptor or other primary obligor of a demand instrument, from the date of demand;

(b) in all other cases from the date of accrual of the cause of action. As amended 1962.

Part 2

Transfer and Negotiation

§3–201. Transfer: Right to Indorsement. (1) Transfer of an instrument vests in the transferee such rights as the transferor has therein, except that a transferee who has himself been a party to any fraud or illegality affecting the instrument or who as a prior holder had notice of a defense or claim against it cannot improve his position by taking from a later holder in due course.

(2) A transfer of a security interest in an instrument vests the foregoing rights in the transferee to the extent of the interest transferred.

(3) Unless otherwise agreed any transfer for value of an instrument not then payable to bearer gives the transferee the specifically enforceable right to have the

A Holder in due cost is one
Who 3-302 –

W

unqualified indorsement of the transferor. Negotiation takes effect only when the indorsement is made and until that time there is no presumption that the transferee is the owner.

§3–202. Negotiation. (1) Negotiation is the transfer of an instrument in such form that the transferee becomes a holder. If the instrument is payable to order it is negotiated by delivery with any necessary indorsement; if payable to bearer it is negotiated by delivery.

(2) An indorsement must be written by or on behalf of the holder and on the instrument or on a paper so firmly affixed thereto as to become a part thereof.

(3) An indorsement is effective for negotiation only when it conveys the entire instrument or any unpaid residue. If it purports to be of less it operates only as a partial assignment.

(4) Words of assignment, condition, waiver, guaranty, limitation or disclaimer of liability and the like accompanying an indorsement do not affect its character as an indorsement.

§3–203. Wrong or Misspelled Name. Where an instrument is made payable to a person under a misspelled name or one other than his own he may indorse in that name or his own or both; but signature in both names may be required by a person paying or giving value for the instrument.

§3–204. Special Indorsement; Blank Indorsement. (1) A special indorsement specifies the person to whom or to whose order it makes the instrument payable. Any instrument specially indorsed becomes payable to the order of the special indorsee and may be further negotiated only by his indorsement.

(2) An indorsement in blank specifies no particular indorsee and may consist of a mere signature. An instrument payable to order and indorsed in blank becomes payable to bearer and may be negotiated by delivery alone until specially indorsed.

(3) The holder may convert a blank indorsement into a special indorsement by writing over the signature of the indorser in blank any contract consistent with the character of the indorsement.

§3–205. Restrictive Indorsements. An indorsement is restrictive which either

(a) is conditional; or

(b) purports to prohibit further transfer of the instrument; or

(c) includes the words "for collection", "for deposit", "pay any bank", or like terms signifying a purpose of deposit or collection; or

(d) otherwise states that it is for the benefit or use of the indorser or of another person.

§3–206. Effect of Restrictive Indorsement. (1) No restrictive indorsement prevents further transfer or negotiation of the instrument.

(2) An intermediary bank, or a payor bank which is not the depositary bank, is neither given notice nor otherwise affected by a restrictive indorsement of any person except the bank's immediate transferor or the person presenting for payment.

(3) Except for an intermediary bank, any transferee under an indorsement which is conditional or includes the words "for collection", "for deposit", "pay any bank", or like terms (subparagraphs (a) and (c) of Section 3–205) must pay or apply any value given by him for or on the security of the instrument consistently with the indorsement and to the extent that he does so he becomes a holder for value. In addition such transferee is a holder in due course if he otherwise complies with the requirements of Section 3–302 on what constitutes a holder in due course.

(4) The first taker under an indorsement for the benefit of the indorser or another person (subparagraph (d) of Section 3–205) must pay or apply any value given by him for or on the security of the instrument consistently with the indorsement and to the extent that he does so he becomes a holder for value. In addition such taker is a holder in due course if

he otherwise complies with the requirements of Section 3–302 on what constitutes a holder in due course. A later holder for value is neither given notice nor otherwise affected by such restrictive indorsement unless he has knowledge that a fiduciary or other person has negotiated the instrument in any transaction for his own benefit or otherwise in breach of duty (subsection (2) of Section 3–304).

§3–207. Negotiation Effective Although It May Be Rescinded. (1) Negotiation is effective to transfer the instrument although the negotiation is

(a) made by an infant, a corporation exceeding its powers, or any other person without capacity; or

(b) obtained by fraud, duress or mistake of any kind; or

(c) part of an illegal transaction; or

(d) made in breach of duty.

(2) Except as against a subsequent holder in due course such negotiation is in an appropriate case subject to rescission, the declaration of a constructive trust or any other remedy permitted by law.

§3–208. Reacquisition. Where an instrument is returned to or reacquired by a prior party he may cancel any indorsement which is not necessary to his title and reissue or further negotiate the instrument, but any intervening party is discharged as against the reacquiring party and subsequent holders not in due course and if his indorsement has been cancelled is discharged as against subsequent holders in due course as well.

Part 3

Rights of a Holder

§3–301. Rights of a Holder. The holder of an instrument whether or not he is the owner may transfer or negotiate it and, except as otherwise provided in Section 3–603 on payment or satisfaction, discharge it or enforce payment in his own name.

§3–302. Holder in Due Course. (1) A holder in due course is a holder who takes the instrument

(a) for value; and

(b) in good faith; and

(c) without notice that it is overdue or has been dishonored or of any defense against or claim to it on the part of any person.

(2) A payee may be a holder in due course.

(3) A holder does not become a holder in due course of an instrument:

(a) by purchase of it at judicial sale or by taking it under legal process; or

(b) by acquiring it in taking over an estate; or

(c) by purchasing it as part of a bulk transaction not in regular course of business of the transferor.

(4) A purchaser of a limited interest can be a holder in due course only to the extent of the interest purchased.

§3–303. Taking for Value. A holder takes the instrument for value

(a) to the extent that the agreed consideration has been performed or that he acquires a security interest in or a lien on the instrument otherwise than by legal process; or

(b) when he takes the instrument in payment of or as security for an antecedent claim against any person whether or not the claim is due; or

(c) when he gives a negotiable instrument for it or makes an irrevocable commitment to a third person.

§3–304. Notice to Purchaser. (1) The purchaser has notice of a claim or defense if

(a) the instrument is so incomplete, bears such visible evidence of forgery or alteration, or is otherwise so irregular as to call into question its validity, terms or ownership or to create an ambiguity as to the party to pay; or

(b) the purchaser has notice that the obligation of any party is voidable in whole or in part, or that all parties have been discharged.

(2) The purchaser has notice of a claim against the instrument when he has knowledge that a fiduciary has negotiated the instrument in payment of or as security for his own debt or in any transaction for his own benefit or otherwise in breach of duty.

(3) The purchaser has notice that an instrument is overdue if he has reason to know

(a) that any part of the principal amount is overdue or that there is an uncured default in payment of another instrument of the same series; or

(b) that acceleration of the instrument has been made; or

(c) that he is taking a demand instrument after demand has been made or more than a reasonable length of time after its issue. A reasonable time for a check drawn and payable within the states and territories of the United States and the District of Columbia is presumed to be thirty days.

(4) Knowledge of the following facts does not of itself give the purchaser notice of a defense or claim

(a) that the instrument is antedated or postdated;

(b) that it was issued or negotiated in return for an executory promise or accompanied by a separate agreement, unless the purchaser has notice that a defense or claim has arisen from the terms thereof;

(c) that any party has signed for accommodation;

(d) that an incomplete instrument has been completed, unless the purchaser has notice of any improper completion;

(e) that any person negotiating the instrument is or was a fiduciary;

(f) that there has been default in payment of interest on the instrument or in payment of any other instrument, except one of the same series.

(5) The filing or recording of a document does not of itself constitute notice within the provisions of this Article to a person who would otherwise be a holder in due course.

(6) To be effective notice must be received at such time and in such manner as to give a reasonable opportunity to act on it.

§3–305. Rights of a Holder in Due Course. To the extent that a holder is a holder in due course he takes the instrument free from

(1) All claims to it on the part of any person; and

(2) all defenses of any party to the instrument with whom the holder has not dealt except

(a) infancy, to the extent that it is a defense to a simple contract; and

(b) such other incapacity, or duress, or illegality of the transaction, as renders the obligation of the party a nullity; and

(c) such misrepresentation as has induced the party to sign the instrument with neither knowledge nor reasonable opportunity to obtain knowledge of its character or its essential terms; and

(d) discharge in insolvency proceedings; and

(e) any other discharge of which the holder has notice when he takes the instrument.

§3–306. Rights of One Not Holder in Due Course. Unless he has the rights of a holder in due course any person takes the instrument subject to

(a) all valid claims to it on the part of any person; and

(b) all defenses of any party which would be available in an action on a simple contract; and

(c) the defenses of want or failure of consideration, nonperformance of any condition precedent, non-delivery, or delivery for a special purpose (Section 3–408); and

(d) the defense that he or a person through whom he holds the instrument acquired it by theft, or that payment or satisfaction to such holder would be inconsistent with the terms of a restrictive indorsement. The claim of any third person to the instrument is not otherwise available as a defense to any party liable thereon unless the third person himself defends the action for such party.

§3–307. Burden of Establishing Signatures, Defenses and Due Course. (1) Unless specifically denied in the pleadings each signature on an instrument is admitted. When the effectiveness of a signature is put in issue

(a) the burden of establishing it is on the party claiming under the signature; but

(b) the signature is presumed to be genuine or authorized except where the action is to enforce the obligation of a purported signer who has died or become incompetent before proof is required.

(2) When signatures are admitted or established, production of the instrument entitles a holder to recover on it unless the defendant establishes a defense.

(3) After it is shown that a defense exists a person claiming the rights of a holder in due course has the burden of establishing that he or some person under whom he claims is in all respects a holder in due course.

Part 4

Liability of Parties

§3–401. Signature. (1) No person is liable on an instrument unless his signature appears thereon.

(2) A signature is made by use of any name, including any trade or assumed name, upon an instrument, or by any word or mark used in lieu of a written signature.

§3–402. Signature in Ambiguous Capacity. Unless the instrument clearly indicates that a signature is made in some other capacity it is an indorsement.

§3–403. Signature by Authorized Representative. (1) A signature may be made by an agent or other representative, and his authority to make it may be established as in other cases of representation. No particular form of appointment is necessary to establish such authority.

(2) An authorized representative who signs his own name to an instrument

(a) is personally obligated if the instrument neither names the person represented nor shows that the representative signed in a representative capacity;

(b) except as otherwise established between the immediate parties, is personally obligated if the instrument names the person represented but does not show that the representative signed in a representative capacity, or if the instrument does not name the person represented but does show that the representative signed in a representative capacity.

(3) Except as otherwise established the name of an organization preceded or followed by the name and office of an authorized individual is a signature made in a representative capacity.

§3–404. Unauthorized Signatures. (1) Any unauthorized signature is wholly inoperative as that of the person whose name is signed unless he ratifies it or is precluded from denying it;

but it operates as the signature of the unauthorized signer in favor of any person who in good faith pays the instrument or takes it for value.

(2) Any unauthorized signature may be ratified for all purposes of this Article. Such ratification does not of itself affect any rights of the person ratifying against the actual signer.

§3–405. Impostors; Signature in Name of Payee. (1) An indorsement by any person in the name of a named payee is effective if

(a) an impostor by use of the mails or otherwise has induced the maker or drawer to issue the instrument to him or his confederate in the name of the payee; or

(b) a person signing as or on behalf of a maker or drawer intends the payee to have no interest in the instrument; or

(c) an agent or employee of the maker or drawer has supplied him with the name of the payee intending the latter to have no such interest.

(2) Nothing in this section shall affect the criminal or civil liability of the person so indorsing.

§3–406. Negligence Contributing to Alteration or Unauthorized Signature. Any person who by his negligence substantially contributes to a material alteration of the instrument or to the making of an unauthorized signature is precluded from asserting the alteration or lack of authority against a holder in due course or against a drawee or other payor who pays the instrument in good faith and in accordance with the reasonable commercial standards of the drawee's or payor's business.

§3–407. Alteration. (1) Any alteration of an instrument is material which changes the contract of any party thereto in any respect, including any such change in

(a) the number or relations of the parties; or

(b) an incomplete instrument, by completing it otherwise than as authorized; or

(c) the writing as signed, by adding to it or by removing any part of it.

(2) As against any person other than a subsequent holder in due course.

(a) alteration by the holder which is both fraudulent and material discharges any party whose contract is thereby changed unless that party assents or is precluded from asserting the defense;

(b) no other alteration discharges any party and the instrument may be enforced according to its original tenor, or as to incomplete instruments according to the authority given.

(3) A subsequent holder in due course may in all cases enforce the instrument according to its original tenor, and when an incomplete instrument has been completed, he may enforce it as completed.

§3–408. Consideration. Want or failure of consideration is a defense as against any person not having the rights of a holder in due course (Section 3–305), except that no consideration is necessary for an instrument or obligation thereon given in payment of or as security for an antecedent obligation of any kind. Nothing in this section shall be taken to displace any statute outside this Act under which a promise is enforceable notwithstanding lack or failure of consideration. Partial failure of consideration is a defense pro tanto whether or not the failure is in an ascertained or liquidated amount.

§3–409. Draft Not an Assignment. (1) A check or other draft does not of itself operate as an assignment of any funds in the hands of the drawee available for its payment, and the drawee is not liable on the instrument until he accepts it.

(2) Nothing in this section shall affect any liability in contract, tort or otherwise arising from any letter of credit or other obligation or representation which is not an acceptance.

§3–410. Definition and Operation of Acceptance. (1) Acceptance is the drawee's signed engagement to honor the draft as presented. It must be written on the draft, and may consist of his signature alone. It becomes operative when completed by delivery or notification.

(2) A draft may be accepted although it has not been signed by the drawer or is otherwise incomplete or is overdue or has been dishonored.

(3) Where the draft is payable at a fixed period after sight and the acceptor fails to date his acceptance the holder may complete it by supplying a date in good faith.

§3–411. Certification of a Check. (1) Certification of a check is acceptance. Where a holder procures certification the drawer and all prior indorsers are discharged.

(2) Unless otherwise agreed a bank has no obligation to certify a check.

(3) A bank may certify a check before returning it for lack of proper indorsement. If it does so the drawer is discharged.

§3–412. Acceptance Varying Draft. (1) Where the drawee's proffered acceptance in any manner varies the draft as presented the holder may refuse the acceptance and treat the draft as dishonored in which case the drawee is entitled to have his acceptance cancelled.

(2) The terms of the draft are not varied by an acceptance to pay at any particular bank or place in the United States, unless the acceptance states that the draft is to be paid only at such bank or place.

(3) Where the holder assents to an acceptance varying the terms of the draft each drawer and indorser who does not affirmatively assent is discharged. As amended 1962.

§3–413. Contract of Maker, Drawer and Acceptor. (1) The maker or acceptor engages that he will pay the instrument according to its tenor at the time of his engagement or as completed pursuant to Section 3–115 on incomplete instruments.

(2) The drawer engages that upon dishonor of the draft and any necessary notice of dishonor or protest he will pay the amount of the draft to the holder or to any indorser who takes it up. The drawer may disclaim this liability by drawing without recourse.

(3) By making, drawing or accepting the party admits as against all subsequent parties including the drawee the existence of the payee and his then capacity to indorse.

§3–414. Contract of Indorser; Order of Liability. (1) Unless the indorsement otherwise specifies (as by such words as "without recourse") every indorser engages that upon dishonor and any necessary notice of dishonor and protest he will pay the instrument according to its tenor at the time of his indorsement to the holder or to any subsequent indorser who takes it up, even though the indorser who takes it up was not obligated to do so.

(2) Unless they otherwise agree indorsers are liable to one another in the order in which they indorse, which is presumed to be the order in which their signatures appear on the instrument.

§3–415. Contract of Accommodation Party. (1) An accommodation party is one who signs the instrument in any capacity for the purpose of lending his name to another party to it.

(2) When the instrument has been taken for value before it is due the accommodation party is liable in the capacity in which he has signed even though the taker knows of the accommodation.

(3) As against a holder in due course and without notice of the accommodation oral proof of the accommodation is not admissible to give the accommodation party the benefit of discharges dependent on his character as such. In other cases the accommodation character may be shown by oral proof.

(4) An indorsement which shows that it is not in the chain of title is notice of its accommodation character.

(5) An accommodation party is not liable to the party accommodated, and if he pays the instrument has a right of recourse on the instrument against such party.

§3–416. Contract of Guarantor. (1) "Payment guaranteed" or equivalent words added to a signature mean that the signer engages that if the instrument is not paid when due he will pay it according to its tenor without resort by the holder to any other party.

(2) "Collection guaranteed" or equivalent words added to a signature mean that the signer engages that if the instrument is not paid when due he will pay it according to its tenor, but only after the holder has reduced his claim against the maker or acceptor to judgment and execution has been returned unsatisfied, or after the maker or acceptor has become insolvent or it is otherwise apparent that it is useless to proceed against him.

(3) Words of guaranty which do not otherwise specify guarantee payment.

(4) No words of guaranty added to the signature of a sole maker or acceptor affect his liability on the instrument. Such words added to the signature of one of two or more makers or acceptors create a presumption that the signature is for the accommodation of the others.

(5) When words of guaranty are used presentment, notice of dishonor and protest are not necessary to charge the user.

(6) Any guaranty written on the instrument is enforcible notwithstanding any statute of frauds.

§3–417. Warranties on Presentment and Transfer. (1) Any person who obtains payment or acceptance and any prior transferor warrants to a person who in good faith pays or accepts that

(a) he has a good title to the instrument or is authorized to obtain payment or acceptance on behalf of one who has a good title; and

(b) he has no knowledge that the signature of the maker or drawer is unauthorized, except that this warranty is not given by a holder in due course acting in good faith.

(i) to a maker with respect to the maker's own signature; or

(ii) to a drawer with respect to the drawer's own signature, whether or not the drawer is also the drawee; or

(iii) to an acceptor of a draft if the holder in due course took the draft after the acceptance or obtained the acceptance without knowledge that the drawer's signature was unauthorized; and

(c) the instrument has not been materially altered, except that this warranty is not given by a holder in due course acting in good faith

(i) to the maker of a note; or

(ii) to the drawer of a draft whether or not the drawer is also the drawee; or

(iii) to the acceptor of a draft with respect to an alteration made prior to the acceptance if the holder in due course took the draft after the acceptance, even though the acceptance provided "payable as originally drawn" or equivalent terms; or

(iv) to the acceptor of a draft with respect to an alteration made after the acceptance.

(2) Any person who transfers an instrument and receives consideration warrants to his transferee and if the transfer is by indorsement to any subsequent holder who takes the instrument in good faith that

(a) he has a good title to the instrument or is authorized to obtain payment or acceptance on behalf of one who has a good title and the transfer is otherwise rightful; and

(b) all signatures are genuine or authorized; and

(c) the instrument has not been materially altered; and

(d) no defense of any party is good against him; and

(e) he has no knowledge of any insolvency proceeding instituted with respect to the maker or acceptor or the drawer of an unaccepted instrument.

(3) By transferring "without recourse" the transferor limits the obligation stated in subsection (2) (d) to a warranty that he has no knowledge of such a defense.

(4) A selling agent or broker who does not disclose the fact that he is acting only as such gives the warranties provided in this section, but if he makes such disclosure warrants only his good faith and authority.

§3–418. Finality of Payment or Acceptance. Except for recovery of bank payments as provided in the Article on Bank Deposits and Collections (Article 4) and except for liability for breach of warranty on presentment under the preceding section, payment or acceptance of any instrument is final in favor of a holder in due course, or a person who has in good faith changed his position in reliance on the payment.

§3–419. Conversion of Instrument; Innocent Representative. (1) An instrument is converted when

(a) a drawee to whom it is delivered for acceptance refuses to return it on demand; or

(b) any person to whom it is delivered for payment refuses on demand either to pay or to return it; or

(c) it is paid on a forged indorsement.

(2) In an action against a drawee under subsection (1) the measure of the drawee's liability is the face amount of the instrument. In any other action under subsection (1) the measure of liability is presumed to be the face amount of the instrument.

(3) Subject to the provisions of this Act concerning restrictive indorsements a representative, including a depositary or collecting bank, who has in good faith and in accordance with the reasonable commercial standards applicable to the business of such representative dealt with an instrument or its proceeds on behalf of one who was not the true owner is not liable in conversion or otherwise to the true owner beyond the amount of any proceeds remaining in his hands.

(4) An intermediary bank or payor bank which is not a depositary bank is not liable in conversion solely by reason of the fact that proceeds of an item indorsed restrictively (Sections 3–205 and 3–206) are not paid or applied consistently with the restrictive indorsement of an indorser other than its immediate transferor.

Part 5

Presentment, Notice of Dishonor and Protest

§3–501. When Presentment, Notice of Dishonor, and Protest Necessary or Permissible. (1) Unless excused (Section 3–511) presentment is necessary to charge secondary parties as follows:

(a) presentment for acceptance is necessary to charge the drawer and indorsers of a draft where the draft so provides, or is payable elsewhere than at the residence or place of business of the drawee, or its date of payment depends upon such presentment. The holder may at his option present for acceptance any other draft payable at a stated date;

(b) presentment for payment is necessary to charge any indorser;

(c) in the case of any drawer, the acceptor of a draft payable at a bank or the maker of a note payable at a bank, presentment for payment is necessary, but failure to make presentment discharges such drawer, acceptor or maker only as stated in Section 3–502(1) (b).

(2) Unless excused (Section 3–511)

(a) notice of any dishonor is necessary to charge any indorser;

(b) in the case of any drawer, the acceptor of a draft payable at a bank or the maker of a note payable at a bank, notice of any dishonor is necessary, but failure to give such notice discharges such drawer, acceptor or maker only as stated in Section 3–502(1) (b).

(3) Unless excused (Section 3–511) protest of any dishonor is necessary to charge the drawer and indorsers of any draft which on its face appears to be drawn or payable outside of the states, territories, dependencies and possessions of the United States, the District of Columbia and the Commonwealth of Puerto Rico. The holder may at his option make protest of any dishonor of any other instrument and in the case of a foreign draft may on insolvency of the acceptor before maturity make protest for better security.

(4) Notwithstanding any provision of this section, neither presentment nor notice of dishonor nor protest is necessary to charge an indorser who has indorsed an instrument after maturity. As amended 1966.

§3–502. Unexcused Delay; Discharge. (1) Where without excuse any necessary presentment or notice of dishonor is delayed beyond the time when it is due

(a) any indorser is discharged; and

(b) any drawer or the acceptor of a draft payable at a bank or the maker of a note payable at a bank who because the drawee or payor bank becomes insolvent during the delay is deprived of funds maintained with the drawee or payor bank to cover the instrument may discharge his liability by written assignment to the holder of his rights against the drawee or payor bank in respect of such funds, but such drawer, acceptor or maker is not otherwise discharged.

(2) Where without excuse a necessary protest is delayed beyond the time when it is due any drawer or indorser is discharged.

§3–503. Time of Presentment. (1) Unless a different time is expressed in the instrument the time for any presentment is determined as follows:

(a) where an instrument is payable at or a fixed period after a stated date any presentment for acceptance must be made on or before the date it is payable;

(b) where an instrument is payable after sight it must either be presented for acceptance or negotiated within a reasonable time after date or issue whichever is later;

(c) where an instrument shows the date on which it is payable presentment for payment is due on that date;

(d) where an instrument is accelerated presentment for payment is due within a reasonable time after the acceleration;

(e) with respect to the liability of any secondary party presentment for acceptance or payment of any other instrument is due within a reasonable time after such party becomes liable thereon.

(2) A reasonable time for presentment is determined by the nature of the instrument, any usage of banking or trade and the facts of the particular case. In the case of an uncertified check which is drawn and payable within the United States and which is not a draft drawn by a bank the following are presumed to be reasonable periods within which to present for payment or to initiate bank collection:

(a) with respect to the liability of the drawer, thirty days after date or issue whichever is later; and

(b) with respect to the liability of an indorser, seven days after his indorsement.

(3) Where any presentment is due on a day which is not a full business day for either the person making presentment or the party to pay or accept, presentment is due on the next following day which is a full business day for both parties.

(4) Presentment to be sufficient must be made at a reasonable hour, and if at a bank during its banking day.

§3–504. How Presentment Made. (1) Presentment is a demand for acceptance or payment made upon the maker, acceptor, drawee or other payor by or on behalf of the holder.

(2) Presentment may be made

(a) by mail, in which event the time of presentment is determined by the time of receipt of the mail; or

(b) through a clearing house; or

(c) at the place of acceptance or payment specified in the instrument or if there be none at the place of business or residence of the party to accept or pay. If neither the party to accept or pay nor anyone authorized to act for him is present or accessible at such place presentment is excused.

(3) It may be made

(a) to any one of two or more makers, acceptors, drawees or other payors; or

(b) to any person who has authority to make or refuse the acceptance or payment.

(4) A draft accepted or a note made payable at a bank in the United States must be presented at such bank.

(5) In the cases described in Section 4–210 presentment may be made in the manner and with the result stated in that section. As amended 1962.

§3–505. Rights of Party to Whom Presentment Is Made. (1) The party to whom presentment is made may without dishonor require

(a) exhibition of the instrument; and

(b) reasonable identification of the person making presentment and evidence of his authority to make it if made for another; and

(c) that the instrument be produced for acceptance or payment at a place specified in it, or if there be none at any place reasonable in the circumstances; and

(d) a signed receipt on the instrument for any partial or full payment and its surrender upon full payment.

(2) Failure to comply with any such requirement invalidates the presentment but the person presenting has a reasonable time in which to comply and the time for acceptance or payment runs from the time of compliance.

§3–506. Time Allowed for Acceptance or Payment. (1) Acceptance may be deferred without dishonor until the close of the next business day following presentment. The holder may also in a good faith effort to obtain acceptance and without either dishonor of the instrument or discharge of secondary parties allow postponement of acceptance for an additional business day.

(2) Except as a longer time is allowed in the case of documentary drafts drawn under a letter of credit, and unless an earlier time is agreed to by the party to pay, payment of an instrument may be deferred without dishonor pending reasonable examination to determine whether it is properly payable, but payment must be made in any event before the close of business on the day of presentment.

§3–507. Dishonor; Holder's Right of Recourse; Term Allowing Re-Presentment. (1) An instrument is dishonored when

(a) a necessary or optional presentment is duly made and due acceptance or payment is refused or cannot be obtained within the prescribed time or in case of bank collections the instrument is seasonably returned by the midnight deadline (Section 4–301); or

(b) presentment is excused and the instrument is not duly accepted or paid.

(2) Subject to any necessary notice of dishonor and protest, the holder has upon dishonor an immediate right of recourse against the drawers and indorsers.

(3) Return of an instrument for lack of proper indorsement is not dishonor.

(4) A term in a draft or an indorsement thereof allowing a stated time for re-presentment in the event of any dishonor of the draft by nonacceptance if a time draft or by nonpayment if a sight draft gives the holder as against any secondary party bound by the term an option to waive the dishonor without affecting the liability of the secondary party and he may present again up to the end of the stated time.

§3–508. Notice of Dishonor. (1) Notice of dishonor may be given to any person who may be liable on the instrument by or on behalf of the holder or any party who has himself received notice, or any other party who can be compelled to pay the instrument. In addition an agent or bank in whose hands the instrument is dishonored may give notice to his principal or customer or to another agent or bank from which the instrument was received.

(2) Any necessary notice must be given by a bank before its midnight deadline and by any other person before midnight of the third business day after dishonor or receipt of notice of dishonor.

(3) Notice may be given in any reasonable manner. It may be oral or written and in any terms which identify the instrument and state that it has been dishonored. A misdescription which does not mislead the party notified does not vitiate the notice. Sending the instrument bearing a stamp, ticket or writing stating that acceptance or payment has been refused or sending a notice of debit with respect to the instrument is sufficient.

(4) Written notice is given when sent although it is not received.

(5) Notice to one partner is notice to each although the firm has been dissolved.

(6) When any party is in insolvency proceedings instituted after the issue of the instrument notice may be given either to the party or to the representative of his estate.

(7) When any party is dead or incompetent notice may be sent to his last known address or given to his personal representative.

(8) Notice operates for the benefit of all parties who have rights on the instrument against the party notified.

§3–509. Protest; Noting for Protest. (1) A protest is a certificate of dishonor made under the hand and seal of a United States consul or vice consul or a notary public or other person authorized to certify dishonor by the law of the place where dishonor occurs. It may be made upon information satisfactory to such person.

(2) The protest must identify the instrument and certify either that due presentment has been made or the reason why it is excused and that the instrument has been dishonored by nonacceptance or nonpayment.

(3) The protest may also certify that notice of dishonor has been given to all parties or to specified parties.

(4) Subject to subsection (5) any necessary protest is due by the time that notice of dishonor is due.

(5) If, before protest is due, an instrument has been noted for protest by the officer to make protest, the protest may be made at any time thereafter as of the date of the noting.

§3–510. Evidence of Dishonor and Notice of Dishonor. The following are admissible as evidence and create a presumption of dishonor and of any notice of dishonor therein shown:

(a) a document regular in form as provided in the preceding section which purports to be a protest;

(b) the purported stamp or writing of the drawee, payor bank or presenting bank on the instrument or accompanying it stating that acceptance or payment has been refused for reasons consistent with dishonor;

(c) any book or record of the drawee, payor bank, or any collecting bank kept in the usual course of business which shows dishonor, even though there is no evidence of who made the entry.

§3–511. Waived or Excused Presentment, Protest or Notice of Dishonor or Delay Therein. (1) Delay in presentment, protest or notice of dishonor is excused when the party is without notice that it is due or when the delay is caused by circumstances beyond his control and he exercises reasonable diligence after the cause of the delay ceases to operate.

(2) Presentment or notice or protest as the case may be is entirely excused when

(a) the party to be charged has waived it expressly or by implication either before or after it is due; or

(b) such party has himself dishonored the instrument or has countermanded payment or otherwise has no reason to expect or right to require that the instrument be accepted or paid; or

(c) by reasonable diligence the presentment or protest cannot be made or the notice given.

(3) Presentment is also entirely excused when

(a) the maker, acceptor or drawee of any instrument except a documentary draft is dead or in insolvency proceedings instituted after the issue of the instrument; or

(b) acceptance or payment is refused but not for want of proper presentment.

(4) Where a draft has been dishonored by nonacceptance a later presentment for payment and any notice of dishonor and protest for nonpayment are excused unless in the meantime the instrument has been accepted.

(5) A waiver of protest is also a waiver of presentment and of notice of dishonor even though protest is not required.

(6) Where a waiver of presentment or notice or protest is embodied in the instrument itself it is binding upon all parties; but where it is written above the signature of an indorser it binds him only.

Part 6

Discharge

§3–601. Discharge of Parties. (1) The extent of the discharge of any party from liability on an instrument is governed by the sections on

(a) payment or satisfaction (Section 3–603); or

(b) tender of payment (Section 3–604); or

(c) cancellation or renunciation (Section 3–605); or

(d) impairment of right of recourse or of collateral (Section 3–606); or

(e) reacquisition of the instrument by a prior party (Section 3–208); or

(f) fraudulent and material alteration (Section 3–407); or

(g) certification of a check (Section 3–411); or

(h) acceptance varying a draft (Section 3–412); or

(i) unexcused delay in presentment or notice of dishonor or protest (Section 3–502).

(2) Any party is also discharged from his liability on an instrument to another party by any other act or agreement with such party which would discharge his simple contract for the payment of money.

(3) The liability of all parties is discharged when any party who has himself no right of action or recourse on the instrument

(a) reacquires the instrument in his own right; or

(b) is discharged under any provision of this Article, except as otherwise provided with respect to discharge for impairment of recourse or of collateral (Section 3–606).

§3–602. Effect of Discharge against Holder in Due Course. No discharge of any party provided by this Article is effective against a subsequent holder in due course unless he has notice thereof when he takes the instrument.

§3–603. Payment or Satisfaction. (1) The liability of any party is discharged to the extent of his payment or satisfaction to the holder even though it is made with knowledge of a claim of another person to the instrument unless prior to such payment or satisfaction the person making the claim either supplies indemnity deemed adequate by the party seeking the discharge or enjoins payment or satisfaction by order of a court of competent jurisdiction in an action in which the adverse claimant and the holder are parties. This subsection does not, however, result in the discharge of the liability

(a) of a party who in bad faith pays or satisfies a holder who acquired the instrument by theft or who (unless having the rights of a holder in due course) holds through one who so acquired it; or

(b) of a party (other than an intermediary bank or a payor bank which is not a depositary bank) who pays or satisfies the holder of an instrument which has been restrictively indorsed in a manner not consistent with the terms of such restrictive indorsement.

(2) Payment or satisfaction may be made with the consent of the holder by any person including a stranger to the instrument. Surrender of the instrument to such a person gives him the rights of a transferee (Section 3–201).

§3–604. Tender of Payment. (1) Any party making tender of full payment to a holder when or after it is due is discharged to the extent of all subsequent liability for interest, costs and attorney's fees.

(2) The holder's refusal of such tender wholly discharges any party who has a right of recourse against the party making the tender.

(3) Where the maker or acceptor of an instrument payable otherwise than on demand is able and ready to pay at every place of payment specified in the instrument when it is due, it is equivalent to tender.

§3–605. Cancellation and Renunciation. (1) The holder of an instrument may even without consideration discharge any party

(a) in any manner apparent on the face of the instrument or the indorsement, as by intentionally cancelling the instrument or the party's signature by destruction or mutilation, or by striking out the party's signature; or

(b) by renouncing his rights by a writing signed and delivered or by surrender of the instrument to the party to be discharged.

(2) Neither cancellation nor renunciation without surrender of the instrument affects the title thereto.

§3–606. Impairment of Recourse or of Collateral. (1) The holder discharges any party to the instrument to the extent that without such party's consent the holder

(a) without express reservation of rights releases or agrees not to sue any person against whom the party has to the knowledge of the holder a right of recourse or agrees to suspend the right to enforce against such person the instrument or collateral or otherwise discharges such person, except that failure or delay in effecting any required presentment, protest or notice of dishonor with respect to any such person does not discharge any party as to whom presentment, protest or notice of dishonor is effective or unnecessary; or

(b) unjustifiably impairs any collateral for the instrument given by or on behalf of the party or any person against whom he has a right of recourse.

(2) By express reservation of rights against a party with a right of recourse the holder preserves

(a) all his rights against such party as of the time when the instrument was originally due; and

(b) the right of the party to pay the instrument as of that time; and

(c) all rights of such party to recourse against others.

Part 7

Advice of International Sight Draft

§3–701. Letter of Advice of International Sight Draft. (1) A "letter of advice" is a drawer's communication to the drawee that a described draft has been drawn.

(2) Unless otherwise agreed when a bank receives from another bank a letter of advice of an international sight draft the drawee bank may immediately debit the drawer's account and stop the running of interest pro tanto. Such a debit and any resulting credit to any account covering outstanding drafts leaves in the drawer full power to stop payment or otherwise dispose of the amount and creates no trust or interest in favor of the holder.

(3) Unless otherwise agreed and except where a draft is drawn under a credit issued by the drawee, the drawee of an international sight draft owes the drawer no duty to pay an unadvised draft but if it does so and the draft is genuine, may appropriately debit the drawer's account.

Part 8

Miscellaneous

§3–801. Drafts in a Set. (1) Where a draft is drawn in a set of parts, each of which is numbered and expressed to be an order only if no other part has been honored, the whole of the parts constitutes one draft but a taker of any part may become a holder in due course of the draft.

(2) Any person who negotiates, indorses or accepts a single part of a draft drawn in a set thereby becomes liable to any holder in due course of that part as if it were the whole set, but as between different holders in due course to whom different parts have been negotiated the holder whose title first accrues has all rights to the draft and its proceeds.

(3) As against the drawee the first presented part of a draft drawn in a set is the part entitled to payment, or if a time draft to acceptance and payment. Acceptance of any subsequently presented part renders the drawee liable thereon under subsection (2). With respect both to a holder and to the drawer payment of a subsequently presented part of a draft payable at sight has the same effect as payment of a check notwithstanding an effective stop order (Section 4–407).

(4) Except as otherwise provided in this section, where any part of a draft in a set is discharged by payment or otherwise the whole draft is discharged.

§3–802. Effect of Instrument on Obligation for Which It Is Given. (1) Unless otherwise agreed where an instrument is taken for an underlying obligation

(a) the obligation is pro tanto discharged if a bank is drawer, maker or acceptor of the instrument and there is no recourse on the instrument against the underlying obligor; and

(b) in any other case the obligation is suspended pro tanto until the instrument is due or if it is payable on demand until its presentment. If the instrument is dishonored action may be maintained on either the instrument or the obligation; discharge of the underlying obligor on the instrument also discharges him on the obligation.

(2) The taking in good faith of a check which is not postdated does not of itself so extend the time on the original obligation as to discharge a surety.

§3–803. Notice to Third Party. Where a defendant is sued for breach of an obligation for which a third person is answerable over under this Article he may give the third person written notice of the litigation, and the person notified may then give similar notice to any other person who is answerable over to him under this Article. If the notice states that the person notified may come in and defend and that if the person notified does not do so he will in any action against him by the person giving the notice be bound by any determination of fact common to the two litigations, then unless after seasonable receipt of the notice the person notified does come in and defend he is so bound.

§3–804. Lost, Destroyed or Stolen Instruments. The owner of an instrument which is lost, whether by destruction, theft or otherwise, may maintain an action in his own name and recover from any party liable thereon upon due proof of his ownership, the facts which prevent his production of the instrument and its terms. The court may require security indemnifying the defendant against loss by reason of further claims on the instrument.

§3–805. Instruments Not Payable to Order or to Bearer. This Article applies to any instrument whose terms do not preclude transfer and which is otherwise negotiable within this Article but which is not payable to order or to bearer, except that there can be no holder in due course of such an instrument.

ARTICLE 4: BANK DEPOSITS AND COLLECTIONS

Part 1

General Provisions and Definitions

§4–101. Short Title. This Article shall be known and may be cited as Uniform Commercial Code—Bank Deposits and Collections.

§4–102. Applicability. (1) To the extent that items within this Article are also within the scope of Articles 3 and 8, they are subject to the provisions of those Articles. In the event of conflict the provisions of this Article govern those of Article 3 but the provisions of Article 8 govern those of this Article.

(2) The liability of a bank for action or non-action with respect to any item handled by it for purposes of presentment, payment or collection is governed by the law of the place where the bank is located. In the case of action or non-action by or at a branch or separate office of a bank, its liability is governed by the law of the place where the branch or separate office is located.

§4–103. Variation by Agreement; Measure of Damages; Certain Action Constituting Ordinary Care. (1) The effect of the provisions of this Article may be varied by agreement except that no agreement can disclaim a bank's responsibility for its own lack of good faith or failure to exercise ordinary care or can limit the measure of damages for such lack or failure; but the parties may by agreement determine the standards by which such responsibility is to be measured if such standards are not manifestly unreasonable.

(2) Federal Reserve regulations and operating letters, clearing house rules, and the like, have the effect of agreements under subsection (1), whether or not specifically assented to by all parties interested in items handled.

(3) Action or non-action approved by this Article or pursuant to Federal Reserve regulations or operating letters constitutes the exercise of ordinary care and, in the absence of special instructions, action or non-action consistent with clearing house rules and the like or with a general banking usage not disapproved by this Article, prima facie constitutes the exercise of ordinary care.

(4) The specification or approval of certain procedures by this Article does not constitute disapproval of other procedures which may be reasonable under the circumstances.

(5) The measure of damages for failure to exercise ordinary care in handling an item is the amount of the item reduced by an amount which could not have been realized by the use of ordinary care, and where there is bad faith it includes other damages, if any, suffered by the party as a proximate consequence.

§4–104. Definitions and Index of Definitions. (1) In this Article unless the context otherwise requires

(a) "Account" means any account with a bank and includes a checking, time, interest or savings account;

(b) "Afternoon" means the period of a day between noon and midnight;

(c) "Banking day" means that part of any day on which a bank is open to the public for carrying on substantially all of its banking functions;

(d) "Clearing house" means any association of banks or other payors regularly clearing items;

(e) "Customer" means any person having an account with a bank or for whom a bank has agreed to collect items and includes a bank carrying an account with another bank;

(f) "Documentary draft" means any negotiable or non-negotiable draft with accompanying documents, securities or other papers to be delivered against honor of the draft;

(g) "Item" means any instrument for the payment of money even though it is not negotiable but does not include money;

(h) "Midnight deadline" with respect to a bank is midnight on its next banking day following the banking day on which it receives the relevant item or notice or from which the time for taking action commences to run, whichever is later;

(i) "Properly payable" includes the availability of funds for payment at the time of decision to pay or dishonor;

(j) "Settle" means to pay in cash, by clearing house settlement, in a charge or credit or by remittance, or otherwise as instructed. A settlement may be either provisional or final;

(k) "Suspends payments" with respect to a bank means that it has been closed by order of the supervisory authorities, that a public officer has been appointed to take it over or that it ceases or refuses to make payments in the ordinary course of business.

(2) Other definitions applying to this Article and the sections in which they appear are:

"Collecting bank". Section 4–105.
"Depositary bank". Section 4–105.
"Intermediary bank". Section 4–105.
"Payor bank". Section 4–105.
"Presenting bank". Section 4–105.
"Remitting bank". Section 4–105.

(3) The following definitions in other Articles apply to this Article:
"Acceptance". Section 3–410.

"Certificate of deposit". Section 3–104.
"Certification". Section 3–411.
"Check". Section 3–104.
"Draft". Section 3–104.
"Holder in due course". Section 3–302.
"Notice of dishonor". Section 3–508.
"Presentment". Section 3–504.
"Protest". Section 3–509.
"Secondary party". Section 3–102.

(4) In addition Article 1 contains general definitions and principles of construction and interpretation applicable throughout this Article.

§4–105. "Depositary Bank"; "Intermediary Bank"; "Collecting Bank"; "Payor Bank"; "Presenting Bank"; "Remitting Bank". In this Article unless the context otherwise requires:

(a) "Depositary bank" means the first bank to which an item is transferred for collection even though it is also the payor bank;

(b) "Payor bank" means a bank by which an item is payable as drawn or accepted;

(c) "Intermediary bank" means any bank to which an item is transferred in course of collection except the depositary or payor bank;

(d) "Collecting bank" means any bank handling the item for collection except the payor bank;

(e) "Presenting bank" means any bank presenting an item except a payor bank;

(f) "Remitting bank" means any payor or intermediary bank remitting for an item.

§4–106. Separate Office of a Bank. A branch or separate office of a bank [maintaining its own deposit ledgers] is a separate bank for the purpose of computing the time within which and determing the place at or to which action may be taken or notices or orders shall be given under this Article and under Article 3. As amended 1962.

Note: *The brackets are to make it optional with the several states whether to require a branch to maintain its own deposit ledgers in order to be considered to be a separate bank for certain purposes under Article 4. In some states "maintaining its own deposit ledgers" is a satisfactory test. In others branch banking practices are such that this test would not be suitable.*

§4–107. Time of Receipt of Items. (1) For the purpose of allowing time to process items, prove balances and make the necessary entries on its books to determine its position for the day, a bank may fix an afternoon hour of 2 P.M. or later as a cut-off hour for the handling of money and items and the making of entries on its books.

(2) Any item or deposit of money received on any day after a cut-off hour so fixed or after the close of the banking day may be treated as being received at the opening of the next banking day.

§4–108. Delays. (1) Unless otherwise instructed, a collecting bank in a good faith effort to secure payment may, in the case of specific items and with or without the approval of any person involved, waive, modify or extend time limits imposed or permitted by this Act for a period not in excess of an additional banking day without discharge of secondary parties and without liability to its transferor or any prior party.

(2) Delay by a collecting bank or payor bank beyond time limits prescribed or permitted by this Act or by instructions is excused if caused by interruption of communication facilities, suspension of payments by another bank, war, emergency conditions or other circumstances beyond the control of the bank provided it exercises such diligence as the circumstances require.

§4–109. Process of Posting. The "process of posting" means the usual procedure followed by a payor bank in determining to pay an item and in recording the payment including one or more of the following or other steps as determined by the bank:

(a) verification of any signature;

(b) ascertaining that sufficient funds are available;

(c) affixing a "paid" or other stamp;

(d) entering a charge or entry to a customer's account;

(e) correcting or reversing an entry or erroneous action with respect to the item. Added 1962.

Part 2

Collection of Items: Depositary and Collecting Banks

§4–201. Presumption and Duration of Agency Status of Collecting Banks and Provisional Status of Credits; Applicability of Article; Item Indorsed "Pay Any Bank". (1) Unless a contrary intent clearly appears and prior to the time that a settlement given by a collecting bank for an item is or becomes final (subsection (3) of Section 4–211 and Sections 4–212 and 4–213) the bank is an agent or sub-agent of the owner of the item and any settlement given for the item is provisional. This provision applies regardless of the form of indorsement or lack of indorsement and even though credit given for the item is subject to immediate withdrawal as of right or is in fact withdrawn; but the continuance of ownership of an item by its owner and any rights of the owner to proceeds of the item are subject to rights of a collecting bank such as those resulting from outstanding advances on the item and valid rights of setoff. When an item is handled by banks for purposes of presentment, payment and collection, the relevant provisions of this Article apply even though action of parties clearly establishes that a particular bank has purchased the item and is the owner of it.

(2) After an item has been indorsed with the words "pay any bank" or the like, only a bank may acquire the rights of a holder

(a) until the item has been returned to the customer initiating collection; or

(b) until the item has been specially indorsed by a bank to a person who is not a bank.

§4–202. Responsibility for Collection; When Action Seasonable. (1) A collecting bank must use ordinary care in

(a) presenting an item or sending it for presentment; and

(b) sending notice of dishonor or non-payment or returning an item other than a documentary draft to the bank's transferor [or directly to the depositary bank under subsection (2) of Section 4–212] (*see note to Section 4–212*) after learning that the item has not been paid or accepted, as the case may be; and

(c) settling for an item when the bank receives final settlement; and

(d) making or providing for any necessary protest; and

(e) notifying its transferor of any loss or delay in transit within a reasonable time after discovery thereof.

(2) A collecting bank taking proper action before its midnight deadline following receipt of an item, notice or payment acts seasonably; taking proper action within a reasonably longer time may be seasonable but the bank has the burden of so establishing.

(3) Subject to subsection (1) (a), a bank is not liable for the insolvency, neglect,

misconduct, mistake or default of another bank or person or for loss or destruction of an item in transit or in the possession of others.

§4–203. Effect of Instructions. Subject to the provisions of Article 3 concerning conversion of instruments (Section 3–419) and the provisions of both Article 3 and this Article concerning restrictive indorsements only a collecting bank's transferor can give instructions which affect the bank or constitute notice to it and a collecting bank is not liable to prior parties for any action taken pursuant to such instructions or in accordance with any agreement with its transferor.

§4–204. Methods of Sending and Presenting; Sending Direct to Payor Bank. (1) A collecting bank must send items by reasonably prompt method taking into consideration any relevant instructions, the nature of the item, the number of such items on hand, and the cost of collection involved and the method generally used by it or others to present such items.

(2) A collecting bank may send

(a) any item direct to the payor bank;

(b) any item to any non-bank payor if authorized by its transferor; and

(c) any item other than documentary drafts to any non-bank payor, if authorized by Federal Reserve regulation or operating letter, clearing house rule or the like.

(3) Presentment may be made by a presenting bank at a place where the payor bank has requested that presentment be made. As amended 1962.

§4–205. Supplying Missing Indorsement; No Notice from Prior Indorsement. (1) A depositary bank which has taken an item for collection may supply any indorsement of the customer which is necessary to title unless the item contains the words "payee's indorsement required" or the like. In the absence of such a requirement a statement placed on the item by the depositary bank to the effect that the item was deposited by a customer or credited to his account is effective as the customer's indorsement.

(2) An intermediary bank, or payor bank which is not a depositary bank, is neither given notice nor otherwise affected by a restrictive indorsement of any person except the bank's immediate transferor.

§4–206. Transfer between Banks. Any agreed method which identifies the transferor bank is sufficient for the item's further transfer to another bank.

§4–207. Warranties of Customer and Collecting Bank on Transfer or Presentment of Items; Time for Claims. (1) Each customer or collecting bank who obtains payment or acceptance of an item and each prior customer and collecting bank warrants to the payor bank or other payor who in good faith pays or accepts the item that

(a) he has a good title to the item or is authorized to obtain payment or acceptance on behalf of one who has a good title; and

(b) he has no knowledge that the signature of the maker or drawer is unauthorized, except that this warranty is not given by any customer or collecting bank that is a holder in due course and acts in good faith

(i) to a maker with respect to the maker's own signature; or

(ii) to a drawer with respect to the drawer's own signature, whether or not the drawer is also the drawee; or

(iii) to an acceptor of an item if the holder in due course took the item after the acceptance or obtained the acceptance without knowledge that the drawer's signature was unauthorized; and

(c) the item has not been materially altered, except that this warranty is not given by any customer or collecting bank that is a holder in due course and acts in good faith

(i) to the maker of a note; or

(ii) to the drawer of a draft whether or not the drawer is also the drawee; or

(iii) to the acceptor of an item with respect to an alteration made prior to the acceptance if the holder in due course took the item after the acceptance, even though the acceptance provided "payable as originally drawn" or equivalent terms; or

(iv) to the acceptor of an item with respect to an alteration made after the acceptance.

(2) Each customer and collecting bank who transfers an item and receives a settlement or other consideration for it warrants to his transferee and to any subsequent collecting bank who takes the item in good faith that

(a) he has a good title to the item or is authorized to obtain payment or acceptance on behalf of one who has a good title and the transfer is otherwise rightful; and

(b) all signatures are genuine or authorized; and

(c) the item has not been materially altered; and

(d) no defense of any party is good against him; and

(e) he has no knowledge of any insolvency proceeding instituted with respect to the maker or acceptor or the drawer of an unaccepted item.

In addition each customer and collecting bank so transferring an item and receiving a settlement or other consideration engages that upon dishonor and any necessary notice of dishonor and protest he will take up the item.

(3) The warranties and the engagement to honor set forth in the two preceding subsections arise notwithstanding the absence of indorsement or words of guaranty or warranty in the transfer or presentment and a collecting bank remains liable for their breach despite remittance to its transferor. Damages for breach of such warranties or engagement to honor shall not exceed the consideration received by the customer or collecting bank responsible plus finance charges and expenses related to the item, if any.

(4) Unless a claim for breach of warranty under this section is made within a reasonable time after the person claiming learns of the breach, the person liable is discharged to the extent of any loss caused by the delay in making claim.

§4–208. Security Interest of Collecting Bank in Items, Accompanying Documents and Proceeds. (1) A bank has a security interest in an item and any accompanying documents or the proceeds of either

(a) in case of an item deposited in an account to the extent to which credit given for the item has been withdrawn or applied;

(b) in case of an item for which it has given credit available for withdrawal as of right, to the extent of the credit given whether or not the credit is drawn upon and whether or not there is a right of charge-back; or

(c) if it makes an advance on or against the item.

(2) When credit which has been given for several items received at one time or pursuant to a single agreement is withdrawn or applied in part the security interest remains upon all the items, any accompanying documents or the proceeds of either. For the purpose of this section, credits first given are first withdrawn.

(3) Receipt by a collecting bank of a final settlement for an item is a realization on its security interest in the item, accompanying documents and proceeds. To the extent and so long as the bank does not receive final settlement for the item or give up possession of the item or accompanying documents for purposes other than collection, the security interest continues and is subject to the provisions of Article 9 except that

(a) no security agreement is necessary to make the security interest enforceable (subsection (1) (b) of Section 9–203); and

(b) no filing is required to perfect the security interest; and

(c) the security interest has priority over conflicting perfected security interests in the item, accompanying documents or proceeds.

§4–209. When Bank Gives Value for Purposes of Holder in Due Course. For purposes of determining its status as a holder in due course, the bank has given value to the extent that it has a security interest in an item provided that the bank otherwise complies with the requirements of Section 3–302 on what constitutes a holder in due course.

§4–210. Presentment by Notice of Item Not Payable by, through or at a Bank; Liability of Secondary Parties. (1) Unless otherwise instructed, a collecting bank may present an item not payable by, through or at a bank by sending to the party to accept or pay a written notice that the bank holds the item for acceptance or payment. The notice must be sent in time to be received on or before the day when presentment is due and the bank must meet any requirement of the party to accept or pay under Section 3–505 by the close of the bank's next banking day after it knows of the requirement.

(2) Where presentment is made by notice and neither honor nor request for compliance with a requirement under Section 3–505 is received by the close of business on the day after maturity or in the case of demand items by the close of business on the third banking day after notice was sent, the presenting bank may treat the item as dishonored and charge any secondary party by sending him notice of the facts.

§4–211. Media of Remittance; Provisional and Final Settlement in Remittance Cases. (1) A collecting bank may take in settlement of an item

(a) a check of the remitting bank or of another bank on any bank except the remitting bank; or

(b) a cashier's check or similar primary obligation of a remitting bank which is a member of or clears through a member of the same clearing house or group as the collecting bank; or

(c) appropriate authority to charge an account of the remitting bank or of another bank with the collecting bank; or

(d) if the item is drawn upon or payable by a person other than a bank, a cashier's check, certified check or other bank check or obligation.

(2) If before its midnight deadline the collecting bank properly dishonors a remittance check or authorization to charge on itself or presents or forwards for collection a remittance instrument of or on another bank which is of a kind approved by subsection (1) or has not been authorized by it, the collecting bank is not liable to prior parties in the event of the dishonor of such check, instrument or authorization.

(3) A settlement for an item by means of a remittance instrument or authorization to charge is or becomes a final settlement as to both the person making and the person receiving the settlement

(a) if the remittance instrument or authorization to charge is of a kind approved by subsection (1) or has not been authorized by the person receiving the settlement and in either case the person receiving the settlement acts seasonably before its midnight deadline in presenting, forwarding for collection or paying the instrument or authorization,—at the time the remittance instrument or authorization is finally paid by the payor by which it is payable;

(b) if the person receiving the settlement has authorized remittance by a non-bank check or obligation or by a cashier's check or similar primary obligation of or a check upon the payor or other remitting bank which is not of a kind approved by subsection (1) (b),—at the time of the receipt of such remittance check or obligation; or

(c) if in a case not covered by sub-paragraphs (a) or (b) the person receiving the settlement fails to seasonably present, forward for collection, pay or return a remittance instrument or authorization to it to charge before its midnight deadline,—at such midnight deadline.

§4–212. Right of Charge-Back or Refund. (1) If a collecting bank has made provisional settlement with its customer for an item and itself fails by reason of dishonor, suspension of payments by a bank or otherwise to receive a settlement for the item which is or becomes final, the bank may revoke the settlement given by it, charge-back the amount of any credit given for the item to its customer's account or obtain refund from its customer whether or not it is able to return the items if by its midnight deadline or within a longer reasonable time after it learns the facts it returns the item or sends notification of the facts. These rights to revoke, charge-back and obtain refund terminate if and when a settlement for the item received by the bank is or becomes final (subsection (3) of Section 4–211 and subsections (2) and (3) of Section 4–213).

[(2) Within the time and manner prescribed by this section and Section 4–301, an intermediary or payor bank, as the case may be, may return an unpaid item directly to the depositary bank and may send for collection a draft on the depositary bank and obtain reimbursement. In such case, if the depositary bank has received provisional settlement for the item, it must reimburse the bank drawing the draft and any provisional credits for the item between banks shall become and remain final.]

Note: *Direct returns is recognized as an innovation that is not yet established bank practice, and therefore, Paragraph 2 has been bracketed. Some lawyers have doubts whether it should be included in legislation or left to development by agreement.*

(3) A depositary bank which is also the payor may charge-back the amount of an item to its customer's account or obtain refund in accordance with the section governing return of an item received by a payor bank for credit on its books. (Section 4–301).

(4) The right to charge-back is not affected by

(a) prior use of the credit given for the item; or

(b) failure by any bank to exercise ordinary care with respect to the item but any bank so failing remains liable.

(5) A failure to charge-back or claim refund does not affect other rights of the bank against the customer or any other party.

(6) If credit is given in dollars as the equivalent of the value of an item payable in a foreign currency the dollar amount of any charge-back or refund shall be calculated on the basis of the buying sight rate for the foreign currency prevailing on the day when the person entitled to the charge-back or refund learns that it will not receive payment in ordinary course.

§4–213. Final Payment of Item by Payor Bank; When Provisional Debits and Credits Become Final; When Certain Credits Become Available for Withdrawal. (1) An item is finally paid by a payor bank when the bank has done any of the following, whichever happens first:

(a) paid the item in cash; or

(b) settled for the item without reserving a right to revoke the settlement and without having such right under statute, clearing house rule or agreement; or

(c) completed the process of posting the item to the indicated account of the drawer, maker or other person to be charged therewith; or

(d) made a provisional settlement for the item and failed to revoke the settlement in the time and manner permitted by statute, clearing house rule or agreement.

Upon a final payment under subparagraphs (b), (c) or (d) the payor bank shall be accountable for the amount of the item.

(2) If provisional settlement for an item between the presenting and payor banks is made through a clearing house or by debits or credits in an account between them, then to the extent that provisional debits or credits for the item are entered in accounts between the presenting and payor banks or between the presenting and successive prior collecting banks seriatim, they become final upon final payment of the item by the payor bank.

(3) If a collecting bank receives a settlement for an item which is or becomes final (subsection (3) of Section 4–211, subsection (2) of Section 4–213) the bank is accountable to

its customer for the amount of the item and any provisional credit given for the item in an account with its customer becomes final.

(4) Subject to any right of the bank to apply the credit to an obligation of the customer, credit given by a bank for an item in an account with its customer becomes available for withdrawal as of right

(a) in any case where the bank has received a provisional settlement for the item,—when such settlement becomes final and the bank has had a reasonable time to learn that the settlement is final;

(b) in any case where the bank is both a depositary bank and a payor bank and the item is finally paid,—at the opening of the bank's second banking day following receipt of the item.

(5) A deposit of money in a bank is final when made but, subject to any right of the bank to apply the deposit to an obligation of the customer, the deposit becomes available for withdrawal as of right at the opening of the bank's next banking day following receipt of the deposit.

§4–214. Insolvency and Preference. (1) Any item in or coming into the possession of a payor or collecting bank which suspends payment and which item is not finally paid shall be returned by the receiver, trustee or agent in charge of the closed bank to the presenting bank or the closed bank's customer.

(2) If a payor bank finally pays an item and suspends payments without making a settlement for the item with its customer or the presenting bank which settlement is or becomes final, the owner of the item has a preferred claim against the payor bank.

(3) If a payor bank gives or a collecting bank gives or receives a provisional settlement for an item and thereafter suspends payments, the suspension does not prevent or interfere with the settlement becoming final if such finality occurs automatically upon the lapse of certain time or the happening of certain events (subsection (3) of Section 4–211, subsections (1) (d), (2) and (3) of Section 4–213).

(4) If a collecting bank receives from subsequent parties settlement for an item which settlement is or becomes final and suspends payments without making a settlement for the item with its customer which is or becomes final, the owner of the item has a preferred claim against such collecting bank.

Part 3

Collection of Items: Payor Banks

§4–301. Deferred Posting; Recovery of Payment by Return of Items; Time of Dishonor. (1) Where an authorized settlement for a demand item (other than a documentary draft) received by a payor bank otherwise than for immediate payment over the counter has been made before midnight of the banking day of receipt the payor bank may revoke the settlement and recover any payment if before it has made final payment (subsection (1) of Section 4–213) and before its midnight deadline it

(a) returns the item; or

(b) sends written notice of dishonor or nonpayment if the item is held for protest or is otherwise unavailable for return.

(2) If a demand item is received by a payor bank for credit on its books it may return such item or send notice of dishonor and may revoke any credit given or recover the amount thereof withdrawn by its customer, if it acts within the time limit and in the manner specified in the preceding subsection.

(3) Unless previous notice of dishonor has been sent an item is dishonored at the time when for purposes of dishonor it is returned or notice sent in accordance with this section.

(4) An item is returned:

(a) as to an item received through a clearing house, when it is delivered to the presenting or last collecting bank or to the clearing house or is sent or delivered in accordance with its rules; or

(b) in all other cases, when it is sent or delivered to the bank's customer or transferor or pursuant to his instructions.

§4–302. Payor Bank's Responsibility for Late Return of Item. In the absence of a valid defense such as breach of a presentment warranty (subsection (1) of Section 4–207), settlement effected or the like, if an item is presented on and received by a payor bank the bank is accountable for the amount of

(a) a demand item other than a documentary draft whether properly payable or not if the bank, in any case where it is not also the depositary bank, retains the item beyond midnight of the banking day of receipt without settling for it or, regardless of whether it is also the depositary bank, does not pay or return the item or send notice of dishonor until after its midnight deadline; or

(b) any other properly payable item unless within the time allowed for acceptance or payment of that item the bank either accepts or pays the item or returns it and accompanying documents.

§4–303. When Items Subject to Notice, Stop-Order, Legal Process or Setoff; Order in Which Items May Be Charged or Certified. (1) Any knowledge, notice or stop-order received by, legal process served upon or setoff exercised by a payor bank, whether or not effective under other rules of law to terminate, suspend or modify the bank's right or duty to pay an item or to charge its customer's account for the item, comes too late to so terminate, suspend or modify such right or duty if the knowledge, notice, stop-order or legal process is received or served and a reasonable time for the bank to act thereon expires or the setoff is exercised after the bank has done any of the following:

(a) accepted or certified the item;

(b) paid the item in cash;

(c) settled for the item without reserving a right to revoke the settlement and without having such right under statute, clearing house rule or agreement;

(d) completed the process of posting the item to the indicated account of the drawer, maker or other person to be charged therewith or otherwise has evidenced by examination of such indicated account and by action its decision to pay the item; or

(e) become accountable for the amount of the item under subsection (1) (d) of Section 4–213 and Section 4–302 dealing with the payor bank's responsibility for late return of items.

(2) Subject to the provisions of subsection (1) items may be accepted, paid, certified or charged to the indicated account of its customer in any order convenient to the bank.

Part 4

Relationship Between Payor Bank and Its Customer

§4–401. When Bank May Charge Customer's Account. (1) As against its customer, a bank may charge against his account any item which is otherwise properly payable from that account even though the charge creates an overdraft.

(2) A bank which in good faith makes payment to a holder may charge the indicated account of its customer according to

(a) the original tenor of his altered item; or

(b) the tenor of his completed item, even though the bank knows the item has been completed unless the bank has notice that the completion was improper.

§4–402. Bank's Liability to Customer for Wrongful Dishonor. A payor bank is liable to its customer for damages proximately caused by the wrongful dishonor of an item. When the dishonor occurs through mistake liability is limited to actual damages proved. If so proximately caused and proved damages may include damages for an arrest or prosecution of the customer or other consequential damages. Whether any consequential damages are proximately caused by the wrongful dishonor is a question of fact to be determined in each case.

§4–403. Customer's Right to Stop Payment; Burden of Proof of Loss. (1) A customer may by order to his bank stop payment of any item payable for his account but the order must be received at such time and in such manner as to afford the bank a reasonable opportunity to act on it prior to any action by the bank with respect to the item described in Section 4–303.

(2) An oral order is binding upon the bank only for fourteen calendar days unless confirmed in writing within that period. A written order is effective for only six months unless renewed in writing.

(3) The burden of establishing the fact and amount of loss resulting from the payment of an item contrary to a binding stop payment order is on the customer.

§4–404. Bank Not Obligated to Pay Check More than Six Months Old. A bank is under no obligation to a customer having a checking account to pay a check, other than a certified check, which is presented more than six months after its date, but it may charge its customer's account for a payment made thereafter in good faith.

§4–405. Death or Incompetence of Customer. (1) A payor or collecting bank's authority to accept, pay or collect an item or to account for proceeds of its collection if otherwise effective is not rendered ineffective by incompetence of a customer of either bank existing at the time the item is issued or its collection is undertaken if the bank does not know of an adjudication of incompetence. Neither death nor incompetence of a customer revokes such authority to accept, pay, collect or account until the bank knows of the fact of death or of an adjudication of incompetence and has reasonable opportunity to act on it.

(2) Even with knowledge a bank may for 10 days after the date of death pay or certify checks drawn on or prior to that date unless ordered to stop payment by a person claiming an interest in the account.

§4–406. Customer's Duty to Discover and Report Unauthorized Signature or Alteration. (1) When a bank sends to its customer a statement of account accompanied by items paid in good faith in support of the debit entries or holds the statement and items pursuant to a request or instructions of its customer or otherwise in a reasonable manner makes the statement and items available to the customer, the customer must exercise reasonable care and promptness to examine the statement and items to discover his unauthorized signature or any alteration on an item and must notify the bank promptly after discovery thereof.

(2) If the bank establishes that the customer failed with respect to an item to comply with the duties imposed on the customer by subsection (1) the customer is precluded from asserting against the bank

(a) his unauthorized signature or any alteration on the item if the bank also establishes that it suffered a loss by reason of such failure; and

(b) an unauthorized signature or alteration by the same wrongdoer on any other item paid in good faith by the bank after the first item and statement was available to the customer for a reasonable period not exceeding fourteen calendar days and before the bank receives notification from the customer of any such unauthorized signature or alteration.

(3) The preclusion under subsection (2) does not apply if the customer establishes lack of ordinary care on the part of the bank in paying the item(s).

(4) Without regard to care or lack of care of either the customer or the bank a customer who does not within one year from the time the statement and items are made available to the customer (subsection (1)) discover and report his unauthorized signature or any alteration on the face or back of the item or does not within 3 years from that time discover and report any unauthorized indorsement is precluded from asserting against the bank such unauthorized signature or indorsement or such alteration.

(5) If under this section a payor bank has a valid defense against a claim of a customer upon or resulting from payment of an item and waives or fails upon request to assert the defense the bank may not assert against any collecting bank or other prior party presenting or transferring the item a claim based upon the unauthorized signature or alteration giving rise to the customer's claim.

§4–407. Payor Bank's Right to Subrogation on Improper Payment. If a payor bank has paid an item over the stop payment order of the drawer or maker or otherwise under circumstances giving a basis for objection by the drawer or maker, to prevent unjust enrichment and only to the extent necessary to prevent loss to the bank by reason of its payment of the item, the payor bank shall be subrogated to the rights

(a) of any holder in due course on the item against the drawer or maker; and

(b) of the payee or any other holder of the item against the drawer or maker either on the item or under the transaction out of which the item arose; and

(c) of the drawer or maker against the payee or any other holder of the item with respect to the transaction out of which the item arose.

Part 5

Collection of Documentary Drafts

§4–501. Handling of Documentary Drafts; Duty to Send for Presentment and to Notify Customer of Dishonor. A bank which takes a documentary draft for collection must present or send the draft and accompanying documents for presentment and upon learning that the draft has not been paid or accepted in due course must seasonably notify its customer of such fact even though it may have discounted or bought the draft or extended credit available for withdrawal as of right.

§4–502. Presentment of "On Arrival Drafts." When a draft or the relevant instructions require presentment "on arrival", "when goods arrive" or the like, the collecting bank need not present until in its judgment a reasonable time for arrival of the goods has expired. Refusal to pay or accept because the goods have not arrived is not dishonor; the bank must notify its transferor of such refusal but need not present the draft again until it is instructed to do so or learns of the arrival of the goods.

§4–503. Responsibility of Presenting Bank for Documents and Goods; Report of Reasons for Dishonor; Referee in Case of Need. Unless otherwise instructed and except as provided in Article 5 a bank presenting a documentary draft

(a) must deliver the documents to the drawee on acceptance of the draft if it is payable more than three days after presentment; otherwise, only on payment; and

(b) upon dishonor, either in the case of presentment for acceptance or presentment for payment, may seek and follow instructions from any referee in case of need designated in the draft or if the presenting bank does not choose to utilize his services it must use diligence and good faith to ascertain the reason for dishonor, must notify its transferor of the dishonor and of the results of its effort to ascertain the reasons therefor and must request instructions.

But the presenting bank is under no obligation with respect to goods represented by the documents except to follow any reasonable instructions seasonably received; it has a right to reimbursement for any expense incurred in following instructions and to prepayment of or indemnity for such expenses.

§4–504. Privilege of Presenting Bank to Deal with Goods; Security Interest for Expenses. (1) A presenting bank which, following the dishonor of a documentary draft, has seasonably requested instructions but does not receive them within a reasonable time may store, sell, or otherwise deal with the goods in any reasonable manner.

(2) For its reasonable expenses incurred by action under subsection (1) the presenting bank has a lien upon the goods or their proceeds, which may be foreclosed in the same manner as an unpaid seller's lien.

ARTICLE 5: LETTERS OF CREDIT

§5–101. Short Title. This Article shall be known and may be cited as Uniform Commercial Code—Letters of Credit.

§5–102. Scope. (1) This Article applies

(a) to a credit issued by a bank if the credit requires a documentary draft or a documentary demand for payment; and

(b) to a credit issued by a person other than a bank if the credit requires that the draft or demand for payment be accompanied by a document of title; and

(c) to a credit issued by a bank or other person if the credit is not within subparagraphs (a) or (b) but conspicuously states that it is a letter of credit or is conspicuously so entitled.

(2) Unless the engagement meets the requirements of subsection (1), this Article does not apply to engagements to make advances or to honor drafts or demands for payment, to authorities to pay or purchase, to guarantees or to general agreements.

(3) This Article deals with some but not all of the rules and concepts of letters of credit as such rules or concepts have developed prior to this act or may hereafter develop. The fact that this Article states a rule does not by itself require, imply or negate application of the same or a converse rule to a situation not provided for or to a person not specified by this Article.

§5–103. Definitions. (1) In this Article unless the context otherwise requires

(a) "Credit" or "letter of credit" means an engagement by a bank or other person made at the request of a customer and of a kind within the scope of this Article (Section 5–102) that the issuer will honor drafts or other demands for payment upon compliance with the conditions specified in the credit. A credit may be either revocable or irrevocable. The engagement may be either an agreement to honor or a statement that the bank or other person is authorized to honor.

(b) A "documentary draft" or a "documentary demand for payment" is one honor of which is conditioned upon the presentation of a document or documents. "Document" means any paper including document of title, security, invoice, certificate, notice of default and the like.

(c) An "issuer" is a bank or other person issuing a credit.

(d) A "beneficiary" of a credit is a person who is entitled under its terms to draw or demand payment.

(e) An "advising bank" is a bank which gives notification of the issuance of a credit by another bank.

(f) A "confirming bank" is a bank which engages either that it will itself honor a credit already issued by another bank or that such a credit will be honored by the issuer or a third bank.

(g) A "customer" is a buyer or other person who causes an issuer to issue a credit. The term also includes a bank which procures issuance or confirmation on behalf of that bank's customer.

(2) Other definitions applying to this Article and the sections in which they appear are:

"Notation of Credit".   Section 5–108.

"Presenter".   Section 5–112(3).

(3) Definitions in other Articles applying to this Article and the sections in which they appear are:

"Accept" or "Acceptance".   Section 3–410.

"Contract for sale".   Section 2–106.

"Draft".   Section 3–104.

"Holder in due course".   Section 3–302.

"Midnight deadline".   Section 4–104.

"Security".   Section 8–102.

(4) In addition, Article 1 contains general definitions and principles of construction and interpretation applicable throughout this Article.

§5–104. Formal Requirements; Signing. (1) Except as otherwise required in subsection (1) (c) of Section 5–102 on scope, no particular form of phrasing is required for a credit. A credit must be in writing and signed by the issuer and a confirmation must be in writing and signed by the confirming bank. A modification of the terms of a credit or confirmation must be signed by the issuer or confirming bank.

(2) A telegram may be a sufficient signed writing if it identifies its sender by an authorized authentication. The authentication may be in code and the authorized naming of the issuer in an advice of credit is a sufficient signing.

§5–105. Consideration. No consideration is necessary to establish a credit or to enlarge or otherwise modify its terms.

§5–106. Time and Effect of Establishment of Credit. (1) Unless otherwise agreed a credit is established

(a) as regards the customer as soon as a letter of credit is sent to him or the letter of credit or an authorized written advice of its issuance is sent to the beneficiary; and

(b) as regards the beneficiary when he receives a letter of credit or an authorized written advice of its issuance.

(2) Unless otherwise agreed once an irrevocable credit is established as regards the customer it can be modified or revoked only with the consent of the customer and once it is established as regards the beneficiary it can be modified or revoked only with his consent.

(3) Unless otherwise agreed after a revocable credit is established it may be modified or revoked by the issuer without notice to or consent from the customer or beneficiary.

(4) Notwithstanding any modification or revocation of a revocable credit any person authorized to honor or negotiate under the terms of the original credit is entitled to

reimbursement for or honor of any draft or demand for payment duly honored or negotiated before receipt of notice of the modification or revocation and the issuer in turn is entitled to reimbursement from its customer.

§5–107. Advice of Credit; Confirmation; Error in Statement of Terms. (1) Unless otherwise specified an advising bank by advising a credit issued by another bank does not assume any obligation to honor drafts drawn or demands for payment made under the credit but it does assume obligation for the accuracy of its own statement.

(2) A confirming bank by confirming a credit becomes directly obligated on the credit to the extent of its confirmation as though it were its issuer and acquires the rights of an issuer.

(3) Even though an advising bank incorrectly advises the terms of a credit it has been authorized to advise the credit is established as against the issuer to the extent of its original terms.

(4) Unless otherwise specified the customer bears as against the issuer all risks of transmission and reasonable translation or interpretation of any message relating to a credit.

§5–108. "Notation Credit"; Exhaustion of Credit. (1) A credit which specifies that any person purchasing or paying drafts drawn or demands for payment made under it must note the amount of the draft or demand on the letter or advice of credit is a "notation credit".

(2) Under a notation credit

(a) a person paying the beneficiary or purchasing a draft or demand for payment from him acquires a right to honor only if the appropriate notation is made and by transferring or forwarding for honor the documents under the credit such a person warrants to the issuer that the notation has been made; and

(b) unless the credit or a signed statement that an appropriate notation has been made accompanies the draft or demand for payment the issuer may delay honor until evidence of notation has been procured which is satisfactory to it but its obligation and that of its customer continue for a reasonable time not exceeding thirty days to obtain such evidence.

(3) If the credit is not a notation credit

(a) the issuer may honor complying drafts or demands for payment presented to it in the order in which they are presented and is discharged pro tanto by honor of any such draft or demand;

(b) as between competing good faith purchasers of complying drafts or demands the person first purchasing has priority over a subsequent purchaser even though the later purchased draft or demand has been first honored.

§5–109. Issuer's Obligation to Its Customer. (1) An issuer's obligation to its customer includes good faith and observance of any general banking usage but unless otherwise agreed does not include liability or responsibility

(a) for performance of the underlying contract for sale or other transaction between the customer and the beneficiary; or

(b) for any act or omission of any person other than itself or its own branch or for loss or destruction of a draft, demand or document in transit or in the possession of others; or

(c) based on knowledge or lack of knowledge of any usage of any particular trade.

(2) An issuer must examine documents with care so as to ascertain that on their face they appear to comply with the terms of the credit but unless otherwise agreed assumes no liability or responsibility for the genuineness, falsification or effect of any document which appears on such examination to be regular on its face.

(3) A non-bank issuer is not bound by any banking usage of which it has no knowledge.

§5–110. Availability of Credit in Portions; Presenter's Reservation of Lien or Claim. (1) Unless otherwise specified a credit may be used in portions in the discretion of the beneficiary.

(2) Unless otherwise specified a person by presenting a documentary draft or demand for payment under a credit relinquishes upon its honor all claims to the documents and a person by transferring such draft or demand or causing such presentment authorizes such relinquishment. An explicit reservation of claim makes the draft or demand non-complying.

§5–111. Warranties on Transfer and Presentment. (1) Unless otherwise agreed the beneficiary by transferring or presenting a documentary draft or demand for payment warrants to all interested parties that the necessary conditions of the credit have been complied with. This is in addition to any warranties arising under Articles 3, 4, 7 and 8.

(2) Unless otherwise agreed a negotiating, advising, confirming, collecting or issuing bank presenting or transferring a draft or demand for payment under a credit warrants only the matters warranted by a collecting bank under Article 4 and any such bank transferring a document warrants only the matters warranted by an intermediary under Articles 7 and 8.

§5–112. Time Allowed for Honor or Rejection; Withholding Honor or Rejection by Consent; "Presenter". (1) A bank to which a documentary draft or demand for payment is presented under a credit may without dishonor of the draft, demand or credit

(a) defer honor until the close of the third banking day following receipt of the documents; and

(b) further defer honor if the presenter has expressly or impliedly consented thereto.

Failure to honor within the time here specified constitutes dishonor of the draft or demand and of the credit [except as otherwise provided in subsection (4) of Section 5–114 on conditional payment].

Note: *The bracketed language in the last sentence of subsection (1) should be included only if the optional provisions of Section 5–114(4) and (5) are included.*

(2) Upon dishonor the bank may unless otherwise instructed fulfill its duty to return the draft or demand and the documents by holding them at the disposal of the presenter and sending him an advice to that effect.

(3) "Presenter" means any person presenting a draft or demand for payment for honor under a credit even though that person is a confirming bank or other correspondent which is acting under an issuer's authorization.

§5–113. Indemnities. (1) A bank seeking to obtain (whether for itself or another) honor, negotiation or reimbursement under a credit may give an indemnity to induce such honor, negotiation or reimbursement.

(2) An indemnity agreement inducing honor, negotiation or reimbursement

(a) unless otherwise explicitly agreed applies to defects in the documents but not in the goods; and

(b) unless a longer time is explicitly agreed expires at the end of ten business days following receipt of the documents by the ultimate customer unless notice of objection is sent before such expiration date. The ultimate customer may send notice of objection to the person from whom he received the documents and any bank receiving such notice is under a duty to send notice to its transferor before its midnight deadline.

§5–114. Issuer's Duty and Privilege to Honor; Right to Reimbursement. (1) An issuer must honor a draft or demand for payment which complies with the terms of the relevant credit regardless of whether the goods or documents conform to the underlying contract for sale or other contract between the customer and the beneficiary. The issuer is not excused from honor of such a draft or demand by reason of an additional general term that all documents must be satisfactory to the issuer, but an issuer may require that specified documents must be satisfactory to it.

(2) Unless otherwise agreed when documents appear on their face to comply with the terms of a credit but a required document does not in fact conform to the warranties made on negotiation or transfer of a document of title (Section 7–507) or of a security (Section 8–306) or is forged or fraudulent or there is fraud in the transaction

(a) the issuer must honor the draft or demand for payment if honor is demanded by a negotiating bank or other holder of the draft or demand which has taken the draft or demand under the credit and under circumstances which would make it a holder in due course (Section 3–302) and in an appropriate case would make it a person to whom a document of title has been duly negotiated (Section 7–502) or a bona fide purchaser of a security (Section 8–302); and

(b) in all other cases as against its customer, an issuer acting in good faith may honor the draft or demand for payment despite notification from the customer of fraud, forgery or other defect not apparent on the face of the documents but a court of appropriate jurisdiction may enjoin such honor.

(3) Unless otherwise agreed an issuer which has duly honored a draft or demand for payment is entitled to immediate reimbursement of any payment made under the credit and to be put in effectively available funds not later than the day before maturity of any acceptance made under the credit.

[(4) When a credit provides for payment by the issuer on receipt of notice that the required documents are in the possession of a correspondent or other agent of the issuer

(a) any payment made on receipt of such notice is conditional; and

(b) the issuer may reject documents which do not comply with the credit if it does so within three banking days following its receipt of the documents; and

(c) in the event of such rejection, the issuer is entitled by charge back or otherwise to return of the payment made.]

[(5) In the case covered by subsection (4) failure to reject documents within the time specified in sub-paragraph (b) constitutes acceptance of the documents and makes the payment final in favor of the beneficiary.]

Note: *Subsections (4) and (5) are bracketed as optional. If they are included the bracketed language in the last sentence of Section 5–112(1) should also be included.*

§5–115. Remedy for Improper Dishonor or Anticipatory Repudiation. (1) When an issuer wrongfully dishonors a draft or demand for payment presented under a credit the person entitled to honor has with respect to any documents the rights of a person in the position of a seller (Section 2–707) and may recover from the issuer the face amount of the draft or demand together with incidental damages under Section 2–710 on seller's incidental damages and interest but less any amount realized by resale or other use or disposition of the subject matter of the transaction. In the event no resale or other utilization is made the documents, goods or other subject matter involved in the transaction must be turned over to the issuer on payment of judgment.

(2) When an issuer wrongfully cancels or otherwise repudiates a credit before presentment of a draft or demand for payment drawn under it the beneficiary has the rights of a seller after anticipatory repudiation by the buyer under Section 2–610 if he learns of the repudiation in time reasonably to avoid procurement of the required documents. Otherwise the beneficiary has an immediate right of action for wrongful dishonor.

§5–116. Transfer and Assignment. (1) The right to draw under a credit can be transferred or assigned only when the credit is expressly designated as transferable or assignable.

(2) Even though the credit specifically states that it is nontransferable or nonassignable the beneficiary may before performance of the conditions of the credit assign his right to proceeds. Such an assignment is an assignment of a contract right under Article 9 on Secured Transactions and is governed by that Article except that

(a) the assignment is ineffective until the letter of credit or advice of credit is delivered to the assignee which delivery constitutes perfection of the security interest under Article 9; and

(b) the issuer may honor drafts or demands for payment drawn under the credit until it receives a notification of the assignment signed by the beneficiary which reasonably identifies the credit involved in the assignment and contains a request to pay the assignee; and

(c) after what reasonably appears to be such a notification has been received the issuer may without dishonor refuse to accept or pay even to a person otherwise entitled to honor until the letter of credit or advice of credit is exhibited to the issuer.

(3) Except where the beneficiary has effectively assigned his right to draw or his right to proceeds, nothing in this section limits his right to transfer or negotiate drafts or demands drawn under the credit. Amended in 1972.

§5–117. Insolvency of Bank Holding Funds for Documentary Credit. (1) Where an issuer or an advising or confirming bank or a bank which has for a customer procured issuance of a credit by another bank becomes insolvent before final payment under the credit and the credit is one to which this Article is made applicable by paragraphs (a) or (b) of Section 5–102(1) on scope, the receipt or allocation of funds or collateral to secure or meet obligations under the credit shall have the following results:

(a) to the extent of any funds or collateral turned over after or before the insolvency as indemnity against or specifically for the purpose of payment of drafts or demands for payment drawn under the designated credit, the drafts or demands are entitled to payment in preference over depositors or other general creditors of the issuer or bank; and

(b) on expiration of the credit or surrender of the beneficiary's rights under it unused any person who has given such funds or collateral is similarly entitled to return thereof; and

(c) a charge to a general or current account with a bank if specifically consented to for the purpose of indemnity against or payment of drafts or demands for payment drawn under the designated credit falls under the same rules as if the funds had been drawn out in cash and then turned over with specific instructions.

(2) After honor or reimbursement under this section the customer or other person for whose account the insolvent bank has acted is entitled to receive the documents involved.

ARTICLE 6: BULK TRANSFERS

§6–101. Short Title. This Article shall be known and may be cited as Uniform Commercial Code—Bulk Transfers.

§6–102. "Bulk Transfers"; Transfers of Equipment; Enterprises Subject to This Article; Bulk Transfers Subject to This Article. (1) A "bulk transfer" is any transfer in bulk and not in the ordinary course of the transferor's business of a major part of the materials, supplies, merchandise or other inventory (Section 9–109) of an enterprise subject to this Article.

(2) A transfer of a substantial part of the equipment (Section 9–109) of such an

enterprise is a bulk transfer if it is made in connection with a bulk transfer of inventory, but not otherwise.

(3) The enterprises subject to this Article are all those whose principal business is the sale of merchandise from stock, including those who manufacture what they sell.

(4) Except as limited by the following section all bulk transfers of goods located within this state are subject to this Article.

§6–103. Transfers Excepted from This Article. The following transfers are not subject to this Article:

(1) Those made to give security for the performance of an obligation;

(2) General assignments for the benefit of all the creditors of the transferor, and subsequent transfers by the assignee thereunder;

(3) Transfers in settlement or realization of a lien or other security interests;

(4) Sales by executors, administrators, receivers, trustees in bankruptcy, or any public officer under judicial process;

(5) Sales made in the course of judicial or administrative proceedings for the dissolution or reorganization of a corporation and of which notice is sent to the creditors of the corporation pursuant to order of the court or administrative agency;

(6) Transfers to a person maintaining a known place of business in this State who becomes bound to pay the debts of the transferor in full and gives public notice of that fact, and who is solvent after becoming so bound;

(7) A transfer to a new business enterprise organized to take over and continue the business, if public notice of the transaction is given and the new enterprise assumes the debts of the transferor and he receives nothing from the transaction except an interest in the new enterprise junior to the claims of creditors;

(8) Transfers of property which is exempt from execution.

Public notice under subsection (6) or subsection (7) may be given by publishing once a week for two consecutive weeks in a newspaper of general circulation where the transferor had its principal place of business in this state an advertisement including the names and addresses of the transferor and transferee and the effective date of the transfer.

§6–104. Schedule of Property, List of Creditors. (1) Except as provided with respect to auction sales (Section 6–108), a bulk transfer subject to this Article is ineffective against any creditor of the transferor unless:

(a) The transferee requires the transferor to furnish a list of his existing creditors prepared as stated in this section; and

(b) The parties prepare a schedule of the property transferred sufficient to identify it; and

(c) The transferee preserves the list and schedule for six months next following the transfer and permits inspection of either or both and copying therefrom at all reasonable hours by any creditor of the transferor, or files the list and schedule in (a public office to be here identified).

(2) The list of creditors must be signed and sworn to or affirmed by the transferor or his agent. It must contain the names and business addresses of all creditors of the transferor, with the amounts when known, and also the names of all persons who are known to the transferor to assert claims against him even though such claims are disputed. If the transferor is the obligor of an outstanding issue of bonds, debentures or the like as to which there is an indenture trustee, the list of creditors need include only the name and address of the indenture trustee and the aggregate outstanding principal amount of the issue.

(3) Responsibility for the completeness and accuracy of the list of creditors rests on

the transferor, and the transfer is not rendered ineffective by errors or omissions therein unless the transferee is shown to have had knowledge.

§6–105. Notice to Creditors. In addition to the requirements of the preceding section, any bulk transfer subject to this Article except one made by auction sale (Section 6–108) is ineffective against any creditor of the transferor unless at least ten days before he takes possession of the goods or pays for them, whichever happens first, the transferee gives notice of the transfer in the manner and to the persons hereafter provided (Section 6–107).

[**§6–106. Application of the Proceeds.** In addition to the requirements of the two preceding sections:

(1) Upon every bulk transfer subject to this Article for which new consideration becomes payable except those made by sale at auction it is the duty of the transferee to assure that such consideration is applied so far as necessary to pay those debts of the transferor which are either shown on the list furnished by the transferor (Section 6–104) or filed in writing in the place stated in the notice (Section 6–107) within thirty days after the mailing of such notice. This duty of the transferee runs to all the holders of such debts, and may be enforced by any of them for the benefit of all.

(2) If any of said debts are in dispute the necessary sum may be withheld from distribution until the dispute is settled or adjudicated.

(3) If the consideration payable is not enough to pay all of the said debts in full distribution shall be made pro rata.]

Note: *This section is bracketed to indicate division of opinion as to whether or not it is a wise provision, and to suggest that this is a point on which State enactments may differ without serious damage to the principle of uniformity.*

In any State where this section is omitted, the following parts of sections, also bracketed in the text, should also be omitted, namely:

Section 6–107(2) (e).

6–108(3) (c).

6–109(2).

In any State where this section is enacted, these other provisions should be also.

Optional Subsection (4)

[(4) The transferee may within ten days after he takes possession of the goods pay the consideration into the (specify court) in the county where the transferor had its principal place of business in this state and thereafter may discharge his duty under this section by giving notice by registered or certified mail to all the persons to whom the duty runs that the consideration has been paid into that court and that they should file their claims there. On motion of any interested party, the court may order the distribution of the consideration to the persons entitled to it.]

Note: *Optional subsection (4) is recommended for those states which do not have a general statute providing for payment of money into court.*

§6–107. The Notice. (1) The notice to creditors (Section 6–105) shall state:

(a) that a bulk transfer is about to be made; and

(b) the names and business addresses of the transferor and transferee, and all other business names and addresses used by the transferor within three years last past so far as known to the transferee; and

(c) whether or not all the debts of the transferor are to be paid in full as they fall due as a result of the transaction, and if so, the address to which creditors should send their bills.

(2) If the debts of the transferor are not to be paid in full as they fall due or if the transferee is in doubt on that point then the notice shall state further:

(a) the location and general description of the property to be transferred and the estimated total of the transferor's debts;

(b) the address where the schedule of property and list of creditors (Section 6–104) may be inspected;

(c) whether the transfer is to pay existing debts and if so the amount of such debts and to whom owing;

(d) whether the transfer is for new consideration and if so the amount of such consideration and the time and place of payment; [and]

[(e) if for new consideration the time and place where creditors of the transferor are to file their claims.]

(3) The notice in any case shall be delivered personally or sent by registered or certified mail to all the persons shown on the list of creditors furnished by the transferor (Section 6–104) and to all other persons who are known to the transferee to hold or assert claims against the transferor.

Note: *The words in brackets are optional. See Note under §6–106.*

§6–108. Auction Sales; "Auctioneer." (1) A bulk transfer is subject to this Article even though it is by sale at auction, but only in the manner and with the results stated in this section.

(2) The transferor shall furnish a list of his creditors and assist in the preparation of a schedule of the property to be sold, both prepared as before stated (Section 6–104).

(3) The person or persons other than the transferor who direct, control or are responsible for the auction are collectively called "the auctioneer". The auctioneer shall:

(a) receive and retain the list of creditors and prepare and retain the schedule of property for the period stated in this Article (Section 6–104);

(b) give notice of the auction personally or by registered or certified mail at least ten days before it occurs to all persons shown on the list of creditors and to all other persons who are known to him to hold or assert claims against the transferor; [and]

[(c) assure that the net proceeds of the auction are applied as provided in this Article (Section 6–106).]

(4) Failure of the auctioneer to perform any of these duties does not affect the validity of the sale or the title of the purchasers, but if the auctioneer knows that the auction constitutes a bulk transfer such failure renders the auctioneer liable to the creditors of the transferor as a class for the sums owing to them from the transferor up to but not exceeding the net proceeds of the auction. If the auctioneer consists of several persons their liability is joint and several.

Note: *The words in brackets are optional. See Note under §6–106.*

§6–109. What Creditors Protected; [Credit for Payment to Particular Creditors]. (1) The creditors of the transferor mentioned in this Article are those holding claims based on transactions or events occurring before the bulk transfer, but creditors who become such after notice to creditors is given (Sections 6–105 and 6–107) are not entitled to notice.

[(2) Against the aggregate obligation imposed by the provisions of this Article concerning the application of the proceeds (Section 6–106 and subsection (3) (c) of 6–108) the transferee or auctioneer is entitled to credit for sums paid to particular creditors of the transferor, not exceeding the sums believed in good faith at the time of the payment to be properly payable to such creditors.]

Note: *The words in brackets are optional. See Note under §6–106.*

§6–110. Subsequent Transfers. When the title of a transferee to property is subject to a defect by reason of his non-compliance with the requirements of this Article, then:

(1) a purchaser of any of such property from such transferee who pays no value or who takes with notice of such non-compliance takes subject to such defect, but

(2) a purchaser for value in good faith and without such notice takes free of such defect.

§6–111. Limitation of Actions and Levies. No action under this Article shall be brought nor levy made more than six months after the date on which the transferee took possession of the goods unless the transfer has been concealed. If the transfer has been concealed, actions may be brought or levies made within six months after its discovery.

ARTICLE 7: WAREHOUSE RECEIPTS, BILLS OF LADING
AND OTHER DOCUMENTS OF TITLE

Part 1

General

§7–101. Short Title. This Article shall be known and may be cited as Uniform Commercial Code—Documents of Title.

§7–102. Definitions and Index of Definitions. (1) In this Article, unless the context otherwise requires:

(a) "Bailee" means the person who by a warehouse receipt, bill of lading or other document of title acknowledges possession of goods and contracts to deliver them.

(b) "Consignee" means the person named in a bill to whom or to whose order the bill promises delivery.

(c) "Consignor" means the person named in a bill as the person from whom the goods have been received for shipment.

(d) "Delivery order" means a written order to deliver goods directed to a warehouseman, carrier or other person who in the ordinary course of business issues warehouse receipts or bills of lading.

(e) "Document" means document of title as defined in the general definitions in Article 1 (Section 1–201).

(f) "Goods" means all things which are treated as movable for the purposes of a contract of storage or transportation.

(g) "Issuer" means a bailee who issues a document except that in relation to an unaccepted delivery order it means the person who orders the possessor of goods to deliver. Issuer includes any person for whom an agent or employee purports to act in issuing a document if the agent or employee has real or apparent authority to issue documents, notwithstanding that the issuer received no goods or that the goods were misdescribed or that in any other respect the agent or employee violated his instructions.

(h) "Warehouseman" is a person engaged in the business of storing goods for hire.

(2) Other definitions applying to this Article or to specified Parts thereof, and the sections in which they appear are:

"Duly negotiate". Section 7–501.

"Person entitled under the document". Section 7–403(4).

(3) Definitions in other Articles applying to this Article and the sections in which they appear are:

"Contract for sale". Section 2–106.

"Overseas". Section 2–323.

"Receipt" of goods. Section 2–103.

(4) In addition Article 1 contains general definitions and principles of construction and interpretation applicable throughout this Article.

§7–103. Relation of Article to Treaty, Statute, Tariff, Classification or Regulation. To the extent that any treaty or statute of the United States, regulatory statute of this State or tariff, classification or regulation filed or issued pursuant thereto is applicable, the provisions of this Article are subject thereto.

§7–104. Negotiable and Non-Negotiable Warehouse Receipt, Bill of Lading or Other Document of Title. (1) A warehouse receipt, bill of lading or other document of title is negotiable

(a) if by its terms the goods are to be delivered to bearer or to the order of a named person; or

(b) where recognized in overseas trade, if it runs to a named person or assigns.

(2) Any other document is non-negotiable. A bill of lading in which it is stated that the goods are consigned to a named person is not made negotiable by a provision that the goods are to be delivered only against a written order signed by the same or another named person.

§7–105. Construction against Negative Implication. The omission from either Part 2 or Part 3 of this Article of a provision corresponding to a provision made in the other Part does not imply that a corresponding rule of law is not applicable.

Part 2

Warehouse Receipts: Special Provisions

§7–201. Who May Issue a Warehouse Receipt; Storage Under Government Bond. (1) A warehouse receipt may be issued by any warehouseman.

(2) Where goods including distilled spirits and agricultural commodities are stored under a statute requiring a bond against withdrawal or a license for the issuance of receipts in the nature of warehouse receipts, a receipt issued for the goods has like effect as a warehouse receipt even though issued by a person who is the owner of the goods and is not a warehouseman.

§7–202. Form of Warehouse Receipt; Essential Terms; Optional Terms. (1) A warehouse receipt need not be in any particular form.

(2) Unless a warehouse receipt embodies within its written or printed terms each of the following, the warehouseman is liable for damages caused by the omission to a person injured thereby:

(a) the location of the warehouse where the goods are stored;

(b) the date of issue of the receipt;

(c) the consecutive number of the receipt;

(d) a statement whether the goods received will be delivered to the bearer, to a specified person, or to a specified person or his order;

(e) the rate of storage and handling charges, except that where goods are stored under a field warehousing arrangement a statement of that fact is sufficient on a non-negotiable receipt;

(f) a description of the goods or of the packages containing them;

(g) the signature of the warehouseman, which may be made by his authorized agent;

(h) if the receipt is issued for goods of which the warehouseman is owner, either solely or jointly or in common with others, the fact of such ownership; and

(i) a statement of the amount of advances made and of liabilities incurred for which the warehouseman claims a lien or security interest (Section 7–209). If the precise amount of such advances made or of such liabilities incurred is, at the time of the issue of the receipt, unknown to the warehouseman or to his agent who issues it, a statement of the fact that advances have been made or liabilities incurred and the purpose thereof is sufficient.

(3) A warehouseman may insert in his receipt any other terms which are not contrary to the provisions of this Act and do not impair his obligation of delivery (Section 7–403) or his duty of care (Section 7–204). Any contrary provisions shall be ineffective.

§7–203. Liability for Non-Receipt or Misdescription. A party to or purchaser for value in good faith of a document of title other than a bill of lading relying in either case upon the description therein of the goods may recover from the issuer damages caused by the non-receipt or misdescription of the goods, except to the extent that the document conspicuously indicates that the issuer does not know whether any part or all of the goods in fact were received or conform to the description, as where the description is in terms of marks or labels or kind, quantity or condition, or the receipt or description is qualified by "contents, condition and quality unknown", "said to contain" or the like, if such indication be true, or the party or purchaser otherwise has notice.

§7–204. Duty of Care; Contractual Limitation of Warehouseman's Liability. (1) A warehouseman is liable for damages for loss of or injury to the goods caused by his failure to exercise such care in regard to them as a reasonably careful man would exercise under like circumstances but unless otherwise agreed he is not liable for damages which could not have been avoided by the exercise of such care.

(2) Damages may be limited by a term in the warehouse receipt or storage agreement limiting the amount of liability in case of loss or damage, and setting forth a specific liability per article or item, or value per unit of weight, beyond which the warehouseman shall not be liable; provided, however, that such liability may on written request of the bailor at the time of signing such storage agreement or within a reasonable time after receipt of the warehouse receipt be increased on part or all of the goods thereunder, in which event increased rates may be charged based on such increased valuation, but that no such increase shall be permitted contrary to a lawful limitation of liability contained in the warehouseman's tariff, if any. No such limitation is effective with respect to the warehouseman's liability for conversion to his own use.

(3) Reasonable provisions as to the time and manner of presenting claims and instituting actions based on the bailment may be included in the warehouse receipt or tariff.

(4) This section does not impair or repeal . . .

Note: *Insert in subsection (4) a reference to any statute which imposes a higher responsibility upon the warehouseman or invalidates contractual limitations which would be permissible under this Article.*

§7–205. Title under Warehouse Receipt Defeated in Certain Cases. A buyer in the ordinary course of business of fungible goods sold and delivered by a warehouseman who is also in the business of buying and selling such goods takes free of any claim under a warehouse receipt even though it has been duly negotiated.

§7–206. Termination of Storage at Warehouseman's Option. (1) A warehouseman may on notifying the person on whose account the goods are held and any other person known to claim an interest in the goods require payment of any charges and removal of the goods from the warehouse at the termination of the period of storage fixed by the document, or, if no period is fixed, within a stated period not less than thirty days after the notification. If the goods are not removed before the date specified in the notification, the warehouseman may sell them in accordance with the provisions of the section on enforcement of a warehouseman's lien (Section 7–210).

(2) If a warehouseman in good faith believes that the goods are about to deteriorate

or decline in value to less than the amount of his lien within the time prescribed in subsection (1) for notification, advertisement and sale, the warehouseman may specify in the notification any reasonable shorter time for removal of the goods and in case the goods are not removed, may sell them at public sale held not less than one week after a single advertisement or posting.

(3) If as a result of a quality or condition of the goods of which the warehouseman had no notice at the time of deposit the goods are a hazard to other property or to the warehouse or to persons, the warehouseman may sell the goods at public or private sale without advertisement on reasonable notification to all persons known to claim an interest in the goods. If the warehouseman after a reasonable effort is unable to sell the goods he may dispose of them in any lawful manner and shall incur no liability by reason of such disposition.

(4) The warehouseman must deliver the goods to any person entitled to them under this Article upon due demand made at any time prior to sale or other disposition under this section.

(5) The warehouseman may satisfy his lien from the proceeds of any sale or disposition under this section but must hold the balance for delivery on the demand of any person to whom he would have been bound to deliver the goods.

§7–207. Goods Must Be Kept Separate; Fungible Goods. (1) Unless the warehouse receipt otherwise provides, a warehouseman must keep separate the goods covered by each receipt so as to permit at all times identification and delivery of those goods except that different lots of fungible goods may be commingled.

(2) Fungible goods so commingled are owned in common by the persons entitled thereto and the warehouseman is severally liable to each owner for that owner's share. Where because of overissue a mass of fungible goods is insufficient to meet all the receipts which the warehouseman has issued against it, the persons entitled include all holders to whom overissued receipts have been duly negotiated.

§7–208. Altered Warehouse Receipts. Where a blank in a negotiable warehouse receipt has been filled in without authority, a purchaser for value and without notice of the want of authority may treat the insertion as authorized. Any other unauthorized alteration leaves any receipt enforceable against the issuer according to its original tenor.

§7–209. Lien of Warehouseman. (1) A warehouseman has a lien against the bailor on the goods covered by a warehouse receipt or on the proceeds thereof in his possession for charges for storage or transportation (including demurrage, and terminal charges), insurance, labor, or charges present or future in relation to the goods, and for expenses necessary for preservation of the goods or reasonably incurred in their sale pursuant to law. If the person on whose account the goods are held is liable for like charges or expenses in relation to other goods whenever deposited and it is stated in the receipt that a lien is claimed for charges and expenses in relation to other goods, the warehouseman also has a lien against him for such charges and expenses whether or not the other goods have been delivered by the warehouseman. But against a person to whom a negotiable warehouse receipt is duly negotiated a warehouseman's lien is limited to charges in an amount or at a rate specified on the receipt or if no charges are so specified then to a reasonable charge for storage of the goods covered by the receipt subsequent to the date of the receipt.

(2) The warehouseman may also reserve a security interest against the bailor for a maximum amount specified on the receipt for charges other than those specified in subsection (1), such as for money advanced and interest. Such a security interest is governed by the Article on Secured Transactions (Article 9).

(3) (a) A warehouseman's lien for charges and expenses under subsection (1) or a

security interest under subsection (2) is also effective against any person who so entrusted the bailor with possession of the goods that a pledge of them by him to a good faith purchaser for value would have been valid but is not effective against a person as to whom the document confers no right in the goods covered by it under Section 7–503.

(b) A warehouseman's lien on household goods for charges and expenses in relation to the goods under subsection (1) is also effective against all persons if the depositor was the legal possessor of the goods at the time of deposit. "Household goods" means furniture, furnishings and personal effects used by the depositor in a dwelling.

(4) A warehouseman loses his lien on any goods which he voluntarily delivers or which he unjustifiably refuses to deliver. (As amended in 1966.)

§7–210. Enforcement of Warehouseman's Lien. (1) Except as provided in subsection (2), a warehouseman's lien may be enforced by public or private sale of the goods in block or in parcels, at any time or place and on any terms which are commercially reasonable, after notifying all persons known to claim an interest in the goods. Such notification must include a statement of the amount due, the nature of the proposed sale and the time and place of any public sale. The fact that a better price could have been obtained by a sale at a different time or in a different method from that selected by the warehouseman is not of itself sufficent to establish that the sale was not made in a commercially reasonable manner. If the warehouseman either sells the goods in the usual manner in any recognized market therefor, or if he sells at the price current in such market at the time of his sale, or if he has otherwise sold in conformity with commercially reasonable practices among dealers in the type of goods sold, he has sold in a commercially reasonable manner. A sale of more goods than apparently necessary to be offered to insure satisfaction of the obligation is not commercially reasonable except in cases covered by the preceding sentence.

(2) A warehouseman's lien on goods other than goods stored by a merchant in the course of his business may be enforced only as follows:

(a) All persons known to claim an interest in the goods must be notified.

(b) The notification must be delivered in person or sent by registered or certified letter to the last known address of any person to be notified.

(c) The notification must include an itemized statement of the claim, a description of the goods subject to the lien, a demand for payment within a specified time not less than ten days after receipt of the notification, and a conspicuous statement that unless the claim is paid within that time the goods will be advertised for sale and sold by auction at a specified time and place.

(d) The sale must conform to the terms of the notification.

(e) The sale must be held at the nearest suitable place to that where the goods are held or stored.

(f) After the expiration of the time given in the notification, an advertisement of the sale must be published once a week for two weeks consecutively in a newspaper of general circulation where the sale is to be held. The advertisement must include a description of the goods, the name of the person on whose account they are being held, and the time and place of the sale. The sale must take place at least fifteen days after the first publication. If there is no newspaper of general circulation where the sale is to be held, the advertisement must be posted at least ten days before the sale in not less than six conspicuous places in the neighborhood of the proposed sale.

(3) Before any sale pursuant to this section any person claiming a right in the goods may pay the amount necessary to satisfy the lien and the reasonable expenses incurred under this section. In that event the goods must not be sold, but must be retained by the warehouseman subject to the terms of the receipt and this Article.

(4) The warehouseman may buy at any public sale pursuant to this section.

(5) A purchaser in good faith of goods sold to enforce a warehouseman's lien takes the goods free of any rights of persons against whom the lien was valid, despite noncompliance by the warehouseman with the requirements of this section.

(6) The warehouseman may satisfy his lien from the proceeds of any sale pursuant to this section but must hold the balance, if any, for delivery on demand to any person to whom he would have been bound to deliver the goods.

(7) The rights provided by this section shall be in addition to all other rights allowed by law to a creditor against his debtor.

(8) Where a lien is on goods stored by a merchant in the course of his business the lien may be enforced in accordance with either subsection (1) or (2).

(9) The warehouseman is liable for damages caused by failure to comply with the requirements for sale under this section and in case of willful violation is liable for conversion. As amended in 1962.

Part 3

Bills of Lading: Special Provisions

§7–301. Liability for Non-Receipt or Misdescription; "Said to Contain"; "Shipper's Load and Count"; Improper Handling. (1) A consignee of a non-negotiable bill who has given value in good faith or a holder to whom a negotiable bill has been duly negotiated relying in either case upon the description therein of the goods, or upon the date therein shown, may recover from the issuer damages caused by the misdating of the bill or the nonreceipt or misdescription of the goods, except to the extent that the document indicates that the issuer does not know whether any part or all of the goods in fact were received or conform to the description, as where the description is in terms of marks or labels or kind, quantity, or condition or the receipt or description is qualified by "contents or condition of contents of packages unknown", "said to contain", "shipper's weight, load and count" or the like, if such indication be true.

(2) When goods are loaded by an issuer who is a common carrier, the issuer must count the packages of goods if package freight and ascertain the kind and quantity if bulk freight. In such cases "shipper's weight, load and count" or other words indicating that the description was made by the shipper are ineffective except as to freight concealed by packages.

(3) When bulk freight is loaded by a shipper who makes available to the issuer adequate facilities for weighing such freight, an issuer who is a common carrier must ascertain the kind and quantity within a reasonable time after receiving the written request of the shipper to do so. In such cases "shipper's weight" or other words of like purport are ineffective.

(4) The issuer may by inserting in the bill the words "shipper's weight, load and count" or other words of like purport indicate that the goods were loaded by the shipper; and if such statement be true the issuer shall not be liable for damages caused by the improper loading. But their ommission does not imply liability for such damages.

(5) The shipper shall be deemed to have guaranteed to the issuer the accuracy at the time of shipment of the description, marks, labels, number, kind, quantity, condition and weight, as furnished by him; and the shipper shall indemnify the issuer against damage caused by inaccuracies in such particulars. The right of the issuer to such indemnity shall in

no way limit his responsibility and liability under the contract of carriage to any person other than the shipper.

§7–302. Through Bills of Lading and Similar Documents. (1) The issuer of a through bill of lading or other document embodying an undertaking to be performed in part by persons acting as its agents or by connecting carriers is liable to anyone entitled to recover on the document for any breach by such other persons or by a connecting carrier of its obligation under the document but to the extent that the bill covers an undertaking to be performed overseas or in territory not contiguous to the continental United States or an undertaking including matters other than transportation this liability may be varied by agreement of the parties.

(2) Where goods covered by a through bill of lading or other document embodying an undertaking to be performed in part by persons other than the issuer are received by any such person, he is subject with respect to his own performance while the goods are in his possession to the obligation of the issuer. His obligation is discharged by delivery of the goods to another such person pursuant to the document, and does not include liability for breach by any other such persons or by the issuer.

(3) The issuer of such through bill of lading or other document shall be entitled to recover from the connecting carrier or such other person in possession of the goods when the breach of the obligation under the document occurred, the amount it may be required to pay to anyone entitled to recover on the document therefor, as may be evidenced by any receipt, judgment, or transcript thereof, and the amount of any expense reasonably incurred by it in defending any action brought by anyone entitled to recover on the document therefor.

§7–303. Diversion; Reconsignment; Change of Instructions. (1) Unless the bill of lading otherwise provides, the carrier may deliver the goods to a person or destination other than that stated in the bill or may otherwise dispose of the goods on instructions from

(a) the holder of a negotiable bill; or

(b) the consignor on a non-negotiable bill notwithstanding contrary instructions from the consignee; or

(c) the consignee on a non-negotiable bill in the absence of contrary instructions from the consignor, if the goods have arrived at the billed destination or if the consignee is in possession of the bill; or

(d) the consignee on a non-negotiable bill if he is entitled as against the consignor to dispose of them.

(2) Unless such instructions are noted on a negotiable bill of lading, a person to whom the bill is duly negotiated can hold the bailee according to the original terms.

§7–304. Bills of Lading in a Set. (1) Except where customary in overseas transportation, a bill of lading must not be issued in a set of parts. The issuer is liable for damages caused by violation of this subsection.

(2) Where a bill of lading is lawfully drawn in a set of parts, each of which is numbered and expressed to be valid only if the goods have not been delivered against any other part, the whole of the parts constitute one bill.

(3) Where a bill of lading is lawfully issued in a set of parts and different parts are negotiated to different persons, the title of the holder to whom the first due negotiation is made prevails as to both the document and the goods even though any later holder may have received the goods from the carrier in good faith and discharged the carrier's obligation by surrender of his part.

(4) Any person who negotiates or transfers a single part of a bill of lading drawn in a set is liable to holders of that part as if it were the whole set.

(5) The bailee is obliged to deliver in accordance with Part 4 of this Article against the first presented part of a bill of lading lawfully drawn in a set. Such delivery discharges the bailee's obligation on the whole bill.

§7–305. Destination Bills. (1) Instead of issuing a bill of lading to the consignor at the place of shipment a carrier may at the request of the consignor procure the bill to be issued at destination or at any other place designated in the request.

(2) Upon request of anyone entitled as against the carrier to control the goods while in transit and on surrender of any outstanding bill of lading or other receipt covering such goods, the issuer may procure a substitute bill to be issued at any place designated in the request.

§7–306. Altered Bills of Lading. An unauthorized alteration or filling in of a blank in a bill of lading leaves the bill enforceable according to its original tenor.

§7–307. Lien of Carrier. (1) A carrier has a lien on the goods covered by a bill of lading for charges subsequent to the date of its receipt of the goods for storage or transportation (including demurrage and terminal charges) and for expenses necessary for preservation of the goods incident to their transportation or reasonably incurred in their sale pursuant to law. But against a purchaser for value of a negotiable bill of lading a carrier's lien is limited to charges stated in the bill or the applicable tariffs, or if no charges are stated then to a reasonable charge.

(2) A lien for charges and expenses under subsection (1) on goods which the carrier was required by law to receive for transportation is effective against the consignor or any person entitled to the goods unless the carrier had notice that the consignor lacked authority to subject the goods to such charges and expenses. Any other lien under subsection (1) is effective against the consignor and any person who permitted the bailor to have control or possession of the goods unless the carrier had notice that the bailor lacked such authority.

(3) A carrier loses his lien on any goods which he voluntarily delivers or which he unjustifiably refuses to deliver.

§7–308. Enforcement of Carrier's Lien. (1) A carrier's lien may be enforced by public or private sale of the goods, in block or in parcels, at any time or place and on any terms which are commercially reasonable, after notifying all persons known to claim an interest in the goods. Such notification must include a statement of the amount due, the nature of the proposed sale and the time and place of any public sale. The fact that a better price could have been obtained by a sale at a different time or in a different method from that selected by the carrier is not of itself sufficient to establish that the sale was not made in a commercially reasonable manner. If the carrier either sells the goods in the usual manner in any recognized market therefor or if he sells at the price current in such market at the time of his sale or if he has otherwise sold in conformity with commercially reasonable practices among dealers in the type of goods sold he has sold in a commercially reasonable manner. A sale of more goods than apparently necessary to be offered to ensure satisfaction of the obligation is not commercially reasonable except in cases covered by the preceding sentence.

(2) Before any sale pursuant to this section any person claiming a right in the goods may pay the amount necessary to satisfy the lien and the reasonable expenses incurred under this section. In that event the goods must not be sold, but must be retained by the carrier subject to the terms of the bill and this Article.

(3) The carrier may buy at any public sale pursuant to this section.

(4) A purchaser in good faith of goods sold to enforce a carrier's lien takes the goods free of any rights of persons against whom the lien was valid, despite noncompliance by the carrier with the requirements of this section.

(5) The carrier may satisfy his lien from the proceeds of any sale pursuant to this section but must hold the balance, if any, for delivery on demand to any person to whom he would have been bound to deliver the goods.

(6) The rights provided by this section shall be in addition to all other rights allowed by law to a creditor against his debtor.

(7) A carrier's lien may be enforced in accordance with either subsection (1) or the procedure set forth in subsection (2) of Section 7–210.

(8) The carrier is liable for damages caused by failure to comply with the requirements for sale under this section and in case of willful violation is liable for conversion.

§7–309. Duty of Care; Contractual Limitation of Carrier's Liability. (1) A carrier who issues a bill of lading whether negotiable or non-negotiable must exercise the degree of care in relation to the goods which a reasonably careful man would exercise under like circumstances. This subsection does not repeal or change any law or rule of law which imposes liability upon a common carrier for damages not caused by its negligence.

(2) Damages may be limited by a provision that the carrier's liability shall not exceed a value stated in the document if the carrier's rates are dependent upon value and the consignor by the carrier's tariff is afforded an opportunity to declare a higher value or a value as lawfully provided in the tariff, or where no tariff is filed he is otherwise advised of such opportunity; but no such limitation is effective with respect to the carrier's liability for conversion to its own use.

(3) Reasonable provisions as to the time and manner of presenting claims and instituting actions based on the shipment may be included in a bill of lading or tariff.

Part 4

Warehouse Receipts and Bills of Lading:
General Obligations

§7–401. Irregularities in Issue of Receipt or Bill or Conduct of Issuer. The obligations imposed by this Article on an issuer apply to a document of title regardless of the fact that

(a) the document may not comply with the requirements of this Article or of any other law or regulation regarding its issue, form or content; or

(b) the issuer may have violated laws regulating the conduct of his business; or

(c) the goods covered by the document were owned by the bailee at the time the document was issued; or

(d) the person issuing the document does not come within the definition of warehouseman if it purports to be a warehouse receipt.

§7–402. Duplicate Receipt or Bill; Overissue. Neither a duplicate nor any other document of title purporting to cover goods already represented by an outstanding document of the same issuer confers any right in the goods, except as provided in the case of bills in a set, overissue of documents for fungible goods and substitutes for lost, stolen or destroyed documents. But the issuer is liable for damages caused by his overissue or failure to identify a duplicate document as such by conspicuous notation on its face.

§7–403. Obligation of Warehouseman or Carrier to Deliver; Excuse. (1) The bailee must deliver the goods to a person entitled under the document who complies with subsections (2) and (3), unless and to the extent that the bailee establishes any of the following:

(a) delivery of the goods to a person whose receipt was rightful as against the claimant;

(b) damage to or delay, loss or destruction of the goods for which the bailee is not liable [, but the burden of establishing negligence in such cases is on the person entitled under the document];

Note: *The brackets in (1) (b) indicate that State enactments may differ on this point without serious damage to the principle of uniformity.*

(c) previous sale or other disposition of the goods in lawful enforcement of a lien or on warehouseman's lawful termination of storage;

(d) the exercise by a seller of his right to stop delivery pursuant to the provisions of the Article on Sales (Section 2–705);

(e) a diversion, reconsignment or other disposition pursuant to the provisions of this Article (Section 7–303) or tariff regulating such right;

(f) release, satisfaction or any other fact affording a personal defense against the claimant;

(g) any other lawful excuse.

(2) A person claiming goods covered by a document of title must satisfy the bailee's lien where the bailee so requests or where the bailee is prohibited by law from delivering the goods until the charges are paid.

(3) Unless the person claiming is one against whom the document confers no right under Sec. 7–503(1), he must surrender for cancellation or notation of partial deliveries any outstanding negotiable document covering the goods, and the bailee must cancel the document or conspicuously note the partial delivery thereon or be liable to any person to whom the document is duly negotiated.

(4) "Person entitled under the document" means holder in the case of a negotiable document, or the person to whom delivery is to be made by the terms of or pursuant to written instructions under a non-negotiable document.

§7–404. No Liability for Good Faith Delivery Pursuant to Receipt or Bill. A bailee who in good faith including observance of reasonable commercial standards has received goods and delivered or otherwise disposed of them according to the terms of the document of title or pursuant to this Article is not liable therefor. This rule applies even though the person from whom he received the goods had no authority to procure the document or to dispose of the goods and even though the person to whom he delivered the goods had no authority to receive them.

Part 5

Warehouse Receipts and Bills of Lading:
Negotiations and Transfer

§7–501. Form of Negotiation and Requirements of "Due Negotiation". (1) A negotiable document of title running to the order of a named person is negotiated by his indorsement and delivery. After his indorsement in blank or to bearer any person can negotiate it by delivery alone.

(2) (a) A negotiable document of title is also negotiated by delivery alone when by its original terms it runs to bearer.

(b) When a document running to the order of a named person is delivered to him the effect is the same as if the document had been negotiated.

(3) Negotiation of a negotiable document of title after it has been indorsed to a specified person requires indorsement by the special indorsee as well as delivery.

(4) A negotiable document of title is "duly negotiated" when it is negotiated in the manner stated in this section to a holder who purchases it in good faith without

notice of any defense against or claim to it on the part of any person and for value, unless it is established that the negotiation is not in the regular course of business or financing or involves receiving the document in settlement or payment of a money obligation.

(5) Indorsement of a non-negotiable document neither makes it negotiable nor adds to the transferee's rights.

(6) The naming in a negotiable bill of a person to be notified of the arrival of the goods does not limit the negotiability of the bill nor constitute notice to a purchaser thereof of any interest of such person in the goods.

§7–502. Rights Acquired by Due Negotiation. (1) Subject to the following section and to the provisions of Section 7–205 on fungible goods, a holder to whom a negotiable document of title has been duly negotiated acquires thereby:

(a) title to the document;

(b) title to the goods;

(c) all rights accruing under the law of agency or estoppel, including rights to goods delivered to the bailee after the document was issued; and

(d) the direct obligation of the issuer to hold or deliver the goods according to the terms of the document free of any defense or claim by him except those arising under the terms of the document or under this Article. In the case of a delivery order the bailee's obligation accrues only upon acceptance and the obligation acquired by the holder is that the issuer and any indorser will procure the acceptance of the bailee.

(2) Subject to the following section, title and rights so acquired are not defeated by any stoppage of the goods represented by the document or by surrender of such goods by the bailee, and are not impaired even though the negotiation or any prior negotiation constituted a breach of duty or even though any person has been deprived of possession of the document by misrepresentation, fraud, accident, mistake, duress, loss, theft or conversion, or even though a previous sale or other transfer of the goods or document has been made to a third person.

§7–503. Document of Title to Goods Defeated in Certain Cases. (1) A document of title confers no right in goods against a person who before issuance of the document had a legal interest or a perfected security interest in them and who neither

(a) delivered or entrusted them or any document of title covering them to the bailor or his nominee with actual or apparent authority to ship, store or sell or with power to obtain delivery under this Article (Section 7–403) or with power of disposition under this Act (Sections 2–403 and 9–307) or other statute or rule of law; nor

(b) acquiesced in the procurement by the bailor or his nominee of any document of title.

(2) Title to goods based upon an unaccepted delivery order is subject to the rights of anyone to whom a negotiable warehouse receipt or bill of lading covering the goods has been duly negotiated. Such a title may be defeated under the next section to the same extent as the rights of the issuer or a transferee from the issuer.

(3) Title to goods based upon a bill of lading issued to a freight forwarder is subject to the rights of anyone to whom a bill issued by the freight forwarder is duly negotiated; but delivery by the carrier in accordance with Part 4 of this Article pursuant to its own bill of lading discharges the carrier's obligation to deliver.

§7–504. Rights Acquired in the Absence of Due Negotiation; Effect of Diversion; Seller's Stoppage of Delivery (1) A transferee of a document, whether negotiable or non-negotiable, to whom the document has been delivered but not duly negotiated, acquires the title and rights which his transferor had or had actual authority to convey.

(2) In the case of a non-negotiable document, until but not after the bailee receives notification of the transfer, the rights of the transferee may be defeated

(a) by those creditors of the transferor who could treat the sale as void under Section 2–402; or

(b) by a buyer from the transferor in ordinary course of business if the bailee has delivered the goods to the buyer or received notification of his rights; or

(c) as against the bailee by good faith dealings of the bailee with the transferor.

(3) A diversion or other change of shipping instructions by the consignor in a non-negotiable bill of lading which causes the bailee not to deliver to the consignee defeats the consignee's title to the goods if they have been delivered to a buyer in ordinary course of business and in any event defeats the consignee's rights against the bailee.

(4) Delivery pursuant to a non-negotiable document may be stopped by a seller under Section 2–705, and subject to the requirement of due notification there provided. A bailee honoring the seller's instructions is entitled to be indemnified by the seller against any resulting loss or expense.

§7–505. Indorser Not a Guarantor for Other Parties. The indorsement of a document of title issued by a bailee does not make the indorser liable for any default by the bailee or by previous indorsers.

§7–506. Delivery Without Indorsement: Right to Compel Indorsement. The transferee of a negotiable document of title has a specifically enforceable right to have his transferor supply any necessary indorsement but the transfer becomes a negotiation only as of the time the indorsement is supplied.

§7–507. Warranties on Negotiation or Transfer of Receipt or Bill. Where a person negotiates or transfers a document of title for value otherwise than as a mere intermediary under the next following section, then unless otherwise agreed he warrants to his immediate purchaser only in addition to any warranty made in selling the goods

(a) that the document is genuine; and

(b) that he has no knowledge of any fact which would impair its validity or worth; and

(c) that his negotiation or transfer is rightful and fully effective with respect to the title to the document and the goods it represents.

§7–508. Warranties of Collecting Bank as to Documents. A collecting bank or other intermediary known to be entrusted with documents on behalf of another or with collection of a draft or other claim against delivery of documents warrants by such delivery of the documents only its own good faith and authority. This rule applies even though the intermediary has purchased or made advances against the claim or draft to be collected.

§7–509. Receipt or Bill: When Adequate Compliance with Commercial Contract. The question whether a document is adequate to fulfill the obligations of a contract for sale or the conditions of a credit is governed by the Articles on Sales (Article 2) and on Letters of Credit (Article 5).

Part 6

Warehouse Receipts and Bills of Lading:
Miscellaneous Provisions

§7–601. Lost and Missing Documents. (1) If a document has been lost, stolen or destroyed, a court may order delivery of the goods or issuance of a substitute document and the bailee may without liability to any person comply with such order. If the document was negotiable the claimant must post security approved by the court to indemnify any person who may suffer loss as a result of non-surrender of the document. If the document was not negotiable, such security may be required at the discretion of the court. The court may also in its discretion order payment of the bailee's reasonable costs and counsel fees.

(2) A bailee who without court order delivers goods to a person claiming under a missing negotiable document is liable to any person injured thereby, and if the delivery is not in good faith becomes liable for conversion. Delivery in good faith is not conversion if made in accordance with a filed classification or tariff or, where no classification or tariff is filed, if the claimant posts security with the bailee in an amount at least double the value of the goods at the time of posting to indemnify any person injured by the delivery who files a notice of claim within one year after the delivery.

§7–602. Attachment of Goods Covered by a Negotiable Document. Except where the document was originally issued upon delivery of the goods by a person who had no power to dispose of them, no lien attaches by virtue of any judicial process to goods in the possession of a bailee for which a negotiable document of title is outstanding unless the document be first surrendered to the bailee or its negotiation enjoined, and the bailee shall not be compelled to deliver the goods pursuant to process until the document is surrendered to him or impounded by the court. One who purchases the document for value without notice of the process or injunction takes free of the lien imposed by judicial process.

§7–603. Conflicting Claims; Interpleader. If more than one person claims title or possession of the goods, the bailee is excused from delivery until he has had a reasonable time to ascertain the validity of the adverse claims or to bring an action to compel all claimants to interplead and may compel such interpleader, either in defending an action for non-delivery of the goods, or by original action, whichever is appropriate.

ARTICLE 8: INVESTMENT SECURITIES

Part 1

Short Title and General Matters

§8–101. Short Title. This Article shall be known and may be cited as Uniform Commercial Code—Investment Securities.

§8–102. Definitions and Index of Definitions. (1) In this Article unless the context otherwise requires

(a) A "security" is an instrument which

(i) is issued in bearer or registered form; and

(ii) is of a type commonly dealt in upon securities exchanges or markets or commonly recognized in any area in which it is issued or dealt in as a medium for investment; and

(iii) is either one of a class or series or by its terms is divisible into a class or series of instruments; and

(iv) evidences a share, participation or other interest in property or in an enterprise or evidences an obligation of the issuer.

(b) A writing which is a security is governed by this Article and not by Uniform Commercial Code—Commercial Paper even though it also meets the requirements of that Article. This Article does not apply to money.

(c) A security is in "registered form" when it specifies a person entitled to the security or to the rights it evidences and when its transfer may be registered upon books maintained for that purpose by or on behalf of an issuer or the security so states.

(d) A security is in "bearer form" when it runs to bearer according to its terms and not by reason of any indorsement.

(2) A "subsequent purchaser" is a person who takes other than by original issue.

(3) A "clearing corporation" is a corporation all of the capital stock of which is held by or for a national securities exchange or association registered under a statute of the United States such as the Securities Exchange Act of 1934.

(4) A "custodian bank" is any bank or trust company which is supervised and examined by state or federal authority having supervision over banks and which is acting as custodian for a clearing corporation.

(5) Other definitions applying to this Article or to specified Parts thereof and the sections in which they appear are:

"Adverse claim". Section 8–301.
"Bona fide purchaser". Section 8–302.
"Broker". Section 8–303.
"Guarantee of the signature". Section 8–402.
"Intermediary Bank". Section 4–105.
"Issuer". Section 8–201.
"Overissue". Section 8–104.

(6) In addition Article 1 contains general definitions and principles of construction and interpretation applicable throughout this Article.

§8–103. Issuer's Lien. A lien upon a security in favor of an issuer thereof is valid against a purchaser only if the right of the issuer to such lien is noted conspicuously on the security.

§8–104. Effect of Overissue; "Overissue." (1) The provisions of this Article which validate a security or compel its issue or reissue do not apply to the extent that validation, issue or reissue would result in overissue; but

(a) if an identical security which does not constitute an overissue is reasonably available for purchase, the person entitled to issue or validation may compel the issuer to purchase and deliver such a security to him against surrender of the security, if any, which he holds; or

(b) if a security is not so available for purchase, the person entitled to issue or validation may recover from the issuer the price he or the last purchaser for value paid for it with interest from the date of his demand.

(2) "Overissue" means the issue of securities in excess of the amount which the issuer has corporate power to issue.

§8–105. Securities Negotiable; Presumptions. (1) Securities governed by this Article are negotiable instruments.

(2) In any action on a security

(a) unless specifically denied in the pleadings, each signature on the security or in a necessary indorsement is admitted;

(b) when the effectiveness of a signature is put in issue the burden of establishing it is on the party claiming under the signature but the signature is presumed to be genuine or authorized;

(c) when signatures are admitted or established production of the instrument entitles a holder to recover on it unless the defendant establishes a defense or a defect going to the validity of the security; and

(d) after it is shown that a defense or defect exists the plaintiff has the burden of establishing that he or some person under whom he claims is a person against whom the defense or defect is ineffective (Section 8–202).

§8–106. Applicability. The validity of a security and the rights and duties of the issuer with respect to registration of transfer are governed by the law (including the conflict of laws rules) of the jurisdiction of organization of the issuer.

§8–107. Securities Deliverable; Action for Price. (1) Unless otherwise agreed and subject to any applicable law or regulation respecting short sales, a person obligated to deliver securities may deliver any security of the specified issue in bearer form or registered in the name of the transferee or indorsed to him or in blank.

(2) When the buyer fails to pay the price as it comes due under a contract of sale the seller may recover the price

(a) of securities accepted by the buyer; and

(b) of other securities if efforts at their resale would be unduly burdensome or if there is no readily available market for their resale.

Part 2

Issue—Issuer

§8–201. "Issuer". (1) With respect to obligations on or defenses to a security "issuer" includes a person who

(a) places or authorizes the placing of his name on a security (otherwise than as authenticating trustee, registrar, transfer agent or the like) to evidence that it represents a share, participation or other interest in his property or in an enterprise or to evidence his duty to perform an obligation evidenced by the security; or

(b) directly or indirectly creates fractional interests in his rights or property which fractional interests are evidenced by securities; or

(c) becomes responsible for or in place of any other person described as an issuer in this section.

(2) With respect to obligations on or defenses to a security a guarantor is an issuer to the extent of his guaranty whether or not his obligation is noted on the security.

(3) With respect to registration of transfer (Part 4 of this Article) "issuer" means a person on whose behalf transfer books are maintained.

§8–202. Issuer's Responsibility and Defenses; Notice of Defect or Defense. (1) Even against a purchaser for value and without notice, the terms of a security include those stated on the security and those made part of the security by reference to another instrument, indenture or document or to a constitution, statute, ordinance, rule, regulation, order or the like to the extent that the terms so referred to do not conflict with the stated terms. Such a reference does not of itself charge a purchaser for value with notice of a defect going to the validity of the security even though the security expressly states that a person accepting it admits such notice.

(2) (a) A security other than one issued by a government or governmental agency or unit even though issued with a defect going to its validity is valid in the hands of a purchaser for value and without notice of the particular defect unless the defect involves a violation of constitutional provisions in which case the security is valid in the hands of a subsequent purchaser for value and without notice of the defect.

(b) The rule of subparagraph (a) applies to an issuer which is a government or governmental agency or unit only if either there has been substantial compliance with the legal requirements governing the issue or the issuer has received a substantial consideration for the issue as a whole or for the particular security and a stated purpose of the issue is one for which the issuer has power to borrow money or issue the security.

(3) Except as otherwise provided in the case of certain unauthorized signatures on

issue (Section 8–205), lack of genuineness of a security is a complete defense even against a purchaser for value and without notice.

(4) All other defenses of the issuer including nondelivery and conditional delivery of the security are ineffective against a purchaser for value who has taken without notice of the particular defense.

(5) Nothing in this section shall be construed to affect the right of a party to a "when, as and if issued" or a "when distributed" contract to cancel the contract in the event of a material change in the character of the security which is the subject of the contract or in the plan or arrangement pursuant to which such security is to be issued or distributed.

§8–203. Staleness as Notice of Defects or Defenses. (1) After an act or event which creates a right to immediate performance of the principal obligation evidenced by the security or which sets a date on or after which the security is to be presented or surrendered for redemption or exchange, a purchaser is charged with notice of any defect in its issue or defense of the issuer.

(a) if the act or event is one requiring the payment of money or the delivery of securities or both on presentation or surrender of the security and such funds or securities are available on the date set for payment or exchange and he takes the security more than one year after that date; and

(b) if the act or event is not covered by paragraph (a) and he takes the security more than two years after the date set for surrender or presentation or the date on which such performance became due.

(2) A call which has been revoked is not within subsection (1).

§8–204. Effect of Issuer's Restrictions on Transfer. Unless noted conspicuously on the security a restriction on transfer imposed by the issuer even though otherwise lawful is ineffective except against a person with actual knowledge of it.

§8–205. Effect of Unauthorized Signature on Issue. An unauthorized signature placed on a security prior to or in the course of issue is ineffective except that the signature is effective in favor of a purchaser for value and without notice of the lack of authority if the signing has been done by

(a) an authenticating trustee, registrar, transfer agent or other person entrusted by the issuer with the signing of the security or of similar securities or their immediate preparation for signing; or

(b) an employee of the issuer or of any of the foregoing entrusted with responsible handling of the security.

§8–206. Completion or Alteration of Instrument. (1) Where a security contains the signatures necessary to its issue or transfer but is incomplete in any other respect

(a) any person may complete it by filling in the blanks as authorized; and

(b) even though the blanks are incorrectly filled in, the security as completed is enforceable by a purchaser who took it for value and without notice of such incorrectness.

(2) A complete security which has been improperly altered even though fraudulently remains enforceable but only according to its original terms.

§8–207. Rights of Issuer with Respect to Registered Owners. (1) Prior to due presentment for registration of transfer of a security in registered form the issuer or indenture trustee may treat the registered owner as the person exclusively entitled to vote, to receive notifications and otherwise to exercise all the rights and powers of an owner.

(2) Nothing in this Article shall be construed to affect the liability of the registered owner of a security for calls, assessments or the like.

§8–208. Effect of Signature of Authenticating Trustee, Registrar or Transfer Agent. (1) A person placing his signature upon a security as authenticating trustee, registrar, transfer agent or the like warrants to a purchaser for value without notice of the particular defect that

(a) the security is genuine; and

(b) his own participation in the issue of the security is within his capacity and within the scope of the authorization received by him from the issuer; and

(c) he has reasonable grounds to believe that the security is in the form and within the amount the issuer is authorized to issue.

(2) Unless otherwise agreed, a person by so placing his signature does not assume responsibility for the validity of the security in other respects.

Part 3

Purchase

§8–301. Rights Acquired by Purchaser; "Adverse Claim"; Title Acquired by Bona Fide Purchaser. (1) Upon delivery of a security the purchaser acquires the rights in the security which his transferor had or had actual authority to convey except that a purchaser who has himself been a party to any fraud or illegality affecting the security or who as a prior holder had notice of an adverse claim cannot improve his position by taking from a later bona fide purchaser. "Adverse claim" includes a claim that a transfer was or would be wrongful or that a particular adverse person is the owner of or has an interest in the security.

(2) A bona fide purchaser in addition to acquiring the rights of a purchaser also acquires the security free of any adverse claim.

(3) A purchaser of a limited interest acquires rights only to the extent of the interest purchased.

§8–302. "Bona Fide Purchaser". A "bona fide purchaser" is a purchaser for value in good faith and without notice of any adverse claim who takes delivery of a security in bearer form or of one in registered form issued to him or indorsed to him or in blank.

§8–303. "Broker". "Broker" means a person engaged for all or part of his time in the business of buying and selling securities, who in the transaction concerned acts for, or buys a security from or sells a security to a customer. Nothing in this Article determines the capacity in which a person acts for purposes of any other statute or rule to which such person is subject.

§8–304. Notice to Purchaser of Adverse Claims. (1) A purchaser (including a broker for the seller or buyer but excluding an intermediary bank) of a security is charged with notice of adverse claims if

(a) the security whether in bearer or registered form has been indorsed "for collection" or "for surrender" or for some other purpose not involving transfer; or

(b) the security is in bearer form and has on it an unambiguous statement that it is the property of a person other than the transferor. The mere writing of a name on a security is not such a statement.

(2) The fact that the purchaser (including a broker for the seller or buyer) has notice that the security is held for a third person or is registered in the name of or indorsed by a fiduciary does not create a duty of inquiry into the rightfulness of the transfer or constitute notice of adverse claims. If, however, the purchaser (excluding an intermediary bank) has knowledge that the proceeds are being used or that the transaction is for the individual benefit of the fiduciary or otherwise in breach of duty, the purchaser is charged with notice of adverse claims.

§8–305. Staleness as Notice of Adverse Claims. An act or event which creates a right to immediate performance of the principal obligation evidenced by the security or which sets a date on or after which the security is to be presented or surrendered for redemption or exchange does not of itself constitute any notice of adverse claims except in the case of a purchase

(a) after one year from any date set for such presentment or surrender for redemption or exchange; or

(b) after six months from any date set for payment of money against presentation or surrender of the security if funds are available for payment on that date.

§8–306. Warranties on Presentment and Transfer. (1) A person who presents a security for registration of transfer or for payment or exchange warrants to the issuer that he is entitled to the registration, payment or exchange. But a purchaser for value without notice of adverse claims who receives a new, reissued or re-registered security on registration of transfer warrants only that he has no knowledge of any unauthorized signature (Section 8–311) in a necessary indorsement.

(2) A person by transferring a security to a purchaser for value warrants only that

(a) his transfer is effective and rightful; and

(b) the security is genuine and has not been materially altered; and

(c) he knows no fact which might impair the validity of the security.

(3) Where a security is delivered by an intermediary known to be entrusted with delivery of the security on behalf of another or with collection of a draft or other claim against such delivery, the intermediary by such delivery warrants only his own good faith and authority even though he has purchased or made advances against the claim to be collected against the delivery.

(4) A pledgee or other holder for security who redelivers the security received, or after payment and on order of the debtor delivers that security to a third person makes only the warranties of an intermediary under subsection (3).

(5) A broker gives to his customer and to the issuer and a purchaser the warranties provided in this section and has the rights and privileges of a purchaser under this section. The warranties of and in favor of the broker acting as an agent are in addition to applicable warranties given by and in favor of his customer.

§8–307. Effect of Delivery without Indorsement; Right to Compel Indorsement. Where a security in registered form has been delivered to a purchaser without a necessary indorsement he may become a bona fide purchaser only as of the time the indorsement is supplied, but against the transferor the transfer is complete upon delivery and the purchaser has a specifically enforceable right to have any necessary indorsement supplied.

§8–308. Indorsement, How Made; Special Indorsement; Indorser Not a Guarantor; Partial Assignment. (1) An indorsement of a security in registered form is made when an appropriate person signs on it or on a separate document an assignment or transfer of the security or a power to assign or transfer it or when the signature of such person is written without more upon the back of the security.

(2) An indorsement may be in blank or special. An indorsement in blank includes an indorsement to bearer. A special indorsement specifies the person to whom the security is to be transferred, or who has power to transfer it. A holder may convert a blank indorsement into a special indorsement.

(3) "An appropriate person" in subsection (1) means

(a) the person specified by the security or by special indorsement to be entitled to the security; or

(b) where the person so specified is described as a fiduciary but is no longer serving in the described capacity,—either that person or his successor; or

(c) where the security or indorsement so specifies more than one person as fiduciaries and one or more are no longer serving in the described capacity,—the remaining fiduciary or fiduciaries, whether or not a successor has been appointed or qualified; or

(d) where the person so specified is an individual and is without capacity to act by virtue of death, incompetence, infancy or otherwise,—his executor, administrator, guardian or like fiduciary; or

(e) where the security or indorsement so specifies more than one person as tenants by the entirety or with right of survivorship and by reason of death all cannot sign,—the survivor or survivors; or

(f) a person having power to sign under applicable law or controlling instrument; or

(g) to the extent that any of the foregoing persons may act through an agent,—his authorized agent.

(4) Unless otherwise agreed the indorser by his indorsement assumes no obligation that the security will be honored by the issuer.

(5) An indorsement purporting to be only of part of a security representing units intended by the issuer to be separately transferable is effective to the extent of the indorsement.

(6) Whether the person signing is appropriate is determined as of the date of signing and an indorsement by such a person does not become unauthorized for the purposes of this Article by virtue of any subsequent change of circumstances.

(7) Failure of a fiduciary to comply with a controlling instrument or with the law of the state having jurisdiction of the fiduciary relationship, including any law requiring the fiduciary to obtain court approval of the transfer, does not render his indorsement unauthorized for the purposes of this Article.

§8–309. Effect of Indorsement without Delivery. An indorsement of a security whether special or in blank does not constitute a transfer until delivery of the security on which it appears or if the indorsement is on a separate document until delivery of both the document and the security.

§8–310. Indorsement of Security in Bearer Form. An indorsement of a security in bearer form may give notice of adverse claims (Section 8–304) but does not otherwise affect any right to registration the holder may possess.

§8–311. Effect of Unauthorized Indorsement. Unless the owner has ratified an unauthorized indorsement or is otherwise precluded from asserting its ineffectiveness

(a) he may assert its ineffectiveness against the issuer or any purchaser other than a purchaser for value and without notice of adverse claims who has in good faith received a new, reissued or re-registered security on registration of transfer; and

(b) an issuer who registers the transfer of a security upon the unauthorized indorsement is subject to liability for improper registration (Section 8–404).

§8–312. Effect of Guaranteeing Signature or Indorsement. (1) Any person guaranteeing a signature of an indorser of a security warrants that at the time of signing

(a) the signature was genuine; and

(b) the signer was an appropriate person to indorse (Section 8–308); and

(c) the signer had legal capacity to sign.

But the guarantor does not otherwise warrant the rightfulness of the particular transfer.

(2) Any person may guarantee an indorsement of a security and by so doing warrants not only the signature (subsection 1) but also the rightfulness of the particular transfer in all respects. But no issuer may require a guarantee of indorsement as a condition to registration of transfer.

(3) The foregoing warranties are made to any person taking or dealing with the

security in reliance on the guarantee and the guarantor is liable to such person for any loss resulting from breach of the warranties.

§8–313. When Delivery to the Purchaser Occurs; Purchaser's Broker as Holder. (1) Delivery to a purchaser occurs when

(a) he or a person designated by him acquires possession of a security; or

(b) his broker acquires possession of a security specially indorsed to or issued in the name of the purchaser; or

(c) his broker sends him confirmation of the purchase and also by book entry or otherwise identifies a specific security in the broker's possession as belonging to the purchaser; or

(d) with respect to an identified security to be delivered while still in the possession of a third person when that person acknowledges that he holds for the purchaser; or

(e) appropriate entries on the books of a clearing corporation are made under Section 8–320.

(2) The purchaser is the owner of a security held for him by his broker, but is not the holder except as specified in subparagraphs (b), (c) and (e) of subsection (1). Where a security is part of a fungible bulk the purchaser is the owner of a proportionate property interest in the fungible bulk.

(3) Notice of an adverse claim received by the broker or by the purchaser after the broker takes delivery as a holder for value is not effective either as to the broker or as to the purchaser. However, as between the broker and the purchaser the purchaser may demand delivery of an equivalent security as to which no notice of an adverse claim has been received.

§8–314. Duty to Deliver, When Completed. (1) Unless otherwise agreed where a sale of a security is made on an exchange or otherwise through brokers

(a) the selling customer fulfills his duty to deliver when he places such a security in the possession of the selling broker or of a person designated by the broker or if requested causes an acknowledgment to be made to the selling broker that it is held for him; and

(b) the selling broker including a correspondent broker acting for a selling customer fulfills his duty to deliver by placing the security or a like security in the possession of the buying broker or a person designated by him or by effecting clearance of the sale in accordance with the rules of the exchange on which the transaction took place.

(2) Except as otherwise provided in this section and unless otherwise agreed, a transferor's duty to deliver a security under a contract of purchase is not fulfilled until he places the security in form to be negotiated by the purchaser in the possession of the purchaser or of a person designated by him or at the purchaser's request causes an acknowledgment to be made to the purchaser that it is held for him. Unless made on an exchange a sale to a broker purchasing for his own account is within this subsection and not within subsection (1).

§8–315. Action against Purchaser Based upon Wrongful Transfer. (1) Any person against whom the transfer of a security is wrongful for any reason, including his incapacity, may against anyone except a bona fide purchaser reclaim possession of the security or obtain possession of any new security evidencing all or part of the same rights or have damages.

(2) If the transfer is wrongful because of an unauthorized indorsement, the owner may also reclaim or obtain possession of the security or new security even from a bona fide purchaser if the ineffectiveness of the purported indorsement can be asserted against him under the provisions of this Article on unauthorized indorsements (Section 8–311).

(3) The right to obtain or reclaim possession of a security may be specifically enforced and its transfer enjoined and the security impounded pending the litigation.

§8–316. Purchaser's Right to Requisites for Registration of Transfer on Books. Unless otherwise agreed the transferor must on due demand supply his purchaser with any proof of his authority to transfer or with any other requisite which may be necessary to obtain registration of the transfer of the security but if the transfer is not for value a transferor need not do so unless the purchaser furnishes the necessary expenses. Failure to comply with a demand made within a reasonable time gives the purchaser the right to reject or rescind the transfer.

§8–317. Attachment or Levy upon Security. (1) No attachment or levy upon a security or any share or other interest evidenced thereby which is outstanding shall be valid until the security is actually seized by the officer making the attachment or levy but a security which has been surrendered to the issuer may be attached or levied upon at the source.

(2) A creditor whose debtor is the owner of a security shall be entitled to such aid from courts of appropriate jurisdiction, by injunction or otherwise, in reaching such security or in satisfying the claim by means thereof as is allowed at law or in equity in regard to property which cannot readily be attached or levied upon by ordinary legal process.

§8–318. No Conversion by Good Faith Delivery. An agent or bailee who in good faith (including observance of reasonable commercial standards if he is in the business of buying, selling or otherwise dealing with securities) has received securities and sold, pledged or delivered them according to the instructions of his principal is not liable for conversion or for participation in breach of fiduciary duty although the principal had no right to dispose of them.

§8–319. Statute of Frauds. A contract for the sale of securities is not enforceable by way of action or defense unless

(a) there is some writing signed by the party against whom enforcement is sought or by his authorized agent or broker sufficient to indicate that a contract has been made for sale of a stated quantity of described securities at a defined or stated price; or

(b) delivery of the security has been accepted or payment has been made but the contract is enforceable under this provision only to the extent of such delivery or payment; or

(c) within a reasonable time a writing in confirmation of the sale or purchase and sufficient against the sender under paragraph (a) has been received by the party against whom enforcement is sought and he has failed to send written objection to its contents within ten days after its receipt; or

(d) the party against whom enforcement is sought admits in his pleading, testimony or otherwise in court that a contract was made for a sale of a stated quantity of described securities at a defined or stated price.

§8–320. Transfer or Pledge within a Central Depository System. (1) If a security

(a) is in the custody of a clearing corporation or of a custodian bank or a nominee of either subject to the instructions of the clearing corporation; and

(b) is in bearer form or indorsed in blank by an appropriate person or registered in the name of the clearing corporation or custodian bank or a nominee of either; and

(c) is shown on the account of a transferor or pledgor on the books of the clearing corporation;

then, in addition to other methods, a transfer or pledge of the security or any interest therein may be effected by the making of appropriate entries on the books of the clearing corporation reducing the account of the transferor or pledgor and increasing the account of the transferee or pledgee by the amount of the obligation or the number of shares or rights transferred or pledged.

(2) Under this section entries may be with respect to like securities or interests therein as a part of a fungible bulk and may refer merely to a quantity of a particular security without reference to the name of the registered owner, certificate or bond number or the like and, in appropriate cases, may be on a net basis taking into account other transfers or pledges of the same security.

(3) A transfer or pledge under this section has the effect of a delivery of a security in bearer form or duly indorsed in blank (Section 8–301) representing the amount of the obligation or the number of shares or rights transferred or pledged. If a pledge or the creation of a security interest is intended, the making of entries has the effect of a taking of delivery by the pledgee or a secured party (Sections 9–304 and 9–305). A transferee or pledgee under this section is a holder.

(4) A transfer or pledge under this section does not constitute a registration of transfer under Part 4 of this Article.

(5) That entries made on the books of the clearing corporation as provided in subsection (1) are not appropriate does not affect the validity or effect of the entries nor the liabilities or obligations of the clearing corporation to any person adversely affected thereby.

Part 4

Registration

§8–401. Duty of Issuer to Register Transfer. (1) Where a security in registered form is presented to the issuer with a request to register transfer, the issuer is under a duty to register the transfer as requested if

(a) the security is indorsed by the appropriate person or persons (Section 8–308); and

(b) reasonable assurance is given that those indorsements are genuine and effective (Section 8–402); and

(c) the issuer has no duty to inquire into adverse claims or has discharged any such duty (Section 8–403); and

(d) any applicable law relating to the collection of taxes has been complied with; and

(e) the transfer is in fact rightful or is to a bona fide purchaser.

(2) Where an issuer is under a duty to register a transfer of a security the issuer is also liable to the person presenting it for registration or his principal for loss resulting from any unreasonable delay in registration or from failure or refusal to register the transfer.

§8–402. Assurance That Indorsements Are Effective. (1) The issuer may require the following assurance that each necessary indorsement (Section 8–308) is genuine and effective

(a) in all cases, a guarantee of the signature (subsection (1) of Section 8–312) of the person indorsing; and

(b) where the indorsement is by an agent, appropriate assurance of authority to sign;

(c) where the indorsement is by a fiduciary, appropriate evidence of appointment or incumbency;

(d) where there is more than one fiduciary, reasonable assurance that all who are required to sign have done so;

(e) where the indorsement is by a person not covered by any of the foregoing, assurance appropriate to the case corresponding as nearly as may be to the foregoing.

(2) A "guarantee of the signature" in subsection (1) means a guarantee signed by or on behalf of a person reasonably believed by the issuer to be responsible. The issuer may adopt standards with respect to responsibility provided such standards are not manifestly unreasonable.

(3) "Appropriate evidence of appointment or incumbency" in subsection (1) means

(a) in the case of a fiduciary appointed or qualified by a court, a certificate issued by or under the direction or supervision of that court or an officer thereof and dated within sixty days before the date of presentation for transfer; or

(b) in any other case, a copy of a document showing the appointment or a certificate issued by or on behalf of a person reasonably believed by the issuer to be responsible or, in the absence of such a document or certificate, other evidence reasonably deemed by the issuer to be appropriate. The issuer may adopt standards with respect to such evidence provided such standards are not manifestly unreasonable. The issuer is not charged with notice of the contents of any document obtained pursuant to this paragraph (b) except to the extent that the contents relate directly to the appointment or incumbency.

(4) The issuer may elect to require reasonable assurance beyond that specified in this section but if it does so and for a purpose other than that specified in subsection 3(b) both requires and obtains a copy of a will, trust, indenture, articles of co-partnership, by-laws or other controlling instrument it is charged with notice of all matters contained therein affecting the transfer.

§8–403. Limited Duty of Inquiry. (1) An issuer to whom a security is presented for registration is under a duty to inquire into adverse claims if

(a) a written notification of an adverse claim is received at a time and in a manner which affords the issuer a reasonable opportunity to act on it prior to the issuance of a new, reissued or re-registered security and the notification identifies the claimant, the registered owner and the issue of which the security is a part and provides an address for communications directed to the claimant; or

(b) the issuer is charged with notice of an adverse claim from a controlling instrument which it has elected to require under subsection (4) of Section 8–402.

(2) The issuer may discharge any duty of inquiry by any reasonable means, including notifying an adverse claimant by registered or certified mail at the address furnished by him or if there be no such address at his residence or regular place of business that the security has been presented for registration of transfer by a named person, and that the transfer will be registered unless within thirty days from the date of mailing the notification, either

(a) an appropriate restraining order, injunction or other process issues from a court of competent jurisdiction; or

(b) an indemnity bond sufficient in the issuer's judgment to protect the issuer and any transfer agent, registrar or other agent of the issuer involved, from any loss which it or they may suffer by complying with the adverse claim is filed with the issuer.

(3) Unless an issuer is charged with notice of an adverse claim from a controlling instrument which it has elected to require under subsection (4) of Section 8–402 or receives notification of an adverse claim under subsection (1) of this section, where a security presented for registration is indorsed by the appropriate person or persons the issuer is under no duty to inquire into adverse claims. In particular

(a) an issuer registering a security in the name of a person who is a fiduciary or who is described as a fiduciary is not bound to inquire into the existence, extent, or correct description of the fiduciary relationship and thereafter the issuer may assume without inquiry that the newly registered owner continues to be the fiduciary until the issuer receives written notice that the fiduciary is no longer acting as such with respect to the particular security;

(b) an issuer registering transfer on an indorsement by a fiduciary is not bound to inquire whether the transfer is made in compliance with a controlling instrument or with the law of the state having jurisdiction of the fiduciary relationship, including any law requiring the fiduciary to obtain court approval of the transfer; and

(c) the issuer is not charged with notice of the contents of any court record or file or other recorded or unrecorded document even though the document is in its possession and even though the transfer is made on the indorsement of a fiduciary to the fiduciary himself or to his nominee.

§8–404. Liability and Non-Liability for Registration. (1) Except as otherwise provided in any law relating to the collection of taxes, the issuer is not liable to the owner or any other person suffering loss as a result of the registration of a transfer of a security if

(a) there were on or with the security the necessary indorsements (Section 8–308); and

(b) the issuer had no duty to inquire into adverse claims or has discharged any such duty (Section 8–403).

(2) Where an issuer has registered a transfer of a security to a person not entitled to it the issuer on demand must deliver a like security to the true owner unless

(a) the registration was pursuant to subsection (1); or

(b) the owner is precluded from asserting any claim for registering the transfer under subsection (1) of the following section; or

(c) such delivery would result in overissue, in which case the issuer's liability is governed by Section 8–104.

§8–405. Lost, Destroyed and Stolen Securities. (1) Where a security has been lost, apparently destroyed or wrongfully taken and the owner fails to notify the issuer of that fact within a reasonable time after he has notice of it and the issuer registers a transfer of the security before receiving such a notification, the owner is precluded from asserting against the issuer any claim for registering the transfer under the preceding section or any claim to a new security under this section.

(2) Where the owner of a security claims that the security has been lost, destroyed, or wrongfully taken, the issuer must issue a new security in place of the original security if the owner

(a) so requests before the issuer has notice that the security has been acquired by a bona fide purchaser; and

(b) files with the issuer a sufficient indemnity bond; and

(c) satisfies any other reasonable requirements imposed by the issuer.

(3) If, after the issue of the new security, a bona fide purchaser of the original security presents it for registration of transfer, the issuer must register the transfer unless registration would result in overissue, in which event the issuer's liability is governed by Section 8–104. In addition to any rights on the indemnity bond, the issuer may recover the new security from the person to whom it was issued or any person taking under him except a bona fide purchaser.

§8–406. Duty of Authenticating Trustee, Transfer Agent or Registrar. (1) Where a person acts as authenticating trustee, transfer agent, registrar, or other agent for an issuer in the registration of transfers of its securities or in the issue of new securities or in the cancellation of surrendered securities

(a) he is under a duty to the issuer to exercise good faith and due diligence in performing his functions; and

(b) he has with regard to the particular functions he performs the same obligation to the holder or owner of the security and has the same rights and privileges as the issuer has in regard to those functions.

(2) Notice to an authenticating trustee, transfer agent, registrar or other such agent is notice to the issuer with respect to the functions performed by the agent.

ARTICLE 9: SECURED TRANSACTIONS: SALES OF ACCOUNTS AND CHATTEL PAPER

Part 1

Short Title, Applicability and Definitions

§9–101. Short Title. This Article shall be known and may be cited as Uniform Commercial Code—Secured Transactions.

§9–102. Policy and Subject Matter of Article. (1) Except as otherwise provided in Section 9–104 on excluded transactions, this Article applies

(a) to any transaction (regardless of its form) which is intended to create a security interest in personal property or fixtures including goods, documents, instruments, general intangibles, chattel paper or accounts; and also

(b) to any sale of accounts or chattel paper.

(2) This Article applies to security interests created by contract including pledge, assignment, chattel mortgage, chattel trust, trust deed, factor's lien, equipment trust, conditional sale, trust receipt, other lien or title retention contract and lease or consignment intended as security. This Article does not apply to statutory liens except as provided in Section 9–310.

(3) The application of this Article to a security interest in a secured obligation is not affected by the fact that the obligation is itself secured by a transaction or interest to which this Article does not apply. Amended in 1972.

Note: *The adoption of this Article should be accompanied by the repeal of existing statutes dealing with conditional sales, trust receipts, factor's liens where the factor is given a non-possessory lien, chattel mortgages, crop mortgages, mortgages on railroad equipment, assignment of accounts and generally statutes regulating security interests in personal property.*

Where the state has a retail installment selling act or small loan act, that legislation should be carefully examined to determine what changes in those acts are needed to conform them to this Article. This Article primarily sets out rules defining rights of a secured party against persons dealing with the debtor; it does not prescribe regulations and controls which may be necessary to curb abuses arising in the small loan business or in the financing of consumer purchases on credit. Accordingly there is no intention to repeal existing regulatory acts in those fields by enactment or re-enactment of Article 9. See Section 9–203(4) and the Note thereto.

§9–103. Perfection of Security Interests in Multiple State Transactions. (1) Documents, instruments and ordinary goods. (a) This subsection applies to documents and instruments and to goods other than those covered by a certificate of title described in subsection (2), mobile goods described in subsection (3), and minerals described in subsection (5).

(b) Except as otherwise provided in this subsection, perfection and the effect of perfection or non-perfection of a security interest in collateral are governed by the law of the jurisdiction where the collateral is when the last event occurs on which is based the assertion that the security interest is perfected or unperfected.

(c) If the parties to a transaction creating a purchase money security interest in goods in one jurisdiction understand at the time that the security interest attaches that the goods will be kept in another jurisdiction, then the law of the other jurisdiction governs the perfection and the effect of perfection or non-perfection of the security interest from the time it attaches until thirty days after the debtor receives possession of the goods and thereafter if the goods are taken to the other jurisdiction before the end of the thirty-day period.

(d) When collateral is brought into and kept in this state while subject to a security interest perfected under the law of the jurisdiction from which the collateral was removed, the security interest remains perfected, but if action is required by Part 3 of this Article to perfect the security interest,

(i) if the action is not taken before the expiration of the period of perfection in the other jurisdiction or the end of four months after the collateral is brought into this state, whichever period first expires, the security interest becomes unperfected at the end of that period and is thereafter deemed to have been unperfected as against a person who became a purchaser after removal;

(ii) if the action is taken before the expiration of the period specified in sub-paragraph (i), the security interest continues perfected thereafter;

(iii) for the purpose of priority over a buyer of consumer goods (subsection (2) of Section 9–307), the period of the effectiveness of a filing in the jurisdiction from which the collateral is removed is governed by the rules with respect to perfection in subparagraphs (i) and (ii).

(2) Certificate of title. (a) This subsection applies to goods covered by a certificate of title issued under a statute of this state or of another jurisdiction under the law of which indication of a security interest on the certificate is required as a condition of perfection.

(b) Except as otherwise provided in this subsection, perfection and the effect of perfection or non-perfection of the security interest are governed by the law (including the conflict of laws rules) of the jurisdiction issuing the certificate until four months after the goods are removed from that jurisdiction and thereafter until the goods are registered in another jurisdiction, but in any event not beyond surrender of the certificate. After the expiration of that period, the goods are not covered by the certificate of title within the meaning of this section.

(c) Except with respect to the rights of a buyer described in the next paragraph, a security interest, perfected in another jurisdiction otherwise than by notation on a certificate of title, in goods brought into this state and thereafter covered by a certificate of title issued by this state is subject to the rules stated in paragraph (d) of subsection (1).

(d) If goods are brought into this state while a security interest therein is perfected in any manner under the law of the jurisdiction from which the goods are removed and a certificate of title is issued by this state and the certificate does not show that the goods are subject to the security interest or that they may be subject to security interests not shown on the certificate, the security interest is subordinate to the rights of a buyer of the goods who is not in the business of selling goods of that kind to the extent that he gives value and receives delivery of the goods after issuance of the certificate and without knowledge of the security interest.

(3) Accounts, general intangibles and mobile goods. (a) This subsection applies to accounts (other than an account described in subsection (5) on minerals) and general

intangibles and to goods which are mobile and which are of a type normally used in more than one jurisdiction, such as motor vehicles, trailers, rolling stock, airplanes, shipping containers, road building and construction machinery and commercial harvesting machinery and the like, if the goods are equipment or are inventory leased or held for lease by the debtor to others, and are not covered by a certificate of title described in subsection (2).

(b) The law (including the conflict of laws rules) of the jurisdiction in which the debtor is located governs the perfection and the effect of perfection or non-perfection of the security interest.

(c) If, however, the debtor is located in a jurisdiction which is not a part of the United States, and which does not provide for perfection of the security interest by filing or recording in that jurisdiction, the law of the jurisdiction in the United States in which the debtor has its major executive office in the United States governs the perfection and the effect of perfection or non-perfection of the security interest through filing. In the alternative, if the debtor is located in a jurisdiction which is not a part of the United States or Canada and the collateral is accounts or general intangibles for money due or to become due, the security interest may be perfected by notification to the account debtor. As used in this paragraph, "United States" includes its territories and possessions and the Commonwealth of Puerto Rico.

(d) A debtor shall be deemed located at his place of business if he has one, at his chief executive office if he has more than one place of business, otherwise at his residence. If, however, the debtor is a foreign air carrier under the Federal Aviation Act of 1958, as amended, it shall be deemed located at the designated office of the agent upon whom service of process may be made on behalf of the foreign air carrier.

(e) A security interest perfected under the law of the jurisdiction of the location of the debtor is perfected until the expiration of four months after a change of the debtor's location to another jurisdiction, or until perfection would have ceased by the law of the first jurisdiction, whichever period first expires. Unless perfected in the new jurisdiction before the end of that period, it becomes unperfected thereafter and is deemed to have been unperfected as against a person who became a purchaser after the change.

(4) Chattel paper. The rules stated for goods in subsection (1) apply to a possessory security interest in chattel paper. The rules stated for accounts in subsection (3) apply to a non-possessory security interest in chattel paper, but the security interest may not be perfected by notification to the account debtor.

(5) Minerals. Perfection and the effect of perfection or non-perfection of a security interest which is created by a debtor who has an interest in minerals or the like (including oil and gas) before extraction and which attaches thereto as extracted, or which attaches to an account resulting from the sale thereof at the wellhead or minehead are governed by the law (including the conflict of laws rules) of the jurisdiction wherein the wellhead or minehead is located. Amended in 1972.

§9–104. Transactions Excluded from Article. This Article does not apply

(a) to a security interest subject to any statute of the United States, to the extent that such statute governs the rights of parties to and third parties affected by transactions in particular types of property; or

(b) to a landlord's lien; or

(c) to a lien given by statute or other rule of law for services or materials except as provided in Section 9–310 on priority of such liens; or

(d) to a transfer of a claim for wages, salary or other compensation of an employee; or

(e) to a transfer by a government or governmental subdivision or agency; or

(f) to a sale of accounts of chattel paper as part of a sale of the business out of which they arose, or an assignment of accounts or chattel paper which is for the purpose of collection only, or a transfer of a right to payment under a contract to an assignee who is also to do the performance under the contract or a transfer of a single account to an assignee in whole or partial satisfaction of a preexisting indebtedness; or

(g) to a transfer of an interest in or claim in or under any policy of insurance, except as provided with respect to proceeds (Section 9–306) and priorities in proceeds (Section 9–312); or

(h) to a right represented by a judgment (other than a judgment taken on a right to payment which was collateral); or

(i) to any right of set-off; or

(j) except to the extent that provision is made for fixtures in Section 9–313, to the creation or transfer of an interest in or lien on real estate, including a lease or rents thereunder; or

(k) to a transfer in whole or in part of any claim arising out of tort; or

(l) to a transfer of an interest in any deposit account (subsection (1) of Section 9–105), except as provided with respect to proceeds (Section 9–306) and priorities in proceeds (Section 9–312).
Amended in 1972.

§9–105. Definitions and Index of Definitions. (1) In this Article unless the context otherwise requires:

(a) "Account debtor" means the person who is obligated on an account, chattel paper or general intangible;

(b) "Chattel paper" means a writing or writings which evidence both a monetary obligation and a security interest in or a lease of specific goods, but a charter or other contract involving the use or hire of a vessel is not chattel paper. When a transaction is evidenced both by such a security agreement or a lease and by an instrument or a series of instruments, the group of writings taken together constitutes chattel paper;

(c) "Collateral" means the property subject to a security interest, and includes accounts and chattel paper which have been sold;

(d) "Debtor" means the person who owes payment or other performance of the obligation secured, whether or not he owns or has rights in the collateral, and includes the seller of accounts or chattel paper. Where the debtor and the owner of the collateral are not the same person, the term "debtor" means the owner of the collateral in any provision of the Article dealing with the collateral, the obligor in any provision dealing with the obligation, and may include both where the context so requires;

(e) "Deposit account" means a demand, time, savings, passbook or like account maintained with a bank, savings and loan association, credit union or like organization, other than an account evidenced by a certificate of deposit;

(f) "Document" means document of title as defined in the general definitions of Article 1 (Section 1–201), and a receipt of the kind described in subsection (2) of Section 7–201;

(g) "Encumbrance" includes real estate mortgages and other liens on real estate and all other rights in real estate that are not ownership interests;

(h) "Goods" includes all things which are movable at the time the security interest attaches or which are fixtures (Section 9–313), but does not include money, documents, instruments, accounts, chattel paper, general intangibles, or minerals or the like (including oil and gas) before extraction. "Goods" also includes standing timber which is to be cut and removed under a conveyance or contract for sale, the unborn young of animals, and growing crops;

(i) "Instrument" means a negotiable instrument (defined in Section 3–104), or a security (defined in Section 8–102) or any other writing which evidences a right to the payment of money and is not itself a security agreement or lease and is of a type which is in ordinary course of business transferred by delivery with any necessary indorsement or assignment;

(j) "Mortgage" means a consensual interest created by a real estate mortgage, a trust deed on real estate, or the like;

(k) An advance is made "pursuant to commitment" if the secured party has bound himself to make it, whether or not a subsequent event of default or other event not within his control has relieved or may relieve him from his obligation;

(l) "Security agreement" means an agreement which creates or provides for a security interest;

(m) "Secured party" means a lender, seller or other person in whose favor there is a security interest, including a person to whom accounts or chattel paper have been sold. When the holders of obligations issued under an indenture of trust, equipment trust agreement or the like are represented by a trustee or other person, the representative is the secured party;

(n) "Transmitting utility" means any person primarily engaged in the railroad, street railway or trolley bus business, the electric or electronics communications transmission business, the transmission of goods by pipeline, or the transmission or the production and transmission of electricity, steam, gas or water, or the provision of sewer service.

(2) Other definitions applying to this Article and the sections in which they appear are:

"Account". Section 9–106.
"Attach". Section 9–203.
"Construction mortgage". Section 9–313(1).
"Consumer goods". Section 9–109(1).
"Equipment". Section 9–109(2).
"Farm products". Section 9–109(3).
"Fixture". Section 9–313(1).
"Fixture filing". Section 9–313(1).
"General intangibles". Section 9–106.
"Inventory". Section 9–109(4).
"Lien creditor". Section 9–301(3).
"Proceeds". Section 9–306(1).
"Purchase money security interest". Section 9–107.
"United States". Section 9–103.

(3) The following definitions in other Articles apply to this Article:

"Check". Section 3–104.
"Contract for sale". Section 2–106.
"Holder in due course". Section 3–302.
"Note". Section 3–104.
"Sale". Section 2–106.

(4) In addition Article 1 contains general definitions and principles of construction and interpretation applicable throughout this Article. Amended in 1966, 1972.

§9–106. Definitions: "Account"; "General Intangibles." "Account" means any right to payment for goods sold or leased or for services rendered which is not evidenced by an instrument or chattel paper, whether or not it has been earned by performance. "General intangibles" means any personal property (including things in action) other than goods, accounts, chattel paper, documents, instruments, and money. All rights to payment earned or unearned under a charter or other contract involving the use or hire of a vessel and all rights incident to the charter or contract are accounts. Amended in 1966, 1972.

§9–107. Definitions: "Purchase Money Security Interest." A security interest is a "purchase money security interest" to the extent that it is

(a) taken or retained by the seller of the collateral to secure all or part of its price; or

(b) taken by a person who by making advances or incurring an obligation gives value to enable the debtor to acquire rights in or the use of collateral if such value is in fact so used.

§9–108. When After-Acquired Collateral Not Security for Antecedent Debt. Where a secured party makes an advance, incurs an obligation, releases a perfected security interest, or otherwise gives new value which is to be secured in whole or in part by after-acquired property his security interest in the after-acquired collateral shall be deemed to be taken for new value and not as security for an antecedent debt if the debtor acquires his rights in such collateral either in the ordinary course of his business or under a contract of purchase made pursuant to the security agreement within a reasonable time after new value is given.

§9–109. Classification of Goods; "Consumer Goods"; "Equipment"; "Farm Products"; "Inventory." Goods are

(1) "consumer goods" if they are used or bought for use primarily for personal, family or household purposes;

(2) "equipment" if they are used or bought for use primarily in business (including farming or a profession) or by a debtor who is a non-profit organization or a governmental subdivision or agency or if the goods are not included in the definitions of inventory, farm products or consumer goods;

(3) "farm products" if they are crops or livestock or supplies used or produced in farming operations or if they are products of crops or livestock in their unmanufactured states (such as ginned cotton, wool-clip, maple syrup, milk and eggs), and if they are in the possession of a debtor engaged in raising, fattening, grazing or other farming operations. If goods are farm products they are neither equipment nor inventory;

(4) "inventory" if they are held by a person who holds them for sale or lease or to be furnished under contracts of service or if he has so furnished them, or if they are raw materials, work in process or materials used or consumed in a business. Inventory of a person is not to be classified as his equipment.

§9–110. Sufficiency of Description. For the purposes of this Article any description of personal property or real estate is sufficient whether or not it is specific if it reasonably identifies what is described.

§9–111. Applicability of Bulk Transfer Laws. The creation of a security interest is not a bulk transfer under Article 6 (see Section 6–103).

§9–112. Where Collateral Is Not Owned by Debtor. Unless otherwise agreed, when a secured party knows that collateral is owned by a person who is not the debtor, the owner of the collateral is entitled to receive from the secured party any surplus under Section 9–502(2) or under Section 9–504(1), and is not liable for the debt or for any deficiency after resale, and he has the same right as the debtor

(a) to receive statements under Section 9–208;

(b) to receive notice of and to object to a secured party's proposal to retain the collateral in satisfaction of the indebtedness under Section 9–505;

(c) to redeem the collateral under Section 9–506;

(d) to obtain injunctive or other relief under Section 9–507(1); and

(e) to recover losses caused to him under Section 9–208(2).

§9–113. Security Interests Arising under Article on Sales. A security interest arising solely under the Article on Sales (Article 2) is subject to the provisions of this Article except that to the extent that and so long as the debtor does not have or does not lawfully obtain possession of the goods

(a) no security agreement is necessary to make the security interest enforceable; and

(b) no filing is required to perfect the security interest; and

(c) the rights of the secured party on default by the debtor are governed by the Article on Sales (Article 2).

§9–114. Consignment. (1) A person who delivers goods under a consignment which is not a security interest and who would be required to file under this Article by paragraph (3) (c) of Section 2–326 has priority over a secured party who is or becomes a creditor of the consignee and who would have a perfected security interest in the goods if they were the property of the consignee, and also has priority with respect to identifiable cash proceeds received on or before delivery of the goods to a buyer, if

(a) the consignor complies with the filing provision of the Article on Sales with respect to consignments (paragraph (3) (c) of Section 2–326) before the consignee receives possession of the goods; and

(b) the consignor gives notification in writing to the holder of the security interest if the holder has filed a financing statement covering the same types of goods before the date of the filing made by the consignor; and

(c) the holder of the security interest receives the notification within five years before the consignee receives possession of the goods; and

(d) the notification states that the consignor expects to deliver goods on consignment to the consignee, describing the goods by item or type.

(2) In the case of a consignment which is not a security interest and in which the requirements of the preceding subsection have not been met, a person who delivers goods to another is subordinate to a person who would have a perfected security interest in the goods if they were the property of the debtor. Added in 1972.

Part 2

*Validity of Security Agreement and Rights
of Parties Thereto*

§9–201. General Validity of Security Agreement. Except as otherwise provided by this act a security agreement is effective according to its terms between the parties, against purchasers of the collateral and against creditors. Nothing in this Article validates any charge or practice illegal under any statute or regulation thereunder governing usury, small loans, retail installment sales, or the like, or extends the application of any such statute or regulation to any transaction not otherwise subject thereto.

§9–202. Title to Collateral Immaterial. Each provision of this Article with regard to rights, obligations and remedies applies whether title to collateral is in the secured party or in the debtor.

§9–203. Attachment and Enforceability of Security Interest; Proceeds; Formal Requisites. (1) Subject to the provisions of Section 4–208 on the security interest of a collecting bank and Section 9–113 on a security interest arising under the Article on Sales, a security interest is not enforceable against the debtor or third parties with respect to the collateral and does not attach unless

(a) the collateral is in the possession of the secured party pursuant to agreement, or the debtor has signed a security agreement which contains a description of the collateral and in addition, when the security interest covers crops growing or to be grown or timber to be cut, a description of the land concerned; and

(b) value has been given; and

(c) the debtor has rights in the collateral.

(2) A security interest attaches when it becomes enforceable against the debtor with respect to the collateral. Attachment occurs as soon as all of the events specified in subsection (1) have taken place unless explicit agreement postpones the time of attaching.

(3) Unless otherwise agreed a security agreement gives the secured party the rights to proceeds provided by Section 9–306.

(4) A transaction; although subject to this Article, is also subject to . . . .*, and in the case of conflict between the provisions of this Article and any such statute, the provisions of such statute control. Failure to comply with any applicable statute has only the effect which is specified therein. Amended in 1972.

Note: *At * in subsection (4) insert reference to any local statute regulating: small loans, retail installment sales and the like.*

The foregoing subsection (4) is designed to make it clear that certain transactions, although subject to this Article, must also comply with other applicable legislation.

This Article is designed to regulate all the "security" aspects of transactions within its scope. There is, however, much regulatory legislation, particularly in the consumer field, which supplements this Article and should not be repealed by its enactment. Examples are small loan acts, retail installment selling acts and the like. Such acts may provide for licensing and rate regulation and may prescribe particular forms of contract. Such provisions should remain in force despite the enactment of this Article. On the other hand if a retail installment selling act contains provisions on filing, rights on default, etc., such provisions should be repealed as inconsistent with this Article except that inconsistent provisions as to deficiencies, penalties, etc., in the Uniform Consumer Credit Code and other recent related legislation should remain because those statutes were drafted after the substantial enactment of the Article and with the intention of modifying certain provisions of this Article as to consumer credit.

§9–204. After-Acquired Property; Future Advances. (1) Except as provided in subsection (2), a security agreement may provide that any or all obligations covered by the security agreement are to be secured by after-acquired collateral.

(2) No security interest attaches under an after-acquired property clause to consumer goods other than accessions (Section 9–314) when given as additional security unless the debtor acquires rights in them within ten days after the secured party gives value.

(3) Obligations covered by a security agreement may include future advances or other value whether or not the advances or value are given pursuant to commitment (subsection (1) of Section 9–105). Amended in 1972.

§9–205. Use or Disposition of Collateral without Accounting Permissible. A security interest is not invalid or fraudulent against creditors by reason of liberty in the debtor to use, commingle or dispose of all or part of the collateral (including returned or repossessed goods) or to collect or compromise accounts or chattel paper, or to accept the return of goods or make repossessions, or to use, commingle or dispose of proceeds, or by reason of the failure of the secured party to require the debtor to account for proceeds or replace collateral. This section does not relax the requirements of possession where perfection of a security interest depends upon possession of the collateral by the secured party or by a bailee. Amended in 1972.

§9–206. Agreement Not to Assert Defenses against Assignee; Modification of Sales Warranties Where Security Agreement Exists. (1) Subject to any statute or decision which establishes a different rule for buyers or lessees of consumer goods, an agreement by a buyer or lessee that he will not assert against an assignee any claim or defense which he may have against the seller or lessor is enforceable by an assignee who takes his assignment for value, in good faith and without notice of a claim or defense, except as to defenses of a type which may be asserted against a holder in due course of a negotiable instrument under the Article on Commercial Paper (Article 3). A buyer who as part of one transaction signs both a negotiable instrument and a security agreement makes such an agreement.

(2) When a seller retains a purchase money security interest in goods the Article on Sales (Article 2) governs the sale and any disclaimer, limitation or modification of the seller's warranties. Amended in 1962.

§9–207. Rights and Duties When Collateral Is in Secured Party's Possession. (1) A secured party must use reasonable care in the custody and preservation of collateral in his possession. In the case of an instrument or chattel paper reasonable care includes taking necessary steps to preserve rights against prior parties unless otherwise agreed.

(2) Unless otherwise agreed, when collateral is in the secured party's possession

(a) reasonable expenses (including the cost of any insurance and payment of taxes or other charges) incurred in the custody, preservation, use or operation of the collateral are chargeable to the debtor and are secured by the collateral;

(b) the risk of accidental loss or damage is on the debtor to the extent of any deficiency in any effective insurance coverage;

(c) the secured party may hold as additional security any increase or profits (except money) received from the collateral, but money so received, unless remitted to the debtor, shall be applied in reduction of the secured obligation;

(d) the secured party must keep the collateral identifiable but fungible collateral may be commingled;

(e) the secured party may repledge the collateral upon terms which do not impair the debtor's right to redeem it.

(3) A secured party is liable for any loss caused by his failure to meet any obligation imposed by the preceding subsections but does not lose his security interest.

(4) A secured party may use or operate the collateral for the purpose of preserving the collateral or its value or pursuant to the order of a court of appropriate jurisdiction or, except in the case of consumer goods, in the manner and to the extent provided in the security agreement.

§9–208. Request for Statement of Account or List of Collateral. (1) A debtor may sign a statement indicating what he believes to be the aggregate amount of unpaid indebtedness as of a specified date and may send it to the secured party with a request that the statement be approved or corrected and returned to the debtor. When the security agreement or any other record kept by the secured party identifies the collateral a debtor may similarly request the secured party to approve or correct a list of the collateral.

(2) The secured party must comply with such a request within two weeks after receipt by sending a written correction or approval. If the secured party claims a security interest in all of a particular type of collateral owned by the debtor he may indicate that fact in his reply and need not approve or correct an itemized list of such collateral. If the secured party without reasonable excuse fails to comply he is liable for any loss caused to the debtor thereby; and if the debtor has properly included in his request a good faith statement of the obligation or a list of the collateral or both the secured party may claim a security interest only as shown in the statement against persons misled by his failure to comply. If he no longer has an interest in the obligation or collateral at the time the request

is received he must disclose the name and address of any successor in interest known to him and he is liable for any loss caused to the debtor as a result of failure to disclose. A successor in interest is not subject to this section until a request is received by him.

(3) A debtor is entitled to such a statement once every six months without charge. The secured party may require payments of a charge not exceeding $10 for each additional statement furnished.

Part 3

Rights of Third Parties; Perfected and
Unperfected Security Interests;
Rules of Priority

§9–301. Persons Who Take Priority over Unperfected Security Interests; Rights of "Lien Creditor." (1) Except as otherwise provided in subsection (2), an unperfected security interest is subordinate to the rights of

(a) persons entitled to priority under Section 9–312;

(b) a person who becomes a lien creditor before the security interest is perfected;

(c) in the case of goods, instruments, documents, and chattel paper, a person who is not a secured party and who is a transferee in bulk or other buyer not in ordinary course of business or is a buyer of farm products in ordinary course of business, to the extent that he gives value and receives delivery of the collateral without knowledge of the security interest and before it is perfected;

(d) in the case of accounts and general intangibles, a person who is not a secured party and who is a transferee to the extent that he gives value without knowledge of the security interest and before it is perfected.

(2) If the secured party files with respect to a purchase money security interest before or within ten days after the debtor receives possession of the collateral, he takes priority over the rights of a transferee in bulk or of a lien creditor which arise between the time the security interest attaches and the time of filing.

(3) A "lien creditor" means a creditor who has acquired a lien on the property involved by attachment, levy or the like and includes an assignee for benefit of creditors from the time of assignment, and a trustee in bankruptcy from the date of the filing of the petition or a receiver in equity from the time of appointment.

(4) A person who becomes a lien creditor while a security interest is perfected takes subject to the security interest only to the extent that it secures advances made before he becomes a lien creditor or within 45 days thereafter or made without knowledge of the lien or pursuant to a commitment entered into without knowledge of the lien. Amended in 1972.

§9–302. When Filing Is Required to Perfect Security Interest; Security Interests to Which Filing Provisions of This Article Do Not Apply. (1) A financing statement must be filed to perfect all security interests except the following:

(a) a security interest in collateral in possession of the secured party under Section 9–305;

(b) a security interest temporarily perfected in instruments or documents without delivery under Section 9–304 or in proceeds for a 10 day period under Section 9–306;

(c) a security interest created by an assignment of a beneficial interest in a trust or a decedent's estate;

(d) a purchase money security interest in consumer goods; but filing is required for a motor vehicle required to be registered; and fixture filing is required for priority over conflicting interests in fixtures to the extent provided in Section 9–313;

(e) an assignment of accounts which does not alone or in conjunction with other assignments to the same assignee transfer a significant part of the outstanding accounts of the assignor;

(f) a security interest of a collecting bank (Section 4–208) or arising under the Article on Sales (see Section 9–113) or covered in subsection (3) of this section;

(g) an assignment for the benefit of all the creditors of the transferor, and subsequent transfers by the assignee thereunder.

(2) If a secured party assigns a perfected security interest, no filing under this Article is required in order to continue the perfected status of the security interest against creditors of and transferees from the original debtor.

(3) The filing of a financing statement otherwise required by this Article is not necessary or effective to perfect a security interest in property subject to

(a) a statute or treaty of the United States which provides for a national or international registration or a national or international certificate of title or which specifies a place of filing different from that specified in this Article for filing of the security interest; or

(b) the following statutes of this state; [list any certificate of title statute covering automobiles, trailers, mobile homes, boats, farm tractors, or the like, and any central filing statute*.]; but during any period in which collateral is inventory held for sale by a person who is in the business of selling goods of that kind, the filing provisions of this Article (Part 4) apply to a security interest in that collateral created by him as debtor; or

(c) a certificate of title statute of another jurisdiction under the law of which indication of a security interest on the certificate is required as a condition of perfection (subsection (2) of Section 9–103).

(4) Compliance with a statute or treaty described in subsection (3) is equivalent to the filing of a financing statement under this Article, and a security interest in property subject to the statute or treaty can be perfected only by compliance therewith except as provided in Section 9–103 on multiple state transactions. Duration and renewal of perfection of a security interest perfected by compliance with the statute or treaty are governed by the provisions of the statute or treaty; in other respects the security interest is subject to this Article. Amended in 1972.

*Note: *It is recommended that the provisions of certificate of title acts for perfection of security interests by notation on the certificates should be amended to exclude coverage of inventory held for sale.*

§9–303. When Security Interest Is Perfected; Continuity of Perfection. (1) A security interest is perfected when it has attached and when all of the applicable steps required for perfection have been taken. Such steps are specified in Sections 9–302, 9–304, 9–305 and 9–306. If such steps are taken before the security interest attaches, it is perfected at the time when it attaches.

(2) If a security interest is originally perfected in any way permitted under this Article and is subsequently perfected in some other way under this Article, without an intermediate period when it was unperfected, the security interest shall be deemed to be perfected continuously for the purposes of this Article.

§9–304. Perfection of Security Interest in Instruments, Documents, and Goods Covered by Documents; Perfection by Permissive Filing; Temporary Perfection without Filing or Transfer of Possession. (1) A security interest in chattel paper or negotiable documents may be perfected by filing. A security interest in money or instruments (other than instruments which constitute part of chattel paper) can be perfected only by the secured party's taking possession, except as provided in subsections (4) and (5) of this section and subsections (2) and (3) of Section 9–306 on proceeds.

(2) During the period that goods are in the possession of the issuer of a negotiable document therefor, a security interest in the goods is perfected by perfecting a security interest in the document, and any security interest in the goods otherwise perfected during such period is subject thereto.

(3) A security interest in goods in the possession of a bailee other than one who has issued a negotiable document therefor is perfected by issuance of a document in the name of the secured party or by the bailee's receipt of notification of the secured party's interest or by filing as to the goods.

(4) A security interest in instruments or negotiable documents is perfected without filing or the taking of possession for a period of 21 days from the time it attaches to the extent that it arises for new value given under a written security agreement.

(5) A security interest remains perfected for a period of 21 days without filing where a secured party having a perfected security interest in an instrument, a negotiable document or goods in possession of a bailee other than one who has issued a negotiable document therefor

(a) makes available to the debtor the goods or documents representing the goods for the purpose of ultimate sale or exchange or for the purpose of loading, unloading, storing, shipping, transshipping, manufacturing, processing or otherwise dealing with them in a manner preliminary to their sale or exchange, but priority between conflicting security interests in the goods is subject to subsection (3) of Section 9–312; or

(b) delivers the instrument to the debtor for the purpose of ultimate sale or exchange or of presentation, collection, renewal or registration of transfer.

(6) After the 21 day period in subsections (4) and (5) perfection depends upon compliance with applicable provisions of this Article. Amended in 1972.

§9–305. When Possession by Secured Party Perfects Security Interest without Filing. A security interest in letters of credit and advices of credit (subsection (2) (a) of Section 5–116), goods, instruments, money, negotiable documents or chattel paper may be perfected by the secured party's taking possession of the collateral. If such collateral other than goods covered by a negotiable document is held by a bailee, the secured party is deemed to have possession from the time the bailee receives notification of the secured party's interest. A security interest is perfected by possession from the time possession is taken without relation back and continues only so long as possession is retained, unless otherwise specified in this Article. The security interest may be otherwise perfected as provided in this Article before or after the period of possession by the secured party. Amended in 1972.

§9–306. "Proceeds"; Secured Party's Rights on Disposition of Collateral. (1) "Proceeds" includes whatever is received upon the sale, exchange, collection or other disposition of collateral or proceeds. Insurance payable by reason of loss or damage to the collateral is proceeds, except to the extent that it is payable to a person other than a party to the security agreement. Money, checks, deposit accounts, and the like are "cash proceeds". All other proceeds are "non-cash proceeds."

(2) Except where this Article otherwise provides, a security interest continues in collateral notwithstanding sale, exchange or other disposition thereof unless the disposition was authorized by the secured party in the security agreement or otherwise, and also continues in any identifiable proceeds including collections received by the debtor.

(3) The security interest in proceeds is a continuously perfected security interest if

the interest in the original collateral was perfected but it ceases to be a perfected security interest and becomes unperfected ten days after receipt of the proceeds by the debtor unless

(a) a filed financing statement covers the original collateral and the proceeds are collateral in which a security interest may be perfected by filing in the office or offices where the financing statement has been filed and, if the proceeds are acquired with cash proceeds, the description of collateral in the financing statement indicates the types of property constituting the proceeds; or

(b) a filed financing statement covers the original collateral and the proceeds are identifiable cash proceeds; or

(c) the security interest in the proceeds is perfected before the expiration of the ten day period.

Except as provided in this section, a security interest in proceeds can be perfected only by the methods or under the circumstances permitted in this Article for original collateral of the same type.

(4) In the event of insolvency proceedings instituted by or against a debtor, a secured party with a perfected security interest in proceeds has a perfected security interest only in the following proceeds:

(a) in identifiable non-cash proceeds and in separate deposit accounts containing only proceeds;

(b) in identifiable cash proceeds in the form of money which is neither commingled with other money nor deposited in a deposit account prior to the insolvency proceedings;

(c) in identifiable cash proceeds in the form of checks and the like which are not deposited in a deposit account prior to the insolvency proceedings; and

(d) in all cash and deposit accounts of the debtor in which proceeds have been commingled with other funds, but the perfected security interest under this paragraph (d) is

(i) subject to any right to set-off; and

(ii) limited to an amount not greater than the amount of any cash proceeds received by the debtor within ten days before the institution of the insolvency proceedings less the sum of (I) the payments to the secured party on account of cash proceeds received by the debtor during such period and (II) the cash proceeds received by the debtor during such period to which the secured party is entitled under paragraphs (a) through (c) of this subsection (4).

(5) If a sale of goods results in an account or chattel paper which is transferred by the seller to a secured party, and if the goods are returned to or are repossessed by the seller or the secured party, the following rules determine priorities:

(a) If the goods were collateral at the time of sale, for an indebtedness of the seller which is still unpaid, the original security interest attaches again to the goods and continues as a perfected security interest if it was perfected at the time when the goods were sold. If the security interest was originally perfected by a filing which is still effective, nothing further is required to continue the perfected status; in any other case, the secured party must take possession of the returned or repossessed goods or must file.

(b) An unpaid transferee of the chattel paper has a security interest in the goods against the transferor. Such security interest is prior to a security interest asserted under paragraph (a) to the extent that the transferee of the chattel paper was entitled to priority under Section 9–308.

(c) An unpaid transferee of the account has a security interest in the goods against the transferor. Such security interest is subordinate to a security interest asserted under paragraph (a).

(d) A security interest of an unpaid transferee asserted under paragraph (b) or (c) must be perfected for protection against creditors of the transferor and purchasers of the returned or repossessed goods.

Amended in 1972.

§9–307. Protection of Buyers of Goods. (1) A buyer in ordinary course of business (subsection (9) of Section 1–201) other than a person buying farm products from a person engaged in farming operations takes free of a security interest created by his seller even though the security interest is perfected and even though the buyer knows of its existence.

(2) In the case of consumer goods, a buyer takes free of a security interest even though perfected if he buys without knowledge of the security interest, for value and for his own personal, family or household purposes unless prior to the purchase the secured party has filed a financing statement covering such goods.

(3) A buyer other than a buyer in ordinary course of business (subsection (1) of this section) takes free of a security interest to the extent that it secures future advances made after the secured party acquires knowledge of the purchase, or more than 45 days after the purchase, whichever first occurs, unless made pursuant to a commitment entered into without knowledge of the purchase and before the expiration of the 45 day period. Amended in 1972.

§9–308. Purchase of Chattel Paper and Instruments. A purchaser of chattel paper or an instrument who gives new value and takes possession of it in the ordinary course of his business has priority over a security interest in the chattel paper or instrument

(a) which is perfected under Section 9–304 (permissive filing and temporary perfection) or under Section 9–306 (perfection as to proceeds) if he acts without knowledge that the specific paper or instrument is subject to a security interest; or

(b) which is claimed merely as proceeds of inventory subject to a security interest (Section 9–306) even though he knows that the specific paper or instrument is subject to the security interest.

Amended in 1972.

§9–309. Protection of Purchasers of Instruments and Documents. Nothing in this Article limits the rights of a holder in due course of a negotiable instrument (Section 3–302) or a holder to whom a negotiable document of title has been duly negotiated (Section 7–501) or a bona fide purchaser of a security (Section 8–301) and such holders or purchasers take priority over an earlier security interest even though perfected. Filing under this Article does not constitute notice of the security interest to such holders or purchasers.

§9–310. Priority of Certain Liens Arising by Operation of Law. When a person in the ordinary course of his business furnishes services or materials with respect to goods subject to a security interest, a lien upon goods in the possession of such person given by statute or rule of law for such materials or services takes priority over a perfected security interest unless the lien is statutory and the statute expressly provides otherwise.

§9–311. Alienability of Debtor's Rights: Judicial Process. The debtor's rights in collateral may be voluntarily or involuntarily transferred (by way of sale, creation of a security interest, attachment, levy, garnishment or other judicial process) notwithstanding a provision in the security agreement prohibiting any transfer or making the transfer constitute a default.

§9–312. Priorities among Conflicting Security Interests in the Same Collateral. (1) The rules of priority stated in other sections of this Part and in the following sections shall govern when applicable: Section 4–208 with respect to the security interests of collecting banks in items being collected, accompanying documents and proceeds; Section 9–103 on security interests related to other jurisdictions; Section 9–114 on consignments.

(2) A perfected security interest in crops for new value given to enable the debtor to produce the crops during the production season and given not more than three months before the crops become growing crops by planting or otherwise takes priority over an earlier perfected security interest to the extent that such earlier interest secures obligations due more than six months before the crops become growing crops by planting or otherwise, even though the person giving new value had knowledge of the earlier security interest.

(3) A perfected purchase money security interest in inventory has priority over a conflicting security interest in the same inventory and also has priority in identifiable cash proceeds received on or before the delivery of the inventory to a buyer if

(a) the purchase money security interest is perfected at the time the debtor receives possession of the inventory; and

(b) the purchase money secured party gives notification in writing to the holder of the conflicting security interest if the holder had filed a financing statement covering the same types of inventory (i) before the date of the filing made by the purchase money secured party, or (ii) before the beginning of the 21 day period where the purchase money security interest is temporarily perfected without filing or possession (subsection (5) of Section 9–304); and

(c) the holder of the conflicting security interest receives the notification within five years before the debtor receives possession of the inventory; and

(d) the notification states that the person giving the notice has or expects to acquire a purchase money security interest in inventory of the debtor, describing such inventory by item or type.

(4) A purchase money security interest in collateral other than inventory has priority over a conflicting security interest in the same collateral or its proceeds if the purchase money security interest is perfected at the time the debtor receives possession of the collateral or within ten days thereafter.

(5) In all cases not governed by other rules stated in this section (including cases of purchase money security interests which do not qualify for the special priorities set forth in subsections (3) and (4) of this section), priority between conflicting security interests in the same collateral shall be determined according to the following rules:

(a) Conflicting security interests rank according to priority in time of filing or perfection. Priority dates from the time a filing is first made covering the collateral or the time the security interest is first perfected, whichever is earlier, provided that there is no period thereafter when there is neither filing nor perfection.

(b) So long as conflicting security interests are unperfected, the first to attach has priority.

(6) For the purposes of subsection (5) a date of filing or perfection as to collateral is also a date of filing or perfection as to proceeds.

(7) If future advances are made while a security interest is perfected by filing or the taking of possession, the security interest has the same priority for the purposes of subsection (5) with respect to the future advances as it does with respect to the first advance. If a commitment is made before or while the security interest is so perfected, the security interest has the same priority with respect to advances made pursuant thereto. In other cases a perfected security interest has priority from the date the advance is made. Amended in 1972.

§9–313. Priority of Security Interests in Fixtures. (1) In this section and in the provisions of Part 4 of this Article referring to fixture filing, unless the context otherwise requires

(a) goods are "fixtures" when they become so related to particular real estate that an interest in them arises under real estate law

(b) a "fixture filing" is the filing in the office where a mortgage on the real estate would be filed or recorded of a financing statement covering goods which are or are to become fixtures and conforming to the requirements of subsection (5) of Section 9–402

(c) a mortgage is a "construction mortgage" to the extent that it secures an obligation incurred for the construction of an improvement on land including the acquisition cost of the land, if the recorded writing so indicates.

(2) A security interest under this Article may be created in goods which are fixtures or may continue in goods which become fixtures, but no security interest exists under this Article in ordinary building materials incorporated into an improvement on land.

(3) This Article does not prevent creation of an encumbrance upon fixtures pursuant to real estate law.

(4) A perfected security interest in fixtures has priority over the conflicting interest of an encumbrancer or owner of the real estate where

(a) the security interest is a purchase money security interest, the interest of the encumbrancer or owner arises before the goods become fixtures, the security interest is perfected by a fixture filing before the goods become fixtures or within ten days thereafter, and the debtor has an interest of record in the real estate or is in possession of the real estate; or

(b) the security interest is perfected by a fixture filing before the interest of the encumbrancer or owner is of record, the security interest has priority over any conflicting interest of a predecessor in title of the encumbrancer or owner, and the debtor has an interest of record in the real estate or is in possession of the real estate; or

(c) the fixtures are readily removable factory or office machines or readily removable replacements of domestic appliances which are consumer goods, and before the goods become fixtures the security interest is perfected by any method permitted by this Article; or

(d) the conflicting interest is a lien on the real estate obtained by legal or equitable proceedings after the security interest was perfected by any method permitted by this Article.

(5) A security interest in fixtures, whether or not perfected, has priority over the conflicting interest of an encumbrancer or owner of the real estate where

(a) the encumbrancer or owner has consented in writing to the security interest or has disclaimed an interest in the goods as fixtures; or

(b) the debtor has a right to remove the goods as against the encumbrancer or owner. If the debtor's right terminates, the priority of the security interest continues for a reasonable time.

(6) Notwithstanding paragraph (a) of subsection (4) but otherwise subject to subsections (4) and (5), a security interest in fixtures is subordinate to a construction mortgage recorded before the goods become fixtures if the goods become fixtures before the completion of the construction. To the extent that it is given to refinance a construction mortgage, a mortgage has this priority to the same extent as the construction mortgage.

(7) In cases not within the preceding subsections, a security interest in fixtures is subordinate to the conflicting interest of an encumbrancer or owner of the related real estate who is not the debtor.

(8) When the secured party has priority over all owners and encumbrancers of the real estate, he may, on default, subject to the provisions of Part 5, remove his collateral from the real estate but he must reimburse any encumbrancer or owner of the real estate who is not the debtor and who has not otherwise agreed for the cost of repair of any physical injury, but not for any diminution in value of the real estate caused by the absence

of the goods removed or by any necessity of replacing them. A person entitled to reimbursement may refuse permission to remove until the secured party gives adequate security for the performance of this obligation. Amended in 1972.

§9–314. Accessions. (1) A security interest in goods which attaches before they are installed in or affixed to other goods takes priority as to the goods installed or affixed (called in this section "accessions") over the claims of all persons to the whole except as stated in subsection (3) and subject to Section 9–315(1).

(2) A security interest which attaches to goods after they become part of a whole is valid against all persons subsequently acquiring interests in the whole except as stated in subsection (3) but is invalid against any person with an interest in the whole at the time the security interest attaches to the goods who has not in writing consented to the security interest or disclaimed an interest in the goods as part of the whole.

(3) The security interests described in subsections (1) and (2) do not take priority over

(a) a subsequent purchaser for value of any interest in the whole; or

(b) a creditor with a lien on the whole subsequently obtained by judicial proceedings; or

(c) a creditor with a prior perfected security interest in the whole to the extent that he makes subsequent advances

if the subsequent purchase is made, the lien by judicial proceedings obtained or the subsequent advance under the prior perfected security interest is made or contracted for without knowledge of the security interest and before it is perfected. A purchaser of the whole at a foreclosure sale other than the holder of a perfected security interest purchasing at his own foreclosure sale is a subsequent purchaser within this section.

(4) When under subsections (1) or (2) and (3) a secured party has an interest in accessions which has priority over the claims of all persons who have interests in the whole, he may on default subject to the provisions of Part 5 remove his collateral from the whole but he must reimburse any encumbrancer or owner of the whole who is not the debtor and who has not otherwise agreed for the cost of repair of any physical injury but not for any diminution in value of the whole caused by the absence of the goods removed or by any necessity for replacing them. A person entitled to reimbursement may refuse permission to remove until the secured party gives adequate security for the performance of this obligation.

§9–315. Priority When Goods Are Commingled or Processed. (1) If a security interest in goods was perfected and subsequently the goods or a part thereof have become part of a product or mass, the security interest continues in the product or mass if

(a) the goods are so manufactured, processed, assembled or commingled that their identity is lost in the product or mass; or

(b) a financing statement covering the original goods also covers the product into which the goods have been manufactured, processed or assembled.

In a case to which paragraph (b) applies, no separate security interest in that part of the original goods which has been manufactured, processed or assembled into the product may be claimed under Section 9–314.

(2) When under subsection (1) more than one security interest attaches to the product or mass, they rank equally according to the ratio that the cost of the goods to which each interest originally attached bears to the cost of the total product or mass.

§9–316. Priority Subject to Subordination. Nothing in this Article prevents subordination by agreement by any person entitled to priority.

§9–317. Secured Party Not Obligated on Contract of Debtor. The mere existence of a security interest or authority given to the debtor to dispose of or use collateral does not impose contract or tort liability upon the secured party for the debtor's acts or omissions.

§9–318. Defenses against Assignee; Modification of Contract after Notification of Assignment; Term Prohibiting Assignment Ineffective; Identification and Proof of Assignment (1) Unless an account debtor has made an enforceable agreement not to assert defenses or claims arising out of a sale as provided in Section 9–206 the rights of an assignee are subject to

(a) all the terms of the contract between the account debtor and assignor and any defense or claim arising therefrom; and

(b) any other defense or claim of the account debtor against the assignor which accrues before the account debtor receives notification of the assignment.

(2) So far as the right to payment or a part thereof under an assigned contract has not been fully earned by performance, and notwithstanding notification of the assignment, any modification of or substitution for the contract made in good faith and in accordance with reasonable commercial standards is effective against an assignee unless the account debtor has otherwise agreed but the assignee acquires corresponding rights under the modified or substituted contract. The assignment may provide that such modification or substitution is a breach by the assignor.

(3) The account debtor is authorized to pay the assignor until the account debtor receives notification that the amount due or to become due has been assigned and that payment is to be made to the assignee. A notification which does not reasonably identify the rights assigned is ineffective. If requested by the account debtor, the assignee must seasonably furnish reasonable proof that the assignment has been made and unless he does so the account debtor may pay the assignor.

(4) A term in any contract between an account debtor and an assignor is ineffective if it prohibits assignment of an account or prohibits creation of a security interest in a general intangible for money due or to become due or requires the account debtor's consent to such assignment or security interest. Amended in 1972.

Part 4

Filing

§9–401. Place of Filing; Erroneous Filing; Removal of Collateral

First Alternative Subsection (1)

(1) The proper place to file in order to perfect a security interest is as follows:

(a) when the collateral is timber to be cut or is minerals or the like (including oil and gas) or accounts subject to subsection (5) of Section 9–103, or when the financing statement is filed as a fixture filing (Section 9–313) and the collateral is goods which are or are to become fixtures, then in the office where a mortgage on the real estate would be filed or recorded;

(b) in all other cases, in the office of the [Secretary of State].

Second Alternative Subsection (1)

(1) The proper place to file in order to perfect a security interest is as follows:

(a) when the collateral is equipment used in farming operations, or farm products, or accounts or general intangibles arising from or relating to the sale of farm products by a farmer, or consumer goods, then in the office of the . . . . in the county of the debtor's residence or if the debtor is not a resident of this state then in the office of the . . . . in the county where the goods are kept, and in addition when the collateral is crops growing or to be grown in the office of the . . . . in the county where the land is located;

(b) when the collateral is timber to be cut or is minerals or the like (including oil and gas) or accounts subject to subsection (5) of Section 9–103, or when the financing statement is filed as a fixture filing (Section 9–313) and the collateral is goods which are or are to become fixtures, then in the office where a mortgage on the real estate would be filed or recorded;

(c) in all other cases, in the office of the [Secretary of State].

Third Alternative Subsection (1)

(1) The proper place to file in order to perfect a security interest is as follows:

(a) when the collateral is equipment used in farming operations, or farm products, or accounts or general intangibles arising from or relating to the sale of farm products by a farmer, or consumer goods, then in the office of the . . . . in the county of the debtor's residence or if the debtor is not a resident of this state then in the office of the . . . . in the county where the goods are kept, and in addition when the collateral is crops growing or to be grown in the office of the . . . . in the county were the land is located;

(b) when the collateral is timber to be cut or is minerals or the like (including oil and gas) or accounts subject to subsection (5) of Section 9–103, or when the financing statement is filed as a fixture filing (Section 9–313) and the collateral is goods which are or are to become fixtures, then in the office where a mortgage on the real estate would be filed or recorded;

(c) in all other cases, in the office of the [Secretary of State] and in addition, if the debtor has a place of business in only one county of this state, also in the office of . . . . of such county, or, if the debtor has no place of business in this state, but resides in the state, also in the office of . . . . of the county in which he resides.

Note: *One of the three alternatives should be selected as subsection (1).*

(2) A filing which is made in good faith in an improper place or not in all of the places required by this section is nevertheless effective with regard to any collateral as to which the filing complied with the requirements of this Article and is also effective with regard to collateral covered by the financing statement against any person who has knowledge of the contents of such financing statement.

(3) A filing which is made in the proper place in this state continues effective even though the debtor's residence or place of business or the location of the collateral or its use, whichever controlled the original filing, is thereafter changed.

Alternative Subsection (3)

[(3) A filing which is made in the proper county continues effective for four months after a change to another county of the debtor's residence or place of business or the location of the collateral, whichever controlled the original filing. It becomes ineffective thereafter unless a copy of the financing statement signed by the secured party is filed in the new county within said period. The security interest may also be perfected in the new county after the expiration of the four-month period; in such case perfection dates from the time of perfection in the new county. A change in the use of the collateral does not impair the effectiveness of the original filing.]

(4) The rules stated in Section 9–103 determine whether filing is necessary in this State.

(5) Notwithstanding the preceding subsections, and subject to subsection (3) of Section 9–302, the proper place to file in order to perfect a security interest in collateral, including fixtures, of a transmitting utility is the office of the [Secretary of State]. This filing constitutes a fixture filing (Section 9–313) as to the collateral described therein which is or is to become fixtures.

(6) For the purposes of this section, the residence of an organization is its place of business if it has one or its chief executive office if it has more than one place of business. Amended in 1962 and 1972.

Note: *Subsection (6) should be used only if the state chooses the Second or Third Alternative Subsection (1).*

§9–402. Formal Requisites of Financing Statement; Amendments; Mortgage as Financing Statement (1) A financing statement is sufficient if it gives the names of the debtor and the secured party, is signed by the debtor, gives an address of the secured party from which information concerning the security interest may be obtained, gives a mailing address of the debtor and contains a statement indicating the types, or describing the items, of collateral. A financing statement may be filed before a security agreement is made or a security interest otherwise attaches. When the financing statement covers crops growing or to be grown, the statement must also contain a description of the real estate concerned. When the financing statement covers timber to be cut or covers minerals or the like (including oil and gas) or accounts subject to subsection (5) of Section 9–103, or when the financing statement is filed as a fixture filing (Section 9–313) and the collateral is goods which are or are to become fixtures, the statement must also comply with subsection (5). A copy of the security agreement is sufficient as a financing statement if it contains the above information and is signed by the debtor. A carbon, photographic or other reproduction of a security agreement or a financing statement is sufficient as a financing statement if the security agreement so provides or if the original has been filed in this state.

(2) A financing statement which otherwise complies with subsection (1) is sufficient when it is signed by the secured party instead of the debtor if it is filed to perfect a security interest in

(a) collateral already subject to a security interest in another jurisdiction when it is brought into this state, or when the debtor's location is changed to this state. Such a financing statement must state that the collateral was brought into this state or that the debtor's location was changed to this state under such circumstances; or

(b) proceeds under Section 9–306 if the security interest in the original collateral was perfected. Such a financing statement must describe the original collateral; or

(c) collateral as to which the filing has lapsed; or

(d) collateral acquired after a change of name, identity or corporate structure of the debtor (subsection (7)).

(3) A form substantially as follows is sufficient to comply with subsection (1):
Name of debtor (or assignor). . . . .
Address . . . .
Name of secured party (or assignee) . . . .
Address . . . .
1. This financing statement covers the following types (or items) of property:
(Describe) . . . .
2. (If collateral is crops) The above described crops are growing or are to be grown on:
(Describe Real Estate) . . . .

3. (If applicable) The above goods are to become fixtures on*
(Describe Real Estate) . . . . and this financing statement is to be filed [for record] in the real estate records. (If the debtor does not have an interest of record) The name of a record owner is . . . .

4. (If products of collateral are claimed) Products of the collateral are also covered.

(use . . . .
whichever Signature of Debtor (or Assignor)
is . . . .
applicable) Signature of Secured Party (or Assignee)

(4) A financing statement may be amended by filing a writing signed by both the debtor and the secured party. An amendment does not extend the period of effectiveness of a financing statement. If any amendment adds collateral, it is effective as to the added collateral only from the filing date of the amendment. In this Article, unless the context otherwise requires, the term "financing statement" means the original financing statement and any amendments.

(5) A financing statement covering timber to be cut or covering minerals or the like (including oil and gas) or accounts subject to subsection (5) of Section 9–103, or a financing statement filed as a fixture filing (Section 9–313) where the debtor is not a transmitting utility, must show that it covers this type of collateral, must recite that it is to be filed [for record] in the real estate records, and the financing statement must contain a description of the real estate [sufficient if it were contained in a mortgage of the real estate to give constructive notice of the mortgage under the law of this state]. If the debtor does not have an interest of record in the real estate, the financing statement must show the name of a record owner.

(6) A mortgage is effective as a financing statement filed as a fixture filing from the date of its recording if

(a) the goods are described in the mortgage by item or type; and

(b) the goods are or are to become fixtures related to the real estate described in the mortgage; and

(c) the mortgage complies with the requirements for a financing statement in this section other than a recital that it is to be filed in the real estate records; and

(d) the mortgage is duly recorded.

No fee with reference to the financing statement is required other than the regular recording and satisfaction fees with respect to the mortgage.

(7) A financing statement sufficiently shows the name of the debtor if it gives the individual, partnership or corporate name of the debtor, whether or not it adds other trade names or names of partners. Where the debtor so changes his name or in the case of an organization its name, identity or corporate structure that a filed financing statement becomes seriously misleading, the filing is not effective to perfect a security interest in collateral acquired by the debtor more than four months after the change, unless a new appropriate financing statement is filed before the expiration of that time. A filed financing statement remains effective with respect to collateral transferred by the debtor even though the secured party knows of or consents to the transfer.

(8) A financing statement substantially complying with the requirements of this section is effective even though it contains minor errors which are not seriously misleading. Amended in 1972.

*Where appropriate substitute either "The above timber is standing on. . . ." or "The above minerals or the like (including oil and gas) or accounts will be financed at the wellhead or minehead of the well or mine located on. . . ."

Note: *Language in brackets is optional.*

Note: *Where the state has any special recording system for real estate other than the usual grantor-grantee index (as, for instance, a tract system or a title registration or Torrens system) local adaptations of subsection (5) and Section 9–403(7) may be necessary. See Mass. Gen. Laws Chapter 106, Section 9–409.*

§9–403. What Constitutes Filing; Duration of Filing; Effect of Lapsed Filing; Duties of Filing Officer. (1) Presentation for filing of a financing statement and tender of the filing fee or acceptance of the statement by the filing officer constitutes filing under this Article.

(2) Except as provided in subsection (6) a filed financing statement is effective for a period of five years from the date of filing. The effectiveness of a filed financing statement lapses on the expiration of the five year period unless a continuation statement is filed prior to the lapse. If a security interest perfected by filing exists at the time insolvency proceedings are commenced by or against the debtor, the security interest remains perfected until termination of the insolvency proceedings and thereafter for a period of sixty days or until expiration of the five year period, whichever occurs later. Upon lapse the security interest becomes unperfected, unless it is perfected without filing. If the security interest becomes unperfected upon lapse, it is deemed to have been unperfected as against a person who became a purchaser or lien creditor before lapse.

(3) A continuation statement may be filed by the secured party within six months prior to the expiration of the five year period specified in subsection (2). Any such continuation statement must be signed by the secured party, identify the original statement by file number and state that the original statement is still effective. A continuation statement signed by a person other than the secured party of record must be accompanied by a separate written statement of assignment signed by the secured party of record and complying with subsection (2) of Section 9–405, including payment of the required fee. Upon timely filing of the continuation statement, the effectiveness of the original statement is continued for five years after the last date to which the filing was effective whereupon it lapses in the same manner as provided in subsection (2) unless another continuation statement is filed prior to such lapse. Succeeding continuation statements may be filed in the same manner to continue the effectiveness of the original statement. Unless a statute on disposition of public records provides otherwise, the filing officer may remove a lapsed statement from the files and destroy it immediately if he has retained a microfilm or other photographic record, or in other cases after one year after the lapse. The filing officer shall so arrange matters by physical annexation of financing statements to continuation statements or other related filings, or by other means, that if he physically destroys the financing statements of a period more than five years past, those which have been continued by a continuation statement or which are still effective under subsection (6) shall be retained.

(4) Except as provided in subsection (7) a filing officer shall mark each statement with a file number and with the date and hour of filing and shall hold the statement or a microfilm or other photographic copy thereof for public inspection. In addition the filing officer shall index the statement according to the name of the debtor and shall note in the index the file number and the address of the debtor given in the statement.

(5) The uniform fee for filing and indexing and for stamping a copy furnished by the secured party to show the date and place of filing for an original financing statement or for a continuation statement shall be $ . . . . if the statement is in the standard form prescribed by the [Secretary of State] and otherwise shall be $ . . . . , plus in each case, if the financing statement is subject to subsection (5) of Section 9–402, $ . . . . The uniform fee for each name more than one required to be indexed shall be $ . . . . The secured party may at his option show a trade name for any person

and an extra uniform indexing fee of $ . . . . shall be paid with respect thereto.

(6) If the debtor is a transmitting utility (subsection (5) of Section 9–401) and a filed financing statement so states, it is effective until a termination statement is filed. A real estate mortgage which is effective as a fixture filing under subsection (6) of Section 9–402 remains effective as a fixture filing until the mortgage is released or satisfied of record or its effectiveness otherwise terminates as to the real estate.

(7) When a financing statement covers timber to be cut or covers minerals or the like (including oil and gas) or accounts subject to subsection (5) of Section 9–103, or is filed as a fixture filing, [it shall be filed for record and] the filing officer shall index it under the names of the debtor and any owner of record shown on the financing statement in the same fashion as if they were the mortgagors in a mortgage of the real estate described, and, to the extent that the law of this state provides for indexing of mortgages under the name of the mortgagee, under the name of the secured party as if he were the mortgagee thereunder, or where indexing is by description in the same fashion as if the financing statement were a mortgage of the real estate described. Amended in 1972.

Note: *In states in which writings will not appear in the real estate records and indices unless actually recorded the bracketed language in subsection (7) should be used.*

§9–404. Termination Statement. (1) If a financing statement covering consumer goods is filed on or after . . . . , then within one month or within ten days following written demand by the debtor after there is no outstanding secured obligation and no commitment to make advances, incur obligations or otherwise give value, the secured party must file with each filing officer with whom the financing statement was filed, a termination statement to the effect that he no longer claims a security interest under the financing statement, which shall be identified by file number. In other cases whenever there is no outstanding secured obligation and no commitment to make advances, incur obligations or otherwise give value, the secured party must on written demand by the debtor send the debtor, for each filing officer with whom the financing statement was filed, a termination statement to the effect that he no longer claims a security interest under the financing statement, which shall be identified by file number. A termination statement signed by a person other than the secured party of record must be accompanied by a separate written statement of assignment signed by the secured party of record complying with subsection (2) of Section 9–405, including payment of the required fee. If the affected secured party fails to file such a termination statement as required by this subsection, or to send such a termination statement within ten days after proper demand therefor, he shall be liable to the debtor for one hundred dollars, and in addition for any loss caused to the debtor by such failure.

(2) On presentation to the filing officer of such a termination statement he must note it in the index. If he has received the termination statement in duplicate, he shall return one copy of the termination statement to the secured party stamped to show the time of receipt thereof. If the filing officer has a microfilm or other photographic record of the financing statement, and of any related continuation statement, statement of assignment and statement of release, he may remove the originals from the files at any time after receipt of the termination statement, or if he has no such record, he may remove them from the files at any time after one year after receipt of the termination statement.

(3) If the termination statement is in the standard form prescribed by the [Secretary of State], the uniform fee for filing and indexing the termination statement shall be $ . . . . , and otherwise shall be $ . . . . , plus in each case an additional fee of $ . . . . for each name more than one against which the termination statement is required to be indexed. Amended in 1972.

Note: *The date to be inserted should be the effective date of the revised Article 9.*

§9–405. Assignment of Security Interest; Duties of Filing Officer; Fees. (1) A financing statement may disclose an assignment of a security interest in the collateral described in the financing statement by indication in the financing statement of the name and address of the assignee or by an assignment itself or a copy thereof on the face or back of the statement. On presentation to the filing officer of such a financing statement the filing officer shall mark the same as provided in Section 9–403(4). The uniform fee for filing, indexing and furnishing filing data for a financing statement so indicating an assignment shall be $ . . . . if the statement is in the standard form prescribed by the [Secretary of State] and otherwise shall be $ . . . . , plus in each case an additional fee of $ . . . . for each name more than one against which the financing statement is required to be indexed.

(2) A secured party may assign of record all or part of his rights under a financing statement by the filing in the place where the original financing statement was filed of a separate written statement of assignment signed by the secured party of record and setting forth the name of the secured party of record and the debtor, the file number and the date of filing of the financing statement and the name and address of the assignee and containing a description of the collateral assigned. A copy of the assignment is sufficient as a separate statement if it complies with the preceding sentence. On presentation to the filing officer of such a separate statement, the filing officer shall mark such separate statement with the date and hour of the filing. He shall note the assignment on the index of the financing statement, or in the case of a fixture filing, or a filing covering timber to be cut, or covering minerals or the like (including oil and gas) or accounts subject to subsection (5) of Section 9–103, he shall index the assignment under the name of the assignor as grantor and, to the extent that the law of this state provides for indexing the assignment of a mortgage under the name of the assignee, he shall index the assignment of the financing statement under the name of the assignee. The uniform fee for filing, indexing and furnishing filing data about such a separate statement of assignment shall be $ . . . . if the statement is in the standard form prescribed by the [Secretary of State] and otherwise shall be $ . . . . , plus in each case an additional fee of $ . . . . for each name more than one against which the statement of assignment is required to be indexed. Notwithstanding the provisions of this subsection, an assignment of record of a security interest in a fixture contained in a mortgage effective as a fixture filing (subsection (6) of Section 9–402) may be made only by an assignment of the mortgage in the manner provided by the law of this state other than this Act.

(3) After the disclosure or filing of an assignment under this section, the assignee is the secured party of record. Amended in 1972.

§9–406. Release of Collateral; Duties of Filing Officer; Fees. A secured party of record may by his signed statement release all or a part of any collateral described in a filed financing statement. The statement of release is sufficient if it contains a description of the collateral being released, the name and address of the debtor, the name and address of the secured party, and the file number of the financing statement. A statement of release signed by a person other than the secured party of record must be accompanied by a separate written statement of assignment signed by the secured party of record and complying with subsection (2) of Section 9–405, including payment of the required fee. Upon presentation of such a statement of release to the filing officer he shall mark the statement with the hour and date of filing and shall note the same upon the margin of the index of the filing of the financing statement. The uniform fee for filing and noting such a statement of release shall be $ . . . . if the statement is in the standard form prescribed by the [Secretary of State] and otherwise shall be $ . . . . , plus in each case an additional fee of

$ . . . . for each name more than one against which the statement of release is required to be indexed. Amended in 1972.

[§9–407. Information from Filing Officer]. [(1) If the person filing any financing statement, termination statement, statement of assignment, or statement of release, furnishes the filing officer a copy thereof, the filing officer shall upon request note upon the copy the file number and date and hour of the filing of the original and deliver or send the copy to such person.]

[(2) Upon request of any person, the filing officer shall issue his certificate showing whether there is on file on the date and hour stated therein, any presently effective financing statement naming a particular debtor and any statement of assignment thereof and if there is, giving the date and hour of filing of each such statement and the names and addresses of each secured party therein. The uniform fee for such a certificate shall be $ . . . . if the request for the certificate is in the standard form prescribed by the [Secretary of State] and otherwise shall be $ . . . . Upon request the filing officer shall furnish a copy of any filed financing statement or statement of assignment for a uniform fee of $ . . . . per page.] Amended in 1972.

Note: *This section is proposed as an optional provision to require filing officers to furnish certificates. Local law and practices should be consulted with regard to the advisability of adoption.*

§9–408. Financing Statements Covering Consigned or Leased Goods. A consignor or lessor of goods may file a financing statement using the terms "consignor," "consignee," "lessor," "lessee" or the like instead of the terms specified in Section 9–402. The provisions of this Part shall apply as appropriate to such a financing statement but its filing shall not of itself be a factor in determining whether or not the consignment or lease is intended as security (Section 1–201(37)). However, if it is determined for other reasons that the consignment or lease is so intended, a security interest of the consignor or lessor which attaches to the consigned or leased goods is perfected by such filing. Added in 1972.

Part 5

Default

§9–501. Default; Procedure When Security Agreement Covers Both Real and Personal Property. (1) When a debtor is in default under a security agreement, a secured party has the rights and remedies provided in this Part and except as limited by subsection (3) those provided in the security agreement. He may reduce his claim to judgment, foreclose or otherwise enforce the security interest by any available judicial procedure. If the collateral is documents the secured party may proceed either as to the documents or as to the goods covered thereby. A secured party in possession has the rights, remedies and duties provided in Section 9–207. The rights and remedies referred to in this subsection are cumulative.

(2) After default, the debtor has the rights and remedies provided in this Part, those provided in the security agreement and those provided in Section 9–207.

(3) To the extent that they give rights to the debtor and impose duties on the secured party, the rules stated in the subsections referred to below may not be waived or varied except as provided with respect to compulsory disposition of collateral (subsection (3) of Section 9–504 and Section 9–505) and with respect to redemption of collateral (Section 9–506) but the parties may by agreement determine the standards by which the fulfillment

of these rights and duties is to be measured if such standards are not manifestly unreasonable:

(a) subsection (2) of Section 9–502 and subsection (2) of Section 9–504 insofar as they require accounting for surplus proceeds of collateral;

(b) subsection (3) of Section 9–504 and subsection (1) of Section 9–505 which deal with disposition of collateral;

(c) subsection (2) of Section 9–505 which deals with acceptance of collateral as discharge of obligation;

(d) Section 9–506 which deals with redemption of collateral; and

(e) subsection (1) of Section 9–507 which deals with the secured party's liability for failure to comply with this Part.

(4) If the security agreement covers both real and personal property, the secured party may proceed under this Part as to the personal property or he may proceed as to both the real and the personal property in accordance with his rights and remedies in respect of the real property in which case the provisions of this Part do not apply.

(5) When a secured party has reduced his claim to judgment the lien of any levy which may be made upon his collateral by virtue of any execution based upon the judgment shall relate back to the date of the perfection of the security interest in such collateral. A judicial sale, pursuant to such execution, is a foreclosure of the security interest by judicial procedure within the meaning of this section, and the secured party may purchase at the sale and thereafter hold the collateral free of any other requirements of this Article. Amended in 1972.

§9–502. Collection Rights of Secured Party. (1) When so agreed and in any event on default the secured party is entitled to notify an account debtor or the obligor on an instrument to make payment to him whether or not the assignor was theretofore making collections on the collateral, and also to take control of any proceeds to which he is entitled under Section 9–306.

(2) A secured party who by agreement is entitled to charge back uncollected collateral or otherwise to full or limited recourse against the debtor and who undertakes to collect from the account debtors or obligors must proceed in a commercially reasonable manner and may deduct his reasonable expenses of realization from the collections. If the security agreement secures an indebtedness, the secured party must account to the debtor for any surplus, and unless otherwise agreed, the debtor is liable for any deficiency. But, if the underlying transaction was a sale of accounts or chattel paper, the debtor is entitled to any surplus or is liable for any deficiency only if the security agreement so provides. Amended in 1972.

§9–503. Secured Party's Right to Take Possession after Default. Unless otherwise agreed a secured party has on default the right to take possession of the collateral. In taking possession a secured party may proceed without judicial process if this can be done without breach of the peace or may proceed by action. If the security agreement so provides the secured party may require the debtor to assemble the collateral and make it available to the secured party at a place to be designated by the secured party which is reasonably convenient to both parties. Without removal a secured party may render equipment unusable, and may dispose of collateral on the debtor's premises under Section 9–504.

§9–504. Secured Party's Right to Dispose of Collateral after Default; Effect of Disposition. (1) A secured party after default may sell, lease or otherwise dispose of any or all of the collateral in its then condition or following any commercially reasonable preparation or processing. Any sale of goods is subject to the Article on Sales (Article 2). The proceeds of disposition shall be applied in the order following to

(a) the reasonable expenses of retaking, holding, preparing for sale or lease, selling, leasing and the like and, to the extent provided for in the agreement and not prohibited by law, the reasonable attorneys' fees and legal expenses incurred by the secured party;

(b) the satisfaction of indebtedness secured by the security interest under which the disposition is made;

(c) the satisfaction of indebtedness secured by any subordinate security interest in the collateral if written notification of demand therefor is received before distribution of the proceeds is completed. If requested by the secured party, the holder of a subordinate security interest must seasonably furnish reasonable proof of his interest, and unless he does so, the secured party need not comply with his demand.

(2) If the security interest secures an indebtedness, the secured party must account to the debtor for any surplus, and unless otherwise agreed, the debtor is liable for any deficiency. But if the underlying transaction was a sale of accounts or chattel paper, the debtor is entitled to any surplus or is liable for any deficiency only if the security agreement so provides.

(3) Disposition of the collateral may be by public or private proceedings and may be made by way of one or more contracts. Sale or other disposition may be as a unit or in parcels and at any time and place and on any terms but every aspect of the disposition including the method, manner, time, place and terms must be commercially reasonable. Unless collateral is perishable or threatens to decline speedily in value or is of a type customarily sold on a recognized market, reasonable notification of the time and place of any public sale or reasonable notification of the time after which any private sale or other intended disposition is to be made shall be sent by the secured party to the debtor, if he has not signed after default a statement renouncing or modifying his right to notification of sale. In the case of consumer goods no other notification need be sent. In other cases notification shall be sent to any other secured party from whom the secured party has received (before sending his notification to the debtor or before the debtor's renunciation of his rights) written notice of a claim of an interest in the collateral. The secured party may buy at any public sale and if the collateral is of a type customarily sold in a recognized market or is of a type which is the subject of widely distributed standard price quotations he may buy at private sale.

(4) When collateral is disposed of by a secured party after default, the disposition transfers to a purchaser for value all of the debtor's rights therein, discharges the security interest under which it is made and any security interest or lien subordinate thereto. The purchaser takes free of all such rights and interests even though the secured party fails to comply with the requirements of this Part or of any judicial proceedings

(a) in the case of a public sale, if the purchaser has no knowledge of any defects in the sale and if he does not buy in collusion with the secured party, other bidders or the person conducting the sale; or

(b) in any other case, if the purchaser acts in good faith.

(5) A person who is liable to a secured party under a guaranty, indorsement, repurchase agreement or the like and who receives a transfer of collateral from the secured party or is subrogated to his rights has thereafter the rights and duties of the secured party. Such a transfer of collateral is not a sale or disposition of the collateral under this Article. Amended in 1972.

§9–505. Compulsory Disposition of Collateral; Acceptance of the Collateral as Discharge of Obligation. (1) If the debtor has paid sixty per cent of the cash price in the case of a purchase money security interest in consumer goods or sixty per cent of the loan in the case of another security interest in consumer goods, and has not signed after default a statement renouncing or modifying his rights under this Part a secured party who has taken possession of collateral must dispose of it under Section 9–504 and if he fails to do so within ninety days after he takes possession the debtor at his option may recover in conversion or under Section 9–507(1) on secured party's liability.

(2) In any other case involving consumer goods or any other collateral a secured party in possession may, after default, propose to retain the collateral in satisfaction of the obligation. Written notice of such proposal shall be sent to the debtor if he has not signed after default a statement renouncing or modifying his rights under this subsection. In the case of consumer goods no other notice need be given. In other cases notice shall be sent to any other secured party from whom the secured party has received (before sending his notice to the debtor or before the debtor's renunciation of his rights) written notice of a claim of an interest in the collateral. If the secured party receives objection in writing from a person entitled to receive notification within twenty-one days after the notice was sent, the secured party must dispose of the collateral under Section 9–504. In the absence of such written objection the secured party may retain the collateral in satisfaction of the debtor's obligation. Amended in 1972.

§9–506. Debtor's Right to Redeem Collateral. At any time before the secured party has disposed of collateral or entered into a contract for its disposition under Section 9–504 or before the obligation has been discharged under Section 9–505(2) the debtor or any other secured party may unless otherwise agreed in writing after default redeem the collateral by tendering fulfillment of all obligations secured by the collateral as well as the expenses reasonably incurred by the secured party in retaking, holding and preparing the collateral for disposition, in arranging for the sale, and to the extent provided in the agreement and not prohibited by law, his reasonable attorneys' fees and legal expenses.

§9–507. Secured Party's Liability for Failure to Comply with This Part. (1) If it is established that the secured party is not proceeding in accordance with the provisions of this Part disposition may be ordered or restrained on appropriate terms and conditions. If the disposition has occurred the debtor or any person entitled to notification or whose security interest has been made known to the secured party prior to the disposition has a right to recover from the secured party any loss caused by a failure to comply with the provisions of this Part. If the collateral is consumer goods, the debtor has a right to recover in any event an amount not less than the credit service charge plus ten per cent of the principal amount of the debt or the time price differential plus 10 per cent of the cash price.

(2) The fact that a better price could have been obtained by a sale at a different time or in a different method from that selected by the secured party is not of itself sufficient to establish that the sale was not made in a commercially reasonable manner. If the secured party either sells the collateral in the usual manner in any recognized market therefor or if he sells at the price current in such market at the time of his sale or if he has otherwise sold in conformity with reasonable commercial practices among dealers in the type of property sold he has sold in a commercially reasonable manner. The principles stated in the two preceding sentences with respect to sales also apply as may be appropriate to other types of disposition. A disposition which has been approved in any judicial proceeding or by any bona fide creditors' committee or representative of creditors shall conclusively be deemed to be commercially reasonable, but this sentence does not indicate that any such approval must be obtained in any case nor does it indicate that any disposition not so approved is not commercially reasonable.

ARTICLE 10: EFFECTIVE DATE AND REPEALER

See Article 11 for Transition Provisions for those jurisdictions adopting the 1972 amendments.

Section

10–101. Effective Date.

10–102. Specific Repealer; Provision for Transition.

10–103. General Repealer.

10–104. Laws Not Repealed.

§10–101. Effective Date. This Act shall become effective at midnight on December 31st following its enactment. It applies to transactions entered into and events occurring after that date.

§10–102. Specific Repealer; Provision for Transition. (1) The following acts and all other acts and parts of acts inconsistent herewith are hereby repealed:

(Here should follow the acts to be specifically repealed including the following:

Uniform Negotiable Instruments Act

Uniform Warehouse Receipts Act

Uniform Sales Act

Uniform Bills of Lading Act

Uniform Stock Transfer Act

Uniform Conditional Sales Act

Uniform Trust Receipts Act

Also any acts regulating:

Bank collections

Bulk sales

Chattel mortgages

Conditional sales

Factor's lien acts

Farm storage of grain and similar acts

Assignment of accounts receivable)

(2) Transactions validly entered into before the effective date specified in Section 10–101 and the rights, duties and interests flowing from them remain valid thereafter and may be terminated, completed, consummated or enforced as required or permitted by any statute or other law amended or repealed by this Act as though such repeal or amendment had not occurred.

Note

Subsection (1) should be separately prepared for each state. The foregoing is a list of statutes to be checked.

§10–103. General Repealer. Except as provided in the following section, all acts and parts of acts inconsistent with this Act are hereby repealed.

§10–104. Laws Not Repealed. [(1)] The Article on Documents of Title (Article 7) does not repeal or modify any laws prescribing the form or contents of documents of title or the services or facilities to be afforded by bailees, or otherwise regulating bailees' businesses in respects not specifically dealt with herein; but the fact that such laws are violated does not affect the status of a document of title which otherwise complies with the definition of a document of title (Section 1–201).

[(2) This Act does not repeal . . . . *, cited as the Uniform Act for the Simplification of Fiduciary Security Transfers, and if in any respect there is any inconsistency between that Act and the Article of this Act on investment securities (Article 8) the provisions of the former Act shall control.] As amended 1962.

Note: *At * in subsection (2) insert the statutory reference to the Uniform Act for the*

Simplification of Fiduciary Security Transfers if such Act has previously been enacted. If it has not been enacted, omit subsection (2).

ARTICLE 11: EFFECTIVE DATE AND TRANSITION PROVISIONS

Notes

This material has been numbered Article 11 to distinguish it from Article 10, the transition provision of the 1962 Code, which may still remain in effect in some states to cover transition problems from pre-Code law to the original Uniform Commercial Code. Adaptation may be necessary in particular states. The terms "[old Code]" and "[new Code]" and "[old U.C.C.]" and "[new U.C.C.]" are used herein, and should be suitably changed in each state.

This draft was prepared by the Reporters and has not been passed upon by the Review Committee, the Permanent Editorial Board, the American Law Institute, or the National Conference of Commissioners on Uniform State Laws. It is submitted as a working draft which may be adapted as appropriate in each state. The "Discussions" were written by the Reporters to assist in understanding the purpose of the drafts.

§11–101. Effective Date. This Act shall become effective at 12:01 A.M. on   19 .

§11–102. Preservation of Old Transition Provision. The provisions of [here insert reference to the original transition provision in the particular state] shall continue to apply to [the new U.C.C.] and for this purpose the [old U.C.C. and new U.C.C.] shall be considered one continuous statute.

§11–103. Transition to [New Code]—General Rule. Transactions validly entered into after [effective date of old U.C.C.] and before [effective date of new U.C.C.], and which were subject to the provisions of [old U.C.C.] and which would be subject to this Act as amended if they had been entered into after the effective date of [new U.C.C.] and the rights, duties and interests flowing from such transactions remain valid after the latter date and may be terminated, completed, consummated or enforced as required or permitted by the [new U.C.C.]. Security interests arising out of such transactions which are perfected when [new U.C.C. becomes effective shall remain perfected until they lapse as provided in [new U.C.C.], and may be continued as permitted by [new U.C.C.], except as stated in Section 11–105.

§11–104. Transition Provision on Change of Requirement of Filing. A security interest for the perfection of which filing or the taking of possession was required under [old U.C.C.] and which attached prior to the effective date of [new U.C.C.] but was not perfected shall be deemed perfected on the effective date of [new U.C.C.] if [new U.C.C.] permits perfection without filing or authorizes filing in the office or offices where a prior ineffective filing was made.

§11–105. Transition Provision on Change of Place of Filing. (1) A financing statement or continuation statement filed prior to [effective date of new U.C.C.] which shall not have lapsed prior to [the effective date of new U.C.C.] shall remain effective for the period provided in the [old Code], but not less than five years after the filing.

(2) With respect to any collateral acquired by the debtor subsequent to the effective date of [new U.C.C.], any effective financing statement or continuation statement described in this section shall apply only if the filing or filings are in the office or offices that would be appropriate to perfect the security interests in the new collateral under [new U.C.C.].

(3) The effectiveness of any financing statement or continuation statement filed prior to [effective date of new U.C.C.] may be continued by a continuation statement as permitted by [new U.C.C.], except that if [new U.C.C.] requires a filing in an office where there was no previous financing statement, a new financing statement conforming to Section 11–106 shall be filed in that office.

(4) If the record of a mortgage of real estate would have been effective as a fixture filing of goods described therein if [new U.C.C.] had been in effect on the date of recording the mortgage, the mortgage shall be deemed effective as a fixture filing as to such goods under subsection (6) of Section 9–402 of the [new U.C.C.] on the effective date of [new U.C.C.].

§11–106. Required Refilings. (1) If a security interest is perfected or has priority when this Act takes effect as to all persons or as to certain persons without any filing or recording, and if the filing of a financing statement would be required for the perfection or priority of the security interest against those persons under [new U.C.C.], the perfection and priority rights of the security interest continue until 3 years after the effective date of [new U.C.C.]. The perfection will then lapse unless a financing statement is filed as provided in subsection (4) or unless the security interest is perfected otherwise than by filing.

(2) If a security interest is perfected when [new U.C.C.] takes effect under a law other than [U.C.C.] which requires no further filing, refiling or recording to continue its perfection, perfection continues until and will lapse 3 years after [new U.C.C.] takes effect, unless a financing statement is filed as provided in subsection (4) or unless the security interest is perfected otherwise than by filing, or unless under subsection (3) of Section 9–302 the other law continues to govern filing.

(3) If a security interest is perfected by a filing, refiling or recording under a law repealed by this Act which required further filing, refiling or recording to continue its perfection, perfection continues and will lapse on the date provided by the law so repealed for such further filing, refiling or recording unless a financing statement is filed as provided in subsection (4) or unless the security interest is perfected otherwise than by filing.

(4) A financing statement may be filed within six months before the perfection of a security interest would otherwise lapse. Any such financing statement may be signed by either the debtor or the secured party. It must identify the security agreement, statement or notice (however denominated in any statute or other law repealed or modified by this Act), state the office where and the date when the last filing, refiling or recording, if any, was made with respect thereto, and the filing number, if any, or book and page, if any, of recording and further state that the security agreement, statement or notice, however denominated, in another filing office under the [U.C.C.] or under any statute or other law repealed or modified by this Act is still effective. Section 9–401 and Section 9–103 determine the proper place to file such a financing statement. Except as specified in this subsection, the provisions of Section 9–403(3) for continuation statements apply to such a financing statement.

§11–107. Transition Provisions as to Priorities. Except as otherwise provided in [Article 11], [old U.C.C.] shall apply to any questions of priority if the positions of the parties were fixed prior to the effective date of [new U.C.C.]. In other cases questions of priority shall be determined by [new U.C.C.].

§11–108. Presumption that Rule of Law Continues Unchanged. Unless a change in law has clearly been made, the provisions of [new U.C.C.] shall be deemed declaratory of the meaning of the [old U.C.C.].

APPENDIX 2
UNIFORM PARTNERSHIP ACT

Part I

Preliminary Provisions

§1. Name of Act. This act may be cited as Uniform Partnership Act.

§2. Definition of Terms. In this act, "Court" includes every court and judge having jurisdiction in the case.

"Business" includes every trade, occupation, or profession.

"Person" includes individuals, partnerships, corporations, and other associations.

"Bankrupt" includes bankrupt under the Federal Bankruptcy Act or insolvent under any state insolvent act.

"Conveyance" includes every assignment, lease, mortgage, or encumbrance.

"Real property" includes land and any interest or estate in land.

§3. Interpretation of Knowledge and Notice. (1) A person has "knowledge" of a fact within the meaning of this act not only when he has actual knowledge thereof, but also when he has knowledge of such other facts as in the circumstances shows bad faith.

(2) A person has "notice" of a fact within the meaning of this act when the person who claims the benefit of the notice:

(a) States the fact to such person, or

(b) Delivers through the mail, or by other means of communication, a written statement of the fact to such person or to a proper person at his place of business or residence.

§4. Rules of Construction. (1) The rule that statutes in derogation of the common law are to be strictly construed shall have no application to this act.

(2) The law of estoppel shall apply under this act.

(3) The law of agency shall apply under this act.

(4) This act shall be so interpreted and construed as to effect its general purpose to make uniform the law of those states which enact it.

(5) This act shall not be construed so as to impair the obligations of any contract existing when the act goes into effect, nor to affect any action or proceedings begun or right accrued before this act takes effect.

§5. Rules for Cases Not Provided for in This Act. In any case not provided for in this act the rules of law and equity, including the law merchant, shall govern.

Part II

Nature of Partnership

§6. Partnership Defined. (1) A partnership is an association of two or more persons to carry on as co-owners a business for profit.

(2) But any association formed under any other statute of this state, or any statute adopted by authority, other than the authority of this state, is not a partnership under this act, unless such association would have been a partnership in this state prior to the adoption of this act; but this act shall apply to limited partnerships except in so far as the statutes relating to such partnerships are inconsistent herewith.

§7. Rules for Determining the Existence of a Partnership. In determining whether a partnership exists, these rules shall apply:

(1) Except as provided by Section 16 persons who are not partners as to each other are not partners as to third persons.

(2) Joint tenancy, tenancy in common, tenancy by the entireties, joint property, common property, or part ownership does not of itself establish a partnership, whether such co-owners do or do not share any profits made by the use of the property.

(3) The sharing of gross returns does not of itself establish a partnership, whether or not the persons sharing them have a joint or common right or interest in any property from which the returns are derived.

(4) The receipt by a person of a share of the profits of a business is prima facie evidence that he is a partner in the business, but no such inference shall be drawn if such profits were received in payment:

(a) As a debt by installments or otherwise,

(b) As wages of an employee or rent to a landlord,

(c) As an annuity to a widow or representative of a deceased partner,

(d) As interest on a loan, though the amount of payment vary with the profits of the business,

(e) As the consideration for the sale of a good-will of a business or other property by installments or otherwise.

§8. Partnership Property. (1) All property originally brought into the partnership stock or subsequently acquired by purchase or otherwise, on account of the partnership, is partnership property.

(2) Unless the contrary intention appears, property acquired with partnership funds is partnership property.

(3) Any estate in real property may be acquired in the partnership name. Title so acquired can be conveyed only in the partnership name.

(4) A conveyance to a partnership in the partnership name, though without words of inheritance, passes the entire estate of the grantor unless a contrary intent appears.

Part III

Relations of Partners to Persons Dealing with the Partnership

§9. Partner Agent of Partnership as to Partnership Business. (1) Every partner is an agent of the partnership for the purpose of its business, and the act of every partner, including the execution in the partnership name of any instrument, for apparently carrying on in the usual way the business of the partnership of which he is a member binds the partnership, unless the partner so acting has in fact no authority to act for the partnership in the particular matter, and the person with whom he is dealing has knowledge of the fact that he has no such authority.

(2) An act of a partner which is not apparently for the carrying on of the business of the partnership in the usual way does not bind the partnership unless authorized by the other partners.

(3) Unless authorized by the other partners or unless they have abandoned the business, one or more but less than all the partners have no authority to:

(a) Assign the partnership property in trust for creditors or on the assignee's promise to pay the debts of the partnership,

(b) Dispose of the good-will of the business,

(c) Do any other act which would make it impossible to carry on the ordinary business of a partnership,

(d) Confess a judgment,

(e) Submit a partnership claim or liability to arbitration or reference.

(4) No act of a partner in contravention of a restriction on authority shall bind the partnership to persons having knowledge of the restriction.

§10. Conveyance of Real Property of the Partnership. (1) Where title to real property is in the partnership name, any partner may convey title to such property by a conveyance executed in the partnership name; but the partnership may recover such property unless the partner's act binds the partnership under the provisions of paragraph (1) of section 9, or unless such property has been conveyed by the grantee or a person claiming through such grantee to a holder for value without knowledge that the partner, in making the conveyance, has exceeded his authority.

(2) Where title to real property is in the name of the partnership, a conveyance executed by a partner, in his own name, passes the equitable interest of the partnership, provided the act is one within the authority of the partner under the provisions of paragraph (1) of section 9.

(3) Where title to real property is in the name of one or more but not all the partners, and the record does not disclose the right of the partnership, the partners in whose name the title stands may convey title to such property, but the partnership may recover such property if the partner's act does not bind the partnership under the provisions of paragraph (1) of section 9, unless the purchaser or his assignee, is a holder for value, without knowledge.

(4) Where the title to real property is in the name of one or more or all the partners, or in a third person in trust for the partnership, a conveyance executed by a partner in the partnership name, or in his own name, passes the equitable interest of the partnership, provided the act is one within the authority of the partner under the provisions of paragraph (1) of section 9.

(5) Where the title to real property is in the names of all the partners a conveyance executed by all the partners passes all their rights in such property.

§11. Partnership Bound by Admission of Partner. An admission or representation made by any partner concerning partnership affairs within the scope of his authority as conferred by this act is evidence against the partnership.

§12. Partnership Charged with Knowledge of or Notice to Partner. Notice to any partner of any matter relating to partnership affairs, and the knowledge of the partner acting in the particular matter, acquired while a partner or then present to his mind, and the knowledge of any other partner who reasonably could and should have communicated it to the acting partner, operate as notice to or knowledge of the partnership, except in the case of a fraud on the partnership committed by or with the consent of that partner.

§13. Partnership Bound by Partner's Wrongful Act. Where, by any wrongful act or omission of any partner acting in the ordinary course of the business of the partnership or with the authority of his co-partners, loss or injury is caused to any person, not being a partner in the partnership, or any penalty is incurred, the partnership is liable therefor to the same extent as the partner so acting or omitting to act.

§14. Partnership Bound by Partner's Breach of Trust. The partnership is bound to make good the loss:

(a) Where one partner acting within the scope of his apparent authority receives money or property of a third person and misapplies it; and

(b) Where the partnership in the course of its business receives money or property of a third person and the money or property so received is misapplied by any partner while it is in the custody of the partnership.

§15. Nature of Partner's Liability. All partners are liable

(a) Jointly and severally for everything chargeable to the partnership under sections 13 and 14.

(b) Jointly for all other debts and obligations of the partnership; but any partner may enter into a separate obligation to perform a partnership contract.

§16. Partner by Estoppel. (1) When a person, by words spoken or written or by conduct, represents himself, or consents to another representing him to any one, as a partner in an existing partnership or with one or more persons not actual partners, he is liable to any such person to whom such representation has been made, who has, on the faith of such representation, given credit to the actual or apparent partnership, and if he has made such representation or consented to its being made in a public manner he is liable to such person, whether the representation has or has not been made or communicated to such person so giving credit by or with the knowledge of the apparent partner making the representation or consenting to its being made.

(a) When a partnership liability results, he is liable as though he were an actual member of the partnership.

(b) When no partnership liability results, he is liable jointly with the other persons, if any, so consenting to the contract or representation as to incur liability, otherwise separately.

(2) When a person has been thus represented to be a partner in an existing partnership, or with one or more persons not actual partners, he is an agent of the persons

consenting to such representation to bind them to the same extent and in the same manner as though he were a partner in fact, with respect to persons who rely upon the representation. Where all the members of the existing partnership consent to the representation, a partnership act or obligation results; but in all other cases it is the joint act or obligation of the person acting and the persons consenting to the representation.

§17. Liability of Incoming Partner. A person admitted as a partner into an existing partnership is liable for all the obligations of the partnership arising before his admission as though he had been a partner when such obligations were incurred, except that this liability shall be satisfied only out of partnership property.

Part IV

Relations of Partners to One Another

§18. Rules Determining Rights and Duties of Partners. The rights and duties of the partners in relation to the partnership shall be determined, subject to any agreement between them, by the following rules:

(a) Each partner shall be repaid his contributions, whether by way of capital or advances to the partnership property and share equally in the profits and surplus remaining after all liabilities, including those to partners, are satisfied; and must contribute towards the losses, whether of capital or otherwise, sustained by the partnership according to his share in the profits.

(b) The partnership must indemnify every partner in respect of payments made and personal liabilities reasonably incurred by him in the ordinary and proper conduct of its business, or for the preservation of its business or property.

(c) A partner, who in aid of the partnership makes any payment or advance beyond the amount of capital which he agreed to contribute, shall be paid interest from the date of the payment.

(d) A partner shall receive interest on the capital contributed by him only from the date when repayment should be made.

(e) All partners have equal rights in the management and conduct of the partnership business.

(f) No partner is entitled to remuneration for acting in the partnership business, except that a surviving partner is entitled to reasonable compensation for his services in winding up the partnership affairs.

(g) No person can become a member of a partnership without the consent of all the partners.

(h) Any difference arising as to ordinary matters connected with the partnership business may be decided by a majority of the partners; but no act in contravention of any agreement between the partners may be done rightfully without the consent of all the partners.

§19. Partnership Books. The partnership books shall be kept, subject to any agreement between the partners, at the principal place of business of the partnership, and every partner shall at all times have access to and may inspect and copy any of them.

§20. Duty of Partners to Render Information. Partners shall render on demand true and full information of all things affecting the partnership to any partner or the legal representative of any deceased partner or partner under legal disability.

§21. Partner Accountable as a Fiduciary. (1) Every partner must account to the partnership for any benefit, and hold as trustee for it any profits derived by him without the consent of the other partners from any transaction connected with the formation, conduct, or liquidation of the partnership or from any use by him of its property.

(2) This section applies also to the representatives of a deceased partner engaged in the liquidation of the affairs of the partnership as the personal representatives of the last surviving partner.

§22. Right to an Account. Any partner shall have the right to a formal account as to partnership affairs:

(a) If he is wrongfully excluded from the partnership business or possession of its property by his co-partners,

(b) If the right exists under the terms of any agreement,

(c) As provided by section 21.

(d) Whenever other circumstances render it just and reasonable.

§23. Continuation of Partnership beyond Fixed Term. (1) When a partnership for a fixed term or particular undertaking is continued after the termination of such term or particular undertaking without any express agreement, the rights and duties of the partners remain the same as they were at such termination, so far as is consistent with a partnership at will.

(2) A continuation of the business by the partners or such of them as habitually acted therein during the term, without any settlement or liquidation of the partnership affairs, is prima facie evidence of a continuation of the partnership.

Part V

Property Rights of a Partner

§24. Extent of Property Rights of a Partner. The property rights of a partner are (1) his rights in specific partnership property, (2) his interest in the partnership, and (3) his right to participate in the management.

§25. Nature of a Partner's Right in Specific Partnership Property. (1) A partner is co-owner with his partners of specific partnership property holding as a tenant in partnership.

(2) The incidents of this tenancy are such that:

(a) A partner, subject to the provisions of this act and to any agreement between the partners, has an equal right with his partners to possess specific partnership property for partnership purposes; but he has no right to possess such property for any other purpose without the consent of his partners.

(b) A partner's right in specific partnership property is not assignable except in connection with the assignment of rights of all the partners in the same property.

(c) A partner's right in specific partnership property is not subject to attachment or execution, except on a claim against the partnership. When partnership property is attached for a partnership debt the partners, or any of them, or the representatives of a deceased partner, cannot claim any right under the homestead or exemption laws.

(d) On the death of a partner his right in specific partnership property vests in the surviving partner or partners, except where the deceased was the last surviving partner, when his right in such property vests in his legal representative. Such surviving partner or partners, or the legal representative of the last surviving partner, has no right to possess the partnership property for any but a partnership purpose.

(e) A partner's right in specific partnership property is not subject to dower, curtesy, or allowances to widows, heirs, or next of kin.

§26. Nature of Partner's Interest in the Partnership. A partner's interest in the partnership is his share of the profits and surplus, and the same is personal property.

§27. Assignment of Partner's Interest. (1) A conveyance by a partner of his interest in the partnership does not of itself dissolve the partnership, nor, as against the other partners in the absence of agreement, entitle the assignee, during the continuance of the partnership, to interfere in the management or administration of the partnership business or affairs, or to require any information or account of partnership transactions, or to inspect the partnership books; but it merely entitles the assignee to receive in accordance with his contract the profits to which the assigning partner would otherwise be entitled.

(2) In case of a dissolution of the partnership, the assignee is entitled to receive his assignor's interest and may require an account from the date only of the last account agreed to by all the partners.

§28. Partner's Interest Subject to Charging Order. (1) On due application to a competent court by any judgment creditor of a partner, the court which entered the judgment, order, or decree, or any other court, may charge the interest of the debtor partner with payment of the unsatisfied amount of such judgment debt with interest thereon; and may then or later appoint a receiver of his share of the profits, and of any other money due or to fall due to him in respect of the partnership, and make all other orders, directions, accounts and inquiries which the debtor partner might have made, or which the circumstances of the case may require.

(2) The interest charged may be redeemed at any time before foreclosure, or in case of a sale being directed by the court may be purchased without thereby causing a dissolution:

(a) With separate property, by any one or more of the partners, or

(b) With partnership property, by any one or more of the partners with the consent of all the partners whose interests are not so charged or sold.

(3) Nothing in this act shall be held to deprive a partner of his right, if any, under the exemption laws, as regards his interest in the partnership.

Part VI

Dissolution and Winding Up

§29. Dissolution Defined. The dissolution of a partnership is the change in the relation of the partners caused by any partner ceasing to be associated in the carrying on as distinguished from the winding up of the business.

§30. Partnership not Terminated by Dissolution. On dissolution the partnership is not terminated, but continues until the winding up of partnership affairs is completed.

§31. Causes of Dissolution. Dissolution is caused:

(1) Without violation of the agreement between the partners,

(a) By the termination of the definite term or particular undertaking specified in the agreement,

(b) By the express will of any partner when no definite term or particular undertaking is specified,

(c) By the express will of all the partners who have not assigned their interests or suffered them to be charged for their separate debts, either before or after the termination of any specified term or particular undertaking,

(d) By the expulsion of any partner from the business bona fide in accordance with such a power conferred by the agreement between the partners;

(2) In contravention of the agreement between the partners, where the circumstances do not permit a dissolution under any other provision of this section, by the express will of any partner at any time;

(3) By any event which makes it unlawful for the business of the partnership to be carried on or for the members to carry it on in partnership;

(4) By the death of any partner;

(5) By the bankruptcy of any partner or the partnership;

(6) By decree of court under section 32.

§32. Dissolution by Decree of Court. (1) On application by or for a partner the court shall decree a dissolution whenever:

(a) A partner has been declared a lunatic in any judicial proceeding or is shown to be of unsound mind,

(b) A partner becomes in any other way incapable of performing his part of the partnership contract,

(c) A partner has been guilty of such conduct as tends to affect prejudicially the carrying on of the business,

(d) A partner wilfully or persistently commits a breach of the partnership agreement, or otherwise so conducts himself in matters relating to the partnership business that it is not reasonably practicable to carry on the business in partnership with him,

(e) The business of the partnership can only be carried on at a loss,

(f) Other circumstances render a dissolution equitable.

(2) On the application of the purchaser of a partner's interest under sections 28 or 29:

(a) After the termination of the specified term or particular undertaking,

(b) At any time if the partnership was a partnership at will when the interest was assigned or when the charging order was issued.

§33. General Effect of Dissolution on Authority of Partner. Except so far as may be necessary to wind up partnership affairs or to complete transactions begun but not then finished, dissolution terminates all authority of any partner to act for the partnership,

(1) With respect to the partners,

(a) When the dissolution is not by the act, bankruptcy or death of a partner; or

(b) When the dissolution is by such act, bankruptcy or death of a partner, in cases where section 34 so requires.

(2) With respect to persons not partners, as declared in section 35.

§34. Right of Partner to Contribution from Co-partners after Dissolution. Where the dissolution is caused by the act, death or bankruptcy of a partner, each partner is liable to his co-partners for his share of any liability created by any partner acting for the partnership as if the partnership had not been dissolved unless

(a) The dissolution being by act of any partner, the partner acting for the partnership had knowledge of the dissolution, or

(b) The dissolution being by the death or bankruptcy of a partner, the partner acting for the partnership had knowledge or notice of the death or bankruptcy.

§35. Power of Partner to Bind Partnership to Third Persons after Dissolution. (1) After dissolution a partner can bind the partnership except as provided in Paragraph (3).

(a) By any act appropriate for winding up partnership affairs or completing transactions unfinished at dissolution;

(b) By any transaction which would bind the partnership if dissolution had not taken place, provided the other party to the transaction

(I) Had extended credit to the partnership prior to dissolution and had no knowledge or notice of the dissolution; or

(II) Though he had not so extended credit, had nevertheless known of the partnership prior to dissolution, and, having no knowledge or notice of dissolution, the fact of dissolution had not been advertised in a newspaper of general circulation in the place (or in each place if more than one) at which the partnership business was regularly carried on.

(2) The liability of a partner under Paragraph (1b) shall be satisfied out of partnership assets alone when such partner had been prior to dissolution

(a) Unknown as a partner to the person with whom the contract is made; and

(b) So far unknown and inactive in partnership affairs that the business reputation of the partnership could not be said to have been in any degree due to his connection with it.

(3) The partnership is in no case bound by any act of a partner after dissolution

(a) Where the partnership is dissolved because it is unlawful to carry on the business, unless the act is appropriate for winding up partnership affairs; or

(b) Where the partner has become bankrupt; or

(c) Where the partner has no authority to wind up partnership affairs; except by a transaction with one who

(I) Had extended credit to the partnership prior to dissolution and had no knowledge or notice of his want of authority; or

(II) Had not extended credit to the partnership prior to dissolution, and, having no knowledge or notice of his want of authority, the fact of his want of authority has not been advertised in the manner provided for advertising the fact of dissolution in Paragraph (1bII).

(4) Nothing in this section shall affect the liability under Section 16 of any person who after dissolution represents himself or consents to another representing him as a partner in a partnership engaged in carrying on business.

§36. Effect of Dissolution on Partner's Existing Liability. (1) The dissolution of the partnership does not of itself discharge the existing liability of any partner.

(2) A partner is discharged from any existing liability upon dissolution of the partnership by an agreement to that effect between himself, the partnership creditor and the person or partnership continuing the business; and such agreement may be inferred from the course of dealing between the creditor having knowledge of the dissolution and the person or partnership continuing the business.

(3) Where a person agrees to assume the existing obligations of a dissolved partnership, the partners whose obligations have been assumed shall be discharged from any liability to any creditor of the partnership who, knowing of the agreement, consents to a material alteration in the nature or time of payment of such obligations.

(4) The individual property of a deceased partner shall be liable for all obligations of the partnership incurred while he was a partner but subject to the prior payment of his separate debts.

§37. Right to Wind Up. Unless otherwise agreed the partners who have not wrongfully dissolved the partnership or the legal representative of the last surviving partner, not bankrupt, has the right to wind up the partnership affairs; provided, however, that any partner, his legal representative or his assignee, upon cause shown, may obtain winding up by the court.

§38. Rights of Partners to Application of Partnership Property. (1) When dissolution is caused in any way, except in contravention of the partnership agreement, each partner, as against his co-partners and all persons claiming through them in respect of their interests in the partnership, unless otherwise agreed, may have the partnership property applied to discharge its liabilities, and the surplus applied to pay in cash the net amount owing to the respective partners. But if dissolution is caused by expulsion of a partner, bona fide under the partnership agreement and if the expelled partner is discharged from all partnership liabilities, either by payment or agreement under section 36(2), he shall receive in cash only the net amount due him from the partnership.

(2) When dissolution is caused in contravention of the partnership agreement the rights of the partners shall be as follows:

(a) Each partner who has not caused dissolution wrongfully shall have,

(I) All the rights specified in paragraph (1) of this section, and

(II) The right, as against each partner who has caused the dissolution wrongfully, to damages for breach of the agreement.

(b) The partners who have not caused the dissolution wrongfully, if they all desire to continue the business in the same name, either by themselves or jointly with others, may do so, during the agreed term for the partnership and for that purpose may possess the partnership property, provided they secure the payment by bond approved by the court, or pay to any partner who has caused the dissolution wrongfully, the value of his interest in the partnership at the dissolution, less any damages recoverable under clause (2aII) of this section, and in like manner indemnify him against all present or future partnership liabilities.

(c) A partner who has caused the dissolution wrongfully shall have:

(I) If the business is not continued under the provisions of paragraph (2b) all the rights of a partner under paragraph (1), subject to clause (2aII), of this section,

(II) If the business is continued under paragraph (2b) of this section the right as against his co-partners and all claiming through them in respect of their interests in the partnership, to have the value of his interest in the partnership, less any damages caused to his co-partners by the dissolution, ascertained and paid to him in cash, or the payment secured by bond approved by the court, and to be released from all existing liabilities of the partnership; but in ascertaining the value of the partner's interest the value of the good-will of the business shall not be considered.

§39. Rights Where Partnership Is Dissolved for Fraud or Misrepresentation. Where a partnership contract is rescinded on the ground of the fraud or misrepresentation of one of the parties thereto, the party entitled to rescind is, without prejudice to any other right, entitled,

(a) To a lien on, or a right of retention of, the surplus of the partnership property after satisfying the partnership liabilities to third persons for any sum of money paid by him for the purchase of an interest in the partnership and for any capital or advances contributed by him; and

(b) To stand, after all liabilities to third persons have been satisfied, in the place of the creditors of the partnership for any payments made by him in respect of the partnership liabilities; and

(c) To be indemnified by the person guilty of the fraud or making the representation against all debts and liabilities of the partnership.

§40. Rules for Distribution. In settling accounts between the partners after dissolution, the following rules shall be observed, subject to any agreement to the contrary:

(a) The assets of the partnership are:

(I) The partnership property,

(II) The contributions of the partners necessary for the payment of all the liabilities specified in clause (b) of this paragraph.

(b) The liabilities of the partnership shall rank in order of payment, as follows:

(I) Those owing to creditors other than partners,

(II) Those owing to partners other than for capital and profits,

(III) Those owing to partners in respect of capital,

(IV) Those owing to partners in respect of profits.

(c) The assets shall be applied in order of their declaration in clause (a) of this paragraph to the satisfaction of the liabilities.

(d) The partners shall contribute, as provided by section 18 (a) the amount necessary to satisfy the liabilities; but if any, but not all, of the partners are insolvent, or, not being subject to process, refuse to contribute, the other partners shall contribute their share of the liabilities, and, in the relative proportions in which they share the profits, the additional amount necessary to pay the liabilities.

(e) An assignee for the benefit of creditors or any person appointed by the court shall have the right to enforce the contributions specified in clause (d) of this paragraph.

(f) Any partner or his legal representative shall have the right to enforce the contributions specified in clause (d) of this paragraph, to the extent of the amount which he has paid in excess of his share of the liability.

(g) The individual property of a deceased partner shall be liable for the contributions specified in clause (d) of this paragraph.

(h) When partnership property and the individual properties of the partners are in possession of a court for distribution, partnership creditors shall have priority on partnership property and separate creditors on individual property, saving the rights of lien or secured creditors as heretofore.

(i) Where a partner has become bankrupt or his estate is insolvent the claims against his separate property shall rank in the following order:

(I) Those owing to separate creditors,

(II) Those owing to partnership creditors,

(III) Those owing to partners by way of contribution.

§41. Liability of Persons Continuing the Business in Certain Cases. (1) When any new partner is admitted into an existing partnership, or when any partner retires and assigns (or the representative of the deceased partner assigns) his rights in partnership property to two or more of the partners, or to one or more of the partners and one or more third persons, if the business is continued without liquidation of the partnership affairs, creditors of the first or dissolved partnership are also creditors of the partnership so continuing the business.

(2) When all but one partner retire and assign (or the representative of a deceased partner assigns) their rights in partnership property to the remaining partner, who continues the business without liquidation of partnership affairs, either alone or with others, creditors of the dissolved partnership are also creditors of the person or partnership so continuing the business.

(3) When any partner retires or dies and the business of the dissolved partnership is continued as set forth in paragraphs (1) and (2) of this section, with the consent of the retired partners or the representative of the deceased partner, but without any assignment of his right in partnership property, rights of creditors of the dissolved partnership and of the creditors of the person or partnership continuing the business shall be as if such assignment had been made.

(4) When all the partners or their representatives assign their rights in partnership property to one or more third persons who promise to pay the debts and who continue the business of the dissolved partnership, creditors of the dissolved partnership are also creditors of the person or partnership continuing the business.

(5) When any partner wrongfully causes a dissolution and the remaining partners continue the business under the provisions of section 38(2b), either alone or with others,

and without liquidation of the partnership affairs, creditors of the dissolved partnership are also creditors of the person or partnership continuing the business.

(6) When a partner is expelled and the remaining partners continue the business either alone or with others, without liquidation of the partnership affairs, creditors of the dissolved partnership are also creditors of the person or partnership continuing the business.

(7) The liability of a third person becoming a partner in the partnership continuing the business, under this section, to the creditors of the dissolved partnership shall be satisfied out of partnership property only.

(8) When the business of a partnership after dissolution is continued under any conditions set forth in this section the creditors of the dissolved partnership, as against the separate creditors of the retiring or deceased partner or the representative of the deceased partner, have a prior right to any claim of the retired partner or the representative of the deceased partner against the person or partnership continuing the business, on account of the retired or deceased partner's interest in the dissolved partnership or on account of any consideration promised for such interest or for his right in partnership property.

(9) Nothing in this section shall be held to modify any right of creditors to set aside any assignment on the ground of fraud.

(10) The use by the person or partnership continuing the business of the partnership name, or the name of a deceased partner as part thereof, shall not of itself make the individual property of the deceased partner liable for any debts contracted by such person or partnership.

§42. Rights of Retiring or Estate of Deceased Partner When the Business Is Continued. When any partner retires or dies, and the business is continued under any of the conditions set forth in section 41 (1, 2, 3, 5, 6), or section 38(2b) without any settlement of accounts as between him or his estate and the person or partnership continuing the business, unless otherwise agreed, he or his legal representative as against such persons or partnership may have the value of his interest at the date of dissolution ascertained, and shall receive as an ordinary creditor an amount equal to the value of his interest in the dissolved partnership with interest, or, at his option or at the option of his legal representative, in lieu of interest, the profits attributable to the use of his right in the property of the dissolved partnership; provided that the creditors of the dissolved partnership as against the separate creditors, or the representative of the retired or deceased partner, shall have priority on any claim arising under this section, as provided by section 41(8) of this act.

§43. Accrual of Actions. The right to an account of his interest shall accrue to any partner, or his legal representative, as against the winding up partners or the surviving partners or the person or partnership continuing the business, at the date of dissolution, in the absence of any agreement to the contrary.

Part VII

Miscellaneous Provisions

§44. When Act Takes Effect. This act shall take effect on the . . . . day of . . . . one thousand nine hundred and . . . .

§45. Legislation Repealed. All acts or parts of acts inconsistent with this act are hereby repealed.

GLOSSARY

Abandonment In the law of property, the voluntary relinquishment of possession of personal property with the intention of terminating ownership, but without vesting the ownership in any other person.

Ab initio (ab i-nish′i-o) From the beginning. A contract which at no time had any legal validity is void ab initio.

Abrogate To annul; to repeal; to annul or repeal a former rule, order, or law. A rule of the common law may be abrogated by a statute.

Abscond To hide, conceal, or absent oneself with the intent of avoiding legal process.

Abstract of title A condensed history of the title to land, including a synopsis of all conveyances which affect said land, as well as a statement of all liens, charges, and encumbrances to which the same may be subject.

Accession (ak-sesh′ on) Acquisition of title to property by an increase of the original property or by production from such property.

Accommodation party In the law of commercial paper, a person who signs a negotiable instrument to lend credit to the accommodated party.

Accord and satisfaction An accord is an agreement to discharge an earlier agreement on different and ordinarily easier terms. The satisfaction is the performance of the accord.

Account debtor In the law of secured transactions, a person who is obligated on an account, chattel paper, or general intangible.

Accounts   In the law of secured transactions, any right to payment for goods sold or leased or for services rendered which is not evidenced by an instrument or chattel paper.

Accretion   (a-kre′ shun)   An increase by the gradual deposit by water of solid material so as to cause land which was covered by water to become dry land.

Acknowledgment   A statement made by a person before an authorized public officer that he signed a certain legal paper. The word is also used as an admission of an obligation of responsibility.

Act of God   An act that is caused exclusively by the forces of nature, as a hurricane, tornado, flood, lightning, drought, or blight which could not have been foreseen and prevented.

Action   The word in legal parlance refers to a proceeding in a court whereby a person seeks to enforce some right.

Action in personam   (ak′ shon in per-so′ nam)   An action brought to enforce some personal liability, as the recovery of some debt or of damages for some personal injury.

Action in rem   (ak′ shon in rem)   An action brought directly against property, as an action to foreclose a lien or to partition real property. In a more general sense, an action in rem is brought against individuals where the direct object is to reach and dispose of property owned by them or some interest in the property.

Adjudication   A judgment; the giving or pronouncing of a judgment or decree. The word is used mostly in bankruptcy proceedings. The adjudication is the order which declares the debtor to be a bankrupt.

Administrator, administratrix   In the law of probate, the person appointed to administer the estate of a person who has died without leaving a will. Administrator refers to a man, and administratrix refers to a woman. *See* Executor, executrix.

Affiant   (a-fi′ ant)   The person who makes, or subscribes to, an affidavit.

Affidavit   (af-i-da′ vit)   A declaration or statement of facts reduced to writing and sworn to or affirmed by the party making it before an authorized public officer.

Alienation   In the law of real property, the transfer of the title to real property. Real property may be sold, but the estate is not alienated unless the title is conveyed to the buyer.

Allegation   The assertion, declaration, or statement of a party to an action setting out in a pleading what he expects to prove.

Allege   To make an allegation.

Allonge   (a-lunj)   In the law of commercial paper, a paper securely fastened to a negotiable instrument for the purpose of providing additional space for indorsements.

Amicus curiae   (a-mi′ kus ku′ ri-e)   A friend of the court. A person who is appointed, or permitted, by the court to take part in a pending litigation by furnishing his opinion, or preparing a legal brief, in the matter.

Antedate   In the law of commercial paper, to date an instrument as of a time before the time it was written.

Anticipatory breach   An announcement by one of the parties to a contract, before the time for performance arrives, that he will not perform his part of the contract.

Appeal   The removal of a case to a higher court from a lower court whose judgment or decision the higher court is called upon to review.

Appellant (a-pel' ant)   The person who appeals a case from one court to another.

Appellee (ap-e-le')   The person against whom an appeal is taken.

Arbitration   A method whereby differences may be settled without litigation in court.

Arson   At common law, the willful and malicious burning, or causing to be burned, of the house of another, or any part thereof or adjoining or belonging to the house. The common-law definition has been enlarged by statute to include the burning of buildings and property.

Artisan   A person in some kind of mechanical craft or art, as an automobile mechanic.

Assignee (as-i-ne')   A person to whom an assignment has been made.

Assignment (as-sign' ment)   A transfer of property; ordinarily limited to rights in, or connected with, property, as rights under a contract.

Assignor (as-i-nor')   A person who makes an assignment.

Attachment   A seizure or taking into custody by virtue of legal process, used either for the purpose of bringing a person before the court or for acquiring jurisdiction over the property seized; to compel an appearance; to furnish security for debts or costs; or to arrest a fund in the hands of a third person who may become liable to pay it over; used also to designate the writ of process for the accomplishment of the purposes enumerated.

Attestation   The act of witnessing the signing of a paper.

Attestation clause   The clause in which witnesses certify that the instrument has been executed before them; commonly placed at the conclusion of a writing.

Attorney-in-fact   An agent who is authorized by his principal for some particular purpose, or to do some particular act, not of a legal character.

Attractive nuisance doctrine   A rule imposing liability on a landowner who maintains upon his premises a condition which is dangerous to children of tender years and which may reasonably be expected to attract children of tender years.

Auction   A public sale of land or goods to the highest bidder.

Auctioneer   The person who conducts an auction.

Avulsion   A sudden addition to land by the action of water, as a flood.

Bailee   The person to whom personal property is delivered under a contract of bailment.

Bailment   The transfer of possession of personal property from the bailor to the bailee, without a transfer of title, for some temporary purpose, the possession to revert to the bailor or the property to be otherwise disposed of as directed by the bailor.

Bailor   The person who delivers personal property to another person in a contract of bailment.

Bankrupt   A person who, by a formal decree of a court, has been declared subject to be proceeded against under the bankruptcy laws or entitled, on his voluntary application, to take the benefit of the bankruptcy laws.

Barratry (bar' a-tri)   In the law of admiralty, some fraudulent act of the master or mariners, intended to be for their own benefit, to the prejudice of the owner of the vessel.

Bearer   The person in possession of an instrument, document of title, or security payable to bearer or indorsed in blank.

Beneficiary   A person given property by will; a person to whom the proceeds of a life insurance policy are payable; a person for whom a trust is created; a person for whose benefit a contract was entered into.

Bequeath   To give personal property by will. A word which in its ordinary legal meaning, also in common usage, refers to real as well as personal property.

Bill of lading   A document evidencing the receipt of goods for shipment issued by a person engaged in the business of transporting or forwarding goods.

Binder   In the law of insurance, a temporary contract of insurance looking toward the actual, subsequent issuance of the policy.

Blue-sky laws   Statutes providing for the regulation and supervision of investment companies for the protection of persons investing in fraudulent companies.

Bona fide   (bo′ na fi′ de)   In or with good faith; without any fraud or deceit.

Bond   An obligation or promise in writing for the payment of money, or acknowledgment of being bound for money, conditioned to be void on the performance of some duty.

Bulk transfer   Any transfer in bulk which is not made in the ordinary course of business, but which consists of a major part of the materials, supplies, merchandise, or other inventory.

Cause of action   The grounds for which a judicial proceeding may be brought.

Caveat emptor   (ka′ ve-at emp′ tor)   Let the buyer beware; the duty imposed on the buyer to examine the article he is buying and act on his own judgment and at his own risk.

Cestui que trust   (ses′ twe ke trust)   The person for whose benefit property is held in trust.

Chancery court   (chan′ se-ri court)   A court of equity.

Charter   In the law of admiralty, to hire or lease a vessel for a voyage. In the law of corporations, a grant of authority from the government to a corporation to exist as a corporation.

Chattel mortgage   A writing whereby an owner creates a lien upon, or transfers title to, personal property as security for the performance of some act, usually the payment of money, with the lien or title subject to defeasance upon performance.

Chattel paper   In the law of secured transactions, a writing or writings which evidence both a monetary obligation and a security in or lease of specific goods. Chattel paper is, in most instances, a "security agreement."

Chattels personal   All movable property, as animals, automobiles, and money.

Chattels real   Rights in land which are less than a freehold, as a lease.

Chose in action   (shoz in ak′ shon)   A right to a thing personal not in one's possession but recoverable by a judicial proceeding, as a claim for wages.

Codicil   (kod′ i-sil)   An addition to or modification of an executed will. A codicil must be executed with the same formality as a will.

Coinsurance   A clause requiring the insured to carry insurance in an amount equal to a stated percentage of the value of the property insured, and providing that if he fails to do so, the insured is an insurer for the uninsured excess.

Collateral security   A separate obligation given to guarantee the performance of another contract.

Color of title   Circumstances that have the appearance of supporting a claim of a present title to real property, but which fall short of supporting the claim, as a deed appearing to convey title to a person but failing to do so because the grantor was not the owner of the land.

Commission merchant   A term which is synonymous with "factor." One whose business is to receive and sell goods for a commission, being entrusted with the possession of the goods to be sold and usually selling in his own name.

Common carrier   A carrier that holds out its facilities to the general public as being in the business of transporting goods and passengers for compensation without unjust discrimination.

Common law   As distinguished from law enacted by legislative enactments, the body of law based on usages and customs and enforced by the courts.

Community property   Property acquired by a husband and wife during their marriage.

Complaint   In civil practice, the initial pleading in which the plaintiff alleges the general facts constituting his claim and requests the desired legal relief.

Composition of creditors   An agreement between a debtor and some or all of his creditors whereby the creditors agree to accept less than the whole amount of their claims in full settlement of the whole.

Conditional sale   A contract for the sale of goods under which possession of the goods is delivered to the buyer but the seller reserves the title until the buyer has performed the condition of the contract, which usually consists of payment of the purchase price.

Confession of judgment   A written and acknowledged consent of a person permitting judgment to be entered against him for the amount stated in the consent.

Confusion of goods   The intermingling of goods of different owners to such an extent that the property of each can no longer be distinguished.

Consanguinity   (kon-sang-gwin' i-ti)   The blood relation of persons descended from the same common ancestor.

Conservator   A person appointed by the court to protect the interests of the estate of an insane or other incompetent person.

Consignee   The person to whom a consignment is made.

Consignment   Goods or property sent by a common carrier by a person (the consignor) in one place to another person (the consignee) in another place sometimes to be sold by the consignee.

Consignor   The person who makes a consignment.

Constructive notice   Information or knowledge of a fact imputed by law to a person. A recorded deed is an instance of constructive notice.

Consumer goods   In the law of secured transactions, goods which are used or bought primarily for personal, family, or household purposes.

Contra   (kon' tra)   Disagreeing with; contrary to.

Contract carrier   A private carrier. A carrier that engages to transport goods or passengers on a particular instance, but that does not hold out its facilities to the general public.

Contract right   In the law of secured transactions, any right to payment under a contract not yet earned by performance. This is now an "account" under the 1972 Code changes.

Conversion   In the law of torts, an unlawful act occurring when a person deals with chattels not belonging to him in a manner inconsistent with the ownership of the lawful owner.

Conveyance   An instrument in writing by which an interest in real property is transferred from one person to another, ordinarily by the execution and delivery of a deed. In its broadest meaning, "conveyance" also includes the transfer of personal property.

Copyright An exclusive right granted to authors or originators to publish and sell their writings and discoveries for a period of twenty-eight years, renewable for a second period of twenty-eight years. The word "writings" has been construed to include such materials as books, maps, charts, music, prints, engravings, drawings, paintings, and photoplays.

Coterminous Having the same or coincident boundaries; covering the same area, as Washington, D.C., and the District of Columbia.

Counterclaim A claim constituting a distinct cause of action asserted by a defendant in opposition to, or deduction from the claim of the plaintiff. *See* Setoff.

Covenant A word now used principally in connection with promises contained in a mortgage, lease, deed, or other contract incidental to the main purpose of the contract, as a covenant against encumbrances.

Covenantee The person to whom the promise of a covenant is made.

Covenantor The person who makes a covenant.

Curtesy (ker′ te-si) A right held by a married man in part of the land owned by his wife, which right becomes effective upon the death of his wife.

Cy pres doctrine In the law of trusts, a rule for the construction of instruments whereby the intention of the donor is carried out as nearly as possible when it would be impossible or illegal to give the instrument literal effect.

Damages Compensation or indemnity which may be recovered by any person who has suffered loss, detriment, or injury through the unlawful act, omission, or negligence of another.

Deceit A species of fraud; a fraudulent misrepresentation or contrivance used by one person to deceive and trick another person who has no means of detecting the fraud perpetrated to his prejudice and damage.

Declaration In pleading, the first or initial pleading in which a plaintiff in an action at law alleges his cause of action.

Decree A decision of a court of equity; comparable to a judgment in a court of law. In many states which have adopted code procedure, the distinction between decrees and judgments are abolished for all practical purposes.

De facto (de fak′ to) In fact. A corporation de facto is one whose organization is defective to the extent that it may be successfully attacked by the state.

Defeasance clause A provision which will of itself render an instrument null and void. A clause in a deed conveying real property which provides that the deed shall be null and void upon the payment of the obligation by the debtor.

Defendant The person against whom a legal action is brought.

De jure (de ju′ re) Of right. A corporation de jure is one which exists by reason of full compliance with the requirements of law permitting organization of such a corporation.

Del credere (del kre′ de-re) An agreement by which a factor, in selling goods on credit for an additional commission, guarantees that the purchase price will be paid the seller.

Demurrage (de-mer′ aj) In the law of admiralty, the amount paid to the master or owner of a vessel for detention of the vessel beyond the time allowed for loading, unloading, and sailing.

Demurrer (de-mer′ er) A form of pleading which disputes the sufficiency in law of the pleading of the other party; in effect, an allegation that, even if the other party's statements are correct, a cause of action has not been stated which would require the demurring party to answer them or proceed further with the cause.

Derivative   Something derived from something else.

Descent   Hereditary succession. The transfer of the title to real property to the heirs upon the death of an ancestor who dies without making a will. The word is used loosely to refer to either real or personal property.

Devise   To make a gift of real property by will. The word is used loosely to refer to either real or personal property.

Devisee   The beneficiary named in a will which in legal usage is a testamentary gift of real property.

Dictum   (dik′ tum)   A remark by a judge in pronouncing an opinion concerning some rule which is not necessarily involved in the case or essential to its determination.

Directed verdict   A verdict which the jury returns in favor of a specified party as directed by the trial judge.

Discharge in bankruptcy   An order of the court whereby the bankrupt debtor is discharged from the unpaid balance of provable claims against him. Certain tax claims, tort claims, fines, and penalties are not provable claims.

Diuturnal   Of long continuance; lasting.

Divestiture   Act of divesting; to cease; to annul; to take away.

Document   In the law of secured transactions, a document of title, including bills of lading, dock warrants, dock receipts, warehouse receipts, or orders for the delivery of goods.

Domicile   That place where a person has his or her true, fixed, and permanent home and principal establishment, and to which, whenever he is absent, he has an intention of returning.

Donee   A person to whom a gift is made.

Donor   A person who makes a gift.

Dower   (dou′ er)   A right held by a married woman in part of the land owned by her husband, which right becomes effective upon the death of her husband.

Draft   In the law of commercial paper, an order from one person to another person to pay a third person a sum of money.

Drawee   The person upon whom a draft is drawn by the drawer.

Drawer   The person who draws a draft.

Duress   (du′ res)   Compulsion by which a person is illegally forced to do or forbear to do some act.

Easement   The right of one person to use the land of another for a special purpose, as a right of way for a pipeline.

Eleemosynary corporation   (el-e-mos′ i-na-ri kor-po-ra′ shon)   A corporation organized for a charitable purpose or for charitable purposes.

Emancipate   To release; to set free. The word is used primarily with reference to the emancipation of a minor child by his parents, which involves the renunciation of parental duties and a surrender of the right to the care, custody, and earnings of such child.

Embezzlement   (em-bez′ lment)   The fraudulent appropriation of another's personal property or money by one acting in a fiduciary capacity, as an agent, employee, or corporate officer to whom the property or money has been entrusted.

Eminent domain   The power of the government, governmental agencies, and government corporations to take private property for a public purpose upon the payment of just compensation.

Encumbrance   (en-kum' brans)   A claim or lien upon property which may diminish its value, as a mortgage encumbering real property.

Eo instante   (e' o in-stan' te)   At the same instant; immediately.

Equipment   In the law of secured transactions, goods which are used or bought for use primarily in business, including farming, a profession, a nonprofit organization, or a governmental agency.

Escrow   A written deed, or other instrument, delivered to a third person to be delivered by the third person to the grantee upon the performance of some condition. The deposit of the escrow places it beyond the control of the grantor, but the title does not pass until the fulfillment of the condition.

Estoppel   A rule of law which precludes a person from alleging or denying certain facts as a result of his previous allegation, denial, conduct, or admission.

Eviction   Dispossession of a person of the possession of his lands or tenements. Dispossession of a tenant by a landlord.

Evidence   Any records, documents, testimony, or other species of proof presented to the court and jury for the purpose of ascertaining the truth of any alleged matter of fact.

Ex contractu   (ex kon-trak' tu)   From or out of a contract. A right or cause of action arising out of a contract.

Ex delicto   (ex de-lik' to)   From or out of a tort. A right or cause of action arising out of a tort.

Executor, executrix   In the law of wills, the person named in a will to administer the estate of a deceased person. Executor refers to a man, and executrix refers to a woman. *See* Administrator, administratrix.

Exemption   Freedom from some charge or burden to which others are subject; also used to designate a privilege allowed a judgment debtor to hold a certain amount of property free from a forced sale at the instance of a creditor.

Ex post facto law   (ex post fak' to law)   A law passed after the commission of an act which retrospectively changes the legal consequences of such act. The phrase "ex post facto" in constitutions pertains to criminal cases, and is a law that inflicts a greater punishment than the law pertaining to the crime when committed.

Factor   Synonymous with "commission merchant." One whose business is to receive and sell goods for a commission, being entrusted with the possession of the goods to be sold, and usually selling in his own name.

Farm products   In the law of secured transactions, goods which are in the possession of a debtor engaged in raising, fattening, or grazing livestock or other farming operations.

Fee-simple estate   A freehold estate of inheritance in which the owner is entitled to the entire property, with unconditional power of disposition during his life, and descending to his heirs upon his death.

Felony   A criminal offense for which the offender is punishable by death or imprisonment in a state prison or penitentiary, or that offense which is stated by a constitution or statute to be a felony.

Fiduciary (fi-du′ shi-a-ri) A person who occupies a position of trust and confidence in relation to another person.

Foreclosure A proceeding by which the rights of the mortgagee of real property are enforced and the rights of the mortgagor to redeem the mortgaged property are cut off. Foreclosure is also applied to other liens, as a mechanic's lien.

Forgery The fraudulent making or materially altering of any writing with the intent to deceive or injure another person.

Fraud A fraudulent misrepresentation or contrivance used by one person to deceive and trick another who has no means of detecting the fraud, perpetrated to his prejudice and damage. *See* Deceit.

Freehold An estate of inheritance, or an estate for life, existing in or arising from real property.

Fructus industriales (fruk′ tus in-dus-tri-a′ lez) Fruits of industry; crops that must be sown or planted each year and which require the labor of man to produce them.

Fructus naturales (fruk′ tus na-tu-ra′ lez) Products that are produced by the power of nature, as the fruits and produce of perennial trees and bushes.

Fungible goods (fun′ ji-bl) Goods of such kind or nature that one part may be used in place of another equal part, as grains and oils.

Future advance mortgage A mortgage given to secure future additional loans as well as the original loan.

Garnishment A proceeding in which money or property due the defendant and in the hands of a third person is attached for the purpose of applying it to the debt of the defendant.

General intangibles In the law of secured transactions, any personal property other than goods, accounts, chattel paper, documents, and instruments. General intangibles include such things as goodwill, copyrights, trade-marks, and patents.

Gift causa mortis (gift ka′ za mor′ tis) A conditional gift made by the donor in contemplation of death, generally with the understanding that the donee will return the gift if the donor survives.

Gift inter vivos (gift in′ ter vi′ vos) An irrevocable gift among the living.

Goods In the law of secured transactions, all things which are movable at the time the security interest attaches, excluding money, documents, instruments, accounts, chattel paper, general intangibles, the unborn young of animals, and growing crops.

Grantee In the law of real property, the person to whom real property is granted and conveyed.

Grantor In the law of real property, the person who grants and conveys real property to the grantee.

Guarantee The creditor under a contract of guaranty.

Guarantor A person bound by a contract of guaranty.

Guaranty An undertaking by one person to pay some debt of, or the performance of some contract by, another person, who himself remains liable to pay the debt or perform the contract.

Guardian   A person lawfully charged with the duty of taking care of and protecting the rights and property of another person who is considered incapable of administering his own affairs.

Habendum   (ha-ben′ dum)   The clause in a deed which defines the extent of the ownership granted.

Heirs   Those persons designated by law to succeed to the estate in case of intestacy.

Hereditaments   (her-e-dit′ a-ments)   Anything capable of being inherited.

Holding company   A corporation organized to hold the stock of another corporation or corporations.

Holographic will   A will written and signed by the testator in his own handwriting.

Illusory   Tending to deceive. An illusory promise is a promise which appears to be binding but which in fact is not for such reasons as indefiniteness.

Inchoate   (in-ko′ at)   Imperfect, begun but not completed, as the inchoate interest a wife has in the lands of her husband during his life, which may become a right of dower upon his death.

Indemnity   A contract by which one person engages to secure another against loss or damage, as a contract of insurance.

Indorsee   The person to whom negotiable instruments, documents, and securities (drafts, checks, promissory notes, bills of lading, warehouse receipts, and shares of stock) are transferred by indorsement.

Indorsement   The act of a person in writing his name upon a negotiable instrument or document—usually on the back thereof—for the purpose of passing title to another person.

Indorser   The person who writes his name on negotiable instruments, documents, and securities for the purpose of passing title to another person.

Infant   In the legal meaning of the word, any person who has not attained his or her majority. At common law, any person who has not attained the age of twenty-one years.

Inheritance   In a restricted sense, the estate which passes from the decedent to his heirs by descent. The word is commonly used to include property obtained by both devise and descent.

Injunction   A restraining order issued by the court which prohibits the performance of an act by the defendant. A mandatory injunction requires the defendant to do or undo a certain act.

In pari delicto   (in pa′ ri de-lik′ to)   In equal fault or guilt. The courts will not assist persons in carrying out their illegal objects nor award damages when the parties are in pari delicto.

In personam   Against the person. Actions or rights in personam are contrasted with actions or rights in rem.

In re   In the matter of. "In re Brown" means "in the matter of Brown."

In rem   Against the thing; against the status; directed at specific property or at a specific right or status, as a proceeding against a vessel in a court of admiralty.

Insolvency   The financial condition of a person which is such that all his assets are not enough to pay all his debts, or a failure to pay one's debts as they mature.

In status quo   (in sta′ tus quo)   In the condition or situation in which it was. The requirement that before a contract may be rescinded, the parties must be placed in their original position prior to the creation of the contract.

Instrument   In the law of secured transactions, a negotiable instrument or security, which includes drafts, promissory notes, checks, certificates of deposit, bonds, and shares of stock.

Insured   The person whose life or property is insured.

Insurer   The person or company who promises to pay a sum of money to another if the latter sustains a loss.

Intangible property   In the law of property, property which has no physical existence but is only a right to receive property, as patent rights and shares of stock. In the law of secured transactions, instruments, documents, chattel paper, accounts, contract rights, and general intangibles.

Inter alia   (in-ter a' li-a)   Among other things.

Interlocutory   Temporary. An interlocutory decree between the commencement and end of a case which decides some point or matter but is not the final decision of the entire case.

Intervener   A person who, with the permission of the court, voluntarily interposes in an action or other proceeding.

Intestate   A person is said to die intestate when he dies without making a will. The word is also used to signify a person who dies without making a will.

In transitu   (in tran' si-tu)   In transit. Goods are in transit while they are in the possession of a carrier traveling from the place of business of the seller to the place of business of the buyer.

Inventory   In the law of secured transactions, goods held for sale or lease in the ordinary course of business.

Ipso facto   (ip' so fak' to)   By the fact itself. By the fact itself without any further facts on the part of anyone.

Issuer   With respect to the registration of a transfer of a security, the person on whose behalf transfer books are maintained. With respect to obligations on or defenses to a security, the person who places or authorizes the placing of his name on a security. With respect to documents of title, the person on whose behalf a bill of lading or a warehouse receipt is issued.

Jettison   (jet' i-son)   The act of throwing overboard a part of a cargo to lighten a vessel in danger of being lost or wrecked.

Joint-and-several liability   Persons are jointly and severally liable when the creditor may sue one or more of the promisors to such liability separately, or he may sue all of them together at his option.

Joint liability   Persons are jointly liable when both or all of the promisors must be sued in one action by the creditor. The creditor may not sue either one of the promisors at his option.

Judgment   The final determination by a court as a result of an action or proceeding instituted in such court.

Jury   A body of persons selected and summoned by law and sworn to try the facts of a case in order to render a verdict according to the law and the evidence.

Laches   (lach' ez)   Undue delay to the extent that it would be inequitable to accord the relief sought because rights of third persons have intervened or witnesses have disappeared.

Latent Concealed. The word is used with respect to a defect in materials not apparent by examination.

Lease A contract whereby one person, the lessor, agrees to give possession of property ordinarily for a period of time—but sometimes at will or for the life of the tenant—to another person, the lessee, in consideration of the payment of money. The parties are frequently referred to as "landlord" and "tenant" where real property is involved.

Legacy A bequest, or gift, of personal property by will. The courts, however, will construe the word to include real property when this is necessary to effectuate the purpose of the testator as expressed in his will.

Lessee The person to whom a lease is granted.

Lessor The person who grants a lease.

Letter of credit An engagement by a bank or other person made at the request of a customer that the bank will honor drafts or other demands for payment.

Levy Attachment of property. The act of an officer of the court in seizing property of the defendant to satisfy a judgment of the plaintiff.

License In the law of real property, a privilege to go upon or temporarily use the land of another in a limited manner, as where a landowner gives his neighbor permission to walk across his land for the purpose of going back and forth from work.

Lien A claim or encumbrance by one person upon the property of another person to enforce the performance of an obligation which is usually the payment of money. A seller may have a lien upon the property sold to the buyer for the balance of the purchase price.

Life estate An interest in land which begins with its creation and, unless it is terminated sooner, continues for the duration of the life by which it is measured. A life estate is not an estate of inheritance.

Life tenant The person who holds an estate in lands the duration of which is measured by the life of some person.

Lis pendens (lis pen' denz) A suit pending. A "notice of lis pendens" is filed for the purpose of warning all persons dealing with the defendant regarding the subject matter of the suit that they do so subject to the final determination of the suit.

Litigation A judicial controversy; to prosecute or defend a cause in court; to carry on a legal contest by judicial process.

Locus sigilli (lo' kus si-jil' li) The place occupied by the seal on written instruments. The words are usually abbreviated "L.S."

Malice The doing of a wrongful act intentionally, without just cause or excuse.

Mandamus We command. A command issued from a court, in the name of the state, directed to some corporation, to an executive, administrator, or judicial officer, or to an inferior court commanding the performance of a particular act.

Manslaughter The unlawful killing of a human creature without malice, either express or implied, which may be done voluntarily upon a sudden heat of passion, or involuntarily.

Materialman A person who furnishes materials to be used in the construction or repair of a building, vessel, or other structure.

Mechanic's lien   A lien upon real property to secure the payment of debts owed those persons who contribute labor or materials to the improvement of the property.

Minor   At common law, a person who has not attained the age of twenty-one years. An infant, or person, who has not attained his or her majority.

Misdemeanor   A criminal offense generally defined by statute to be all crimes other than treason or felony.

Necessaries   With reference to an infant, the word includes such things as food, clothing, lodging, medical attention, and whatever is reasonably necessary for his proper and suitable maintenance, according to his circumstances and station in life.

Non compos mentis   (non kom′ pos men′ tis)   Mentally incompetent; not sound of mind; insane.

Non obstante veredicto   (non ob-stan′ te ve-re-dik′ to)   Notwithstanding the verdict. A judgment entered by order of the court which is contrary to the verdict of the jury.

Notary public   A public officer whose chief function is to administer oaths and to authenticate and certify copies of certain documents so that such documents will have credit and authenticity in foreign jurisdictions; also to take acknowledgments of deeds and other conveyances.

Nudum pactum   (nu′ dum pak′ tum)   A promise for which there is no consideration; a naked promise.

Nuncupative will   (nung ku-pa-tiv wil)   An oral will made by the testator during his last illness in the presence of witnesses.

Oath   Any form of attestation by which a person affirms the truth of a statement which he is about to make; an outward pledge made under an immediate sense of responsibility to God. If taken as a part of a judicial proceeding, a willful false statement made in violation of such an oath is perjury.

Obligee   The person to whom another is obligated.

Obligor   The person who has engaged to perform some obligation.

Offeree   The person to whom an offer is made.

Offeror   The person who makes an offer.

Operation of law   The manner in which rights and liabilities devolve upon a person by the mere application of rules of law, without any act of the person himself.

Opinion of the court   The reasons given by the court for its decision.

Option   An agreement, supported by sufficient consideration, to sell property for a stipulated price within a specified period of time.

Ordinance   The word, as used in a limited sense, designates a legislative enactment of a municipality.

Partition   A method whereby those who own property as joint tenants or as tenants in common are enabled to put an end to the tenancy and vest in each a share in specific property or an allotment of the land.

Patent   As an adjective, not hidden from the eyes; open to view on ordinary inspection.

Payee   In the law of commercial paper, the person to whom a negotiable instrument is made payable.

Penalty   In the law of contracts, a sum of money stated in a contract by way of security for actual damages and involving the idea of punishment.

Per capita By the head; share and share alike. In the law of wills, a method of dividing an intestate estate whereby an equal share is given to a number of heirs who stand in equal degree to the decedent.

Per curiam (per ku′ ri-am) By the court. An opinion of the whole court as distinguished from an opinion written by any one justice.

Perjury The willful and intentional giving of false evidence in court after having sworn or affirmed to make a truthful statement. The definition of the word "perjury" has been expanded by statute to include false swearing in affidavits and depositions, such as those made with respect to tax returns.

Per se In itself; taken alone; unconnected with other matters.

Personal representative In the law of wills, the executor, executrix, administrator, or administratrix who administers the estate of a deceased person.

Per stirpes By representation. A method of dividing an intestate estate where a class of heirs take the share which their deceased would have been entitled to, thus inheriting by right of representing such ancestor.

Plaintiff A person who brings an action seeking a remedy in court.

Pledge In the law of bailments, a pawn. The bailment of personal property as security for a debt or engagement.

Pledgee The person to whom personal property is pledged.

Pledgor The person delivering personal property in pledge.

Postdate To date an instrument as of a time later than the date on which it was executed.

Power of attorney A written authorization by which one person appoints another person to act as agent of the person making the appointment.

Precatory Indicating a desire or wish.

Presumption The word is used to mean that the trier of the facts must find the existence of the fact presumed unless evidence is introduced which would support a finding of the nonexistence of the fact.

Prima facie (pri′ ma fa′ shi-e) At first sight. A litigating party is said to have a prima-facie case when the evidence is sufficient for proof until it is rebutted or contradicted.

Principal In the law of agency, the person who gives authority to an agent to do some act for him.

Privileged communication In the law of evidence, a communication which a witness is not permitted to divulge because of the relationship with the person furnishing the communication, as attorney and client, physician and patient.

Probate Formerly, relating to proof or relating to proof of wills. The word is now generally used to include all matters of which probate courts have jurisdiction, the most common of which are estates of deceased persons and persons under guardianship.

Profit a prendre A nonpossessory interest in land; a right to take substance from the soil of another, as coal or minerals.

Pro rata (pro ra′ ta) Proportionately; according to share, interest, or liability of each.

Prospectus A published document setting forth the nature and object of shares of stock or other securities of a company or corporation and inviting the public to subscribe to the issue.

Pro tempore   Temporarily; for the time being. Abbreviation: Pro tem.

Proxy   Authority to act for another; used by absent shareholders to authorize another to vote the stock owned by the shareholders.

Quantum meruit   (kwon' tum me' ru-it)   As much as he deserves; one of the common counts for work and labor founded on an implied promise on the part of the defendant to pay the plaintiff for the value of the services rendered.

Quasi contract   (kwa' si kon-trakt)   Sometimes referred to as a "contract implied in law," but more properly an obligation imposed by law to prevent injustice irrespective of the intention of the parties, and not properly a contract at all.

Quitclaim deed   A deed that is intended to pass any title or interest which the grantor may have in the premises, but not professing that he has any title.

Quorum   The minimum number of persons who may lawfully transact the business at a meeting.

Quo warranto   (kwo wo-ran' to)   A proceeding commenced by the government to dissolve a corporation or to remove a person from public office.

Rebuttal   (re-but' al)   In the law of evidence, the introduction of rebutting evidence by the opposite party.

Receiver   An impartial person appointed by the court to receive and preserve the property or funds in litigation for the protection of all persons concerned.

Recognizance   (re-kog' ni-zans)   A contract of record. An obligation entered into before a court to do some act, usually to appear at a later date and answer to a criminal accusation.

Redemption   A repurchase. The buying back of one's property after it has been sold, as the right of the mortgagor to redeem his land upon default.

Referee   In the law of bankruptcy, the person in charge of the proceedings during the administration of the estate of the bankrupt.

Registered bonds   Bonds registered upon the books maintained for that purpose.

Reimbursement   The act of paying back; to make restoration, as to reimburse one for his losses.

Replevin   A proceeding by which the owner recovers his own property in the possession of another person.

Repudiate   To reject; disclaim; to disclaim some privilege, duty, obligation, or right.

Res   (rez)   The thing; the subject matter of the litigation. In the law of trusts, the subject matter is the *res*.

Respondeat superior   (re-spon' de-at su-pe' ri or)   Let the master answer. In the law of agency, this maxim means that the principal is liable in certain cases for the wrongful acts of his agent.

Rider   In the law of insurance, a provision added to the policy whereby the scope of the coverage is restricted or enlarged.

Riparian   (ri-pa' ri-an)   Relating to the bank of a river. A riparian owner is one who owns land on the bank of a river.

Scienter   (si-en' ter)   Knowledge on the part of a person making a representation, at the time the representation is made, that the representation is false. The courts generally hold that scienter must be proved in a tort action of deceit.

Seal   An impression upon a written instrument to show that the instrument was executed in a formal manner. The United States, each of the states, and corporations have and use seals. At early common law, a seal was an imprint on a wafer, soft wax, or some other substance with a signet ring or other device. Under modern law, the written letters "L.S." (locus sigili), the written word "SEAL," or any mark not ordinarily a part of the signature is a seal when so intended.

Security agreement   In the law of secured transactions, an agreement which provides for a security interest. A and B enter into a security agreement where A borrows money from B and gives B a security interest in his television set as collateral for the loan.

Setoff   A claim constituting a distinct cause of action asserted by a defendant in opposition to or deduction from the claim of the plaintiff. *See* Counterclaim.

Settlor   In the law of trusts, the donor of a trust deed.

Several liability   Persons are severally liable when the creditor may sue each promisor separately.

Slander   The use of spoken defamatory words which injure the reputation of a person.

Specific performance   An equitable remedy to compel a person to do precisely what he ought to have done under the terms of contract.

Spendthrift trust   A term applied when the settlor desires to protect a beneficiary who is incompetent, inexperienced, or immature. Provision against alienation of the trust fund by the voluntary act of the beneficiary or by his creditors is the usual incident of a spendthrift trust.

Spoilation   The erasure or alteration of a writing by a stranger. Spoilation does not destroy the legal effect of a writing.

Stare decisis   (sta′ re de-si′ sis)   A doctrine declaring that once a decision is reached by a superior court in a particular case, it becomes a precedent and all other cases of a similar kind are to be decided according to the same rule.

Status quo   (sta′ tus kwo)   The situation in which he was. In the law of contracts, the requirement that the parties must be placed in their original position before a contract may be rescinded.

Statute of limitations   A statute declaring that no action shall be maintained on certain causes of action unless brought within a specified period after the right of action accrued.

Stoppage in transitu   (stop′ aj in tran′ zi-tu)   A resumption of possession of goods by an unpaid seller while such goods are in transit and not delivered to the insolvent buyer.

Subpoena   A writ commanding the person designated in the subpoena to attend court for the purpose of testifying as a witness.

Subrogation   In the law of insurance, the right of the insurer, upon paying the loss, to recover from the third person who caused the loss. In the law of suretyship, the right of the surety, upon paying the creditor, to recover from the debtor.

Sui juris   (su′ i ju′ ris)   Of his own right; not under any legal disability or guardianship.

Summons   A writ, or process, notifying the person named therein that an action has been commenced against him and requiring him to appear and answer the allegations in such action.

Surety   A person who binds himself for the payment of a sum of money, or for the performance of some obligation, with another person, called the principal, in respect to which the principal is already bound.

Survivorship   The right whereby a person becomes entitled to property by reason of his having survived another person who had an interest in the property. Common examples are property owned by persons as joint tenants and property owned by a husband and wife as tenants by the entirety.

Symbolic delivery   The constructive delivery of the subject matter of a sale or gift by delivering the means of control, as a present gift of an automobile accompanied by a transfer of the key.

Tacking   In the law of real property, the attaching of successive periods of possession of one occupant to that of another for the purpose of computing the statutory period of continuous adverse possession to vest legal title. The occupants must be in privity, as a grantor and grantee or a devisor and devisee.

Tangible property   In the law of property, property which has a physical existence, as land, buildings, furniture, and animals. In the law of secured transactions, consumer goods, equipment, farm products, and inventory.

Tender   The act by which one person produces and offers to another person, in satisfaction of some claim or demand, the amount of money which the former considers and admits to be due; used also in connection with a tender of performance of a duty or obligation.

Testate   Leaving a will upon death. A person who dies testate dies leaving a will.

Testator   A deceased person who died leaving a valid will.

Title insurance   A policy of insurance which, for all practical purposes, insures the buyer of real property against loss should the title be defective.

Torrens System   A system of land registration developed by Sir Robert Torrens in Australia in 1858. This system has met with little success in the United States.

Tort-feasor   A wrongdoer; a person who commits a tort.

Trade fixture   An article of personal property attached to buildings by the tenant which is necessary or is used in connection with the business of the tenant.

Trade-mark   A distinctive mark, device, or emblem which a manufacturer affixes to the goods he sells so they may be identified in the market.

Trade name   A name under which a business is carried on.

Treason   Treason against the United States shall consist only in levying war against them, or in adhering to their enemies, giving them aid and comfort. [U.S. Constitution, Art. III, sec. 3.] The offense of attempting to overthrow the government of the state to which the offender owes allegiance.

Trespass   An unlawful act by one person committed with violence and causing injury to another person or to his property or relative rights.

Trust corpus   The subject matter of the trust; definite and ascertainable property that is transferred to the trustee.

Trustee   A person who, under an express or implied agreement, holds some estate or interest for the purpose of administering the trust for the benefit of another or to the use of another.

Ultra vires   (ul' tra vi' rez)   Beyond the powers of; commonly used to designate an act beyond the powers of a corporation.

Undisclosed principal   A principal who is represented by an agent who does not reveal that he is acting in a representative capacity.

Undue influence   The mental coercion of one person over another.

Usury   Unlawful interest; the lending of money at a rate of interest in excess of the maximum rate allowed by law.

Valid   Of binding force; an instrument which has received all the formalities required by law; incapable of being rightfully overthrown or set aside, as a valid deed.

Vendee   A purchaser, or buyer, of property; a person to whom anything is sold. The word is more commonly used in the sale of real property.

Vendor   A person who sells property to a vendee. The words "vendor" and "vendee" are more commonly used in the sale of real property.

Verdict   The decision, or finding, made by a jury and given to the court concerning matters of fact submitted to the jury for deliberation and determination.

Vested   Fixed; settled; a complete and consummated right of present or future enjoyment. The word is generally applied to the title to, or an interest in, real property.

Void   Null; having no legal force or binding effect.

Voidable   That which may be avoided, but which is not absolutely void or void of itself. Most of the contracts of infants are voidable only, rather than absolutely void.

Voting trust   The transfer by two or more shareholders of the legal title of their shares of stock to a specified trustee for the purpose of voting the shares.

Waiver   A voluntary relinquishment of a known right. The word implies an election to forgo some advantage which a person could have demanded.

Warehouse receipt   A receipt issued by a person engaged in the business of storing goods for hire.

Warranty   (wor' an-ti)   A collateral undertaking that a certain fact regarding the subject matter of a contract is, or shall be, as it is promised to be.

Warranty of authority   An implied warranty of an agent that he has the authority which he assumes to exercise.

Waste   The destruction, misuse, alteration, or neglect of the premises by a tenant to the prejudice of the reversionary interest of the landlord.

Watered stock   Shares of stock issued by a corporation as fully paid, when in fact the shares are not fully paid for.

Will   In the law of wills, the legal declaration of a person's mind or wishes as to the disposition of his property after his death.

Writ   An order running in the name of the state, issued from a court of justice, for the purpose of requiring the performance of a specified act. The writ may be addressed to the sheriff or other officer of the law, or directly to the person whose action the court desires to command.

INDEX